DOCUMENTS IN EUROPEAN CO
ENVIRONMENTAL LAV

G000055094

This is the companion volume to the second edition of Philippe Sands' *Principles of International Environmental Law* and Sands and Galizzi's *Documents in International Environmental Law*. It comprises extracts from those EC Treaties, Regulations, Directives, Decisions and other Acts of EC institutions which are essential for anyone interested in environmental protection in the European Community and its Member States. EC environmental legislation represents one of the most complex and challenging legal regimes for the protection of the environment. The significant body of legislation which now exists has given rise to numerous disputes over its application and interpretation. This collection brings together the principal documents in an accessible form, providing practitioners, scholars and students with the essentials necessary to understand, advise upon and apply this body of law. Concise editorial notes summarise the main provisions of the instruments reproduced and place them in their wider context.

PHILIPPE SANDS QC is Professor of Laws and Director of the Centre for International Courts and Tribunals at University College London and a Barrister at Matrix Chambers. He was co-founder of FIELD (Foundation for International Environmental Law and Development).

PAOLO GALIZZI is Marie Curie Fellow at Imperial College London and a Visiting Scholar and Adjunct Professor of Law at Fordham University School of Law in New York. He is also a Fellow in International and European Environmental Law at the British Institute of International and Comparative Law, London. He has taught international law and environmental law in several countries, in particular Italy, the United Kingdom, Ghana and the United States, and has published extensively on international and European environmental law.

DOCUMENTS IN EUROPEAN COMMUNITY ENVIRONMENTAL LAW

Second edition

Edited by

PHILIPPE SANDS AND
PAOLO GALIZZI

CAMBRIDGE
UNIVERSITY PRESS

CAMBRIDGE UNIVERSITY PRESS
Cambridge, New York, Melbourne, Madrid, Cape Town, Singapore, São Paulo

Cambridge University Press
The Edinburgh Building, Cambridge CB2 2RU, UK

Published in the United States of America by Cambridge University Press, New York

www.cambridge.org
Information on this title: www.cambridge.org/9780521540612

First edition published by Manchester University Press 1995
This edition published by Cambridge University Press 2006

Printed in the United Kingdom at the University Press, Cambridge

A catalogue record for this publication is available from the British Library

ISBN-13   978-0-521-83303-5 hardback
ISBN-10   0-521-83303-5 hardback

ISBN-13   978-0-521-54061-2 paperback
ISBN-10   0-521-54061-5 paperback

To my students, past, present and future
PS

To my mentors, past, present and future
(Nerina Boschiero, Tullio Treves, Tullio Scovazzi, Philippe Sands,
Stephen Girvin, Erika Szyszczak, Zen Makuch and Roger Goebel)
PG

CONTENTS

PREFACE

The protection of the environment is arguably one of the most successful policies in the European integration project. When originally conceived, the instrument establishing the European Economic Community included no specific provision on the environment. However, this did not prevent the Community's institutions from adopting environmental legislation as early as the 1970s. The original Treaty of Rome has been amended several times since its adoption and the protection of the environment is now one of the key policies of the European Community.

EC environmental legislation has grown over the years and now represents one of the most complex and challenging legal regimes for the protection of the environment. The significant body of legislation which now exists has given rise to numerous disputes over its application and interpretation.

This collection of documents in EC environmental law comprises extracts from those EC Treaties, Regulations, Directives, Decisions and other acts of EC institutions which are essential for anyone interested in environmental protection in the law of the Member States and at the EC and international levels. This collection aims to provide practitioners, scholars and students with the essentials necessary to understand, advise upon and apply this body of law. The main objective of the volume is to bring together the principal documents in an accessible form that provides the reader with the key information on the relevant areas of law. This book also serves as a companion to the second edition of Philippe Sands' textbook *Principles of International Environmental Law* (2nd edition, 2003, Cambridge University Press) and to Sands and Galizzi's *Documents in International Environmental Law* (2nd edition, 2004, Cambridge University Press).

This volume builds on a previous edition published in 1995 by Manchester University Press and edited by Philippe Sands and Richard Tarasofsky. Since then, the EC Treaty has been fundamentally amended on several occasions and numerous pieces of new legislation have been adopted. This volume represents an up-to-date collection of the most important documents in EC environmental law and, like its predecessor, aims to make easily accessible the text and key information on the documents reproduced. The documents reproduced in this volume are available on the web, but we nevertheless consider that advantages may be obtained in reproducing them in a single volume. Books can follow us around. Over time we can highlight key provisions, insert notes, and compare texts wherever we are and as much as we like.

The success and demand for similar volumes in other fields testifies that books still have a fundamental role to play in the internet era.

   This volume does not purport to be comprehensive and the documents selected are those that we felt are of more general interest and that we use more frequently in our courses on EC environmental law and in our professional life. Making a selection of the documents to be included did require some difficult choices, but this was necessary to produce a volume that we hope will be easily manageable, suitable and accessible to a wide audience.[1] The documents that have been included reflect a wide spectrum of approaches taken in the development of EC environmental law. They address each of the main environmental media and sectors (air, water, flora and fauna) and particular sources of pollution (hazardous substances and wastes), some of the rules governing the economic aspects of the Community legal order and some of the emerging techniques for applying environmental standards (for example, environmental impact assessment, access to environmental information). Each document is presented according to the same format and is introduced with a short Editorial Note, which summarises the main provisions of the instrument and places it in its wider context. The legal status of the legislative acts, including amendments, is generally current to December 2004. If available, consolidated versions of documents have been provided.[2] In other cases, the original text of a document and the text of amendments have been reproduced. For most of the documents, the entirety of the text is provided. In some cases, however, we have provided only those extracts of instruments which relate specifically to environmental matters (e.g. the EC Treaty as amended) or we have omitted annexes or appendices which include detailed technical arrangements of less interest to the general reader or which do not relate expressly to environmental issues.

Acknowledgements

Many people deserve recognition for the successful conclusion of this project. We would like to recognize the assistance provided by Angela Williams, and also Zen Makuch and Karen McDonald. Our colleagues in the Department of Environmental Science and Technology at Imperial College (and particularly the then Head of Department, Professor John Beddington) and at the Faculty of Law at University College London (in particular Professors Jeffrey Jowell and Richard Macrory and Dr Jane Holder) have provided strong support and encouragement, for which we are enormously grateful. We extend our thanks also to Fordham University School of Law in New York City, and in particular to Professors Sheila Foster and Roger Goebel, to Associate Dean Matthew Diller and to Dean William Treanor, to Peter Davies at

---

[1] A complete list of EC environmental legislation in force and the full text of such legislation can be found at http://www.europa.eu.int/eur-lex/en/lif/ind/en_analytical_index_15.html.

[2] Consolidated versions of the various documents are provided by the Community's institutions purely as a documentation tool and the institutions do not assume any liability for their contents.

the University of Nottingham, and to all the students who have taken our courses on EC and international environmental law for their forbearance and insights. Thanks also for the generous support and assistance received from the EU Sixth European Framework Research Programme and its Marie Curie Fellowship.

A special thanks is owed to Cambridge University Press and more specifically to Finola O'Sullivan and Jane O'Regan for their support, help and patience (particularly for this volume) throughout this project.

Last but not least, this collection could not have been published without the assistance of Edem Kuenyehia and Natalia Schiffrin, unique friends and sources of constant inspiration and joy in our lives.

Needless to say, such errors and omissions as might have crept in remain the full responsibility of the co-editors.

PHILIPPE SANDS
University College London

PAOLO GALIZZI
Imperial College London and Fordham University School of Law New York

February 2005

PART I

General principles of EC environmental law

Treaty establishing the European Community 27 March 1957 (extracts; as amended by the 1986 Single European Act, the 1992 Treaty on European Union, the 1997 Treaty of Amsterdam and the 2001 Treaty of Nice)

Editorial note

The Treaty establishing the European Community (formerly European Economic Community, EEC) was designed to create a common market among Western European Member States. When adopted in 1957, it included no rules on environmental protection. The Treaty has been amended several times: it was amended in 1986 by the Single European Act (SEA) and in 1992 by the Treaty on the European Union (TEU). It was further amended in 1997 and in 2001 (respectively by the Treaty of Amsterdam and the Treaty of Nice). The EC Treaty has also been amended by the various accession treaties following the several enlargements of the Community, which over the years has expanded from its original six founding Members to the current twenty-five Member States. Of particular significance are the changes to the Treaty made as a result of the Treaty on the Accession of ten new Member States, which was signed on 16 April 2003 and came into force on 1 May 2004.

In particular, the SEA, adopted in February 1986 and entered into force on 1 July 1987, included new specific rules on environmental protection (the then Title VII of the EEC Treaty), which were further expanded upon by the Treaty on European Union, signed on 7 February 1992 and entered into force on 1 November 1993. The TEU, also known as the Maastricht Treaty, changed the name of the European Economic Community to simply 'the European Community'. It also introduced new forms of co-operation between the Member States – for example on defence, and in the area of 'justice and home affairs'. By adding this inter-governmental co-operation to the existing 'Community' system, the Maastricht Treaty created a new structure with three so-called 'pillars' which is political as well as economic, known as the European Union (EU). The Treaty of Amsterdam, signed on 2 October 1997, entered into force on 1 May 1999, amended and renumbered the EU and EC Treaties (for example, Articles 130r, 130s and 130t, the three provisions on the Title on the Environment, have respectively become Articles 174, 175 and 176). The Treaty of Nice, signed on 26 February 2001, entered into force on 1 February 2003.

The EC Treaty will be superseded by the Treaty establishing a Constitution for Europe adopted at an Intergovernmental Conference by the Heads of States and Governments of the Member States of the European Union on 18 June 2004. The final text of the Treaty establishing a Constitution for Europe was signed in Rome on 29 October 2004 and will then be subject to ratification (parliamentary approval and/or referendum) by the twenty-five Member States of the Union. If approved by all the Member States, the Treaty will enter into force on 1 November 2006.

The EC Treaty prohibits, subject to certain qualifications, quantitative restrictions on imports from Member States and measures having equivalent effect (Articles 23–25 and 28). Quantitative restrictions on exports are also prohibited between Member States (Article 29). All these provisions are subject to exceptions based on the protection of the health and life of humans, animals or plants, so long as such measures do not arbitrarily discriminate or act as a disguised restriction to trade (Article 30). EC rules on competition specifically prohibit any practice which has as its object or effect 'the prevention, restriction or distortion of competition' (Article 81), and the abuse by an undertaking of its dominant position is prohibited if trade between Member States is affected (Article 82). The Treaty also prohibits State aids (subsidies) which distort or threaten to distort competition, but certain exceptions are allowed (Article 87).

The SEA introduced specific provisions relating to the protection of the environment which, as mentioned earlier, have been further expanded upon by the subsequent amending treaties. Article 2 now specifies that the Community shall have as its task, *inter alia*, the promotion of 'balanced and sustainable development of economic activities' and of 'a high level of protection and improvement of the quality of the environment'. For this purpose, the Treaty specifically recognises that the Community's activities include 'a policy in the sphere of the environment' (Article 3(l)). The principles of subsidiarity and proportionality shall guide the Community action (Article 5). Article 6 requires that 'Environmental protection requirements must be integrated into the definition and implementation of the Community policies' for the promotion of sustainable development. Prohibitions or restrictions on imports and exports may be justified under Article 30, *inter alia*, for 'the protection of health and life of humans, animals or plants'. Article 95 allows Member States to enact stricter national measures following harmonisation legislation for the protection of the environment subject to specific conditions and procedures. Article 174(1) specifies the objectives of the Community's environmental policy: preservation, protection and improvement of the quality of the environment; protection of human health; prudent and rational utilisation of natural resources; promotion of international measures to deal with regional and global environmental problems. The Community's action shall aim at a high level of protection and shall be based on the precautionary principle, the principle of prevention, the proximity principle and the polluter pays principle (Article 174(2)). The Community's policy shall take into account, *inter alia*, available scientific and technical data and the costs of action (or inaction) according to

Article 174(3). The Community's environmental legislation shall be adopted by qualified majority under the so-called co-decision procedure (Article 175(1)), although in specified cases unanimity is still required (Article 175(2)). Member States may adopt more stringent protective measures, if compatible with the Treaty (Article 176).

This section reproduces the text of the EC Treaty as amended by the SEA, the TEU, the Treaty of Amsterdam and the Treaty of Nice, which has been in force from 1 February 2003 (Document 1).

It is followed by selected provisions from the 1957 EC Treaty as modified by the Treaty of Amsterdam (Document 1A), the 1957 EC Treaty as modified by the TEU (Document 1B) and the EEC Treaty as modified by the SEA (Document 1C). These provisions have been reproduced to allow the reader to compare the relevant provisions and assess the amendments, and also to provide the necessary background for understanding the legal basis upon which the European Court of Justice has interpreted and applied the law from time to time. Extracts from the Treaty establishing a Constitution for Europe have also been included (Document 1D).

With effect from 1 May 2004 there are twenty-five members of the European Community: Austria, Belgium, Cyprus, Czech Republic, Denmark, Estonia, Germany, Greece, Finland, France, Hungary, Ireland, Italy, Latvia, Lithuania, Luxembourg, Malta, The Netherlands, Poland, Portugal, Slovakia, Slovenia, Spain, Sweden, United Kingdom.

Source: C/235/40 Official Journal of the European Communities 24.12.2002

Treaty establishing the European Community 27 March 1957 (extracts; as amended by the 1986 Single European Act, the 1992 Treaty on European Union, the 1997 Treaty of Amsterdam and the 2001 Treaty of Nice)

Preamble

[*The Heads of State,*]

Determined to lay the foundations of an ever closer union among the peoples of Europe,

Resolved to ensure the economic and social progress of their countries by common action to eliminate the barriers which divide Europe,

Affirming as the essential objective of their efforts the constant improvements of the living and working conditions of their peoples,

Recognising that the removal of existing obstacles calls for concerted action in order to guarantee steady expansion, balanced trade and fair competition,

Anxious to strengthen the unity of their economies and to ensure their harmonious development by reducing the differences existing between the various regions and the backwardness of the less favoured regions,

Desiring to contribute, by means of a common commercial policy, to the progressive abolition of restrictions on international trade,

Intending to confirm the solidarity which binds Europe and the overseas countries and desiring to ensure the development of their prosperity, in accordance with the principles of the Charter of the United Nations,

Resolved by thus pooling their resources to preserve and strengthen peace and liberty, and calling upon the other peoples of Europe who share their ideal to join in their efforts,

Determined to promote the development of the highest possible level of knowledge for their peoples through a wide access to education and through its continuous updating,

Have decided to create a *EUROPEAN COMMUNITY* and to this end . . . have agreed as follows:

Part one
Principles

Article 1

By this Treaty, the *High Contracting Parties* establish among themselves a *European Community*.

Article 2

The Community shall have as its task, by establishing a common market and an economic and monetary union and by implementing common policies or activities referred to in Articles 3 and 4, to promote throughout the Community a harmonious, balanced and sustainable development of economic activities, a high level of employment and of social protection, equality between men and women, sustainable and non-inflationary growth, a high degree of competitiveness and convergence of economic performance, a high level of protection and improvement of the quality of the environment, the raising of the standard of living and quality of life, and economic and social cohesion and solidarity among Member States.

Article 3

1. For the purposes set out in Article 2, the activities of the Community shall include, as provided in this Treaty and in accordance with the timetable set out therein:

(a) the prohibition, as between Member States, of customs duties and quantitative restrictions on the import and export of goods, and of all other measures having equivalent effect;
(b) a common commercial policy;
(c) an internal market characterised by the abolition, as between Member States, of obstacles to the free movement of goods, persons, services and capital;
(d) measures concerning the entry and movement of persons as provided for in Title IV;

(e) a common policy in the sphere of agriculture and fisheries;

(f) a common policy in the sphere of transport;

(g) a system ensuring that competition in the internal market is not distorted;

(h) the approximation of the laws of Member States to the extent required for the functioning of the common market;

 (i) the promotion of coordination between employment policies of the Member States with a view to enhancing their effectiveness by developing a coordinated strategy for employment;

 (j) a policy in the social sphere comprising a European Social Fund;

(k) the strengthening of economic and social cohesion;

 (l) a policy in the sphere of the environment;

(m) the strengthening of the competitiveness of Community industry;

(n) the promotion of research and technological development;

(o) encouragement for the establishment and development of trans-European networks;

(p) a contribution to the attainment of a high level of health protection;

(q) a contribution to education and training of quality and to the flowering of the cultures of the Member States;

(r) a policy in the sphere of development cooperation;

(s) the association of the overseas countries and territories in order to increase trade and promote jointly economic and social development;

(t) a contribution to the strengthening of consumer protection;

(u) measures in the spheres of energy, civil protection and tourism.

2. In all the activities referred to in this Article, the Community shall aim to eliminate inequalities, and to promote equality, between men and women.

Article 4

1. For the purposes set out in Article 2, the activities of the Member States and the Community shall include, as provided in this Treaty and in accordance with the timetable set out therein, the adoption of an economic policy which is based on the close coordination of Member States' economic policies, on the internal market and on the definition of common objectives, and conducted in accordance with the principle of an open market economy with free competition.

2. Concurrently with the foregoing, and as provided in this Treaty and in accordance with the timetable and the procedures set out therein, these activities shall include the irrevocable fixing of exchange rates leading to the introduction of a single currency, the ecu, and the definition and conduct of a single monetary policy and exchange-rate policy the primary objective of both of which shall be to maintain price stability and, without prejudice to this objective, to support the general economic policies in the Community, in accordance with the principle of an open market economy with free competition.

3. These activities of the Member States and the Community shall entail compliance with the following guiding principles: stable prices, sound public finances and monetary conditions and a sustainable balance of payments.

Article 5

The Community shall act within the limits of the powers conferred upon it by this Treaty and of the objectives assigned to it therein.

In areas which do not fall within its exclusive competence, the Community shall take action, in accordance with the principle of subsidiarity, only if and in so far as the objectives of the proposed action cannot be sufficiently achieved by the Member States and can therefore, by reason of the scale or effects of the proposed action, be better achieved by the Community. Any action by the Community shall not go beyond what is necessary to achieve the objectives of this Treaty.

Article 6

Environmental protection requirements must be integrated into the definition and implementation of the Community policies and activities referred to in Article 3, in particular with a view to promoting sustainable development.

Article 7

1. The tasks entrusted to the Community shall be carried out by the following institutions:

— a European Parliament,
— a Council,
— a Commission,
— a Court of Justice,
— a Court of Auditors.

Each institution shall act within the limits of the powers conferred upon it by this Treaty.

2. The Council and the Commission shall be assisted by an Economic and Social Committee and a Committee of the Regions acting in an advisory capacity.

Article 8

A European system of central banks (hereinafter referred to as 'ESCB') and a European Central Bank (hereinafter referred to as 'ECB') shall be established in accordance with the procedures laid down in this Treaty; they shall act within the limits of the powers conferred upon them by this Treaty and by the Statute of the ESCB and of the ECB (hereinafter referred to as 'Statute of the ESCB') annexed thereto.

Article 9

A European Investment Bank is hereby established, which shall act within the limits of the powers conferred upon it by this Treaty and the Statute annexed thereto.

Article 10

Member States shall take all appropriate measures, whether general or particular, to ensure fulfilment of the obligations arising out of this Treaty or resulting from action taken by the institutions of the Community. They shall facilitate the achievement of the Community's tasks.

They shall abstain from any measure which could jeopardise the attainment of the objectives of this Treaty.

Article 11

1. Member States which intend to establish enhanced cooperation between themselves in one of the areas referred to in this Treaty shall address a request to the Commission, which may submit a proposal to the Council to that effect. In the event of the Commission not submitting a proposal, it shall inform the Member States concerned of the reasons for not doing so.

2. Authorisation to establish enhanced cooperation as referred to in paragraph 1 shall be granted, in compliance with Articles 43 to 45 of the Treaty on European Union, by the Council, acting by a qualified majority on a proposal from the Commission and after consulting the European Parliament. When enhanced cooperation relates to an area covered by the procedure referred to in Article 251 of this Treaty, the assent of the European Parliament shall be required.

A member of the Council may request that the matter be referred to the European Council. After that matter has been raised before the European Council, the Council may act in accordance with the first subparagraph of this paragraph.

3. The acts and decisions necessary for the implementation of enhanced cooperation activities shall be subject to all the relevant provisions of this Treaty, save as otherwise provided in this Article and in Articles 43 to 45 of the Treaty on European Union.

Article 11a

Any Member State which wishes to participate in enhanced cooperation established in accordance with Article 11 shall notify its intention to the Council and to the Commission, which shall give an opinion to the Council within three months of the date of receipt of that notification. Within four months of the date of receipt of that notification, the Commission shall take a decision on it, and on such specific arrangements as it may deem necessary.

Article 12

Within the scope of application of this Treaty, and without prejudice to any special provisions contained therein, any discrimination on grounds of nationality shall be prohibited. The Council, acting in accordance with the procedure referred to in Article 251, may adopt rules designed to prohibit such discrimination.

Article 13

1. Without prejudice to the other provisions of this Treaty and within the limits of the powers conferred by it upon the Community, the Council, acting unanimously on a proposal from the Commission and after consulting the European Parliament, may take appropriate action to combat discrimination based on sex, racial or ethnic origin, religion or belief, disability, age or sexual orientation.

2. By way of derogation from paragraph 1, when the Council adopts Community incentive measures, excluding any harmonisation of the laws and regulations of the Member States, to support action taken by the Member States in order to contribute to the achievement of the objectives referred to in paragraph 1, it shall act in accordance with the procedure referred to in Article 251.

Article 14

1. The Community shall adopt measures with the aim of progressively establishing the internal market over a period expiring on 31 December 1992, in accordance with the provisions of this Article and of Articles 15, 26, 47(2), 49, 80, 93 and 95 and without prejudice to the other provisions of this Treaty.

2. The internal market shall comprise an area without internal frontiers in which the free movement of goods, persons, services and capital is ensured in accordance with the provisions of this Treaty.

3. The Council, acting by a qualified majority on a proposal from the Commission, shall determine the guidelines and conditions necessary to ensure balanced progress in all the sectors concerned.

Article 15

When drawing up its proposals with a view to achieving the objectives set out in Article 14, the Commission shall take into account the extent of the effort that certain economies showing differences in development will have to sustain during the period of establishment of the internal market and it may propose appropriate provisions.

If these provisions take the form of derogations, they must be of a temporary nature and must cause the least possible disturbance to the functioning of the common market.

Article 16

Without prejudice to Articles 73, 86 and 87, and given the place occupied by services of general economic interest in the shared values of the Union as well as their role in promoting social and territorial cohesion, the Community and the Member States, each within their respective powers and within the scope of application of this Treaty, shall take care that such services operate on the basis of principles and conditions which enable them to fulfil their missions.
[...]

Part three
Community policies

Title I
Free movement of goods

Article 23

1. The Community shall be based upon a customs union which shall cover all trade in goods and which shall involve the prohibition between Member States of customs duties on imports and exports and of all charges having equivalent effect, and the adoption of a common customs tariff in their relations with third countries.

2. The provisions of Article 25 and of Chapter 2 of this title shall apply to products originating in Member States and to products coming from third countries which are in free circulation in Member States.

Article 24

Products coming from a third country shall be considered to be in free circulation in a Member State if the import formalities have been complied with and any customs duties or charges having equivalent effect which are payable have been levied in that Member State, and if they have not benefited from a total or partial drawback of such duties or charges.

Chapter 1
The customs union

Article 25

Customs duties on imports and exports and charges having equivalent effect shall be prohibited between Member States. This prohibition shall also apply to customs duties of a fiscal nature.

Article 26

Common Customs Tariff duties shall be fixed by the Council acting by a qualified majority on a proposal from the Commission.

Article 27

In carrying out the tasks entrusted to it under this chapter the Commission shall be guided by:

(a) the need to promote trade between Member States and third countries;
(b) developments in conditions of competition within the Community in so far as they lead to an improvement in the competitive capacity of undertakings;
(c) the requirements of the Community as regards the supply of raw materials and semi-finished goods; in this connection the Commission shall take care to avoid distorting conditions of competition between Member States in respect of finished goods;
(d) the need to avoid serious disturbances in the economies of Member States and to ensure rational development of production and an expansion of consumption within the Community.

Chapter 2
Prohibition of quantitative restrictions between Member States

Article 28

Quantitative restrictions on imports and all measures having equivalent effect shall be prohibited between Member States.

Article 29

Quantitative restrictions on exports, and all measures having equivalent effect, shall be prohibited between Member States.

Article 30

The provisions of Articles 28 and 29 shall not preclude prohibitions or restrictions on imports, exports or goods in transit justified on grounds of public morality, public policy or public security; the protection of health and life of humans, animals or plants; the protection of national treasures possessing artistic, historic or archaeological value; or the protection of industrial and commercial property. Such prohibitions or restrictions shall not, however, constitute a means of arbitrary discrimination or a disguised restriction on trade between Member States.

Article 31

1. Member States shall adjust any State monopolies of a commercial character so as to ensure that no discrimination regarding the conditions under which goods are procured and marketed exists between nationals of Member States.

The provisions of this Article shall apply to any body through which a Member State, in law or in fact, either directly or indirectly supervises, determines or appreciably influences imports or exports between Member States. These provisions shall likewise apply to monopolies delegated by the State to others.

2. Member States shall refrain from introducing any new measure which is contrary to the principles laid down in paragraph 1 or which restricts the scope of the articles dealing with the prohibition of customs duties and quantitative restrictions between Member States.

3. If a State monopoly of a commercial character has rules which are designed to make it easier to dispose of agricultural products or obtain for them the best return, steps should be taken in applying the rules contained in this article to ensure equivalent safeguards for the employment and standard of living of the producers concerned.
[...]

Title VI
Common rules on competition, taxation and approximation of laws

Chapter 1
Rules on competition

Section 1
Rules applying to undertakings

Article 81

1. The following shall be prohibited as incompatible with the common market: all agreements between undertakings, decisions by associations of undertakings and concerted practices which may affect trade between Member States and which have as their object or effect the prevention, restriction or distortion of competition within the common market, and in particular those which:

(a) directly or indirectly fix purchase or selling prices or any other trading conditions;
(b) limit or control production, markets, technical development, or investment;
(c) share markets or sources of supply;
(d) apply dissimilar conditions to equivalent transactions with other trading parties, thereby placing them at a competitive disadvantage;
(e) make the conclusion of contracts subject to acceptance by the other parties of supplementary obligations which, by their nature or according to commercial usage, have no connection with the subject of such contracts.

2. Any agreements or decisions prohibited pursuant to this article shall be automatically void.

3. The provisions of paragraph 1 may, however, be declared inapplicable in the case of:

– any agreement or category of agreements between undertakings,
– any decision or category of decisions by associations of undertakings,
– any concerted practice or category of concerted practices,

which contributes to improving the production or distribution of goods or to promoting technical or economic progress, while allowing consumers a fair share of the resulting benefit, and which does not:

(a) impose on the undertakings concerned restrictions which are not indispensable to the attainment of these objectives;
(b) afford such undertakings the possibility of eliminating competition in respect of a substantial part of the products in question.

Article 82

Any abuse by one or more undertakings of a dominant position within the common market or in a substantial part of it shall be prohibited as incompatible with the common market in so far as it may affect trade between Member States. Such abuse may, in particular, consist in:

(a) directly or indirectly imposing unfair purchase or selling prices or other unfair trading conditions;
(b) limiting production, markets or technical development to the prejudice of consumers;
(c) applying dissimilar conditions to equivalent transactions with other trading parties, thereby placing them at a competitive disadvantage;
(d) making the conclusion of contracts subject to acceptance by the other parties of supplementary obligations which, by their nature or according to commercial usage, have no connection with the subject of such contracts.

Article 83

1. The appropriate regulations or directives to give effect to the principles set out in Articles 81 and 82 shall be laid down by the Council, acting by a qualified majority on a proposal from the Commission and after consulting the European Parliament.

2. The regulations or directives referred to in paragraph 1 shall be designed in particular:

(a) to ensure compliance with the prohibitions laid down in Article 81(1) and in Article 82 by making provision for fines and periodic penalty payments;
(b) to lay down detailed rules for the application of Article 81(3), taking into account the need to ensure effective supervision on the one hand, and to simplify administration to the greatest possible extent on the other;
(c) to define, if need be, in the various branches of the economy, the scope of the provisions of Articles 81 and 82;
(d) to define the respective functions of the Commission and of the Court of Justice in applying the provisions laid down in this paragraph;
(e) to determine the relationship between national laws and the provisions contained in this section or adopted pursuant to this article.

Article 84

Until the entry into force of the provisions adopted in pursuance of Article 83, the authorities in Member States shall rule on the admissibility of agreements, decisions and concerted practices and on abuse of a dominant position in the common market in accordance with the law of their country and with the provisions of Article 81, in particular paragraph 3, and of Article 82.

Article 85

1. Without prejudice to Article 84, the Commission shall ensure the application of the principles laid down in Articles 81 and 82. On application by a Member State or on its own initiative, and in cooperation with the competent authorities in the Member States, which shall give it their assistance, the Commission shall investigate cases of suspected infringement of these principles. If it finds that there has been an infringement, it shall propose appropriate measures to bring it to an end.

2. If the infringement is not brought to an end, the Commission shall record such infringement of the principles in a reasoned decision. The Commission may publish its decision and authorise Member States to take the measures, the conditions and details of which it shall determine, needed to remedy the situation.

Article 86

1. In the case of public undertakings and undertakings to which Member States grant special or exclusive rights, Member States shall neither enact nor maintain in force any measure contrary to the rules contained in this Treaty, in particular to those rules provided for in Article 12 and Articles 81 to 89.

2. Undertakings entrusted with the operation of services of general economic interest or having the character of a revenue-producing monopoly shall be subject to the rules contained in this Treaty, in particular to the rules on competition, in so far as the application of such rules does not obstruct the performance, in law or in fact, of the particular tasks assigned to them. The development of trade must not be affected to such an extent as would be contrary to the interests of the Community.

3. The Commission shall ensure the application of the provisions of this Article and shall, where necessary, address appropriate directives or decisions to Member States.

Section 2
Aids granted by States

Article 87

1. Save as otherwise provided in this Treaty, any aid granted by a Member State or through State resources in any form whatsoever which distorts or threatens to distort competition by favouring certain undertakings or the production of certain goods

shall, in so far as it affects trade between Member States, be incompatible with the common market.

2. The following shall be compatible with the common market:

(a) aid having a social character, granted to individual consumers, provided that such aid is granted without discrimination related to the origin of the products concerned;
(b) aid to make good the damage caused by natural disasters or exceptional occurrences;
(c) aid granted to the economy of certain areas of the Federal Republic of Germany affected by the division of Germany, in so far as such aid is required in order to compensate for the economic disadvantages caused by that division.

3. The following may be considered to be compatible with the common market:

(a) aid to promote the economic development of areas where the standard of living is abnormally low or where there is serious underemployment;
(b) aid to promote the execution of an important project of common European interest or to remedy a serious disturbance in the economy of a Member State;
(c) aid to facilitate the development of certain economic activities or of certain economic areas, where such aid does not adversely affect trading conditions to an extent contrary to the common interest;
(d) aid to promote culture and heritage conservation where such aid does not affect trading conditions and competition in the Community to an extent that is contrary to the common interest;
(e) such other categories of aid as may be specified by decision of the Council acting by a qualified majority on a proposal from the Commission.

Article 88

1. The Commission shall, in cooperation with Member States, keep under constant review all systems of aid existing in those States. It shall propose to the latter any appropriate measures required by the progressive development or by the functioning of the common market.

2. If, after giving notice to the parties concerned to submit their comments, the Commission finds that aid granted by a State or through State resources is not compatible with the common market having regard to Article 87, or that such aid is being misused, it shall decide that the State concerned shall abolish or alter such aid within a period of time to be determined by the Commission.

If the State concerned does not comply with this decision within the prescribed time, the Commission or any other interested State may, in derogation from the provisions of Articles 226 and 227, refer the matter to the Court of Justice direct.

On application by a Member State, the Council may, acting unanimously, decide that aid which that State is granting or intends to grant shall be considered to be compatible with the common market, in derogation from the provisions of Article 87 or from the regulations provided for in Article 89, if such a decision is justified by exceptional circumstances. If, as regards the aid in question, the Commission has already initiated the procedure provided for in the first subparagraph of this paragraph, the fact that the State concerned has made its application to the Council shall have the effect of suspending that procedure until the Council has made its attitude known.

If, however, the Council has not made its attitude known within three months of the said application being made, the Commission shall give its decision on the case.

3. The Commission shall be informed, in sufficient time to enable it to submit its comments, of any plans to grant or alter aid. If it considers that any such plan is not compatible with the common market having regard to Article 87, it shall without delay initiate the procedure provided for in paragraph 2.

The Member State concerned shall not put its proposed measures into effect until this procedure has resulted in a final decision.

Article 89

The Council, acting by a qualified majority on a proposal from the Commission and after consulting the European Parliament, may make any appropriate regulations for the application of Articles 87 and 88 and may in particular determine the conditions in which Article 88(3) shall apply and the categories of aid exempted from this procedure.

Chapter 2
Tax provisions

Article 90

No Member State shall impose, directly or indirectly, on the products of other Member States any internal taxation of any kind in excess of that imposed directly or indirectly on similar domestic products.

Furthermore, no Member State shall impose on the products of other Member States any internal taxation of such a nature as to afford indirect protection to other products.

Article 91

Where products are exported to the territory of any Member State, any repayment of internal taxation shall not exceed the internal taxation imposed on them whether directly or indirectly.

Article 92

In the case of charges other than turnover taxes, excise duties and other forms of indirect taxation, remissions and repayments in respect of exports to other Member

States may not be granted and countervailing charges in respect of imports from Member States may not be imposed unless the measures contemplated have been previously approved for a limited period by the Council acting by a qualified majority on a proposal from the Commission.

Article 93

The Council shall, acting unanimously on a proposal from the Commission and after consulting the European Parliament and the Economic and Social Committee, adopt provisions for the harmonisation of legislation concerning turnover taxes, excise duties and other forms of indirect taxation to the extent that such harmonisation is necessary to ensure the establishment and the functioning of the internal market within the time limit laid down in Article 14.

Chapter 3
Approximation of laws

Article 94

The Council shall, acting unanimously on a proposal from the Commission and after consulting the European Parliament and the Economic and Social Committee, issue directives for the approximation of such laws, regulations or administrative provisions of the Member States as directly affect the establishment or functioning of the common market.

Article 95

1. By way of derogation from Article 94 and save where otherwise provided in this Treaty, the following provisions shall apply for the achievement of the objectives set out in Article 14. The Council shall, acting in accordance with the procedure referred to in Article 251 and after consulting the Economic and Social Committee, adopt the measures for the approximation of the provisions laid down by law, regulation or administrative action in Member States which have as their object the establishment and functioning of the internal market.

2. Paragraph 1 shall not apply to fiscal provisions, to those relating to the free movement of persons nor to those relating to the rights and interests of employed persons.

3. The Commission, in its proposals envisaged in paragraph 1 concerning health, safety, environmental protection and consumer protection, will take as a base a high level of protection, taking account in particular of any new development based on scientific facts. Within their respective powers, the European Parliament and the Council will also seek to achieve this objective.

4. If, after the adoption by the Council or by the Commission of a harmonisation measure, a Member State deems it necessary to maintain national provisions on

grounds of major needs referred to in Article 30, or relating to the protection of the environment or the working environment, it shall notify the Commission of these provisions as well as the grounds for maintaining them.

5. Moreover, without prejudice to paragraph 4, if, after the adoption by the Council or by the Commission of a harmonisation measure, a Member State deems it necessary to introduce national provisions based on new scientific evidence relating to the protection of the environment or the working environment on grounds of a problem specific to that Member State arising after the adoption of the harmonisation measure, it shall notify the Commission of the envisaged provisions as well as the grounds for introducing them.

6. The Commission shall, within six months of the notifications as referred to in paragraphs 4 and 5, approve or reject the national provisions involved after having verified whether or not they are a means of arbitrary discrimination or a disguised restriction on trade between Member States and whether or not they shall constitute an obstacle to the functioning of the internal market.

In the absence of a decision by the Commission within this period the national provisions referred to in paragraphs 4 and 5 shall be deemed to have been approved.

When justified by the complexity of the matter and in the absence of danger for human health, the Commission may notify the Member State concerned that the period referred to in this paragraph may be extended for a further period of up to six months.

7. When, pursuant to paragraph 6, a Member State is authorised to maintain or introduce national provisions derogating from a harmonisation measure, the Commission shall immediately examine whether to propose an adaptation to that measure.

8. When a Member State raises a specific problem on public health in a field which has been the subject of prior harmonisation measures, it shall bring it to the attention of the Commission which shall immediately examine whether to propose appropriate measures to the Council.

9. By way of derogation from the procedure laid down in Articles 226 and 227, the Commission and any Member State may bring the matter directly before the Court of Justice if it considers that another Member State is making improper use of the powers provided for in this Article.

10. The harmonisation measures referred to above shall, in appropriate cases, include a safeguard clause authorising the Member States to take, for one or more of the non-economic reasons referred to in Article 30, provisional measures subject to a Community control procedure.

Article 96

Where the Commission finds that a difference between the provisions laid down by law, regulation or administrative action in Member States is distorting the conditions of competition in the common market and that the resultant distortion needs to be eliminated, it shall consult the Member States concerned.

If such consultation does not result in an agreement eliminating the distortion in question, the Council shall, on a proposal from the Commission, acting by a qualified majority, issue the necessary directives.

The Commission and the Council may take any other appropriate measures provided for in this Treaty.

Article 97

1. Where there is a reason to fear that the adoption or amendment of a provision laid down by law, regulation or administrative action may cause distortion within the meaning of Article 96, a Member State desiring to proceed therewith shall consult the Commission. After consulting the Member States, the Commission shall recommend to the States concerned such measures as may be appropriate to avoid the distortion in question.

2. If a State desiring to introduce or amend its own provisions does not comply with the recommendation addressed to it by the Commission, other Member States shall not be required, pursuant to Article 96, to amend their own provisions in order to eliminate such distortion. If the Member State which has ignored the recommendation of the Commission causes distortion detrimental only to itself, the provisions of Article 96 shall not apply.

[...]

Title XVII
Economic and social cohesion

Article 158

In order to promote its overall harmonious development, the Community shall develop and pursue its actions leading to the strengthening of its economic and social cohesion. In particular, the Community shall aim at reducing disparities between the levels of development of the various regions and the backwardness of the least favoured regions or islands, including rural areas.

Article 159

Member States shall conduct their economic policies and shall coordinate them in such a way as, in addition, to attain the objectives set out in Article 158. The formulation and implementation of the Community's policies and actions and the implementation of the internal market shall take into account the objectives set out in Article 158 and shall contribute to their achievement. The Community shall also support the achievement of these objectives by the action it takes through the Structural Funds (European Agricultural Guidance and Guarantee Fund, Guidance Section; European Social Fund; European Regional Development Fund), the European Investment Bank and the other existing Financial Instruments.

The Commission shall submit a report to the European Parliament, the Council, the Economic and Social Committee and the Committee of the Regions every three years on the progress made towards achieving economic and social cohesion and on the manner in which the various means provided for in this Article have contributed to it. This report shall, if necessary, be accompanied by appropriate proposals.

If specific actions prove necessary outside the Funds and without prejudice to the measures decided upon within the framework of the other Community policies, such actions may be adopted by the Council acting in accordance with the procedure referred to in Article 251 and after consulting the Economic and Social Committee and the Committee of the Regions.

Article 160

The European Regional Development Fund is intended to help to redress the main regional imbalances in the Community through participation in the development and structural adjustment of regions whose development is lagging behind and in the conversion of declining industrial regions.

Article 161

Without prejudice to Article 162, the Council, acting unanimously on a proposal from the Commission and after obtaining the assent of the European Parliament and consulting the Economic and Social Committee and the Committee of the Regions, shall define the tasks, priority objectives and the organisation of the Structural Funds, which may involve grouping the Funds. The Council, acting by the same procedure, shall also define the general rules applicable to them and the provisions necessary to ensure their effectiveness and the coordination of the Funds with one another and with the other existing Financial Instruments. A Cohesion Fund set up by the Council in accordance with the same procedure shall provide a financial contribution to projects in the fields of environment and trans-European networks in the area of transport infrastructure.

From 1 January 2007, the Council shall act by a qualified majority on a proposal from the Commission after obtaining the assent of the European Parliament and after consulting the Economic and Social Committee and the Committee of the Regions if, by that date, the multiannual financial perspective applicable from 1 January 2007 and the Interinstitutional Agreement relating thereto have been adopted. If such is not the case, the procedure laid down by this paragraph shall apply from the date of their adoption.

Article 162

Implementing decisions relating to the European Regional Development Fund shall be taken by the Council, acting in accordance with the procedure referred to in Article 251 and after consulting the Economic and Social Committee and the Committee of the Regions. With regard to the European Agricultural Guidance and Guarantee Fund,

Guidance Section, and the European Social Fund, Articles 37 and 148 respectively shall continue to apply.

[...]

Title XIX
Environment

Article 174

1. Community policy on the environment shall contribute to pursuit of the following objectives:

– preserving, protecting and improving the quality of the environment,
– protecting human health,
– prudent and rational utilisation of natural resources,
– promoting measures at international level to deal with regional or worldwide environmental problems.

2. Community policy on the environment shall aim at a high level of protection taking into account the diversity of situations in the various regions of the Community. It shall be based on the precautionary principle and on the principles that preventive action should be taken, that environmental damage should as a priority be rectified at source and that the polluter should pay.

In this context, harmonisation measures answering environmental protection requirements shall include, where appropriate, a safeguard clause allowing Member States to take provisional measures, for non-economic environmental reasons, subject to a Community inspection procedure.

3. In preparing its policy on the environment, the Community shall take account of:

– available scientific and technical data,
– environmental conditions in the various regions of the Community,
– the potential benefits and costs of action or lack of action,
– the economic and social development of the Community as a whole and the balanced development of its regions.

4. Within their respective spheres of competence, the Community and the Member States shall cooperate with third countries and with the competent international organisations. The arrangements for Community cooperation may be the subject of agreements between the Community and the third parties concerned, which shall be negotiated and concluded in accordance with Article 300.

The previous subparagraph shall be without prejudice to Member States' competence to negotiate in international bodies and to conclude international agreements.

Article 175

1. The Council, acting in accordance with the procedure referred to in Article 251 and after consulting the Economic and Social Committee and the Committee of the Regions, shall decide what action is to be taken by the Community in order to achieve the objectives referred to in Article 174.

2. By way of derogation from the decision-making procedure provided for in paragraph 1 and without prejudice to Article 95, the Council, acting unanimously on a proposal from the Commission and after consulting the European Parliament, the Economic and Social Committee and the Committee of the Regions, shall adopt:

(a) provisions primarily of a fiscal nature;
(b) measures affecting:
  – town and country planning,
  – quantitative management of water resources or affecting, directly or indirectly, the availability of those resources,
  – land use, with the exception of waste management;
(c) measures significantly affecting a Member State's choice between different energy sources and the general structure of its energy supply.

The Council may, under the conditions laid down in the first subparagraph, define those matters referred to in this paragraph on which decisions are to be taken by a qualified majority.

3. In other areas, general action programmes setting out priority objectives to be attained shall be adopted by the Council, acting in accordance with the procedure referred to in Article 251 and after consulting the Economic and Social Committee and the Committee of the Regions. The Council, acting under the terms of paragraph 1 or paragraph 2 according to the case, shall adopt the measures necessary for the implementation of these programmes.

4. Without prejudice to certain measures of a Community nature, the Member States shall finance and implement the environment policy.

5. Without prejudice to the principle that the polluter should pay, if a measure based on the provisions of paragraph 1 involves costs deemed disproportionate for the public authorities of a Member State, the Council shall, in the act adopting that measure, lay down appropriate provisions in the form of:

– temporary derogations, and/or
– financial support from the Cohesion Fund set up pursuant to Article 161.

Article 176

The protective measures adopted pursuant to Article 175 shall not prevent any Member State from maintaining or introducing more stringent protective measures.

Such measures must be compatible with this Treaty. They shall be notified to the Commission.

[...]

1. Part six
General and final provisions

[...]

Article 300

1. Where this Treaty provides for the conclusion of agreements between the Community and one or more States or international organisations, the Commission shall make recommendations to the Council, which shall authorise the Commission to open the necessary negotiations. The Commission shall conduct these negotiations in consultation with special committees appointed by the Council to assist it in this task and within the framework of such directives as the Council may issue to it.

In exercising the powers conferred upon it by this paragraph, the Council shall act by a qualified majority, except in the cases where the first subparagraph of paragraph 2 provides that the Council shall act unanimously.

2. Subject to the powers vested in the Commission in this field, the signing, which may be accompanied by a decision on provisional application before entry into force, and the conclusion of the agreements shall be decided on by the Council, acting by a qualified majority on a proposal from the Commission. The Council shall act unanimously when the agreement covers a field for which unanimity is required for the adoption of internal rules and for the agreements referred to in Article 310.

By way of derogation from the rules laid down in paragraph 3, the same procedures shall apply for a decision to suspend the application of an agreement, and for the purpose of establishing the positions to be adopted on behalf of the Community in a body set up by an agreement, when that body is called upon to adopt decisions having legal effects, with the exception of decisions supplementing or amending the institutional framework of the agreement.

The European Parliament shall be immediately and fully informed of any decision under this paragraph concerning the provisional application or the suspension of agreements, or the establishment of the Community position in a body set up by an agreement.

3. The Council shall conclude agreements after consulting the European Parliament, except for the agreements referred to in Article 133(3), including cases where the agreement covers a field for which the procedure referred to in Article 251 or that referred to in Article 252 is required for the adoption of internal rules. The European Parliament shall deliver its opinion within a time limit which the Council may lay down according to the urgency of the matter. In the absence of an opinion within that time limit, the Council may act.

By way of derogation from the previous subparagraph, agreements referred to in Article 310, other agreements establishing a specific institutional framework by organising cooperation procedures, agreements having important budgetary implications for the Community and agreements entailing amendment of an act adopted under the procedure referred to in Article 251 shall be concluded after the assent of the European Parliament has been obtained.

The Council and the European Parliament may, in an urgent situation, agree upon a time limit for the assent.

4. When concluding an agreement, the Council may, by way of derogation from paragraph 2, authorise the Commission to approve modifications on behalf of the Community where the agreement provides for them to be adopted by a simplified procedure or by a body set up by the agreement; it may attach specific conditions to such authorisation.

5. When the Council envisages concluding an agreement which calls for amendments to this Treaty, the amendments must first be adopted in accordance with the procedure laid down in Article 48 of the Treaty on European Union.

6. The European Parliament, the Council, the Commission or a Member State may obtain the opinion of the Court of Justice as to whether an agreement envisaged is compatible with the provisions of this Treaty. Where the opinion of the Court of Justice is adverse, the agreement may enter into force only in accordance with Article 48 of the Treaty on European Union.

7. Agreements concluded under the conditions set out in this Article shall be binding on the institutions of the Community and on Member States.

Article 301

Where it is provided, in a common position or in a joint action adopted according to the provisions of the Treaty on European Union relating to the common foreign and security policy, for an action by the Community to interrupt or to reduce, in part or completely, economic relations with one or more third countries, the Council shall take the necessary urgent measures. The Council shall act by a qualified majority on a proposal from the Commission.

Article 302

It shall be for the Commission to ensure the maintenance of all appropriate relations with the organs of the United Nations and of its specialised agencies.

The Commission shall also maintain such relations as are appropriate with all international organisations.

Article 303

The Community shall establish all appropriate forms of cooperation with the Council of Europe.

Article 304

The Community shall establish close cooperation with the Organisation for Economic Cooperation and Development, the details of which shall be determined by common accord.
[...]

Article 307

The rights and obligations arising from agreements concluded before 1 January 1958 or, for acceding States, before the date of their accession, between one or more Member States on the one hand, and one or more third countries on the other, shall not be affected by the provisions of this Treaty.

To the extent that such agreements are not compatible with this Treaty, the Member State or States concerned shall take all appropriate steps to eliminate the incompatibilities established. Member States shall, where necessary, assist each other to this end and shall, where appropriate, adopt a common attitude.

In applying the agreements referred to in the first paragraph, Member States shall take into account the fact that the advantages accorded under this Treaty by each Member State form an integral part of the establishment of the Community and are thereby inseparably linked with the creation of common institutions, the conferring of powers upon them and the granting of the same advantages by all the other Member States.

Article 308

If action by the Community should prove necessary to attain, in the course of the operation of the common market, one of the objectives of the Community, and this Treaty has not provided the necessary powers, the Council shall, acting unanimously on a proposal from the Commission and after consulting the European Parliament, take the appropriate measures.
[...]

Article 310

The Community may conclude with one or more States or international organisations agreements establishing an association involving reciprocal rights and obligations, common action and special procedure.
[...]

EC Treaty, incorporating amendments introduced by the Treaty of Amsterdam, the TEU and the SEA (extracts; superseded by the entry into force of the Treaty of Nice on 1 February 2003)

Part one
Principles

Article 1 (ex Article 1)

By this Treaty, the *High Contracting Parties* establish among themselves a *European Community*.

Article 2 (ex Article 2)

The Community shall have as its task, by establishing a common market and an economic and monetary union and by implementing common policies or activities referred to in Articles 3 and 4, to promote throughout the Community a harmonious, balanced and sustainable development of economic activities, a high level of employment and of social protection, equality between men and women, sustainable and non-inflationary growth, a high degree of competitiveness and convergence of economic performance, a high level of protection and improvement of the quality of the environment, the raising of the standard of living and quality of life, and economic and social cohesion and solidarity among Member States.

Article 3 (ex Article 3)

1. For the purposes set out in Article 2, the activities of the Community shall include, as provided in this Treaty and in accordance with the timetable set out therein:

(a) the prohibition, as between Member States, of customs duties and quantitative restrictions on the import and export of goods, and of all other measures having equivalent effect;
(b) a common commercial policy;
(c) an internal market characterised by the abolition, as between Member States, of obstacles to the free movement of goods, persons, services and capital;
(d) measures concerning the entry and movement of persons as provided for in Title IV;

(e) a common policy in the sphere of agriculture and fisheries;
(f) a common policy in the sphere of transport;
(g) a system ensuring that competition in the internal market is not distorted;
(h) the approximation of the laws of Member States to the extent required for the functioning of the common market;
(i) the promotion of coordination between employment policies of the Member States with a view to enhancing their effectiveness by developing a coordinated strategy for employment;
(j) a policy in the social sphere comprising a European Social Fund;
(k) the strengthening of economic and social cohesion;
(l) a policy in the sphere of the environment;
(m) the strengthening of the competitiveness of Community industry;
(n) the promotion of research and technological development;
(o) encouragement for the establishment and development of trans-European networks;
(p) a contribution to the attainment of a high level of health protection;
(q) a contribution to education and training of quality and to the flowering of the cultures of the Member States;
(r) a policy in the sphere of development cooperation;
(s) the association of the overseas countries and territories in order to increase trade and promote jointly economic and social development;
(t) a contribution to the strengthening of consumer protection;
(u) measures in the spheres of energy, civil protection and tourism.

2. In all the activities referred to in this Article, the Community shall aim to eliminate inequalities, and to promote equality, between men and women.

Article 4 (ex Article 3a)

1. For the purposes set out in Article 2, the activities of the Member States and the Community shall include, as provided in this Treaty and in accordance with the timetable set out therein, the adoption of an economic policy which is based on the close coordination of Member States' economic policies, on the internal market and on the definition of common objectives, and conducted in accordance with the principle of an open market economy with free competition.

2. Concurrently with the foregoing, and as provided in this Treaty and in accordance with the timetable and the procedures set out therein, these activities shall include the irrevocable fixing of exchange rates leading to the introduction of a single currency, the ECU, and the definition and conduct of a single monetary policy and exchange-rate policy the primary objective of both of which shall be to maintain price stability and, without prejudice to this objective, to support the general economic policies in the Community, in accordance with the principle of an open market economy with free competition.

3. These activities of the Member States and the Community shall entail compliance with the following guiding principles: stable prices, sound public finances and monetary conditions and a sustainable balance of payments.

Article 5 (ex Article 3b)

The Community shall act within the limits of the powers conferred upon it by this Treaty and of the objectives assigned to it therein.

In areas which do not fall within its exclusive competence, the Community shall take action, in accordance with the principle of subsidiarity, only if and insofar as the objectives of the proposed action cannot be sufficiently achieved by the Member States and can therefore, by reason of the scale or effects of the proposed action, be better achieved by the Community.

Any action by the Community shall not go beyond what is necessary to achieve the objectives of this Treaty.

Article 6 (ex Article 3c)

Environmental protection requirements must be integrated into the definition and implementation of the Community policies and activities referred to in Article 3, in particular with a view to promoting sustainable development.

Article 7 (ex Article 4)

1. The tasks entrusted to the Community shall be carried out by the following institutions:

– a EUROPEAN PARLIAMENT,
– a COUNCIL,
– a COMMISSION,
– a COURT OF JUSTICE,
[...]

Chapter 2
Prohibition of quantitative restrictions between Member States

Article 28 (ex Article 30)

Quantitative restrictions on imports and all measures having equivalent effect shall be prohibited between Member States.

Article 29 (ex Article 34)

Quantitative restrictions on exports, and all measures having equivalent effect, shall be prohibited between Member States.

Article 30 (ex Article 36)

The provisions of Articles 28 and 29 shall not preclude prohibitions or restrictions on imports, exports or goods in transit justified on grounds of public morality, public policy or public security; the protection of health and life of humans, animals or plants; the protection of national treasures possessing artistic, historic or archaeological value; or the protection of industrial and commercial property. Such prohibitions or restrictions shall not, however, constitute a means of arbitrary discrimination or a disguised restriction on trade between Member States.

[...]

Section 2
Aids granted by States

Article 87 (ex Article 92)

1. Save as otherwise provided in this Treaty, any aid granted by a Member State or through State resources in any form whatsoever which distorts or threatens to distort competition by favouring certain undertakings or the production of certain goods shall, insofar as it affects trade between Member States, be incompatible with the common market.

2. The following shall be compatible with the common market:

(a) aid having a social character, granted to individual consumers, provided that such aid is granted without discrimination related to the origin of the products concerned;

(b) aid to make good the damage caused by natural disasters or exceptional occurrences;

(c) aid granted to the economy of certain areas of the Federal Republic of Germany affected by the division of Germany, insofar as such aid is required in order to compensate for the economic disadvantages caused by that division.

3. The following may be considered to be compatible with the common market:

(a) aid to promote the economic development of areas where the standard of living is abnormally low or where there is serious under-employment;

(b) aid to promote the execution of an important project of common European interest or to remedy a serious disturbance in the economy of a Member State;

(c) aid to facilitate the development of certain economic activities or of certain economic areas, where such aid does not adversely affect trading conditions to an extent contrary to the common interest;

(d) aid to promote culture and heritage conservation where such aid does not affect trading conditions and competition in the Community to an extent that is contrary to the common interest;

(e) such other categories of aid as may be specified by decision of the Council acting
by a qualified majority on a proposal from the Commission.

[...]

Chapter 3
Approximation of laws

Article 94 (ex Article 100)

The Council shall, acting unanimously on a proposal from the Commission and after
consulting the European Parliament and the Economic and Social Committee, issue
directives for the approximation of such laws, regulations or administrative provisions
of the Member States as directly affect the establishment or functioning of the common
market.

Article 95 (ex Article 100a)

1. By way of derogation from Article 94 and save where otherwise provided in this
Treaty, the following provisions shall apply for the achievement of the objectives set
out in Article 14. The Council shall, acting in accordance with the procedure referred
to in Article 251 and after consulting the Economic and Social Committee, adopt the
measures for the approximation of the provisions laid down by law, regulation or
administrative action in Member States which have as their object the establishment
and functioning of the internal market.

2. Paragraph 1 shall not apply to fiscal provisions, to those relating to the free
movement of persons nor to those relating to the rights and interests of employed
persons.

3. The Commission, in its proposals envisaged in paragraph 1 concerning health,
safety, environmental protection and consumer protection, will take as a base a high
level of protection, taking account in particular of any new development based on
scientific facts. Within their respective powers, the European Parliament and the
Council will also seek to achieve this objective.

4. If, after the adoption by the Council or by the Commission of a harmonisation
measure, a Member State deems it necessary to maintain national provisions on
grounds of major needs referred to in Article 30, or relating to the protection of the
environment or the working environment, it shall notify the Commission of these
provisions as well as the grounds for maintaining them.

5. Moreover, without prejudice to paragraph 4, if, after the adoption by the Council
or by the Commission of a harmonisation measure, a Member State deems it necessary
to introduce national provisions based on new scientific evidence relating to the
protection of the environment or the working environment on grounds of a problem
specific to that Member State arising after the adoption of the harmonisation measure,

it shall notify the Commission of the envisaged provisions as well as the grounds for introducing them.

6. The Commission shall, within six months of the notifications as referred to in paragraphs 4 and 5, approve or reject the national provisions involved after having verified whether or not they are a means of arbitrary discrimination or a disguised restriction on trade between Member States and whether or not they shall constitute an obstacle to the functioning of the internal market.

In the absence of a decision by the Commission within this period the national provisions referred to in paragraphs 4 and 5 shall be deemed to have been approved.

When justified by the complexity of the matter and in the absence of danger for human health, the Commission may notify the Member State concerned that the period referred to in this paragraph may be extended for a further period of up to six months.

7. When, pursuant to paragraph 6, a Member State is authorised to maintain or introduce national provisions derogating from a harmonisation measure, the Commission shall immediately examine whether to propose an adaptation to that measure.

8. When a Member State raises a specific problem on public health in a field which has been the subject of prior harmonisation measures, it shall bring it to the attention of the Commission which shall immediately examine whether to propose appropriate measures to the Council.

9. By way of derogation from the procedure laid down in Articles 226 and 227, the Commission and any Member State may bring the matter directly before the Court of Justice if it considers that another Member State is making improper use of the powers provided for in this Article.

10. The harmonisation measures referred to above shall, in appropriate cases, include a safeguard clause authorising the Member States to take, for one or more of the non-economic reasons referred to in Article 30, provisional measures subject to a Community control procedure.

[...]

Title XIX (ex Title XVI)
Environment

Article 174 (ex Article 130r)

1. Community policy on the environment shall contribute to pursuit of the following objectives:

– preserving, protecting and improving the quality of the environment;
– protecting human health;
– prudent and rational utilisation of natural resources;
– promoting measures at international level to deal with regional or worldwide environmental problems.

2. Community policy on the environment shall aim at a high level of protection taking into account the diversity of situations in the various regions of the Community. It shall be based on the precautionary principle and on the principles that preventive action should be taken, that environmental damage should as a priority be rectified at source and that the polluter should pay.

In this context, harmonisation measures answering environmental protection requirements shall include, where appropriate, a safeguard clause allowing Member States to take provisional measures, for non-economic environmental reasons, subject to a Community inspection procedure.

3. In preparing its policy on the environment, the Community shall take account of:

– available scientific and technical data;
– environmental conditions in the various regions of the Community;
– the potential benefits and costs of action or lack of action;
– the economic and social development of the Community as a whole and the balanced development of its regions.

4. Within their respective spheres of competence, the Community and the Member States shall cooperate with third countries and with the competent international organisations. The arrangements for Community cooperation may be the subject of agreements between the Community and the third parties concerned, which shall be negotiated and concluded in accordance with Article 300.

The previous subparagraph shall be without prejudice to Member States' competence to negotiate in international bodies and to conclude international agreements.

Article 175 (ex Article 130s)

1. The Council, acting in accordance with the procedure referred to in Article 251 and after consulting the Economic and Social Committee and the Committee of the Regions, shall decide what action is to be taken by the Community in order to achieve the objectives referred to in Article 174.

2. By way of derogation from the decision-making procedure provided for in paragraph 1 and without prejudice to Article 95, the Council, acting unanimously on a proposal from the Commission and after consulting the European Parliament, the Economic and Social Committee and the Committee of the Regions, shall adopt:

– provisions primarily of a fiscal nature;
– measures concerning town and country planning, land use with the exception of waste management and measures of a general nature, and management of water resources;
– measures significantly affecting a Member State's choice between different energy sources and the general structure of its energy supply.

The Council may, under the conditions laid down in the preceding subparagraph, define those matters referred to in this paragraph on which decisions are to be taken by a qualified majority.

3. In other areas, general action programmes setting out priority objectives to be attained shall be adopted by the Council, acting in accordance with the procedure referred to in Article 251 and after consulting the Economic and Social Committee and the Committee of the Regions. The Council, acting under the terms of paragraph 1 or paragraph 2 according to the case, shall adopt the measures necessary for the implementation of these programmes.

4. Without prejudice to certain measures of a Community nature, the Member States shall finance and implement the environment policy.

5. Without prejudice to the principle that the polluter should pay, if a measure based on the provisions of paragraph 1 involves costs deemed disproportionate for the public authorities of a Member State, the Council shall, in the act adopting that measure, lay down appropriate provisions in the form of:

– temporary derogations, and/or
– financial support from the Cohesion Fund set up pursuant to Article 161.

Article 176 (ex Article 130t)

The protective measures adopted pursuant to Article 175 shall not prevent any Member State from maintaining or introducing more stringent protective measures. Such measures must be compatible with this Treaty. They shall be notified to the Commission.

[...]

Chapter 2
Provisions common to several institutions

Article 249 (ex Article 189)

In order to carry out their task and in accordance with the provisions of this Treaty, the European Parliament acting jointly with the Council, the Council and the Commission shall make regulations and issue directives, take decisions, make recommendations or deliver opinions.

A regulation shall have general application. It shall be binding in its entirety and directly applicable in all Member States.

A directive shall be binding, as to the result to be achieved, upon each Member State to which it is addressed, but shall leave to the national authorities the choice of form and methods.

A decision shall be binding in its entirety upon those to whom it is addressed. Recommendations and opinions shall have no binding force.

Article 250 (ex Article 189a)

1. Where, in pursuance of this Treaty, the Council acts on a proposal from the Commission, unanimity shall be required for an act constituting an amendment to that proposal, subject to Article 251(4) and (5).

2. As long as the Council has not acted, the Commission may alter its proposal at any time during the procedures leading to the adoption of a Community act.

Article 251 (ex Article 189b)

1. Where reference is made in this Treaty to this Article for the adoption of an act, the following procedure shall apply.

2. The Commission shall submit a proposal to the European Parliament and the Council. The Council, acting by a qualified majority after obtaining the opinion of the European Parliament,

- if it approves all the amendments contained in the European Parliament's opinion, may adopt the proposed act thus amended;
- if the European Parliament does not propose any amendments, may adopt the proposed act;
- shall otherwise adopt a common position and communicate it to the European Parliament. The Council shall inform the European Parliament fully of the reasons which led it to adopt its common position. The Commission shall inform the European Parliament fully of its position.

If, within three months of such communication, the European Parliament:

(a) approves the common position or has not taken a decision, the act in question shall be deemed to have been adopted in accordance with that common position;
(b) rejects, by an absolute majority of its component members, the common position, the proposed act shall be deemed not to have been adopted;
(c) proposes amendments to the common position by an absolute majority of its component members, the amended text shall be forwarded to the Council and to the Commission, which shall deliver an opinion on those amendments.

3. If, within three months of the matter being referred to it, the Council, acting by a qualified majority, approves all the amendments of the European Parliament, the act in question shall be deemed to have been adopted in the form of the common position thus amended; however, the Council shall act unanimously on the amendments on which the Commission has delivered a negative opinion. If the Council does not approve all the amendments, the President of the Council, in agreement with the President of the European Parliament, shall within six weeks convene a meeting of the Conciliation Committee.

4. The Conciliation Committee, which shall be composed of the members of the Council or their representatives and an equal number of representatives of the

European Parliament, shall have the task of reaching agreement on a joint text, by a qualified majority of the members of the Council or their representatives and by a majority of the representatives of the European Parliament. The Commission shall take part in the Conciliation Committee's proceedings and shall take all the necessary initiatives with a view to reconciling the positions of the European Parliament and the Council. In fulfilling this task, the Conciliation Committee shall address the common position on the basis of the amendments proposed by the European Parliament.

5. If, within six weeks of its being convened, the Conciliation Committee approves a joint text, the European Parliament, acting by an absolute majority of the votes cast, and the Council, acting by a qualified majority, shall each have a period of six weeks from that approval in which to adopt the act in question in accordance with the joint text. If either of the two institutions fails to approve the proposed act within that period, it shall be deemed not to have been adopted.

6. Where the Conciliation Committee does not approve a joint text, the proposed act shall be deemed not to have been adopted.

7. The periods of three months and six weeks referred to in this Article shall be extended by a maximum of one month and two weeks respectively at the initiative of the European Parliament or the Council.

Article 252 (ex Article 189c)

Where reference is made in this Treaty to this Article for the adoption of an act, the following procedure shall apply:

(a) The Council, acting by a qualified majority on a proposal from the Commission and after obtaining the opinion of the European Parliament, shall adopt a common position.
(b) The Council's common position shall be communicated to the European Parliament. The Council and the Commission shall inform the European Parliament fully of the reasons which led the Council to adopt its common position and also of the Commission's position.

    If, within three months of such communication, the European Parliament approves this common position or has not taken a decision within that period, the Council shall definitively adopt the act in question in accordance with the common position.
(c) The European Parliament may, within the period of three months referred to in point (b), by an absolute majority of its component Members, propose amendments to the Council's common position. The European Parliament may also, by the same majority, reject the Council's common position. The result of the proceedings shall be transmitted to the Council and the Commission.

    If the European Parliament has rejected the Council's common position, unanimity shall be required for the Council to act on a second reading.

(d) The Commission shall, within a period of one month, reexamine the proposal on the basis of which the Council adopted its common position, by taking into account the amendments proposed by the European Parliament.

    The Commission shall forward to the Council, at the same time as its re-examined proposal, the amendments of the European Parliament which it has not accepted, and shall express its opinion on them. The Council may adopt these amendments unanimously.

(e) The Council, acting by a qualified majority, shall adopt the proposal as re-examined by the Commission.

    Unanimity shall be required for the Council to amend the proposal as re-examined by the Commission.

(f) In the cases referred to in points (c), (d) and (e), the Council shall be required to act within a period of three months. If no decision is taken within this period, the Commission proposal shall be deemed not to have been adopted.

(g) The periods referred to in points (b) and (f) may be extended by a maximum of one month by common accord between the Council and the European Parliament.

[. . .]

Article 308 (ex Article 235)

If action by the Community should prove necessary to attain, in the course of the operation of the common market, one of the objectives of the Community and this Treaty has not provided the necessary powers, the Council shall, acting unanimously on a proposal from the Commission and after consulting the European Parliament, take the appropriate measures.

[. . .]

EC Treaty, incorporating amendments introduced by the TEU and the SEA (extracts; superseded by the entry into force of the Treaty of Nice on 1 February 2003)

Part one
Principles

Article 1

By this Treaty, the *High Contracting Parties* establish among themselves a *European Community.*

Article 2

The Community shall have as its task, by establishing a common market and an economic and monetary union and by implementing the common policies or activities referred to in Articles 3 and 3a, to promote throughout the Community an harmonious and balanced development of economic activities, sustainable and non-inflationary growth respecting the environment, a high degree of convergence of economic performance, a high level of employment and social protection, the raising of standard of living and quality of life, and economic and social cohesion and solidarity among member-States.

Article 3

For the purposes set out in Article 2, the activities of the Community shall include, as provided in this Treaty and in accordance with the timetable set out therein:

(a) the elimination, as between Member States, of customs duties and quantitative restrictions on the import and export of goods, and of all other measures having equivalent effect;
(b) a common commercial policy;
(c) an internal market characterized by the abolition, as between Member States, of obstacles to the free movement of goods, persons, services and capital;
(d) measures concerning the entry and movement of persons in the internal market as provided for in Article 100c;
(e) a common policy in the sphere of agriculture and fisheries;

(f) a common policy in the sphere of transport;

(g) a system ensuring that competition in the internal market is not distorted;

(h) the approximation of the laws of Member States to the extent required for the functioning of the common market;

(i) a policy in the social sphere comprising a European Social Fund;

(j) the strengthening of economic and social cohesion;

(k) a policy in the sphere of the environment;

(l) the strengthening of the competitiveness of Community industry;

(m) the promotion of research and technological development;

(n) encouragement for the establishment and development of trans-European networks;

(o) a contribution to the attainment of a high level of health protection;

(p) a contribution to education and training of quality and to the flowering of the cultures of the Member States;

(q) a policy in the sphere of development cooperation;

(r) the association of the overseas countries and territories in order to increase trade and promote jointly economic and social development;

(s) a contribution to the strengthening of consumer protection;

(t) measures in the spheres of energy, civil protection and tourism.

Article 3a

1. For the purposes set out in Article 2, the activities of the Member States and the Community shall include, as provided in this Treaty and in accordance with the timetable set out therein, the adoption of an economic policy which is based on the close coordination of Member States' economic policies, on the internal market and on the definition of common objectives, and conducted in accordance with the principle of an open market economy with free competition.

2. Concurrently with the foregoing, and as provided in this Treaty and in accordance with the timetable and the procedures set out therein, these activities shall include the irrevocable fixing of exchange rates leading to the introduction of a single currency, the ECU, and the definition and conduct of a single monetary policy and exchange rate policy the primary objective of both of which shall be to maintain price stability and, without prejudice to this objective, to support the general economic policies in the Community, in accordance with the principle of an open market economy with free competition.

3. These activities of the Member States and the Community shall entail compliance with the following guiding principles: stable prices, sound public finances and monetary conditions and a sustainable balance of payments.

Article 3b

The Community shall act within the limits of the powers conferred upon it by this Treaty and of the objectives assigned to it therein.

In areas which do not fall within its exclusive competence, the Community shall take action, in accordance with the principle of subsidiarity, only if and in so far as the objectives of the proposed action cannot be sufficiently achieved by the Member States and can therefore, by reason of the scale or effects of the proposed action, be better achieved by the Community.

Any action by the Community shall not go beyond what is necessary to achieve the objectives of this Treaty.

Article 4

1. The tasks entrusted to the Community shall be carried out by the following institutions:

– a EUROPEAN PARLIAMENT,
– a COUNCIL,
– a COMMISSION,
– a COURT OF JUSTICE,
[. . .]

Article 7

1. The common market shall be progressively established during a transitional period of 12 years.

This transitional period shall be divided into three stages of four years each; the length of each stage may be altered in accordance with the provisions set out below.
[. . .]

Chapter 2
Elimination of quantitative restrictions between member-States

Article 30

Quantitative restrictions on imports and all measures having equivalent effect shall, without prejudice to the following provisions, be prohibited between member-States.
[. . .]

Article 34

1. Quantitative restrictions on exports, an all measures having equivalent effect, shall be prohibited between member-States.

2. Member-States shall, by the end of the first stage at the latest, abolish all quantitative restrictions on exports and any measures having equivalent effect which are in existence when this Treaty enters into force.
[. . .]

Article 36

The provisions of Articles 30 to 34 shall not preclude prohibitions or restrictions on imports, exports or goods in transit justified on the grounds of public morality, public policy or public security; the protection of health and life of humans, animals or plants; the protection of national treasures possessing artistic, historic or archaeological value; or the protection of industrial and commercial property. Such prohibitions or restrictions shall not, however, constitute a means of arbitrary discrimination or a disguised restriction on trade between member-States.

[...]

Article 100

The Council shall, acting unanimously on a proposal from the Commission and after consulting the European Parliament and the Economic and Social Committee, issue directives for the approximation of such laws, regulations or administrative provisions of the Member States as directly affect the establishment or functioning of the common market.

Article 100A

1. By way of derogation from Article 100 and save where otherwise provided in this Treaty, the following provisions shall apply for the achievement of the objectives set out in Article 7a. The Council shall, acting in accordance with the procedure referred to in Article 189b and after consulting the Economic and Social Committee, adopt the measures for the approximation of the provisions laid down by law, regulation or administrative action in Member States which have as their object the establishment and functioning of the internal market.

2.

[...]

Title XVI
Environment

Article 130r

1. Community policy on the environment shall contribute to pursuit of the following objectives:

- preserving, protecting and improving the quality of the environment;
- protecting human health;
- prudent and rational utilization of natural resources;
- promoting measures at international level to deal with regional or worldwide environmental problems.

2. Community policy on the environment shall aim at a high level of protection taking into account the diversity of situations in the various regions of the Community. It shall be based on the precautionary principle and on the principles that preventive action should be taken, that environmental damage should as a priority be rectified at source and that the polluter should pay. Environmental protection requirements must be integrated into the definition and implementation of other Community policies.

In this context, harmonization measures answering these requirements shall include, where appropriate, a safeguard clause allowing Member States to take provisional measures, for non-economic environmental reasons, subject to a Community inspection procedure.

3. In preparing its policy on the environment, the Community shall take account of:

– available scientific and technical data;
– environmental conditions in the various regions of the Community;
– the potential benefits and costs of action or lack of action;
– the economic and social development of the Community as a whole and the balanced development of its regions.

4. Within their respective spheres of competence, the Community and the Member States shall cooperate with third countries and with the competent international organizations.

The arrangements for Community cooperation may be the subject of agreements between the Community and the third parties concerned, which shall be negotiated and concluded in accordance with Article 228.

The previous subparagraph shall be without prejudice to Member States' competence to negotiate in international bodies and to conclude international agreements.

Article 130s

1. The Council, acting in accordance with the procedure referred to in Article 189c and after consulting the Economic and Social Committee, shall decide what action is to be taken by the Community in order to achieve the objectives referred to in Article 130r.

2. By way of derogation from the decision-making procedure provided for in paragraph 1 and without prejudice to Article 100a, the Council, acting unanimously on a proposal from the Commission and after consulting the European Parliament and the Economic and Social Committee, shall adopt:

– provisions primarily of a fiscal nature;
– measures concerning town and country planning, land use with the exception of waste management and measures of a general nature, and management of water resources;

– measures significantly affecting a Member State's choice between different energy sources and the general structure of its energy supply.

The Council may, under the conditions laid down in the preceding subparagraph, define those matters referred to in this paragraph on which decisions are to be taken by a qualified majority.

3. In other areas, general action programmes setting out priority objectives to be attained shall be adopted by the Council, acting in accordance with the procedure referred to in Article 189b and after consulting the Economic and Social Committee.

The Council, acting under the terms of paragraph 1 or paragraph 2 according to the case, shall adopt the measures necessary for the implementation of these programmes.

4. Without prejudice to certain measures of a Community nature, the Member States shall finance and implement the environment policy.

5. Without prejudice to the principle that the polluter should pay, if a measure based on the provisions of paragraph 1 involves costs deemed disproportionate for the public authorities of a Member State, the Council shall, in the act adopting that measure, lay down appropriate provisions in the form of:

– temporary derogations and/or
– financial support from the Cohesion Fund to be set up no later than 31 December 1993 pursuant to Article 130d.

Article 130t

The protective measures adopted pursuant to Article 130s shall not prevent any Member State from maintaining or introducing more stringent protective measures. Such measures must be compatible with this Treaty. They shall be notified to the Commission.

[...]

Article 189

In order to carry out their task and in accordance with the provisions of this Treaty, the European Parliament acting jointly with the Council, the Council and the Commission shall make regulations and issue directives, take decisions, make recommendations or deliver opinions.

A regulation shall have general application. It shall be binding in its entirety and directly applicable in all Member States.

A directive shall be binding, as to the result to be achieved, upon each Member State to which it is addressed, but shall leave to the national authorities the choice of form and methods.

A decision shall be binding in its entirety upon those to whom it is addressed.

Recommendations and opinions shall have no binding force.

Article 189a

1. Where, in pursuance of this Treaty, the Council acts on a proposal from the Commission, unanimity shall be required for an act constituting an amendment to that proposal, subject to Article 189b(4) and (5).

2. As long as the Council has not acted, the Commission may alter its proposal at any time during the procedures leading to the adoption of a Community act.

Article 189b

1. Where reference is made in this Treaty to this Article for the adoption of an act, the following procedure shall apply.

2. The Commission shall submit a proposal to the European Parliament and the Council.

The Council, acting by a qualified majority after obtaining the opinion of the European Parliament, shall adopt a common position. The common position shall be communicated to the European Parliament. The Council shall inform the European Parliament fully of the reasons which led it to adopt its common position. The Commission shall inform the European Parliament fully of its position.

If, within three months of such communication, the European Parliament:

(a) approves the common position, the Council shall definitively adopt the act in question in accordance with that common position;
(b) has not taken a decision, the Council shall adopt the act in question in accordance with its common position;
(c) indicates, by an absolute majority of its component members, that it intends to reject the common position, it shall immediately inform the Council. The Council may convene a meeting of the Conciliation Committee referred to in paragraph 4 to explain further its position. The European Parliament shall thereafter either confirm, by an absolute majority of its component members, its rejection of the common position, in which event the proposed act shall be deemed not to have been adopted, or propose amendments in accordance with subparagraph (d) of this paragraph;
(d) proposes amendments to the common position by an absolute majority of its component members, the amended text shall be forwarded to the Council and to the Commission, which shall deliver an opinion on those amendments.

3. If, within three months of the matter being referred to it, the Council, acting by a qualified majority, approves all the amendments of the European Parliament, it shall amend its common position accordingly and adopt the act in question; however, the Council shall act unanimously on the amendments on which the Commission has delivered a negative opinion. If the Council does not approve the act in question, the President of the Council, in agreement with the President of the European Parliament, shall forthwith convene a meeting of the Conciliation Committee.

4. The Conciliation Committee, which shall be composed of the members of the Council or their representatives and an equal number of representatives of the European Parliament, shall have the task of reaching agreement on a joint text, by a qualified majority of the members of the Council or their representatives and by a majority of the representatives of the European Parliament. The Commission shall take part in the Conciliation Committee's proceedings and shall take all the necessary initiatives with a view to reconciling the positions of the European Parliament and the Council.

5. If, within six weeks of its being convened, the Conciliation Committee approves a joint text, the European Parliament, acting by an absolute majority of the votes cast, and the Council, acting by a qualified majority, shall have a period of six weeks from that approval in which to adopt the act in question in accordance with the joint text. If one of the two institutions fails to approve the proposed act, it shall be deemed not to have been adopted.

6. Where the Conciliation Committee does not approve a joint text, the proposed act shall be deemed not to have been adopted unless the Council, acting by a qualified majority within six weeks of expiry of the period granted to the Conciliation Committee, confirms the common position to which it agreed before the conciliation procedure was initiated, possibly with amendments proposed by the European Parliament. In this case, the act in question shall be finally adopted unless the European Parliament, within six weeks of the date of confirmation by the Council, rejects the text by an absolute majority of its component members, in which case the proposed act shall be deemed not to have been adopted.

7. The periods of three months and six weeks referred to in this Article may be extended by a maximum of one month and two weeks respectively by common accord of the European Parliament and the Council. The period of three months referred to in paragraph 2 shall be automatically extended by two months where paragraph 2(c) applies.

8. The scope of the procedure under this Article may be widened, in accordance with the procedure provided for in Article N(2) of the Treaty on European Union, on the basis of a report to be submitted to the Council by the Commission by 1996 at the latest.

Article 189c

Where reference is made in this Treaty to this Article for the adoption of an act, the following procedure shall apply:

(a) The Council, acting by a qualified majority on a proposal from the Commission and after obtaining the opinion of the European Parliament, shall adopt a common position.

(b) The Council's common position shall be communicated to the European Parliament. The Council and the Commission shall inform the European Parliament

fully of the reasons which led the Council to adopt its common position and also
of the Commission's position.

If, within three months of such communication, the European Parliament
approves this common position or has not taken a decision within that period,
the Council shall definitively adopt the act in question in accordance with the
common position.

(c) The European Parliament may, within the period of three months referred to in
point (b), by an absolute majority of its component members, propose amendments to the Council's common position. The European Parliament may also,
by the same majority, reject the Council's common position. The result of the
proceedings shall be transmitted to the Council and the Commission.

If the European Parliament has rejected the Council's common position, unanimity shall be required for the Council to act on a second reading.

(d) The Commission shall, within a period of one month, re-examine the proposal
on the basis of which the Council adopted its common position, by taking into
account the amendments proposed by the European Parliament.

The Commission shall forward to the Council, at the same time as its re-
examined proposal, the amendments of the European Parliament which it has
not accepted, and shall express its opinion on them. The Council may adopt these
amendments unanimously.

(e) The Council, acting by a qualified majority, shall adopt the proposal as re-
examined by the Commission.

Unanimity shall be required for the Council to amend the proposal as re-
examined by the Commission.

(f) In the cases referred to in points (c), (d) and (e), the Council shall be required to
act within a period of three months. If no decision is taken within this period, the
Commission proposal shall be deemed not to have been adopted.

(g) The periods referred to in points (b) and (f) may be extended by a maximum of
one month by common accord between the Council and the European Parliament.

[...]

EEC Treaty, incorporating amendments introduced by the SEA (extracts; superseded by the entry into force of the Treaty of Nice on 1 February 2003)

Part one
Principles

Article 1

By this Treaty, the High Contracting Parties establish among themselves a *European Economic Community.*

Article 2

The Community shall have as its task, by establishing a common market and progressively approximating the economic policies of Member States, to promote throughout the Community a harmonious development of economic activities, a continuous and balanced expansion, an increase in stability, an accelerated raising of the standard of living and closer relations between the States belonging to it.

Article 3

For the purposes set out in Article 2, the activities of the Community shall include, as provided in this Treaty and in accordance with the timetable set out therein:

(a) the elimination, as between Member States, of custom duties and of quantitative restrictions to the import and export of goods, and of all other measures having equivalent effect;
(b) the establishment of a common custom tariff and of a common commercial policy towards third countries;
(c) the abolition, as between Member States, of obstacles to freedom of movement for persons, services and capital;
(d) the adoption of a common policy in the sphere of agriculture;
(e) the adoption of a common policy in the sphere of transport;
(f) the institution of a system ensuring that competition in the common market is not distorted;
(g) the application of procedures by which the economic policies of Member States can be co-ordinated and disequilibria in their balances of payments remedied;

(h) the approximation of laws of Member States to the extent required for the proper functioning of the common market;

(i) the creation of a European Social Fund in order to improve employment opportunities for workers and contribute to the raising of their standard of living;

(j) the establishment of a European Investment Bank to facilitate economic expansion of the Community by opening up fresh resources;

(k) the association of the overseas countries and territories in order to increase trade and to promote jointly economic and social development.

Article 4

1. The tasks entrusted to the Community shall be carried out by the following institutions:

a European Parliament,
a Council,
a Commission,
a Court of Justice.

Each institution shall act within the limits of the powers conferred upon it by this Treaty.
[....]

Article 8A

The Community shall adopt measures with the aim of progressively establishing the internal market over a period expiring on 31 December 1992, in accordance with the provisions of this Article and of Articles 8B, 8C, 28, 57(2), 59, 70(1), 84, 99, 100A and 100B and without prejudice to the operation of this Treaty.

The internal market shall comprise an area without internal frontiers in which the free movement of goods, persons, services and capital is ensured in accordance with the provisions of this Treaty.
[...]

Chapter 3
Approximation of laws

Article 100

The Council shall, acting unanimously on a proposal from the Commission, issue directives for the approximation of such provisions laid down by law, regulation or administrative action in Member States as directly affecting the establishment and functioning of the common market.

The European Parliament and the Economic and Social Committee shall be consulted in the case of directives whose implementation would, in one or more Member States, involve the amendment of legislation.

Article 100A

1. By way of derogation from Article 100 and save where otherwise provided in this Treaty, the following provisions shall apply for the achievement of the objectives set out in Article 8A. The Council shall, acting by a qualified majority on a proposal from the Commission in co-operation with the European Parliament and after consulting the Economic and Social Committee, adopt the measures for the approximation of the provisions laid down by law, regulation or administrative action in Member States which have as their object the establishment and functioning of the internal market.

2. Paragraph 1 shall not apply to fiscal provisions, to those relating to the free movement of persons nor to those relating to the rights and interests of employed persons.

3. The Commission, in its proposals envisaged in paragraph 1 concerning health, safety, environmental protection and consumer protection, will take as a base a high level of protection.

4. If, after the adoption of a harmonization measure by the Council acting by a qualified majority, a Member State deems it necessary to apply national provisions on grounds of major needs referred to in Article 36, or relating to the protection of the environment or the working environment, it shall notify the Commission of these provisions.

The Commission shall confirm the provisions involved after having verified that they are not a means of arbitrary discrimination or a disguised restriction on trade between Member States.

By way of derogation from the procedure laid down in Articles 169 and 170, the Commission or any Member State may bring the matter directly before the Court of Justice if it considers that another Member State is making improper use of the powers provided for in this Article.

5. The harmonization measures referred to above shall, in appropriate cases, include a safeguard clause authorizing the Member States to take, for one or more of the non-economic reasons referred to in Article 36, provisional measures subject to a Community control procedure.

[...]

Title VII
Environment

Article 130r

1. Action by the Community relating to the environment shall have the following objectives:

 (i) to preserve, protect and improve the quality of the environment;
 (ii) to contribute towards protecting human health;
(iii) to ensure a prudent and rational utilization of natural resources.

2. Action by the Community relating to the environment shall be based on the principles that preventive action should be taken, that environmental damage should as a priority be rectified at source, and that the polluter should pay. Environmental protection requirements shall be a component of the Community's other policies.

3. In preparing its action relating to the environment, the Community shall take account of:

(i)   available scientific and technical data;
(ii) environmental conditions in the various regions of the Community;
(iii) the potential benefits and costs of action or lack of action;
(iv) the economic and social development of the Community as a whole and the balanced development of its regions.

4. The Community shall take action relating to the environment to the extent to which the objectives referred to in paragraph 1 can be attained better at Community level than at the level of the individual Member States. Without prejudice to certain measures of a Community nature, the Member States shall finance and implement the other measures.

5. Within their respective spheres of competence, the Community and the Member States shall co-operate with third countries and with the competent international organizations.

The arrangements for Community co-operation may be the subject of agreements between the Community and the third parties concerned, which shall be negotiated and concluded in accordance with Article 228.

The previous subparagraph shall be without prejudice to Member States' competence to negotiate in international bodies and to conclude international agreements.

Article 130s

The Council, acting unanimously on a proposal from the Commission and after consulting the European Parliament and the Economic and Social Committee, shall decide what action is to be taken by the Community.

The Council shall, under the conditions laid down in the preceding subparagraph, define those matters on which decisions are to be taken by a qualified majority.

Article 130t

The protective measures adopted in common pursuant to Article 130s shall not prevent any Member State from maintaining or introducing more stringent protective measures compatible with this Treaty.

[...]

Treaty establishing a Constitution for Europe, 28 October 2004 (extracts)

Source: OJ C310 16 December 2004 p. 1

Treaty establishing a Constitution for Europe

[...]

Part I
Title I
Definition and objectives of the Union

Article I-1
Establishment of the Union

1. Reflecting the will of the citizens and States of Europe to build a common future, this Constitution establishes the European Union, on which the Member States confer competences to attain objectives they have in common. The Union shall coordinate the policies by which the Member States aim to achieve these objectives, and shall exercise on a Community basis the competences they confer on it.

2. The Union shall be open to all European States which respect its values and are committed to promoting them together.

Article I-2
The Union's values

The Union is founded on the values of respect for human dignity, freedom, democracy, equality, the rule of law and respect for human rights, including the rights of persons belonging to minorities. These values are common to the Member States in a society in which pluralism, non-discrimination, tolerance, justice, solidarity and equality between women and men prevail.

Article I-3
The Union's objectives

1. The Union's aim is to promote peace, its values and the well-being of its peoples.

2. The Union shall offer its citizens an area of freedom, security and justice without internal frontiers, and an internal market where competition is free and undistorted.

3. The Union shall work for the sustainable development of Europe based on balanced economic growth and price stability, a highly competitive social market economy, aiming at full employment and social progress, and a high level of protection and improvement of the quality of the environment. It shall promote scientific and technological advance.

It shall combat social exclusion and discrimination, and shall promote social justice and protection, equality between women and men, solidarity between generations and protection of the rights of the child.

It shall promote economic, social and territorial cohesion, and solidarity among Member States.

It shall respect its rich cultural and linguistic diversity, and shall ensure that Europe's cultural heritage is safeguarded and enhanced.

4. In its relations with the wider world, the Union shall uphold and promote its values and interests. It shall contribute to peace, security, the sustainable development of the Earth, solidarity and mutual respect among peoples, free and fair trade, eradication of poverty and the protection of human rights, in particular the rights of the child, as well as to the strict observance and the development of international law, including respect for the principles of the United Nations Charter.

5. The Union shall pursue its objectives by appropriate means commensurate with the competences which are conferred upon it in the Constitution.

Article I-4
Fundamental freedoms and non-discrimination

1. The free movement of persons, services, goods and capital, and freedom of establishment shall be guaranteed within and by the Union, in accordance with the Constitution.

2. Within the scope of the Constitution, and without prejudice to any of its specific provisions, any discrimination on grounds of nationality shall be prohibited.

Article I-5
Relations between the Union and the Member States

1. The Union shall respect the equality of Member States before the Constitution as well as their national identities, inherent in their fundamental structures, political and constitutional, inclusive of regional and local self-government. It shall respect their essential State functions, including ensuring the territorial integrity of the State, maintaining law and order and safeguarding national security.

2. Pursuant to the principle of sincere cooperation, the Union and the Member States shall, in full mutual respect, assist each other in carrying out tasks which flow from the Constitution.

The Member States shall take any appropriate measure, general or particular, to ensure fulfilment of the obligations arising out of the Constitution or resulting from the acts of the institutions of the Union.

The Member States shall facilitate the achievement of the Union's tasks and refrain from any measure which could jeopardise the attainment of the Union's objectives.

Article I-6
Union law

The Constitution and law adopted by the institutions of the Union in exercising competences conferred on it shall have primacy over the law of the Member States.

Article I-7
Legal personality

The Union shall have legal personality.

Article I-8
The symbols of the Union

The flag of the Union shall be a circle of twelve golden stars on a blue background.

The anthem of the Union shall be based on the 'Ode to Joy' from the Ninth Symphony by Ludwig van Beethoven.

The motto of the Union shall be: 'United in diversity'.

The currency of the Union shall be the euro.

Europe day shall be celebrated on 9 May throughout the Union.

Title II
Fundamental rights and citizenship of the Union

Article I-9
Fundamental rights

1. The Union shall recognise the rights, freedoms and principles set out in the Charter of Fundamental Rights which constitutes Part II.

2. The Union shall accede to the European Convention for the Protection of Human Rights and Fundamental Freedoms. Such accession shall not affect the Union's competences as defined in the Constitution.

3. Fundamental rights, as guaranteed by the European Convention for the Protection of Human Rights and Fundamental Freedoms and as they result from the constitutional traditions common to the Member States, shall constitute general principles of the Union's law.

Article I-10
Citizenship of the Union

1. Every national of a Member State shall be a citizen of the Union. Citizenship of the Union shall be additional to national citizenship and shall not replace it.

2. Citizens of the Union shall enjoy the rights and be subject to the duties provided for in the Constitution. They shall have:

(a) the right to move and reside freely within the territory of the Member States;

(b) the right to vote and to stand as candidates in elections to the European Parliament and in municipal elections in their Member State of residence, under the same conditions as nationals of that State;

(c) the right to enjoy, in the territory of a third country in which the Member State of which they are nationals is not represented, the protection of the diplomatic and consular authorities of any Member State on the same conditions as the nationals of that State;

(d) the right to petition the European Parliament, to apply to the European Ombudsman, and to address the institutions and advisory bodies of the Union in any of the Constitution's languages and to obtain a reply in the same language.

These rights shall be exercised in accordance with the conditions and limits defined by the Constitution and by the measures adopted thereunder.

Title III
Union competences

Article I-11
Fundamental principles

1. The limits of Union competences are governed by the principle of conferral. The use of Union competences is governed by the principles of subsidiarity and proportionality.

2. Under the principle of conferral, the Union shall act within the limits of the competences conferred upon it by the Member States in the Constitution to attain the objectives set out in the Constitution. Competences not conferred upon the Union in the Constitution remain with the Member States.

3. Under the principle of subsidiarity, in areas which do not fall within its exclusive competence, the Union shall act only if and insofar as the objectives of the proposed action cannot be sufficiently achieved by the Member States, either at central level or at regional and local level, but can rather, by reason of the scale or effects of the proposed action, be better achieved at Union level.

The institutions of the Union shall apply the principle of subsidiarity as laid down in the Protocol on the application of the principles of subsidiarity and proportionality.

National Parliaments shall ensure compliance with that principle in accordance with the procedure set out in that Protocol.

4. Under the principle of proportionality, the content and form of Union action shall not exceed what is necessary to achieve the objectives of the Constitution.

The institutions of the Union shall apply the principle of proportionality as laid down in the Protocol on the application of the principles of subsidiarity and proportionality.

Article I-12
Categories of competence

1. When the Constitution confers on the Union exclusive competence in a specific area, only the Union may legislate and adopt legally binding acts, the Member States being able to do so themselves only if so empowered by the Union or for the implementation of Union acts.

2. When the Constitution confers on the Union a competence shared with the Member States in a specific area, the Union and the Member States may legislate and adopt legally binding acts in that area. The Member States shall exercise their competence to the extent that the Union has not exercised, or has decided to cease exercising, its competence.

3. The Member States shall coordinate their economic and employment policies within arrangements as determined by Part III, which the Union shall have competence to provide.

4. The Union shall have competence to define and implement a common foreign and security policy, including the progressive framing of a common defence policy.

5. In certain areas and under the conditions laid down in the Constitution, the Union shall have competence to carry out actions to support, coordinate or supplement the actions of the Member States, without thereby superseding their competence in these areas.

Legally binding acts of the Union adopted on the basis of the provisions in Part III relating to these areas shall not entail harmonisation of Member States' laws or regulations.

6. The scope of and arrangements for exercising the Union's competences shall be determined by the provisions relating to each area in Part III.

Article I-13
Areas of exclusive competence

1. The Union shall have exclusive competence in the following areas:

(a) customs union;
(b) the establishing of the competition rules necessary for the functioning of the internal market;

(c) monetary policy for the Member States whose currency is the euro;
(d) the conservation of marine biological resources under the common fisheries policy;
(e) common commercial policy.

2. The Union shall also have exclusive competence for the conclusion of an international agreement when its conclusion is provided for in a legislative act of the Union or is necessary to enable the Union to exercise its internal competence, or insofar as its conclusion may affect common rules or alter their scope.

Article I-14
Areas of shared competence

1. The Union shall share competence with the Member States where the Constitution confers on it a competence which does not relate to the areas referred to in Articles I-13 and I-17.

2. Shared competence between the Union and the Member States applies in the following principal areas:

(a) internal market;
(b) social policy, for the aspects defined in Part III;
(c) economic, social and territorial cohesion;
(d) agriculture and fisheries, excluding the conservation of marine biological resources;
(e) environment;
(f) consumer protection;
(g) transport;
(h) trans-European networks;
(i) energy;
(j) area of freedom, security and justice;
(k) common safety concerns in public health matters, for the aspects defined in Part III.

3. In the areas of research, technological development and space, the Union shall have competence to carry out activities, in particular to define and implement programmes; however, the exercise of that competence shall not result in Member States being prevented from exercising theirs.

4. In the areas of development cooperation and humanitarian aid, the Union shall have competence to carry out activities and conduct a common policy; however, the exercise of that competence shall not result in Member States being prevented from exercising theirs.

[...]

Article I-17
Areas of supporting, coordinating or complementary action

The Union shall have competence to carry out supporting, coordinating or complementary action.

The areas of such action shall, at European level, be:

(a) protection and improvement of human health;
(b) industry;
(c) culture;
(d) tourism;
(e) education, youth, sport and vocational training;
(f) civil protection;
(g) administrative cooperation.

Article I-18
Flexibility clause

1. If action by the Union should prove necessary, within the framework of the policies defined in Part III, to attain one of the objectives set out in the Constitution, and the Constitution has not provided the necessary powers, the Council of Ministers, acting unanimously on a proposal from the European Commission and after obtaining the consent of the European Parliament, shall adopt the appropriate measures.

2. Using the procedure for monitoring the subsidiarity principle referred to in Article I-11(3), the European Commission shall draw national Parliaments' attention to proposals based on this Article.

3. Measures based on this Article shall not entail harmonisation of Member States' laws or regulations in cases where the Constitution excludes such harmonisation.

Title IV
The Union's institutions and bodies

Chapter I
The institutional framework

Article I-19
The Union's institutions

1. The Union shall have an institutional framework which shall aim to:

– promote its values,
– advance its objectives,
– serve its interests, those of its citizens and those of the Member States,
– ensure the consistency, effectiveness and continuity of its policies and actions.

This institutional framework comprises:

- The European Parliament,
- The European Council,
- The Council of Ministers (hereinafter referred to as the "Council"),
- The European Commission (hereinafter referred to as the "Commission"),
- The Court of Justice of the European Union.

2. Each institution shall act within the limits of the powers conferred on it in the Constitution, and in conformity with the procedures and conditions set out in it. The institutions shall practice mutual sincere cooperation.
[...]

Part II
The charter of Fundamental Rights of the Union

[...]

Article II-97
Environmental protection

A high level of environmental protection and the improvement of the quality of the environment must be integrated into the policies of the Union and ensured in accordance with the principle of sustainable development.
[...]

Part III
The policies and functioning of the Union

[...]

Article III-119

Environmental protection requirements must be integrated into the definition and implementation of the policies and activities referred to in this Part, in particular with a view to promoting sustainable development.
[...]

Section 3
Free movement of goods

Subsection 1
Customs union

Article III-151

1. The Union shall comprise a customs union which shall cover all trade in goods and which shall involve the prohibition between Member States of customs duties on

imports and exports and of all charges having equivalent effect, and the adoption of a common customs tariff in their relations with third countries.

2. Paragraph 4 and Subsection 3 on the prohibition of quantitative restrictions shall apply to products originating in Member States and to products coming from third countries which are in free circulation in Member States.

3. Products coming from a third country shall be considered to be in free circulation in a Member State if the import formalities have been complied with and any customs duties or charges having equivalent effect which are payable have been levied in that Member State, and if they have not benefited from a total or partial drawback of such duties or charges.

4. Customs duties on imports and exports and charges having equivalent effect shall be prohibited between Member States. This prohibition shall also apply to customs duties of a fiscal nature.

5. The Council, on a proposal from the Commission, shall adopt the European regulations and decisions fixing Common Customs Tariff duties.

6. In carrying out the tasks entrusted to it under this Article the Commission shall be guided by:

(a) the need to promote trade between Member States and third countries;
(b) developments in conditions of competition within the Union insofar as they lead to an improvement in the competitive capacity of undertakings;
(c) the requirements of the Union as regards the supply of raw materials and semi-finished goods; in this connection the Commission shall take care to avoid distorting conditions of competition between Member States in respect of finished goods;
(d) the need to avoid serious disturbances in the economies of Member States and to ensure rational development of production and an expansion of consumption within the Union.

[...]

Subsection 3
Prohibition of quantitative restrictions

Article III-153

Quantitative restrictions on imports and exports and all measures having equivalent effect shall be prohibited between Member States.

Article III-154

Article III-153 shall not preclude prohibitions or restrictions on imports, exports or goods in transit justified on grounds of public morality, public policy or public security; the protection of health and life of humans, animals or plants; the protection of national treasures possessing artistic, historic or archaeological value; or the protection of industrial and commercial property. Such prohibitions or restrictions shall not, however, constitute a means of arbitrary discrimination or a disguised restriction on trade between Member States.

[...]

Article III-172

1. Save where otherwise provided in the Constitution, this Article shall apply for the achievement of the objectives set out in Article III-130. European laws or framework laws shall establish measures for the approximation of the provisions laid down by law, regulation or administrative action in Member States which have as their object the establishment and functioning of the internal market. Such laws shall be adopted after consultation of the Economic and Social Committee.

2. Paragraph 1 shall not apply to fiscal provisions, to those relating to the free movement of persons or to those relating to the rights and interests of employed persons.

3. The Commission, in its proposals submitted under paragraph 1 concerning health, safety, environmental protection and consumer protection, shall take as a base a high level of protection, taking account in particular of any new development based on scientific facts. Within their respective powers, the European Parliament and the Council shall also seek to achieve this objective.

4. If, after the adoption of a harmonisation measure by means of a European law or framework law or by means of a European regulation of the Commission, a Member State deems it necessary to maintain national provisions on grounds of major needs referred to in Article III-154, or relating to the protection of the environment or the working environment, it shall notify the Commission of these provisions as well as the grounds for maintaining them.

5. Moreover, without prejudice to paragraph 4, if, after the adoption of a harmonisation measure by means of a European law or framework law or by means of a European regulation of the Commission, a Member State deems it necessary to introduce national provisions based on new scientific evidence relating to the protection of the environment or the working environment on grounds of a problem specific to that Member State arising after the adoption of the harmonization measure, it shall notify the Commission of the envisaged provisions and the reasons for them.

6. The Commission shall, within six months of the notifications referred to in paragraphs 4 and 5, adopt a European decision approving or rejecting the national provisions involved after having verified whether or not they are a means of arbitrary discrimination or a disguised restriction on trade between Member States and whether or not they constitute an obstacle to the functioning of the internal market.

In the absence of a decision by the Commission within this period the national provisions referred to in paragraphs 4 and 5 shall be deemed to have been approved.

[...]

Chapter III
Policies in other areas

[...]

Section 5
Environment

Article III-233

1. Union policy on the environment shall contribute to the pursuit of the following objectives:

(a) preserving, protecting and improving the quality of the environment;
(b) protecting human health;
(c) prudent and rational utilisation of natural resources;
(d) promoting measures at international level to deal with regional or worldwide environmental problems.

2. Union policy on the environment shall aim at a high level of protection taking into account the diversity of situations in the various regions of the Union. It shall be based on the precautionary principle and on the principles that preventive action should be taken, that environmental damage should as a priority be rectified at source and that the polluter should pay.

In this context, harmonisation measures answering environmental protection requirements shall include, where appropriate, a safeguard clause allowing Member States to take provisional steps, for non-economic environmental reasons, subject to a procedure of inspection by the Union.

3. In preparing its policy on the environment, the Union shall take account of:

(a) available scientific and technical data;
(b) environmental conditions in the various regions of the Union;
(c) the potential benefits and costs of action or lack of action;
(d) the economic and social development of the Union as a whole and the balanced development of its regions.

4. Within their respective spheres of competence, the Union and the Member States shall cooperate with third countries and with the competent international organisations. The arrangements for the Union's cooperation may be the subject of agreements between the Union and the third parties concerned.

The first subparagraph shall be without prejudice to Member States' competence to negotiate in international bodies and to conclude international agreements.

Article III-234

1. European laws or framework laws shall establish what action is to be taken in order to achieve the objectives referred to in Article III-233. They shall be adopted after consultation of the Committee of the Regions and the Economic and Social Committee.

2. By way of derogation from paragraph 1 and without prejudice to Article III-172, the Council shall unanimously adopt European laws or framework laws establishing:

(a) provisions primarily of a fiscal nature;
(b) measures affecting:
   (i) town and country planning;
   (ii) quantitative management of water resources or affecting, directly or indirectly, the availability of those resources;
   (iii) land use, with the exception of waste management;
(c) measures significantly affecting a Member State's choice between different energy sources and the general structure of its energy supply.

The Council, on a proposal from the Commission, may unanimously adopt a European decision making the ordinary legislative procedure applicable to the matters referred to in the first subparagraph.

In all cases, the Council shall act after consulting the European Parliament, the Committee of the Regions and the Economic and Social Committee.

3. European laws shall establish general action programmes which set out priority objectives to be attained. Such laws shall be adopted after consultation of the Committee of the Regions and the Economic and Social Committee.

The measures necessary for the implementation of these programmes shall be adopted under the terms of paragraph 1 or 2, as the case may be.

4. Without prejudice to certain measures adopted by the Union, the Member States shall finance and implement the environment policy.

5. Without prejudice to the principle that the polluter should pay, if a measure based on paragraph 1 involves costs deemed disproportionate for the public authorities of a Member State, such measure shall provide in appropriate form for:

(a) temporary derogations, and/or
(b) financial support from the Cohesion Fund.

6. The protective measures adopted pursuant to this Article shall not prevent any Member State from maintaining or introducing more stringent protective measures. Such measures must be compatible with the Constitution. They shall be notified to the Commission.

[...]

Decision No 1600/2002/EC of the European Parliament and of the Council of 22 July 2002 laying down the Sixth Community Environment Action Programme

Editorial note

The Sixth Community Environment Action Programme sets out the strategic direction of EC environmental law and policy over the next decade. Earlier action programmes were adopted for the periods 1973–1977 (OJ C 112 20.12.1973 p. 1), 1977–1983 (OJ C 139 13.06.1977 p. 1), 1983–1987 (OJ C 46 17.02.1983 p. 1), 1987–1992 (OJ C 70 18.03.1987 p. 3) and 1993–2000 (OJ C 138 17.05.1993 p. 1). The Sixth Community Environment Action Programme was adopted in July 2002 and covers a period of ten years (Article 1(3)). The Programme addresses the key environmental priorities and objectives of the Community (Article 1(1)). It integrates environmental concerns in all Community policies and contributes to sustainable development (Article 1(1)). The Programme sets out key environmental objectives to be attained and, where appropriate, targets and timetables are also established (Article 1(2)). It identifies four key environmental priorities: climate change; nature and biodiversity; environment and health and quality of life; natural resources and waste (Article 1(4)). The Programme aims to ensure a high level of protection, taking into account the principle of subsidiarity and the diversity of situations in the various regions of the Community. It is based, *inter alia*, on the polluter-pays principle, the precautionary principle and preventive action, and the principle of rectification of pollution at source (Article 2(1)).

The Programme is to ensure that the most effective and appropriate means be used to achieve its aims, in particular in the four key environmental priorities identified above (Article 2(3)). The aims and objectives of the Programme are to be pursued according to approaches outlined in Article 3 of the Programme, which include, *inter alia*, developing new legislation and amending existing legislation, where appropriate; encouraging more effective implementation and enforcement; integrating environmental protection requirements into the initiatives in other Community policy areas; promoting market-based economic instruments; improving collaboration and partnership with enterprises (Article 3).

Thematic strategies, developed and implemented in consultation with the relevant parties, are to be adopted for priority environmental problems requiring a broad approach (Article 4). Article 5 outlines the objectives and priority areas for action on tackling climate change. Article 6 outlines the Community's objectives and priority areas for action on nature and biodiversity. Objectives and priority areas for action on environment and health and quality of life are identified in Article 7. Article 8 deals with the objective and priority areas for action on the sustainable use and management of natural resources and waste, the fourth key environmental priority identified in the Programme. Article 9 outlines the objectives and priority areas for action on international issues and international dimensions of the four environmental priority areas of the Programme, whilst Article 10 sets out the priority actions to be followed in the pursuit of the objectives set out in Article 2 on environment policy-making. The progress made in the implementation of the Programme is to be monitored by the Commission in the fourth year of the operation of the Programme. A final assessment of the Programme and the state of and prospects for the environment is to be submitted by the Commission to Parliament in the course of the final year of the Programme (Article 11(2)).

Source: OJ L 242 10.09.2002 p. 1

Decision No 1600/2002/EC of the European Parliament and of the Council of 22 July 2002 laying down the Sixth Community Environment Action Programme

The European Parliament and the Council of the European Union,
    Having regard to the Treaty establishing the European Community, and in partic-
ular Article 175(3) thereof,
    Having regard to the proposal from the Commission,[1]
    Having regard to the opinion of the Economic and Social Committee,[2]
    Having regard to the opinion of the Committee of the Regions,[3]
    Acting in accordance with the procedure laid down in Article 251 of the Treaty,[4] in
the light of the joint text approved by the Conciliation Committee on 1 May 2002,
    Whereas:

(1) A clean and healthy environment is essential for the well-being and prosperity of society, yet continued growth at a global level will lead to continuing pressures on the environment.

----

[1] OJ C 154 E, 29.5.2001, p. 218.   [2] OJ C 221, 7.8.2001, p. 80.   [3] OJ C 357, 14.12.2001, p. 44.
[4] Opinion of the European Parliament of 31 May 2001 (OJ C 47 E, 21.2.2002, p. 113), Council Common Position of 27 September 2001 (OJ C 4, 7.1.2002, p. 52) and Decision of the European Parliament of 17 January 2002 (not yet published in the Official Journal). Decision of the European Parliament of 30 May 2002 and Decision of the Council of 11 June 2002.

(2) The Community's fifth environmental action programme 'Towards Sustainability' ended on 31 December 2000 having delivered a number of important improvements.

(3) Continued effort is required in order to meet the environmental objectives and targets already established by the Community and there is a need for the Sixth Environmental Action Programme (the 'Programme') set out in this Decision.

(4) A number of serious environmental problems persist and new ones are emerging which require further action.

(5) Greater focus on prevention and the implementation of the precautionary principle is required in developing an approach to protect human health and the environment.

(6) A prudent use of natural resources and the protection of the global eco-system together with economic prosperity and a balanced social development are a condition for sustainable development.

(7) The Programme aims at a high level of protection of the environment and human health and at a general improvement in the environment and quality of life, indicates priorities for the environmental dimension of the Sustainable Development Strategy and should be taken into account when bringing forward actions under the Strategy.

(8) The Programme aims to achieve a decoupling between environmental pressures and economic growth whilst being consistent with the principle of subsidiarity and respecting the diversity of conditions across the various regions of the European Union.

(9) The Programme establishes environmental priorities for a Community response focusing in particular on climate change, nature and biodiversity, environment and health and quality of life, and natural resources and wastes.

(10) For each of these areas key objectives and certain targets are indicated and a number of actions are identified with a view to achieving the said targets. These objectives and targets constitute performance levels or achievements to be aimed at.

(11) The objectives, priorities and actions of the Programme should contribute to sustainable development in the candidate countries and endeavour to ensure the protection of the natural assets of these countries.

(12) Legislation remains central to meeting environmental challenges and full and correct implementation of the existing legislation is a priority. Other options for achieving environmental objectives should also be considered.

(13) The Programme should promote the process of integration of environmental concerns into all Community policies and activities in line with Article 6 of the Treaty in order to reduce the pressures on the environment from various sources.

(14) A strategic integrated approach, incorporating new ways of working with the market, involving citizens, enterprises and other stakeholders is needed in order to induce necessary changes in both production and public and private

consumption patterns that influence negatively the state of, and trends in, the environment. This approach should encourage sustainable use and management of land and sea.

(15) Provision for access to environmental information and to justice and for public participation in policy-making will be important to the success of the Programme.

(16) Thematic strategies will consider the range of options and instruments required for dealing with a series of complex issues that require a broad and multi-dimensional approach and will propose the necessary actions, involving where appropriate the European Parliament and the Council.

(17) There is scientific consensus that human activity is causing increases in concentrations of greenhouse gases, leading to higher global temperatures and disruption to the climate.

(18) The implications of climate change for human society and for nature are severe and necessitate mitigation. Measures to reduce emissions of greenhouse gases can be implemented without a reduction in levels of growth and prosperity.

(19) Regardless of the success of mitigation, society needs to adapt to and prepare for the effects of climate change.

(20) Healthy and balanced natural systems are essential for supporting life on the planet.

(21) There is considerable pressure from human activity on nature and biodiversity. Action is necessary to counteract pressures arising notably from pollution, the introduction of non-native species, potential risks from releasing genetically modified organisms and the way in which the land and sea are exploited.

(22) Soil is a finite resource that is under environmental pressure.

(23) Despite improvements in environmental standards, there is increased likelihood of a link between environmental degradation and certain human illnesses. Therefore the potential risks arising, for example, from emissions and hazardous chemicals, pesticides, and from noise should be addressed.

(24) Greater knowledge is required on the potential negative impacts arising from the use of chemicals and the responsibility for generating knowledge should be placed on producers, importers and downstream users.

(25) Chemicals that are dangerous should be replaced by safer chemicals or safer alternative technologies not entailing the use of chemicals, with the aim of reducing risks to man and the environment.

(26) Pesticides should be used in a sustainable way so as to minimise negative impacts for human health and the environment.

(27) The urban environment is home to some 70% of the population and concerted efforts are needed to ensure a better environment and quality of life in towns and cities.

(28) There is a limited capacity of the planet to meet the increasing demand for resources and to absorb the emissions and waste resulting from their use and

there is evidence that the existing demand exceeds the carrying capacity of the environment in several cases.

(29) Waste volumes in the Community continue to rise, a significant quantity of these being hazardous, leading to loss of resources and to increased pollution risks.

(30) Economic globalisation means that environmental action is increasingly needed at international level, including on transport policies, requiring new responses from the Community linked to policy related to trade, development and external affairs enabling sustainable development to be pursued in other countries. Good governance should make a contribution to this end.

(31) Trade, international investment flows and export credits should make a more positive contribution to the pursuit of environmental protection and sustainable development.

(32) Environmental policy-making, given the complexities of the issues, needs to be based on best available scientific and economic assessment, and on knowledge of the state and trends of the environment, in line with Article 174 of the Treaty.

(33) Information to policy makers, stakeholders and the general public has to be relevant, transparent, up to date and easily understandable.

(34) Progress towards meeting environmental objectives needs to be measured and evaluated.

(35) On the basis of an assessment of the state of the environment, taking account of the regular information provided by the European Environment Agency, a review of progress and an assessment of the need to change orientation should be made at the mid term point of the Programme,

Have decided as follows:

Article 1
Scope of the Programme

1. This Decision establishes a programme of Community action on the environment (hereinafter referred to as the 'Programme'). It addresses the key environmental objectives and priorities based on an assessment of the state of the environment and of prevailing trends including emerging issues that require a lead from the Community. The Programme should promote the integration of environmental concerns in all Community policies and contribute to the achievement of sustainable development throughout the current and future enlarged Community. The Programme furthermore provides for continuous efforts to achieve environmental objectives and targets already established by the Community.

2. The Programme sets out the key environmental objectives to be attained. It establishes, where appropriate, targets and timetables. The objectives and targets should be fulfilled before expiry of the Programme, unless otherwise specified.

3. The Programme shall cover a period of ten years starting from 22 July 2002. Appropriate initiatives in the different policy areas with the aim of meeting the

objectives shall consist of a range of measures including legislation and the strategic approaches outlined in Article 3. These initiatives should be presented progressively and at the latest by four years after the adoption of this Decision.

4. The objectives respond to the key environmental priorities to be met by the Community in the following areas:

— climate change,
— nature and biodiversity,
— environment and health and quality of life,
— natural resources and wastes.

Article 2
Principles and overall aims

1. The Programme constitutes a framework for the Community's environmental policy during the period of the Programme with the aim of ensuring a high level of protection, taking into account the principle of subsidiarity and the diversity of situations in the various regions of the Community, and of achieving a decoupling between environmental pressures and economic growth. It shall be based particularly on the polluter pays principle, the precautionary principle and preventive action, and the principle of rectification of pollution at source.

The Programme shall form a basis for the environmental dimension of the European Sustainable Development Strategy and contribute to the integration of environmental concerns into all Community policies, *inter alia* by setting out environmental priorities for the Strategy.

2. The Programme aims at:

— emphasising climate change as an outstanding challenge of the next 10 years and beyond and contributing to the long term objective of stabilising greenhouse gas concentrations in the atmosphere at a level that would prevent dangerous anthropogenic interference with the climate system. Thus a long term objective of a maximum global temperature increase of $2°$Celsius over pre-industrial levels and a CO_2 concentration below 550 ppm shall guide the Programme. In the longer term this is likely to require a global reduction in emissions of greenhouse gases by 70% as compared to 1990 as identified by the Intergovernmental Panel on Climate Change (IPCC);
— protecting, conserving, restoring and developing the functioning of natural systems, natural habitats, wild flora and fauna with the aim of halting desertification and the loss of biodiversity, including diversity of genetic resources, both in the European Union and on a global scale;
— contributing to a high level of quality of life and social well being for citizens by providing an environment where the level of pollution does not give rise to harmful effects on human health and the environment and by encouraging a sustainable urban development;

— better resource efficiency and resource and waste management to bring about more sustainable production and consumption patterns, thereby decoupling the use of resources and the generation of waste from the rate of economic growth and aiming to ensure that the consumption of renewable and non-renewable resources does not exceed the carrying capacity of the environment.

3. The Programme shall ensure that environmental objectives, which should focus on the environmental outcomes to be achieved, are met by the most effective and appropriate means available, in the light of the principles set out in paragraph 1 and the strategic approaches set out in Article 3. Full consideration shall be given to ensuring that the Community's environmental policy-making is undertaken in an integrated way and to all available options and instruments, taking into account regional and local differences, as well as ecologically sensitive areas, with an emphasis on:

— developing European initiatives to raise the awareness of citizens and local authorities;
— extensive dialogue with stakeholders, raising environmental awareness and public participation;
— analysis of benefits and costs, taking into account the need to internalise environmental costs;
— the best available scientific evidence, and the further improvement of scientific knowledge through research and technological development;
— data and information on the state and trends of the environment.

4. The Programme shall promote the full integration of environmental protection requirements into all Community policies and actions by establishing environmental objectives and, where appropriate, targets and timetables to be taken into account in relevant policy areas.

Furthermore, measures proposed and adopted in favour of the environment should be coherent with the objectives of the economic and social dimensions of sustainable development and vice versa.

5. The Programme shall promote the adoption of policies and approaches that contribute to the achievement of sustainable development in the countries which are candidates for accession ('Candidate Countries') building on the transposition and implementation of the acquis. The enlargement process should sustain and protect the environmental assets of the Candidate Countries such as wealth of biodiversity, and should maintain and strengthen sustainable production and consumption and land use patterns and environmentally sound transport structures through:

— integration of environmental protection requirements into Community Programmes including those related to development of infrastructure;
— promotion of transfer of clean technologies to the Candidate Countries;

– extended dialogue and exchange of experience with the national and local adminis-
  trations in the Candidate Countries on sustainable development and preservation
  of their environmental assets;
– cooperation with civil society, environmental non-governmental organisations
  (NGOs) and business in the Candidate Countries to help raise public awareness
  and participation;
– encouraging international financing institutions and the private sector to support
  the implementation of and compliance with the environmental acquis in the Candidate Countries and to pay due attention to integrating environmental concerns
  into the activities of the economic sector.

6. The Programme shall stimulate:

– the positive and constructive role of the European Union as a leading partner
  in the protection of the global environment and in the pursuit of a sustainable
  development;
– the development of a global partnership for environment and sustainable development;
– the integration of environmental concerns and objectives into all aspects of the
  Community's external relations.

Article 3
Strategic approaches to meeting environmental objectives

The aims and objectives set out in the Programme shall be pursued, *inter alia*, by the
following means:

1. Development of new Community legislation and amendment of existing legislation, where appropriate;

2. Encouraging more effective implementation and enforcement of Community
legislation on the environment and without prejudice to the Commission's right to
initiate infringement proceedings. This requires:

– increased measures to improve respect for Community rules on the protection of
  the environment and addressing infringements of environmental legislation;
– promotion of improved standards of permitting, inspection, monitoring and
  enforcement by Member States;
– a more systematic review of the application of environmental legislation across the
  Member States;
– improved exchange of information on best practice on implementation including by
  the European Network for the Implementation and Enforcement of Environmental
  Law (IMPEL network) within the framework of its competencies;

3. Further efforts for integration of environmental protection requirements into the
preparation, definition and implementation of Community policies and activities in
the different policy areas are needed. Further efforts are necessary in different sectors

including consideration of their specific environmental objectives, targets, timetables and indicators. This requires:

– ensuring that the integration strategies produced by the Council in different policy areas are translated into effective action and contribute to the implementation of the environmental aims and objectives of the Programme;
– consideration, prior to their adoption, of whether action in the economic and social fields, contribute to and are coherent with the objectives, targets and time frame of the Programme;
– establishing appropriate regular internal mechanisms in the Community institutions, taking full account of the need to promote transparency and access to information, to ensure that environmental considerations are fully reflected in Commission policy initiatives, including relevant decisions and legislative proposals;
– regular monitoring, via relevant indicators, elaborated where possible on the basis of a common methodology for each sector, and reporting on the process of sectoral integration;
– further integration of environmental criteria into Community funding programmes without prejudice to existing ones;
– full and effective use and implementation of Environmental Impact Assessment and Strategic Environmental Assessment;
– that the objectives of the Programme should be taken into account in future financial perspective reviews of Community financial instruments;

4. Promotion of sustainable production and consumption patterns by effective implementation of the principles set out in Article 2, to internalise the negative as well as the positive impacts on the environment through the use of a blend of instruments, including market based and economic instruments. This requires, *inter alia*:

– encouraging reforms of subsidies that have considerable negative effects on the environment and are incompatible with sustainable development, *inter alia* by establishing, by the mid-term review, a list of criteria allowing such environmentally negative subsidies to be recorded, with a view to gradually eliminating them;
– analysing the environmental efficiency of tradable environmental permits as a generic instrument and of emission trading with a view to promoting and implementing their use where feasible;
– promoting and encouraging the use of fiscal measures such as environmentally related taxes and incentives, at the appropriate national or Community level;
– promoting the integration of environmental protection requirements in standardisation activities;

5. Improving collaboration and partnership with enterprises and their representative bodies and involving the social partners, consumers and their organisations, as

appropriate, with a view to improving the environmental performance of enterprises and aiming at sustainable production patterns. This requires:

- promoting an integrated product policy approach throughout the Programme that will encourage the taking into account of environmental requirements throughout the life-cycle of products, and more widespread application of environmentally friendly processes and products;
- encouraging wider uptake of the Community's Eco-Management and Audit Scheme (EMAS)[1] and developing initiatives to encourage companies to publish rigorous and independently verified environmental or sustainable development performance reports;
- establishing a compliance assistance programme, with specific help for small and medium enterprises;
- stimulating the introduction of company environmental performance award schemes;
- stimulating product innovation with the aim of greening the market including through improved dissemination of results of the LIFE Programme;[2]

- encouraging voluntary commitments or agreements to achieve clear environmental objectives, including setting out procedures in the event of non-compliance;

6. To help ensure that individual consumers, enterprises and public bodies in their roles as purchasers, are better informed about the processes and products in terms of their environmental impact with a view to achieving sustainable consumption patterns. This requires:

- encouraging the uptake of eco-labels and other forms of environmental information and labelling that allow consumers to compare environmental performance between products of the same type;
- encouraging the use of reliable self-declared environmental claims and preventing misleading claims;
- promoting a green public procurement policy, allowing environmental characteristics to be taken into account and the possible integration of environmental life cycle, including the production phase, concerns in the procurement procedures while respecting Community competition rules and the internal market, with guidelines on best practice and starting a review of green procurement in Community Institutions;

---

[1] Regulation (EC) No 761/2001 of the European Parliament and of the Council of 19 March 2001 allowing voluntary participation by organisations in a Community eco-management and audit scheme (EMAS) (OJ L 114, 24.4.2001, p. 1).
[2] Regulation (EC) No 1655/2000 of the European Parliament and of the Council of 17 July 2000 concerning the Financial Instrument for the Environment (LIFE) (OJ L 192, 28.7.2000, p. 1).

7. To support environmental integration in the financial sector. This requires:

- considering a voluntary initiative with the financial sector, covering guide-lines for the incorporation of data on environmental cost in company annual financial reports, and the exchange of best policy practices between Member States;
- calling on the European Investment Bank to strengthen the integration of environmental objectives and considerations into its lending activities in particular with a view to supporting a sustainable development of Candidate Countries;
- promoting integration of environmental objectives and considerations into the activities of other financial institutions such as the European Bank for Reconstruction and Development;

8. To create a Community liability regime requires *inter alia*:

- legislation on environmental liability;

9. To improve collaboration and partnership with consumer groups and NGOs and promote better understanding of and participation in environmental issues amongst European citizens requires: – ensuring access to information, participation and justice through early ratification of the Aarhus Convention[1] by the Community and by Member States;

- supporting the provision of accessible information to citizens on the state and trends of the environment in relation to social, economic and health trends;
- general raising of environmental awareness;
- developing general rules and principles for good environmental governance in dialogue processes;

10. To encourage and promote effective and sustainable use and management of land and sea taking account of environmental concerns. This requires, while fully respecting the subsidiarity principle, the following:

- promoting best practice with respect to sustainable land use planning, which takes account of specific regional circumstances with particular emphasis on the Integrated Coastal Zone Management programme;
- promoting best practices and supporting networks fostering the exchange of experience on sustainable development including urban areas, sea, coastline, mountain areas, wetlands and other areas of a sensitive nature;
- enhancing the use, increasing resources and giving broader scope for agri-environment measures under the Common Agricultural Policy;
- encouraging Member States to consider using regional planning as an instrument for improving environmental protection for the citizen and promoting the

[1] Convention on Access to Information, Public Participation in Decision-Making and Access to Justice in Environmental Matters, Aarhus, 25 June 1998.

exchange of experience on sustainable regional development, particularly in urban and densely populated areas.

Article 4
Thematic strategies

1. Actions in Articles 5 to 8 shall include the development of thematic strategies and the evaluation of existing strategies for priority environmental problems requiring a broad approach. These strategies should include an identification of the proposals that are required to reach the objectives set out in the Programme and the procedures foreseen for their adoption. These strategies shall be submitted to the European Parliament and Council and shall, where appropriate take the form of a Decision of the European Parliament and of the Council to be adopted in accordance with the procedure laid down in Article 251 of the Treaty. Subject to the legal base of the proposal, the legislative proposals arising from these strategies shall be adopted in accordance with the procedure laid down in Article 251 of the Treaty.

2. The thematic strategies may include approaches among those outlined in Article 3 and in Article 9 and relevant qualitative and quantitative environmental targets and timetables against which the measures foreseen can be measured and evaluated.

3. The thematic strategies should be developed and implemented in close consultation with the relevant parties, such as NGOs, industry, other social partners and public authorities, while ensuring, as appropriate, consultation of Candidate Countries in this process.

4. The thematic strategies should be presented to the European Parliament and the Council within 3 years of the adoption of the Programme at the latest. The mid term report, in which the Commission evaluates the progress made in implementing the Programme, shall include a review of the thematic strategies.

5. The Commission shall report annually to the European Parliament and the Council on the progress in the development and implementation of the strategies and on their effectiveness.

Article 5
Objectives and priority areas for action on tackling climate change

1. The aims set out in Article 2 should be pursued by the following objectives:

– ratification and entering into force of the Kyoto Protocol to the United Nations framework Convention on climate change by 2002 and fulfilment of its commitment of an 8% reduction in emissions by 2008–12 compared to 1990 levels for the European Community as a whole, in accordance with the commitment of each Member State set out in the Council Conclusions of 16 and 17 June 1998;
– realisation by 2005 of demonstrable progress in achieving the commitments under the Kyoto Protocol;

— placing the Community in a credible position to advocate an international agreement on more stringent reduction targets for the second commitment period provided for by the Kyoto Protocol. This agreement should aim at cutting emissions significantly, taking full account, *inter alia*, of the findings of the IPCC 3rd Assessment Report, and take into account the necessity to move towards a global equitable distribution of greenhouse gas emissions.

2. These objectives shall be pursued by means, *inter alia*, of the following priority actions:

(i) Implementing international climate commitments including the Kyoto Protocol by means of:
- (a) examining the results of the European Climate Change Programme and adopting effective common and coordinated policies and measures on its basis, as appropriate, for various sectors complementary to domestic actions in the Member States;
- (b) working towards the establishment of a Community framework for the development of effective CO_2 emissions trading with the possible extension to other greenhouse gases;
- (c) improving monitoring of greenhouse gases and of progress towards delivering Member States commitments made under the Internal Burden Sharing Agreement;

(ii) Reducing greenhouse gas emissions in the energy sector:
- (a) undertaking as soon as possible an inventory and review of subsidies that counteract an efficient and sustainable use of energy with a view to gradually phasing them out;
- (b) encouraging renewable and lower carbon fossil fuels for power generation;
- (c) encouraging the use of renewable energy sources, including the use of incentives, including at the local level, with a view to meeting the indicative target of 12% of total energy use by 2010;
- (d) introducing incentives to increase Combined Heat and Power and implement measures aiming at doubling the overall share of Combined Heat and Power in the Community as a whole to 18% of the total gross electricity generation;
- (e) prevent and reduce methane emissions from energy production and distribution;
- (f) promoting energy efficiency;

(iii) Reducing greenhouse gas emissions in the transport sector:
- (a) identifying and undertaking specific actions to reduce greenhouse gas emissions from aviation if no such action is agreed within the International Civil Aviation Organisation by 2002;
- (b) identifying and undertaking specific actions to reduce greenhouse gas emissions from marine shipping if no such action is agreed within the International Maritime Organisation by 2003;

(c) encouraging a switch to more efficient and cleaner forms of transport including better organisation and logistics;

(d) in the context of the EU target of an 8% reduction in greenhouse gas emissions, inviting the Commission to submit by the end of 2002 a Communication on quantified environmental objectives for a sustainable transport system;

(e) identifying and undertaking further specific action, including any appropriate legislation, to reduce greenhouse gas emissions from motor vehicles including N_2O;

(f) promoting the development and use of alternative fuels and of low-fuel-consuming vehicles with the aim of substantially and continually increasing their share;

(g) promoting measures to reflect the full environmental costs in the price of transport;

(h) decoupling economic growth and the demand for transport with the aim of reducing environmental impacts;

(iv) Reducing greenhouse gas emissions in industrial production:

(a) promoting eco-efficiency practices and techniques in industry;

(b) developing means to assist SMEs to adapt, innovate and improve performance;

(c) encouraging the development of more environmentally sound and technically feasible alternatives, including the establishment of Community measures, aiming at reducing emissions, phasing out the production where appropriate and feasible and reducing the use of industrial fluorinated gases HFCs (hydrofluorocarbons), PFCs (Perfluorocarbons) and SF6 (sulphur hexafluoride);

(v) Reducing greenhouse gas emissions in other sectors:

(a) promoting energy efficiency notably for heating, cooling and hot tap water in the design of buildings;

(b) taking into account the need to reduce greenhouse gas emissions, alongside with other environmental considerations, in the Common agricultural policy and in the Community's waste management strategy;

(vi) Using other appropriate instruments such as:

(a) promoting the use of fiscal measures, including a timely and appropriate Community framework for energy taxation, to encourage a switch to more efficient energy use, cleaner energy and transport and to encourage technological innovation;

(b) encouraging environmental agreements with industry sectors on greenhouse gas emission reductions;

(c) ensuring climate change as a major theme of Community policy for research and technological development and for national research programmes.

3. In addition to the mitigation of climate change, the Community should prepare for measures aimed at adaptation to the consequences of climate change, by:

- reviewing Community policies, in particular those relevant to climate change, so that adaptation is addressed adequately in investment decisions;
- encouraging regional climate modelling and assessments both to prepare regional adaptation measures such as water resources management, conservation of biodiversity, desertification and flooding prevention and to support awareness raising among citizens and business.

4. It must be ensured that the climate challenge is taken into account in the Community's enlargement. This will require, *inter alia*, the following actions with Candidate Countries:

- supporting capacity building, for the application of domestic measures for the use of the Kyoto mechanisms and improved reporting and emission monitoring;
- supporting a more sustainable transport and energy sector;
- ensuring that cooperation with candidate countries is further strengthened on climate change issues.

5. Combating climate change will form an integral part of the European Union's external relations policies and will constitute one of the priorities in its sustainable development policy. This will require concerted and coordinated efforts on the part of the Community and its Member States with a view to:

- capacity-building to assist developing countries and countries with economies in transition for example through encouraging projects in connection with the Clean Development Mechanism (CDM) in the Kyoto Protocol and joint implementation;
- responding to identified technology-transfer needs;
- assisting with the challenge of adapting to climate change in the countries concerned.

Article 6
Objectives and priority areas for action on nature and biodiversity
1. The aims set out in Article 2 should be pursued by the following objectives:

- halting biodiversity decline with the aim to reach this objective by 2010, including prevention and mitigation of impacts of invasive alien species and genotypes;
- protection and appropriate restoration of nature and biodiversity from damaging pollution;
- conservation, appropriate restoration and sustainable use of marine environment, coasts and wetlands;

- conservation and appropriate restoration of areas of significant landscape values including cultivated as well as sensitive areas;
- conservation of species and habitats, with special concern to preventing habitat fragmentation;
- promotion of a sustainable use of the soil, with particular attention to preventing erosion, deterioration, contamination and desertification.

2. These objectives shall be pursued by means of the following priority actions, taking into account the principle of subsidiarity, based on the existing global and regional conventions and strategies and full implementation of the relevant Community acts. The ecosystem approach, as adopted in the Convention on Biological Diversity,[1] should be applied whenever appropriate:

(a) on biodiversity:
  - ensuring the implementation and promoting the monitoring and assessment of the Community's biodiversity strategy and the relevant action plans, including through a programme for gathering data and information, developing the appropriate indicators, and promoting the use of best available techniques and of best environmental practices;
  - promoting research on biodiversity, genetic resources, ecosystems and interactions with human activities;
  - developing measures to enhance sustainable use, sustainable production and sustainable investments in relation to biodiversity;
  - encouraging coherent assessment, further research and cooperation on threatened species;
  - promoting at the global level a fair and equitable sharing of benefits arising from the use of genetic resources to implement Article 15 of the Convention on Biological Diversity on access to genetic resources originating from third countries;
  - developing measures aimed at the prevention and control of invasive alien species including alien genotypes;
  - establishing the Natura 2000 network and implementing the necessary technical and financial instruments and measures required for its full implementation and for the protection, outside the Natura 2000 areas, of species protected under the Habitats and Birds Directives;
  - promoting the extension of the Natura 2000 network to the Candidate Countries;
(b) on accidents and disasters:
  - promoting Community coordination to actions by Member States in relation to accidents and natural disasters by, for example, setting up a network for exchange of prevention practices and tools;

[1] OJ L 309, 13.12.1993, p. 1.

    – developing further measures to help prevent the major accident hazards with special regards to those arising from pipelines, mining, marine transport of hazardous substances and developing measures on mining waste;

(c) a thematic strategy on soil protection, addressing the prevention of, *inter alia*, pollution, erosion, desertification, land degradation, land-take and hydrogeological risks taking into account regional diversity, including specificities of mountain and arid areas;

(d) promoting sustainable management of extractive industries with a view to reduce their environmental impact;

(e) promoting the integration of conservation and restoration of the landscape values into other policies including tourism, taking account of relevant international instruments;

(f) promoting the integration of biodiversity considerations in agricultural policies and encouraging sustainable rural development, multifunctional and sustainable agriculture, through:

    – encouraging full use of current opportunities of the Common Agriculture Policy and other policy measures;

    – encouraging more environmentally responsible farming, including, where appropriate, extensive production methods, integrated farming practices, organic farming and agro-biodiversity, in future reviews of the Common Agricultural Policy, taking account of the need for a balanced approach to the multifunctional role of rural communities;

(g) promoting sustainable use of the seas and conservation of marine ecosystems, including sea beds, estuarine and coastal areas, paying special attention to sites holding a high biodiversity value, through:

    – promoting greater integration of environmental considerations in the Common Fisheries Policy, taking the opportunity of its review in 2002;

    – a thematic strategy for the protection and conservation of the marine environment taking into account, *inter alia*, the terms and implementation obligations of marine Conventions, and the need to reduce emissions and impacts of sea transport and other sea and landbased activities;

    – promoting integrated management of coastal zones;

    – further promote the protection of marine areas, in particular with the Natura 2000 network as well as by other feasible Community means;

(h) implementing and further developing strategies and measures on forests in line with the forest strategy for the European Union, taking account the principle of subsidiarity and biodiversity considerations, incorporating the following elements:

    – improving existing Community measures which protect forests and implementing sustainable forest management, *inter alia*, through national forest programmes, in connection with rural development plans, with increased emphasis on the monitoring of the multiple roles of forests in line with recommendations adopted by the Ministerial Conference on the Protection of Forests in Europe and the United Nations Forum on Forests and the Convention on Biodiversity and other fora;

- encouraging the effective coordination between all policy sectors involved in forestry, including the private sector, as well as the coordination of all stakeholders involved in forestry issues;
- stimulating the increase of the market share for sustainably produced wood, *inter alia*, through encouraging certification for sustainable forest management and encouraging labelling of related products;
- continuing the active participation of the Community and of Member States in the implementation of global and regional resolutions and in discussions and negotiations on forest-related issues;
- examining the possibilities to take active measures to prevent and combat trade of illegally harvested wood;
- encouraging consideration of climate change effects in forestry;

(i) on genetically modified organisms (GMOs):

- developing the provisions and methods for risk assessment, identification, labelling and traceability of GMOs in order to enable effective monitoring and controls of health and environmental effects;
- aiming for swift ratification and implementation of the Cartagena Protocol on Biosafety and supporting the build up of regulatory frameworks in third countries where needed through technical and financial assistance.

Article 7
Objectives and priority areas for action on environment and health
and quality of life

1. The aims set out in Article 2 should be pursued by the following objectives, taking into account relevant World Health Organisation (WHO) standards, guidelines and programmes:

- achieving better understanding of the threats to environment and human health in order to take action to prevent and reduce these threats;
- contributing to a better quality of life through an integrated approach concentrating on urban areas;
- aiming to achieve within one generation (2020) that chemicals are only produced and used in ways that do not lead to a significant negative impact on health and the environment, recognising that the present gaps of knowledge on the properties, use, disposal and exposure of chemicals need to be overcome;
- chemicals that are dangerous should be substituted by safer chemicals or safer alternative technologies not entailing the use of chemicals, with the aim of reducing risks to man and the environment;

- reducing the impacts of pesticides on human health and the environment and more generally to achieve a more sustainable use of pesticides as well as a significant overall reduction in risks and of the use of pesticides consistent with the necessary crop protection. Pesticides in use which are persistent or bio-accumulative or toxic or have other properties of concern should be substituted by less dangerous ones where possible;
- achieving quality levels of ground and surface water that do not give rise to significant impacts on and risks to human health and the environment, and to ensure that the rates of extraction from water resources are sustainable over the long term;
- achieving levels of air quality that do not give rise to significant negative impacts on and risks to human health and the environment;
- substantially reducing the number of people regularly affected by long-term average levels of noise, in particular from traffic which, according to scientific studies, cause detrimental effects on human health and preparing the next step in the work with the noise directive.

2. These objectives shall be pursued by means of the following priority actions:

(a) reinforcement of Community research programmes and scientific expertise, and encouragement to the international coordination of national research programmes, to support achievement of objectives on health and environment, and in particular the:
  - identification and recommendations on the priority areas for research and action including among others the potential health impacts of electromagnetic pollution sources and including particular attention to the development and validation of alternative methods to animal testing in particular in the field of chemical safety;
  - definition and development of indicators of health and environment;
  - re-examination, development and updating of current health standards and limit values, including where appropriate, the effects on potentially vulnerable groups, for example children or the elderly and the synergies and the reciprocal impact of various pollutants;
  - review of trends and the provision of an early warning mechanism for new or emerging problems;
(b) on chemicals:
  - placing the responsibility on manufacturers, importers and downstream users for generating knowledge about all chemicals (duty of care) and assessing risks of their use, including in products, as well as recovery and disposal;
  - developing a coherent system based on a tiered approach, excluding chemical substances used in very low quantities, for the testing, risk assessment and risk management of new and existing substances with testing procedures that minimise the need for animal testing and develop alternative testing methods;

- ensuring that the chemical substances of concern are subject to accelerated risk management procedures and that substances of very high concern, including carcinogenic, mutagenic or toxic for reproduction substances and those which have POPs (persistent organic pollutants) characteristics, are used only in justified and well defined cases and must be subject to authorisation before their use;
- ensuring that the results of the risk assessments of chemicals are taken fully into account in all areas of Community legislation where chemicals are regulated and to avoid duplication of work;
- providing criteria for including among the substances of very high concern those that are persistent and bioaccumulating and toxic and substances that are very persistent and very bio-accumulative and envisaging the addition of known endocrine disrupters when agreed test methods and criteria are established;
- ensuring that the main measures that are necessary in view of the identified objectives are developed speedily so that they can come into force before the mid-term review;
- ensuring public access to the non-confidential information in the Community Register on Chemicals (REACH Register);

(c) on pesticides:

- full implementation and review of the effectiveness of the applicable legal framework[1] in order to ensure a high level of protection, when amended. This revision might include, where appropriate, comparative assessment and the development of Community authorisation procedures for placing on the market;

- a thematic strategy on the sustainable use of pesticides that addresses:
  (i)   minimising the hazards and risks to health and environment from the use of pesticides;
  (ii) improved controls on the use and distribution of pesticides;
  (iii) reducing the levels of harmful active substances including through substituting the most dangerous with safer, including non-chemical, alternatives;
  (iv) encouragement of the use of low input or pesticide free cultivation among others through raising users' awareness, promoting the use of codes of good practices, and promoting consideration of the possible application of financial instruments;
  (v)   a transparent system for reporting and monitoring progress made in fulfilling the objectives of the strategy including the development of suitable indicators;

---

[1] Council Directive 91/414/EEC of 15 July 1991 concerning the placing of plant protection products on the market (OJ L 230, 19.8.1991, p. 1). Directive as last amended by Commission Directive 2001/49/EC (OJ L 176, 29.6.2001, p. 61).

(d) on chemicals and pesticides:
  - aiming at swift ratification of the Rotterdam Convention on the Prior Informed Consent Procedure for Certain Hazardous Chemicals and Pesticides in International Trade and of the Stockholm Convention on Persistent Organic Pollutants (POPs);
  - amending Council Regulation (EEC) No 2455/92 of 23 July 1992 concerning the export and import of certain dangerous chemicals[1] with the aim of bringing it into line with the Rotterdam Convention, improving its procedural mechanisms and improving information to developing countries;
  - support the improvement of the management of chemicals and pesticides in developing and candidate countries, including the elimination of stocks of obsolete pesticides, *inter alia*, by supporting projects aimed at such elimination;
  - contributing to international efforts on the elaboration of a strategic approach on international chemicals management;
(e) on the sustainable use and high quality of water:
  - ensuring a high level of protection of surface and groundwater, preventing pollution and promoting sustainable water use;
  - working towards ensuring full implementation of the Water Framework Directive,[2] aiming at a good ecological, chemical and quantitative water status and a coherent and sustainable water management;
  - developing measures aimed at cessation of discharges, emissions and losses of Priority Hazardous Substances, in line with the provisions of the Water Framework Directive;
  - ensuring a high level of protection of bathing water, including revising the Bathing Water Directive;[3]
  - ensuring the integration of the concepts and approaches of the Water Framework Directive and of other water protection directives in other Community policies;
(f) on air quality, development and implementation of the measures in Article 5 in the transport, industry and energy sectors should be compatible with and contribute to improvement of quality of air. Further measures envisaged are:
  - improving the monitoring and assessment of air quality, including the deposition of pollutants, and the provision of information to the public, including the development and use of indicators;

---

[1] OJ L 251, 29.8.1992, p. 13. Regulation as last amended by Commission Regulation (EC) No 2247/98 (OJ L 282, 20.10.1998, p. 12).

[2] Directive 2000/60/EC of the European Parliament and of the Council of 23 October 2000 establishing a framework for Community action in the field of water policy (OJ L 327, 22.12.2000, p. 1).

[3] Council Directive 76/160/EEC of 8 December 1975 concerning the quality of bathing water (OJ L 31, 5.2.1976, p. 1). Directive as last amended by the 1994 Act of Accession.

    – a thematic strategy to strengthen a coherent and integrated policy on air pollution to cover priorities for further actions, the review and updating where appropriate of air quality standards and national emission ceilings with a view to reach the long term objective of no-excedence of critical loads and levels and the development of better systems for gathering information, modelling and forecasting;

    – adopting appropriate measures concerning ground-level ozone and particulates;

    – considering indoor air quality and the impacts on health, with recommendations for future measures where appropriate;

    – playing a leading role in the negotiations and the implementation of the Montreal Protocol on ozone depleting substances;

    – playing a leading role in the negotiations on and strengthening the links and interactions with international processes contributing to clean air in Europe;

    – further development of specific Community instruments for reducing emissions from relevant source categories;

(g) on noise:

    – supplementing and further improving measures, including appropriate type-approval procedures, on noise emissions from services and products, in particular motor vehicles including measures to reduce noise from the interaction between tyre and road surface that do not compromise road safety, from railway vehicles, aircraft and stationary machinery;

    – developing and implementing instruments to mitigate traffic noise where appropriate, for example by means of transport demand reduction, shifts to less noisy modes of transport, the promotion of technical measures and of sustainable transport planning;

(h) on urban environment:

    – a thematic strategy promoting an integrated horizontal approach across Community policies and improving the quality of urban environment, taking into account progress made in implementing the existing cooperation framework[1] reviewing it where necessary, and addressing:

    – the promotion of Local Agenda 21;

    – the reduction of the link between economic growth and passenger transport demand;

    – the need for an increased share in public transport, rail, inland waterways, walking and cycling modes;

    – the need to tackle rising volumes of traffic and to bring about a significant decoupling of transport growth and GDP growth;

---

[1] Decision No 1141/2001/EC of the European Parliament and of the Council of 27 June 2001 on a Community framework for cooperation to promote sustainable urban development (OJ L 191, 13.7.2001, p. 1).

– the need to promote the use of low emission vehicles in public transports;
– the consideration of urban environment indicators.

Article 8
Objectives and priority areas for action on the sustainable use and management
of natural resources and wastes

1. The aims set out in Article 2 should be pursued by the following objectives:

– aiming at ensuring that the consumption of resources and their associated impacts do not exceed the carrying capacity of the environment and breaking the linkages between economic growth and resource use. In this context the indicative target to achieve a percentage of 22% of the electricity production from renewable energies by 2010 in the Community is recalled with a view to increasing drastically resource and energy efficiency;
– achieving a significant overall reduction in the volumes of waste generated through waste prevention initiatives, better resource efficiency and a shift towards more sustainable production and consumption patterns;
– a significant reduction in the quantity of waste going to disposal and the volumes of hazardous waste produced while avoiding an increase of emissions to air, water and soil;
– encouraging re-use and for wastes that are still generated: the level of their hazardousness should be reduced and they should present as little risk as possible; preference should be given to recovery and especially to recycling; the quantity of waste for disposal should be minimised and should be safely disposed of; waste intended for disposal should be treated as closely as possible to the place of its generation, to the extent that this does not lead to a decrease in the efficiency in waste treatment operations.

2. These objectives shall be pursued taking into consideration the Integrated Product Policy approach and the Community's strategy for waste management[1] by means of the following priority actions:

(i) developing a thematic strategy on the sustainable use and management of resources, including *inter alia*:
  (a) an estimate of materials and waste streams in the Community, including imports and exports for example by using the instrument of material flow analysis;
  (b) a review of the efficiency of policy measures and the impact of subsidies relating to natural resources and waste;

---

[1] Council Resolution of 24 February 1997 on a Community strategy for waste management (OJ C 76, 11.3.1997, p. 1).

(c) establishment of goals and targets for resource efficiency and the diminished use of resources, decoupling the link between economic growth and negative environmental impacts;

(d) promotion of extraction and production methods and techniques to encourage eco-efficiency and the sustainable use of raw-materials, energy, water and other resources;

(e) development and implementation of a broad range of instruments including research, technology transfer, market-based and economic instruments, programmes of best practice and indicators of resource efficiency;

(ii) Developing and implementing measures on waste prevention and management by, *inter alia*:

    (a) developing a set of quantitative and qualitative reduction targets covering all relevant waste, to be achieved at Community level by 2010. The Commission is invited to prepare a proposal for such targets by 2002;

    (b) encourage ecologically sound and sustainable product design;

    (c) raising awareness of the public's potential contribution on waste reduction;

    (d) the formulation of operational measures to encourage waste prevention, e.g. stimulating re-use and recovery, the phasing out of certain substances and materials through product-related measures;

    (e) developing further indicators in the field of waste management;

(iii) Developing a thematic strategy on waste recycling, including *inter alia*:

    (a) measures aimed at ensuring source separation, the collection and recycling of priority waste streams;

    (b) further development of producer responsibility;

    (c) development and transfer of environmentally sound waste recycling and treatment technology;

(iv) Developing or revising the legislation on wastes, including, *inter alia*, construction and demolition waste, sewage sludge,[1] biodegradable wastes, packaging,[2] batteries[3] and waste shipments,[4] clarification of the distinction between waste and non-waste and development of adequate criteria for the further elaboration of Annex IIA and IIB of the framework directive on wastes.[5]

---

[1] Council Directive 86/278/EEC of 12 June 1986 on the protection of the environment, and in particular of the soil, when sewage sludge is used in agriculture (OJ L 181, 4.7.1986, p. 6). Directive as last amended by the 1994 Act of Accession.

[2] Directive 94/62/EC of the European Parliament and of the Council of 20 December 1994 on packaging and packaging waste (OJ L 365, 31.12.1994, p. 10). Directive as last amended by Commission Decision 1999/177/EC (OJ L 56, 4.3.1999, p. 47).

[3] Commission Directive 93/86/EEC of 4 October 1993 adapting to technical progress Council Directive 91/157/EEC on batteries and accumulators containing certain dangerous substances (OJ L 264, 23.10.1993, p. 51).

[4] Council Regulation (EEC) No 259/93 of 1 February 1993 on the supervision and control of shipments of waste within, into and out of the European Community (OJ L 30, 6.2.1993, p. 1). Regulation as last amended by Commission Decision 1999/816/EEC (OJ L 316, 10.12.1999, p. 45).

[5] Council Directive 75/442/EEC of 15 July 1975 on waste (OJ L 194, 25.7.1975, p. 39). Directive as last amended by Commission Decision 96/350/EC (OJ L 135, 6.6.1996, p. 32).

Article 9
Objectives and priority areas for action on international issues

1. The aim set out in Article 2 on international issues and the international dimensions of the four environmental priority areas of this Programme involve the following objectives:

- the pursuit of ambitious environmental policies at the international level paying particular attention to the carrying capacity of the global environment;
- the further promotion of sustainable consumption and production patterns at the international level;
- making progress to ensure that trade and environment policies and measures are mutually supportive.

2. These objectives shall be pursued by means of the following priority actions:

(a) integrating environment protection requirements into all the Community's external policies, including trade and development cooperation, in order to achieve sustainable development by *inter alia* the elaboration of guidelines;
(b) establishing a coherent set of environment and development targets to be promoted for adoption as part of 'a new global deal or pact' at the World Summit on Sustainable Development in 2002;
(c) work towards strengthening international environmental governance by the gradual reinforcement of the multilateral cooperation and the institutional framework including resources;
(d) aiming for swift ratification, effective compliance and enforcement of international conventions and agreements relating to the environment where the Community is a Party;
(e) promoting sustainable environmental practices in foreign investment and export credits;
(f) intensify efforts at the international level to arrive at consensus on methods for the evaluation of risks to health and the environment, as well as approaches of risk management including the precautionary principle;
(g) achieving mutual supportiveness between trade and the needs for environmental protection, by taking due account of the environmental dimension in Sustainability Impact Assessments of multilateral trade agreements to be carried out at an early stage of their negotiation and by acting accordingly;
(h) further promoting a world trade system that fully recognises Multilateral or Regional Environmental Agreements and the precautionary principle, enhancing opportunities for trade in sustainable and environmentally friendly products and services;
(i) promoting cross-border environmental cooperation with neighbouring countries and regions;
(j) promoting a better policy coherence by linking the work done within the framework of the different conventions, including the assessment of interlinkages

between biodiversity and climate change, and the integration of biodiversity considerations into the implementation of the United Nations Framework Convention on Climate Change and the Kyoto Protocol.

Article 10
Environment policy making

The objectives set out in Article 2 on environment policy making based on participation and best available scientific knowledge and the strategic approaches set out in Article 3 shall be pursued by means of the following priority actions:

(a) development of improved mechanisms and of general rules and principles of good governance within which stakeholders are widely and extensively consulted at all stages so as to facilitate the most effective choices for the best results for the environment and sustainable development in regard to the measures to be proposed;

(b) strengthening participation in the dialogue process by environmental NGOs through appropriate support, including Community finance;

(c) improvement of the process of policy making through:
   – *ex-ante* evaluation of the possible impacts, in particular the environmental impacts, of new policies including the alternative of no action and of the proposals for legislation and publication of the results;
   – *ex-post* evaluation of the effectiveness of existing measures in meeting their environmental objectives;

(d) ensuring that environment and notably the priority areas identified in this Programme are a major priority for Community research programmes. Regular reviews of environmental research needs and priorities should be undertaken within the context of the Community Framework Programme of research and technological development. Ensuring better coordination of research related to the environment conducted in Member States *inter alia* to improve the application of results; development of bridges between environmental and other actors in the fields of information, training, research, education and policies;

(e) ensuring regular information, to be provided starting from 2003, that can help to provide the basis for:
   – policy decisions on the environment and sustainable development;
   – the follow-up and review of sector integration strategies as well as of the Sustainable Development Strategy;
   – information to the wider public. The production of this information will be supported by regular reports from the European Environment Agency and other relevant bodies. The information shall consist notably of:
     – headline environmental indicators;
     – indicators on the state and trends of the environment;
     – integration indicators;

(f) reviewing and regularly monitoring information and reporting systems with a view to a more coherent and effective system to ensure streamlined reporting of high quality, comparable and relevant environmental data and information. The Commission is invited, as soon as possible, to provide a proposal as appropriate to this end. Monitoring, data collection and reporting requirements should be addressed efficiently in future environmental legislation;

(g) reinforcing the development and the use of earth monitoring (e.g. satellite technology) applications and tools in support of policy-making and implementation.

Article 11

Monitoring and evaluation of results

1. In the fourth year of operation of the Programme the Commission shall evaluate the progress made in its implementation together with associated environmental trends and prospects. This should be done on the basis of a comprehensive set of indicators. The Commission shall submit this mid-term report together with any proposal for amendment that it may consider appropriate to the European Parliament and the Council.

2. The Commission shall submit to the European Parliament and the Council a final assessment of the Programme and the state and prospects for the environment in the course of the final year of the Programme.

Article 12

This Decision shall be published in the *Official Journal of the European Communities*.

Done at Brussels, 22 July 2002.

Commission Communication of 2 February 2000 on the precautionary principle

Editorial note

Article 174(2) of the EC Treaty specifies that Community policy on the environment shall be based on the precautionary principle. The principle is not defined in the Treaty. In 1999 the Council asked the Commission to develop clear and effective guidelines for its application. The Commission responded to the Council request by adopting a Communication on the Precautionary Principle in February 2000. The Commission recognises in its Communication of 2 February 2000 that 'the issue of when and how to use the precautionary principle, both within the European Union and internationally, is giving rise to much debate, and to mixed, and sometimes contradictory views. Thus, decision-makers are constantly faced with the dilemma of balancing the freedom and rights of individuals, industry and organisations with the need to reduce the risk of adverse effects to the environment, human, animal or plant health. Therefore, finding the correct balance so that the proportionate, non-discriminatory, transparent and coherent actions can be taken, requires a structured decision-making process with detailed scientific and other objective information' (paragraph 1). The Communication's aim is fourfold according to the Commission: to outline the Commission's approach to using the precautionary principle; to establish Commission guidelines for applying it; to build a common understanding of how to assess, appraise, manage and communicate risks that science is not yet able to evaluate fully; and to avoid unwarranted recourse to the precautionary principle, as a disguised form of protectionism (paragraph 2).

The Communication examines the precautionary principle in the European Union (paragraph 3) and in international law (paragraph 4). It identifies the constituent parts of the precautionary principle (paragraph 5). According to the Commission, measures applying the precautionary principle belong in the general framework of risk analysis, and in particular risk management (paragraph 5). The Communication continues with the analysis of factors triggering its application, which can never be justified to adopt arbitrary decisions (paragraph 5.1). Among the factors triggering recourse to the principle, the Communication examines the identification of potentially negative effects; scientific evaluation; and scientific uncertainty.

Once the factors that may trigger the application of the principle have been evaluated, a decision is usually made on whether action should be taken. Paragraph 5.2

of the Communication examines the measures resulting from reliance on the precautionary principle and, in particular, the decision whether or not to act and the nature of the action ultimately to be taken.

Paragraph 6 outlines guidelines for the application of the principle. The principle should be applied according to the general principles of risk management: proportionality; non-discrimination; consistency; examination of the benefits and costs of action or lack of action; and examination of scientific developments. The question of the burden of proof for the application of the principle is dealt with in paragraph 6.4.

The Communication, as specified by the Commission, has a general scope. It reflects the Commission's position on the precautionary principle and is designed to provide concrete guidance for its application. The Communication, however, should not be seen as a last word on the subject, but rather as a point of departure for broader studies on the conditions in which risks should be assessed, appraised, managed and communicated (paragraph 7).

Source: COM (2000) 12 February 2000

Commission Communication of 2 February 2000 on the precautionary principle

Summary

1. The issue of when and how to use the precautionary principle, both within the European Union and internationally, is giving rise to much debate, and to mixed, and sometimes contradictory views. Thus, decision-makers are constantly faced with the dilemma of balancing the freedom and rights of individuals, industry and organisations with the need to reduce the risk of adverse effects to the environment, human, animal or plant health. Therefore, finding the correct balance so that the proportionate, non-discriminatory, transparent and coherent actions can be taken, requires a structured decision-making process with detailed scientific and other objective information.

2. The Communication's fourfold aim is to:

- outline the Commission's approach to using the precautionary principle,
- establish Commission guidelines for applying it,
- build a common understanding of how to assess, appraise, manage and communicate risks that science is not yet able to evaluate fully, and
- avoid unwarranted recourse to the precautionary principle, as a disguised form of protectionism.

It also seeks to provide an input to the ongoing debate on this issue, both within the Community and internationally.

3. The precautionary principle is not defined in the Treaty, which prescribes it only once – to protect the environment. But in practice, its scope is much wider,

and specifically where preliminary objective scientific evaluation, indicates that there are reasonable grounds for concern that the potentially dangerous effects on the environment, human, animal or plant health may be inconsistent with the high level of protection chosen for the Community.

The Commission considers that the Community, like other WTO members, has the right to establish the level of protection – particularly of the environment, human, animal and plant health, – that it deems appropriate. Applying the precautionary principle is a key tenet of its policy, and the choices it makes to this end will continue to affect the views it defends internationally, on how this principle should be applied.

4. The precautionary principle should be considered within a structured approach to the analysis of risk which comprises three elements: risk assessment, risk management, risk communication. The precautionary principle is particularly relevant to the management of risk.

The precautionary principle, which is essentially used by decision-makers in the management of risk, should not be confused with the element of caution that scientists apply in their assessment of scientific data.

Recourse to the precautionary principle presupposes that potentially dangerous effects deriving from a phenomenon, product or process have been identified, and that scientific evaluation does not allow the risk to be determined with sufficient certainty. The implementation of an approach based on the precautionary principle should start with a scientific evaluation, as complete as possible, and where possible, identifying at each stage the degree of scientific uncertainty.

5. Decision-makers need to be aware of the degree of uncertainty attached to the results of the evaluation of the available scientific information. Judging what is an "acceptable" level of risk for society is an eminently political responsibility. Decision-makers faced with an unacceptable risk, scientific uncertainty and public concerns have a duty to find answers. Therefore, all these factors have to be taken into consideration.

In some cases, the right answer may be not to act or at least not to introduce a binding legal measure. A wide range of initiatives is available in the case of action, going from a legally binding measure to a research project or a recommendation.

The decision-making procedure should be transparent and should involve as early as possible and to the extent reasonably possible all interested parties.

6. Where action is deemed necessary, measures based on the precautionary principle should be, inter alia:

- proportional to the chosen level of protection,
- non-discriminatory in their application,
- consistent with similar measures already taken,
- based on an examination of the potential benefits and costs of action or lack of action (including, where appropriate and feasible, an economic cost/benefit analysis),

– subject to review, in the light of new scientific data, and
– capable of assigning responsibility for producing the scientific evidence necessary for a more comprehensive risk assessment.

Proportionality means tailoring measures to the chosen level of protection. Risk can rarely be reduced to zero, but incomplete risk assessments may greatly reduce the range of options open to risk managers. A total ban may not be a proportional response to a potential risk in all cases. However, in certain cases, it is the sole possible response to a given risk.

Non-discrimination means that comparable situations should not be treated differently, and that different situations should not be treated in the same way, unless there are objective grounds for doing so.

Consistency means that measures should be of comparable scope and nature to those already taken in equivalent areas in which all scientific data are available.

Examining costs and benefits entails comparing the overall cost to the Community of action and lack of action, in both the short and long term. This is not simply an economic cost-benefit analysis: its scope is much broader, and includes non-economic considerations, such as the efficacy of possible options and their acceptability to the public. In the conduct of such an examination, account should be taken of the general principle and the case law of the Court that the protection of health takes precedence over economic considerations.

Subject to review in the light of new scientific data, means measures based on the precautionary principle should be maintained so long as scientific information is incomplete or inconclusive, and the risk is still considered too high to be imposed on society, in view of chosen level of protection. Measures should be periodically reviewed in the light of scientific progress, and amended as necessary.

Assigning responsibility for producing scientific evidence is already a common consequence of these measures. Countries that impose a prior approval (marketing authorisation) requirement on products that they deem dangerous a priori reverse the burden of proving injury, by treating them as dangerous unless and until businesses do the scientific work necessary to demonstrate that they are safe.

Where there is no prior authorisation procedure, it may be up to the user or to public authorities to demonstrate the nature of a danger and the level of risk of a product or process. In such cases, a specific precautionary measure might be taken to place the burden of proof upon the producer, manufacturer or importer, but this cannot be made a general rule.

Table of contents

1. Introduction

A number of recent events has shown that public opinion is becoming increasingly aware of the potential risks to which the population or their environment are potentially exposed. Enormous advances in communications technology have fostered this growing sensitivity to the emergence of new risks, before scientific research has been able to fully illuminate the problems. Decision-makers have to take account of the fears generated by these perceptions and to put in place preventive measures to eliminate the risk or at least reduce it to the minimum acceptable level. On 13 April 1999 the Council adopted a resolution urging the Commission inter alia 'to be in the future even more determined to be guided by the precautionary principle in preparing proposals for legislation and in its other consumer-related activities and develop as priority clear and effective guidelines for the application of this principle'. This Communication is part of the Commission's response.

The dimension of the precautionary principle goes beyond the problems associated with a short or medium-term approach to risks. It also concerns the longer run and the well-being of future generations.

A decision to take measures without waiting until all the necessary scientific knowledge is available is clearly a precaution-based approach.

Decision-makers are constantly faced with the dilemma of balancing the freedoms and rights of individuals, industry and organisations with the need to reduce or eliminate the risk of adverse effects to the environment or to health.

Finding the correct balance so that proportionate, non-discriminatory, transparent and coherent decisions can be arrived at, which at the same time provide the chosen level of protection, requires a structured decision making process with detailed scientific and other objective information. This structure is provided by the three elements of risk analysis: the assessment of risk, the choice of risk management strategy and the communication of the risk. Any assessment of risk that is made should be based on the existing body of scientific and statistical data. Most decisions are taken where there is sufficient information available for appropriate preventive measures to be taken but in other circumstances, these data may be wanting in some respects.

Whether or not to invoke the precautionary principle is a decision exercised where scientific information is insufficient, inconclusive, or uncertain and where there are indications that the possible effects on the environment, or human, animal or plant health may be potentially dangerous and inconsistent with the chosen level of protection.

2. The goals of this communication

The aim of this Communication is to inform all interested parties, in particular the European Parliament the Council and Member States of the manner in which the Commission applies or intends to apply the precautionary principle when faced with taking decisions relating to the containment of risk. However, this general Communication does not claim to be the final word – rather, the idea is to provide input to the ongoing debate both at Community and international level.

This Communication seeks to establish a common understanding of the factors leading to recourse to the precautionary principle and its place in decision making, and to establish guidelines for its application based on reasoned and coherent principles.

The guidelines outlined in this Communication are only intended to serve as general guidance and in no way to modify or affect the provisions of the Treaty or secondary Community legislation.

Another objective is to avoid unwarranted recourse to the precautionary principle, which in certain cases could serve as a justification for disguised protectionism. Accordingly the development of international guidelines could facilitate the achievement of this end. The Commission also wishes to stress in this Communication that, far from being a way of evading obligations arising from the WTO Agreements, the envisaged use of the precautionary principle complies with these obligations.

It is also necessary to clarify a misunderstanding as regards the distinction between reliance on the precautionary principle and the search for zero risk, which in reality is rarely to be found. The search for a high level of health and safety and environmental and consumer protection belongs in the framework of the single market, which is a cornerstone of the Community.

The Community has already relied on the precautionary principle. Abundant experience has been gained over many years in the environmental field, where many measures have been inspired by the precautionary principle, such as measures to protect the ozone layer or concerning climate change.

3. *The precautionary principle in the European Union*

The Community has consistently endeavoured to achieve a high level of protection, among others in environment and human, animal or plant health. In most cases, measures making it possible to achieve this high level of protection can be determined on a satisfactory scientific basis. However, when there are reasonable grounds for concern that potential hazards may affect the environment or human, animal or plant health, and when at the same time the available data preclude a detailed risk evaluation, the precautionary principle has been politically accepted as a risk management strategy in several fields. To understand fully the use of the precautionary principle in the European Union, it is necessary to examine the legislative texts, the case law of the Court of Justice and the Court of First Instance, and the policy approaches that have emerged.

Legal texts

The analysis starts with the legal texts which explicitly or implicitly refer to the precautionary principle (Annex I, Ref. 1).

At Community level the only explicit reference to the precautionary principle is to be found in the environment title of the EC Treaty, and more specifically Article 174. However, one cannot conclude from this that the principle applies only to the environment (Annex I, Refs. 2 and 3). Although the principle is adumbrated in the Treaty, it is not defined there. Like other general notions contained in the legislation, such as subsidiarity or proportionality, it is for the decision-makers and ultimately the courts to flesh out the principle. In other words, the scope of the precautionary principle also depends on trends in case law, which to some degree are influenced by prevailing social and political values. However, it would be wrong to conclude that the absence of a definition has to lead to legal uncertainty. The Community authorities' practical experience with the precautionary principle and its judicial review make it possible to get an ever-better handle on the precautionary principle.

Case law

The Court of Justice of the European Communities and the Court of First Instance have already had occasion to review the application of the precautionary principle in cases they have adjudicated and hence to develop case law in this area. (see Annex I, Refs. 5, 6 and 7)

Policy orientations

Policy orientations were set out by the Commission in the Green Paper on the General Principles of Food Safety and the Communication of 30 April 1997 on Consumer Health and Food Safety, by Parliament in its Resolution of 10 March 1998 concerning the Green Paper, by the Council in its Resolution of 13 April 1999 and by the Joint Parliamentary Committee of the EEA (European Economic Area) in its Resolution of 16 March 1999 (Annex I, Refs. 8-12).

Hence the Commission considers that the precautionary principle is a general one which should in particular be taken into consideration in the fields of environmental protection and human, animal and plant health.

> Although the precautionary principle is not explicitly mentioned in the Treaty except in the environmental field, its scope is far wider and covers those specific circumstances where scientific evidence is insufficient, inconclusive or uncertain and there are indications through preliminary objective scientific evaluation that there are reasonable grounds for concern that the potentially dangerous effects on the environment, human, animal or plant health may be inconsistent with the chosen level of protection.

4. The precautionary principle in international law

At international level, the precautionary principle was first recognised in the World Charter for Nature, adopted by the UN General Assembly in 1982. It was subsequently incorporated into various international conventions on the protection of the environment (cf. Annex II).

This principle was enshrined at the 1992 Rio Conference on the Environment and Development, during which the Rio Declaration was adopted, whose principle 15 states that: '*in order to protect the environment, the precautionary approach shall be widely applied by States according to their capability. Where there are threats of serious or irreversible damage, lack of full scientific certainty shall not be used as a reason for postponing cost-effective measures to prevent environmental degradation*'. Besides, the United Nations' Framework Convention on Climate Change and the Convention of Biological Diversity both refer to the precautionary principle. Recently, on 28 January 2000, at the Conference of the Parties to the Convention on Biological Diversity, the Protocol on Biosafety concerning the safe transfer, handling and use of living modified organisms resulting from modern biotechnology confirmed the key function of the Precautionary Principle (see Annex II).

Hence this principle has been progressively consolidated in international environmental law, and so it has since become a full-fledged and general principle of international law.

The WTO agreements confirm this observation. The preamble to the WTO Agreement highlights the ever closer links between international trade and environmental protection.[1] A consistent approach means that the precautionary principle must be taken into account in these agreements, notably in the Agreement on Sanitary and Phytosanitary Measures (SPS) and in the Agreement on Technical Barriers to Trade (TBT), to ensure that this general principle is duly enforced in this legal order.

Hence, each Member of the WTO has the independent right to determine the level of environmental or health protection they consider appropriate. Consequently a member may apply measures, including measures based on the precautionary principle, which lead to a higher level of protection than that provided for in the relevant international standards or recommendations.

The Agreement on the Application of Sanitary and Phytosanitary Measures (SPS Agreement) clearly sanctions the use of the precautionary principle, although the term itself is not explicitly used. Although the general rule is that all sanitary and phytosanitary measures must be based on scientific principles and that they should not be maintained without adequate scientific evidence, a derogation from these principles is provided for in Article 5(7) which stipulates that: '*in cases where relevant scientific evidence is insufficient, a Member may provisionally adopt sanitary or phytosanitary measures on the basis of available pertinent information, including that from the relevant international organizations as well as from sanitary or phytosanitary measures applied by other Members. In such circumstances, Members shall seek to obtain the additional information necessary for a more objective assessment of risk and review the sanitary or phytosanitary measure accordingly within a reasonable period of time.*'

Hence, according to the SPS Agreement, measures adopted in application of a precautionary principle when the scientific data are inadequate, are provisional and imply that efforts be undertaken to elicit or generate the necessary scientific data. It is important to stress that the provisional nature is not bound up with a time limit but with the development of scientific knowledge.

The use of the term 'more objective assessment of risk' in Article 5.7 infers that a precautionary measure may be based on a less objective appraisal but must nevertheless include an evaluation of risk.

---

[1] 'The parties to this agreement . . . recognising that their relations in the field of trade and economic endeavour should be conducted with a view to raising standards of living, ensuring full employment and a large and steadily growing volume of real income and effective demand, and expanding the production of and trade in goods and services, while allowing for the optimal use of the world's resources in accordance with the objective of sustainable development, seeking both to protect and preserve the environment and to enhance the means for doing to in a manner consistent with their respective needs and concerns at different levels of economic development . . . '

The concept of risk assessment in the SPS leaves leeway for interpretation of what could be used as a basis for a precautionary approach. The risk assessment on which a measure is based may include non-quantifiable data of a factual or qualitative nature and is not uniquely confined to purely quantitative scientific data. This interpretation has been confirmed by the WTO's Appellate body in the case of growth hormones, which rejected the panel's initial interpretation that the risk assessment had to be quantitative and had to establish a minimum degree of risk.

The principles enshrined in Article 5.7 of the SPS must be respected in the field of sanitary and phytosanitary measures; however, because of the specific nature of other areas, such as the environment, it may be that somewhat different principles will have to be applied. International guidelines are being considered in relation to the application of the Precautionary Principle in Codex Alimentarius. Such guidance in this, and other sectors, could pave the way to a harmonised approach by the WTO Members, to drawing up health or environment protection measures, while avoiding the misuse of the precautionary principle which could otherwise lead to unjustifiable barriers to trade.

In the light of these observations, the Commission considers that, following the example set by other Members of the WTO, the Community is entitled to prescribe the level of protection, notably as regards the environment and human, animal and plant health, which it considers appropriate. In this context, the Community must respect Articles 6, 95, 152 and 174 of the Treaty. To this end, reliance on the precautionary principle constitutes an essential plank of its policy. It is clear that the choices made will affect its positions at international and notably multilateral level, as regards recourse to the precautionary principle.

Bearing in mind the very origins of the precautionary principle and its growing role in international law, and notably in the agreements of the World Trade Organisation, this principle must be duly addressed at international level in the various areas in which it is likely to be of relevance.

Following the example set by the other members of the WTO, the Commission considers that the Community is entitled to prescribe the level of protection, notably as regards environmental protection and human, animal and plant health, that it considers appropriate. Recourse to the precautionary principle is a central plank of Community policy. The choices made to this end will continue to influence its positions at international level, and notably at multinational level, as regards the precautionary principle.

---

5. The constituent parts of the precautionary principle

An analysis of the precautionary principle reveals two quite distinct aspects: (i) the political decision to act or not to act as such, which is linked to the factors triggering recourse to the precautionary principle; (ii) in the affirmative, how to act, i.e. the measures resulting from application of the precautionary principle.

There is a controversy as to the role of scientific uncertainty in risk analysis, and notably as to whether it belongs under risk assessment or risk management. This controversy springs from a confusion between a prudential approach and application of the precautionary principle. These two aspects are complementary but should not be confounded.

The prudential approach is part of risk assessment policy which is determined before any risk assessment takes place and which is based on the elements described in 5.1.3; it is therefore an integral part of the scientific opinion delivered by the risk evaluators.

On the other hand, application of the precautionary principle is part of risk management, when scientific uncertainty precludes a full assessment of the risk and when decision-makers consider that the chosen level of environmental protection or of human, animal and plant health may be in jeopardy.

The Commission considers that measures applying the precautionary principle belong in the general framework of risk analysis, and in particular risk management.

5.1. Factors triggering recourse to the precautionary principle

The precautionary principle is relevant only in the event of a potential risk, even if this risk cannot be fully demonstrated or quantified or its effects determined because of the insufficiency or inclusive nature of the scientific data.

It should however be noted that the precautionary principle can under no circumstances be used to justify the adoption of arbitrary decisions.

5.1.1. Identification of potentially negative effects   Before the precautionary principle is invoked, the scientific data relevant to the risks must first be evaluated. However, one factor logically and chronologically precedes the decision to act, namely identification of the potentially negative effects of a phenomenon. To understand these effects more thoroughly it is necessary to conduct a scientific examination. The decision to conduct this examination without awaiting additional information is bound up with a less theoretical and more concrete perception of the risk.

5.1.2. Scientific evaluation   A scientific evaluation of the potential adverse effects should be undertaken based on the available data when considering whether measures are necessary to protect the environment, the human, animal or plant health. An assessment of risk should be considered where feasible when deciding whether or not to invoke the precautionary principle. This requires reliable scientific data and logical reasoning, leading to a conclusion which expresses the possibility of occurrence and the severity of a hazard's impact on the environment, or health of a given population including the extent of possible damage, persistency, reversibility and delayed effect. However it is not possible in all cases to complete a comprehensive assessment of risk, but all effort should be made to evaluate the available scientific information. Where possible, a report should be made which indicates the assessment of the existing knowledge and the available information, providing the views of the scientists on the reliability of the assessment as well as on the remaining uncertainties. If necessary, it should also contain the identification of topics for further scientific research. Risk assessment consists of four components – namely hazard identification, hazard characterisation, appraisal of exposure and risk characterisation (Annex III). The limits of scientific knowledge may affect each of these components, influencing the overall level of attendant uncertainty and ultimately affecting the foundation for protective or preventive action. An attempt to complete these four steps should be performed before decision to act is taken.

5.1.3. Scientific uncertainty Scientific uncertainty results usually from five characteristics of the scientific method: the variable chosen, the measurements made, the samples drawn, the models used and the causal relationship employed. Scientific uncertainty may also arise from a controversy on existing data or lack of some relevant data. Uncertainty may relate to qualitative or quantitative elements of the analysis.

A more abstract and generalised approach preferred by some scientists is to separate all uncertainties into three categories of – Bias, Randomness and True Variability. Some other experts categorise uncertainty in terms of estimation of confidence interval of the probability of occurrence and of the severity of the hazard's impact.

This issue is very complex and the Commission launched a project 'Technological Risk and the Management of Uncertainty' conducted under the auspices of the European Scientific Technology Observatory. The four ESTO reports will be published shortly and will give a comprehensive description of scientific uncertainty.

Risk evaluators accommodate these uncertainty factors by incorporating prudential aspects such as:

– relying on animal models to establish potential effects in man; using body weight ranges to make inter-species comparisons;
– adopting a safety factor in evaluating an acceptable daily intake to account for intra- and inter-species variability; the magnitude of this factor depends on the degree of uncertainty of the available data;
– not adopting an acceptable daily intake for substances recognised as genotoxic or carcinogenic;
– adopting the 'ALARA' (as low as reasonably achievable) level as a basis for certain toxic contaminants.

Risk managers should be fully aware of these uncertainty factors when they adopt measures based on the scientific opinion delivered by the evaluators.

However, in some situations the scientific data are not sufficient to allow one to apply these prudential aspects in practice, i.e. in cases in which extrapolations cannot be made because of the absence of parameter modelling and where cause-effect relationships are suspected but have not been demonstrated. It is in situations like these that decision-makers face the dilemma of having to act or not to act.

> Recourse to the precautionary principle presupposes:
>   – identification of potentially negative effects resulting from a phenomenon, product or procedure;
>   – a scientific evaluation of the risk which because of the insufficiency of the data, their inconclusive or imprecise nature, makes it impossible to determine with sufficient certainty the risk in question.

5.2. Measures resulting from reliance on the precautionary principle

5.2.1. The decision whether or not to act   In the kind of situation described above – sometimes under varying degrees of pressure from public opinion – decision-makers have to respond. However, responding does not necessarily mean that measures always have to be adopted. The decision to do nothing may be a response in its own right.

> The appropriate response in a given situation is thus the result of an eminently political decision, a function of the risk level that is 'acceptable' to the society on which the risk is imposed.

5.2.2. Nature of the action ultimately taken   The nature of the decision influences the type of control that can be carried out. Recourse to the precautionary principle does not necessarily mean adopting final instruments designed to produce legal effects that are open to judicial review. There is a whole range of actions available to decision-makers under the head of the precautionary principle. The decision to fund a research programme or even the decision to inform the public about the possible adverse effects of a product or procedure may themselves be inspired by the precautionary principle.

It is for the Court of Justice to pronounce on the legality of any measures taken by the Community institutions. The Court has consistently held that when the Commission or any other Community institution has broad discretionary powers, notably as regards the nature and scope of the measures it adopts, review by the Court must be limited to examining whether the institution committed a manifest error or misuse of power or manifestly exceed the limits of its powers of appraisal.

Hence the measures may not be of an arbitrary nature.

> Recourse to the precautionary principle does not necessarily mean adopting final instruments designed to produce legal effects, which are subject to judicial review.

6. Guidelines for applying the precautionary principle.

6.1. Implementation

When decision-makers become aware of a risk to the environment or human, animal or plant health that in the event of non-action may have serious consequences, the question of appropriate protective measures arise. Decision-makers have to obtain, through a structured approach, a scientific evaluation, as complete as possible, of the risk to the environment, or health, in order to select the most appropriate course of action.

The determination of appropriate action including measures based on the precautionary principle should start with a scientific evaluation and, if necessary, the decision to commission scientists to perform an as objective and complete as possible scientific evaluation. It will cast light on the existing objective evidence, the gaps in knowledge and the scientific uncertainties.

The implementation of an approach based on the precautionary principle should start with a scientific evaluation, as complete as possible, and where possible, identifying at each stage the degree of scientific uncertainty.

6.2. The triggering factor

Once the scientific evaluation has been performed as best as possible, it may provide a basis for triggering a decision to invoke the precautionary principle. The conclusions of this evaluation should show that the desired level of protection for the environment or a population group could be jeopardised. The conclusions should also include an assessment of the scientific uncertainties and a description of the hypotheses used to compensate for the lack of the scientific or statistical data. An assessment of the potential consequences of inaction should be considered and may be used as a trigger by the decision-makers. The decision to wait or not to wait for new scientific data before considering possible measures should be taken by the decision-makers with a maximum of transparency. The absence of scientific proof of the existence of a cause-effect relationship, a quantifiable dose/response relationship or a quantitative evaluation of the probability of the emergence of adverse effects following exposure should not be used to justify inaction. Even if scientific advice is supported only by a minority fraction of the scientific community, due account should be taken of their views, provided the credibility and reputation of this fraction are recognised.[2]

---

[2] Cf The WTO Appellate Body report on hormones, paragraph 124: 'In some cases, the very existence of divergent views presented by qualified scientists who have investigated the particular issue at hand, may indicate a state of scientific uncertainty'.

The Commission has confirmed its wish to rely on procedures as transparent as possible and to involve all interested parties at the earliest possible stage.[3] This will assist decision-makers in taking legitimate measures which are likely to achieve the society's chosen level of health or environmental protection.

[3] A considerable effort has already been made notably as regards public health and the environment. As regards the latter, the Community and the Member States have demonstrated the importance they attach to access to information and justice by signing the Aarhus Convention of June 1998.

An assessment of the potential consequences of inaction and of the uncertainties of the scientific evaluation should be considered by decision-makers when determining whether to trigger action based on the precautionary principle.

All interested parties should be involved to the fullest extent possible in the study of various risk management options that may be envisaged once the results of the scientific evaluation and/or risk assessment are available and the procedure be as transparent as possible.

6.3. The general principles of application

The general principles are not limited to application of the precautionary principle. They apply to all risk management measures. An approach inspired by the precautionary principle does not exempt one from applying wherever possible these criteria, which are generally used when a complete risk assessment is at hand.

Thus reliance on the precautionary principle is no excuse for derogating from the general principles of risk management.

These general principles include:

– proportionality,
– non-discrimination,
– consistency,
– examination of the benefits and costs of action or lack of action,
– examination of scientific developments.

6.3.1. Proportionality   The measures envisaged must make it possible to achieve the appropriate level of protection. Measures based on the precautionary principle must not be disproportionate to the desired level of protection and must not aim at zero risk, something which rarely exists. However, in certain cases, an incomplete assessment of the risk may considerably limit the number of options available to the risk managers.

In some cases a total ban may not be a proportional response to a potential risk. In other cases, it may be the sole possible response to a potential risk. Risk reduction measures should include less restrictive alternatives which make it possible to achieve an equivalent level of protection, such as appropriate treatment, reduction of exposure, tightening of controls, adoption of provisional limits, recommendations for populations at risk, etc. One should also consider replacing the products or procedures concerned by safer products or procedures.

The risk reduction measure should not be limited to immediate risks where the proportionality of the action is easier to assess. It is in situations in which the adverse effects do not emerge until long after exposure that the cause-effect relationships are more difficult to prove scientifically and that – for this reason – the precautionary principle often has to be invoked. In this case the potential long-term effects must be taken into account in evaluating the proportionality of measures in the form of rapid action to limit or eliminate a risk whose effects will not surface until ten or twenty years later or will affect future generations. This applies in particular to effects on the eco-system. Risks that are carried forward into the future cannot be eliminated or reduced except at the time of exposure, that is to say immediately.

> Measures should be proportional to the desired level of protection.

6.3.2. Non-discrimination The principle of non-discrimination means that comparable situations should not be treated differently and that different situations should not be treated in the same way, unless there are objective grounds for doing so.

Measures taken under the precautionary principle should be designed to achieve an equivalent level of protection without invoking the geographical origin or the nature of the production process to apply different treatments in an arbitrary manner.

> Measures should not be discriminatory in their application.

6.3.3. Consistency Measures should be consistent with the measures already adopted in similar circumstances or using similar approaches. Risk evaluations include a series of factors to be taken into account to ensure that they are as thorough as possible. The goal here is to identify and characterise the hazards, notably by establishing a relationship between the dose and the effect and assessing the exposure of the target population or the environment. If the absence of certain scientific data makes it impossible to characterise the risk, taking into account the uncertainties inherent to the evaluation, the measures taken under the precautionary principle should be comparable in nature and scope with measures already taken in equivalent areas in which all the scientific data are available.

> Measures should be consistent with the measures already adopted in similar circumstances or using similar approaches.

6.3.4. Examination of the benefits and costs of action and lack of action

A comparison must be made between the most likely positive or negative consequences of the envisaged action and those of inaction in terms of the overall cost to the Community, both in the long- and short-term. The measures envisaged must produce an overall advantage as regards reducing risks to an acceptable level.

Examination of the pros and cons cannot be reduced to an economic cost-benefit analysis. It is wider in scope and includes non-economic considerations.

However, examination of the pros and cons should include an economic cost-benefit analysis where this is appropriate and possible.

Besides, other analysis methods, such as those concerning the efficacy of possible options and their acceptability to the public may also have to be taken into account. A society may be willing to pay a higher cost to protect an interest, such as the environment or health, to which it attaches priority.

The Commission affirms, in accordance with the case law of the Court that requirements linked to the protection of public health should undoubtedly be given greater weight than economic considerations.

The measures adopted presuppose examination of the benefits and costs of action and lack of action. This examination should include an economic cost/benefit analysis when this is appropriate and feasible. However, other analysis methods, such as those concerning efficacy and the socio-economic impact of the various options, may also be relevant. Besides the decision-maker may, in certain circumstances, by guided by non-economic considerations such as the protection of health.

6.3.5. Examination of scientific developments

The measures should be maintained as long as the scientific data are inadequate, imprecise or inconclusive and as long as the risk is considered too high to be imposed on society. The measures may have to be modified or abolished by a particular deadline, in the light of new scientific findings. However, this is not always linked to the time factor, but to the development of scientific knowledge.

Besides, scientific research should be carried out with a view to obtaining a more advanced or more complete scientific assessment. In this context, the measures should be subjected to regular scientific monitoring, so that they can be reevaluated in the light of new scientific information.

The Agreement on Sanitary and Phytosanitary Measures (SPS) provides that measures adopted in the context of inadequate scientific evidence must respect certain conditions. Hence these conditions concern only the scope of the SPS Agreement, but the specific nature of certain sectors, such as the environment, may mean that somewhat different principles have to be applied.

Article 5(7) of the SPS agreement includes certain specific rules:

- The measures must be of a provisional nature pending the availability of more reliable scientific data. However this provisional nature is linked to the development of scientific knowledge rather than to a time factor.
- Research must be carried out to elicit the additional scientific data required for a more objective assessment of the risk.
- The measures must be periodically reviewed to take account of new scientific data. The results of scientific research should make it possible to complete the risk evaluation and if necessary to review the measures on the basis of the conclusions.
- Hence the reasonable period envisaged in the SPS Agreement includes the time needed for completion of the necessary scientific work and, besides, the time needed for performance of a risk evaluation based on the conclusions of this scientific work. It should not be possible to invoke budgetary constraints or political priorities to justify excessive delays in obtaining results, re-evaluating the risk or amending the provisional measures.

Research could also be conducted for the improvement of the methodologies and instruments for assessing risk, including greater integration of all pertinent factors (e.g. socio-economic information, technological perspectives).

> The measures, although provisional, shall be maintained as long as the scientific data remain incomplete, imprecise or inconclusive and as long as the risk is considered too high to be imposed on society.
>
> Maintenance of the measures depends on the development of scientific knowledge, in the light of which they should be reevaluated. This means that scientific research shall be continued with a view to obtaining more complete data.
>
> Measures based on the precautionary principle shall be reexamined and if necessary modified depending on the results of the scientific research and the follow up of their impact.

6.4. The burden of proof

- Community rules and those of many third countries enshrine the principle of prior approval (positive list) before the placing on the market of certain products, such as drugs, pesticides or food additives. This is one way of applying the precautionary principle, by shifting responsibility for producing scientific evidence. This applies in particular to substances deemed 'a priori' hazardous or which are potentially hazardous at a certain level of absorption. In this case the legislator, by way of precaution, has clearly reversed the burden of proof by requiring that the substances be deemed hazardous until proven otherwise. Hence it is up to the business community to carry out the scientific work needed to evaluate the risk. As long as the human health risk cannot be evaluated with sufficient certainty, the legislator is not legally entitled to authorise use of the substance, unless exceptionally for test purposes.

– In other cases, where such a prior approval procedure does not exist, it may be for the user, a private individual, a consumer association, citizens or the public authorities to demonstrate the nature of a danger and the level of risk posed by a product or process. Action taken under the head of the precautionary principle must in certain cases include a clause reversing the burden of proof and placing it on the producer, manufacturer or importer, but such an obligation cannot be systematically entertained as a general principle. This possibility should be examined on a case-by-case basis when a measure is adopted under the precautionary principle, pending supplementary scientific data, so as to give professionals who have an economic interest in the production and/or marketing of the procedure or product in question the opportunity to finance the necessary research on a voluntary basis.

Measures based on the precautionary principle may assign responsibility for producing the scientific evidence necessary for a comprehensive risk evaluation.

---

7. Conclusion

This Communication of a general scope sets out the Commission's position as regards recourse to the precautionary principle. The Communication reflects the Commission's desire for transparency and dialogue with all stakeholders. At the same time it provides concrete guidance for applying the precautionary principle.

The Commission wishes to reaffirm the crucial importance it attaches to the distinction between the decision to act or not to act, which is of an eminently political nature, and the measures resulting from recourse to the precautionary principle, which must comply with the general principles applicable to all risk management measures. The Commission also considers that every decision must be preceded by an examination of all the available scientific data and, if possible, a risk evaluation that is as objective and comprehensive as possible. A decision to invoke the precautionary principle does not mean that the measures will be adopted on an arbitrary or discriminatory basis.

This Communication should also contribute to reaffirming the Community's position at international level, where the precautionary principle is receiving increasing attention. However the Commission wishes to stress that this Communication is not meant to be the last word; rather, it should be seen as the point of departure for a broader study of the conditions in which risks should be assessed, appraised, managed and communicated.

Annex I
Legal and other bases for EC decisions on precautionary measures
The legislative texts

Ref. 1

The EC Treaty, incorporating provisions already introduced by the Maastricht Treaty of 1992, and more specifically Article 174 thereof, states:

- '2. Community policy on the environment shall aim at a high level of protection taking into account the diversity of situations in the various regions of the Community. It shall be based on the precautionary principle and on the principles that preventive action should be taken, that environmental damage should as a priority be rectified at source and that the polluter should pay...
- 3. In preparing its policy on the environment, the Community shall take account of:
  - Available scientific and technical data, ...
  - The potential benefits and costs of action or lack of action ...'.

Ref. 2

Article 6 of the EC Treaty provides that 'environmental protection requirements must be integrated into the definition and implementation of the Community policies and activities referred to in Article 3, in particular with a view to promoting sustainable development'.

Ref. 3

Hence, Article 95(3) of the EC Treaty provides that: 'The Commission, in its proposals envisaged in paragraph 1 concerning health, safety, environmental protection and consumer protection, will take as a base a high level of protection, taking account in particular of any new development based on scientific facts. Within their respective powers, the European Parliament and the Council will also seek to achieve this objective'.

Ref. 4

The first paragraph of Article 152 of the EC Treaty provides that: 'A high level of human health protection shall be ensured in the definition and implementation of all Community policies and activities'.

Case law

Ref. 5

In its judgement on the validity of the Commission's decision banning the exportation of beef from the United Kingdom to reduce the risk of BSE transmission (Judgements of 5 May 1998, cases C-157/96 and C-180/96), the Court held:

> 'Where there is uncertainty as to the existence or extent of risks to human health, the institutions may take protective measures without having to wait until the reality and seriousness of those risks become fully apparent.' (Ground 63). The next section fleshes out the Court's reasoning: 'That approach is borne out by Article 130r(1) of the EC Treaty, according to which Community policy on the environment is to pursue the objective inter alia of protecting human health. Article 130r(2) provides that that policy is to aim at a high level of protection and is to be based in particular on the principles that preventive action should be taken and that environmental protection requirements must be integrated into the definition and implementation of other Community policies.' (Ground 64).

Ref. 6

In another judgement concerning protection of consumer health (Judgement of 16 July 1998, case T-199/96), the Court of First Instance cites the above passage from the BSE judgement (see Grounds 66 and 67).

Ref. 7

Recently, in the Order of 30 June 1999 (Case T-70/99), the President of the Court of First Instance confirmed the positions expressed in the abovementioned judgements. Note that this judgement contains an explicit reference to the precautionary principle and affirms that 'requirements linked to the protection of public health should undoubtedly be given greater weight that economic considerations.'

Policy orientations

Ref. 8

In its Communication of 30 April 1997 on consumer health and food safety (COM(97) 183 final), the Commission states: 'the Commission will be guided in its risk analysis by the precautionary principle, in cases where the scientific basis is insufficient or some uncertainty exists'.

Ref. 9

In its Green Paper on the General Principles of Food Law in the European Union of 30 April 1997 (COM(97) 176 final), the Commission reiterates this point:

> 'The Treaty requires the Community to contribute to the maintenance of a high level of protection of public health, the environment and consumers. In order to ensure a high level of protection and coherence, protective measures should be based on risk assessment, taking into account all relevant risk factors, including technological aspects, the best available scientific evidence and the availability of inspection sampling and testing methods. Where a full risk assessment is not possible, measures should be based on the precautionary principle.'

Ref. 10

In its Resolution of 10 March 1998 on the Green Paper, the European Parliament states:

> 'European food law is based on the principle of preventive protection of consumer health;
>
> stresses that policy in this area must be founded on a scientifically-based risk analysis supplemented, where necessary, by appropriate risk management based on the precautionary principle;
>
> invites the Commission to anticipate possible challenges to Community food law by WTO bodies by requesting the scientific committees to present a full set of arguments based on the precautionary principle.'

Ref. 11

The Joint Parliamentary Committee of the EEA (European Economic Area), adopted a Resolution on Food Safety in the EEA on 16 March 1999. In this connection, on the one hand, it *'emphasises the importance of application of the precautionary principle'* (point 5) and, on the other, *'reaffirms the over-riding need for a precautionary approach within the EEA to the assessment and evaluation of applications for the marketing of GMOs intended to enter the food chain . . .' (point 13).*

Ref. 12

On 13 April 1999, the Council adopted a Resolution urging the Commission, *inter alia, 'to be in the future even more determined to be guided by the precautionary principle in preparing proposals for legislation and in its other consumer-related activities and develop as a priority clear and effective guidelines for the application of this principle'.*

Annex II
The precautionary principle in international law

The environment

Although applied more broadly, the precautionary principle has been developed primarily in the context of environmental policy.

Hence, the Ministerial Declaration of the Second International Conference on the Protection of the North Sea (1987) states that *'in order to protect the North Sea from possibly damaging effects of the most dangerous substances, a precautionary approach is necessary which may require action to control inputs of such substances even before a causal link has been established by absolutely clear scientific evidence'.* A new Ministerial Declaration was delivered at the Third International Conference on the Protection of the North Sea (1990). It fleshes out the earlier declaration, stating that '*the participants... will continue to apply the precautionary principle, that is to take action to avoid potentially damaging impacts of substances that are persistent, toxic and liable to bioaccumulate even where there is no scientific evidence to prove a causal link between emissions and effects*'.

The precautionary principle was explicitly recognised during the UN Conference on Environment and Development (UNCED) in Rio de Janeiro 1992 and included in the so-called Rio Declaration. Since then the precautionary principle has been implemented in various environmental instruments, and in particular in global climate change, ozone depleting substances and biodiversity conservation.

The precautionary principle is listed as Principle 15 of the Rio Declaration among the principles of general rights and obligations of national authorities:

> '*In order to protect the environment, the precautionary approach should be widely applied by States according to their capabilities. Where there are threats of serious or irreversible damage, lack of full scientific certainty shall not be used as a reason for postponing cost-effective measures to prevent environmental degradation*'.

Principle 15 is reproduced in similar wording in:

1. The preamble of the Convention of Biological Diversity (1992):

   > *(...) Noting also that where there is a threat of significant reduction or loss of biological diversity, lack of full scientific certainty should not be used as a reason for postponing measures to avoid or minimise such a threat (...)*

2. In article 3 (Principles) of the Convention of Climate Change (1992):

   > *(..) The Parties should take precautionary measures to anticipate, prevent or minimise the causes of climate change and mitigate its adverse effects. Where there are threats of serious or irreversible damage, lack of full scientific certainty should not be used as a reason for postponing such measures, taking into account that policies and measures to deal with climate change should be cost-effective so as to ensure global benefits at the lowest possible cost. To achieve this, such policies and measures should take into account different socio-economic contexts, be comprehensive, cover all relevant sources, sinks and reservoirs of greenhouse gases and adaptation, and comprise all economic sectors. Efforts to address climate change may be carried out cooperatively by interested Parties.*

In the Paris Convention for the protection of the marine environment of the northeast Atlantic (September 1992), the precautionary principle is defined as the principle '*by virtue of which preventive measures are to be taken when there are reasonable grounds for concern that substances or energy introduced, directly or indirectly, into the marine environment may bring about hazards to human health, harm living resources and marine ecosystems, damage amenities or interfere with other legitimate uses of the sea, even when there is no conclusive evidence of a causal relationship between the inputs and the effects.'*

Recently, on 28 January 2000, at the Conference of the Parties to the Convention on Biological diversity, the Protocol on Biosafety concerning the safe transfer, handling and use of living modified organisms resulting from modern biotechnology confirmed the key function of the precautionary principle. In fact, Article 10, paragraph 6 states: *'Lack of scientific certainty due to insufficient relevant scientific information and knowledge regarding the extent of the potential adverse effects of a living modified organism on the conservation and sustainable use of biological diversity in the Party of import, taking also into account risks to human health, shall not prevent that Party from taking a decision, as appropriate, with regard to the import of living modified organism in question as referred to in paragraph 3 above, in order to avoid or minimize such potential adverse effects'.*

Besides, the preamble to the WTO Agreement highlights the ever closer links between international trade and environmental protection.

The WTO SPS Agreement

Although the term 'precautionary principle' is not explicitly used in the WTO Agreement on the Application of Sanitary and Phytosanitary Measures (SPS), the Appellate Body on EC measures concerning meat and meat products (Hormones) (AB-1997-4, paragraph 124) states that it finds reflection in Article 5.7 of this Agreement. Art 5.7 reads: *'In cases where relevant scientific evidence is insufficient, a Member may provisionally adopt sanitary or phytosanitary measures on the basis of available scientific information, including that from the relevant international organizations as well as from sanitary and phytosanitary measures applied by other Members. In such circumstances, Members shall seek to obtain the additional information necessary for a more objective assessment of risk and review the sanitary or phytosanitary measure accordingly within a reasonable period of time.'*

The Appellate Body on Hormones (Paragraph 124) recognises . . . 'that there is no need to assume that Article 5.7 exhausts the relevance of a precautionary principle'. Moreover, Members have the 'right to establish their own level of sanitary protection, which level may be higher (i.e. more cautious) than that implied in existing international standards, guidelines and recommendations'. Furthermore, it accepts that 'responsible, representative governments commonly act from perspectives of prudence and precaution where risks of irreversible, e.g. life-terminating, damage to human health are concerned.' The Appellate Body on Japan-Measures affecting agricultural products (AB-1998-8, paragraph 89) clarifies the four requirements which must be met in order to adopt and maintain provisional SPS measures. A Member may provisionally adopt an SPS measure if this measure is:

1) imposed in respect of a situation where 'relevant scientific information is insufficient'; and

2) adopted 'on the basis of available pertinent information'.

Such a provisional measure may not be maintained unless the Member which adopted the measure:

1) 'seek(s) to obtain the additional information necessary for a more objective risk assessment'; and
2) 'review(s) the ... measure accordingly within a reasonable period of time.'

These four requirements are clearly cumulative and are equally important for the purpose of determining consistency with the provision of Art 5.7. Whenever one of these four requirements is not met, the measure at issue is inconsistent with Art 5.7. As to what constitutes a 'reasonable period of time' to review the measure, the Appellate Body points out (Paragraph 93), that this has to be established on a case-by-case basis and depends on the specific circumstances of each case, including the difficulty of obtaining the additional information necessary for the review *and* the characteristics of the provisional SPS measure.

Annex III
The four components of risk assessment

An attempt to complete as far as possible these four components should be performed before action is taken.

Hazard identification means identifying the biological, chemical or physical agents that may have adverse effects. A new substance or biological agent may reveal itself through its effects on the population (illness or death), or on the environment and it may be possible to describe the actual or potential effects on the population or environment before the cause is identified beyond doubt.

Hazard characterisation consists of determining, in quantitative and/or qualitative terms, the nature and severity of the adverse effects associated with the causal agents or activity. It is at this stage that a relationship between the amount of the hazardous substance and the effect has to be established. However, the relationship is sometimes difficult or impossible to prove, for instance because the causal link has not been established beyond doubt.

Appraisal of exposure consists of quantitatively or qualitatively evaluating the probability of exposure to the agent under study. Apart from information on the agents themselves (source, distribution, concentrations, characteristics, etc.), there is a need for data on the probability of contamination or exposure of the population or environment to the hazard.

Risk characterisation corresponds to the qualitative and/or quantitative estimation, taking account of inherent uncertainties, of the probability, of the frequency and severity of the known or potential adverse environmental or health effects liable to occur. It is established on the basis of the three preceding and closely depends on the uncertainties, variations, working hypotheses and conjectures made at each stage of the process. When the available data are inadequate or non-conclusive, a prudent and cautious approach to environmental protection, health or safety could be to opt for the worst-case hypothesis. When such hypotheses are accumulated, this will lead to an exaggeration of the real risk, but gives a certain assurance that it will not be underestimated.

Decision No 466/2002/EC of the European Parliament and of the Council of 1 March 2002 laying down a Community action programme promoting non-governmental organisations primarily active in the field of environmental protection (as amended)

Editorial note

Decision 446/2002/EC lays down an action programme promoting non-governmental organisations (NGOs) primarily active in the field of environmental protection (Article 1). The Programme is also to promote the systematic involvement of NGOs at all stages of the Community environmental policy-making process (Article 1(3)). An NGO, in order to qualify for a grant, is to be an independent and non-profit-making legal person primarily active in the field of environmental protection; it is to be active at the European level; its activities must meet the principles underlying the Sixth Environment Action Programme; and it must have been legally constituted for more than two years (Article 2). The Programme is open to the participation of NGOs established in the Member States, the Associated Countries and the other countries listed in Article 3.

Calls for proposals for grants are to be published each year in the Official Journal of the European Communities by the Commission. Proposals are to be assessed by the Commission, which will decide which organisations are to receive financing in the following year (Article 4). Support from the Programme is to target in particular the priority areas identified by the Sixth Environment Action Programme: limiting climate change; nature and biodiversity – protecting a unique resource; health and environment; and ensuring the sustainable management of natural resources and waste (Article 5).

In the case of NGOs based in the Community, grants are not to exceed 70 percent of the applicant's average audited annual eligible expenses during the two previous years (with exceptions made for NGOs based in candidate countries and the Balkan countries) (Article 6). Beneficiaries are free to use the grant to cover their expenses as deemed appropriate (Article 6(2)). Reasons for failure to obtain a grant are to be given to unsuccessful applicants with sufficient explanation to enable them to identify reforms needed before making new applications (Article 6(6)). The Programme started on 1 January 2002 and will end on 31 December 2006. The financial framework for its implementation was set at EUR 34.3 million for the period 2002 to 2006 (Article 7). On-the-spot checks may be carried out by the Commission to protect the Communities' financial interests against fraud and other irregularities (Article 8). Administrative measures and penalties are to be applied in cases of irregularities, mismanagement or fraud, depending on the severity of the case (Article 9(3)). Failure to meet expected results, as evidenced by obligatory reports, may lead to ineligibility for funding under the Programme (Article 9). A list of beneficiaries of grants is to be published each year in the Official Journal of the European Communities (Article 10). The Commission is to publish a report each year on the process of allocating grants and outcomes of grants (Article 11). A report on the achievement of the objectives of this Programme during the first three years is to be submitted to the European Parliament by the Commission. A decision on the continuation of the Programme as from 1 January 2007 will be made by the European Parliament and Council following a proposal of the Commission and on the basis of an external evaluation of the results of this Programme (Article 11). The Annex to the Decision specifies the four steps of the selection and award process; the characteristics against which applicants are assessed; the determination of grants and eligible expenses under the Programme.

Source: OJ L 75, 16.03.2002, p. 1 Amended by: Decision No 786/2004/EC of the European Parliament and of the Council of 21 April 2004 L 138 7 30.04.2004

Decision No 466/2002/EC of the European Parliament and of the Council of 1 March 2002 laying down a Community action programme promoting non-governmental organisations primarily active in the field of environmental protection (as amended)

The European Parliament and the Council of the European Union,

Having regard to the Treaty establishing the European Community, and in particular Article 175(1) thereof, Having regard to the proposal from the Commission,[1]

Having regard to the opinion of the Economic and Social Committee,[2]

Following consultation of the Committee of the Regions,

Acting in accordance with the procedure laid down in Article 251 of the Treaty,[3]

---

[1] OJ C 270 E, 25.9.2001, p. 125.
[2] Opinion delivered on 18 October 2001 (not yet published in the Official Journal).
[3] Opinion of the European Parliament of 23 October 2001 (not yet published in the Official Journal), Council Common Position of 6 December 2001 (not yet published in the Official Journal) and Decision of the European Parliament of 16 January 2002 (not yet published in the Official Journal).

Whereas:

(1) The Treaty provides for the development and the implementation of a Community environment policy and sets out the objectives and principles which guide that policy.

(2) The Action Programme introduced by Council Decision 97/872/EC of 16 December 1997 on a Community action programme promoting nongovernmental organisations primarily active in the field of environmental protection[1] comes to an end on 31 December 2001. The Programme has been evaluated by the Commission and present and previous beneficiaries, revealing a strong support for its renewal or revision.

(3) The Sixth Environment Action Programme recognises the need for empowering citizens, and the measures proposed include extensive and wide-ranging dialogue with stakeholders in environmental policy-making. In order to make it possible for nongovernmental organisations (hereinafter referred to as 'NGOs') to take part in such a dialogue, the Sixth Environment Action Programme envisages the need for appropriate support, including Community finance, to NGOs.

(4) NGOs active in the field of environmental protection have already demonstrated that they can contribute to the environment policy of the Community, as laid down in Article 174 of the Treaty, by active involvement in concrete environmental protection measures and in activities to increase the general awareness of the need for the protection of the environment with a view to sustainable development. NGOs also active in the field of animal protection, provided that such activities serve to achieve environmental protection objectives, may also participate in this Programme.

(5) NGOs are essential to coordinate and channel to the Commission information and views on the new and emerging perspectives, such as on nature protection and transboundary environmental problems, which cannot be, or are not being, fully dealt with at the Member State or subordinate level. NGOs have good understanding of public concerns on the environment and can thus promote these views and channel them back to the Commission.

(6) Environmental NGOs participate in experts groups, in preparatory and implementation committees of the Community institutions, providing important input to Community policies, programmes and initiatives and necessary balance in relation to the interests of other actors in the environment, including industry/business, trade unions and consumer groups.

(7) NGOs with a capacity to stimulate exchange of perspectives, problems and possible solutions and to implement relevant activities related to environmental problems with a Community dimension, involving stakeholders at national,

---

[1] OJ L 354, 30.12.1997, p. 25.

regional and local level, should be promoted. For this purpose only NGOs and NGO networks active at a European level will be targeted.

(8) The geographical expansion of the Programme is necessary in order to include Candidate Countries' NGOs in the light of their importance in gaining public acceptance for the environmental 'acquis' and strengthening its implementation.

(9) In the light of the experience gained in the first three years of implementation of this Decision, an assessment of the operation of the Programme should be undertaken in order to decide on its continuation.

(10) The annual appropriations should be decided upon by the budgetary authority in the budgetary procedure.

(11) This Decision lays down, for the entire duration of the Programme, a financial framework constituting the prime reference, within the meaning of point 33 of the Interinstitutional Agreement of 6 May 1999 between the European Parliament, the Council and the Commission on budgetary discipline and improvement of the budgetary procedure,[1] for the budgetary authority during the annual budgetary procedure,

Have decided as follows:

Article 1

1. A Community action programme promoting non-governmental organisations (NGOs) primarily active in the field of environmental protection is hereby established.

2. The general objective of this Programme shall be to promote NGOs which are primarily active in the field of environmental protection and enhancement at a European level. Such activities should involve contributing, or being able to contribute, to the development and implementation of Community environmental policy and legislation in different regions of Europe.

3. The Programme shall also promote the systematic involvement of NGOs at all stages of the Community environmental policy-making process, by ensuring relevant representation in stakeholder consultation meetings and public hearings. The Programme shall also contribute to the strengthening of small regional or local associations working to apply the *acquis communautaire* in relation to the environment and sustainable development in their local area.

Article 2

In order to qualify for a grant, an NGO shall have the following characteristics and comply with the Annex:

(a) it must be an independent and non-profit-making legal person primarily active in the field of environmental protection and enhancement with an environmental objective aimed at the public good and with a view to sustainable development;

[1] OJ C 172, 18.6.1999, p. 1.

(b) it must be active at a European level, either singly or in the form of several coordinated associations with a structure (membership base) and activities covering at least three European countries. However, coverage of two European countries is acceptable, provided that the primary objective of the activities is to support the development and implementation of Community environmental policy, as detailed in Article 1(2) and (3);

(c) its activities must meet, in particular, the principles underlying the Sixth Environment Action Programme and be in line with the priority areas identified in Article 5;

(d) it must have been legally constituted for more than two years and have had its annual statement of accounts for the two preceding years certified by a registered auditor. In cases of exceptional circumstances, the Commission may grant a derogation from these two requirements, provided that to do so would not compromise the protection of Community financial interests.

Article 3

The Programme shall be open to the participation of European NGOs established in either:

(a) the Member States;

(b) the Associated Countries[1] in accordance with the conditions established in the respective Europe Agreements, in the additional protocols thereto and in the decisions of the respective Association Councils;

(c) Cyprus, Malta or Turkey in accordance with conditions and procedures to be agreed with those countries; or

(d) the Balkan countries forming part of the Stabilisation and Association process for countries of South-Eastern Europe[2] in accordance with conditions and procedures to be agreed with those countries.

Article 4

1. The Commission shall publish a Call for Proposals in the *Official Journal of the European Communities* by 30 September each year, for grants in the following calendar year. In addition, the Commission shall use other appropriate means available to make the programme known to potential beneficiaries, including the electronic media.

2. The Call for Proposals shall include an information package and set out the eligibility, selection and award criteria (including details of the proposed weighting system) and the application, assessment and approval procedure.

---

[1] Bulgaria, the Czech Republic, Estonia, Hungary, Latvia, Lithuania, Poland, Romania, the Slovak Republic and Slovenia.

[2] Former Yugoslav Republic of Macedonia, Albania, Federal Republic of Yugoslavia, Bosnia-Herzegovina, and Croatia.

3. After assessing the proposals, the Commission shall decide which organisations are to receive financing in the following year, by 31 December each year, save for a delay in the adoption of the Community budget. The decision shall give rise to an agreement between the Commission and the beneficiary, fixing the maximum amount of the grant, the methods of payment, the control and monitoring measures and the objectives to be achieved by the grant. Payments shall be made immediately.

Article 5

1. Given the importance of sustainable development and the health and quality of life of European citizens, support from this Programme shall target in particular the priority areas from the Sixth Environment Action Programme, grouped under four main headings as follows:

(a) limiting climate change;
(b) nature and bio-diversity – protecting a unique resource;
(c) health and environment;
(d) ensuring the sustainable management of natural resources and waste.

The Sixth Environment Action Programme will be subject to a review in the fourth year of operation and revised and updated, as necessary, to take account of new developments and information. In addition to the abovementioned areas, environmental education and implementation and enforcement of Community environmental legislation shall also be priorities.

2. The selection and award process shall be carried out in four steps, as detailed in A of the Annex.

Article 6

1. A grant shall not exceed 70% of the applicant's average audited annual eligible expenses during the preceding two years, in the case of NGOs based in the Community, or 80% in the case of NGOs based in the candidate countries and the Balkan countries, nor 80% of the applicant's eligible expenses for the current year. The amount shall be determined annually according to a fixed weighting system, which takes into account the score values resulting from the assessment referred to in Article 5(2) and described in A of the Annex and the principles as outlined in C of the Annex.

2. A beneficiary under this Programme shall be free to use the grant to cover its eligible expenses as it deems appropriate, over the grant year. All expenses incurred by the beneficiary during the grant year shall be considered eligible, except for those specified in section 2 of D of the Annex. Beneficiaries may also disburse funds to partners or member organisations in accordance with details specified in the approved work programme.

3. The amount of the grant shall become final only once the audited financial statement has been accepted by the Commission, ensuring that Community funds have been used in accordance with the relevant provisions of the Financial Regulation

of 21 December 1977 applicable to the general budget of the European Communities.[1] The final payment shall be reduced accordingly if the total of Community grants, from this and any other programmes, exceeds 80% of the audited eligible expenses of the beneficiary for the year.

4. Moreover, if the audited financial statement of the grant year shows that the total revenues of the beneficiary, save revenues regularly earmarked for ineligible expenses, exceed the eligible expenses, the final payment shall be reduced or, if necessary, the excess amount shall be recovered accordingly. Pursuant to Article 256 of the Treaty, recovery orders shall be enforceable.

5. In order to ensure the effectiveness of the grants to environmental NGOs, the Commission shall take the necessary measures to verify that a selected organisation still satisfies the requirements for being awarded the grant throughout the grant year. In particular, a systematic scheme to monitor the beneficiaries' performance during the grant year, as well as an ex-post performance evaluation, shall be put in place.

6. The Commission shall provide unsuccessful applicants with reasons for the failure of the NGO to meet the requirements, giving sufficient explanation to enable them to identify reforms needed before making new applications

Article 7

1. This Programme shall start on 1 January 2002 and end on 31 December 2006.

2. The financial framework for the implementation of this Programme for the period 2002 to 2006 is hereby set at EUR 34,3 million.

3. The annual appropriations shall be authorised by the budgetary authority within the limits of the financial perspective.

Article 8

1. In order to protect the Communities' financial interests against fraud and other irregularities, the Commission may carry out on-the-spot checks and inspections under this Programme in accordance with Council Regulation (Euratom, EC) No 2185/96.[2] If appropriate, the European Anti-Fraud Office (OLAF) shall carry out investigations, which shall be governed by Regulation (EC) No 1073/1999 of the European Parliament and of the Council.[3]

2. The beneficiary of a grant shall keep available for the Commission all the supporting documents, including the audited financial statement, regarding expenditure incurred during the grant year for a period of five years following the last payment. The

---

[1] OJ L 356, 31.12.1977, p. 1. Regulation as last amended by Regulation (EC) No 762/2001 (OJ L 111, 20.4.2001, p. 1).

[2] OJ L 292, 15.11.1996, p. 2.   [3] OJ L 136, 31.5.1999, p. 1.

beneficiary of a grant shall see to it that, where appropriate, supporting documents that are in the hands of partners or members are available for the Commission.

Article 9

1. Failure to meet expected results, as evidenced by obligatory reports, may lead to ineligibility for funding under this Programme in the following year. Repeated failure in two successive years shall result in ineligibility for the remaining years of the programme.

2. If an NGO becomes the subject of a Commission recovery order due to intentional irregularities, irregularities caused by negligence or fraud, it shall automatically be excluded from funding under the remaining years of the Programme.

3. If the Commission discovers irregularities, mismanagement or fraud in relation to a grant, either by audits or on-the-spot checks, the beneficiary shall be subject to one or several of the following administrative measures and penalties in proportion to the severity of the case (and with a right to appeal against the decision):

(a) annulment of the grant;
(b) payment of a fine of up to 50% of the amount of the recovery order;
(c) exclusion from other Community funding opportunity, for the remaining years of the Programme;
(d) exclusion from the relevant dialogue mechanisms of the Commission, for the remaining years of the Programme.

Article 10

A list of the beneficiaries to be financed under this Programme, together with the amount allocated, shall be published each year in the *Official Journal of the European Communities.*

Article 11

The Commission shall provide a report to the Member States and the European Parliament by 30 April each year on the process of allocating grants for the current year, and outcomes from grants for the previous year. The report shall include an explanation of how the Commission has selected beneficiaries for the current year. The Commission shall convene a meeting of stakeholders to discuss this report by 30 June each year. By 31 December 2004 at the latest, the Commission shall submit a report to the European Parliament and the Council on the achievement of the objectives of this Programme during the first three years and shall, if appropriate, make proposals for any adjustment to be made with a view to continuing or not continuing the Programme. This Report shall be based on the reports concerning beneficiaries' performance and assess, in particular, their effectiveness in contributing to the objectives stated in Article 1 and the Annex. The European Parliament and the Council, in accordance with the Treaty, shall decide on the continuation of the Programme as from 1 January 2007. Before putting forward proposals to this end, the Commission shall conduct an external evaluation of the results achieved by the Programme.

Article 12

This Decision shall enter into force on the day following that of its publication in the *Official Journal of the European Communities.*

ANNEX

A. *The four steps of the selection and award process*

1. Elimination of applications which do not comply with the technical/ administrative requirements for submitting a request for funding under this Programme. In particular, incomplete or insufficiently detailed applications, or applications which have not been filled in according to the instructions given on the application form or which have been submitted after the publicised deadline, shall be ineligible under this Programme.

2. Elimination of applications which do not comply with the eligibility criteria as outlined in Articles 2 and 3.

3. Comparative assessment of the remaining eligible applications evaluated against the following criteria, which are further specified in B:

(a) extent to which the application and, more specifically, the proposed work programme meet the objectives of the Programme as described in Article 1 and the priorities of the Programme as described in Article 5;

(b) management and product quality;

(c) outreach, effectiveness and efficiency. Comparative score values will be assigned to each retained applicant.

4. Fixing the set of applications, which will enter the award procedure by retaining only those which have received score values above thresholds defined by the Commission.

B. *Characteristics against which applicants will be assessed*

Applicants having successfully passed the first two selection steps accounted for in A shall be measured against the following criteria:

1. Extent to which the application meets the objectives of the Programme Characteristics of the applicant, including his proposed work programme, which will be evaluated, shall include:

(a) Policy relevance (in relation to the Sixth Environment Action programme, a new European Governance, Sustainable Development, Enlargement, the Stabilisation and Association process for countries of South-Eastern Europe, the development of the Euro-Mediterranean Partnership, Integration, Gender Mainstreaming).
(b) Relevance and potential impact of involvement in Community environmental policy-shaping and implementation.
(c) Representational ability as to voicing the public's concerns from different regions of Europe and as to feeding in these ideas and proposals for the solution of environmental problems.
(d) Relevance in environment-awareness raising and knowledge-enhancement activities, both in general and in relation to Community environmental policies.
(e) Ability to: develop networks between organisations in Member States and in candidate countries; encourage cooperation with organisations in the public and private sector; and attract part financing from external sources. For each of the abovementioned characteristics, consideration shall be given to the strength of the applicant with regard to fulfilling the associated NGO roles indicated in the examples given in D.

2. Management and product quality Characteristics to be assessed shall include:

(a) Organisational structure, adequacy in staffing and management of human resources.
(b) Internal decision-making process, relationship with members, including arrangements to ensure involvement of membership in policy development and policy pronouncements.
(c) Strategic approach, goal-orientation and planning practices.
(d) Administration, budget control and financial management.
(e) Reporting practices (internal and external).
(f) Self-assessment and quality control, feedback of experience (learning).
(g) Technical/scientific competence.

3. Outreach, effectiveness, efficiency Characteristics to be assessed shall include:

(a) General visibility of the organisation and its activities.
(b) External relations and effectiveness (with other actors in the field of the environment, such as local and regional authorities, business and industry, consumer groups, trade unions, other NGOs and the general public).

C. Determination of grants

The grant is calculated on the applicant's forecasted total eligible expenses for the grant year, taking explicitly into account his average audited expenses over the preceding two years, according to the following principles:

1. When all other parameters are equal, the grant amount for NGOs with larger volumes of relevant activities (as measured by the average value of their preceding two years' audited annual expenses and the forecasted total eligible expenses for the grant year) will normally be higher than the grant amounts for NGOs with smaller volumes of relevant activities. However, the distribution will be made on a non-linear basis and so beneficiaries with smaller volumes of relevant activities will receive a relatively higher rate of support.

2. When all other parameters are equal, NGOs getting higher comparative assessment scores will receive larger amounts than lower scoring applicants.

3. When an NGO has requested a specified amount, under no circumstances shall the grant awarded exceed that amount.

D. Eligible expenses

1. All expenses incurred by the beneficiary during the grant year shall be considered eligible except those listed in section 2. Eligible expenses could include some of the following, illustrative, examples of activities:

(a) coordinating and channelling to the Commission information and views, based on the concerns and opinions of the general public, on new and emerging perspectives, which cannot be, or are not being, fully dealt with at the Member State or appropriate level;

(b) preparatory work and research required for participation in experts groups, in preparatory and implementation committees of the Community institutions, providing important input to Community policies, programmes and initiatives and the necessary balance in relation to the interests of other actors in the environment, including industry/business, trade unions and consumer groups;

(c) stimulation of exchange of views, problems and possible solutions, related to environmental problems with a Community dimension, involving stakeholders at national, regional and local level. This could also include transfer of knowledge and ensuring synergy via networking;

(d) awareness-raising and knowledge-enhancement regarding both general aspects of the environment and Community environmental policy;

(e) capacity building, in particular to reinforce the involvement of small NGOs, new NGO networks and NGOs in the candidate countries and the Balkan countries at European level.

2. Payments made by the beneficiary and contracts awarded to third parties, which comprise elements of the categories below, will be deemed ineligible:

(a) entertainment, hospitality, unnecessary or ill considered expenses;

(b) expenses clearly outside the agreed work programme of the beneficiary for the grant year;

(c) debt reimbursements, interest owed, carried over deficits;
(d) costs related to the capital employed, investments or reserves set aside to strengthen the assets of the beneficiary;
(e) contributions in kind;
(f) private expenses;
(g) criminal/illegal activities.

Regulation (EC) No 2493/2000 of the European Parliament and of the Council of 7 November 2000 on measures to promote the full integration of the environmental dimension in the development process of developing countries

Editorial note

Regulation EC 2493/2000 aims at promoting the full integration of environmental dimensions in the development process of developing countries. The Regulation specifies rules under which activities promoting sustainable development can receive assistance from the Community.

The Community is to provide financial assistance and appropriate expertise aimed at drawing up and promoting the implementation of policies, strategies, tools and technologies for the pursuit of sustainable development (Article 1). Community support is to be provided directly and indirectly. Assistance and expertise are to complement and reinforce that provided under other instruments of development cooperation (Article 1(2) and (3)).

Article 2 defines sustainable development for the purposes of the Regulation as: 'the improvement of the standard of living and welfare of the relevant populations within the limits of the capacity of the ecosystems by maintaining natural assets and their biological diversity for the benefit of present and future generations'. The activities to be carried out are in particular to address global environmental issues; transboundary environmental issues; environmental impacts related to the integration of developing countries in the world economy; sustainable patterns of production and consumption; sustainable production and use of energy; etc. (Article 3(1)). Activities eligible for financing include: support for the drawing up of national, regional and local policies, plans and strategies; schemes to build up institutional and operational capacities of actors in the development process; pilot projects; promotion of trade in products produced in a sustainable manner; etc. (Article 3(2)). Particular attention, in the selection, preparation, implementation and evaluation of activities, is to be paid to: the contribution to the overall objective of poverty eradication; local initiatives; active involvement of local populations, including indigenous communities, etc. (Article 3(3)).

Cooperation partners that may receive assistance include international organisations, States, regions and regional bodies, decentralised departments, public agencies, private operators and industries cooperatives, local communities, NGOs and associations representing local people, in particular indigenous people (Article 4). Article 5 specifies the activities that may be covered by Community financing. It also stresses that cofinancing shall be sought from each cooperation activity from cooperation partners. Coordination measures shall be adopted to attain consistency and complementarity and to guarantee the optimum efficiency of the activities (Article 5(5)).

Financial assistance under the Regulation is to take the form of grants (Article 6). EUR 93 million are provided as the financial framework for implementing the Regulation for the period 2000 to 2006 (Article 7).

The appraisal, decisions on financing and administrative activities covered by the Regulation are to be carried out by the Commission (Article 8). The Commission is to be assisted by a Committee (Article 9). An annual report is to be submitted by the Commission to the European Parliament and the Council (Article 10). The Regulation is to apply until 31 December 2006 (Article 11(1)). Four years after the entry into force of the Regulation, an overall evaluation of the Programme is to be submitted by the Commission to the European Parliament and to the Council, together with proposals concerning the future of the Programme (Article 11(2)).

Source: OJ L 288 15.11.2000 p. 1

Regulation (EC) No 2493/2000 of the European Parliament and of the Council of 7 November 2000 on measures to promote the full integration of the environmental dimension in the development process of developing countries

The European Parliament and the Council of the European Union,

Having regard to the Treaty establishing the European Community, and in particular Articles 175 and 179 thereof,

Having regard to the proposal from the Commission,[1]

Having regard to the opinion of the Economic and Social Committee,[2]

After consulting the Committee of the Regions,

Acting in accordance with the procedure laid down in Article 251 of the Treaty,[3] in the light of the joint text approved by the Conciliation Committee on 27 July 2000.

---

[1] OJ C 47, 20.2.1999, p. 10 and OJ C 274 E, 26.9.2000, p. 1.

[2] OJ C 258, 10.9.1999, p. 16.

[3] Opinion of the European Parliament of 5 May 1999 (OJ C 279, 01.10.1999, p. 173), Council Common Position of 16 December 1999 (OJ C 64, 06.03.2000, p. 47) and Decision of the European Parliament of 15 March 2000 (not yet published in the Official Journal). Decision of the European Parliament of 20 September 2000 and Council Decision of 7 September 2000.

Whereas:

(1) Depletion of natural resources and environmental degradation have direct effects on economic development and especially on the livelihoods of local communities, including indigenous peoples, and thus counteract the alleviation of poverty through sustainable development.

(2) Current patterns of production and consumption have undeniable transboundary and global consequences, in particular where the atmosphere, the hydrosphere, soil condition and biological diversity are concerned.

(3) The Community and its Member States are signatories to the Rio Declaration and the Agenda 21 action programme and are committed to the United Nations General Assembly Special Session (Ungass) Resolution 'Programme for the further implementation of Agenda 21'.

(4) The Community and its Member States are parties to Multilateral Environment Agreements, notably the Convention on Biological Diversity, the Framework Convention on Climate Change and the Convention to Combat Desertification. They are thus committed to take into account the common but differentiated responsibilities of developed parties and developing parties on these subjects.

(5) The internal and external aspects of the European Community's environment policy need to be coherent in order to effectively respond to the challenges identified in the United Nations Conference on Environment and Development (UNCED) and its follow-up processes.

(6) The Community and its Member States are committed to the Organisation of Economic Cooperation and Development/Development Assistance Committee's (OECD/DAC) 'Shaping the 21st Century Strategy' which calls for the support for the implementation of national strategies for sustainable development in all countries by 2005, so as to ensure that current trends in the loss of environmental resources are effectively reversed at both global and national levels by 2015.

(7) The European Parliament and the Council have adopted Decision No 2179/98/EC of 24 September 1998 on the review of the European Community Programme of policy and action in relation to the environment and sustainable development 'Towards Sustainability',[1] which calls for a strengthened role for the Community in international cooperation in environment and sustainable development. The basic strategy of the Programme is to achieve full integration of environmental policy in other policies, including development policy.

(8) The European Council held in Cardiff in June 1998 welcomed the Commission Communication 'Partnership for Integration' setting out a strategy

[1] OJ L 275, 10.10.1998, p. 1.

for integrating environment considerations into European Union policies and endorsed the principle that major policy proposals should be accompanied by the appraisal of their environmental impact.

(9) The Council and the Member States adopted on 15 July 1996 a Resolution on Environmental Assessment in Development Cooperation.

(10) In its Resolution of 30 November 1998, the Council acknowledges the key role that indigenous peoples play in the conservation and sustainable use of natural resources.

(11) Sustainable development relies on the integration of the environmental dimension into the development process.

(12) Since resources are limited, the creation of suitable policies, strategies and tools and the implementation of experimental schemes are essential elements for such integration in economic and development cooperation.

(13) The financial instruments available to the Community for supporting sustainable development in developing countries should be supplemented.

(14) Coordination of operations financed under Community instruments should be improved.

(15) Council Regulation (EC) No 722/97 of 22 April 1997 on environmental measures in developing countries in the context of sustainable development[1] set out the framework for Community assistance aimed at enabling developing countries to integrate the environmental dimension in their development process. Regulation (EC) No 722/97 was applicable until 31 December 1999. The experience acquired during the implementation of Regulation (EC) No 722/97 should be reflected in this Regulation.

(16) Provision should be made for funding the activities referred to in this Regulation.

(17) This Regulation lays down, for the entire duration of the programme it establishes, a financial framework constituting the prime reference, within the meaning of point 33 of the Interinstitutional Agreement between the European Parliament, the Council and the Commission of 6 May 1999, on budgetary discipline and improvement of the budgetary procedure,[2] for the budgetary authority during the annual budgetary procedure.

(18) Detailed rules for implementation should be laid down, in particular the form of action, the cooperation partners and the decision-making procedure.

(19) The measures necessary for the implementation of this Regulation should be adopted in accordance with Council Decision 1999/468/EC of 28 June 1999, laying down the procedures for the exercise of implementing powers conferred on the Commission,[3]

---

[1] OJ L 108, 25.4.1997, p.1.   [2] OJ C 172, 18.6.1999, p. 1.   [3] OJ L 184, 17.7.1999, p. 23.

Have adopted this regulation:

Article 1

1. The Community shall support developing countries in their efforts to integrate the environmental dimension into their development process. To this end, the Community shall provide financial assistance and appropriate expertise aimed at drawing up and promoting the implementation of policies, strategies, tools and technologies for the pursuit of sustainable development.

2. Community support shall be provided directly to developing country stakeholders as well as indirectly through the strengthening of the environmental dimension of Community economic and development cooperation in order to ensure that full account is taken of environmental considerations in Community programmes.

3. The assistance and expertise provided under this Regulation shall complement and reinforce that provided through other instruments of development cooperation.

Article 2

For the purposes of this Regulation:

'sustainable development' means the improvement of the standard of living and welfare of the relevant populations within the limits of the capacity of the ecosystems by maintaining natural assets and their biological diversity for the benefit of present and future generations.

Article 3

1. The activities to be carried out under this Regulation shall address in particular:

– global environmental issues, in particular those covered by multilateral environmental agreements, such as climate change, desertification and biological diversity,
– transboundary environmental issues, in particular air, soil and water pollution,
– environmental impacts related to the integration of developing countries into the world economy,
– the inclusion in development cooperation projects of environmental considerations enabling the sustainable dimension of these projects to be distinguished, identified and assessed,
– environmental impacts of macroeconomic and sectoral policies in developing countries,
– sustainable patterns of production and consumption,
– sustainable management and use of natural and environmental resources in all productive sectors such as agriculture, fisheries and industry,
– environmental problems caused by the non-sustainable use of resources due to poverty,

- sustainable production and use of energy and in particular encouragement of the use of renewable energy sources, increased energy efficiency, energy saving and the replacement of especially damaging energy sources by others which are less so,
- sustainable production and use of chemical products, in particular hazardous and toxic substances,
- conservation of biological diversity – especially by protecting ecosystems and habitats and the conservation of species diversity – the sustainable use of its components, the involvement of holders of traditional knowledge on the use of biological diversity, and the fair and equitable sharing of the benefits arising out of the utilisation of genetic resources,
- the management of fresh water resources,
- coastal zone, estuary and wetland management,
- desertification,
- urban environment problems relating, *inter alia*, to transport, waste, waste water, air pollution and noise, and the quality of drinking water,
- environmental problems related to industrial activities.

2. Activities eligible for financing include, amongst others:

- support for the drawing up of national, regional and local policies, plans and strategies, programmes and projects for sustainable development,
- schemes to build up the institutional and operational capacities of actors in the development process, i.e. government, non-governmental organisations, private sector, civil society, indigenous peoples, at national, regional and local level,
- pilot projects in the field including those involving environmentally sound technologies adapted to local constraints and needs,
- the promotion of trade in products that have been produced in a sustainable manner,
- the creation of instruments for sustainable development, *inter alia*, trade-related instruments such as labelling and certification schemes and green trade initiatives,
- the formulation of guidelines, operating manuals and instruments aimed at promoting sustainable development and environmental integration in particular in the form of public databases and databanks on the internet (open to the public),
- information campaigns on hazardous substances, and toxic waste and pesticides in particular,
- support for the development and application of environment assessment tools in the preparation and implementation of policies, strategies, programmes and projects,
- raising awareness of local populations and key actors in the development process and development cooperation with regard to the implications of sustainable development, in particular through information campaigns and training,
- inventory, accounting and statistical work, in order to improve the quality of environmental data and environmental indicators.

3. In the selection, preparation, implementation and evaluation of activities, particular attention shall be paid to:

– the contribution to the overall objective of eradicating poverty,
– local initiatives involving innovative measures aimed at sustainable development,
– active involvement, support and ownership of local populations, including indigenous communities,
– gender-specific roles, knowledge, perspectives and contributions of women/girls and men/boys in the sustainable management and use of natural resources,
– the potential for integration into the wider context of Community development cooperation policies and programmes,
– the internalisation of environmental costs, including through economic instruments,
– the contribution to strengthening regional cooperation in the area of sustainable development.

Lesson-learning and dissemination of the results of the activities carried out will be essential elements of implementing this Regulation, including support of the implementation of international environmental agreements.

Article 4

Cooperation partners which may receive assistance under this Regulation shall include international organisations, States, regions and regional bodies, decentralised departments, public agencies, private operators and industries, cooperatives, local communities, non-governmental organisations and associations representing local people, in particular indigenous peoples.

Article 5

1. Community financing may cover studies, technical assistance, education, training or other services, minor supplies and works, small grant funds as well as appraisals, audits and evaluation and monitoring missions. It may cover, within the limit established annually by the budgetary authority, technical and administrative assistance costs, to the benefit of the Commission and the beneficiary, related to operations other than the permanent tasks of the public administration, linked to the identification, preparation, management, monitoring, auditing and control of programmes or projects. Community financing may cover both investment, linked to a specific activity, with the exception of the purchase of real estate, and recurrent expenditure (including administrative, maintenance and operating expenditure). With the exception of training, education and research programmes, recurrent expenditure may normally be covered only during the start-up phase and on a gradually decreasing basis.

2. A contribution from the cooperation partners defined in Article 4 shall be sought for each cooperation activity. Their contribution shall be requested according to their means and the nature of the activity concerned.

3. Opportunities may be sought for cofinancing with other donors, especially with Member States and the international organisations concerned. In this respect, coordination with the measures taken by other donors shall be sought.

4. The necessary measures shall be taken to emphasise the Community character of the assistance provided under this Regulation.

5. In order to attain the objectives of consistency and complementarity laid down in the Treaty and with the aim of guaranteeing optimum efficiency for all these activities, the Commission shall, in liaison with Member States, take all coordination measures necessary, including in particular: (a) the systematic exchange and analysis of information on activities financed or being considered for financing by the Community and the Member States; (b) the spot coordination of these activities by means of regular meetings and exchange of information between representatives of the Commission and of the Member States in the beneficiary countries.

6. In order to obtain the greatest possible impact of the activities at global, national and local levels, the Commission, in liaison with the Member States, shall take any initiative necessary for ensuring proper coordination and close collaboration with the cooperation partners, the local partners (non governmental organisations, grassroots communities and associations), donors and other international organisations involved, in particular those forming part of the United Nations system.

Article 6

Financial assistance under this Regulation shall take the form of grants.

Article 7

The financial framework for implementing this Regulation during the period from 2000 to 2006 shall be EUR 93 million. The annual appropriations shall be authorised by the budgetary authority within the limits of the financial perspective.

Article 8

1. The Commission shall be responsible for appraising, taking decisions to finance and administering activities covered by this Regulation according to the budgetary and other procedures in force, and in particular those laid down in the Financial Regulation applicable to the general budget of the European Communities.

2. Every second year, the Commission shall adopt, in accordance with the procedure laid down in Article 9(2) strategic guidelines and priorities for implementing the activities to be carried out in the following years. It shall inform the European Parliament thereof.

3. Decisions relating to grants of EUR 2,5 million or more for individual activities financed under this Regulation shall be adopted by the Commission under the procedure laid down in Article 9(2).

4. The Commission shall inform the Committee referred to in Article 9(1) succinctly of any financing decisions it intends to take with regard to grants of less than EUR 2,5 million for activities covered by this Regulation. The information shall be made available not later than one week before the decision is taken.

5. The Commission shall be authorised to approve any extra commitments needed for covering any expected or real cost overruns or additional requirements in connection with the activities, provided that the overrun or additional requirement is less than or equal to 20% of the initial commitment fixed by the financing decision.

6. All financing agreements or contracts concluded under this Regulation shall provide for the Commission and the Court of Auditors to conduct on-the-spot checks according to the usual procedures laid down by the Commission under the rules in force, in particular those of the Financial Regulation applicable to the general budget of the European Communities.

7. Where operations are the subject of financing agreements between the Community and the recipient country, such agreements shall stipulate that the payment of taxes, duties or any other charges is not to be covered by the Community.

8. Participation in invitations to tender and the award of contracts shall be open on equal terms to all natural and legal persons of the Member States and of the recipient country. It may be extended to other developing countries and, in exceptional cases, which are fully justified, to other third countries.

9. Supplies shall originate in the Member States, the recipient country or other developing countries. In exceptional cases, where circumstances warrant, supplies may originate in other countries.

10. Particular attention shall be paid to:
– the pursuit of cost-effectiveness and sustainable impact of activities,
– the clear definition and monitoring of objectives and indicators of achievement for all activities.

Article 9

1. The Commission shall be assisted by the appropriate geographically determined committee responsible for development, hereinafter referred to as the 'Committee'.

2. Where reference is made to this paragraph, Articles 4 and 7 of Decision 1999/468/EC shall apply, having regard to the provisions of Article 8 thereof. The period laid down in Article 4(3) of Decision 1999/468/EC shall be set at one month.

3. The Committee shall adopt its rules of procedure.

Article 10

1. By 1 September after each budget year, the Commission shall submit an annual report to the European Parliament and the Council, summarising the activities financed in the course of that year and evaluating the implementation of this Regulation over that period. The summary shall in particular provide information about the number and nature of activities financed, the cooperation partners and the countries concerned. The report shall also indicate the number of external evaluations carried out, regarding specific activities.

2. The Commission shall regularly evaluate activities financed by the Community with a view to establishing whether the objectives aimed at by those activities have been achieved and to providing guidelines for improving the effectiveness of future activities. The Commission shall submit to the Committee referred to in Article 9(1) a summary of the evaluations made. The evaluation reports shall be available to any Member State, to the European Parliament and to other interested parties.

3. The Commission shall inform the Member States, at the latest one month after its decision, of the activities that have been approved, stating their cost and nature, the country concerned and the cooperation partners.

4. A financing guide specifying the guidelines and criteria applicable to the selection of activities shall be published and communicated to the interested parties by the Commission services including Commission delegations in the countries concerned.

Article 11

1. This Regulation shall enter into force on the third day following that of its publication in the *Official Journal of the European Communities*. It shall apply until 31 December 2006.

2. Four years after the entry into force of this Regulation, the Commission shall submit to the European Parliament and the Council an overall evaluation of the activities financed by the Community under this Regulation, in the context of overall Community development cooperation, together with proposals concerning the future of this Regulation, including its possible modification or termination.

This Regulation shall be binding in its entirety and directly applicable in all Member States.

Done at Brussels, 7 November 2000.

PART II

European Community institutions and legislation

EC Treaty, as amended by the 1986 Single European Act, the 1992 Treaty on European Union, the 1997 Treaty of Amsterdam, the 2001 Treaty of Nice and the 2003 Act of Accession[1] (selected articles)

Editorial note

The main EC institutions with responsibilities for development of EC environmental law under the EC Treaty (as amended by the 1986 Single European Act, the 1992 Treaty on European Union, the 1997 Treaty of Amsterdam and the 2001 Treaty of Nice) are the European Parliament (Articles 189–201); the Council (Articles 202–210); the Commission (Articles 211–219); and the European Court of Justice (to which is attached a Court of First Instance (Articles 220–245)). The Economic and Social Committee (Articles 257–262) and the Committee of the Regions (Articles 263–265) also play a role.

Secondary environmental legislation adopted by the Community comprises regulations, directives and decisions, which are binding, and non-binding recommendations and opinions (Article 249).

Source: OJ 24.12.2002 C 325/23

EC Treaty, as amended by the 1986 Single European Act, the 1992 Treaty on European Union, the 1997 Treaty of Amsterdam, the 2001 Treaty of Nice and the 2003 Act of Accession (selected articles)

[. . .]

Part five
Institutions of the Community

Title I
Provisions governing the institutions

---

[1] Act concerning the conditions of accession of the Czech Republic, the Republic of Estonia, the Republic of Cyprus, the Republic of Latvia, the Republic of Lithuania, the Republic of Hungary, the Republic of Malta, the Republic of Poland, the Republic of Slovenia and the Slovak Republic and the adjustments to the Treaties on which the European Union is founded (OJ L 236 23.09.2003 p. 33).

Chapter 1
The institutions

Section 1
The European Parliament

Article 189

The European Parliament, which shall consist of representatives of the peoples of the States brought together in the Community, shall exercise the powers conferred upon it by this Treaty.

The number of Members of the European Parliament shall not exceed 732.

Article 190

1. The representatives in the European Parliament of the peoples of the States brought together in the Community shall be elected by direct universal suffrage.

2. The number of representatives elected in each Member State shall be as follows:[1]

Belgium 24
Czech Republic 24
Denmark 14
Germany 99
Estonia 6
Greece 24
Spain 54
France 78
Ireland 13
Italy 78
Cyprus 6
Latvia 9
Lithuania 13
Luxembourg 6
Hungary 24
Malta 5
Netherlands 27
Austria 18
Poland 54
Portugal 24
Slovenia 7
Slovakia 14

---

[1] Paragraph replaced by Article 11 of the Act concerning the conditions of accession of the Czech Republic, the Republic of Estonia, the Republic of Cyprus, the Republic of Latvia, the Republic of Lithuania, the Republic of Hungary, the Republic of Malta, the Republic of Poland, the Republic of Slovenia and the Slovak Republic and the adjustments to the Treaties on which the European Union is founded (OJ 23.9.2003 L 236 p. 36)

Finland 14
Sweden 19
United Kingdom 78.

In the event of amendments to this paragraph, the number of representatives elected in each Member State must ensure appropriate representation of the peoples of the States brought together in the Community.

3. Representatives shall be elected for a term of five years.

4. The European Parliament shall draw up a proposal for elections by direct universal suffrage in accordance with a uniform procedure in all Member States or in accordance with principles common to all Member States.

The Council shall, acting unanimously after obtaining the assent of the European Parliament, which shall act by a majority of its component members, lay down the appropriate provisions, which it shall recommend to Member States for adoption in accordance with their respective constitutional requirements.

5. The European Parliament, after seeking an opinion from the Commission and with the approval of the Council acting by a qualified majority, shall lay down the regulations and general conditions governing the performance of the duties of its Members. All rules or conditions relating to the taxation of Members or former Members shall require unanimity within the Council.

Article 191

Political parties at European level are important as a factor for integration within the Union. They contribute to forming a European awareness and to expressing the political will of the citizens of the Union.

The Council, acting in accordance with the procedure referred to in Article 251, shall lay down the regulations governing political parties at European level and in particular the rules regarding their funding.

Article 192

In so far as provided in this Treaty, the European Parliament shall participate in the process leading up to the adoption of Community acts by exercising its powers under the procedures laid down in Articles 251 and 252 and by giving its assent or delivering advisory opinions.

The European Parliament may, acting by a majority of its Members, request the Commission to submit any appropriate proposal on matters on which it considers that a Community act is required for the purpose of implementing this Treaty.

Article 193

In the course of its duties, the European Parliament may, at the request of a quarter of its Members, set up a temporary Committee of Inquiry to investigate, without prejudice to the powers conferred by this Treaty on other institutions or bodies, alleged contraventions or maladministration in the implementation of Community law, except where the alleged facts are being examined before a court and while the case is still subject to legal proceedings.

The temporary Committee of Inquiry shall cease to exist on the submission of its report.

The detailed provisions governing the exercise of the right of inquiry shall be determined by common accord of the European Parliament, the Council and the Commission.

Article 194

Any citizen of the Union, and any natural or legal person residing or having its registered office in a Member State, shall have the right to address, individually or in association with other citizens or persons, a petition to the European Parliament on a matter which comes within the Community's fields of activity and which affects him, her or it directly.

Article 195

1. The European Parliament shall appoint an Ombudsman empowered to receive complaints from any citizen of the Union or any natural or legal person residing or having its registered office in a Member State concerning instances of maladministration in the activities of the Community institutions or bodies, with the exception of the Court of Justice and the Court of First Instance acting in their judicial role.

In accordance with his duties, the Ombudsman shall conduct inquiries for which he finds grounds, either on his own initiative or on the basis of complaints submitted to him direct or through a Member of the European Parliament, except where the alleged facts are or have been the subject of legal proceedings. Where the Ombudsman establishes an instance of maladministration, he shall refer the matter to the institution concerned, which shall have a period of three months in which to inform him of its views. The Ombudsman shall then forward a report to the European Parliament and the institution concerned. The person lodging the complaint shall be informed of the outcome of such inquiries.

The Ombudsman shall submit an annual report to the European Parliament on the outcome of his inquiries.

2. The Ombudsman shall be appointed after each election of the European Parliament for the duration of its term of office. The Ombudsman shall be eligible for reappointment.

The Ombudsman may be dismissed by the Court of Justice at the request of the European Parliament if he no longer fulfils the conditions required for the performance of his duties or if he is guilty of serious misconduct.

3. The Ombudsman shall be completely independent in the performance of his duties. In the performance of those duties he shall neither seek nor take instructions from any body. The Ombudsman may not, during his term of office, engage in any other occupation, whether gainful or not.

4. The European Parliament shall, after seeking an opinion from the Commission and with the approval of the Council acting by a qualified majority, lay down the regulations and general conditions governing the performance of the Ombudsman's duties.

Article 196

The European Parliament shall hold an annual session. It shall meet, without requiring to be convened, on the second Tuesday in March.

The European Parliament may meet in extraordinary session at the request of a majority of its Members or at the request of the Council or of the Commission.

Article 197

The European Parliament shall elect its President and its officers from among its Members.

Members of the Commission may attend all meetings and shall, at their request, be heard on behalf of the Commission.

The Commission shall reply orally or in writing to questions put to it by the European Parliament or by its Members.

The Council shall be heard by the European Parliament in accordance with the conditions laid down by the Council in its Rules of Procedure.

Article 198

Save as otherwise provided in this Treaty, the European Parliament shall act by an absolute majority of the votes cast.

The Rules of Procedure shall determine the quorum.

Article 199

The European Parliament shall adopt its Rules of Procedure, acting by a majority of its Members.

The proceedings of the European Parliament shall be published in the manner laid down in its Rules of Procedure.

Article 200

The European Parliament shall discuss in open session the annual general report submitted to it by the Commission.

Article 201

If a motion of censure on the activities of the Commission is tabled before it, the European Parliament shall not vote thereon until at least three days after the motion has been tabled and only by open vote.

If the motion of censure is carried by a two-thirds majority of the votes cast, representing a majority of the Members of the European Parliament, the Members of the Commission shall resign as a body. They shall continue to deal with current business until they are replaced in accordance with Article 214. In this case, the term of office of the Members of the Commission appointed to replace them shall expire on the date on which the term of office of the Members of the Commission obliged to resign as a body would have expired.

Section 2
The Council

Article 202

To ensure that the objectives set out in this Treaty are attained the Council shall, in accordance with the provisions of this Treaty:

— ensure coordination of the general economic policies of the Member States,
— have power to take decisions,
— confer on the Commission, in the acts which the Council adopts, powers for the implementation of the rules which the Council lays down. The Council may impose certain requirements in respect of the exercise of these powers. The Council may also reserve the right, in specific cases, to exercise directly implementing powers itself. The procedures referred to above must be consonant with principles and rules to be laid down in advance by the Council, acting unanimously on a proposal from the Commission and after obtaining the opinion of the European Parliament.

Article 203

The Council shall consist of a representative of each Member State at ministerial level, authorised to commit the government of that Member State.

The office of President shall be held in turn by each Member State in the Council for a term of six months in the order decided by the Council acting unanimously.

Article 204

The Council shall meet when convened by its President on his own initiative or at the request of one of its Members or of the Commission.

Article 205

1. Save as otherwise provided in this Treaty, the Council shall act by a majority of its Members.

2. Where the Council is required to act by a qualified majority, the votes of its members shall be weighted as follows:

Belgium 12
Czech Republic 12
Denmark 7
Germany 29
Estonia 4
Greece 12
Spain 27
France 29
Ireland 7
Italy 29
Cyprus 4
Latvia 4
Lithuania 7
Luxembourg 4
Hungary 12
Malta 3
Netherlands 13
Austria 10
Poland 27
Portugal 12
Slovenia 4
Slovakia 7
Finland 7
Sweden 10
United Kingdom 29.

Acts of the Council shall require for their adoption at least 232 votes in favour cast by a majority of the members where this Treaty requires them to be adopted on a proposal from the Commission.

In other cases, for their adoption acts of the Council shall require at least 232 votes in favour, cast by at least two-thirds of the members.[1]

3. Abstentions by Members present in person or represented shall not prevent the adoption by the Council of acts which require unanimity.

4. When a decision is to be adopted by the Council by a qualified majority, a member of the Council may request verification that the Member States constituting the qualified majority represent at least 62% of the total population of the Union.

---

[1] Paragraph replaced by Article 12 of the Act concerning the conditions of accession of the Czech Republic, the Republic of Estonia, the Republic of Cyprus, the Republic of Latvia, the Republic of Lithuania, the Republic of Hungary, the Republic of Malta, the Republic of Poland, the Republic of Slovenia and the Slovak Republic and the adjustments to the Treaties on which the European Union is founded (OJ 23.9.2003 L 236 p. 36)

If that condition is shown not to have been met, the decision in question shall not be adopted.

Article 206

Where a vote is taken, any Member of the Council may also act on behalf of not more than one other member.

Article 207

1. A committee consisting of the Permanent Representatives of the Member States shall be responsible for preparing the work of the Council and for carrying out the tasks assigned to it by the Council. The Committee may adopt procedural decisions in cases provided for in the Council's Rules of Procedure.

2. The Council shall be assisted by a General Secretariat, under the responsibility of a Secretary-General, High Representative for the common foreign and security policy, who shall be assisted by a Deputy Secretary-General responsible for the running of the General Secretariat. The Secretary-General and the Deputy Secretary-General shall be appointed by the Council acting by a qualified majority.

The Council shall decide on the organisation of the General Secretariat.

3. The Council shall adopt its Rules of Procedure.

For the purpose of applying Article 255(3), the Council shall elaborate in these Rules the conditions under which the public shall have access to Council documents. For the purpose of this paragraph, the Council shall define the cases in which it is to be regarded as acting in its legislative capacity, with a view to allowing greater access to documents in those cases, while at the same time preserving the effectiveness of its decision-making process. In any event, when the Council acts in its legislative capacity, the results of votes and explanations of vote as well as statements in the minutes shall be made public.

Article 208

The Council may request the Commission to undertake any studies the Council considers desirable for the attainment of the common objectives, and to submit to it any appropriate proposals.

Article 209

The Council shall, after receiving an opinion from the Commission, determine the rules governing the committees provided for in this Treaty.

Article 210

The Council shall, acting by a qualified majority, determine the salaries, allowances and pensions of the President and Members of the Commission, and of the President, Judges, Advocates-General and Registrar of the Court of Justice and of the Members and Registrar of the Court of First Instance. It shall also, again by a qualified majority, determine any payment to be made instead of remuneration.

Section 3
The Commission

Article 211

In order to ensure the proper functioning and development of the common market, the Commission shall:

- ensure that the provisions of this Treaty and the measures taken by the institutions pursuant thereto are applied,
- formulate recommendations or deliver opinions on matters dealt with in this Treaty, if it expressly so provides or if the Commission considers it necessary,
- have its own power of decision and participate in the shaping of measures taken by the Council and by the European Parliament in the manner provided for in this Treaty,
- exercise the powers conferred on it by the Council for the implementation of the rules laid down by the latter.

Article 212

The Commission shall publish annually, not later than one month before the opening of the session of the European Parliament, a general report on the activities of the Community.

Article 213

1. The Commission shall consist of 20 Members,[1] who shall be chosen on the grounds of their general competence and whose independence is beyond doubt.

The number of Members of the Commission may be altered by the Council, acting unanimously.

Only nationals of Member States may be Members of the Commission.

The Commission must include at least one national of each of the Member States, but may not include more than two Members having the nationality of the same State.

2. The Members of the Commission shall, in the general interest of the Community, be completely independent in the performance of their duties.

---

[1] Until 1 May 2004 there were 20 commissioners – two from each of the most heavily populated member states and one from each of the other EU countries. When ten more countries joined the EU on 1 May 2004, the number of commissioners rose to 30. From the date when the 2004–2009 Commission takes office (1 November 2004), there will be only 25 commissioners – one per country. Once Bulgaria and Romania join, the Union will have 27 member states. At that point, the Council – by a unanimous decision – will fix the maximum number of commissioners. There must be fewer than 27 of them, and their nationality will be determined by a system of rotation that must be fair to all countries.

In the performance of these duties, they shall neither seek nor take instructions from any government or from any other body. They shall refrain from any action incompatible with their duties. Each Member State undertakes to respect this principle and not to seek to influence the Members of the Commission in the performance of their tasks.

The Members of the Commission may not, during their term of office, engage in any other occupation, whether gainful or not. When entering upon their duties they shall give a solemn undertaking that, both during and after their term of office, they will respect the obligations arising therefrom and in particular their duty to behave with integrity and discretion as regards the acceptance, after they have ceased to hold office, of certain appointments or benefits. In the event of any breach of these obligations, the Court of Justice may, on application by the Council or the Commission, rule that the Member concerned be, according to the circumstances, either compulsorily retired in accordance with Article 216 or deprived of his right to a pension or other benefits in its stead.

Article 214

1. The Members of the Commission shall be appointed, in accordance with the procedure referred to in paragraph 2, for a period of five years, subject, if need be, to Article 201.
Their term of office shall be renewable.

2. The Council, meeting in the composition of Heads of State or Government and acting by a qualified majority, shall nominate the person it intends to appoint as President of the Commission; the nomination shall be approved by the European Parliament.

The Council, acting by a qualified majority and by common accord with the nominee for President, shall adopt the list of the other persons whom it intends to appoint as Members of the Commission, drawn up in accordance with the proposals made by each Member State.

The President and the other Members of the Commission thus nominated shall be subject as a body to a vote of approval by the European Parliament. After approval by the European Parliament, the President and the other Members of the Commission shall be appointed by the Council, acting by a qualified majority.

Article 215

Apart from normal replacement, or death, the duties of a Member of the Commission shall end when he resigns or is compulsorily retired.

A vacancy caused by resignation, compulsory retirement or death shall be filled for the remainder of the Member's term of office by a new Member appointed by the Council, acting by a qualified majority. The Council may, acting unanimously, decide that such a vacancy need not be filled.

In the event of resignation, compulsory retirement or death, the President shall be replaced for the remainder of his term of office. The procedure laid down in Article 214(2) shall be applicable for the replacement of the President.

Save in the case of compulsory retirement under Article 216, Members of the Commission shall remain in office until they have been replaced or until the Council has decided that the vacancy need not be filled, as provided for in the second paragraph of this Article.

Article 216

If any Member of the Commission no longer fulfils the conditions required for the performance of his duties or if he has been guilty of serious misconduct, the Court of Justice may, on application by the Council or the Commission, compulsorily retire him.

Article 217

1. The Commission shall work under the political guidance of its President, who shall decide on its internal organisation in order to ensure that it acts consistently, efficiently and on the basis of collegiality.

2. The responsibilities incumbent upon the Commission shall be structured and allocated among its Members by its President. The President may reshuffle the allocation of those responsibilities during the Commission's term of office. The Members of the Commission shall carry out the duties devolved upon them by the President under his authority.

3. After obtaining the approval of the College, the President shall appoint Vice-Presidents from among its Members.

4. A Member of the Commission shall resign if the President so requests, after obtaining the approval of the College.

Article 218

1. The Council and the Commission shall consult each other and shall settle by common accord their methods of cooperation.

2. The Commission shall adopt its Rules of Procedure so as to ensure that both it and its departments operate in accordance with the provisions of this Treaty. It shall ensure that these Rules are published.

Article 219

The Commission shall act by a majority of the number of Members provided for in Article 213.

A meeting of the Commission shall be valid only if the number of Members laid down in its Rules of Procedure is present.

Section 4
The Court of Justice

Article 220

The Court of Justice and the Court of First Instance, each within its jurisdiction, shall ensure that in the interpretation and application of this Treaty the law is observed.

In addition, judicial panels may be attached to the Court of First Instance under the conditions laid down in Article 225a in order to exercise, in certain specific areas, the judicial competence laid down in this Treaty.

Article 221

The Court of Justice shall consist of one judge per Member State.

The Court of Justice shall sit in chambers or in a Grand Chamber, in accordance with the rules laid down for that purpose in the Statute of the Court of Justice.

When provided for in the Statute, the Court of Justice may also sit as a full Court.

Article 222

The Court of Justice shall be assisted by eight Advocates-General. Should the Court of Justice so request, the Council, acting unanimously, may increase the number of Advocates-General.

It shall be the duty of the Advocate-General, acting with complete impartiality and independence, to make, in open court, reasoned submissions on cases which, in accordance with the Statute of the Court of Justice, require his involvement.

Article 223

The Judges and Advocates-General of the Court of Justice shall be chosen from persons whose independence is beyond doubt and who possess the qualifications required for appointment to the highest judicial offices in their respective countries or who are jurisconsults of recognised competence; they shall be appointed by common accord of the governments of the Member States for a term of six years.

Every three years there shall be a partial replacement of the Judges and Advocates-General, in accordance with the conditions laid down in the Statute of the Court of Justice.

The Judges shall elect the President of the Court of Justice from among their number for a term of three years. He may be re-elected.

Retiring Judges and Advocates-General may be reappointed.

The Court of Justice shall appoint its Registrar and lay down the rules governing his service.

The Court of Justice shall establish its Rules of Procedure. Those Rules shall require the approval of the Council, acting by a qualified majority.

Article 224

The Court of First Instance shall comprise at least one judge per Member State. The number of Judges shall be determined by the Statute of the Court of Justice. The Statute may provide for the Court of First Instance to be assisted by Advocates-General.

The members of the Court of First Instance shall be chosen from persons whose independence is beyond doubt and who possess the ability required for appointment to high judicial office. They shall be appointed by common accord of the governments of the Member States for a term of six years. The membership shall be partially renewed every three years. Retiring members shall be eligible for reappointment.

The Judges shall elect the President of the Court of First Instance from among their number for a term of three years. He may be re-elected.

The Court of First Instance shall appoint its Registrar and lay down the rules governing his service.

The Court of First Instance shall establish its Rules of Procedure in agreement with the Court of Justice.

Those Rules shall require the approval of the Council, acting by a qualified majority.

Unless the Statute of the Court of Justice provides otherwise, the provisions of this Treaty relating to the Court of Justice shall apply to the Court of First Instance.

Article 225

1. The Court of First Instance shall have jurisdiction to hear and determine at first instance actions or proceedings referred to in Articles 230, 232, 235, 236 and 238, with the exception of those assigned to a judicial panel and those reserved in the Statute for the Court of Justice. The Statute may provide for the Court of First Instance to have jurisdiction for other classes of action or proceeding.

Decisions given by the Court of First Instance under this paragraph may be subject to a right of appeal to the Court of Justice on points of law only, under the conditions and within the limits laid down by the Statute.

2. The Court of First Instance shall have jurisdiction to hear and determine actions or proceedings brought against decisions of the judicial panels set up under Article 225a.

Decisions given by the Court of First Instance under this paragraph may exceptionally be subject to review by the Court of Justice, under the conditions and within the limits laid down by the Statute, where there is a serious risk of the unity or consistency of Community law being affected.

3. The Court of First Instance shall have jurisdiction to hear and determine questions referred for a preliminary ruling under Article 234, in specific areas laid down by the Statute.

Where the Court of First Instance considers that the case requires a decision of principle likely to affect the unity or consistency of Community law, it may refer the case to the Court of Justice for a ruling.

Decisions given by the Court of First Instance on questions referred for a preliminary ruling may exceptionally be subject to review by the Court of Justice, under the conditions and within the limits laid down by the Statute, where there is a serious risk of the unity or consistency of Community law being affected.

Article 225a

The Council, acting unanimously on a proposal from the Commission and after consulting the European Parliament and the Court of Justice or at the request of the Court of Justice and after consulting the European Parliament and the Commission, may create judicial panels to hear and determine at first instance certain classes of action or proceeding brought in specific areas.

The decision establishing a judicial panel shall lay down the rules on the organisation of the panel and the extent of the jurisdiction conferred upon it.

Decisions given by judicial panels may be subject to a right of appeal on points of law only or, when provided for in the decision establishing the panel, a right of appeal also on matters of fact, before the Court of First Instance.

The members of the judicial panels shall be chosen from persons whose independence is beyond doubt and who possess the ability required for appointment to judicial office. They shall be appointed by the Council, acting unanimously.

The judicial panels shall establish their Rules of Procedure in agreement with the Court of Justice. Those Rules shall require the approval of the Council, acting by a qualified majority.

Unless the decision establishing the judicial panel provides otherwise, the provisions of this Treaty relating to the Court of Justice and the provisions of the Statute of the Court of Justice shall apply to the judicial panels.

Article 226

If the Commission considers that a Member State has failed to fulfil an obligation under this Treaty, it shall deliver a reasoned opinion on the matter after giving the State concerned the opportunity to submit its observations.

If the State concerned does not comply with the opinion within the period laid down by the Commission, the latter may bring the matter before the Court of Justice.

Article 227

A Member State which considers that another Member State has failed to fulfil an obligation under this Treaty may bring the matter before the Court of Justice.

Before a Member State brings an action against another Member State for an alleged infringement of an obligation under this Treaty, it shall bring the matter before the Commission.

The Commission shall deliver a reasoned opinion after each of the States concerned has been given the opportunity to submit its own case and its observations on the other party's case both orally and in writing.

If the Commission has not delivered an opinion within three months of the date on which the matter was brought before it, the absence of such opinion shall not prevent the matter from being brought before the Court of Justice.

Article 228

1. If the Court of Justice finds that a Member State has failed to fulfil an obligation under this Treaty, the State shall be required to take the necessary measures to comply with the judgment of the Court of Justice.

2. If the Commission considers that the Member State concerned has not taken such measures it shall, after giving that State the opportunity to submit its observations, issue a reasoned opinion specifying the points on which the Member State concerned has not complied with the judgment of the Court of Justice.

If the Member State concerned fails to take the necessary measures to comply with the Court's judgment within the time limit laid down by the Commission, the latter may bring the case before the Court of Justice. In so doing it shall specify the amount of the lump sum or penalty payment to be paid by the Member State concerned which it considers appropriate in the circumstances.

If the Court of Justice finds that the Member State concerned has not complied with its judgment it may impose a lump sum or penalty payment on it.

This procedure shall be without prejudice to Article 227.

Article 229

Regulations adopted jointly by the European Parliament and the Council, and by the Council, pursuant to the provisions of this Treaty, may give the Court of Justice unlimited jurisdiction with regard to the penalties provided for in such regulations.

Article 229a

Without prejudice to the other provisions of this Treaty, the Council, acting unanimously on a proposal from the Commission and after consulting the European Parliament, may adopt provisions to confer jurisdiction, to the extent that it shall determine, on the Court of Justice in disputes relating to the application of acts adopted on the basis of this Treaty which create Community industrial property rights. The Council shall recommend those provisions to the Member States for adoption in accordance with their respective constitutional requirements.

Article 230

The Court of Justice shall review the legality of acts adopted jointly by the European Parliament and the Council, of acts of the Council, of the Commission and of the ECB, other than recommendations and opinions, and of acts of the European Parliament intended to produce legal effects vis-à-vis third parties.

It shall for this purpose have jurisdiction in actions brought by a Member State, the European Parliament, the Council or the Commission on grounds of lack of competence, infringement of an essential procedural requirement, infringement of this Treaty or of any rule of law relating to its application, or misuse of powers.

The Court of Justice shall have jurisdiction under the same conditions in actions brought by the Court of Auditors and by the ECB for the purpose of protecting their prerogatives.

Any natural or legal person may, under the same conditions, institute proceedings against a decision addressed to that person or against a decision which, although in the form of a regulation or a decision addressed to another person, is of direct and individual concern to the former.

The proceedings provided for in this article shall be instituted within two months of the publication of the measure, or of its notification to the plaintiff, or, in the absence thereof, of the day on which it came to the knowledge of the latter, as the case may be.

Article 231

If the action is well founded, the Court of Justice shall declare the act concerned to be void.

In the case of a regulation, however, the Court of Justice shall, if it considers this necessary, state which of the effects of the regulation which it has declared void shall be considered as definitive.

Article 232

Should the European Parliament, the Council or the Commission, in infringement of this Treaty, fail to act, the Member States and the other institutions of the Community may bring an action before the Court of Justice to have the infringement established.

The action shall be admissible only if the institution concerned has first been called upon to act. If, within two months of being so called upon, the institution concerned has not defined its position, the action may be brought within a further period of two months.

Any natural or legal person may, under the conditions laid down in the preceding paragraphs, complain to the Court of Justice that an institution of the Community has failed to address to that person any act other than a recommendation or an opinion.

The Court of Justice shall have jurisdiction, under the same conditions, in actions or proceedings brought by the ECB in the areas falling within the latter's field of competence and in actions or proceedings brought against the latter.

Article 233

The institution or institutions whose act has been declared void or whose failure to act has been declared contrary to this Treaty shall be required to take the necessary measures to comply with the judgment of the Court of Justice.

This obligation shall not affect any obligation which may result from the application of the second paragraph of Article 288.

This article shall also apply to the ECB.

Article 234

The Court of Justice shall have jurisdiction to give preliminary rulings concerning:

(a) the interpretation of this Treaty;
(b) the validity and interpretation of acts of the institutions of the Community and of the ECB;
(c) the interpretation of the statutes of bodies established by an act of the Council, where those statutes so provide.

Where such a question is raised before any court or tribunal of a Member State, that court or tribunal may, if it considers that a decision on the question is necessary to enable it to give judgment, request the Court of Justice to give a ruling thereon.

Where any such question is raised in a case pending before a court or tribunal of a Member State against whose decisions there is no judicial remedy under national law, that court or tribunal shall bring the matter before the Court of Justice.

Article 235

The Court of Justice shall have jurisdiction in disputes relating to compensation for damage provided for in the second paragraph of Article 288.

Article 236

The Court of Justice shall have jurisdiction in any dispute between the Community and its servants within the limits and under the conditions laid down in the Staff Regulations or the Conditions of employment.

Article 237

The Court of Justice shall, within the limits hereinafter laid down, have jurisdiction in disputes concerning:

(a) the fulfilment by Member States of obligations under the Statute of the European Investment Bank.
   In this connection, the Board of Directors of the Bank shall enjoy the powers conferred upon the Commission by Article 226;
(b) measures adopted by the Board of Governors of the European Investment Bank. In this connection, any Member State, the Commission or the Board of Directors of the Bank may institute proceedings under the conditions laid down in Article 230;
(c) measures adopted by the Board of Directors of the European Investment Bank. Proceedings against such measures may be instituted only by Member States or by the Commission, under the conditions laid down in Article 230, and solely on the grounds of non-compliance with the procedure provided for in Article 21(2), (5), (6) and (7) of the Statute of the Bank;

(d) the fulfilment by national central banks of obligations under this Treaty and the Statute of the ESCB. In this connection the powers of the Council of the ECB in respect of national central banks shall be the same as those conferred upon the Commission in respect of Member States by Article 226. If the Court of Justice finds that a national central bank has failed to fulfil an obligation under this Treaty, that bank shall be required to take the necessary measures to comply with the judgment of the Court of Justice.

Article 238

The Court of Justice shall have jurisdiction to give judgment pursuant to any arbitration clause contained in a contract concluded by or on behalf of the Community, whether that contract be governed by public or private law.

Article 239

The Court of Justice shall have jurisdiction in any dispute between Member States which relates to the subject matter of this Treaty if the dispute is submitted to it under a special agreement between the parties.

Article 240

Save where jurisdiction is conferred on the Court of Justice by this Treaty, disputes to which the Community is a party shall not on that ground be excluded from the jurisdiction of the courts or tribunals of the Member States.

Article 241

Notwithstanding the expiry of the period laid down in the fifth paragraph of Article 230, any party may, in proceedings in which a regulation adopted jointly by the European Parliament and the Council, or a regulation of the Council, of the Commission, or of the ECB is at issue, plead the grounds specified in the second paragraph of Article 230 in order to invoke before the Court of Justice the inapplicability of that regulation.

Article 242

Actions brought before the Court of Justice shall not have suspensory effect. The Court of Justice may, however, if it considers that circumstances so require, order that application of the contested act be suspended.

Article 243

The Court of Justice may in any cases before it prescribe any necessary interim measures.

Article 244

The judgments of the Court of Justice shall be enforceable under the conditions laid down in Article 256.

Article 245

The Statute of the Court of Justice shall be laid down in a separate Protocol.

The Council, acting unanimously at the request of the Court of Justice and after consulting the European Parliament and the Commission, or at the request of the Commission and after consulting the European Parliament and the Court of Justice, may amend the provisions of the Statute, with the exception of Title I.
[. . .]

Chapter 2
Provisions common to several institutions

Article 249

In order to carry out their task and in accordance with the provisions of this Treaty, the European Parliament acting jointly with the Council, the Council and the Commission shall make regulations and issue directives, take decisions, make recommendations or deliver opinions.

A regulation shall have general application. It shall be binding in its entirety and directly applicable in all Member States.

A directive shall be binding, as to the result to be achieved, upon each Member State to which it is addressed, but shall leave to the national authorities the choice of form and methods.

A decision shall be binding in its entirety upon those to whom it is addressed.

Recommendations and opinions shall have no binding force.

Article 250

1. Where, in pursuance of this Treaty, the Council acts on a proposal from the Commission, unanimity shall be required for an act constituting an amendment to that proposal, subject to Article 251(4) and (5).

2. As long as the Council has not acted, the Commission may alter its proposal at any time during the procedures leading to the adoption of a Community act.

Article 251

1. Where reference is made in this Treaty to this Article for the adoption of an act, the following procedure shall apply.

2. The Commission shall submit a proposal to the European Parliament and the Council.

The Council, acting by a qualified majority after obtaining the opinion of the European Parliament:

– if it approves all the amendments contained in the European Parliament's opinion, may adopt the proposed act thus amended,
– if the European Parliament does not propose any amendments, may adopt the proposed act,
– shall otherwise adopt a common position and communicate it to the European Parliament.
  The Council shall inform the European Parliament fully of the reasons which led it to adopt its common position. The Commission shall inform the European Parliament fully of its position.
  If, within three months of such communication, the European Parliament:

(a) approves the common position or has not taken a decision, the act in question shall be deemed to have been adopted in accordance with that common position;
(b) rejects, by an absolute majority of its component members, the common position, the proposed act shall be deemed not to have been adopted;
(c) proposes amendments to the common position by an absolute majority of its component members, the amended text shall be forwarded to the Council and to the Commission, which shall deliver an opinion on those amendments.

3. If, within three months of the matter being referred to it, the Council, acting by a qualified majority, approves all the amendments of the European Parliament, the act in question shall be deemed to have been adopted in the form of the common position thus amended; however, the Council shall act unanimously on the amendments on which the Commission has delivered a negative opinion. If the Council does not approve all the amendments, the President of the Council, in agreement with the President of the European Parliament, shall within six weeks convene a meeting of the Conciliation Committee.

4. The Conciliation Committee, which shall be composed of the Members of the Council or their representatives and an equal number of representatives of the European Parliament, shall have the task of reaching agreement on a joint text, by a qualified majority of the Members of the Council or their representatives and by a majority of the representatives of the European Parliament. The Commission shall take part in the Conciliation Committee's proceedings and shall take all the necessary initiatives with a view to reconciling the positions of the European Parliament and the Council. In fulfilling this task, the Conciliation Committee shall address the common position on the basis of the amendments proposed by the European Parliament.

5. If, within six weeks of its being convened, the Conciliation Committee approves a joint text, the European Parliament, acting by an absolute majority of the votes cast, and the Council, acting by a qualified majority, shall each have a period of six weeks from that approval in which to adopt the act in question in accordance with the joint

text. If either of the two institutions fails to approve the proposed act within that period, it shall be deemed not to have been adopted.

6. Where the Conciliation Committee does not approve a joint text, the proposed act shall be deemed not to have been adopted.

7. The periods of three months and six weeks referred to in this Article shall be extended by a maximum of one month and two weeks respectively at the initiative of the European Parliament or the Council.

Article 252

Where reference is made in this Treaty to this Article for the adoption of an act, the following procedure shall apply.

(a) The Council, acting by a qualified majority on a proposal from the Commission and after obtaining the opinion of the European Parliament, shall adopt a common position.

(b) The Council's common position shall be communicated to the European Parliament. The Council and the Commission shall inform the European Parliament fully of the reasons which led the Council to adopt its common position and also of the Commission's position.

If, within three months of such communication, the European Parliament approves this common position or has not taken a decision within that period, the Council shall definitively adopt the act in question in accordance with the common position.

(c) The European Parliament may, within the period of three months referred to in point (b), by an absolute majority of its component Members, propose amendments to the Council's common position. The European Parliament may also, by the same majority, reject the Council's common position. The result of the proceedings shall be transmitted to the Council and the Commission.

If the European Parliament has rejected the Council's common position, unanimity shall be required for the Council to act on a second reading.

(d) The Commission shall, within a period of one month, re-examine the proposal on the basis of which the Council adopted its common position, by taking into account the amendments proposed by the European Parliament.

The Commission shall forward to the Council, at the same time as its re-examined proposal, the amendments of the European Parliament which it has not accepted, and shall express its opinion on them. The Council may adopt these amendments unanimously.

(e) The Council, acting by a qualified majority, shall adopt the proposal as re-examined by the Commission.

Unanimity shall be required for the Council to amend the proposal as re-examined by the Commission.

(f) In the cases referred to in points (c), (d) and (e), the Council shall be required to act within a period of three months. If no decision is taken within this period, the Commission proposal shall be deemed not to have been adopted.

(g) The periods referred to in points (b) and (f) may be extended by a maximum of one month by common accord between the Council and the European Parliament.

Article 253

Regulations, directives and decisions adopted jointly by the European Parliament and the Council, and such acts adopted by the Council or the Commission, shall state the reasons on which they are based and shall refer to any proposals or opinions which were required to be obtained pursuant to this Treaty.

Article 254

1. Regulations, directives and decisions adopted in accordance with the procedure referred to in Article 251 shall be signed by the President of the European Parliament and by the President of the Council and published in the *Official Journal of the European Union*. They shall enter into force on the date specified in them or, in the absence thereof, on the 20th day following that of their publication.

2. Regulations of the Council and of the Commission, as well as directives of those institutions which are addressed to all Member States, shall be published in the *Official Journal of the European Union*.

They shall enter into force on the date specified in them or, in the absence thereof, on the 20th day following that of their publication.

3. Other directives, and decisions, shall be notified to those to whom they are addressed and shall take effect upon such notification.

Article 255

1. Any citizen of the Union, and any natural or legal person residing or having its registered office in a Member State, shall have a right of access to European Parliament, Council and Commission documents, subject to the principles and the conditions to be defined in accordance with paragraphs 2 and 3.

2. General principles and limits on grounds of public or private interest governing this right of access to documents shall be determined by the Council, acting in accordance with the procedure referred to in Article 251 within two years of the entry into force of the Treaty of Amsterdam.

3. Each institution referred to above shall elaborate in its own Rules of Procedure specific provisions regarding access to its documents.

Article 256

Decisions of the Council or of the Commission which impose a pecuniary obligation on persons other than States, shall be enforceable.

Enforcement shall be governed by the rules of civil procedure in force in the State in the territory of which it is carried out. The order for its enforcement shall be appended to the decision, without other formality than verification of the authenticity of the decision, by the national authority which the government of each Member State shall designate for this purpose and shall make known to the Commission and to the Court of Justice.

When these formalities have been completed on application by the party concerned, the latter may proceed to enforcement in accordance with the national law, by bringing the matter directly before the competent authority.

Enforcement may be suspended only by a decision of the Court of Justice. However, the courts of the country concerned shall have jurisdiction over complaints that enforcement is being carried out in an irregular manner.

Chapter 3
The Economic and Social Committee

Article 257

An Economic and Social Committee is hereby established. It shall have advisory status.

The Committee shall consist of representatives of the various economic and social components of organised civil society, and in particular representatives of producers, farmers, carriers, workers, dealers, craftsmen, professional occupations, consumers and the general interest.

Article 258

The number of members of the Economic and Social Committee shall not exceed 350.

The number of members of the Committee shall be as follows:

Belgium 12
Czech Republic 12
Denmark 9
Germany 24
Estonia 7
Greece 12
Spain 21
France 24
Ireland 9
Italy 24
Cyprus 6
Latvia 7
Lithuania 9
Luxembourg 6
Hungary 12

Malta 5
Netherlands 12
Austria 12
Poland 21
Portugal 12
Slovenia 7
Slovakia 9
Finland 9
Sweden 12
United Kingdom 24.[1]

The members of the Committee may not be bound by any mandatory instructions. They shall be completely independent in the performance of their duties, in the general interest of the Community.

The Council, acting by a qualified majority, shall determine the allowances of members of the Committee.

Article 259

1. The members of the Committee shall be appointed for four years, on proposals from the Member States. The Council, acting by a qualified majority, shall adopt the list of members drawn up in accordance with the proposals made by each Member State. The term of office of the members of the Committee shall be renewable.

2. The Council shall consult the Commission. It may obtain the opinion of European bodies which are representative of the various economic and social sectors to which the activities of the Community are of concern.

Article 260

The Committee shall elect its chairman and officers from among its members for a term of two years.

It shall adopt its Rules of Procedure.

The Committee shall be convened by its chairman at the request of the Council or of the Commission. It may also meet on its own initiative.

Article 261

The Committee shall include specialised sections for the principal fields covered by this Treaty.

These specialised sections shall operate within the general terms of reference of the Committee. They may not be consulted independently of the Committee.

---

[1] Paragraph replaced by Article 14 of the Act concerning the conditions of accession of the Czech Republic, the Republic of Estonia, the Republic of Cyprus, the Republic of Latvia, the Republic of Lithuania, the Republic of Hungary, the Republic of Malta, the Republic of Poland, the Republic of Slovenia and the Slovak Republic and the adjustments to the Treaties on which the European Union is founded (OJ 23.9.2003 L 236 p. 37).

Subcommittees may also be established within the Committee to prepare on specific questions or in specific fields, draft opinions to be submitted to the Committee for its consideration.

The Rules of Procedure shall lay down the methods of composition and the terms of reference of the specialised sections and of the subcommittees.

Article 262

The Committee must be consulted by the Council or by the Commission where this Treaty so provides.

The Committee may be consulted by these institutions in all cases in which they consider it appropriate.

It may issue an opinion on its own initiative in cases in which it considers such action appropriate.

The Council or the Commission shall, if it considers it necessary, set the Committee, for the submission of its opinion, a time limit which may not be less than one month from the date on which the chairman receives notification to this effect. Upon expiry of the time limit, the absence of an opinion shall not prevent further action.

The opinion of the Committee and that of the specialised section, together with a record of the proceedings, shall be forwarded to the Council and to the Commission.

The Committee may be consulted by the European Parliament.

Chapter 4
The Committee of the Regions

Article 263

A committee, hereinafter referred to as 'the Committee of the Regions', consisting of representatives of regional and local bodies who either hold a regional or local authority electoral mandate or are politically accountable to an elected assembly, is hereby established with advisory status.

The number of members of the Committee of the Regions shall not exceed 350.

The number of members of the Committee shall be as follows:

Belgium 12
Czech Republic 12
Denmark 9
Germany 24
Estonia 7
Greece 12
Spain 21
France 24
Ireland 9
Italy 24

Cyprus 6
Latvia 7
Lithuania 9
Luxembourg 6
Hungary 12
Malta 5
Netherlands 12
Austria 12
Poland 21
Portugal 12
Slovenia 7
Slovakia 9
Finland 9
Sweden 12
United Kingdom 24.[1]

The members of the Committee and an equal number of alternate members shall be appointed for four years, on proposals from the respective Member States. Their term of office shall be renewable. The Council, acting by a qualified majority, shall adopt the list of members and alternate members drawn up in accordance with the proposals made by each Member State. When the mandate referred to in the first paragraph on the basis of which they were proposed comes to an end, the term of office of members of the Committee shall terminate automatically and they shall then be replaced for the remainder of the said term of office in accordance with the same procedure. No member of the Committee shall at the same time be a Member of the European Parliament.

The members of the Committee may not be bound by any mandatory instructions. They shall be completely independent in the performance of their duties, in the general interest of the Community.

Article 264

The Committee of the Regions shall elect its chairman and officers from among its members for a term of two years.

It shall adopt its Rules of Procedure.

The Committee shall be convened by its chairman at the request of the Council or of the Commission. It may also meet on its own initiative.

---

[1] Paragraph replaced by Article 15 of the Act concerning the conditions of accession of the Czech Republic, the Republic of Estonia, the Republic of Cyprus, the Republic of Latvia, the Republic of Lithuania, the Republic of Hungary, the Republic of Malta, the Republic of Poland, the Republic of Slovenia and the Slovak Republic and the adjustments to the Treaties on which the European Union is founded (OJ 23.9.2003 L 236 p. 37).

Article 265

The Committee of the Regions shall be consulted by the Council or by the Commission where this Treaty so provides and in all other cases, in particular those which concern cross-border cooperation, in which one of these two institutions considers it appropriate.

The Council or the Commission shall, if it considers it necessary, set the Committee, for the submission of its opinion, a time limit which may not be less than one month from the date on which the chairman receives notification to this effect. Upon expiry of the time limit, the absence of an opinion shall not prevent further action.

Where the Economic and Social Committee is consulted pursuant to Article 262, the Committee of the Regions shall be informed by the Council or the Commission of the request for an opinion. Where it considers that specific regional interests are involved, the Committee of the Regions may issue an opinion on the matter.

The Committee of the Regions may be consulted by the European Parliament.

It may issue an opinion on its own initiative in cases in which it considers such action appropriate.

The opinion of the Committee, together with a record of the proceedings, shall be forwarded to the Council and to the Commission.

[...]

Council Regulation (EEC) No 1210/90 of 7 May 1990 on the establishment of the European Environment Agency and the European environment information and observation network (as amended)

Editorial note

The European Environment Agency (EEA – www.eea.eu.int), which is based in Copenhagen, is aimed at providing the Community and the Member States with objective, reliable and comparable information at the European level to enable environmental protection measures to be taken, to assess the results of such measures, and to ensure that the public is properly informed about the state of the environment (Article 1). The Agency co-ordinates the European environment network and records, collates and assesses data on the state of the environment (Article 2). In addition, the Agency is to provide the Community and individual Member States with objective information necessary to frame and implement effective environmental policies; assist the monitoring of environmental measures; ensure that environmental data at the European level are comparable; promote the incorporation of European environmental information into international environmental monitoring programmes; publish a report on the state, trends and prospects for the environment; stimulate the development of environmental forecasting; etc. (Article 2(i) to (xiii)). Agency activity is to include assessment of the pressures on, and quality and sensitivity of, the environment, and to be directed to certain priority areas (Article 3(1) and (2)). The Agency is an autonomous legal entity run by a management board, an Executive Director and a scientific committee (Articles 7–10), which is open to countries that are not EC members (Article 19).

Source: OJ L 120 11.05.1990, p. 1. Amended by: Council Regulation (EC) No 933/1999 of 29 April 1999 (L 117 1 05.05.1999); Regulation (EC) No 1641/2003 of the European Parliament and of the Council of 22 July 2003 (L 245 1 29.09.2003)

Council Regulation (EEC) No 1210/90 of 7 May 1990 on the establishment of the European Environment Agency and the European environment information and observation network (as amended)

The Council of the European Communities,

Having regard to the Treaty establishing the European Economic Community, and in particular Article 130s thereof,

Having regard to the proposal from the Commission,[1]

Having regard to the opinion of the European Parliament,[2]

Having regard to the opinion of the Economic and Social Committee, [3]

Whereas the Treaty provides for the development and implementation of a Community policy on the environment, and lays down the objectives and principles which should govern such policy;

Whereas environmental protection requirements shall be a component of the Community's other policies;

Whereas, according to Article 130r of the Treaty, in preparing its action relating to the environment the Community shall take account, *inter alia,* of the available scientific and technical data;

Whereas, in accordance with Decision 85/338/EEC,[4] the Commission has undertaken a work programme concerning an experimental project for gathering, coordinating and ensuring the consistency of information on the state of the environment and natural resources in the Community; whereas it is now appropriate to take the necessary decisions regarding a permanent environmental information and observation system;

Whereas collection, processing and analysis of environmental data at European level are necessary in order to provide objective, reliable and comparable information which will enable the Community and the Member States to take the requisite measures to protect the environment, to assess the results of such measures and to ensure that the public is properly informed about the state of the environment;

Whereas there already exist in the Community and the Member States facilities providing such information and services;

Whereas they should form the basis for setting up a European environment information and observation network which would be coordinated at Community level by a European Environment Agency;

Whereas the Agency should cooperate with existing structures at Community level to enable the Commission to ensure full application of Community legislation on the environment;

Whereas the status and structure of such an Agency should correspond to the objective character of the results it is intended to produce and allow it to carry out its functions in close cooperation with the existing national and international facilities;

Whereas the Agency should be granted legal autonomy while maintaining close links with the Community institutions and the Member States;

Whereas it is desirable to provide for the Agency to be open to other countries which share the concern of the Community and the Member States for the

[1] OJ No C 217, 23.8.1989, p. 7. [2] OJ No C 96, 17.4.1990.

[3] OJ No C 56, 7.3.1990, p. 20. [4] OJ No L 176, 6.7.1985, p. 14.

objectives of the Agency under agreements to be concluded between them and the Community;

Whereas this Regulation should be reviewed after two years, with a view to deciding on further tasks for the Agency,

Has adopted this Regulation:

Article 1

1. This Regulation establishes the European Environment Agency and aims at the setting-up of a European environment information and observation network.

2. To achieve the aims of environmental protection and improvement laid down by the Treaty and by successive Community action programmes on the environment, as well as of sustainable development, the objective shall be to provide the Community and the Member States with:

– objective, reliable and comparable information at European level enabling them to take the requisite measures to protect the environment, to assess the results of such measures and to ensure that the public is properly informed about the state of the environment,
– to that end, the necessary technical and scientific support.

Article 2

For the purposes of achieving the objective set out in Article 1, the tasks of the Agency shall be:

(i) to establish, in cooperation with the Member States, and coordinate the network referred to in Article 4. In this context, the Agency shall be responsible for the collection, processing and analysis of data, in particular in the fields referred to in Article 3. It shall also be responsible for continuing the work started under Decision 85/338/EEC;

(ii)
– to provide the Community and the Member States with the objective information necessary for framing and implementing sound and effective environmental policies; to that end, in particular to provide the Commission with the information that it needs to be able to carry out successfully its tasks of identifying, preparing and evaluating measures and legislation in the field of the environment;
– to assist the monitoring of environmental measures through appropriate support for reporting requirements (including through involvement in the development of questionnaires, the processing of reports from Member States and the distribution of results), in accordance with its multiannual work programme and with the aim of coordinating reporting;
– to advise individual Member States, upon their request and where this is consistent with the Agency's annual work programme, on the development,

establishment and expansion of their systems for the monitoring of environmental measures, provided such activities do not endanger the fulfillment of the other tasks established by this Article. Such advice may also include peer reviews by experts at the specific request of Member States;

(iii) to record, collate and assess data on the state of the environment, to draw up expert reports on the quality, sensitivity and pressures on the environment within the territory of the Community, to provide uniform assessment criteria for environmental data to be applied in all Member States, to develop further and maintain a reference centre of information on the environment. The Commission shall use this information in its task of ensuring the implementation of Community legislation on the environment;

(iv) to help ensure that environmental data at European level are comparable and, if necessary, to encourage by appropriate means improved harmonization of methods of measurement;

(v) to promote the incorporation of European environmental information into international environment monitoring programmes such as those established by the United Nations and its specialized agencies;

(vi) to publish a report on the state of, trends in and prospects for the environment every five years, supplemented by indicator reports focusing upon specific issues;

(vii) to stimulate the development and application of environmental forecasting techniques so that adequate preventive measures can be taken in good time;

(viii) to stimulate the development of methods of assessing the cost of damage to the environment and the costs of environmental preventive, protection and restoration policies;

(ix) to stimulate the exchange of information on the best technologies available for preventing or reducing damage to the environment;

(x) to cooperate with the bodies and programmes referred to in Article 15;

(xi) to ensure the broad dissemination of reliable and comparable environmental information, in particular on the state of the environment, to the general public and, to this end, to promote the use of new telematics technology for this purpose;

(xii) to support the Commission in the process of exchange of information on the development of Environmental Assessment methodologies and best practice;

(xiii) to assist the Commission in the diffusion of information on the results of relevant environmental research and in a form which can best assist policy development.

Article 3

1. The principal areas of activity of the Agency shall, as far as possible, include all elements enabling it to gather the information making it possible to describe the

present and foreseeable state of the environment from the following points of view:

(i) the quality of the environment;
(ii) the pressures on the environment;
(iii) the sensitivity of the environment; including placing these in the context of sustainable development.

2. The Agency shall furnish information which can be directly used in the implementation of Community environmental policy. Priority will be given to the following areas of work:

− air quality and atmospheric emissions,
− water quality, pollutants and water resources,
− the state of the soil, of the fauna and flora, and of biotopes,
− land use and natural resources,
− waste management,
− noise emissions,
− chemical substances which are hazardous for the environment,
− coastal and marine protection.

In particular, transfrontier, plurinational and global phenomena shall be covered. The socioeconomic dimension shall also be taken into account.

3. The Agency may also cooperate in the exchange of information with other bodies, including with the IMPEL network. In its activities the Agency shall avoid duplicating the existing activities of other institutions and bodies.

Article 4

1. The network shall comprise:

− the main component elements of the national information networks,
− the national focal points,
− the topic centres.

2. To enable the network to be set up as rapidly and as efficiently as possible, the Member States shall, within six months of the entry into force of this Regulation, inform the Agency of the main component elements of their national environment information networks, especially in the priority areas referred to in Article 3(2), including any institution which in their judgement could contribute to the work of the Agency, taking into account the need to ensure the fullest possible geographical coverage of their territory.

Member States shall keep the Agency informed of the main component elements of their national environment information networks. Member States shall, as appropriate, cooperate with the Agency and contribute to the work of the European environment information and observation network in accordance with the work programme of the Agency by collecting, collating and analysing data nationwide. Member States may also join to cooperate in these activities at a transnational level.

3. Member States may in particular designate from among the institutions referred to in paragraph 2 or other organizations established in their territory a 'national focal point' for coordinating and/or transmitting the information to be supplied at national level to the Agency and to the institutions or bodies forming part of the network including the topic centres referred to in paragraph 4.

4. Member States may also, within the period laid down in paragraph 2, identify the institutions or other organizations established in their territory which could be specifically entrusted with the task of cooperating with the Agency as regards certain topics of particular interest. An institution thus identified should be in a position to conclude an agreement with the Agency to act as a topic centre of the network for specific tasks. These centres shall cooperate with other institutions which form part of the network.

5. Within six months of receiving the information referred to in paragraph 2, the Agency shall confirm the main elements of the network on the basis of a decision by the management board and the arrangements referred to in Article 5.

The topic centres shall be designated by the management board as defined in Article 8(1), for a period not exceeding the duration of each multiannual work programme as referred to in Article 8(4). Each designation may, however, be renewed.

6. The allocation of specific tasks to the topic centres shall appear in the Agency's multiannual work programme mentioned in Article 8(4).

7. In the light in particular of the multiannual work programme, the Agency shall periodically re-examine the component elements of the network as referred to in paragraph 2 and shall make such changes as may be decided on by the management board, taking account of any new designations made by the Member States.

Article 5

The Agency may agree with the institutions or bodies which form part of the network, as referred to in Article 4, upon the necessary arrangements, in particular contracts, for successfully carrying out the tasks which it may entrust to them. A Member State may provide, as regards the national institutions or organizations in its territory, that such arrangements with the Agency shall be made in agreement with the national focal point.

Article 6

1. Regulation (EC) No 1049/2001 of the European Parliament and of the Council of 30 May 2001 regarding access to European Parliament, Council and Commission documents[1] shall apply to documents held by the Agency.

---

[1] OJ L 145, 31.5.2001, p. 43.

2. The Management Board shall adopt the practical arrangements for implementing Regulation (EC) No 1049/2001 within six months after the entry into force of Regulation (EC) No 1641/2003 of the European Parliament and of the Council of 22 July 2003 amending Council Regulation (EC) No 1210/90 on the establishment of the European Environment Agency and the European Environment Information and Observation Network.[1]

3. Decisions taken by the Agency pursuant to Article 8 of Regulation (EC) No 1049/2001 may form the subject of a complaint to the Ombudsman or of an action before the Court of Justice, under the conditions laid down in Articles 195 and 230 of the EC Treaty respectively;

Article 7

The Agency shall have legal personality. It shall enjoy in all the Member States the most extensive legal capacity accorded to legal persons under their laws.

Article 8

1. The Agency shall have a management board consisting of one representative of each Member State and two representatives of the Commission. In addition, there may be one representative of each other country which participates in the Agency, in accordance with the relevant provisions.

In addition, the European Parliament shall designate, as members of the management board, two scientific personalities particularly qualified in the field of environmental protection, who shall be chosen on the basis of the personal contribution they are likely to make to the Agency's work.

Each member of the management board may be represented by an alternate member.

2. The management board shall elect its chairman from among its members for a period of three years and shall adopt its rules of procedure.

Each member of the management board shall have a vote.

The management board shall elect a bureau to which it may delegate executive decisions, according to the rules that it shall adopt.

3. Decisions of the management board shall require for their adoption a two-thirds majority of the members of the board.

4. The management board shall adopt a multiannual work programme based on the priority areas referred to in Article 3(2), using as its basis a draft submitted by the Executive Director referred to in Article 9, after consulting the scientific committee, referred to in Article 10, and receiving the Commission's opinion. The multiannual work programme shall, without prejudice to the annual Community budgetary procedure, include a multiannual budget estimate.

---

[1] OJ L 245, 29.9.2003, p. 1.

5. Under the multiannual programme, the management board shall each year adopt the Agency's work programme on the basis of a draft submitted by the Executive Director after consulting the scientific committee and receiving the Commission's opinion. The programme may be adjusted in the course of the year by the same procedure.

6. The Management Board shall adopt the annual report on the Agency's activities and forward it by 15 June at the latest to the European Parliament, the Council, the Commission, the Court of Auditors and the Member States.

7. The Agency shall forward annually to the budgetary authority all information relevant to the outcome of the evaluation procedures.

Article 9

1. The Agency shall be headed by an Executive Director appointed by the management board on a proposal from the Commission for a period of five years, which shall be renewable. The Executive Director shall be the legal representative of the Agency. He shall be responsible:

- for the proper preparation and execution of the decisions and programmes adopted by the management board,
- for the day-to-day administration of the Agency,
- for the performance of the tasks defined in Articles 12 and 13,
- for the preparation and publication of the reports specified in Article 2 (vi),
- for all staff matters, for the performance of the tasks referred to in Article 8(4) and (5).

He shall obtain the opinion of the scientific committee, referred to in Article 10, for the purposes of recruitment of the Agency's scientific staff.

2. The Executive Director shall be accountable to the management board for his activities.

Article 10

1. The management board and the Executive Director shall be assisted by a scientific committee which shall deliver an opinion where provided for in this Regulation and on any scientific matter concerning the Agency's activity which the management board or the Executive Director may submit to it.

The opinions of the scientific committee shall be published.

2. The scientific committee shall be made up of members particularly qualified in the field of the environment, designated by the management board for a term of four years renewable once, taking into account, *inter alia*, the scientific areas which need to be represented in the committee in order to assist the Agency in its areas of activity. It shall function as determined by the rules of procedure provided for in Article 8(2).

Article 11

1. Estimates shall be drawn up of all the Agency's revenue and expenditure for each financial year, which shall correspond to the calendar year, and shall be entered in the Agency's budget.

2. The revenue and expenditure shown in the budget shall be in balance.

3. The revenue of the Agency shall, without prejudice to other resources, consist of a subsidy from the Community entered in the general budget of the European Communities and payments for services rendered.

4. The expenditure of the Agency shall include, *inter alia,* staff remuneration, administrative and infrastructure expenses, operating costs and expenditure relating to contracts concluded with institutions or bodies forming part of the network and with third parties.

Article 12

1. Each year the Management Board, on the basis of a draft drawn up by the Executive Director, shall produce a statement of estimates of revenue and expenditure of the Agency for the following financial year. This statement of estimates, which shall include a draft establishment plan, shall be forwarded by the Management Board to the Commission by 31 March at the latest.

2. The statement of estimates shall be forwarded by the Commission to the European Parliament and the Council (hereinafter referred to as the budgetary authority) together with the preliminary draft general budget of the European Union.

3. On the basis of the statement of estimates, the Commission shall enter in the preliminary draft general budget of the European Union the estimates it deems necessary for the establishment plan and the amount of the subsidy to be charged to the general budget, which it shall place before the budgetary authority in accordance with Article 272 of the Treaty.

4. The budgetary authority shall authorise the appropriations for the subsidy to the Agency. The budgetary authority shall adopt the establishment plan for the Agency.

5. The budget shall be adopted by the Management Board. It shall become final following final adoption of the general budget of the European Union. Where appropriate, it shall be adjusted accordingly.

6. The Management Board shall, as soon as possible, notify the budgetary authority of its intention to implement any project which may have significant financial implications for the funding of the budget, in particular any projects relating to property such as the rental or purchase of buildings. It shall inform the Commission thereof.

Where a branch of the budgetary authority has notified its intention to deliver an opinion, it shall forward its opinion to the Management Board within a period of six weeks after the date of notification of the project.

Article 13

1. The Executive Director shall implement the budget of the Agency.

2. By 1 March at the latest following each financial year, the Agency's accounting officer shall communicate the provisional accounts to the Commission's accounting officer together with a report on the budgetary and financial management for that financial year. The Commission's accounting officer shall consolidate the provisional accounts of the institutions and decentralised bodies in accordance with Article 128 of the general Financial Regulation.

3. By 31 March at the latest following each financial year, the Commission's accounting officer shall forward the Agency's provisional accounts to the Court of Auditors, together with a report on the budgetary and financial management for that financial year. The report on the budgetary and financial management for the financial year shall also be forwarded to the European Parliament and the Council.

4. On receipt of the Court of Auditors' observations on the Agency's provisional accounts under Article 129 of the general Financial Regulation, the Executive Director shall draw up the Agency's final accounts under his own responsibility and submit them to the Management Board for an opinion.

5. The Management Board shall deliver an opinion on the Agency's final accounts.

6. The Executive Director shall, by 1 July at the latest following each financial year, forward the final accounts to the European Parliament, the Council, the Commission and the Court of Auditors, together with the Management Board's opinion.

7. The final accounts shall be published.

8. The Executive Director shall send the Court of Auditors a reply to its observations by 30 September at the latest. He shall also send this reply to the Management Board.

9. The Executive Director shall submit to the European Parliament, at the latter's request, all information necessary for the smooth application of the discharge procedure for the financial year in question, as laid down in Article 146(3) of the general Financial Regulation.

10. The European Parliament, on a recommendation from the Council acting by a qualified majority, shall, before 30 April of year N + 2, give a discharge to the Executive Director in respect of the implementation of the budget for year N.

Article 14

The financial rules applicable to the Agency shall be adopted by the Management Board after the Commission has been consulted. They may not depart from Commission Regulation (EC, Euratom) No 2343/2002 of 19 November 2002 on the framework Financial Regulation for the bodies referred to in Article 185 of Council Regulation (EC, Euratom) No 1605/2002 on the Financial Regulation applicable to the general budget of the European Communities[1] unless such departure is specifically required for the Agency's operation and the Commission has given its prior consent.

---

[1] OJ L 357, 31.12.2002, p. 72; corrigendum in OJ L 2, 7.1.2003, p. 39.

Article 15

1. The Agency shall actively seek the cooperation of other Community bodies and programmes, and notably the Joint Research Centre, the Statistical Office and the Community's environmental research and development programmes. In particular:

- cooperation with the Joint Research Centre shall include the tasks set out in the Annex under A,
- coordination with the Statistical Office of the European Communities (Eurostat) and the statistical programme of the European Communities will follow the guidelines outlined in the Annex under B.

2. The Agency shall also cooperate actively with other bodies such as the European Space Agency, the Organization for Economic Cooperation and Development, the Council of Europe and the International Energy Agency as well as the United Nations and its specialized agencies, particularly the United Nations Environment Programme (UNEP), the World Meteorological Organization and the International Atomic Energy Authority.

2a. The Agency may cooperate in areas of common interest with those institutions in countries which are not members of the European Communities which can provide data, information and expertise, methodologies of data collection, analysis and assessment which are of mutual interest and which are necessary for the successful completion of the Agency's work.

3. The cooperation referred to in paragraphs 1, 2 and 2a must in particular take account of the need to avoid any duplication of effort.

Article 16

The Protocol on the Privileges and Immunities of the European Communities shall apply to the Agency.

Article 17

The staff of the Agency shall be subject to the Regulations and Rules applicable to officials and other servants of the European Communities.

The Agency shall exercise in respect of its staff the powers devolved to the Appointing Authority.

The management board shall, in agreement with the Commission, adopt the appropriate implementing rules.

Article 18

1. The contractual liability of the Agency shall be governed by the law applicable to the contract in question. The Court of Justice of the European Communities shall have jurisdiction to give judgment pursuant to an arbitration clause contained in a contract concluded by the Agency.

2. In the case of non-contractual liability, the Agency shall, in accordance with the general principles common to the laws of the Member States, make good any damage caused by the Agency or its servants in the performance of their duties.

The Court of Justice shall have jurisdiction in disputes relating to compensation for any such damage.

3. The personal liability of servants towards the Agency shall be governed by the provisions applying to the staff of the Agency.

Article 19

The Agency is open to countries which are not members of the European Communities but which share the concern of the Communities and the Member States for the objectives of the Agency under agreements concluded between them and the Community following the procedure in Article 228 of the Treaty.

Article 20

1. The Agency shall conduct an evaluation of its performance and efficiency before 15 September 1999 and submit a report to the management board, the Commission, the Council and the European Parliament.

2. Not later than 31 December 2003, on the basis of a report from the Commission, the Council shall review the progress of, and tasks undertaken by, the Agency in relation to the Community's overall policy on the environment.

Article 21

This Regulation shall enter into force on the day following that on which the competent authorities have decided the seat of the Agency[1]

This Regulation shall be binding in its entirety and directly applicable in all Member States.

[1] The date of entry into force of the Regulation shall be published in the Official Journal.

Annex

A. Cooperation with the Joint Research Centre

- Harmonization of environmental measurement methods.[1]
- Intercalibration of instruments.[1]
- Standardization of data formats.
- Development of new environmental measurement methods and instruments.
- Other tasks as agreed between the Executive Director of the Agency and the Director-General of the Joint Research Centre.

[1] Cooperation in these areas shall also take account of the work carried out by the Community Bureau of Reference.

B. Cooperation with Eurostat

1. The Agency will use, as far as possible, information collected via the official Community statistical services. These result from the work of Eurostat and the national statistical services in collecting, validating and disseminating social and economic statistics, including national accounts and related information. In particular, the Agency will make use of work done by Eurostat and the national statistical offices under Decision 94/808/EEC,[1] covering statistics on (a) human activities resulting in pressure on the environment and (b) societal and economic responses to such pressures.

2. The statistical programme in the field of the environment will be agreed between the Executive Director of the Agency and the Director-General of Eurostat and will be submitted for approval to the management board of the Agency and the Statistical Programme Committee.

3. The statistical programme shall be conceived and implemented within the framework established by the international statistical bodies, such as the UN Statistical Commission, the Conference of European Statisticians and the OECD.

[1] Council Decision 94/808/EEC of 15 December 1994 adopting a four-year development programme (1994 to 1997) relating to the environmental component of Community statistics (OJ L 328, 20.12.1994, p. 58).

Decision of 21 March 1997 on public access to European Environment Agency documents

Editorial note

The European Environment Agency has, *inter alia*, the task to ensure that the public is properly informed about the state of the environment (Article 1(2) Regulation EEC 1210/1990). This Decision provides for the public to have the widest possible access to Agency documents and specifies the conditions for such access (paragraph I). Applicants are to send a request in writing to the Executive Director of the Agency. They do not have to prove an interest. Applications must be sufficiently precise to allow the identification of the document requested (paragraph II). In some circumstances, charges may be made to access Agency documents, but they are not to exceed what is reasonable (paragraph III). Applications are to be dealt with as quickly as possible (paragraph IV). Access to an Agency document can be denied in specific circumstances (paragraph V).

Source: OJ C 282 18.09.1997 p. 5

Decision of 21 March 1997 on public access to European Environment Agency documents

Explanatory memorandum

1. Pursuant to Council Regulation (EEC) No 1210/90 of 7 May 1990 on the establishment of the European Environment Agency and the European environment information and observation network[1] it is one of the tasks of the Agency 'to ensure that the public is properly informed about the state of the environment' (Article 1(2)). In conformity with this general statement, the Agency is in charge of ensuring 'the broad dissemination of reliable environmental information' (Article 2, point (vi)).

2. Considering that free access to available information on the environment held by public authorities of Member States will improve environmental protection, access to documents held by Member States has been ensured by Council Directive 90/313/EEC of 7 June 1990 on the freedom of access to information on the environment.[2]

---

[1] OJ L 120, 11. 5. 1990, p. 1.   [2] OJ L 158, 23. 6. 1990, p. 56.

3. On 6 December 1993 the Council and the Commission approved a code of conduct concerning public access to Council and Commission documents.[1] Shortly afterwards, both institutions, implementing this code of conduct, adopted decisions on public access to their respective documents.[2]

4. The Agency has until now applied the Commission decision by analogy. However, having been granted legal personality and legal autonomy, it is not bound by the abovementioned decisions and it is therefore necessary for the Agency to adopt its own set of rules on public access to European Environment Agency documents.

It is strongly indicated that these rules follow closely those adopted by the Council and the Commission. In conformity with the principle of legal autonomy, the decision does not refer to the abovementioned code of conduct but is to be applied on an independent basis.

5. As to the substance of the decision, the point of departure should be, and this should be made perfectly clear, that the Agency is determined to grant access to existing documents in the widest possible way. The purpose of the decision is to set up the rules following which the public is entitled to apply for available documents without having to prove an interest. It must be understood that the applicants are only entitled to receive or to consult existing documents. There will be no obligation for the Agency to undertake research work or to produce new documents at the request of the public.

6. Access to documents (whatever their format) will normally be restricted to documents emanating from the Agency. For all other documents requested, applicants should be invited to apply to the authority from which these documents emanate.

7. While consultation of Agency documents on Agency premises will normally be free of charge, the Agency should have the possibility to charge a small fee for photocopies of documents exceeding 30 pages.

8. Access to Agency documents should be refused under certain conditions, especially in cases where public interest, the protection of the individual and of privacy, the protection of commercial and industrial secrecy so require. For reasons of coherence, it was found advisable to draft these exceptions (Article 5) exactly the same way as did the code of conduct adopted by the Council and the Commission.

9. The procedure set up by the decision is as follows:

– all applications should be addressed to the Office Executive Director. All requests should be handled under the responsibility of the Executive Director,
– if the Agency intends to refuse access to documents, the applicant is to be informed in writing of the reasons motivating this intention. Against this decision, the applicant

---

[1] OJ L 340, 31. 12. 1993, p. 41.
[2] Council Decision of 20. 12. 1993 on public access to Council Documents (OJ L 340, 31. 12. 1993, p. 43), Commission Decision of 08.2.1994 on public access to Commission documents (OJ L 46, 18. 2. 1994, p. 58), as modified by Decision of 19. 9. 1996 (OJ L 247, 28. 9. 1996, p. 45).

may lodge an appeal to the Management Board chairperson. It is expected that this will take place only on very exceptional occasions.
– if the Management Board chairperson decides to reject the appeal, its decision shall state the reasons thereof and inform the applicant of the possibility of referring the matter to the Ombudsman pursuant to Article 138c of the EC Treaty.

10. The decision of the Management Board of the European Environment Agency has been adopted and should be reviewed after two years by the same body. It should be published in the Official Journal of the European Communities ('C' series) and made available to the public.

Text of the decision

I. The public shall have the widest possible access to Agency documents under the conditions laid down in this decision.

'Agency documents' means any existing written text, whatever its format, containing existing data and emanating from the European Environment Agency. This decision is not applicable to documents already published.

II. An application for access to an Agency document shall be sent in writing to the Executive Director of the Agency.[1] Applicants do not have to prove an interest. Applications must be made in a sufficiently precise manner and must contain information enabling the particular document requested to be identified. Where necessary, the applicant shall be asked for further details.

III. The applicant shall have access to Agency documents either by consulting them on Agency premises or by having a copy sent at his own expense. For photocopies exceeding 30 sheets of paper, the Agency may charge a fee of ECU 10, plus ECU 0,036 per sheet. Charges for information in other formats shall be set on a case-by-case basis but shall not exceed what is reasonable.

Documents shall be provided in the language available, taking account of the applicant's preference.

Anyone given access to an Agency document may not sell the document, or distribute it for commercial purposes without prior authorization. Reproduction of published documents is authorized, provided the source is acknowledged.

IV. Applications shall be dealt with as quickly as possible under the responsibility of the Executive Director.

The applicant shall be informed in writing within one month whether his application is granted or whether the intention is to refuse access. In the latter case, the applicant shall be informed of the reasons for this intention. He shall also be informed that he has one month in which to apply to the Management Board chairperson for

---

[1] European Environment Agency, Kongens Nytorv 6, DK-1050 Copenhague, Fax (45 33) 36 71 99.

review of the intention to refuse access failing which he will be deemed to have withdrawn his application.

Failure to reply to an application within a month of submission shall be equivalent to a refusal. In this case the applicant may apply to the Management Board chairperson within one month, failing which he will be deemed to have withdrawn his application.

The decision on the application for review shall be taken as soon as possible and within two months of submission of such application, at the latest. If the application is rejected, the decision shall state the grounds on which it is based. At the same time, the applicant shall be informed of the possibility of referring the matter of the Ombudsman pursuant to the provisions of Article 138e of the EC Treaty.

V. Access to an Agency document shall not be granted where its disclosure could undermine

- the protection of the public interest (public security, international relations, monetary stability, court proceedings, inspections and investigations),
- the protection of the individual and of privacy,
- the protection of commercial and industrial secrecy,
- the protection of the Community's financial interests,
- the protection of confidentiality as requested by the natural or legal person who supplied any of the information contained in the document or as required by the legislation of the member country which supplied any of that information.

Access to an Agency document may be refused in order to protect the confidentiality of the Agency's proceedings.

VI. This decision shall be reviewed after two years of operation. In preparation for that review, the Executive Director shall submit in due time a report to the Management Board on the implementation of this Decision.

VII. This Decision shall take effect on 1 June 1997. It shall be published in the Official Journal of the European Communities and made available to the public.

Council Resolution of 7 October 1997 on the drafting, implementation and enforcement of Community environmental law

Editorial note

The Council Resolution on the drafting, implementation and enforcement of Community environmental law (7 October 1997) recognises the importance of the quality of drafting of Community legislation to make it more accessible. It also affirms that environmental legislation will only be effective if fully implemented and enforced. The Resolution recognises the peculiarity of environmental legislation and acknowledges that its distinct nature is to be taken into consideration when drafting, implementing and enforcing environmental law (paragraph 2). The characteristics and circumstances of environmental protection help explain the complex and not always satisfactory implementation and enforcement of environmental law (paragraph 4). Paragraphs 5-10 deal specifically with the drafting of environmental legislation and the Council invites the Commission to, *inter alia*, consult the main actors concerned at an early stage of a draft proposal, provide explanatory memoranda of proposals with detailed information, study the overall coherence of Community environmental legislation and suggest possible improvements without lowering the level of environmental protection. Paragraphs 11-14 deal with the transposition and practical application of environmental law and stress the need to deal systematically with problems encountered in this respect. Paragraphs 15-18 stress the importance of inspections to achieve the objective of application and enforcement of environmental law in the Member States. Paragraphs 19-23 recognise the role IMPEL[1] plays in the improvement of implementation of environmental law and call for its further development. Paragraphs 24-28 finally deal with complaints of, and legal protection for, citizens and non-governmental organisations and call for the development of existing and new initiatives to improve awareness, knowledge and application of Community environmental law.

Source: OJ C 321 22.10.1997 p. 1

---

[1] The European Union Network for the **Implementation and Enforcement of Environmental Law (IMPEL)** an informal Network of the environmental authorities of the Member States, acceding and candidate countries of the European Union and Norway. The network is commonly known as the IMPEL Network. The European Commission is also a member of IMPEL and shares the chairmanship of meetings.

Council Resolution of 7 October 1997 on the drafting, implementation and enforcement of Community environmental law

The Council of the European Union,

Having regard to the Treaty establishing the European Community,

Having regard to the declaration of the European Council, meeting in Dublin on 25 and 26 June 1990, on the environmental imperative, where the Heads of State or Government stressed *inter alia* that Community environmental legislation will only be effective if it is fully implemented and enforced by Member States, and renewed their commitment in this respect,

Having regard to the Council resolution of 8 June 1993 on the quality of drafting of Community legislation[1] and its general objective of making Community legislation more accessible,

Having regard to the resolution of the Council and the representatives of the Governments of the Member States, meeting within the Council, of 1 February 1993 on a Community programme of policy and action in relation to the environment and sustainable development,[2] hereinafter referred to as "the fifth environmental action programme", and to the proposal from the Commission for its review,

Having regard to the Commission communication of 5 November 1996 on implementing Community environmental law,

Taking note of the European Parliament resolution of 14 May 1997 on a communication from the Commission on implementing Community environmental law,

Whereas the Conference of the representatives of the Governments of the Member States, in their declaration (No 19) on the treaty of the European Union on the implementation of Community law stressed that each Member State should fully and accurately transpose into national law the Community directives addressed to it within the deadlines laid down therein and, while recognizing that it must be for each Member State to determine how the provisions of Community law can best be enforced in the light of its own particular institutions, legal system and other circumstances, but in any event in compliance with Article 189 of the treaty establishing the European Community, further considered it essential for the proper functioning of the Community that the measures taken by the different Member States should result in Community law being applied with the same effectiveness and rigour as in the application of their national law;

Whereas the Community, while further developing legislation to address major environmental problems, needs in parallel to focus strengthening and consolidating the implementation of the existing *acquis communautaire*, also with respect to current trends, practices and attitudes;

Whereas the European Union network for the implementation and enforcement of environmental law (Impel), having regard to chapter 9 of the fifth environmental

---

[1] OJ C 166, 17.6.1993, p. 1.   [2] OJ C 138, 17.5.1993, p. 1.

action programme, has so far played a useful role as an informal network for the improvement of the implementation, inspection and enforcement of environmental law, focusing on issues relating to industrial pollution;

Whereas the implementation and enforcement of Community environmental law through shared responsibility is one of the key elements of the Community's environmental policy;

Whereas subsidiarity is a fundamental general principle of Community policy and legislation as established by Article 3b of the Treaty;

Whereas the diversity of situations and environmental conditions in the various regions of the Community needs to be duly taken into account in drafting legislation in accordance with Article 130r(2) of the Treaty, and whereas the different legal and administrative systems and practices of the Member States should be taken more into consideration;

Whereas openness and access to information are important means to ensure the involvement of citizens, non-governmental organizations (NGOs) and other interested actors in the area covered by this resolution;

Whereas increased efforts are needed by all actors in the different links of the regulatory chain to improve the drafting, implementation and enforcement of Community environmental law,

1. *Welcomes* the communication from the Commission on implementing Community environmental law and *considers* it a useful initiative in order to promote and improve the effective and even implementation and enforcement of environmental law throughout the Community.

Specificity of environmental protection and its impact on environmental law

2. *Acknowledges* that environmental protection implies particular challenges that make it in many ways distinct from other subjects of policy and legislation, and that should be taken into account when drafting, implementing and enforcing environmental law.

3. *Stresses* that environmental protection has, in fact, to take into account, *inter alia*, the environmental media (air, water, soil) and living organisms (human, flora and fauna) as well as their inter-relationships, constantly changing environmental situations, the developing state of scientific knowledge and the close relation of environmental protection with complex and developing technology, a broad number of public and private actors involved, powers for the transposition and practical application of the law often devolved to, and shared between, different levels of public administration, and, last but not least, the fact that the environment is a common good frequently not linked to a private interest.

4. *Considers* that these characteristics and circumstances, although not entirely exclusive of environmental protection, help to explain why the implementation and

enforcement of environmental law, and in particular of Community environmental law, are so complex and not always satisfactory and why they require particular efforts from all actors involved in order to achieve the objectives set by environmental law.

Drafting of Community environmental legislation

5. *Invites* the Commission to consult the main actors concerned, including those likely to be involved at national level and within the Commission in the transposition and practical application, at an early stage on concrete legislative draft proposals so as to, apart from facilitating subsequent discussions, make legislation easier to implement and enforce.

In this context, furthermore *invites* the Commission to give due consideration in this consultation process to the linguistic diversity within the European Union so as to ensure an effective and non-discriminatory involvement of the main actors concerned.

Invites Member States similarly to conduct consultations of the main actors concerned throughout all the legislative, transposition and practical application stages.

6. *Considers* that transparency in the development of policy and the drafting of proposals should also be improved by other means and *invites*, therefore, the Commission to keep the other institutions and Member States regularly informed in an appropriate manner of its preparatory work and in this context make available studies and relevant documentation.

7. *Asks* the Commission to provide in the explanatory memoranda of its proposals more detailed information on:

– their scope,
– the choice of the type of instrument,
– the legal basis and other legal aspects,
– the proposed deadline for bringing into force,
– the practical and other aspects of implementation and enforcement by the Member States,
– the potential benefits and costs of action or lack of action,
– the coherence of the proposed measure with existing Community legislation,
– the overall strategy clearly presenting the environmental problem that is to be solved,
– the application of the principles enshrined in Article 3b of the Treaty.

8. *Stresses* that increased efforts should be made to ensure that texts resulting from the different phases of the Community legislative process are not unnecessarily ambiguous or complicated so as to reduce problems of transposition and of practical application which lead to incomplete or uneven implementation throughout the Community.

9. *Recalls* the importance of coherence of the whole system of Community environmental legislation; *invites* therefore the Commission to study the overall coherence

of Community environmental legislation and suggest to Council possible improve-ments without lowering the level of environmental protection. In this respect, it is important to take into account the interlinkage between the environmental media.

10. *Invites* the Commission to improve the coherence of community legislation by the use, *inter alia*, of framework directives and of codification or consolidation of legislation. In this context, account should also be taken of the work of the committees established by Council directives and especially those charged with the adaptation and execution of Community legislation. The legislation in other Community sectors should also be taken into consideration.

Notes furthermore the importance to ensure also coherence of the Community environmental legislation with international environmental instruments.

Invites Member States to ensure the coherence of their environmental legislation, and in particular their compatibility with Community legislation.

Transposition and practical application

11. *Emphasizes* the need to tackle more systematically concrete problems with regard to transposition and practical application of Community environmental legislation. The exchange of experiences between Member States on common concrete problems constitute in this regard an important basis to consider possible solutions, including, where appropriate, the review of existing legislation.

In this context, the system of harmonized reporting as set up in Council Directive 91/692/EEC of 23 December 1991 standardizing and rationalizing reports on the implementation of certain directives relating to the environment[1] should assist in examining the common and individual problems Member States have in the field of transposition and application and encouraging the exchanges of views between Member States.

12. *Considers* that in implementing Community legislation on the environment, Member States should provide for appropriate sanctions to ensure a more even enforcement of Community environmental law. Sanctions, which would remain within the power of Member States, should be transparent, dissuasive, proportionate and be actually applied in practice. The Council resolution of 29 June 1995 on the effective uniform application of Community law and on the penalties applicable for breaches of Community law in the internal market[2] should be taken into consideration in this context.

13. *Invites* the Commission to consider the inclusion in its future proposals for envi-ronmental measures, where appropriate and on a case-by-case basis, of a provision requiring national implementing measures to include appropriately dissuasive sanc-tions for non-compliance with the requirements of the relevant Community acts and having regard to the principle of subsidiarity.

---

[1] OJ L 377, 31.12.1991, p. 48. [2] OJ C 188, 22.7.1995, p. 1.

14. *Invites* the Commission to ensure that the Community's environmental objectives and the requirements of Community environmental law are fully integrated into the Community's existing financial support mechanisms and into the monitoring of projects financed by the Community.

Recalls furthermore that all projects, whether requiring Community or national funding or not, must comply, *inter alia*, with Community environmental legislation.

Inspections

15. *Stresses* the fact that inspection is an essential prerequisite to achieve the objective of an even practical application and enforcement of environmental law in all Member States.

16. *Notes* that different systems and practices of inspection already exist in Member States and *considers* that such differences should be acknowledged; *considers* furthermore that these should not be replaced by a system of inspection at Community level.

Also notes that the broader application of voluntary environmental management and audit schemes in line with the Community environment management and audit system Regulation could be helpful for improving the practical application of Community environmental law by means of enhanced self-control and self-monitoring.

17. *Asks* the Commission, taking into account the variety of existing systems, to propose for further consideration in the Council, in particular on the basis of the work of Impel, minimum criteria and/or guidelines for inspection tasks carried out at Member State level and the possible ways in which their application in practice could be monitored by Member States in order to ensure an even practical application and enforcement of environmental legislation.

18. *Invites* Member States to encourage, in the appropriate framework, *inter alia* by promoting initiatives of the Impel network, cooperation between and within Member States to combat illegal practices with a transboundary character in the field of the environment.

Impel

19. *Recognizes* that Impel, where all Member States and the Commission are represented, is a very useful informal instrument for the improvement of implementation, inspection and enforcement, *inter alia* through exchange of information and experiences on different administrative levels, as well as through training and in-depth discussions on environmental issues and enforcement aspects.

20. *Considers* that the Impel network should also play in the future an important role during the different stages of the regulatory chain and could in particular give advice, on request or on its own initiative, on general questions regarding implementation

and enforcement as well as on new draft proposals for Community legislation, in particular where the input of practical experience is necessary.

21. *Considers* also that Impel could be further developed, *inter alia* by asking it to consider whether it should or not broaden the scope of its mandate and the focus of its current work.

The structure of Impel should reflect its main tasks concerning legal policy, implementation and enforcement issues as well as technical issues, practical enforcement, inspections and environmental management, while maintaining its informal character.

22. *Invites* Member States to encourage the creation of national coordination networks involving the main relevant authorities at different levels of public administration.

23. *Considers* further that, in order to be able to carry out the above-mentioned functions, the Impel network will require appropriate financial means and a secretariat.

Dealing with complaints of, and legal protection for, citizens and non-governmental organizations

24. *Encourages* Member States, the Commission and other actors, to develop existing and new initiatives for improving awareness, knowledge and application of Community environmental law by the main actors involved in the practical application and enforcement in the Member States.

25. *Stresses* the importance that, in order to settle environmental disputes more efficiently (i.e. more speedily and at low cost) and with greater ease for citizens and national authorities alike, all Member States consider appropriate mechanisms at the appropriate levels to deal with complaints of citizens and NGOs regarding non-compliance with environmental legislation and make available information regarding the opportunities for complaints to be dealt with at the Member State level.

26. *Invites* the Commission to submit to the Council a report on the existing administrative and judicial mechanisms to deal with complaints of citizens and NGOs and other interested actors and also on the existing systems of legal protection, including access to justice for citizens and NGOs. The report should be presented before the finalization of the negotiations in the ad hoc Working Group on the ECE-Convention on access to environmental information and public participation in environmental decision-making at the end of 1997.

Further invites the Commission to assess, on the basis of this report, whether there is a need for the development of minimum criteria or guidelines regarding:

– the handling of complaints both at national and Community level, and
– improved access to courts and administrative tribunals, in the light of the subsidiarity principle and taking into account the different legal systems of the Member States.

In this particular context, attention should be paid, if appropriate, to the outcome of ongoing discussions on access to justice in the field of consumer protection.

27. *Invites* the Commission, in addition to submitting its annual report on Monitoring the Application of Community Law, to submit to the Council an annual survey of the environment containing, *inter alia*, detailed information on transposition and practical application by Member States of Community environmental law and furthermore on the principal activities and concrete results of the Impel network, including its current and future work programme, on the basis of a report by Impel.

28. *Undertakes* to examine regularly on this basis the state of implementation and enforcement of Community environmental law.

PART III

The relationship between environmental protection, financial assistance and free trade

Council Recommendation 75/436/Euratom, ECSC, EEC of 3 March 1975 regarding cost allocation and action by public authorities on environmental matters

Editorial note

Council Recommendation 75/436 Euratom, ECSC, EEC of 3 March 1975 regarding cost allocation and action by public authorities on environmental matters seeks to apply the 'polluter pays' principle at both the Community and the Member State level. The operative elements are in the Annex. The principle, intended to induce reductions in pollution levels and a more rational use of environmental resources, is considered to be effective and equitable; if applied uniformly throughout the Community, it should avoid trade and investment distortions (paragraph 1). The polluter pays principle is defined as requiring the party responsible for pollution to meet the cost of measures to eliminate or reduce pollution according to quality objectives or standards set by public authorities – in other words, environmental protection should not be dependent on state aid (paragraph 2). The 'polluter' is the person who damages the environment directly or indirectly or creates the conditions for damage to occur; where it proves too difficult to identify the polluter, the costs are to be borne by the person whose penalisation will yield the optimal result from an economic, administrative and environmental point of view (paragraph 3).

Two economic instruments are identified as capable of implementing the polluter pays principle: standards and charges (paragraph 4). The Recommendation specifies which particular expenditures the polluter must bear in order to comply with the polluter pays principle and outlines two permissible exceptions (paragraphs 5 and 6). Other circumstances where subsidisation would not conflict with the polluter pays principle are listed in paragraph 7.

Source: OJ L 194 25.07.1975 p. 1

Council Recommendation 75/436/Euratom ECSC, EEC of 3 March 1975 regarding cost allocation and action by public authorities on environmental matters

The Council of the European Communities,

Having regard to the Treaty establishing the European Coal and Steel Community;

Having regard to the Treaty establishing the European Economic Community;

Having regard to the Treaty establishing the European Atomic Energy Community;

Having regard to the draft recommendation submitted by the Commission;

Having regard to the Opinion of the European Parliament;[1]

Having regard to the Opinion of the Economic and Social Committee;[2]

Whereas in the framework of the declaration of the Council of the European Communities and of the representatives of the Governments of the Member States meeting with the Council of 22 November 1973[3] on the programme of action of the European Communities on the environment, the "polluter pays" principle was adopted;

Whereas the costs associated with the protection of the environment against pollution should be allocated according to the same principles throughout the Community, in order to avoid distortions in trade and competition incompatible with the proper functioning of the common market and with the aim of balanced economic expansion pursued by the Community and in order to further the aims set out in the programme of action of the European Communities on the environment;

Whereas in order to facilitate application of the said principle, the European Communities and the Member States must define it more clearly by laying down procedures for its application, and by making provision for certain exceptions to be made to it such as may be made on grounds of difficulties encountered in its application and because of the interplay between other policies and the environmental protection policy;

Recommends, within the meaning of the EEC Treaty, that in respect of allocation of costs and of action by public authorities in the field of environmental protection, the Member States conform to the principles and the rules governing their application which are contained in the Commission communication annexed to this recommendation.

Done at Brussels, 3 March 1975.

Annex

Communication from the Commission to the Council regarding cost allocation and action by public authorities on environmental matters

Principles and detailed rules governing their application

1. In the framework of the declaration of the Council of the European Communities and of the representatives of the Governments of the Member States meeting within

---

[1] OJ No C 76, 3.7.1974, p. 31.   [2] OJ No C 116, 30.9.1974, p. 35.   [3] OJ No C 112, 20.12.1973, p. 1.

the Council of 22 November 1973 on the programme of action of the European Communities on the environment, the "polluter pays" principle was adopted. The programme of action provides that the Commission submit to the Council a proposal concerning the application of this principle, including possible exceptions thereto.

Charging to polluters the costs of action taken to combat the pollution which they cause encourages them to reduce that pollution and to endeavour to find less polluting products or technologies thereby enabling a more rational use to be made of the resources of the environment. Moreover, it satisfies the criteria of effectiveness and equitable practice.

In order to avoid distortions of competition affecting trade and the location of investments which would be incompatible with the proper functioning of the common market, the costs connected with the protection of the environment against pollution should be allocated according to the same principles throughout the Community.

2. To achieve this, the European Communities at Community level and the Member States in their national legislation on environmental protection must apply the "polluter pays" principle, under which natural or legal persons governed by public or private law who are responsible for pollution must pay the costs of such measures as are necessary to eliminate that pollution or to reduce it so as to comply with the standards or equivalent measures which enable quality objectives to be met or, where there are no such objectives, so as to comply with the standards or equivalent measures laid down by the public authorities.[1]

Consequently, environmental protection should not in principle depend on policies which rely on grants of aid and place the burden of combating pollution on the Community.

3. A polluter is someone who directly or indirectly damages the environment or who creates conditions leading to such damage.[2]

If identifying the polluter proves impossible or too difficult, and hence arbitrary, particularly where environmental pollution arises from several simultaneous causes ("cumulative pollution")[3] or from several consecutive causes ("pollution chain"),[4] the cost of combating pollution should be borne at the point in the pollution chain or in the cumulative pollution process, and by the legal or administrative means which offer the best solution from the administrative and economic points of view and which make the most effective contribution towards improving the environment.

Thus, in the case of pollution chains, costs could be charged at the point at which the number of economic operators is least and control is easiest or else at the point

---

[1] As long as such a level has not been laid down by the public authorities, measures taken by such authorities to avoid pollution should also be paid for by the polluters, in accordance with the 'polluter pays principle'.

[2] The concept of polluter, as defined in this sentence, does not affect Provisions concerning third-party liability.

[3] Where, in a built-up area, for example, several polluters, such as householders, users of motor vehicles and industrial plants, are simultaneously responsible for polluting the atmosphere with SO_2.

[4] For example, in cases of environmental pollution by motor vehicle exhaust fumes, not only the user of the vehicle but also the manufacturer of the vehicle and of the fuel are responsible for causing atmospheric pollution.

where the most effective contribution is made towards improving the environment, and where distortions to competition are avoided.

4. Under the "polluter pays" principle, standards and charges, or a possible combination of the two, are the major instruments of action available to public authorities for the avoidance of pollution.

(a) Standards include:
    (i) "environmental quality standards" which, with legally binding force, prescribe the levels of pollution or nuisance not to be exceeded in a given environment or part thereof;
    (ii) "product standards" (the term product is used here in its broadest meaning) which:
       – set levels for pollutants or nuisance which are not to be exceeded in the composition or the emissions of a product, or
       – specify properties or characteristics of design of a product, or
       – are concerned with the way in which products are used.[1]
    Where appropriate, product standards include specifications for testing, packaging, marking and labelling products;
    (iii) standards for fixed installations, sometimes called "process standards", such as:
       (a) "emission standards", which set levels for pollutants or nuisances not to be exceeded in emissions from fixed installations;
       (b) "installation design standards", which determine the requirements[2] to be met in the design and construction of fixed installations in order to protect the environment;
       (c) "operating standards", which determine the requirements to be met in the operation of fixed installations in order to protect the environment.

(b) The purpose of charges shall be to encourage the polluter to take the necessary measures to reduce the pollution he is causing as cheaply as possible (incentive function) and/or to make him pay his share of the costs of collective measures, for example purification costs (redistribution function). The charges should be applied, according to the extent of pollution emitted, on the basis of an appropriate administrative procedure.

Charges should be fixed so that primarily they fulfil their incentive function. In so far as the main function of charges is redistribution, they should at least be fixed within the context of the abovementioned measures so that, for a given region and/or qualitative objective, the aggregate amount of the charges is equal to the total cost to the Community of eliminating nuisances.

---

[1] Such methods of use and specifications may be issued in the form of "codes of practice".
[2] Such methods of use and specifications may be issued in the form of "codes of practice".

Income from charges may be used to finance either measures taken by public authorities or to help finance installations set up by an individual polluter, provided that the latter, at the specific request of the public authorities, is seen to render a particular service to the Community, by reducing his pollution level to below that set by the competent authorities. In the latter instance, the financial aid granted must be limited to compensating for the services thus rendered by the polluter to the Community.

In line with Article 92 et seq. of the EEC Treaty, income from charges may also be used to finance the installations of individual polluters for protecting the environment, in order actively to reduce existing pollution. In this case, the measures for financing should be incorporated in an official multi-annual finance programme by the competent authorities.

Where the overall revenue exceeds the total expenditure by the public authorities when applying the two preceding paragraphs, the surplus should preferably be used by each government for its national environmental policies; however, the surplus may be used for granting aid only under the conditions specified in paragraphs 6 and 7 below.

As far as possible, the Community should endeavour to standardize the methods of calculation used by the Member States to set charges.

(c) In order to avoid distortions of competition affecting trade and the location of investment in the Community, it will undoubtedly be necessary to harmonize more and more closely at Community level the various instruments where they are applied in similar cases.

Until this is achieved, the question of the allocation of anti-pollution costs will never be entirely resolved at Community level. This Commission communication therefore constitutes merely a first step in the application of the "polluter pays" principle. The first step must be followed up as quickly as possible by the harmonization within the Community of the instruments for implementing the said principle when they are applied to similar cases, as stated in the third subparagraph of paragraph 8 of this document.

5. Depending on the instruments used and without prejudice to any compensation due under national law or international law, and/or regulations to be drawn up within the Community, polluters will be obliged to bear:

(a) expenditure on pollution control measures (investment in anti-pollution installations and equipment, introduction of new processes, cost of running anti-pollution installations, etc.), even when these go beyond the standards laid down by the public authorities;

(b) the charges.

The costs to be borne by the polluter (under the "polluter pays" principle) should include all the expenditure necessary to achieve an environmental quality objective, including the administrative costs directly linked to the implementation of anti-pollution measures. The cost to the public authorities of constructing, buying and operating pollution monitoring and supervision installations may, however, be borne by those authorities.

6. Exceptions to the "polluter pays" principle may be justified in limited cases:

(a) Where the immediate application of very stringent standards or the imposition of substantial charges is likely to lead to serious economic disturbances, the rapid incorporation of pollution control costs into production costs may give rise to greater social costs. It may then prove necessary:
   – to allow some polluters time to adapt their products or production processes to the new standards;
   – and/or to grant aid for a limited period and possibly of a degressive nature. Such measures may, in any case, apply only to existing production plants[1] and existing products.
(b) Where, in the context of other policies (e.g. regional, industrial, social, and agricultural policies or scientific research and development policy), investment affecting environmental protection benefit from aid intended to solve certain industrial, agricultural or regional structural problems.

Aids referred to under (a) and (b) may, of course, only be granted by Member States in compliance with the provisions on State aid set out in the Treaties establishing the European Communities, and in particular Articles 92 et seq. of the EEC Treaty. In applying Articles 92 et seq. of the EEC Treaty to these aids, account will be taken of the requirements which such aids satisfy as regards environmental protection.

7. The following shall not be considered contrary to the "polluter pays" principle:[2]

(a) financial contributions which might be granted to local authorities for the construction and operation of public installations for the protection of the environment, the cost of which could not be wholly covered in the short term from the charges paid by polluters using them. In so far as other effluent as well as household waste is treated in these installations, the service thus rendered to undertakings should be charged to them on the basis of the actual cost of the treatment concerned;
(b) financing designed to compensate for the particularly heavy costs which some polluters would be obliged to meet in order to achieve an exceptional degree of environmental cleanliness;
(c) contributions granted to foster activities concerning research and development with a view to implementing techniques, manufacturing processes and products causing less pollution.

---

[1] The enlargement or the transfer of existing production plants will be considered as the creation of new plants where this represents an increase in productivity capacity.
[2] This list may be modified by the Council, on a proposal from the Commission.

8. In carrying out its tasks within the framework of the Community environment policy, the Commission will comply particularly with the abovementioned definitions and methods of application of the abovementioned "polluter pays" principle.

The Commission asks the Council to take note of these definitions and conditions of application and to recommend that the Member States conform to them in their legislation and administrative measures involving the allocation of costs in the environmental field.

The Commission will submit all the necessary proposals in this field to the Council in due course, particularly as regards the harmonization of instruments for administering the "polluter pays" principle, and its specific application to the problems of transfrontier pollution.

Each Member State should apply the "polluter pays" principle to all forms of pollution within its own country and without making any distinction as to whether the pollution affects that country or another.

Council Regulation (EC) No 1164/94 of 16 May 1994 establishing a Cohesion Fund (as amended)

Editorial note

Regulation 1164/94 establishes a Cohesion Fund in addition to the other Community development instruments, to provide assistance in the fields of the environment and transport infrastructure of common interest with a view to promoting economic and social cohesion and solidarity between Member States. The Fund may contribute to projects, stages of a project or groups of projects (Article 1). The Fund is to provide financial contributions to projects in the fields of the environment and trans-European transport infrastructure networks (Article 3) in the Member States that meet the criteria specified under Article 2 (Greece, Ireland, Spain, Portugal and the ten newest Member States). Article 4 specifies the financial resources available to the Fund. The rate of Community assistance granted by the Fund is to be 80 to 85 per cent of public or equivalent expenditure (Article 7). Projects financed by the Fund are to be adopted by the Commission in agreement with the Member State (Article 10(1)). Applications are to be submitted by the beneficiary Member State and are to contain detailed information, including information enabling impact on the environment to be assessed (Article 10(3) and (4)). Without prejudice to the Commission's responsibilities, Member States are to take responsibility in the first instance for the financial controls of projects (Article 12(1)). The Commission is to ensure that funds are efficiently and correctly used (Article 12(2)). The Member States and the Commission are to ensure that implementation of projects is effectively monitored and evaluated (Article 13). The Commission is to present an annual report on the activities of the Fund (Article 14).

Annex I to the Regulation contains indicative allocations among the beneficiary Member States of the total resources of the Cohesion Fund. Annex II specifies implementing provisions for the Regulation (Article 15) (on the designation of projects, stages or group of projects; ex-ante evaluation; commitments; payments; use of the euro; monitoring; checks; financial corrections; public contracts; information; review). The Council is to re-examine the Regulation, acting on a proposal from the Commission, by 31 December 2006 at the latest.

Source: OJ L 130 25.05.1994 p. 1. Amended by: Council Regulation (EC) No 1264/1999 of 21 June 1999 L 161 57 26.06.1999; Council Regulation (EC) No 1265/1999 of 21

June 1999 L 161 62 26.06.1999: Act concerning the conditions of accession of the Czech Republic, the Republic of Estonia, the Republic of Cyprus, the Republic of Latvia, the Republic of Lithuania, the Republic of Hungary, the Republic of Malta, the Republic of Poland, the Republic of Slovenia and the Slovak Republic and the adjustments to the Treaties on which the European Union is founded L 236 33 23.09.2003

Council Regulation (EC) No 1164/94 of 16 May 1994 establishing a Cohesion Fund (as amended)

The Council of the European Union,

Having regard to the Treaty establishing the European Economic Community, and in particular the second subparagraph of Article 130d thereof,

Having regard to the proposal from the Commission,[1]

Having regard to the assent of the European Parliament,[2]

Having regard to the opinion of the Economic and Social Committee,[3]

Having regard to the opinion of the Committee of the Regions,[4]

Whereas Article 2 of the Treaty includes the task of promoting economic and social cohesion and solidarity among Member States as objectives essential to the Community's development and success; whereas the strengthening of such cohesion is referred to in point (j) of Article 3 of the Treaty as one of the activities of the Community for the purposes set out in Article 2 of the Treaty;

Whereas Article 130a of the Treaty provides for the Community to develop and pursue its actions leading to the strengthening of its economic and social cohesion, and provides in particular that it shall aim at reducing disparities between the levels of development of the various regions and the backwardness of the least-favoured regions; whereas Community action through the Cohesion Fund should support the achievement of the objectives set out in Article 130a;

Whereas the conclusions of the European Councils held in Lisbon on 26 and 27 June 1992 and in Edinburgh on 11 and 12 December 1992 concerning the establishment of the Cohesion Fund set out the principles governing it;

Whereas the promotion of economic and social cohesion requires action by the Cohesion Fund in addition to that taken through the Structural Funds, the European Investment Bank and the other financial instruments in the fields of the environment and transport infrastructure of common interest;

Whereas the Protocol on economic and social cohesion annexed to the Treaty establishing the European Community reaffirms the Community's task of promoting economic and social cohesion and solidarity between Member States and specifies

---

[1] OJ No C 39, 9. 2. 1994, p. 6.
[2] Assent given on 5 May 1994 (not yet published in the Official Journal).
[3] OJ No C 133, 16. 5. 1994.
[4] Opinion delivered on 5 April 1994 (not yet published in the Official Journal).

that a Cohesion Fund will provide a financial contribution to projects in the fields of the environment and trans-European networks in the Member States subject to two conditions: firstly that they have a per capita gross national product (GNP) of less than 90% of the Community average and secondly that they have a programme leading to the fulfilment of the conditions of economic convergence as set out in Article 104c of the Treaty; whereas the relative prosperity of Member States is best assessed on the basis of per capita GNP, measured in purchasing power parities;

Whereas meeting the convergence criteria which are a precondition for moving to the third stage of economic and monetary union calls for a determined effort from the Member States concerned; whereas, in this context, all of the beneficiary Member States are to submit to the Council a convergence programme designed for that purpose and to avoid excessive government deficits;

Whereas, with regard to the economic convergence criterion, the current macroeconomic conditionality provisions will continue to apply; whereas, accordingly, no new projects or new project stages shall be financed by the Fund in a Member State in the event of the Council, acting by qualified majority on a recommendation from the Commission, finding that the Member State has not respected the Stability Growth Pact;

Whereas the provisions to speed up and clarify the excessive deficit procedure, having as its objective to deter excessive general government deficits and, if they occur, to further their prompt correction were set out in Council Regulation (EC) No 1467/97;[1]

Whereas the second subparagraph of Article 130d of the Treaty states that the Council is to set up a Cohesion Fund before 31 December 1993 to provide a financial contribution to projects in the fields of environment and trans-European networks in the area of transport infrastructure;

Whereas Article 129c(1) of the Treaty provides that the Community may contribute through the Cohesion Fund to the financing of specific projects in the Member States in the area of transport infrastructure, whilst taking into account the potential economic viability of the projects; whereas projects financed by the Fund should form part of trans-European network guidelines which have been adopted by the Council including those covered by the plans for trans-European networks approved by the Council or proposed by the Commission before the entry into force of the Treaty on European Union; whereas, however, other transport infrastructure projects contributing to the attainment of the objectives of Article 129b of the Treaty may be financed until the Council has adopted the appropriate guidelines;

Whereas Article 130r of the Treaty defines the objectives and principles of the Community in the field of the environment; whereas the Community may contribute, through the Cohesion Fund, to actions designed to achieve those objectives; whereas, in accordance with Article 130s(5) of the Treaty and without prejudice

---

[1] OJ L 209, 2.8.1997, p. 6.

to the principle that the polluter should pay, the Council may decide on financial assistance from the Cohesion Fund where a measure based on paragraph 1 of that Article involves costs deemed disproportionate for the public authorities of a Member State;

Whereas the principles and objectives of sustainable development are established in the Community's programme of policy and action in relation to the environment and sustainable development as set out in the Council Resolution of 1 February 1993;[1]

Whereas a suitable balance must be struck between financing for transport infrastructure projects and financing for environmental projects;

Whereas the Commission's Green Paper on the Impact of Transport on the Environment reiterates the need to develop a more environment friendly transport system which takes into account the sustainable development needs of the Member States;

Whereas any calculation of the cost of transport infrastructure projects must encompass environmental costs;

Whereas, in the light of the undertaking by the Member States concerned not to decrease their investment efforts in the fields of environmental protection and transport infrastructure, the principle of additionality within the meaning of Article 9 of Council Regulation (EEC) No 4253/88 of 19 December 1988 laying down provisions for implementing Regulation (EEC) No 2052/88 as regards coordination of the activities of the different Structural Funds between themselves and with the operations of the European Investment Bank and the other existing financial instruments[2] will not apply to the Cohesion Fund;

Whereas, in accordance with Article 198e of the Treaty, the European Investment Bank (EIB) is to facilitate the financing of investments in conjunction with assistance from the other Community financial instruments;

Whereas it is necessary to coordinate action taken in the fields of the environment and of trans-European transport infrastructure networks through the Cohesion Fund, the Structural Funds, the EIB and the other financial instruments in order to enhance the effectiveness of Community assistance;

Whereas with a view, in particular, to helping Member States in the preparation of their projects, the Commission should be in a position to ensure that the necessary technical support is available to them, particularly in order to contribute to the preparation, implementation, monitoring and evaluation of projects;

Whereas, particularly in order to ensure value for money, a thorough appraisal should precede the commitment of Community resources in order to ensure that they yield socio-economic benefits in keeping with the resources deployed;

Whereas assistance from the Cohesion Fund must be consistent with Community policies, including environmental protection, transport, trans-European networks,

---

[1] OJ No C 138, 17. 5. 1993, p. 1.
[2] OJ No L 374, 31. 12. 1988, p. 1. Regulation as amended by Regulation (EEC) No 2082/93 (OJ No L 193, 31. 7. 1993, p. 20).

competition and the award of public contracts; whereas environmental protection includes the assessment of environmental impact;

Whereas there should be provision for an indicative allocation of the global resources available for commitment between the Member States in order to facilitate the preparation of projects;

Whereas total annual receipt in any Member State from the Cohesion Fund under this Regulation, in combination with assistance provided under the Structural Funds, should be limited under a general capping dependent on the national absorption capacity;

Whereas provision should be made, in conjunction with the fulfillment of the conditions of economic convergence as set out in Article 104 of the Treaty and with the need for sound management of the government deficit, for a form of conditionality in the granting of financial assistance; whereas, in that context, compliance with the obligations arising from the Treaty must also be assessed having due regard to the guidelines adopted in the Resolution of the European Council of 17 June 1997 on the Stability and Growth Pact[1] and whereas the concept of excessive deficit is to be interpreted in the light of that Resolution; whereas, for each participating Member State, macroeconomic conditionality should be assessed taking account of the responsibilities of that Member State in respect of the stability of the euro;

Whereas it is necessary, given the requirements of economic and social cohesion, to provide a high rate of assistance;

Whereas, in order to facilitate the management of assistance from the Fund, there should be provision for identifying the stages of projects which may be considered technically and financially separate and for grouping the projects together, if necessary;

Whereas it should be possible to opt for assistance from the Fund either by annual instalments or for the whole of the project; and whereas, in accordance with the principle laid down by the European Council meeting at Edinburgh on 11 and 12 December 1992, payment instalments following an initial advance should be closely and transparently linked with progress towards the completion of projects;

Whereas the respective powers and responsibilities of the Member States and the Commission concerning financial control over the Fund's operations should be specified;

Whereas, in the interests of the proper management of the Cohesion Fund, provision should be made for effective methods of evaluating, monitoring and checking Community operations, specifying the principles governing the evaluation, defining the nature of and the rules governing the monitoring, and laying down the action to be taken in response to irregularities or failure to comply with one of the conditions laid down when assistance from that Fund was approved;

---

[1] OJ C 236, 2.8.1997, p. 1.

Whereas adequate information should be provided, *inter alia*, in the form of an annual report;

Whereas provision should be made to give adequate publicity to Community assistance from the Cohesion Fund;

Whereas publication in the *Official Journal of the European Communities* of calls for public tenders concerning projects receiving assistance from the Fund should mention the assistance;

Whereas in order to facilitate the application of this Regulation, the implementing provisions should be defined in Annex II; whereas to ensure the necessary flexibility in their application, the Council, acting by a qualified majority on a proposal from the Commission, should be able, if necessary, in the light of experience gained, to amend those provisions;

Whereas this Regulation should, without interruption, replace Council Regulation (EEC) No 792/93 of 30 March 1993 establishing a cohesion financial instrument,[1]

Has adopted this Regulation:

Article 1
Definition and objective

1. A Cohesion Fund, hereinafter referred to as 'the Fund', is hereby established.

2. The Fund shall contribute to the strengthening of the economic and social cohesion of the Community and shall operate according to the provisions set out in this Regulation.

3. The Fund may contribute to the financing of:

– projects, or
– stages of a project which are technically and financially independent, or
– groups of projects linked to a visible strategy which form a coherent whole.

Article 2
Scope

1. The Fund shall provide financial contributions to projects, which contribute to achieving the objectives laid down in the Treaty on European Union, in the fields of the environment and trans-European transport infrastructure networks in Member States with a per capita gross national product (GNP), measured in purchasing power parities, of less than 90% of the Community average which have a programme leading to the fulfilment of the conditions of economic convergence referred to in Article 104c of the Treaty.

2. Until the end of 1999, only the four Member States which currently meet the criterion regarding per capita GNP referred to in paragraph 1 shall be eligible

---

[1] OJ No L 79, 1. 4. 1993, p. 74.

for assistance from the Fund. Those Member States are Greece, Spain, Ireland and Portugal.

3. With regard to the GNP criterion referred to in paragraph 1, the Member States referred to in paragraph 2 shall continue to be eligible for assistance from the Fund provided that, after a mid-term review in 1996, their GNP remains below 90% of the Community average. Any eligible Member State whose GNP exceeds the 90% threshold at that time shall lose its entitlement to assistance from the Fund for new projects or, in the case of important projects split into several technically and financially separate stages, for new stages of a project.

4. To be eligible under the Fund from 1 January 2000, the beneficiary Member States must have introduced a programme as provided for in Articles 3 and 7 of Council Regulation (EC) No 1466/97.[1]

The four Member States meeting the GNP criterion referred to in paragraph 1 are Spain, Greece, Portugal and Ireland.

A mid-term review as provided for in paragraph 3 shall be carried out before the end of 2003 based on per capita GNP as shown by Community data for the period 2000 to 2002.

5. From the date of accession until 31 December 2006 the Czech Republic, Estonia, Cyprus, Latvia, Lithuania, Hungary, Malta, Poland, Slovenia and Slovakia shall also be eligible for assistance from the Fund.

6. For the purposes of applying this Regulation, GNP shall mean GNI for the year at market prices as provided by the Commission in application of the ESA 95 in accordance with Regulation (EC) No 2223/96.

Article 3

Eligible measures

1. The Fund may provide assistance for the following:

− environmental projects contributing to the achievement of the objectives of Article 130r of the Treaty, including projects resulting from measures adopted pursuant to Article 130s of the Treaty and, in particular, projects in line with the priorities conferred on Community environmental policy by the Programme of Policy and Action in relation to the Environment and Sustainable Development,
− transport infrastructure projects of common interest, supported by Member States, which are identified within the framework of the guidelines adopted by Decision No 1692/96/EC of the European Parliament and the Council of 23 July 1996 on the development of the trans-European transport network.[2]

2. Assistance may also be granted for:

---

[1] OJ L 209, 2.8.1997, p. 2.   [2] OJ L 228, 9.9.1996, p. 1.

– preliminary studies related to eligible projects, including those necessary for their implementation, technical support measures, including publicity and information campaigns, particularly:

(a)   horizontal measures such as comparative studies to assess the impact of Community assistance;

(b)   measures and studies which contribute to the appraisal, monitoring, supervision or evaluation, of projects, and to strengthening and ensuring the coordination and consistency of projects, particularly their consistency with other Community policies;

(c)   measures and studies helping to make the necessary adjustments to the implementation of projects.

Article 4
Financial resources

For the period 1993 to 1999, the total resources available for commitment for the Fund under this Regulation and Regulation (EEC) No 792/93, as set out in the Interinstitutional Agreement of 29 October 1993, shall be ECU 15 150 million at 1992 prices.

The financial perspectives established with regard to the commitment appropriations available for each year of the period under the Regulations referred to in the first paragraph are as follows:

– 1993: ECU 1 500 million,
– 1994: ECU 1 750 million,
– 1995: ECU 2 000 million,
– 1996: ECU 2 250 million,
– 1997: ECU 2 500 million,
– 1998: ECU 2 550 million,
– 1999: ECU 2 600 million.

From 1 January 2000, total resources available for commitments for Greece, Spain, Portugal and Ireland in the period 2000 to 2006 should be EUR 18 billion at 1999 prices.

Commitment appropriations for each year of that period should be:

– 2000: EUR 2,615 billion,
– 2001: EUR 2,615 billion,
– 2002: EUR 2,615 billion,
– 2003: EUR 2,615 billion,
– 2004: EUR 2,515 billion,
– 2005: EUR 2,515 billion,
– 2006: EUR 2,510 billion.

Total resources available for commitments for the Czech Republic, Estonia, Cyprus, Latvia, Lithuania, Hungary, Malta, Poland, Slovenia and Slovakia in the period from the date of accession to 2006 should be EUR 7,5905 billion at 1999 prices.

Commitment appropriations for each year of that period should be:

– 2004: EUR 2,6168 billion
– 2005: EUR 2,1517 billion
– 2006: EUR 2,8220 billion

In the event of a Member State becoming ineligible, resources for the Cohesion Fund will be reduced accordingly.

Article 5
Indicative allocation

An indicative allocation of the total resources of the Fund shall be made on the basis of precise and objective criteria, principally population, per capita GNP taking account of the improvement in national prosperity attained over the previous period, and surface area; it shall also take account of other socioeconomic factors such as deficiencies in transport infrastructure.

The indicative allocation of the total resources resulting from the application of those criteria is set out in Annex I.

Total annual receipts from the Cohesion Fund under this Regulation, in combination with assistance provided under the Structural Funds, should not exceed 4% of national GDP.

Article 6
Conditional assistance

1. No new projects or, in the event of important projects, no new project stages shall be financed by the Fund in a Member State in the event of the Council, acting by a qualified majority on a recommendation from the Commission, finding that the Member State in the application of this Regulation has not implemented the programme referred to in Article 2(4) in such a way as to avoid an excessive government deficit.

The suspension of financing shall cease when the Council, acting under the same conditions, finds that the Member State concerned has taken measures to implement that programme in such a way as to avoid an excessive government deficit.

2. Exceptionally, in the case of projects directly effecting more than one Member State, the Council acting by a qualified majority on a recommendation from the Commission may decide to defer suspension of financing.

Article 7
Rate of assistance

1. The rate of Community assistance granted by the Fund shall be 80% to 85% of public or equivalent expenditure, including expenditure by bodies whose activities

are undertaken within an administrative or legal framework by virtue of which they may be deemed to be equivalent to public bodies.

However, from 1 January 2000 this rate may be reduced to take account, in cooperation with the Member State concerned, of the estimated revenue generated by projects and of any application of the polluter-pays principle.

To achieve this, the Commission shall support beneficiary Member States' efforts to maximise the leverage of Fund resources by encouraging greater use of private sources of funding.

2. Where assistance is granted for a project which generates revenue, the amount of the assistance from the Fund shall be established by the Commission, taking account of revenue where it constitutes substantial net revenue for the promoters and in close collaboration with the beneficiary Member State.

'Project which generates revenue' means:

– infrastructures the use of which involves fees borne directly by users,
– productive investments in the environment sector.

3. The beneficiary Member States may submit proposals for preparatory studies and technical support measures.

4. Preliminary studies and technical support measures, including those undertaken at the Commission's initiative, may be financed exceptionally at 100% of the total cost.

Total expenditure carried out pursuant to this paragraph may not exceed 0,5% of the total allocation to the Fund.

Article 8
Coordination and compatibility with Community policies

1. Projects financed by the Fund shall be in keeping with the provisions of the Treaties, with the instruments adopted pursuant thereto and with Community policies, including those concerning environmental protection, transport, trans-European networks, competition and the award of public contracts.

2. The Commission shall ensure coordination and consistency between projects undertaken pursuant to this Regulation and measures undertaken with contributions from the Community budget, the European Investment Bank (EIB) and the other financial instruments of the Community.

Article 9
Cumulation and overlapping

1. No item of expenditure may benefit both from the Fund and from the European Agricultural Guidance and Guarantee Fund, the European Social Fund, the European Regional Development Fund or the financial instrument of fisheries guidance.

2. The combined assistance of the Fund and other Community aid for a project shall not exceed 90% of the total expenditure relating to that project.

Article 10

Approval of projects

1. The projects to be financed by the Fund shall be adopted by the Commission in agreement with the beneficiary Member State.

2. A suitable balance shall be struck between projects in the field of the environment and projects relating to transport infrastructure. This balance shall take account of Article 130s(5) of the Treaty.

3. Applications for assistance for projects under Article 3(1) shall be submitted by the beneficiary Member State. Projects, including groups of related projects, shall be of a sufficient scale to have a significant impact in the field of environmental protection or in the improvement of trans-European transport infrastructure networks. In any event, the total cost of projects or groups of projects may in principle not be less than EUR 10 million. Projects or groups of projects costing less than this may be approved in duly justified cases.

4. Applications shall contain the following information: the body responsible for implementation, the nature of the investment and a description thereof, its costs and location, including, where applicable, an indication of projects of common interest situated on the same transport axis, the timetable for implementation of the work, a cost-benefit analysis, including the direct and indirect effects on employment, information enabling impact on the environment to be assessed, information on public contracts, the financing plan including, where possible, information on the economic viability of the project, and the total financing the Member State is seeking from the Fund and any other Community source.

They shall also contain all relevant information providing the required proof that the projects comply with the Regulation and with the criteria set out in paragraph 5, and particularly that there are medium-term economic and social benefits commensurate with the resources deployed.

5. The following criteria shall be applied to ensure the high quality of projects:

- their medium-term economic and social benefits, which shall be commensurate with the resources deployed; an assessment shall be made in the light of a cost-benefit analysis,
- the priorities established by the beneficiary Member States,
- the contribution which projects can make to the implementation of Community policies on the environment including the polluter-pays principle and trans-European networks,
- the compatibility of projects with Community policies and their consistency with other Community structural measures,
- the establishment of an appropriate balance between the fields of the environment and transport infrastructure.

6. Subject to Article 6 and to the availability of commitment appropriations, the Commission shall decide on the grant of assistance from the Fund provided that the

requirements of this Article are fulfilled, as a general rule within three months of receipt of the application.

Commission decisions approving projects, stages of projects or groups of related projects shall determine the amount of financial support and lay down a financing plan together with all the provisions and conditions necessary for the implementation of the projects.

7. The key details of the Commission's decisions shall be published in the *Official Journal of the European Communities*.

Article 11
Financial provisions

1. The commitment appropriations entered in the budget shall be granted on the basis of the decisions approving the measures concerned, in accordance with Article 10.

2. Assistance relating to the projects referred to in Article 3(1) shall as a general rule be committed by annual instalments. However, in appropriate cases, the Commission may commit the total amount of the assistance granted when it adopts the decision granting the assistance.

3. Expenditure within the meaning of Article 7(1) shall not be deemed eligible for assistance from the Fund if incurred by the beneficiary Member State before the date on which the Commission receives the relevant application.

For the Czech Republic, Estonia, Cyprus, Latvia, Lithuania, Hungary, Malta, Poland, Slovenia and Slovakia, expenditure within the meaning of Article 7(1) shall be deemed eligible for assistance from the Fund only if incurred after 1 January 2004 and provided that all requirements of this Regulation have been fulfilled.

4. Payments made after an initial advance must be closely and transparently linked to progress made in the implementation of the projects.

5. Payments shall be made in euro and shall be subject to the specific provisions set out in Annex II.

Article 12
Financial checks

1. Without prejudice to the Commission's responsibility for implementing the Community budget, Member States shall take responsibility in the first instance for the financial control of projects.

To that end, the measures they take shall include:

(a) verifying that management and control arrangements have been set up and are being implemented in such a way as to ensure that Community funds are being used efficiently and correctly;

(b) providing the Commission with a description of these arrangments;

(c) ensuring that projects are managed in accordance with all the applicable Community rules and that the funds placed at their disposal are used in accordance with the principles of sound financial management;

(d) certifying that the declarations of expenditure presented to the Commission are accurate and guaranteeing that they result from accounting systems based on verifiable supporting documents;

(e) preventing and detecting irregularities, notifying these to the Commission, in accordance with the rules, and keeping the Commission informed of the progress of administrative and legal proceedings. In that context, the Member States and the Commission shall take the necessary steps to ensure that the information exchanged remains confidential;

(f) presenting to the Commission, when each project, step of project or group of projects is wound up, a declaration drawn up by a person or department having a function independent of the designated authority. This declaration shall summarise the conclusions of the checks carried out during previous years and shall assess the validity of the application for payment of the final balance and the legality and regularity of the expenditure covered by the final certificate. The Member States may attach their own opinion to this declaration if they consider it necessary;

(g) cooperating with the Commission to ensure that Community funds are used in accordance with the principles of sound financial management;

(h) recovering any amounts lost as a result of an irregularity detected and, where appropriate, charging interest on late payments.

2. The Commission in its responsibility for the implementation of the Community budget shall ensure that Member States have smoothly functioning management and control systems so that Community funds are efficiently and correctly used.

To that end, without prejudice to checks carried out by the Member States in accordance with national laws, regulations and administrative provisions, Commission officials or servants may, in accordance with arrangements agreed with the Member State in the framework of cooperation described in Article G(1) of Annex II, carry out on-the-spot checks, including sample checks, on the projects financed by the Fund and on management and control systems with a minimum of one working day's notice. The Commission shall give notice to the Member State concerned with a view to obtaining all the assistance necessary.

Officials or servants of the Member State concerned may take part in such checks.

The Commission may require the Member State concerned to carry out an on-the-spot check to verify the correctness of one or more transactions.

Commission officials or servants may take part in such checks.

Before carrying out an on-the-spot check, the Commission shall give notice to the Member State concerned with a view to obtaining all the assistance necessary.

On-the-spot checks by the Commission without notice shall be subject to agreements reached in accordance with the Financial Regulation. Officials or agents of the Member State concerned may take part in checks.

The Commission may require the Member State concerned to carry out an on-the-spot check to verify the correctness of payment applications.

Officials or agents of the Commission may take part in such checks, and must do so if the Member State concerned so requests.

The Commission shall ensure that any checks that it carries out are performed in a coordinated manner so as to avoid repeating checks in respect of the same subject matter during the same period. The Member State concerned and the Commission shall immediately exchange any relevant information concerning the results of the checks carried out.

3. Member States shall make available to the Commission any appropriate national control reports on the projects concerned.

4. As soon as this Regulation enters into force, the Commission shall adopt detailed rules for the application of this Article and shall inform the European Parliament thereof.

Article 13
Appraisal, monitoring and evaluation

1. The Member States and the Commission shall ensure that the implementation of projects under this Regulation is effectively monitored and evaluated. Projects must be adjusted on the basis of the results of monitoring and evaluation.

2. In order to ensure the effectiveness of Community assistance, the Commission and the beneficiary Member States shall, in cooperation with the EIB where appropriate, carry out a systematic appraisal and evaluation of projects.

3. On receipt of a request for assistance and before approving a project, the Commission shall carry out a thorough appraisal in order to assess the project's consistency with the criteria laid down in Article 10(5). The Commission shall invite the EIB to contribute to the assessment of projects as necessary.

4. During the implementation of projects and after their completion, the Commission and the beneficiary Member States shall evaluate the manner in which they have been carried out and the potential and actual impact of their implementation in order to assess whether the original objectives can be, or have been, achieved. This evaluation shall, *inter alia,* address the environmental impact of the projects, in compliance with the existing Community rules.

5. In vetting individual applications for assistance, the Commission shall take into account the findings of appraisals and evaluations made in accordance with this Article.

6. The detailed rules for monitoring and evaluation, as provided for in paragraph 4, shall be laid down in the decisions approving projects.

Article 14
Information and publicity

1. The Commission shall present an annual report on the activities of the Fund, for the purposes of examination and their opinion, to the European Parliament, the Council, the Economic and Social Committee and the Committee of the Regions.

The European Parliament shall deliver an opinion on the report as soon as possible. The Commission shall report on how it has applied the observations contained in the European Parliament's opinion.

The Commission shall ensure that Member States are informed of the activities of the Fund.

2. The Member States responsible for implementing a measure receiving a financial contribution from the Fund shall ensure that adequate publicity is given to the measure with a view to:

– making the general public aware of the role played by the Community in relation to the measure,
– making potential beneficiaries and professional organizations aware of the possibilities afforded by the measure.

Member States shall ensure, in particular, that directly visible display panels are erected showing the percentage of the total cost of a given project which is being financed by the Community, together with the Community logo, and that representatives of the Community institutions are duly involved in the most important public activities connected with the Fund.

They shall inform the Commission of the initiatives taken under this paragraph.

3. As soon as this Regulation enters into force, the Commission shall adopt detailed rules on information and publicity, shall inform the European Parliament thereof and shall publish them in the *Official Journal of the European Communities.*

Article 15
Implementation

The provisions for the implementation of this Regulation are set out in Annex II hereto.

Article 16
Final and transitional provisions

1. The Council, acting on a proposal from the Commission in accordance with the procedure laid down in Article 130d of the Treaty, shall re-examine this Regulation by 31 December 2006 at the latest.

2. As soon as it enters into force, this Regulation shall replace Regulation (EEC) No 792/93.

3. This Regulation shall not affect the continuation of measures approved by the Commission on the basis of the provisions of Regulation (EEC) No 792/93 applicable before the entry into force of this Regulation, which shall consequently apply thereafter to those measures.

4. Applications presented within the framework of Regulation (EEC) No 792/93 before the entry into force of this Regulation shall remain valid provided such applications are supplemented, where necessary, so as to comply with the requirements of this Regulation within not more than two months of the entry into force of this Regulation.

Article 16a
Specific provisions following the accession to the European Union of a new Member State which has benefited from pre-accession aid under the Instrument for Structural Policies for Pre-Accession (ISPA)

1. Measures which, on the date of accession of the Czech Republic, Estonia, Latvia, Lithuania, Hungary, Poland, Slovenia and Slovakia, have been the subject of Commission decisions on assistance under Regulation (EC) No 1267/99 establishing an instrument for Structural Policies for Pre-accession[1] and the implementation of which has not been completed by that date shall be considered to have been approved by the Commission Regulation. Unless stated otherwise in paragraphs 2 to 5, the provisions governing the implementation of measures approved pursuant to this Regulation shall apply to these measures.

2. Any procurement procedure relating to a measure referred to in paragraph 1 which, on the date of accession, has already been the subject of an invitation to tender published in the Official Journal of the European Union shall be implemented in accordance with the rules laid down in that invitation to tender. The provisions contained in Article 165 of Council Regulation (EC, Euratom) No 1605/2002 on the Financial Regulation applicable to the general budget of the European Communities[2] shall not apply.

Any procurement procedure relating to a measure referred to in paragraph 1 which has not yet been the subject of an invitation to tender published in the Official Journal of the European Union shall follow the rules and provisions referred to in Article 8.

3. The Commission may decide, in duly justified cases, on request from the Member State concerned and only in respect of the annual instalments still to be committed under the general budget, to modify the Community assistance to be granted, taking account of the criteria laid down in Article 7. The modification of the Community assistance shall not affect the part of the measure already covered by a loan signed

---

[1] OJ L 161, 26.6.1999, p. 73 as amended.   [2] OJ L 248, 16.9.2002, p. 1.

with the EIB, the European Bank for Reconstruction and Development or another international financial institution.

Payments made by the Commission under a measure referred to in paragraph 1 shall be posted to the earliest open commitment made in first instance pursuant to Regulation (EC) No 1267/1999, and then pursuant to this Regulation.

4. For the measures referred to in paragraph 1, the rules governing the eligibility of expenditure pursuant to Regulation (EC) No 1267/1999 shall remain applicable, except in duly justified cases to be decided on by the Commission at the request of the Member State concerned.

5. The Commission may decide, in exceptional and duly justified cases, to authorise specific exemptions from the rules applicable pursuant to this Regulation for the measures referred to in paragraph 1.

Article 17
Entry into force

This Regulation shall enter into force on the day following its publication in the *Official Journal of the European Communities.*

This Regulation shall be binding in its entirety and directly applicable in all Member States.

Annex I

Indicative allocation among the beneficiary Member States of the total resources of the Cohesion Fund, as referred to in the third paragraph of Article 4:

– Greece: 16% to 18% of the total
– Spain: 61% to 63,5% of the total
– Ireland: 2% to 6% of the total
– Portugal: 16% to 18% of the total.

Indicative allocation among the beneficiary Member States of the total resources of the Cohesion Fund, as referred to in the fifth paragraph of Article 4:

– Czech Republic: 9,76% to 12,28% of the total
– Estonia: 2,88% to 4,39% of the total
– Cyprus: 0,43% to 0,84% of the total
– Latvia: 5,07% to 7,08% of the total
– Lithuania: 6,15% to 8,17% of the total
– Hungary: 11,58% to 14,61% of the total
– Malta: 0,16% to 0,36% of the total
– Poland: 45,65% to 52,72% of the total
– Slovenia: 1,72% to 2,73% of the total
– Slovakia: 5,71% to 7,72% of the total.

Annex II
Implementing provisions

Article A
Designation of projects, of stages or groups of projects

1. The Commission may, in agreement with the beneficiary Member State, group projects together and designate technically and financially separate stages of a project for the purpose of granting assistance.

2. For the purpose of this Regulation, the following definitions shall apply:

(a) a 'project' shall be an economically indivisible series of works fulfilling a precise technical function and with clearly identified aims from which to judge whether the project complies with the criterion laid down in the first indent of Article 10(5);
(b) a 'technically and financially independent stage' shall be a stage which can be identified as operational in its own right.

3. A stage may also cover preliminary, feasibility and technical studies needed for carrying out a project.

4. To comply with the criterion in the third indent of Article 1(3), projects meeting the following three conditions may be grouped:

(a) they must be located in the same area or situated along the same transport corridor;
(b) they must be carried out under an overall plan for the area or corridor with clearly identified goals, as provided for in Article 1(3);
(c) they must be supervised by a body responsible for coordinating and monitoring the group of projects in cases where the projects are carried out by different competent authorities.

Article B
Ex-ante evaluation

1. The Commission shall examine applications for assistance to verify in particular that the administrative and financial mechanisms are adequate for the effective implementation of the project.

2. Pursuant to Article 13(3), the Commission shall appraise projects to determine their anticipated impact in terms of the objectives of the Fund, quantified using appropriate indicators.

The beneficiary Member States shall provide all necessary information, as set out in Article 10(4), including the results of feasibility studies and *ex ante* appraisals. In order to make this appraisal as effective as possible, Member States shall also provide the results of the environmental impact assessment in conformity with the Community legislation, and their consistency with a general environmental or transport strategy at administrative unit or sector level, and, where appropriate:

– an indication of the possible alternatives that were not chosen, and
– the links between projects of common interest located along the same transport corridor.

Article C
Commitments

1. Budgetary commitments shall be made on the basis of the Commission decisions approving the measures concerned (project, stage of project, group of projects, study or technical support measure). Commitments shall be valid for a period determined by the nature of the measure and the specific conditions for its implementation.

2. Budgetary commitments in respect of assistance granted to projects, stages of projects or groups of projects shall be carried out in one of two ways:

(a) commitments in respect of the projects referred to in Article 3(1) to be carried out over a period of two or more years shall, as a general rule and subject to the provisions of subparagraph (b), be effected in annual instalments. The commitments in respect of the first annual instalment shall be made when the decision granting Community assistance is adopted by the Commission. Commitments in respect of subsequent annual instalments shall be based on the initial or revised financing plan for the project and shall normally be made at the beginning of each budget year and as a general rule by 30 April each year, based on the expenditure forecasts for the project for that current year;

(b) for projects to be carried out over a period of less than two years or where Community assistance is less than EUR 50 million, an initial commitment of 80% of assistance may be made when the Commission adopts the decision to grant Community assistance.

The balance shall be committed according to the implementation of the project.

3. In the case of the studies and technical support measures referred to in Article 3(2), the assistance shall be committed when the Commission approves the measure concerned.

4. The arrangements for commitments shall be specified in the Commission decisions approving the measures concerned.

5. Except in duly justified cases, the assistance granted to a project, group of projects or project stage on which work has not begun within two years from the date of its expected start as indicated in the decision granting assistance or the date of its approval if later, shall be cancelled.

In any case the Commission shall inform in good time the Member States and the designated authority whenever there is a risk of cancellation.

Article D
Payments

1. Payments of financial assistance shall be made in accordance with the corresponding budget commitments, to the authority or body designated for the purpose in the application submitted by the beneficiary Member State concerned. Payments may take the form of payments on account, interim payments or payments of the

final balance. Interim payments and payments of the balance shall relate to expenditure actually paid out, which must be supported by receipted invoices or accounting documents of equivalent probative value.

2. Payments shall be made as follows:

(a) a single payment on account of 20% of the Fund assistance as initially decided shall be paid when the decision granting Community assistance is adopted and, except where duly justified, after signature of the contracts relating to public procurement.

All or part of a payment on account shall be repaid by the designated authority or body referred to in paragraph 1 if no payment application is sent to the Commission within 12 months from the date on which the payment on account is paid;

(b) interim payments may be paid provided that the project is progressing satisfactorily towards completion and shall be made to refund the expenditure certified and actually paid, subject to the following conditions:

– the Member State has submitted an application describing the progress of the project in terms of its physical and financial indicators and its conformity with the decision to grant asssistance, including where appropriate any specific conditions attached to the assistance,

– the observations and recommendations of the national and/or Community inspection authorities have been acted on, in particular as regards the correction of any observed or presumed irregularities,

– the main technical, financial and legal problems that have arisen and the measures taken to correct them have been indicated,

– any departures from the original financing plan have been analysed,

– the steps taken to publicise the project have been described.

The Member States shall be informed without delay by the Commission if one of the abovementioned conditions is not fulfilled;

(c) the total amount of the payments made under (a) and (b) may not exceed 80% of the total assistance granted. This percentage may be increased to 90% for important projects committed in annual instalments and in justified cases;

(d) the final balance of Community assistance calculated on the basis of expenditure certified and actually paid shall be paid provided that:

– the project, stage of project, or group of projects has been carried out according to its objectives,

– the designated authority or body referred to in paragraph 1 submits an application for payment to the Commission within six months of the deadline for completion of the work and for expenditure laid down in the decision granting assistance to the project, stage of project or group of projects,

– the final report referred to in Article F(4) is submitted to the Commission,

– the Member State certifies to the Commission that the information given in the application for payment and in the report is correct,

- the Member State has sent the Commission the declaration referred to in Article 12(1),
- all the information and publicity measures drawn up by the Commission under Article 14(3) have been implemented.

3. If the final report referred to in paragraph 2 is not sent to the Commission within 18 months of the final date for completion of the works and payments as given in the decision granting assistance, that part of the assistance representing the remaining balance for the project shall be cancelled.

4. Member States shall designate the authorities empowered to issue the certificates referred to in paragraph 2(d).

4a. Member States shall ensure that applications for payment are submitted to the Commission as a general rule three times a year, by 1 March, 1 July and 1 November at the latest.

5. Payment shall be made to the authority or body designated by the Member State, as a general rule not later than two months after receipt of an admissible application for payment provided budget funds are available.

6. In the case of the studies and other measures referred to in Article 3(2), the Commission shall determine the appropriate payment procedures.

7. The Commission shall lay down common rules on the eligibility of expenditure.

Article E
Use of the euro

1. Applications for assistance, together with the relevant financing plan, shall be submitted to the Commission in euro.

2. The amounts of assistance and the financing plans approved by the Commission shall be expressed in euro.

3. Declarations of expenditure in support of the corresponding payment applications shall be expressed in euro.

4. Payments of financial assistance by the Commission shall be made in euro to the authority designated by the Member State to receive such payments.

5. For Member States not participating in the euro, the conversion rate shall be the Commission's financial accounting rate.

Article F
Monitoring

1. The Commission and the Member State shall ensure effective monitoring of implementation of Community projects part-financed by the Fund. Monitoring shall be carried out by way of jointly agreed reporting procedures, sample checks and the establishment of *ad hoc* committees.

2. Monitoring shall be carried out by reference to physical and financial indicators.

The indicators shall relate to the specific character of the project and its objectives. They shall be arranged in such a way as to show:

— the stage reached in the receipt in relation to the plan and objectives originally laid down;
— the progress achieved on the management side and any related problems.

3. Monitoring committees shall be set up by arrangement between the Member State concerned and the Commission.

The authorities or bodies designated by the Member State, the Commission and, where appropriate, the EIB shall be represented on the committees.

Where regional and local authorities are competent for the execution of a project and, where appropriate, where they are directly concerned by a project they shall also be represented on such committees.

4. For each project, the authority or body designated for the purpose by the Member State shall submit progress reports to the Commission within three months of the end of each full year of implementation. A final report shall be submitted to the Commission within six months of completion of the project or stage of project.

This report shall include:

(a) a description of the work carried out, accompanied by the physical indicators, the expenditure by category of work and any measures taken under specific clauses in the decision granting assistance;
(b) information on all publicity measures;
(c) certification that the work conforms to the decision granting assistance;
(d) an initial assessment as to whether the anticipated results as indicated in Article 13(4) are likely to be achieved, including in particular:
 — the actual starting date of the project,
 — the way in which it will be managed once finished,
 — confirmation, if appropriate, of the financial forecasts, especially as regards the operating costs and expected revenue,
 — confirmation of the socioeconomic forecasts, in particular the expected costs and benefits,
 — an indication of the environmental protection measures taken, and their cost, including compliance with the polluter-pays principle.

5. On the basis of the results of monitoring, and taking account of the comments of the monitoring committee, the Commission shall adjust the amounts and conditions for granting assistance as initially approved, as well as the financing plan envisaged, if necessary on a proposal by the Member States.

The decision granting assistance shall include appropriate arrangements for making the modifications, differentiating between them on the basis of their nature and importance.

6. For the greater effectiveness of the Fund, the Commission shall ensure that when the Fund is administered particular attention is paid to transparency of management.

7. The monitoring arrangements shall be laid down in the Commission decisions approving the projects.

Article G
Checks

1. The Commission and the Member State shall on the basis of bilateral administrative arrangements cooperate to coordinate plans, methods and implementation of checks so as to maximise the usefulness of those carried out. They shall immediately exchange the results of the checks carried out. At least once a year the following shall be examined and evaluated:

(a) the results of the checks carried out by the Member State and the Commission;
(b) any comments made by other national or Community control bodies or institutions;
(c) the financial impact of the irregularities noted, the steps already taken or still required to correct them and, where necessary, adjustments to the management and control systems.

Following this examination and evaluation and without prejudice to the measures to be taken immediately by the Member State under Article H, the Commission may make observations, particularly regarding the financial impact of any irregularities detected. These observations shall be addressed to the Member State and the designated authority of the project concerned. The observations shall be accompanied, where necessary, by requests for corrective measures to remedy the management shortcomings found and correct those irregularities detected which have not already been corrected. The Member State shall have the opportunity to comment on these observations.

Where following or in the absence of comments of the Member State the Commission adopts conclusions, the Member State shall take the necessary steps within the deadline set to comply with the Commission's request and inform the Commission of its actions.

2. Without prejudice to this Article, the Commission may suspend all or part of an interim payment if it finds that the expenditure concerned is linked to a serious irregularity. The Commission shall inform the Member State concerned of the action taken and the reasons for it.

3. For a period of three years, unless otherwise decided in the bilateral administrative arrangements, following the payment by the Commission of the final balance in respect of a project, the responsible body and authorities shall keep available for the Commission all the supporting documents (either the originals or versions certified to be in conformity with the originals on commonly accepted data carriers) regarding expenditure and checks on the project concerned.

This period shall be interrupted either in the case of legal proceedings or at the duly substantiated request of the Commission.

Article H
Financial corrections

1. If, after completing the necessary verifications, the Commission concludes that:

(a) the implementation of a project does not justify either part or the whole of the assistance granted to it, including a failure to comply with one of the conditions in the decision to grant assistance and in particular any significant change affecting the nature or conditions of implementation of the project for which the Commission's approval has not been sought, or
(b) (b) there is an irregularity with regard to assistance from the Fund and that the Member State concerned has not taken the necessary corrective measures, the Commission shall suspend the assistance in respect of the project concerned and stating its reason, request that the Member State submits its comments within a specified period of time.

If the Member State objects to the observations made by the Commission, the Member State shall be invited to a hearing by the Commission, in which both sides make efforts to reach an agreement about the observations and the conclusions to be drawn from them.

2. At the end of the period set by the Commission, the Commission shall, subject to the respect of due procedure, if no agreement has been reached within three months, taking into account any comments made by the Member State, decide to:

(a) reduce the payment on account referred to in Article D(2), or
(b) make the financial corrections required. This shall mean cancelling all or part of the assistance granted to the project.

These decisions shall respect the principle of proportionality. The Commission shall, when deciding the amount of a correction, take account of the type of irregularity or change and the extent of the potential financial impact of any shortcomings in the management or control systems. Any reduction or cancellation shall give rise to recovery of the sums paid.

3. Any sum received unduly and to be recovered shall be paid to the Commission. Interest on account of late repayment shall be charged in accordance with the rules to be adopted by the Commission.

4. The Commission shall lay down the detailed rules for implementing paragraphs 1 to 3 and shall inform the Member States and the European Parliament thereof.

Article I
Public contracts

In the context of the application of Community rules on the award of public contracts, notices sent for publication in the *Official Journal of the European Communities* shall specify those projects for which Community assistance has been applied for or granted.

Article J
Information

The information to be given in the annual report provided for in Article 14 shall be as set out in the Annex to this Annex.

The Commission shall be responsible for organizing an information meeting with the Member States every six months. At this meeting the Commission shall inform the Member States in particular of the relevant subjects for the annual report and its actions and decisions taken. The Commission shall send the Member States the appropriate documents in good time before the meeting is held.

Article K
Review

If necessary, in the light of experience gained, the Council may, acting by a qualified majority on a proposal from the Commission and after consulting the European Parliament, amend the provisions of this Annex.

Annex to Annex II

The annual report shall provide information on the following:
1. financial assistance committed and paid by the Fund, with an annual breakdown by Member State and by type of project (environment or transport);
2. the economic and social impact of the Fund in the Member States and on economic and social cohesion in the Union, including the impact on employment;
3. summary of information on the programmes implemented in the beneficiary Member States to fulfil the conditions of economic convergence referred to in Article 104c of the Treaty and on the application of Article 6 of the Regulation;
4. information on the conclusions drawn by the Commission, with regard to the suspension of financing, from decisions taken by the Commission, such as those mentioned in Article 6;
5. the contribution which the Fund has made to the efforts of the beneficiary Member States to implement Community environment policy and to strengthen trans-European transport infrastructure networks; the balance between projects in the field of the environment and projects relating to transport infrastructure;
6. assessment of the compatibility of operations of the Fund with Community policies, including those concerning environmental protection, transport, competition and the award of public contracts;

7. the measures taken to ensure coordination and consistency between projects financed by the Fund and measures financed with contributions from the Community budget, the European Investment Bank and the other financial instruments of the Community;

8. the investment efforts of the beneficiary Member States in the fields of environmental protection and transport infrastructure;

9. the preparatory studies and technical support measures financed, including a specification of the types of such studies and measures;

10. the results of appraisal, monitoring and evaluation of projects, including information on any adjustment of projects to accord with the results of appraisal, monitoring and evaluation;

11. the contribution of the EIB to the evaluation of projects;

12. summary of information on the results of checks carried out, irregularities found and administrative and judicial proceedings in progress.

Regulation (EC) No 1655/2000 of the European Parliament and of the Council of 17 July 2000 concerning the Financial Instrument for the Environment (LIFE)

Editorial note

Council Regulation 1655/2000 establishing the Financial Instrument for the Environment (LIFE) repealed Regulation EEC/1973/92 of 21 May 1992 which established LIFE and was the product of efforts to unify the several existing financial instruments in the Community. The general objective of LIFE is to contribute to the implementation, updating and development of Community environmental policy and legislation (Article 1). LIFE consists of three thematic components: LIFE-nature, LIFE-environment and LIFE-third countries (Article 2(1)). Projects financed by LIFE shall be of Community interest; be carried out by technically and financially sound participants; be feasible in terms of technical proposals, timetable, budget and value for money (Article 2(2)). Article 3 sets out the specific objective of LIFE-nature; Article 4 sets out the specific objective for LIFE-environment and Article 5 sets out the specific objective for LIFE-third countries. LIFE is open to the participation of accession candidates and east European countries in accordance with their Association Agreements (Article 6). Technical and financial reports for projects funded by LIFE are to be sent to the Commission by the beneficiary for the monitoring of the compliance of the project with the provisions of this Regulation (Article 9). The Commission may reduce, suspend or recover the amount of financial assistance granted in case of irregularities (Article 10).

LIFE is implemented in phases. The first phase, which ran from 23 July 1992 to 31 December 1995, was granted EUR 400 million. The second phase, which ran from 1 January 1996 to 31 December 1999, was granted approximately EUR 450 million. The third phase started on 1 January 2000 and its anticipated deadline was 31 December 2004 (Article 8). Taking account of the Commission report on the Mid-term Review of Regulation (EC) No 1655/2000 LIFE, Regulation (EC) No 1682/2004 (reproduced below) extended this phase until 31 December 2006 and modified other provisions of the original Regulation. The Regulation was further amended by Regulation (EC) No 788/2004 of the European Parliament and of the Council of 21 April 2004 amending Council Regulation (EC) No 2236/95 and Regulations (EC) No 1655/2000, (EC) No 1382/2003 and (EC) No 2152/2003 with a view to adapting the reference amounts to take account of the enlargement of the European Union (not reproduced).

Source: OJ L 192 28.07.2000 p. 1

Regulation (EC) No 1655/2000 of the European Parliament and of the Council of 17 July 2000 concerning the Financial Instrument for the Environment (LIFE)

The European Parliament and the Council of the European Union,
Having regard to the Treaty establishing the European Community and in particular Article 175(1) thereof,
Having regard to the proposal from the Commission,[1]
Having regard to the opinion of the Economic and Social Committee,[2]
Having regard to the opinion of the Committee of the Regions,[3]
Acting in accordance with the procedure laid down in Article 251 of the Treaty, in the light of the joint text approved by the Conciliation Committee on 23 May 2000,[4]
Whereas:

(1) Council Regulation (EEC) No 1973/92 of 21 May 1992 establishing a Financial Instrument for the Environment (LIFE)[5] was adopted to contribute to the implementation and development of Community environment policy and of environmental legislation.

(2) Council Regulation (EEC) No 1973/92 was substantially amended by Regulation (EC) No 1404/96;[6] with a view to further contributing to the implementation, updating and development of Community environment policy and of environmental legislation, in particular as regards the integration of the environment into other policies, and to sustainable development in the Community, amendments are to be made to Council Regulation (EEC) No 1973/72, which should, for reasons of clarity, be recast and replaced by this Regulation.

(3) The Financial Instrument for the Environment, LIFE, is being implemented in phases; the second phase ended on 31 December 1999.

(4) Given the positive contribution of LIFE to the attainment of the objectives of Community policy on the environment and in accordance with Article 14 of

---

[1] OJ C 15, 20.1.1999, p. 4.   [2] OJ C 209, 22.7.1999, p. 14.   [3] OJ C 374, 23.12.1999, p. 45.
[4] Opinion of the European Parliament of 14 April 1999 (OJ C 219,30.7.1999, p. 265), confirmed on 6 May 1999 (OJ C 279, 01.10.1999, p. 275), Council Common Position of 22 October 1999 (OJ C 346, 02.12.1999, p. 1), Decision of the European Parliament of 16 February 2000 (not yet published in the Official Journal), Decision of the Council of 29 June 2000 and Decision of the European Parliament of 5 July 2000.
[5] OJ L 206, 22.7.1992, p. 1.   [6] OJ L 181, 20.7.1996, p. 1.

Regulation (EEC) No 1973/92, a third phase for a period of five years ending on 31 December 2004 should be set in motion.

(5) LIFE should be reinforced as a specific financial instrument, complementary with other Community instruments, without however limiting LIFE interventions to areas not covered by other Community financial instruments.

(6) The efficiency and transparency of the various procedures for LIFE should be improved by identifying clearly the three component parts which constitute the instrument.

(7) It is necessary to ensure effective monitoring and evaluation of the actions undertaken under LIFE.

(8) The experience gained with LIFE during the second phase has highlighted the need to concentrate efforts by specifying more clearly the areas of activity able to benefit from Community financial aid, simplifying the management burden and improving the measures to disseminate information concerning the experience gained, the results achieved and their long-term impact, with a view to promoting the transfer of these results.

(9) The development of Community environmental policy must take account of the results achieved and the experience gained from the individual actions implemented under LIFE.

(10) Consideration should be given to migration routes and the role of buffer zones in the context of projects contributing to the implementation of 'Natura 2000'.

(11) Preparatory projects should concern the development of new Community environmental actions and instruments, and/or the updating of environmental legislation and policies.

(12) Decision No 2179/98/EC of the European Parliament and of the Council of 24 September 1998 on the review of the European Community programme of policy and action in relation to the environment and sustainable development, 'Towards sustainability'[1] sets, among the priority objectives of the Community, the development of programmes for the further promotion of environmental awareness on the part of industry, including, in particular, small and medium-sized enterprises (SMEs), and giving priority to the problems of SMEs as regards technical and financial obstacles to the development and use of clean technology in relation to the environment.

(13) The employment implications of proposals considered for financial support under LIFE-environment should be taken into account, where appropriate.

(14) For third countries bordering on the Mediterranean and the Baltic Sea other than the countries of central and eastern Europe which have concluded Association Agreements with the European Community, technical assistance activities are needed to create capacities and administrative structures in the field of the environment.

---

[1] OJ L 275, 10.10.1998, p. 1.

(15) The Europe Agreements between the European Communities and their Member States, of the one part, and the accession candidate central and east European countries, of the other part, provide for the participation of those countries in Community programmes, in particular in the field of the environment.

(16) While the abovementioned central and east European countries should normally themselves meet the costs arising from their participation, the Community may decide, if necessary, for specific cases and in conformity with the rules applicable to the general budget of the European Union and the relevant Association Agreements, to supplement the national contribution of the country concerned.

(17) The other accession candidate countries may, where they make a financial contribution to LIFE, participate under conditions equivalent to those laid down for the accession candidate central and east European countries.

(18) Receipts from third countries constitute resources earmarked for the instrument in question and are entered as such in the corresponding expenditure item.

(19) Selection mechanisms should be established so that Community assistance may be adapted to the particular features of the projects to be supported; guidelines should promote synergy between demonstration actions and the guiding principles of Community environmental policy with a view to sustainable development.

(20) The measures necessary for the implementation of this Regulation should be adopted in accordance with Council Decision 1999/468/EC of 28 June 1999 laying down the procedures for the exercise of implementing powers conferred on the Commission.[1]

(21) This Regulation lays down, for the entire duration of the third phase, a financial framework constituting the prime reference, within the meaning of point 33 of the Interinstitutional Agreement of 6 May 1999 between the European Parliament, the Council and the Commission,[2] for the budgetary authority during the annual budgetary procedure.

(22) The European Parliament and the Council should examine the advisability of continuing the LIFE action beyond the third phase, acting on the basis of a proposal from the Commission,

Have adopted this Regulation:

Article 1
General objective

A Financial Instrument for the Environment, hereinafter referred to as 'LIFE', is hereby established.

---

[1] OJ L 184, 17.7.1999, p. 23.   [2] OJ C 172, 18.6.1999, p. 1.

The general objective of LIFE shall be to contribute to the implementation, updating and development of Community environment policy and of environmental legislation, in particular as regards the integration of the environment into other policies, and to sustainable development in the Community.

Article 2
Thematic components and general criteria

LIFE shall consist of the three thematic components: LIFE-nature, LIFE-environment and LIFE-third countries.

The projects financed by LIFE shall meet the following general criteria:

(a) be of Community interest by making a significant contribution to the general objective laid down in Article 1;
(b) be carried out by technically and financially sound participants;
(c) be feasible in terms of technical proposals, timetable, budget and value for money.

Priority may be given to projects based on a multinational approach when this is likely to have more effective results in terms of achievement of objectives taking into account feasibility and costs.

Article 3
LIFE-nature

1. The specific objective of LIFE-nature shall be to contribute to the implementation of Council Directive 79/409/EEC of 2 April 1979 on the conservation of wild birds,[1] Council Directive 92/43/EEC of 21 May 1992 on the conservation of natural habitats and of wild fauna and flora[2] and, in particular, the Natura 2000 European network established by the latter Directive.

2. The following shall be eligible for LIFE-nature:

(a) nature conservation projects which further the specific objective set out in paragraph 1 and contribute to maintaining or restoring natural habitats and/or species populations to a favourable conservation status within the meaning of Directive 92/43/EEC;
(b) accompanying measures which further the specific objective set out in paragraph 1 and are required:
(i) to prepare projects involving partners in several Member States ('starter' measure);
(ii) to exchange experiences between projects ('co-op' measure);

[1] OJ L 103, 25.04.1979, p. 1. Directive as last amended by Council Directive 97/49/EC, (OJ L 223, 13.08.1997, p. 9).
[2] OJ L 206, 22.07.1992, p. 7. Directive as last amended by Council Directive 97/62/EC, (OJ L 305, 08.11.1997, p. 42).

(iii) to monitor and evaluate projects and disseminate their results, including the results of projects decided upon during the preceding phases of LIFE ('assist' measure).

3. Financial assistance shall be provided by co-financing of projects. The maximum rate shall be:

(a) 50% for nature conservation projects and 100% for accompanying measures;
(b) by way of exception, the rate of 50% provided for in (a) shall be a maximum of 75% for projects concerning priority natural habitats or priority species within the meaning of Directive 92/43/EEC or the species of birds considered as priority for funding under LIFE-nature by the committee set up pursuant to Article 16 of Directive 79/409/EEC.

4. Proposals for projects to be financed pursuant to paragraph 2(a) shall be forwarded to the Commission by the Member States. Where projects involve more than one Member State, proposals shall be forwarded by the Member State in which the project coordinating body is located. The Commission shall fix annually the date of forwarding of proposals and shall decide on the proposals in accordance with paragraph 7.

5. Proposals shall be considered for financial support, in accordance with paragraph 7, only where they comply with the requirements of Article 2 and paragraph 2(a) of this Article, and meet the following criteria:

(a) projects in the European territory of the Member States relating to:
    (i) a site proposed by a Member State under Article 4 of Directive 92/43/EEC, or
   (ii) a site classified pursuant to Article 4 of Directive 79/409/EEC, or
  (iii) a species in Annexes II or IV to Directive 92/43/EEC or in Annex I to Directive 79/409/EEC;
(b) projects in accession candidate countries to which Article 6 applies relating to:
    (i) a site of international importance hosting a type of habitat cited in Annex I or a species cited in Annex II to Directive 92/43/EEC or a type of habitat or species not present in the Community but classified in the relevant Berne Convention resolutions as being in need of specific conservation measures, or
   (ii) a site of international importance hosting a bird species cited in Annex I to Directive 79/409/EEC or a migratory bird species present in the Community or a bird species not present in the Community but classified in the relevant Berne Convention resolutions as being in need of specific conservation measures, or
  (iii) a species cited in Annexes II or IV to Directive 92/43/EEC or in Annex I to Directive 79/409/EEC or a species not present in the Community but classified in Appendix I or II to the Berne Convention.

6. A summary of the proposals received shall be sent to the Member States by the Commission. On request, it shall place the original documents at the disposal of the Member States for consultation.

7. Projects considered for financial support under LIFE-nature shall be subject to the procedure set out in Article 11. For the purposes of this paragraph, the committee shall be that referred to in Article 20 of Directive 92/43/EEC. An outline decision shall be adopted by the Commission and addressed to the Member States on the projects which have been accepted, and individual decisions shall be addressed to the beneficiaries laying down the amount of financial assistance, the financial procedures and controls, and the specific technical conditions of the project approved.

8. At the Commission's initiative:

(a) accompanying measures to be financed pursuant to paragraph 2(b)(i) and (ii) shall, after consultation of the committee mentioned in Article 21 of Directive 92/43/EEC, be the subject of calls for expressions of interest. Member States may submit proposals on accompanying measures to the Commission;

(b) accompanying measures to be financed pursuant to paragraph 2(b)(iii) shall be the subject of calls for expression of interest.

All calls for expression of interest shall be published in the *Official Journal of the European Communities* where the specific criteria to be met will be set out.

Article 4
LIFE-environment

1. The specific objective of LIFE-environment shall be to contribute to the development of innovative and integrated techniques and methods and to the further development of Community environment policy.

2. The following projects and/or measures shall be eligible for LIFE-environment:

(a) demonstration projects which further the objective set out in paragraph 1 and:
   - integrate considerations on the environment and on sustainable development in land-use development and planning, including in urban and coastal areas, or
   - promote the sustainable management of groundwater and surface water, or
   - minimise the environmental impact of economic activities, notably through the development of clean technologies and by placing the emphasis on prevention, including the reduction of emission of gases having a greenhouse effect, or
   - prevent, reuse, recover and recycle waste of all kinds and ensure the sound management of waste streams, or
   - reduce the environmental impact of products through an integrated approach to production, distribution, consumption and handling at the end of their lifetime, including the development of environmentally-friendly products;

(b) projects which are preparatory to the development of new Community environmental actions and instruments, and/or to the updating of environmental legislation and policies;

(c) accompanying measures required:

   (i) to disseminate information on the exchange of experience between projects;

   (ii) to evaluate, monitor, and promote the actions undertaken during this implementation phase of the LIFE instrument and during the first two phases, and disseminate information on the experience gained and on the transfer of results obtained with such actions.

3. Financial assistance shall be provided by co-financing of projects.

The rate of Community financial support shall be a maximum of 30% of the eligible cost of the project for projects generating substantial net revenue. In this case, the beneficiaries' contribution to the financing shall be at least as much as the Community support.

The rate of Community financial support to all other applicants shall be a maximum of 50% of the eligible cost of the project. The rate of Community financial support for the accompanying measures shall be a maximum of 100% of their cost.

4. As far as demonstration projects are concerned, guidelines will be established by the Commission, after being subject to the procedure set out in Article 11, and published in the *Official Journal of the European Communities*. The guidelines shall promote synergy between demonstration actions and the guiding principles of Community environmental policy with a view to sustainable development.

5. Proposals for projects to be financed pursuant to paragraph 2(a) shall be forwarded to the Commission by the Member States. Where projects involve more than one Member State, proposals shall be forwarded by the Member State in which the project coordinating body is located.

The Commission shall fix annually the date of forwarding of proposals and shall decide on the proposals in accordance with paragraph 10.

6. Proposals shall only be considered for financial support, in accordance with paragraph 10, where they comply with the requirements of Article 2 and paragraph (2)(a) of this Article and meet the following criteria:

(a) providing solutions to a problem which arises very often in the Community or is of great concern to some Member States

(b) being innovative by virtue of the technology or the method applied

(c) setting an example and representing progress compared with the current situation

(d) being capable of promoting the dissemination and widest possible application of practices technologies and/or products conducive to environmental protection

(e) aiming at developing and transferring know-how which can be used in identical or similar situations

(f) promoting cooperation in the environmental field

(g) having a potential satisfactory cost-benefit ratio from an environmental point of view
(h) promoting integration of environmental considerations into activities whose main aims are economic and social.

When these proposals are considered, their employment implications should also be taken into account, where appropriate.

7. The following costs shall be considered ineligible:

(a) land purchase
(b) studies not specifically addressing the objective aimed at by the financed projects
(c) investments in major infrastructures or investments of a non-innovative structural nature, including activities already confirmed on an industrial scale
(d) research and technological development activities.

8. At the Commission's initiative:

(a) projects to be financed pursuant to paragraph 2(b) and accompanying measures to be financed pursuant to paragraph 2(c)(i) shall, after consultation of the committee mentioned in Article 11, be the subject of calls for expression of interest. Member States may submit proposals on projects to be financed pursuant to paragraph 2(b) to the Commission;
(b) accompanying measures to be financed pursuant to paragraph 2(c)(ii) shall be the subject of calls for expression of interest.

All calls for expression of interest shall be published in the *Official Journal of the European Communities* where the specific criteria to be met will be set out.

9. A summary of the main points and of the content of the proposals received under paragraph 2(a) and (b) shall be sent to the Member States by the Commission. On request, it shall place the original documents at the disposal of the Member States for consultation.

10. Projects considered for financial support shall be subject to the procedure set out in Article 11.

11. An outline decision shall be adopted by the Commission and addressed to the Member States on the projects which have been accepted and individual decisions shall be addressed to the beneficiaries laying down the amount of financial assistance, the financial procedures and controls, and the specific technical conditions of the project approved.

Article 5
LIFE-third countries

1. The specific objective of LIFE-third countries shall be to contribute to the establishment of capacities and administrative structures needed in the environmental sector and in the development of environmental policy and action programmes in

third countries bordering on the Mediterranean and the Baltic Sea other than the countries of central and eastern Europe which have concluded Association Agreements with the European Community and are referred to in Article 6(1).

2. The following shall be eligible for LIFE-third countries:

(a) technical assistance projects which further the objective set out in paragraph 1;
(b) accompanying measures required for evaluating, monitoring and promoting the actions undertaken during this implementation phase of the LIFE instrument and during the first two phases thereof, for the exchange of experience between projects and for the dissemination of information on the experience gained and on the results obtained with such actions.

3. Financial assistance shall be provided by co-financing of projects and accompanying measures. The rate of Community financial support shall be a maximum of 70% of the cost of the projects referred to in paragraph 2(a) and a maximum of 100% of the cost of the accompanying measures referred to in paragraph 2(b).

4. Proposals for projects to be financed under paragraph 2(a) from third countries shall be submitted to the Commission by the relevant national authorities. Where projects involve more than one country, proposals shall be submitted by the country in which the project coordinating body is located or by the international organisation acting to protect the environment in the geographical area concerned.

The Commission shall fix annually the date of forwarding of proposals and shall decide on the proposals in accordance with paragraph 7.

5. Proposals shall be considered for financial support, in accordance with paragraph 7, only where they comply with the requirements of Article 2 and paragraph (2)(a) of this Article and meet the following criteria:

(a) be of interest to the Community, notably through their contribution to implementing regional and international guidelines and agreements;
(b) contribute to an approach promoting sustainable development at international, national or regional level;
(c) provide solutions to major environmental problems in the region and the relevant sector. Priority will be given to projects which will promote cooperation at the transfrontier, transnational or regional level.

6. A summary of the main points and the content of the proposals received from the third countries shall be sent to the Member States by the Commission. On request, it shall place the original documents at the disposal of the Member States for consultation.

7. Projects considered for financial support shall be subject to the procedure set out in Article 11. Without prejudice to this procedure, the committee set up by Article 21 of Directive 92/43/EEC shall be consulted before a decision is taken on projects concerning nature protection. The Commission shall adopt a decision concerning the list of projects selected.

8. The projects approved shall give rise to a contract between the Commission and the beneficiaries setting out the amount of financial assistance, the financial procedures and controls, as well as all the specific technical conditions of the approved project. The list of proposals accepted shall be sent to the Member States.

9. At the Commission's initiative, accompanying measures to be financed under paragraph 2(b) shall be the subject of calls for expression of interest published in the *Official Journal of the European Communities* and setting out the specific criteria to be met.

Article 6
Participation of accession candidate countries

1. LIFE shall be open to the accession candidate central and east European countries in accordance with the conditions referred to in the Association Agreements concluded with those countries and on the basis of provisions of the decision of the Association Council competent for each country concerned.

2. Proposals for projects to be financed under LIFE-nature and LIFE-environment shall be forwarded to the Commission by the national authorities of the countries concerned within the time limits fixed by the Commission in accordance with Article 3(4) and Article 4(5) respectively. Where projects involve more than one country, proposals shall be forwarded by the country in which the project coordinating body is located.

3. Proposals which meet the general criteria set out in Article 2 and the specific criteria set out in Article 3(5)(b) and Article 4(6) and (8) shall be taken into consideration for Community financial support.

4. A summary of the main points and of the content of the proposals received from the national authorities of the countries concerned shall be sent to the Member States by the Commission. On request, it shall place the original documents at the disposal of the Member States for consultation.

5. Projects considered for LIFE financial support shall be subject either to the procedure set out in Article 3(7) or to that set out in Article 11 according to the type of project proposed.

6. The projects approved shall give rise to a contract or an agreement between the Commission and the beneficiaries setting out the amount of financial assistance, the financial procedures and controls, as well as all the specific technical conditions of the approved action. The list of proposals accepted shall be sent to the Member States.

7. Where conditions and provisions equivalent to those referred to in paragraph 1 have been established for the other accession candidate countries, LIFE will be open for participation by those countries in accordance with paragraphs 2 to 6.

Countries participating under this Article may not participate under Article 5.

8. The annual breakdown of appropriations for the cofinancing of the instrument by the countries referred to in paragraphs 1 and 7 is published in the general budget of the European Union, Section III, Part B, Annex IV.

Article 7
Consistency between financial instruments

1. Without prejudice to the conditions for accession candidate countries set out in Article 6, projects receiving aid provided for under the Structural Funds or other Community budget instruments shall not be eligible for financial assistance under this Regulation.

2. The Commission shall ensure that actions undertaken in the framework of this Regulation are consistent with those undertaken under the Structural Funds, research, technological development and demonstration programmes or other Community financial instruments.

Article 8
Duration of the third phase and budgetary resources

1. LIFE shall be implemented in phases. The third phase shall start on 1 January 2000 and shall end on 31 December 2004. The financial framework for the implementation of the third phase for the period 2000 to 2004 is hereby set at EUR 640 million.

2. The budgetary resources allocated to the actions provided for in this Regulation shall be entered in the annual appropriations of the general budget of the European Union. The available annual appropriations shall be authorised by the budgetary authority within the limits of the financial perspective.

3. The amount of resources to be allocated to each of the areas of activity shall be as follows:

(a) 47% for actions undertaken under Article 3;
(b) 47% for actions undertaken under Article 4;
(c) 6% for actions undertaken under Article 5.

The accompanying measures shall be limited to 5% of the available appropriations.

Article 9
Monitoring of projects

1. For any project financed by LIFE, the beneficiary shall send the Commission and, on request, the Member State concerned, technical and financial reports on the progress of work. Reports sent to Member States could be sent in summarized form. A final report shall also be sent to the Commission and the Member State concerned within three months of completion of the project.

The Commission shall determine the form and content of the reports. The report shall be based on the physical and financial indicators set out in the Commission Decision approving the projects or in the contract or agreement concluded with the beneficiaries. These indicators shall be such as to indicate the progress of the work and the objectives to be attained within a specified time limit.

2. Without prejudice to the audits carried out by the Court of Auditors in liaison with the competent national audit bodies or departments pursuant to Article 248 of the Treaty, or any inspection carried out pursuant to Article 279(c) of the Treaty, officials and other staff of the Commission may carry out on-the-spot checks, including sample checks, on projects financed under LIFE. Before carrying out an on-the-spot check, the Commission shall inform the beneficiary and its Member State unless there are good reasons to suspect fraud and/or improper use.

3. For a period of five years following the last payment in respect of any action, the beneficiary of financial assistance shall keep available for the Commission all the supporting documents regarding expenditure on the action.

4. On the basis of the results of the reports and sample checks referred to in paragraphs 1 and 2, the Commission shall, if necessary, adjust the scale or the conditions of allocation of the financial assistance originally approved and also the timetable for payments.

5. The Commission shall take every other step necessary to verify that the projects financed are carried out properly and in compliance with the provisions of this Regulation.

Article 10
Protection of Community financial interests

1. The Commission may reduce, suspend or recover the amount of financial assistance granted for a project if it finds irregularities, including non-compliance with the provisions of this Regulation or the individual decision or the contract or agreement granting the financial support in question, or if it transpires that, without Commission approval having been sought, the project has undergone a major change which conflicts with the nature or implementing conditions of the project.

2. If the time limits have not been observed or if only part of the allocated financial assistance is justified by the progress made with implementing a project, the Commission shall request the beneficiary to submit its observations within a specified period. If the beneficiary does not give a satisfactory answer, the Commission may cancel the remaining financial assistance and demand repayment of sums already paid.

3. Any undue payment shall be repaid to the Commission. Interest may be added to any sums not repaid in good time.The Commission shall lay down detailed rules for the implementation of this paragraph.

Article 11
Committee

1. The Commission shall be assisted by a committee (hereinafter referred to as 'the Committee').

2. Where reference is made to this paragraph, Articles 5 and 7 of Decision 1999/468/EC shall apply, having regard to the provisions of Article 8 thereof.

The period referred to in Article 5(6) of Decision 1999/468/EC shall be set at three months.

3. The Committee shall adopt its rules of procedure.

Article 12
Evaluation of the third phase and continuation of LIFE

1. Not later than 30 September 2003, the Commission shall submit to the European Parliament and the Council:

(a) a report on the implementation of this Regulation, its contribution to the development of Community environmental policy, and the use made of the appropriations as well as, where appropriate, proposals for any adjustments to be made with a view to continuing the action beyond the third phase;

(b) if appropriate, a proposal concerning a fourth phase of LIFE.

2. The European Parliament and the Council, acting in accordance with the Treaty, shall decide no later than 1 July 2004 on the implementation of the fourth phase as from 1 January 2005.

Article 13
Repeal of Council Regulation (EEC) No 1973/92

1. Council Regulation (EEC) No 1973/92 shall be repealed without prejudice to decisions taken and contracts or agreements concluded concerning the granting of financial assistance pursuant to that Regulation.

2. References to the repealed Regulation shall be understood as referring to this Regulation and shall be read in accordance with the table of equivalence set out in the Annex to this Regulation.

Article 14
Entry into force

This Regulation shall enter into force on the third day following its publication in the *Official Journal of the European Communities*.

This Regulation shall be binding in its entirety and directly applicable in all Member States. Done at Brussels, 17 July 2000.

Annex
Table of Equivalence (Regulation (EEC) No 1973/92)

[Omitted]

Regulation (EC) No 1682/2004 of the European Parliament and of the Council of 15 September 2004 amending Regulation (EC) No 1655/2000 concerning the Financial Instrument for the Environment (LIFE)

Source: OJ L 308 05.10.2004 p. 1

Regulation (EC) No 1682/2004 of the European Parliament and of the Council of 15 September 2004 amending Regulation (EC) No 1655/2000 concerning the Financial Instrument for the Environment (LIFE)

The European Parliament and the Council of the European Union,

Having regard to the Treaty establishing the European Community and in particular Article 175(1) thereof,

Having regard to the proposal from the Commission,

Having regard to the opinion of the European Economic and Social Committee,[1]

After consulting the Committee of the Regions,

Acting in accordance with the procedure laid down in Article 251 of the Treaty,[2]

Whereas

(1) The financial instrument for the environment, LIFE, as established by Regulation (EC) No 1655/2000 of the European Parliament and of the Council,[3] is being implemented in phases the third of which will end on 31 December 2004.

(2) Given the positive contribution of LIFE to the attainment of the objectives of Community policy on the environment and with a view to further contributing to the implementation, updating and development of Community environment policy and of environment legislation, in particular as regards the integration of the environment into other policies, and to sustainable development, the duration of the third phase should be extended until 31 December 2006.

---

[1] OJ C 80, 30.3.2004, p. 57.

[2] Opinion of the European Parliament of 21 April 2004 (not yet published in the Official Journal) and Decision of the Council of 26 July 2004.

[3] OJ L 192, 28.7.2000, p. 1. Regulation as amended by Regulation (EC) No 788/2004 (OJ L 138, 30.4.2004, p. 17).

(3) A Sixth Community Environment Action Programme was adopted on 22 July 2002 by Decision No 1600/2002/EC of the European Parliament and of the Council.[1] It is necessary to adapt Regulation (EC) No 1655/2000 to the objectives and priorities laid down in that Programme.

(4) There is a need to bridge the gap between the expiry of the third phase of LIFE and the new, post-2006 financial perspectives, for a period of two years ending on 31 December 2006.

(5) LIFE should be reinforced as a specific financial instrument, complementary to the Community research programmes and to the Structural Funds and rural development programmes. Efforts should be made to encourage more efficient use of these Community financial instruments for the funding of elements of environment and nature projects. Appropriate measures should also be put in place to prevent the possibility of double funding.

(6) The Communication entitled 'Developing an action plan for environmental technology' was adopted by the Commission on 25 March 2003. This Communication was followed by an environmental technology action plan adopted on 28 January 2004, which should serve as a reference for the guidelines for LIFE Environment.

(7) The Court of Auditors' special report No 11/2003[2] examined the conception, management and implementation of LIFE. It is appropriate to have regard to the Court's recommendations.

(8) On 1 May 2004 10 new Member States joined the European Union and this should be reflected accordingly in the budget allocation to LIFE.

(9) The exploitation and dissemination of results should be improved and the amount allocated in the budget for that purpose should be increased.

(10) Projects still ongoing at the end of 2006 should continue to be monitored and audited.

(11) In its Judgment of 21 January 2003[3] the Court of Justice of the European Communities annulled Article 11 (2) of Regulation (EC) No 1655/2000. The Court declared that 'the effects of Article 11(2) of Regulation (EC) No 1655/2000 are to be fully maintained until the Parliament and the Council adopt new provisions concerning the committee procedure to which the measures for the implementation of that Regulation are subject'.

(12) In accordance with Article 233 of the Treaty, the institutions whose act has been declared void are required to take the necessary measures to comply with the judgment of the Court of Justice.

(13) The measures that the Commission is empowered to adopt under the implementing powers conferred on it by Regulation (EC) No 1655/2000 are management

[1] OJ L 242, 10.9.2002, p. 1.   [2] OJ C 61, 10.3.2004, p. 1.
[3] Case C-378/00 *Commission* v *European Parliament and Council* [2003] ECR I-937.

measures relating to the implementation of a programme with substantial budgetary implications within the meaning of Article 2(a) of Council Decision 1999/468/EC of 28 June 1999 laying down the procedures for the exercise of implementing powers conferred on the Commission.[1] Those measures should therefore be adopted in accordance with the management procedure provided for in Article 4 of that Decision, without prejudice to the committee procedure to be chosen for any further development of LIFE or a financial instrument exclusively in the environmental field.

(14) This Regulation lays down, for the entire duration of the programme, a financial framework constituting the prime reference, within the meaning of point 33 of the Interinstitutional Agreement of 6 May 1999 between the European Parliament, the Council and the Commission on budgetary discipline and improvement of the budgetary procedure,[2] for the budgetary authority during the annual budgetary procedure.

Have adopted this Regulation:

Article 1

Regulation (EC) No 1655/2000 is amended as follows:
   1. Article 3 shall be amended as follows:

(a) in paragraph 3:
   (i) point (a) shall be replaced by the following:
       '(a) 50% for nature conservation projects, 100% of eligible costs excluding overheads and durable goods for accompanying measures pursuant to paragraph 2(b)(i) and (ii) and 100% of costs for accompanying measures pursuant to paragraph 2(b)(iii);'
   (ii) the following point shall be added:
       '(c) the salary costs of a civil servant shall be considered eligible only to the extent that they relate to the cost of activities that the relevant public authority would not carry out if the project concerned were not undertaken.';
(b) the following paragraph shall be inserted:
       '3a. The grant of assistance in respect of a project that involves the acquisition of land shall be subject to the condition that the land purchased is reserved in the long term for uses of land consistent with the objective of LIFE-nature set out in paragraph 1. Member States shall, by way of transfer or otherwise, ensure the long-term reservation of such land for nature conservation purposes.';

---

[1] OJ L 184, 17.7.1999, p. 23.
[2] OJ C 172, 18.6.1999, p. 1. Agreement as amended by Decision 2003/429/EC of the European Parliament and of the Council (OJ L 147, 14.06.2003, p. 25).

(c) in paragraph 7 the second subparagraph shall be replaced by the following:
'In accordance with Article 116 of Council Regulation (EC, Euratom) No 1605/2002 of 25 June 2002 on the Financial Regulation applicable to the general budget of the European Communities,* a decision shall be adopted by the Commission on the projects which have been accepted and grant agreements shall be concluded with the beneficiaries laying down the amount of financial assistance, the financial procedures and controls, and the specific technical conditions of the project approved.'

* OJ L 248, 16.9.2002, p. 1.

(d) paragraph 8 shall be replaced by the following:
'8. At the Commission's initiative:
(a) accompanying measures to be financed pursuant to paragraph 2(b)(i) and (ii) shall, after consultation of the committee mentioned in Article 21 of Directive 92/43/EEC, be the subject of calls for proposal. Member States may submit proposals on accompanying measures to the Commission,
(b) accompanying measures to be financed pursuant to paragraph 2(b)(iii) shall be the subject of calls for tender. All calls for tender shall be published in the Official Journal of the European Union where the specific criteria to be met shall be set out.';

2. Article 4 shall be amended as follows:

(a) in paragraph 3
(i) the fourth subparagraph shall be replaced by the following:
'The rate of Community financial support shall be 100% of eligible costs excluding overheads and durable goods for accompanying measures pursuant to paragraph 2(c)(i) and 100% of costs for accompanying measures pursuant to paragraph 2(c)(ii).';
(ii) the following subparagraph shall be added:
'The salary costs of a civil servant shall be considered eligible only to the extent that they relate to the cost of activities that the relevant public authority would not carry out if the project concerned were not undertaken.';
(b) paragraph 4 shall be replaced by the following:
'4. As far as demonstration projects referred to in paragraph 2(a) are concerned, guidelines shall be established by the Commission, in accordance with the procedure referred to in Article 11(2), and published in the Official Journal of the European Union.

Those guidelines shall indicate the priority areas and objectives for demonstration projects with an explicit reference to the priorities set out in Decision No 1600/2002/EC.*

* OJ L 242, 10.9.2002, p. 1.

The guidelines shall ensure that LIFE-Environment is complementary to the Community research programmes and to the Structural Funds and rural development programmes.

The Commission shall also establish guidelines on preparatory projects referred to in paragraph 2(b). It shall publish such guidelines in the Official Journal of the European Union and inform the committee referred to in Article 11(1) of their publication.

(c) in paragraph 6, points (d) and (e) shall be replaced by the following:

'(d) being capable of promoting the wide application and dissemination of practices, technologies and/or products conducive to environmental protection;

(e) aiming at developing and transferring innovative technologies or methods which can be used in identical or similar situations, particularly in new Member States;'

(d) paragraph 8 shall be replaced by the following:

'8. At the Commission's initiative:

(a) projects to be financed pursuant to paragraph 2(b) and accompanying measures to be financed pursuant to paragraph 2(c)(i) shall, after consultation of the committee mentioned in Article 11(1), be the subject of calls for proposal. Member States may submit proposals for projects to be financed pursuant to paragraph 2(b) and accompanying measures to be financed pursuant to paragraph 2(c)(i) to the Commission;

(b) accompanying measures to be financed pursuant to paragraph 2(c)(ii) shall be the subject of calls for tender. All calls for tender shall be published in the Official Journal of the European Union where the specific criteria to be met shall be set out.';

(e) paragraph 11 shall be replaced by the following:

'11. In accordance with Article 116 of Regulation (EC, Euratom) No 1605/2002, a decision shall be adopted by the Commission on the projects which have been accepted and grant agreements shall be concluded with the beneficiaries laying down the amount of financial assistance, the financial procedures and controls, and the specific technical conditions of the project approved.';

3. in Article 5, paragraph 9, shall be replaced by the following:

'9. At the Commission's initiative, accompanying measures to be financed under paragraph 2(b) shall be the subject of calls for tender published in the Official Journal of the European Union where the specific criteria to be met shall be set out.';

4. in Article 7, the title and paragraph 1 shall be replaced by the following:

'Article 7
Consistency and complementarity between financial instruments

1. Without prejudice to the conditions for accession candidate countries set out in Article 6, projects receiving aid provided for under the Structural Funds or other

Community budget instruments shall not be eligible for financial assistance under this Regulation. The Commission shall ensure that applicants' attention is drawn to the fact that they cannot cumulate subsidies from different Community funds. Appropriate measures shall be put in place to prevent the possibility of double funding.

The Commission and Member States shall inform applicants of the different Community financial instruments available for the funding of elements of environment and nature projects.';

5. Article 8 shall be amended as follows:

(a) in paragraph 1, the following subparagraph shall be added:
'The third phase shall be extended by two years until 31 December 2006. The financial framework for the implementation of this Regulation is hereby set at EUR 317,2 million. The budgetary authority shall authorise annual appropriations in the context of the annual budgetary procedure and within the limits of the applicable financial perspective.';

(b) in paragraph 3, the second subparagraph shall be replaced by the following:
'For the period 1 January 2005 to 31 December 2006, the accompanying measures shall be limited to 6% of the available appropriations.';

6. Article 9 shall be amended as follows:

(a) in paragraph 1, the following subparagraph shall be added:
'The Commission shall ensure that the results of all funded projects are disseminated to the general public and shall further demonstrate how the skills and experience gained may be reproduced elsewhere.';

(b) the following paragraph shall be added:
'6. The Commission shall publish annually a complete list of projects financed including a short description and a summary of funds expended in each case.';

7. Article 11(2) shall be replaced by the following:

'2. Where reference is made to this paragraph, Articles 4 and 7 of Decision 1999/468/EC shall apply, having regard to the provisions of Article 8 thereof.

The period referred to in Article 4(3) of Decision 1999/468/EC shall be set at three months.'

8. Article 12 shall be replaced by the following:

'Article 12
Evaluation of the third phase and continuation of LIFE

1. Not later than 30 September 2005, the Commission shall submit to the European Parliament and the Council:

(a) a report updating the mid-term review submitted in November 2003 and evaluating the implementation of this Regulation, its contribution to the development of Community environmental policy, and the use made of the appropriations; and

(b) if appropriate, a proposal for the further development of LIFE or a financial instrument exclusively in the environmental field that, inter alia, shall take account of the recommendations of the review of LIFE, to apply from 2007 onwards.

2. Following the Commission's adoption of such a proposal, the European Parliament and the Council, acting in accordance with the Treaty, shall decide no later than 1 May 2006 on the implementation of that financial instrument, as from 1 January 2007.

3. The amount needed within the financial framework to provide for monitoring and auditing measures in the period following 31 December 2006 shall be deemed to be confirmed only if it is consistent with the new financial perspectives commencing in 2007.'

Article 2

This Regulation shall enter into force on the third day following that of its publication in the Official Journal of the European Union.

This Regulation shall be binding in its entirety and directly applicable in all Member States.

Done at Strasbourg, 15 September 2004.

Commission Communication: Community guidelines on State aid for environmental protection (3 February 2001)

Editorial note

In 1994, the Commission adopted the Community guidelines on State aid for environmental protection. The 1994 Guidelines expired on 31 December 1999 and the Commission extended their validity until 31 December 2000. The current Community guidelines became applicable when published in the Official Journal on 3 February 2001 and will expire on 31 December 2007 (paragraph 81).

The data in the eighth survey on State aid in the European Union in the manufacturing and certain other sectors show that between 1996 and 1998 environmental aid accounted on average for only 1.85 percent of total aid granted to the manufacturing and service sectors (paragraph 25). The Commission guidelines determine whether and under what conditions State aid may be regarded as necessary to ensure environmental protection and sustainable development without having disproportionate effects on competition and economic growth (paragraph 5). The guidelines apply to aid to protect the environment in all sectors governed by the EC Treaty, including those subject to specific Community rules on state aid (steel processing, shipbuilding, motor vehicles, synthetic fibres, transport and fisheries), but *excluding state aid for research and development, training aid* and the area covered by the guidelines for *state aid in the agricultural sector*. However, the guidelines do apply to the fisheries and aquaculture sector (paragraph 7).

The general conditions for authorising environmental aid are set out in chapter E. Paragraph 29 specifies that investment aid enabling firms to improve on the Community standards applicable may be authorised up to not more than 30 percent gross of the eligible investment costs as defined in paragraph 37. These conditions also apply to aid where firms undertake investment in the absence of mandatory Community standards or where they have to undertake investment in order to comply with national standards that are more stringent than the applicable Community standards. Specific guidelines are provided for investment aid in energy (paragraphs 30–32); firms located in assisted regions (paragraphs 33–34); and small or medium-sized enterprises (SMEs) (paragraph 35). The investments concerned are investments in land which are strictly necessary in order to meet environmental objectives, investments in buildings, plant and equipment intended to reduce or eliminate pollution and nuisances, and investments to adapt production methods with a view to protecting the environment. Spending on technology transfer through the acquisition of operating licences or of patented and non-patented know-how may also qualify (paragraph 36). Eligible costs must be confined strictly to the extra investment necessary to meet the environmental objectives (paragraph 37).

As a rule, the relocation of firms to new sites does not constitute environmental protection and does not therefore confer entitlement to aid under the guidelines. The granting of aid may, however, be justified when a firm established, say, in an urban area or in a Natura 2000 designated area lawfully carries on an activity that creates major pollution and must, on account of this location, move from its place of establishment to a more suitable area (paragraph 39). Specific provisions are applicable to aid to SMEs for advisory/consultancy services in the environmental field (paragraph 41); and to operating aid to promote waste management and energy savings (paragraphs 42–46). Paragraphs 47–53 provide rules for all operating aid in the form of tax reductions and exemptions. Rules applicable to operating aid for renewable energy sources are to be found in paragraphs 54–65 and rules on operating aid for the combined production of electric power and heat in paragraphs 66–67.

Subject to the limits and conditions set out in these guidelines, environmental aid will be authorised by the Commission pursuant to Article 87(3)(c) of the EC Treaty for 'aid to facilitate the development of certain economic activities or of certain economic areas, where such aid does not adversely affect trading conditions to an extent contrary to the common interest'. Aid to promote the execution of important projects of common European interest which are an environmental priority and will often have beneficial effects beyond the frontiers of the Member State(s) concerned can be authorised under the exemption provided for in Article 87(3)(b) of the EC Treaty. However, the aid must be necessary for the project to proceed, and the project must be specific, well defined and qualitatively important and must make an exemplary and clearly identifiable contribution to the common European interest. When this exemption is applied, the Commission may authorise aid at higher rates than the limits laid down for aid authorised pursuant to Article 87(3)(c) (paragraphs 72 and 73). In order to enable the Commission to assess any substantial amounts of aid granted under authorised schemes and to decide whether such aid is compatible with the common market, any individual case of investment aid must be notified in advance to the Commission where the eligible costs exceed EUR 25 million and where the aid exceeds the gross grant equivalent of EUR 5 million (paragraph 76).

Source: OJ C 37 03.02.2001 p. 3

Commission Communication: Community guidelines on State aid for environmental protection

A. Introduction

1. In 1994 the Commission adopted the Community guidelines on State aid for environmental protection,[1] which expired on 31 December 1999. In accordance with point 4.3 of the guidelines, it conducted a review in 1996 and concluded that there was no need to make any amendments in the meantime. On 22 December 1999 it decided to extend the validity of the guidelines until 30 June 2000.[2] On 28 June 2000 the Commission decided to extend the validity of the guidelines to 31 December 2000.[3]

2. Since the guidelines were adopted in 1994, action in the field of the environment has evolved at the initiative of the Member States and the Community and at world level, in particular following the adoption of the Kyoto Protocol. Member States are granting State aid more frequently in the energy sector, for example, and the aid they provide is frequently in forms which have been rather uncommon until recently, such as tax reductions and exemptions. New forms of operating aid are also on the increase. The Commission ought therefore to adopt new guidelines, which will be needed in order to familiarise Member States and firms with the criteria that it will apply in deciding whether or not aid measures planned by the Member States are compatible with the common market.

3. Under Article 6 of the EC Treaty, environmental policy objectives must be integrated into the Commission's policy on aid controls in the environmental sector, in particular with a view to promoting sustainable development. Accordingly, competition policy and environmental policy are not mutually antagonistic, but the requirements of environmental protection need to be integrated into the definition and implementation of competition policy, in particular so as to promote sustainable development.[4]

4. However, taking long-term environmental requirements into account does not mean that all aid must be authorised. Consideration has to be given to the effects the aid may have in terms of sustainable development and full application of the 'polluter pays' principle. Some forms of aid certainly do satisfy these tests, particularly where they make it possible to achieve a high level of environmental protection while avoiding any conflict with the principle of the internalisation of costs. But other forms of aid, as well as having adverse effects on trade between Member States and on competition, may run counter to the polluter pays principle and may hinder the establishment

---

[1] OJ C 72, 10.3.1994, p. 3.   [2] OJ C 14, 19.1.2000, p. 8.   [3] OJ C 184, 01.7.2000, p. 25.

[4] The Commission also set out its commitment to integrating environmental policy into other policy areas in its working paper of 26 May 1999 entitled 'Integrating environmental aspects into all relevant policy areas' and in its report to the Helsinki European Council on integrating environmental concerns and sustainable development into Community policies (SEC(1999) 1941 final).

of a process of sustainable development. This might be the case, for example, where aid is designed merely to facilitate compliance with new mandatory Community standards.

5. The Commission's approach in these guidelines therefore consists in determining whether, and under what conditions, State aid may be regarded as necessary to ensure environmental protection and sustainable development without having disproportionate effects on competition and economic growth. This analysis must be carried out in the light of the lessons that can be drawn from the functioning of the 1994 guidelines and in the light of the changes in environmental policy that have occurred since then.

B. Definitions and scope

6. *The concept of environmental protection*: for the purposes of these guidelines, the Commission takes 'environmental protection' to mean any action designed to remedy or prevent damage to our physical surroundings or natural resources, or to encourage the efficient use of these resources. The Commission regards energy-saving measures and the use of renewable sources of energy as action to protect the environment. Energy-saving measures should be understood as meaning among other things action which enables companies to reduce the amount of energy used in their production cycle. The design and manufacture of machines or means of transport which can be operated with fewer natural resources are not covered by these guidelines. Action taken within plants or other production units with a view to improving safety or hygiene is important and may be eligible for certain types of aid, but it is not covered by these guidelines.

The concept of the 'internalisation of costs': in these guidelines the 'internalisation of costs' means the principle that all costs associated with the protection of the environment should be included in firms' production costs.

The 'polluter pays' principle: this is the principle that the costs of measures to deal with pollution should be borne by the polluter who causes the pollution.

Polluter: a polluter is someone who directly or indirectly damages the environment or who creates conditions leading to such damage.[1]

Prices to reflect costs: this principle states that the prices of goods or services should incorporate the external costs associated with the negative impact on the environment of their production and marketing. Community standard: mandatory Community standard setting the levels to be attained in environmental terms and the obligation under Community law to use the best available techniques (BAT).[2] which do not entail

---

[1] Council Recommendation of 3 March 1975 regarding cost allocation and action by public authorities on environmental matters (OJ L 194, 25.7.1975, p. 1).

[2] The concept of best available techniques was introduced into Community legislation by Council Directive 76/464/EEC of 4 May 1976 on pollution caused by certain dangerous substances discharged into the aquatic

excessive costs. Renewable energy sources: renewable non-fossil energy sources, viz. wind energy, solar energy, geothermal energy, wave energy, tidal energy, hydroelectric installations with a capacity below 10 MW and biomass, where biomass is defined as products from agriculture and forestry, vegetable waste from agriculture, forestry and the food production industry, and untreated wood waste and cork waste.[1] Electric power generated from renewable energy sources: electric power generated by plant using only renewable energy sources, and that share of electric power generated from renewable energy sources in hybrid plant using traditional energy sources, in particular for contingency purposes.[2] Environmental tax: One likely feature for a levy to be considered as environmental would be that the taxable base of the levy has a clear negative effect on the environment. However, a levy could also be regarded as environmental if it has a less clear, but nevertheless discernible positive environmental effect. [. . .] In general, it is up to the Member State to show the estimated environmental effect of the levy [. . .].[3]

7. *Scope*: These guidelines apply to aid[4] to protect the environment in all sectors governed by the EC Treaty, including those subject to specific Community rules on State aid (steel processing,[5] shipbuilding, motor vehicles, synthetic fibres, transport, and fisheries), but excluding the field covered by the Community guidelines for State aid in the agriculture sector.[6] These guidelines apply to fisheries and aquaculture, without prejudice to the application of the provisions set out in Council Regulation (EC) No 2792/99 of 17 December 1999 laying down the detailed rules and arrangements regarding Community structural assistance in the fisheries sector[7] and in the guidelines for examining State aid in the fisheries and aquaculture

environment of the Community (OJ L 129, 18.5.1976, p. 23) and appeared again, in slightly amended form, in Council Directive 84/360/EEC of 28 June 1984 on the combating of air pollution from industrial plants (OJ L 188, 16.7.1984, p. 20). Council Directive 96/61/EEC of 24 September 1996 concerning integrated pollution prevention and control (OJ L 257, 10.10.1996, p. 26; 'the IPPC Directive') developed and confirmed this concept. The scope of the IPPC Directive covers industrial installations with a high pollution potential. The Directive has applied since November 1999 to new installations or existing installations which have undergone substantial changes. Existing installations must comply with the rules of the IPPC Directive by October 2007. Until that date the provisions of the two abovementioned directives relating to the concept of BAT continue to apply. As a rule, the concrete standards – i.e. the emission or consumption limit values based on the use of the best available techniques – are not set by the Community but by the national authorities.

[1] This definition is contained in the Commission proposal for a Parliament and Council Directive on the promotion of electricity from renewable sources in the internal electricity market (OJ C 311 E, 31.10.2000, p. 320). Once the Directive has been adopted by Parliament and the Council, the Commission will apply the definition given in the final text.

[2] Same observation as for footnote 7.

[3] Environmental taxes and charges in the single market (COM(97) 9 final, 26.3.1997).

[4] The purpose of these guidelines is not to discuss the concept of State aid, which derives from Article 87(1) of the EC Treaty and from the case law of the Court of Justice and the Court of First Instance.

[5] Within the limits laid down in the second paragraph of point 7.

[6] OJ C 28, 1.2.2000, p. 2.   [7] OJ L 337, 30.12.1999, p. 10.

sector.[1] State aid for R & D in the environmental field is subject to the rules set out in the Community framework for State aid for research and development.[2] Similarly, the Commission considers that the characteristics of aid for environmental training activities do not justify such aid being treated separately, and it will therefore examine it in accordance with the provisions of Commission Regulation (EC) No 68/2001 of 12 January 2001 on the application of Articles 87 and 88 of the EC Treaty to training aid.[3]

By virtue of Article 3 of Commission Decision No 2496/96/ECSC of 18 December 1996 establishing Community rules for State aid to the steel industry,[4] aid for environmental protection in the steel industry will continue to be analysed in accordance with the Community guidelines on State aid for environmental protection published in Official Journal C 72 of 10 March 1994 until the expiry of the ECSC Treaty. These guidelines do not apply to stranded costs, which will be dealt with separately.[5] The Commission would point out that, by virtue of Commission Regulation (EC) No 69/2001 of 12 January 2001 on the application of Articles 87 and 88 of the EC Treaty to de minimis[6] aid, aid of not more than EUR 100 000 granted to a firm for a period of three years is not caught by Article 87. That Regulation does not, however, apply to agriculture, fisheries, and transport, nor to the sectors covered by the ECSC Treaty.

C. Policy for controlling State aid and environmental policy

8. During the 1970s and 1980s Community policy on the environment took an essentially corrective approach. The emphasis was on standards intended to reflect the main concerns of environmental policy.

9. The fifth action programme on the environment, entitled 'Towards sustainability' and adopted in 1993,[7] represents something of a break with that approach. It emphasises the need to conduct a long-term policy with the aim of promoting sustainable development. The objective is to reconcile on a lasting basis the development of the European economy with the need to protect the environment. Community action must no longer be limited to reacting to environmental problems but, as explicitly provided for in Article 6 of the EC Treaty as amended by the Treaty of Amsterdam, environmental protection requirements must be integrated into the definition and implementation of all Community policies and activities, and must foster the active involvement of socioeconomic operators.

---

[1] The Commission would point out that these guidelines concern only environmental aid, without prejudice to the applicability of other provisions governing State aid, subject to the limitations of the rules on combinations of aid in point 74 below.

[2] OJ C 45, 17.2.1996, p. 5.   [3] OJ L 10, 13.1.2001, p. 20.   [4] OJ L 338, 28.12.1996, p. 42.

[5] Stranded costs are costs which firms must bear because of commitments they made and are no longer able to honour as a result of the liberalisation of the sector in question.

[6] OJ L 10, 13.1.2001, p. 30.   [7] OJ C 138, 17.5.1993, p. 1.

10. Article 174 of the Treaty also provides for Community policy to be based on the 'polluter pays' principle. The costs associated with protecting the environment should be internalised by firms just like other production costs. In order to implement this policy, the Community will have to use a series of instruments: regulation, and in particular the adoption of standards, but also voluntary agreements or economic instruments.

11. In 1996 the Commission drew up a progress report on the fifth action programme on the environment. The report states that the programme's overall strategy and objectives are still valid. There can be no doubt that progress has been made in integrating environmental and sustainability aspects into the other Community policies. However, what has still not occurred is a genuine change in attitude on the part of all the interested parties: policymakers, firms and the general public. It is important to develop the concept of shared responsibility for the environment and to make the general public aware of the issues at stake.

12. In 1999 the Commission adopted a global assessment of the fifth action programme. The assessment noted that, although the programme raised awareness of the need for stakeholders, citizens and decision-makers in other sectors to pursue environmental objectives actively, less progress had been made overall in changing economic trends and modes of conduct which were harmful to the environment.

13. The assessment also noted that 'it is increasingly clear that damages to the environment have costs to society as a whole and, conversely, that environmental action can generate benefits in the form of economic growth, employment and competitiveness' and that 'the effective application of the "polluter pays" principle and the full internalisation of environmental costs onto polluters remains a critical process'.[1]

14. The Commission's policy on the control of State aid for environmental purposes therefore needs to satisfy a double imperative:

(a) to ensure the competitive functioning of markets, while promoting the completion of the single market and increased competitiveness in firms;
(b) to ensure that the requirements of environmental protection are integrated into the definition and implementation of competition policy, in particular in order to promote sustainable development. The Commission here believes that internalisation of costs is a priority objective that can be achieved in various ways, including by way of instruments based on market laws or those based on a regulatory approach, these being the most effective tools for achieving the objectives described above.

15. Cost internalisation helps to ensure that prices accurately reflect costs in so far as economic operators allocate their financial resources on the basis of the prices of the goods and services they wish to buy. The progress report on the fifth programme

---

[1] Europe's environment: what directions for the future? The global assessment of the European Community programme of policy and action in relation to the environment and sustainable development, 'Towards sustainability' (COM(1999) 543 final of 24.11.1999).

emphasises that this aim has not been realised because prices do not reflect ecological costs. This in turn makes it more difficult to raise public awareness and promotes overexploitation of natural resources.

16. Ensuring that prices reflect costs at all stages of the economic process is the best way of making all parties aware of the cost of protecting the environment. Apart from its potentially adverse effects on trade and competition, State aid generally undermines that aim because it enables certain firms to reduce costs artificially and not to reveal the costs of environmental protection to consumers. In the long term, therefore, some forms of State aid run counter to the objectives of sustainable development.

17. The Community guidelines on State aid adopted by the Commission in 1994 form an integral part of this Community policy. In general, the 'polluter pays' principle and the need for firms to internalise the costs associated with protecting the environment would appear to militate against the granting of State aid.

18. Nevertheless, the guidelines state that aid can be justified in two instances:

(a) in certain specific circumstances in which it is not yet possible for all costs to be internalised by firms and the aid can therefore represent a temporary second-best solution by encouraging firms to adapt to standards;
(b) the aid may also act as an incentive to firms to improve on standards or to undertake further investment designed to reduce pollution from their plants.

19. In the Community guidelines adopted in 1994, the Commission took the view that, in certain cases, total cost internalisation was not yet possible and that aid might be necessary on a temporary basis. The following changes have nevertheless taken place since 1994:

(a) since the adoption of the fifth action programme on the environment, which was already based on the 'polluter pays' principle and cost internalisation, firms have had seven years in which to adapt to the gradual application of the principle;
(b) the Commission's 1996 progress report on the fifth action programme and the 1999 evaluation report restate the need to provide for cost internalisation and to use market instruments in order to make significant progress in improving the environment;
(c) the use of market instruments and proper pricing is also advocated by the Kyoto Protocol on climate change.

20. The Commission's position is therefore that aid should no longer be used to make up for the absence of cost internalisation. If environmental requirements are to be taken into account in the long term, prices must accurately reflect costs and environmental protection costs must be fully internalised. Consequently, the Commission takes the view that aid is not justified in the case of investments designed merely to bring companies into line with new or existing Community technical standards. In its view, however, in order to address the special difficulties encountered by SMEs, it should be possible to grant them aid for adapting to new Community standards for a period of three years from the adoption of such standards. Aid may

though be useful where it serves as an incentive to achieve levels of protection which are higher than those required by Community standards. This is the case when a Member State decides to adopt standards which are more stringent than the Community standards so as to achieve a higher level of environmental protection. It will also apply when a firm invests in environmental protection over and above the strictest existing Community standards or where no Community standards exist.

21. However, it has not been shown that aid has an incentive effect of this kind where it is designed merely to help firms to comply with existing or new Community technical standards. Such standards constitute the ordinary law with which firms must comply, and it is not necessary to provide them with aid in order to encourage them to obey the law.[1] Specific case of the energy sector and tax reductions

22. Since the guidelines were adopted in 1994, the energy sector has undergone major changes which need to be taken into consideration.

23. Certain Member States have adopted, are in the process of adopting or might consider adopting taxes the effects of which are conducive to environmental protection. In some cases, exemptions from or reductions in taxes are granted to firms in particular categories in order to avoid placing them in a difficult competitive situation. The Commission takes the view that such measures may constitute State aid within the meaning of Article 87 of the Treaty. However, the adverse effects of such aid can be offset by the positive effects of adopting taxes. Accordingly, if such exemptions are necessary to ensure the adoption or continued application of taxes applicable to all products, the Commission takes the view that they are acceptable, subject to certain conditions and for a limited period of time. This period may last for 10 years if the conditions are met. Thereafter, Member States will remain free to renotify the measures in question to the Commission, which could adopt the same approach in its analysis while taking into consideration the positive results obtained in environmental terms.

24. Member States have also taken action in recent years to promote the use of renewable sources of energy and combined heat and energy production, which has the encouragement of the Commission given the major advantages for the environment. The Commission therefore takes the view that, where measures to promote renewable sources of energy and the combined production of electric power and heat constitute State aid, they are acceptable subject to certain conditions. It must be certain, however, that such aid is not in breach of other provisions of the Treaty or secondary legislation.

D. Relative importance of environmental aid

25. The data in the eighth survey on State aid in the European Union in the manufacturing and certain other sectors[2] show that between 1996 and 1998 environmental aid accounted on average for only 1.85% of total aid granted to the manufacturing and service sectors.

---

[1] With the exception of SMEs, as provided for in point 20.
[2] COM(2000) 205 final, 11.4.2000.

26. In the period 1994–1999 environmental aid was provided predominantly in the form of grants. Proportionally speaking, little use was made of the other forms of aid: low-interest loans, State guarantees, etc.

27. As to the sectors receiving aid, the period 1998–1999 saw an increase in aid for measures in the energy sector, whether in support of energy saving or to promote the use of new or renewable sources of energy, especially in the form of ecotaxes.

E. General conditions for authorising environmental aid

E.1. Investment aid

E.1.1. Transitional investment aid to help SMEs adapt to new Community standards

28. For a period of three years from the adoption of new compulsory Community standards, investment aid to help SMEs meet new standards may be authorised up to a maximum of 15% gross of eligible costs.

E.1.2. General conditions for authorising investment aid to firms improving on Community standards

29. Investment aid enabling firms to improve on the Community standards applicable may be authorised up to not more than 30% gross of the eligible investment costs as defined in point 37. These conditions also apply to aid where firms undertake investment in the absence of mandatory Community standards or where they have to undertake investment in order to comply with national standards that are more stringent than the applicable Community standards.

E.1.3. Investment in energy

30. Investments in energy saving as defined in point 6 are deemed equivalent to investments to promote environmental protection. Such investments play a major role in achieving economically the Community objectives for the environment.[1] They are, therefore, eligible for investment aid at the basic rate of 40% of eligible costs.

31. Investments in the combined production of electric power and heat may also qualify under these guidelines if it can be shown that the measures beneficial in terms of the protection of the environment because the conversion efficiency[2] is particularly high, because the measures will allow energy consumption to be reduced or because the production process will be less damaging to the environment. In this connection, the Commission will take into particular consideration the type of primary energy used in the production process. It should also be borne in mind that increased energy

---

[1] Action plan to improve energy efficiency in the European Community (COM (2000) 247 final, 26.4.2000).

[2] By 'conversion efficiency' is meant the ratio between the quantity of primary energy used to produce a secondary form of energy and the quantity of secondary energy actually produced. It is calculated as follows: electric energy produced + thermal energy produced/energy used.

use from combined production of heat and power is a Community priority for the environment.[1] Such investment may, therefore, be given aid at the basic rate of 40% of eligible cost.

32. Investments to promote renewable sources of energy are deemed equivalent to environmental investments undertaken in the absence of mandatory Community standards. It should also be borne in mind that measures in support of renewable sources of energy are one of the Community's environmental priorities[2] and one of the long-term objectives that should be encouraged most. The rate of aid for investment in support of these forms of energy is therefore 40% of eligible costs.

The Commission takes the view that renewable energy installations serving all the needs of an entire community such as an island or residential area should also benefit. Investments made in this connection may qualify for a bonus of 10 percentage points on top of the basic rate of 40% of eligible costs.

The Commission considers that, where it can be shown to be necessary, Member States will be able to grant investment aid to support renewable energy, up to 100% of eligible costs. The installations concerned will not be entitled to receive any further support.

E.1.4. Bonus for firms located in assisted regions

33. In regions which are eligible for national regional aid, firms may receive aid to promote regional development. To encourage them to invest further in the environment, it should be possible, where appropriate, to provide additional aid towards any environmental investment carried out in accordance with point 29.[3]

34. Consequently, in regions eligible for regional aid, the maximum rate of environmental aid applicable to eligible costs as defined in point 37 below is determined as follows.

In assisted regions the maximum rate of aid applicable is the higher of the following two options:

(a) either the basic rate for environmental investment aid, i.e. 30% gross (standard system), 40% gross (investments in energy saving, in renewable sources of energy or to promote the combined production of electric power and heat) or 50% gross (investments in renewable sources of energy that supply an entire community), plus 5 percentage points gross in the regions covered by Article 87(3)(c) and 10 percentage points in the regions covered by Article 87(3)(a)[4]

(b) or the regional aid rate plus 10 percentage points gross.

---

[1] Council Resolution of 18 December 1997 on a Community strategy to promote combined heat and power (OJ C 4, 8.1.1998, p. 1).

[2] Council Resolution of 8 June 1998 on renewable sources of energy (OJ C 198, 24.6.1998, p. 1).

[3] These bonuses are not available where the Member State grants investment aid in accordance with the third paragraph of point 32 (aid of up to 100% of eligible costs).

[4] Investments in assisted regions are eligible for investment aid if the conditions of the guidelines on regional State aid (OJ C 74, 10.3.1998, p. 9) are met.

E.1.5. Bonus for SMEs

35. Where investments of the kind referred to in points 29 to 32 are carried out by small or medium-sized enterprises, an increase of 10 percentage points gross may be authorized.[1] For the purposes of these guidelines, the definition of SMEs is that given by the relevant Community texts.[2]

The above bonuses for assisted regions and SMEs may be combined, but the maximum rate of environmental aid may never exceed 100% gross of the eligible costs. SMEs do not qualify for a double bonus either under the provisions applicable to regional aid or under those applicable in the environmental field.[3]

E.1.6. The investments concerned

36. The investments concerned are investments in land which are strictly necessary in order to meet environmental objectives, investments in buildings, plant and equipment intended to reduce or eliminate pollution and nuisances, and investments to adapt production methods with a view to protecting the environment.

Spending on technology transfer through the acquisition of operating licences or of patented and non-patented know-how may also qualify. But any such intangible asset must satisfy the following tests:

(a) it must be regarded as a depreciable asset;
(b) it must be purchased on market terms, from a firm in which the acquirer has no power of direct or indirect control;
(c) it must be included in the assets of the firm, and remain in the establishment of the recipient of the aid and be used there for at least five years. This condition does not apply if these intangible assets are technically out of date. If it is sold during those five years, the yield from the sale must be deducted from the eligible costs and all or part of the amount of aid must, where appropriate, be reimbursed.

E.1.7. Eligible costs

37. Eligible costs must be confined strictly to the extra investment costs necessary to meet the environmental objectives.

This has the following consequences: where the cost of investment in environmental protection cannot be easily identified in the total cost, the Commission will take account of objective and transparent methods of calculation, e.g. the cost of a technically comparable investment that does not though provide the same degree of environmental protection.

---

[1] This bonus is not available where the Member State grants investment aid in accordance with the third paragraph of point 32 (aid of up to 100% of eligible costs).
[2] Commission Recommendation 96/280/EC of 3 April 1996 concerning the definition of small and medium-sized enterprises (OJ L 107, 30.4.1996, p. 4).
[3] Investments by SMEs are eligible for investment aid under the provisions of Commission Regulation (EC) No 70/2001 of 12 January 2001 on the application of Articles 87 and 88 of the EC Treaty to State aid for small and medium-sized enterprises (OJ L 10, 13.1.2001, p. 33).

In all cases, eligible costs must be calculated net of the benefits accruing from any increase in capacity, cost savings engendered during the first five years of the life of the investment and additional ancillary production during that five-year period.[1]

For renewable energy, eligible investment costs are normally the extra costs borne by the firm compared with a conventional power plant with the same capacity in terms of the effective production of energy.

Where SMEs adapt to new Community standards, eligible costs include additional investments needed to attain the level of environmental protection required by those standards.

Where the firm is adapting to national standards adopted in the absence of Community standards, the eligible costs consist of the additional investment costs necessary to achieve the level of environmental protection required by the national standards.

Where the firm is adapting to national standards which are more stringent than the Community standards or undertakes a voluntary improvement on Community standards, the eligible costs consist of the additional investment costs necessary to achieve a level of environmental protection higher than the level required by the Community standards. The cost of investments needed to reach the level of protection required by the Community standards is not eligible.

Where no standards exist, eligible costs consist of the investment costs necessary to achieve a higher level of environmental protection than that which the firm or firms in question would achieve in the absence of any environmental aid.

38. Interventions made by firms repairing environmental damage by rehabilitating polluted industrial sites may come within the scope of these guidelines.[2] The environmental damage concerned may be damage to the quality of the soil or of surface water or groundwater.[3] Where the person responsible for the pollution is clearly identified, that person must finance the rehabilitation in accordance with the 'polluter pays' principle, and no State aid may be given. By person responsible for the pollution. is meant the person liable under the law applicable in each Member State, without prejudice to the adoption of Community rules in the matter. Where the person responsible for the pollution is not identified or cannot be made to bear the cost, the person responsible for the work may receive aid.[4] Aid for the rehabilitation of polluted industrial sites may amount to up to 100% of the eligible costs, plus 15%

---

[1] If the investments are concerned solely with environmental protection without any other economic benefits, no additional reduction will be applied in determining the eligible costs. E.1.8. Rehabilitation of polluted industrial sites.

[2] The Commission would point out that rehabilitation work carried out by public authorities is not as such caught by Article 87 of the Treaty. Problems of State aid may, however, arise if the land is sold after rehabilitation at a price below its market value.

[3] All expenditure incurred by a firm in rehabilitating its site, whether or not such expenditure can be shown as a fixed asset on its balance sheet, ranks as eligible investment in the case of the rehabilitation of polluted sites.

[4] The person responsible for performing the work need not necessarily be the person responsible for the pollution in the meaning in which that expression is used here.

of the cost of the work. The eligible costs are equal to the cost of the work less the increase in the value of the land. The total amount of aid may under no circumstances exceed the actual expenditure incurred by the firm.

E.1.9. Relocation of firms

39. The Commission takes the view that as a rule the relocation of firms to new sites does not constitute environmental protection and does not therefore give entitlement to aid under these guidelines. The granting of aid may, however, be justified when a firm established in an urban area or in a Natura 2000 designated area lawfully carries on an activity that creates major pollution and must, on account of this location, move from its place of establishment to a more suitable area. All the following criteria must be satisfied at the same time:

(a) The change of location must be dictated on environmental protection grounds and must have been ordered by administrative or judicial decision.
(b) The firm must comply with the strictest environmental standards applicable in the new region where it is located.

A firm satisfying the above conditions may receive investment aid in accordance with point 29. The provisions of point 35 concerning the granting of a bonus for SMEs will apply. In order to determine the amount of eligible costs in the case of relocation aid, the Commission will take into account the yield from the sale or renting of the plant or land abandoned, the compensation paid in the event of expropriation and the costs connected with the purchase of land or the construction or purchase of new plant of the same capacity as the plant abandoned. Account may also be taken of any other gains connected with the transfer of the plant, notably gains resulting from an improvement, on the occasion of the transfer, in the technology used and accounting gains associated with better use of the plant. Investments relating to any capacity increase may not be taken into consideration in calculating the eligible costs conferring entitlement to the granting of environmental aid. If the administrative or judicial decision ordering the change of location results in the early termination of a contract for the renting of land or buildings, any penalties imposed on the firm for having terminated the contract may be taken into consideration in calculating the eligible costs.

E.1.10. Common rules

40. Aid for investment to improve on Community standards or undertaken where no Community standards exist may not be granted where such improvements merely bring companies into line with Community standards already adopted but not yet in force. A firm may be given aid to enable it to comply with national standards which are more stringent than Community standards or where no Community standards exist only if it complies with the national standards by the final date laid down

in the relevant national measures. Investments carried out after that date do not qualify.[1]

E.2. Aid to SMEs for advisory/consultancy services in the environmental field

41. Advisory/consultancy services play an important part in helping SMEs to make progress in environmental protection. The Commission therefore takes the view that aid may be granted under the provisions of Regulation (EC) No 70/200138.[2]

E.3. Operating aid

E.3.1. Rules applicable to all operating aid to promote waste management and energy saving

42. The following rules apply to two types of operating aid, namely:

(a) aid for the management of waste where such management is in line with the hierarchical classification of the principles of waste management;[3]
(b) aid in the energy-saving field.

43. Where such aid is shown to be absolutely necessary, it should be strictly limited to compensating for extra production costs by comparison with the market prices of the relevant products or services.[4] Such aid must also be temporary and, as a general rule, must be wound down over time, so as to provide an incentive for prices to reflect costs reasonably rapidly.

44. The Commission takes the view that firms should normally bear the costs of treating industrial waste in accordance with the 'polluter pays' principle. However, operating aid may be necessary where national standards are introduced which are more stringent than the applicable Community rules, or where national standards are introduced in the absence of Community rules, so that firms temporarily lose competitiveness at international level.

Firms receiving operating aid towards the treatment of industrial or non-industrial waste must finance the service provided in proportion to the amount of waste they produce and/or the cost of treatment.

45. All such operating aid is subject to a limited duration of five years where the aid is 'degressive'. Its intensity may amount to 100% of the extra costs in the first year but must have fallen in a linear fashion to zero by the end of the fifth year.

---

[1] The rules set out in this point are without prejudice to point 28 concerning aid for SMEs.
[2] Reference given in footnote 32.
[3] Classification given in the Community strategy for waste management (COM(96) 399 final of 30.7.1996). In this communication, the Commission recalls that waste management is a priority objective for the Community in order to reduce the risks to the environment. The concept of waste treatment must be looked at from three angles: re-utilisation, recycling and recovery. Waste whose production is unavoidable must be treated and eliminated without danger.
[4] The concept of production costs must be understood as being net of any aid but inclusive of a normal level of profit.

46. In the case of 'non-degressive' aid, its duration is limited to five years and its intensity must not exceed 50% of the extra costs.

E.3.2. Rules applicable to all operating aid in the form of tax reductions or exemptions

47. When adopting taxes that are to be levied on certain activities for reasons of environmental protection, Member States may deem it necessary to make provision for temporary exemptions for certain firms notably because of the absence of harmonisation at European level or because of the temporary risks of a loss of international competitiveness. In general, such exemptions constitute operating aid caught by Article 87 of the EC Treaty. In analysing these measures, it has to be ascertained among other things whether the tax is to be levied as the result of a Community decision or an autonomous decision on the part of a Member State.

48. If the tax is to be levied as the result of an autonomous decision on the part of a Member State, the firms affected may have some difficulty in adapting rapidly to the new tax burden. In such circumstances there may be justification for a temporary exemption enabling certain firms to adapt to the new situation.

49. If the tax is to be levied as the result of a Community directive, there are two possible scenarios:

(a) a Member State applies tax to certain products at a rate higher than the minimum rate laid down in the Community directive and grants an exemption to certain firms, which, as a result, pay tax at a rate which is lower but nevertheless at least equal to the minimum rate set by the directive. The Commission takes the view that, in those circumstances, a temporary exemption may be justified to enable firms to adapt to higher taxation and to provide them with an incentive to act in a more environmentally friendly manner;

(b) a Member State applies tax to certain products at the minimum rate laid down in the Community directive and grants an exemption to certain firms, which are thus subject to taxation at a rate below the minimum rate. If such an exemption is not authorised by the directive in question, it will constitute aid which is incompatible with Article 87 of the Treaty. If it is authorised by the directive, the Commission may take the view that it is compatible with Article 87 in so far as it is necessary and is not disproportionate in the light of the Community objectives pursued. The Commission will be specially concerned to ensure that any such exemption is strictly limited in time.

50. In general, the tax measures in question should make a significant contribution to protecting the environment. Care should be taken to ensure that the exemptions do not, by their very nature, undermine the general objectives pursued.

51. These exemptions can constitute operating aid which may be authorised on the following conditions:

1. When, for environmental reasons, a Member State introduces a new tax in a sector of activity or on products in respect of which no Community tax harmonisation has been carried out or when the tax envisaged by the Member State exceeds that laid down by Community legislation, the Commission takes the view that exemption decisions covering a 10-year period with no degressivity may be justified in two cases:

   (a) these exemptions are conditional on the conclusion of agreements between the Member State concerned and the recipient firms whereby the firms or associations of firms undertake to achieve environmental protection objectives during the period for which the exemptions apply or when firms conclude voluntary agreements which have the same effect. Such agreements or undertakings may relate, among other things, to a reduction in energy consumption, a reduction in emissions or any other environmental measure. The substance of the agreements must be negotiated by each Member State and will be assessed by the Commission when the aid projects are notified to it. Member States must ensure strict monitoring of the commitments entered into by the firms or associations of firms. The agreements concluded between a Member State and the firms concerned must stipulate the penalty arrangements applicable if the commitments are not met.

   These provisions also apply where a Member State makes a tax reduction subject to conditions that have the same effect as the agreements or commitments referred to above;

   (b) these exemptions need not be conditional on the conclusion of agreements between the Member State concerned and the recipient firms if the following alternative conditions are satisfied:
   - where the reduction concerns a Community tax, the amount effectively paid by the firms after the reduction must remain higher than the Community minimum in order to provide the firms with an incentive to improve environmental protection,
   - where the reduction concerns a domestic tax imposed in the absence of a Community tax, the firms eligible for the reduction must nevertheless pay a significant proportion of the national tax.

2. The provisions in point 51.1 may be applied to existing taxes if the following two conditions are satisfied at the same time:

   (a) the tax in question must have an appreciable positive impact in terms of environmental protection;

   (b) the derogations for the firms concerned must have been decided on when the tax was adopted or must have become necessary as a result of a significant change in economic conditions that placed the firms in a particularly difficult competitive situation. In the latter instance, the amount of the reduction may not exceed the increase in costs resulting from the change in economic conditions. Once there is no longer any increase in costs, the reduction must no longer apply.

3. Member States may also encourage the development of processes for producing electric power from conventional energy sources such as gas that have an energy efficiency very much higher than the energy efficiency obtained with conventional production processes. In such cases, given the importance of such techniques for environmental protection and provided that the primary energy used reduces significantly the negative effects in terms of environmental protection, the Commission takes the view that total exemptions from taxes may be justified for a period of five years where aid is non-degressive. Derogations for 10 years may also be granted in accordance with the conditions set out in points 51.1 and 51.2.

52. Where an existing tax is increased significantly and where the Member State concerned takes the view that derogations are needed for certain firms, the conditions set out in point 51.1 as regards new taxes are applicable by analogy.

53. When the reductions concern a tax that has not been harmonised at Community level and when the domestic tax is lower than or equal to the Community minimum, the Commission takes the view that long-term exemptions are not justified. In this case, any exemptions granted must satisfy the conditions laid down in points 45 and 46 and must, in any event, be covered by an express authorisation to derogate from the Community minimum. In all cases of reduction of tax, the Member State may grant operating aid in accordance with points 45 and 46.

E.3.3. Rules applicable to operating aid for renewable energy sources

54. As regards the production of renewable energy, operating aid will usually be allowable under these guidelines.

55. The Commission takes the view that such aid qualifies for special treatment because of the difficulties these sources of energy have sometimes encountered in competing effectively with conventional sources. It must also be borne in mind that it is Community policy to encourage the development of these sources of energy, notably on environmental grounds. Aid may be necessary in particular where the technical processes available do not allow energy to be produced at unit costs comparable to those of conventional sources.

56. Operating aid may be justified here in order to cover the difference between the cost of producing energy from renewable energy sources and the market price of that energy. The form of such aid may vary depending on the kind of energy involved and the support mechanism worked out by the Member State. Moreover, when studying cases, the Commission will take account of the competitive position of each form of energy involved.

57. Member States may grant aid for renewable energy sources as follows:

E.3.3.1. Option 1

58. In the renewable energy field, unit investment costs are particularly high and generally account for a significant proportion of firms' costs and do not allow firms to charge competitive prices on the markets where they sell energy.

59. In order to take better account of this market-access barrier for renewable energies, Member States may grant aid to compensate for the difference between the production cost of renewable energy and the market price of the form of power concerned. Any operating aid may then be granted only for plant depreciation. Any further energy produced by the plant will not qualify for any assistance. However, the aid may also cover a fair return on capital if Member States can show that this is indispensable given the poor competitiveness of certain renewable energy sources.

In determining the amount of operating aid, account should also be taken of any investment aid granted to the firm in question in respect of the new plant.

When notifying aid schemes to the Commission, Member States must state the precise support mechanisms and in particular the methods of calculating the amount of aid. If the Commission authorises the scheme, the Member State must then apply those mechanisms and methods of calculation when it comes to granting aid to firms.

60. Unlike most other renewable sources of energy, biomass requires relatively less investment but brings higher operating costs. The Commission will, therefore, be amenable to operating aid exceeding the amount of investment where Member States can show that the aggregate costs borne by the firms after plant depreciation are still higher than the market prices of the energy.

E.3.3.2. Option 2

61. Member States may grant support for renewable energy sources by using market mechanisms such as green certificates or tenders. These systems allow all renewable energy producers to benefit indirectly from guaranteed demand for their energy, at a price above the market price for conventional power. The price of these green certificates is not fixed in advance but depends on supply and demand.

62. Where they constitute State aid, these systems may be authorised by the Commission if Member States can show that support is essential to ensure the viability of the renewable energy sources concerned, does not in the aggregate result in overcompensation for renewable energy and does not dissuade renewable energy producers from becoming more competitive. With a view to verifying that these criteria are met, the Commission intends to authorise these aid systems for a period of ten years, after which it will have to be assessed whether the support measure needs to be continued.

E.3.3.3. Option 3

63. Member States may grant operating aid to new plants producing renewable energy that will be calculated on the basis of the external costs avoided. These are the

environmental costs that society would have to bear if the same quantity of energy were produced by a production plant operating with conventional forms of energy. They will be calculated on the basis of the difference between, on the one hand, the external costs produced and not paid by renewable energy producers and, on the other hand, the external costs produced and not paid by non-renewable energy producers. To carry out these calculations, the Member State will have to use a method of calculation that is internationally recognised and has been communicated to the Commission. It will have to provide among other things a reasoned and quantified comparative cost analysis, together with an assessment of competing energy producers' external costs, so as to demonstrate that the aid does genuinely compensate for external costs not covered.

At any event, the amount of the aid thus granted to the renewable energy producer must not exceed EUR 0,05 per kWh.

Furthermore, the amount of aid granted to producers that exceeds the amount of aid resulting from option 1 must be reinvested by the firms in renewable sources of energy. It will be taken into account by the Commission if this activity also qualifies for State aid.

64. If Option 3 is to remain consistent with the general rules on competition, the Commission must be certain that the aid does not give rise to any distortion of competition contrary to the common interest. In other words, it must be certain that the aid will result in an actual overall increase in the use of renewable energy sources at the expense of conventional energy sources, and not in a simple transfer of market shares between renewable energy sources. The following conditions will therefore have to be met:

– aid granted under this option must form part of a scheme which treats firms in the renewable energy sector on an equal footing;
– the scheme must provide for aid to be granted without discrimination as between firms producing the same renewable energy;
– the scheme must be re-examined by the Commission every five years.

E.3.3.4. Option 4

65. Member States may still grant operating aid in accordance with the general rules governing such aid in points 45 and 46.

E.3.4. Rules applicable to operating aid for the combined production of electric power and heat

66. The Commission takes the view that operating aid for the combined production of electric power and heat may be justified provided that the conditions set out in point 31 are met. Such aid may be granted to firms distributing electric power and heat to the public where the costs of producing such electric power or heat exceed its market price. In similar circumstances, operating aid may be granted in accordance

with the rules in points 58 to 65. The decision as to whether the aid is essential will take account of the costs and revenue resulting from the production and sale of the electric power or heat.

67. Operating aid may be granted on the same conditions as for the industrial use of the combined production of electric power and heat where it can be shown that the production cost of one unit of energy using that technique exceeds the market price of one unit of conventional energy. The production cost may include the plant's normal return on capital, but any gains by the firm in terms of heat production must be deducted from production costs.

F. Policies, measures and instruments for reducing greenhouse gases

68. The Kyoto Protocol, signed by the Member States and by the Community, provides that the parties undertake to limit or reduce greenhouse gas emissions during the period 2008–2012. For the Community as a whole, the target is to reduce greenhouse gas emissions by 8% of their 1990 level.

69. Member States and the Community, as parties to the Protocol, will have to achieve the greenhouse gas reductions by means of common and coordinated policies and measures,[1] including economic instruments, and also by means of the instruments established by the Kyoto Protocol itself, namely international emissions trading, joint implementation, and the clean development mechanism.

70. In the absence of any Community provisions in this area and without prejudice to the Commission's right of initiative in proposing such provisions, it is for each Member State to formulate the policies, measures and instruments it wishes to adopt in order to comply with the targets set under the Kyoto Protocol.

71. The Commission takes the view that some of the means adopted by Member States to comply with the objectives of the Protocol could constitute State aid but it is still too early to lay down the conditions for authorising any such aid.

G. Basis of exemption for all projects examined by the Commission

72. Subject to the limits and conditions set out in these guidelines, environmental aid will be authorised by the Commission pursuant to Article 87(3)(c) of the EC Treaty for 'aid to facilitate the development of certain economic activities or of certain economic areas, where such aid does not adversely affect trading conditions to an extent contrary to the common interest'.

73. Aid to promote the execution of important projects of common European interest which are an environmental priority and will often have beneficial effects beyond the frontiers of the Member State(s) concerned can be authorised under the

---

[1] For details of common and coordinated policies and measures see in particular. Preparing for Implementation of the Kyoto Protocol. (COM(1999) 230 of 19.5.1999).

exemption provided for in Article 87(3)(b) of the EC Treaty. However, the aid must be necessary for the project to proceed, and the project must be specific, well defined and qualitatively important and must make an exemplary and clearly identifiable contribution to the common European interest. When this exemption is applied, the Commission may authorise aid at higher rates than the limits laid down for aid authorised pursuant to Article 87(3)(c).

H. Overlapping aid from different sources

74. The aid ceilings stipulated in these guidelines are applicable irrespective of whether the aid in question is financed wholly or in part from State resources or from Community resources. Aid authorised under these guidelines may not be combined with other forms of State aid within the meaning of Article 87(1) of the Treaty or with other forms of Community financing if such overlapping produces an aid intensity higher than that laid down in these guidelines.

In the case of aid serving different purposes and involving the same eligible costs, the most favourable aid ceiling will apply.

I. 'Appropriate measures' within the meaning of Article 88(1) of the EC Treaty

75. Acting under Article 88(1) of the Treaty, the Commission will propose the following appropriate measures to the Member States in respect of their existing systems of aid.

76. In order to enable it to assess any substantial amounts of aid granted under authorised schemes and to decide whether such aid is compatible with the common market, the Commission will propose, as an appropriate measure under Article 88(1) of the Treaty, that Member States should notify it in advance of any individual case of investment aid granted under an authorised scheme where the eligible costs exceed EUR 25 million and where the aid exceeds the gross grant equivalent of EUR 5 million. Notification will be given by means of the form of which a model is shown in the Annex.

77. The Commission will also propose, as an appropriate measure under Article 88(1), that Member States should bring their existing environmental aid schemes into line with these guidelines before 1 January 2002.

78. The Commission will ask the Member States to confirm within one month of receipt of the proposed measures referred to in points 75 to 77 that they agree to the proposals. In the absence of any reply, the Commission will take it that the relevant Member State does not agree.

79. The Commission would point out that, with the exception of aid classed as de minimis aid under Regulation (EC) No 69/2001,[1] these guidelines do not affect the obligation incumbent on Member States under Article 88(3) of the Treaty to notify

---

[1] OJ L 10, 13.1.2001, p. 30.

any aid schemes, any changes to those schemes and any individual aid granted to firms outside the framework of authorised schemes.

80. The Commission intends to ensure that any authorisation for a future scheme complies with these guidelines.

J. Application of the guidelines

81. These guidelines will become applicable when they are published in the Official Journal of the European Communities. They will cease to be applicable on 31 December 2007. After consulting the Member States, the Commission may amend them before that date on the basis of important competition policy or environmental policy considerations or in order to take account of other Community policies or international commitments.

82. The Commission will apply these guidelines to all aid projects notified in respect of which it is called upon to take a decision after the guidelines are published in the Official Journal, even where the projects were notified prior to their publication. In the case of non-notified aid, the Commission will apply:

(a) these guidelines if the aid was granted after their publication in the Official Journal of the European Communities;

(b) the guidelines in force when aid is granted in all other cases.

K. Integration of environmental policy into other State aid guidelines

83. Article 6 of the Treaty states that:

> Environmental protection requirements must be integrated into the definition and implementation of the Community policies and activities referred to in Article 3, in particular with a view to promoting sustainable development.

When the Commission adopts or revises other Community guidelines or frameworks on State aid, it will consider how those requirements can best be taken into account. It will also examine whether it would not be expedient to ask the Member States to provide an environmental impact study whenever they notify it of an important aid project, irrespective of the sector involved.

Annex
Additional information ordinarily to be supplied when notifying State aid for environmental purposes under Article 88(3) of the Treaty

(Schemes, cases of aid granted under an approved scheme, and one-off aid measures)

To be attached to the general questionnaire in Section A of Annex II to the Commission letter to Member States of 2 August 1995 on notifications and standardised annual reports:

1. Objectives

Detailed description of the objectives of the measure, and of the type of environmental protection it is intended to promote.

2. Description of the measure

Detailed description of the measure and of the recipients.

Description of the total costs of the investments involved and of the eligible costs.

If the measure in question has already been applied in the past, what environmental results have been obtained?

If the measure is a new one, what environmental results are anticipated, and over what period?

If the aid is to be granted towards an improvement on standards, what are the standards applicable, and in what way does the measure allow an appreciably higher level of environmental protection to be achieved?

If the aid is to be granted in the absence of mandatory standards, please give a detailed description of the way.

PART IV

Procedural techniques of environmental protection

Council Directive 85/337/EEC of 27 June 1985 on the assessment of the effects of certain public and private projects on the environment (as amended)

Editorial note

Council Directive 85/337/EEC on the Assessment of the Effects of Certain Public and Private Projects on the Environment (as amended by Directives 97/11 and 2003/35) is intended to establish an assessment process whereby a minimum amount of information is to be considered by decision-makers before granting development consents.

All projects, public or private, likely to have 'significant effects on the environment' are to be assessed (Article 1(1) and Article 2). Member States may decide, on a case-by-case basis, not to apply the Directive to projects serving national defence (Article 1(4)). The Directive does not apply to projects the details of which are approved by a specific act of legislation (Article 1(5)). In exceptional cases, Member States may exempt a specific project from the provisions of the Directive (Article 2(3)). The environmental impact assessment shall identify, describe and assess the direct and indirect effect of a project on: human beings, fauna and flora; soil, water, air, climate change and the landscape; material assets and the cultural heritage; and the interaction between the factors mentioned before (Article 3). The projects listed in Annex I to the Directive are to be subject to an assessment (Article 4(1)). For the projects listed under Annex II, Member States are to determine whether an assessment is required through a case-by-case examination or thresholds or criteria (Article 4(2)).

The environmental impact assessment must be carried out in accordance with Articles 5 to 10 of the Directive. Developers must supply to the competent authority in an appropriate form the information necessary to evaluate the impact of the proposed project. The information is to include at least a description of the project (site, design and size); a description of the measures envisaged to avoid, reduce and, if possible, remedy significant adverse effects; data required to identify and assess the main effects on the environment; an outline of the main alternatives and the reasons for the choice of the project; and a non-technical summary (Article 5(3)).

Member States must ensure that national authorities with environmental responsibilities are given an opportunity to express their views on the development proposal (Article 6(1)). The public are to be informed early in the environmental decision-making process and, at the latest, as soon as the information can be reasonably provided, of, *inter alia*, the request for development consent, the fact that the project is subject to environmental impact assessment, times and places where the information will be made available, and details of arrangements for public participation (Article 6(2)). The public concerned are to have access to the information provided by the developer and other information as specified by Article 6(3)). They are to be given an early and effective opportunity to participate in the environmental decision-making procedure and are to be entitled to express comments and opinions (Article 6(4)). Information exchange is required should a project be likely to have significant effects on the environment in another Member State (Article 7). The Directive requires all the information gathered pursuant to its provisions and from the consultation process to be taken into consideration in the development consent procedure (Article 8). All these requirements are subject to national regulations governing industrial and commercial secrecy and the safeguarding of public interest (Article 10).

The final decision to grant or refuse development consent must be conveyed to the public, in particular its content and any conditions attached, and the reasons therefor, a description where necessary of the main measures to avoid, reduce and, if possible, offset the major adverse effects. The competent authority is to inform any Member State consulted under Article 7 (Article 9). Member States are to ensure that members of the public concerned having a sufficient interest, or, alternatively, maintaining the impairment of a right, where administrative law of a Member State so requires as a precondition, have access to a review procedure before a court of law or another independent and impartial body (Article 10a).

Source: OJ L 175 05.07.1985 p. 40. Amended by: Council Directive 97/11/EC of 3 March 1997 (L 73 5 14.03.1997); Directive 2003/35/EC of the European Parliament and of the Council of 26 May 2003 (L 156 17 25.06.2003).

Council Directive 85/337/EEC of 27 June 1985 on the assessment of the effects of certain public and private projects on the environment (as amended)

The Council of the European Communities,

Having regard to the Treaty establishing the European Economic Community, and in particular Articles 100 and 235 thereof,

Having regard to the proposal from the Commission,[1]

Having regard to the opinion of the European Parliament,[2]

Having regard to the opinion of the Economic and Social Committee,[3]

---

[1] OJ No C 169, 9.7.1980, p. 14.   [2] OJ No C 66, 15.3.1982, p. 89.   [3] OJ No C 185, 27.7.1981, p. 8.

Whereas the 1973[1] and 1977[2] action programmes of the European Communities on the environment, as well as the 1983[3] action programme, the main outlines of which have been approved by the Council of the European Communities and the representatives of the Governments of the Member States, stress that the best environmental policy consists in preventing the creation of pollution or nuisances at source, rather than subsequently trying to counteract their effects; whereas they affirm the need to take effects on the environment into account at the earliest possible stage in all the technical planning and decision-making processes; whereas to that end, they provide for the implementation of procedures to evaluate such effects;

Whereas the disparities between the laws in force in the various Member States with regard to the assessment of the environmental effects of public and private projects may create unfavourable competitive conditions and thereby directly affect the functioning of the common market; whereas, therefore, it is necessary to approximate national laws in this field pursuant to Article 100 of the Treaty;

Whereas, in addition, it is necessary to achieve one of the Community's objectives in the sphere of the protection of the environment and the quality of life;

Whereas, since the Treaty has not provided the powers required for this end, recourse should be had to Article 235 of the Treaty;

Whereas general principles for the assessment of environmental effects should be introduced with a view to supplementing and coordinating development consent procedures governing public and private projects likely to have a major effect on the environment;

Whereas development consent for public and private projects which are likely to have significant effects on the environment should be granted only after prior assessment of the likely significant environmental effects of these projects has been carried out; whereas this assessment must be conducted on the basis of the appropriate information supplied by the developer, which may be supplemented by the authorities and by the people who may be concerned by the project in question;

Whereas the principles of the assessment of environmental effects should be harmonized, in particular with reference to the projects which should be subject to assessment, the main obligations of the developers and the content of the assessment;

Whereas projects belonging to certain types have significant effects on the environment and these projects must as a rule be subject to systematic assessment;

Whereas projects of other types may not have significant effects on the environment in every case and whereas these projects should be assessed where the Member States consider that their characteristics so require;

Whereas, for projects which are subject to assessment, a certain minimal amount of information must be supplied, concerning the project and its effects;

[1] OJ No C 112, 20.12.1973, p. 1.   [2] OJ No C 139, 13.6.1977, p. 1.   [3] OJ No C 46, 17.2.1983, p. 1.

Whereas the effects of a project on the environment must be assessed in order to take account of concerns to protect human health, to contribute by means of a better environment to the quality of life, to ensure maintenance of the diversity of species and to maintain the reproductive capacity of the ecosystem as a basic resource for life;

Whereas, however, this Directive should not be applied to projects the details of which are adopted by a specific act of national legislation, since the objectives of this Directive, including that of supplying information, are achieved through the legislative process;

Whereas, furthermore, it may be appropriate in exceptional cases to exempt a specific project from the assessment procedures laid down by this Directive, subject to appropriate information being supplied to the Commission,

Has adopted this Directive:

Article 1

1. This Directive shall apply to the assessment of the environmental effects of those public and private projects which are likely to have significant effects on the environment.

2. For the purposes of this Directive:

'project' means:

- the execution of construction works or of other installations or schemes,
- other interventions in the natural surroundings and landscape including those involving the extraction of mineral resources;

'developer' means:

the applicant for authorization for a private project or the public authority which initiates a project;

'development consent' means:

the decision of the competent authority or authorities which entitles the developer to proceed with the project;

'public' means:

one or more natural or legal persons and, in accordance with national legislation or practice, their associations, organisations or groups;

'public concerned' means:

the public affected or likely to be affected by, or having an interest in, the environmental decision-making procedures referred to in Article 2(2); for the purposes of this definition, non-governmental organizations promoting environmental protection and meeting any requirements under national law shall be deemed to have an interest.

3. The competent authority or authorities shall be that or those which the Member States designate as responsible for performing the duties arising from this Directive.

4. Member States may decide, on a case-by-case basis if so provided under national law, not to apply this Directive to projects serving national defence purposes, if they deem that such application would have an adverse effect on these purposes.

5. This Directive shall not apply to projects the details of which are adopted by a specific act of national legislation, since the objectives of this Directive, including that of supplying information, are achieved through the legislative process.

Article 2

1. Member States shall adopt all measures necessary to ensure that, before consent is given, projects likely to have significant effects on the environment by virtue, *inter alia*, of their nature, size or location are made subject to a requirement for development consent and an assessment with regard to their effects. These projects are defined in Article 4.

2. The environmental impact assessment may be integrated into the existing procedures for consent to projects in the Member States, or, failing this, into other procedures or into procedures to be established to comply with the aims of this Directive.

2a. Member States may provide for a single procedure in order to fulfil the requirements of this Directive and the requirements of Council Directive 96/61/EC of 24 September 1996 on integrated pollution prevention and control.[1]

3. Without prejudice to Article 7, Member States may, in exceptional cases, exempt a specific project in whole or in part from the provisions laid down in this Directive.

In this event, the Member States shall:

(a) consider whether another form of assessment would be appropriate;
(b) make available to the public concerned the information obtained under other forms of assessment referred to in point (a), the information relating to the exemption decision and the reasons for granting it;
(c) inform the Commission, prior to granting consent, of the reasons justifying the exemption granted, and provide it with the information made available, where applicable, to their own nationals.

The Commission shall immediately forward the documents received to the other Member States.

The Commission shall report annually to the Council on the application of this paragraph.

---

[1] OJ No L 257, 10.10.1996, p. 26.

Article 3

The environmental impact assessment shall identify, describe and assess in an appropriate manner, in the light of each individual case and in accordance with Articles 4 to 11, the direct and indirect effects of a project on the following factors:

- human beings, fauna and flora;
- soil, water, air, climate and the landscape;
- material assets and the cultural heritage;
- the interaction between the factors mentioned in the first, second and third indents.

Article 4

1. Subject to Article 2(3), projects listed in Annex I shall be made subject to an assessment in accordance with Articles 5 to 10.

2. Subject to Article 2(3), for projects listed in Annex II, the Member States shall determine through:

(a) a case-by-case examination, or
(b) thresholds or criteria set by the Member State

whether the project shall be made subject to an assessment in accordance with Articles 5 to 10.

Member States may decide to apply both procedures referred to in (a) and (b).

3. When a case-by-case examination is carried out or thresholds or criteria are set for the purpose of paragraph 2, the relevant selection criteria set out in Annex III shall be taken into account.

4. Member States shall ensure that the determination made by the competent authorities under paragraph 2 is made available to the public.

Article 5

1. In the case of projects which, pursuant to Article 4, must be subjected to an environmental impact assessment in accordance with Articles 5 to 10, Member States shall adopt the necessary measures to ensure that the developer supplies in an appropriate form the information specified in Annex IV inasmuch as:

(a) the Member States consider that the information is relevant to a given stage of the consent procedure and to the specific characteristics of a particular project or type of project and of the environmental features likely to be affected;
(b) the Member States consider that a developer may reasonably be required to compile this information having regard *inter alia* to current knowledge and methods of assessment.

2. Member States shall take the necessary measures to ensure that, if the developer so requests before submitting an application for development consent, the competent authority shall give an opinion on the information to be supplied by the developer

in accordance with paragraph 1. The competent authority shall consult the developer and authorities referred to in Article 6(1) before it gives its opinion. The fact that the authority has given an opinion under this paragraph shall not preclude it from subsequently requiring the developer to submit further information. Member States may require the competent authorities to give such an opinion, irrespective of whether the developer so requests.

3. The information to be provided by the developer in accordance with paragraph 1 shall include at least:

- a description of the project comprising information on the site, design and size of the project,
- a description of the measures envisaged in order to avoid, reduce and, if possible, remedy significant adverse effects,
- the data required to identify and assess the main effects which the project is likely to have on the environment,
- an outline of the main alternatives studied by the developer and an indication of the main reasons for his choice, taking into account the environmental effects,
- a non-technical summary of the information mentioned in the previous indents.

4. Member States shall, if necessary, ensure that any authorities holding relevant information, with particular reference to Article 3, shall make this information available to the developer.

Article 6

1. Member States shall take the measures necessary to ensure that the authorities likely to be concerned by the project by reason of their specific environmental responsibilities are given an opportunity to express their opinion on the information supplied by the developer and on the request for development consent. To this end, Member States shall designate the authorities to be consulted, either in general terms or on a case-by-case basis. The information gathered pursuant to Article 5 shall be forwarded to those authorities. Detailed arrangements for consultation shall be laid down by the Member States.

2. The public shall be informed, whether by public notices or other appropriate means such as electronic media where available, of the following matters early in the environmental decision-making procedures referred to in Article 2(2) and, at the latest, as soon as information can reasonably be provided:

(a) the request for development consent;
(b) the fact that the project is subject to an environmental impact assessment procedure and, where relevant, the fact that Article 7 applies;
(c) details of the competent authorities responsible for taking the decision, those from which relevant information can be obtained, those to which comments or

questions can be submitted, and details of the time schedule for transmitting comments or questions;

(d) the nature of possible decisions or, where there is one, the draft decision;
(e) an indication of the availability of the information gathered pursuant to Article 5;
(f) an indication of the times and places where and means by which the relevant information will be made available;
(g) details of the arrangements for public participation made pursuant to paragraph 5 of this Article.

3. Member States shall ensure that, within reasonable time-frames, the following is made available to the public concerned:

(a) any information gathered pursuant to Article 5;
(b) in accordance with national legislation, the main reports and advice issued to the competent authority or authorities at the time when the public concerned is informed in accordance with paragraph 2 of this Article;
(c) in accordance with the provisions of Directive 2003/4/EC of the European Parliament and of the Council of 28 January 2003 on public access to environmental information,[1] information other than that referred to in paragraph 2 of this Article which is relevant for the decision in accordance with Article 8 and which only becomes available after the time the public concerned was informed in accordance with paragraph 2 of this Article.

4. The public concerned shall be given early and effective opportunities to participate in the environmental decision-making procedures referred to in Article 2(2) and shall, for that purpose, be entitled to express comments and opinions when all options are open to the competent authority or authorities before the decision on the request for development consent is taken.

5. The detailed arrangements for informing the public (for example by bill posting within a certain radius or publication in local newspapers) and for consulting the public concerned (for example by written submissions or by way of a public inquiry) shall be determined by the Member States.

6. Reasonable time-frames for the different phases shall be provided, allowing sufficient time for informing the public and for the public concerned to prepare and participate effectively in environmental decision-making subject to the provisions of this Article.

Article 7

1. Where a Member State is aware that a project is likely to have significant effects on the environment in another Member State or where a Member State likely to be significantly affected so requests, the Member State in whose territory the project is

[1] OJ L 41, 14.02.2003, p. 26.

intended to be carried out shall send to the affected Member State as soon as possible and no later than when informing its own public, *inter alia*:

(a) a description of the project, together with any available information on its possible transboundary impact;
(b) information on the nature of the decision which may be taken, and shall give the other Member State a reasonable time in which to indicate whether it wishes to participate in the environmental decision-making procedures referred to in Article 2(2), and may include the information referred to in paragraph 2 of this Article.

2. If a Member State which receives information pursuant to paragraph 1 indicates that it intends to participate in the environmental decision-making procedures referred to in Article 2(2), the Member State in whose territory the project is intended to be carried out shall, if it has not already done so, send to the affected Member State the information required to be given pursuant to Article 6(2) and made available pursuant to Article 6(3)(a) and (b).

3. The Member States concerned, each insofar as it is concerned, shall also:

(a) arrange for the information referred to in paragraphs 1 and 2 to be made available, within a reasonable time, to the authorities referred to in Article 6(1) and the public concerned in the territory of the Member State likely to be significantly affected; and
(b) ensure that those authorities and the public concerned are given an opportunity, before development consent for the project is granted, to forward their opinion within a reasonable time on the information supplied to the competent authority in the Member State in whose territory the project is intended to be carried out.

4. The Member States concerned shall enter into consultations regarding, *inter alia*, the potential transboundary effects of the project and the measures envisaged to reduce or eliminate such effects and shall agree on a reasonable time frame for the duration of the consultation period.

5. The detailed arrangements for implementing this Article may be determined by the Member States concerned and shall be such as to enable the public concerned in the territory of the affected Member State to participate effectively in the environmental decision-making procedures referred to in Article 2(2) for the project.

Article 8

The results of consultations and the information gathered pursuant to Articles 5, 6 and 7 must be taken into consideration in the development consent procedure.

Article 9

1. When a decision to grant or refuse development consent has been taken, the competent authority or authorities shall inform the public thereof in accordance

with the appropriate procedures and shall make available to the public the following information:

– the content of the decision and any conditions attached thereto,
– having examined the concerns and opinions expressed by the public concerned, the main reasons and considerations on which the decision is based, including information about the public participation process,
– a description, where necessary, of the main measures to avoid, reduce and, if possible, offset the major adverse effects.

2. The competent authority or authorities shall inform any Member State which has been consulted pursuant to Article 7, forwarding to it the information referred to in paragraph 1 of this Article. The consulted Member States shall ensure that that information is made available in an appropriate manner to the public concerned in their own territory.

Article 10

The provisions of this Directive shall not affect the obligation on the competent authorities to respect the limitations imposed by national regulations and administrative provisions and accepted legal practices with regard to commercial and industrial confidentiality, including intellectual property, and the safeguarding of the public interest. Where Article 7 applies, the transmission of information to another Member State and the receipt of information by another Member State shall be subject to the limitations inforce in the Member State in which the project is proposed.

Article 10a

Member States shall ensure that, in accordance with the relevant national legal system, members of the public concerned:

(a) having a sufficient interest, or alternatively,
(b) maintaining the impairment of a right, where administrative procedural law of a Member State requires this as a precondition,

have access to a review procedure before a court of law or another independent and impartial body established by law to challenge the substantive or procedural legality of decisions, acts or omissions subject to the public participation provision s of this Directive.

Member States shall determine at what stage the decisions, acts or omissions may be challenged.

What constitutes a sufficient interest and impairment of a right shall be determined by the Member States, consistently with the objective of giving the public concerned wide access to justice. To this end, the interest of any non-governmental organisation meeting the requirements referred to in Article 1(2), shall be deemed sufficient for the purpose of subparagraph (a) of this Article. Such organisations shall also be deemed to have rights capable of being impaired for the purpose of subparagraph (b) of this Article.

The provisions of this Article shall not exclude the possibility of a preliminary review procedure before an administrative authority and shall not affect the requirement of exhaustion of administrative review procedures prior to recourse to judicial review procedures, where such a requirement exists under national law.

Any such procedure shall be fair, equitable, timely and not prohibitively expensive.

In order to further the effectiveness of the provisions of this article, Member States shall ensure that practical information is made available to the public on access to administrative and judicial review procedures.

Article 11

1. The Member States and the Commission shall exchange information on the experience gained in applying this Directive.

2. In particular, Member States shall inform the Commission of any criteria and/or thresholds adopted for the selection of the projects in question, in accordance with Article 4(2).

3. Five years after notification of this Directive, the Commission shall send the European Parliament and the Council a report on its application and effectiveness. The report shall be based on the aforementioned exchange of information.

4. On the basis of this exchange of information, the Commission shall submit to the Council additional proposals, should this be necessary, with a view to this Directive's being applied in a sufficiently coordinated manner.

Article 12

1. Member States shall take the measures necessary to comply with this Directive within three years of its notification.[1]

2. Member States shall communicate to the Commission the texts of the provisions of national law which they adopt in the field covered by this Directive.

Article 14

This Directive is addressed to the Member States.

Annex I
Projects subject to Article 4(1)

1. Crude-oil refineries (excluding undertakings manufacturing only lubricants from crude oil) and installations for the gasification and liquefaction of 500 tonnes or more of coal or bituminous shale per day.

---

[1] This Directive was notified to the Member States on 3 July 1985.

2.

– Thermal power stations and other combustion installations with a heat output of 300 megawatts or more, and
– nuclear power stations and other nuclear reactors including the dismantling or decommissioning of such power stations or reactors* (except research installations for the production and conversion of fissionable and fertile materials, whose maximum power does not exceed 1 kilowatt continuous thermal load).

3.

(a) Installations for the reprocessing of irradiated nuclear fuel.
(b) Installations designed:
    – for the production or enrichment of nuclear fuel,
    – for the processing of irradiated nuclear fuel or high-level radioactive waste,
    – for the final disposal of irradiated nuclear fuel,
    – solely for the final disposal of radioactive waste,
    – solely for the storage (planned for more than 10 years) of irradiated nuclear fuels or radioactive waste in a different site than the production site.

4.

– Integrated works for the initial smelting of cast-iron and steel;
– Installations for the production of non-ferrous crude metals from ore, concentrates or secondary raw materials by metallurgical, chemical or electrolytic processes.

5. Installations for the extraction of asbestos and for the processing and transformation of asbestos and products containing asbestos: for asbestos-cement products, with an annual production of more than 20,000 tonnes of finished products, for friction material, with an annual production of more than 50 tonnes of finished products, and for other uses of asbestos, utilization of more than 200 tonnes per year.

6. Integrated chemical installations, i.e. those installations for the manufacture on an industrial scale of substances using chemical conversion processes, in which several units are juxtaposed and are functionally linked to one another and which are:

  (i) for the productionof basic organic chemicals;
 (ii) for the production of basic inorganic chemicals;
(iii) for the production of phosphorous-, nitrogen- or potassium-based fertilizers (simple or compound fertilizers);
(iv) for the production of basic plant health products and of biocides;
 (v) for the productionof basic pharmaceutical products using a chemical or biological process;
(vi) for the production of explosives.

---

* Nuclear power stations and other nuclear reactors cease to be such an installation when all nuclear fuel and other radioactively contaminated elements have been removed permanently from the installation site.

7.

(a) Construction of lines for long-distance railway traffic and of airports[1] with a basic runway length of 2 100 m or more;
(b) Construction of motorways and express roads;[2]
(c) Construction of a new road of four or more lanes, or realignment and/or widening of an existing road of two lanes or less so as to provide four or more lanes, where such new road, or realigned and/or widened section of road would be 10 km or more in a continuous length.

8.

(a) Inland waterways and ports for inland-waterway traffic which permit the passage of vessels of over 1 350 tonnes;
(b) Trading ports, piers for loading and unloading connected to land and outside ports (excluding ferry piers) which can take vessels of over 1 350 tonnes.

9. Waste disposal installations for the incineration, chemical treatment as defined in Annex IIA to Directive 75/442/EEC[3] under heading D9, or landfill of hazardous waste (i.e. waste to which Directive 91/689/EEC[4] applies).

10. Waste disposal installations for the incineration or chemical treatment as defined in Annex IIA to Directive 75/442/EEC under heading D9 of non hazardous waste with a capacity exceeding 100 tonnes per day.

11. Groundwater abstraction or artificial groundwater recharge schemes where the annual volume of water abstracted or recharged is equivalent to or exceeds 10 million cubic metres.

12.

(a) Works for the transfer of water resources between river basins where this transfer aims at preventing possible shortages of water and where the amount of water transferred exceeds 100 million cubic metres/year;
(b) In all other cases, works for the transfer of water resources between river basins where the multi-annual average flow of the basin of abstraction exceeds 2 000 million cubic metres/year and where the amount of water transferred exceeds 5% of this flow.

In both cases transfers of piped drinking water are excluded.

---

[1] For the purposes of this Directive, 'airport' means airports which comply with the definition in the 1944 Chicago Convention setting up the International Civil Aviation Organization (Annex 14).
[2] For the purposes of the Directive, 'express road' means a road which complies with the definition in the European Agreement on Main International Traffic Arteries of 15 November 1975.
[3] OJ No L 194, 25.7.1975, p. 39. Directive as last amended by Commission Decision 94/3/EC (OJ No L 5, 7.1.1994, p. 15).
[4] OJ No L 377, 31.12.1991, p. 20. Directive as last amended by Directive 94/31/EC (OJ No L 168, 2.7.1994, p. 28).

13. Waste water treatment plants with a capacity exceeding 150 000 population equivalent as defined in Article 2 point (6) of Directive 91/271/EEC.[1]

14. Extraction of petroleum and natural gas for commercial purposes where the amount extracted exceeds 500 tonnes/day in the case of petroleum and 500 000 m^3/day in the case of gas.

15. Dams and other installations designed for the holding back or permanent storage of water, where a new or additional amount of water held back or stored exceeds 10 million cubic metres.

16. Pipelines for the transport of gas, oil or chemicals with a diameter of more than 800 mm and a length of more than 40 km.

17. Installations for the intensive rearing of poultry or pigs with more than:

(a) 85 000 places for broilers, 60 000 places for hens;
(b) 3 000 places for production pigs (over 30 kg); or
(c) 900 places for sows.

18. Industrial plants for the

(a) production of pulp from timber or similar fibrous materials;
(b) production of paper and board with a production capacity exceeding 200 tonnes per day.

19. Quarries and open-cast mining where the surface of the site exceeds 25 hectares, or peat extraction, where the surface of the site exceeds 150 hectares.

20. Construction of overhead electrical power lines with a voltage of 220 kV or more and a length of more than 15 km.

21. Installations for storage of petroleum, petrochemical, or chemical products with a capacity of 200 000 tonnes or more.

22. Any change to or extension of projects listed in this Annex where such a change or extension in itself meets the thresholds, if any, set out in this Annex.

Annex II
Projects subject to Article 4(2)

1. Agriculture, silviculture and aquaculture

(a) Projects for the restructuring of rural land holdings;
(b) Projects for the use of uncultivated land or semi-natural areas for intensive agricultural purposes;
(c) Water management projects for agriculture, including irrigation and land drainage projects;

---

[1] OJ No L 135, 30.5.1991, p. 40. Directive as last amended by the 1994 Act of Accession.

(d) Initial afforestation and deforestation for the purposes of conversion to another type of land use;
(e) Intensive livestock installations (projects not included in Annex I);
(f) Intensive fish farming;
(g) Reclamation of land from the sea.

2. Extractive industry

(a) Quarries, open-cast mining and peat extraction (projects not included in Annex I);
(b) Underground mining;
(c) Extraction of minerals by marine or fluvial dredging;
(d) Deep drillings, in particular:
  – geothermal drilling,
  – drilling for the storage of nuclear waste material,
  – drilling for water supplies, with the exception of drillings for investigating the stability of the soil;
(e) Surface industrial installations for the extraction of coal, petroleum, natural gas and ores, as well as bituminous shale.

3. Energy industry

(a) Industrial installations for the production of electricity, steam and hot water (projects not included in Annex I);
(b) Industrial installations for carrying gas, steam and hot water; transmission of electrical energy by overhead cables (projects not included in Annex I);
(c) Surface storage of natural gas;
(d) Underground storage of combustible gases;
(e) Surface storage of fossil fuels;
(f) Industrial briquetting of coal and lignite;
(g) Installations for the processing and storage of radioactive waste (unless included in Annex I);
(h) Installations for hydroelectric energy production;
 (i) Installations for the harnessing of wind power for energy production (wind farms).

4. Production and processing of metals

(a) Installations for the production of pig iron or steel (primary or secondary fusion) including continuous casting;
(b) Installations for the processing of ferrous metals:
   (i) hot-rolling mills;
  (ii) smitheries with hammers;
  (iii) application of protective fused metal coats;
(c) Ferrous metal foundries;

(d) Installations for the smelting, including the alloyage, of non-ferrous metals, excluding precious metals, including recovered products (refining, foundry casting, etc.);
(e) Installations for surface treatment of metals and plastic materials using anelectrolytic or chemical process;
(f) Manufacture and assembly of motor vehicles and manufacture of motor vehicle engines;
(g) Shipyards;
(h) Installations for the construction and repair of aircraft;
 (i) Manufacture of railway equipment;
 (j) Swaging by explosives;
(k) Installations for the roasting and sintering of metallic ores.

5. Mineral industry

(a) Coke ovens (dry coal distillation);
(b) Installations for the manufacture of cement;
(c) Installations for the production of asbestos and the manufacture of asbestos-products (projects not included in Annex I);
(d) Installations for the manufacture of glass including glass fibre;
(e) Installations for smelting mineral substances including the production of mineral fibres;
(f) Manufacture of ceramic products by burning, in particular roofing tiles, bricks, refractory bricks, tiles, stoneware or porcelain.

6. Chemical industry (Projects not included in Annex I)

(a) Treatment of intermediate products and production of chemicals;
(b) Production of pesticides and pharmaceutical products, paint and varnishes, elastomers and peroxides;
(c) Storage facilities for petroleum, petrochemical and chemical products.

7. Food industry

(a) Manufacture of vegetable and animal oils and fats;
(b) Packing and canning of animal and vegetable products;
(c) Manufacture of dairy products;
(d) Brewing and malting;
(e) Confectionery and syrup manufacture;
(f) Installations for the slaughter of animals;
(g) Industrial starch manufacturing installations;
(h) Fish-meal and fish-oil factories;
 (i) Sugar factories.

8. Textile, leather, wood and paper industries

(a) Industrial plants for the production of paper and board (projects not included in Annex I);
(b) Plants for the pretreatment (operations such as washing, bleaching, mercerization) or dyeing of fibres or textiles;
(c) Plants for the tanning of hides and skins;
(d) Cellulose-processing and production installations.

9. Rubber industry Manufacture and treatment of elastomer-based products.

10. Infrastructure projects

(a) Industrial estate development projects;
(b) Urban development projects, including the construction of shopping centres and car parks;
(c) Construction of railways and intermodal transshipment facilities, and of intermodal terminals (projects not included in Annex I);
(d) Construction of airfields (projects not included in Annex I);
(e) Construction of roads, harbours and port installations, including fishing harbours (projects not included in Annex I);
(f) Inland-waterway construction not included in Annex I, canalization and flood-relief works;
(g) Dams and other installations designed to hold water or store it on a long-term basis (projects not included in Annex I);
(h) Tramways, elevated and underground railways, suspended lines or similar lines of a particular type, used exclusively or mainly for passenger transport;
(i) Oil and gas pipeline installations (projects not included in Annex I);
(j) Installations of long-distance aqueducts;
(k) Coastal work to combat erosion and maritime works capable of altering the coast through the construction, for example, of dykes, moles, jetties and other sea defence works, excluding the maintenance and reconstruction of such works;
(l) Groundwater abstraction and artificial groundwater recharge schemes not included in Annex I;
(m) Works for the transfer of water resources between river basins not included in Annex I.

11. Other projects

(a) Permanent racing and test tracks for motorized vehicles;
(b) Installations for the disposal of waste (projects not included in Annex I);
(c) Waste-water treatment plants (projects not included in Annex I);

(d) Sludge-deposition sites;
(e) Storage of scrap iron, including scrap vehicles;
(f) Test benches for engines, turbines or reactors;
(g) Installations for the manufacture of artificial mineral fibres;
(h) Installations for the recovery or destruction of explosive substances;
(i) Knackers' yards.

12. Tourism and leisure

(a) Ski-runs, ski-lifts and cable-cars and associated developments;
(b) Marinas;
(c) Holiday villages and hotel complexes outside urban areas and associated developments;
(d) Permanent camp sites and caravan sites;
(e) Theme parks.

13.

– Any change or extension of projects listed in Annex I or Annex II, already authorized, executed or in the process of being executed, which may have significant adverse effects on the environment (change or extension not included in Annex I);
– Projects in Annex I, undertaken exclusively or mainly for the development and testing of new methods or products and not used for more than two years.

Annex III
Selection criteria referredto in Article 4(3)

1. Characteristics of projects   The characteristics of projects must be considered having regard, in particular, to:

– the size of the project,
– the cumulation with other projects,
– the use of natural resources,
– the production of waste,
– pollution and nuisances,
– the risk of accidents, having regard in particular to substances or technologies used.

2. Location of projects   The environmental sensitivity of geographical areas likely to be affected by projects must be considered, having regard, in particular, to:

– the existing land use,
– the relative abundance, quality and regenerative capacity of natural resources in the area,

– the absorption capacity of the natural environment, paying particular attention to the following areas:

(a) wetlands;
(b) coastal zones;
(c) mountain and forest areas;
(d) nature reserves and parks;
(e) areas classified or protected under Member States' legislation; special protection areas designated by Member States pursuant to Directive 79/409/EEC and 92/43/EEC;
(f) areas in which the environmental quality standards laid down in Community legislation have already been exceeded;
(g) densely populated areas;
(h) landscapes of historical, cultural or archaeological significance.

3. Characteristics of the potential impact The potential significant effects of projects must be considered in relation to criteria set out under 1 and 2 above, and having regard in particular to:

– the extent of the impact (geographical area and size of the affected population),
– the transfrontier nature of the impact,
– the magnitude and complexity of the impact,
– the probability of the impact,
– the duration, frequency and reversibility of the impact.

Annex IV
Information referred to in Article 5(1)

1. Description of the project, including in particular:

– a description of the physical characteristics of the whole project and the land-use requirements during the construction and operational phases,
– a description of the main characteristics of the production processes, for instance, nature and quantity of the materials used,
– an estimate, by type and quantity, of expected residues and emissions (water, air and soil pollution, noise, vibration, light, heat, radiation, etc.) resulting from the operation of the proposed project.

2. An outline of the main alternatives studied by the developer and an indication of the main reasons for this choice, taking into account the environmental effects.

3. A description of the aspects of the environment likely to be significantly affected by the proposed project, including, in particular, population, fauna, flora, soil, water,

air, climatic factors, material assets, including the architectural and archaeological heritage, landscape and the inter-relationship between the above factors.

4. A description[1] of the likely significant effects of the proposed project on the environment resulting from:

– the existence of the project,
– the use of natural resources,
– the emission of pollutants, the creation of nuisances and the elimination of waste, and the description by the developer of the forecasting methods used to assess the effects on the environment.

5. A description of the measures envisaged to prevent, reduce and where possible offset any significant adverse effects on the environment.

6. A non-technical summary of the information provided under the above headings.

7. An indication of any difficulties (technical deficiencies or lack of know-how) encountered by the developer in compiling the required information.

---

[1] This description should cover the direct effects and any indirect, secondary, cumulative, short, medium and long-term, permanent and temporary, positive and negative effects of the project.

Directive 2001/42/EC of the European Parliament and of the Council of 27 June 2001 on the assessment of the effects of certain plans and programmes on the environment

Editorial note

Council Directive 2001/42 of 27 June 2001 on the assessment of certain plans and programmes on the environment is aimed at providing a high level of protection of the environment and at promoting sustainable development, by ensuring that an environmental impact assessment is carried out on certain plans and programmes which are likely to have significant effects on the environment (Article 1 and Article 3). Plans and programmes for the purposes of the Directive are 'plans and programmes, including those co-financed by the European Community, as well as any modifications to them: which are subject to preparation and/or adoption by an authority at national, regional or local level or which are prepared by an authority for adoption, through a legislative procedure by Parliament or Government, and which are required by legislative, regulatory or administrative provisions' (Article 2(a)).

An environmental assessment is to be carried out for all plans and programmes which are prepared for agriculture, forestry, fisheries, energy, industry, transport, waste management, water management, telecommunications, tourism, town and country planning or land use and which set the framework for future development consent of projects listed in Annexes I and II to Directive 85/337/EEC, or which, in view of the likely effect on sites, have been determined to require an assessment pursuant to Article 6 or 7 of Directive 92/43/EEC (Habitat Directive) (Article 3(1)). If such plans and programmes determine the use of small areas at local level and minor modifications to plans and programmes, they are to require an environmental assessment only where the Member States determine that they are likely to have significant environmental effects (Article 3(2)). Member States are to determine whether plans and programmes, other than those referred to in Article 3(2), which set the framework for future development consent of projects, are likely to have significant environmental effects (Article 3(3)). Member States are to determine whether plans or programmes referred to in Article 3(3) and (4) are likely to have significant environmental effects either through case-by-case examination or by specifying types of plans and programmes or by combining both approaches. For this purpose Member States are in all cases to take into account relevant criteria set out in Annex II, in order to ensure that plans and programmes with likely significant effects on the environment are covered by this Directive (Article 3(5)). Plans and programmes, the sole purpose of which is to serve national defence or civil emergency, financial or budget plans and programmes, are not subject to the Directive (Article 3(8)).

The environmental assessment is to be carried out according to the provisions set out in Articles 4 to 9. It is to be carried out during the preparation of the plan or programme and before its adoption (Article 4(1)). An environmental report is to be prepared in which the likely significant effects on the environment of implementing the plan or progamme and reasonable alternatives are identified, described and evaluated (Article 5). The draft plan and programme and the environmental report are to be made available to the relevant authorities and to the public for information and consultation (Article 6). Transboundary consultations are required when the implementation of a plan or programme is likely to have significant effects on the environment of another Member State (Article 7). The environmental report, the opinion expressed during consultation with the public and competent authorities and with transboundary States, if any, is to be taken into account during the preparation of the plan or programme and before its adoption or submission to the legislative procedure (Article 8). When a plan or progamme is adopted the public, the competent authorities and any Member State consulted are to be informed of the decision (Article 9). Member States are to monitor the significant environmental effects of the implementation of plans and programmes (Article 10). They are to ensure that environmental reports are of a sufficient quality (Article 11(2)). The Directive is to be implemented by the Member States before 21 July 2004 (Article 13).

Source: OJ L 197 21.07.2001 p. 30

Directive 2001/42/EC of the European Parliament and of the Council of 27 June 2001 on the assessment of the effects of certain plans and programmes on the environment

The European Parliament and the Council of the European Union,
    Having regard to the Treaty establishing the European Community, and in particular Article 175(1) thereof,
    Having regard to the proposal from the Commission,[1]
    Having regard to the opinion of the Economic and Social Committee,[2]
    Having regard to the opinion of the Committee of the Regions,[3]

---

[1] OJ C 129, 25.4.1997, p. 14 and OJ C 83, 25.3.1999, p. 13.
[2] OJ C 287, 22.9.1997, p. 101.
[3] OJ C 64, 27.2.1998, p. 63 and OJ C 374, 23.12.1999, p. 9.

Acting in accordance with the procedure laid down in Article 251 of the Treaty,[1] in the light of the joint text approved by the Conciliation Committee on 21 March 2001, Whereas:

(1) Article 174 of the Treaty provides that Community policy on the environment is to contribute to, *inter alia*, the preservation, protection and improvement of the quality of the environment, the protection of human health and the prudent and rational utilisation of natural resources and that it is to be based on the precautionary principle. Article 6 of the Treaty provides that environmental protection requirements are to be integrated into the definition of Community policies and activities, in particular with a view to promoting sustainable development.

(2) The Fifth Environment Action Programme: Towards sustainability – A European Community programme of policy and action in relation to the environment and sustainable development,[2] supplemented by Council Decision No 2179/98/EC[3] on its review, affirms the importance of assessing the likely environmental effects of plans and programmes.

(3) The Convention on Biological Diversity requires Parties to integrate as far as possible and as appropriate the conservation and sustainable use of biological diversity into relevant sectoral or cross-sectoral plans and programmes.

(4) Environmental assessment is an important tool for integrating environmental considerations into the preparation and adoption of certain plans and programmes which are likely to have significant effects on the environment in the Member States, because it ensures that such effects of implementing plans and programmes are taken into account during their preparation and before their adoption.

(5) The adoption of environmental assessment procedures at the planning and programming level should benefit undertakings by providing a more consistent framework in which to operate by the inclusion of the relevant environmental information into decision making. The inclusion of a wider set of factors in decision making should contribute to more sustainable and effective solutions.

(6) The different environmental assessment systems operating within Member States should contain a set of common procedural requirements necessary to contribute to a high level of protection of the environment.

(7) The United Nations/Economic Commission for Europe Convention on Environmental Impact Assessment in a Transboundary Context of 25 February 1991, which applies to both Member States and other States, encourages the parties to the Convention to apply its principles to plans and programmes as well; at the

---

[1] Opinion of the European Parliament of 20 October 1998 (OJ C 341, 9.11.1998, p. 18), confirmed on 16 September 1999 (OJ C 54, 25.2.2000, p. 76), Council Common Position of 30 March 2000 (OJ C 137, 16.5.2000, p. 11) and Decision of the European Parliament of 6 September 2000 (OJ C 135, 7.5.2001, p. 155). Decision of the European Parliament of 31 May 2001 and Decision of the Council of 5 June 2001.
[2] OJ C 138, 17.5.1993, p. 5.   [3] OJ L 275, 10.10.1998, p. 1.

second meeting of the Parties to the Convention in Sofia on 26 and 27 February 2001, it was decided to prepare a legally binding protocol on strategic environmental assessment which would supplement the existing provisions on environmental impact assessment in a transboundary context, with a view to its possible adoption on the occasion of the 5th Ministerial Conference 'Environment for Europe' at an extraordinary meeting of the Parties to the Convention, scheduled for May 2003 in Kiev, Ukraine. The systems operating within the Community for environmental assessment of plans and programmes should ensure that there are adequate transboundary consultations where the implementation of a plan or programme being prepared in one Member State is likely to have significant effects on the environment of another Member State. The information on plans and programmes having significant effects on the environment of other States should be forwarded on a reciprocal and equivalent basis within an appropriate legal framework between Member States and these other States.

(8) Action is therefore required at Community level to lay down a minimum environmental assessment framework, which would set out the broad principles of the environmental assessment system and leave the details to the Member States, having regard to the principle of subsidiarity. Action by the Community should not go beyond what is necessary to achieve the objectives set out in the Treaty.

(9) This Directive is of a procedural nature, and its requirements should either be integrated into existing procedures in Member States or incorporated in specifically established procedures. With a view to avoiding duplication of the assessment, Member States should take account, where appropriate, of the fact that assessments will be carried out at different levels of a hierarchy of plans and programmes.

(10) All plans and programmes which are prepared for a number of sectors and which set a framework for future development consent of projects listed in Annexes I and II to Council Directive 85/337/EEC of 27 June 1985 on the assessment of the effects of certain public and private projects on the environment,[1] and all plans and programmes which have been determined to require assessment pursuant to Council Directive 92/43/EEC of 21 May 1992 on the conservation of natural habitats and of wild flora and fauna,[2] are likely to have significant effects on the environment, and should as a rule be made subject to systematic environmental assessment. When they determine the use of small areas at local level or are minor modifications to the above plans or programmes, they should be assessed only where Member States determine that they are likely to have significant effects on the environment.

(11) Other plans and programmes which set the framework for future development consent of projects may not have significant effects on the environment in all

[1] OJ L 175, 5.7.1985, p. 40. Directive as amended by Directive 97/11/EC (OJ L 73, 14.3.1997, p. 5).
[2] OJ L 206, 22.7.1992, p. 7. Directive as last amended by Directive 97/62/EC (OJ L 305, 8.11.1997, p. 42).

cases and should be assessed only where Member States determine that they are likely to have such effects.

(12) When Member States make such determinations, they should take into account the relevant criteria set out in this Directive.

(13) Some plans or programmes are not subject to this Directive because of their particular characteristics.

(14) Where an assessment is required by this Directive, an environmental report should be prepared containing relevant information as set out in this Directive, identifying, describing and evaluating the likely significant environmental effects of implementing the plan or programme, and reasonable alternatives taking into account the objectives and the geographical scope of the plan or programme; Member States should communicate to the Commission any measures they take concerning the quality of environmental reports.

(15) In order to contribute to more transparent decision making and with the aim of ensuring that the information supplied for the assessment is comprehensive and reliable, it is necessary to provide that authorities with relevant environmental responsibilities and the public are to be consulted during the assessment of plans and programmes, and that appropriate time frames are set, allowing sufficient time for consultations, including the expression of opinion.

(16) Where the implementation of a plan or programme prepared in one Member State is likely to have a significant effect on the environment of other Member States, provision should be made for the Member States concerned to enter into consultations and for the relevant authorities and the public to be informed and enabled to express their opinion.

(17) The environmental report and the opinions expressed by the relevant authorities and the public, as well as the results of any transboundary consultation, should be taken into account during the preparation of the plan or programme and before its adoption or submission to the legislative procedure.

(18) Member States should ensure that, when a plan or programme is adopted, the relevant authorities and the public are informed and relevant information is made available to them.

(19) Where the obligation to carry out assessments of the effects on the environment arises simultaneously from this Directive and other Community legislation, such as Council Directive 79/409/EEC of 2 April 1979 on the conservation of wild birds,[1] Directive 92/43/EEC, or Directive 2000/60/EC of the European Parliament and the Council of 23 October 2000 establishing a framework for Community action in the field of water policy,[2] in order to avoid duplication of the assessment, Member States may provide for coordinated or joint procedures fulfilling the requirements of the relevant Community legislation.

---

[1] OJ L 103, 25.4.1979, p. 1. Directive as last amended by Directive 97/49/EC (OJ L 223, 13.8.1997, p. 9).
[2] OJ L 327, 22.12.2000, p. 1.

(20) A first report on the application and effectiveness of this Directive should be carried out by the Commission five years after its entry into force, and at seven-year intervals thereafter. With a view to further integrating environmental protection requirements, and taking into account the experience acquired, the first report should, if appropriate, be accompanied by proposals for amendment of this Directive, in particular as regards the possibility of extending its scope to other areas/sectors and other types of plans and programmes,

Have adopted this Directive:

Article 1
Objectives

The objective of this Directive is to provide for a high level of protection of the environment and to contribute to the integration of environmental considerations into the preparation and adoption of plans and programmes with a view to promoting sustainable development, by ensuring that, in accordance with this Directive, an environmental assessment is carried out of certain plans and programmes which are likely to have significant effects on the environment.

Article 2
Definitions

For the purposes of this Directive:

(a) 'plans and programmes' shall mean plans and programmes, including those co-financed by the European Community, as well as any modifications to them:
  – which are subject to preparation and/or adoption by an authority at national, regional or local level or which are prepared by an authority for adoption, through a legislative procedure by Parliament or Government, and
  – which are required by legislative, regulatory or administrative provisions;
(b) 'environmental assessment' shall mean the preparation of an environmental report, the carrying out of consultations, the taking into account of the environmental report and the results of the consultations in decision-making and the provision of information on the decision in accordance with Articles 4 to 9;
(c) 'environmental report' shall mean the part of the plan or programme documentation containing the information required in Article 5 and Annex I;
(d) 'The public' shall mean one or more natural or legal persons and, in accordance with national legislation or practice, their associations, organisations or groups.

Article 3
Scope

1. An environmental assessment, in accordance with Articles 4 to 9, shall be carried out for plans and programmes referred to in paragraphs 2 to 4 which are likely to have significant environmental effects.

2. Subject to paragraph 3, an environmental assessment shall be carried out for all plans and programmes, (a) which are prepared for agriculture, forestry, fisheries, energy, industry, transport, waste management, water management, telecommunications, tourism, town and country planning or land use and which set the framework for future development consent of projects listed in Annexes I and II to Directive 85/337/EEC, or (b) which, in view of the likely effect on sites, have been determined to require an assessment pursuant to Article 6 or 7 of Directive 92/43/EEC.

3. Plans and programmes referred to in paragraph 2 which determine the use of small areas at local level and minor modifications to plans and programmes referred to in paragraph 2 shall require an environmental assessment only where the Member States determine that they are likely to have significant environmental effects.

4. Member States shall determine whether plans and programmes, other than those referred to in paragraph 2, which set the framework for future development consent of projects, are likely to have significant environmental effects.

5. Member States shall determine whether plans or programmes referred to in paragraphs 3 and 4 are likely to have significant environmental effects either through case-by-case examination or by specifying types of plans and programmes or by combining both approaches. For this purpose Member States shall in all cases take into account relevant criteria set out in Annex II, in order to ensure that plans and programmes with likely significant effects on the environment are covered by this Directive.

6. In the case-by-case examination and in specifying types of plans and programmes in accordance with paragraph 5, the authorities referred to in Article 6(3) shall be consulted.

7. Member States shall ensure that their conclusions pursuant to paragraph 5, including the reasons for not requiring an environmental assessment pursuant to Articles 4 to 9, are made available to the public.

8. The following plans and programmes are not subject to this Directive: – plans and programmes the sole purpose of which is to serve national defence or civil emergency, – financial or budget plans and programmes.

9. This Directive does not apply to plans and programmes co-financed under the current respective programming periods[1] for Council Regulations (EC) No 1260/1999[2] and (EC) No 1257/1999.[3]

---

[1] The 2000–2006 programming period for Council Regulation (EC) No 1260/1999 and the 2000–2006 and 2000–2007 programming periods for Council Regulation (EC) No 1257/1999.

[2] Council Regulation (EC) No 1260/1999 of 21 June 1999 laying down general provisions on the Structural Funds (OJ L 161, 26.6.1999, p. 1).

[3] Council Regulation (EC) No 1257/1999 of 17 May 1999 on support for rural development from the European Agricultural Guidance and Guarantee Fund (EAGGF) and amending and repealing certain regulations (OJ L 160, 26.6.1999, p. 80).

Article 4
General obligations

1. The environmental assessment referred to in Article 3 shall be carried out during the preparation of a plan or programme and before its adoption or submission to the legislative procedure.

2. The requirements of this Directive shall either be integrated into existing procedures in Member States for the adoption of plans and programmes or incorporated in procedures established to comply with this Directive.

3. Where plans and programmes form part of a hierarchy, Member States shall, with a view to avoiding duplication of the assessment, take into account the fact that the assessment will be carried out, in accordance with this Directive, at different levels of the hierarchy. For the purpose of, *inter alia*, avoiding duplication of assessment, Member States shall apply Article 5(2) and (3).

Article 5
Environmental report

1. Where an environmental assessment is required under Article 3(1), an environmental report shall be prepared in which the likely significant effects on the environment of implementing the plan or programme, and reasonable alternatives taking into account the objectives and the geographical scope of the plan or programme, are identified, described and evaluated. The information to be given for this purpose is referred to in Annex I.

2. The environmental report prepared pursuant to paragraph 1 shall include the information that may reasonably be required taking into account current knowledge and methods of assessment, the contents and level of detail in the plan or programme, its stage in the decision-making process and the extent to which certain matters are more appropriately assessed at different levels in that process in order to avoid duplication of the assessment.

3. Relevant information available on environmental effects of the plans and programmes and obtained at other levels of decision-making or through other Community legislation may be used for providing the information referred to in Annex I.

4. The authorities referred to in Article 6(3) shall be consulted when deciding on the scope and level of detail of the information which must be included in the environmental report.

Article 6
Consultations

1. The draft plan or programme and the environmental report prepared in accordance with Article 5 shall be made available to the authorities referred to in paragraph 3 of this Article and the public.

2. The authorities referred to in paragraph 3 and the public referred to in paragraph 4 shall be given an early and effective opportunity within appropriate time frames

to express their opinion on the draft plan or programme and the accompanying environmental report before the adoption of the plan or programme or its submission to the legislative procedure.

3. Member States shall designate the authorities to be consulted which, by reason of their specific environmental responsibilities, are likely to be concerned by the environmental effects of implementing plans and programmes.

4. Member States shall identify the public for the purposes of paragraph 2, including the public affected or likely to be affected by, or having an interest in, the decision-making subject to this Directive, including relevant non-governmental organisations, such as those promoting environmental protection and other organisations concerned.

5. The detailed arrangements for the information and consultation of the authorities and the public shall be determined by the Member States.

Article 7
Transboundary consultations

1. Where a Member State considers that the implementation of a plan or programme being prepared in relation to its territory is likely to have significant effects on the environment in another Member State, or where a Member State likely to be significantly affected so requests, the Member State in whose territory the plan or programme is being prepared shall, before its adoption or submission to the legislative procedure, forward a copy of the draft plan or programme and the relevant environmental report to the other Member State.

2. Where a Member State is sent a copy of a draft plan or programme and an environmental report under paragraph 1, it shall indicate to the other Member State whether it wishes to enter into consultations before the adoption of the plan or programme or its submission to the legislative procedure and, if it so indicates, the Member States concerned shall enter into consultations concerning the likely transboundary environmental effects of implementing the plan or programme and the measures envisaged to reduce or eliminate such effects. Where such consultations take place, the Member States concerned shall agree on detailed arrangements to ensure that the authorities referred to in Article 6(3) and the public referred to in Article 6(4) in the Member State likely to be significantly affected are informed and given an opportunity to forward their opinion within a reasonable time-frame.

3. Where Member States are required under this Article to enter into consultations, they shall agree, at the beginning of such consultations, on a reasonable timeframe for the duration of the consultations.

Article 8
Decision making

The environmental report prepared pursuant to Article 5, the opinions expressed pursuant to Article 6 and the results of any transboundary consultations entered into pursuant to Article 7 shall be taken into account during the preparation of the plan or programme and before its adoption or submission to the legislative procedure.

Article 9
Information on the decision

1. Member States shall ensure that, when a plan or programme is adopted, the authorities referred to in Article 6(3), the public and any Member State consulted under Article 7 are informed and the following items are made available to those so informed:

(a) the plan or programme as adopted;
(b) a statement summarising how environmental considerations have been integrated into the plan or programme and how the environmental report prepared pursuant to Article 5, the opinions expressed pursuant to Article 6 and the results of consultations entered into pursuant to Article 7 have been taken into account in accordance with Article 8 and the reasons for choosing the plan or programme as adopted, in the light of the other reasonable alternatives dealt with, and
(c) the measures decided concerning monitoring in accordance with Article 10.

2. The detailed arrangements concerning the information referred to in paragraph 1 shall be determined by the Member States.

Article 10
Monitoring

1. Member States shall monitor the significant environmental effects of the implementation of plans and programmes in order, *inter alia*, to identify at an early stage unforeseen adverse effects, and to be able to undertake appropriate remedial action.

2. In order to comply with paragraph 1, existing monitoring arrangements may be used if appropriate, with a view to avoiding duplication of monitoring.

Article 11
Relationship with other Community legislation

1. An environmental assessment carried out under this Directive shall be without prejudice to any requirements under Directive 85/337/EEC and to any other Community law requirements.

2. For plans and programmes for which the obligation to carry out assessments of the effects on the environment arises simultaneously from this Directive and other Community legislation, Member States may provide for coordinated or joint procedures fulfilling the requirements of the relevant Community legislation in order, *inter alia*, to avoid duplication of assessment.

3. For plans and programmes co-financed by the European Community, the environmental assessment in accordance with this Directive shall be carried out in conformity with the specific provisions in relevant Community legislation.

Article 12
Information, reporting and review

1. Member States and the Commission shall exchange information on the experience gained in applying this Directive.

2. Member States shall ensure that environmental reports are of a sufficient quality to meet the requirements of this Directive and shall communicate to the Commission any measures they take concerning the quality of these reports.

3. Before 21 July 2006 the Commission shall send a first report on the application and effectiveness of this Directive to the European Parliament and to the Council. With a view further to integrating environmental protection requirements, in accordance with Article 6 of the Treaty, and taking into account the experience acquired in the application of this Directive in the Member States, such a report will be accompanied by proposals for amendment of this Directive, if appropriate. In particular, the Commission will consider the possibility of extending the scope of this Directive to other areas/sectors and other types of plans and programmes. A new evaluation report shall follow at seven-year intervals.

4. The Commission shall report on the relationship between this Directive and Regulations (EC) No 1260/1999 and (EC) No 1257/1999 well ahead of the expiry of the programming periods provided for in those Regulations, with a view to ensuring a coherent approach with regard to this Directive and subsequent Community Regulations.

Article 13
Implementation of the Directive

1. Member States shall bring into force the laws, regulations and administrative provisions necessary to comply with this Directive before 21 July 2004. They shall forthwith inform the Commission thereof.

2. When Member States adopt the measures, they shall contain a reference to this Directive or shall be accompanied by such reference on the occasion of their official publication. The methods of making such reference shall be laid down by Member States.

3. The obligation referred to in Article 4(1) shall apply to the plans and programmes of which the first formal preparatory act is subsequent to the date referred to in paragraph 1. Plans and programmes of which the first formal preparatory act is before that date and which are adopted or submitted to the legislative procedure more than 24 months thereafter, shall be made subject to the obligation referred to in Article 4(1) unless Member States decide on a case by case basis that this is not feasible and inform the public of their decision.

4. Before 21 July 2004, Member States shall communicate to the Commission, in addition to the measures referred to in paragraph 1, separate information on the types of plans and programmes which, in accordance with Article 3, would be subject to

an environmental assessment pursuant to this Directive. The Commission shall make this information available to the Member States. The information will be updated on a regular basis.

Article 14
Entry into force

This Directive shall enter into force on the day of its publication in the *Official Journal of the European Communities.*

Article 15
Addressees

This Directive is addressed to the Member States.
Done at Luxembourg, 27 June 2001.

Annex I
Information referred to in Article 5(1)

The information to be provided under Article 5(1), subject to Article 5(2) and (3), is the following:

(a) an outline of the contents, main objectives of the plan or programme and relationship with other relevant plans and programmes;
(b) the relevant aspects of the current state of the environment and the likely evolution thereof without implementation of the plan or programme;
(c) the environmental characteristics of areas likely to be significantly affected;
(d) any existing environmental problems which are relevant to the plan or programme including, in particular, those relating to any areas of a particular environmental importance, such as areas designated pursuant to Directives 79/409/EEC and 92/43/EEC;
(e) the environmental protection objectives, established at international, Community or Member State level, which are relevant to the plan or programme and the way those objectives and any environmental considerations have been taken into account during its preparation;
(f) the likely significant effects[1] on the environment, including on issues such as biodiversity, population, human health, fauna, flora, soil, water, air, climatic factors, material assets, cultural heritage including architectural and archaeological heritage, landscape and the interrelationship between the above factors;
(g) the measures envisaged to prevent, reduce and as fully as possible offset any significant adverse effects on the environment of implementing the plan or programme;

---

[1] These effects should include secondary, cumulative, synergistic, short, medium and long-term permanent and temporary, positive and negative effects.

(h) an outline of the reasons for selecting the alternatives dealt with, and a description of how the assessment was undertaken including any difficulties (such as technical deficiencies or lack of know-how) encountered in compiling the required information;
(i) a description of the measures envisaged concerning monitoring in accordance with Article 10;
(j) a non-technical summary of the information provided under the above headings.

Annex II
Criteria for determining the likely significance of effects referred to in Article 3(5)

1. The characteristics of plans and programmes, having regard, in particular, to

— the degree to which the plan or programme sets a framework for projects and other activities, either with regard to the location, nature, size and operating conditions or by allocating resources,
— the degree to which the plan or programme influences other plans and programmes including those in a hierarchy,
— the relevance of the plan or programme for the integration of environmental considerations in particular with a view to promoting sustainable development,
— environmental problems relevant to the plan or programme,
— the relevance of the plan or programme for the implementation of Community legislation on the environment (e.g. plans and programmes linked to waste-management or water protection).

2. Characteristics of the effects and of the area likely to be affected, having regard, in particular, to

— the probability, duration, frequency and reversibility of the effects,
— the cumulative nature of the effects,
— the transboundary nature of the effects,
— the risks to human health or the environment (e.g. due to accidents),
— the magnitude and spatial extent of the effects (geographical area and size of the population likely to be affected),
— the value and vulnerability of the area likely to be affected due to:
    — special natural characteristics or cultural heritage,
    — exceeded environmental quality standards or limit values,
    — intensive land-use,
— the effects on areas or landscapes which have a recognised national, Community or international protection status.

Council Directive 96/61/EC of 24 September 1996 concerning integrated pollution prevention and control (as amended)

Editorial note

Council Directive 96/61 on integrated pollution prevention and control (IPPC) is designed to achieve integrated prevention and control of pollution arising from activities listed in Annex I to the Directive (energy industries, production and processing of metals, mineral industry, chemical industry, waste management, livestock farming, etc.). The Directive lays down measures designed to prevent or, where that is not practicable, to reduce emissions in the air, water and land from the above-mentioned activities, including measures concerning waste, in order to achieve a high level of protection of the environment taken as a whole (Article 1). The competent authorities of Member States are to ensure that installations subject to the Directive are operated in such a way that all the appropriate preventive measures are taken against pollution, in particular through application of the best available techniques; no significant pollution is caused; waste production is avoided or, where waste is produced, it is recovered or, where that is technically and economically impossible, it is disposed of while avoiding or reducing any impact on the environment; energy is used efficiently; the necessary measures are taken to prevent accidents and limit their consequences; and the necessary measures are taken upon definitive cessation of activities to avoid any pollution risk and return the site of operation to a satisfactory state (Article 3). New installations regulated by the Directive are to operate only with a permit issued in accordance with the Directive (Article 4). A transitional period (30 October 1999 to 30 October 2007) is laid down during which existing installations are to comply with the Directive.

Member States are to ensure that applications for permits include, *inter alia*, a description of the installation and its activities; the raw and auxiliary materials, substances and energy used; sources of emissions, etc. (Article 6). They are to ensure that an integrated approach is followed by the competent authorities (Article 7). The competent authority can grant or refuse a permit for the installation and all permits are to include details of the arrangements made for air, water and land protection (Article 8). Permits are to include all measures necessary for compliance with the Directive in order to achieve a high level of protection of the environment as a whole by means of protection of the air, water and land (Article 9). In particular, permits are to include emission limit values, which shall be based on the best available techniques (Article 9(3) and (4)). The operator must inform the competent authorities of changes and, where appropriate, the permit is to be updated. No substantial change in the operation of the activity is to be made without a permit issued in accordance with the Directive (Article 12). Permits shall be periodically reconsidered and updated in specific circumstances (Article 13). Member States are to ensure that operators of installations comply with the permit and the conditions attached thereto (Article 14). The public concerned are to be given an early and effective opportunity to participate in the procedure for issuing a new permit, substantial changes and updating of existing permits (Article 15(1)). The public are to be informed of the decision on applications for permits and are to have access to information, including results of monitoring of releases from installations (Article 15(2), (3), (4) and (5)). Member States are to ensure that the public concerned, having a sufficient interest or, alternatively, maintaining the impairment of a right, where the administrative law of a Member State so requires as a precondition, have access to a review procedure before a court of law or another independent and impartial body established by law (Article 15a). Member States are to exchange information with another Member State where the operation of an installation is likely to have significant negative effects on the environment of such other Member State (Article 17).

Source: OJ L 257 10.10.1996 p. 26. Amended by: Directive 2003/35/EC of the European Parliament and of the Council of 26 May 2003 L 156 17 25.06.2003; Directive 2003/87/EC of the European Parliament and of the Council of 13 October 2003 L 275 32 25.10.2003; Regulation (EC) No 1882/2003 of the European Parliament and of the Council of 29 September 2003 L 284 1 31.10.2003

Council Directive 96/61/EC of 24 September 1996 concerning integrated pollution prevention and control (as amended)

The council of the European Union,

Having regard to the Treaty establishing the European Community, and in particular Article 130s(1) thereof,

Having regard to the proposal from the Commission,[1]

Having regard to the opinion of the Economic and Social Committee,[2]

Acting in accordance with the procedure laid down in Article 189c of the Treaty,[3]

---

[1] OJ No C 311, 17. 11. 1993 p. 6 and OJ No C 165, 1. 7. 1995, p. 9.

[2] OJ No C 195, 18. 7. 1995, p. 54.

[3] Opinion of the European Parliament of 14 December 1994 (OJ No C 18, 23. 1. 1995 p. 96), Council common position of 27 November 1995 (OJ No C87, 25. 3. 1996, p. 8) and Decision of the European Parliament of 22 May 1996 (OJ No C 166, 10. 6. 1996).

1. Whereas the objectives and principles of the Community's environment policy, as set out in Article 130r of the Treaty, consist in particular of preventing, reducing and as far as possible eliminating pollution by giving priority to intervention at source and ensuring prudent management of natural resources, in compliance with the 'polluter pays' principle and the principle of pollution prevention;

2. Whereas the Fifth Environmental Action Programme, the broad outline of which was approved by the Council and the Representatives of the Governments of the Member States, meeting within the Council, in the resolution of 1 February 1993 on a Community programme of policy and action in relation to the environment and sustainable development,[1] accords priority to integrated pollution control as an important part of the move towards a more sustainable balance between human activity and socio-economic development, on the one hand, and the resources and regenerative capacity of nature, on the other;

3. Whereas the implementation of an integrated approach to reduce pollution requires action at Community level in order to modify and supplement existing Community legislation concerning the prevention and control of pollution from industrial plants;

4. Whereas Council Directive 84/360/EEC of 28 June 1984 on the combating of air pollution from industrial plants[2] introduced a general framework requiring authorization prior to any operation or substantial modification of industrial installations which may cause air pollution;

5. Whereas Council Directive 76/464/EEC of 4 May 1976 on pollution caused by certain dangerous substances discharged into the aquatic environment of the Community[3] introduced an authorization requirement for the discharge of those substances;

6. Whereas, although Community legislation exists on the combating of air pollution and the prevention or minimization of the discharge of dangerous substances into water, there is no comparable Community legislation aimed at preventing or minimizing emissions into soil;

7. Whereas different approaches to controlling emissions into the air, water or soil separately may encourage the shifting of pollution between the various environmental media rather than protecting the environment as a whole;

8. Whereas the objective of an integrated approach to pollution control is to prevent emissions into air, water or soil wherever this is practicable, taking into account waste management, and, where it is not, to minimize them in order to achieve a high level of protection for the environment as a whole;

---

[1] OJ No C 138, 17. 5. 1993, p. 1.
[2] OJ No L 188, 16. 7. 1984, p. 20. Directive as last amended by Directive 91/692/EEC (OJ No L 377, 31. 12. 1991, p. 48).
[3] OJ No L 129, 18. 5. 1976, p. 23. Directive as last amended by Directive 91/692/EEC.

9. Whereas this Directive establishes a general framework for integrated pollution prevention and control; whereas it lays down the measures necessary to implement integrated pollution prevention and control in order to achieve a high level of protection for the environment as a whole; whereas application of the principle of sustainable development will be promoted by an integrated approach to pollution control;

10. Whereas the provisions of this Directive apply without prejudice to the provisions of Council Directive 85/337/EEC of 27 June 1985 on the assessment of the effects of public and private projects on the environment;[1] whereas, when information or conclusions obtained further to the application of that Directive have to be taken into consideration for the granting of authorization, this Directive does not affect the implementation of Directive 85/337/EEC;

11. Whereas the necessary steps must be taken by the Member States in order to ensure that the operator of the industrial activities referred to in Annex I is complying with the general principles of certain basic obligations; whereas for that purpose it would suffice for the competent authorities to take those general principles into account when laying down the authorization conditions;

12. Whereas some of the provisions adopted pursuant to this Directive must be applied to existing installations after a fixed period and others as from the date of implementation of this Directive;

13. Whereas, in order to tackle pollution problems more effectively and efficiently, environmental aspects should be taken into consideration by the operator; whereas those aspects should be communicated to the competent authority or authorities so that they can satisfy themselves, before granting a permit, that all appropriate preventive or pollution-control measures have been laid down; whereas very different application procedures may give rise to different levels of environmental protection and public awareness; whereas, therefore, applications for permits under this Directive should include minimum data;

14. Whereas full coordination of the authorization procedure and conditions between competent authorities will make it possible to achieve the highest practicable level of protection for the environment as a whole;

15. Whereas the competent authority or authorities will grant or amend a permit only when integrated environmental protection measures for air, water and land have been laid down;

16. Whereas the permit is to include all necessary measures to fulfil the authorization conditions in order thus to achieve a high level of protection for the environment as a whole; whereas, without prejudice to the authorization procedure, those measures may also be the subject of general binding requirements;

---

[1] OJ No L 175, 5. 7. 1985, p. 40.

17. Whereas emission limit values, parameters or equivalent technical measures should be based on the best available techniques, without prescribing the use of one specific technique or technology and taking into consideration the technical characteristics of the installation concerned, its geographical location and local environmental conditions; whereas in all cases the authorization conditions will lay down provisions on minimizing long-distance or transfrontier pollution and ensure a high level of protection for the environment as a whole;

18. Whereas it is for the Member States to determine how the technical characteristics of the installation concerned, its geographical location and local environmental conditions can, where appropriate, be taken into consideration;

19. Whereas, when an environmental quality standard requires more stringent conditions than those that can be achieved by using the best available techniques, supplementary conditions will in particular be required by the permit, without prejudice to other measures that may be taken to comply with the environmental quality standards;

20. Whereas, because best available techniques will change with time, particularly in the light of technical advances, the competent authorities must monitor or be informed of such progress;

21. Whereas, changes to an installation may give rise to pollution; whereas the competent authority or authorities must therefore be notified of any change which might affect the environment; whereas substantial changes to plant must be subject to the granting of prior authorization in accordance with this Directive;

22. Whereas the authorization conditions must be periodically reviewed and if necessary updated; whereas, under certain conditions, they will in any event be re-examined;

23. Whereas, in order to inform the public of the operation of installations and their potential effect on the environment, and in order to ensure the transparency of the licensing process throughout the Community, the public must have access, before any decision is taken, to information relating to applications for permits for new installations or substantial changes and to the permits themselves, their updating and the relevant monitoring data;

24. Whereas the establishment of an inventory of principal emissions and sources responsible may be regarded as an important instrument making it possible in particular to compare pollution activities in the Community; whereas such an inventory will be prepared by the Commission, assisted by a regulatory committee;

25. Whereas the development and exchange of information at Community level about best available techniques will help to redress the technological imbalances in the Community, will promote the worldwide dissemination of limit values and techniques used in the Community and will help the Member States in the efficient implementation of this Directive;

26. Whereas reports on the implementation and effectiveness of this Directive will have to be drawn up regularly;

27. Whereas this Directive is concerned with installations whose potential for pollution, and therefore transfrontier pollution, is significant; whereas transboundary consultation is to be organized where applications relate to the licensing of new installations or substantial changes to installations which are likely to have significant negative environmental effects; whereas the applications relating to such proposals or substantial changes will be available to the public of the Member State likely to be affected;

28. Whereas the need for action may be identified at Community level to lay down emission limit values for certain categories of installation and pollutant covered by this Directive; whereas the Council will set such emission limit values in accordance with the provisions of the Treaty;

29. Whereas the provisions of this Directive apply without prejudice to Community provisions on health and safety at the workplace,

Has adopted this Directive:

Article 1
Purpose and scope

The purpose of this Directive is to achieve integrated prevention and control of pollution arising from the activities listed in Annex I. It lays down measures designed to prevent or, where that is not practicable, to reduce emissions in the air, water and land from the abovementioned activities, including measures concerning waste, in order to achieve a high level of protection of the environment taken as a whole, without prejudice to Directive 85/337/EEC and other relevant Community provisions.

Article 2
Definitions

For the purposes of this Directive:

1. 'substance' shall mean any chemical element and its compounds, with the exception of radioactive substances within the meaning of Directive 80/836/Euratom[1] and genetically modified organisms within the meaning of Directive 90/219/EEC[2] and Directive 90/220/EEC;[3]

---

[1] Council Directive 80/836/Euratom of 15 July 1980 amending the Directives laying down the basic safety standards for the health protection of the general public and workers against the dangers of ionizing radiation (OJ No L 246, 17. 9. 1980, p. 1). Directive as amended by Directive 84/467/ EEC (OJ No L 265, 5. 10. 1984, p. 4).

[2] Council Directive 90/219/EEC of 23 April 1990 on the contained use of genetically modified micro-organisms (OJ No L 117, 8. 5. 90, p. 1). Directive as amended by Commission Directive 94/51/EC (OJ No L 297, 18. 11. 1994, p. 29).

[3] Council Directive 90/220/EEC of 23 April 1990 on the deliberate release into the environment of genetically modified organisms (OJ No L 117, 8. 5. 1990, p. 15). Directive as amended by Commission Directive 94/15/EC (OJ No L 103, 22. 4. 1994, p. 20).

2. 'pollution' shall mean the direct or indirect introduction as a result of human activity, of substances, vibrations, heat or noise into the air, water or land which may be harmful to human health or the quality of the environment, result in damage to material property, or impair or interfere with amenities and other legitimate uses of the environment;

3. 'installation' shall mean a stationary technical unit where one or more activities listed in Annex I are carried out, and any other directly associated activities which have a technical connection with the activities carried out on that site and which could have an effect on emissions and pollution;

4. 'existing installation' shall mean an installation in operation or, in accordance with legislation existing before the date on which this Directive is brought into effect, an installation authorized or in the view of the competent authority the subject of a full request for authorization, provided that that installation is put into operation no later than one year after the date on which this Directive is brought into effect;

5. 'emission' shall mean the direct or indirect release of substances, vibrations, heat or noise from individual or diffuse sources in the installation into the air, water or land;

6. 'emission limit values' shall mean the mass, expressed in terms of certain specific parameters, concentration and/or level of an emission, which may not be exceeded during one or more periods of time. Emission limit values may also be laid down for certain groups, families or categories of substances, in particular for those listed in Annex III.

   The emission limit values for substances shall normally apply at the point where the emissions leave the installation, any dilution being disregarded when determining them. With regard to indirect releases into water, the effect of a water treatment plant may be taken into account when determining the emission limit values of the installation involved, provided that an equivalent level is guaranteed for the protection of the environment as a whole and provided this does not lead to higher levels of pollution in the environment, without prejudice to Directive 76/464/EEC or the Directives implementing it;

7. 'environmental quality standard' shall mean the set of requirements which must be fulfilled at a given time by a given environment or particular part thereof, as set out in Community legislation;

8. 'competent authority' shall mean the authority or authorities or bodies responsible under the legal provisions of the Member States for carrying out the obligations arising from this Directive;

9. 'permit' shall mean that part or the whole of a written decision (or several such decisions) granting authorization to operate all or part of an installation, subject to certain conditions which guarantee that the installation complies with the requirements of this Directive. A permit may cover one or more installations or parts of installations on the same site operated by the same operator;

10. (a) 'change in operation' shall mean a change in the nature or functioning, or an extension, of the installation which may have consequences for the environment;

 (b) 'substantial change' shall mean a change in operation which, in the opinion of the competent authority, may have significant negative effects on human beings or the environment. For the purposes of this definition, any change to or extension of an operation shall be deemed to be substantial if the change or extension in itself meets the thresholds, if any, set out in Annex I;

11. 'best available techniques' shall mean the most effective and advanced stage in the development of activities and their methods of operation which indicate the practical suitability of particular techniques for providing in principle the basis for emission limit values designed to prevent and, where that is not practicable, generally to reduce emissions and the impact on the environment as a whole:

 − 'techniques' shall include both the technology used and the way in which the installation is designed, built, maintained, operated and decommissioned,

 − 'available' techniques shall mean those developed on a scale which allows implementation in the relevant industrial sector, under economically and technically viable conditions, taking into consideration the costs and advantages, whether or not the techniques are used or produced inside the Member State in question, as long as they are reasonably accessible to the operator,

 − 'best' shall mean most effective in achieving a high general level of protection of the environment as a whole. In determining the best available techniques, special consideration should be given to the items listed in Annex IV;

12. 'operator' shall mean any natural or legal person who operates or controls the installation or, where this is provided for in national legislation, to whom decisive economic power over the technical functioning of the installation has been delegated;

13. 'the public' shall mean one or more natural or legal persons and, in accordance with national legislation or practice, their associations, organisations or groups;

14. 'the public concerned' shall mean the public affected or likely to be affected by, or having an interest in, the taking of a decision on the issuing or the updating of a permit or of permit conditions; for the purposes of this definition, non-governmental organisations promoting environmental protection and meeting any requirements under national law shall be deemed to have an interest.

Article 3
General principles governing the basic obligations of the operator

Member States shall take the necessary measures to provide that the competent authorities ensure that installations are operated in such a way that:

(a) all the appropriate preventive measures are taken against pollution, in particular through application of the best available techniques;

(b) no significant pollution is caused;
(c) waste production is avoided in accordance with Council Directive 75/442/EEC of 15 July 1975 on waste;[1] where waste is produced, it is recovered or, where that is technically and economically impossible, it is disposed of while avoiding or reducing any impact on the environment;
(d) energy is used efficiently;
(e) the necessary measures are taken to prevent accidents and limit their consequences;
(f) the necessary measures are taken upon definitive cessation of activities to avoid any pollution risk and return the site of operation to a satisfactory state.

For the purposes of compliance with this Article, it shall be sufficient if Member States ensure that the competent authorities take account of the general principles set out in this Article when they determine the conditions of the permit.

Article 4
Permits for new installations

Member States shall take the necessary measures to ensure that no new installation is operated without a permit issued in accordance with this Directive, without prejudice to the exceptions provided for in Council Directive 88/609/EEC of 24 November 1988 on the limitation of emissions of certain pollutants into the air from large combustion plants.[2]

Article 5
Requirements for the granting of permits for existing installations

1. Member States shall take the necessary measures to ensure that the competent authorities see to it, by means of permits in accordance with Articles 6 and 8 or, as appropriate, by reconsidering and, where necessary, by updating the conditions, that existing installations operate in accordance with the requirements of Articles 3, 7, 9, 10, 13, the first and second indents of 14, and 15(2) not later than eight years after the date on which this Directive is brought into effect, without prejudice to specific Community legislation.

2. Member States shall take the necessary measures to apply the provisions of Articles 1, 2, 11, 12, 14, third indent, 15(1), (3) and (4), 16, 17 and 18(2) to existing installations as from the date on which this Directive is brought into effect.

---

[1] OJ No L 194, 25. 7. 1975, p. 39. Directive as last amended by Directive 91/692/EEC (OJ No L 377, 31. 12. 1991, p. 48).
[2] OJ No L 336, 7. 12. 1988, p. 1. Directive as last amended by Directive 90/656/EEC (OJ No L 353, 17. 12. 1990, p. 59).

Article 6
Applications for permits

1. Member States shall take the necessary measures to ensure that an application to the competent authority for a permit includes a description of:

- the installation and its activities,
- the raw and auxiliary materials, other substances and the energy used in or generated by the installation,
- the sources of emissions from the installation,
- the conditions of the site of the installation,
- the nature and quantities of foreseeable emissions from the installation into each medium as well as identification of significant effects of the emissions on the environment,
- the proposed technology and other techniques for preventing or, where this not possible, reducing emissions from the installation,
- where necessary, measures for the prevention and recovery of waste generated by the installation,
- further measures planned to comply with the general principles of the basic obligations of the operator as provided for in Article 3,
- measures planned to monitor emissions into the environment,
- the main alternatives, if any, studied by the applicant in outline.

An application for a permit shall also include a non-technical summary of the details referred to in the above indents.

2. Where information supplied in accordance with the requirements provided for in Directive 85/337/EEC or a safety report prepared in accordance with Council Directive 82/501/EEC of 24 June 1982 on the major-accident hazards of certain industrial activities[1] or other information produced in response to other legislation fulfils any of the requirements of this Article, that information may be included in, or attached to, the application.

Article 7
Integrated approach to issuing permits

Member States shall take the measures necessary to ensure that the conditions of, and procedure for the grant of, the permit are fully coordinated where more than one competent authority is involved, in order to guarantee an effective integrated approach by all authorities competent for this procedure.

---

[1] OJ No L 230, 5. 8. 1982, p. 1. Directive as last amended by Directive 91/692/EEC (OJ No L 377, 31. 12. 1991, p. 48).

Article 8
Decisions

Without prejudice to other requirements laid down in national or Community legislation, the competent authority shall grant a permit containing conditions guaranteeing that the installation complies with the requirements of this Directive or, if it does not, shall refuse to grant the permit. All permits granted and modified permits must include details of the arrangements made for air, water and land protection as referred to in this Directive.

Article 9
Conditions of the permit

1. Member States shall ensure that the permit includes all measures necessary for compliance with the requirements of Articles 3 and 10 for the granting of permits in order to achieve a high level of protection for the environment as a whole by means of protection of the air, water and land.

2. In the case of a new installation or a substantial change where Article 4 of Directive 85/337/EEC applies, any relevant information obtained or conclusion arrived at pursuant to Articles 5, 6 and 7 of that Directive shall be taken into consideration for the purposes of granting the permit.

3. The permit shall include emission limit values for pollutants, in particular, those listed in in Annex III, likely to be emitted from the installation concerned in significant quantities, having regard to their nature and their potential to transfer pollution from one medium to another (water, air and land). If necessary, the permit shall include appropriate requirements ensuring protection of the soil and ground water and measures concerning the management of waste generated by the installation. Where appropriate, limit values may be supplemented or replaced by equivalent parameters or technical measures.

For installations under subheading 6.6 in Annex I, emission limit values laid down in accordance with this paragraph shall take into account practical considerations appropriate to these categories of installation.

Where emissions of a greenhouse gas from an installation are specified in Annex I to Directive 2003/87/EC of the European Parliament and of the Council of 13 October 2003 establishing a scheme for greenhouse gas emission allowance trading within the Community and amending Council Directive 96/61/EC[1] in relation to an activity carried out in that installation, the permit shall not include an emission limit value for direct emissions of that gas unless it is necessary to ensure that no significant local pollution is caused.

For activities listed in Annex I to Directive 2003/87/EC, Member States may choose not to impose requirements relating to energy efficiency in respect of combustion units or other units emitting carbon dioxide on the site.

---

[1] OJ L 275, 25. 10. 2003, p. 32.

Where necessary, the competent authorities shall amend the permit as appropriate.

The three preceding subparagraphs shall not apply to installations temporarily excluded from the scheme for greenhouse gas emission allowance trading within the Community in accordance with Article 27 of Directive 2003/87/EC.

4. Without prejudice to Article 10, the emission limit values and the equivalent parameters and technical measures referred to in paragraph 3 shall be based on the best available techniques, without prescribing the use of any technique or specific technology, but taking into account the technical characteristics of the installation concerned, its geographical location and the local environmental conditions. In all circumstances, the conditions of the permit shall contain provisions on the minimization of long-distance or transboundary pollution and ensure a high level of protection for the environment as a whole.

5. The permit shall contain suitable release monitoring requirements, specifying measurement methodology and frequency, evaluation procedure and an obligation to supply the competent authority with data required for checking compliance with the permit.

For installations under subheading 6.6 in Annex I, the measures referred to in this paragraph may take account of costs and benefits.

6. The permit shall contain measures relating to conditions other than normal operating conditions. Thus, where there is a risk that the environment may be affected, appropriate provision shall be made for start-up, leaks malfunctions, momentary stoppages and definitive cessation of operations. The permit may also contain temporary derogations from the requirements of paragraph 4 if a rehabilitation plan approved by the competent authority ensures that these requirements will be met within six months and if the project leads to a reduction of pollution.

7. The permit may contain such other specific conditions for the purposes of this Directive as the Member State or competent authority may think fit.

8. Without prejudice to the obligation to implement a permit procedure pursuant to this Directive, Member States may prescribe certain requirements for certain categories of installations in general binding rules instead of including them in individual permit conditions, provided that an integrated approach and an equivalent high level of environmental protection as a whole are ensured.

Article 10
Best available techniques and environmental quality standards

Where an environmental quality standard requires stricter conditions than those achievable by the use of the best available techniques, additional measures shall in particular be required in the permit, without prejudice to other measures which might be taken to comply with environmental quality standards.

Article 11
Developments in best available techniques

Member States shall ensure that the competent authority follows or is informed of developments in best available techniques.

Article 12
Changes by operators to installations

1. Member States shall take the necessary measures to ensure that the operator informs the competent authorities of any changes planned in the operation of the installation as referred to in Article 2(10)(a). Where appropriate, the competent authorities shall update the permit or the conditions.

2. Member States shall take the necessary measures to ensure that no substantial change in the operation of the installation within the meaning of Article 2(10)(b) planned by the operator is made without a permit issued in accordance with this Directive. The application for a permit and the decision by the competent authority must cover those parts of the installation and those aspects listed in Article 6 that may be affected by the change. The relevant provisions of Articles 3 and 6 to 10 and Article 15(1), (2) and (4) shall apply *mutatis mutandis*.

Article 13
Reconsideration and updating of permit conditions by the competent authority

1. Member States shall take the necessary measures to ensure that competent authorities periodically reconsider and, where necessary, update permit conditions.

2. The reconsideration shall be undertaken in any event where:

- the pollution caused by the installation is of such significance that the existing emission limit values of the permit need to be revised or new such values need to be included in the permit,
- substantial changes in the best available techniques make it possible to reduce emissions significantly without imposing excessive costs,
- the operational safety of the process or activity requires other techniques to be used,
- new provisions of Community or national legislation so dictate.

Article 14
Compliance with permit conditions

Member States shall take the necessary measures to ensure that:

- the conditions of the permit are complied with by the operator when operating the installation,
- the operator regularly informs the competent authority of the results of the monitoring of releases and without delay of any incident or accident significantly affecting the environment,

— operators of installations afford the representatives of the competent authority all necessary assistance to enable them to carry out any inspections within the installation, to take samples and to gather any information necessary for the performance of their duties for the purposes of this Directive.

Article 15
Access to information and public participation in the permit procedure

1. Member States shall ensure that the public concerned are given early and effective opportunities to participate in the procedure for:

— issuing a permit for new installations,
— issuing a permit for any substantial change in the operation of an installation,
— updating of a permit or permit conditions for an installation in accordance with Article 13, paragraph 2, first indent. The procedure set out in Annex V shall apply for the purposes of such participation.

2. The results of monitoring of releases as required under the permit conditions referred to in Article 9 and held by the competent authority must be made available to the public.

3. An inventory of the principal emissions and sources responsible shall be published every three years by the Commission on the basis of the data supplied by the Member States. The Commission shall establish the format and particulars needed for the transmission of information in accordance with the procedure laid down in Article 19. In accordance with the same procedure, the Commission may propose measures to ensure inter-comparability and complementarity between data concerning the inventory of emissions referred to in the first subparagraph and data from other registers and sources of data on emissions.

4. Paragraphs 1, 2 and 3 shall apply subject to the restrictions laid down in Article 3(2) and (3) of Directive 90/313/EEC.

5. When a decision has been taken, the competent authority shall inform the public in accordance with the appropriate procedures and shall make available to the public the following information:

(a) the content of the decision, including a copy of the permit and of any conditions and any subsequent updates; and
(b) having examined the concerns and opinions expressed by the public concerned, the reasons and considerations on which the decision is based, including information on the public participation process.

Article 15a
Access to justice

Member States shall ensure that, in accordance with the relevant national legal system, members of the public concerned:

(a) having a sufficient interest, or alternatively,

(b) maintaining the impairment of a right, where administrative procedural law of a Member State requires this as a precondition;

have access to a review procedure before a court of law or another independent and impartial body established by law to challenge the substantive or procedural legality of decisions, acts or omissions subject to the public participation provisions of this Directive.

Member States shall determine at what stage the decisions, acts or omissions may be challenged.

What constitutes a sufficient interest and impairment of a right shall be determined by the Member States, consistently with the objective of giving the public concerned wide access to justice. To this end, the interest of any non-governmental organization meeting the requirements referred to in Article 2(14) shall be deemed sufficient for the purpose of subparagraph (a) of this Article. Such organisations shall also be deemed to have rights capable of being impaired for the purpose of subparagraph (b) of this Article.

The provisions of this Article shall not exclude the possibility of a preliminary review procedure before an administrative authority and shall not affect the requirement of exhaustion of administrative review procedures prior to recourse to judicial review procedures, where such a requirement exists under national law.

Any such procedure shall be fair, equitable, timely and not prohibitively expensive.

In order to further the effectiveness of the provisions of this Article, Member States shall ensure that practical information is made available to the public on access to administrative and judicial review procedures.

Article 16
Exchange of information

1. With a view to exchanging information, Member States shall take the necessary measures to send the Commission every three years, and for the first time within 18 months of the date on which this Directive is brought into effect, the available representative data on the limit values laid down by specific category of activities in accordance with Annex I and, if appropriate, the best available techniques from which those values are derived in accordance with, in particular, Article 9. On subsequent occasions the data shall be supplemented in accordance with the procedures laid down in paragraph 3 of this Article.

2. The Commission shall organize an exchange of information between Member States and the industries concerned on best available techniques, associated monitoring, and developments in them. Every three years the Commission shall publish the results of the exchanges of information.

3. Reports on the implementation of this Directive and its effectiveness compared with other Community environmental instruments shall be established in accordance with the procedure laid down in Articles 5 and 6 of Directive 91/692/EEC. The first

report shall cover the three years following the date on which this present Directive is brought into effect as referred to in Article 21. The Commission shall submit the report to the Council, accompanied by proposals if necessary.

4. Member States shall establish or designate the authority or authorities which are to be responsible for the exchange of information under paragraphs 1, 2 and 3 and shall inform the Commission accordingly.

Article 17
Transboundary effects

1. Where a Member State is aware that the operation of an installation is likely to have significant negative effects on the environment of another Member State, or where a Member State likely to be significantly affected so requests, the Member State in whose territory the application for a permit pursuant to Article 4 or Article 12(2) was submitted shall forward to the other Member State any information required to be given or made available pursuant to Annex V at the same time as it makes it available to its own nationals. Such information shall serve as a basis for any consultations necessary in the framework of the bilateral relations between the two Member States on a reciprocal and equivalent basis.

2. Within the framework of their bilateral relations, Member States shall see to it that in the cases referred to in paragraph 1 the applications are also made available for an appropriate period of time to the public of the Member State likely to be affected so that it will have the right to comment on them before the competent authority reaches its decision.

3. The results of any consultations pursuant to paragraphs 1 and 2 must be taken into consideration when the competent authority reaches a decision on the application.

4. The competent authority shall inform any Member State, which has been consulted pursuant to paragraph 1, of the decision reached on the application and shall forward to it the information referred to in Article 15(5). That Member State shall take the measures necessary to ensure that that information is made available in an appropriate manner to the public concerned in its own territory.

Article 18
Community emission limit values

1. Acting on a proposal from the Commission, the Council will set emission limit values, in accordance with the procedures laid down in the Treaty, for:

- the categories of installations listed in Annex I except for the landfills covered by categories 5.1 and 5.4 of that Annex, and
- the polluting substances referred to in Annex III, for which the need for Community action has been identified, on the basis, in particular, of the exchange of information provided for in Article 16.

2. In the absence of Community emission limit values defined pursuant to this Directive, the relevant emission limit values contained in the Directives referred to in Annex II and in other Community legislation shall be applied as minimum emission limit values pursuant to this Directive for the installations listed in Annex I.

Without prejudice to the requirements of this Directive, the technical requirements applicable for the landfills covered by categories 5.1 and 5.4 of Annex I, shall be fixed by the Council, acting on a proposal by the Commission, in accordance with the procedures laid down in the Treaty.

Article 19
Committee procedure

1. The Commission shall be assisted by a committee.

2. Where reference is made to this Article, Articles 5 and 7 of Decision 1999/468/EC[1] shall apply, having regard to the provisions of Article 8 thereof.

The period laid down in Article 5(6) of Decision 1999/468/EC shall be set at three months.

3. The Committee shall adopt its rules of procedure.

Article 20
Transitional provisions

1. The provisions of Directive 84/360/EEC, the provisions of Articles 3, 5, 6(3) and 7(2) of Directive 76/464/EEC and the relevant provisions concerning authorization systems in the Directives listed in Annex II shall apply, without prejudice to the exceptions provided for in Directive 88/609/EEC, to existing installations in respect of activities listed in Annex I until the measures required pursuant to Article 5 of this Directive have been taken by the competent authorities.

2. The relevant provisions concerning authorization systems in the Directives referred to in paragraph 1 shall not apply to installations which are new in respect of the activities listed in Annex I on the date on which this Directive is brought into effect.

3. Directive 84/360/EEC shall be repealed 11 years after the date of entry into force of this Directive.

As soon as the measures provided for in Article 4, 5 or 12 have been taken in respect of an installation, the exception provided for in Article 6(3) of Directive 76/464/EEC shall no longer apply to installations covered by this Directive.

Acting on a proposal from the Commission, the Council shall, where necessary, amend the relevant provisions of the Directives referred to in Annex II in order to adapt them to the requirements of this Directive before the date of repeal of Directive 84/360/EEC, referred to in the first subparagraph.

---

[1] Council Decision 1999/468/EC of 28 June 1999 laying down the procedures for the exercise of implementing powers conferred on the Commission (OJ L 184, 17. 7. 1999, p. 23).

Article 21
Bringing into effect

1. Member States shall adopt the laws, regulations and administrative provisions necessary to comply with this Directive no later than three years after its entry into force. They shall forthwith inform the Commission thereof. When Member States adopt these measures, they shall contain a reference to this Directive or shall be accompanied by such reference on the occasion of their official publication. The methods of making such reference shall be laid down by Member States.

2. Member States shall communicate to the Commission the texts of the main provisions of national law which they adopt in the field covered by this Directive.

Article 22

This Directive shall enter into force on the 20th day following its publication.

Article 23

This Directive is addressed to the Member States.

Annex I
Categories of industrial activities referred to in Article 1

1. Installations or parts of installations used for research, development and testing of new products and processes are not covered by this Directive.

2. The threshold values given below generally refer to production capacities or outputs. Where one operator carries out several activities falling under the same subheading in the same installation or on the same site, the capacities of such activities are added together.

1. *Energy industries*

1.1. Combustion installations with a rated thermal input exceeding 50 MW[1]
1.2. Mineral oil and gas refineries
1.3. Coke ovens
1.4. Coal gasification and liquefaction plants

2. *Production and processing of metals*

2.1. Metal ore (including sulphide ore) roasting or sintering installations
2.2. Installations for the production of pig iron or steel (primary or secondary fusion) including continuous casting, with a capacity exceeding 2,5 tonnes per hour

---

[1] The material requirements of Directive 88/609/EEC for existing installations still apply until 31 December 2003.

2.3. Installations for the processing of ferrous metals:
  (a) hot-rolling mills with a capacity exceeding 20 tonnes of crude steel per hour
  (b) smitheries with hammers the energy of which exceeds 50 kilojoule per hammer, where the calorific power used exceeds 20 MW
  (c) application of protective fused metal coats with an input exceeding 2 tonnes of crude steel per hour
2.4. Ferrous metal foundries with a production capacity exceeding 20 tonnes per day
2.5. Installations
  (a) for the production of non-ferrous crude metals from ore, concentrates or secondary raw materials by metallurgical, chemical or electrolytic processes
  (b) for the smelting, including the alloyage, of non-ferrous metals, including recovered products, (refining, foundry casting, etc.) with a melting capacity exceeding 4 tonnes per day for lead and cadmium or 20 tonnes per day for all other metals
2.6. Installations for surface treatment of metals and plastic materials using an electrolytic or chemical process where the volume of the treatment vats exceeds 30 m^3

  3. *Mineral industry*

3.1. Installations for the production of cement clinker in rotary kilns with a production capacity exceeding 500 tonnes per day or lime in rotary kilns with a production capacity exceeding 50 tonnes per day or in other furnaces with a production capacity exceeding 50 tonnes per day
3.2. Installations for the production of asbestos and the manufacture of asbestos-based products
3.3. Installations for the manufacture of glass including glass fibre with a melting capacity exceeding 20 tonnes per day
3.4. Installations for melting mineral substances including the production of mineral fibres with a melting capacity exceeding 20 tonnes per day
3.5. Installations for the manufacture of ceramic products by firing, in particular roofing tiles, bricks, refractory bricks, tiles, stoneware or porcelain, with a. production capacity exceeding 75 tonnes per day, and/or with a kiln capacity exceeding 4 m^3 and with a setting density per kiln exceeding 300 kg/m^3

  4. *Chemical industry*
Production within the meaning of the categories of activities contained in this section means the production on an industrial scale by chemical processing of substances or groups of substances listed in Sections 4.1 to 4.6

4.1. Chemical installations for the production of basic organic chemicals, such as:
  (a) simple hydrocarbons (linear or cyclic, saturated or unsaturated, aliphatic or aromatic)

(b) oxygen-containing hydrocarbons such as alcohols, aldehydes, ketones, carboxylic acids, esters, acetates, ethers, peroxides, epoxy resins

(c) sulphurous hydrocarbons

(d) nitrogenous hydrocarbons such as amines, amides, nitrous compounds, nitro compounds or nitrate compounds, nitriles, cyanates, isocyanates

(e) phosphorus-containing hydrocarbons

(f) halogenic hydrocarbons

(g) organometallic compounds

(h) basic plastic materials (polymers synthetic fibres and cellulose-based fibres)

(i) synthetic rubbers

(j) dyes and pigments

(k) surface-active agents and surfactants

4.2. Chemical installations for the production of basic inorganic chemicals, such as:

(a) gases, such as ammonia, chlorine or hydrogen chloride, fluorine or hydrogen fluoride, carbon oxides, sulphur compounds, nitrogen oxides, hydrogen, sulphur dioxide, carbonyl chloride

(b) acids, such as chromic acid, hydrofluoric acid, phosphoric acid, nitric acid, hydrochloric acid, sulphuric acid, oleum, sulphurous acids

(c) bases, such as ammonium hydroxide, potassium hydroxide, sodium hydroxide

(d) salts, such as ammonium chloride, potassium chlorate, potassium carbonate, sodium carbonate, perborate, silver nitrate

(e) non-metals, metal oxides or other inorganic compounds such as calcium carbide, silicon, silicon carbide

4.3. Chemical installations for the production of phosphorous-, nitrogen- or potassium-based fertilizers (simple or compound fertilizers)

4.4. Chemical installations for the production of basic plant health products and of biocides

4.5. Installations using a chemical or biological process for the production of basic pharmaceutial products

4.6. Chemical installations for the production of explosives

5. *Waste management*

Without prejudice of Article 11 of Directive 75/442/EEC or Article 3 of Council Directive 91/689/EEC of 12 December 1991 on hazardous waste:[1]

5.1. Installations for the disposal or recovery of hazardous waste as defined in the list referred to in Article 1(4) of Directive 91/689/EEC, as defined in Annexes

---

[1] OJ No L 377, 31. 12. 1991, p. 20. Directive as amended by Directive 94/31/EC (OJ No L 168, 2. 7. 1994, p. 28).

II A and II B (operations R1, R5, R6, R8 and R9) to Directive 75/442/EEC and in Council Directive 75/439/EEC of 16 June 1975 on the disposal of waste oils,[1] with a capacity exceeding 10 tonnes per day

5.2. Installations for the incineration of municipal waste as defined in Council Directive 89/369/EEC of 8 June 1989 on the prevention of air pollution from new municipal waste incineration plants[2] and Council Directive 89/429/EEC of 21 June 1989 on the reduction of air pollution from existing municipal waste-incineration plants[3] with a capacity exceeding 3 tonnes per hour

5.3. Installations for the disposal of non-hazardous waste as defined in Annex II A to Directive 75/442/EEC under headings D8 and D9, with a capacity exceeding 50 tonnes per day

5.4. Landfills receiving more than 10 tonnes per day or with a total capacity exceeding 25 000 tonnes, excluding landfills of inert waste

6. *Other activities*

6.1. Industrial plants for the production of:
   (a) pulp from timber or other fibrous materials
   (b) paper and board with a production capacity exceeding 20 tonnes per day

6.2. Plants for the pre-treatment (operations such as washing, bleaching, mercerization) or dyeing of fibres or textiles where the treatment capacity exceeds 10 tonnes per day

6.3. Plants for the tanning of hides and skins where the treatment capacity exceeds 12 tonnes of finished products per day

6.4. (a) Slaughterhouses with a carcase production capacity greater than 50 tonnes per day
   (b) Treatment and processing intended for the production of food products from:
      – animal raw materials (other than milk) with a finished product production capacity greater than 75 tonnes per day
      – vegetable raw materials with a finished product production capacity greater than 300 tonnes per day (average value on a quarterly basis)
   (c) Treatment and processing of milk, the quantity of milk received being greater than 200 tonnes per day (average value on an annual basis)

6.5. Installations for the disposal or recycling of animal carcases and animal waste with a treatment capacity exceeding 10 tonnes per day

6.6. Installations for the intensive rearing of poultry or pigs with more than:
   (a) 40,000 places for poultry

---

[1] OJ No L 194, 25. 7. 1975, p. 23. Directive as last amended by Directive 91/692/EEC (OJ No L 377, 31. 12. 1991, p. 48).
[2] OJ No L 163, 14. 6. 1989, p. 32.   [3] OJ No L 203, 15. 7. 1989, p. 50.

(b) 2,000 places for production pigs (over 30 kg), or

(c) 750 places for sows

6.7. Installations for the surface treatment of substances, objects or products using organic solvents, in particular for dressing, printing, coating, degreasing, waterproofing, sizing, painting, cleaning or impregnating, with a consumption capacity of more than 150 kg per hour or more than 200 tonnes per year

6.8. Installations for the production of carbon (hard-burnt coal) or electrographite by means of incineration or graphitization

Annex II
List of the Directives referred to in Articles 18(2) and 20

1. Directive 87/217/EEC on the prevention and reduction of environmental pollution by asbestos

2. Directive 82/176/EEC on limit values and quality objectives for mercury discharges by the chlor-alkali electrolysis industry

3. Directive 83/513/EEC on limit values and quality objectives for cadmium discharges

4. Directive 84/156/EEC on limit values and quality objectives for mercury discharges by sectors other than the chlor-alkali electrolysis industry

5. Directive 84/491/EEC on limit values and quality objectives for discharges of hexachlorocyclohexane

6. Directive 86/280/EEC on limit values and quality objectives for discharges of certain dangerous substances included in List 1 of the Annex to Directive 76/464/EEC, subsequently amended by Directives 88/347/EEC and 90/415/EEC amending Annex II to Directive 86/280/EEC

7. Directive 89/369/EEC on the prevention of air pollution from new municipal waste-incineration plants

8. Directive 89/429/EEC on the reduction of air pollution from existing municipal waste-incineration plants

9. Directive 94/67/EC on the incineration of hazardous waste

10. Directive 92/112/EEC on procedures for harmonizing the programmes for the reduction and eventual elimination of pollution caused by waste from the titanium oxide industry

11. Directive 88/609/EEC on the limitation of emissions of certain pollutants into the air from large combustion plants, as last amended by Directive 94/66/EC

12. Directive 76/464/EEC on pollution caused by certain dangerous substances discharged into the aquatic environment of the Community

13. Directive 75/442/EEC on waste, as amended by Directive 91/156/EEC

14. Directive 75/439/EEC on the disposal of waste oils

15. Directive 91/689/EEC on hazardous waste

Annex III
Indicative list of the main polluting substances to be taken into account if they are relevant for fixing emission limit values

Air

1. Sulphur dioxide and other sulphur compounds
2. Oxides of nitrogen and other nitrogen compounds
3. Carbon monoxide
4. Volatile organic compounds
5. Metals and their compounds
6. Dust
7. Asbestos (suspended particulates, fibres)
8. Chlorine and its compounds
9. Fluorine and its compounds
10. Arsenic and its compounds
11. Cyanides
12. Substances and preparations which have been proved to possess carcinogenic or mutagenic properties or properties which may affect reproduction via the air
13. Polychlorinated dibenzodioxins and polychlorinated dibenzofurans

Water

1. Organohalogen compounds and substances which may form such compounds in the aquatic environment
2. Organophosphorus compounds
3. Organotin compounds
4. Substances and preparations which have been proved to possess carcinogenic or mutagenic properties or properties which may affect reproduction in or via the aquatic environment
5. Persistent hydrocarbons and persistent and bioaccumulable organic toxic substances
6. Cyanides
7. Metals and their compounds
8. Arsenic and its compounds
9. Biocides and plant health products
10. Materials in suspension
11. Substances which contribute to eutrophication (in particular, nitrates and phosphates)
12. Substances which have an unfavourable influence on the oxygen balance (and can be measured using parameters such as BOD, COD, etc.).

Annex IV

Considerations to be taken into account generally or in specific cases when determining best available techniques, as defined in Article 2(11), bearing in mind the likely costs and benefits of a measure and the principles of precaution and prevention:

1. the use of low-waste technology;
2. the use of less hazardous substances;
3. the furthering of recovery and recycling of substances generated and used in the process and of waste, where appropriate;
4. comparable processes, facilities or methods of operation which have been tried with success on an industrial scale;
5. technological advances and changes in scientific knowledge and understanding;
6. the nature, effects and volume of the emissions concerned;
7. the commissioning dates for new or existing installations;
8. the length of time needed to introduce the best available technique;
9. the consumption and nature of raw materials (including water) used in the process and their energy efficiency;
10. the need to prevent or reduce to a minimum the overall impact of the emissions on the environment and the risks to it;
11. the need to prevent accidents and to minimize the consequences for the environment;
12. the information published by the Commission pursuant to Article 16(2) or by international organizations.

Annex V
Public participation in decision-making

1. The public shall be informed (by public notices or other appropriate means such as electronic media where available) of the following matters early in the procedure for the taking of a decision or, at the latest, as soon as the information can reasonably be provided:

(a) the application for a permit or, as the case may be, the proposal for the updating of a permit or of permit conditions in accordance with Article 15(1), including the description of the elements listed in Article 6(1);
(b) where applicable, the fact that a decision is subject to a national or transboundary environmental impact assessment or to consultations between Member States in accordance with Article 17;
(c) details of the competent authorities responsible for taking the decision, those from which relevant information can be obtained, those to which comments or questions can be submitted, and details of the time schedule for transmitting comments or questions;
(d) the nature of possible decisions or, where there is one, the draft decision;
(e) where applicable, the details relating to a proposal for the updating of a permit or of permit conditions;

(f) an indication of the times and places where, or means by which, the relevant information will be made available;
(g) details of the arrangements for public participation and consultation made pursuant to point 5.

2. Member States shall ensure that, within appropriate time-frames, the following is made available to the public concerned:

(a) in accordance with national legislation, the main reports and advice issued to the competent authority or authorities at the time when the public concerned were informed in accordance with point 1;
(b) in accordance with the provisions of Directive 2003/4/EC of the European Parliament and of the Council of 28 January 2003 on public access to environmental information,[1] information other than that referred to in point 1 which is relevant for the decision in accordance with Article 8 and which only becomes available after the time the public concerned was informed in accordance with point 1.

3. The public concerned shall be entitled to express comments and opinions to the competent authority before a decision is taken.

4. The results of the consultations held pursuant to this Annex must be taken into due account in the taking of a decision.

5. The detailed arrangements for informing the public (for example by bill posting within a certain radius or publication in local newspapers) and consulting the public concerned (for example by written submissions or by way of a public inquiry) shall be determined by the Member States. Reasonable time-frames for the different phases shall be provided, allowing sufficient time for informing the public and for the public concerned to prepare and participate effectively in environmental decision-making subject to the provisions of this Annex.

---

[1] OJ L 41, 14. 2. 2003, p. 26.

Recommendation 2001/331/EC of the European Parliament and of the Council of 4 April 2001 providing for minimum criteria for environmental inspections in the Member States

Editorial note

Recommendation 2001/331 of 4 April 2001 provides minimum criteria for environmental inspection in the Member States. The Recommendation recognises the role that inspection plays in strengthening compliance with and contributing to the implementation and enforcement of environmental legislation (Article I). The Recommendation applies to environmental inspections of all industrial installations and other enterprises and facilities whose emissions/discharges are subject to authorisation, permit or licensing requirements (Article II). Member States are to ensure that environmental inspections are carried out to achieve a high level of environmental protection (Article III). Environmental inspections activities should be planned in advance (Article IV). The Recommendations set out the criteria to be applied to site visits (Article V). Reports and conclusions are to be processed or stored by the inspecting authorities after each site visit; such reports should be properly recorded and maintained in a readily accessible database (Article VI). Member States are to ensure that the relevant authority carries out investigation of serious accidents, incidents and occurrences of non-compliance with EC legislation (Article VII). Member States are required to report to the Commission on their experience on the operation of the Recommendation two years after its entry into force (Article VIII) and the Commission should review the operation and effectiveness of the Recommendation (Article IX).

Source: OJ L 118 27.04.2001 p. 41

Recommendation 2001/331/EC of the European Parliament and of the Council of 4 April 2001 providing for minimum criteria for environmental inspections in the Member States

The European Parliament and the Council of the European Union,
   Having regard to the Treaty establishing the European Community and in particular Article 175(1) thereof,

Having regard to the proposal from the Commission,
Having regard to the opinion of the Economic and Social Committee,[1]
Having regard to the opinion of the Committee of the Regions,[2]
Acting in accordance with the procedure laid down in Article 251 of the Treaty,[3] and in the light of the joint text approved by the Conciliation Committee on 8 January 2001,
Whereas:

(1) The resolution of the Council and of the Representatives of the Governments of the Member States, meeting within the Council, of 1 February 1993 on a Community programme of policy and action in relation to the environment and sustainable development[4] and the Decision of the European Parliament and the Council on its review[5] emphasised the importance of implementation of Community environmental law through the concept of shared responsibility.

(2) The Commission Communication of 5 November 1996 to the Council of the European Union and the European Parliament on implementing Community environmental law, in particular paragraph 29 thereof, proposed the establishment of guidelines at Community level in order to assist Member States in carrying out inspection tasks, thereby reducing the currently-existing wide disparity among Member States' inspections.

(3) The Council in its resolution of 7 October 1997 on the drafting, implementation and enforcement of Community environmental law[6] invited the Commission to propose, for further consideration by the Council, in particular on the basis of the work of the European Union network for the implementation and enforcement of environmental law (IMPEL), minimum criteria and/or guidelines for inspection tasks carried out at Member State level and the possible ways in which their application in practice could be monitored by Member States, in order to ensure an even practical application and enforcement of environmental legislation, and the Commission's proposal has taken into account a paper produced by IMPEL in November 1997 and entitled 'Minimum Criteria for Inspections'.

(4) The European Parliament by its resolution of 14 May 1997 on the Commission's Communication called for Community legislation on environmental inspections, and the Economic and Social Committee and the Committee of the

---

[1] OJ C 169, 16.6.1999, p. 12.   [2] OJ C 374, 23.12.1999, p. 48.
[3] Opinion of the European Parliament of 16 September 1999 (OJ C54, 25.2.2000, p. 92), Council Common Position of 30 March 2000 (OJ C 137, 16.5.2000, p. 1) and Decision of the European Parliament of 6 July 2000 (not yet published in the Official Journal). Decision of the European Parliament of 1 February 2001 and Council Decision of 26 February 2001.
[4] OJ C 138, 17.5.1993, p. 1.   [5] OJ L 275, 10.10.1998, p. 1.   [6] OJ C 321, 22.10.1997, p. 1.

Regions gave favourable opinions on the Commission's Communication and stressed the importance of environmental inspections.

(5) Different systems and practices of inspection already exist in Member States and should not be replaced by a system of inspection at Community level, as was considered in the Council resolution of 7 October 1997, and Member States should retain responsibility for environmental inspection tasks.

(6) The European Environment Agency can advise the Member States on developing, setting up and extending their systems for monitoring environmental provisions and can assist the Commission and the Member States in monitoring environmental provisions by giving support in respect of the reporting process, so that reporting is coordinated.

(7) The existence of inspection systems and the effective carrying out of inspections is a deterrent to environmental violations since it enables authorities to identify breaches and enforce environmental laws through sanctions or other means; thus inspections are an indispensable link in the regulatory chain and an efficient instrument to contribute to a more consistent implementation and enforcement of Community environmental legislation across the Community and to avoid distortions of competition.

(8) There is currently a wide disparity in the inspection systems and mechanisms among Member States in terms not only of their capacities for carrying out inspection tasks but also of the scope and contents of the inspection tasks undertaken and even in the very existence of inspection tasks in a few Member States, and this is a situation which cannot be considered satisfactory with reference to the objective of an effective and more consistent implementation, practical application and enforcement of Community legislation on environmental protection.

(9) It is necessary, therefore, to provide, at this stage, guidelines in the form of minimum criteria to be applied as a common basis for the performance of environmental inspection tasks within the Member States.

(10) Community environmental legislation obliges Member States to apply requirements in relation to certain emissions, discharges and activities; minimum criteria on the organisation and carrying out of inspections should be met in the Member States, as a first stage, for all industrial installations and other enterprises and facilities whose air emissions and/or water discharges and/or waste disposal or recovery activities are subject to authorisation, permit or licensing requirements under Community law.

(11) Inspections should take place taking into account the division of responsibilities in the Member States between authorisation and inspection services.

(12) In order to make this system of inspections efficient, Member States should ensure that environmental inspections activities are planned in advance.

(13) Site visits form an important part of environmental inspection activities.

(14) The data and documentation provided by industrial operators registered under the Community eco-management and audit scheme could be a useful source of information in the context of environmental inspections.

(15) In order to draw conclusions from site visits, regular reports should be established.

(16) Reporting on inspection activities, and public access to information thereon, are important means to ensure through transparency the involvement of citizens, nongovernmental organisations and other interested actors in the implementation of Community environmental legislation; access to such information should be in line with the provisions of Council Directive 90/313/EEC of 7 June 1990 on the freedom of access to information on the environment.[1]

(17) Member States should assist each other administratively in operating this recommendation. The establishment by Member States in cooperation with IMPEL of reporting and advice schemes relating to inspectorates and inspection procedures would help to promote best practice across the Community.

(18) Member States should report to the Council and the Commission on their experience in operating this recommendation and the Commission should regularly inform the European Parliament.

(19) The Commission should keep the operation and effectiveness of this recommendation under review and report thereon to the European Parliament and the Council as soon as possible after the receipt of the Member States' reports.

(20) Further work by IMPEL and Member States, in cooperation with the Commission, should be encouraged in respect of best practices concerning the qualifications and training of environmental inspectors.

(21) In accordance with the principles of subsidiarity and proportionality as set out in Article 5 of the Treaty, and given the differences in inspection systems and mechanisms in the Member States, the objectives of the proposed action can best be achieved by guidance set out at Community level.

(22) In the light of the experience gained in the operation of this recommendation and taking account of IMPEL's further work, as well as of the results of any schemes provided for in this recommendation, the Commission should, upon receipt of Member States' reports, give consideration to developing the minimum criteria in terms of their scope and substance and to making further proposals which might include a proposal for a directive, if appropriate,

Hereby recommend:

I Purpose

Environmental inspection tasks should be carried out in the Member States, according to minimum criteria to be applied in the organising, carrying out, following up and

---

[1] OJ L 158, 23.6.1990, p. 56

publicising of the results of such tasks, thereby strengthening compliance with, and contributing to a more consistent implementation and enforcement of Community environmental law in all Member States.

II Scope and definitions

1.

(a) This recommendation applies to environmental inspections of all industrial installations and other enterprises and facilities, whose air emissions and/or water discharges and/or waste disposal or recovery activities are subject to authorisation, permit or licensing requirements under Community law, without prejudice to specific inspection provisions in existing Community legislation.
(b) For the purposes of this recommendation, all the installations and other enterprises and facilities referred to in point (a) are 'controlled installations'.

2. For the purposes of this recommendation, 'environmental inspection' is an activity which entails, as appropriate:

(a) checking and promoting the compliance of controlled installations with relevant environmental requirements set out in Community legislation as transposed into national legislation or applied in the national legal order (referred to hereinafter as 'EC legal requirements');
(b) monitoring the impact of controlled installations on the environment to determine whether further inspection or enforcement action (including issuing, modification or revocation of any authorisation, permit or licence) is required to secure compliance with EC legal requirements;
(c) the carrying out of activities for the above purposes including:
   – site visits,
   – monitoring achievement of environmental quality standards,
   – consideration of environmental audit reports and statements,
   – consideration and verification of any self monitoring carried out by or on behalf of operators of controlled installations,
   – assessing the activities and operations carried out at the controlled installation,
   – checking the premises and the relevant equipment (including the adequacy with which it is maintained) and the adequacy of the environmental management at the site,
   – checking the relevant records kept by the operators of controlled installations.

3. Environmental inspections, including site visits, may be:

(a) routine, that is, carried out as part of a planned inspections programme; or
(b) non-routine, that is, carried out in such cases in response to complaints, in connection with the issuing, renewal or modification of an authorisation, permit or

licence, or in the investigation of accidents, incidents and occurrences of non-compliance.

4.

(a) Environmental inspections may be carried out by any public authority at either national, regional or local level, which is established or designated by the Member State and responsible for the matters covered by this recommendation.
(b) The bodies referred to in point (a) may, in accordance with their national legislation, delegate the tasks provided for in this recommendation to be accomplished, under their authority and supervision, to any legal person whether governed by public or private law provided such person has no personal interest in the outcome of the inspections it undertakes.
(c) The bodies referred to in points (a) and (b) are defined as 'inspecting authorities'.

5. For the purposes of this recommendation, an 'operator of a controlled installation' is any natural or legal person who operates or controls the controlled installation or, where this is provided for in national legislation, to whom decisive economic power over the technical functioning of the controlled installation has been delegated.

III Organisation and carrying out of environmental inspections

1. Member States should ensure that environmental inspections aim to achieve a high level of environmental protection and to this end should take the necessary measures to ensure that environmental inspections of controlled installations are organised and carried out in accordance with points IV to VIII of this recommendation.

2. Member States should assist each other administratively in carrying out the guidelines of this recommendation by the exchange of relevant information and, where appropriate, inspecting officials.

3. To prevent illegal cross-border environmental practices, Member States should encourage, in cooperation with IMPEL, the coordination of inspections with regard to installations and activities which might have significant transboundary impact.

4. In order to promote best practice across the Community, Member States may, in cooperation with IMPEL, consider the establishment of a scheme, under which Member States report and offer advice on inspectorates and inspection procedures in Member States, paying due regard to the different systems and contexts in which they operate, and report to the Member States concerned on their findings.

IV Plans for environmental inspections

1. Member States should ensure that environmental inspection activities are planned in advance, by having at all times a plan or plans for environmental

inspections providing coverage of all the territory of the Member State and of the controlled installations within it. Such a plan or plans should be available to the public according to Directive 90/313/EEC.

2. Such plan or plans may be established at national, regional or local levels, but Member States should ensure that the plan or plans apply to all environmental inspections of controlled installations within their territory and that the authorities mentioned in point II(4) are designated to carry out such inspections.

3. Plans for environmental inspections should be produced on the basis of the following:

(a) the EC legal requirements to be complied with;
(b) a register of controlled installations within the plan area;
(c) a general assessment of major environmental issues within the plan area and a general appraisal of the state of compliance by the controlled installations with EC legal requirements;
(d) data on and from previous inspection activities, if any.

4. Plans for environmental inspections should:

(a) be appropriate to the inspection tasks of the relevant authorities, and should take account of the controlled installations concerned and the risks and environmental impacts of emissions and discharges from them;
(b) take into account relevant available information in relation to specific sites or types of controlled installations, such as reports by operators of controlled installations made to the authorities, self monitoring data, environmental audit information and environmental statements, in particular those produced by controlled installations registered according to the Community eco-management and audit scheme (EMAS), results of previous inspections and reports of environmental quality monitoring.

5. Each plan for environmental inspections should as a minimum:

(a) define the geographical area which it covers, which may be for all or part of the territory of a Member State;
(b) cover a defined time period, for example one year;
(c) include specific provisions for its revision;
(d) identify the specific sites or types of controlled installations covered;
(e) prescribe the programmes for routine environmental inspections, taking into account environmental risks; these programmes should include, where appropriate, the frequency of site visits for different types of or specified controlled installations;
(f) provide for and outline the procedures for non-routine environmental inspections, in such cases in response to complaints, accidents, incidents and occurrences of noncompliance and for purposes of granting permission;

(g) provide for coordination between the different inspecting authorities, where relevant.

V Site visits

1. Member States should ensure that the following criteria are applied in respect of all site visits:

(a) that an appropriate check is made of compliance with the EC legal requirements relevant to the particular inspection;
(b) that if site visits are to be carried out by more than one environmental inspecting authority, they exchange information on each others' activities and, as far as possible, coordinate site visits and other environmental inspection work;
(c) that the findings of site visits are contained in reports made in accordance with point VI and exchanged, as necessary, between relevant inspection, enforcement and other authorities, whether national, regional or local;
(d) that inspectors or other officials entitled to carry out site visits have a legal right of access to sites and information, for the purposes of environmental inspection.

2. Member States should ensure that site visits are regularly carried out by inspecting authorities as part of their routine environmental inspections and that the following additional criteria are applied for such site visits:

(a) that the full range of relevant environmental impacts is examined, in conformity with the applicable EC legal requirements, the environmental inspection programmes and the inspecting bodies' organisational arrangements;
(b) that such site visits should aim to promote and reinforce operators' knowledge and understanding of relevant EC legal requirements and environmental sensitivities, and of the environmental impacts of their activities;
(c) that the risks to and impact on the environment of the controlled installation are considered in order to evaluate the effectiveness of existing authorisation, permit or licensing requirements and to assess whether improvements or other changes to such requirements are necessary.

3. Member States should also ensure that non-routine site visits are carried out in the following circumstances:

(a) in the investigation by the relevant inspecting authorities of serious environmental complaints, and as soon as possible after such complaints are received by the authorities;
(b) in the investigation of serious environmental accidents, incidents and occurrences of non-compliance, and as soon as possible after these come to the notice of the relevant inspecting authorities;

(c) where appropriate, as part of the determination as to whether and on what terms to issue a first authorisation, permit or licence for a process or activity at a controlled installation or the proposed site thereof or to ensure the compliance with the requirements of authorisation, permit or licence after it has been issued and before the start of activity;

(d) where appropriate, before the reissue, renewal or modification of authorisations, permits or licences.

VI Reports and conclusions following site visits

1. Member States should ensure that after every site visit the inspecting authorities process or store, in identifiable form and in data files, the inspection data and their findings as to compliance with EC legal requirements, an evaluation thereof and a conclusion on whether any further action should follow, such as enforcement proceedings, including sanctions, the issuing of a new or revised authorisation, permit or licence or follow-up inspection activities, including further site visits. Reports should be finalised as soon as possible.

2. Member States should ensure that such reports are properly recorded in writing and maintained in a readily accessible database. The full reports, and wherever this is not practicable the conclusions of such reports, should be communicated to the operator of the controlled installation in question according to Directive 90/313/EEC; these reports should be publicly available within two months of the inspection taking place.

VII Investigations of serious accidents, incidents and occurrences of non-compliance

Member States should ensure that the investigation of serious accidents, incidents and occurrences of non-compliance with EC legislation, whether these come to the attention of the authorities through a complaint or otherwise, is carried out by the relevant authority in order to:

(a) clarify the causes of the event and its impact on the environment, and as appropriate, the responsibilities and possible liabilities for the event and its consequences, and to forward conclusions to the authority responsible for enforcement, if different from the inspecting authority;

(b) mitigate and, where possible, remedy the environmental impacts of the event through a determination of the appropriate actions to be taken by the operator(s) and the authorities;

(c) determine action to be taken to prevent further accidents, incidents and occurrences of non-compliance;

(d) enable enforcement action or sanctions to proceed, if appropriate; and

(e) ensure that the operator takes appropriate follow-up actions.

VIII Reporting on environmental inspection activities in general

1. Member States should report to the Commission on their experience of the operation of this recommendation two years after the date of its publication in the *Official Journal of the European Communities*, using, to the extent possible, any data available from regional and local inspecting authorities.

2. Such reports should be available to the public and should include in particular the following information:

(a) data about the staffing and other resources of the inspecting authorities;
(b) details of the inspecting authority's role and performance in the establishment and implementation of relevant plan(s) for inspections;
(c) summary details of the environmental inspections carried out, including the number of site visits made, the proportion of controlled installations inspected (by type) and estimated length of time before all controlled installations of that type have been inspected;
(d) brief data on the degree of compliance by controlled installations with EC legal requirements as appears from inspections carried out;
(e) a summary, including numbers, of the actions taken as a result of serious complaints, accidents, incidents and occurrences of non-compliance;
(f) an evaluation of the success or failure of the plans for inspections as applicable to the inspecting body, with any recommendations for future plans.

IX Review and development of the recommendation

1. The Commission should review the operation and effectiveness of this recommendation, as soon as possible after receipt of the Member States' reports mentioned in point VIII above, with the intention of developing the minimum criteria further in terms of their scope in the light of the experience gained from their application, and taking into account any further contributions from interested parties, including IMPEL and the European Environment Agency. The Commission should then submit to the European Parliament and the Council a report accompanied, if appropriate, by a proposal for a directive. The European Parliament and the Council will consider such a proposal without delay.

2. The Commission is invited to draw up, as quickly as possible, in cooperation with IMPEL and other interested parties, minimum criteria concerning the qualifications of environmental inspectors who are authorised to carry out inspections for or under the authority or supervision of inspecting authorities.

3. Member States should, as quickly as possible, in cooperation with IMPEL, the Commission and other interested parties, develop training programmes in order to meet the demand for qualified environmental inspectors.

X Implementation

Member States should inform the Commission of the implementation of this recommendation together with details of environmental inspection mechanisms already existing or foreseen not later than twelve months after its publication in the *Official Journal of the European Communities.*

Done at Luxembourg, 4 April 2001.

Directive 2003/4/EC of the European Parliament and of the Council of 28 January 2003 on public access to environmental information and repealing Council Directive 90/313/EEC

Editorial note

Directive 2003/4 of 28 January 2003 regulates public access to environmental information and repeals the earlier Directive 90/313/EEC of 7 June 1990 on the freedom of access to information on the environment. The objective of the Directive is to guarantee the right of access to environmental information held by or for public authorities and to ensure that environmental information is progressively made available and disseminated to the public (Article 1). 'Environmental information' is specifically defined by the Directive, as are the terms 'public authority', 'information held by a public authority', 'information held for a public authority', 'applicant' and 'public' (Article 2). Member States are to ensure that public authorities make available environmental information held by, or for, them to any applicant without him having to state his interest. Information is to be made available as soon as possible or, at the latest, within one month of the applicant's request or within two months in case of complex requests. Information is to be made available in the format requested by the applicant, with some exceptions. Member States are required to ensure that public authorities and the public are adequately informed of their rights under the Directive (Article 3).

The Directive lists a series of exceptions to the right to access information and states that grounds for refusal are to be interpreted in a restrictive way (Article 4). If possible, information is to be made available in part where it is possible to separate out any information which cannot be disclosed (Article 4(4)). Refusals are to be notified to the applicant and are to state the reasons for refusal and include information on the review procedure to be provided under the Directive (Article 4(5)). Charges for supplying environmental information shall not exceed a reasonable amount (Article 5). Any applicant who considers that his request for information has been ignored, wrongfully refused, inadequately answered or otherwise not dealt with as provided for by the Directive, is to have access to a procedure where the acts or omissions of the public authority concerned can be reconsidered or reviewed in an expeditious manner and free of charge (Article 6(1)). In addition, applicants are to have access to a review procedure before a court of law or another independent body established by law (Article 6(2)).

Member States are required to organise environmental information with a view to its active and systematic dissemination (Article 7). Member States shall also ensure that any information that is compiled by them or on their behalf is up to date, accurate and comparable (Article 8). The Directive is to be implemented by 14 February 2005 (Article 10).

Source: OJ L 41 14.02.2003 p. 26.

Directive 2003/4/EC of the European Parliament and of the Council of 28 January 2003 on public access to environmental information and repealing Council Directive 90/313/EEC

The European Parliament and the Council of the European Union,
Having regard to the Treaty establishing the European Community, and in particular Article 175(1) thereof,
Having regard to the proposal from the Commission,[1]
Having regard to the opinion of the European Economic and Social Committee,[2]
Having regard to the opinion of the Committee of the Regions,[3]
Acting in accordance with the procedure laid down in Article 251 of the Treaty[4] in the light of the joint text approved by the Conciliation Committee on 8 November 2002,
Whereas:

(1) Increased public access to environmental information and the dissemination of such information contribute to a greater awareness of environmental matters, a free exchange of views, more effective participation by the public in environmental decision-making and, eventually, to a better environment.

(2) Council Directive 90/313/EEC of 7 June 1990 on the freedom of access to information on the environment[5] initiated a process of change in the manner in which public authorities approach the issue of openness and transparency, establishing measures for the exercise of the right of public access to environmental information which should be developed and continued. This Directive expands the existing access granted under Directive 90/313/EEC.

---

[1] OJ C 337 E, 28.11.2000, p. 156 and OJ C 240 E, 28.8.2001, p. 289.
[2] OJ C 116, 20.4.2001, p. 43.   [3] OJ C 148, 18.5.2001, p. 9.
[4] Opinion of the European Parliament of 14 March 2001 (OJ C 343, 5.12.2001, p. 165), Council Common Position of 28 January 2002 (OJ C 113 E, 14.5.2002, p. 1) and Decision of the European Parliament of 30 May 2002 (not yet published in the Official Journal). Decision of the Council of 16 December 2002 and decision the European Parliament of 18 December 2002.
[5] OJ L 158, 23.6.1990, p. 56.

(3) Article 8 of that Directive requires Member States to report to the Commission on the experience gained, in the light of which the Commission is required to make a report to the European Parliament and to the Council together with any proposal for revision of the Directive which it may consider appropriate.

(4) The report produced under Article 8 of that Directive identifies concrete problems encountered in the practical application of the Directive.

(5) On 25 June 1998 the European Community signed the UN/ECE Convention on Access to Information, Public Participation in Decision-Making and Access to Justice in Environmental Matters ('the Aarhus Convention'). Provisions of Community law must be consistent with that Convention with a view to its conclusion by the European Community.

(6) It is appropriate in the interest of increased transparency to replace Directive 90/313/EEC rather than to amend it, so as to provide interested parties with a single, clear and coherent legislative text.

(7) Disparities between the laws in force in the Member States concerning access to environmental information held by public authorities can create inequality within the Community as regards access to such information or as regards conditions of competition.

(8) It is necessary to ensure that any natural and legal person has a right of access to environmental information held by or for public authorities without his having to state an interest.

(9) It is also necessary that public authorities make available and disseminate environmental information to the general public to the widest extent possible, in particular by using information and communication technologies. The future development of these technologies should be taken into account in the reporting on, and reviewing of, this Directive.

(10) The definition of environmental information should be clarified so as to encompass information in any form on the state of the environment, on factors, measures or activities affecting or likely to affect the environment or designed to protect it, on cost-benefit and economic analyses used within the framework of such measures or activities and also information on the state of human health and safety, including the contamination of the food chain, conditions of human life, cultural sites and built structures in as much as they are, or may be, affected by any of those matters.

(11) To take account of the principle in Article 6 of the Treaty, that environmental protection requirements should be integrated into the definition and implementation of Community policies and activities, the definition of public authorities should be expanded so as to encompass government or other public administration at national, regional or local level whether or not they have specific responsibilities for the environment. The definition should likewise be expanded to include other persons or bodies performing public administrative functions

in relation to the environment under national law, as well as other persons or bodies acting under their control and having public responsibilities or functions in relation to the environment.

(12) Environmental information which is physically held by other bodies on behalf of public authorities should also fall within the scope of this Directive.

(13) Environmental information should be made available to applicants as soon as possible and within a reasonable time and having regard to any timescale specified by the applicant.

(14) Public authorities should make environmental information available in the form or format requested by an applicant unless it is already publicly available in another form or format or it is reasonable to make it available in another form or format. In addition, public authorities should be required to make all reasonable efforts to maintain the environmental information held by or for them in forms or formats that are readily reproducible and accessible by electronic means.

(15) Member States should determine the practical arrangements under which such information is effectively made available. These arrangements shall guarantee that the information is effectively and easily accessible and progressively becomes available to the public through public telecommunications networks, including publicly accessible lists of public authorities and registers or lists of environmental information held by or for public authorities.

(16) The right to information means that the disclosure of information should be the general rule and that public authorities should be permitted to refuse a request for environmental information in specific and clearly defined cases. Grounds for refusal should be interpreted in a restrictive way, whereby the public interest served by disclosure should be weighed against the interest served by the refusal. The reasons for a refusal should be provided to the applicant within the time limit laid down in this Directive.

(17) Public authorities should make environmental information available in part where it is possible to separate out any information falling within the scope of the exceptions from the rest of the information requested.

(18) Public authorities should be able to make a charge for supplying environmental information but such a charge should be reasonable. This implies that, as a general rule, charges may not exceed actual costs of producing the material in question. Instances where advance payment will be required should be limited. In particular cases, where public authorities make available environmental information on a commercial basis, and where this is necessary in order to guarantee the continuation of collecting and publishing such information, a marketbased charge is considered to be reasonable; an advance payment may be required. A schedule of charges should be published and made available to applicants together with information on the circumstances in which a charge may be levied or waived.

(19) Applicants should be able to seek an administrative or judicial review of the acts or omissions of a public authority in relation to a request.

(20) Public authorities should seek to guarantee that when environmental information is compiled by them or on their behalf, the information is comprehensible, accurate and comparable. As this is an important factor in assessing the quality of the information supplied the method used in compiling the information should also be disclosed upon request.

(21) In order to increase public awareness in environmental matters and to improve environmental protection, public authorities should, as appropriate, make available and disseminate information on the environment which is relevant to their functions, in particular by means of computer telecommunication and/or electronic technology, where available.

(22) This Directive should be evaluated every four years, after its entry into force, in the light of experience and after submission of the relevant reports by the Member States, and be subject to revision on that basis. The Commission should submit an evaluation report to the European Parliament and the Council.

(23) Since the objectives of the proposed Directive cannot be sufficiently achieved by the Member States and can therefore be better achieved at Community level, the Community may adopt measures, in accordance with the principle of subsidiarity as set out in Article 5 of the Treaty. In accordance with the principle of proportionality, as set out in that Article, this Directive does not go beyond what is necessary in order to achieve those objectives.

(24) The provisions of this Directive shall not affect the right of a Member State to maintain or introduce measures providing for broader access to information than required by this Directive,

Have adopted this Directive:

Article 1
Objectives

The objectives of this Directive are:

(a) to guarantee the right of access to environmental information held by or for public authorities and to set out the basic terms and conditions of, and practical arrangements for, its exercise; and

(b) to ensure that, as a matter of course, environmental information is progressively made available and disseminated to the public in order to achieve the widest possible systematic availability and dissemination to the public of environmental information. To this end the use, in particular, of computer telecommunication and/or electronic technology, where available, shall be promoted.

Article 2
Definitions

For the purposes of this Directive:

1. 'Environmental information' shall mean any information in written, visual, aural, electronic or any other material form on:

(a) the state of the elements of the environment, such as air and atmosphere, water, soil, land, landscape and natural sites including wetlands, coastal and marine areas, biological diversity and its components, including genetically modified organisms, and the interaction among these elements;

(b) factors, such as substances, energy, noise, radiation or waste, including radioactive waste, emissions, discharges and other releases into the environment, affecting or likely to affect the elements of the environment referred to in (a);

(c) measures (including administrative measures), such as policies, legislation, plans, programmes, environmental agreements, and activities affecting or likely to affect the elements and factors referred to in (a) and (b) as well as measures or activities designed to protect those elements;

(d) reports on the implementation of environmental legislation;

(e) cost-benefit and other economic analyses and assumptions used within the framework of the measures and activities referred to in (c); and

(f) the state of human health and safety, including the contamination of the food chain, where relevant, conditions of human life, cultural sites and built structures inasmuch as they are or may be affected by the state of the elements of the environment referred to in (a) or, through those elements, by any of the matters referred to in (b) and (c).

2. 'Public authority' shall mean:

(a) government or other public administration, including public advisory bodies, at national, regional or local level;

(b) any natural or legal person performing public administrative functions under national law, including specific duties, activities or services in relation to the environment; and

(c) any natural or legal person having public responsibilities or functions, or providing public services, relating to the environment under the control of a body or person falling within (a) or (b).

Member States may provide that this definition shall not include bodies or institutions when acting in a judicial or legislative capacity. If their constitutional provisions at the date of adoption of this Directive make no provision for a review procedure within the meaning of Article 6, Member States may exclude those bodies or institutions from that definition.

3. 'Information held by a public authority' shall mean environmental information in its possession which has been produced or received by that authority.

4. 'Information held for a public authority' shall mean environmental information which is physically held by a natural or legal person on behalf of a public authority.

5. 'Applicant' shall mean any natural or legal person requesting environmental information.

6. 'Public' shall mean one or more natural or legal persons, and, in accordance with national legislation or practice, their associations, organisations or groups.

Article 3
Access to environmental information upon request

1. Member States shall ensure that public authorities are required, in accordance with the provisions of this Directive, to make available environmental information held by or for them to any applicant at his request and without his having to state an interest.

2. Subject to Article 4 and having regard to any timescale specified by the applicant, environmental information shall be made available to an applicant:

(a) as soon as possible or, at the latest, within one month after the receipt by the public authority referred to in paragraph 1 of the applicant's request; or
(b) within two months after the receipt of the request by the public authority if the volume and the complexity of the information is such that the one-month period referred to in (a) cannot be complied with. In such cases, the applicant shall be informed as soon as possible, and in any case before the end of that one-month period, of any such extension and of the reasons for it.

3. If a request is formulated in too general a manner, the public authority shall as soon as possible, and at the latest within the timeframe laid down in paragraph 2(a), ask the applicant to specify the request and shall assist the applicant in doing so, e.g. by providing information on the use of the public registers referred to in paragraph 5(c). The public authorities may, where they deem it appropriate, refuse the request under Article 4(1)(c).

4. Where an applicant requests a public authority to make environmental information available in a specific form or format (including in the form of copies), the public authority shall make it so available unless:

(a) it is already publicly available in another form or format, in particular under Article 7, which is easily accessible by applicants; or
(b) it is reasonable for the public authority to make it available in another form or format, in which case reasons shall be given for making it available in that form or format.
    For the purposes of this paragraph, public authorities shall make all reasonable efforts to maintain environmental information held by or for them in forms or

formats that are readily reproducible and accessible by computer telecommunications or by other electronic means.

The reasons for a refusal to make information available, in full or in part, in the form or format requested shall be provided to the applicant within the time limit referred to in paragraph 2(a).

5. For the purposes of this Article, Member States shall ensure that:

(a) officials are required to support the public in seeking access to information;
(b) lists of public authorities are publicly accessible; and
(c) the practical arrangements are defined for ensuring that the right of access to environmental information can be effectively exercised, such as:
  – the designation of information officers;
  – the establishment and maintenance of facilities for the examination of the information required,
  – registers or lists of the environmental information held by public authorities or information points, with clear indications of where such information can be found.

Member States shall ensure that public authorities inform the public adequately of the rights they enjoy as a result of this Directive and to an appropriate extent provide information, guidance and advice to this end.

Article 4
Exceptions

1. Member States may provide for a request for environmental information to be refused if:

(a) the information requested is not held by or for the public authority to which the request is addressed. In such a case, where that public authority is aware that the information is held by or for another public authority, it shall, as soon as possible, transfer the request to that other authority and inform the applicant accordingly or inform the applicant of the public authority to which it believes it is possible to apply for the information requested;
(b) the request is manifestly unreasonable;
(c) the request is formulated in too general a manner, taking into account Article 3(3);
(d) the request concerns material in the course of completion or unfinished documents or data;
(e) the request concerns internal communications, taking into account the public interest served by disclosure.

Where a request is refused on the basis that it concerns material in the course of completion, the public authority shall state the name of the authority preparing the material and the estimated time needed for completion.

2. Member States may provide for a request for environmental information to be refused if disclosure of the information would adversely affect:

(a) the confidentiality of the proceedings of public authorities, where such confidentiality is provided for by law;
(b) international relations, public security or national defence;
(c) the course of justice, the ability of any person to receive a fair trial or the ability of a public authority to conduct an enquiry of a criminal or disciplinary nature;
(d) the confidentiality of commercial or industrial information where such confidentiality is provided for by national or Community law to protect a legitimate economic interest, including the public interest in maintaining statistical confidentiality and tax secrecy;
(e) intellectual property rights;
(f) the confidentiality of personal data and/or files relating to a natural person where that person has not consented to the disclosure of the information to the public, where such confidentiality is provided for by national or Community law;
(g) the interests or protection of any person who supplied the information requested on a voluntary basis without being under, or capable of being put under, a legal obligation to do so, unless that person has consented to the release of the information concerned;
(h) the protection of the environment to which such information relates, such as the location of rare species.

The grounds for refusal mentioned in paragraphs 1 and 2 shall be interpreted in a restrictive way, taking into account for the particular case the public interest served by disclosure. In every particular case, the public interest served by disclosure shall be weighed against the interest served by the refusal. Member States may not, by virtue of paragraph 2(a), (d), (f), (g) and (h), provide for a request to be refused where the request relates to information on emissions into the environment.

Within this framework, and for the purposes of the application of subparagraph (f), Member States shall ensure that the requirements of Directive 95/46/EC of the European Parliament and of the Council of 24 October 1995 on the protection of individuals with regard to the processing of personal data and on the free movement of such data are complied with.[1]

3. Where a Member State provides for exceptions, it may draw up a publicly accessible list of criteria on the basis of which the authority concerned may decide how to handle requests.

---

[1] OJ L 281, 23.11.1995, p. 31.

4. Environmental information held by or for public authorities which has been requested by an applicant shall be made available in part where it is possible to separate out any information falling within the scope of paragraphs 1(d) and (e) or 2 from the rest of the information requested.

5. A refusal to make available all or part of the information requested shall be notified to the applicant in writing or electronically, if the request was in writing or if the applicant so requests, within the time limits referred to in Article 3(2)(a) or, as the case may be, (b). The notification shall state the reasons for the refusal and include information on the review procedure provided for in accordance with Article 6.

Article 5
Charges

1. Access to any public registers or lists established and maintained as mentioned in Article 3(5) and examination *in situ* of the information requested shall be free of charge.

2. Public authorities may make a charge for supplying any environmental information but such charge shall not exceed a reasonable amount.

3. Where charges are made, public authorities shall publish and make available to applicants a schedule of such charges as well as information on the circumstances in which a charge may be levied or waived.

Article 6
Access to justice

1. Member States shall ensure that any applicant who considers that his request for information has been ignored, wrongfully refused (whether in full or in part), inadequately answered or otherwise not dealt with in accordance with the provisions of Articles 3, 4 or 5, has access to a procedure in which the acts or omissions of the public authority concerned can be reconsidered by that or another public authority or reviewed administratively by an independent and impartial body established by law. Any such procedure shall be expeditious and either free of charge or inexpensive.

2. In addition to the review procedure referred to in paragraph 1, Member States shall ensure that an applicant has access to a review procedure before a court of law or another independent and impartial body established by law, in which the acts or omissions of the public authority concerned can be reviewed and whose decisions may become final. Member States may furthermore provide that third parties incriminated by the disclosure of information may also have access to legal recourse.

3. Final decisions under paragraph 2 shall be binding on the public authority holding the information. Reasons shall be stated in writing, at least where access to information is refused under this Article.

Article 7
Dissemination of environmental information

1. Member States shall take the necessary measures to ensure that public authorities organise the environmental information which is relevant to their functions and which is held by or for them, with a view to its active and systematic dissemination to the public, in particular by means of computer telecommunication and/or electronic technology, where available.

The information made available by means of computer telecommunication and/or electronic technology need not include information collected before the entry into force of this Directive unless it is already available in electronic form.

Member States shall ensure that environmental information progressively becomes available in electronic databases which are easily accessible to the public through public telecommunication networks.

2. The information to be made available and disseminated shall be updated as appropriate and shall include at least:

(a) texts of international treaties, conventions or agreements, and of Community, national, regional or local legislation, on the environment or relating to it;
(b) policies, plans and programmes relating to the environment;
(c) progress reports on the implementation of the items referred to in (a) and (b) when prepared or held in electronic form by public authorities;
(d) the reports on the state of the environment referred to in paragraph 3;
(e) data or summaries of data derived from the monitoring of activities affecting, or likely to affect, the environment;
(f) authorisations with a significant impact on the environment and environmental agreements or a reference to the place where such information can be requested or found in the framework of Article 3;
(g) environmental impact studies and risk assessments concerning the environmental elements referred to in Article 2(1)(a) or a reference to the place where the information can be requested or found in the framework of Article 3.

3. Without prejudice to any specific reporting obligations laid down by Community legislation, Member States shall take the necessary measures to ensure that national, and, where appropriate, regional or local reports on the state of the environment are published at regular intervals not exceeding four years; such reports shall include information on the quality of, and pressures on, the environment.

4. Without prejudice to any specific obligation laid down by Community legislation, Member States shall take the necessary measures to ensure that, in the event of an imminent threat to human health or the environment, whether caused by human activities or due to natural causes, all information held by or for public authorities which could enable the public likely to be affected to take measures to prevent or mitigate harm arising from the threat is disseminated, immediately and without delay.

5. The exceptions in Article 4(1) and (2) may apply in relation to the duties imposed by this Article.

6. Member States may satisfy the requirements of this Article by creating links to Internet sites where the information can be found.

Article 8
Quality of environmental information

1. Member States shall, so far as is within their power, ensure that any information that is compiled by them or on their behalf is up to date, accurate and comparable.

2. Upon request, public authorities shall reply to requests for information pursuant to Article 2(1)b, reporting to the applicant on the place where information, if available, can be found on the measurement procedures, including methods of analysis, sampling, and pre-treatment of samples, used in compiling the information, or referring to a standardised procedure used.

Article 9
Review procedure

1. Not later than 14 February 2009, Member States shall report on the experience gained in the application of this Directive.

They shall communicate the report to the Commission not later than 14 August 2009.

No later than 14 February 2004, the Commission shall forward to the Member States a guidance document setting out clearly the manner in which it wishes the Member States to report.

2. In the light of experience and taking into account developments in computer telecommunication and/or electronic technology, the Commission shall make a report to the European Parliament and to the Council together with any proposal for revision, which it may consider appropriate.

Article 10
Implementation

Member States shall bring into force the laws, regulations and administrative provisions necessary to comply with this Directive by 14 February 2005. They shall forthwith inform the Commission thereof.

When Member States adopt these measures, they shall contain a reference to this Directive or shall be accompanied by such reference on the occasion of their official publication. The methods of making such reference shall be laid down by Member States.

Article 11
Repeal

Directive 90/313/EEC is hereby repealed with effect from 14 February 2005.

References to the repealed Directive shall be construed as referring to this Directive and shall be read in accordance with the correlation table in the Annex.

Article 12

Entry into force

This Directive shall enter into force on the day of its publication in the *Official Journal of the European Union.*

Article 13

Addressees

This Directive is addressed to the Member States.
Done at Brussels, 28 January 2003.

Annex

Correlation table (Directive 90/313/EEC and Directive 2003/4/EC)

[omitted]

Directive 2003/35/EC of the European Parliament and of the Council of 26 May 2003 providing for public participation in respect of the drawing up of certain plans and programmes relating to the environment and amending with regard to public participation and access to justice Council Directives 85/337/EEC and 96/61/EC

Editorial note

Directive 2003/35 of 26 May 2003 aims at contributing to the implementation of the UN/ECE Convention on Access to Information, Public Participation in Decision-Making and Access to Justice in Environmental Matters (the Århus Convention). In particular, the Directive provides for public participation in respect of the drawing up of certain plans and programmes relevant to the environment (Article 2); improves public participation and provides for provisions on access to justice within Council Directives 85/337/EEC (Environmental Impact Assessment) (Article 3) and 96/61/EC (Integrated Pollution Prevention and Control) (Article 4).

Source: OJ L 156 25.06.2003 p. 17

Directive 2003/35/EC of the European Parliament and of the Council of 26 May 2003 providing for public participation in respect of the drawing up of certain plans and programmes relating to the environment and amending with regard to public participation and access to justice Council Directives 85/337/EEC and 96/61/EC

The European Parliament and the Council of the European Union,

Having regard to the Treaty establishing the European Community, and in particular Article 175 thereof,

Having regard to the proposal from the Commission,[1]

Having regard to the opinion of the European Economic and Social Committee,[2]

---

[1] OJ C 154 E, 29.5.2001, p. 123.   [2] OJ C 221, 7.8.2001, p. 65.

Having regard to the opinion of the Committee of the Regions,[1]

Acting in accordance with the procedure laid down in Article 251 of the Treaty,[2] in the light of the joint text approved by the Conciliation Committee on 15 January 2003,

Whereas:

(1) Community legislation in the field of the environment aims to contribute to preserving, protecting and improving the quality of the environment and protecting human health.

(2) Community environmental legislation includes provisions for public authorities and other bodies to take decisions which may have a significant effect on the environment as well as on personal health and wellbeing.

(3) Effective public participation in the taking of decisions enables the public to express, and the decision-maker to take account of, opinions and concerns which may be relevant to those decisions, thereby increasing the accountability and transparency of the decision-making process and contributing to public awareness of environmental issues and support for the decisions taken.

(4) Participation, including participation by associations, organisations and groups, in particular non-governmental organisations promoting environmental protection, should accordingly be fostered, including *inter alia* by promoting environmental education of the public.

(5) On 25 June 1998 the Community signed the UN/ECE Convention on Access to Information, Public Participation in Decision-Making and Access to Justice in Environmental Matters (the Århus Convention). Community law should be properly aligned with that Convention with a view to its ratification by the Community.

(6) Among the objectives of the Århus Convention is the desire to guarantee rights of public participation in decision-making in environmental matters in order to contribute to the protection of the right to live in an environment which is adequate for personal health and wellbeing.

(7) Article 6 of the Århus Convention provides for public participation in decisions on the specific activities listed in Annex I thereto and on activities not so listed which may have a significant effect on the environment.

(8) Article 7 of the Århus Convention provides for public participation concerning plans and programmes relating to the environment.

---

[1] OJ C 357, 14.12.2001, p. 58.

[2] Opinion of the European Parliament of 23 October 2001 (OJ C 112, 9.5.2002, p. 125(E)), Council Common Position of 25 April 2002 (OJ C 170 E, 16.7.2002, p. 22) and Decision of the European Parliament of 5 September 2002 (not yet published in the Official Journal). Decision of the European Parliament of 30 January 2003 and Decision of the Council of 4 March 2003.

(9) Article 9(2) and (4) of the Århus Convention provides for access to judicial or other procedures for challenging the substantive or procedural legality of decisions, acts or omissions subject to the public participation provisions of Article 6 of the Convention.

(10) Provision should be made in respect of certain Directives in the environmental area which require Member States to produce plans and programmes relating to the environment but which do not contain sufficient provisions on public participation, so as to ensure public participation consistent with the provisions of the Århus Convention, in particular Article 7 thereof. Other relevant Community legislation already provides for public participation in the preparation of plans and programmes and, for the future, public participation requirements in line with the Århus Convention will be incorporated into the relevant legislation from the outset.

(11) Council Directive 85/337/EEC of 27 June 1985 on the assessment of the effects of certain public and private projects on the environment,[1] and Council Directive 96/61/EC of 24 September 1996 concerning integrated pollution prevention and control[2] should be amended to ensure that they are fully compatible with the provisions of the Århus Convention, in particular Article 6 and Article 9(2) and (4) thereof.

(12) Since the objective of the proposed action, namely to contribute to the implementation of the obligations arising under the Århus Convention, cannot be sufficiently achieved by the Member States and can therefore, by reason of the scale and effects of the action, be better achieved at Community level, the Community may adopt measures in accordance with the principle of subsidiarity as set out in Article 5 of the Treaty. In accordance with the principle of proportionality, as set out in that Article, this Directive does not go beyond what is necessary in order to achieve that objective,

Have Adopted this Directive:

Article 1
Objective

The objective of this Directive is to contribute to the implementation of the obligations arising under the Århus Convention, in particular by:

(a) providing for public participation in respect of the drawing up of certain plans and programmes relating to the environment;

(b) improving the public participation and providing for provisions on access to justice within Council Directives 85/337/ EEC and 96/61/EC.

---

[1] OJ L 175, 5.7.1985, p. 40. Directive as amended by Directive 97/11/EC (OJ L 73, 14.3.1997, p. 5).
[2] OJ L 257, 10.10.1996, p. 26.

Article 2
Public participation concerning plans and programmes

1. For the purposes of this Article, 'the public' shall mean one or more natural or legal persons and, in accordance with national legislation or practice, their associations, organisations or groups.

2. Member States shall ensure that the public is given early and effective opportunities to participate in the preparation and modification or review of the plans or programmes required to be drawn up under the provisions listed in Annex I.

To that end, Member States shall ensure that:

(a) the public is informed, whether by public notices or other appropriate means such as electronic media where available, about any proposals for such plans or programmes or for their modification or review and that relevant information about such proposals is made available to the public including *inter alia* information about the right to participate in decision-making and about the competent authority to which comments or questions may be submitted;
(b) the public is entitled to express comments and opinions when all options are open before decisions on the plans and programmes are made;
(c) in making those decisions, due account shall be taken of the results of the public participation;
(d) having examined the comments and opinions expressed by the public, the competent authority makes reasonable efforts to inform the public about the decisions taken and the reasons and considerations upon which those decisions are based, including information about the public participation process.

3. Member States shall identify the public entitled to participate for the purposes of paragraph 2, including relevant nongovernmental organisations meeting any requirements imposed under national law, such as those promoting environmental protection.

The detailed arrangements for public participation under this Article shall be determined by the Member States so as to enable the public to prepare and participate effectively.

Reasonable time-frames shall be provided allowing sufficient time for each of the different stages of public participation required by this Article.

4. This Article shall not apply to plans and programmes designed for the sole purpose of serving national defence or taken in case of civil emergencies.

5. This Article shall not apply to plans and programmes set out in Annex I for which a public participation procedure is carried out under Directive 2001/42/EC of the European Parliament and of the Council of 27 June 2001 on the assessment of the effects of certain plans and programmes on the environment[1] or under Directive

---

[1] OJ L 197, 21.7.2001, p. 30.

2000/60/EC of the European Parliament and of the Council of 23 October 2000 establishing a framework for Community action in the field of water policy.[1]

Article 3
Amendment of Directive 85/337/EEC

[Omitted – amendments incorporated in the text of the Directive 85/337/EEC reproduced above]

Article 4
Amendment of Directive 96/61/EC

[Omitted – amendments incorporated in the text of the Directive 96/61/EC reproduced above]

Article 5
Reporting and review

By 25 June 2009, the Commission shall send a report on the application and effectiveness of this Directive to the European Parliament and to the Council. With a view to further integrating environmental protection requirements, in accordance with Article 6 of the Treaty, and taking into account the experience acquired in the application of this Directive in the Member States, such a report will be accompanied by proposals for amendment of this Directive, if appropriate. In particular, the Commission will consider the possibility of extending the scope of this Directive to other plans and programmes relating to the environment.

Article 6
Implementation

Member States shall bring into force the laws, regulations and administrative provisions necessary to comply with this Directive by 25 June 2005 at the latest. They shall forthwith inform the Commission thereof.

When Member States adopt these measures, they shall contain a reference to this Directive or shall be accompanied by such a reference on the occasion of their official publication. The methods of making such reference shall be laid down by Member States.

Article 7
Entry into force

This Directive shall enter into force on the day of its publication in the *Official Journal of the European Union*.

---

[1] OJ L 327, 22.12.2000, p. 1. Directive as amended by Decision No 2455/2001/EC (OJ L 331, 15.12.2001, p. 1).

Article 8

Addressees

This Directive is addressed to the Member States.

Done at Brussels, 26 May 2003.

Annex I

Provisions for Plans and Programmes Referred to in Article 2

(a) Article 7(1) of Council Directive 75/442/EEC of 15 July 1975 on waste.[1]
(b) Article 6 of Council Directive 91/157/EEC of 18 March 1991 on batteries and accumulators containing certain dangerous substances.[2]
(c) Article 5(1) of Council Directive 91/676/EEC of 12 December 1991 concerning the protection of waters against pollution caused by nitrates from agricultural sources.[3]
(d) Article 6(1) of Council Directive 91/689/EEC of 12 December 1991 on hazardous waste.[4]
(e) Article 14 of Directive 94/62/EC of the European Parliament and of the Council of 20 December 1994 on packaging and packaging waste.[5]
(f) Article 8(3) of Council Directive 96/62/EC of 27 September 1996 on ambient air quality assessment and management.[6]

Annex II

In Directive 96/61/EC, the following Annex shall be added:

[Omitted – Amendment incorporated in Directive 96/61/EC reproduced above]

---

[1] OJ L 194, 25.7.1975, p. 39. Directive as last amended by Commission Decision 96/350/EC (OJ L 135, 6.6.1996, p. 32).
[2] OJ L 78, 26.3.1991, p. 38. Directive as last amended by Commission Directive 98/101/EC (OJ L 1, 5.1.1999, p. 1).
[3] OJ L 375, 31.12.1991, p. 1.
[4] OJ L 377, 31.12.1991, p. 20. Directive as last amended by Directive 94/31/EC (OJ L 168, 2.7.1994, p. 28).
[5] OJ L 365, 31.12.1994, p. 10.   [6] OJ L 296, 21.11.1996, p. 55.

Directive 2004/35/EC of the European Parliament and of the Council of 21 April 2004 on environmental liability with regard to the prevention and remedying of environmental damage

Editorial note

Directive 2004/35/EC of 21 April 2004 establishes a framework of environmental liability based on the polluter pays principle, to prevent and remedy environmental damage (Article 1). The Directive defines several terms to be used in its applications, including 'environmental damage' (Article 2(1)); 'damage' (Article 2(2)); 'occupational activity' (Article 2(7)); 'preventive measures' (Article 2(10)); 'remedial measures' (Article 2(11)); and 'costs' (Article 2(16)).

The Directive applies to environmental damage and to any imminent threat of such damage caused by any of the occupational activities listed in Annex III. Damage to protected species and natural habitats caused by any occupational activities other than those listed in Annex III, and any imminent threat of such damage, is also covered whenever the operator has been at fault or negligent (Article 3). The Directive does not cover environmental damage resulting from an armed conflict or a natural phenomenon (Article 4(1)). The Directive does not apply to environmental damage or threat of such damage in respect of which liability is regulated under any of the international conventions listed in Annex IV (Article 4(2)). Other exceptions include nuclear damage (covered by either the Euratom Treaty or falling under one of the international liability regimes listed in Annex V) (Article 4(4)). The Directive applies to damage caused by pollution of a diffuse character only if it is possible to establish a causal link with activities of an individual operator (Article 4(5)). Activities whose main purpose is to serve national defence or international security or the sole purpose of which is to protect from natural disasters are excluded from the application of the Directive (Article 4(6)).

The operator is to take the necessary preventive measures where environmental damage has not yet occurred but there is an imminent threat (Article 5(1)). Where appropriate, and in any event whenever an imminent threat of damage is not dispelled despite the preventive measures taken, the operator is to inform the competent authority of all the relevant aspects of the situation, as soon as possible (Article 5(2)). Where environmental damage has occurred, the operator is, without delay, to inform

the competent authority and take all practicable steps immediately to control, contain, remove or otherwise manage the relevant containment and/or any other damage
factors to limit or to prevent further environmental damage (Article 6). The operator
is to take the necessary remedial measures (Article 6(2) and Article 7).

The operator is to bear the costs of the preventive and remedial actions taken in the
application of the Directive. Costs incurred by the competent authority should also
be recovered from the operator (Article 8). The public authority is to be entitled to
initiate cost recovery proceedings within five years (Article 10). However, the operator
should not bear the costs of preventive or remedial actions if the damage was caused
by a third party and occurred despite the presence of appropriate safety measures,
or resulted from compliance with a compulsory order or instruction from a public
authority (Article 8). Member States may allow the operator not to bear such costs
where the operator demonstrates that he was not at fault or negligent if the environmental damage was caused by an emission or event expressly authorised, or an
emission or activity that the operator demonstrates was not considered likely to cause
environmental damage according to the state of scientific and technical knowledge at
the time the emission or activity took place (Article 8(4)).

Member States are to designate the competent authority(ies) responsible for the
application of the Directive (Article 11).

Natural or legal persons affected or likely to be affected by environmental damage; or
having a sufficient interest in environmental decision-making relating to the damage;
or, alternatively, alleging the impairment of a right, where administrative procedural
law of a Member State requires this as a precondition, are to be entitled to submit
to the competent authority any observations relating to instances of environmental
damage or an imminent threat of such damage of which they are aware, and are to
be entitled to request the competent authority to take action under this Directive
(Article 12). Natural or legal persons identified under Article 12(1) are to have access
to a court or other independent impartial public body to review the procedural and
substantive legality of the decisions, acts or failure to act of the competent authority
(Article 13).

Member States are to take measures to encourage the development of financial
instruments with the aim of enabling the operators to use financial guarantees to
cover their responsibilities (Article 14(1)). The Commission is to present a report
before 30 April 2010 on the effectiveness of the Directive, on the availability at reasonable cost and on conditions of insurance and other types of financial security
for the activities covered by Annex III (Article 14(2)). Member States are to cooperate where environmental damage is likely to affect several Member States (Article
15). Member States may maintain or adopt more stringent provisions (Article 16).
Temporal exceptions to the application of the Directive are specified in Article 17.

The Directive is to be implemented by 30 April 2007 (Article 19).

Source: OJ L 143 30.04.2004 p. 56

Directive 2004/35/EC of the European Parliament and of the Council of 21 April 2004 on environmental liability with regard to the prevention and remedying of environmental damage

The European Parliament and the Council of the European Union,

Having regard to the Treaty establishing the European Community, and in particular Article 175(1) thereof,

Having regard to the proposal from the Commission,[1]

Having regard to the Opinion of the European Economic and Social Committee,[2]

After consulting the Committee of the Regions,

Acting in accordance with the procedure laid down in Article 251 of the Treaty,[3] in the light of the joint text approved by the Conciliation Committee on 10 March 2004,

Whereas:

(1) There are currently many contaminated sites in the Community, posing significant health risks, and the loss of biodiversity has dramatically accelerated over the last decades. Failure to act could result in increased site contamination and greater loss of biodiversity in the future. Preventing and remedying, insofar as is possible, environmental damage contributes to implementing the objectives and principles of the Community's environment policy as set out in the Treaty. Local conditions should be taken into account when deciding how to remedy damage.

(2) The prevention and remedying of environmental damage should be implemented through the furtherance of the 'polluter pays' principle, as indicated in the Treaty and in line with the principle of sustainable development. The fundamental principle of this Directive should therefore be that an operator whose activity has caused the environmental damage or the imminent threat of such damage is to be held financially liable, in order to induce operators to adopt measures and develop practices to minimise the risks of environmental damage so that their exposure to financial liabilities is reduced.

(3) Since the objective of this Directive, namely to establish a common framework for the prevention and remedying of environmental damage at a reasonable cost to society, cannot be sufficiently achieved by the Member States and can therefore be better achieved at Community level by reason of the scale of this Directive and its implications in respect of other Community legislation, namely Council Directive 79/409/EEC of 2 April 1979 on the conservation of wild

---

[1] OJ C 151 E, 25.6.2002, p. 132.   [2] OJ C 241, 7.10.2002, p. 162.

[3] Opinion of the European Parliament of 14 May 2003 (not yet published in the Official Journal), Council Common Position of 18 September 2003 (OJ C 277 E, 18.11.2003, p. 10) and Position of the European Parliament of 17 December 2003 (not yet published in the Official Journal). Legislative resolution of the European Parliament of 31 March 2004 and Council Decision of 30 March 2004.

birds,[1] Council Directive 92/43/EEC of 21 May 1992 on the conservation of natural habitats and of wild fauna and flora,[2] and Directive 2000/60/EC of the European Parliament and of the Council of 23 October 2000 establishing a framework for Community action in the field of water policy,[3] the Community may adopt measures in accordance with the principle of subsidiarity as set out in Article 5 of the Treaty. In accordance with the principle of proportionality, as set out in that Article, this Directive does not go beyond what is necessary in order to achieve that objective.

(4) Environmental damage also includes damage caused by airborne elements as far as they cause damage to water, land or protected species or natural habitats.

(5) Concepts instrumental for the correct interpretation and application of the scheme provided for by this Directive should be defined especially as regards the definition of environmental damage. When the concept in question derives from other relevant Community legislation, the same definition should be used so that common criteria can be used and uniform application promoted.

(6) Protected species and natural habitats might also be defined by reference to species and habitats protected in pursuance of national legislation on nature conservation. Account should nevertheless be taken of specific situations where Community, or equivalent national, legislation allows for certain derogations from the level of protection afforded to the environment.

(7) For the purposes of assessing damage to land as defined in this Directive the use of risk assessment procedures to determine to what extent human health is likely to be adversely affected is desirable.

(8) This Directive should apply, as far as environmental damage is concerned, to occupational activities which present a risk for human health or the environment. Those activities should be identified, in principle, by reference to the relevant Community legislation which provides for regulatory requirements in relation to certain activities or practices considered as posing a potential or actual risk for human health or the environment.

(9) This Directive should also apply, as regards damage to protected species and natural habitats, to any occupational activities other than those already directly or indirectly identified by reference to Community legislation as posing an actual or potential risk for human health or the environment. In such cases the operator should only be liable under this Directive whenever he is at fault or negligent.

(10) Express account should be taken of the Euratom Treaty and relevant international conventions and of Community legislation regulating more comprehensively

---

[1] OJ L 103, 25.4.1979, p. 1. Directive as last amended by Regulation (EC) No 807/2003 (OJ L 122, 16.5.2003, p. 36).

[2] OJ L 206, 22.7.1992, p. 7. Directive as last amended by Regulation (EC) No 1882/2003 of the European Parliament and of the Council (OJ L 284, 31.10.2003, p. 1).

[3] OJ L 327, 22.12.2000, p. 1. Directive as amended by Decision No 2455/2001/EC (OJ L 331, 15.12.2001, p. 1).

and more stringently the operation of any of the activities falling under the scope of this Directive. This Directive, which does not provide for additional rules of conflict of laws when it specifies the powers of the competent authorities, is without prejudice to the rules on international jurisdiction of courts as provided, *inter alia*, in Council Regulation (EC) No 44/2001 of 22 December 2000 on jurisdiction and the recognition and enforcement of judgments in civil and commercial matters.[1] This Directive should not apply to activities the main purpose of which is to serve national defence or international security.

(11) This Directive aims at preventing and remedying environmental damage, and does not affect rights of compensation for traditional damage granted under any relevant international agreement regulating civil liability.

(12) Many Member States are party to international agreements dealing with civil liability in relation to specific fields. These Member States should be able to remain so after the entry into force of this Directive, whereas other Member States should not lose their freedom to become parties to these agreements.

(13) Not all forms of environmental damage can be remedied by means of the liability mechanism. For the latter to be effective, there need to be one or more identifiable polluters, the damage should be concrete and quantifiable, and a causal link should be established between the damage and the identified polluter(s). Liability is therefore not a suitable instrument for dealing with pollution of a widespread, diffuse character, where it is impossible to link the negative environmental effects with acts or failure to act of certain individual actors.

(14) This Directive does not apply to cases of personal injury, to damage to private property or to any economic loss and does not affect any right regarding these types of damages.

(15) Since the prevention and remedying of environmental damage is a task directly contributing to the pursuit of the Community's environment policy, public authorities should ensure the proper implementation and enforcement of the scheme provided for by this Directive.

(16) Restoration of the environment should take place in an effective manner ensuring that the relevant restoration objectives are achieved. A common framework should be defined to that end, the proper application of which should be supervised by the competent authority.

(17) Appropriate provision should be made for those situations where several instances of environmental damage have occurred in such a manner that the competent authority cannot ensure that all the necessary remedial measures are taken at the same time. In such a case, the competent authority should be entitled to decide which instance of environmental damage is to be remedied first.

---

[1] OJ L 12, 16.1.2001, p. 1. Regulation as amended by Commission Regulation (EC) No 1496/2002 (OJ L 225, 22.8.2002, p. 13).

(18) According to the 'polluter-pays' principle, an operator causing environmental damage or creating an imminent threat of such damage should, in principle, bear the cost of the necessary preventive or remedial measures. In cases where a competent authority acts, itself or through a third party, in the place of an operator, that authority should ensure that the cost incurred by it is recovered from the operator. It is also appropriate that the operators should ultimately bear the cost of assessing environmental damage and, as the case may be, assessing an imminent threat of such damage occurring.

(19) Member States may provide for flat-rate calculation of administrative, legal, enforcement and other general costs to be recovered.

(20) An operator should not be required to bear the costs of preventive or remedial actions taken pursuant to this Directive in situations where the damage in question or imminent threat thereof is the result of certain events beyond the operator's control. Member States may allow that operators who are not at fault or negligent shall not bear the cost of remedial measures, in situations where the damage in question is the result of emissions or events explicitly authorised or where the potential for damage could not have been known when the event or emission took place.

(21) Operators should bear the costs relating to preventive measures when those measures should have been taken as a matter of course in order to comply with the legislative, regulatory and administrative provisions regulating their activities or the terms of any permit or authorisation.

(22) Member States may establish national rules covering cost allocation in cases of multiple party causation. Member States may take into account, in particular, the specific situation of users of products who might not be held responsible for environmental damage in the same conditions as those producing such products. In this case, apportionment of liability should be determined in accordance with national law.

(23) Competent authorities should be entitled to recover the cost of preventive or remedial measures from an operator within a reasonable period of time from the date on which those measures were completed.

(24) It is necessary to ensure that effective means of implementation and enforcement are available, while ensuring that the legitimate interests of the relevant operators and other interested parties are adequately safeguarded. Competent authorities should be in charge of specific tasks entailing appropriate administrative discretion, namely the duty to assess the significance of the damage and to determine which remedial measures should be taken.

(25) Persons adversely affected or likely to be adversely affected by environmental damage should be entitled to ask the competent authority to take action. Environmental protection is, however, a diffuse interest on behalf of which individuals will not always act or will not be in a position to act. Non-governmental organisations promoting environmental protection should therefore also be

given the opportunity to properly contribute to the effective implementation of this Directive.

(26) The relevant natural or legal persons concerned should have access to procedures for the review of the competent authority's decisions, acts or failure to act.

(27) Member States should take measures to encourage the use by operators of any appropriate insurance or other forms of financial security and the development of financial security instruments and markets in order to provide effective cover for financial obligations under this Directive.

(28) Where environmental damage affects or is likely to affect several Member States, those Member States should cooperate with a view to ensuring proper and effective preventive or remedial action in respect of any environmental damage. Member States may seek to recover the costs for preventive or remedial actions.

(29) This Directive should not prevent Member States from maintaining or enacting more stringent provisions in relation to the prevention and remedying of environmental damage; nor should it prevent the adoption by Member States of appropriate measures in relation to situations where double recovery of costs could occur as a result of concurrent action by a competent authority under this Directive and by a person whose property is affected by the environmental damage.

(30) Damage caused before the expiry of the deadline for implementation of this Directive should not be covered by its provisions.

(31) Member States should report to the Commission on the experience gained in the application of this Directive so as to enable the Commission to consider, taking into account the impact on sustainable development and future risks to the environment, whether any review of this Directive is appropriate,

Have adopted this Directive:

Article 1
Subject matter

The purpose of this Directive is to establish a framework of environmental liability based on the 'polluter-pays' principle, to prevent and remedy environmental damage.

Article 2
Definitions

For the purpose of this Directive the following definitions shall apply:

1. 'environmental damage' means:
   (a) damage to protected species and natural habitats, which is any damage that has significant adverse effects on reaching or maintaining the favourable conservation status of such habitats or species. The significance of such effects is to be assessed with reference to the baseline condition, taking account of the criteria set out in Annex I; Damage to protected species and natural habitats

does not include previously identified adverse effects which result from an act by an operator which was expressly authorised by the relevant authorities in accordance with provisions implementing Article 6(3) and (4) or Article 16 of Directive 92/43/EEC or Article 9 of Directive 79/409/EEC or, in the case of habitats and species not covered by Community law, in accordance with equivalent provisions of national law on nature conservation.

(b) water damage, which is any damage that significantly adversely affects the ecological, chemical and/or quantitative status and/or ecological potential, as defined in Directive 2000/60/EC, of the waters concerned, with the exception of adverse effects where Article 4(7) of that Directive applies;

(c) land damage, which is any land contamination that creates a significant risk of human health being adversely affected as a result of the direct or indirect introduction, in, on or under land, of substances, preparations, organisms or micro-organisms;

2. 'damage' means a measurable adverse change in a natural resource or measurable impairment of a natural resource service which may occur directly or indirectly;

3. 'protected species and natural habitats' means:

(a) the species mentioned in Article 4(2) of Directive 79/409/EEC or listed in Annex I thereto or listed in Annexes II and IV to Directive 92/43/EEC;

(b) the habitats of species mentioned in Article 4(2) of Directive 79/409/EEC or listed in Annex I thereto or listed in Annex II to Directive 92/43/EEC, and the natural habitats listed in Annex I to Directive 92/43/EEC and the breeding sites or resting places of the species listed in Annex IV to Directive 92/43/EEC; and

(c) where a Member State so determines, any habitat or species, not listed in those Annexes which the Member State designates for equivalent purposes as those laid down in these two Directives;

4. 'conservation status' means:

(a) in respect of a natural habitat, the sum of the influences acting on a natural habitat and its typical species that may affect its long-term natural distribution, structure and functions as well as the long-term survival of its typical species within, as the case may be, the European territory of the Member States to which the Treaty applies or the territory of a Member State or the natural range of that habitat; The conservation status of a natural habitat will be taken as 'favourable' when:

– its natural range and areas it covers within that range are stable or increasing,

– the specific structure and functions which are necessary for its long-term maintenance exist and are likely to continue to exist for the foreseeable future, and

– the conservation status of its typical species is favourable, as defined in (b);

(b) in respect of a species, the sum of the influences acting on the species concerned that may affect the long-term distribution and abundance of its populations within, as the case may be, the European territory of the Member States to which the Treaty applies or the territory of a Member State or the natural range of that species;

The conservation status of a species will be taken as 'favourable' when:
- population dynamics data on the species concerned indicate that it is maintaining itself on a long-term basis as a viable component of its natural habitats,
- the natural range of the species is neither being reduced nor is likely to be reduced for the foreseeable future, and
- there is, and will probably continue to be, a sufficiently large habitat to maintain its populations on a long-term basis;

5. 'waters' mean all waters covered by Directive 2000/60/EC;

6. 'operator' means any natural or legal, private or public person who operates or controls the occupational activity or, where this is provided for in national legislation, to whom decisive economic power over the technical functioning of such an activity has been delegated, including the holder of a permit or authorisation for such an activity or the person registering or notifying such an activity;

7. 'occupational activity' means any activity carried out in the course of an economic activity, a business or an undertaking, irrespectively of its private or public, profit or non-profit character;

8. 'emission' means the release in the environment, as a result of human activities, of substances, preparations, organisms or micro-organisms;

9. 'imminent threat of damage' means a sufficient likelihood that environmental damage will occur in the near future;

10. 'preventive measures' means any measures taken in response to an event, act or omission that has created an imminent threat of environmental damage, with a view to preventing or minimising that damage;

11. 'remedial measures' means any action, or combination of actions, including mitigating or interim measures to restore, rehabilitate or replace damaged natural resources and/or impaired services, or to provide an equivalent alternative to those resources or services as foreseen in Annex II;

12. 'natural resource' means protected species and natural habitats, water and land;

13. 'services' and 'natural resources services' mean the functions performed by a natural resource for the benefit of another natural resource or the public;

14. 'baseline condition' means the condition at the time of the damage of the natural resources and services that would have existed had the environmental damage not occurred, estimated on the basis of the best information available;

15. 'recovery', including 'natural recovery', means, in the case of water, protected species and natural habitats the return of damaged natural resources and/or impaired services to baseline condition and in the case of land damage, the elimination of any significant risk of adversely affecting human health;

16. 'costs' means costs which are justified by the need to ensure the proper and effective implementation of this Directive including the costs of assessing environmental damage, an imminent threat of such damage, alternatives for action as well as

the administrative, legal, and enforcement costs, the costs of data collection and other general costs, monitoring and supervision costs.

Article 3
Scope

1. This Directive shall apply to:

(a) environmental damage caused by any of the occupational activities listed in Annex III, and to any imminent threat of such damage occurring by reason of any of those activities;
(b) damage to protected species and natural habitats caused by any occupational activities other than those listed in Annex III, and to any imminent threat of such damage occurring by reason of any of those activities, whenever the operator has been at fault or negligent.

2. This Directive shall apply without prejudice to more stringent Community legislation regulating the operation of any of the activities falling within the scope of this Directive and without prejudice to Community legislation containing rules on conflicts of jurisdiction.

3. Without prejudice to relevant national legislation, this Directive shall not give private parties a right of compensation as a consequence of environmental damage or of an imminent threat of such damage.

Article 4
Exceptions

1. This Directive shall not cover environmental damage or an imminent threat of such damage caused by:

(a) an act of armed conflict, hostilities, civil war or insurrection;
(b) a natural phenomenon of exceptional, inevitable and irresistible character.

2. This Directive shall not apply to environmental damage or to any imminent threat of such damage arising from an incident in respect of which liability or compensation falls within the scope of any of the International Conventions listed in Annex IV, including any future amendments thereof, which is in force in the Member State concerned.

3. This Directive shall be without prejudice to the right of the operator to limit his liability in accordance with national legislation implementing the Convention on Limitation of Liability for Maritime Claims (LLMC), 1976, including any future amendment to the Convention, or the Strasbourg Convention on Limitation of Liability in Inland Navigation (CLNI), 1988, including any future amendment to the Convention.

4. This Directive shall not apply to such nuclear risks or environmental damage or imminent threat of such damage as may be caused by the activities covered by the Treaty establishing the European Atomic Energy Community or caused by an incident

or activity in respect of which liability or compensation falls within the scope of any of the international instruments listed in Annex V, including any future amendments thereof.

5. This Directive shall only apply to environmental damage or to an imminent threat of such damage caused by pollution of a diffuse character, where it is possible to establish a causal link between the damage and the activities of individual operators.

6. This Directive shall not apply to activities the main purpose of which is to serve national defence or international security nor to activities the sole purpose of which is to protect from natural disasters.

Article 5
Preventive action

1. Where environmental damage has not yet occurred but there is an imminent threat of such damage occurring, the operator shall, without delay, take the necessary preventive measures.

2. Member States shall provide that, where appropriate, and in any case whenever an imminent threat of environmental damage is not dispelled despite the preventive measures taken by the operator, operators are to inform the competent authority of all relevant aspects of the situation, as soon as possible.

3. The competent authority may, at any time:

(a) require the operator to provide information on any imminent threat of environmental damage or in suspected cases of such an imminent threat;
(b) require the operator to take the necessary preventive measures;
(c) give instructions to the operator to be followed on the necessary preventive measures to be taken; or
(d) itself take the necessary preventive measures.

4. The competent authority shall require that the preventive measures are taken by the operator. If the operator fails to comply with the obligations laid down in paragraph 1 or 3(b) or (c), cannot be identified or is not required to bear the costs under this Directive, the competent authority may take these measures itself.

Article 6
Remedial action

1. Where environmental damage has occurred the operator shall, without delay, inform the competent authority of all relevant aspects of the situation and take:

(a) all practicable steps to immediately control, contain, remove or otherwise manage the relevant contaminants and/or any other damage factors in order to limit or to prevent further environmental damage and adverse effects on human health or further impairment of services and
(b) the necessary remedial measures, in accordance with Article 7.

2. The competent authority may, at any time:

(a) require the operator to provide supplementary information on any damage that has occurred;
(b) take, require the operator to take or give instructions to the operator concerning, all practicable steps to immediately control, contain, remove or otherwise manage the relevant contaminants and/or any other damage factors in order to limit or to prevent further environmental damage and adverse effect on human health, or further impairment of services;
(c) require the operator to take the necessary remedial measures;
(d) give instructions to the operator to be followed on the necessary remedial measures to be taken; or
(e) itself take the necessary remedial measures.

3. The competent authority shall require that the remedial measures are taken by the operator. If the operator fails to comply with the obligations laid down in paragraph 1 or 2(b), (c) or (d), cannot be identified or is not required to bear the costs under this Directive, the competent authority may take these measures itself, as a means of last resort.

Article 7
Determination of remedial measures

1. Operators shall identify, in accordance with Annex II, potential remedial measures and submit them to the competent authority for its approval, unless the competent authority has taken action under Article 6(2)(e) and (3).

2. The competent authority shall decide which remedial measures shall be implemented in accordance with Annex II, and with the cooperation of the relevant operator, as required.

3. Where several instances of environmental damage have occurred in such a manner that the competent authority cannot ensure that the necessary remedial measures are taken at the same time, the competent authority shall be entitled to decide which instance of environmental damage must be remedied first. In making that decision, the competent authority shall have regard, inter alia, to the nature, extent and gravity of the various instances of environmental damage concerned, and to the possibility of natural recovery. Risks to human health shall also be taken into account.

4. The competent authority shall invite the persons referred to in Article 12(1) and in any case the persons on whose land remedial measures would be carried out to submit their observations and shall take them into account.

Article 8
Prevention and remediation costs

1. The operator shall bear the costs for the preventive and remedial actions taken pursuant to this Directive.

2. Subject to paragraphs 3 and 4, the competent authority shall recover, inter alia, via security over property or other appropriate guarantees from the operator who has caused the damage or the imminent threat of damage, the costs it has incurred in relation to the preventive or remedial actions taken under this Directive. However, the competent authority may decide not to recover the full costs where the expenditure required to do so would be greater than the recoverable sum or where the operator cannot be identified.

3. An operator shall not be required to bear the cost of preventive or remedial actions taken pursuant to this Directive when he can prove that the environmental damage or imminent threat of such damage:

(a) was caused by a third party and occurred despite the fact that appropriate safety measures were in place; or

(b) resulted from compliance with a compulsory order or instruction emanating from a public authority other than an order or instruction consequent upon an emission or incident caused by the operator's own activities. In such cases Member States shall take the appropriate measures to enable the operator to recover the costs incurred.

4. The Member States may allow the operator not to bear the cost of remedial actions taken pursuant to this Directive where he demonstrates that he was not at fault or negligent and that the environmental damage was caused by:

(a) an emission or event expressly authorised by, and fully in accordance with the conditions of, an authorisation conferred by or given under applicable national laws and regulations which implement those legislative measures adopted by the Community specified in Annex III, as applied at the date of the emission or event;

(b) an emission or activity or any manner of using a product in the course of an activity which the operator demonstrates was not considered likely to cause environmental damage according to the state of scientific and technical knowledge at the time when the emission was released or the activity took place.

5. Measures taken by the competent authority in pursuance of Article 5(3) and (4) and Article 6(2) and (3) shall be without prejudice to the liability of the relevant operator under this Directive and without prejudice to Articles 87 and 88 of the Treaty.

Article 9
Cost allocation in cases of multiple party causation

This Directive is without prejudice to any provisions of national regulations concerning cost allocation in cases of multiple party causation especially concerning the apportionment of liability between the producer and the user of a product.

Article 10

Limitation period for recovery of costs

The competent authority shall be entitled to initiate cost recovery proceedings against the operator, or if appropriate, a third party who has caused the damage or the imminent threat of damage in relation to any measures taken in pursuance of this Directive within five years from the date on which those measures have been completed or the liable operator, or third party, has been identified, whichever is the later.

Article 11

Competent authority

1. Member States shall designate the competent authority(ies) responsible for fulfilling the duties provided for in this Directive.

2. The duty to establish which operator has caused the damage or the imminent threat of damage, to assess the significance of the damage and to determine which remedial measures should be taken with reference to Annex II shall rest with the competent authority. To that effect, the competent authority shall be entitled to require the relevant operator to carry out his own assessment and to supply any information and data necessary.

3. Member States shall ensure that the competent authority may empower or require third parties to carry out the necessary preventive or remedial measures.

4. Any decision taken pursuant to this Directive which imposes preventive or remedial measures shall state the exact grounds on which it is based. Such decision shall be notified forthwith to the operator concerned, who shall at the same time be informed of the legal remedies available to him under the laws in force in the Member State concerned and of the time-limits to which such remedies are subject.

Article 12

Request for action

1. Natural or legal persons:

(a) affected or likely to be affected by environmental damage or
(b) having a sufficient interest in environmental decision-making relating to the damage or, alternatively,
(c) alleging the impairment of a right, where administrative procedural law of a Member State requires this as a precondition,

shall be entitled to submit to the competent authority any observations relating to instances of environmental damage or an imminent threat of such damage of which they are aware and shall be entitled to request the competent authority to take action under this Directive. What constitutes a 'sufficient interest' and 'impairment of a right' shall be determined by the Member States. To this end, the interest of any non-governmental organisation promoting environmental protection and meeting any requirements under national law shall be deemed sufficient for the purpose of subparagraph (b). Such organisations shall also be deemed to have rights capable of being impaired for the purpose of subparagraph (c).

2. The request for action shall be accompanied by the relevant information and data supporting the observations submitted in relation to the environmental damage in question.

3. Where the request for action and the accompanying observations show in a plausible manner that environmental damage exists, the competent authority shall consider any such observations and requests for action. In such circumstances the competent authority shall give the relevant operator an opportunity to make his views known with respect to the request for action and the accompanying observations.

4. The competent authority shall, as soon as possible and in any case in accordance with the relevant provisions of national law, inform the persons referred to in paragraph 1, which submitted observations to the authority, of its decision to accede to or refuse the request for action and shall provide the reasons for it.

5. Member States may decide not to apply paragraphs 1 and 4 to cases of imminent threat of damage.

Article 13
Review procedures

1. The persons referred to in Article 12(1) shall have access to a court or other independent and impartial public body competent to review the procedural and substantive legality of the decisions, acts or failure to act of the competent authority under this Directive.

2. This Directive shall be without prejudice to any provisions of national law which regulate access to justice and those which require that administrative review procedures be exhausted prior to recourse to judicial proceedings.

Article 14
Financial security

1. Member States shall take measures to encourage the development of financial security instruments and markets by the appropriate economic and financial operators, including financial mechanisms in case of insolvency, with the aim of enabling operators to use financial guarantees to cover their responsibilities under this Directive.

2. The Commission, before 30 April 2010 shall present a report on the effectiveness of the Directive in terms of actual remediation of environmental damages, on the availability at reasonable costs and on conditions of insurance and other types of financial security for the activities covered by Annex III. The report shall also consider in relation to financial security the following aspects: a gradual approach, a ceiling for the financial guarantee and the exclusion of low-risk activities. In the light of that report, and of an extended impact assessment, including a cost-benefit analysis,

the Commission shall, if appropriate, submit proposals for a system of harmonised mandatory financial security.

Article 15
Cooperation between Member States

1. Where environmental damage affects or is likely to affect several Member States, those Member States shall cooperate, including through the appropriate exchange of information, with a view to ensuring that preventive action and, where necessary, remedial action is taken in respect of any such environmental damage.

2. Where environmental damage has occurred, the Member State in whose territory the damage originates shall provide sufficient information to the potentially affected Member States.

3. Where a Member State identifies damage within its borders which has not been caused within them it may report the issue to the Commission and any other Member State concerned; it may make recommendations for the adoption of preventive or remedial measures and it may seek, in accordance with this Directive, to recover the costs it has incurred in relation to the adoption of preventive or remedial measures.

Article 16
Relationship with national law

1. This Directive shall not prevent Member States from maintaining or adopting more stringent provisions in relation to the prevention and remedying of environmental damage, including the identification of additional activities to be subject to the prevention and remediation requirements of this Directive and the identification of additional responsible parties.

2. This Directive shall not prevent Member States from adopting appropriate measures, such as the prohibition of double recovery of costs, in relation to situations where double recovery could occur as a result of concurrent action by a competent authority under this Directive and by a person whose property is affected by environmental damage.

Article 17
Temporal application

This Directive shall not apply to:

- damage caused by an emission, event or incident that took place before the date referred to in Article 19(1),
- damage caused by an emission, event or incident which takes place subsequent to the date referred to in Article 19(1) when it derives from a specific activity that took place and finished before the said date,
- damage, if more than 30 years have passed since the emission, event or incident, resulting in the damage, occurred.

Article 18
Reports and review

1. Member States shall report to the Commission on the experience gained in the application of this Directive by 30 April 2013 at the latest. The reports shall include the information and data set out in Annex VI.

2. On that basis, the Commission shall submit a report to the European Parliament and to the Council before 30 April 2014, which shall include any appropriate proposals for amendment.

3. The report, referred to in paragraph 2, shall include a review of:

(a) the application of:
  - Article 4(2) and (4) in relation to the exclusion of pollution covered by the international instruments listed in Annexes IV and V from the scope of this Directive, and
  - Article 4(3) in relation to the right of an operator to limit his liability in accordance with the international conventions referred to in Article 4(3).

    The Commission shall take into account experience gained within the relevant international fora, such as the IMO and Euratom and the relevant international agreements, as well as the extent to which these instruments have entered into force and/or have been implemented by Member States and/or have been modified, taking account of all relevant instances of environmental damage resulting from such activities and the remedial action taken and the differences between the liability levels in Member States, and considering the relationship between shipowners' liability and oil receivers' contributions, having due regard to any relevant study undertaken by the International Oil Pollution Compensation Funds.

(b) the application of this Directive to environmental damage caused by genetically modified organisms (GMOs), particularly in the light of experience gained within relevant international fora and Conventions, such as the Convention on Biological Diversity and the Cartagena Protocol on Biosafety, as well as the results of any incidents of environmental damage caused by GMOs;

(c) the application of this Directive in relation to protected species and natural habitats;

(d) the instruments that may be eligible for incorporation into Annexes III, IV and V.

Article 19
Implementation

1. Member States shall bring into force the laws, regulations and administrative provisions necessary to comply with this Directive by 30 April 2007. They shall forthwith inform the Commission thereof. When Member States adopt those measures, they shall contain a reference to this Directive or shall be accompanied by such a reference on the occasion of their official publication. The methods of making such reference shall be laid down by Member States.

2. Member States shall communicate to the Commission the text of the main provisions of national law which they adopt in the field covered by this Directive together with a table showing how the provisions of this Directive correspond to the national provisions adopted.

Article 20
Entry into force

This Directive shall enter into force on the day of its publication in the *Official Journal of the European Union.*

Article 21
Addressees

This Directive is addressed to the Member States.
Done at Strasbourg, 21 April 2004.

Annex I
Criteria referred to in Article 2(1)(A)

The significance of any damage that has adverse effects on reaching or maintaining the favourable conservation status of habitats or species has to be assessed by reference to the conservation status at the time of the damage, the services provided by the amenities they produce and their capacity for natural regeneration. Significant adverse changes to the baseline condition should be determined by means of measurable data such as:

- the number of individuals, their density or the area covered,
- the role of the particular individuals or of the damaged area in relation to the species or to the habitat conservation, the rarity of the species or habitat (assessed at local, regional and higher level including at Community level),
- the species' capacity for propagation (according to the dynamics specific to that species or to that population), its viability or the habitat's capacity for natural regeneration (according to the dynamics specific to its characteristic species or to their populations),
- the species' or habitat's capacity, after damage has occurred, to recover within a short time, without any intervention other than increased protection measures, to a condition which leads, solely by virtue of the dynamics of the species or habitat, to a condition deemed equivalent or superior to the baseline condition.

Damage with a proven effect on human health must be classified as significant damage.
The following does not have to be classified as significant damage:

- negative variations that are smaller than natural fluctuations regarded as normal for the species or habitat in question,

- negative variations due to natural causes or resulting from intervention relating to the normal management of sites, as defined in habitat records or target documents or as carried on previously by owners or operators,
- damage to species or habitats for which it is established that they will recover, within a short time and without intervention, either to the baseline condition or to a condition which leads, solely by virtue of the dynamics of the species or habitat, to a condition deemed equivalent or superior to the baseline condition.

Annex II
Remedying of environmental damage

This Annex sets out a common framework to be followed in order to choose the most appropriate measures to ensure the remedying of environmental damage.

1. Remediation of damage to water or protected species or natural habitats

Remedying of environmental damage, in relation to water or protected species or natural habitats, is achieved through the restoration of the environment to its baseline condition by way of primary, complementary and compensatory remediation, where:

(a) 'Primary' remediation is any remedial measure which returns the damaged natural resources and/or impaired services to, or towards, baseline condition;
(b) 'Complementary' remediation is any remedial measure taken in relation to natural resources and/or services to compensate for the fact that primary remediation does not result in fully restoring the damaged natural resources and/or services;
(c) 'Compensatory' remediation is any action taken to compensate for interim losses of natural resources and/or services that occur from the date of damage occurring until primary remediation has achieved its full effect;
(d) 'Interim losses' means losses which result from the fact that the damaged natural resources and/or services are not able to perform their ecological functions or provide services to other natural resources or to the public until the primary or complementary measures have taken effect. It does not consist of financial compensation to members of the public.

Where primary remediation does not result in the restoration of the environment to its baseline condition, then complementary remediation will be undertaken. In addition, compensatory remediation will be undertaken to compensate for the interim losses.

Remedying of environmental damage, in terms of damage to water or protected species or natural habitats, also implies that any significant risk of human health being adversely affected be removed.

1.1. *Remediation objectives*

Purpose of primary remediation

1.1.1. The purpose of primary remediation is to restore the damaged natural resources and/or services to, or towards, baseline condition.

Purpose of complementary remediation

1.1.2. Where the damaged natural resources and/or services do not return to their baseline condition, then complementary remediation will be undertaken. The purpose of complementary remediation is to provide a similar level of natural resources and/or services, including, as appropriate, at an alternative site, as would have been provided if the damaged site had been returned to its baseline condition. Where possible and appropriate the alternative site should be geographically linked to the damaged site, taking into account the interests of the affected population.

Purpose of compensatory remediation

1.1.3. Compensatory remediation shall be undertaken to compensate for the interim loss of natural resources and services pending recovery. This compensation consists of additional improvements to protected natural habitats and species or water at either the damaged site or at an alternative site. It does not consist of financial compensation to members of the public.

1.2. *Identification of remedial measures*

Identification of primary remedial measures

1.2.1. Options comprised of actions to directly restore the natural resources and services towards baseline condition on an accelerated time frame, or through natural recovery, shall be considered.

Identification of complementary and compensatory remedial measures

1.2.2. When determining the scale of complementary and compensatory remedial measures, the use of resource-to-resource or service-to-service equivalence approaches shall be considered first. Under these approaches, actions that provide natural resources and/or services of the same type, quality and quantity as those damaged shall be considered first. Where this is not possible, then alternative natural resources and/or services shall be provided. For example, a reduction in quality could be offset by an increase in the quantity of remedial measures.

1.2.3. If it is not possible to use the first choice resource-to-resource or service-to-service equivalence approaches, then alternative valuation techniques shall be used. The competent authority may prescribe the method, for example monetary valuation, to determine the extent of the necessary complementary and compensatory remedial measures. If valuation of the lost resources and/or services is practicable, but valuation of the replacement natural resources and/or services cannot be performed within a reasonable time-frame or at a reasonable cost, then the competent authority may choose remedial measures whose cost is equivalent to the estimated monetary value of the lost natural resources and/or services.

The complementary and compensatory remedial measures should be so designed that they provide for additional natural resources and/or services to reflect time preferences and the time profile of the remedial measures. For example, the longer the period of time before the baseline condition is reached, the greater the amount of compensatory remedial measures that will be undertaken (other things being equal).

1.3. *Choice of the remedial options*

1.3.1. The reasonable remedial options should be evaluated, using best available technologies, based on the following criteria:

- The effect of each option on public health and safety,
- The cost of implementing the option,
- The likelihood of success of each option,
- The extent to which each option will prevent future damage, and avoid collateral damage as a result of implementing the option,
- The extent to which each option benefits to each component of the natural resource and/or service,
- The extent to which each option takes account of relevant social, economic and cultural concerns and other relevant factors specific to the locality,
- The length of time it will take for the restoration of the environmental damage to be effective,
- The extent to which each option achieves the restoration of site of the environmental damage,
- The geographical linkage to the damaged site.

1.3.2. When evaluating the different identified remedial options, primary remedial measures that do not fully restore the damaged water or protected species or natural habitat to baseline or that restore it more slowly can be chosen. This decision can be taken only if the natural resources and/or services foregone at the primary site as a result of the decision are compensated for by increasing complementary or compensatory actions to provide a similar level of natural resources and/or services as were foregone. This will be the case, for example, when the equivalent natural resources and/or services could be provided elsewhere at a lower cost. These additional remedial measures shall be determined in accordance with the rules set out in section 1.2.2.

1.3.3. Notwithstanding the rules set out in section 1.3.2. and in accordance with Article 7(3), the competent authority is entitled to decide that no further remedial measures should be taken if:

(a) the remedial measures already taken secure that there is no longer any significant risk of adversely affecting human health, water or protected species and natural habitats, and
(b) the cost of the remedial measures that should be taken to reach baseline condition or similar level would be disproportionate to the environmental benefits to be obtained.

2. Remediation of land damage

The necessary measures shall be taken to ensure, as a minimum, that the relevant contaminants are removed, controlled, contained or diminished so that the contaminated land, taking account of its current use or approved future use at the time of the damage, no longer poses any significant risk of adversely affecting human health. The presence of such risks shall be assessed through risk-assessment procedures taking into account the characteristic and function of the soil, the type and concentration of the harmful substances, preparations, organisms or micro-organisms, their risk and the possibility of their dispersion. Use shall be ascertained on the basis of the land use regulations, or other relevant regulations, in force, if any, when the damage occurred. If the use of the land is changed, all necessary measures shall be taken to prevent any adverse effects on human health. If land use regulations, or other relevant regulations, are lacking, the nature of the relevant area where the damage occurred, taking into account its expected development, shall determine the use of the specific area. A natural recovery option, that is to say an option in which no direct human intervention in the recovery process would be taken, shall be considered.

Annex III
Activities referred to in Article 3(1)

1. The operation of installations subject to permit in pursuance of Council Directive 96/61/EC of 24 September 1996 concerning integrated pollution prevention and control.[1] That means all activities listed in Annex I of Directive 96/61/EC with the exception of installations or parts of installations used for research, development and testing of new products and processes.

2. Waste management operations, including the collection, transport, recovery and disposal of waste and hazardous waste, including the supervision of such operations and after-care of disposal sites, subject to permit or registration in pursuance of Council Directive 75/442/EEC of 15 July 1975 on waste[2] and Council Directive 91/689/EEC of 12 December 1991 on hazardous waste.[3]

Those operations include, *inter alia,* the operation of landfill sites under Council Directive 1999/31/EC of 26 April 1999 on the landfill of waste[4] and the operation of incineration plants under Directive 2000/76/EC of the European Parliament and of the Council of 4 December 2000 on the incineration of waste.[5]

For the purpose of this Directive, Member States may decide that those operations shall not include the spreading of sewage sludge from urban waste water treatment plants, treated to an approved standard, for agricultural purposes.

---

[1] OJ L 257, 10.10.1996, p. 26. Directive as last amended by Regulation (EC) No 1882/2003.
[2] OJ L 194, 25.7.1975, p. 39. Directive as last amended by Regulation (EC) No 1882/2003.
[3] OJ L 377, 31.12.1991, p. 20. Directive as amended by Directive 94/31/EC (OJ L 168, 2.7.1994, p. 28).
[4] OJ L 182, 16.7.1999, p. 1 Directive as amended by Regulation (EC) No 1882/2003.
[5] OJ L 332, 28.12.2000, p. 91.

3. All discharges into the inland surface water, which require prior authorisation in pursuance of Council Directive 76/464/EEC of 4 May 1976 on pollution caused by certain dangerous substances, discharged into the aquatic environment of the Community.[1]

4. All discharges of substances into groundwater which require prior authorisation in pursuance of Council Directive 80/68/EEC of 17 December 1979 on the protection of groundwater against pollution caused by certain dangerous substances.[2]

5. The discharge or injection of pollutants into surface water or groundwater which require a permit, authorisation or registration in pursuance of Directive 2000/60/EC.

6. Water abstraction and impoundment of water subject to prior authorisation in pursuance of Directive 2000/60/EC.

7. Manufacture, use, storage, processing, filling, release into the environment and onsite transport of

(a) dangerous substances as defined in Article 2(2) of Council Directive 67/548/EEC of 27 June 1967 on the approximation of the laws, regulations and administrative provisions of the Member States relating to the classification, packaging and labelling of dangerous substances;[3]

(b) dangerous preparations as defined in Article 2(2) of Directive 1999/45/EC of the European Parliament and of the Council of 31 May 1999 concerning the approximation of the laws, regulations and administrative provisions of the Member States relating to the classification, packaging and labelling of dangerous preparations;[4]

(c) plant protection products as defined in Article 2(1) of Council Directive 91/414/EEC of 15 July 1991 concerning the placing of plant protection products on the market;[5]

(d) biocidal products as defined in Article 2(1)(a) of Directive 98/8/EC of the European Parliament and of the Council of 16 February 1998 concerning the placing of biocidal products on the market.[6]

8. Transport by road, rail, inland waterways, sea or air of dangerous goods or polluting goods as defined either in Annex A to Council Directive 94/55/EC of 21 November 1994 on the approximation of the laws of the Member States with regard to the

---

[1] OJ L 129, 18.5.1976, p. 23. Directive as last amended by Directive 2000/60/EC.

[2] OJ L 20, 26.1.1980, p. 43. Directive as amended by Directive 91/692/EEC (OJ L 377, 31.12.1991, p. 48).

[3] OJ 196, 16.8.1967, p. 1. Directive as last amended by Regulation (EC) No 807/2003.

[4] OJ L 200, 30.7.1999, p. 1. Directive as last amended by Regulation (EC) No 1882/2003.

[5] OJ L 230, 19.8.1991, p. 1. Directive as last amended by Regulation (EC) No 806/2003 (OJ L 122, 16.5.2003, p. 1).

[6] OJ L 123, 24.4.1998, p. 1. Directive as amended by Regulation (EC) No 1882/2003.

transport of dangerous goods by road[1] or in the Annex to Council Directive 96/49/EC of 23 July 1996 on the approximation of the laws of the Member States with regard to the transport of dangerous goods by rail[2] or as defined in Council Directive 93/75/EEC of 13 September 1993 concerning minimum requirements for vessels bound for or leaving Community ports and carrying dangerous or polluting goods.[3]

9. The operation of installations subject to authorisation in pursuance of Council Directive 84/360/EEC of 28 June 1984 on the combating of air pollution from industrial plants[4] in relation to the release into air of any of the polluting substances covered by the aforementioned Directive.

10. Any contained use, including transport, involving genetically modified micro-organisms as defined by Council Directive 90/219/EEC of 23 April 1990 on the contained use of genetically modified micro-organisms.[5]

11. Any deliberate release into the environment, transport and placing on the market of genetically modified organisms as defined by Directive 2001/18/EC of the European Parliament and of the Council.[6]

12. Transboundary shipment of waste within, into or out of the European Union, requiring an authorisation or prohibited in the meaning of Council Regulation (EEC) No 259/93 of 1 February 1993 on the supervision and control of shipments of waste within, into and out of the European Community.[7]

Annex IV
International conventions referred to in Article 4(2)

(a) the International Convention of 27 November 1992 on Civil Liability for Oil Pollution Damage;
(b) the International Convention of 27 November 1992 on the Establishment of an International Fund for Compensation for Oil Pollution Damage;
(c) the International Convention of 23 March 2001 on Civil Liability for Bunker Oil Pollution Damage;
(d) the International Convention of 3 May 1996 on Liability and Compensation for Damage in Connection with the Carriage of Hazardous and Noxious Substances by Sea;

---

[1] OJ L 319, 12.12.1994, p. 7. Directive as last amended by Commission Directive 2003/28/EC (OJ L 90, 8.4.2003, p. 45).
[2] OJ L 235, 17.9.1996, p. 25. Directive as last amended by Commission Directive 2003/29/EC (OJ L 90, 8.4.2003, p. 47).
[3] OJ L 247, 5.10.1993, p. 19. Directive as last amended by Directive 2002/84/EC of the European Parliament and of the Council (OJ L 324, 29.11.2002, p. 53).
[4] OJ L 188, 16.7.1984, p. 20. Directive as amended by Directive 91/692/EEC (OJ L 377, 31.12.1991, p. 48).
[5] OJ L 117, 8.5.1990, p. 1. Directive as last amended by Regulation (EC) No 1882/2003.
[6] OJ L 106, 17.4.2001, p. 1. Directive as last amended by Regulation (EC) No 1830/2003 (OJ L 268, 18.10.2003, p. 24).
[7] OJ L 30, 6.2.1993, p. 1. Regulation as last amended by Commission Regulation (EC) No 2557/2001 (OJ L 349, 31.12.2001, p. 1).

(e) the Convention of 10 October 1989 on Civil Liability for Damage Caused during Carriage of Dangerous Goods by Road, Rail and Inland Navigation Vessels.

Annex V
International instruments referred to in Article 4(4)

(a) the Paris Convention of 29 July 1960 on Third Party Liability in the Field of Nuclear Energy and the Brussels Supplementary Convention of 31 January 1963;
(b) the Vienna Convention of 21 May 1963 on Civil Liability for Nuclear Damage;
(c) the Convention of 12 September 1997 on Supplementary Compensation for Nuclear Damage;
(d) the Joint Protocol of 21 September 1988 relating to the Application of the Vienna Convention and the Paris Convention;
(e) the Brussels Convention of 17 December 1971 relating to Civil Liability in the Field of Maritime Carriage of Nuclear Material.

Annex VI
Information and data referred to in Article 18(1)

The reports referred to in Article 18(1) shall include a list of instances of environmental damage and instances of liability under this Directive, with the following information and data for each instance:

1. Type of environmental damage, date of occurrence and/or discovery of the damage and date on which proceedings were initiated under this Directive.
2. Activity classification code of the liable legal person(s).[1]
3. Whether there has been resort to judicial review proceedings either by liable parties or qualified entities. (The type of claimants and the outcome of proceedings shall be specified.)
4. Outcome of the remediation process.
5. Date of closure of proceedings.

Member States may include in their reports any other information and data they deem useful to allow a proper assessment of the functioning of this Directive, for example:

1. Costs incurred with remediation and prevention measures, as defined in this Directive:
   – paid for directly by liable parties, when this information is available;
   – recovered ex post facto from liable parties;
   – unrecovered from liable parties. (Reasons for non-recovery should be specified.)

---

[1] The NACE code can be used (Council Regulation (EEC) No 3037/90 of 9 October 1990 on the statistical classification of economic activities in the European Community (OJ L 293, 24.10.1990, p. 1).

2. Results of the actions to promote and the implementation of the financial security instruments used in accordance with this Directive.
3. An assessment of the additional administrative costs incurred annually by the public administration in setting up and operating the administrative structures needed to implement and enforce this Directive.

Commission declaration on Article 14(2) – Environmental Liability Directive

The Commission takes note of Article 14(2). In accordance with this article, the Commission will present a report, six years after the entry into force of the Directive, covering, *inter alia*, the availability at reasonable costs and conditions of insurance and other types of financial security. The report will in particular take into account the development by the market forces of appropriate financial security products in relation to the aspects referred to. It will also consider a gradual approach according to the type of damage and the nature of the risks. In the light of the report, the Commission will, if appropriate, submit as soon as possible proposals. The Commission will carry out an impact assessment, extended to the economic, social and environmental aspects, in accordance with the relevant existing rules and in particular the inter-institutional agreement on Better Law-Making and its Communication on Impact Assessment [COM(2002) 276 final].

PART V

Protection of air quality

Council Directive 84/360/EEC of 28 June 1984 on the combating of air pollution from industrial plants (as amended)

Editorial note

Council Directive 84/360/EEC of 28 June 1984 requires Member States to combat air pollution from stationary industrial plants. The purpose of the Directive is to provide further measures and procedures for the prevention and reduction of air pollution from industrial plants, especially those listed in Annex I (Article 1). The Directive defines 'emission limit values' to be the concentration and/or mass of polluting substances in emissions from plants during a specified period which is not to be exceeded (Article 2(5)). Prior authorisation by competent authorities is required for the operation or substantial alteration of the plants listed in Annex I (Article 3). Such authorisation can only be issued where all appropriate preventive measures against air pollution have been taken, the use of the plant will not cause significant air pollution particularly from the emission of Annex II substances, the emission limit values will not be exceeded, and the applicable air quality limit values will be taken into account (Article 4). Member States may define particularly polluted areas for which more stringent emission limit values may be fixed, or areas to be specially protected for which more stringent air quality limit values and emission limit values may be fixed (Article 5).

The Directive provides that applications for authorisation must include a description of the plant and the necessary information for the decision to be made (Article 6). Subject to the provisions regarding commercial secrecy, Member States are required to exchange information among themselves and with the Commission regarding their experience and knowledge of measures for the prevention and reduction of air pollution, as well as information regarding technical processes and equipment (Article 7). The Directive allows for the Council to fix emission limit values based on the best available technology not entailing excessive costs and stipulates suitable measurement and assessment techniques and methods (Article 8). Member States must take the necessary steps to ensure that applications for authorisation and the decisions of the competent authorities are made available to the public (Article 9(1)) and, within the framework of bilateral relations, other Member States (Article 10).

For the purpose of monitoring compliance, emissions from plants must be determined in accordance with the obligations referred to in Article 4 (Article 11). Member
States should follow developments as regards the best available technology and the
environmental situation (Article 12) and implement policies and strategies for the
gradual adaptation of existing Annex I plants (Article 13). In order to protect public
health and the environment, Member States may adopt provisions stricter than those
provided for in the Directive (Article 14). The Directive does not apply to industrial
plants serving national defence purposes (Article 15). Member States are required
to report to the Commission at three-yearly intervals on the implementation of the
Directive (Article 15a). Member States must transpose the Directive into national law
by 30 June 1987 (Article 16).

Source: OJ L 188 16.07.1984 p. 20. Amended by: Council Directive 91/692/EEC of
23 December 1991 L 377 48 31.12.1991

Council Directive (84/360/EEC) of 28 June 1984 on the combating of air pollution from industrial plants (as amended)

The Council of the European Communities,
    Having regard to the Treaty establishing the European Economic Community, and
in particular Articles 100 and 235 thereof, Having regard to the proposal from the
Commission,[1]
    Having regard to the opinion of the European Parliament,[2]
    Having regard to the opinion of the Economic and Social Committee,[3]
    Whereas the 1973,[4] 1977[5] and 1983[6] action programmes of the European Commu-
nities on the environment stress the importance of the prevention and reduction of air
pollution; Whereas the 1973 and 1977 action programmes in particular provide not
only for the objective evaluation of the risks to human health and to the environment
from air pollution but also for the formulation of quality objectives and the setting
of quality standards, especially for a number of air pollutants regarded as the most
hazardous;
    Whereas the Council has already adopted several Directives under these pro-
grammes;
    Whereas, moreover, under Decision 81/462/EEC[7] the Community is a party to the
Convention on long-range transboundary air pollution;
    Whereas the 1983 action programme, the general guidelines of which have been
approved by the Council of the European Communities and by the representatives
of the Member States meeting within the Council, envisages that the Commission

[1] OJ No C 139, 27. 5. 1983, p. 5.   [2] OJ No C 342, 19. 12. 1983, p. 160.   [3] OJ No C 23, 30. 1. 1984, p. 27.
[4] OJ No C 112, 20. 12. 1973, p. 1.   [5] OJ No C 139, 13. 6. 1977, p. 1.   [6] OJ No C 46, 17. 2. 1983. p. 1.
[7] OJ No L 171, 27. 6. 1981, p. 11.

will continue its efforts to establish air quality standards and that where appropriate emission standards for certain types of source should be laid down;

Whereas all the Member States have laws, regulations and administrative provisions concerning the combating of air pollution from stationary industrial plants; whereas several Member States are in the process of amending the existing provisions;

Whereas the disparities between the provisions concerning the combating of air pollution from industrial installations currently in force, or in the process of amendment, in the different Member States are liable to create unequal conditions of competition and thus have a direct effect on the functioning of the common market; whereas, therefore, approximation of the law in this field is required, as provided for by Article 100 of the Treaty;

Whereas one of the essential tasks of the Community is to promote throughout the Community a harmonious development of economic activities and a continuous and balanced expansion, tasks which are inconceivable in the absence of a campaign to combat pollution and nuisances or of an improvement in the quality of life and in the protection of the environment;

Whereas the Community should and must help increase the effectiveness of action undertaken by the Member States to combat air pollution from stationary industrial plants;

Whereas in order to achieve this end certain principles aiming at the implementation of a series of measures and procedures designed to prevent and reduce air pollution from industrial plants within the Community should be introduced;

Whereas the Community's endeavours to introduce these principles can be only gradual, bearing in mind the complexity of the situations and the fundamental principles on which the various national policies are based;

Whereas initially a general framework should be introduced to permit the Member States to adapt, where necessary, their existing rules to the principles adopted at Community level; whereas the Member States should therefore introduce a system of prior authorization for the operation and substantial alteration of stationary industrial plants which can cause air pollution;

Whereas, moreover, the competent national authorities cannot grant such authorization unless a number of conditions have been fulfilled, including the requirements that all appropriate preventive measures are taken, and that the operation of the plant does not result in a significant level of air pollution;

Whereas it should be possible to apply special provisions in particularly polluted areas and in areas in need of special protection;

Whereas the rules applicable to the authorization procedures and to the determination of emissions must satisfy certain requirements;

Whereas in certain situations the competent authorities must explore the need to impose further requirements, which, however, must not result in excessive costs for the undertaking concerned;

Whereas the provisions taken pursuant to this Directive are to be applied gradually to existing plants, taking due account of technical factors and the economic effects;

Whereas provision must be made for cooperation between the Member States themselves and with the Commission to facilitate implementation of the measures designed to prevent and to reduce air pollution and to develop preventive technology,

Has Adopted this Directive:

Article 1

The purpose of this Directive is to provide for further measures and procedures designed to prevent or reduce air pollution from industrial plants within the Community, particularly those belonging to the categories set out in Annex I.

Article 2

For the purposes of this Directive:

1. 'Air pollution' means the introduction by man, directly or indirectly, of substances or energy into the air resulting in deleterious effects of such a nature as to endanger human health, harm living resources and ecosystems and material property and impair or interfere with amenities and other legitimate uses of the environment.
2. 'Plant' means any establishment or other stationary plant used for industrial or public utility purposes which is likely to cause air pollution.
3. 'Existing plant' means a plant in operation before 1 July 1987 or built or authorized before that date.
4. 'Air quality limit values' means the concentration of polluting substances in the air during a specified period which is not to be exceeded.
5. 'Emission limit values' means the concentration and/or mass of polluting substances in emissions from plants during a specified period which is not to be exceeded.

Article 3

1. Member States shall take the necessary measures to ensure that the operation of plants belonging to the categories listed in Annex I requires prior authorization by the competent authorities. The necessity to meet the requirements prescribed for such authorization must be taken into account at the plant's design stage.

2. Authorization is also required in the case of substantial alteration of all plants which belong to the categories listed in Annex I or which, as a result of the alteration, will fall within those categories.

3. Member States may require other categories of plants to be subject to authorization or, where national legislation so provides, prior notification.

Article 4

Without prejudice to the requirements laid down by national and Community provisions with a purpose other than that of this Directive, an authorization may be issued only when the competent authority is satisfied that:

1. all appropriate preventive measures against air pollution have been taken, including the application of the best available technology, provided that the application of such measures does not entail excessive costs;
2. the use of plant will not cause significant air pollution particularly from the emission of substances referred to in Annex 11;
3. none of the emission limit values applicable will be exceeded;
4. all the air quality limit values applicable will be taken into account.

Article 5

Member States may:

– define particularly polluted areas for which emission limit values more stringent than those referred to in Article 4 may be fixed,
– define areas to be specially protected for which air quality limit values and emission limit values more stringent than those referred to in Article 4 may be fixed,
– decide that, within the abovementioned areas, specified categories of plants set out in Annex 1 may not be built or operated unless special conditions are complied with.

Article 6

Applications for authorization shall include a description of the plant containing the necessary information for the purposes of the decision whether to grant authorization in accordance with Articles 3 and 4.

Article 7

Subject to the provisions regarding commercial secrecy, Member States shall exchange information among themselves and with the Commission regarding their experience and knowledge of measures for prevention and reduction of air pollution, as well as technical processes and equipment and air quality and emission limit values.

Article 8

1. The Council, acting unanimously on a proposal from the Commission, shall if necessary fix emission limit values based on the best available technology not entailing excessive costs, and taking into account the nature, quantities and harmfulness of the emissions concerned.

2. The Council, acting unanimously on a proposal from the Commission, shall stipulate suitable measurement and assessment techniques and methods.

Article 9

1. Member States shall take the necessary measures to ensure that applications for authorization and the decisions of the competent authorities are made available to the public concerned in accordance with procedures provided for in the national law.

2. Paragraph 1 shall apply without prejudice to specific national or Community provisions concerning the assessment of the environmental effects of public and private projects and subject to observance of the provisions regarding commercial secrecy.

Article 10

The Member States shall make available to the other Member States concerned, as a basis for all necessary consultation within the framework of their bilateral relations, the same information as is furnished to their own nationals.

Article 11

Member States shall take the necessary measures to ensure that emissions from plants are determined for the purpose of monitoring compliance with the obligations referred to in Article 4. The determination methods must be approved by the competent authorities.

Article 12

The Member States shall follow developments as regards the best available technology and the environmental situation. in the light of this examination they shall, if necessary, impose appropriate conditions on plants authorized in accordance with this Directive, on the basis both of those developments and of the desirability of avoiding excessive costs for the plants in question, having regard in particular to the economic situation of the plants belonging to the category concerned.

Article 13

In the light of an examination of developments as regards the best available technology and the environmental situation, the Member States shall implement policies and strategies, including appropriate measures, for the gradual adaptation of existing plants belonging to the categories given in Annex I to the best available technology, taking into account in particular:

- the plant's technical characteristics,
- its rate of utilization and length of its remaining life,
- the nature and volume of polluting emissions from it,
- the desirability of not entailing excessive costs for the plant concerned, having regard in particular to the economic situation of undertakings belonging to the category in question.

Article 14

Member States may, in order to protect public health and the environment, adopt provisions stricter than those provided for in this Directive.

Article 15

The Directive does not apply to industrial plants serving national defence purposes.

Article 15a

At intervals of three years the Member States shall send information to the Commission on the implementation of this Directive, in the form of a sectoral report which shall also cover other pertinent Community Directives. This report shall be drawn up on the basis of a questionnaire or outline drafted by the Commission in accordance with the procedure laid down in Article 6 of Directive 91/692/EEC.[1] The questionnaire or outline shall be sent to the Member States six months before the start of the period covered by the report. The report shall be sent to the Commission within nine months of the end of the three-year period covered by it.

The first report shall cover the period from 1994 to 1996 inclusive.

The Commission shall publish a Community report on the implementation of the Directive within nine months of receiving the reports from the Member States.

Article 16

1. Member States shall bring into force the laws, regulations and administrative provisions necessary to comply with this Directive not later than 30 June 1987.

2. Member States shall communicate to the Commission the texts of the provisions of national law which they adopt in the field governed by this Directive.

Article 17

This Directive is addressed to the Member States.

Annex I
Categories of plants[2] (covered by Article 3)

1. *Energy industry*

1.1. Coke ovens
1.2. Oil refineries (excluding undertakings manufacturing only lubricants from crude oil)
1.3. Coal gasification and liquefaction plants

---

[1] OJ No L 377, 31. 12. 1991, p. 48.
[2] The thresholds given in this Annex refer to production capacities.

1.4. Thermal power stations (excluding nuclear power stations) and other combustion installations with a nominal heat output of more than 50 MW.

2. *Production and processing of metals*

2.1. Roasting and sintering plants with a capacity of more than 1 000 tonnes of metal ore per year
2.2. Integrated plants for the production of pig iron and crude steel
2.3. Ferrous metal foundries having melting installations with a total capacity of over 5 tonnes
2.4. Plants for the production and melting of non-ferrous metals having installations with a total capacity of over 1 tonne for heavy metals or 0,5 tonne for light metals.

3. *Manufacture of non-metallic mineral products*

3.1. Plants for the production of cement and rotary kiln lime production
3.2. Plants for the production and processing of asbestos and manufacture of asbestos-based products
3.3. Plants for the manufacture of glass fibre or mineral fibre
3.4. Plants for the production of glass (ordinary and special) with a capacity of more than 5 000 tonnes per year
3.5. Plants for the manufacture of coarse ceramics notably refractory bricks, stoneware pipes, facing and floor bricks and roof tiles.

4. *Chemical industry*

4.1. Chemical plants for the production of olefins, derivatives of olefins, monomers and polymers
4.2. Chemical plants for the manufacture of other organic intermediate products
4.3. Plants for the manufacture of basic inorganic chemicals.

5. *Waste disposal*

5.1. Plants for the disposal of toxic and dangerous waste by incineration
5.2. Plants for the treatment by incineration of other solid and liquid waste.

6. *Other industries*

Plants for the manufacture of paper pulp by chemical methods with a production capacity of 25 000 tonnes or more per year.

Annex II
List of most important polluting substances (within the meaning of Article 4(2))

1. Sulphur dioxide and other sulphur compounds
2. Oxides of nitrogen and other nitrogen compounds
3. Carbon monoxide

4. Organic compounds, in particular hydrocarbons (except methane)
5. Heavy metals and their compounds
6. Dust; asbestos (suspended particulates and fibres), glass and mineral fibres
7. Chlorine and its compounds
8. Fluorine and its compounds

Council Directive 93/76/EEC of 13 September 1993 to limit carbon dioxide emissions by improving energy efficiency (SAVE)

Editorial note

Council Directive 93/76/EEC of 13 September 1993 aims to limit carbon dioxide emissions by improving energy efficiency, primarily by drawing up and implementing programmes such as laws, regulations, economic and administrative instruments, information, education and voluntary agreements (Article 1). Member States are to draw up and implement programmes on the energy certification of buildings in order to provide information for prospective users concerning a building's energy efficiency (Article 2), and also on the billing of heating, air-conditioning and hot water costs calculated on the basis of actual consumption, enabling the cost of these services to be apportioned among the users of all or part of a building (Article 3). Member States are to draw up and implement programmes to permit third-party financing for energy efficiency investments in the public sector (Article 4); so that new buildings receive effective thermal insulation, taking into account climatic conditions and the intended use of the building (Article 5); on the regular inspection of heating installations of an effective rated output of more than 15 kW with the aim of improving operating conditions regarding energy consumption and limiting carbon dioxide emissions (Article 6); and with the aim of promoting the regular completion of energy audits of industrial undertakings with high energy consumption (Article 7). The scope of each of these programmes should be determined on the basis of potential improvements in energy efficiency, cost effectiveness, technical feasibility and environmental impact (Article 8).

Member States are required to report to the Commission every two years on the result of the measures taken to implement the programmes provided for in the Directive (Article 9). Member States must transpose the Directive into national law by 31 December 1994 (Article 10).

Source: OJ L 237 22.09.1993 p. 28

Council Directive 93/76/EEC of 13 September 1993 to limit carbon dioxide emissions by improving energy efficiency (SAVE)

The Council of the European Communities,

Having regard to the Treaty establishing the European Economic Community, and in particular Articles 130s and 235 thereof,

Having regard to the proposal from the Commission,[1]

Having regard to the opinion of the European Parliament,[2]

Having regard to the opinion of the Economic and Social Committee,[3]

Whereas, by its resolution of 16 September 1986,[4] the Council set new Community energy policy objectives for 1995 and convergence of the policies of the Member States;

Whereas the Council of Environment and Energy Ministers agreed at their meeting on 29 October 1990 that the Community and the Member States, assuming that other leading countries undertook similar commitments, and acknowledging the targets identified by a number of Member States for stabilizing or reducing emissions by different dates, were willing to take actions aimed at reaching stabilization of the total carbon dioxide emissions by the year 2000 at the 1990 level in the Community as a whole; whereas it was also agreed that Member States which start from relatively low levels of energy consumption and therefore low emissions measured on a per capita or other appropriate basis are entitled to have carbon dioxide targets and/or strategies corresponding to their economic and social development, while improving the energy efficiency of their economic activities;

Whereas by Decision 91/565/EEC the Council adopted the SAVE programme aimed at promoting energy efficiency in the Community;[5]

Whereas Article 130r of the Treaty stipulates that the objective of action by the Community relating to the environment shall be to ensure a prudent and rational utilization of natural resources; whereas these natural resources include oil products, natural gas and solid fuels, which are essential sources of energy but also the leading sources of carbon dioxide emissions;

Whereas, since the Treaty has not provided elsewhere the powers required to legislate on energy-related aspects of the programmes laid down in this Directive, recourse should be had also to Article 235 of the Treaty;

Whereas the residential and tertiary sectors account for nearly 40% of final energy consumption in the Community and are expanding, a trend which is bound to increase their energy consumption and hence also their carbon dioxide emissions;

Whereas this Directive aims to preserve the quality of the environment and to ensure a prudent and rational utilization of natural resources, which are matters of non-exclusive Community competence;

Whereas a collective effort by all Member States, implying measures at Community level, is necessary in order to limit carbon dioxide emissions and to promote the rational use of energy;

[1] OJ No C 179, 16. 7. 1992, p. 8.   [2] OJ No C 176, 28. 6. 1993.   [3] OJ No C 19, 25. 1. 1993, p. 134.
[4] OJ No C 241, 25. 9. 1986, p. 1.   [5] OJ No L 307, 8. 11. 1991, p. 34.

Whereas the measures are to be determined according to the principle of subsidiarity by Member States on the basis of potential improvements in energy efficiency, cost effectiveness, technical feasibility and environmental impact;

Whereas, by providing objective information on the energy characteristics of buildings, energy certification will help to improve transparency of the property market and to encourage investment in energy savings;

Whereas the billing, to occupiers of buildings, of heating, air-conditioning and hot water costs calculated, in an appropriate proportion, on the basis of actual consumption will contribute towards energy saving in the residential sector; whereas it is desirable that occupants of such buildings should be enabled to regulate their own consumption of heat, cold and hot water; whereas the recommendations and resolutions adopted by the Council on the billing of heating and hot water costs[1] have been applied in only two Member States; whereas a significant proportion of heating, air-conditioning and hot water costs are still being billed on the basis of factors other than energy consumption;

Whereas new methods of financial support are needed to promote investments in energy saving in the public sector; whereas, with that in mind, the Member States should permit and make full use of the possibilities offered by third-party financing;

Whereas buildings will have an impact on long-term energy consumption; whereas new buildings should therefore be fitted with efficient thermal insulation tailored to the local climate; whereas this applies also to public authority buildings where the public authorities should set an example in taking environmental and energy considerations into account;

Whereas regular maintenance of boilers contributes to maintaining their correct adjustment in accordance with the product specification and in that way to an optimal performance from an environmental and energy point of view;

Whereas industry is generally willing to make more efficient use of energy to meet its own economic objectives; whereas energy audits in particular in undertakings with high energy consumption should be promoted to bring about significant improvements in energy efficiency in this sector;

Whereas improving energy efficiency in all regions of the Community will strengthen economic and social cohesion in the Community, as provided for in Article 130a of the Treaty,

Has adopted this Directive:

Article 1

The purpose of this Directive is the attainment by Member States of the objective of limiting carbon dioxide emissions by improving energy efficiency, notably by means

---

[1] Recommendation 76/493/EEC (OJ No L 140, 28. 5. 1976, p. 12). Recommendation 77/712/EEC (OJ No L 295, 18. 11. 1977, p. 1). Resolution of 9. 6. 1980 (OJ No C 149, 18. 6. 1980, p. 3). Resolution of 15. 1. 1985 (OJ No C 20, 22. 1. 1985, p. 1).

of drawing up and implementing programmes in the following fields:

- energy certification of buildings,
- the billing of heating, air-conditioning and hot water costs on the basis of actual consumption,
- third-party financing for energy efficiency investments in the public sector,
- thermal insulation of new buildings,
- regular inspection of boilers,
- energy audits of undertakings with high energy consumption.

Programmes can include laws, regulations, economic and administrative instruments, information, education and voluntary agreements whose impact can be objectively assessed.

Article 2

Member States shall draw up and implement programmes on the energy certification of buildings. Energy certification of buildings, which shall consist of a description of their energy characteristics, must provide information for prospective users concerning a building's energy efficiency.

Whereas appropriate, certification may also include options for the improvement of these energy characteristics.

Article 3

Member States shall draw up and implement programmes on the billing of heating, air-conditioning and hot water costs calculated, in an appropriate proportion, on the basis of actual consumption. These programmes shall enable the cost of these services to be apportioned among the users of all or part of a building on the basis of the specific quantities of heat, of cold and of hot water consumed by each occupier. This shall apply to buildings or parts of buildings supplied by a collective heating, air-conditioning or domestic hot water installation. Occupants of such buildings should be enabled to regulate their own consumption of heat, cold or hot water.

Article 4

Member States shall draw up and implement programmes to permit third-party financing for energy efficiency investments in the public sector.

For the purposes of this Directive, 'third-party financing' means the overall provision of auditing, installation, operation, maintenance and financing services for an energy efficiency investment, with recovery of the cost of these services being contingent, either wholly or in part, on the level of energy savings.

Article 5

Member States shall draw up and implement programmes so that new buildings receive effective thermal insulation, taking a long-term view, on the basis of standards laid down by the Member States, taking account of climatic conditions or climatic areas and the intended use of the building.

Article 6

Member States shall draw up and implement programmes on the regular inspection of heating installations of an effective rated output of more than 15 Kw with the aim of improving operating conditions from the point of view of energy consumption and of limiting carbon dioxide emissions.

Article 7

Member States shall draw up and implement programmes with the aim of promoting the regular completion of energy audits of industrial undertakings with high energy consumption to improve their energy efficiency and limit emissions of carbon dioxide, and may make similar provisions for other undertakings with high energy consumption.

Article 8

Member States shall determine the scope of the programmes referred to in Articles 1 to 7 on the basis of potential improvements in energy efficiency, cost-effectiveness, technical feasibility and environmental impact.

Article 9

Member States shall report to the Commission every two years on the results of the measures taken to implement the programmes provided for in this Directive. In so doing, they shall inform the Commission of the choices they have made in their package of measures. In addition, they shall, on request, provide the Commission with justification for the content of the programmes, taking Article 8 into account.

In considering Member States' reports, the Commission shall be assisted by the advisory committee referred to in Decision 91/565/EEC following the procedure referred to in Article 6 of that Decision.

Article 10

1. Member States shall bring into force the laws, regulations and/or other measures as mentioned in Article 1 as necessary to comply with this Directive as soon as possible and not later than 31 December 1994. Member States are required to make all the necessary provisions to enable them to fulfil the objectives of this Directive.

When Member States adopt laws or regulations for this purpose, such laws or regulations shall contain a reference to this Directive or shall be accompanied by such reference on the occasion of their official publication. The methods of making such a reference shall be laid down by the Member States. This shall apply by analogy where the programmes are transposed in another form.

2. Member States shall communicate to the Commission the provisions of national law and/or other measures as mentioned in Article 1 which they adopt in the field covered by this Directive.

Article 11

This Directive is addressed to the Member States.

Done at Brussels, 13 September 1993.

Council Directive 96/62/EC of 27 September 1996 on ambient air quality assessment and management (as amended)

Editorial note

Council Directive 96/62/EC recognises the need to assess ambient air quality needs against limit values and/or alert thresholds. The general aim of the Directive is to define the basic principles of a common strategy regarding ambient air quality, including defining and establishing objectives, assessing quality and obtaining information (Article 1). 'Ambient air' is defined as outdoor air in the troposphere, excluding work places (Article 2(1)). Member States are required to designate competent authorities in order to ensure the implementation of the Directive (Article 3). The Directive establishes a timetable for the Commission to propose the setting of limit values and alert thresholds for pollutants listed in Annex I (Article 4(1)), which must take into account the most recent scientific-research data and the most recent advances in metrology (Article 4(2)). When the limit values and alert thresholds are set, criteria and techniques must be established for the measurement and use of other techniques for assessing ambient air quality (Article 4(3)). Member States which do not have representative measurements of the levels of pollutants for all zones and agglomerations must undertake a series of representative measurements, surveys or assessments in order to have data available in time for implementation of legislation (Article 5). Once limit values and alert thresholds have been set, ambient air quality must be assessed throughout the territory of the Member States (Article 6).

Member States must take the necessary measures to ensure compliance with the limit values, and draw up action plans indicating the measures to be taken in the short term where there is a risk of the limit values and/or alert thresholds being exceeded (Article 7). The Directive requires Member States to draw up a list of zones and agglomerations where the levels of one or more pollutants are either higher than the limit value plus the margin of tolerance, or are between the limit value and the limit value plus the margin of tolerance (Article 8). Member States must also draw up a list of zones and agglomerations where the levels of pollutants are below the limit values (Article 9). Where the alert thresholds are exceeded, Member States must ensure that the necessary steps are taken to inform the public and provide information to the Commission (Article 10). Member States must notify the Commission of the competent authorities appointed in accordance with Article 3, and, in respect of zones where levels are higher than the limit value, inform the Commission of certain specified information (Article 11). The Commission will be assisted by a committee (Article 12) and Member States must transpose the Directive into national law no later than eighteen months after it comes into force with regard to the provisions relating to the timetable established in Articles 1 to 4 and 12 of the Directive (Article 13).

Source: OJ L 296 21.11.1996 p. 55. Amended by: Regulation (EC) No 1882/2003 of the European Parliament and of the Council of 29 September 2003 L 284 1 31.10.2003

Council Directive 96/62/EC of 27 September 1996 on ambient air quality assessment and management (as amended)

The Council of the European Union,

Having regard to the Treaty establishing the European Community, and in particular Article 130s(1) thereof,

Having regard to the proposal from the Commission,[1]

Having regard to the opinion of the Economic and Social Committee,[2]

Acting in accordance with the procedure laid down in Article 189c of the Treaty,[3]

Whereas the fifth action programme of 1992 on the environment, the general approach of which was endorsed by the Council and the Representatives of the Governments of the Member States, meeting within the Council, in their resolution 93/C 138/01 of 1 February 1993,[4] envisages amendments to existing legislation on air pollutants; whereas the said programme recommends the establishment of long-term air quality objectives;

Whereas, in order to protect the environment as a whole and human health, concentrations of harmful air pollutants should be avoided, prevented or reduced and limit values and/or alert thresholds set for ambient air pollution levels;

Whereas, in order to take into account the specific formation mechanisms of ozone, these limit values and alert thresholds may need to be complemented or replaced by target values;

Whereas the numerical values for limit values, alert thresholds and, as regards ozone, target values and/or limit values and alert thresholds are to be based on the findings of work carried out by international scientific groups active in the field;

Whereas the Commission is to carry out studies to analyse the effects of the combined action of various pollutants or sources of pollution and the effect of climate on the activity of the various pollutants examined in the context of this Directive;

---

[1] OJ No C 216, 6. 8. 1994, p. 4.   [2] OJ No C 110, 2. 5. 1995, p. 5.

[3] Opinion of the European Parliament of 16 June 1995 (OJ No C 166, 3. 7. 1995, p. 173), Council common position of 30 November 1995 (OJ No C 59, 28. 2. 1996, p. 24) and decision of the European Parliament of 22 May 1996 (OJ No C 166, 10. 6. 1996, p. 63).

[4] OJ No C 138, 17. 5. 1993, p. 1.

Whereas the ambient air quality needs to be assessed against limit values and/or alert thresholds, and, as regards ozone, target values and/or limit values taking into account the size of populations and ecosystems exposed to air pollution, as well as the environment;

Whereas, in order for assessment of ambient air quality based on measurements made in Member States to be comparable, the location and number of sampling points and reference methods of measurement used should be specified when values are set for alert thresholds, limit values and target values;

Whereas, to allow for the use of other techniques of estimation of ambient air quality besides direct measurement, it is necessary to define the criteria for use and required accuracy of these techniques;

Whereas the general measures set up under this Directive have to be supplemented by others specific to individual substances covered;

Whereas these specific measures need to be adopted as soon as possible in order to fulfil the overall objectives of this Directive;

Whereas preliminary representative data on the levels of pollutants should be collected;

Whereas, in order to protect the environment as a whole and human health, it is necessary that Member States take action when limit values are exceeded in order to comply with these values within the time fixed;

Whereas the measures taken by Member States must take into account the requirements set by regulations concerning the operation of industrial installations in conformity with Community legislation in the field of integrated prevention and reduction of pollution when this legislation applies;

Whereas, because these actions require time to be implemented and become effective, temporary margins of tolerance of the limit value may need to be set;

Whereas areas may exist in Member States where pollution levels are greater than the limit value but within the allowed margin of tolerance; whereas the limit value must be complied with within the time specified;

Whereas Member States must consult with one another if the level of a pollutant exceeds, or is likely to exceed, the limit value plus the margin of tolerance or, as the case may be, the alert threshold, following significant pollution originating in another Member State;

Whereas the setting of alert thresholds at which precautionary measures should be taken will make it possible to limit the impact of pollution episodes on human health;

Whereas, in zones and agglomerations where the levels of pollutants are below the limit values, Member States must endeavour to preserve the best ambient air quality compatible with sustainable development; Whereas, in order to facilitate the handling and comparison of data received, such data should be provided to the Commission in standardized form;

Whereas the implementation of a wide and comprehensive policy of ambient air quality assessment and management needs to be based on strong technical and scientific grounds and permanent exchange of views between the Member States;

Whereas there is a need to avoid increasing unnecessarily the amount of information to be transmitted by Member States; whereas the information gathered by the Commission pursuant to the implementation of this Directive is useful to the European Environment Agency (EEA) and may therefore be transmitted to it by the Commission;

Whereas the adaptation of criteria and techniques used for the assessment of the ambient air quality to scientific and technical progress and the arrangements needed to exchange the information to be provided pursuant to this Directive may be desirable; whereas, in order to facilitate implementation of the work necessary to this end, a procedure should be set up to establish close cooperation between the Member States and the Commission within a committee;

Whereas, in order to promote the reciprocal exchange of information between Member States and the EEA, the Commission, with the assistance of the EEA, is to publish a report on ambient air quality in the Community every three years;

Whereas the substances already covered by Council Directive 80/779/ EEC of 15 July 1980 on air quality limit values and guide values for sulphur dioxide and suspended particulates,[1] Council Directive 82/ 884/EEC of 3 December 1982 on a limit value for lead in the air,[2] Council Directive 85/203/EEC of 7 March 1985 on air quality standards for nitrogen dioxide[3] and Council Directive 92/72/EEC of 21 September 1992 on air pollution by ozone[4] should be dealt with first,

Has adopted this Directive:

Article 1
Objectives

The general aim of this Directive is to define the basic principles of a common strategy to:

- define and establish objectives for ambient air quality in the Community designed to avoid, prevent or reduce harmful effects on human health and the environment as a whole,
- assess the ambient air quality in Member States on the basis of common methods and criteria,
- obtain adequate information on ambient air quality and ensure that it is made available to the public, *inter alia* by means of alert thresholds,
- maintain ambient air quality where it is good and improve it in other cases.

---

[1] OJ No L 229, 30. 8. 1980, p. 30. Directive as last amended by Directive 91/692/EEC (OJ No L 377, 31. 12. 1991, p. 48).
[2] OJ No L 378, 31. 12. 1982, p. 15. Directive as last amended by Directive 91/692/EEC.
[3] OJ No L 87, 27. 3. 1985, p. 1. Directive as last amended by Directive 91/692/EEC.
[4] OJ No L 297, 13. 10. 1992, p. 1.

Article 2
Definitions

For the purposes of this Directive:

1. 'ambient air' shall mean outdoor air in the troposphere, excluding work places;
2. 'pollutant' shall mean any substance introduced directly or indirectly by man into the ambient air and likely to have harmful effects on human health and/or the environment as a whole;
3. 'level' shall mean the concentration of a pollutant in ambient air or the deposition thereof on surfaces in a given time;
4. 'assessment' shall mean any method used to measure, calculate, predict or estimate the level of a pollutant in the ambient air;
5. 'limit value' shall mean a level fixed on the basis of scientific knowledge, with the aim of avoiding, preventing or reducing harmful effects on human health and/or the environment as a whole, to be attained within a given period and not to be exceeded once attained;
6. 'target value' shall mean a level fixed with the aim of avoiding more long-term harmful effects on human health and/or the environment as a whole, to be attained where possible over a given period;
7. 'alert threshold' shall mean a level beyond which there is a risk to human health from brief exposure and at which immediate steps shall be taken by the Member States as laid down in this Directive;
8. 'margin of tolerance' shall mean the percentage of the limit value by which this value may be exceeded subject to the conditions laid down in this Directive;
9. 'zone' shall mean part of their territory delimited by the Member States;
10. 'agglomeration' shall mean a zone with a population concentration in excess of 250 000 inhabitants or, where the population concentration is 250 000 inhabitants or less, a population density per km^2 which for the Member States justifies the need for ambient air quality to be assessed and managed.

Article 3
Implementation and responsibilities

For the implementation of this Directive, the Member States shall designate at the appropriate levels the competent authorities and bodies responsible for:

– implementation of this Directive,
– assessment of ambient air quality,
– approval of the measuring devices (methods, equipment, networks, laboratories),
– ensuring accuracy of measurement by measuring devices and checking the maintenance of such accuracy by those devices, in particular by internal quality controls carried out in accordance, *inter alia*, with the requirements of European quality assurance standards,

– analysis of assessment methods,
– coordination on their territory of Community-wide quality assurance programmes organized by the Commission. When they supply it to the Commission, the Member States shall make the information referred to in the first subparagraph available to the public.

Article 4
Setting of the limit values and alert thresholds for ambient air

1. For those pollutants listed in Annex I, the Commission shall submit to the Council proposals for the setting of limit values and, as appropriate, alert thresholds according to the following timetable:

– no later than 31 December 1996 for pollutants 1 to 5,
– in accordance with Article 8 of Directive 92/72/EEC for ozone,
– no later than 31 December 1997 for pollutants 7 and 8,
– as soon as possible, and no later than 31 December 1999, for pollutants 9 to 13.

In fixing the limit values and, as appropriate, alert thresholds, account shall be taken, by way of example, of the factors laid down in Annex II.

Regarding ozone, these proposals will take account of the specific formation mechanisms of this pollutant and, to this end, provision may be made for target values and/or limit values.

If a target value fixed for ozone is exceeded, Member States shall inform the Commission of the measures taken in order to attain that value. On the basis of this information the Commission shall evaluate whether additional measures are necessary at Community level and, should the need arise, shall submit proposals to the Council.

For other pollutants, the Commission shall submit to the Council proposals for fixing limit values and, as appropriate, alert thresholds if, on the basis of scientific progress and taking into account the criteria laid down in Annex III, it appears necessary to avoid, prevent or reduce the harmful effects of such pollutants on human health and/or the environment as a whole within the Community.

2. The Commission shall be responsible, taking account of the most recent scientific-research data in the epidemiological and environmental fields concerned and of the most recent advances in metrology, for re-examining the elements on which the limit values and alert thresholds referred to in paragraph 1 are based.

3. When limit values and alert thresholds are set, criteria and techniques shall be established for:

(a) the measurement to be used in implementing the legislation referred to in paragraph 1:
   – the location of the sampling points,
   – the minimum number of sampling points,
   – the reference measurement and sampling techniques;

(b) the use of other techniques for assessing ambient air quality, particularly modelling:
  – spatial resolution for modelling and objective assessment methods,
  – reference modelling techniques.

These criteria and techniques shall be established in respect of each pollutant according to the size of agglomerations or to the levels of pollutants in the zones examined.

4. To take into account the actual levels of a given pollutant when setting limit values and the time needed to implement measures for improving the ambient air quality, the Council may also set a temporary margin of tolerance for the limit value.

This margin shall be reduced according to procedures to be defined for each pollutant in order to attain the level of the limit value at the latest at the end of a period to be determined for each pollutant when that value is set.

5. In accordance with the Treaty, the Council shall adopt the legislation provided for in paragraph 1 and the provisions laid down in paragraphs 3 and 4.

6. When a Member State takes more stringent measures than those laid down in the provisions referred to in paragraph 5, it shall inform the Commission thereof.

7. When a Member State intends to set limit values or alert thresholds for pollutants not referred to in Annex I and not covered by Community provisions concerning ambient air quality in the Community, it shall inform the Commission thereof in sufficient time. The Commission shall be required to supply, in sufficient time, an answer to the question of the need to act at Community level following the criteria laid down in Annex III.

Article 5
Preliminary assessment of ambient air quality

Member States which do not have representative measurements of the levels of pollutants for all zones and agglomerations shall undertake series of representative measurements, surveys or assessments in order to have the data available in time for implementation of the legislation referred to in Article 4(1).

Article 6
Assessment of ambient air quality

1. Once limit values and alert thresholds have been set, ambient air quality shall be assessed throughout the territory of the Member States, in accordance with this Article.

2. In accordance with the criteria referred to in Article 4(3), and in respect of the relevant pollutants under Article 4(3), measurement is mandatory in the following zones:

– agglomerations as defined in Article 2(10),
– zones in which levels are between the limit values and the levels provided for in paragraph 3, and
– other zones where levels exceed the limit values.

The measures provided for may be supplemented by modelling techniques to provide an adequate level of information on ambient air quality.

3. A combination of measurements and modelling techniques may be used to assess ambient air quality where the levels over a representative period are below a level lower than the limit value, to be determined according to the provisions referred to in Article 4(5).

4. Where the levels are below a level to be determined according to the provisions referred to in Article 4(5), the sole use of modelling or objective estimation techniques for assessing levels shall be possible. This provision shall not apply to agglomerations in the case of pollutants for which alert thresholds have been fixed according to the provisions referred to in Article 4(5).

5. Where pollutants have to be measured, the measurements shall be taken at fixed sites either continuously or by random sampling; the number of measurements shall be sufficiently large to enable the levels observed to be determined.

Article 7
Improvement of ambient air quality – General requirements

1. Member States shall take the necessary measures to ensure compliance with the limit values.

2. Measures taken in order to achieve the aims of this Directive shall:

(a) take into account an integrated approach to the protection of air, water and soil;
(b) not contravene Community legislation on the protection of safety and health of workers at work;
(c) have no significant negative effects on the environment in the other Member States.

3. Member States shall draw up action plans indicating the measures to be taken in the short term where there is a risk of the limit values and/or alert thresholds being exceeded, in order to reduce that risk and to limit the duration of such an occurrence. Such plans may, depending on the individual case, provide for measures to control and, where necessary, suspend activities, including motor-vehicle traffic, which contribute to the limit values being exceeded.

Article 8
Measures applicable in zones where levels are higher than the limit value

1. Member States shall draw up a list of zones and agglomerations in which the levels of one or more pollutants are higher than the limit value plus the margin of tolerance.

Where no margin of tolerance has been fixed for a specific pollutant, zones and agglomerations in which the level of that pollutant exceeds the limit value shall be treated in the same way as the zones and agglomerations referred to in the first subparagraph, and paragraphs 3, 4 and 5 shall apply to them.

2. Member States shall draw up a list of zones and agglomerations in which the levels of one or more pollutants are between the limit value and the limit value plus the margin of tolerance.

3. In the zones and agglomerations referred to in paragraph 1, Member States shall take measures to ensure that a plan or programme is prepared or implemented for attaining the limit value within the specific time limit. The said plan or programme, which must be made available to the public, shall incorporate at least the information listed in Annex IV.

4. In the zones and agglomerations referred to in paragraph 1, where the level of more than one pollutant is higher than the limit values, Member States shall provide an integrated plan covering all the pollutants concerned.

5. The Commission shall regularly check the implementation of the plans or programmes submitted under paragraph 3 by examining their progress and the trends in air pollution.

6. When the level of a pollutant exceeds, or is likely to exceed, the limit value plus the margin of tolerance or, as the case may be, the alert threshold following significant pollution originating in another Member State, the Member States concerned shall consult with one another with a view to finding a solution. The Commission may be present at such consultations.

Article 9
Requirements in zones where the levels are lower than the limit value

Member States shall draw up a list of zones and agglomerations in which the levels of pollutants are below the limit values.

Member States shall maintain the levels of pollutants in these zones and agglomerations below the limit values and shall endeavour to preserve the best ambient air quality, compatible with sustainable development.

Article 10
Measures applicable in the event of the alert thresholds being exceeded

When the alert thresholds are exceeded, Member States shall undertake to ensure that the necessary steps are taken to inform the public (e.g. by means of radio, television and the press). Member States shall also forward to the Commission on a provisional basis information concerning the levels recorded and the duration of the episode(s) of pollution no later than three months following their occurrence. A list of minimum details to be supplied to the public shall be drawn up together with the alert thresholds.

Article 11
Transmission of information and reports

After adoption by the Council of the first proposal referred to in the first indent of Article 4(1):

1. Member States shall notify to the Commission the competent authorities, laboratories and bodies referred to in Article 3 and

(a) in the zones referred to in Article 8(1) shall:
   (i) inform the Commission of the occurrence of levels exceeding the limit value plus the margin of tolerance, of the dates or periods when such levels were observed and the values recorded in the nine-month period after the end of each year. When no margin of tolerance has been fixed for a given pollutant, the zones and agglomerations where the level of such pollutant exceeds the limit value shall be treated in the same way as the zones and agglomerations referred to in the first subparagraph;
   (ii) inform the Commission of the reasons for each recorded instance, in the nine-month period after the end of each year;
   (iii) send to the Commission the plans or programmes referred to in Article 8(3) no later than two years after the end of the year during which the levels were observed;
   (iv) inform the Commission every three years of the progress of the plan or programme;
(b) shall forward to the Commission annually, and no later than nine months after the end of each year, the list of zones and agglomerations referred to in Article 8(1) and (2) and in Article 9;
(c) shall forward to the Commission every three years within the framework of the sectoral report referred to in Article 4 of Council Directive 91/692/EEC of 23 December 1991 standardizing and rationalizing reports on the implementation of certain Directives relating to the environment,[1] and no later than nine months after the end of each three-year period, information reviewing the levels observed or assessed, as appropriate, in the zones and agglomerations referred to in Article 8 and Article 9;
(d) shall inform the Commission of the methods used for the preliminary assessment of air quality provided for in Article 5.

2. The Commission shall publish:

(a) annually, a list of the zones and agglomerations referred to in Article 8(1);
(b) every three years, a report on the ambient air quality in the Community. This report shall show in summary form the information received through a mechanism for the exchange of information between the Commission and the Member States.

3. The Commission will call upon as necessary the expertise available in the European Environment Agency in drafting the report referred to in paragraph 2(b).

---

[1] OJ No L 377, 31. 12. 1991, p. 48.

Article 12
Committee and its functions

1. The amendments necessary to adapt the criteria and techniques referred to in Article 4(2) to scientific and technical progress, and the detailed arrangements for forwarding the information to be provided under Article 11, and other tasks specified in the provisions referred to in Article 4(3), shall be adopted in accordance with the procedure laid down in paragraph 2 of this Article. Such adaptation must not have the effect of modifying the limit values or the alert thresholds either directly or indirectly.

2. The Commission shall be assisted by a committee.

3. Where reference is made to this Article, Articles 5 and 7 of Decision 1999/468/EC[1] shall apply, having regard to the provisions of Article 8 thereof.

The period laid down in Article 5(6) of Decision 1999/468/EC shall be set at three months.

4. The Committee shall adopt its rules of procedure.

Article 13

1. Member States shall bring into force the laws, regulations and administrative provisions necessary to comply with this Directive not later than 18 months after it comes into force with regard to the provisions relating to Articles 1 to 4 and 12 and Annexes I, II, III and IV, and at the latest on the date on which the provisions referred to in Article 4(5) apply, with regard to the provisions relating to the other Articles.

When Member States adopt these measures, they shall contain a reference to this Directive or shall be accompanied by such a reference at the time of their official publication. The procedures for such a reference shall be adopted by Member States.

2. Member States shall communicate to the Commission the text of the main provisions of national law which they adopt in the field covered by this Directive.

Article 14

This Directive shall enter into force on the day of its publication in the *Official Journal of the European Communities*.

Article 15

This Directive is addressed to the Member States.

---

[1] Council Decision 1999/468/EC of 28 June 1999 laying down the procedures for the exercise of implementing powers conferred on the Commission (OJ L 184, 17. 7. 1999, p. 23).

Annex I
List of atmospheric pollutants to be taken into consideration in the assessment and management of ambient air quality

I. *Pollutants to be studied at an initial stage, including pollutants governed by existing ambient air quality directives*

1. Sulphur dioxide
2. Nitrogen dioxide
3. Fine particulate matter such as soot (including mw 10)
4. Suspended particulate matter
5. Lead
6. Ozone

II. *Other air pollutants*

7. Benzene
8. Carbon monoxide
9. Poly-aromatic hydrocarbons
10. Cadmium
11. Arsenic
12. Nickel
13. Mercury

Annex II
Factors to be taken into account when setting limit values and alert thresholds

When setting the limit value and, as appropriate, alert threshold, the following factors may, by way of example, be taken into account:

— degree of exposure of sectors of the population, and in particular sensitive sub-groups,
— climatic conditions,
— sensitivity of flora and fauna and their habitats,
— historic heritage exposed to pollutants,
— economic and technical feasibility,
— long-range transmission of pollutants, of which secondary pollutants, including ozone.

Annex III
Guidelines for selecting air pollutants for consideration

1. Possibility, severity and frequency of effects; with regard to human health and the environment as a whole, the irreversible effects must be of special concern.

2. Ubiquity and high concentration of the pollutant in the atmosphere.
3. Environmental transformations or metabolic alterations, as these alterations may lead to the production of chemicals with greater toxicity.
4. Persistence in the environment, particularly if the pollutant is not biodegradable and can accumulate in humans, the environment or food chains.
5. Impact of the pollutant:
   – size of exposed population, living resources or ecosystems,
   – existence of particularly sensitive targets in the zone concerned.
6. Risk-assessment methods may also be used.

The pertinent danger criteria established under Directive 67/548/EEC[1] and its successive adaptations must be taken into account in the selection of the pollutants.

Annex IV
Information to be included in the local, regional or national Programmes for improvement in the ambient air quality

Information to be provided under Article 8(3)

1. *Localization of excess pollution*

– region
– city (map)
– measuring station (map, geographical coordinates).

2. *General information*

– type of zone (city, industrial or rural area)
– estimate of the polluted area (km^2) and of the population exposed to the pollution
– useful climatic data
– relevant data on topography
– sufficient information on the type of targets requiring protection in the zone.

3. *Responsible authorities*
   Names and addresses of persons responsible for the development and implementation of improvement plans.

4. *Nature and assessment of pollution*

– concentrations observed over previous years (before the implementation of the improvement measures)
– concentrations measured since the beginning of the project
– techniques used for the assessment.

---

[1] OJ No 196, 16. 8. 1967, p. 1/670. Directive as last amended by Commission Directive 91/632/EEC (OJ No L 338, 10. 12. 1991, p. 23)

5. *Origin of pollution*

– list of the main emission sources responsible for pollution (map)
– total quantity of emissions from these sources (tonnes/year)
– information on pollution imported from other regions.

6. *Analysis of the situation*

– details of those factors responsible for the excess (transport, including cross-border transport, formation)
– details of possible measures for improvement of air quality.

7. *Details of those measures or projects for improvement which existed prior to the entry into force of this Directive i.e.*

– local, regional, national, international measures
– observed effects of these measures.

8. *Details of those measures or projects adopted with a view to reducing pollution following the entry into force of this Directive*

– listing and description of all the measures set out in the project
– timetable for implementation
– estimate of the improvement of air quality planned and of the expected time required to attain these objectives.

9. *Details of the measures or projects planned or being researched for the long term.*
10. *List of the publications, documents, work, etc., used to supplement information requested in this Annex.*

Regulation (EC) No 2037/2000 of the European Parliament and of the Council of 29 June 2000 on substances that deplete the ozone layer (as amended)

Editorial note

Regulation (EC) No 2037/2000 on substances that deplete the ozone layer updates earlier Community legislation regarding ozone depleting substances and implements recent amendments to the Montreal Protocol. This Regulation applies to the production, importation, exportation, placing on the market, use, recovery, recycling and reclamation, and destruction of certain substances that deplete the ozone layer (Article 1). The Regulation prohibits the production (Article 3(1)) as well as the placing on the market and use (Article 4(1)) of chlorofluorocarbons, other fully halogenated chlorofluorocarbons, halons, carbon tetrachloride, 1,1,1-trichloroethane, hydrobromofluorocarbons and bromochloromethane. It identifies 'controlled substances' as those being the most dangerous in respect of depleting the ozone layer and defines each individually (Article 2 and Annex I). It prohibits the use of hydrochlorofluorocarbons, except in a number of specified situations (Article 5).

The importation into the European Community of controlled substances requires a licence (Article 6) and is subject to quantitative limits (Article 7). However, the importation of controlled substances (Article 8) or products containing controlled substances (Article 9) from a State not party to the Montreal Protocol is prohibited. The Council will adopt specific rules on the importation of products produced using controlled substances from a State not party to the Montreal Protocol (Article 10). The Regulation prohibits the export of certain controlled substances (Article 11), whilst other controlled substances, or products containing controlled substances, are subject to export authorisation (Article 12). In exceptional circumstances, the Commission has the right to authorise trade in controlled substances, including products which contain controlled substances or are produced by controlled substances, with States not party to the Montreal Protocol (Article 13). Trade with territories not covered by the Protocol is subject to the same arrangements as those set out for States not party to the Montreal Protocol (Article 14). The Commission must immediately notify the Member States of any measures adopted regarding the import or export of controlled substances (Article 15). The Regulation provides for the recovery and destruction of used controlled substances, including recycling and reclamation (Article 16(1)).

Member States are obliged to promote the recovery, recycling, reclamation and destruction of controlled substances (Article 16(5)) and must report annually on the systems established and facilities available in respect of this obligation (Article 16(6)). The Regulations require all practicable precautionary measures to be taken to prevent and minimise leakages of controlled and other specified substances (Article 17).

The Commission is assisted in its work by a Committee (Article 18), and requires each producer, importer and exporter of controlled substances to report annually (Article 19). The Commission may obtain information from the governments and competent authorities of Member States and require competent authorities to undertake investigations (Article 20). Member States shall determine the necessary penalties applicable to breaches of the Regulation (Article 21). The production, release for free circulation in the European Community, import, placing on the market, and use of new substances which are listed in Annex II is prohibited (Article 22(1)). The Commission can make proposals to include new substances in Annex II (Article 22(2)).

Source: OJ L 244 29.09.2000 p. 1. Amended by: Regulation (EC) No 2038/2000 of the European Parliament and of the Council of 28 September 2000 (L 244 25 29.09.2000); Regulation (EC) No 2039/2000 of the European Parliament and of the Council of 28 September 2000 (L 244 26 29.09.2000); Commission Decision 2003/160/EC of 7 March 2003 (L 65 29 08.03.2003); Regulation (EC) No 1804/2003 of the European Parliament and of the Council of 22 September 2003 (L 265 1 16.10.2003); Commission Decision 2004/232/EC of 3 March 2004 (L 71 28 10.03.2004)

Regulation (EC) No 2037/2000 of the European Parliament and of the Council of 29 June 2000 on substances that deplete the ozone layer (as amended)

The European Parliament and the Council of the European Union,

Having regard to the Treaty establishing the European Community, and in particular Article 175(1) thereof,

Having regard to the proposal from the Commission,[1]

Having regard to the opinion of the Economic and Social Committee,[2]

After consulting the Committee of the Regions,

Acting in accordance with the procedure laid down in Article 251 of the Treaty,[3] in the light of the joint text approved on 5 May 2000 by the Conciliation Committee,

---

[1] OJ C 286, 15.9.1998, p. 6 and OJ C 83, 25.3.1999, p. 4.   [2] OJ C 40, 15.2.1999, p. 34.

[3] Opinion of the European Parliament of 17 December 1998 (OJ C 98, 9.4.1999, p. 266), confirmed on 16 September 1999, Council Common Position of 23 February 1999 (OJ C 123, 4.5.1999, p. 28) and Decision of the European Parliament of 15 December 1999 (not yet published in the Official Journal). Decision of the European Parliament of 13 June 2000 and Decision of the Council of 16 June 2000.

Whereas:

(1) It is established that continued emissions of ozone-depleting substances at current levels continue to cause significant damage to the ozone layer. Ozone depletion in the southern hemisphere reached unprecedented levels in 1998. In three out of four recent springs severe ozone depletion has occurred in the Arctic region.

Increased UV-B radiation resulting from ozone depletion poses a significant threat to health and environment. Further efficient measures need therefore to be taken in order to protect human health and the environment against adverse effects resulting from such emissions.

(2) In view of its responsibilities for the environment and trade, the Community, pursuant to Decision 88/540/EEC,[1] has become a Party to the Vienna Convention for the Protection of the Ozone Layer and the Montreal Protocol on Substances that Deplete the Ozone Layer, as amended by the Parties to the Protocol at their second meeting in London and at their fourth meeting in Copenhagen.

(3) Additional measures for the protection of the ozone layer were adopted by the Parties to the Montreal Protocol at their seventh meeting in Vienna in December 1995 and at their ninth meeting in Montreal in September 1997, in which the Community participated.

(4) It is necessary for action to be taken at Community level to carry out the Community's obligations under the Vienna Convention and the latest amendments and adjustments to the Montreal Protocol, in particular to phase out the production and the placing on the market of methyl bromide within the Community and to provide for a system for the licensing not only of imports but also of exports of ozone-depleting substances.

(5) In view of the earlier than anticipated availability of technologies for replacing ozone-depleting substances, it is appropriate in certain cases to provide for control measures which are stricter than those provided for in Council Regulation (EC) No 3093/94 of 15 December 1994 on substances that deplete the ozone layer[2] and stricter than those of the Montreal Protocol.

(6) Regulation (EC) No 3093/94 must be modified substantially. It is in the interest of legal clarity and transparency to revise that Regulation completely.

(7) Under Regulation (EC) No 3093/94 the production of chlorofluorocarbons, other fully halogenated chlorofluorocarbons, halons, carbon tetrachloride, 1,1,1-trichloroethane and hydrobromofluorocarbons has been phased out. The production of those controlled substances is thus prohibited, subject to possible derogation for essential uses and to meet the basic domestic needs of Parties pursuant to Article 5 of the Montreal Protocol. It is now also appropriate

[1] OJ L 297, 31.10.1988, p. 8.   [2] OJ L 333, 22.12.1994, p. 1.

progressively to prohibit the placing on the market and use of those substances and of products and equipment containing those substances.

(8) Even after the phase-out of controlled substances the Commission may under certain conditions grant exemptions for essential uses.

(9) The growing availability of alternatives to methyl bromide should be reflected in more substantial reductions in its production and consumption compared to the Montreal Protocol. The production and consumption of methyl bromide should cease completely subject to possible derogations for critical uses determined at Community level following the criteria established under the Montreal Protocol. Also the use of methyl bromide for quarantine and preshipment applications should be controlled. Such use should not exceed current levels and ultimately be reduced in the light of technical development and developments under the Montreal Protocol.

(10) Regulation (EC) No 3093/94 provides for controls on the production of all other ozone-depleting substances but not for controls on the production of hydrochlorofluorocarbons. It is appropriate to introduce such provision to ensure that hydrochlorofluorocarbons do not continue to be used where nonozone-depleting alternatives exist. Measures for the control of the production of hydrochlorofluorocarbons should be taken by all Parties to the Montreal Protocol. A freeze on production of hydrochlorofluorocarbons would reflect that need and the Community's determination to take a leading role in this respect.

The quantities produced should be adapted to the reductions envisaged for the placing on the Community market of hydrochlorofluorocarbons and to the declining demand worldwide as a consequence of reductions in the consumption of hydrochlorofluorocarbons required by the Protocol.

(11) The Montreal Protocol, in Article 2F(7), requires the Parties to endeavour to ensure that the use of hydrochlorofluorocarbons is limited to those applications where other more environmentally suitable alternative substances or technologies are not available.

In view of the availability of alternative and substitute technologies, the placing on the market and use of hydrochlorofluorocarbons and products containing hydrochlorofluorocarbons can be further limited. Decision VI/13 of the Meeting of the Parties to the Montreal Protocol provides that the evaluation of alternatives to hydrochlorofluorocarbons should take into account such factors as ozone-depleting potential, energy efficiency, potential flammability, toxicity and global warming and the potential impacts on the effective use and phase-out of chlorofluorocarbons and halons. Hydrochlorofluorocarbon controls under the Montreal Protocol should be considerably tightened to protect the ozone layer and to reflect the availability of alternatives.

(12) Quotas for the release for free circulation in the Community of controlled substances should be allocated only for limited uses of controlled substances.

Controlled substances and products containing controlled substances from States not party to the Montreal Protocol should not be imported.

(13) The licensing system for controlled substances should be extended to include the authorisation of exports of controlled substances, in order to monitor trade in ozone-depleting substances and to allow for exchange of information between Parties.

(14) Provision should be made for the recovery of used controlled substances, and to prevent leakages of controlled substances.

(15) The Montreal Protocol requires reporting on trade in ozone-depleting substances. Annual reporting should therefore be required from producers, importers and exporters of controlled substances.

(16) The measures necessary for the implementation of this Regulation should be adopted in accordance with Council Decision 1999/468/EC of 28 June 1999 laying down the procedures for the exercise of implementing powers conferred on the Commission.[1]

(17) Decision X/8 of the 10th meeting of the Parties to the Montreal Protocol encourages Parties to take measures actively, as appropriate, to discourage the production and marketing of new ozone-depleting substances and in particular of bromochloromethane. To this end a mechanism should be established to provide for new substances to be addressed by this Regulation.The production, importation, placing on the market and use of bromochloromethane should be prohibited.

(18) The switch to new technologies or alternative products, required because the production and use of controlled substances are to be phased out, could lead to problems for small and medium-sized enterprises (SMEs) in particular. The Member States should therefore consider providing appropriate forms of assistance specifically to enable SMEs to make the necessary changes,

Have adopted this Regulation:

Chapter I
Introductory provisions

Article 1
Scope

This Regulation shall apply to the production, importation, exportation, placing on the market, use, recovery, recycling and reclamation and destruction of chlorofluorocarbons, other fully halogenated chlorofluorocarbons, halons, carbon tetrachloride, 1,1,1-trichloroethane, methyl bromide, hydrobromofluorocarbons,

---

[1] OJ L 184, 17.7.1999, p. 23.

hydrochlorofluorocarbons and bromochloromethane, to the reporting of information on these substances and to the importation, exportation, placing on the market and use of products and equipment containing those substances.

This Regulation shall also apply to the production, importation, placing on the market and use of substances in Annex II.

Article 2
Definitions

For the purposes of this Regulation:

- 'Protocol' means the 1987 Montreal Protocol on Substances that Deplete the Ozone Layer, as last amended and adjusted,
- 'Party' means any party to the Protocol,
- 'State not party to the Protocol', with respect to a particular controlled substance, includes any State or regional economic integration organisation that has not agreed to be bound by the provisions of the Protocol applicable to that substance,
- 'controlled substances' means chlorofluorocarbons, other fully halogenated chlorofluorocarbons, halons, carbon tetrachloride, 1,1,1-trichloroethane, methyl bromide, hydrobromofluorocarbons, hydrochlorofluorocarbons and bromochloromethane, whether alone or in a mixture, and whether they are virgin, recovered, recycled or reclaimed. This definition shall not cover any controlled substance which is in a manufactured product other than a container used for the transportation or storage of that substance, or insignificant quantities of any controlled substance, originating from inadvertent or coincidental production during a manufacturing process, from unreacted feedstock, or from use as a processing agent which is present in chemical substances as trace impurities, or that is emitted during product manufacture or handling,
- 'chlorofluorocarbons' (CFCs) means the controlled substances listed in Group I of Annex I, including their isomers,
- 'other fully halogenated chlorofluorocarbons' means the controlled substances listed in Group II of Annex I, including their isomers,
- 'halons' means the controlled substances listed in Group III of Annex I, including their isomers,
- 'carbon tetrachloride' means the controlled substance specified in Group IV of Annex I,
- '1,1,1-trichloroethane' means the controlled substance specified in Group V of Annex I,
- 'methyl bromide' means the controlled substance specified in Group VI of Annex I,
- 'hydrobromofluorocarbons' means the controlled substances listed in Group VII of Annex I, including their isomers,
- 'bromochloromethane' means the controlled substance indicated in Group IX of Annex I,

- 'hydrochlorofluorocarbons' (HCFCs) means the controlled substances listed in Group VIII of Annex I, including their isomers,
- 'new substances' means substances listed in Annex II. This definition shall cover substances whether alone or in a mixture, and whether they are virgin, recovered, recycled or reclaimed. This definition shall not cover any substance which is in a manufactured product other than a container used for transportation or storage of that substance, or insignificant quantities of any new substance, originating from inadvertent or coincidental production during a manufacturing process or from unreacted feedstock,
- 'feedstock' means any controlled substance or new substance that undergoes chemical transformation in a process in which it is entirely converted from its original composition and whose emissions are insignificant,
- 'processing agent' means controlled substances used as chemical processing agents in those applications listed in Annex VI, in installations existing at 1 September 1997, and where emissions are insignificant. The Commission shall, in the light of those criteria and in accordance with the procedure referred to in Article 18(2), establish a list of undertakings in which the use of controlled substances as processing agents shall be permitted, laying down maximum emission levels for each of the undertakings concerned.

  It may, in accordance with the procedure referred to in Article 18(2), amend Annex VI as well as the list of undertakings referred to above in the light of new information or technical developments, including the review provided for in Decision X/14 of the Meeting of the Parties to the Protocol,
- 'producer' means any natural or legal person manufacturing controlled substances within the Community,
- 'production' means the amount of controlled substances produced, less the amount destroyed by technologies approved by the Parties and less the amount entirely used as feedstock or as a processing agent in the manufacture of other chemicals. No amount recovered, recycled or reclaimed shall be considered as 'production',
- 'ozone-depleting potential' means the figure specified in the third column of Annex I representing the potential effect of each controlled substance on the ozone layer,
- 'calculated level' means a quantity determined by multiplying the quantity of each controlled substance by its ozone-depleting potential and by adding together, for each group of controlled substances in Annex I separately, the resulting figures,
- 'industrial rationalisation' means the transfer either between Parties or within a Member State of all or a portion of the calculated level of production of one producer to another, for the purpose of optimizing economic efficiency or responding to anticipated shortfalls in supply as a result of plant closures,
- 'placing on the market' means the supplying or making available to third persons, against payment or free of charge, of controlled substances or products containing controlled substances covered by this Regulation,

- 'use' means the utilisation of controlled substances in the production or maintenance, in particular refilling, of products or equipment or in other processes except for feedstock and processing agent uses,
- 'reversible air-conditioning/heat pump system' means a combination of interconnected refrigerant-containing parts constituting one closed refrigeration circuit, in which the refrigerant is circulated for the purpose of extracting and rejecting heat (i.e. cooling, heating), processes which are reversible in that the evaporators and condensers are designed to be interchangeable in their functions,
- 'inward processing' means a procedure provided for in Article 114(1)(a) of Council Regulation (EEC) No 2913/92 of 12 October 1992 establishing the Community Customs Code,[1]
- 'recovery' means the collection and the storage of controlled substances from, for example, machinery, equipment and containment vessels during servicing or before disposal,
- 'recycling' means the reuse of a recovered controlled substance following a basic cleaning process such as filtering and drying.

    For refrigerants, recycling normally involves recharge back into equipment as is often carried out on site,
- 'reclamation' means the reprocessing and upgrading of a recovered controlled substance through such processes as filtering, drying, distillation and chemical treatment in order to restore the substance to a specified standard of performance, which often involves processing off site at a central facility,
- 'undertaking' means any natural or legal person who produces, recycles for placing on the market or uses controlled substances for industrial or commercial purposes in the Community, who releases such imported substances for free circulation in the Community, or who exports such substances from the Community for industrial or commercial purposes.

Chapter II
Phase-out schedule

Article 3
Control of production of controlled substances

1. Subject to paragraphs 5 to 10, the production of the following shall be prohibited:

(a) chlorofluorocarbons;
(b) other fully halogenated chlorofluorocarbons;
(c) halons;
(d) carbon tetrachloride;

---

[1] OJ L 302, 19.10.1992, p. 1. Regulation as last amended by Regulation (EC) No 955/1999 (OJ L 119, 7.5.1999, p. 1).

(e) 1,1,1-trichloroethane;
(f) hydrobromofluorocarbons;
(g) bromochloromethane.

In the light of the proposals made by Member States, the Commission shall, in accordance with the procedure referred to in Article 18(2), apply the criteria set out in Decision IV/25 of the Parties in order to determine every year any essential uses for which the production and importation of controlled substances referred to in the first subparagraph may be permitted in the Community and those users who may take advantage of those essential uses. Such production and importation shall be allowed only if no adequate alternatives or recycled or reclaimed controlled substances referred to in the first subparagraph are available from any of the Parties.

2.

(i) Subject to paragraphs 5 to 10, each producer shall ensure that:
    (a) the calculated level of its production of methyl bromide in the period 1 January to 31 December 1999 and in each 12-month period thereafter does not exceed 75% of the calculated level of its production of methyl bromide in 1991;
    (b) the calculated level of its production of methyl bromide in the period 1 January to 31 December 2001 and in each 12-month period thereafter does not exceed 40% of the calculated level of its production of methyl bromide in 1991;
    (c) the calculated level of its production of methyl bromide in the period 1 January to 31 December 2003 and in each 12-month period thereafter does not exceed 25% of the calculated level of its production of methyl bromide in 1991;
    (d) it produces no methyl bromide after 31 December 2004.
    The calculated levels referred to in subparagraphs (a), (b), (c) and (d) shall not include the amount of methyl bromide produced for quarantine and preshipment applications.

(ii) In the light of the proposals made by Member States, the Commission shall, in accordance with the procedure referred to in Article 18(2), apply the criteria set out in Decision IX/6 of the Parties, together with any other relevant criteria agreed by the Parties, in order to determine every year any critical uses for which the production, importation and use of methyl bromide may be permitted in the Community after 31 December 2004, the quantities and uses to be permitted and those users who may take advantage of the critical exemption. Such production and importation shall be allowed only if no adequate alternatives or recycled or reclaimed methyl bromide is available from any of the Parties.

In an emergency, where unexpected outbreaks of particular pests or diseases so require, the Commission, at the request of the competent authority of a Member State, may authorise the temporary use of methyl bromide. Such authorisation shall apply for a period not exceeding 120 days and to a quantity not exceeding 20 tonnes.

3. Subject to paragraphs 8, 9 and 10, each producer shall ensure that:

(a) the calculated level of its production of hydrochlorofluorocarbons in the period 1 January 2000 to 31 December 2000 and in each 12-month period thereafter does not exceed the calculated level of its production of hydrochlorofluorocarbons in 1997;

(b) the calculated level of its production of hydrochlorofluorocarbons in the period 1 January 2008 to 31 December 2008 and in each 12-month period thereafter does not exceed 35% of the calculated level of its production of hydrochlorofluorocarbons in 1997;

(c) the calculated level of its production of hydrochlorofluorocarbons in the period 1 January 2014 to 31 December 2014 and in each 12-month period thereafter does not exceed 20% of the calculated level of its production of hydrochlorofluorocarbons in 1997;

(d) the calculated level of its production of hydrochlorofluorocarbons in the period 1 January 2020 to 31 December 2020 and in each 12-month period thereafter does not exceed 15% of the calculated level of its production of hydrochlorofluorocarbons in 1997;

(e) it produces no hydrochlorofluorocarbons after 31 December 2025.

Before 31 December 2002, the Commission shall review the level of production of hydrochlorofluorocarbons with a view to determining:

– whether a production cut ahead of the year 2008 should be proposed, and/or
– whether a change to the levels of production provided for under (b), (c) and (d) should be proposed.

This review will take into account the development of hydrochlorofluorocarbon consumption worldwide, the hydrochlorofluorocarbon exports from the Community and other OECD countries and the technical and economic availability of alternative substances or technologies as well as relevant international developments under the Protocol.

4. The Commission shall issue licences to those users identified in accordance with the second subparagraph of paragraph 1 and paragraph 2(ii) and shall notify them of the use for which they have authorisation and the substances and quantities thereof that they are authorised to use.

5. A producer may be authorised by the competent authority of the Member State in which that producer's relevant production is situated to produce the controlled substances referred to in paragraphs 1 and 2 for the purpose of meeting the requests licensed in accordance with paragraph 4. The competent authority of the Member State concerned shall notify the Commission in advance of its intention to issue any such authorisation.

6. The competent authority of the Member State in which a producer's relevant production is situated may authorise that producer to exceed the calculated levels of

production laid down in paragraphs 1 and 2 in order to satisfy the basic domestic needs of Parties pursuant to Article 5 of the Protocol, provided that the additional calculated levels of production of the Member State concerned do not exceed those permitted for that purpose by Articles 2A to 2E and 2H of the Protocol for the periods in question. The competent authority of the Member State concerned shall notify the Commission in advance of its intention to issue any such authorisation.

7. To the extent permitted by the Protocol, the competent authority of the Member State in which a producer's relevant production is situated may authorise that producer to exceed the calculated levels of production laid down in paragraphs 1 and 2 in order to satisfy any essential, or critical, uses of Parties at their request. The competent authority of the Member State concerned shall notify the Commission in advance of its intention to issue any such authorisation.

8. To the extent permitted by the Protocol, the competent authority of the Member State in which a producer's relevant production is situated may authorise that producer to exceed the calculated levels of production laid down in paragraphs 1 to 7 for the purpose of industrial rationalisation within the Member State concerned, provided that the calculated levels of production of that Member State do not exceed the sum of the calculated levels of production of its domestic producers as laid down in paragraphs 1 to 7 for the periods in question. The competent authority of the Member State concerned shall notify the Commission in advance of its intention to issue any such authorisation.

9. To the extent permitted by the Protocol, the Commission may, in agreement with the competent authority of the Member State in which a producer's relevant production is situated, authorise that producer to exceed the calculated levels of production laid down in paragraphs 1 to 8 for the purpose of industrial rationalisation between Member States, provided that the combined calculated levels of production of the Member States concerned do not exceed the sum of the calculated levels of production of their domestic producers as laid down in paragraphs 1 to 8 for the periods in question. The agreement of the competent authority of the Member State in which it is intended to reduce production shall also be required.

10. To the extent permitted by the Protocol, the Commission may, in agreement with both the competent authority of the Member State in which a producer's relevant production is situated and the government of the third Party concerned, authorise a producer to combine the calculated levels of production laid down in paragraphs 1 to 9 with the calculated levels of production allowed to a producer in a third Party under the Protocol and that producer's national legislation for the purpose of industrial rationalisation with a third Party, provided that the combined calculated levels of production by the two producers do not exceed the sum of the calculated levels of production allowed to the Community producer under paragraphs 1 to 9 and the calculated levels of production allowed to the third Party producer under the Protocol and any relevant national legislation.

Article 4

Control of the placing on the market and use of controlled substances

1. Subject to paragraphs 4 and 5, the placing on the market and the use of the following controlled substances shall be prohibited:

(a) chlorofluorocarbons;
(b) other fully halogenated chlorofluorocarbons;
(c) halons;
(d) carbon tetrachloride;
(e) 1,1,1-trichloroethane;
(f) hydrobromofluorocarbons; and
(g) bromochloromethane.

The Commission may, following a request by a competent authority of a Member State and in accordance with the procedure referred to in Article 18(2), authorise a temporary exemption to allow the use of chlorofluorocarbons until 31 December 2004 in delivery mechanisms for hermetically sealed devices designed for implantation in the human body for delivery of measured doses of medication, and until 31 December 2008, in existing military applications, where it is demonstrated that, for a particular use, technically and economically feasible alternative substances or technologies are not available or cannot be used.

2.

(i) Subject to paragraphs 4 and 5, each producer and importer shall ensure that:
  (a) the calculated level of methyl bromide which it places on the market or uses for its own account in the period 1 January 1999 to 31 December 1999 and in each 12-month period thereafter does not exceed 75% of the calculated level of methyl bromide which it placed on the market or used for its own account in 1991;
  (b) the calculated level of methyl bromide which it places on the market or uses for its own account in the period 1 January 2001 to 31 December 2001 and in each 12-month period thereafter does not exceed 40% of the calculated level of methyl bromide which it placed on the market or used for its own account in 1991;
  (c) the calculated level of methyl bromide which it places on the market or uses for its own account in the period 1 January 2003 to 31 December 2003 and in each 12-month period thereafter does not exceed 25% of the calculated level of methyl bromide which it placed on the market or used for its own account in 1991;
  (d) it does not place any methyl bromide on the market or use any for its own account after 31 December 2004.

To the extent permitted by the Protocol, the Commission shall, following a request by a competent authority of a Member State and in accordance with the procedure referred to in Article 18(2), adjust the calculated level of methyl bromide referred to in Article 3(2) (i) (c) and subparagraph(c) where it is demonstrated that this is necessary to meet the needs of that Member State, because technically and economically feasible alternatives or substitutes that are acceptable from the standpoint of environment and health are not available or cannot be used.

The Commission, in consultation with Member States, shall encourage the development, including research, and the use of alternatives to methyl bromide as soon as possible.

(ii) Subject to paragraph 4, the placing on the market and the use of methyl bromide by undertakings other than producers and importers shall be prohibited after 31 December 2005.

(iii) The calculated levels referred to in subparagraphs (i) (a), (b), (c) and (d) and (ii) shall not include the amount of methyl bromide produced or imported for quarantine and preshipment applications. For the period 1 January 2001 to 31 December 2001 and for each 12-month period thereafter, each producer and importer shall ensure that the calculated level of methyl bromide which it places on the market or uses for its own account for quarantine and preshipment applications shall not exceed the average of the calculated level of methyl bromide which it placed on the market or used for its own account for quarantine and preshipment in the years 1996, 1997 and 1998.

Each year Member States shall report to the Commission the quantities of methyl bromide authorised for quarantine and preshipment used in their territory, the purposes for which methyl bromide was used, and the progress in evaluating and using alternatives.

The Commission shall, in accordance with the procedure referred to in Article 18(2), take measures to reduce the calculated level of methyl bromide which producers and importers may place on the market or use for their own account for quarantine and preshipment in the light of technical and economic availability of alternative substances or technologies and of the relevant international developments under the Protocol.

(iv) The total quantitative limits for the placing on the market or use for their own account by producers and importers of methyl bromide are set out in Annex III.

3.

(i) Subject to paragraphs 4 and 5 and to Article 5(5):
    (a) the calculated level of hydrochlorofluorocarbons which producers and importers place on the market or use for their own account in the period

1 January 1999 to 31 December 1999 and in the 12-month period thereafter shall not exceed the sum of:
- – 2,6% of the calculated level of chlorofluorocarbons which producers and importers placed on the market or used for their own account in 1989, and
- – the calculated level of hydrochlorofluorocarbons which producers and importers placed on the market or used for their own account in 1989;

(b) the calculated level of hydrochlorofluorocarbons which producers and importers place on the market or use for their own account in the period 1 January 2001 to 31 December 2001 shall not exceed the sum of:
- – 2,0% of the calculated level of chlorofluorocarbons which producers and importers placed on the market or used for their own account in 1989, and
- – the calculated level of hydrochlorofluorocarbons which producers and importers placed on the market or used for their own account in 1989;

(c) the calculated level of hydrochlorofluorocarbons which producers and importers place on the market or use for their own account in the period 1 January 2002 to 31 December 2002 shall not exceed 85% of the level calculated pursuant to subparagraph (b);

(d) the calculated level of hydrochlorofluorocarbons which producers and importers place on the market or use for their own account in the period 1 January 2003 to 31 December 2003 shall not exceed 45% of the level calculated pursuant to subparagraph (b);

(e) the calculated level of hydrochlorofluorocarbons which producers and importers place on the market or use for their own account in the period 1 January 2004 to 31 December 2004 and in each 12-month period thereafter shall not exceed 30% of the level calculated pursuant to subparagraph (b);

(f) the calculated level of hydrochlorofluorocarbons which producers and importers place on the market or use for their own account in the period 1 January 2008 to 31 December 2008 and in each 12-month period thereafter shall not exceed 25% of the level calculated pursuant to subparagraph (b);

(g) producers and importers shall not place hydrochlorofluorocarbons on the market or use them for their own account after 31 December 2009;

(h) each producer and importer shall ensure that the calculated level of hydrochlorofluorocarbons which it places on the market or uses for its own account in the period 1 January 2001 to 31 December 2001 and in the 12-month period thereafter shall not exceed, as a percentage of the calculated levels set out in (a) to (c), the percentage share assigned to it in 1999.

(ii) Before 1 January 2001, the Commission shall, in accordance with the procedure referred to in Article 18(2), determine a mechanism for the allocation of quotas to each producer and importer of the calculated levels set out in (d) to (f), applicable for the period 1 January 2003 to 31 December 2003 and for each 12-month period thereafter.

(iii) In the case of producers, the quantities referred to in this paragraph shall apply to the amounts of virgin hydrochlorofluorocarbons which they place on the market or use for their own account within the Community and which were produced in the Community.

(iv) The total quantitative limits for the placing on the market or use for their own account by producers and importers of hydrochlorofluorocarbons are set out in Annex III.

4.

(i) (a) Paragraphs 1, 2 and 3 shall not apply to the placing on the market of controlled substances for destruction within the Community by technologies approved by the Parties;

(b) paragraphs 1, 2 and 3 shall not apply to the placing on the market and use of controlled substances if:
   – they are used for feedstock or as a processing agent; or
   – they are used to meet the licensed requests for essential uses of those users identified as laid down in Article 3(1) and to meet the licensed requests for critical uses of those users identified as laid down in Article 3(2) or to meet the requests for temporary emergency applications authorised in accordance with Article 3(2) (ii).

(ii) Paragraph 1 shall not apply to the placing on the market, by undertakings other than producers, of controlled substances for the maintenance or servicing of refrigeration and air-conditioning equipment until 31 December 1999.

(iii) Paragraph 1 shall not apply to the use of controlled substances for the maintenance or servicing of refrigeration and air-conditioning equipment or in finger-printing processes until 31 December 2000.

(iv) Paragraph 1(c) shall not apply to the placing on the market and use of halons that have been recovered, recycled or reclaimed in existing fire protection systems until 31 December 2002 or to the placing on the market and use of halons for critical uses as set out in Annex VII. Each year the competent authorities of the Member States shall notify to the Commission the quantities of halons used for critical uses, the measures taken to reduce their emissions and an estimate of such emissions, and the current activities to identify and use adequate alternatives.

Each year the Commission shall review the critical uses listed in Annex VII and, if necessary, adopt modifications and, where appropriate, time-frames for phase-out, taking into account the availability of both technically and economically feasible alternatives or technologies that are acceptable from the standpoint of environment and health, in accordance with the procedure referred to in Article 18(2).

(v) Except for uses listed in Annex VII, fire protection systems and fire extinguishers containing halons shall be decommissioned before 31 December 2003, and halons shall be recovered in accordance with Article 16.

5. Any producer or importer entitled to place controlled substances referred to in this Article on the market or use them for its own account may transfer that right in respect of all or any quantities of that group of substances fixed in accordance with this Article to any other producer or importer of that group of substances within the Community. Any such transfer shall be notified in advance to the Commission. The transfer of the right to place on the market or use shall not imply the further right to produce or to import.

6. The importation and placing on the market of products and equipment containing chlorofluorocarbons, other fully halogenated chlorofluorocarbons, halons, carbon tetrachloride, 1,1,1-trichloroethane, hydrobromofluorocarbons and bromochloromethane shall be prohibited, with the exception of products and equipment for which the use of the respective controlled substance has been authorised in accordance with the second subparagraph of Article 3(1) or is listed in Annex VII.

Products and equipment shown to be manufactured before the entry into force of this Regulation shall not be covered by this prohibition.

Article 5
Control of the use of hydrochlorofluorocarbons

1. Subject to the following conditions, the use of hydrochlorofluorocarbons shall be prohibited:

(a) in aerosols;
(b) as solvents:
    (i) in non-contained solvent uses including open-top cleaners and open-top dewatering systems without refrigerated areas, in adhesives and mould-release agents when not employed in closed equipment, for drain cleaning where hydrochlorofluorocarbons are not recovered;
    (ii) from 1 January 2002, in all solvent uses, with the exception of precision cleaning of electrical and other components in aerospace and aeronautics applications where the prohibition shall enter into force on 31 December 2008;
(c) as refrigerants:
    (i) in equipment produced after 31 December 1995 for the following uses:
        – in non-confined direct-evaporation systems,
        – in domestic refrigerators and freezers,
        – in motor vehicle, tractor and off-road vehicle or trailer air conditioning systems operating on any energy source, except for military uses where the prohibition shall enter into force on 31 December 2008,
        – in road public-transport air-conditioning,

(ii) in rail transport air-conditioning, in equipment produced after 31 December 1997;

(iii) from 1 January 2000, in equipment produced after 31 December 1999 for the following uses:
- in public and distribution cold stores and warehouses,
- for equipment of 150 kw and over, shaft input,

(iv) from 1 January 2001, in all other refrigeration and air-conditioning equipment produced after 31 December 2000, with the exception of fixed air-conditioning equipment, with a cooling capacity of less than 100 kW, where the use of hydrochlofluorocarbons shall be prohibited from 1 July 2002 in equipment produced after 30 June 2002 and of reversible airconditioning/heat pump systems where the use of hydrochlorofluorocarbons shall be prohibited from 1 January 2004 in all equipment produced after 31 December 2003;

(v) from 1 January 2010, the use of virgin hydrochlorofluorocarbons shall be prohibited in the maintenance and servicing of refrigeration and air-conditioning equipment existing at that date; all hydrochlorofluorocarbons shall be prohibited from 1 January 2015.

Before 31 December 2008 the Commission shall review the technical and economic availability of alternatives to recycled hydrochlorofluorocarbons.

The review shall take into account the availability of technically and economically feasible alternatives to hydrochlorofluorocarbons in existing refrigeration equipment with the view to avoiding undue abandonment of equipment.

Alternatives for consideration should have a significantly less harmful effect on the environment than hydrochlorofluorocarbons.

The Commission shall submit the result of the review to the European Parliament and to the Council. It shall, as appropriate, in accordance with the procedure referred to in Article 18(2), take a decision on whether to adapt the date of 1 January 2015;

(d) for the production of foams:

(i) for the production of all foams except integral skin foams for use in safety applications and rigid insulating foams;

(ii) from 1 October 2000, for the production of integral skin foams for use in safety applications and polyethylene rigid insulating foams;

(iii) from 1 January 2002, for the production of extruded polystyrene rigid insulating foams, except where used for insulated transport;

(iv) from 1 January 2003, for the production of polyurethane foams for appliances, of polyurethane flexible faced laminate foams and of polyurethane sandwich panels, except where these last two are used for insulated transport;

(v) from 1 January 2004, for the production of all foams, including polyurethane spray and block foams;

(e) as carrier gas for sterilisation substances in closed systems, in equipment produced after 31 December 1997;

(f) in all other applications.

2. By way of derogation from paragraph l, the use of hydrochlorofluorocarbons shall be permitted:

(a) in laboratory uses, including research and development;

(b) as feedstock;

(c) as a processing agent.

3. By way of derogation from paragraph 1, the use of hydrochlorofluorocarbons as fire-fighting agents in existing fire protection systems may be permitted for replacing halons in applications listed in Annex VII under the following conditions:

– halons contained in such fire protection systems shall be replaced completely,
– halons withdrawn shall be destroyed,
– 70% of the destruction costs shall be covered by the supplier of the hydrochloro-fluorocarbons,
– each year, Member States making use of this provision shall notify to the Commission the number of installations and the quantities of halons concerned.

4. The importation and placing on the market of products and equipment containing hydrochlorofluorocarbons for which a use restriction is in force under this Article shall be prohibited from the date on which the use restriction comes into force. Products and equipment shown to be manufactured before the date of that use restriction shall not be covered by this prohibition.

5. Until 31 December 2009, the use restrictions under this Article shall not apply to the use of hydrochlorofluorocarbons for the production of products for export to countries where the use of hydrochlorofluorocarbons in those products is still permitted.

6. The Commission may, in accordance with the procedure referred to in Article 18(2), in the light of experience with the operation of this Regulation or to reflect technical progress, modify the list and the dates set out in paragraph 1, but in no case extend the periods set out therein, without prejudice to the exemptions provided for in paragraph 7.

7. The Commission may, following a request by a competent authority of a Member State and in accordance with the procedure referred to in Article 18(2), authorise a time-limited exemption to allow the use and placing on the market of hydrochlorofluorocarbons in derogation from paragraph 1 and Article 4(3) where it is demonstrated that, for a particular use, technically and economically feasible alternative substances or technologies are not available or cannot be used. The Commission shall immediately inform the Member States of any exemptions granted.

Chapter III
Trade

Article 6
Licences to import from third countries

1. The release for free circulation in the Community or inward processing of controlled substances shall be subject to the presentation of an import licence. Such licences shall be issued by the Commission after verification of compliance with Articles 6, 7, 8 and 13. The Commission shall forward a copy of each licence to the competent authority of the Member State into which the substances concerned are to be imported. Each Member State shall appoint a competent authority for that purpose. Controlled substances listed in groups I, II, III, IV, V and IX as listed in Annex I shall not be imported for inward processing.

2. The licence, when related to an inward-processing procedure, shall be issued only if the controlled substances are to be used in the customs territory of the Community under the system of suspension provided for in Article 114(2)(a) of Regulation (EEC) No 2913/92, and under the condition that the compensating products are re-exported to a State where the production, consumption or import of that controlled substance is not prohibited. The licence shall only be issued following approval of the competent authority of the Member State in which the inward-processing operation is to take place.

3. A request for a licence shall state:

(a) the names and the addresses of the importer and the exporter;
(b) the country of exportation;
(c) the country of final destination if controlled substances are to be used in the customs territory of the Community under the inward processing procedure as referred to in paragraph 2;
(d) a description of each controlled substance, including:
 – the commercial description,
 – the description and the CN code as laid down in Annex IV,
 – the nature of the substance (virgin, recovered or reclaimed),
 – the quantity of the substance in kilograms;
(e) the purpose of the proposed import;
(f) if known, the place and date of the proposed importation and,

where relevant, any changes to these data.

4. The Commission may require a certificate attesting the nature of substances to be imported.

5. The Commission may, in accordance with the procedure referred to in Article 18(2), modify the list of items mentioned in paragraph 3 and Annex IV.

Article 7
Imports of controlled substances from third countries

The release for free circulation in the Community of controlled substances imported from third countries shall be subject to quantitative limits. Those limits shall be determined and quotas allocated to undertakings for the period 1 January to 31 December 1999 and for each 12-month period thereafter in accordance with the procedure referred to in Article 18(2). They shall be allocated only:

(a) for controlled substances of groups VI and VIII as referred to in Annex I;
(b) for controlled substances if they are used for essential or critical uses or for quarantine and preshipment applications;
(c) for controlled substances if they are used for feedstock or as processing agents; or
(d) to undertakings having destruction facilities for recovered controlled substances if the controlled substances are used for destruction in the Community by technologies approved by the Parties.

Article 8
Imports of controlled substances from a State not party to the Protocol

The release for free circulation in the Community or inward processing of controlled substances imported from any State not party to the Protocol shall be prohibited.

Article 9
Imports of products containing controlled substances from a State not party to the Protocol

1. The release for free circulation in the Community of products and equipment containing controlled substances imported from any State not Party to the Protocol shall be prohibited.

2. A list of products containing controlled substances and of Combined Nomenclature codes is given in Annex V for guidance of the Member States' customs authorities. The Commission may, in accordance with the procedure referred to in Article 18(2), add to, delete items from or amend this list in the light of the lists established by the Parties.

Article 10
Imports of products produced using controlled substances from a State not party to the Protocol

In the light of the decision of the Parties, the Council shall, on a proposal from the Commission, adopt rules applicable to the release for free circulation in the Community of products which were produced using controlled substances but do not contain substances which can be positively identified as controlled substances, imported from any State not party to the Protocol. The identification of such products shall comply with periodical technical advice given to the Parties. The Council shall act by a qualified majority.

Article 11
Export of controlled substances or products containing controlled substances

1. Exports from the Community of chlorofluorocarbons, other fully halogenated chlorofluorocarbons, halons, carbon tetrachloride, 1,1,1-trichloroethane, hydrobromofluorocarbons and bromochloromethane or products and equipment, other than personal effects, containing those substances or whose continuing function relies on supply of those substances shall be prohibited. This prohibition shall not apply to exports of:

(a) controlled substances produced under Article 3(6) to satisfy the basic domestic needs of Parties pursuant to Article 5 of the Protocol;
(b) controlled substances produced under Article 3(7) to satisfy essential or critical uses of Parties;
(c) products and equipment containing controlled substances produced under Article 3(5) or imported under Article 7(b);
(d) recovered, recycled and reclaimed halon stored for critical uses in facilities authorised or operated by the competent authority to satisfy critical uses listed in Annex VII until 31 December 2009, and products and equipment containing halon to satisfy critical uses listed in Annex VII. By 1 January 2005, the Commission shall undertake a review of exports of such recovered, recycled and reclaimed halon for critical uses and, in accordance with the procedure referred to in Article 18(2), shall take a decision, if appropriate, to prohibit such exports earlier than 31 December 2009;
(e) controlled substances to be used for feedstock and processing agent applications;
(f) metered dose inhalers and delivery mechanisms containing chlorofluorcarbons for hermetically sealed devices for implantation in the human body for delivery of measured doses of medication which, under Article 4(1), may be given a temporary authorisation in accordance with the procedure referred to in Article 18(2);
(g) used products and equipment that contain rigid insulating foam or integral skin foam which have been produced with chlorofluorocarbons.

This exemption does not apply to:

– refrigeration and air-conditioning equipment and products;
– refrigeration and air-conditioning equipment and products which contain chlorofluorocarbons used as refrigerants, or whose continuing function relies on the

supply of chlorofluorocarbons used as refrigerants, in other equipment and products;
− building insulation foam and products.

2. Exports from the Community of methyl bromide to any State not party to the Protocol shall be prohibited.

3. From 1 January 2004, exports from the Community of hydrochlorofluorocarbons to any State not party to the Protocol shall be prohibited. The Commission shall, in accordance with the procedure referred to in Article 18(2), examine the above date in the light of relevant international developments under the Protocol and modify it as appropriate.

4. From 31 December 2003, exports from the Community of halon for critical uses not from storage facilities authorised or operated by the competent authority to store halon for critical uses shall be prohibited.

Article 12
Export authorisation

1. Exports from the Community of controlled substances shall be subject to authorisation. Such export authorisation shall be issued by the Commission to undertakings for the period 1 January to 31 December 2001 and for each 12-month period thereafter after verification of compliance with Article 11. Provisions governing the export authorisation of halon as a controlled substance are set out in paragraph 4. The Commission shall forward a copy of each export authorisation to the competent authority of the Member State concerned.

2. An application for an export authorisation shall state:

(a) the name and address of the exporter and of the producer, where it is not the same;
(b) a description of the controlled substance(s) intended for export, including:
  − the commercial description,
  − the description and the CN code as laid down in Annex IV,
  − the nature of the substance (virgin, recovered or reclaimed);
(c) the total quantity of each substance to be exported;
(d) the country/countries of final destination of the controlled substance(s);
(e) the purpose of the exports.

3. Each exporter shall notify the Commission of any changes which might occur during the period of validity of the authorisation in relation to the data notified under paragraph 2. Each exporter shall report to the Commission in accordance with Article 19.

4. Exports from the Community of halon, and products and equipment containing halon, to satisfy critical uses listed in Annex VII shall be subject to authorisation for the period 1 January to 31 December 2004 and each 12-month period thereafter.

Such export authorisation shall be issued by the Commission to the exporter after verification of compliance with Article 11(1)(d) by the competent authority of the Member State concerned. An application for an export authorisation shall record:

- the name and address of the exporter,
- a commercial description of the export,
- the total quantity of halon,
- the country/countries of final destination of the products and equipment,
- a declaration that the halon is to be exported for a specific critical use listed in Annex VII,
- any further information deemed necessary by the competent authority.

Article 13
Exceptional authorisation to trade with a State not party to the Protocol

By way of derogation from Articles 8, 9(1), 10, 11(2) and (3), trade with any State not party to the Protocol in controlled substances and products which contain or are produced by means of one or more such substances may be authorised by the Commission, to the extent that the State not party to the Protocol is determined by a meeting of the Parties to be in full compliance with the Protocol and has submitted data to that effect as specified in Article 7 of the Protocol. The Commission shall act in accordance with the procedure referred to in Article 18(2) of this Regulation.

Article 14
Trade with a territory not covered by the Protocol

1. Subject to any decision taken under paragraph 2, Articles 8, 9, 11(2) and (3) shall apply to any territory not covered by the Protocol as they apply to any State not party to the Protocol.

2. Where the authorities of a territory not covered by the Protocol are in full compliance with the Protocol and have submitted data to that effect as specified in Article 7 of the Protocol, the Commission may decide that some or all of the provisions of Articles 8, 9 and 11 of this Regulation shall not apply in respect of that territory.

The Commission shall take its decision in accordance with the procedure referred to in Article 18(2).

Article 15
Notification of Member States

The Commission shall immediately notify the Member States of any measures it adopts pursuant to Articles 6, 7, 9, 12, 13 and 14.

Chapter IV
Emission control

Article 16
Recovery of used controlled substances

1. Controlled substances contained in:

- refrigeration, air-conditioning and heat pump equipment, except domestic refrigerators and freezers,
- equipment containing solvents,
- fire protection systems and fire extinguishers, shall be recovered for destruction by technologies approved by the Parties or by any other environmentally acceptable destruction technology, or for recycling or reclamation during the servicing and maintenance of equipment or before the dismantling or disposal of equipment.

2. Controlled substances contained in domestic refrigerators and freezers shall be recovered and dealt with as provided for in paragraph 1 after 31 December 2001.

3. Controlled substances contained in products, installations and equipment other than those mentioned in paragraphs 1 and 2 shall be recovered, if practicable, and dealt with as provided in paragraph 1.

4. Controlled substances shall not be placed on the market in disposable containers, except for essential uses.

5. Member States shall take steps to promote the recovery, recycling, reclamation and destruction of controlled substances and shall assign to users, refrigeration technicians or other appropriate bodies responsibility for ensuring compliance with the provisions of paragraph 1. Member States shall define the minimum qualification requirements for the personnel involved. By 31 December 2001 at the latest, Member States shall report to the Commission on the programmes related to the above qualification requirements. The Commission shall evaluate the measures taken by the Member States. In the light of this evaluation and of technical and other relevant information, the Commission, as appropriate, shall propose measures regarding those minimum qualification requirements.

6. Member States shall report to the Commission by 31 December 2001, and for each 12-month period thereafter, on the systems established to promote the recovery of used controlled substances, including the facilities available and the quantities of used controlled substances recovered, recycled, reclaimed or destroyed.

7. This Article shall be without prejudice to Council Directive 75/442/EEC of 15 July 1975 on waste[1] or to measures adopted following Article 2(2) of that Directive.

---

[1] OJ L 194, 25.7.1975, p. 39. Directive as last amended by Commission Decision 96/350/EC (OJ L 135, 6.6.1996, p. 32).

Article 17
Leakages of controlled substances

1. All precautionary measures practicable shall be taken to prevent and minimise leakages of controlled substances. In particular, fixed equipment with a refrigerating fluid charge of more than 3 kg shall be checked for leakages annually. Member States shall define the minimum qualification requirements for the personnel involved. By 31 December 2001 at the latest, Member States shall report to the Commission on the programmes related to the above qualification requirements. The Commission shall evaluate the measures taken by the Member States. In the light of this evaluation and of technical and other relevant information, the Commission, as appropriate, shall propose measures regarding those minimum qualification requirements.

The Commission shall promote the preparation of European standards relating to the control of leakages and to the recovery of substances leaking from commercial and industrial air-conditioning and refrigeration equipment, from fire-protection systems and from equipment containing solvents as well as, as appropriate, to technical requirements with respect to the leakproofness of refrigeration systems.

2. All precautionary measures practicable shall be taken to prevent and minimise leakages of methyl bromide from fumigation installations and operations in which methyl bromide is used. Whenever methyl bromide is used in soil fumigation, the use of virtually impermeable films for a sufficient time, or other techniques ensuring at least the same level of environmental protection shall be mandatory. Member States shall define the minimum qualification requirements for the personnel involved.

3. All precautionary measures practicable shall be taken to prevent and minimise leakages of controlled substances used as feedstock and as processing agents.

4. All precautionary measures practicable shall be taken to prevent and minimise any leakage of controlled substances inadvertently produced in the course of the manufacture of other chemicals.

5. The Commission shall develop as appropriate and ensure the dissemination of notes describing best available technologies and best environmental practices concerning the prevention and minimisation of leakages and emissions of controlled substances.

Chapter V
Committee, reporting, inspection and penalties

Article 18
Committee

1. The Commission shall be assisted by a Committee.

2. Where reference is made to this paragraph, Articles 4 and 7 of Decision 1999/468/EC shall apply, having regard to the provisions of Article 8 thereof.

The period laid down in Article 4(3) of Decision 1999/468/EC shall be set at one month.

3. The Committee shall adopt its rules of procedure.

Article 19

Reporting

1. Every year before 31 March, each producer, importer and exporter of controlled substances shall communicate to the Commission, sending a copy to the competent authority of the Member State concerned, data as specified below for each controlled substance in respect of the period 1 January to 31 December of the preceding year.

The format of this report shall be established in accordance with the procedure referred to in Article 18(2).

(a) Each producer shall communicate:
  - its total production of each controlled substance,
  - any production placed on the market or used for the producer's own account within the Community, separately identifying production for feedstock, processing agent, quarantine and preshipment and other uses,
  - any production to meet the essential uses in the Community, licensed in accordance with Article 3(4),
  - any production authorised under Article 3(6) to satisfy basic domestic needs of Parties pursuant to Article 5 of the Protocol,
  - any production authorised under Article 3(7) to satisfy essential, or critical, uses of Parties,
  - any increase in production authorised under Article 3(8), (9) and (10) in connection with industrial rationalisation,
  - any quantities recycled, reclaimed or destroyed,
  - any stocks.
(b) Each importer, including any producers who also import, shall communicate:
  - any quantities released for free circulation in the Community, separately identifying imports for feedstock and processing agent uses, for essential or critical uses licensed in accordance with Article 3(4), for use in quarantine and preshipment applications and for destruction,
  - any quantities of controlled substances entering the Community under the inward-processing procedure,
  - any quantities of used controlled substances imported for recycling or reclamation,
  - any stocks.
(c) Each exporter, including any producers who also export, shall communicate:
  - any quantities of controlled substances exported from the Community, including substances which are re-exported under the inward processing procedure, separately identifying quantities exported to each country of destination and

quantities exported for feedstock and processing agent uses, essential uses, critical uses, quarantine and preshipment uses, to meet the basic domestic needs of Parties pursuant to Article 5 of the Protocol and for destruction,
– any quantities of used controlled substances exported for recycling or reclamation,
– any stocks.

2. Every year before 31 December, Member States' customs authorities shall return to the Commission the stamped used licence documents.

3. Every year before 31 March, each user who has been authorised to take advantage of an essential use exemption under Article 3(1) shall, for each substance for which an authorisation has been received, report to the Commission, sending a copy to the competent authority of the Member State concerned, the nature of the use, the quantities used during the previous year, the quantities held in stock, any quantities recycled or destroyed, and the quantity of products containing those substances placed on the Community market and/or exported.

4. Every year before 31 March, each undertaking which has been authorised to use controlled substances as a processing agent shall report to the Commission the quantities used during the previous year, and an estimate of the emissions which occurred during such use.

4a. Every year before 31 March, the exporter shall communicate to the Commission, sending a copy of the data to the competent authority of the Member State concerned, the records provided by each applicant in accordance with Article 12(4), in respect of the period 1 January to 31 December of the preceding year.

5. The Commission shall take appropriate steps to protect the confidentiality of the information submitted to it.

6. The Commission may, in accordance with the procedure referred to in Article 18(2), modify the reporting requirements laid down in paragraphs 1 to 4, to meet commitments under the Protocol or to improve the practical application of those reporting requirements.

Article 20
Inspection

1. In carrying out the tasks assigned to it by this Regulation, the Commission may obtain all the information from the governments and competent authorities of the Member States and from undertakings.

2. When requesting information from an undertaking the Commission shall at the same time forward a copy of the request to the competent authority of the Member State within the territory of which the undertaking's seat is situated, together with a statement of the reasons why that information is required.

3. The competent authorities of the Member States shall carry out the investigations which the Commission considers necessary under this Regulation. Member States shall

also conduct random checks on imports of controlled substances, and communicate the schedules and results of those checks to the Commission.

4. Subject to the agreement of the Commission and of the competent authority of the Member State within the territory of which the investigations are to be made, the officials of the Commission shall assist the officials of that authority in the performance of their duties.

5. The Commission shall take appropriate action to promote adequate exchange of information and cooperation between national authorities and between national authorities and the Commission. The Commission shall take appropriate steps to protect the confidentiality of information obtained under this Article.

Article 21
Penalties

Member States shall determine the necessary penalties applicable to breaches of this Regulation. The penalties shall be effective, proportionate and dissuasive. Member States shall notify the provisions regarding penalties to the Commission by 31 December 2000 at the latest and shall also notify it without delay of any subsequent amendment affecting such provisions.

Chapter VI
New substances

Article 22
New substances

1. The production, release for free circulation in the Community and inward processing, placing on the market and use of new substances in Annex II are prohibited. This prohibition does not apply to new substances if they are used as feedstock.

2. The Commission shall, as appropriate, make proposals to include in Annex II any substances that are not controlled substances but that are found by the Scientific Assessment Panel under the Protocol to have a significant ozone-depleting potential, including on possible exemptions from paragraph 1.

Chapter VII
Final provisions

Article 23
Repeal

Regulation (EC) No 3093/94 shall be repealed as from 1 October 2000.

References to the repealed Regulation shall be construed as references to this Regulation.

Article 24
Entry into force

This Regulation shall enter into force on the day following that of its publication in the *Official Journal of the European Communities.*

It shall apply from 1 October 2000.

This Regulation shall be binding in its entirety and directly applicable in all Member States.

Annex I
Controlled substances covered

Group		Substance	Ozone-depleting potential[1]
Group I	$CFCl_3$	(CFC-11)	1,0
	CF_2Cl_2	(CFC-12)	1,0
	$C_2F_3Cl_3$	(CFC-113)	0,8
	$C_4F_4Cl_2$	(CFC-114)	1,0
	C_2F_5Cl	(CFC-115)	0,6
Group II	CF_3Cl	(CFC-13)	1,0
	C_2FCl_5	(CFC-111)	1,0
	$C_2F_2Cl_4$	(CFC-112)	1,0
	C_3FCl_7	(CFC-211)	1,0
	$C_3F_2Cl_6$	(CFC-212)	1,0
	$C_3F_3Cl_5$	(CFC-213)	1,0
	$C_3F_4Cl_4$	(CFC-214)	1,0
	$C_3F_5Cl_3$	(CFC-215)	1,0
	$C_3F_6Cl_2$	(CFC-216)	1,0
	C_3F_7Cl	(CFC-217)	1,0
Group III	CF_2BrCl	(halon-1211)	3,0
	CF_3Br	(halon-1301)	10,0
	$C_2F_4Br_2$	(halon-2402)	6,0
Group IV	CCl_4	(carbon tetrachloride)	1,1
Group V	$C_2H_3Cl_3^{[2]}$	(1,1,1-trichloroethane)	0,1
Group VI	CH_3Br	(methyl bromide)	0,6
Group VII	$CHFBr_2$		1,00
	CHF_2Br		0,74
	CH_2FBr		0,73
	C_2HFBr_4		0,8
	$C_2HF_2Br_3$		1,8
	$C_2HF_3Br_2$		1,6
	C_2HF_4Br		1,2
	$C_2H_2FBr_3$		1,1

Group	Substance		Ozone-depleting potential[1]
	$C_2H_2F_2Br_2$		1,5
	$C_2H_2F_3Br$		1,6
	$C_2H_3FBr_2$		1,7
	$C_2H_3F_2Br$		1,1
	C_2H_4FBr		0,1
	C_3HFBr_6		1,5
	$C_3HF_2Br_5$		1,9
	$C_3HF_3Br_4$		1,8
	$C_3HF_4Br_3$		2,2
	$C_3HF_5Br_2$		2,0
	C_3HF_6Br		3,3
	$C_3H_2FBr_5$		1,9
	$C_3H_2F_2Br_4$		2,1
	$C_3H_2F_3Br_3$		5,6
	$C_3H_2F_4Br_2$		7,5
	$C_3H_2F_5Br$		1,4
	$C_3H_3FBr_4$		1,9
	$C_3H_3F_2Br_3$		3,1
	$C_3H_3F_3Br_2$		2,5
	$C_3H_3F_4Br$		4,4
	$C_3H_4FBr_3$		0,3
	$C_3H_4F_2Br_2$		1,0
	$C_3H_4F_3Br$		0,8
	$C_3H_5FBr_2$		0,4
	$C_3H_5F_2Br$		0,8
	C_3H_6FBr		0,7
Group VIII	$CHFCl_2$	(HCFC-21)[3]	0,040
	CHF_2Cl	(HCFC-22)[3]	0,055
	CH_2FCl	(HCFC-31)	0,020
	C_2HFCl_4	(HCFC-121)	0,040
	$C_2HF_2Cl_3$	(HCFC-122)	0,080
	$C_2HF_3Cl_2$	(HCFC-123)[3]	0,020
	C_2HF_4Cl	(HCFC-124)[3]	0,022
	$C_2H_2FCl_3$	(HCFC-131)	0,050
	$C_2H_2F_2Cl_2$	(HCFC-132)	0,050
	$C_2H_2F_3Cl$	(HCFC-133)	0,060
	$C_2H_3FCl_2$	(HCFC-141)	0,070
	CH_3CFCl_2	(HCFC-141b)[3]	0,110
	$C_2H_3F_2Cl$	(HCFC-142)	0,070

(*cont.*)

Group		Substance	Ozone-depleting potential[1]
	CH_3CF_2Cl	(HCFC-142b)[3]	0,065
	C_2H_4FCl	(HCFC-151)	0,005
	C_3HFCl_6	(HCFC-221)	0,070
	$C_3HF_2Cl_5$	(HCFC-222)	0,090
	$C_3HF_3Cl_4$	(HCFC-223)	0,080
	$C_3HF_4Cl_3$	(HCFC-224)	0,090
	$C_3HF_5Cl_2$	(HCFC-225)	0,070
	$CF_3CF_2CHCl_2$	(HCFC-225ca)[3]	0,025
	CF_2ClCF_2CHClF	(HCFC-225cb)[3]	0,033
	C_3HF_6Cl	(HCFC-226)	0,100
	$C_3H_2FCl_5$	(HCFC-231)	0,090
	$C_3H_2F_2Cl_4$	(HCFC-232)	0,100
	$C_3H_2F_3Cl_3$	(HCFC-233)	0,230
	$C_3H_2F_4Cl_2$	(HCFC-234)	0,280
	$C_3H_2F_5Cl$	(HCFC-235)	0,520
	$C_3H_3FCl_4$	(HCFC-241)	0,090
	$C_3H_3F_2Cl_3$	(HCFC-242)	0,130
	$C_3H_3F_3Cl_2$	(HCFC-243)	0,120
	$C_3H_3F_4Cl$	(HCFC-244)	0,140
	$C_3H_4FCl_3$	(HCFC-251)	0,010
	$C_3H_4F_2Cl_2$	(HCFC-252)	0,040
	$C_3H_4F_3Cl$	(HCFC-253)	0,030
	$C_3H_5FCl_2$	(HCFC-261)	0,020
	$C_3H_5F_2Cl$	(HCFC-262)	0,020
	C_3H_6FCl	(HCFC-271)	0,030
Group IX	CH_2BrCl	(halon 1011 bromochloro-methane)	0,12

[1] These ozone-depleting potentials are estimates based on existing knowledge and will be reviewed and revised periodically in the light of decisions taken by the Parties.

[2] This formula does not refer to 1,1,2-trichloroethane.

[3] Identifies the most commercially viable substance as prescribed in the Protocol.

Annex III

Total quantitative limits on producers and importers placing controlled substances on the market and using them for their own account in the Community (calculated levels expressed in ODP tonnes)

Substance For 12-month periods from 1 January to 31 December	Group I	Group II	Group III	Group IV	Group V	Group VI[1] For uses other than quarantine and preshipment applications	Group VI[1] For quarantine and pre-shipment applications	Group VII	Group VIII
1999	0	0	0	0	0	8 665		0	8 079
2000						8 665			8 079
2001						4 621	607		6 678
2002						4 621	607		5 676
2003						2 888	607		3 005
2004						2 888	607		2 003
2005						0	607		2 003
2006							607		2 003
2007							607		2 003
2008							607		1 669
2009							607		1 669
2010							607		0
2011							607		0
2012							607		0
2013							607		0
2014							607		0
2015							607		0

[1] Calculated on the basis of ODP = 0,6.

Annex IV
Groups, Combined Nomenclature 1999 (CN 99) Codes[1] and descriptions
for the substances referred to in Annexes I and III

Group	CN 99 code	Description
Group 1	2903 41 00	– – Trichlorofluoromethane
	2903 42 00	– – Dichlorodifluoromethane
	2903 43 00	– – Trichlorotrifluoroethanes
	2903 44 10	– – – Dichlorotetrafluoroethanes
	2903 44 90	– – – Chloropentafluoroethane
Group II	2903 45 10	– – – Chlorotrifluoromethane
	2903 45 15	– – – Pentachlorofluoroethane
	2903 45 20	– – – Tetrachlorodifluoroethanes
	2903 45 25	– – – Heptachlorofluoropropanes
	2903 45 30	– – – Hexachlerodifluoropropanes
	2903 45 35	– – – Pentachlorotrifluoropropanes
	2903 45 40	– – – Tetrachlorotetrafluoropropanes
	2903 45 45	– – – Trichloropentafluoropropanes
	2903 45 50	– – – Dichlorohexafluoropropanes
	2903 45 55	– – – Chloroheptafluoropropanes
Group III	2903 46 10	– – – Bromochlorodifluoromethane
	2903 46 20	– – – Bromotrifluoromethane
	2903 46 90	– – – Dibromotetrafluoroethanes
Group IV	2903 14 00	– – Carbon tetrachloride
Group V	2903 19 10	– – – 1,1,1-Trichloroethane (methylchloroform)
Group VI	2903 30 33	– – – Bromomethane (methyl bromide)
Group VII	2903 49 30	– – – – Hydrobromofluoromethanes, -ethanes or -propanes
Group VIII	2903 49 10	– – – – Hydrochlorofluoromethanes, -ethanes or -propanes
	ex 3824 71 00	– – Mixtures containing one or more substances falling within CN codes 2903 41 00 to 2903 45 55.
	ex 3824 79 00	– – Mixtures containing one or more substances falling within CN codes 2903 46 10 to 2903 46 90
	ex 3824 90 95	– – – – Mixtures containing one or more substances falling within CN codes 2903 14 00, 2903 19 10, 2903 30 33, 2903 49 10 or 2903 49 30

[1] An 'ex' before a code implies that other products than those referred to in the column 'Description' may fall under that subheading.

Annex V
Combined Nomenclature (CN) codes for products containing controlled substances*

1. Automobiles and trucks equipped with air-conditioning units

CN codes
8701 20 10 – 8701 90 90
8702 10 11 – 8702 90 90
8703 10 11 – 8703 90 90
8704 10 11 – 8704 90 00
8705 10 00 – 8705 90 90
8706 00 11 – 8706 00 99

2. Domestic and commercial refrigeration and air-conditioning/heat-pump equipment

Refrigerators:

CN codes
8418 10 10 – 8418 29 00
8418 50 11 – 8418 50 99
8418 61 10 – 8418 69 99

Freezers:

CN codes
8418 10 10 – 8418 29 00
8418 30 10 – 8418 30 99
8418 40 10 – 8418 40 99
8418 50 11 – 8418 50 99
8418 61 10 – 8418 61 90
8418 69 10 – 8418 69 99

Dehumidifiers:

CN codes
8415 10 00 – 8415 83 90
8479 60 00
8479 89 10
8479 89 98

Water coolers and gas liquefying units:

CN codes
8419 60 00
8419 89 98

* These customs codes are given for the guidance of the Member States' customs authorities

Ice machines:

CN codes
8418 10 10 – 8418 29 00
8418 30 10 – 8418 30 99
8418 40 10 – 8418 40 99
8418 50 11 – 8418 50 99
8418 61 10 – 8418 61 90
8418 69 10 – 8418 69 99

Air-conditioning and heat-pump units:

CN codes
8415 10 00 – 8415 83 90
8418 61 10 – 8418 61 90
8418 69 10 – 8418 69 99
8418 99 10 – 8418 99 90

3. *Aerosol products, except medical aerosols*

Food products:

CN codes
0404 90 21 – 0404 90 89
1517 90 10 – 1517 90 99
2106 90 92
2106 90 98

Paints and varnishes, prepared water pigments and dyes:

CN codes
3208 10 10 – 3208 10 90
3208 20 10 – 3208 20 90
3208 90 11 – 3208 90 99
3209 10 00 – 3209 90 00
3210 00 10 – 3210 00 90
3212 90 90

Perfumery, cosmetic or toilet preparations:

CN codes
3303 00 10 – 3303 00 90
3304 30 00
3304 99 00
3305 10 00 – 3305 90 90
3306 10 00 – 3306 90 00
3307 10 00 – 3307 30 00
3307 49 00
3307 90 00

Surface-active preparations:

CN codes
3402 20 10 – 3402 20 90

Lubricating preparations:

CN codes
2710 00 81
2710 00 97
3403 11 00
3403 19 10 – 3403 19 99
3403 91 00
3403 99 10 – 3403 99 90

Household preparations:

CN codes
3405 10 00
3405 20 00
3405 30 00
3405 40 00
3405 90 10 – 3405 90 90

Articles of combustible materials:

CN codes
3606 10 00

Insecticides, rodenticides, fungicides, herbicides, etc.:

CN codes
3808 10 10 – 3808 10 90
3808 20 10 – 3808 20 80
3808 30 11 – 3808 30 90
3808 40 10 – 3808 40 90
3808 90 10 – 3808 90 90

Finishing agents, etc.:

CN codes
3809 10 10 – 3809 10 90
3809 91 00 – 3809 93 00

Preparations and charges for fire-extinguishers; charged fire-extinguishing grenades:

CN codes
3813 00 00

Organic composite solvents, etc.:

CN codes
3814 00 10 – 3814 00 90

Prepared de-icing fluids:

CN codes
3820 00 00

Products of the chemical or allied industries:

CN codes
3824 90 10
3824 90 35
3824 90 40
3824 90 45 – 3824 90 95

Silicones in primary forms:

CN codes
3910 00 00

Arms:

CN codes
9304 00 00

4. *Portable fire extinguishers*

CN codes
8424 10 10 – 8424 10 99

5. *Insulation boards, panels and pipe covers*

CN codes
3917 21 10 – 3917 40 90
3920 10 23 – 3920 99 90
3921 11 00 – 3921 90 90
3925 10 00 – 3925 90 80
3926 90 10 – 3926 90 99

6. *Pre-polymers*

CN codes
3901 10 10 – 3911 90 99

Annex VI
Processes in which controlled substances are used as processing agents

- Use of carbon tetrachloride for the elimination of nitrogen trichloride in the production of chlorine and caustic soda,
- Use of carbon tetrachloride in the recovery of chlorine in tail gas from production of chlorine,
- Use of carbon tetrachloride in the manufacture of chlorinated rubber,
- Use of carbon tetrachloride in the manufacture of isobutyl acetophenone (ibuprofen-analgesic),
- Use of carbon tetrachloride in the manufacture of polyphenyleneterephtalamide,
- Use of CFC-11 in manufacture of fine synthetic polyolefin fibre sheet,
- Use of CFC-113 in the manufacture of vinorelbine (pharmaceutical product),
- Use of CFC-12 in the photochemical synthesis of perfluoropolyetherpolyperoxide precursors of Z-perfluoropolyethers and difunctional derivatives,
- Use of CFC-113 in the reduction of perfluoropolyetherpolyperoxide intermediate for production of perfluoropolyether diesters,
- Use of CFC-113 in the preparation of perfluoropolyether diols with high functionality,
- Use of carbon tetrachloride in the production of tralomethrine (insecticide).

Also the use of HCFCs in the above processes when used to replace CFC or carbon tetrachloride.

Annex VII
Critical uses of halon

Use of halon 1301:

- in aircraft for the protection of crew compartments, engine nacelles, cargo bays and dry bays, and fuel tank inerting,
- in military land vehicles and naval vessels for the protection of spaces occupied by personnel and engine compartments,
- for the making inert of occupied spaces where flammable liquid and/or gas release could occur in the military and oil, gas and petrochemical sector, and in existing cargo ships,
- for the making inert of existing manned communication and command centres of the armed forces or others, essential for national security,
- for the making inert of spaces where there may be a risk of dispersion of radioactive matter,
- in the Channel Tunnel and associated installations and rolling stock.

Use of halon 1211:

- in military land vehicles and naval vessels for the protection of spaces occupied by personnel and engine compartments,
- in hand-held fire extinguishers and fixed extinguisher equipment for engines for use on board aircraft,
- in aircraft for the protection of crew compartments, engine nacelles, cargo bays and dry bays,
- in fire extinguishers essential to personal safety used for initial extinguishing by fire brigades,
- in military and police fire extinguishers for use on persons.

Use of halon 2402 only in Cyprus, the Czech Republic, Estonia, Hungary, Latvia, Lithunia, Malta, Poland, Slovakia and Slovenia:

- in aircraft for the protection of crew compartments, engine nacelles, cargo bays and dry bays and fuel tank inerting,
- in military land vehicles and naval vessels for the protection of spaces occupied by personnel and engine compartments,
- for the making inert of occupied spaces where flammable liquid and/or gas release could occur in the military and oil, gas and petrochemical sectors, and in existing cargo ships,
- for the making inert of existing manned communication and command centres of the armed forces or others, essential for national security,
- for the making inert of spaces where there may be a risk of dispersion of radioactive matter,
- in hand-held fire extinguishers and fixed extinguisher equipment for engines for use on board aircraft,
- in fire extinguishers essential to personal safety used for initial extinguishing by fire brigades,
- in military and police fire extinguishers for use on persons.

Directive 2002/3/EC of the European Parliament and of the Council of 12 February 2002 relating to ozone in ambient air

Editorial note

Directive 2002/3/EC of 12 February 2002 relating to ozone in ambient air requires Member States to take action in order to ensure effective protection from harmful effects on human health from exposure to ozone. The main purpose of this Directive is to establish long-term objectives, target values, an alert threshold and an information threshold for concentration of ozone in ambient air (Article 1). Ambient air means outdoor air in the troposphere, excluding the work place (Article 2(1)).

Target values for 2010 in respect of ozone concentrations in ambient air are set out in Section II of Annex I (Article 3(1)). The Directive requires Member States to draw up a list of zones and agglomerations (zones with certain population density) where the levels of ozone in ambient air are higher than the target values, and ensure a plan is implemented in order to attain the target value (Article 3(2) and (3)). The long-term objectives for ozone concentrations in ambient air are set out in Section III of Annex I (Article 4(1)). Member States are to draw up a list of zones and agglomerations where the levels of ozone in ambient air are higher than the long-term objectives, but below or equal to the target values set out in Section II of Annex I, and implement cost-effective measures with the aim of achieving the long-term measures (Article 4(1)). In zones and agglomerations where ozone levels meet the long-term objectives, Member States must maintain the levels of ozone below the long-term objectives and preserve the best ambient air quality (Article 5).

The Directive requires Member States to ensure that up-to-date information on concentrations of ozone in ambient air is made available to the public, with Section I of Annex II setting out the information threshold and the alert threshold for concentrations of ozone in ambient air (Article 6). Member States are required to draw up action plans indicating specific measures to be taken in the short term for zones where there is a risk of exceedances of the alert threshold – if there is a significant potential for reducing that risk, or for reducing the duration or severity of any exceedance of the alert threshold (Article 7). The Directive requires cooperation between Member States in drawing up joint plans and programmes where ozone concentrations exceeding target values or long-term objectives are due largely to transboundary pollution

(Article 8). Fixed, continuous measurement is mandatory in zones and agglomerations where concentrations of ozone have exceeded a long-term objective during the last five years, whilst the Directive sets out the techniques for assessing concentrations of ozone and precursor substances in ambient air (Article 9). The criteria for determining the location of sampling points for the measurement of ozone are outlined in Annex IV. The Directive requires that each Member State comply with reporting requirements (Article 10) and, in particular, send to the Commission lists of identified zones and agglomerations for each year along with a report giving an overview of the situation regarding exceedance of the target values (Article 10(1)).

The Commission is required to submit to the European Parliament and the Council, by 31 December 2004, a report based on experience of the application of this Directive (Article 11), and develop guidance for the implementation of this Directive by 9 September 2002 (Article 12). Member States are to determine penalties for the breach of national provisions adopted in accordance with this Directive (Article 14) and must transpose the Directive into national law by 9 September 2003 (Article 15).

Source: OJ L 67 09.03.2002 p. 14

Directive 2002/3/EC of the European Parliament and of the Council of 12 February 2002 relating to ozone in ambient air

The European Parliament and the Council of the European Union,
    Having regard to the Treaty establishing the European Community, and in particular Article 175(1) thereof,
    Having regard to the proposal from the Commission,[1]
    Having regard to the opinion of the Economic and Social Committee,[2]
    Having regard to the opinion of the Committee of the Regions,[3]
    Acting in accordance with the procedure laid down in Article 251 of the Treaty,[4] in light of the joint text approved by the Conciliation Committee on 10 December 2001,
    Whereas:

(1) On the basis of principles enshrined in Article 174 of the Treaty, the Fifth Environmental Action Programme, approved by the Resolution of the Council and the Representatives of the Governments of the Member States meeting within the Council of 1 February 1993 on a European Community programme of policy and action in relation to the environment and sustainable development[5]

---

[1] OJ C 56 E, 29.2.2000, p. 40, and OJ C 29 E, 30.1.2001, p. 291.
[2] OJ C 51, 23.2.2000, p. 11.   [3] OJ C 317, 6.11.2000, p. 35.
[4] Opinion of the European Parliament of 15 March 2000 (OJ C 377, 29.12.2000, p. 154), Council Common Position of 8 March 2001 (OJ C 126, 26.4.2001, p. 1) and Decision of the European Parliament of 13 June 2001 (not yet published in the Official Journal). Decision of the European Parliament of 17 January 2002 and Decision of the Council of 19 December 2001.
[5] OJ C 138, 17.5.1993, p. 1.

and supplemented by Decision No 2179/98/EC[1] envisages, in particular, amendments to existing legislation on air pollutants. The said programme recommends
the establishment of long-term air quality objectives.

(2) Pursuant to Article 4(5) of Council Directive 96/62/EC of 27 September 1996
on ambient air quality assessment and management,[2] the Council is to adopt
the legislation provided for in paragraph 1 and the provisions laid down in
paragraphs 3 and 4 of that Article.

(3) It is important to ensure effective protection against harmful effects on human
health from exposure to ozone. The adverse effects of ozone on vegetation,
ecosystems and the environment as a whole should be reduced, as far as possible.
The transboundary nature of ozone pollution requires measures to be taken at
Community level.

(4) Directive 96/62/EC provides that numerical thresholds are to be based on the
findings of work carried out by international scientific groups active in the field.
The Commission is to take account of the most recent scientific research data in
the epidemiological and environmental fields concerned and of the most recent
advances in metrology with a view to re-examining the elements on which such
thresholds are based.

(5) Directive 96/62/EC requires limit and/or target values to be set for ozone. In
view of the transboundary nature of ozone pollution, target values should be set
at Community level for the protection of human health and for the protection
of vegetation. Those target values should relate to the interim objectives derived
from the Community integrated strategy to combat acidification and ground-
level ozone, which also form the basis of Directive 2001/81/EC of the European
Parliament and of the Council of 23 October 2001 on national emission ceilings
for certain atmospheric pollutants.[3]

(6) In accordance with Directive 96/62/EC, plans and programmes should be implemented in respect of zones and agglomerations within which ozone concentrations exceed target values in order to ensure that target values are met as far
as possible by the date specified. Such plans and programmes should to a large
extent refer to control measures to be implemented in accordance with relevant
Community legislation.

(7) Long-term objectives should be set with the aim of providing effective protection
of human health and the environment. Long-term objectives should relate to
the ozone and acidification abatement strategy and its aim of closing the gap
between current ozone levels and the long-term objectives.

(8) Measurements should be mandatory in zones with exceedances of the long-
term objectives. Supplementary means of assessment may reduce the required
number of fixed sampling points.

---

[1] OJ L 275, 10.10.1998, p. 1.   [2] OJ L 296, 21.11.1996, p. 55.   [3] OJ L 309, 27.11.2001, p. 22.

(9) An alert threshold for ozone should be set for the protection of the general population. An information threshold should be set to protect sensitive sections of the population. Up-to-date information on concentrations of ozone in ambient air should be routinely made available to the public.

(10) Short-term action plans should be drawn up where the risk of exceedances of the alert threshold can be reduced significantly. The potential for reducing the risk, duration and severity of exceedances should be investigated and assessed. Local measures should not be required where examination of benefits and costs shows them to be disproportionate.

(11) The transboundary nature of ozone pollution may require some coordination between neighbouring Member States in drawing up and implementing plans, programmes and short-term action plans and in informing the public. Where appropriate, Member States should pursue cooperation with third countries, with particular emphasis on early involvement of accession candidate countries.

(12) As a basis for regular reports, information on measured concentrations should be submitted to the Commission.

(13) The Commission should review the provisions of this Directive in the light of the most recent scientific research concerning, in particular, the effects of ozone on human health and the environment. The Commission's report should be presented as an integral part of an air quality strategy designed to review and propose Community air quality objectives and develop implementing strategies to ensure achievement of those objectives. In this context, the report should take into account the potential to achieve the long-term objectives within a specified time period.

(14) The measures necessary for the implementation of this Directive should be adopted in accordance with Council Decision 1999/468/EC of 28 June 1999 laying down the procedures for the exercise of implementing powers conferred on the Commission.[1]

(15) Since the objectives of the proposed action ensuring effective protection against harmful effects on human health from ozone and reducing the adverse effect of ozone on vegetation, ecosystems and the environment as a whole cannot be sufficiently achieved by the Member States because of the transboundary nature of ozone pollution and can therefore be better achieved at Community level, the Community may adopt measures, in accordance with the principle of subsidiarity as set out in Article 5 of the Treaty. In accordance with the principle of proportionality, as set out in that Article, this Directive does not go beyond what is necessary in order to achieve those objectives.

(16) Council Directive 92/72/EEC of 21 September 1992 on air pollution by ozone[2] should be repealed,

---

[1] OJ L 184, 17.7.1999, p. 23. [2] OJ L 297, 13.10.1992, p. 1.

Have adopted this Directive:

Article 1
Objectives

The purpose of this Directive is:

(a) to establish long-term objectives, target values, an alert threshold and an information threshold for concentrations of ozone in ambient air in the Community, designed to avoid, prevent or reduce harmful effects on human health and the environment as a whole;
(b) to ensure that common methods and criteria are used to assess concentrations of ozone and, as appropriate, ozone precursors (oxides of nitrogen and volatile organic compounds) in ambient air in the Member States;
(c) to ensure that adequate information is obtained on ambient levels of ozone and that it is made available to the public;
(d) to ensure that, with respect to ozone, ambient air quality is maintained where it is good, and improved in other cases;
(e) to promote increased cooperation between the Member States, in reducing ozone levels, use of the potential of transboundary measures and agreement on such measures.

Article 2
Definitions

For the purposes of this Directive:

1. 'ambient air' means outdoor air in the troposphere, excluding work places;
2. 'pollutant' means any substance introduced directly or indirectly by man into the ambient air and likely to have harmful effects on human health and/or the environment as a whole;
3. 'ozone precursor substances', means substances which contribute to the formation of ground-level ozone, some of which are listed in Annex VI;
4. 'level' means the concentration of a pollutant in ambient air or the deposition thereof on surfaces in a given time;
5. 'assessment' means any method used to measure, calculate, predict or estimate the level of a pollutant in the ambient air;
6. 'fixed measurements' means measurements taken in accordance with Article 6(5) of Directive 96/62/EC;
7. 'zone' means part of the territory of a Member State as delimited by it;
8. 'agglomeration' means a zone with a population concentration in excess of 250 000 inhabitants or, where the population concentration is 250 000 inhabitants or less, a population density per km^2 which for the Member State justifies the need for ambient air quality to be assessed and managed;

9. 'target value' means a level fixed with the aim, in the long term, of avoiding harmful effects on human health and/or the environment as a whole, to be attained where possible over a given period;

10. 'long-term objective' means an ozone concentration in the ambient air below which, according to current scientific knowledge, direct adverse effects on human health and/or the environment as a whole are unlikely. This objective is to be attained in the long term, save where not achievable through proportionate measures, with the aim of providing effective protection of human health and the environment;

11. 'alert threshold' means a level beyond which there is a risk to human health from brief exposure for the general population and at which immediate steps shall be taken by the Member States as laid down in Articles 6 and 7;

12. 'information threshold' means a level beyond which there is a risk to human health from brief exposure for particularly sensitive sections of the population and at which up-to-date information is necessary;

13. 'volatile organic compounds' (VOC) means all organic compounds from anthropogenic and biogenic sources, other than methane, that are capable of producing photochemical oxidants by reactions with nitrogen oxides in the presence of sunlight.

Article 3
Target values

1. The target values for 2010 in respect of ozone concentrations in ambient air are those set out in Section II of Annex I.

2. Member States shall draw up a list of zones and agglomerations in which the levels of ozone in ambient air, as assessed in accordance with Article 9, are higher than the target values referred to in paragraph 1.

3. For the zones and agglomerations referred to in paragraph 2, Member States shall take measures to ensure, in accordance with the provisions of Directive 2001/81/EC, that a plan or programme is prepared and implemented in order to attain the target value, save where not achievable through proportionate measures, as from the date specified in Section II of Annex I. Where, in accordance with Article 8(3) of Directive 96/62/EC, plans or programmes must be prepared or implemented in respect of pollutants other than ozone, Member States shall, where appropriate, prepare and implement integrated plans or programmes covering all the pollutants concerned.

4. The plans or programmes, referred to in paragraph 3, shall incorporate at least the information listed in Annex IV to Directive 96/62/EC and shall be made available to the public and to appropriate organisations such as environmental organisations, consumer organisations, organisations representing the interests of sensitive population groups and other relevant health care bodies.

Article 4
Long-term objectives

1. The long-term objectives for ozone concentrations in ambient air are those set out in Section III of Annex I.

2. Member States shall draw up a list of the zones and agglomerations in which the levels of ozone in ambient air, as assessed in accordance with Article 9, are higher than the long-term objectives referred to in paragraph 1 but below, or equal to, the target values set out in Section II of Annex I. For such zones and agglomerations, Member States shall prepare and implement cost-effective measures with the aim of achieving the long-term objectives. The measures taken shall, at least, be consistent with all plans or programmes specified in Article 3(3). Furthermore, they shall build upon measures taken under the provisions of Directive 2001/81/EC and other relevant existing and future EC legislation.

3. Community progress towards attaining the long-term objectives shall be subject to successive reviews, as part of the process set out in Article 11 and in connection with Directive 2001/81/EC, using the year 2020 as a benchmark and taking account of progress towards attaining the national emission ceilings set out in the said Directive.

Article 5
Requirements in zones and agglomerations where ozone levels meet the long-term objectives

Member States shall draw up a list of zones and agglomerations in which ozone levels meet the long-term objectives. In so far as factors including the transboundary nature of ozone pollution and meteorological conditions permit, they shall maintain the levels of ozone in those zones and agglomerations below the long-term objectives and shall preserve through proportionate measures the best ambient air quality compatible with sustainable development and a high level of environmental and human health protection.

Article 6
Information to the public

1. Member States shall take appropriate steps to:

(a) ensure that up-to-date information on concentrations of ozone in ambient air is routinely made available to the public as well as to appropriate organisations such as environmental organisations, consumer organisations, organisations representing the interests of sensitive population groups and other relevant health care bodies.

   This information shall be updated on at least a daily basis and, wherever appropriate and practicable, on an hourly basis.

Such information shall at least indicate all exceedances of the concentrations in the long-term objective for the protection of health, the information threshold and the alert threshold for the relevant averaging period. It should also provide a short assessment in relation to effects on health.

The information threshold and the alert threshold for concentrations of ozone in ambient air are given in Section I of Annex II;

(b) make available to the public and to appropriate organisations such as environmental organisations, consumer organisations, organisations representing the interests of sensitive population groups and other relevant health care bodies comprehensive annual reports which shall at least indicate, in the case of human health, all exceedances of concentrations in the target value and the long-term objective, the information threshold and the alert threshold, for the relevant averaging period, and in the case of vegetation, any exceedance of the target value and the long-term objective, combined with, as appropriate, a short assessment of the effects of these exceedances. They may include, where appropriate, further information and assessments on forest protection, as specified in section I of Annex III. They may also include information on relevant precursor substances, in so far as these are not covered by existing Community legislation;

(c) ensure that timely information about actual or predicted exceedances of the alert threshold is provided to health care institutions and the population.

The information and reports referred to above shall be published by appropriate means, depending on the case, for example the broadcasting media, the press or publications, information screens or computer network services, such as the internet.

2. Details supplied to the public in accordance with Article 10 of Directive 96/62/EC when either threshold is exceeded shall include the items listed in Section II of Annex II. Member States shall, where practicable, also take steps to supply such information when an exceedance of the information threshold or alert threshold is predicted.

3. Information supplied under paragraphs 1 and 2 shall be clear, comprehensible and accessible.

Article 7
Short-term action plans

1. In accordance with Article 7(3) of Directive 96/62/EC, Member States shall draw up action plans, at appropriate administrative levels, indicating specific measures to be taken in the short term, taking into account particular local circumstances, for the zones where there is a risk of exceedances of the alert threshold, if there is a significant potential for reducing that risk or for reducing the duration or severity of

any exceedance of the alert threshold. Where it is found that there is no significant potential for reducing the risk, duration or severity of any exceedance in the relevant zones, Member States shall be exempt from the provisions of Article 7(3) of Directive 96/62/EC. It is for Member States to identify whether there is significant potential for reducing the risk, duration or severity of any exceedance, taking account of the national geographical, meteorological and economic conditions.

2. The design of short-term action plans, including trigger levels for specific actions, is the responsibility of Member States. Depending on the individual case, the plans may provide for graduated, cost-effective measures to control and, where necessary, reduce or suspend certain activities, including motor vehicle traffic, which contribute to emissions which result in the alert threshold being exceeded. These may also include effective measures in relation to the use of industrial plants or products.

3. When developing and implementing the short-term action plans, Member States shall consider examples of measures (the effectiveness of which has been assessed), which should be included in the guidance referred to in Article 12.

4. Member States shall make available to the public and to appropriate organisations such as environmental organisations, consumer organisations, organisations representing the interests of sensitive population groups and other relevant health care bodies both the results of their investigations and the content of specific short-term action plans as well as information on the implementation of these plans.

Article 8
Transboundary pollution

1. Where ozone concentrations exceeding target values or long-term objectives are due largely to precursor emissions in other Member States, the Member States concerned shall cooperate, where appropriate, in drawing up joint plans and programmes in order to attain the target values or long-term objectives, save where not achievable through proportionate measures. The Commission shall assist in those efforts. In carrying out its obligations under Article 11, the Commission shall consider, taking into account Directive 2001/81/EC, in particular Article 9 thereof, whether further action should be taken at Community level in order to reduce precursor emissions responsible for such transboundary ozone pollution.

2. Member States shall, if appropriate according to Article 7, prepare and implement joint short-term action plans covering neighbouring zones in different Member States. Member States shall ensure that neighbouring zones in different Member States, which have developed short-term action plans, receive all appropriate information.

3. Where exceedances of the information threshold or alert threshold occur in zones close to national borders, information should be provided as soon as possible

to the competent authorities in the neighbouring Member States concerned in order to facilitate the provision of information to the public in those States.

4. In drawing up the plans and programmes referred to in paragraph 1 and 2 and in informing the public as referred to in paragraph 3, Member States shall, where appropriate, pursue cooperation with third countries, with particular emphasis on accession candidate countries.

Article 9
Assessment of concentrations of ozone and precursor substances in ambient air

1. In zones and agglomerations where, during any of the previous five years of measurement, concentrations of ozone have exceeded a long-term objective, fixed continuous measurement is mandatory.

Where fewer than five years' data are available, Member States may, to determine exceedances, combine measurement campaigns of short duration at times and locations likely to be typical of the highest pollution levels with results obtained from emission inventories and modelling.

Annex IV sets out criteria for determining the location of sampling points for the measurement of ozone.

Section I of Annex V sets out the minimum number of fixed sampling points for continuous measurement of ozone in each zone or agglomeration within which measurement is the sole source of information for assessing air quality. Measurements of nitrogen dioxide shall also be made at a minimum of 50% of the ozone sampling points required by Section I of Annex V.

Measurement of nitrogen dioxide shall be continuous, except at rural background stations, as defined in section I of Annex IV, where other measurement methods may be used.

For zones and agglomerations within which information from sampling points for fixed measurement is supplemented by information from modelling and/or indicative measurement, the total number of sampling points specified in Section I of Annex V may be reduced, provided that:

(a) the supplementary methods provide an adequate level of information for the assessment of air quality with regard to target values, information and alert thresholds;

(b) the number of sampling points to be installed and the spatial resolution of other techniques are sufficient for the concentration of ozone to be established in accordance with the data quality objectives specified in Section I of Annex VII and lead to assessment results as specified in Section II of Annex VII;

(c) the number of sampling points in each zone or agglomeration amounts to at least one sampling point per two million inhabitants or one sampling point per 50 000 km^2, whichever produces the greater number of sampling points;

(d) each zone or agglomeration contains at least one sampling point, and

(e) nitrogen dioxide is measured at all remaining sampling points except at rural background stations.

In this case, the results of modelling and/or indicative measurement shall be taken into account for the assessment of air quality with respect to the target values.

2. In zones and agglomerations where, during each of the previous five years of measurement, concentrations are below the long-term objectives, the number of continuous measurement stations shall be determined in accordance with Section II of Annex V.

3. Each Member State shall ensure that at least one measuring station to supply data on concentrations of the ozone precursor substances listed in Annex VI is installed and operated in its territory. Each Member State shall choose the number and siting of the stations at which ozone precursor substances are to be measured, taking into account the objectives, methods and recommendations laid down in the said Annex.

As part of the guidance developed under Article 12, guidelines for an appropriate strategy to measure ozone precursor substances shall be laid down, taking into account existing requirements in Community legislation and the cooperative programme for monitoring and evaluation of the long-range transmission of air pollutants in Europe (EMEP).

4. Reference methods for analysis of ozone are set out in Section I of Annex VIII. Section II of Annex VIII provides for reference modelling techniques for ozone.

5. Any amendments necessary to adapt this Article and Annexes IV to VIII to scientific and technical progress shall be adopted in accordance with the procedure laid down in Article 13(2).

Article 10
Transmission of information and reports

1. When forwarding information to the Commission under Article 11 of Directive 96/62/EC, Member States shall also, and, for the first time, for the calendar year following the date referred to in Article 15(1):

(a) send to the Commission for each calendar year no later than 30 September of the following year the lists of zones and agglomerations referred to in Article 3(2), Article 4(2) and Article 5;
(b) send to the Commission a report giving an overview of the situation as regards exceedance of the target values as laid down in section II of Annex I. This report shall provide an explanation of annual exceedances of the target value for the protection of human health. The report shall also contain the plans and programmes referred to in Article 3(3). The report shall be sent no later than two years after the end of the period during which exceedances of the target values for ozone were observed;

(c) inform the Commission every three years of the progress of any such plan or programme.

2. Furthermore, Member States shall, for the first time, for the calendar year following the date referred to in Article 15(1):

(a) for each month from April to September each year, send to the Commission, on a provisional basis,
   (i) by no later than the end of the following month, for each day with exceedance(s) of the information and/or the alert threshold, the following information: date, total hours of exceedance, maximum 1 h ozone value(s);
  (ii) by no later than 31 October each year, any other information specified in Annex III;
(b) for each calendar year no later than 30 September of the following year, send to the Commission the validated information specified in Annex III and the annual average concentrations for that year of the ozone precursor substances specified in Annex VI;
(c) forward to the Commission every three years, within the framework of the sectoral report referred to in Article 4 of Council Directive 91/692/EEC,[1] and no later than 30 September following the end of each three-year period:
   (i) information reviewing the levels of ozone observed or assessed, as appropriate, in the zones and agglomerations referred to in Articles 3(2), Article 4(2) and Article 5;
  (ii) information on any measures taken or planned under Article 4(2), and
  (iii) information regarding decisions on short-term action plans and concerning the design and content, and an assessment of the effects, of any such plans prepared in accordance with Article 7.

3. The Commission shall:

(a) ensure that the information submitted pursuant to paragraph 2(a) is promptly made available by appropriate means and is transmitted to the European Environment Agency;
(b) publish annually a list of the zones and agglomerations submitted pursuant to paragraph 1(a) and, by 30 November each year, a report on the ozone situation during the current summer and the preceding calendar year, aiming to provide overviews, in a comparable format, of each Member State's situation, taking into account the different meteorological conditions and transboundary pollution, and an overview of all the exceedances of the long-term objective in the Member States;

---

[1] OJ L 377, 31.12.1991, p. 48.

(c) check regularly the implementation of the plans or programmes submitted pursuant to paragraph 1(b) by examining their progress and the trends in air pollution, taking account of meteorological conditions and the origin of the ozone precursors (biogenic or anthropogenic);

(d) take into account the information provided under paragraphs 1 and 2 in preparing three-yearly reports on ambient air quality in accordance with Article 11(2) of Directive 96/62/EC;

(e) arrange appropriate exchange of information and experience forwarded in accordance with paragraph 2(c)(iii) regarding the design and implementation of short-term action plans.

4. When carrying out the tasks referred to in paragraph 3, the Commission shall, as necessary, call upon the expertise available in the European Environment Agency.

5. The date by which Member States shall inform the Commission of the methods used for the preliminary assessment of air quality under Article 11(1)(d) of Directive 96/62/EC shall be no later than 9 September 2003.

Article 11
Review and reporting

1. The Commission shall submit to the European Parliament and the Council by 31 December 2004, at the latest, a report based on experience of the application of this Directive. It shall report, in particular, on:

(a) the findings of the most recent scientific research, in the light of the World Health Organisation's Guidelines, into the effects of exposure to ozone on the environment and human health, specifically taking into account sensitive population groups; the development of more accurate models shall be taken into account;

(b) technological developments, including progress achieved in methods of measuring and otherwise assessing concentrations and evolution of ozone concentrations throughout Europe;

(c) comparison of model predictions with actual measurements;

(d) the setting of, and levels for, long-term objectives, for target values, for information and alert thresholds;

(e) the results on the effects of ozone on crops and natural vegetation of the International Cooperative Programme under UN/ECE Convention on Long-range Transboundary Air Pollution.

2. The report shall be presented as an integral part of an air quality strategy designed to review and propose Community air quality objectives and develop implementing

strategies to ensure achievement of those objectives. In this context the report shall take into account:

(a) the broad scope for making further reductions in polluting emissions across all relevant sources, taking account of technical feasibility and cost-effectiveness;
(b) relationships between pollutants, and opportunities for combined strategies to achieve Community air quality and related objectives;
(c) the potential for further action to be taken at Community level in order to reduce precursor emissions;
(d) the progress in implementing the target values in Annex I, including the plans and programmes developed and implemented in accordance with Articles 3 and 4, the experience in implementing short-term action plans under Article 7 and the conditions, as laid down under Annex IV, under which air quality measurement has been carried out;
(e) the potential to achieve the long-term objectives, set out in Section III of Annex I, within a specified time period;
(f) current and future requirements for informing the public and for the exchange of information between Member States and the Commission;
(g) the relationship between this Directive and expected changes resulting from measures to be taken by the Community and Member States in order to fulfil commitments relating to climate change;
(h) transport of pollution across national boundaries taking account of measures taken in accession candidate countries.

3. The report shall also include a review of the provisions of this Directive in the light of its findings and it shall be accompanied, if appropriate, by proposals to amend this Directive, paying special attention to the effects of ozone on the environment and on human health, with particular reference to sensitive population groups.

Article 12
Guidance

1. The Commission shall develop guidance for implementing this Directive by 9 September 2002. In so doing, it will call upon the expertise available in the Member States, the European Environment Agency and other expert bodies, as appropriate and taking into account existing requirements in Community legislation and EMEP.

2. The guidance shall be adopted in accordance with the procedure laid down in Article 13(2). Such guidance shall not have the effect of modifying the target values, long-term objectives, alert threshold or information threshold either directly or indirectly.

Article 13
Committee procedure

1. The Commission shall be assisted by the committee established by Article 12(2) of Directive 96/62/EC.

2. Where reference is made to this paragraph, Articles 5 and 7 of Decision 1999/468/EC shall apply, having regard to the provisions of Article 8 thereof.

The period laid down in Article 5(6) of Decision 1999/468/EC shall be set at three months.

3. The committee shall adopt its rules of procedure.

Article 14
Penalties

Member States shall determine the penalties applicable to breaches of the national provisions adopted pursuant to this Directive. The penalties shall be effective, proportionate and dissuasive.

Article 15
Transposition

1. Member States shall bring into force the laws, regulations and administrative provisions necessary to comply with this Directive by 9 September 2003.They shall forthwith inform the Commission thereof.

When Member States adopt those measures, they shall contain a reference to this Directive or be accompanied by such a reference on the occasion of their official publication. Member States shall determine how such reference is to be made.

2. Member States shall communicate to the Commission the text of the main provisions of national law, which they adopt in the field covered by this Directive.

Article 16
Repeal

Directive 92/72/EEC shall be repealed from 9 September 2003.

Article 17
Entry into force

This Directive shall enter into force on the day of its publication in the *Official Journal of the European Communities.*

Article 18
Addressees

This Directive is addressed to the Member States.

Done at Brussels, 12 February 2002.

Annex I
Definitions, target values and long-term objectives for ozone

I. *Definitions*

All values are to be expressed in μg/m³. The volume must be standardised at the following conditions of temperature and pressure: 293 K and 101.3 kPa. The time is to be specified in Central European Time.

AOT40 (expressed in (μg/m³)· hours) means the sum of the difference between hourly concentrations greater than 80 μg/m³ (= 40 parts per billion) and 80 μg/m³ over a given period using only the 1 hour values measured between 8:00 and 20:00 Central European Time each day.[*]

In order to be valid, the annual data on exceedances used to check compliance with the target values and long-term objectives below must meet the criteria laid down in Section II of Annex III.

II. *Target values for ozone*

	Parameter	Target value for 2010[a,1]
1. Target value for the protection of human health	Maximum daily 8-hour mean[b]	120 μg/m³ not to be exceeded on more than 25 days per calender year averaged over three years[c]
2. Target value for the protection of vegetation	AOT40, calculated from 1 h values from May to July	18 000 μg/m³·h averaged over five years[c]

[a] Compliance with target values will be assessed as of this value. That is, 2010 will be the first year the data for which is used in calculating compliance over the following three or five years, as appropriate.

[b] The maximum daily 8-hour mean concentration shall be selected by examining 8-hour running averages, calculated from hourly data and updated each hour. Each 8-hour average so calculated shall be assigned to the day on which it ends, i.e. the first calculation period for any one day will be the period from 17:00 on the previous day to 01:00 on that day; the last calculation period for any one day will be the period from 16:00 to 24:00 on the day.

[c] If the three or five year averages cannot be determined on the basis of a full and consecutive set of annual data, the minimum annual data required for checking compliance with the target values will be as follows:

– for the target value for the protection of human health: valid data for one year,
– for the target value for the protection of vegetation: valid data for three years.

[1] These target values and permitted exceedance are set without prejudice to the results of the studies and of the review, provided for in Article 11, which will take account of the different geographical and climatic situations in the European Community.

[*] Or the appropriate time for ultra-peripheral regions.

III. *Long-term objectives for ozone*

	Parameter	Long-term objective[a]
1. Long-term objective for the protection of human health	Maximum daily 8-hour mean within a calender year	120 µg/m^3
2. Long-term objective for the protection of vegetation	AOT40, calculated from 1 h values from May to July	6000 µg/m^3·h

[a] Community progress towards attaining the long-term objective using the year 2020 as a benchmark shall be reviewed as part of the process set out in Article 11.

Annex II
Information and alert thresholds

I. *Information and alert thresholds for ozone*

	Parameter	Threshold
Information threshold	1 hour average	180 µg/m^3
Alert threshold	1 hour average[a]	240 µg/m^3

[a] For the implementation of Article 7, the exceedance of the threshold is to be measured or predicted for three consecutive hours.

II. *Minimum details to be supplied to the public when the information or alert threshold is exceeded or exceedance is predicted*

Details to be supplied to the public on a sufficiently large scale as soon as possible should include:

1. information on observed exceedance(s):
   - location or area of the exceedance,
   - type of threshold exceeded (information or alert),
   - start time and duration of the exceedance,
   - highest 1-hour and 8-hour mean concentration;
2. forecast for the following afternoon/day(s):
   - geographical area of expected exceedances of information and/or alert threshold,
   - expected change in pollution (improvement, stabilisation or deterioration);
3. information on type of population concerned, possible health effects and recommended conduct:
   - information on population groups at risk,
   - description of likely symptoms,
   - recommended precautions to be taken by the population concerned,
   - where to find further information;
4. information on preventive action to reduce pollution and/or exposure to it: indication of main source sectors; recommendations for action to reduce emissions.

Annex III

Information submitted by Member States to the Commission and criteria for aggregating data and calculating statistical parameters

I. *Information to be submitted to the Commission*

The following table stipulates the type and amount of data Member States are to submit to the Commission:

	Type of station	Level	Averaging/ accumulation time	Provisional data for each month from April to September	Report for each year
Information threshold	Any	180 μg/m^3	1 hour	– for each day with exceedance(s): date, total hours of exceedance, maximum 1 hour ozone and related NO$_2$ values when required, – monthly 1 hour maximum ozone	– for each day with exceedance(s): date, total hours of exceedance, maximum 1 hour ozone and related NO$_2$ values, when required
Alert threshold	Any	240 μg/m^3	1 hour	– for each day with exceedance(s): date, total hours of exceedance, maximum 1 hour ozone and related NO$_2$ values, when required	– for each day with exceedance(s): date, total hours of exceedance, maximum 1 hour ozone and related NO$_2$ values when required
Health protection	Any	120 μg/m^3	8 hours	– for each day with exceedance(s): date, 8 hours maximum^b	– for each day with exceedance(s): date, 8 hours maximum^b
Vegetation protection	Suburban, rural, rural background	AOT40 (a) = 6000 μg/m^3·h	1 hour, accumulated from May to July	–	Value
Forest protection	Suburban, rural, rural background	AOT40 (a) = 20 000 μg/m^3·h	1hour, accumulated from April to September	–	Value
Materials	Any	40 μg/m$^{3\,c}$	1 year	–	Value

^{a} See definition of AOT40 in Section I of Annex I.

^{b} Maximum daily 8-hour mean (see section II of Annex I note (a)).

^{c} Value to be reviewed, pursuant to Article 11(3), in the light of developing scientific knowledge.

As part of the yearly reporting, the following must also be provided, if all available hourly data for ozone, nitrogen dioxide and nitrogen oxides of the year in question have not already been delivered under the framework of Council Decision 97/101/EC:[1]

- for ozone, nitrogen dioxide, nitrogen oxides and the sums of ozone and nitrogen dioxide (added as parts per billion and expressed in μg/m³ ozone) the maximum, 99.9th, 98th, 50th percentile and annual average and number of valid data from hourly series,
- the maximum, 98th, 50th percentile and annual average from series of daily 8-hour ozone maxima.

Data submitted in the monthly reports are considered provisional and are to be updated, if necessary, in subsequent submissions.

II. *Criteria for aggregating data and calculating statistical parameters*
Percentiles are to be calculated using the method specified in Council Decision 97/101/EC.

The following criteria are to be used for checking validity when aggregating data and calculating statistical parameters:

Parameter	Required proportion of valid data
1 hour values	75% (i.e. 45 minutes)
8 hour values	75% of values (i.e. 6 hours)
Maximum daily 8 hours mean from hourly running 8 hours averages	75% of the hourly running 8 hours averages (i.e. 18 8 hours averages per day)
AOT40	90% of the 1 hour values over the time period defined for calculating the AOT40 value[a]
Annual mean	75% of the 1 hour values over summer (April to September) and winter (January to March, October to December) seasons separately
Number of exceedances and maximum values per month	90% of the daily maximum 8 hours mean values (27 available daily values per month)
	90% of the 1 hour values between 8:00 and 20:00 Central European Time
Number of exceedances and maximum values per year	five out of six months over the summer season (April to September)

[a] In cases where all possible measured data are not available, the following factor shall be used to calculated AOT40 values:

$$\text{AOT40[estimate]} = \text{AOT40}_{measured} \times \frac{\text{total possible number of hours*}}{\text{number of measured hourly values}}$$

* being the number of hours within the time period of AOT40 definition, (i.e. 08:00 to 20:00 h CET from 1 May to 31 July each year, for vegetation protection and from 1 April to 30 September each year for forest protection).

[1] OJ L 35, 5.2.1997, p. 14.

Annex IV
Criteria for classifying and locating sampling points for assessments of ozone
concentrations

The following considerations apply to fixed measurements:
I. *Macroscale siting*

Type of station	Objectives of measurement	Representativeness[a]	Macroscale siting criteria
Urban	**Protection of human health:** to assess the exposure of the urban population to ozone, i.e. where population density and ozone concentration are relatively high and representative of the exposure of the general population	A few km^2	Away from the influence of local emissions such as traffic, petrol stations, etc.; Vented locations where well mixed levels can be measured; Locations such as residential and commercial areas of cities, parks (away from the trees), big streets or squares with very little or no traffic, open areas characteristic of educational, sports or recreation facilities
Suburban	**Protection of human health and vegetation:** to assess the exposure of the population and vegetation located in the outskirts of the agglomeration, where the highest ozone levels, to which the population and vegetation is likely to be directly or indirectly exposed, occur	Some tens of km^2	At a certain distance from the area of maximum emissions, downwind following the main wind direction/direction during conditions favourable to ozone formation; Where population, sensitive crops or natural ecosystems located in the outer fringe of an agglomeration are exposed to high ozone levels; Where appropriate, some suburban stations also upwind of the area of maximum emissions, in order to determine the regional background levels of ozone
Rural	**Protection of human health and vegetation:** to assess the exposure of population, crops and natural ecosystems to sub-regional scale ozone concentrations	Sub-regional levels (a few km^2)	Stations can be located in small settlements and/or areas with natural ecosystems, forests or crops; Representative for ozone away from the influence of immediate local emissions such as industrial installations and roads; At open area sites, but not on higher mountaintops

Type of station	Objectives of measurement	Representativeness[a]	Macroscale siting criteria
Rural background	**Protection of vegetation and human health:** to assess the exposure of crops and natural ecosystems to regional-scale ozone concentrations as well as exposure of the population	Regional/national/ continental levels (1 000 to 10 000 km^2)	Station located in areas with lower population density, e.g. with natural ecosystems, forests, far removed from urban and industrial areas and away from local emissions; Avoid locations which are subject to locally enhanced formation of ground-near inversion conditions, also summits of higher mountains; Coastal sites with pronounced diurnal wind cycles of local character are not recommended.

[a] Sampling points should also, where possible, be representative of similar locations not in their immediate vicinity.

For rural and rural background stations, consideration should be given, where appropriate, to coordination with the monitoring requirements of Commission Regulation (EC) No 1091/94[1] concerning protection of the Community's forests against atmospheric pollution.

II. *Microscale siting*
The following guidelines should be followed, as far as practicable:

1. The flow around the inlet sampling probe should be unrestricted (free in an arc of at least 270°) without any obstructions affecting the air flow in the vicinity of the sampler, i.e. away from buildings, balconies, trees and other obstacles by more than twice the height the obstacle protrudes above the sampler.
2. In general, the inlet sampling point should be between 1.5 m (the breathing zone) and 4 m above the ground. Higher positions are possible for urban stations in some circumstances and in wooded areas.
3. The inlet probe should be positioned well away from such sources as furnaces and incineration flues and more than 10 m from the nearest road, with distance increasing as a function of traffic intensity.
4. The sampler's exhaust outlet should be positioned so as to avoid recirculation of exhaust air to the sampler inlet.

The following factors may also be taken into account:

1. interfering sources;
2. security;

[1] OJ L 125, 18.5.1994, p. 1.

3. access;
4. availability of electrical power and telephone communications;
5. visibility of the site in relation to its surroundings;
6. safety of public and operators;
7. the desirability of colocating sampling points for different pollutants;
8. planning requirements.

III. *Documentation and review of site selection*
Site selection procedures should be fully documented at the classification stage by such means as compass point photographs of the surroundings and a detailed map. Sites should be reviewed at regular intervals with repeated documentation to ensure that selection criteria are still being met.

This requires proper screening and interpretation of the monitoring data in the context of the meteorological and photochemical processes affecting the ozone concentrations measured at the respective sites.

Annex V
Criteria for determining the minimum number of sampling points for fixed measurement of concentrations of ozone

I. *Minimum number of sampling points for fixed continuous measurements to assess air quality in view of compliance with the target values, long-term objectives and information and alert thresholds where continuous measurement is the sole source of information*

Population (× 1 000)	Agglomerations (urban and suburban)[a]	Other zones (suburban and rural)[a]	Rural background
< 250		1	1 station/50 000 km² as an average density over all zones per country[b]
< 500	1	2	
< 1 000	2	2	
< 1 500	3	3	
< 2 000	3	4	
< 2 750	4	5	
< 3 750	5	6	
> 3 750	1 additional station per 2 million inhabitants	1 additional station per 2 million inhabitants	

[a] At least 1 station in suburban areas, where the highest exposure of the population is likely to occur. In agglomerations at least 50% of the stations should be located in suburban areas.
[b] 1 station per 25 000 km² for complex terrain is recommended.

II. *Minimum number of sampling points for fixed measurements for zones and agglomerations attaining the long-term objectives*
The number of sampling points for ozone must, in combination with other means of supplementary assessment such as air quality modelling and colocated nitrogen dioxide measurements, be sufficient to examine the trend of ozone pollution and check compliance with the long-term objectives. The number of stations located in agglomerations and other zones may be reduced to one-third of the number specified in Section I. Where information from fixed measurements stations is the sole source of information, at least one monitoring station should be kept. If, in zones where there is supplementary assessment, the result of this is that a zone has no remaining station, coordination with the number of stations in neighbouring zones must ensure adequate assessment of ozone concentrations against long-term objectives. The number of rural background stations should be 1 per 100 000 km^2.

Annex VI
Measurements of ozone precursor substances

Objectives
The main objectives of such measurements are to analyse any trend in ozone precursors, to check the efficiency of emission reduction strategies, to check the consistency of emission inventories and to help attribute emission sources to pollution concentration.

An additional aim is to support the understanding of ozone formation and precursor dispersion processes, as well as the application of photochemical models.

Substances
Measurements of ozone precursor substances must include at least nitrogen oxides, and appropriate volatile organic compounds (VOC). A list of volatile organic compounds recommended for measurement is given below.

	1-Butene	Isoprene	Ethyl benzene
Ethane	trans-2-Butene	n-Hexane	m+p-Xylene
Ethylene	cis-2-Butene	i-Hexane	o-Xylene
Acetylene	1.3-Butadiene	n-Heptane	1,2,4-Trimeth. benzene
Propane	n-Pentane	n-Octane	1,2,3-Trimeth. benzene
Propene	i-Pentane	i-Octane	1,3,5-Trimeth. benzene
n-Butane	1-Pentene	Benzene	Formaldehyde
i-Butane	2-Pentene	Toluene	Total non-methane hydrocarbons

Reference methods
The reference method specified in Directive 1999/30/CE[1] or in subsequent Community legislation will apply for nitrogen oxides.

[1] OJ L 163, 29.6.1999, p. 41.

Each Member State must inform the Commission of the methods it uses to sample and measure VOC. The Commission must carry out inter-comparison exercises as soon as possible and investigate the potential for defining reference methods for precursor sampling and measurement in order to improve the comparability and precision of measurements for the review of this Directive in accordance with Article 11.

Siting

Measurements should be taken in particular in urban and suburban areas at any monitoring site set up in accordance with the requirements of Directive 96/62/EC and considered appropriate with regard to the above monitoring objectives.

Annex VII

Data quality objectives and compilation of the results of air quality assessment

I. *Data quality objectives*

The following data quality objectives, for allowed uncertainty of assessment methods, and of minimum time coverage and of data capture of measurement are provided to guide quality-assurance programmes.

	For ozone, NO and NO_2
Continuous fixed measurement	
Uncertainty of individual measurements	15%
Minimum data capture	90% during summer
	75% during winter
Indicative measurement	
Uncertainty of individual measurements	30%
Minimum data capture	90%
Minimum time coverage	> 10% during summer
Modelling	
Uncertainty	
1 hour averages (daytime)	50%
8 hours daily maximum	50%
Objective estimation	
Uncertainty	75%

The uncertainty (on a 95% confidence interval) of the measurement methods will be evaluated in accordance with the principles of the ISO 'Guide to the Expression of Uncertainty in Measurement' (1993), or the methodology of ISO 5725-1 'Accuracy (trueness and precision) of measurement methods and results' (1994) or equivalent. The percentages for uncertainty in the table are given for individual measurements, averaged over the period for calculating target values and long-term objectives, for a 95% confidence interval. The uncertainty for continuous fixed measurements should be interpreted as being applicable in the region of the concentration used for the appropriate threshold.

The uncertainty for modelling and objective estimation is defined as the maximum deviation of the measured and calculated concentration levels, over the period for calculating the appropriate threshold, without taking into account the timing of the events.

'Time coverage' is defined as the percentage of the time considered for setting the threshold value during which the pollutant is measured.

'Data capture' is defined as the ratio of the time for which the instrument produces valid data, to the time for which the statistical parameter or aggregated value is to be calculated.

The requirements for minimum data capture and time coverage do not include losses of data due to the regular calibration or normal maintenance of the instrumentation.

II. *Results of air quality assessment*

The following information should be compiled for zones or agglomerations within which sources other than measurement are employed to supplement information from measurement:

— a description of the assessment activities carried out,
— specific methods used, with references to descriptions of the method,
— sources of data and information,
— a description of results, including uncertainties and, in particular, the extent of any area within the zone or agglomeration over which concentrations exceed long-term objectives or target values,
— for long-term objectives or target values whose object is the protection of human health, the population potentially exposed to concentrations in excess of the threshold.

Where possible, Member States should compile maps showing concentration distributions within each zone and agglomeration.

III. *Standardisation*

For ozone the volume must be standardised at the following conditions of temperature and pressure: 293 K, 101,3 kPa. For nitrogen oxides the standardisation specified in Directive 1999/30/EC will apply.

Annex VIII
Reference method for analysis of ozone and calibration of ozone instruments

I. *Reference method for analysis of ozone and calibration of ozone instruments*

— Analysis method: UV photometric method (ISO FDIS 13964),
— Calibration method: Reference UV photometer (ISO FDIS 13964, VDI 2468, B1.6).

This method is being standardised by the European Committee for Standardisation (CEN). Once the latter has published the relevant standard, the method and techniques described therein will constitute the reference and calibration method in this Directive.

A Member State may also used any other method which it can demonstrate gives results equivalent to the above method.

II. *Reference modelling technique for ozone*

Reference modelling techniques cannot be specified at present. Any amendments to adapt this point to scientific and technical progress will be adopted in accordance with the procedure laid down in Article 13(2).

Directive 2002/91/EC of the European Parliament and of the Council of 16 December 2002 on the energy performance of buildings

Editorial note

Directive 2002/91/EC of 16 December 2002 on the energy performance of buildings acknowledges the high levels of energy consumption associated with buildings and recognises that increased energy efficiency constitutes an important part of the package of policies and measures needed to comply with the Kyoto Protocol. The objective of this Directive is to promote the improvement of the energy performance of buildings, taking into consideration outdoor climate and local conditions, together with indoor climate requirements and cost effectiveness (Article 1). The Directive applies to buildings where energy is used to condition the indoor climate (Article 2). Member States are required to apply a methodology to calculate the energy performance of buildings based upon the framework set out in the Annex, which includes aspects such as thermal characteristics of the building, heating installation, air-conditioning, ventilation, built-in lighting, position and orientation of the building, passive solar systems, and indoor climatic conditions (Article 3).

Member States must take necessary measures to ensure that requirements for minimum energy consumption for buildings are set, taking into account general indoor climate conditions as well as local conditions and the designated function and age of the building. These energy performance requirements must be reviewed at least at five-yearly intervals and updated in order to reflect technical progress (Article 4(1)). Member States may decide not to set energy performance requirements for certain categories of buildings, including those that are officially protected, those used as places of worship, temporary buildings and those with low energy demands, residential buildings which are used for less than four months of the year, and stand-alone buildings with a total useful floor area of less than 50 m^2 (Article 4(3)). The Directive requires Member States to ensure that new buildings meet the minimum energy performance requirements (Article 5), whilst existing buildings with a total useful floor area over 1,000 m^2 must have their energy performance upgraded in order to meet minimum requirements when they have any major renovation (Article 6). Member States must ensure that when buildings are constructed, sold or rented out, an energy performance certificate is made available, the validity of which is not to exceed ten years (Article 7(1)). The energy performance certificates are to include reference values in order for consumers to compare and assess the energy performance of the building, and are to be accompanied by recommendations for the cost-effective improvement of the energy performance (Article 7(2)).

The Directive requires Member States to lay down measures establishing a regular inspection of boilers fired by non-renewable liquid or solid fuel of an effective rated output of 20 kW to 100 kW (Article 8). Similarly, Member States are also to lay down the necessary measures to establish a regular inspection of air-conditioning systems of an effective rated output of more than 12 kW (Article 9). The certification of buildings, drafting of accompanying recommendations and the inspection of boilers and air-conditioning systems must be carried out in an independent manner by qualified and/or accredited experts (Article 10).

The Directive is to be evaluated by the Commission, and a committee established by this Directive, with a view to making proposals regarding possible complementary measures referring to renovation in buildings and general incentives for further energy efficiency measures (Article 11). The Directive provides for Member States to inform users of buildings as to the different methods and practices that serve to enhance energy performance (Article 12) and makes provision for the periodic review and adaptation of points 1 and 2 of the Annex (Article 13). Member States must transpose the Directive into national law by 4 January 2006 at the latest (Article 15).

Source: OJ L 001 04.01.2003 p. 65

Directive 2002/91/EC of the European Parliament and of the Council of 16 December 2002 on the energy performance of buildings

The European Parliament and the Council of the European Union,
    Having regard to the Treaty establishing the European Community, and in particular Article 175(1) thereof,
    Having regard to the proposal from the Commission,[1]
    Having regard to the opinion of the Economic and Social Committee,[2]
    Having regard to the opinion of the Committee of the Regions,[3]
    Acting in accordance with the procedure laid down in Article 251 of the Treaty,[4]
    Whereas:

(1) Article 6 of the Treaty requires environmental protection requirements to be integrated into the definition and implementation of Community policies and actions.

---

[1] OJ C 213 E, 31.7.2001, p. 266 and OJ C 203 E, 27.8.2002, p. 69.   [2] OJ C 36, 8.2.2002, p. 20.
[3] OJ C 107, 3.5.2002, p. 76.
[4] Opinion of the European Parliament of 6 February 2002 (not yet published in the Official Journal), Council Common Position of 7 June 2002 (OJ C 197, 20.8.2002, p. 6) and decision of the European Parliament of 10 October 2002 (not yet published in the Official Journal).

(2) The natural resources, to the prudent and rational utilization of which Article 174 of the Treaty refers, include oil products, natural gas and solid fuels, which are essential sources of energy but also the leading sources of carbon dioxide emissions.

(3) Increased energy efficiency constitutes an important part of the package of policies and measures needed to comply with the Kyoto Protocol and should appear in any policy package to meet further commitments.

(4) Demand management of energy is an important tool enabling the Community to influence the global energy market and hence the security of energy supply in the medium and long term.

(5) In its conclusions of 30 May 2000 and of 5 December 2000, the Council endorsed the Commission's action plan on energy efficiency and requested specific measures in the building sector.

(6) The residential and tertiary sector, the major part of which is buildings, accounts for more than 40% of final energy consumption in the Community and is expanding, a trend which is bound to increase its energy consumption and hence also its carbon dioxide emissions.

(7) Council Directive 93/76/EEC of 13 September 1993 to limit carbon dioxide emissions by improving energy efficiency (SAVE),[1] which requires Member States to develop, implement and report on programmes in the field of energy efficiency in the building sector, is now starting to show some important benefits. However, a complementary legal instrument is needed to lay down more concrete actions with a view to achieving the great unrealised potential for energy savings and reducing the large differences between Member States' results in this sector.

(8) Council Directive 89/106/EEC of 21 December 1988 on the approximation of laws, regulations and administrative provisions of the Member States relating to construction products[2] requires construction works and their heating, cooling and ventilation installations to be designed and built in such a way that the amount of energy required in use will be low, having regard to the climatic conditions of the location and the occupants.

(9) The measures further to improve the energy performance of buildings should take into account climatic and local conditions as well as indoor climate environment and cost-effectiveness. They should not contravene other essential requirements concerning buildings such as accessibility, prudence and the intended use of the building.

(10) The energy performance of buildings should be calculated on the basis of a methodology, which may be differentiated at regional level, that includes, in addition to thermal insulation other factors that play an increasingly important role such as heating and air-conditioning installations, application of renewable

[1] OJ L 237, 22.9.1993, p. 28.
[2] OJ L 40, 11.2.1989, p. 12. Directive as amended by Directive 93/68/EEC (OJ L 220, 30.8.1993, p.1).

energy sources and design of the building. A common approach to this process, carried out by qualified and/or accredited experts, whose independence is to be guaranteed on the basis of objective criteria, will contribute to a level playing field as regards efforts made in Member States to energy saving in the buildings sector and will introduce transparency for prospective owners or users with regard to the energy performance in the Community property market.

(11) The Commission intends further to develop standards such as EN 832 and prEN 13790, also including consideration of air-conditioning systems and lighting.

(12) Buildings will have an impact on long-term energy consumption and new buildings should therefore meet minimum energy performance requirements tailored to the local climate. Best practice should in this respect be geared to the optimum use of factors relevant to enhancing energy performance. As the application of alternative energy supply systems is generally not explored to its full potential, the technical, environmental and economic feasibility of alternative energy supply systems should be considered; this can be carried out once, by the Member State, through a study which produces a list of energy conservation measures, for average local market conditions, meeting cost-effectiveness criteria.

Before construction starts, specific studies may be requested if the measure, or measures, are deemed feasible.

(13) Major renovations of existing buildings above a certain size should be regarded as an opportunity to take cost effective measures to enhance energy performance.

Major renovations are cases such as those where the total cost of the renovation related to the building shell and/or energy installations such as heating, hot water supply, air-conditioning, ventilation and lighting is higher than 25% of the value of the building, excluding the value of the land upon which the building is situated, or those where more than 25% of the building shell undergoes renovation.

(14) However, the improvement of the overall energy performance of an existing building does not necessarily mean a total renovation of the building but could be confined to those parts that are most relevant for the energy performance of the building and are cost-effective.

(15) Renovation requirements for existing buildings should not be incompatible with the intended function, quality or character of the building. It should be possible to recover additional costs involved in such renovation within a reasonable period of time in relation to the expected technical lifetime of the investment by accrued energy savings.

(16) The certification process may be supported by programmes to facilitate equal access to improved energy performance; based upon agreements between organisations of stakeholders and a body appointed by the Member States; carried out by energy service companies which agree to commit themselves to undertake the identified investments. The schemes adopted should be supervised and followed up by Member States, which should also facilitate the use of incentive

systems. To the extent possible, the certificate should describe the actual energy-performance situation of the building and may be revised accordingly. Public authority buildings and buildings frequently visited by the public should set an example by taking environmental and energy considerations into account and therefore should be subject to energy certification on a regular basis. The dissemination to the public of this information on energy performance should be enhanced by clearly displaying these energy certificates. Moreover, the displaying of officially recommended indoor temperatures, together with the actual measured temperature, should discourage the misuse of heating, air-conditioning and ventilation systems. This should contribute to avoiding unnecessary use of energy and to safeguarding comfortable indoor climatic conditions (thermal comfort) in relation to the outside temperature.

(17) Member States may also employ other means/measures, not provided for in this Directive, to encourage enhanced energy performance. Member States should encourage good energy management, taking into account the intensity of use of buildings.

(18) Recent years have seen a rise in the number of air-conditioning systems in southern European countries. This creates considerable problems at peak load times, increasing the cost of electricity and disrupting the energy balance in those countries. Priority should be given to strategies which enhance the thermal performance of buildings during the summer period. To this end there should be further development of passive cooling techniques, primarily those that improve indoor climatic conditions and the microclimate around buildings.

(19) Regular maintenance of boilers and of air-conditioning systems by qualified personnel contributes to maintaining their correct adjustment in accordance with the product specification and in that way will ensure optimal performance from an environmental, safety and energy point of view. An independent assessment of the total heating installation is appropriate whenever replacement could be considered on the basis of cost-effectiveness.

(20) The billing, to occupants of buildings, of the costs of heating, air-conditioning and hot water, calculated in proportion to actual consumption, could contribute towards energy saving in the residential sector. Occupants should be enabled to regulate their own consumption of heat and hot water, in so far as such measures are cost effective.

(21) In accordance with the principles of subsidiarity and proportionality as set out in Article 5 of the Treaty, general principles providing for a system of energy performance requirements and its objectives should be established at Community level, but the detailed implementation should be left to Member States, thus allowing each Member State to choose the regime which corresponds best to its particular situation. This Directive confines itself to the minimum required in order to achieve those objectives and does not go beyond what is necessary for that purpose.

(22) Provision should be made for the possibility of rapidly adapting the methodology of calculation and of Member States regularly reviewing minimum requirements in the field of energy performance of buildings with regard to technical progress, *inter alia*, as concerns the insulation properties (or quality) of the construction material, and to future developments in standardisation.

(23) The measures necessary for the implementation of this Directive should be adopted in accordance with Council Decision 1999/468/EC of 28 June 1999 laying down the procedures for the exercise of implementing powers conferred on the Commission,[1]

Have adopted this Directive:

Article 1
Objective

The objective of this Directive is to promote the improvement of the energy performance of buildings within the Community, taking into account outdoor climatic and local conditions, as well as indoor climate requirements and cost-effectiveness.

This Directive lays down requirements as regards:

(a) the general framework for a methodology of calculation of the integrated energy performance of buildings;
(b) the application of minimum requirements on the energy performance of new buildings;
(c) the application of minimum requirements on the energy performance of large existing buildings that are subject to major renovation;
(d) energy certification of buildings; and
(e) regular inspection of boilers and of air-conditioning systems in buildings and in addition an assessment of the heating installation in which the boilers are more than 15 years old.

Article 2
Definitions

For the purpose of this Directive, the following definitions shall apply:

1. 'building': a roofed construction having walls, for which energy is used to condition the indoor climate; a building may refer to the building as a whole or parts thereof that have been designed or altered to be used separately;
2. 'energy performance of a building': the amount of energy actually consumed or estimated to meet the different needs associated with a standardised use of the building, which may include, *inter alia*, heating, hot water heating, cooling, ventilation and lighting. This amount shall be reflected in one or more numeric indicators

---

[1] OJ L 184, 17.7.1999, p. 23.

which have been calculated, taking into account insulation, technical and installation characteristics, design and positioning in relation to climatic aspects, solar exposure and influence of neighbouring structures, own-energy generation and other factors, including indoor climate, that influence the energy demand;

3. 'energy performance certificate of a building': a certificate recognised by the Member State or a legal person designated by it, which includes the energy performance of a building calculated according to a methodology based on the general framework set out in the Annex;

4. 'CHP' (combined heat and power): the simultaneous conversion of primary fuels into mechanical or electrical and thermal energy, meeting certain quality criteria of energy efficiency;

5. 'air-conditioning system': a combination of all components required to provide a form of air treatment in which temperature is controlled or can be lowered, possibly in combination with the control of ventilation, humidity and air cleanliness;

6. 'boiler': the combined boiler body and burner-unit designed to transmit to water the heat released from combustion;

7. 'effective rated output (expressed in kW)': the maximum calorific output specified and guaranteed by the manufacturer as being deliverable during continuous operation while complying with the useful efficiency indicated by the manufacturer;

8. 'heat pump': a device or installation that extracts heat at low temperature from air, water or earth and supplies the heat to the building.

Article 3
Adoption of a methodology

Member States shall apply a methodology, at national or regional level, of calculation of the energy performance of buildings on the basis of the general framework set out in the Annex. Parts 1 and 2 of this framework shall be adapted to technical progress in accordance with the procedure referred to in Article 14(2), taking into account standards or norms applied in Member State legislation.

This methodology shall be set at national or regional level.

The energy performance of a building shall be expressed in a transparent manner and may include a CO_2 emission indicator.

Article 4
Setting of energy performance requirements

1. Member States shall take the necessary measures to ensure that minimum energy performance requirements for buildings are set, based on the methodology referred to in Article 3. When setting requirements, Member States may differentiate between new and existing buildings and different categories of buildings. These requirements shall take account of general indoor climate conditions, in order to avoid possible negative effects such as inadequate ventilation, as well as local conditions and the designated

function and the age of the building. These requirements shall be reviewed at regular intervals which should not be longer than five years and, if necessary, updated in order to reflect technical progress in the building sector.

2. The energy performance requirements shall be applied in accordance with Articles 5 and 6.

3. Member States may decide not to set or apply the requirements referred to in paragraph 1 for the following categories of buildings:

- buildings and monuments officially protected as part of a designated environment or because of their special architectural or historic merit, where compliance with the requirements would unacceptably alter their character or appearance,
- buildings used as places of worship and for religious activities,
- temporary buildings with a planned time of use of two years or less, industrial sites, workshops and non-residential agricultural buildings with low energy demand and nonresidential agricultural buildings which are in use by a sector covered by a national sectoral agreement on energy performance,
- residential buildings which are intended to be used less than four months of the year,
- stand-alone buildings with a total useful floor area of less than 50 m^2.

Article 5
New buildings

Member States shall take the necessary measures to ensure that new buildings meet the minimum energy performance requirements referred to in Article 4.

For new buildings with a total useful floor area over 1 000 m^2, Member States shall ensure that the technical, environmental and economic feasibility of alternative systems such as:

- decentralised energy supply systems based on renewable energy,
- CHP,
- district or block heating or cooling, if available,
- heat pumps, under certain conditions,

is considered and is taken into account before construction starts.

Article 6
Existing buildings

Member States shall take the necessary measures to ensure that when buildings with a total useful floor area over 1 000 m^2 undergo major renovation, their energy performance is upgraded in order to meet minimum requirements in so far as this is technically, functionally and economically feasible.

Member States shall derive these minimum energy performance requirements on the basis of the energy performance requirements set for buildings in accordance with

Article 4. The requirements may be set either for the renovated building as a whole or for the renovated systems or components when these are part of a renovation to be carried out within a limited time period, with the abovementioned objective of improving the overall energy performance of the building.

Article 7
Energy performance certificate

1. Member States shall ensure that, when buildings are constructed, sold or rented out, an energy performance certificate is made available to the owner or by the owner to the prospective buyer or tenant, as the case might be. The validity of the certificate shall not exceed 10 years.

Certification for apartments or units designed for separate use in blocks may be based:

- on a common certification of the whole building for blocks with a common heating system, or
- on the assessment of another representative apartment in the same block.

Member States may exclude the categories referred to in Article 4(3) from the application of this paragraph.

2. The energy performance certificate for buildings shall include reference values such as current legal standards and benchmarks in order to make it possible for consumers to compare and assess the energy performance of the building. The certificate shall be accompanied by recommendations for the cost-effective improvement of the energy performance.

The objective of the certificates shall be limited to the provision of information and any effects of these certificates in terms of legal proceedings or otherwise shall be decided in accordance with national rules.

3. Member States shall take measures to ensure that for buildings with a total useful floor area over 1 000 m^2 occupied by public authorities and by institutions providing public services to a large number of persons and therefore frequently visited by these persons an energy certificate, not older than 10 years, is placed in a prominent place clearly visible to the public.

The range of recommended and current indoor temperatures and, when appropriate, other relevant climatic factors may also be clearly displayed.

Article 8
Inspection of boilers

With regard to reducing energy consumption and limiting carbon dioxide emissions, Member States shall either:

(a) lay down the necessary measures to establish a regular inspection of boilers fired by non-renewable liquid or solid fuel of an effective rated output of 20 kW to 100 kW. Such inspection may also be applied to boilers using other fuels.

Boilers of an effective rated output of more than 100 kW shall be inspected at least every two years. For gas boilers, this period may be extended to four years.

For heating installations with boilers of an effective rated output of more than 20 kW which are older than 15 years, Member States shall lay down the necessary measures to establish a one-off inspection of the whole heating installation. On the basis of this inspection, which shall include an assessment of the boiler efficiency and the boiler sizing compared to the heating requirements of the building, the experts shall provide advice to the users on the replacement of the boilers, other modifications to the heating system and on alternative solutions; or

(b) take steps to ensure the provision of advice to the users on the replacement of boilers, other modifications to the heating system and on alternative solutions which may include inspections to assess the efficiency and appropriate size of the boiler. The overall impact of this approach should be broadly equivalent to that arising from the provisions set out in (a). Member States that choose this option shall submit a report on the equivalence of their approach to the Commission every two years.

Article 9
Inspection of air-conditioning systems

With regard to reducing energy consumption and limiting carbon dioxide emissions, Member States shall lay down the necessary measures to establish a regular inspection of air conditioning systems of an effective rated output of more than 12 kW.

This inspection shall include an assessment of the air-conditioning efficiency and the sizing compared to the cooling requirements of the building. Appropriate advice shall be provided to the users on possible improvement or replacement of the air-conditioning system and on alternative solutions.

Article 10
Independent experts

Member States shall ensure that the certification of buildings, the drafting of the accompanying recommendations and the inspection of boilers and air-conditioning systems are carried out in an independent manner by qualified and/or accredited experts, whether operating as sole traders or employed by public or private enterprise bodies.

Article 11
Review

The Commission, assisted by the Committee established by Article 14, shall evaluate this Directive in the light of experience gained during its application, and, if necessary, make proposals with respect to, *inter alia*:

(a) possible complementary measures referring to the renovations in buildings with a total useful floor area less than 1 000 m²;

(b) general incentives for further energy efficiency measures in buildings.

Article 12
Information

Member States may take the necessary measures to inform the users of buildings as to the different methods and practices that serve to enhance energy performance. Upon Member States' request, the Commission shall assist Member States in staging the information campaigns concerned, which may be dealt with in Community programmes.

Article 13
Adaptation of the framework

Points 1 and 2 of the Annex shall be reviewed at regular intervals, which shall not be shorter than two years.

Any amendments necessary in order to adapt points 1 and 2 of the Annex to technical progress shall be adopted in accordance with the procedure referred to in Article 14(2).

Article 14
Committee

1. The Commission shall be assisted by a Committee.

2. Where reference is made to this paragraph, Articles 5 and 7 of Decision 1999/468/EC shall apply, having regard to the provisions of Article 8 thereof.

The period laid down in Article 5(6) of Decision 1999/468/EC shall be set at three months.

3. The Committee shall adopt its Rules of Procedure.

Article 15
Transposition

1. Member States shall bring into force the laws, regulations and administrative provisions necessary to comply with this Directive at the latest on 4 January 2006. They shall forthwith inform the Commission thereof.

When Member States adopt these measures, they shall contain a reference to this Directive or shall be accompanied by such reference on the occasion of their official publication. Member States shall determine how such reference is to be made.

2. Member States may, because of lack of qualified and/or accredited experts, have an additional period of three years to apply fully the provisions of Articles 7, 8 and

9. When making use of this option, Member States shall notify the Commission, providing the appropriate justification together with a time schedule with respect to the further implementation of this Directive.

Article 16
Entry into force

This Directive shall enter into force on the day of its publication in the *Official Journal of the European Communities.*

Article 17
Addressees

This Directive is addressed to the Member States.

Done at Brussels, 16 December 2002.

Annex

General framework for the calculation of energy performance of buildings (Article 3)

1. The methodology of calculation of energy performances of buildings shall include at least the following aspects:

(a) thermal characteristics of the building (shell and internal partitions, etc.). These characteristics may also include air-tightness;
(b) heating installation and hot water supply, including their insulation characteristics;
(c) air-conditioning installation;
(d) ventilation;
(e) built-in lighting installation (mainly the non-residential sector);
(f) position and orientation of buildings, including outdoor climate;
(g) passive solar systems and solar protection;
(h) natural ventilation;
(i) indoor climatic conditions, including the designed indoor climate.

2. The positive influence of the following aspects shall, where relevant in this calculation, be taken into account:

(a) active solar systems and other heating and electricity systems based on renewable energy sources;
(b) electricity produced by CHP;
(c) district or block heating and cooling systems;
(d) natural lighting.

3. For the purpose of this calculation buildings should be adequately classified into categories such as:

(a) single-family houses of different types;
(b) apartment blocks;
(c) offices;
(d) education buildings;
(e) hospitals;
(f) hotels and restaurants;
(g) sports facilities;
(h) wholesale and retail trade services buildings;
(i) other types of energy-consuming buildings.

Directive 2003/30/EC of the European Parliament and of the Council of 8 May 2003 on the promotion of the use of biofuels or other renewable fuels for transport

Editorial note

Directive 2003/30/EC of 8 May 2003 is concerned with the promotion of the use of biofuels or other renewable fuels to replace diesel or petrol for transport purposes in each Member State (Article 1). The term 'biofuels' is defined to mean liquid or gaseous fuel for transport produced from biomass (Article 2(1)) and a list of some products considered to be biofuels is provided in Article 2(2). Member States should set national indicative targets to ensure that a minimum proportion of biofuels and other renewable fuels are placed on their markets, with a reference value for these targets of 2 percent and 5.75 percent for 31 December 2005 and 31 December 2010 respectively (Article 3(1)). The Directive provides that biofuels can be made available either as pure biofuels (or at high concentration in mineral oil derivatives), as biofuels blended in mineral oil derivatives, or as liquids derived from biofuels (Article 3(2)). Member States should consider the overall climate and environmental balance of the various types of biofuels and other renewable fuels and may give priority to the promotion of fuels which demonstrate a very good cost-effective environmental balance (Article 3(4)). Information should be given to the public on the availability of biofuels and other renewable fuels (Article 3(5)).

Member States are required to report to the Commission on the measures taken to promote the use of biofuels or other renewable fuels, the national resources allocated to the production of biomass for energy uses other than transport, and the total sale of transport fuel and the share of biofuels and other renewable fuels placed on the market (Article 4(1)). The Commission must report to the European Parliament and the Council by 31 December 2006 on the progress made in the use of biofuels and other renewable fuels in the Member States (Article 4(2)). The Directive allows for the list contained in Article 2(2) detailing the products considered to be biofuels to be adapted to technical progress (Article 5). The Commission will be assisted by a committee (Article 6), and Member States must transpose the Directive into national law by 31 December 2004 at the latest (Article 7).

Source: OJ L 123 17.05.2003 p. 42

Directive 2003/30/EC of the European Parliament and of the Council of 8 May 2003 on the promotion of the use of biofuels or other renewable fuels for transport

The European Parliament and the Council of the European Union,

Having regard to the Treaty establishing the European Community, and in particular Article 175(1) thereof,

Having regard to the proposal from the Commission,[1]

Having regard to the opinion of the European Economic and Social Committee,[2]

Having regard to the opinion of the Committee of the Regions,[3]

Acting in accordance with the procedure laid down in Article 251 of the Treaty,[4]

Whereas:

(1) The European Council meeting at Gothenburg on 15 and 16 June 2001 agreed on a Community strategy for sustainable development consisting in a set of measures, which include the development of biofuels.

(2) Natural resources, and their prudent and rational utilisation as referred to in Article 174(1) of the Treaty, include oil, natural gas and solid fuels, which are essential sources of energy but also the leading sources of carbon dioxide emissions.

(3) However, there is a wide range of biomass that could be used to produce biofuels, deriving from agricultural and forestry products, as well as from residues and waste from forestry and the forestry and agrifoodstuffs industry.

(4) The transport sector accounts for more than 30% of final energy consumption in the Community and is expanding, a trend which is bound to increase, along with carbon dioxide emissions and this expansion will be greater in percentage terms in the candidate countries following their accession to the European Union.

(5) The Commission White Paper 'European transport policy for 2010: time to decide' expects CO_2 emissions from transport to rise by 50% between 1990 and 2010, to around 1 113 million tonnes, the main responsibility resting with road transport, which accounts for 84% of transport-related CO_2 emissions. From an ecological point of view, the White Paper therefore calls for dependence on oil (currently 98%) in the transport sector to be reduced by using alternative fuels such as biofuels.

(6) Greater use of biofuels for transport forms a part of the package of measures needed to comply with the Kyoto Protocol, and of any policy package to meet further commitments in this respect.

---

[1] OJ C 103 E, 30.4.2002, p. 205 and OJ C 331 E, 31.12.2002, p. 291.

[2] OJ C 149, 21.6.2002, p. 7.   [3] OJ C 278, 14.11.2002, p. 29.

[4] Opinion of the European Parliament of 4 July 2002 (not yet published in the Official Journal), Council Common Position of 18 November 2002 (OJ C 32 E, 11.2.2003, p. 1) and decision of the European Parliament of 12 March 2003 (not yet published in the Official Journal).

(7) Increased use of biofuels for transport, without ruling out other possible alternative fuels, including automotive LPG and CNG, is one of the tools by which the Community can reduce its dependence on imported energy and influence the fuel market for transport and hence the security of energy supply in the medium and long term. However, this consideration should not detract in any way from the importance of compliance with Community legislation on fuel quality, vehicle emissions and air quality.

(8) As a result of technological advances, most vehicles currently in circulation in the European Union are capable of using a low biofuel blend without any problem. The most recent technological developments make it possible to use higher percentages of biofuel in the blend. Some countries are already using biofuel blends of 10% and higher.

(9) Captive fleets offer the potential of using a higher concentration of biofuels. In some cities captive fleets are already operating on pure biofuels and, in some cases, this has helped to improve air quality in urban areas. Member States could therefore further promote the use of biofuels in public transport modes.

(10) Promoting the use of biofuels in transport constitutes a step towards a wider application of biomass which will enable biofuel to be more extensively developed in the future, whilst not excluding other options and, in particular, the hydrogen option.

(11) The research policy pursued by the Member States relating to increased use of biofuels should incorporate the hydrogen sector to a significant degree and promote this option, taking into account the relevant Community framework programmes.

(12) Pure vegetable oil from oil plants produced through pressing, extraction or comparable procedures, crude or refined but chemically unmodified, can also be used as biofuel in specific cases where its use is compatible with the type of engines involved and the corresponding emission requirements.

(13) New types of fuel should conform to recognised technical standards if they are to be accepted to a greater extent by customers and vehicle manufacturers and hence penetrate the market. Technical standards also form the basis for requirements concerning emissions and the monitoring of emissions. Difficulties may be encountered in ensuring that new types of fuel meet current technical standards, which, to a large extent, have been developed for conventional fossil fuels. The Commission and standardisation bodies should monitor developments and adapt and develop actively standards, particularly volatility aspects, so that new types of fuel can be introduced, whilst maintaining environmental performance requirements.

(14) Bioethanol and biodiesel, when used for vehicles in pure form or as a blend, should comply with the quality standards laid down to ensure optimum engine performance. It is noted that in the case of biodiesel for diesel engines, where the processing option is esterification, the standard prEN 14214 of the European Committee for Standardisation (CEN) on fatty acid methyl esters (FAME) could

be applied. Accordingly, the CEN should establish appropriate standards for other transport biofuel products in the European Union.

(15) Promoting the use of biofuels in keeping with sustainable farming and forestry practices laid down in the rules governing the common agricultural policy could create new opportunities for sustainable rural development in a more market-orientated common agriculture policy geared more to the European market and to respect for flourishing country life and multifunctional agriculture, and could open a new market for innovative agricultural products with regard to present and future Member States.

(16) In its resolution of 8 June 1998,[1] the Council endorsed the Commission's strategy and action plan for renewable energy sources and requested specific measures in the biofuels sector.

(17) The Commission Green Paper 'Towards a European strategy for the security of energy supply' sets the objective of 20% substitution of conventional fuels by alternative fuels in the road transport sector by the year 2020.

(18) Alternative fuels will only be able to achieve market penetration if they are widely available and competitive.

(19) In its resolution of 18 June 1998,[2] the European Parliament called for an increase in the market share of biofuels to 2% over five years through a package of measures, including tax exemption, financial assistance for the processing industry and the establishment of a compulsory rate of biofuels for oil companies.

(20) The optimum method for increasing the share of biofuels in the national and Community markets depends on the availability of resources and raw materials, on national and Community policies to promote biofuels and on tax arrangements, and on the appropriate involvement of all stakeholders/parties.

(21) National policies to promote the use of biofuels should not lead to prohibition of the free movement of fuels that meet the harmonised environmental specifications as laid down in Community legislation.

(22) Promotion of the production and use of biofuels could contribute to a reduction in energy import dependency and in emissions of greenhouse gases. In addition, biofuels, in pure form or as a blend, may in principle be used in existing motor vehicles and use the current motor vehicle fuel distribution system. The blending of biofuel with fossil fuels could facilitate a potential cost reduction in the distribution system in the Community.

(23) Since the objective of the proposed action, namely the introduction of general principles providing for a minimum percentage of biofuels to be marketed and distributed, cannot be achieved sufficiently by the Member States by reason of the scale of the action, and can therefore be achieved better at Community level, the Community may adopt measures, in accordance with the principle of subsidiarity as set out in Article 5 of the Treaty. In accordance with the principle

---

[1] OJ C 198, 24.6.1998, p. 1.   [2] OJ C 210, 6.7.1998, p. 215.

of proportionality, as set out in that Article, this Directive does not go beyond what is necessary in order to achieve that objective.

(24) Research and technological development in the field of the sustainability of biofuels should be promoted.

(25) An increase in the use of biofuels should be accompanied by a detailed analysis of the environmental, economic and social impact in order to decide whether it is advisable to increase the proportion of biofuels in relation to conventional fuels.

(26) Provision should be made for the possibility of adapting rapidly the list of bio-fuels, the percentage of renewable contents, and the schedule for introducing biofuels in the transport fuel market, to technical progress and to the results of an environmental impact assessment of the first phase of introduction.

(27) Measures should be introduced for developing rapidly the quality standards for the biofuels to be used in the automotive sector, both as pure biofuels and as a blending component in the conventional fuels. Although the biodegradable fraction of waste is a potentially useful source for producing biofuels, the quality standard has to take into account the possible contamination present in the waste to avoid special components damaging the vehicle or causing emissions to deteriorate.

(28) Encouragement of the promotion of biofuels should be consistent with secu-rity of supply and environmental objectives and related policy objectives and measures within each Member State. In doing so, Member States may consider cost-effective ways of publicising the possibilities of using biofuels.

(29) The measures necessary for the implementation of this Directive should be adopted in accordance with Council Decision 1999/468/EC of 28 June 1999 laying down the procedures for the exercise of implementing powers conferred on the Commission,[1]

Have Adopted this Directive:

Article 1

This Directive aims at promoting the use of biofuels or other renewable fuels to replace diesel or petrol for transport purposes in each Member State, with a view to contributing to objectives such as meeting climate change commitments, environ-mentally friendly security of supply and promoting renewable energy sources.

Article 2

1. For the purpose of this Directive, the following definitions shall apply:

(a) 'biofuels' means liquid or gaseous fuel for transport produced from biomass;
(b) 'biomass' means the biodegradable fraction of products, waste and residues from agriculture (including vegetal and animal substances), forestry and related

---

[1] OJ L 184, 17.7.1999, p. 23.

industries, as well as the biodegradable fraction of industrial and municipal waste;

(c) 'other renewable fuels' means renewable fuels, other than biofuels, which originate from renewable energy sources as defined in Directive 2001/77/EC[1] and used for transport purposes;

(d) 'energy content' means the lower calorific value of a fuel.

2. At least the products listed below shall be considered biofuels:

(a) 'bioethanol': ethanol produced from biomass and/or the biodegradable fraction of waste, to be used as biofuel;

(b) 'biodiesel': a methyl-ester produced from vegetable or animal oil, of diesel quality, to be used as biofuel;

(c) 'biogas': a fuel gas produced from biomass and/or from the biodegradable fraction of waste, that can be purified to natural gas quality, to be used as biofuel, or woodgas;

(d) 'biomethanol': methanol produced from biomass, to be used as biofuel;

(e) 'biodimethylether': dimethylether produced from biomass, to be used as biofuel;

(f) 'bio-ETBE (ethyl-tertio-butyl-ether)': ETBE produced on the basis of bioethanol. The percentage by volume of bio-ETBE that is calculated as biofuel is 47%;

(g) 'bio-MTBE (methyl-tertio-butyl-ether)': a fuel produced on the basis of biomethanol. The percentage by volume of bio-MTBE that is calculated as biofuel is 36%;

(h) 'synthetic biofuels': synthetic hydrocarbons or mixtures of synthetic hydrocarbons, which have been produced from biomass;

(i) 'biohydrogen': hydrogen produced from biomass, and/or from the biodegradable fraction of waste, to be used as biofuel;

(j) 'pure vegetable oil': oil produced from oil plants through pressing, extraction or comparable procedures, crude or refined but chemically unmodified, when compatible with the type of engines involved and the corresponding emission requirements.

Article 3

1.

(a) Member States should ensure that a minimum proportion of biofuels and other renewable fuels is placed on their markets, and, to that effect, shall set national indicative targets.

---

[1] Directive 2001/77/EC of the European Parliament and of the Council of 27 September 2001 on the promotion of electricity produced from renewable energy sources in the internal electricity market (OJ L 283, 27.10.2001, p. 33).

(b)
  (i) A reference value for these targets shall be 2%, calculated on the basis of energy content, of all petrol and diesel for transport purposes placed on their markets by 31 December 2005.
  (ii) A reference value for these targets shall be 5,75%, calculated on the basis of energy content, of all petrol and diesel for transport purposes placed on their markets by 31 December 2010.

2. Biofuels may be made available in any of the following forms:

(a) as pure biofuels or at high concentration in mineral oil derivatives, in accordance with specific quality standards for transport applications;
(b) as biofuels blended in mineral oil derivatives, in accordance with the appropriate European norms describing the technical specifications for transport fuels (EN 228 and EN 590);
(c) as liquids derived from biofuels, such as ETBE (ethyl-tertiobutyl-ether), where the percentage of biofuel is as specified in Article 2(2).

3. Member States shall monitor the effect of the use of biofuels in diesel blends above 5% by non-adapted vehicles and shall, where appropriate, take measures to ensure compliance with the relevant Community legislation on emission standards.

4. In the measures that they take, the Member States should consider the overall climate and environmental balance of the various types of biofuels and other renewable fuels and may give priority to the promotion of those fuels showing a very good cost-effective environmental balance, while also taking into account competitiveness and security of supply.

5. Member States shall ensure that information is given to the public on the availability of biofuels and other renewable fuels. For percentages of biofuels, blended in mineral oil derivatives, exceeding the limit value of 5% of fatty acid methyl ester (FAME) or of 5% of bioethanol, a specific labelling at the sales points shall be imposed.

Article 4

1. Member States shall report to the Commission, before 1 July each year, on:

— the measures taken to promote the use of biofuels or other renewable fuels to replace diesel or petrol for transport purposes,
— the national resources allocated to the production of biomass for energy uses other than transport, and
— the total sales of transport fuel and the share of biofuels, pure or blended, and other renewable fuels placed on the market for the preceding year.

Where appropriate, Member States shall report on any exceptional conditions in the supply of crude oil or oil products that have affected the marketing of biofuels and other renewable fuels. In their first report following the entry into force of this

Directive, Member States shall indicate the level of their national indicative targets for the first phase. In the report covering the year 2006, Member States shall indicate their national indicative targets for the second phase. In these reports, differentiation of the national targets, as compared to the reference values referred to in Article 3(1)(b), shall be motivated and could be based on the following elements:

(a) objective factors such as the limited national potential for production of biofuels from biomass;
(b) the amount of resources allocated to the production of biomass for energy uses other than transport and the specific technical or climatic characteristics of the national market for transport fuels;
(c) national policies allocating comparable resources to the production of other transport fuels based on renewable energy sources and consistent with the objectives of this Directive.

2. By 31 December 2006 at the latest, and every two years thereafter, the Commission shall draw up an evaluation report for the European Parliament and for the Council on the progress made in the use of biofuels and other renewable fuels in the Member States. This report shall cover at least the following:

(a) the cost-effectiveness of the measures taken by Member States in order to promote the use of biofuels and other renewable fuels;
(b) the economic aspects and the environmental impact of further increasing the share of biofuels and other renewable fuels;
(c) the life-cycle perspective of biofuels and other renewable fuels, with a view to indicating possible measures for the future promotion of those fuels that are climate and environmentally friendly, and that have the potential of becoming competitive and cost-efficient;
(d) the sustainability of crops used for the production of biofuels, particularly land use, degree of intensity of cultivation, crop rotation and use of pesticides;
(e) the assessment of the use of biofuels and other renewable fuels with respect to their differentiating effects on climate change and their impact on CO_2 emissions reduction;
(f) a review of further more long-term options concerning energy efficiency measures in transport.

On the basis of this report, the Commission shall submit, where appropriate, proposals to the European Parliament and to the Council on the adaptation of the system of targets, as laid down in Article 3(1). If this report concludes that the indicative targets are not likely to be achieved for reasons that are unjustified and/or do not relate to new scientific evidence, these proposals shall address national targets, including possible mandatory targets, in the appropriate form.

Article 5

The list contained in Article 2(2) may be adapted to technical progress in accordance with the procedure referred to in Article 6(2). When adapting this list, the environmental impact of biofuels shall be taken into account.

Article 6

1. The Commission shall be assisted by a Committee.

2. Where reference is made to this paragraph, Articles 5 and 7 of Decision 1999/468/EC shall apply, having regard to the provisions of Article 8 thereof. The period laid down in Article 5(6) of Decision 1999/468/EC shall be set at three months.

3. The Committee shall adopt its Rules of Procedure.

Article 7

1. Member States shall bring into force the laws, regulations and administrative provisions necessary to comply with this Directive by 31 December 2004 at the latest. They shall forthwith inform the Commission thereof. When Member States adopt these measures, they shall contain a reference to this Directive or be accompanied by such reference on the occasion of their official publication. The methods of making such a reference shall be laid down by the Member States.

2. Member States shall communicate to the Commission the provisions of national law which they adopt in the field covered by this Directive.

Article 8

This Directive shall enter into force on the day of its publication in the *Official Journal of the European Union.*

Article 9

This Directive is addressed to the Member States.

Done at Brussels, 8 May 2003.

Directive 2003/87/EC of the European Parliament and of the Council of 13 October 2003 establishing a scheme for greenhouse gas emission allowance trading within the Community and amending Council Directive 96/61/EC

Editorial note

The Directive establishes a scheme for greenhouse gas emission allowance trading within the Community (the 'Community scheme') in order to promote reductions of greenhouse gas emissions in a cost-effective and economically efficient manner (Article 1). The Directive applies to emissions from the activities listed in Annex I and greenhouse gases listed in Annex II (Article 2(1)). It applies without prejudice to any requirements pursuant to Directive 96/61/EC (Article 2(2)). The specific terms used throughout the Directive are defined in Article 3.

The Directive requires that from 1 January 2005, no installation undertakes any activity listed in Annex I resulting in emissions specified in relation to that activity unless its operator holds a permit issued by a competent authority (Article 4). Detailed guidance is provided on what an application for a greenhouse gas emissions permit must include (Article 5), along with the conditions for and contents of a greenhouse gas emissions permit when issued by a competent authority (Article 6). The operator of an installation must inform the competent authority of any changes planned in the nature or functioning, or an extension, of the installation which may require updating of the greenhouse gas emissions permit (Article 7). Member States must ensure that where installations carry out activities that are included in Annex I to Directive 96/61/EC, the conditions of, and procedure for, the issue of a greenhouse gas emissions permit are coordinated with those for the permit provided for in that Directive (Article 8).

Member States must develop a national plan stating the total quantity of allowances that they intend to allocate for that period and how they propose to allocate them, based on the criteria set out in Annex III (Article 9). The Directive provides that for the three-year period beginning 1 January 2005, Member States must allocate at least 95 per cent of the allowances free of charge, whilst for the five-year period beginning 1 January 2008, Member States must allocate at least 90 per cent of the allowances free of charge (Article 10). Member States are required to determine the total quantity of allowances they will allocate for each specified period and the allocation of those allowances to the operator of each installation (Article 11). Member States may also allow operators to use certified emission reductions and emission reduction units from project activities in the Community scheme in some circumstances (Article 11a). Provision is also made for the transfer, surrender and cancellation of allowances (Article 12), which are valid for emissions during a specified period (Article 13). The Commission must adopt guidelines for the monitoring and reporting of emissions resulting from the activities listed in Annex I and Member States must ensure that emissions are monitored in accordance with these guidelines (Article 14(1)). Member States must ensure that each operator of an installation reports the emissions from that installation to the competent authority (Article 14(3)), and that the reports submitted by operators are verified in accordance with the criteria set out in Annex V (Article 15).

The Directive requires that Member States lay down rules on penalties applicable to infringements of the national provisions and take all measures necessary to ensure that such rules are implemented (Article 16). Decisions relating to the allocation of allowances, information on project activities in which a Member State participates or authorises other entities to participate, and the reports of emissions required under the greenhouse gas emissions permit must be made available to the public (Article 17). Member States must designate a competent authority (Article 18) and provide for the establishment and maintenance of a registry in order to ensure the accurate accounting of the issue, holding, transfer and cancellation of allowances (Article 19). The Commission must designate a Central Administrator to maintain an independent transaction log recording the issue, transfer and cancellation of allowances (Article 20). The Directive requires that Member States make an annual report to the Commission on the application of this Directive (Article 21). The Commission and the Member States must endeavour to support capacity-building activities in developing countries and countries with economies in transition in order to help them take full advantage of Joint Implementation and the Clean Development Mechanism (Article 21a). The Commission has some scope to make amendments to Annex III (Article 22) and will be assisted in its work by the committee instituted by Article 8 of Decision 93/389/EEC (Article 23).

From 2008, Member States may apply emission allowance trading to activities, installations and greenhouse gases which are not listed in Annex I, provided that inclusion of such activities, installations and greenhouse gases is approved by the Commission, whilst from 2005 Member States may under the same conditions apply emissions allowance trading to installations carrying out activities listed in Annex I below the capacity limits referred to in that Annex (Article 24).

The Directive stipulates that agreements should be concluded with third countries listed in Annex B to the Kyoto Protocol which have ratified the Protocol to provide for the mutual recognition of allowances between the Community scheme and other greenhouse gas emissions trading schemes (Article 25). Member States may apply to the Commission for installations to be temporarily excluded until 31 December 2007 at the latest from the Community scheme (Article 27), and amendments are made to Directive 96/61/EC (Article 26). Member States may allow operators of installations carrying out one of the activities listed in Annex I to form a pool of installations from the same activity (Article 28) and, in some circumstances, Member States may apply to the Commission for certain installations to be issued with additional allowances in cases of *force majeure* (Article 29). The Directive makes provision for the review and development of specific areas with a view to further developing the emission allowance trading scheme, including the benefits of Joint Implementation and Clean Development Mechanism projects (Article 30). Member States must transpose the Directive into national law by 31 December 2003 at the latest (Article 31).

The Directive 2003/87/EC has been amended by Directive 2004/101/EC of 27 October 2004 (the so-called Linking Directive) in respect of the Kyoto Protocol's project mechanisms (Joint Implementation and Clean Development Mechanisms). The text of the amending Directive is reproduced after the text of the Emission Trading Directive.

Source: OJ L 275 25.10.2003 p. 32

Directive 2003/87/EC of the European Parliament and of the Council of 13 October 2003 establishing a scheme for greenhouse gas emission allowance trading within the Community and amending Council Directive 96/61/EC

The European Parliament and the Council of the European Union,
    Having regard to the Treaty establishing the European Community, and in particular Article 175(1) thereof,
    Having regard to the proposal from the Commission,[1]
    Having regard to the opinion of the European Economic and Social Committee,[2]
    Having regard to the opinion of the Committee of the Regions,[3]
    Acting in accordance with the procedure laid down in Article 251 of the Treaty,[4]
    Whereas:

(1) The Green Paper on greenhouse gas emissions trading within the European Union launched a debate across Europe on the suitability and possible functioning of greenhouse gas emissions trading within the European Union. The

---

[1] OJ C 75 E, 26.3.2002, p. 33.   [2] OJ C 221, 17.9.2002, p. 27.   [3] OJ C 192, 12.8.2002, p. 59.
[4] Opinion of the European Parliament of 10 October 2002 (not yet published in the Official Journal), Council Common Position of 18 March 2003 (OJ C 125 E, 27.5.2003, p. 72), Decision of the European Parliament of 2 July 2003 (not yet published in the Official Journal) and Council Decision of 22 July 2003.

European Climate Change Programme has considered Community policies and measures through a multi-stakeholder process, including a scheme for greenhouse gas emission allowance trading within the Community (the Community scheme) based on the Green Paper. In its Conclusions of 8 March 2001, the Council recognised the particular importance of the European Climate Change Programme and of work based on the Green Paper, and underlined the urgent need for concrete action at Community level.

(2) The Sixth Community Environment Action Programme established by Decision No 1600/2002/EC of the European Parliament and of the Council[1] identifies climate change as a priority for action and provides for the establishment of a Community-wide emissions trading scheme by 2005. That Programme recognises that the Community is committed to achieving an 8% reduction in emissions of greenhouse gases by 2008 to 2012 compared to 1990 levels, and that, in the longer term, global emissions of greenhouse gases will need to be reduced by approximately 70% compared to 1990 levels.

(3) The ultimate objective of the United Nations Framework Convention on Climate Change, which was approved by Council Decision 94/69/EC of 15 December 1993 concerning the conclusion of the United Nations Framework Convention on Climate Change,[2] is to achieve stabilisation of greenhouse gas concentrations in the atmosphere at a level which prevents dangerous anthropogenic interference with the climate system.

(4) Once it enters into force, the Kyoto Protocol, which was approved by Council Decision 2002/358/EC of 25 April 2002 concerning the approval, on behalf of the European Community, of the Kyoto Protocol to the United Nations Framework Convention on Climate Change and the joint fulfilment of commitments thereunder,[3] will commit the Community and its Member States to reducing their aggregate anthropogenic emissions of greenhouse gases listed in Annex A to the Protocol by 8% compared to 1990 levels in the period 2008 to 2012.

(5) The Community and its Member States have agreed to fulfil their commitments to reduce anthropogenic greenhouse gas emissions under the Kyoto Protocol jointly, in accordance with Decision 2002/358/EC. This Directive aims to contribute to fulfilling the commitments of the European Community and its Member States more effectively, through an efficient European market in greenhouse gas emission allowances, with the least possible diminution of economic development and employment.

(6) Council Decision 93/389/EEC of 24 June 1993 for a monitoring mechanism of Community CO_2 and other greenhouse gas emissions,[4] established a

---

[1] OJ L 242, 10.9.2002, p. 1.   [2] OJ L 33, 7.2.1994, p. 11.   [3] OJ L 130, 15.5.2002, p. 1.
[4] OJ L 167, 09.7.1993, p. 31. Decision as amended by Decision 1999/296/EC (OJ L 117, 5.5.1999, p. 35).

mechanism for monitoring greenhouse gas emissions and evaluating progress towards meeting commitments in respect of these emissions. This mechanism will assist Member States in determining the total quantity of allowances to allocate.

(7) Community provisions relating to allocation of allowances by the Member States are necessary to contribute to preserving the integrity of the internal market and to avoid distortions of competition.

(8) Member States should have regard when allocating allowances to the potential for industrial process activities to reduce emissions.

(9) Member States may provide that they only issue allowances valid for a five-year period beginning in 2008 to persons in respect of allowances cancelled, corresponding to emission reductions made by those persons on their national territory during a three-year period beginning in 2005.

(10) Starting with the said five-year period, transfers of allowances to another Member State will involve corresponding adjustments of assigned amount units under the Kyoto Protocol.

(11) Member States should ensure that the operators of certain specified activities hold a greenhouse gas emissions permit and that they monitor and report their emissions of greenhouse gases specified in relation to those activities.

(12) Member States should lay down rules on penalties applicable to infringements of this Directive and ensure that they are implemented. Those penalties must be effective, proportionate and dissuasive.

(13) In order to ensure transparency, the public should have access to information relating to the allocation of allowances and to the results of monitoring of emissions, subject only to restrictions provided for in Directive 2003/4/EC of the European Parliament and of the Council of 28 January 2003 on public access to environmental information.[1]

(14) Member States should submit a report on the implementation of this Directive drawn up on the basis of Council Directive 91/692/EEC of 23 December 1991 standardising and rationalising reports on the implementation of certain Directives relating to the environment.[2]

(15) The inclusion of additional installations in the Community scheme should be in accordance with the provisions laid down in this Directive, and the coverage of the Community scheme may thereby be extended to emissions of greenhouse gases other than carbon dioxide, *inter alia* from aluminium and chemicals activities.

(16) This Directive should not prevent any Member State from maintaining or establishing national trading schemes regulating emissions of greenhouse gases from activities other than those listed in Annex I or included in the Community

---

[1] OJ L 41, 14.2.2003, p. 26.   [2] OJ L 377, 31.12.1991, p. 48.

scheme, or from installations temporarily excluded from the Community scheme.

(17) Member States may participate in international emissions trading as Parties to the Kyoto Protocol with any other Party included in Annex B thereto.

(18) Linking the Community scheme to greenhouse gas emission trading schemes in third countries will increase the cost-effectiveness of achieving the Community emission reductions target as laid down in Decision 2002/358/EC on the joint fulfilment of commitments.

(19) Project-based mechanisms including Joint Implementation (JI) and the Clean Development Mechanism (CDM) are important to achieve the goals of both reducing global greenhouse gas emissions and increasing the cost effective functioning of the Community scheme. In accordance with the relevant provisions of the Kyoto Protocol and Marrakech Accords, the use of the mechanisms should be supplemental to domestic action and domestic action will thus constitute a significant element of the effort made.

(20) This Directive will encourage the use of more energy efficient technologies, including combined heat and power technology, producing less emissions per unit of output, while the future directive of the European Parliament and of the Council on the promotion of cogeneration based on useful heat demand in the internal energy market will specifically promote combined heat and power technology.

(21) Council Directive 96/61/EC of 24 September 1996 concerning integrated pollution prevention and control[1] establishes a general framework for pollution prevention and control, through which greenhouse gas emissions permits may be issued. Directive 96/61/EC should be amended to ensure that emission limit values are not set for direct emissions of greenhouse gases from an installation subject to this Directive and that Member States may choose not to impose requirements relating to energy efficiency in respect of combustion units or other units emitting carbon dioxide on the site, without prejudice to any other requirements pursuant to Directive 96/61/EC.

(22) This Directive is compatible with the United Nations Framework Convention on Climate Change and the Kyoto Protocol. It should be reviewed in the light of developments in that context and to take into account experience in its implementation and progress achieved in monitoring of emissions of greenhouse gases.

(23) Emission allowance trading should form part of a comprehensive and coherent package of policies and measures implemented at Member State and Community level. Without prejudice to the application of Articles 87 and 88 of the Treaty, where activities are covered by the Community scheme, Member States may consider the implications of regulatory, fiscal or other policies that pursue the

[1] OJ L 257, 10.10.1996, p. 26.

same objectives. The review of the Directive should consider the extent to which these objectives have been attained.

(24) The instrument of taxation can be a national policy to limit emissions from installations temporarily excluded.

(25) Policies and measures should be implemented at Member State and Community level across all sectors of the European Union economy, and not only within the industry and energy sectors, in order to generate substantial emissions reductions. The Commission should, in particular, consider policies and measures at Community level in order that the transport sector makes a substantial contribution to the Community and its Member States meeting their climate change obligations under the Kyoto Protocol.

(26) Notwithstanding the multifaceted potential of market based mechanisms, the European Union strategy for climate change mitigation should be built on a balance between the Community scheme and other types of Community, domestic and international action.

(27) This Directive respects the fundamental rights and observes the principles recognised in particular by the Charter of Fundamental Rights of the European Union.

(28) The measures necessary for the implementation of this Directive should be adopted in accordance with Council Decision 1999/468/EC of 28 June 1999 laying down the procedures for the exercise of implementing powers conferred on the Commission.[1]

(29) As the criteria (1), (5) and (7) of Annex III cannot be amended through comitology, amendments in respect of periods after 2012 should only be made through codecision.

(30) Since the objective of the proposed action, the establishment of a Community scheme, cannot be sufficiently achieved by the Member States acting individually, and can therefore by reason of the scale and effects of the proposed action be better achieved at Community level, the Community may adopt measures, in accordance with the principle of subsidiarity as set out in Article 5 of the Treaty. In accordance with the principle of proportionality, as set out in that Article, this Directive does not go beyond what is necessary in order to achieve that objective,

Have Adopted this Directive:

Article 1
Subject matter

This Directive establishes a scheme for greenhouse gas emission allowance trading within the Community (hereinafter referred to as the 'Community scheme') in order

---

[1] OJ L 184, 17.7.1999, p. 23.

to promote reductions of greenhouse gas emissions in a cost-effective and economically efficient manner.

Article 2
Scope

1. This Directive shall apply to emissions from the activities listed in Annex I and greenhouse gases listed in Annex II.

2. This Directive shall apply without prejudice to any requirements pursuant to Directive 96/61/EC.

Article 3
Definitions

For the purposes of this Directive the following definitions shall apply:

(a) 'allowance' means an allowance to emit one tonne of carbon dioxide equivalent during a specified period, which shall be valid only for the purposes of meeting the requirements of this Directive and shall be transferable in accordance with the provisions of this Directive;

(b) 'emissions' means the release of greenhouse gases into the atmosphere from sources in an installation;

(c) 'greenhouse gases' means the gases listed in Annex II;

(d) 'greenhouse gas emissions permit' means the permit issued in accordance with Articles 5 and 6;

(e) 'installation' means a stationary technical unit where one or more activities listed in Annex I are carried out and any other directly associated activities which have a technical connection with the activities carried out on that site and which could have an effect on emissions and pollution;

(f) 'operator' means any person who operates or controls an installation or, where this is provided for in national legislation, to whom decisive economic power over the technical functioning of the installation has been delegated;

(g) 'person' means any natural or legal person;

(h) 'new entrant' means any installation carrying out one or more of the activities indicated in Annex I, which has obtained a greenhouse gas emissions permit or an update of its greenhouse gas emissions permit because of a change in the nature or functioning or an extension of the installation, subsequent to the notification to the Commission of the national allocation plan;

(i) 'the public' means one or more persons and, in accordance with national legislation or practice, associations, organisations or groups of persons;

(j) 'tonne of carbon dioxide equivalent' means one metric tonne of carbon dioxide (CO_2) or an amount of any other greenhouse gas listed in Annex II with an equivalent global-warming potential.

Article 4
Greenhouse gas emissions permits

Member States shall ensure that, from 1 January 2005, no installation undertakes any activity listed in Annex I resulting in emissions specified in relation to that activity unless its operator holds a permit issued by a competent authority in accordance with Articles 5 and 6, or the installation is temporarily excluded from the Community scheme pursuant to Article 27.

Article 5
Applications for greenhouse gas emissions permits

An application to the competent authority for a greenhouse gas emissions permit shall include a description of:

(a) the installation and its activities including the technology used;
(b) the raw and auxiliary materials, the use of which is likely to lead to emissions of gases listed in Annex I;
(c) the sources of emissions of gases listed in Annex I from the installation; and
(d) the measures planned to monitor and report emissions in accordance with the guidelines adopted pursuant to Article 14. The application shall also include a non-technical summary of the details referred to in the first subparagraph.

Article 6
Conditions for and contents of the greenhouse gas emissions permit

1. The competent authority shall issue a greenhouse gas emissions permit granting authorisation to emit greenhouse gases from all or part of an installation if it is satisfied that the operator is capable of monitoring and reporting emissions. A greenhouse gas emissions permit may cover one or more installations on the same site operated by the same operator.

2. Greenhouse gas emissions permits shall contain the following:

(a) the name and address of the operator;
(b) a description of the activities and emissions from the installation;
(c) monitoring requirements, specifying monitoring methodology and frequency;
(d) reporting requirements; and
(e) an obligation to surrender allowances equal to the total emissions of the installation in each calendar year, as verified in accordance with Article 15, within four months following the end of that year.

Article 7
Changes relating to installations

The operator shall inform the competent authority of any changes planned in the nature or functioning, or an extension, of the installation which may require updating of the greenhouse gas emissions permit. Where appropriate, the competent authority shall update the permit. Where there is a change in the identity of the installation's operator, the competent authority shall update the permit to include the name and address of the new operator.

Article 8
Coordination with Directive 96/61/EC

Member States shall take the necessary measures to ensure that, where installations carry out activities that are included in Annex I to Directive 96/61/EC, the conditions of, and procedure for, the issue of a greenhouse gas emissions permit are coordinated with those for the permit provided for in that Directive. The requirements of Articles 5, 6 and 7 of this Directive may be integrated into the procedures provided for in Directive 96/61/EC.

Article 9
National allocation plan

1. For each period referred to in Article 11(1) and (2), each Member State shall develop a national plan stating the total quantity of allowances that it intends to allocate for that period and how it proposes to allocate them. The plan shall be based on objective and transparent criteria, including those listed in Annex III, taking due account of comments from the public. The Commission shall, without prejudice to the Treaty, by 31 December 2003 at the latest develop guidance on the implementation of the criteria listed in Annex III. For the period referred to in Article 11(1), the plan shall be published and notified to the Commission and to the other Member States by 31 March 2004 at the latest. For subsequent periods, the plan shall be published and notified to the Commission and to the other Member States at least 18 months before the beginning of the relevant period.

2. National allocation plans shall be considered within the committee referred to in Article 23(1).

3. Within three months of notification of a national allocation plan by a Member State under paragraph 1, the Commission may reject that plan, or any aspect thereof, on the basis that it is incompatible with the criteria listed in Annex III or with Article 10. The Member State shall only take a decision under Article 11(1) or (2) if proposed amendments are accepted by the Commission. Reasons shall be given for any rejection decision by the Commission.

Article 10
Method of allocation

For the three-year period beginning 1 January 2005 Member States shall allocate at least 95% of the allowances free of charge. For the five-year period beginning 1 January 2008, Member States shall allocate at least 90% of the allowances free of charge.

Article 11
Allocation and issue of allowances

1. For the three-year period beginning 1 January 2005, each Member State shall decide upon the total quantity of allowances it will allocate for that period and the allocation of those allowances to the operator of each installation. This decision shall be taken at least three months before the beginning of the period and be based on its national allocation plan developed pursuant to Article 9 and in accordance with Article 10, taking due account of comments from the public.

2. For the five-year period beginning 1 January 2008, and for each subsequent five-year period, each Member State shall decide upon the total quantity of allowances it will allocate for that period and initiate the process for the allocation of those allowances to the operator of each installation. This decision shall be taken at least 12 months before the beginning of the relevant period and be based on the Member State's national allocation plan developed pursuant to Article 9 and in accordance with Article 10, taking due account of comments from the public.

3. Decisions taken pursuant to paragraph 1 or 2 shall be in accordance with the requirements of the Treaty, in particular Articles 87 and 88 thereof. When deciding upon allocation, Member States shall take into account the need to provide access to allowances for new entrants.

4. The competent authority shall issue a proportion of the total quantity of allowances each year of the period referred to in paragraph 1 or 2, by 28 February of that year.

Article 12
Transfer, surrender and cancellation of allowances

1. Member States shall ensure that allowances can be transferred between:

(a) persons within the Community;
(b) persons within the Community and persons in third countries, where such allowances are recognised in accordance with the procedure referred to in Article 25 without restrictions other than those contained in, or adopted pursuant to, this Directive.

2. Member States shall ensure that allowances issued by a competent authority of another Member State are recognised for the purpose of meeting an operator's obligations under paragraph 3.

3. Member States shall ensure that, by 30 April each year at the latest, the operator of each installation surrenders a number of allowances equal to the total emissions from that installation during the preceding calendar year as verified in accordance with Article 15, and that these are subsequently cancelled.

4. Member States shall take the necessary steps to ensure that allowances will be cancelled at any time at the request of the person holding them.

Article 13
Validity of allowances

1. Allowances shall be valid for emissions during the period referred to in Article 11(1) or (2) for which they are issued.

2. Four months after the beginning of the first five-year period referred to in Article 11(2), allowances which are no longer valid and have not been surrendered and cancelled in accordance with Article 12(3) shall be cancelled by the competent authority. Member States may issue allowances to persons for the current period to replace any allowances held by them which are cancelled in accordance with the first subparagraph.

3. Four months after the beginning of each subsequent five-year period referred to in Article 11(2), allowances which are no longer valid and have not been surrendered and cancelled in accordance with Article 12(3) shall be cancelled by the competent authority.

Member States shall issue allowances to persons for the current period to replace any allowances held by them which are cancelled in accordance with the first subparagraph.

Article 14
Guidelines for monitoring and reporting of emissions

1. The Commission shall adopt guidelines for monitoring and reporting of emissions resulting from the activities listed in Annex I of greenhouse gases specified in relation to those activities, in accordance with the procedure referred to in Article 23(2), by 30 September 2003. The guidelines shall be based on the principles for monitoring and reporting set out in Annex IV.

2. Member States shall ensure that emissions are monitored in accordance with the guidelines.

3. Member States shall ensure that each operator of an installation reports the emissions from that installation during each calendar year to the competent authority after the end of that year in accordance with the guidelines.

Article 15
Verification

Member States shall ensure that the reports submitted by operators pursuant to Article 14(3) are verified in accordance with the criteria set out in Annex V, and that the competent authority is informed thereof. Member States shall ensure that an operator whose report has not been verified as satisfactory in accordance with the criteria set out in Annex V by 31 March each year for emissions during the preceding year cannot make further transfers of allowances until a report from that operator has been verified as satisfactory.

Article 16
Penalties

1. Member States shall lay down the rules on penalties applicable to infringements of the national provisions adopted pursuant to this Directive and shall take all measures necessary to ensure that such rules are implemented. The penalties provided for must be effective, proportionate and dissuasive. Member States shall notify these provisions to the Commission by 31 December 2003 at the latest, and shall notify it without delay of any subsequent amendment affecting them.

2. Member States shall ensure publication of the names of operators who are in breach of requirements to surrender sufficient allowances under Article 12(3).

3. Member States shall ensure that any operator who does not surrender sufficient allowances by 30 April of each year to cover its emissions during the preceding year shall be held liable for the payment of an excess emissions penalty. The excess emissions penalty shall be EUR 100 for each tonne of carbon dioxide equivalent emitted by that installation for which the operator has not surrendered allowances. Payment of the excess emissions penalty shall not release the operator from the obligation to surrender an amount of allowances equal to those excess emissions when surrendering allowances in relation to the following calendar year.

4. During the three-year period beginning 1 January 2005, Member States shall apply a lower excess emissions penalty of EUR 40 for each tonne of carbon dioxide equivalent emitted by that installation for which the operator has not surrendered allowances. Payment of the excess emissions penalty shall not release the operator from the obligation to surrender an amount of allowances equal to those excess emissions when surrendering allowances in relation to the following calendar year.

Article 17
Access to information

Decisions relating to the allocation of allowances and the reports of emissions required under the greenhouse gas emissions permit and held by the competent authority shall be made available to the public by that authority subject to the restrictions laid down in Article 3(3) and Article 4 of Directive 2003/4/EC.

Article 18
Competent authority

Member States shall make the appropriate administrative arrangements, including the designation of the appropriate competent authority or authorities, for the implementation of the rules of this Directive. Where more than one competent authority is designated, the work of these authorities undertaken pursuant to this Directive must be coordinated.

Article 19
Registries

1. Member States shall provide for the establishment and maintenance of a registry in order to ensure the accurate accounting of the issue, holding, transfer and cancellation of allowances. Member States may maintain their registries in a consolidated system, together with one or more other Member States.

2. Any person may hold allowances. The registry shall be accessible to the public and shall contain separate accounts to record the allowances held by each person to whom and from whom allowances are issued or transferred.

3. In order to implement this Directive, the Commission shall adopt a Regulation in accordance with the procedure referred to in Article 23(2) for a standardised and secured system of registries in the form of standardised electronic databases containing common data elements to track the issue, holding, transfer and cancellation of allowances, to provide for public access and confidentiality as appropriate and to ensure that there are no transfers incompatible with obligations resulting from the Kyoto Protocol.

Article 20
Central Administrator

1. The Commission shall designate a Central Administrator to maintain an independent transaction log recording the issue, transfer and cancellation of allowances.

2. The Central Administrator shall conduct an automated check on each transaction in registries through the independent transaction log to ensure there are no irregularities in the issue, transfer and cancellation of allowances.

3. If irregularities are identified through the automated check, the Central Administrator shall inform the Member State or Member States concerned who shall not register the transactions in question or any further transactions relating to the allowances concerned until the irregularities have been resolved.

Article 21
Reporting by Member States

1. Each year the Member States shall submit to the Commission a report on the application of this Directive. This report shall pay particular attention to the arrangements for the allocation of allowances, the operation of registries, the application of the monitoring and reporting guidelines, verification and issues relating to compliance with the Directive and on the fiscal treatment of allowances, if any. The first report shall be sent to the Commission by 30 June 2005. The report shall be drawn up on the basis of a questionnaire or outline drafted by the Commission in accordance with the procedure laid down in Article 6 of Directive 91/692/EEC. The questionnaire or outline shall be sent to Member States at least six months before the deadline for the submission of the first report.

2. On the basis of the reports referred to in paragraph 1, the Commission shall publish a report on the application of this Directive within three months of receiving the reports from the Member States.

3. The Commission shall organise an exchange of information between the competent authorities of the Member States concerning developments relating to issues of allocation, the operation of registries, monitoring, reporting, verification and compliance.

Article 22
Amendments to Annex III

The Commission may amend Annex III, with the exception of criteria (1), (5) and (7), for the period from 2008 to 2012 in the light of the reports provided for in Article 21 and of the experience of the application of this Directive, in accordance with the procedure referred to in Article 23(2).

Article 23
Committee

1. The Commission shall be assisted by the committee instituted by Article 8 of Decision 93/389/EEC.

2. Where reference is made to this paragraph, Articles 5 and 7 of Decision 1999/468/EC shall apply, having regard to the provisions of Article 8 thereof. The period laid down in Article 5(6) of Decision 1999/468/EC shall be set at three months.

3. The Committee shall adopt its rules of procedure.

Article 24
Procedures for unilateral inclusion of additional activities and gases

1. From 2008, Member States may apply emission allowance trading in accordance with this Directive to activities, installations and greenhouse gases which are not listed in Annex I, provided that inclusion of such activities, installations and greenhouse gases is approved by the Commission in accordance with the procedure referred to in Article 23(2), taking into account all relevant criteria, in particular effects on the internal market, potential distortions of competition, the environmental integrity of the scheme and reliability of the planned monitoring and reporting system. From 2005 Member States may under the same conditions apply emissions allowance trading to installations carrying out activities listed in Annex I below the capacity limits referred to in that Annex.

2. Allocations made to installations carrying out such activities shall be specified in the national allocation plan referred to in Article 9.

3. The Commission may, on its own initiative, or shall, on request by a Member State, adopt monitoring and reporting guidelines for emissions from activities, installations and greenhouse gases which are not listed in Annex I in accordance with the procedure

referred to in Article 23(2), if monitoring and reporting of these emissions can be carried out with sufficient accuracy.

4. In the event that such measures are introduced, reviews carried out pursuant to Article 30 shall also consider whether Annex I should be amended to include emissions from these activities in a harmonised way throughout the Community.

Article 25
Links with other greenhouse gas emissions trading schemes

1. Agreements should be concluded with third countries listed in Annex B to the Kyoto Protocol which have ratified the Protocol to provide for the mutual recognition of allowances between the Community scheme and other greenhouse gas emissions trading schemes in accordance with the rules set out in Article 300 of the Treaty.

2. Where an agreement referred to in paragraph 1 has been concluded, the Commission shall draw up any necessary provisions relating to the mutual recognition of allowances under that agreement in accordance with the procedure referred to in Article 23(2).

Article 26
Amendment of Directive 96/61/EC

In Article 9(3) of Directive 96/61/EC the following subparagraphs shall be added: 'Where emissions of a greenhouse gas from an installation are specified in Annex I to Directive 2003/87/EC of the European Parliament and of the Council of 13 October 2003 establishing a scheme for greenhouse gas emission allowance trading within the Community and amending Council Directive 96/61/EC[*] in relation to an activity carried out in that installation, the permit shall not include an emission limit value for direct emissions of that gas unless it is necessary to ensure that no significant local pollution is caused. For activities listed in Annex I to Directive 2003/87/EC, Member States may choose not to impose requirements relating to energy efficiency in respect of combustion units or other units emitting carbon dioxide on the site. Where necessary, the competent authorities shall amend the permit as appropriate. The three preceding subparagraphs shall not apply to installations temporarily excluded from the scheme for greenhouse gas emission allowance trading within the Community in accordance with Article 27 of Directive 2003/87/EC.

Article 27
Temporary exclusion of certain installations

1. Member States may apply to the Commission for installations to be temporarily excluded until 31 December 2007 at the latest from the Community scheme. Any such application shall list each such installation and shall be published.

[*] OJ L 275, 25.10.2003, p. 32.

2. If, having considered any comments made by the public on that application, the Commission decides, in accordance with the procedure referred to in Article 23(2), that the installations will:

(a) as a result of national policies, limit their emissions as much as would be the case if they were subject to the provisions of this Directive;
(b) be subject to monitoring, reporting and verification requirements which are equivalent to those provided for pursuant to Articles 14 and 15; and
(c) be subject to penalties at least equivalent to those referred to in Article 16(1) and (4) in the case of non-fulfilment of national requirements; it shall provide for the temporary exclusion of those installations from the Community scheme. It must be ensured that there will be no distortion of the internal market.

Article 28
Pooling

1. Member States may allow operators of installations carrying out one of the activities listed in Annex I to form a pool of installations from the same activity for the period referred to in Article 11(1) and/or the first five-year period referred to in Article 11(2) in accordance with paragraphs 2 to 6 of this Article.

2. Operators carrying out an activity listed in Annex I who wish to form a pool shall apply to the competent authority, specifying the installations and the period for which they want the pool and supplying evidence that a trustee will be able to fulfil the obligations referred to in paragraphs 3 and 4.

3. Operators wishing to form a pool shall nominate a trustee:

(a) to be issued with the total quantity of allowances calculated by installation of the operators, by way of derogation from Article 11;
(b) to be responsible for surrendering allowances equal to the total emissions from installations in the pool, by way of derogation from Articles 6(2)(e) and 12(3); and
(c) to be restricted from making further transfers in the event that an operator's report has not been verified as satisfactory in accordance with the second paragraph of Article 15.

4. The trustee shall be subject to the penalties applicable for breaches of requirements to surrender sufficient allowances to cover the total emissions from installations in the pool, by way of derogation from Article 16(2), (3) and (4).

5. A Member State that wishes to allow one or more pools to be formed shall submit the application referred to in paragraph 2 to the Commission. Without prejudice to the Treaty, the Commission may within three months of receipt reject an application that does not fulfil the requirements of this Directive. Reasons shall be given for any

such decision. In the case of rejection the Member State may only allow the pool to be formed if proposed amendments are accepted by the Commission.

6. In the event that the trustee fails to comply with penalties referred to in paragraph 4, each operator of an installation in the pool shall be responsible under Articles 12(3) and 16 in respect of emissions from its own installation.

Article 29
Force majeure

1. During the period referred to in Article 11(1), Member States may apply to the Commission for certain installations to be issued with additional allowances in cases of *force majeure*. The Commission shall determine whether *force majeure* is demonstrated, in which case it shall authorise the issue of additional and non-transferable allowances by that Member State to the operators of those installations.

2. The Commission shall, without prejudice to the Treaty, develop guidance to describe the circumstances under which *force majeure* is demonstrated, by 31 December 2003 at the latest.

Article 30
Review and further development

1. On the basis of progress achieved in the monitoring of emissions of greenhouse gases, the Commission may make a proposal to the European Parliament and the Council by 31 December 2004 to amend Annex I to include other activities and emissions of other greenhouse gases listed in Annex II.

2. On the basis of experience of the application of this Directive and of progress achieved in the monitoring of emissions of greenhouse gases and in the light of developments in the international context, the Commission shall draw up a report on the application of this Directive, considering:

(a) how and whether Annex I should be amended to include other relevant sectors, *inter alia* the chemicals, aluminium and transport sectors, activities and emissions of other greenhouse gases listed in Annex II, with a view to further improving the economic efficiency of the scheme;
(b) the relationship of Community emission allowance trading with the international emissions trading that will start in 2008;
(c) further harmonisation of the method of allocation (including auctioning for the time after 2012) and of the criteria for national allocation plans referred to in Annex III;
(d) the use of credits from project mechanisms;
(e) the relationship of emissions trading with other policies and measures implemented at Member State and Community level, including taxation, that pursue the same objectives;

(f) whether it is appropriate for there to be a single Community registry;
(g) the level of excess emissions penalties, taking into account, *inter alia*, inflation;
(h) the functioning of the allowance market, covering in particular any possible market disturbances;
(i) how to adapt the Community scheme to an enlarged European Union;
(j) pooling;
(k) the practicality of developing Community-wide benchmarks as a basis for allocation, taking into account the best available techniques and cost-benefit analysis.

The Commission shall submit this report to the European Parliament and the Council by 30 June 2006, accompanied by proposals as appropriate.

3. Linking the project-based mechanisms, including Joint Implementation (JI) and the Clean Development Mechanism (CDM), with the Community scheme is desirable and important to achieve the goals of both reducing global greenhouse gas emissions and increasing the cost-effective functioning of the Community scheme. Therefore, the emission credits from the project-based mechanisms will be recognised for their use in this scheme subject to provisions adopted by the European Parliament and the Council on a proposal from the Commission, which should apply in parallel with the Community scheme in 2005. The use of the mechanisms shall be supplemental to domestic action, in accordance with the relevant provisions of the Kyoto Protocol and Marrakesh Accords.

Article 31
Implementation

1. Member States shall bring into force the laws, regulations and administrative provisions necessary to comply with this Directive by 31 December 2003 at the latest. They shall forthwith inform the Commission thereof. The Commission shall notify the other Member States of these laws, regulations and administrative provisions. When Member States adopt these measures, they shall contain a reference to this Directive or be accompanied by such a reference on the occasion of their official publication. The methods of making such reference shall be laid down by Member States.

2. Member States shall communicate to the Commission the text of the provisions of national law which they adopt in the field covered by this Directive. The Commission shall inform the other Member States thereof.

Article 32
Entry into force

This Directive shall enter into force on the day of its publication in the *Official Journal of the European Union*.

Article 33
Addressees

This Directive is addressed to the Member States.

Done at Luxembourg, 13 October 2003.

Annex I

Categories of activities referred to in Articles 2(1), 3, 4, 14(1), 28 and 30

1. Installations or parts of installations used for research, development and testing of new products and processes are not covered by this Directive.

2. The threshold values given below generally refer to production capacities or outputs. Where one operator carries out several activities falling under the same subheading in the same installation or on the same site, the capacities of such activities are added together.

Activities	Greenhouse gases
Energy activities	
Combustion installations with a rated thermal input exceeding 20 MW (except hazardous or municipal waste installations)	Carbon dioxide
Mineral oil refineries	Carbon dioxide
Coke ovens	Carbon dioxide
Production and processing of ferrous metals	
Metal ore (including sulphide ore) roasting or sintering installations	Carbon dioxide
Installations for the production of pig iron or steel (primary or secondary fusion) including continuous casting, with a capacity exceeding 2,5 tonnes per hour	Carbon dioxide
Mineral industry	
Installations for the production of cement clinker in rotary kilns with a production capacity exceeding 500 tonnes per day or lime in rotary kilns with a production capacity exceeding 50 tonnes per day or in other furnaces with a production capacity exceeding 50 tonnes per day	Carbon dioxide
Installations for the manufacture of glass including glass fibre with a melting capacity exceeding 20 tonnes per day	Carbon dioxide
Installations for the manufacture of ceramic products by firing, in particular roofing tiles, bricks, refractory bricks, tiles, stoneware or porcelain, with a production capacity exceeding 75 tonnes per day, and/or with a kiln capacity exceeding 4 m^3 and with a setting density per kiln exceeding 300 kg/m^3	Carbon dioxide
Other activities	
Industrial plants for the production of	Carbon dioxide
(a) pulp from timber or other fibrous materials	
(b) paper and board with a production capacity exceeding 20 tonnes per day	Carbon dioxide

Annex II
Greenhouse gases referred to in Articles 3 and 30

Carbon dioxide (CO_2)
Methane (CH_4)
Nitrous Oxide (N_2O)
Hydrofluorocarbons (HFCs)
Perfluorocarbons (PFCs)
Sulphur Hexafluoride (SF_6)

Annex III
Criteria for national allocation plans referred to in Articles 9, 22 and 30

1. The total quantity of allowances to be allocated for the relevant period shall be consistent with the Member State's obligation to limit its emissions pursuant to Decision 2002/358/EC and the Kyoto Protocol, taking into account, on the one hand, the proportion of overall emissions that these allowances represent in comparison with emissions from sources not covered by this Directive and, on the other hand, national energy policies, and should be consistent with the national climate change programme. The total quantity of allowances to be allocated shall not be more than is likely to be needed for the strict application of the criteria of this Annex. Prior to 2008, the quantity shall be consistent with a path towards achieving or over-achieving each Member State's target under Decision 2002/358/EC and the Kyoto Protocol.

2. The total quantity of allowances to be allocated shall be consistent with assessments of actual and projected progress towards fulfilling the Member States' contributions to the Community's commitments made pursuant to Decision 93/389/EEC.

3. Quantities of allowances to be allocated shall be consistent with the potential, including the technological potential, of activities covered by this scheme to reduce emissions. Member States may base their distribution of allowances on average emissions of greenhouse gases by product in each activity and achievable progress in each activity.

4. The plan shall be consistent with other Community legislative and policy instruments. Account should be taken of unavoidable increases in emissions resulting from new legislative requirements.

5. The plan shall not discriminate between companies or sectors in such a way as to unduly favour certain undertakings or activities in accordance with the requirements of the Treaty, in particular Articles 87 and 88 thereof.

6. The plan shall contain information on the manner in which new entrants will be able to begin participating in the Community scheme in the Member State concerned.

7. The plan may accommodate early action and shall contain information on the manner in which early action is taken into account. Benchmarks derived from reference documents concerning the best available technologies may be employed by

Member States in developing their National Allocation Plans, and these benchmarks can incorporate an element of accommodating early action.

8. The plan shall contain information on the manner in which clean technology, including energy efficient technologies, are taken into account.

9. The plan shall include provisions for comments to be expressed by the public, and contain information on the arrangements by which due account will be taken of these comments before a decision on the allocation of allowances is taken.

10. The plan shall contain a list of the installations covered by this Directive with the quantities of allowances intended to be allocated to each.

11. The plan may contain information on the manner in which the existence of competition from countries or entities outside the Union will be taken into account.

Annex IV
Principles for monitoring and reporting referred to in Article 14(1)

Monitoring of carbon dioxide emissions
Emissions shall be monitored either by calculation or on the basis of measurement.

Calculation
Calculations of emissions shall be performed using the formula: Activity data × Emission factor × Oxidation factor. Activity data (fuel used, production rate etc.) shall be monitored on the basis of supply data or measurement. Accepted emission factors shall be used. Activity-specific emission factors are acceptable for all fuels. Default factors are acceptable for all fuels except non-commercial ones (waste fuels such as tyres and industrial process gases). Seam-specific defaults for coal, and EU-specific or producer country-specific defaults for natural gas shall be further elaborated. IPCC default values are acceptable for refinery products. The emission factor for biomass shall be zero. If the emission factor does not take account of the fact that some of the carbon is not oxidised, then an additional oxidation factor shall be used. If activity-specific emission factors have been calculated and already take oxidation into account, then an oxidation factor need not be applied. Default oxidation factors developed pursuant to Directive 96/61/EC shall be used, unless the operator can demonstrate that activity-specific factors are more accurate. A separate calculation shall be made for each activity, installation and for each fuel.

Measurement
Measurement of emissions shall use standardised or accepted methods, and shall be corroborated by a supporting calculation of emissions.

Monitoring of emissions of other greenhouse gases
Standardised or accepted methods shall be used, developed by the Commission in collaboration with all relevant stakeholders and adopted in accordance with the procedure referred to in Article 23(2).

Reporting of emissions

Each operator shall include the following information in the report for an installation:

A. Data identifying the installation, including:
   – Name of the installation;
   – Its address, including postcode and country;
   – Type and number of Annex I activities carried out in the installation;
   – Address, telephone, fax and email details for a contact person; and
   – Name of the owner of the installation, and of any parent company.
B. For each Annex I activity carried out on the site for which emissions are calculated:
   – Activity data;
   – Emission factors;
   – Oxidation factors;
   – Total emissions; and
   – Uncertainty.
C. For each Annex I activity carried out on the site for which emissions are measured:
   – Total emissions;
   – Information on the reliability of measurement methods; and
   – Uncertainty.
D. For emissions from combustion, the report shall also include the oxidation factor, unless oxidation has already been taken into account in the development of an activity-specific emission factor. Member States shall take measures to coordinate reporting requirements with any existing reporting requirements in order to minimise the reporting burden on businesses.

Annex V

Criteria for verification referred to in Article 15

General principles

1. Emissions from each activity listed in Annex I shall be subject to verification.

2. The verification process shall include consideration of the report pursuant to Article 14(3) and of monitoring during the preceding year. It shall address the reliability, credibility and accuracy of monitoring systems and the reported data and information relating to emissions, in particular:

(a) the reported activity data and related measurements and calculations;
(b) the choice and the employment of emission factors;
(c) the calculations leading to the determination of the overall emissions; and
(d) if measurement is used, the appropriateness of the choice and the employment of measuring methods.

3. Reported emissions may only be validated if reliable and credible data and information allow the emissions to be determined with a high degree of certainty. A high degree of certainty requires the operator to show that:

(a) the reported data is free of inconsistencies;
(b) the collection of the data has been carried out in accordance with the applicable scientific standards; and
(c) the relevant records of the installation are complete and consistent.

4. The verifier shall be given access to all sites and information in relation to the subject of the verification.

5. The verifier shall take into account whether the installation is registered under the Community eco-management and audit scheme (EMAS).

Methodology

Strategic analysis

6. The verification shall be based on a strategic analysis of all the activities carried out in the installation. This requires the verifier to have an overview of all the activities and their significance for emissions.

Process analysis

7. The verification of the information submitted shall, where appropriate, be carried out on the site of the installation. The verifier shall use spot-checks to determine the reliability of the reported data and information.

Risk analysis

8. The verifier shall submit all the sources of emissions in the installation to an evaluation with regard to the reliability of the data of each source contributing to the overall emissions of the installation.

9. On the basis of this analysis the verifier shall explicitly identify those sources with a high risk of error and other aspects of the monitoring and reporting procedure which are likely to contribute to errors in the determination of the overall emissions. This especially involves the choice of the emission factors and the calculations necessary to determine the level of the emissions from individual sources. Particular attention shall be given to those sources with a high risk of error and the abovementioned aspects of the monitoring procedure.

10. The verifier shall take into consideration any effective risk control methods applied by the operator with a view to minimising the degree of uncertainty.

Report

11. The verifier shall prepare a report on the validation process stating whether the report pursuant to Article 14(3) is satisfactory. This report shall specify all issues relevant to the work carried out. A statement that the report pursuant to Article 14(3)

is satisfactory may be made if, in the opinion of the verifier, the total emissions are not materially misstated.

Minimum competency requirements for the verifier

12. The verifier shall be independent of the operator, carry out his activities in a sound and objective professional manner, and understand:

(a) the provisions of this Directive, as well as relevant standards and guidance adopted by the Commission pursuant to Article 14(1);
(b) the legislative, regulatory, and administrative requirements relevant to the activities being verified; and
(c) the generation of all information related to each source of emissions in the installation, in particular, relating to the collection, measurement, calculation and reporting of data.

Directive 2004/101/EC of the European Parliament and of the Council of 27 October 2004 amending Directive 2003/87/EC establishing a scheme for greenhouse gas emission allowance trading within the Community, in respect of the Kyoto Protocol's project mechanisms

Source: OJ L 338 13.11.2004 p. 18

Directive 2004/101/EC of the European Parliament and of the Council of 27 October 2004 amending Directive 2003/87/EC establishing a scheme for greenhouse gas emission allowance trading within the Community, in respect of the Kyoto Protocol's project mechanisms

The European Parliament and the Council of the European Union,

Having regard to the Treaty establishing the European Community, and in particular Article 175(1) thereof,

Having regard to the proposal from the Commission,

Having regard to the opinion of the European Economic and Social Committee,[1]

After consulting the Committee of the Regions,

Acting in accordance with the procedure laid down in Article 251 of the Treaty,[2]

Whereas:

(1) Directive 2003/87/EC[3] establishes a scheme for greenhouse gas emission allowance trading within the Community (the Community scheme) in order to promote reductions of greenhouse gas emissions in a cost-effective and economically efficient manner, recognising that, in the longer-term, global emissions of greenhouse gases will need to be reduced by approximately 70% compared to 1990 levels. It aims at contributing towards fulfilling the commitments of the Community and its Member States to reduce anthropogenic greenhouse gas emissions under the Kyoto Protocol which was approved by Council

---

[1] OJ C 80, 30.3.2004, p. 61.

[2] Opinion of the European Parliament of 20 April 2004 (not yet published in the Official Journal) and Council Decision of 13 September 2004 (not yet published in the Official Journal).

[3] OJ L 275, 25.10.2003, p. 32.

Decision 2002/358/EC of 25 April 2002 concerning the approval, on behalf of the European Community, of the Kyoto Protocol to the United Nations Framework Convention on Climate Change and the joint fulfilment of commitments thereunder.[1]

(2) Directive 2003/87/EC states that the recognition of credits from project-based mechanisms for fulfilling obligations as from 2005 will increase the cost-effectiveness of achieving reductions of global greenhouse gas emissions and shall be provided for by provisions for linking the Kyoto project-based mechanisms, including joint implementation (JI) and the clean development mechanism (CDM), with the Community scheme.

(3) Linking the Kyoto project-based mechanisms to the Community scheme, while safeguarding the latter's environmental integrity, gives the opportunity to use emission credits generated through project activities eligible pursuant to Articles 6 and 12 of the Kyoto Protocol in order to fulfil Member States' obligations in accordance with Article 12(3) of Directive 2003/87/EC. As a result, this will increase the diversity of low-cost compliance options within the Community scheme leading to a reduction of the overall costs of compliance with the Kyoto Protocol while improving the liquidity of the Community market in greenhouse gas emission allowances. By stimulating demand for JI credits, Community companies will invest in the development and transfer of advanced environmentally sound technologies and know-how. The demand for CDM credits will also be stimulated and thus developing countries hosting CDM projects will be assisted in achieving their sustainable development goals.

(4) In addition to the use of the Kyoto project-based mechanisms by the Community and its Member States, and by companies and individuals outside the Community scheme, those mechanisms should be linked to the Community scheme in such a way as to ensure consistency with the United Nations Framework Convention on Climate Change (UNFCCC) and the Kyoto Protocol and subsequent decisions adopted thereunder as well as with the objectives and architecture of the Community scheme and provisions laid down by Directive 2003/87/EC.

(5) Member States may allow operators to use, in the Community scheme, certified emission reductions (CERs) from 2005 and emission reduction units (ERUs) from 2008. The use of CERs and ERUs by operators from 2008 may be allowed up to a percentage of the allocation to each installation, to be specified by each Member State in its national allocation plan. The use will take place through the issue and immediate surrender of one allowance in exchange for one CER or ERU. An allowance issued in exchange for a CER or ERU will correspond to that CER or ERU.

(6) The Commission Regulation for a standardised and secured system of registries, to be adopted pursuant to Article 19(3) of Directive 2003/87/EC and Article 6(1)

---

[1] OJ L 130, 15.5.2002, p. 1. L 338/18 EN Official Journal of the European Union 13.11.2004

of Decision No 280/2004/EC of the European Parliament and of the Council of 11 February 2004 concerning a mechanism for monitoring Community greenhouse gas emissions and for implementing the Kyoto Protocol (1), will provide for the relevant processes and procedures in the registries system for the use of CERs during the period 2005 to 2007 and subsequent periods, and for the use of ERUs during the period 2008 to 2012 and subsequent periods.

(7) Each Member State will decide on the limit for the use of CERs and ERUs from project activities, having due regard to the relevant provisions of the Kyoto Protocol and the Marrakesh Accords, to meet the requirements therein that the use of the mechanisms should be supplemental to domestic action. Domestic action will thus constitute a significant element of the effort made.

(8) In accordance with the UNFCCC and the Kyoto Protocol and subsequent decisions adopted thereunder, Member States are to refrain from using CERs and ERUs generated from nuclear facilities to meet their commitments pursuant to Article 3(1) of the Kyoto Protocol and pursuant to Decision 2002/358/EC.

(9) Decisions 15/CP.7 and 19/CP.7 adopted pursuant to the UNFCCC and the Kyoto Protocol emphasise that environmental integrity is to be achieved, *inter alia*, through sound modalities, rules and guidelines for the mechanisms, and through sound and strong principles and rules governing land use, land-use change and forestry activities, and that the issues of non-permanence, additionality, leakage, uncertainties and socioeconomic and environmental impacts, including impacts on biodiversity and natural ecosystems, associated with afforestation and reforestation project activities are to be taken into account. The Commission should consider, in its review of Directive 2003/87/EC in 2006, technical provisions relating to the temporary nature of credits and the limit of 1% for eligibility for land use, land-use change and forestry project activities as established in Decision 17/CP.7, and also provisions relating to the outcome of the evaluation of potential risks associated with the use of genetically modified organisms and potentially invasive alien species in afforestation and reforestation project activities, to allow operators to use CERs and ERUs resulting from land use, land use change and forestry project activities in the Community scheme from 2008, in accordance with the decisions adopted pursuant to the UNFCCC or the Kyoto Protocol.

(10) In order to avoid double counting, CERs and ERUs should not be issued as a result of project activities undertaken within the Community that also lead to a reduction in, or limitation of, emissions from installations covered by Directive 2003/87/EC, unless an equal number of allowances is cancelled from the registry of the Member State of the CERs' or ERUs' origin.

(11) In accordance with the relevant treaties of accession, the *acquis communautaire* should be taken into account in the establishment of baselines for project activities undertaken in countries acceding to the Union.

(12) Any Member State that authorises private or public entities to participate in project activities remains responsible for the fulfilment of its obligations under

the UNFCCC and the Kyoto Protocol and should therefore ensure that such participation is consistent with the relevant guidelines, modalities and procedures adopted pursuant to the UNFCCC or the Kyoto Protocol.

(13) In accordance with the UNFCCC, the Kyoto Protocol and subsequent decisions adopted for their implementation, the Commission and the Member States should support capacity building activities in developing countries and countries with economies in transition in order to help them take full advantage of JI and the CDM in a manner that supports their sustainable development strategies. The Commission should review and report on efforts in this regard.

(14) Criteria and guidelines that are relevant to considering whether hydroelectric power production projects have negative environmental or social impacts have been identified by the World Commission on Dams in its November 2000 Report 'Dams and Development – A New Framework for Decision-Making', by the OECD and by the World Bank. (1) OJ L 49, 19.2.2004, p. 1.

(15) Since participation in JI and CDM project activities is voluntary, corporate environmental and social responsibility and accountability should be enhanced in accordance with paragraph 17 of the Plan of implementation of the world summit on sustainable development. In this connection, companies should be encouraged to improve the social and environmental performance of JI and CDM activities in which they participate.

(16) Information on project activities in which a Member State participates or authorises private or public entities to participate should be made available to the public in accordance with Directive 2003/4/EC of the European Parliament and of the Council of 28 January 2003 on public access to environmental information.[1]

(17) The Commission may mention impacts on the electricity market in its reports on emission allowance trading and the use of credits from project activities.

(18) Following entry into force of the Kyoto Protocol, the Commission should examine whether it could be possible to conclude agreements with countries listed in Annex B to the Kyoto Protocol which have yet to ratify the Protocol, to provide for the recognition of allowances between the Community scheme and mandatory greenhouse gas emissions trading schemes capping absolute emissions established within those countries.

(19) Since the objective of the proposed action, namely the establishment of a link between the Kyoto project-based mechanisms and the Community scheme, cannot be sufficiently achieved by the Member States acting individually, and can therefore by reason of the scale and effects of this action be better achieved at Community level, the Community may adopt measures, in accordance with the principle of subsidiarity as set out in Article 5 of the Treaty. In accordance with the principle of proportionality, as set out in that Article, this Directive does not go beyond what is necessary in order to achieve that objective.

(20) Directive 2003/87/EC should therefore be amended accordingly,

---

[1] OJ L 41, 14.2.2003, p. 26.

Have adopted this Directive:

Article 1
Amendments to Directive 2003/87/EC

Directive 2003/87/EC is hereby amended as follows:

1. In Article 3, the following points are added:

'(k) "Annex I Party" means a Party listed in Annex I to the United Nations Framework
Convention on Climate Change (UNFCCC) that has ratified the Kyoto Protocol
as specified in Article 1(7) of the Kyoto Protocol;

 (l) "project activity" means a project activity approved by one or more Annex I
Parties in accordance with Article 6 or Article 12 of the Kyoto Protocol and the
decisions adopted pursuant to the UNFCCC or the Kyoto Protocol;

(m) "emission reduction unit" or "ERU" means a unit issued pursuant to Article 6 of
the Kyoto Protocol and the decisions adopted pursuant to the UNFCCC or the
Kyoto Protocol;

 (n) "certified emission reduction" or "CER" means a unit issued pursuant to Article 12 of the Kyoto Protocol and the decisions adopted pursuant to the UNFCCC
or the Kyoto Protocol.'

2. The following Articles are inserted after Article 11:

'Article 11a
Use of CERs and ERUs from project activities in the Community scheme

1. Subject to paragraph 3, during each period referred to in Article 11(2), Member
States may allow operators to use CERs and ERUs from project activities in the Community scheme up to a percentage of the allocation of allowances to each installation,
to be specified by each Member State in its national allocation plan for that period.
This shall take place through the issue and immediate surrender of one allowance
by the Member State in exchange for one CER or ERU held by the operator in the
national registry of its Member State.

2. Subject to paragraph 3, during the period referred to in Article 11(1), Member
States may allow operators to use CERs from project activities in the Community
scheme. This shall take place through the issue and immediate surrender of one
allowance by the Member State in exchange for one CER. Member States shall cancel
CERs that have been used by operators during the period referred to in Article 11(1).

3. All CERs and ERUs that are issued and may be used in accordance with the
UNFCCC and the Kyoto Protocol and subsequent decisions adopted thereunder may
be used in the Community scheme:

(a) except that, in recognition of the fact that, in accordance with the UNFCCC and
the Kyoto Protocol and subsequent decisions adopted thereunder, Member States
are to refrain from using CERs and ERUs generated from nuclear facilities to

meet their commitments pursuant to Article 3(1) of the Kyoto Protocol and in accordance with Decision 2002/358/EC, operators are to refrain from using CERs and ERUs generated from such facilities in the Community scheme during the period referred to in Article 11(1) and the first five-year period referred to in Article 11(2); and

(b) except for CERs and ERUs from land use, land use change and forestry activities.

Article 11b
Project activities

1. Member States shall take all necessary measures to ensure that baselines for project activities, as defined by subsequent decisions adopted under the UNFCCC or the Kyoto Protocol, undertaken in countries having signed a Treaty of Accession with the Union fully comply with the *acquis communautaire*, including the temporary derogations set out in that Treaty of Accession.

2. Except as provided for in paragraphs 3 and 4, Member States hosting project activities shall ensure that no ERUs or CERs are issued for reductions or limitations of greenhouse gas emissions from installations falling within the scope of this Directive.

3. Until 31 December 2012, for JI and CDM project activities which reduce or limit directly the emissions of an installation falling within the scope of this Directive, ERUs and CERs may be issued only if an equal number of allowances is cancelled by the operator of that installation.

4. Until 31 December 2012, for JI and CDM project activities which reduce or limit indirectly the emission level of installations falling within the scope of this Directive, ERUs and CERs may be issued only if an equal number of allowances is cancelled from the national registry of the Member State of the ERUs' or CERs' origin.

5. A Member State that authorises private or public entities to participate in project activities shall remain responsible for the fulfilment of its obligations under the UNFCCC and the Kyoto Protocol and shall ensure that such participation is consistent with the relevant guidelines, modalities and procedures adopted pursuant to the UNFCCC or the Kyoto Protocol.

6. In the case of hydroelectric power production project activities with a generating capacity exceeding 20 MW, Member States shall, when approving such project activities, ensure that relevant international criteria and guidelines, including those contained in the World Commission on Dams November 2000 Report "Dams and Development – A New Framework for Decision-Making", will be respected during the development of such project activities.

7. Provisions for the implementation of paragraphs 3 and 4, particularly in respect of the avoidance of double counting, and any provisions necessary for the implementation of paragraph 5 where the host party meets all eligibility requirements for JI project activities shall be adopted in accordance with Article 23(2).'

3. Article 17 is replaced by the following:

'Article 17
Access to information

Decisions relating to the allocation of allowances, information on project activities in which a Member State participates or authorises private or public entities to participate, and the reports of emissions required under the greenhouse gas emissions permit and held by the competent authority, shall be made available to the public in accordance with Directive 2003/4/EC.'

4. In Article 18 the following subparagraph is added:

'Member States shall in particular ensure coordination between their designated focal point for approving project activities pursuant to Article 6(1)(a) of the Kyoto Protocol and their designated national authority for the implementation of Article 12 of the Kyoto Protocol respectively designated in accordance with subsequent decisions adopted under the UNFCCC or the Kyoto Protocol.'

5. In Article 19(3) the following sentence is added:

'That Regulation shall also include provisions concerning the use and identification of CERs and ERUs in the Community scheme and the monitoring of the level of such use.'

6. Article 21 is amended as follows:

(a) in paragraph 1 the second sentence is replaced by the following:

'This report shall pay particular attention to the arrangements for the allocation of allowances, the use of ERUs and CERs in the Community scheme, the operation of registries, the application of the monitoring and reporting guidelines, verification and issues relating to compliance with the Directive and the fiscal treatment of allowances, if any.'

(b) paragraph 3 is replaced by the following:

'3. The Commission shall organise an exchange of information between the competent authorities of the Member States concerning developments relating to issues of allocation, the use of ERUs and CERs in the Community scheme, the operation of registries, monitoring, reporting, verification and compliance with this Directive.'

7. The following Article is inserted after Article 21:

'Article 21a
Support of capacity-building activities

In accordance with the UNFCCC, the Kyoto Protocol and any subsequent decision adopted for their implementation, the Commission and the Member States shall endeavour to support capacity-building activities in developing countries and countries with economies in transition in order to help them take full advantage of JI and the CDM in a manner that supports their sustainable development strategies and to facilitate the engagement of entities in JI and CDM project development and implementation.'

8. Article 30 is amended as follows:

(a) in paragraph 2, point (d) is replaced by the following:

'(d) the use of credits from project activities, including the need for harmonisation of the allowed use of ERUs and CERs in the Community scheme;'

(b) in paragraph 2 the following points are added:

'(l) the impact of project mechanisms on host countries, particularly on their development objectives, whether JI and CDM hydroelectric power production project activities with a generating capacity exceeding 500 MW and having negative environmental or social impacts have been approved, and the future use of CERs or ERUs resulting from any such hydroelectric power production project activities in the Community scheme;

(m) the support for capacity-building efforts in developing countries and countries with economies in transition;

(n) the modalities and procedures for Member States' approval of domestic project activities and for the issuing of allowances in respect of emission reductions or limitations resulting from such activities from 2008;

(o) technical provisions relating to the temporary nature of credits and the limit of 1% for eligibility for land use, land-use change and forestry project activities as established in Decision 17/CP.7, and provisions relating to the outcome of the evaluation of potential risks associated with the use of genetically modified organisms and potentially invasive alien species by afforestation and reforestation project activities, to allow operators to use CERs and ERUs resulting from land use, land-use change and forestry project activities in the Community scheme from 2008, in accordance with the decisions adopted pursuant to the UNFCCC or the Kyoto Protocol.'

(c) paragraph 3 is replaced by the following:

'3. In advance of each period referred to in Article 11(2), each Member State shall publish in its national allocation plan its intended use of ERUs and CERs and the percentage of the allocation to each installation up to which operators are allowed to use ERUs and CERs in the Community scheme for that period. The total use of ERUs and CERs shall be consistent with the relevant supplementarity obligations under the Kyoto Protocol and the UNFCCC and the decisions adopted thereunder.

Member States shall, in accordance with Article 3 of Decision No 280/2004/EC of the European Parliament and of the Council of 11 February 2004 concerning a mechanism for monitoring Community greenhouse gas emissions and for implementing the

Kyoto Protocol,* report to the Commission every two years on the extent to which domestic action actually constitutes a significant element of the efforts undertaken at national level, as well as the extent to which use of the project mechanisms is actually supplemental to domestic action, and the ratio between them, in accordance with the relevant provisions of the Kyoto Protocol and the decisions adopted thereunder. The Commission shall report on this in accordance with Article 5 of the said Decision. In the light of this report, the Commission shall, if appropriate, make legislative or other proposals to complement provisions adopted by Member States to ensure that use of the mechanisms is supplemental to domestic action within the Community.'

9. In Annex III the following point is added:

'12. The plan shall specify the maximum amount of CERs and ERUs which may be used by operators in the Community scheme as a percentage of the allocation of the allowances to each installation. The percentage shall be consistent with the Member State's supplementarity obligations under the Kyoto Protocol and decisions adopted pursuant to the UNFCCC or the Kyoto Protocol.'

Article 2
Implementation

1. Member States shall bring into force the laws, regulations and administrative provisions necessary to comply with this Directive by 13 November 2005. They shall forthwith inform the Commission thereof.

When Member States adopt these measures, they shall contain a reference to this Directive or be accompanied by such a reference on the occasion of their official publication. The methods of making such reference shall be laid down by the Member States.

2. Member States shall communicate to the Commission the text of the provisions of national law which they adopt in the field covered by this Directive. The Commission shall inform the other Member States thereof.

Article 3
Entry into force

This Directive shall enter into force on the day of its publication in the *Official Journal of the European Union.*

Article 4
Addressees

This Directive is addressed to the Member States.

Done at Strasbourg, 27 October 2004.

---

* OJ L 49, 19.2.2004, p. 1.

Decision No 280/2004/EC of the European Parliament and of the Council of 11 February 2004 concerning a mechanism for monitoring Community greenhouse gas emissions and for implementing the Kyoto Protocol

Editorial note

Decision 280/2004 of 11 February 2004 establishes a mechanism for monitoring Community greenhouse gas emissions and for implementing the Kyoto Protocol. It establishes a mechanism for monitoring all anthropogenic emissions by sources and by removals by sinks; evaluating progress towards meeting commitments in respect of these sources; implementing the United Nations Framework Convention on Climate Change (UNFCCC) and the Kyoto Protocol; and ensuring the timeliness, accuracy, consistency, comparability and transparency of reporting by the Community (Article 1). National and Community programmes are to be devised to fulfil the Community's and Member States' commitments under the UNFCCC and the Kyoto Protocol (Article 2). Member States' reporting obligations to the Commission are outlined in Article 3. Member States' reports are to enable the Commission to assess actual progress and to prepare annual reports (Article 3). The Commission is to compile annually a Community greenhouse gas inventory and a Community greenhouse gas inventory report (Article 4). The Commission, in consultation with Member States, is to assess annually the progress of the Community in fulfilling its obligations under the UNFCCC and the Kyoto Protocol (Article 5). National registries are to be established by the Community and its Member States to ensure the accurate accounting of the issue, holding, transfer, acquisition, cancellation and withdrawal of assigned amount units, removal units, emission reduction units, etc. (Article 6). The Community and each Member State are to submit a report to the UNFCCC Secretariat determining their assigned amount (Article 7). The Commission will be assisted by a 'Climate Change Committee' in the implementation of this Decision.

Source: OJ L 49 19.02.2004 p. 1

Decision No 280/2004/EC of the European Parliament and of the Council of 11 February 2004 concerning a mechanism for monitoring Community greenhouse gas emissions and for implementing the Kyoto Protocol

The European Parliament and the Council of the European Union,

Having regard to the Treaty establishing the European Community, and in particular Article 175(1) thereof,

Having regard to the proposal from the Commission,

Having regard to the opinion of the European Economic and Social Committee,[1]

After consulting the Committee of the Regions,

Acting in accordance with the procedure laid down in Article 251 of the Treaty,[2]

Whereas:

(1) Council Decision 93/389/EEC of 24 June 1993 for a monitoring mechanism of Community CO_2 and other greenhouse gas emissions[3] established a mechanism for monitoring anthropogenic greenhouse gas emissions and evaluating progress towards meeting commitments in respect of these emissions. In order to take into account developments on the international level and on the grounds of clarity, it is appropriate for that Decision to be replaced.

(2) The ultimate objective of the United Nations Framework Convention on Climate Change (UNFCCC), which was approved by Council Decision 94/69/EC,[4] is to achieve stabilisation of greenhouse gas concentrations in the atmosphere at a level which prevents dangerous anthropogenic interference with the climate system.

(3) The UNFCCC commits the Community and its Member States to develop, periodically update, publish and report to the Conference of the Parties national inventories of anthropogenic emissions by sources and removals by sinks of all greenhouse gases not controlled by the Montreal Protocol on substances that deplete the ozone layer (hereinafter greenhouse gases), using comparable methodologies agreed upon by the Conference of the Parties.

(4) There is a need for thorough monitoring and regular assessment of Community greenhouse gas emissions. The measures taken by the Community and its Member States in the field of climate change policy also need to be analysed in good time.

(5) Accurate reporting under this Decision at an early stage would allow early determination of emissions levels pursuant to Council Decision 2002/358/EC of

---

[1] OJ C 234, 30.9.2003, p. 51.

[2] Opinion of the European Parliament of 21 October 2003 (not yet published in the Official Journal) and Council Decision of 26 January 2004.

[3] OJ L 167, 9.7.1993, p. 31. Decision as last amended by Regulation (EC) No 1882/2003 of the European Parliament and of the Council (OJ L 284, 31.10.2003, p. 1).

[4] OJ L 33, 7.2.1994, p. 11.

25 April 2002 concerning the approval, on behalf of the European Community, of the Kyoto Protocol to the United Nations Framework Convention on Climate Change and the joint fulfilment of commitments thereunder,[1] and thereby enable early establishment of eligibility to participate in the Kyoto Protocol's flexible mechanisms.

(6) The UNFCCC commits all Parties to formulate, implement, publish and regularly update national, and where appropriate, regional programmes containing measures to mitigate climate change by addressing anthropogenic emissions by sources and removals by sinks of all greenhouse gases.

(7) The Kyoto Protocol to the UNFCCC was approved by Decision 2002/358/EC. Article 3(2) of the Kyoto Protocol requires Parties to the Protocol included in Annex I to the UNFCCC to have made demonstrable progress in achieving their commitments under the Protocol by 2005.

(8) In accordance with part II, section A, of the Annex to Decision 19/CP.7 of the Conference of the Parties, each Party to the Kyoto Protocol included in Annex I to the UNFCCC is required to establish and maintain a national registry in order to ensure the accurate accounting of the issue, holding, transfer, cancellation and withdrawal of emission reduction units, certified emission reductions, assigned amount units and removal units.

(9) In accordance with Decision 19/CP.7, each emission reduction unit, certified emission reduction, assigned amount unit and removal unit should be held only in one account at any given time.

(10) The Community's registry may be used to hold emission reduction units and certified emission reductions generated by projects funded by the Community, thereby providing a stimulus for Community action in third countries to address climate change more widely, and may be maintained in a consolidated system together with Member States' registries.

(11) The purchase and use of emission reduction units and certified emission reductions by the Community should be subject to further provisions to be adopted by the European Parliament and by the Council on a proposal from the Commission.

(12) The Community and the Member States have the obligation, under Decision 2002/358/EC, to take the necessary measures to comply with their emission levels determined pursuant to that Decision. Provisions laid down on the use of emission reduction units and certified emission reductions held in the Community's registry should take into account Member States' responsibilities to fulfil their own commitments in accordance with Decision 2002/358/EC.

(13) The Community and its Member States have made use of Article 4 of the Kyoto Protocol, which allows Parties to the Protocol to meet their emission limitation

---

[1] OJ L 130, 15.5.2002, p. 1.

and reduction commitments jointly. Therefore, it is appropriate to provide for effective cooperation and coordination in relation to obligations under this Decision, including the compilation of the Community greenhouse gas inventory, the evaluation of progress, the preparation of reports, as well as review and compliance procedures enabling the Community to comply with its reporting obligations under the Kyoto Protocol, as laid down in the political agreements and legal decisions taken at the seventh Conference of the Parties to the UNFCCC in Marrakech (hereinafter the Marrakech Accords).

(14) The Community and the Member States are all Parties to the UNFCCC and the Kyoto Protocol, and are each responsible thereunder for reporting, establishing and accounting for their assigned amounts and establishing and maintaining their eligibility to participate in the Kyoto Protocol's mechanisms.

(15) In accordance with Decision 19/CP.7, each Party included in Annex I to the UNFCCC should issue a quantity of assigned amount units equivalent to its assigned amount in its national registry, corresponding to its emission levels determined pursuant to Decision 2002/358/EC and the Kyoto Protocol.

(16) Pursuant to Decision 2002/358/EC, the Community is not to issue assigned amount units.

(17) The European Environment Agency assists the Commission, as appropriate, with monitoring activities, especially in the ambit of the Community inventory system, and in the analysis by the Commission of progress towards the fulfilment of the commitments under the UNFCCC and the Kyoto Protocol.

(18) In the light of the role played by the European Environment Agency in compiling the annual Community inventory, it would be appropriate for Member States to design their own national systems in a manner that facilitates the work of the Agency.

(19) Since the objectives of the proposed action, namely to comply with the Community's commitments under the Kyoto Protocol, in particular the monitoring and reporting requirements laid down therein, cannot, by their very nature, be sufficiently achieved by the Member States and can therefore be better achieved at Community level, the Community may adopt measures, in accordance with the principle of subsidiarity as set out in Article 5 of the Treaty. In accordance with the principle of proportionality, as set out in that Article, this Decision does not go beyond what is necessary in order to achieve those objectives.

(20) The measures necessary for the implementation of this Decision should be adopted in accordance with Council Decision 1999/468/EC of 28 June 1999 laying down the procedures for the exercise of implementing powers conferred on the Commission,[1]

---

[1] OJ L 184, 17.7.1999, p. 23.

Have adopted this Decision:

Article 1
Subject matter

This Decision establishes a mechanism for:

(a) monitoring all anthropogenic emissions by sources and removals by sinks of greenhouse gases not controlled by the Montreal Protocol on substances that deplete the ozone layer in the Member States;
(b) evaluating progress towards meeting commitments in respect of these emissions by sources and removals by sinks;
(c) implementing the UNFCCC and the Kyoto Protocol, as regards national programmes, greenhouse gas inventories, national systems and registries of the Community and its Member States, and the relevant procedures under the Kyoto Protocol; and
(d) ensuring the timeliness, completeness, accuracy, consistency, comparability and transparency of reporting by the Community and its Member States to the UNFCCC Secretariat.

Article 2
National and Community programmes

1. Member States and the Commission shall devise and implement national programmes and a Community programme respectively, in order to contribute to:

(a) the fulfilment of the Community's and its Member States' commitments relating to the limitation and/or reduction of all greenhouse gas emissions under the UNFCCC and the Kyoto Protocol; and
(b) transparent and accurate monitoring of the actual and projected progress made by Member States, including the contribution made by Community measures, in meeting the Community's and its Member States' commitments relating to the limitation and/or reduction of all greenhouse gas emissions under the UNFCCC and the Kyoto Protocol.

These programmes shall include the information referred to in Article 3(2) and shall be updated accordingly.

2. To this effect, the use of joint implementation, the clean development mechanism and international emissions trading shall be supplemental to domestic action, in accordance with the relevant provisions of the Kyoto Protocol and the Marrakech Accords.

3. Member States shall make national programmes and updates thereof available to the public, and within three months of their adoption shall inform the Commission.

At subsequent meetings of the committee referred to in Article 9(1), the Commission shall inform the Member States of any such national programmes and updates thereof that it has received.

Article 3
Reporting by Member States

1. Member States shall, for the assessment of actual progress and to enable the preparation of annual reports by the Community, in accordance with obligations under the UNFCCC and the Kyoto Protocol, determine and report to the Commission by 15 January each year (year X):

(a) their anthropogenic emissions of greenhouse gases listed in Annex A to the Kyoto Protocol (carbon dioxide (CO_2), methane (CH_4), nitrous oxide (N_2O), hydrofluorocarbons (HFCs), perfluorocarbons (PFCs) and sulphur hexafluoride (SF_6)) during the year before last (year X-2);

(b) provisional data on their emissions of carbon monoxide (CO), sulphur dioxide (SO_2), nitrogen oxides (NOx) and volatile organic compounds (VOC) during the year before last (year X-2), together with final data for the year three years previous (year X-3);

(c) their anthropogenic greenhouse gas emissions by sources and removals of carbon dioxide by sinks resulting from land-use, land-use change and forestry during the year before last (year X-2);

(d) information with regard to the accounting of emissions and removals from land-use, land-use change and forestry, in accordance with Article 3(3) and, where a Member State decides to make use of it, Article 3(4) of the Kyoto Protocol, and the relevant decisions thereunder, for the years between 1990 and the year before last (year X-2);

(e) any changes to the information referred to in points (a) to (d) relating to the years between 1990 and the year three years previous (year X-3);

(f) the elements of the national inventory report necessary for the preparation of the Community greenhouse gas inventory report, such as information on the Member State's quality assurance/quality control plan, a general uncertainty evaluation, a general assessment of completeness, and information on recalculations performed;

(g) information from the national registry, once established, on the issue, acquisition, holding, transfer, cancellation, withdrawal and carryover of assigned amount units, removal units, emission reduction units and certified emission reductions during the previous year (year X-1);

(h) information on legal entities authorised to participate in mechanisms under Articles 6, 12 and 17 of the Kyoto Protocol, in compliance with relevant national or Community provisions;

(i) steps taken to improve estimates, for example where areas of the inventory have been subject to adjustments;

(j) information on indicators for the year before last (year X-2); and

(k) any changes to the national inventory system.

Member States shall communicate to the Commission, by 15 March each year (year X), their complete national inventory report.

2. Member States shall, for the assessment of projected progress, report to the Commission, by 15 March 2005 and every two years thereafter:

(a) information on national policies and measures which limit and/or reduce greenhouse gas emissions by sources or enhance removals by sinks, presented on a sectoral basis for each greenhouse gas, including:

  (i) the objective of policies and measure;

  (ii) the type of policy instrument;

  (iii) the status of implementation of the policy or measure;

  (iv) indicators to monitor and evaluate progress with policies and measures over time, including, *inter alia*, those indicators specified in the implementing provisions adopted pursuant to paragraph 3;

  (v) quantitative estimates of the effect of policies and measures on emissions by sources and removals by sinks of greenhouse gases between the base year and subsequent years, including 2005, 2010 and 2015, including their economic impacts to the extent feasible; and

  (vi) the extent to which domestic action actually constitutes a significant element of the efforts undertaken at national level as well as the extent to which the use of joint implementation and the clean development mechanism and international emissions trading, pursuant to Articles 6, 12 and 17 of the Kyoto Protocol, is actually supplemental to domestic actions, in accordance with the relevant provisions of the Kyoto Protocol and the Marrakech Accords;

(b) national projections of greenhouse gas emissions by sources and their removal by sinks as a minimum for the years 2005, 2010, 2015 and 2020, organised by gas and by sector, including:

  (i) 'with measures' and 'with additional measures' projections such as mentioned in the guidelines of the UNFCCC and further specified in the implementing provisions adopted pursuant to paragraph 3;

  (ii) clear identification of the policies and measures included in the projections;

  (iii) results of sensitivity analysis performed for the projections; and

  (iv) descriptions of methodologies, models, underlying assumptions and key input and output parameters.

(c) information on measures being taken or planned for the implementation of relevant Community legislation and policies, and information on legal and institutional steps to prepare to implement commitments under the Kyoto Protocol and information on arrangements for, and national implementation of, compliance and enforcement procedures;

(d) information on institutional and financial arrangements and decision making procedures to coordinate and support activities related to participation in the mechanisms under Articles 6, 12 and 17 of the Kyoto Protocol, including the participation of legal entities.

3. Implementing provisions for the reporting of the information referred to in paragraphs 1 and 2 shall be adopted in accordance with the procedure referred to in Article 9(2).

These implementing provisions may be revised, as appropriate, taking into account decisions taken under the UNFCCC and the Kyoto Protocol.

Article 4
Community inventory system

1. The Commission shall, in cooperation with the Member States, annually compile a Community greenhouse gas inventory and a Community greenhouse gas inventory report, circulate these in draft to the Member States by 28 February, and publish and submit them to the UNFCCC Secretariat by 15 April each year. Estimates for data missing from a national inventory shall be included in accordance with implementing provisions adopted pursuant to paragraph 2(b), unless updated data are received from Member States by 15 March of that year at the latest.

2. The Commission shall, in accordance with the procedure referred to in Article 9(2), and taking into account the national systems of the Member States, adopt by 30 June 2006 at the latest, a Community inventory system for ensuring the accuracy, comparability, consistency, completeness and timeliness of national inventories with regard to the Community greenhouse gas inventory.

This system shall provide for:

(a) a quality assurance/quality control programme including the establishment of quality objectives and an inventory quality assurance and quality control plan. The Commission shall provide assistance to Member States for the implementation of quality assurance/quality control programmes; and

(b) a procedure for the estimation of data missing from a national inventory, including consultation with the Member State concerned.

3. The European Environment Agency shall provide assistance to the Commission for the implementation of paragraphs 1 and 2 as appropriate, *inter alia*, by conducting studies and compiling data, in accordance with its annual work programme.

4. Member States shall, as early as possible and in any case by 31 December 2005 at the latest, establish national inventory systems under the Kyoto Protocol for the estimation of anthropogenic emissions of greenhouse gases by sources and removals of carbon dioxide by sinks.

Article 5
Evaluation of progress and reporting

1. The Commission shall assess annually, in consultation with Member States, the progress of the Community and its Member States towards fulfilling their

commitments under the UNFCCC and the Kyoto Protocol as set out in Decision 2002/358/EC, in order to evaluate whether progress is sufficient to fulfil these commitments.

This assessment shall take into account progress in Community policies and measures and information submitted by Member States in accordance with Article 3 and Article 6(2) of this Decision and with Article 21 of Directive 2003/87/EC of the European Parliament and of the Council of 13 October 2003 establishing a scheme for greenhouse gas emission allowance trading within the Community.[1]

Every two years, the assessment shall also include the projected progress of the Community and its Member States towards fulfilling their commitments under the UNFCCC and the Kyoto Protocol.

2. On the basis of the assessment referred to in paragraph 1, the Commission shall submit annually a report to the European Parliament and the Council.

This report shall contain sections on actual and projected emissions by sources and removals by sinks, policies and measures and on the use of mechanisms pursuant to Articles 6, 12 and 17 of the Kyoto Protocol.

3. The Commission shall prepare a report on the demonstration of progress achieved by 2005 by the Community, taking into account updated information on emission projections submitted by Member States not later than 15 June 2005, in accordance with the implementing provisions adopted pursuant to Article 3(3), and submit this to the UNFCCC Secretariat by 1 January 2006 at the latest.

4. Each Member State shall prepare a report on the demonstration of progress achieved by 2005 by that Member State, taking into account information submitted in accordance with the implementing provisions adopted pursuant to Article 3(3), and submit this to the UNFCCC Secretariat by 1 January 2006 at the latest.

5. The Community and each Member State shall submit a report to the UNFCCC Secretariat on the additional period set in the Marrakech Accords for fulfilling commitments upon the expiry of that period.

6. In accordance with the procedure referred to in Article 9(2), the Commission may adopt provisions containing requirements for reporting on the demonstration of progress as required by Article 3(2) of the Kyoto Protocol and for reporting in relation to the additional period set in the Marrakech Accords for fulfilling commitments.

7. The European Environment Agency shall provide assistance to the Commission for the implementation of paragraphs 1, 2 and 3 as appropriate, in accordance with its annual work programme.

Article 6

National registries

1. The Community and its Member States shall establish and maintain registries in order to ensure the accurate accounting of the issue, holding, transfer, acquisition, cancellation and withdrawal of assigned amount units, removal units, emission reduction

---

[1] OJ L 275, 25.10.2003, p. 32.

units and certified emission reductions and the carryover of assigned amount units, emission reduction units and certified emission reductions. These registries shall incorporate registries established pursuant to Article 19 of Directive 2003/87EC, in accordance with provisions adopted in accordance with the procedure referred to in Article 9(2) of this Decision.

The Community and Member States may maintain their registries in a consolidated system, together with one or more other Member States.

2. The elements referred to in the first sentence of paragraph 1 shall be made available to the central administrator designated under Article 20 of Directive 2003/87/EC.

Article 7
Assigned amount

1. The Community and each Member State shall, by 31 December 2006 at the latest, each submit a report to the UNFCCC Secretariat determining their assigned amount as equal to their respective emission levels determined pursuant to the first paragraph of Article 3 of Decision 2002/358/EC and the Kyoto Protocol. Member States and the Community shall endeavour to submit their reports simultaneously.

2. Member States shall, following the completion of the review of their national inventories under the Kyoto Protocol for each year of the Kyoto Protocol's first commitment period, including the resolution of any questions of implementation, forthwith withdraw assigned amount units, removal units, emission reduction units and certified emission reductions equivalent to their net emissions during that year.

In respect of the last year of the commitment period, retirement shall take place prior to the end of the additional period set in the Marrakech Accords for fulfilling commitments.

3. Member States shall issue assigned amount units in their national registries corresponding to their emission levels determined pursuant to Decision 2002/358/EC and the Kyoto Protocol.

Article 8
Procedures under the Kyoto Protocol

1. Member States and the Community shall ensure full and effective cooperation and coordination with each other in relation to obligations under this Decision concerning:

(a) the compilation of the Community greenhouse gas inventory and the Community greenhouse gas inventory report, pursuant to Article 4(1);
(b) the review and compliance procedures under the Kyoto Protocol in accordance with the relevant decisions thereunder;
(c) any adjustments under the UNFCCC review process or other changes to inventories and inventory reports submitted, or to be submitted, to the UNFCCC Secretariat;

(d) the preparation of the Community's report and the Member States' reports on the demonstration of progress by 2005 pursuant to Article 5(3) and (4);

(e) the preparation and submission of the report referred to in Article 7(1); and

(f) reporting in relation to the additional period set in the Marrakech Accords for fulfilling commitments pursuant to Article 5(5) and (6).

2. Member States shall submit national inventories to the UNFCCC Secretariat by 15 April each year containing information identical to that submitted in accordance with Article 3(1), unless information removing any inconsistencies or gaps has been provided to the Commission by 15 March of that year at the latest.

3. The Commission may, in accordance with the procedure referred to in Article 9(2), lay down procedures and time scales for such cooperation and coordination.

Article 9
Committee

1. The Commission shall be assisted by a 'Climate Change Committee'.

2. Where reference is made to this paragraph, Articles 5 and 7 of Decision 1999/468/EC shall apply, having regard to Article 8 thereof.

The period laid down in Article 5(6) of Decision 1999/468/EC shall be set at three months.

3. The Climate Change Committee shall adopt its Rules of Procedure.

Article 10
Further measures

Following the submission of the report on the demonstration of progress by 2005, in accordance with Article 5(3), the Commission shall forthwith review the extent to which the Community and its Member States are making progress towards their emission levels, determined in accordance with Decision 2002/358/EC and the Kyoto Protocol, and the extent to which they are meeting their commitments under the Kyoto Protocol. In the light of this assessment, the Commission may make proposals, as appropriate, to the European Parliament and the Council to ensure that the Community and its Member States comply with their emission levels and that all their commitments under the Kyoto Protocol are met.

Article 11
Repeal

Decision 93/389/EEC is hereby repealed.

Any references made to the repealed Decision shall be construed as references to this Decision and shall be read in accordance with the correlation table in the Annex.

Article 12
Addressees

This Decision is addressed to the Member States.

Done at Strasbourg, 11 February 2004.

Annex
Correlation table

Decision 93/389/EEC – This decision.
[Omitted]

PART VI

Biodiversity and nature conservation

Council Directive 79/409/EEC of 2 April 1979 on the conservation of wild birds (as amended)

Editorial note

Council Directive 79/409/EEC on the conservation of wild birds seeks to conserve wild birds and establish measures to ensure the protection and control of certain species. The scope of this Directive extends to the conservation of all species of naturally occurring birds in the wild in the European territory of the Member States to which the Treaty applies, and covers the protection, management and control of these species and establishes rules for their exploitation (Article 1(1)). The Directive applies to birds, their eggs, nests and habitats (Article 1(2)). Member States must take the necessary measures to maintain the population of the species described in Article 1 at a level which corresponds to ecological, scientific and cultural requirements, or to adapt the population of the species to that level, taking into consideration economic and recreational requirements (Article 2). Member States must take measures to preserve, maintain or re-establish a sufficient diversity and area of habitats for all species of birds referred to in Article 1, including the creation of protected areas, the upkeep and management of habitats inside and outside the protected areas, the re-establishment of destroyed biotypes, and the creation of new biotypes (Article 3).

Species listed in Annex I to the Directive are subject to special conservation measures regarding their habitat and Member States must classify the most suitable territories as special protection areas for the conservation of these species (Article 4(1)). The Directive requires Member States to adopt similar measures for regularly occurring migratory species not listed in Annex I and, to this end, attention should be paid to the protection of wetlands, particularly wetlands of international importance (Article 4(2)). Member States are also obliged to avoid pollution, the deterioration of habitats, or disturbances affecting birds in respect of protection areas (Article 4(4)). In order to facilitate the necessary coordination to meet the objectives set out in Article 4, Member States must report to the Commission all relevant information (Article 4(3)).

The Directive requires Member States to establish a general system of protection for all species of birds referred to in Article 1, in particular prohibiting the deliberate killing, capture, destruction of nests and eggs, taking of eggs, disturbance, and keeping of species (Article 5). In respect to the bird species referred to in Article 1, Member States must prohibit the sale, transport for sale, keeping for sale, and the offering for sale of live or dead birds, or of any readily recognisable parts or derivatives of such birds (Article 6(1)). Special provisions are set out for species referred to in Annex III/1 and III/2 (Article 6(2) and (3)). The Directive allows for the hunting of species listed in Annex II, although Member States must ensure that such hunting does not jeopardise conservation efforts in their distribution area (Article 7). In respect of the hunting, capture or killing of birds, under this Directive, Member States must prohibit the use of large-scale or non-selective capture or killing of birds, especially those listed in Annex IV(a), and prohibit hunting from the modes of transport and under the conditions mentioned in Annex IV(b) (Article 8). Member States may derogate from the provisions of Articles 5, 6, 7, and 8 in the interests of public health and safety, or for the purposes of research and teaching, or to permit the capture of certain birds in small numbers (Article 9). The Directive encourages research and work required as a basis for the protection, management and use of the population of all species of birds referred to in Article 1 (Article 10). Member States must see that any introduction of species of birds which do not occur naturally in the wild state in the European territory of the Member State does not prejudice the local flora and fauna (Article 11).

Member States are required to report to the Commission every three years on the implementation of the Directive (Article 12). Any measures taken pursuant to the Directive may not lead to deterioration in the present situation as regards the conservation of species of birds referred to in Article 1 (Article 13), and Member States may introduce stricter protective measures than those provided for under the Directive (Article 14). Amendments to the Directive should be adopted in accordance with the procedure laid down in Article 17 (Article 15) and a Committee for the Adaptation to Technical and Scientific Progress is set up (Article 16) in order to assist the Commission (Article 17). Member States must transpose the Directive into national law within two years of its notification (Article 18).

Source: OJ L 103 25.04.1979 p. 1. Amended by: Council Directive 81/854/EEC of 19 October 1981 L 319 3 07.11.1981. Commission Directive 85/411/EEC of 25 July 1985 L 233 33 30.08.1985. Council Directive 86/122/EEC of 8 April 1986 L 100 22 16.04.1986. Commission Directive 91/244/EEC of 6 March 1991 L 115 41 8.05.1991. Council Directive 94/24/EC of 8 June 1994 L 164 9 30.06.1994. Commission Directive 97/49/EC of 29 July 1997 L 223 9 13.08.1997. Council Regulation (EC) No 807/2003 of 14 April 2003 L 122 36 16.05.2003. Amended by: Act of Accession of Greece L 291 17 19.11.1979. Act of Accession of Spain and Portugal L 302 23 15.11.1985. Act of Accession of Austria, Sweden and Finland C 241 21 29.08.1994. Adapted by Council Decision 95/1/EC, Euratom, ECSC) L 1 1 01.01.1995

Council Directive 79/409/EEC of 2 April 1979 on the conservation of wild birds (as amended)

The Council of the European Communities,

Having regard to the Treaty establishing the European Economic Community, and in particular Article 235 thereof,

Having regard to the proposal from the Commission,[1]

Having regard to the opinion of the European Parliament,[2]

Having regard to the opinion of the Economic and Social Committee,[3]

Whereas the Council declaration of 22 November 1973 on the programme of action of the European Communities on the environment[4] calls for specific action to protect birds, supplemented by the resolution of the Council of the European Communities and of the representatives of the Governments of the Member States meeting within the Council of 17 May 1977 on the continuation and implementation of a European Community policy and action programme on the environment;[5]

Whereas a large number of species of wild birds naturally occurring in the European territory of the Member States are declining in number, very rapidly in some cases; whereas this decline represents a serious threat to the conservation of the natural environment, particularly because of the biological balances threatened thereby;

Whereas the species of wild birds naturally occurring in the European territory of the Member States are mainly migratory species; whereas such species constitute a common heritage and whereas effective bird protection is typically a trans-frontier environment problem entailing common responsibilities;

Whereas the conditions of life for birds in Greenland are fundamentally different from those in the other regions of the European territory of the Member States on account of the general circumstances and in particular the climate, the low density of population and the exceptional size and geographical situation of the island;

Whereas therefore this Directive should not apply to Greenland;

Whereas the conservation of the species of wild birds naturally occurring in the European territory of the Member States is necessary to attain, within the operation of the common market, of the Community's objectives regarding the improvement of living conditions, a harmonious development of economic activities throughout the Community and a continuous and balanced expansion, but the necessary specific powers to act have not been provided for in the Treaty;

Whereas the measures to be taken must apply to the various factors which may affect the numbers of birds, namely the repercussions of man's activities and in particular the destruction and pollution of their habitats, capture and killing by man and the trade resulting from such practices; whereas the stringency of such measures should be adapted to the particular situation of the various species within the framework of a conservation policy;

Whereas conservation is aimed at the long-term protection and management of natural resources as an integral part of the heritage of the peoples of Europe; whereas it makes it possible to control natural resources and governs their use on the basis of

[1] OJ No C 24, 1. 2. 1977, p. 3; OJ No C 201, 23. 8. 1977, p. 2.   [2] OJ No C 163, 11. 7. 1977, p. 28.
[3] OJ No C 152, 29. 6. 1977, p. 3.   [4] OJ No C 112 20. 12. 1973, p. 40.   [5] OJ No C 139, 13. 6. 1977, p. 1.

the measures necessary for the maintenance and adjustment of the natural balances between species as far as is reasonably possible;

Whereas the preservation, maintenance or restoration of a sufficient diversity and area of habitats is essential to the conservation of all species of birds; whereas certain species of birds should be the subject of special conservation measures concerning their habitats in order to ensure their survival and reproduction in their area of distribution; whereas such measures must also take account of migratory species and be coordinated with a view to setting up a coherent whole;

Whereas, in order to prevent commercial interests from exerting a possible harmful pressure on exploitation levels it is necessary to impose a general ban on marketing and to restrict all derogation to those species whose biological status so permits, account being taken of the specific conditions obtaining in the different regions;

Whereas, because of their high population level, geographical distribution and reproductive rate in the Community as a whole, certain species may be hunted, which constitutes acceptable exploitation; where certain limits are established and respected, such hunting must be compatible with maintenance of the population of these species at a satisfactory level;

Whereas the various means, devices or methods of large-scale or nonselective capture or killing and hunting with certain forms of transport must be banned because of the excessive pressure which they exert or may exert on the numbers of the species concerned;

Whereas, because of the importance which may be attached to certain specific situations, provision should be made for the possibility of derogations on certain conditions and subject to monitoring by the Commission;

Whereas the conservation of birds and, in particular, migratory birds still presents problems which call for scientific research; whereas such research will also make it possible to assess the effectiveness of the measures taken;

Whereas care should be taken in consultation with the Commission to see that the introduction of any species of wild bird not naturally occurring in the European territory of the Member States does not cause harm to local flora and fauna;

Whereas the Commission will every three years prepare and transmit to the Member States a composite report based on information submitted by the Member States on the application of national provisions introduced pursuant to this Directive;

Whereas it is necessary to adapt certain Annexes rapidly in the light of technical and scientific progress; whereas, to facilitate the implementation of the measures needed for this purpose, provision should be made for a procedure establishing close cooperation between the Member States and the Commission in a Committee for Adaptation to Technical and Scientific Progress,

Has Adopted this Directive:

Article 1

1. This Directive relates to the conservation of all species of naturally occurring birds in the wild state in the European territory of the Member States to which the Treaty applies. It covers the protection, management and control of these species and lays down rules for their exploitation.

2. It shall apply to birds, their eggs, nests and habitats.

3. This Directive shall not apply to Greenland.

Article 2

Member States shall take the requisite measures to maintain the population of the species referred to in Article 1 at a level which corresponds in particular to ecological, scientific and cultural requirements, while taking account of economic and recreational requirements, or to adapt the population of these species to that level.

Article 3

1. In the light of the requirements referred to in Article 2, Member States shall take the requisite measures to preserve, maintain or re-establish a sufficient diversity and area of habitats for all the species of birds referred to in Article 1.

2. The preservation, maintenance and re-establishment of biotopes and habitats shall include primarily the following measures:

(a) creation of protected areas;
(b) upkeep and management in accordance with the ecological needs of habitats inside and outside the protected zones;
(c) re-establishment of destroyed biotopes;
(d) creation of biotopes.

Article 4

1. The species mentioned in Annex I shall be the subject of special conservation measures concerning their habitat in order to ensure their survival and reproduction in their area of distribution. In this connection, account shall be taken of:

(a) species in danger of extinction;
(b) species vulnerable to specific changes in their habitat;
(c) species considered rare because of small populations or restricted local distribution;
(d) other species requiring particular attention for reasons of the specific nature of their habitat. Trends and variations in population levels shall be taken into account as a background for evaluations.

Member States shall classify in particular the most suitable territories in number and size as special protection areas for the conservation of these species, taking into account their protection requirements in the geographical sea and land area where this Directive applies.

2. Member States shall take similar measures for regularly occurring migratory species not listed in Annex I, bearing in mind their need for protection in the geographical sea and land area where this Directive applies, as regards their breeding, moulting and wintering areas and staging posts along their migration routes. To this end, Member States shall pay particular attention to the protection of wetlands and particularly to wetlands of international importance.

3. Member States shall send the Commission all relevant information so that it may take appropriate initiatives with a view to the coordination necessary to ensure that the areas provided for in paragraphs 1 and 2 above form a coherent whole which meets the protection requirements of these species in the geographical sea and land area where this Directive applies.

4. In respect of the protection areas referred to in paragraphs 1 and 2 above, Member States shall take appropriate steps to avoid pollution or deterioration of habitats or any disturbances affecting the birds, in so far as these would be significant having regard to the objectives of this Article. Outside these protection areas, Member States shall also strive to avoid pollution or deterioration of habitats.

Article 5

Without prejudice to Articles 7 and 9, Member States shall take the requisite measures to establish a general system of protection for all species of birds referred to in Article 1, prohibiting in particular:

(a) deliberate killing or capture by any method;
(b) deliberate destruction of, or damage to, their nests and eggs or removal of their nests;
(c) taking their eggs in the wild and keeping these eggs even if empty;
(d) deliberate disturbance of these birds particularly during the period of breeding and rearing, in so far as disturbance would be significant having regard to the objectives of this Directive;
(e) keeping birds of species the hunting and capture of which is prohibited.

Article 6

1. Without prejudice to the provisions of paragraphs 2 and 3, Member States shall prohibit, for all the bird species referred to in Article 1, the sale, transport for sale, keeping for sale and the offering for sale of live or dead birds and of any readily recognizable parts or derivatives of such birds.

2. The activities referred to in paragraph 1 shall not be prohibited in respect of the species referred to in Annex III/1, provided that the birds have been legally killed or captured or otherwise legally acquired.

3. Member States may, for the species listed in Annex III/2, allow within their territory the activities referred to in paragraph 1, making provision for certain restrictions, provided the birds have been legally killed or captured or otherwise legally acquired.

Member States wishing to grant such authorization shall first of all consult the Commission with a view to examining jointly with the latter whether the marketing of specimens of such species would result or could reasonably be expected to result in the population levels, geographical distribution or reproductive rate of the species being endangered throughout the Community. Should this examination prove that the intended authorization will, in the view of the Commission, result in any one of the aforementioned species being thus endangered or in the possibility of their being thus endangered, the Commission shall forward a reasoned recommendation to the Member State concerned stating its opposition to the marketing of the species in question. Should the Commission consider that no such risk exists, it will inform the Member State concerned accordingly.

The Commission's recommendation shall be published in the *Official Journal of the European Communities.*

Member States granting authorization pursuant to this paragraph shall verify at regular intervals that the conditions governing the granting of such authorization continue to be fulfilled.

4. The Commission shall carry out studies on the biological status of the species listed in Annex III/3 and on the effects of marketing on such status.

It shall submit, at the latest four months before the time limit referred to in Article 18(1) of this Directive, a report and its proposals to the Committee referred to in Article 16, with a view to a decision on the entry of such species in Annex III/2.

Pending this decision, the Member States may apply existing national rules to such species without prejudice to paragraph 3 hereof.

Article 7

1. Owing to their population level, geographical distribution and reproductive rate throughout the Community, the species listed in Annex II may be hunted under national legislation. Member States shall ensure that the hunting of these species does not jeopardize conservation efforts in their distribution area.

2. The species referred to in Annex II/1 may be hunted in the geographical sea and land area where this Directive applies.

3. The species referred to in Annex II/2 may be hunted only in the Member States in respect of which they are indicated.

4. Member States shall ensure that the practice of hunting, including falconry if practised, as carried on in accordance with the national measures in force, complies with the principles of wise use and ecologically balanced control of the species of birds concerned and that this practice is compatible as regards the population of these species, in particular migratory species, with the measures resulting from Article 2. They shall see in particular that the species to which hunting laws apply are not hunted

during the rearing season nor during the various stages of reproduction. In the case of migratory species, they shall see in particular that the species to which hunting regulations apply are not hunted during their period of reproduction or during their return to their rearing grounds. Member States shall send the Commission all relevant information on the practical application of their hunting regulations.

Article 8

1. In respect of the hunting, capture or killing of birds under this Directive, Member States shall prohibit the use of all means, arrangements or methods used for the large-scale or non-selective capture or killing of birds or capable of causing the local disappearance of a species, in particular the use of those listed in Annex IV(a).

2. Moreover, Member States shall prohibit any hunting from the modes of transport and under the conditions mentioned in Annex IV(b).

Article 9

1. Member States may derogate from the provisions of Articles 5, 6, 7 and 8, where there is no other satisfactory solution, for the following reasons:

(a) – in the interests of public health and safety,
  – in the interests of air safety,
  – to prevent serious damage to crops, livestock, forests, fisheries and water,
  – for the protection of flora and fauna;
(b) for the purposes of research and teaching, of re-population, of reintroduction and for the breeding necessary for these purposes;
(c) to permit, under strictly supervised conditions and on a selective basis, the capture, keeping or other judicious use of certain birds in small numbers.

2. The derogations must specify:

– the species which are subject to the derogations,
– the means, arrangements or methods authorized for capture or killing,
– the conditions of risk and the circumstances of time and place under which such derogations may be granted,
– the authority empowered to declare that the required conditions obtain and to decide what means, arrangements or methods may be used, within what limits and by whom,
– the controls which will be carried out.

3. Each year the Member States shall send a report to the Commission on the implementation of this Article.

4. On the basis of the information available to it, and in particular the information communicated to it pursuant to paragraph 3, the Commission shall at all times ensure that the consequences of these derogations are not incompatible with this Directive. It shall take appropriate steps to this end.

Article 10

1. Member States shall encourage research and any work required as a basis for the protection, management and use of the population of all species of bird referred to in Article 1.

2. Particular attention shall be paid to research and work on the subjects listed in Annex V. Member States shall send the Commission any information required to enable it to take appropriate measures for the coordination of the research and work referred to in this Article.

Article 11

Member States shall see that any introduction of species of bird which do not occur naturally in the wild state in the European territory of the Member States does not prejudice the local flora and fauna. In this connection they shall consult the Commission.

Article 12

1. Member States shall forward to the Commission every three years, starting from the date of expiry of the time limit referred to in Article 18(1), a report on the implementation of national provisions taken thereunder.

2. The Commission shall prepare every three years a composite report based on the information referred to in paragraph 1. That part of the draft report covering the information supplied by a Member State shall be forwarded to the authorities of the Member State in question for verification. The final version of the report shall be forwarded to the Member States.

Article 13

Application of the measures taken pursuant to this Directive may not lead to deterioration in the present situation as regards the conservation of species of birds referred to in Article 1.

Article 14

Member States may introduce stricter protective measures than those provided for under this Directive.

Article 15

Such amendments as are necessary for adapting Annexes I and V to this Directive to technical and scientific progress and the amendments referred to in the second paragraph of Article 6(4) shall be adopted in accordance with the procedure laid down in Article 17.

Article 16

1. For the purposes of the amendments referred to in Article 15 of this Directive, a Committee for the Adaptation to Technical and Scientific Progress (hereinafter called 'the Committee'), consisting of representatives of the Member States and chaired by a representative of the Commission, is hereby set up.

Article 17

1. The Commission shall be assisted by the Committee for the Adaptation to Technical and Scientific Progress.

2. Where reference is made to this Article, Articles 5 and 7 of Decision 1999/468/EC[1] shall apply.

The period laid down in Article 5(6) of Decision 1999/468/EC shall be set at three months.

3. The committee shall adopt its rules of procedure.

Article 18

1. Member States shall bring into force the laws, regulations and administrative provisions necessary to comply with this Directive within two years of its notification. They shall forthwith inform the Commission thereof.

2. Member States shall communicate to the Commission the texts of the main provisions of national law which they adopt in the field governed by this Directive.

Article 19

This Directive is addressed to the Member States.

Annexes

[omitted]

---

[1] OJ L 184, 17.7.1999, p. 23.

Council Regulation (EEC) No 348/81 of 20 January 1981 on common rules for imports of whales or other cetacean products (as amended)

Editorial note

Council Regulation (EEC) No 348/81 of 20 January 1981 seeks to restrict international trade in order to conserve cetacean species. From 1 January 1982 the introduction into the Community of the products listed in the Annex will be subject to the production of an import licence, although no licence will be issued in respect of products to be used for commercial purposes (Article 1(1)). Member States must notify the Commission by 1 July 1981 of the names and addresses of the authorities competent to issue import licences (Article 1(2)). The Regulation establishes a Committee on Cetacean Products to examine any question relating to the application of the Regulation submitted to it by its chairman (Article 2). The Commission must submit to the Council a report on whether the list of products in the Annex should be extended, and on the possibilities for supervising compliance with its provisions (Article 3(1)). Acting by qualified majority, the Council may decide to extend the list of products in the Annex (Article 3(2)). Pending such a decision by the Council, Member States may take measures concerning whales or other cetacean products not covered by this Regulation for the protection of the species (Article 3(3)).

Source: OJ L 39 12.02.1981 p. 1. Amended by: Act of Accession of Spain and Portugal L 302 23 15.11.1985. Act of Accession of Austria, Sweden and Finland C 241 21 29.08.1994 (adapted by Council Decision 95/1/EC, Euratom, ECSC) L 1 1 01.01.1995. Corrected by: Corrigendum, OJ L 132, 19.05.1981 p. 30 (348/81)

Council Regulation (EEC) No 348/81 of 20 January 1981 on common rules for imports of whales or other cetacean products (as amended)

The Council of the European Communities,
    Having regard to the Treaty establishing the European Economic Community, and in particular Article 235 thereof,
    Having regard to the proposal from the Commission,[1]

---

[1] OJ No C 121, 20. 5. 1980, p. 5.

Having regard to the opinion of the European Parliament,[1]

Having regard to the opinion of the Economic and Social committee,[2]

Whereas the conservation of cetacean species calls for measures which will restrict international trade; whereas these should be Community level measures and should at the same time respect the Community's international obligations;

Whereas, pending the adoption at Community level of more general measures concerning the supervision of trade in species of wild fauna and flora, imports of the main whale or other cetacean products should be subject, in an initial stage, to import permits, while the possibility of extending the list of these products is also reserved; whereas, in order to clarify the situation, it may be useful to note that, pending this possible extension, the Member States continue to be competent for taking, in compliance with the Treaty, measures for the protection of the species relating to imports of products not covered by this Regulation; whereas the competent authorities should not issue such permits unless they have assured themselves that the products in question are not to be used for commercial purposes,

Has adopted this Regulation:

Article 1

1. From 1 January 1982 the introduction into the Community of the products listed in the Annex shall be subject to the production of an import licence. No such licence shall be issued in respect of products to be used for commercial purposes.

2. Member States shall notify the Commission before 1 July 1981 of the names and addresses of the authorities competent to issue the import licences referred to in paragraph 1. The Commission shall immediately inform the other Member States thereof.

Article 2

1. A Committee on Cetacean Products, hereinafter referred to as 'the Committee' is hereby set up, consisting of representatives of the Member States with a representative of the Commission as chairman.

The Committee shall adopt its own rules of procedure.

It may examine any question relating to the application of this Regulation, including the question of control, submitted to it by its chairman either on his own initiative or at the request of the representative of a Member State.

2. The following procedure shall be adopted for implementing this Regulation:

(a) the Commission representative shall submit to the Committee a draft of the provisions to be adopted. The Committee shall deliver an opinion on the draft within a time limit set by the chairman having regard to the urgency of the matter.

---

[1] OJ No C 291, 10. 11. 1980, p. 46.　　　[2] OJ No C 300, 18. 11. 1980, p. 13.

Decisions shall be taken by a majority of 62 votes, the votes of the Member States being weighted as provided for in Article 148(2) of the Treaty. The chairman shall not vote.

(b) the Commission shall adopt the provisions envisaged if they are in accordance with the opinion of the Committee.

(c) if the provisions envisaged are not in accordance with the opinion of the Committee, or if no opinion is delivered, the Commission shall without delay submit to the Council a proposal with regard to the provisions to be adopted. The Council shall act by a qualified majority. If, within three months of the proposal being submitted to it, the Council has not acted, the proposed provisions shall be adopted by the Commission.

Article 3

1. At the earliest opportunity, the Commission shall submit to the Council a report on whether the list of products in the Annex to this Regulation should be extended, and on the possibilities for supervising compliance with its provisions, together with proposals, as the case may be.

2. The Council acting by qualified majority on a proposal from the Commission may decide to extend the list referred to in paragraph 1.

3. Pending such decision, Member States may take, in compliance with the Treaty, measures concerning whales or other cetacean products not covered by this Regulation for the protection of the species.

This Regulation shall be binding in its entirety and directly applicable in all Member States.

Annex

[omitted]

Council Directive 92/43/EEC of 21 May 1992 on the conservation of natural habitats and of wild fauna and flora (as amended)

Editorial note

The aim of Directive 92/43/EEC is to contribute towards ensuring biodiversity through the conservation of natural habitats and of wild fauna and flora (Article 2(1)). Measures taken pursuant to the Directive should maintain or restore natural habitats and species of wild flora and fauna (Article 2(2)), whilst taking account of economic, social and cultural requirements along with regional and local characteristics (Article 2(3)). The definitions relevant for the purpose of the Directive are set out in Article 1.

The Directive establishes a European ecological network of special areas of conservation entitled Natura 2000, comprising sites hosting the natural habitat types listed in Annex I and habitat types of the species listed in Annex II (Article 3(1)). Each Member State must contribute to the creation of Natura 2000 by designating sites as special areas of conservation (Article 3(2)). Based on the criteria set out in Annex III (Stage 1), each Member State must propose a list of sites indicating which natural habitat types in Annex I and which species in Annex II are native to its territory (Article 4(1)). On the basis of the criteria set out in Annex III (Stage 2), the Commission is to establish a draft list of sites of Community importance within six years of the notification of the Directive (Article 4(2) and (3)). Following the adoption of a site of Community importance, the Member State concerned must designate that site as a special area of conservation (Article 4(4)). In exceptional cases where the Commission finds that a national list referred to in Article 4(1) fails to mention a site hosting a priority habitat type or priority species which it considers to be essential for the maintenance of that priority habitat type or priority species, a bilateral consultation procedure must be initiated between that Member State and the Commission (Article 5). For special areas of conservation, Member States must establish the necessary conservation measures involving appropriate management plans and statutory, administrative or contractual measures which correspond to the ecological requirements of the natural habitat types in Annex I and the species in Annex II present on the sites (Article 6(1)). In special areas of conservation Member States must take steps to avoid the deterioration of natural habitats and the disturbance of the species for which the areas have been designated (Article 6(2)). Any plan or project not directly connected with or necessary to the management of the site, but likely to have a significant effect, must be subject to assessment of its implications in view of the site's conservation objectives (Article 6(3)). In certain circumstances, obligations arising under Article 6 of the Directive will replace obligations established by Article 4 of Directive 79/409/EEC (Article 7). Member States must send to the Commission estimates relating to the Community co-financing which they consider necessary to allow them to meet their obligations under Article 6(1) (Article 8(1)), whereby the Commission will identify those measures essential for the maintenance or re-establishment at a favourable conservation status of the priority natural habitat types and priority species on the sites concerned, as well as the total costs arising from those measures (Article 8(2)). The Commission must periodically review the contribution of Natura 2000 towards the achievement of the objectives set out in Articles 2 and 3 (Article 9). Member States should encourage the management of features of the landscape which are of major importance for wild flora and fauna in their land-use planning and development policies (Article 10). Member States are to undertake surveillance of the conservation status of the natural habitats and species referred to in Article 2, with particular regard to priority natural habitat types and priority species (Article 11).

Member States must establish a system of strict protection for the animal species listed in Annex IV(a) in their natural range, prohibiting deliberate capture, killing, disturbance, destruction or taking of eggs, or disturbance of breeding sites (Article 12(1)), along with prohibition of the keeping, transport, sale or exchange of the species (Article 12(2)). Member States must establish a system of strict protection for the plant species listed in Annex IV(b), prohibiting the deliberate picking, collecting, cutting, uprooting or destruction of such plants, along with the keeping, transport, sale or exchange of the species (Article 13). Where it is deemed necessary, Member States can continue with the surveillance provided for by Article 11 by including measures such as regulating access to property, temporary or local prohibition of taking specimens, regulating the periods and/or methods of taking specimens, applying hunting and fishing rules, establishing a licence system, regulating the sale and purchase of specimens, or breeding species in captivity (Article 14). In respect of the capture or killing of species of wild fauna listed in Annex V(a), Member States must prohibit the use of all indiscriminate means capable of causing local disappearance of, or serious disturbance to, populations of such species (Article 15). Provided that there is no satisfactory alternative and the derogation is not detrimental to the maintenance of the populations of the species concerned at a favourable conservation status in their natural range, in some circumstances Member States may derogate from the provisions of Articles 12, 13, 14 and 15(a) and (b) (Article 16(1)). Member States must report to the Commission every two years on any derogations applied under Article 16(1) (Article 16(2)).

Member States are required to report to the Commission on a regular basis regarding the implementation of the Directive (Article 17). Member States and the Commission are to encourage the necessary research and scientific work, having regard to the objectives set out in Article 2 and the obligation referred to in Article 11 (Article 18). Provision is made within the Directive for amendments to be made to the Annexes (Article 19) and for a Committee to be established in order to assist the Commission (Article 20). Where reference is made to Article 21, Articles 5 and 7 of Decision 1999/468/EC shall apply (Article 21). In implementing the Directive, Member States should study the desirability of re-introducing species in Annex IV, ensure that the deliberate introduction into the wild of any species which is not native to their territory is regulated, and promote education and general information on the need to protect species of wild fauna and flora and to conserve their habitats (Article 22). Member States must transpose the Directive into national law within two years of notification (Article 23).

Source: OJ L 206 22.07.1992 p. 7. Amended by: Council Directive 97/62/EC of 27 October 1997 L 305 42 08.11.1997. Regulation (EC) No 1882/2003 of the European Parliament and of the Council of 29 September 2003 L 284 1 31.10.2003. Amended by: Act of Accession of Austria, Sweden and Finland C 241 21 29.08.1994. Adapted by Council Decision 95/1/EC, Euratom, ECSC, L 1 1 01.01.1995. Corrected by: Corrigendum, OJ L 176, 20.07.1993 p. 29

Council Directive 92/43/EEC of 21 May 1992 on the conservation of natural habitats and of wild fauna and flora (as amended)

The Council of the European Communities,
    Having regard to the Treaty establishing the European Economic Community, and in particular Article 130s thereof,
    Having regard to the proposal from the Commission,[1]
    Having regard to the opinion of the European Parliament,[2]
    Having regard to the opinion of the Economic and Social Committee,[3]
    Whereas the preservation, protection and improvement of the quality of the environment, including the conservation of natural habitats and of wild fauna and flora, are an essential objective of general interest pursued by the Community, as stated in Article 130r of the Treaty;
    Whereas the European Community policy and action programme on the environment (1987 to 1992)[4] makes provision for measures regarding the conservation of nature and natural resources;

---

[1] OJ No C 247, 21. 9. 1988, p. 3 and OJ No C 195, 3.8.1990, p. 1.
[2] OJ No C 75, 20. 3. 1991, p. 12.   [3] OJ No C 31, 6. 2. 1991, p. 25.   [4] OJ No C 328, 7. 12. 1987, p. 1.

Whereas, the main aim of this Directive being to promote the maintenance of biodiversity, taking account of economic, social, cultural and regional requirements, this Directive makes a contribution to the general objective of sustainable development; whereas the maintenance of such biodiversity may in certain cases require the maintenance, or indeed the encouragement, of human activities;

Whereas, in the European territory of the Member States, natural habitats are continuing to deteriorate and an increasing number of wild species are seriously threatened; whereas given that the threatened habitats and species form part of the Community's natural heritage and the threats to them are often of a transboundary nature, it is necessary to take measures at Community level in order to conserve them;

Whereas, in view of the threats to certain types of natural habitat and certain species, it is necessary to define them as having priority in order to favour the early implementation of measures to conserve them;

Whereas, in order to ensure the restoration or maintenance of natural habitats and species of Community interest at a favourable conservation status, it is necessary to designate special areas of conservation in order to create a coherent European ecological network according to a specified timetable;

Whereas all the areas designated, including those classified now or in the future as special protection areas pursuant to Council Directive 79/409/EEC of 2 April 1979 on the conservation of wild birds,[1] will have to be incorporated into the coherent European ecological network;

Whereas it is appropriate, in each area designated, to implement the necessary measures having regard to the conservation objectives pursued;

Whereas sites eligible for designation as special areas of conservation are proposed by the Member States but whereas a procedure must nevertheless be laid down to allow the designation in exceptional cases of a site which has not been proposed by a Member State but which the Community considers essential for either the maintenance or the survival of a priority natural habitat type or a priority species;

Whereas an appropriate assessment must be made of any plan or programme likely to have a significant effect on the conservation objectives of a site which has been designated or is designated in future;

Whereas it is recognized that the adoption of measures intended to promote the conservation of priority natural habitats and priority species of Community interest is a common responsibility of all Member States; whereas this may, however, impose an excessive financial burden on certain Member States given, on the one hand, the uneven distribution of such habitats and species throughout the Community and, on the other hand, the fact that the 'polluter pays' principle can have only limited application in the special case of nature conservation;

---

[1] OJ No L 103, 25.4.1979, p. 1. Directive as last amended by Directive 91/244/ECC (OJ No L 115, 8.5.1991, p. 41).

Whereas it is therefore agreed that, in this exceptional case, a contribution by means of Community co-financing should be provided for within the limits of the resources made available under the Community's decisions;

Whereas land-use planning and development policies should encourage the management of features of the landscape which are of major importance for wild fauna and flora;

Whereas a system should be set up for surveillance of the conservation status of the natural habitats and species covered by this Directive;

Whereas a general system of protection is required for certain species of flora and fauna to complement Directive 79/409/EEC; whereas provision should be made for management measures for certain species, if their conservation status so warrants, including the prohibition of certain means of capture or killing, whilst providing for the possibility of derogations on certain conditions;

Whereas, with the aim of ensuring that the implementation of this Directive is monitored, the Commission will periodically prepare a composite report based, *inter alia*, on the information sent to it by the Member States regarding the application of national provisions adopted under this Directive;

Whereas the improvement of scientific and technical knowledge is essential for the implementation of this Directive; whereas it is consequently appropriate to encourage the necessary research and scientific work;

Whereas technical and scientific progress mean that it must be possible to adapt the Annexes; whereas a procedure should be established whereby the Council can amend the Annexes;

Whereas a regulatory committee should be set up to assist the Commission in the implementation of this Directive and in particular when decisions on Community co-financing are taken;

Whereas provision should be made for supplementary measures governing the reintroduction of certain native species of fauna and flora and the possible introduction of non-native species;

Whereas education and general information relating to the objectives of this Directive are essential for ensuring its effective implementation,

Has adopted this Directive:

Definitions

Article 1

For the purpose of this Directive:

  (a) *conservation* means a series of measures required to maintain or restore the natural habitats and the populations of species of wild fauna and flora at a favourable status as defined in (e) and (i);
  (b) *natural habitats* means terrestrial or aquatic areas distinguished by geographic, abiotic and biotic features, whether entirely natural or semi-natural;

(c) *natural habitat types of Community interest* means those which, within the territory referred to in Article 2:
   (i) are in danger of disappearance in their natural range; or
   (ii) have a small natural range following their regression or by reason of their intrinsically restricted area; or
   (iii) present outstanding examples of typical characteristics of one or more of the six following biogeographical regions: Alpine, Atlantic, Boreal, Continental, Macaronesian and Mediterranean. Such habitat types are listed or may be listed in Annex I;

(d) *priority natural habitat types* means natural habitat types in danger of disappearance, which are present on the territory referred to in Article 2 and for the conservation of which the Community has particular responsibility in view of the proportion of their natural range which falls within the territory referred to in Article 2; these priority natural habitat types are indicated by an asterisk (*) in Annex I;

(e) *conservation status of a natural habitat* means the sum of the influences acting on a natural habitat and its typical species that may affect its long-term natural distribution, structure and functions as well as the long-term survival of its typical species within the territory referred to in Article 2.
   The conservation status of a natural habitat will be taken as 'favourable' when:
   – its natural range and areas it covers within that range are stable or increasing, and
   – the specific structure and functions which are necessary for its long-term maintenance exist and are likely to continue to exist for the foreseeable future, and
   – the conservation status of its typical species is favourable as defined in (i);

(f) *habitat of a species* means an environment defined by specific abiotic and biotic factors, in which the species lives at any stage of its biological cycle;

(g) *species of Community interest* means species which, within the territory referred to in Article 2, are:
   (i) endangered, except those species whose natural range is marginal in that territory and which are not endangered or vulnerable in the western palearctic region; or
   (ii) vulnerable, i.e. believed likely to move into the endangered category in the near future if the causal factors continue operating; or
   (iii) rare, i.e. with small populations that are not at present endangered or vulnerable, but are at risk. The species are located within restricted geographical areas or are thinly scattered over a more extensive range; or
   (iv) endemic and requiring particular attention by reason of the specific nature of their habitat and/or the potential impact of their exploitation on their habitat and/or the potential impact of their exploitation on their conservation status. Such species are listed or may be listed in Annex II and/or Annex IV or V;

(h) *priority species* means species referred to in (g)(i) for the conservation of which the Community has particular responsibility in view of the proportion of their natural range which falls within the territory referred to in Article 2; these priority species are indicated by an asterisk (*) in Annex II;

(i) *conservation status of a species* means the sum of the influences acting on the species concerned that may affect the long-term distribution and abundance of its populations within the territory referred to in Article 2;

The *conservation status* will be taken as 'favourable' when:

– population dynamics data on the species concerned indicate that it is maintaining itself on a long-term basis as a viable component of its natural habitats, and

– the natural range of the species is neither being reduced nor is likely to be reduced for the foreseeable future, and

– there is, and will probably continue to be, a sufficiently large habitat to maintain its populations on a long-term basis;

(j) *site* means a geographically defined area whose extent is clearly delineated;

(k) *site of Community importance* means a site which, in the biogeographical region or regions to which it belongs, contributes significantly to the maintenance or restoration at a favourable conservation status of a natural habitat type in Annex I or of a species in Annex II and may also contribute significantly to the coherence of Natura 2000 referred to in Article 3, and/or contributes significantly to the maintenance of biological diversity within the biogeographic region or regions concerned.

For animal species ranging over wide areas, sites of Community importance shall correspond to the places within the natural range of such species which present the physical or biological factors essential to their life and reproduction;

(l) *special area of conservation* means a site of Community importance designated by the Member States through a statutory, administrative and/or contractual act where the necessary conservation measures are applied for the maintenance or restoration, at a favourable conservation status, of the natural habitats and/or the populations of the species for which the site is designated;

(m) *specimen* means any animal or plant, whether alive or dead, of the species listed in Annex IV and Annex V, any part or derivative thereof, as well as any other goods which appear, from an accompanying document, the packaging or a mark or label, or from any other circumstances, to be parts or derivatives of animals or plants of those species;

(n) *the committee* means the committee set up pursuant to Article 20.

Article 2

1. The aim of this Directive shall be to contribute towards ensuring bio-diversity through the conservation of natural habitats and of wild fauna and flora in the European territory of the Member States to which the Treaty applies.

2. Measures taken pursuant to this Directive shall be designed to maintain or restore, at favourable conservation status, natural habitats and species of wild fauna and flora of Community interest.

3. Measures taken pursuant to this Directive shall take account of economic, social and cultural requirements and regional and local characteristics.

Conservation of natural habitats and habitats of species

Article 3

1. A coherent European ecological network of special areas of conservation shall be set up under the title Natura 2000. This network, composed of sites hosting the natural habitat types listed in Annex I and habitats of the species listed in Annex II, shall enable the natural habitat types and the species' habitats concerned to be maintained or, where appropriate, restored at a favourable conservation status in their natural range.

The Natura 2000 network shall include the special protection areas classified by the Member States pursuant to Directive 79/409/EEC.

2. Each Member State shall contribute to the creation of Natura 2000 in proportion to the representation within its territory of the natural habitat types and the habitats of species referred to in paragraph 1. To that effect each Member State shall designate, in accordance with Article 4, sites as special areas of conservation taking account of the objectives set out in paragraph 1.

3. Where they consider it necessary, Member States shall endeavour to improve the ecological coherence of Natura 2000 by maintaining, and where appropriate developing, features of the landscape which are of major importance for wild fauna and flora, as referred to in Article 10.

Article 4

1. On the basis of the criteria set out in Annex III (Stage 1) and relevant scientific information, each Member State shall propose a list of sites indicating which natural habitat types in Annex I and which species in Annex II that are native to its territory the sites host. For animal species ranging over wide areas these sites shall correspond to the places within the natural range of such species which present the physical or biological factors essential to their life and reproduction. For aquatic species which range over wide areas, such sites will be proposed only where there is a clearly identifiable area representing the physical and biological factors essential to their life and reproduction. Where appropriate, Member States shall propose adaptation of the list in the light of the results of the surveillance referred to in Article 11.

The list shall be transmitted to the Commission, within three years of the notification of this Directive, together with information on each site. That information shall include a map of the site, its name, location, extent and the data resulting from application of the criteria specified in Annex III (Stage 1) provided in a format established by the Commission in accordance with the procedure laid down in Article 21.

2. On the basis of the criteria set out in Annex III (Stage 2) and in the framework both of each of the five biogeographical regions referred to in Article 1(c)(iii) and of the whole of the territory referred to in Article 2(1), the Commission shall establish, in agreement with each Member State, a draft list of sites of Community importance drawn from the Member States' lists identifying those which host one or more priority natural habitat types or priority species.

Member States whose sites hosting one or more priority natural habitat types and priority species represent more than 5% of their national territory may, in agreement with the Commission, request that the criteria listed in Annex III (Stage 2) be applied more flexibly in selecting all the sites of Community importance in their territory.

The list of sites selected as sites of Community importance, identifying those which host one or more priority natural habitat types or priority species, shall be adopted by the Commission in accordance with the procedure laid down in Article 21.

3. The list referred to in paragraph 2 shall be established within six years of the notification of this Directive.

4. Once a site of Community importance has been adopted in accordance with the procedure laid down in paragraph 2, the Member State concerned shall designate that site as a special area of conservation as soon as possible and within six years at most, establishing priorities in the light of the importance of the sites for the maintenance or restoration, at a favourable conservation status, of a natural habitat type in Annex I or a species in Annex II and for the coherence of Natura 2000, and in the light of the threats of degradation or destruction to which those sites are exposed.

5. As soon as a site is placed on the list referred to in the third subparagraph of paragraph 2 it shall be subject to Article 6(2), (3) and (4).

Article 5

1. In exceptional cases where the Commission finds that a national list as referred to in Article 4(1) fails to mention a site hosting a priority natural habitat type or priority species which, on the basis of relevant and reliable scientific information, it considers to be essential for the maintenance of that priority natural habitat type or for the survival of that priority species, a bilateral consultation procedure shall be initiated between that Member State and the Commission for the purpose of comparing the scientific data used by each.

2. If, on expiry of a consultation period not exceeding six months, the dispute remains unresolved, the Commission shall forward to the Council a proposal relating to the selection of the site as a site of Community importance.

3. The Council, acting unanimously, shall take a decision within three months of the date of referral.

4. During the consultation period and pending a Council decision, the site concerned shall be subject to Article 6(2).

Article 6

1. For special areas of conservation, Member States shall establish the necessary conservation measures involving, if need be, appropriate management plans specifically designed for the sites or integrated into other development plans, and appropriate statutory, administrative or contractual measures which correspond to the ecological requirements of the natural habitat types in Annex I and the species in Annex II present on the sites.

2. Member States shall take appropriate steps to avoid, in the special areas of conservation, the deterioration of natural habitats and the habitats of species as well as disturbance of the species for which the areas have been designated, in so far as such disturbance could be significant in relation to the objectives of this Directive.

3. Any plan or project not directly connected with or necessary to the management of the site but likely to have a significant effect thereon, either individually or in combination with other plans or projects, shall be subject to appropriate assessment of its implications for the site in view of the site's conservation objectives. In the light of the conclusions of the assessment of the implications for the site and subject to the provisions of paragraph 4, the competent national authorities shall agree to the plan or project only after having ascertained that it will not adversely affect the integrity of the site concerned and, if appropriate, after having obtained the opinion of the general public.

4. If, in spite of a negative assessment of the implications for the site and in the absence of alternative solutions, a plan or project must nevertheless be carried out for imperative reasons of overriding public interest, including those of a social or economic nature, the Member State shall take all compensatory measures necessary to ensure that the overall coherence of Natura 2000 is protected. It shall inform the Commission of the compensatory measures adopted.

Where the site concerned hosts a priority natural habitat type and/or a priority species, the only considerations which may be raised are those relating to human health or public safety, to beneficial consequences of primary importance for the environment or, further to an opinion from the Commission, to other imperative reasons of overriding public interest.

Article 7

Obligations arising under Article 6(2), (3) and (4) of this Directive shall replace any obligations arising under the first sentence of Article 4(4) of Directive 79/409/EEC in respect of areas classified pursuant to Article 4(1) or similarly recognized under Article 4(2) thereof, as from the date of implementation of this Directive or the date of classification or recognition by a Member State under Directive 79/409/EEC, where the latter date is later.

Article 8

1. In parallel with their proposals for sites eligible for designation as special areas of conservation, hosting priority natural habitat types and/ or priority species, the

Member States shall send, as appropriate, to the Commission their estimates relating to the Community co-financing which they consider necessary to allow them to meet their obligations pursuant to Article 6(1).

2. In agreement with each of the Member States concerned, the Commission shall identify, for sites of Community importance for which co-financing is sought, those measures essential for the maintenance or re-establishment at a favourable conservation status of the priority natural habitat types and priority species on the sites concerned, as well as the total costs arising from those measures.

3. The Commission, in agreement with the Member States concerned, shall assess the financing, including co-financing, required for the operation of the measures referred to in paragraph 2, taking into account, amongst other things, the concentration on the Member State's territory of priority natural habitat types and/or priority species and the relative burdens which the required measures entail.

4. According to the assessment referred to in paragraphs 2 and 3, the Commission shall adopt, having regard to the available sources of funding under the relevant Community instruments and according to the procedure set out in Article 21, a prioritized action framework of measures involving co-financing to be taken when the site has been designated under Article 4(4).

5. The measures which have not been retained in the action framework for lack of sufficient resources, as well as those included in the abovementioned action framework which have not received the necessary co-financing or have only been partially co-financed, shall be reconsidered in accordance with the procedure set out in Article 21, in the context of the two-yearly review of the action framework and may, in the main time, be postponed by the Member States pending such review. This review shall take into account, as appropriate, the new situation of the site concerned.

6. In areas where the measures dependent on co-financing are postponed, Member States shall refrain from any new measures likely to result in deterioration of those areas.

Article 9

The Commission, acting in accordance with the procedure laid down in Article 21, shall periodically review the contribution of Natura 2000 towards achievement of the objectives set out in Article 2 and 3. In this context, a special area of conservation may be considered for declassification where this is warranted by natural developments noted as a result of the surveillance provided for in Article 11.

Article 10

Member States shall endeavour, where they consider it necessary, in their land-use planning and development policies and, in particular, with a view to improving the ecological coherence of the Natura 2000 network, to encourage the management of features of the landscape which are of major importance for wild fauna and flora.

Such features are those which, by virtue of their linear and continuous structure (such as rivers with their banks or the traditional systems for marking field boundaries) or their function as stepping stones (such as ponds or small woods), are essential for the migration, dispersal and genetic exchange of wild species.

Article 11

Member States shall undertake surveillance of the conservation status of the natural habitats and species referred to in Article 2 with particular regard to priority natural habitat types and priority species.

Protection of species

Article 12

1. Member States shall take the requisite measures to establish a system of strict protection for the animal species listed in Annex IV(a) in their natural range, prohibiting:

(a) all forms of deliberate capture or killing of specimens of these species in the wild;
(b) deliberate disturbance of these species, particularly during the period of breeding, rearing, hibernation and migration;
(c) deliberate destruction or taking of eggs from the wild;
(d) deterioration or destruction of breeding sites or resting places.

2. For these species, Member States shall prohibit the keeping, transport and sale or exchange, and offering for sale or exchange, of specimens taken from the wild, except for those taken legally before this Directive is implemented.

3. The prohibition referred to in paragraph 1(a) and (b) and paragraph 2 shall apply to all stages of life of the animals to which this Article applies.

4. Member States shall establish a system to monitor the incidential capture and killing of the animal species listed in Annex IV(a). In the light of the information gathered, Member States shall take further research or conservation measures as required to ensure that incidental capture and killing does not have a significant negative impact on the species concerned.

Article 13

1. Member States shall take the requisite measures to establish a system of strict protection for the plant species listed in Annex IV(b), prohibiting:

(a) the deliberate picking, collecting, cutting, uprooting or destruction of such plants in their natural range in the wild;
(b) the keeping, transport and sale or exchange and offering for sale or exchange of specimens of such species taken in the wild, except for those taken legally before this Directive is implemented.

2. The prohibitions referred to in paragraph 1(a) and (b) shall apply to all stages of the biological cycle of the plants to which this Article applies.

Article 14

1. If, in the light of the surveillance provided for in Article 11, Member States deem it necessary, they shall take measures to ensure that the taking in the wild of specimens of species of wild fauna and flora listed in Annex V as well as their exploitation is compatible with their being maintained at a favourable conservation status.

2. Where such measures are deemed necessary, they shall include continuation of the surveillance provided for in Article 11. Such measures may also include in particular:

- regulations regarding access to certain property,
- temporary or local prohibition of the taking of specimens in the wild and exploitation of certain populations,
- regulation of the periods and/or methods of taking specimens,
- application, when specimens are taken, of hunting and fishing rules which take account of the conservation of such populations,
- establishment of a system of licences for taking specimens or of quotas,
- regulation of the purchase, sale, offering for sale, keeping for sale or transport for sale of specimens,
- breeding in captivity of animal species as well as artificial propagation of plant species, under strictly controlled conditions, with a view to reducing the taking of specimens of the wild,
- assessment of the effect of the measures adopted.

Article 15

In respect of the capture or killing of species of wild fauna listed in Annex V(a) and in cases where, in accordance with Article 16, derogations are applied to the taking, capture or killing of species listed in Annex IV(a), Member States shall prohibit the use of all indiscriminate means capable of causing local disappearance of, or serious disturbance to, populations of such species, and in particular:

(a) use of the means of capture and killing listed in Annex VI(a);
(b) any form of capture and killing from the modes of transport referred to in Annex VI(b).

Article 16

1. Provided that there is no satisfactory alternative and the derogation is not detrimental to the maintenance of the populations of the species concerned at a favourable conservation status in their natural range, Member States may derogate from the provisions of Articles 12, 13, 14 and 15(a) and (b):

(a) in the interest of protecting wild fauna and flora and conserving natural habitats;
(b) to prevent serious damage, in particular to crops, livestock, forests, fisheries and water and other types of property;

(c) in the interests of public health and public safety, or for other imperative reasons of overriding public interest, including those of a social or economic nature and beneficial consequences of primary importance for the environment;

(d) for the purpose of research and education, of repopulating and reintroducing these species and for the breedings operations necessary for these purposes, including the artificial propagation of plants;

(e) to allow, under strictly supervised conditions, on a selective basis and to a limited extent, the taking or keeping of certain specimens of the species listed in Annex IV in limited numbers specified by the competent national authorities.

2. Member States shall forward to the Commission every two years a report in accordance with the format established by the Committee on the derogations applied under paragraph 1. The Commission shall give its opinion on these derogations within a maximum time limit of 12 months following receipt of the report and shall give an account to the Committee.

3. The reports shall specify:

(a) the species which are subject to the derogations and the reason for the derogation, including the nature of the risk, with, if appropriate, a reference to alternatives rejected and scientific data used;

(b) the means, devices or methods authorized for the capture or killing of animal species and the reasons for their use;

(c) the circumstances of when and where such derogations are granted;

(d) the authority empowered to declare and check that the required conditions obtain and to decide what means, devices or methods may be used, within what limits and by what agencies, and which persons are to carry out the task;

(e) the supervisory measures used and the results obtained.

Information

Article 17

1. Every six years from the date of expiry of the period laid down in Article 23, Member States shall draw up a report on the implementation of the measures taken under this Directive. This report shall include in particular information concerning the conservation measures referred to in Article 6(1) as well as evaluation of the impact of those measures on the conservation status of the natural habitat types of Annex I and the species in Annex II and the main results of the surveillance referred to in Article 11. The report, in accordance with the format established by the committee, shall be forwarded to the Commission and made accessible to the public.

2. The Commission shall prepare a composite report based on the reports referred to in paragraph 1. This report shall include an appropriate evaluation of the progress achieved and, in particular, of the contribution of Natura 2000 to the achievement of the objectives set out in Article 3. A draft of the part of the report covering the

information supplied by a Member State shall be forwarded to the Member State in question for verification. After submission to the committee, the final version of the report shall be published by the Commission, not later than two years after receipt of the reports referred to in paragraph 1, and shall be forwarded to the Member States, the European Parliament, the Council and the Economic and Social Committee.

3. Member States may mark areas designated under this Directive by means of Community notices designed for that purpose by the committee.

Research

Article 18

1. Member States and the Commission shall encourage the necessary research and scientific work having regard to the objectives set out in Article 2 and the obligation referred to in Article 11. They shall exchange information for the purposes of proper coordination of research carried out at Member State and at Community level.

2. Particular attention shall be paid to scientific work necessary for the implementation of Articles 4 and 10, and transboundary cooperative research between Member States shall be encouraged.

Procedure for amending the Annexes

Article 19

Such amendments as are necessary for adapting Annexes I, II, III, V and VI to technical and scientific progress shall be adopted by the Council acting by qualified majority on a proposal from the Commission.

Such amendments as are necessary for adapting Annex IV to technical and scientific progress shall be adopted by the Council acting unanimously on a proposal from the Commission.

Committee

Article 20

The Commission shall be assisted by a committee.

Article 21

1. Where reference is made to this Article, Articles 5 and 7 of Decision 1999/468/EC[1] shall apply, having regard to the provisions of Article 8 thereof.

The period laid down in Article 5(6) of Decision 1999/468/EC shall be set at three months.

2. The Committee shall adopt its rules of procedure.

---

[1] Council Decision 1999/468/EC of 28 June 1999 laying down the procedures for the exercise of implementing powers conferred on the Commission (OJ L 184, 17.7.1999, p. 23).

Supplementary provisions

Article 22

In implementing the provisions of this Directive, Member States shall:

(a) study the desirability of re-introducing species in Annex IV that are native to their territory where this might contribute to their conservation, provided that an investigation, also taking into account experience in other Member States or elsewhere, has established that such re-introduction contributes effectively to re-establishing these species at a favourable conservation status and that it takes place only after proper consultation of the public concerned;

(b) ensure that the deliberate introduction into the wild of any species which is not native to their territory is regulated so as not to prejudice natural habitats within their natural range or the wild native fauna and flora and, if they consider it necessary, prohibit such introduction. The results of the assessment undertaken shall be forwarded to the committee for information;

(c) promote education and general information on the need to protect species of wild fauna and flora and to conserve their habitats and natural habitats.

Final provisions

Article 23

1. Member States shall bring into force the laws, regulations and administrative provisions necessary to comply with this Directive within two years of its notification. They shall forthwith inform the Commission thereof.

2. When Member States adopt such measures, they shall contain a reference to this Directive or be accompanied by such reference on the occasion of their official publication. The methods of making such a reference shall be laid down by the Member States.

3. Member States shall communicate to the Commission the main provisions of national law which they adopt in the field covered by this Directive.

Article 24

This Directive is addressed to the Member States.

Annexes

[Omitted]

Council Regulation (EC) No 338/97 of 9 December 1996 on the protection of species of wild fauna and flora by regulating trade therein (as amended)

Editorial note

The object of the Regulation is to protect species of wild fauna and flora and to guarantee their conservation by regulating trade therein, and it should be applied in compliance with the Convention (Article 1). The 'Convention' is defined as the Convention on International Trade in Endangered Species of Wild Fauna and Flora (Article 2). Annex A is based on the species listed in Appendix I to the Convention for which Member States have not entered a reservation (Article 3(1)); Annex B includes the species listed in Appendix II to the Convention (Article 3(2)); Annex C includes the species listed in Appendix III to the Convention (Article 3(3)); and Annex D includes species not listed in Annexes A to C which are imported into the Community in such numbers as to warrant monitoring (Article 3(4)).

The Regulation outlines the specific details and procedures required for the granting of an import permit in each of the different situations (Article 4). The introduction into the Community of specimens of the species listed in Annex A is to be subject to completion of the necessary checks and the prior presentation, at the border customs office at the point of introduction, of an import permit issued by a management authority of the Member State of destination (Article 4(1)). The introduction into the Community of specimens of the species listed in Annex B is to be subject to completion of the necessary checks and the prior presentation, at the border customs office at the point of introduction, of an import permit issued by a management authority of the Member State of destination (Article 4(2)). The introduction into the Community of specimens of the species listed in Annex C is to be subject to completion of the necessary checks and the prior presentation, at the border customs office at the point of introduction, of an import notification and certain other information depending on the country of export (Article 4(3)). The introduction into the Community of specimens of the species listed in Annex D is to be subject to completion of the necessary checks and the prior presentation of an import notification at the border customs office at the point of introduction (Article 4(4)). The export or re-export from the Community of specimens of the species listed in Annexes A, B and C must be subject to completion of the necessary checks and the prior presentation, at the customs office at which the export formalities are completed, of an export permit or re-export certificate issued by a management authority of the Member State in which the specimens are located – and must meet the specified conditions for that particular Annex (Article 5).

When a Member State rejects an application for a permit or certificate in a case of significance in respect of the objectives of this Regulation, it shall immediately inform the Commission of the rejection and of the reasons for rejection (Article 6(1)). The Regulation allows for derogations from the main obligations in circumstances involving specimens born and bred in captivity or artificially propagated (Article 7(1)), where a specimen is in transit (Article 7(2)), personal and household effects (Article 7(3)), and in respect of scientific institutions (Article 7(4)). Although some derogations do exist, commercial activities involving species listed in Annex A are generally prohibited, whilst less stringent provisions are set out for species in Annexes B, C and D (Article 8). Any movement within the Community of a live specimen of a species listed in Annex A requires prior authorisation from a management authority of the Member State in which the specimen is located (Article 9(1)). Less stringent provisions are provided for species listed in Annex B (Article 9(4)), whilst the transportation of any live specimens requires those involved to minimise the risk of injury, damage to health or cruel treatment (Article 9(5)).

Certificates are to be issued by the appropriate management authority in the Member States where all the criteria have been satisfied and correct documentation submitted (Article 10). Whilst Member States may adopt or maintain stricter measures, permits and certificates issued by the competent authorities of the Member States in accordance with this Regulation will be valid throughout the Community (Article 11). Member States must designate customs offices for carrying out the checks and formalities for the introduction into and export from the Community (Article 12). Each Member State must designate a management authority with primary responsibility for implementation of this Regulation and for communication with the Commission (Article 13(1)). Each Member State must also designate one or more scientific authorities with appropriate qualifications whose duties shall be separate from those of any designated management authority (Article 13(2)). The competent authorities of the Member States are responsible for monitoring compliance with the provisions of this Regulation and provision is made for the investigation of infringements (Article 14). The Member States and the Commission must communicate to one another the information necessary for implementing this Regulation (Article 15(1)). Member States must take appropriate measures to ensure the imposition of sanctions for certain specified infringements (Article 16). A Scientific Review Group is established to examine any scientific question relating to the application of this Regulation (Article 17). The Commission, assisted by a Committee (Article 18), has certain specific responsibilities regarding the implementation of the Regulation (Article 19). Member States must notify the Commission and the Convention Secretariat of the provisions which they adopt specifically for the implementation of this Regulation and of all legal instruments used and measures taken for its implementation and enforcement (Article 20). The Regulation repealed Regulation (EEC) No 3626/82 (Article 21) and applied from 1 June 1997 (Article 22).

Source: OJ L 61, 03.03.1997 p. 1. Amended by: Commission Regulation (EC) No 938/97 of 26 May 1997 L 140 1 30.05.1997. Commission Regulation (EC) No 2307/97 of 18 November 1997 L 325 1 27.11.1997. Commission Regulation (EC) No 2214/98 of 15 October 1998 L 279 3 16.10.1998. Commission Regulation (EC) No 1476/1999 of 6 July 1999 L 171 5 07.07.1999. Commission Regulation (EC) No 2724/2000 of 30 November 2000 L 320 1 18.12.2000. Commission Regulation (EC) No 1579/2001 of 1 August 2001 L 209 14 02.08.2001. Commission Regulation (EC) No 2476/2001 of 17 December 2001 L 334 3 18.12.2001. Commission Regulation (EC) No 1497/2003 of 18 August 2003 L 215 3 27.08.2003. Regulation (EC) No 1882/2003 of the European Parliament and of the Council of 29 September 2003 L 284 1 31.10.2003. Commission Regulation (EC) No 834/2004 of 28 April 2004 L 127 40 29.04.2004. Corrected by: Corrigendum, OJ L 298, 01.11.1997 p. 70 (338/97)

Council Regulation (EC) No 338/97 of 9 December 1996 on the protection of species of wild fauna and flora by regulating trade therein (as amended)

The Council of the European Union,
    Having regard to the Treaty establishing the European Community, and in particular Article 130s(1) thereof,
    Having regard to the proposal from the Commission,[1]
    Having regard to the opinion of the Economic and Social Committee,[2]
    Acting in accordance with the procedure laid down in Article 189c of the Treaty,[3]

(1) Whereas Regulation (EEC) No 3626/82[4] applies the Convention on International Trade in Endangered Species of Wild Fauna and Flora in the Community with effect from 1 January 1984; whereas the purpose of the Convention is to protect endangered species of fauna and flora through controls on international trade in specimens of those species;

(2) Whereas, in order to improve the protection of species of wild fauna and flora which are threatened by trade or likely to be so threatened, Regulation (EEC) No 3626/82 must be replaced by a Regulation taking account of the scientific knowledge acquired since its adoption and the current structure of trade; whereas,

---

[1] OJ No C 26, 3. 2. 1992, p. 1, and OJ No C 131, 12. 5. 1994, p. 1.   [2] OJ No C 223, 31. 8. 1992, p. 19.
[3] Opinion of the European Parliament of 15 December 1995 (OJ No C 17, 22. 1. 1996, p. 430). Common position of the Council of 26 February 1996 (OJ No C 196, 6. 7. 1996, p. 58) and Decision of the European Parliament of 18 September 1996 (OJ No C 320, 28. 10. 1996).
[4] OJ No L 384, 31. 12. 1982, p. 1. Regulation as last amended by Commission Regulation (EC) No 558/95 (OJ No L 57, 15. 3. 1995, p. 1).

moreover, the abolition of controls at internal borders resulting from the Single Market necessitates the adoption of stricter trade control measures at the Community's external borders, with documents and goods being checked at the customs office at the border where they are introduced;

(3) Whereas the provisions of this Regulation do not prejudice any stricter measures which may be taken or maintained by Member States, in compliance with the Treaty, in particular with regard to the holding of specimens of species covered by this Regulation;

(4) Whereas it is necessary to lay down objective criteria for the inclusion of species of wild fauna and flora in the Annexes to this Regulation;

(5) Whereas the implementation of this Regulation necessitates the application of common conditions for the issue, use and presentation of documents relating to authorization of the introduction into the Community and the export or re-export from the Community of specimens of the species covered by this Regulation; whereas it is necessary to lay down specific provisions relating to the transit of specimens through the Community;

(6) Whereas it is for a management authority of the Member State of destination, assisted by the scientific authority of that Member State and, where appropriate, taking into account any opinion of the Scientific Review Group, to decide on the requests for introduction of specimens into the Community;

(7) Whereas it is necessary to supplement the provisions on reexport with a consultation procedure, in order to limit the risk of infringement;

(8) Whereas, in order to guarantee effective protection of species of wild fauna and flora, additional restrictions may be imposed on the introduction of specimens into, and the export thereof from, the Community; whereas, with regard to live specimens, these restrictions may be supplemented by restrictions at Community level on the holding or movement of such specimens within the Community;

(9) Whereas it is necessary to lay down specific provisions applicable to captive-born and bred, or artificially propagated specimens, to specimens which are personal or household effects, and to non-commercial loans, donations or exchanges between registered scientists and scientific institutions;

(10) Whereas there is a need, in order to ensure the broadest possible protection for species covered by this Regulation, to lay down provisions for controlling trade and movement of specimens within the Community, and the conditions for housing specimens; whereas the certificates issued under this Regulation, which contribute to controlling these activities, must be governed by common rules on their issue, validity and use;

(11) Whereas measures should be taken to minimize the adverse effects on live specimens of transport to their destination, from or within the Community;

(12) Whereas, to ensure effective controls and to facilitate customs procedures, customs offices should be designated, with trained personnel responsible for carrying out the necessary formalities and corresponding checks where specimens are

introduced into the Community, in order to assign them a customs-approved treatment or use within the meaning of Council Regulation (EEC) No 2913/92 of 12 October 1992 establishing the Community Customs Code,[1] or where they are exported or re-exported from the Community; whereas there should also be facilities guaranteeing that live specimens are adequately housed and cared for;

(13) Whereas the implementation of this Regulation also calls for the designation of management and scientific authorities by the Member States;

(14) Whereas informing the public and making them aware of the provisions of this Regulation, particularly at border crossing points, is likely to encourage compliance with these provisions;

(15) Whereas, in order to ensure effective enforcement of this Regulation, Member States should closely monitor compliance with its provisions and, to that end, cooperate closely between themselves and with the Commission; whereas this requires the communication of information relating to the implementation of this Regulation;

(16) Whereas the monitoring of levels of trade in the species of wild fauna and flora covered by this Regulation is of crucial importance for assessing the effects of trade on the conservation status of species; whereas detailed annual reports should be drawn up in a common format;

(17) Whereas, in order to guarantee compliance with this Regulation, it is important that Member States impose sanctions for infringements in a manner which is both sufficient and appropriate to the nature and gravity of the infringement;

(18) Whereas it is essential to lay down a Community procedure enabling the implementing provisions and amendments to the Annexes of this Regulation to be adopted within a suitable period; whereas a Committee must be set up to permit close and effective cooperation between the Member States and the Commission in this field;

(19) Whereas the multitude of biological and ecological aspects to be considered in the implementation of this Regulation requires the setting up of a Scientific Review Group, whose opinions will be forwarded by the Commission to the Committee and the management bodies of the Member States, to assist them in making their decisions,

Has adopted this Regulation:

Article 1

Object

The object of this Regulation is to protect species of wild fauna and flora and to guarantee their conservation by regulating trade therein in accordance with the following

---

[1] OJ No L 302, 19. 10. 1992, p. 1. Regulation as last amended by the 1994 Act of Accession.

Articles. This Regulation shall apply in compliance with the objectives, principles and provisions of the Convention defined in Article 2.

Article 2
Definitions

For the purposes of this Regulation:

(a) 'Committee' shall mean the Committee on Trade in Wild Fauna and Flora, established under Article 18;

(b) 'Convention' shall mean the Convention on International Trade in Endangered Species of Wild Fauna and Flora (Cites);

(c) 'country of origin' shall mean the country in which a specimen was taken from the wild, captive-bred or artificially propagated;

(d) 'import notification' shall mean the notification given by the importer or his agent or representative, at the time of the introduction into the Community of a specimen of a species included in Annexes C or D, on a form prescribed by the Commission in accordance with the procedure laid down in Article 18;

(e) 'introduction from the sea' shall mean the introduction into the Community of any specimen which was taken in, and is being introduced directly from, the marine environment not under the jurisdiction of any State, including the air-space above the sea and the sea-bed and subsoil beneath the sea;

(f) 'issuance' shall mean the completion of all procedures involved in preparing and validating a permit or certificate and its delivery to the applicant;

(g) 'management authority' shall mean a national administrative authority designated, in the case of a Member State, in accordance with Article 13(1)(a) or, in the case of a third country party to the Convention, in accordance with Article IX of the Convention;

(h) 'Member State of destination' shall mean the Member State of destination mentioned in the document used to export or re-export a specimen; in the event of introduction from the sea, it shall mean the Member State within whose jurisdiction the place of destination of a specimen lies;

(i) 'offering for sale' shall mean offering for sale and any action that may reasonably be construed as such, including advertising or causing to be advertised for sale and invitation to treat;

(j) 'personal or household effects' shall mean dead specimens, parts and derivatives thereof, that are the belongings of a private individual and that form, or are intended to form, part of his normal goods and chattels;

(k) 'place of destination' shall mean the place at which at the time of introduction into the Community, it is intended that specimens will normally be kept; in the case of live specimens, this shall be the first place where specimens are intended to be kept following any period of quarantine or other confinement for the purposes of sanitary checks and controls;

(l) 'population' shall mean a biologically or geographically distinct total number of individuals;

(m) 'primarily commercial purposes' shall mean all purposes the noncommercial aspects of which do not clearly predominate;

(n) 're-export from the Community' shall mean export from the Community of any specimen that has previously been introduced;

(o) 'reintroduction into the Community' shall mean introduction into the Community of any specimen that has previously been exported or re-exported;

(p) 'sale' shall mean any form of sale. For the purposes of this Regulation, hire, barter or exchange shall be regarded as sale; cognate expressions shall be similarly construed;

(q) 'scientific authority' shall mean a scientific authority designated, in the case of a Member State, in accordance with Article 13(1)(b) or, in the case of a third country party to the Convention, in accordance with Article IX of the Convention;

(r) 'Scientific Review Group' shall mean the consultative body established under Article 17;

(s) 'species' shall mean a species, subspecies or population thereof;

(t) 'specimen' shall mean any animal or plant, whether alive or dead, of the species listed in Annexes A to D, any part or derivative thereof, whether or not contained in other goods, as well as any other goods which appear from an accompanying document, the packaging or a mark or label, or from any other circumstances, to be or to contain parts or derivatives of animals or plants of those species, unless such parts or derivatives are specifically exempted from the provisions of this Regulation or from the provisions relating to the Annex in which the species concerned is listed by means of an indication to that effect in the Annexes concerned.

A specimen will be considered to be a specimen of a species listed in Annexes A to D if it is, or is part of or derived from, an animal or plant at least one of whose 'parents' is of a species so listed. In cases where the 'parents' of such an animal or plant are of species listed in different Annexes, or of species only one of which is listed, the provisions of the more restrictive Annex shall apply. However, in the case of specimens of hybrid plants, if one of the 'parents' is of a species listed in Annex A, the provisions of the more restrictive Annex shall apply only if that species is annotated to that effect in the Annex;

(u) 'trade' shall mean the introduction into the Community, including introduction from the sea, and the export and re-export therefrom, as well as the use, movement and transfer of possession within the Community, including within a Member State, of specimens subject to the provisions of this Regulation;

(v) 'transit' shall mean the transport of specimens between two points outside the Community through the territory of the Community which are shipped to a named consignee and during which any interruption in the movement arises only from the arrangements necessitated by this form of traffic;

(w) 'worked specimens that were acquired more than 50 years previously' shall mean specimens that were significantly altered from their natural raw state for jewellery, adornment, art, utility, or musical instruments, more than 50 years before the entry into force of this Regulation and that have been, to the satisfaction of the management authority of the Member State concerned, acquired in such conditions. Such specimens shall be considered as worked only if they are clearly in one of the aforementioned categories and require no further carving, crafting or manufacture to effect their purpose;

(x) 'checks at the time of introduction, export, re-export and transit' shall mean documentary checks on the certificates, permits and notifications provided for in this Regulation and
   – in cases where Community provisions so provide or in other cases by representative sampling of the consignments
   – examination of the specimens, where appropriate accompanied by the taking of samples with a view to analysis or more detailed checks.

Article 3

Scope

1. Annex A shall contain:

(a) the species listed in Appendix I to the Convention for which the Member States have not entered a reservation;
(b) any species:
   (i) which is, or may be, in demand for utilization in the Community or for international trade and which is either threatened with extinction or so rare that any level of trade would imperil the survival of the species; or
   (ii) which is in a genus of which most of the species or which is a species of which most of the subspecies are listed in Annex A in accordance with the criteria in subparagraphs (a) or (b)(i) and whose listing in the Annex is essential for the effective protection of those taxa.

2. Annex B shall contain:

(a) the species listed in Appendix II to the Convention, other than those listed in Annex A, for which the Member States have not entered a reservation;
(b) the species listed in Appendix I to the Convention for which a reservation has been entered;
(c) any other species not listed in Appendices I or II to the Convention:
   (i) which is subject to levels of international trade that might not be compatible:
      – with its survival or with the survival of populations in certain countries, or
      – with the maintenance of the total population at a level consistent with the role of the species in the ecosystems in which it occurs:
      or
   (ii) whose listing in the Annex for reasons of similarity in appearance to other species listed in Annex A or Annex B, is essential in order to ensure the effectiveness of controls on trade in specimens of such species;

(d) species in relation to which it has been established that the introduction of live specimens into the natural habitat of the Community would constitute an eco-logical threat to wild species of fauna and flora indigenous to the Community.

3. Annex C shall contain:

(a) the species listed in Appendix III to the Convention, other than those listed in Annexes A or B, for which the Member States have not entered a reservation;
(b) the species listed in Appendix II to the Convention for which a reservation has been entered.

4. Annex D shall contain:

(a) species not listed in Annexes A to C which are imported into the Community in such numbers as to warrant monitoring;
(b) the species listed in Appendix III to the Convention for which a reservation has been entered.

5. Where the conservation status of species covered by this Regulation warrants their inclusion in one of the Appendices to the Convention, the Member States shall contribute to the necessary amendments.

Article 4
Introduction into the Community

1. The introduction into the Community of specimens of the species listed in Annex A shall be subject to completion of the necessary checks and the prior presentation, at the border customs office at the point of introduction, of an import permit issued by a management authority of the Member State of destination.

The import permit may be issued only in accordance with the restrictions estab-lished pursuant to paragraph 6 and when the following conditions have been met:

(a) the competent scientific authority, after considering any opinion by the Scientific Review Group, has advised that the introduction into the Community:
  (i) would not have a harmful effect on the conservation status of the species or on the extent of the territory occupied by the relevant population of the species;
  (ii) is taking place:
    – for one of the purposes referred to in Article 8(3)(e), (f) and (g), or
    – for other purposes which are not detrimental to the survival of the species concerned;
(b) (i) the applicant provides documentary evidence that the specimens have been obtained in accordance with the legislation on the protection of the species concerned which, in the case of import from a third country of specimens of a species listed in the Appendices to the Convention, shall be an export permit or re-export certificate, or copy thereof, issued in accordance with the Convention by a competent authority of the country of exportor re-export;

(ii) however, the issuance of import permits for species listed in Annex A in accordance with Article 3(1)(a) shall not require such documentary evidence, but the original of any such import permit shall be withheld from the applicant pending presentation of the export permit or re-export certificate;

(c) the competent scientific authority is satisfied that the intended accommodation for a live specimen at the place of destination is adequately equipped to conserve and care for it properly;

(d) the management authority is satisfied that the specimen is not to be used for primarily commercial purposes;

(e) the management authority is satisfied, following consultation with the competent scientific authority, that there are no other factors relating to the conservation of the species which militate against issuance of the import permit; and

(f) in the case of introduction from the sea, the management authority is satisfied that any live specimen will be so prepared and shipped as to minimize the risk of injury, damage to health or cruel treatment.

2. The introduction into the Community of specimens of the species listed in Annex B shall be subject to completion of the necessary checks and the prior presentation, at the border customs office at the point of introduction, of an import permit issued by a management authority of the Member State of destination.

The import permit may be issued only in accordance with the restrictions established pursuant to paragraph 6 and when:

(a) the competent scientific authority, after examining available data and considering any opinion from the Scientific Review Group, is of the opinion that the introduction into the Community would not have a harmful effect on the conservation status of the species or on the extent of the territory occupied by the relevant population of the species, taking account of the current or anticipated level of trade. This opinion shall be valid for subsequent imports as long as the abovementioned aspects have not changed significantly;

(b) the applicant provides documentary evidence that the intended accommodation for a live specimen at the place of destination is adequately equipped to conserve and care for it properly;

(c) the conditions referred to in paragraph 1(b)(i), (e) and (f) have been met.

3. The introduction into the Community of specimens of the species listed in Annex C shall be subject to completion of the necessary checks and the prior presentation, at the border customs office at the point of introduction, of an import notification and:

(a) in the case of export from a country mentioned in relation to the species concerned in Annex C, the applicant shall provide documentary evidence, by means of an export permit issued in accordance with the Convention by an authority of that country competent for the purpose, that the specimens have been obtained in accordance with the national legislation on the conservation of the species concerned; or

(b) in the case of export from a country not mentioned in relation to the species concerned in Annex C or re-export from any country, the applicant shall present an export permit, a re-export certificate or a certificate of origin issued in accordance with the Convention by an authority of the exporting or re-exporting country competent for the purpose.

4. The introduction into the Community of specimens of the species listed in Annex D shall be subject to completion of the necessary checks and the prior presentation of an import notification at the border customs office at the point of introduction.

5. The conditions for the issuance of an import permit as referred to in paragraph 1(a) and (d) and in paragraph 2(a), (b) and (c) shall not apply to specimens for which the applicant provides documentary evidence:

(a) that they had previously been legally introduced into or acquired in the Community and that they are, modified or not, being reintroduced into the Community; or

(b) that they are worked specimens that were acquired more than 50 years previously.

6. In consultation with the countries of origin concerned, in accordance with the procedure laid down in Article 18 and taking account of any opinion from the Scientific Review Group, the Commission may establish general restrictions, or restrictions relating to certain countries of origin, on the introduction into the Community:

(a) on the basis of the conditions referred to in paragraph 1(a)(i) or (e), of specimens of species listed in Annex A;

(b) on the basis of the conditions referred to in paragraph 1(e) or paragraph 2(a), of specimens of species listed in Annex B; and

(c) of live specimens of species listed in Annex B which have a high mortality rate during shipment or for which it has been established that they are unlikely to survive in captivity for a considerable proportion of their potential life span; or

(d) of live specimens of species for which it has been established that their introduction into the natural environment of the Community presents an ecological threat to wild species of fauna and flora indigenous to the Community.

The Commission shall on a quarterly basis publish a list of such restrictions, if any, in the *Official Journal of the European Communities*.

7. Where special cases of transhipment, air transfer or rail transport occur following introduction into the Community, derogations from completion of the checks and presentations of import documents at the border customs office at the point of introduction which are referred to in paragraphs 1 to 4 shall be granted in accordance with the procedure laid down in Article 18, in order to permit such checks and

presentations to be made at another customs office designated in accordance with Article 12(1).

Article 5
Export or re-export from the Community

1. The export or re-export from the Community of specimens of the species listed in Annex A shall be subject to completion of the necessary checks and the prior presentation, at the customs office at which the export formalities are completed, of an export permit or re-export certificate issued by a management authority of the Member State in which the specimens are located.

2. An export permit for specimens of the species listed in Annex A may be issued only when the following conditions have been met:

(a) the competent scientific authority has advised in writing that the capture or collection of the specimens in the wild or their export will not have a harmful effect on the conservation status of the species or on the extent of the territory occupied by the relevant population of the species;

(b) the applicant provides documentary evidence that the specimens have been obtained in accordance with the legislation in force on the protection of the species in question; where the application is made to a Member State other than the Member State of origin, such documentary evidence shall be furnished by means of a certificate stating that the specimen was taken from the wild in accordance with the legislation in force on its territory;

(c) the management authority is satisfied that:
  (i) any live specimen will be so prepared and shipped as to minimize the risk of injury, damage to health or cruel treatment; and
  (ii) – the specimens of species not listed in Annex I to the Convention will not be used for primarily commercial purposes, or
      – in the case of export to a State party to the Convention of specimens of the species referred to in Article 3(1)(a) of this Regulation, an import permit has been issued; and

(d) the management authority of the Member State is satisfied, following consultation with the competent scientific authority, that there are no other factors relating to the conservation of the species which militate against issuance of the export permit.

3. A re-export certificate may be issued only when the conditions referred to in paragraph 2(c) and (d) have been met and when the applicant provides documentary evidence that the specimens:

(a) were introduced into the Community in accordance with the provisions of this Regulation;

(b) if introduced into the Community before the entry into force of this Regula-
    tion, were introduced in accordance with the provisions of Regulation (EEC) No
    3626/82; or
(c) if introduced into the Community before 1984, entered international trade in
    accordance with the provisions of the Convention; or
(d) were legally introduced into the territory of a Member State before the provisions
    of the Regulations referred to in (a) and (b) or of the Convention became applicable
    to them, or became applicable in that Member State.

4. The export or re-export from the Community of specimens of the species listed
in Annexes B and C shall be subject to completion of the necessary checks and the
prior presentation, at the customs office at which the export formalities are completed,
of an export permit or reexport certificate issued by a management authority of the
Member State in whose territory the specimens are located.

An export permit may be issued only when the conditions referred to in paragraph
2(a), (b), (c)(i) and (d) have been met.

A re-export certificate may be issued only when the conditions referred to in paragraph 2(c)(i) and (d) and in paragraph 3(a) to (d) have been met.

5. Where an application for a re-export certificate concerns specimens introduced
into the Community under an import permit issued by another Member State, the
management authority must first consult the management authority which issued the
permit. The consultation procedures and the cases in which consultation is necessary
shall be established in accordance with the procedure laid down in Article 18.

6. The conditions for the issuance of an export permit or re-export certificate as
referred to in paragraph 2(a) and (c)(ii) shall not apply to:

 (i) worked specimens that were acquired more than 50 years previously; or
(ii) dead specimens and parts and derivatives thereof for which the applicant provides
     documentary evidence that they were legally acquired before the provisions of
     this Regulation, or of Regulation (EEC) No 3626/82 or of the Convention became
     applicable to them.

   7.

(a) The competent scientific authority in each Member State shall monitor the
    issuance of export permits by that Member State for specimens of species listed in
    Annex B and actual exports of such specimens. Whenever such scientific authority
    determines that the export of specimens of any such species should be limited in
    order to maintain that species throughout its range at a level consistent with its
    role in the ecosystem in which it occurs, and well above the level at which that
    species might become eligible for inclusion in Annex A in accordance with Article
    3(1)(a) or (b)(i), the scientific authority shall advise the competent management
    authority, in writing, of suitable measures to be taken to limit the issuance of
    export permits for specimens of that species

(b) Whenever a management authority is advised of the measures referred to in (a), it shall inform and send comments to the Commission which shall, if appropriate, recommend restrictions on exports of the species concerned in accordance with the procedure laid down in Article 18.

Article 6
Rejection of applications for permits and certificates referred to in Articles 4, 5 and 10

1. When a Member State rejects an application for a permit or certificate in a case of significance in respect of the objectives of this Regulation, it shall immediately inform the Commission of the rejection and of the reasons for rejection.

2. The Commission shall communicate information received in accordance with paragraph 1 to the other Member States in order to ensure uniform application of this Regulation.

3. When an application is made for a permit or certificate relating to specimens for which such an application has previously been rejected, the applicant must inform the competent authority to which the application is submitted of the previous rejection.

4.

(a) Member States shall recognize the rejection of applications by the competent authorities of the other Member States, where such rejection is based on the provisions of this Regulation

(b) However, this need not apply where the circumstances have significantly changed or where new evidence to support an application has become available. In such cases, if a management authority issues a permit or certificate, it shall inform the Commission thereof, stating the reasons for issuance.

Article 7
Derogations

1. *Specimens born and bred in captivity or artificially propagated*

(a) Save where Article 8 applies, specimens of species listed in Annex A that have been born and bred in captivity or artificially propagated shall be treated in accordance with the provisions applicable to specimens of species listed in Annex B.

(b) In the case of artificially propagated plants, the provisions of Articles 4 and 5 may be waived under special conditions laid down by the Commission, relating to:
   (i) the use of phytosanitary certificates;
   (ii) trade by registered commercial traders and by the scientific institutions referred to in paragraph 4 of this Article; and
   (iii) trade in hybrids.

(c) The criteria for determining whether a specimen has been born and bred in captivity or artificially propagated and whether for commercial purposes, as well as the special conditions referred to in (b), shall be specified by the Commission in accordance with the procedure laid down in Article 18.

2. *Transit*

(a) By way of derogation from Article 4, where a specimen is in transit through the Community, checks and presentation at the border customs office at the point of introduction of the prescribed permits, certificates and notifications shall not be required.

(b) In the case of species listed in the Annexes in accordance with Article 3(1) and Article 3(2)(a) and (b), the derogation referred to in (a) shall apply only where a valid export or re-export document provided for by the Convention, relating to the specimens that it accompanies and specifying the destination of the specimens, has been issued by the competent authorities of the exporting or reexporting third country.

(c) If the document referred to in (b) has not been issued before export or re-export, the specimen must be seized and may, where applicable, be confiscated unless the document is submitted retrospectively in compliance with the conditions specified by the Commission in accordance with the procedure laid down in Article 18.

3. *Personal and household effects* By way of derogation from Articles 4 and 5, the provisions therein shall not apply to dead specimens, parts and derivatives of species listed in Annexes A to D which are personal or household effects being introduced into the Community, or exported or re-exported therefrom, in compliance with provisions that shall be specified by the Commission in accordance with the procedure laid down in Article 18.

4. *Scientific institutions* The documents referred to in Articles 4, 5, 8 and 9 shall not be required in the case of non-commercial loans, donations and exchanges between scientists and scientific institutions, registered by the management authorities of the States in which they are located, of herbarium specimens and other preserved, dried or embedded museum specimens, and of live plant material, bearing a label, the model for which has been determined in accordance with the procedure laid down in Article 18 or a similar label issued or approved by a management authority of a third country.

Article 8
Provisions relating to the control of commercial activities

1. The purchase, offer to purchase, acquisition for commercial purposes, display to the public for commercial purposes, use for commercial gain and sale, keeping for sale, offering for sale or transporting for sale of specimens of the species listed in Annex A shall be prohibited.

2. Member States may prohibit the holding of specimens, in particular live animals of the species listed in Annex A.

3. In accordance with the requirements of other Community legislation on the conservation of wild fauna and flora, exemption from the prohibitions referred to in paragraph 1 may be granted by issuance of a certificate to that effect by a management authority of the Member State in which the specimens are located, on a case-by-case basis where the specimens:

(a) were acquired in, or were introduced into, the Community before the provisions relating to species listed in Appendix I to the Convention or in Annex C1 to Regulation (EEC) No 3626/82 or in Annex A became applicable to the specimens; or

(b) are worked specimens that were acquired more than 50 years previously; or

(c) were introduced into the Community in compliance with the provisions of this Regulation and are to be used for purposes which are not detrimental to the survival of the species concerned; or

(d) are captive-born and bred specimens of an animal species or artificially propagated specimens of a plant species or are parts or derivatives of such specimens; or

(e) are required under exceptional circumstances for the advancement of science or for essential biomedical purposes pursuant to Council Directive 86/609/EEC of 24 November 1986 on the approximation of laws, regulations and administrative provisions of the Member States regarding the protection of animals used for experimental and other scientific purposes,[1] where the species in question proves to be the only one suitable for those purposes and where there are no specimens of the species which have been born and bred in captivity; or

(f) are intended for breeding or propagation purposes from which conservation benefits will accrue to the species concerned; or

(g) are intended for research or education aimed at the preservation or conservation of the species; or

(h) originate in a Member State and were taken from the wild in accordance with the legislation in force in that Member State.

4. General derogations from the prohibitions referred to in paragraph 1 based on the conditions referred to in paragraph 3, as well as general derogations with regard to species listed in Annex A in accordance with Article 3(1)(b)(ii) may be defined by the Commission in accordance with the procedure laid down in Article 18. Any such derogations must be in accordance with the requirements of other Community legislation on the conservation of wild fauna and flora.

5. The prohibitions referred to in paragraph 1 shall also apply to specimens of the species listed in Annex B except where it can be proved to the satisfaction of the competent authority of the Member State concerned that such specimens were acquired and, if they originated outside the Community, were introduced into it, in accordance with the legislation in force for the conservation of wild fauna and flora.

---

[1] OJ No L 358, 18. 12. 1986, p. 1.

6. The competent authorities of the Member States shall have discretion to sell any specimen of the species listed in Annexes B to D they have confiscated under this Regulation, provided that it is not thus returned directly to the person or entity from whom it was confiscated or who was party to the offence. Such specimens may then be treated for all purposes as if they had been legally acquired.

Article 9
Movement of live specimens

1. Any movement within the Community of a live specimen of a species listed in Annex A from the location indicated in the import permit or in any certificate issued in compliance with this Regulation shall require prior authorization from a management authority of the Member State in which the specimen is located. In other cases of movement, the person responsible for moving the specimen must be able, where applicable, to provide proof of the legal origin of the specimen.

2. Such authorization shall:

(a) be granted only when the competent scientific authority of such Member State or, where the movement is to another Member State, the competent scientific authority of the latter, is satisfied that the intended accommodation for a live specimen at the place of destination is adequately equipped to conserve and care for it properly;
(b) be confirmed by issuance of a certificate; and
(c) where applicable, be immediately communicated to a management authority of the Member State in which the specimen is to be located.

3. However, no such authorization shall be required if a live animal must be moved for the purpose of urgent veterinary treatment and is returned directly to its authorized location.

4. Where a live specimen of a species listed in Annex B is moved within the Community, the holder of the specimen may relinquish it only after ensuring that the intended recipient is adequately informed of the accommodation, equipment and practices required to ensure the specimen will be properly cared for.

5. When any live specimens are transported into, from or within the Community or are held during any period of transit or transhipment, they shall be prepared, moved and cared for in a manner such as to minimize the risk of injury, damage to health or cruel treatment and, in the case of animals, in conformity with Community legislation on the protection of animals during transport.

6. Under the procedure laid down in Article 18, the Commission may establish restrictions on the holding or movement of live specimens of species in relation to which restrictions on introduction into the Community have been established in accordance with Article 4(6).

Article 10
Certificates to be issued

On receiving an application, together with all the requisite supporting documents, from the person concerned and provided that all the conditions governing their issuance have been fulfilled, a management authority of a Member State may issue a certificate for the purposes referred to in Article 5(2)(b), 5(3) and (4), Article 8(3) and Article 9(2)(b).

Article 11
Validity of and special conditions for permits and certificates

1. Without prejudice to stricter measures which the Member States may adopt or maintain, permits and certificates issued by the competent authorities of the Member States in accordance with this Regulation shall be valid throughout the Community.

2.

(a) However, any such permit or certificate, as well as any permit or certificate issued on the basis of it, shall be deemed void if a competent authority or the Commission, in consultation with the competent authority which issued the permit or certificate, establishes that it was issued on the false premise that the conditions for its issuance were met

(b) Specimens situated in the territory of a Member State and covered by such documents shall be seized by the competent authorities of that Member State and may be confiscated.

3. Any permit or certificate issued in accordance with this Regulation may stipulate conditions and requirements imposed by the issuing authority to ensure compliance with the provisions thereof. Where such conditions or requirements need to be incorporated in the design of permits or certificates, Member States shall inform the Commission thereof.

4. Any import permit issued on the basis of a copy of the corresponding export permit or re-export certificate shall be valid for the introduction of specimens into the Community only when accompanied by the original of the valid export permit or re-export certificate.

5. The Commission shall establish time limits for the issuance of permits and certificates in accordance with the procedure laid down in Article 18.

Article 12
Places of introduction and export

1. Member States shall designate customs offices for carrying out the checks and formalities for the introduction into and export from the Community, in order to assign to them a customs-approved treatment or use, within the meaning of Regulation

(EEC) No 2913/92, of specimens of species covered by this Regulation and shall state which offices are specifically intended to deal with live specimens.

2. All offices designated in accordance with paragraph 1 shall be provided with sufficient and adequately trained staff. Member States shall ensure that accommodation is provided in accordance with relevant Community legislation as regards the transport and accommodation of live animals and that, where necessary, adequate steps are taken for live plants.

3. All offices designated in accordance with paragraph 1 shall be notified to the Commission which shall publish a list of them in the *Official Journal of the European Communities.*

4. In exceptional cases and in accordance with criteria defined under the procedure laid down in Article 18, a management authority may authorize the introduction into the Community or the export or re-export therefrom at a customs office other than one designated in accordance with paragraph 1.

5. Member States shall ensure that at border crossing-points the public are informed of the implementing provisions of this Regulation.

Article 13
Management and scientific authorities and other competent authorities

1.

(a) Each Member State shall designate a management authority with primary responsibility for implementation of this Regulation and for communication with the Commission
(b) Each Member State may also designate additional management authorities and other competent authorities to assist in implementation, in which case the primary management authority shall be responsible for providing the additional authorities with all the information required for correct application of this Regulation.

2. Each Member State shall designate one or more scientific authorities with appropriate qualifications whose duties shall be separate from those of any designated management authority.

3.

(a) Not later than three months before the date of application of this Regulation, Member States shall forward the names and addresses of the designated management authorities, other authorities competent to issue permits or certificates and scientific authorities to the Commission, which shall publish this information in the *Official Journal of the European Communities* within a month
(b) Each management authority referred to in paragraph 1(a) shall, if so requested by the Commission, communicate to it within two months the names and specimen

signatures of people authorized to sign permits or certificates, and impressions of the stamps, seals or other devices used to authenticate permits or certificates.

(c) Member States shall communicate to the Commission any changes in the information already provided, not later than two months after the implementation of such change.

Article 14
Monitoring of compliance and investigation of infringements

1.

(a) The competent authorities of the Member States shall monitor compliance with the provisions of this Regulation

(b) If, at any time, the competent authorities have reason to believe that these provisions are being infringed, they shall take the appropriate steps to ensure compliance or to instigate legal action.

(c) Member States shall inform the Commission and, in the case of species listed in the Appendices to the Convention, the Convention Secretariat of any steps taken by the competent authorities in relation to significant infringements of this Regulation, including seizures and confiscations.

2. The Commission shall draw the attention of the competent authorities of the Member States to matters whose investigation it considers necessary under this Regulation. Member States shall inform the Commission and, in the case of species listed in the Appendices to the Convention, the Convention Secretariat of the outcome of any subsequent investigation.

3.

(a) An enforcement group shall be established consisting of the representatives of each Member State's authorities with responsibility for ensuring the implementation of the provisions of this Regulation. The group shall be chaired by the representative of the Commission

(b) The enforcement group shall examine any technical question relating to the enforcement of this Regulation raised by the chairman, either on his own initiative or at the request of the members of the group or the committee.

(c) The Commission shall convey the opinions expressed in the enforcement group to the committee.

Article 15
Communication of information

1. The Member States and the Commission shall communicate to one another the information necessary for implementing this Regulation. The Member States and the Commission shall ensure that the necessary steps are taken to make the public aware

and inform it of the provisions regarding implementation of the Convention and of this Regulation and of the latter's implementing measures.

2. The Commission shall communicate with the Convention Secretariat so as to ensure that the Convention is effectively implemented throughout the territory to which this Regulation applies.

3. The Commission shall immediately communicate any advice from the Scientific Review Group to the management authorities of the Member States concerned.

4.

(a) The management authorities of the Member States shall communicate to the Commission before 15 June each year all the information relating to the preceding year required for drawing up the reports referred to in Article VIII.7(a) of the Convention and equivalent information on international trade in all specimens of species listed in Annexes A, B and C and on introduction into the Community of specimens of species listed in Annex D. The information to be communicated and the format for its presentation shall be specified by the Commission in accordance with the procedure laid down in Article 18.

(b) On the basis of the information referred to in (a), the Commission shall publish before 31 October each year a statistical report on the introduction into, and the export and re-export from, the Community of specimens of the species to which this Regulation applies and shall forward to the Convention Secretariat information on the species to which the Convention applies.

(c) Without prejudice to Article 20, the management authorities of the Member States shall, before 15 June of each second year, and for the first time in 1999, communicate to the Commission all the information relating to the preceding two years required for drawing up the reports referred to in Article VIII.7(b) of the Convention and equivalent information on the provisions of this Regulation that fall outside the scope of the Convention. The information to be communicated and the format for its presentation shall be specified by the Commission in accordance with the procedure laid down in Article 18.

(d) On the basis of the information referred to in (c), the Commission shall, before 31 October of each second year, and for the first time in 1999, draw up a report on the implementation and enforcement of this Regulation.

5. With a view to the preparation of amendments to the Annexes, the competent authorities of the Member States shall forward all relevant information to the Commission. The Commission shall specify the information required, in accordance with the procedure laid down in Article 18.

Without prejudice to Council Directive 90/313/EEC of 7 June 1990 on the freedom of access to information on the environment,[1] the Commission shall take appropriate measures to protect the confidentiality of information obtained in implementation of this Regulation.

[1] OJ No L 158, 23. 6. 1990, p. 56.

Article 16
Sanctions

1. Member States shall take appropriate measures to ensure the imposition of sanctions for at least the following infringements of this Regulation:

(a) introduction into, or export or re-export from, the Community of specimens without the appropriate permit or certificate or with a false, falsified or invalid permit or certificate or one altered without authorization by the issuing authority;

(b) failure to comply with the stipulations specified on a permit or certificate issued in accordance with this Regulation;

(c) making a false declaration or knowingly providing false information in order to obtain a permit or certificate;

(d) using a false, falsified or invalid permit or certificate or one altered without authorization as a basis for obtaining a Community permit or certificate or for any other official purpose in connection with this Regulation;

(e) making no import notification or a false import notification;

(f) shipment of live specimens not properly prepared so as to minimize the risk of injury, damage to health or cruel treatment;

(g) use of specimens of species listed in Annex A other than in accordance with the authorization given at the time of issuance of the import permit or subsequently;

(h) trade in artificially propagated plants contrary to the provisions laid down in accordance with Article 7(1)(b);

(i) shipment of specimens into or out of or in transit through the territory of the Community without the appropriate permit or certificate issued in accordance with this Regulation and, in the case of export or re-export from a third country party to the Convention, in accordance therewith, or without satisfactory proof of the existence of such permit or certificate;

(j) purchase, offer to purchase, acquisition for commercial purposes, use for commercial gain, display to the public for commercial purposes, sale, keeping for sale, offering for sale or transporting for sale of specimens in contravention of Article 8;

(k) use of a permit or certificate for any specimen other than one for which it was issued;

(l) falsification or alteration of any permit or certificate issued in accordance with this Regulation;

(m) failure to disclose rejection of an application for a Community import, export or re-export permit or certificate, in accordance with Article 6(3).

2. The measures referred to in paragraph 1 shall be appropriate to the nature and gravity of the infringement and shall include provisions relating to the seizure and, where appropriate, confiscation of specimens.

3. Where a specimen is confiscated, it shall be entrusted to a competent authority of the Member State of confiscation which:

(a) following consultation with a scientific authority of that Member State, shall place or otherwise dispose of the specimen under conditions which it deems to be appropriate and consistent with the purposes and provisions of the Convention and this Regulation; and

(b) in the case of a live specimen which has been introduced into the Community, may, after consultation with the State of export, return the specimen to that State at the expense of the convicted person.

4. Where a live specimen of a species listed in Annex B or C arrives at a point of introduction into the Community without the appropriate valid permit or certificate, the specimen must be seized and may be confiscated or, if the consignee refuses to acknowledge the specimen, the competent authorities of the Member State responsible for the point of introduction may, if appropriate, refuse to accept the shipment and require the carrier to return the specimen to its place of departure.

Article 17
The Scientific Review Group

1. A Scientific Review Group is hereby established, consisting of the representatives of each Member State's scientific authority or authorities and chaired by the representative of the Commission.

2.

(a) The Scientific Review Group shall examine any scientific question relating to the application of this Regulation – in particular concerning Article 4(1)(a), (2)(a) and (6) – raised by the chairman, either on his own initiative or at the request of the members of the Group or the Committee.

(b) The Commission shall convey the opinions of the Scientific Review Group to the Committee.

Article 18

1. The Commission shall be assisted by a committee.

2. Where reference is made to this Article, Articles 5 and 7 of Decision 1999/468/EC[1] shall apply, having regard to the provisions of Article 8 thereof.

The period laid down in Article 5(6) of Decision 1999/468/EC shall be set at three months. As regards the Committee's tasks referred to in points 1 and 2 of Article 19, if, on the expiry of a period of three months from the date of referral to the Council, the Council has not acted, the proposed measures shall be adopted by the Commission.

3. The Committee shall adopt its rules of procedure.

[1] Council Decision 1999/468/EC of 28 June 1999 laying down the procedures for the exercise of implementing powers conferred on the Commission (OJ L 184, 17.7.1999, p. 23).

Article 19

In accordance with the procedure laid down in Article 18, the Commission shall:

1. lay down uniform conditions and criteria for:
   (i) the issue, validity and use of the documents referred to in Articles 4, 5, 7(4) and 10; it shall determine the design thereof;
   (ii) the use of phytosanitary certificates; and
   (iii) the establishment of procedures, where necessary, for marking specimens in order to facilitate identification and ensure enforcement of the provisions;
2. adopt the measures referred to in Article 4(6) and (7), Article 5(5) and (7)(b), Article 7(1)(c), (2)(c) and (3), Article 8(4), Article 9(6), Article 11(5), Article 15(4)(a), (c) and (5) and Article 21(3);
3. amend Annexes A to D except in the case of amendments to Annex A which do not result from decisions of the Conference of the Parties to the Convention;
4. adopt, where necessary, additional measures to implement resolutions of the Conference of the Parties to the Convention, decisions or recommendations of the Standing Committee of the Convention and recommendations of the Convention Secretariat.

Article 20
Final provisions

Each Member State shall notify the Commission and the Convention Secretariat of the provisions which it adopts specifically for the implementation of this Regulation and of all legal instruments used and measures taken for its implementation and enforcement.

The Commission shall communicate this information to the other Member States.

Article 21

1. Regulation (EEC) No 3626/82 is hereby repealed.

2. Until the measures provided for in points 1 and 2 of Article 19 have been adopted, Member States may maintain or continue to apply the measures adopted in accordance with Regulation (EEC) No 3626/82 and Commission Regulation (EEC) No 3418/83 of 28 November 1983 laying down provisions for the uniform issue and use of the documents required for the implementation in the Community of the Convention on International Trade in Endangered Species of Wild Fauna and Flora.[1]

3. Two months before this Regulation is implemented the Commission, in accordance with the procedure laid down in Article 18 and in consultation with the Scientific Review Group:

(a) must check that there is no justification for restrictions on the introduction into the Community of the species listed in Annex C1 to Regulation (EEC) No 3626/82 which are not included in Annex A to this Regulation;

---

[1] OJ No L 344, 7. 12. 1983, p. 1.

(b) shall adopt a Regulation amending Annex D into a representative list of species meeting the criteria laid down in Article 3(4)(a).

Article 22

This Regulation shall enter into force on the date of its publication in the *Official Journal of the European Communities.*

It shall apply from 1 June 1997. Articles 12, 13, 14(3), 16, 17, 18, 19 and 21(3) shall apply from the date of entry into force of this Regulation.

This Regulation shall be binding in its entirety and directly applicable in all Member States.

Annex

[omitted]

Council Directive 1999/22/EC of 29 March 1999 relating to the keeping of wild animals in zoos

Editorial note

The aim of Council Directive 1999/22/EC is to protect wild fauna and conserve biodiversity by providing for the adoption of measures by Member States for the licensing and inspection of zoos in the Community, thereby strengthening the role of zoos in the conservation of biodiversity (Article 1). For the purpose of the Directive, 'zoos' are defined as all permanent establishments where animals of wild species are kept for exhibition to the public for seven or more days a year, although there are some exceptions (Article 2). The Directive requires zoos to take certain conservation measures, including participating in research, promoting public education and awareness, accommodating their animals under conditions which aim to satisfy the biological and conservation requirements of the individual species, preventing the escape of animals, and keeping up-to-date records of the zoo's collection (Article 3). Member States must adopt measures for licensing and inspection of existing and new zoos (Article 4), although licensing requirements may not apply where a Member State can demonstrate to the satisfaction of the Commission that the objective of this Directive and the requirements applicable to zoos are being met and continuously maintained by means of a system of regulation and registration (Article 5). In the event of a zoo (or part thereof) being closed, the competent authority must ensure that the animals concerned are treated or disposed of under conditions which the Member State deems appropriate and consistent with the purposes and provisions of the Directive (Article 6). Member States must designate competent authorities (Article 7) and determine effective, proportionate and dissuasive penalties for breaches of the national provisions adopted pursuant to this Directive (Article 8). Member States must transpose the Directive into national law by 9 April 2002 (Article 9).

Source: OJ L 94 09.04.1999 p. 24.

Council Directive 1999/22/EC of 29 March 1999 relating to the keeping of wild animals in zoos

The Council of the European Union,

Having regard to the Treaty establishing the European Community, and in particular Article 130s(1) thereof,

Having regard to the proposal from the Commission,

Having regard to the opinion of the Economic and Social Committee,[1]

Acting in accordance with the procedure laid down in Article 189c of the Treaty,[2]

Whereas Council Regulation (EEC) No 338/97 of 9 December 1996 on the protection of species of wild fauna and flora by regulating trade therein,[3] requires evidence of the availability of adequate facilities for the accommodation and care of live specimens of a great many species before their importation into the Community is authorised; whereas that Regulation prohibits the display to the public for commercial purposes of specimens of species listed in Annex A thereof unless a specific exemption was granted for education, research or breeding purposes;

Whereas Council Directive 79/409/EEC of 2 April 1979 on the conservation of wild birds,[4] and Council Directive 92/43/EEC of 21 May 1992 on the conservation of natural habitats and of wild fauna and flora,[5] prohibit the capture and keeping of and trade in a great number of species, whilst providing for exemptions for specific reasons, such as research and education, repopulation, reintroduction and breeding;

Whereas the proper implementation of existing and future Community legislation on the conservation of wild fauna and the need to ensure that zoos adequately fulfil their important role in the conservation of species, public education, and/or scientific research make it necessary to provide a common basis for Member States' legislation with regard to the licensing and inspection of zoos, the keeping of animals in zoos, the training of staff and the education of the visiting public;

Whereas action at the Community level is required in order to have zoos throughout the Community contributing to the conservation of biodiversity in accordance with the Community's obligation to adopt measures for *ex situ* conservation under Article 9 of the Convention on Biological Diversity;

Whereas a number of organisations such as the European Association of Zoos and Aquaria have produced guidelines for the care and accommodation of animals in zoos which could, where appropriate, assist in the development and adoption of national standards,

Has adopted this Directive:

Article 1

Aim

The objectives of this Directive are to protect wild fauna and to conserve biodiversity by providing for the adoption of measures by Member States for the licensing and

---

[1] OJ C 204, 15.7.1996, p. 63.

[2] Opinion of the European Parliament of 29 January 1998. (OJ C 56, 23.2.1998, p. 34), Council Common Position of 20 July 1998 (OJ C 364, 25.11.1998, p. 9), and Decision of the European Parliament of 10 February 1999 (not yet published in the Official Journal).

[3] OJ L 61, 3.3.1997, p. 1. Regulation as last amended by Commission Regulation (EC) No 2307/97 (OJ L 325, 27.11.1997, p. 1).

[4] OJ L 103, 25.4.1979, p. 1. Directive as last amended by Directive 97/49/EC (OJ L 223, 13.8.1997, p. 9).

[5] OJ L 206, 22.7.1992, p. 7. Directive as last amended by Commission Directive 97/62/EC (OJ L 305, 8.11.1997, p. 42).

inspection of zoos in the Community, thereby strengthening the role of zoos in the conservation of biodiversity.

Article 2
Definition

For the purpose of this Directive, 'zoos' means all permanent establishments where animals of wild species are kept for exhibition to the public for 7 or more days a year, with the exception of circuses, pet shops and establishments which Member States exempt from the requirements of this Directive on the grounds that they do not exhibit a significant number of animals or species to the public and that the exemption will not jeopardise the objectives of this Directive.

Article 3
Requirements applicable to zoos

Member States shall take measures under Articles 4, 5, 6 and 7 to ensure all zoos implement the following conservation measures:

– participating in research from which conservation benefits accrue to the species, and/or training in relevant conservation skills, and/or the exchange of information relating to species conservation and/or, where appropriate, captive breeding, repopulation or reintroduction of species into the wild,
– promoting public education and awareness in relation to the conservation of biodiversity, particularly by providing information about the species exhibited and their natural habitats,
– accommodating their animals under conditions which aim to satisfy the biological and conservation requirements of the individual species, *inter alia*, by providing species specific enrichment of the enclosures; and maintaining a high standard of animal husbandry with a developed programme of preventive and curative veterinary care and nutrition,
– preventing the escape of animals in order to avoid possible ecological threats to indigenous species and preventing intrusion of outside pests and vermin,
– keeping of up-to-date records of the zoo's collection appropriate to the species recorded.

Article 4
Licensing and inspection

1. Member States shall adopt measures for licensing and inspection of existing and new zoos in order to ensure that the requirements of Article 3 are met.

2. Every zoo shall have a licence within four years after the entry into force of this Directive or, in the case of new zoos, before they are open to the public.

3. Each licence shall contain conditions to enforce the requirements of Article 3. Compliance with the conditions shall be monitored *inter alia* by means of regular inspection and appropriate steps shall be taken to ensure such compliance.

4. Before granting, refusing, extending the period of, or significantly amending a licence, an inspection by Member States' competent authorities shall be carried out in order to determine whether or not the licensing conditions or proposed licensing conditions are met.

5. If the zoo is not licensed in accordance with this Directive or the licensing conditions are not met, the zoo or part thereof:

(a) shall be closed to the public by the competent authority; and/or
(b) shall comply with appropriate requirements imposed by the competent authority to ensure that the licensing conditions are met.

Should these requirements not be complied with within an appropriate period to be determined by the competent authorities but not exceeding two years, the competent authority shall withdraw or modify the licence and close the zoo or part thereof.

Article 5

Licensing requirements set out in Article 4 shall not apply where a Member State can demonstrate to the satisfaction of the Commission that the objective of this Directive as set out in Article 1 and the requirements applicable to zoos set out in Article 3 are being met and continously maintained by means of a system or regulation and registration. Such a system should, *inter alia*, contain provisions regarding inspection and closure of zoos equivalent to those in Article 4(4) and (5).

Article 6
Closure of zoos

In the event of a zoo or part thereof being closed, the competent authority shall ensure that the animals concerned are treated or disposed of under conditions which the Member State deems appropriate and consistent with the purposes and provisions of this Directive.

Article 7
Competent authorities

Member States shall designate competent authorities for the purposes of this Directive.

Article 8
Penalties

Member States shall determine the penalties applicable to breaches of the national provisions adopted pursuant to this Directive. The penalties shall be effective, proportionate and dissuasive.

Article 9
Implementation

1. Member States shall bring into force the laws, regulations and administrative provisions necessary to comply with this directive not later than 9 April 2002. They shall forthwith inform the Commission thereof.

When Member States adopt these measures, they shall contain a reference to this Directive or shall be accompanied by such reference on the occasion of their official publication. The methods of making such a reference shall be laid down by the Member States.

2. Member States shall communicate to the Commission the main provisions of national law which they adopt in the field covered by this Directive.

Article 10
Entry in force

This Directive shall enter into force on the day of its publication in the *Official Journal of the European Communities.*

Article 11

This Directive is addressed to the Member States.

Done at Brussels, 29 March 1999.

PART VII

Waste

Council Directive 75/442/EEC of 15 July 1975
on waste (as amended)

Editorial note

Council Directive 75/442 on wastes, as amended, requires Member States to take measures to prevent or reduce waste production and to recover waste by recycling, re-use, reclamation or any other processes, or to use waste as a source of energy (Article 3). Prevention and reduction are to be achieved by the development of clean technologies, products designed to minimise waste and techniques for the final disposal of dangerous substances (Article 3). Waste is defined as 'any substance or object in the categories set out in Annex I which the holder discards or intends or is required to discard' (Article 1(a)). The Directive does not apply to atmospheric emissions of gases or certain categories of waste covered by other legislation (Article 2(1)).

Member States should take measures necessary to ensure the recovery or disposal of waste without endangering human health and causing harm to the environment, including the prohibition of abandonment, dumping and uncontrolled disposal (Article 4). Member States are required to establish an integrated and adequate network of disposal installations, taking into account the best available technology not involving excessive cost (BATNEEC), designed to enable the Community to become self-sufficient in waste disposal (Article 5(1)). The network must enable waste to be disposed of in one of the nearest appropriate installations and ensure a high level of protection of the environment and human health (Article 5(2)). National authorities must draw up waste management plans and prevent movements of waste not in accordance with those plans (Article 7). Subject to certain exceptions, companies carrying out the disposal operations in Annex IIA or the recovery operations in Annex IIB must obtain a permit from the competent national authorities (Articles 9–11). Companies which collect or transport waste, and dealers or brokers who arrange for its disposal or recovery, must be registered (Article 12). Companies carrying out the operations under the provisions of Articles 9–12 are to be subject to inspections (Article 13). Companies referred to in Articles 9 and 10 are to also keep records of the quantity, nature, origin and, where relevant, the destination, frequency of collection, mode of transport and treatment method of the waste referred to in Annex I and the operations referred to in Annex IIA or B (Article 14). In accordance with the polluter pays principle, the cost of disposing of waste is to be borne by the holder who has waste handled by a waste collector or by an undertaking and/or the previous holders or the producer of the product from which the waste came (Article 15).

Source: OJ L 194 25.07.1975 p. 39. Amended by: Council Directive 91/156/EEC of 18 March 1991 L 78 32 26.03.1991; Council Directive 91/692/EEC of 23 December 1991 L 377 48 31.12.1991; Commission Decision 96/350/EC of 24 May 1996 L 135 32 06.06.1996; Regulation (EC) No 1882/2003 of the European Parliament and of the Council of 29 September 2003 L 284 1 31.10.2003. Corrected by: Corrigendum, OJ L 146 13.06.2003 p. 52 (91/692/EEC)

Council Directive 75/442/EEC of 15 July 1975 on waste (as amended)

The Council of the European Communities,
   Having regard to the Treaty establishing the European Economic Community, and in particular Articles 100 and 235 thereof;
   Having regard to the proposal from the Commission;
   Having regard to the Opinion of the European Parliament;[1]
   Having regard to the Opinion of the Economic and Social Committee;[2]
   Whereas any disparity between the provisions on waste disposal already applicable or in preparation in the various Member States may create unequal conditions of competition and thus directly affect the functioning of the common market; whereas it is therefore necessary to approximate laws in this field, as provided for in Article 100 of the Treaty;
   Whereas it seems necessary for this approximation of laws to be accompanied by Community action so that one of the aims of the Community in the sphere of protection of the environment and improvement of the quality of life can be achieved by more extensive rules; whereas certain specific provisions to this effect should therefore be laid down; whereas Article 235 of the Treaty should be invoked as the powers required for this purpose have not been provided for by the Treaty;
   Whereas the essential objective of all provisions relating to waste disposal must be the protection of human health and the environment against harmful effects caused by the collection, transport, treatment, storage and tipping of waste;
   Whereas the recovery of waste and the use of recovered materials should be encouraged in order to conserve natural resources;
   Whereas the programme of action of the European Communities on the environment,[3] stresses the need for Community action, including the harmonization of legislation;
   Whereas effective and consistent regulations on waste disposal which neither obstruct intra-Community trade nor affect conditions of competition should be

---

[1] OJ No C 32, 11. 2. 1975, p. 36.   [2] OJ No C 16, 23. 1. 1975, p. 12.   [3] OJ No C 112, 20. 12. 1973, p. 3.

applied to movable property which the owner disposes of or is required to dispose of under the provisions of national law in force, with the exception of radioactive, mining and agricultural waste, animal carcases, waste waters, gaseous effluents and waste covered by specific Community rules;

Whereas, in order to ensure the protection of the environment, provision should be made for a system of permits for undertakings which treat, store or tip waste on behalf of third parties, for a supervisory system for undertakings which dispose of their own waste and for those which collect the waste of others, and for a plan embracing the essential factors to be taken into consideration in respect of the various waste disposal operations;

Whereas that proportion of the costs not covered by the proceeds of treating the waste must be defrayed in accordance with the 'polluter pays' principle,

Has adopted this Directive:

Article 1

For the purposes of this Directive:

(a) 'waste' shall mean any substance or object in the categories set out in Annex I which the holder discards or intends or is required to discard. The Commission, acting in accordance with the procedure laid down in Article 18, will draw up, not later than 1 April 1993, a list of wastes belonging to the categories listed in Annex I. This list will be periodically reviewed and, if necessary, revised by the same procedure;

(b) 'producer' shall mean anyone whose activities produce waste ('original producer') and/or anyone who carries out pre-processing, mixing or other operations resulting in a change in the nature or composition of this waste;

(c) 'holder' shall mean the producer of the waste or the natural or legal person who is in possession of it;

(d) 'management' shall mean the collection, transport, recovery and disposal of waste, including the supervision of such operations and after-care of disposal sites;

(e) 'disposal' shall mean any of the operations provided for in Annex II, A;

(f) 'recovery' shall mean any of the operations provided for in Annex II, B;

(g) 'collection' shall mean the gathering, sorting and/or mixing of waste for the purpose of transport.

Article 2

1. The following shall be excluded from the scope of this Directive:

(a) gaseous effluents emitted into the atmosphere;

(b) where they are already covered by other legislation:
   (i) radioactive waste;
   (ii) waste resulting from prospecting, extraction, treatment and storage of mineral resources and the working of quarries;

(iii) animal carcases and the following agricultural waste: faecal matter and other natural, non-dangerous substances used in farming;

(iv) waste waters, with the exception of waste in liquid form;

(v) decommissioned explosives.

2. Specific rules for particular instances or supplementing those of this Directive on the management of particular categories of waste may be laid down by means of individual Directives.

Article 3

1. Member States shall take appropriate measures to encourage:

(a) firstly, the prevention or reduction of waste production and its harmfulness, in particular by:
 – the development of clean technologies more sparing in their use of natural resources,
 – the technical development and marketing of products designed so as to make no contribution or to make the smallest possible contribution, by the nature of their manufacture, use or final disposal, to increasing the amount or harmfulness of waste and pollution hazards,
 – the development of appropriate techniques for the final disposal of dangerous substances contained in waste destined for recovery;

(b) secondly:
 (i) the recovery of waste by means of recycling, re-use or reclamation or any other process with a view to extracting secondary raw materials, or
 (ii) the use of waste as a source of energy.

2. Except where Council Directive 83/189/EEC of 28 March 1983 laying down a procedure for the provision of information in the field of technical standards and regulations[1] applies, Member States shall inform the Commission of any measures they intend to take to achieve the aims set out in paragraph 1. The Commission shall inform the other Member States and the committee referred to in Article 18 of such measures.

Article 4

Member States shall take the necessary measures to ensure that waste is recovered or disposed of without endangering human health and without using processes or methods which could harm the environment, and in particular:

– without risk to water, air, soil and plants and animals,
– without causing a nuisance through noise or odours,
– without adversely affecting the countryside or places of special interest.

[1] OJ No L 109, 26. 4. 1983, p. 8.

Member States shall also take the necessary measures to prohibit the abandonment, dumping or uncontrolled disposal of waste.

Article 5

1. Member States shall take appropriate measures, in cooperation with other Member States where this is necessary or advisable, to establish an integrated and adequate network of disposal installations, taking account of the best available technology not involving excessive costs. The network must enable the Community as a whole to become self-sufficient in waste disposal and the Member States to move towards that aim individually, taking into account geographical circumstances or the need for specialized installations for certain types of waste.

2. The network must also enable waste to be disposed of in one of the nearest appropriate installations, by means of the most appropriate methods and technologies in order to ensure a high level of protection for the environment and public health.

Article 6

Member States shall establish or designate the competent authority or authorities to be responsible for the implementation of this Directive.

Article 7

1. In order to attain the objectives referred to in Article 3, 4 and 5, the competent authority or authorities referred to in Article 6 shall be required to draw up as soon as possible one or more waste management plans. Such plans shall relate in particular to:

– the type, quantity and origin of waste to be recovered or disposed of,
– general technical requirements,
– any special arrangements for particular wastes,
– suitable disposal sites or installations.

Such plans may, for example, cover:

– the natural or legal persons empowered to carry out the management of waste,
– the estimated costs of the recovery and disposal operations,
– appropriate measures to encourage rationalization of the collection, sorting and treatment of waste.

2. Member States shall collaborate as appropriate with the other Member States concerned and the Commission to draw up such plans. They shall notify the Commission thereof.

3. Member States may take the measures necessary to prevent movements of waste which are not in accordance with their waste management plans. They shall inform the Commission and the Member States of any such measures.

Article 8

Member States shall take the necessary measures to ensure that any holder of waste:

– has it handled by a private or public waste collector or by an undertaking which carries out the operations listed in Annex II A or B, or
– recovers or disposes of it himself in accordance with the provisions of this Directive.

Article 9

1. For the purposes of implementing Articles 4, 5 and 7, any establishment or undertaking which carries out the operations specified in Annex II A must obtain a permit from the competent authority referred to in Article 6.
   Such permit shall cover:

– the types and quantities of waste,
– the technical requirements,
– the security precautions to be taken,
– the disposal site,
– the treatment method.

2. Permits may be granted for a specified period, they may be renewable, they may be subject to conditions and obligations, or, notably, if the intended method of disposal is unacceptable from the point of view of environmental protection, they may be refused.

Article 10

For the purposes of implementing Article 4, any establishment or undertaking which carries out the operations referred to in Annex II B must obtain a permit.

Article 11

1. Without prejudice to Council Directive 78/319/EEC of 20 March 1978 on toxic and dangerous waste,[1] as last amended by the Act of Accession of Spain and Portugal, the following may be exempted from the permit requirement imposed in Article 9 or Article 10:

(a) establishments or undertakings carrying out their own waste disposal at the place of production; and
(b) establishments or undertakings that carry out waste recovery.
    This exemption may apply only:
    – if the competent authorities have adopted general rules for each type of activity laying down the types and quantities of waste and the conditions under which the activity in question may be exempted from the permit requirements, and

---

[1] OJ No L 84, 31. 3. 1978, p. 43.

— if the types or quantities of waste and methods of disposal or recovery are such that the conditions imposed in Article 4 are complied with.

2. The establishments or undertakings referred to in paragraph 1 shall be registered with the competent authorities.

3. Member States shall inform the Commission of the general rules adopted pursuant to paragraph 1.

Article 12

Establishments or undertakings which collect or transport waste on a professional basis or which arrange for the disposal or recovery of waste on behalf of others (dealers or brokers), where not subject to authorization, shall be registered with the competent authorities.

Article 13

Establishments or undertakings which carry out the operations referred to in Articles 9 to 12 shall be subject to appropriate periodic inspections by the competent authorities.

Article 14

All establishments or undertakings referred to in Articles 9 and 10 shall:

— keep a record of the quantity, nature, origin, and, where relevant, the destination, frequency of collection, mode of transport and treatment method in respect of the waste referred to in Annex I and the operations referred to in Annex II A or B,
— make this information available, on request, to the competent authorities referred to in Article 6.

Member States may also require producers to comply with the provisions of this Article.

Article 15

In accordance with the 'polluter pays' principle, the cost of disposing of waste must be borne by:

— the holder who has waste handled by a waste collector or by an undertaking as referred to in Article 9, and/or
— the previous holders or the producer of the product from which the waste came.

Article 16

At intervals of three years Member States shall send information to the Commission on the implementation of this Directive, in the form of a sectoral report which shall also cover other pertinent Community Directives. The report shall be drawn up on the basis other of a questionnaire or outline drafted by the Commission in accordance with the procedure laid down in Article 6 of Directive 91/692/EEC.[1] The questionnaire or outline shall be sent to the Member States six months before the start of the period covered by the report. The report shall be made to the Commission within nine months of the end of the three-year period covered by it.

The first report shall cover the period 1995 to 1997 inclusive.

The Commission shall publish a Community report on the implementation of the Directive within nine months of receiving the reports from the Member States.

Article 17

The amendments necessary for adapting the Annexes to this Directive to scientific and technical progress shall be adopted in accordance with the procedure laid down in Article 18.

Article 18

1. The Commission shall be assisted by a committee.

2. Where reference is made to this Article, Articles 5 and 7 of Decision 1999/468/EC[2] shall apply, having regard to the provisions of Article 8 thereof.

The period laid down in Article 5(6) of Decision 1999/468/EC shall be set at three months.

3. The Committee shall adopt its rules of procedure.

Article 19

Member States shall bring into force the measures needed in order to comply with this Directive within 24 months of its notification and shall forthwith inform the Commission thereof.

Article 20

Member States shall communicate to the Commission the texts of the main provisions of national law which they adopt in the field covered by this Directive.

Article 21

This Directive is addressed to the Member States.

---

[1] OJ No L 377, 31. 12. 1991, p. 48.
[2] Council Decision 1999/468/EC of 28 June 1999 laying down the procedures for the exercise of implementing powers conferred on the Commission (OJ L 184, 17.7.1999, p. 23).

Annex I
Categories of waste

Q1 Production or consumption residues not otherwise specified below
Q2 Off-specification products
Q3 Products whose date for appropriate use has expired
Q4 Materials spilled, lost or having undergone other mishap, including any materials, equipment, etc., contaminated as a result of the mishap
Q5 Materials contaminated or soiled as a result of planned actions (e.g. residues from cleaning operations, packing materials, containers, etc.)
Q6 Unusable parts (e.g. reject batteries, exhausted catalysts, etc.)
Q7 Substances which no longer perform satisfactorily (e.g. contaminated acids, contaminated solvents, exhausted tempering salts, etc.)
Q8 Residues of industrial processes (e.g. slags, still bottoms, etc.)
Q9 Residues from pollution abatement processes (e.g. scrubber sludges, baghouse dusts, spent filters, etc.)
Q10 Machining/finishing residues (e.g. lathe turnings, mill scales, etc.)
Q11 Residues from raw materials extraction and processing (e.g. mining residues, oil field slops, etc.)
Q12 Adulterated materials(e.g. oils contaminated with PCBs, etc.)
Q13 Any materials, substances or products whose use has been banned by law
Q14 Products for which the holder has no further use (e.g. agricultural, household, office, commercial and shop discards, etc.)
Q15 Contaminated materials, substances or products resulting from remedial action with respect to land
Q16 Any materials, substances or products which are not contained in the above categories.

Annex IIA
Disposal operations

NB: This Annex is intended to list disposal operations such as they occur in practice. In accordance with Article 4 waste must be disposed of without endangering human health and without the use of processes or methods likely to harm the environment.

D 1 Deposit into or onto land (e.g. landfill, etc.)
D 2 Land treatment (e.g. biodegradation of liquid or sludgy discards in soils, etc.)
D 3 Deep injection (e.g. injection of pumpable discards into wells, salt domes or naturally occurring repositories, etc.)
D 4 Surface impoundment (e.g. placement of liquid or sludgy discards into pits, ponds or lagoons, etc.)
D 5 Specially engineered landfill (e.g. placement into lined discrete cells which are capped and isolated from one another and the environment, etc.)

D 6 Release into a water body except seas/oceans

D 7 Release into seas/oceans including sea-bed insertion

D 8 Biological treatment not specified elsewhere in this Annex which results in final compounds or mixtures which are discarded by means of any of the operations numbered D 1 to D 12

D 9 Physico-chemical treatment not specified elsewhere in this Annex which results in final compounds or mixtures which are discarded by means of any of the operations numbered D 1 to D 12 (e.g. evaporation, drying, calcination, etc.)

D 10 Incineration on land

D 11 Incineration at sea

D 12 Permanent storage (e.g. emplacement of containers in a mine, etc.)

D 13 Blending or mixing prior to submission to any of the operations numbered D 1 to D 12

D 14 Repackaging prior to submission to any of the operations numbered D 1 to D 13

D 15 Storage pending any of the operations numbered D 1 to D 14 (excluding temporary storage, pending collection, on the site where it is produced)

Annex IIB
Recovery operations

NB: This Annex is intended to list recovery operations as they occur in practice. In accordance with Article 4 waste must be recovered without endangering human health and without the use of processes or methods likely to harm the environment.

R 1 Use principally as a fuel or other means to generate energy

R 2 Solvent reclamation/regeneration

R 3 Recycling/reclamation of organic substances which are not used as solvents (including composting and other biological transformation processes)

R 4 Recycling/reclamation of metals and metal compounds

R 5 Recycling/reclamation of other inorganic materials

R 6 Regeneration of acids or bases

R 7 Recovery of components used for pollution abatement

R 8 Recovery of components from catalysts

R 9 Oil re-refining or other reuses of oil

R 10 Land treatment resulting in benefit to agriculture or ecological improvement

R 11 Use of wastes obtained from any of the operations numbered R 1 to R 10

R 12 Exchange of wastes for submission to any of the operations numbered R 1 to R 11

R 13 Storage of wastes pending any of the operations numbered R 1 to R 12 (excluding temporary storage, pending collection, on the site where it is produced)

Council Directive 91/689/EEC of 12 December 1991 on hazardous waste (as amended)

Editorial note

Council Directive 91/689 brings the laws of the Member States on the controlled management of hazardous waste closer to each other by applying most of the provisions of Directive 75/442 to hazardous waste and setting out additional obligations for hazardous waste (Article 1(1)–(2)). It establishes a new definition of hazardous waste by reference to three annexes, but does not apply to domestic waste (Article 1(4)–(5)).

Under the Directive all tipping (discharges) on every site must be recorded and the waste identified; there must be no mixing of different categories of hazardous waste or mixing of hazardous and non-hazardous waste, except in prescribed circumstances (Article 2). Hazardous waste must be properly packaged and labelled in accordance with international and EC standards (Article 5(1)). National authorities must draw up public plans for the management of hazardous waste (Article 6(1)). In an emergency of grave danger hazardous waste must be dealt with so as not to constitute a threat to the population or the environment (Article 7). Member States are to provide the Commission with detailed information on, *inter alia*, the establishments and undertakings carrying out disposal and/or recovery of hazardous waste, and the method used to treat waste, and the types and quantities of waste which can be treated (Article 8). Certain derogations allowed by Directive 75/442 cannot be applied to hazardous waste, and certain provisions of Directive 75/442 apply expressly to hazardous waste (Articles 3, 4, 6, 8).

Source: OJ L 377 31.12.1991 p. 20. Amended by: Council Directive 94/31/EC of 27 June 1994 L 168 28 02.07.1994. Corrected by: Corrigendum, OJ L 23 30.01.1998 p. 39 (91/689/EEC)

Council Directive 91/689/EEC of 12 December 1991 on hazardous waste (as amended)

The Council of the European Communities,

Having regard to the Treaty establishing the European Economic Community, and in particluar Article 130s thereof,

Having regard to the proposal from the Commission,[1]

Having regard to the opinion of the European Parliament,[2]

Having regard to the opinion of the Economic and Social Committee,[3]

Whereas Council Directive 78/319/EEC of 20 March 1978 on toxic and dangerous waste,[4] established Community rules on the disposal of dangerous waste; whereas in order to take account of experience gained in the implementation of that Directive by the Member States, it is necessary to amend the rules and to replace Directive 78/319/EEC by this Directive;

Whereas the Council resolution of 7 May 1990 on waste policy[5] and the action programme of the European Communities on the environment, which was the subject of the resolution of the Council of the European Communities and of the representatives of the Government of the Member States, meeting within the Council, of 19 October 1987 on the continuation and implementation of a European Community policy and action programme on the environment (1987 to 1992),[6] envisage Community measures to improve the conditions under which hazardous wastes are disposed of and managed;

Whereas the general rules applying to waste management which are laid down by Council Directive 75/442/EEC of 15 July 1975 on waste,[7] as amended by Directive 91/156/EEC,[8] also apply to the management of hazardous waste;

Whereas the correct management of hazardous waste necessitates additional, more stringent rules to take account of the special nature of such waste;

Whereas it is necessary, in order to improve the effectiveness of the management of hazardous waste in the Community, to use a precise and uniform definition of hazardous waste based on experience;

Whereas it is necessary to ensure that disposal and recovery of hazardous waste is monitored in the fullest manner possible;

Whereas it must be possible rapidly to adapt the provisions of this Directive to scientific and technical progress; whereas the Committee set up by Directive 75/442/EEC must also empowered to adapt the provisions of this Directive to such progress,

Has adopted this Directive:

Article 1

1. The object of this Directive, drawn up pursuant to Article 2(2) of Directive 75/442/EEC, is to approximate the laws of the Member States on the controlled management of hazardous waste.

2. Subject to this Directive, Directive 75/442/EEC shall apply to hazardous waste.

---

[1] OJ No C 295, 19. 11. 1988, p. 8, and OJ No C 42, 22. 2. 1990, p. 19.
[2] OJ No C 158, 26. 6. 1989, p. 238.   [3] OJ No C 56, 6. 3. 1989, p. 2.   [4] OJ No L 84, 31. 3. 1978, p. 43.
[5] OJ No C 122, 18. 5. 1990, p. 2.   [6] OJ No C 328, 07. 12. 1987, p. 1.   [7] OJ No L 194, 25. 7. 1975, p. 39.
[8] OJ No L 78, 26. 3. 1991, p. 32.

3. The definition of 'waste' and of the other terms used in this Directive shall be those in Directive 75/442/EEC.

4. For the purpose of this Directive 'hazardous waste' means:

– wastes featuring on a list to be drawn up in accordance with the procedure laid down in Article 18 of Directive 75/442/EEC on the basis of Annexes I and II to this Directive, not later than six months before the date of implementation of this Directive. These wastes must have one or more of the properties listed in Annex III. The list shall take into account the origin and composition of the waste and, where necessary, limit values of concentration. This list shall be periodically reviewed and if necessary by the same procedure,
– any other waste which is considered by a Member State to display any of the properties listed in Annex III. Such cases shall be notified to the Commission and reviewed in accordance with the procedure laid down in Article 18 of Directive 75/442/EEC with a view to adaptation of the list.

5. Domestic waste shall be exempted from the provisions of this Directive. The Council shall establish, upon a proposal from the Commission, specific rules taking into consideration the particular nature of domestic waste not later than the end of 1992.

Article 2

1. Member States shall take the necessary measures to require that on every site where tipping (discharge) of hazardous waste takes place the waste is recorded and identified.

2. Member States shall take the necessary measures to require that establishment and undertaking which dispose of, recover, collect or transport hazardous waste do not mix different categories of hazardous waste or mix hazardous waste with non-hazardous waste.

3. By way of derogation from paragraph 2, the mixing of hazardous waste with other hazardous waste or with other waste, substances or materials may be permitted only where the conditions laid down in Article 4 of Directive 75/442/EEC are complied with and in particular for the purpose of improving safety during disposal or recovery. Such an operation shall be subject to the permit requirement imposed in Articles 9, 10 and 11 of Directive 75/442/EEC.

4. Where waste is already mixed with other waste, substances or materials, separation must be effected, where technically and economically feasible, and where necessary in order to comply with Article 4 of Directive 75/442/EEC.

Article 3

1. The derogation referred to in Article 11(1)(a) of Directive 75/442/EEC from the permit requirement for establishments or undertakings which carry out their own waste disposal shall not apply to hazardous waste covered by this Directive.

2. In accordance with Article 11(1)(b) of Directive 75/442/EEC, a Member State may waive Article 10 of that Directive for establishments or undertakings which recover waste covered by this Directive:

— if the Member State adopts general rules listing the type and quantity of waste and laying down specific conditions (limit values for the content of hazardous substances in the waste, emission limit values, type of activity) and other necessary requirements for carrying out different forms of recovery, and
— if the types or quantities of waste and methods of recovery are such that the conditions laid down in Article 4 of Directive 75/442/EEC are complied with.

3. The establishments or undertakings referred to in paragraph 2 shall be registered with the competent authorities.

4. If a Member State intends to make use of the provisions of paragraph 2, the rules referred to in that paragraph shall be sent to the Commission not later than three months prior to their coming into force. The Commission shall consult the Member States. In the light of these consultations the Commission shall propose that the rules be finally agreed upon in accordance with the procedure laid down in Article 18 of Directive 75/442/EEC.

Article 4

1. Article 13 of Directive 75/442/EEC shall also apply to producers of hazardous waste.

2. Article 14 of Directive 75/442/EEC shall also apply to producers of hazardous waste and to all establishments and undertakings transporting hazardous waste.

3. The records referred to in Article 14 of Directive 75/442/EEC must be preserved for at least three years except in the case of establishments and undertakings transporting hazardous waste which must keep such records for at least 12 months. Documentary evidence that the management operations have been carried out must be supplied at the request of the competent authorities or of a previous holder.

Article 5

1. Member States shall take the necessary measures to ensure that, in the course of collection, transport and temporary storage, waste is properly packaged and labelled in accordance with the international and Community standards in force.

2. In the case of hazardous waste, inspections concerning collection and transport operations made on the basis of Article 13 of Directive 75/442/EEC shall cover more particularly the origin and destination of such waste.

3. Where hazardous waste is transferred, it shall be accompanied by an identification form containing the details specified in Section A of Annex I to Council Directive 84/631/EEC of 6 December 1984 on the supervision and control within the European

Community of the transfrontier shipment of hazardous waste,[1] as last amended by Directive 86/279/EEC.[2]

Article 6

1. As provided in Article 7 of Directive 75/442/EEC, the competent authorities shall draw up, either separately or in the framework of their general waste management plans, plans for the management of hazardous waste and shall make these plans public.

2. The Commission shall compare these plans, and in particular the methods of disposal and recovery. It shall make this information available to the competent authorities of the Member States which ask for it.

Article 7

In cases of emergency or grave danger, Member States shall take all necessary steps, including, where appropriate, temporary derogations from this Directive, to ensure that hazardous waste is so dealt with as not to constitute a threat to the population or the environment. The Member State shall inform the Commission of any such derogations.

Article 8

1. In the context of the report provided for in Article 16(1) of Directive 75/442/EEC, and on the basis of a questionnaire drawn up in accordance with that Article, the Member States shall send the Commission a report on the implementation of this Directive.

2. In addition to the consolidated report referred to in Article 16(2) of Directive 75/442/EEC, the Commission shall report to the European Parliament and the Council every three years on the implementation of this Directive.

3. In addition, by 12 December 1994, the Member States shall send the Commission the following information for every establishment or undertaking which carries out disposal and/or recovery of hazardous waste principally on behalf of third parties and which is likely to form part of the integrated network referred to in Article 5 of Directive 75/442/EEC:

– name and address,
– the method used to treat waste,
– the types and quantities of waste which can be treated.

Once a year, Member States shall inform the Commission of any changes in this information. The Commission shall make this information available on request to the competent authorities in the Member States.

[1] OJ No L 326, 13. 12. 1984, p. 31.   [2] OJ No L 181, 4. 7. 1986, p. 13.

The format in which this information will be supplied to the Commission shall be agreed upon in accordance with the procedure laid down in Article 18 of Directive 75/442/EEC.

Article 9

The amendments necessary for adapting the Annexes to this Directive to scientific and technical progress and for revising the list of wastes referred to in Article 1(4) shall be adopted in accordance with the procedure laid down in Article 18 of Directive 74/442/EEC.

Article 10

1. Member States shall bring into force the laws, regulations and administrative provisions necessary for them to comply with this Directive by 27 June 1995. They shall immediately inform the Commission thereof.

2. When Member States adopt these measures, they shall contain a reference to this Directive or shall be accompanied by such reference on the occasion of their official publication. The methods of making such a reference shall be laid down by the Member States.

3. Member States shall communicate to the Commission the texts of the main provisions of national law which they adopt in the field governed by this Directive.

Article 11

Directive 78/319/EEC shall be repealed with effect from 27 June 1995.

Article 12

This Directive is addressed to the Member States.

Annex I

Categories or generic types of hazardous waste listed according to their nature or the activity which generated them* (waste may be liquid, sludge or solid in form)

Annex I.A.

Wastes displaying any of the properties listed in Annex III and which consist of:

1. anatomical substances; hospital and other clinical wastes;
2. pharmaceuticals, medicines and veterinary compounds;
3. wood preservatives;
4. biocides and phyto-pharmaceutical substances;
5. residue from substances employed as solvents;

---

* Certain duplications of entries found in Annex II are intentional.

6. halogenated organic substances not employed as solvents excluding inert poly-merized materials;
7. tempering salts containing cyanides;
8. mineral oils and oily substances (e.g. cutting sludges, etc.);
9. oil/water, hydrocarbon/water mixtures, emulsions;
10. substances containing PCBs and/or PCTs (e.g. dielectrics etc.);
11. tarry materials arising from refining, distillation and any pyrolytic treatment (e.g. still bottoms, etc.);
12. inks, dyes, pigments, paints, lacquers, varnishes;
13. resins, latex, plasticizers, glues/adhesives;
14. chemical substances arising from research and development or teaching activities which are not identified and/or are new and whose effects on man and/or the environment are not known (e.g. laboratory residues, etc.);
15. pyrotechnics and other explosive materials;
16. photographic chemicals and processing materials;
17. any material contaminated with any congener of polychlorinated dibenzofuran;
18. any material contaminated with any congener of polychlorinated dibenzo-pdioxin.

Annex I.B.

Wastes which contain any of the constituents listed in Annex II and having any of the properties listed in Annex III and consisting of:

19. animal or vegetable soaps, fats, waxes;
20. non-halogenated organic substances not employed as solvents;
21. inorganic substances without metals or metal compounds;
22. ashes and/or cinders;
23. soil, sand, clay including dredging spoils;
24. non-cyanidic tempering salts;
25. metallic dust, powder;
26. spent catalyst materials;
27. liquids or sludges containing metals or metal compounds;
28. residue from pollution control operations (e.g. baghouse dusts, etc.) except (29), (30) and (33);
29. scrubber sludges;
30. sludges from water purification plants;
31. decarbonization residue;
32. ion-exchange column residue;
33. sewage sludges, untreated or unsuitable for use in agriculture;
34. residue from cleaning of tanks and/or equipment;
35. contaminated equipment;

36. contaminated containers (e.g. packaging, gas cylinders, etc.) whose contents included one or more of the constituents listed in Annex II;

37. batteries and other electrical cells;

38. vegetable oils;

39. materials resulting from selective waste collections from households and which exhibit any of the characteristics listed in Annex III;

40. any other wastes which contain any of the constituents listed in Annex II and any of the properties listed in Annex III.

Annex II

Constituents of the wastes in Annex I.B. which render them hazardous when they have the properties described in Annex III*

Wastes having as constituents:

C1   beryllium; beryllium compounds;
C2   vanadium compounds;
C3   chromium (VI) compounds;
C4   cobalt compounds;
C5   nickel compounds;
C6   copper compounds;
C7   zinc compounds;
C8   arsenic; arsenic compounds;
C9   selenium; selenium compounds;
C10   silver compounds;
C11   cadmium; cadmium compounds;
C12   tin compounds;
C13   antimony; antimony compounds;
C14   tellurium; tellurium compounds;
C15   barium compounds; excluding barium sulfate;
C16   mercury; mercury compounds;
C17   thallium; thallium compounds;
C18   lead; lead compounds;
C19   inorganic sulphides;
C20   inorganic fluorine compounds, excluding calcium fluoride;
C21   inorganic cyanides;
C22   the following alkaline or alkaline earth metals: lithium, sodium, potassium, calcium, magnesium in uncombined form;

---

* Certain duplications of generic types of hazardous wastes listed in Annex I are intentional.

C23   acidic solutions or acids in solid form;
C24   basic solutions or bases in solid form;
C25   asbestos (dust and fibres);
C26   phosphorus: phosphorus compounds, excluding mineral phosphates;
C27   metal carbonyls;
C28   peroxides;
C29   chlorates;
C30   perchlorates;
C31   azides;
C32   PCBs and/or PCTs;
C33   pharmaceutical or veterinary coumpounds;
C34   biocides and phyto-pharmaceutical substances (e.g. pesticides, etc.);
C35   infectious substances;
C36   creosotes;
C37   isocyanates; thiocyanates;
C38   organic cyanides (e.g. nitriles, etc.);
C39   phenols; phenol compounds;
C40   halogenated solvents;
C41   organic solvents, excluding halogenated solvents;
C42   organohalogen compounds, excluding inert polymerized materials and other substances referred to in this Annex;
C43   aromatic compounds; polycyclic and heterocyclic organic compounds;
C44   aliphatic amines;
C45   aromatic amines
C46   ethers;
C47   substances of an explosive character, excluding those listed elsewhere in this Annex;
C48   sulphur organic compounds;
C49   any congener of polychlorinated dibenzo-furan;
C50   any congener of polychlorinated dibenzo-p-dioxin;
C51   hydrocarbons and their oxygen; nitrogen and/or sulphur compounds not otherwise taken into account in this Annex.

Annex III
Properties of wastes which render them hazardous

H1   'Explosive': substances and preparations which may explode under the effect of flame or which are more sensitive to shocks or friction than dinitrobenzene.
H2   'Oxidizing': substances and preparations which exhibit highly exothermic reactions when in contact with other substances, particularly flammable substances.

H3-A   'Highly flammable':
- liquid substances and preparations having a flash point below 21°C (including extremely flammable liquids), or
- substances and preparations which may become hot and finally catch fire in contact with air at ambient temperature without any application of energy, or
- solid substances and preparations which may readily catch fire after brief contact with a source of ignition and which continue to burn or to be consumed after removal of the source of ignition, or
- gaseous substances and preparations which are flammable in air at normal pressure, or
- substances and preparations which, in contact with water or damp air, evolve highly flammable gases in dangerous quantities.

H3-B   'Flammable': liquid substances and preparations having a flash point equal to or greater than 21°C and less than or equal to 55°C.

H4   'Irritant': non-corrosive substances and preparations which, through immediate, prolonged or repeated contact with the skin or mucous membrane, can cause inflammation.

H5   'Harmful': substances and preparations which, if they are inhaled or ingested or if they penetrate the skin, may involve limited health risks.

H6   'Toxic': substances and preparations (including very toxic substances and preparations) which, if they are inhaled or ingested or if they penetrate the skin, may involve serious, acute or chronic health risks and even death.

H7   'Carcinogenic': substances and preparations which, if they are inhaled or ingested or if they penetrate the skin, may induce cancer or increase its incidence.

H8   'Corrosive': substances and preparations which may destroy living tissue on contacts.

H9   'Infectious': substances containing viable micro-organisms or their toxins which are known or reliably believed to cause disease in man or other living organisms.

H10   'Teratogenic': substances and preparations which, if they are inhaled or ingested or if they penetrate the skin, may induce non-hereditary congenital malformations or increase their incidence.

H11   'Mutagenic': substances and preparations which, if they are inhaled or ingested or if they penetrate the skin, may induce hereditary genetic defects or increase their incidence.

H12   Substances and preparations which release toxic or very toxic gases in contact with water, air or an acid.

H13   Substances and preparations capable by any means, after disposal, of yielding another substance, e.g. a leachate, which possesses any of the characteristics listed above.

H14   'Ecotoxic': substances and preparations which present or may present imme-
       diate or delayed risks for one or more sectors of the environment.

Notes

1. Attribution of the hazard properties 'toxic' (and 'very toxic'), 'harmful', 'corrosive'
and 'irritant' is made on the basis of the criteria laid down by Annex VI, part I A and
part II B, of Council Directive 67/548/EEC of 27 June 1967 of the approximation of
laws, regulations and administrative provisions relating to the classification, packaging
and labelling of dangerous substances,[1] in the version as amended by Council Directive
79/831/EEC.[2]

2. With regard to attribution of the properties 'carcinogenic', 'teratogenic' and
'mutagenic', and reflecting the most recent findings, additional criteria are contained
in the Guide to the classification and labelling of dangerous substances and preparations of Annex VI (part II D) to Directive 67/548/EEC in the version as amended by
Commission Directive 83/467/EEC.[3]

Test methods

The test methods serve to give specific meaning to the definitions given in Annex III.

The methods to be used are those described in Annex V to Directive 67/548/EEC,
in the version as amended by Commission Directive 84/449/EEC,[4] or by subsequent
Commission Directives adapting Directive 67/548/EEC to technical progress. These
methods are themselves based on the work and recommendations of the competent
international bodies, in particular the OECD.

[1] OJ No L 196, 16. 8. 1967, p. 1.   [2] OJ No L 259, 15. 10. 1979, p. 10.
[3] OJ No L 257, 16. 9. 1983, p. 1.   [4] OJ No L 251, 19. 9. 1984, p. 1.

Council Regulation (EEC) No 259/93 of 1 February 1993 on the supervision and control of shipments of waste within, into and out of the European Community (as amended)

Editorial note

Regulation 259/93 regulates and prohibits shipments of all waste within, into and out of the Community, except for five categories of waste which are excluded from the application of the Regulation and certain wastes destined for recovery only and listed in Annex II (Article 1). The Regulation establishes rules to govern four situations: (1) shipments of waste between Member States; (2) the movement of wastes between Member States; (3) exports of wastes; and (4) imports of wastes. Additional rules govern transit.

The Regulation allows waste to be moved between Member States for disposal, subject to the rules governing prior notification and authorisation by national authorities (Articles 3–5) and the three general grounds on which a consignment may be stopped (Article 4(3)(a)–(c)). The shipment of waste for recovery listed in Annex III (amber waste) is subject to a system of prior notification and authorisation (Articles 6–8). Consignments of waste for recovery listed in Annex IV (red list) are generally subject to the same procedures as for the amber list (Article 10). The Regulation also provides for certain information requirements in the case of movement between Member States and via non-Member States (Articles 11–12).

The provisions on shipment between Member States (Title II), on common provisions (Title VII) and on other provisions (Title VIII) do not apply to shipments within a Member State, although Member States may decide, and are free, to apply these provisions (Article 13(1) and (4)). As a minimum, they must establish an 'appropriate system' to supervise and control consignments of waste within their jurisdiction (Article 13(2)).

All exports of waste to African, Caribbean and Pacific countries are prohibited, except that a Member State may return to an ACP State waste which that State has chosen to have processed in the EC (Article 18). As regards exports to all other States, the Regulation distinguishes between waste for disposal and waste for recovery. All exports of waste for disposal are prohibited, except to those EFTA countries which are also parties to the Basle Convention (Article 14(1)). Exports to EFTA countries are allowed subject to the notification and authorisation provisions (Article 15) and can be prohibited in certain circumstances (Article 14(2)). Subject to certain exceptions, the Regulation generally prohibits export of waste for recovery (Article 16). Special conditions apply to exports of waste for recovery listed in Annex II (green), Annex III (amber) and Annex IV (red) (Article 17).

On imports into the EC the Regulation distinguishes between waste for disposal and waste for recovery. With certain exceptions the import of waste for disposal is generally prohibited (Article 19(1)); where permitted, it is subject to prior notification and authorisation (Article 20). The import of waste for recovery is also generally prohibited, with certain exceptions (Article 21(1)–(2)). Different control procedures apply to the import of waste for recovery from countries to which the OECD Decision applies (Article 22).

Other rules govern transit (Articles 23 and 24); non-completion of shipments and return (Article 25); illegal traffic (Article 26); financial guarantees (Article 27); general notification procedures (Article 28); the mixing of wastes (Article 29); compliance, including inspection (Article 30); consignment notes (Article 31); compliance with international transport conventions (Article 32 and Annex I); administrative costs (Article 33); relationship with Directives 75/442 and 91/689 (Article 34); the retention of documents (Article 35); and information and advice (Article 37). The Commission has presented a proposal to revise the Regulation and to simplify the current regime (Proposal of 30 June 2003 for a Regulation of the European Parliament and of the Council on shipments of waste (presented by the Commission), COM(2003) 379 final).

Source: OJ L 30 06.02.1993 p. 1. Amended by: Commission Decision 94/721/EC of 21 October 1994 L 288 36 09.11.1994; Commission Decision 96/660/EC of 14 November 1996 L 304 15 27.11.1996; Council Regulation (EC) No 120/97 of 20 January 1997 L 22 14 24.01.1997; Commission Decision 98/368/EC of 18 May 1998 L 165 20 10.06.1998; Commission Regulation (EC) No 2408/98 of 6 November 1998 L 298 19 07.11.1998; Commission Decision 1999/816/EC of 24 November 1999 L 316 45 10.12.1999; Commission Regulation (EC) No 2557/2001 of 28 December 2001 L 349 1 31.12.2001

Council Regulation (EEC)No 259/93 of 1 February 1993 on the supervision and control of shipments of waste within, into and out of the European Community (as amended)

The Council of the European Communities,

Having regard to the Treaty establishing the European Economic Community, and in particular Article 130s thereof,

Having regard to the proposal from the Commission,[1]

Having regard to the opinion of the European Parliament,[2]

Having regard to the opinion of the Economic and Social Committee,[3]

Whereas the Community has signed the Basle Convention of 22 March 1989 on the control of transboundary movements of hazardous wastes and their disposal;

Whereas provisions concerning waste are contained in Article 39 of the ACP-EEC Convention of 15 December 1989;

Whereas the Community has approved the Decision of the OECD Council of 30 March 1992 on the control of transfrontier movements of wastes destined for recovery operations;

Whereas, in the light of the foregoing, Directive 84/631/EEC,[4] which organizes the supervision and control of transfrontier shipments of hazardous waste, needs to be replaced by a Regulation;

Whereas the supervision and control of shipments of waste within a Member State is a national responsibility; whereas, however, national systems for the supervision and control of shipments of waste within a Member State should comply with minimum criteria in order to ensure a high level of protection of the environment and human health;

Whereas it is important to organize the supervision and control of shipments of wastes in a way which takes account of the need to preserve, protect and improve the quality of the environment;

Whereas Council Directive 75/442/EEC of 15 July 1975 on waste[5] lays down in its Article 5(1) that an integrated and adequate network of waste disposal installations, to be established by Member States through appropriate measures, where necessary or advisable in cooperation with other Member States, must enable the Community as a whole to become self-sufficient in waste disposal and the Member States to move towards that aim individually, taking into account geographical circumstances or the need for specialized installations for certain types of waste; whereas Article 7 of the said Directive requests the drawing up of waste management plans, if appropriate in cooperation with the Member States concerned, which shall be notified to the Commission, and stipulates that Member States may take measures necessary to prevent movements of waste which are not in accordance with their waste management plans and that they shall inform the Commission and the other Member States of any such measures;

---

[1] OJ No C 115, 6. 5. 1992, p. 4.

[2] OJ No C 94, 13. 4. 1992, p. 276 and opinion delivered on 20 January 1993 (not yet published in the Official Journal).

[3] OJ No C 269, 14. 10. 1991, p. 10.

[4] OJ No L 326, 13. 12. 1984, p. 31. Directive as last amended by Directive 91/692/EEC (OJ No L 377, 31. 12. 1991, p. 48).

[5] OJ No L 194, 25. 7. 1975, p. 39. Directive as amended by Directive 91/156/EEC (OJ No L 78, 26. 3. 1991, p. 32).

Whereas it is necessary to apply different procedures depending on the type of waste and its destination, including whether it is destined for disposal or recovery;

Whereas shipments of waste must be subject to prior notification to the competent authorities enabling them to be duly informed in particular of the type, movement and disposal or recovery of the waste, so that these authorities may take all necessary measures for the protection of human health and the environment, including the possibility of raising reasoned objections to the shipment;

Whereas Member States should be able to implement the principles of proximity, priority for recovery and self-sufficiency at Community and national levels – in accordance with Directive 75/442/EEC – by taking measures in accordance with the Treaty to prohibit generally or partially or to object systematically to shipments of waste for disposal, except in the case of hazardous waste produced in the Member State of dispatch in such a small quantity that the provision of new specialized disposal installations within that State would be uneconomic; whereas the specific problem of disposal of such small quantities requires cooperation between the Member States concerned and possible recourse to a Community procedure;

Whereas exports of waste for disposal to third countries must be prohibited in order to protect the environment of those countries; whereas exceptions shall apply to exports to EFTA countries which are also Parties to the Basle Convention;

Whereas exports of waste for recovery to countries to which the OECD Decision does not apply must be subject to conditions providing for environmentally sound management of waste;

Whereas agreements or arrangements on exports of waste for recovery with countries to which the OECD Decision does not apply must be subject to periodic review by the Commission leading, if appropriate, to a proposal by the Commission to reconsider the conditions under which such exports take place, including the possibility of a ban;

Whereas shipments of waste for recovery listed on the green list of the OECD Decision shall be generally excluded from the control procedures of this Regulation since such waste should not normally present a risk to the environment if properly recovered in the country of destination; whereas some exceptions to this exclusion are necessary in accordance with Community legislation and the OECD Decision; whereas some exceptions are also necessary in order to facilitate the tracking of such shipments within the Community and to take account of exceptional cases; whereas such waste shall be subject to Directive 75/442/EEC;

Whereas exports of waste for recovery listed on the OECD green list to countries to which the OECD Decision does not apply must be subject to consultation by the Commission with the country of destination; whereas it may be appropriate in the light of such consultation that the Commission make proposals to the Council;

Whereas exports of waste for recovery to countries which are not parties to the Basle Convention must be subject to specific agreements between these countries and the Community; whereas Member States must, in exceptional cases, be able to conclude after the date of application of this Regulation bilateral agreements for the import of specific waste before the Community has concluded such agreements, in the case of waste for recovery in order to avoid any interruption of waste treatment and in the case of waste for disposal where the country of dispatch does not have or cannot reasonably acquire the technical capacity and necessary facilities to dispose of the waste in an environmentally sound manner;

Whereas provision must be made for the waste to be taken back or to be disposed of or recovered in an alternative and environmentally sound manner if the shipment cannot be completed in accordance with the terms of the consignment note or the contract;

Whereas, in the event of illegal traffic, the person whose action is the cause of such traffic must take back and/or dispose of or recover the waste in an alternative and environmentally sound manner; whereas, should he fail to do so, the competent authorities of dispatch or destination, as appropriate, must themselves intervene;

Whereas it is important for a system of financial guarantees or equivalent insurance to be established;

Whereas Member States must provide the Commission with information relevant to the implementation of this Regulation;

Whereas the documents provided for by this Regulation must be established and the Annexes adapted within a Community procedure,

Has adopted this Regulation:

Title I
Scope and definitions

Article 1

1. This Regulation shall apply to shipments of waste within, into and out of the Community.

2. The following shall be excluded from the scope of this Regulation:

(a) the offloading to shore of waste generated by the normal operation of ships and offshore platforms, including waste water and residues, provided that such waste is the subject of a specific binding international instrument;

(b) shipments of civil aviation waste;

(c) shipments of radioactive waste as defined in Article 2 of Directive 92/3/Euratom of 3 February 1992 on the supervision and control of shipments of radioactive waste between Member States and into and out of the Community;[1]

(d) shipments of waste mentioned in Article 2(1)(b) of Directive 75/442/EEC, where they are already covered by other relevant legislation;

(e) shipments of waste into the Community in accordance with the requirements of the Protocol on Environmental Protection to the Antarctic Treaty.

---

[1] OJ No L 35, 12. 2. 1992, p. 24.

3.

(a) Shipments of waste destined for recovery only and listed in Annex II shall also be excluded from the provisions of this Regulation except as provided for in subparagraphs (b), (c), (d) and (e), in Article 11 and in Article 17(1), (2) and (3).

(b) Such waste shall be subject to all provisions of Directive 75/442/EEC. It shall in particular be:
   – destined for duly authorized facilities only, authorized according to Article 10 and 11 of Directive 75/442/EEC,
   – subject to all provisions of Articles 8, 12, 13 and 14 of Directive 75/442/EEC.

(c) However, certain wastes listed in Annex II may be controlled, if, among other reasons, they exhibit any of the hazardous characteristics listed in Annex III of Council Directive 91/689/EEC,[1] as if they had been listed in Annex III or IV.

   These wastes and the decision about which of the two procedures should be followed shall be determined in accordance with the procedure laid down in Article 18 of Directive 75/442/EEC. Such wastes shall be listed in Annex II (a).

(d) In exceptional cases, shipments of wastes listed in Annex II may, for environmental or public health reasons, be controlled by Member States as if they had been listed in Annex III or IV.

   Member States which make use of this possibility shall immediately notify the Commission of such cases and inform other Member States, as appropriate, and give reasons for their decision. The Commission, in accordance with the procedure laid down in Article 18 of Directive 75/442/EEC, may confirm such action including, where appropriate, by adding such wastes to Annex II.A.

(e) Where waste listed in Annex II is shipped in contravention of this Regulation or of Directive 75/442/EEC, Member States may apply appropriate provisions of Articles 25 and 26 of this Regulation.

Article 2

For the purposes of this Regulation:

(a) *waste* is as defined in Article 1(a) of Directive 75/442/EEC;

(b) *competent authorities* means the competent authorities designated by either the Member States in accordance with Article 36 or non-Member States;

(c) *competent authority of dispatch* means the competent authority, designated by the Member States in accordance with Article 36, for the area from which the shipment is dispatched or designated by non-Member States;

(d) *competent authority of destination* means the competent authority, designated by the Member States in accordance with Article 36, for the area in which the shipment is received, or in which waste is loaded on board before disposal at

---

[1] OJ No L 377, 31. 12. 1991, p. 20.

sea without prejudice to existing conventions on disposal at sea or designated by non-Member States;

(e) *competent authority of transit* means the single authority designated by Member States in accordance with Article 36 for the State through which the shipment is in transit;

(f) *correspondent* means the central body designated by each Member State and the Commission, in accordance with Article 37;

(g) *notifier* means any natural person or corporate body to whom or to which the duty to notify is assigned, that is to say the person referred to hereinafter who proposes to ship waste or have waste shipped:

(i) the person whose activities produced the waste (original producer); or

(ii) where this is not possible, a collector licensed to this effect by a Member State or a registered or licensed dealer or broker who arranges for the disposal or the recovery of waste; or

(iii) where these persons are unknown or are not licensed, the person having possession or legal control of the waste (holder); or

(iv) in the case of import into or transit through the Community of waste, the person designated by the laws of the State of dispatch or, when this designation has not taken place, the person having possession or legal control of the waste (holder);

(h) *consignee* means the person or undertaking to whom or to which the waste is shipped for recovery or disposal;

(i) *disposal* is as defined in Article 1(e) of Directive 75/442/EEC;

(j) *authorized centre* means any establishment or undertaking authorized or licensed pursuant to Article 6 of Directive 75/439/EEC,[1] Articles 9, 10 and 11 of Directive 75/442/EEC and Article 6 of Directive 76/403/EEC;[2]

(k) *recovery* is as defined in Article 1(f) of Directive 75/442/EEC;

(l) *State of dispatch* means any State from which a shipment of waste is planned or made;

(m) *State of destination* means any State to which a shipment of waste is planned or made for disposal or recovery, or for loading on board before disposal at sea without prejudice to existing conventions on disposal at sea;

(n) *State of transit* means any State, other than the State of dispatch or destination, through which a shipment of waste is planned or made;

(o) *consignment note* means the standard consignment note to be drawn up in accordance with Article 42;

(p) *the Basle Convention* means the Basle Convention of 22 March 1989 on the control of transboundary movements of hazardous wastes and their disposal;

---

[1] OJ No L 194, 25. 7. 1975, p. 23. Directive as last amended by Directive 91/692/EEC (OJ No L 377, 31. 12. 1991, p. 48).

[2] OJ No L 108, 26. 4. 1976, p. 41.

(q) *the fourth Lomé Convention* means the Lomé Convention of 15 December 1989;
(r) *the OECD Decision* means the decision of the OECD Council of 30 March 1992 on the control of transfrontier movements of wastes destined for recovery operations.

Title II
Shipments of waste between Member States

Chapter A
Waste for disposal

Article 3

1. Where the notifier intends to ship waste for disposal from one Member State to another Member State and/or pass it in transit through one or several other Member States, and without prejudice to Articles 25(2) and 26(2), he shall notify the competent authority of destination and send a copy of the notification to the competent authorities of dispatch and of transit and to the consignee.

2. Notification shall mandatorily cover any intermediate stage of the shipment from the place of dispatch to its final destination.

3. Notification shall be effected by means of the consignment note which shall be issued by the competent authority of dispatch.

4. In making notification, the notifier shall complete the consignment note and shall, if requested by competent authorities, supply additional information and documentation.

5. The notifier shall supply on the consignment note information with particular regard to:

- the source, composition and quantity of the waste for disposal including, in the case of Article 2(g)(ii), the producer's identity and, in the case of waste from various sources a detailed inventory of the waste and, if known, the identity of the original producers,
- the arrangements for routing and for insurance against damage to third parties,
- the measures to be taken to ensure safe transport and, in particular, compliance by the carrier with the conditions laid down for transport by the Member States concerned,
- the identity of the consignee of the waste, the location of the disposal centre and the type and duration of the authorization under which the centre operates. The centre must have adequate technical capacity for the disposal of the waste in question under conditions presenting no danger to human health or to the environment,
- the operations involving disposal as referred to in Annex II.A to Directive 75/442/EEC.

6. The notifier must make a contract with the consignee for the disposal of the waste.

The contract may include some or all of the information referred to in paragraph 5.

The contract must include the obligation:

– of the notifier, in accordance with Articles 25 and 26(2), to take the waste back if the shipment has not been completed as planned or if it has been effected in violation of this Regulation,
– of the consignee, to provide as soon as possible and no later than 180 days following the receipt of the waste a certificate to the notifier that the waste has been disposed of in an environmentally sound manner.

A copy of this contract must be supplied to the competent authority on request.

Should the waste be shipped between two establishments under the control of the same legal entity, this contract may be replaced by a declaration by the entity in question undertaking to dispose of the waste.

7. The information given in accordance with paragraphs 4 to 6 shall be treated confidentially in accordance with existing national regulations.

8. A competent authority of dispatch may, in accordance with national legislation, decide to transmit the notification itself instead of the notifier to the competent authority of destination, with copies to the consignee and to the competent authority of transit.

The competent authority of dispatch may decide not to proceed with notification if it has itself immediate objections to raise against the shipment in accordance with Article 4(3). It shall immediately inform the notifier of these objections.

Article 4

1. On receipt of the notification, the competent authority of destination shall, within three working days, send an acknowledgement to the notifier and copies thereof to the other competent authorities concerned and to the consignee.

2.

(a) The competent authority of destination shall have 30 days following dispatch of the acknowledgement to take its decision authorizing the shipment, with or without conditions, or refusing it. It may also request additional information.

It shall give its authorization only in the absence of objections on its part or on the part of the other competent authorities. The authorization shall be subject to any transport conditions referred to in (d).

The competent authority of destination shall take its decision not earlier than 21 days following the dispatch of the acknowledgement. It may, however, take its decision earlier if it has the written consent of the other competent authorities concerned.

The competent authority of destination shall send its decision to the notifier in writing, with copies to the other competent authorities concerned.

(b) The competent authorities of dispatch and transit may raise objections within 20 days following the dispatch of the acknowledgement. They may also request additional information. These objections shall be conveyed in writing to the notifier, with copies to the other competent authorities concerned.

(c) The objections and conditions referred to in (a) and (b) shall be based on paragraph 3.

(d) The competent authorities of dispatch and transit may, within 20 days following the dispatch of the acknowledgement, lay down conditions in respect of the transport of waste within their jurisdiction.

These conditions must be notified to the notifier in writing, with copies to the competent authorities concerned, and entered in the consignment note. They may not be more stringent than those laid down in respect of similar shipments occurring wholly within their jurisdiction and shall take due account of existing agreements, in particular relevant international conventions.

3.

(a) (i) In order to implement the principles of proximity, priority for recovery and self-sufficiency at Community and national levels in accordance with Directive 75/442/EEC, Member States may take measures in accordance with the Treaty to prohibit generally or partially or to object systematically to shipments of waste. Such measures shall immediately be notified to the Commission, which will inform the other Member States.

 (ii) In the case of hazardous waste (as defined in Article 1(4) of Directive 91/689/EEC) produced in a Member State of dispatch in such a small quantity overall per year that the provision of new specialized disposal installations within that State would be uneconomic, (i) shall not apply.

(iii) The Member State of destination shall cooperate with the Member State of dispatch which considers that (ii) applies, with a view to resolving the issue bilaterally. If there is no satisfactory solution, either Member State may refer the matter to the Commission, which will determine the issue in accordance with the procedure laid down in Article 18 of Directive 75/442/EEC.

(b) The competent authorities of dispatch and destination, while taking into account geographical circumstances or the need for specialized installations for certain types of waste, may raise reasoned objections to planned shipments if they are not in accordance with Directive 75/442/EEC, especially Articles 5 and 7:

 (i) in order to implement the principle of self-sufficiency at Community and national levels;

 (ii) in cases where the installation has to dispose of waste from a nearer source and the competent authority has given priority to this waste;

(iii) in order to ensure that shipments are in accordance with waste management plans.

(c) Furthermore, the competent authorities of dispatch, destination and transit may raise reasoned objections to the planned shipment if:
  – it is not in accordance with national laws and regulations relating to environmental protection, public order, public safety or health protection,
  – the notifier or the consignee was previously guilty of illegal trafficking. In this case, the competent authority of dispatch may refuse all shipments involving the person in question in accordance with national legislation, or
  – the shipment conflicts with obligations resulting from international conventions concluded by the Member State or Member States concerned.

4. If, within the time limits laid down in paragraph 2, the competent authorities are satisfied that the problems giving rise to their objections have been solved and that the conditions in respect of the transport will be met, they shall immediately inform the notifier in writing, with copies to the consignee and to the other competent authorities concerned.

If there is subsequently any essential change in the conditions of the shipment, a new notification must be made.

5. The competent authority of destination shall signify its authorization by appropriately stamping the consignment note.

Article 5

1. The shipment may be effected only after the notifier has received authorization from the competent authority of destination.

2. Once the notifier has received authorization, he shall insert the date of shipment and otherwise complete the consignment note and send copies to the competent authorities concerned three working days before the shipment is made.

3. A copy or, if requested by the competent authorities, a specimen of the consignment note, together with the stamp of authorization, shall accompany each shipment.

4. All undertakings involved in the operation shall complete the consignment note at the points indicated, sign it and retain a copy thereof.

5. Within three working days following receipt of the waste for disposal, the consignee shall send copies of the completed consignment note, except for the certificate referred to in paragraph 6, to the notifier and the competent authorities concerned.

6. As soon as possible and not later than 180 days following the receipt of the waste, the consignee shall, under his responsibility, send a certificate of disposal to the notifier and the other competent authorities concerned. This certificate shall be part of or attached to the consignment note which accompanies the shipment.

Chapter B
Waste for recovery

Article 6

1. Where the notifier intends to ship waste for recovery listed in Annex III from one Member State to another Member State and/or pass it in transit through one or

several other Member States, and without prejudice to Articles 25(2) and 26(2), he shall notify the competent authority of destination and send copies of the notification to the competent authorities of dispatch and transit and to the consignee.

2. Notification shall mandatorily cover any intermediary stage of the shipment from the place of dispatch to its final destination.

3. Notification shall be effected by means of the consignment note which shall be issued by the competent authority of dispatch.

4. In making notification, the notifier shall complete the consignment note and shall, if requested by competent authorities, supply additional information and documentation.

5. The notifier shall supply on the consignment note information with particular regard to:

- the source, composition and quantity of the waste for recovery, including the producer's identity and, in the case of waste from various sources, a detailed inventory of the waste and, if known, the indentity of the original producer,
- the arrangements for routing and for insurance against damage to third parties,
- the measures to be taken to ensure safe transport and, in particular, compliance by the carrier with the conditions laid down for transport by the Member States concerned,
- the identity of the consignee of the waste, the location of the recovery centre and the type and duration of the autorization under which the centre operates. The centre must have adequate technical capacity for the recovery of the waste in question under conditions presenting no danger to human health or to the environment,
- the operations involving recovery as contained in Annex II.B to Directive 75/442/EEC,
- the planned method of disposal for the residual waste after recycling has taken place,
- the amount of the recycled material in relation to the residual waste,
- the estimated value of the recycled material.

6. The notifier must conclude a contract with the consignee for the recovery of the waste.

The contract may include some or all of the information referred to in paragraph 5.

The contract must include the obligation:

- of the notifier, in accordance with Articles 25 and 26(2), to take the waste back if the shipment has not been completed as planned or if it has been effected in violation of this Regulation,
- of the consignee to provide, in the case of retransfer of the waste for recovery to another Member State or to a third country, the notification of the initial country of dispatch,

– of the consignee to provide, as soon as possible and not later than 180 days following the receipt of the waste, a certificate to the notifier that the waste has been recovered in an environmentally sound manner.

A copy of this contract must be supplied to the competent authority on request.

Should the waste be shipped between two establishments under the control of the same legal entity, this contract may be replaced by a declaration by the entity in question undertaking to recover the waste.

7. The information given in accordance with paragraphs 4 to 6 shall be treated confidentially in accordance with existing national regulations.

8. A competent authority of dispatch may, in accordance with national legislation, decide to transmit the notification itself instead of the notifier to the competent authority of destination, with copies to the consignee and to the competent authority of transit.

Article 7

1. On receipt of the notification the competent authority of destination shall send, within three working days, an acknowledgement to the notifier and copies thereof to the other competent authorities and to the consignee.

2. The competent authorities of destination, dispatch and transit shall have 30 days following dispatch of the acknowledgement to object to the shipment. Such objection shall be based on paragraph 4. Any objection must be provided in writing to the notifier and to other competent authorities concerned within the 30-day period.

The competent authorities concerned may decide to provide written consent in a period less than the 30 days.

Written consent or objection may be provided by post, or by telefax followed by post. Such consent shall expire within one year unless otherwise specified.

3. The competent authorities of dispatch, destination and transit shall have 20 days following the dispatch of the acknowledgement in which to lay down conditions in respect of the transport of waste within their jurisdiction.

These conditions must be notified to the notifier in writing, with copies to the competent authorities concerned, and entered in the consignment note. They may not be more stringent that those laid down in respect of similar shipments occurring wholly within their jurisdiction and shall take due account of existing agreements, in particular relevant international conventions.

4.

(a) The competent authorities of destination and dispatch may raise reasoned objections to the planned shipment:
  – in accordance with Directive 75/442/EEC, in particular Article 7 thereof, or
  – if it is not in accordance with national laws and regulations relating to environmental protection, public order, public safety or health protection, or

- if the notifier or the consignee has previously been guilty of illegal trafficking. In this case, the competent authority of dispatch may refuse all shipments involving the person in question in accordance with national legislation, or
- if the shipment conflicts with obligations resulting from international conventions concluded by the Member State or Member States concerned, or
- if the ratio of the recoverable and non-recoverable waste, the estimated value of the materials to be finally recovered or the cost of the recovery and the cost of the disposal of the non recoverable fraction do not justify the recovery under economic and environmental considerations.

(b) The competent authorities of transit may raise reasoned objections to the planned shipment based on the second, third and fourth indents of (a).

5. If within the time limit laid down in paragraph 2 the competent authorities are satisfied that the problems giving rise to their objections have been solved and that the conditions in respect of the transport will be met, they shall immediately inform the notifier in writing, with copies to the consignee and to the other competent authorities concerned. If there is subsequently any essential change in the conditions of the shipment, a new notification must be made.

6. In case of prior written consent, the competent authority shall signify its authorization by appropriately stamping the consignment note.

Article 8

1. The shipment may be effected after the 30-day period has passed if no objection has been lodged. Tacit consent, however, expires within one year from that date.

Where the competent authorities decide to provide written consent, the shipment may be effected immediately after all necessary consents have been received.

2. The notifier shall insert the date of shipment and otherwise complete the consignment note and send copies to the competent authorities concerned three working days before the shipment is made.

3. A copy or, if requested by the competent authorities, a specimen of the consignment note shall accompany each shipment.

4. All undertakings involved in the operation shall complete the consignment note at the points indicated, sign it and retain a copy thereof.

5. Within three working days following receipt of the waste for recovery, the consignee shall send copies of the completed consignment note, except for the certificate referred to in paragraph 6, to the notifier and to the competent authorities concerned.

6. As soon as possible and not later than 180 days following receipt of the waste the consignee, under his responsability, shall send a certificate of recovery of the waste to the notifier and the other competent authorities concerned. This certificate shall be part of or attached to the consignment note which accompanies the shipment.

Article 9

1. The competent authorities having jurisdiction over specific recovery facilities may decide, notwithstanding Article 7, that they will not raise objections concerning shipments of certain types of waste to a specific recovery facility. Such decisions may be limited to a specific period of time; however, they may be revoked at any time.

2. Competent authorities which select this option shall inform the Commission of the recovery facility name, address, technologies employed, waste types to which the decision applies and the period covered. Any revocations must also be notified to the Commission.

The Commission shall send this information without delay to the other competent authorities concerned in the Community and to the OECD Secretariat.

3. All intended shipments to such facilities shall require notification to the competent authorities concerned, in accordance with Article 6. Such notification shall arrive prior to the time the shipment is dispatched.

The competent authorities of the Member States of dispatch and transit may raise objections to any such shipment, based on Article 7(4), or impose conditions in respect of the transport.

4. In instances where competent authorities acting under terms of their domestic laws are required to review the contract referred to in Article 6(6), these authorities shall so inform the Commission. In such cases, the notification plus the contracts or portions thereof to be reviewed must arrive seven days prior to the time the shipment is dispatched in order that such review may be appropriately performed.

5. For the actual shipment, Article 8(2) to (6) shall apply.

Article 10

Shipments of waste for recovery listed in Annex IV and of waste for recovery which has not yet been assigned to Annex II, Annex III or Annex IV shall be subject to the same procedures as referred to in Articles 6 to 8 except that the consent of the competent authorities concerned must be provided in writing prior to commencement of shipment.

Article 11

1. In order to assist the tracking of shipments of waste for recovery listed in Annex II, they shall be accompanied by the following information, signed by the holder:

(a) the name and address of the holder;
(b) the usual commercial description of the waste;
(c) the quantity of the waste;
(d) the name and address of the consignee;

(e) the operations involving recovery, as listed in Annex II.B to Directive 75/442/EEC;
(f) the anticipated date of shipment.

2. The information specified in paragraph 1 shall be treated confidentially in accordance with existing national regulations.

Chapter C
Shipment of waste for disposal and recovery between Member States with transit via third States

Article 12

Without prejudice to Articles 3 to 10, where a shipment of waste takes place between Member States with transit via one or more third States,

(a) the notifier shall send a copy of the notification to the competent authority(ies) of the third State(s);
(b) the competent authority of destination shall ask the competent authority in the third State(s) whether it wishes to send its written consent to the planned shipment:
  – in the case of parties to the Basle Convention, within 60 days, unless it has waived this right in accordance with the terms of that Convention, or
  – in the case of countries not parties to the Basle Convention, within a period agreed between the competent authorities.

In both cases the competent authority of destination shall, where appropriate, wait for consent before giving its authorization.

Title III
Shipments of waste within Member States

Article 13

1. Titles II, VII and VIII shall not apply to shipments within a Member State.

2. Member States shall, however, establish an appropriate system for the supervision and control of shipments of waste within their jurisdiction. This system should take account of the need for coherence with the Community system established by this Regulation.

3. Member States shall inform the Commission of their system for the supervision and control of shipments of waste. The Commission shall inform the other Member States thereof.

4. Member States may apply the system provided for in Titles II, VII and VIII within their jurisdiction.

Title IV
Exports of waste

Chapter A
Waste for disposal

Article 14

1. All exports of waste for disposal shall be prohibited, except those to EFTA countries which are also parties to the Basle Convention.

2. However, without prejudice to Articles 25(2), and 26(2), exports of waste for disposal to an EFTA country shall also be banned:

(a) where the EFTA country of destination prohibits imports of such wastes or where it has not given its written consent to the specific import of this waste;
(b) if the competent authority of dispatch in the Community has reason to believe that the waste will not be managed in accordance with environmentally sound methods in the EFTA country of destination concerned.

3. The competent authority of dispatch shall require that any waste for disposal authorized for export to EFTA countries be managed in an environmentally sound matter throughout the period of shipment and in the State of destination.

Article 15

1. The notifier shall send the notification to the competent authority of dispatch by means of the consignment note in accordance with Article 3(5), with copies to the other competent authorities concerned and to the consignee. The consignment note shall be issued by the competent authority of dispatch.

On receipt of the notification, the competent authority of dispatch shall within three working days send the notifier a written acknowledgement of the notification, with copies to the other competent authorities concerned.

2. The competent authority of dispatch shall have 70 days following dispatch of the acknowledgement to take its decision authorizing the shipment, with or without conditions, or refusing it. It may also request additional information.

It shall give its authorization only in the absence of objections on its part or on the part of the other competent authorities and if it has received from the notifier the copies referred to in paragraph 4. The authorization shall, where applicable, be subject to any transport conditions referred to in paragraph 5.

The competent authority of dispatch shall take its decision no earlier than 61 days following the dispatch of the acknowledgement.

It may, however, take its decision earlier if it has the written consent of the other competent authorities.

It shall send a certified copy of the decision to the other competent authorities concerned, to the customs office of departure from the Community and to the consignee.

3. The competent authorities of dispatch and transit in the Community may, within 60 days following the dispatch of the acknowledgement, raise objections based on Article 4(3). They may also request additional information. Any objection must be provided in writing to the notifier, with copies to the other competent authorities concerned.

4. The notifier shall provide to the competent authority of dispatch a copy of:

(a) the written consent of the EFTA country of destination to the planned shipment;
(b) the confirmation from the EFTA country of destination of the existence of a contract between the notifier and the consignee specifying environmentally sound management of the waste in question; a copy of the contract must be supplied, if requested.

    The contract shall also specify that the consignee be required to provide:
– within three working days following the receipt of the waste for disposal, copies of the fully completed consignment note, except for the certification referred to in the second indent, to the notifier and to the competent authority concerned,
– as soon as possible and not later than 180 days following the receipt of the waste, a certificate of disposal under his responsability to the notifier and to the competent authority concerned. The form of this certificate shall be part of the consignment note which accompanies the shipment.

    The contract shall, in addition, stipulate that if a consignee issues an incorrect certificate with the consequence that the financial guarantee is released he shall bear the costs arising from the duty to return the waste to the area of jurisdiction of the competent authority of dispatch and its disposal in an alternative and environmentally sound manner;
(c) written consent to the planned shipment from the other State(s) of transit, unless this (these) State(s) is (are) a Party (Parties) to the Basle Convention and has (have) waived this in accordance with the terms of that Convention.

5. The competent authorities of transit in the Community shall have 60 days following the dispatch of the acknowledgement in which to lay down conditions in respect of the shipments of waste in their area of jurisdiction. These conditions, which shall be forwarded to the notifier, with copies to the other competent authorities concerned, may not be more stringent than those laid down in respect of similar shipments effected wholly within the area of jurisdiction of the competent authority in question.

6. The competent authority of dispatch shall signify its authorization by appropriately stamping the consignment note.

7. The shipment may be effected only after the notifier has received authorization from the competent authority of dispatch.

8. Once the notifier has received authorization, he shall insert the date of shipment and otherwise complete the consignment note and send copies to the competent authorities concerned three working days before the shipment is made. A copy or, if requested by the competent authorities, a specimen of the consignment note, together

with the stamp of authorization, shall accompany each shipment. All undertakings involved in the operation shall complete the consignment note at the points indicated, sign it and retain a copy thereof. A specimen of the consignment note shall be delivered by the carrier to the last customs office of departure when the waste leaves the Community.

9. As soon as the waste has left the Community, the customs office of departure shall send a copy of the consignment note to the competent authority which issued the authorization.

10. If, 42 days after the waste has left the Community, the competent authority which gave the authorization has received no information from the consignee about his receipt of the waste, it shall inform without delay the competent authority of destination. It shall take action in a similar way if, 180 days after the waste has left the Community, the competent authority which gave the authorization has not received from the consignee the certificate of disposal referred to in paragraph 4.

11. A competent authority of dispatch may, in accordance with national legislation, decide to transmit the notification itself instead of the notifier, with copies to the consignee and the competent authority of transit. The competent authority of dispatch may decide to proceed with any notification if it has itself immediate objections to raise against the shipment in accordance with Article 4(3). It shall immediately inform the notifier of these objections.

12. The information given in paragraphs 1 to 4 shall be treated confidentially in accordance with existing national regulations.

Chapter B
Waste for recovery

Article 16

1. All exports for recovery of waste listed in Annex V for recovery shall be prohibited except those to:

(a) countries to which the OECD Decision applies;
(b) other countries:
  - which are Parties to the Basle Convention and/or with which the Community, or the Community and its Member States, have concluded bilateral or multi-lateral or regional agreements or arrangements in accordance with Article 11 of the Basle Convention and paragraph 2 of this Article. Any such exports shall however be prohibited from 1 January 1998 onwards,
  - with which individual Member States have concluded bilateral agreements and arrangements prior to the date of application of this Regulation, insofar as these are compatible with Community legislation and in accordance with Article 11 of the Basle Convention and paragraph 2 of this Article. These agreements and arrangements shall be notified to the Commission within three months of

the date of application of this Regulation or of the date that such agreements
are brought into effect, whichever is earlier, and shall expire when agreements
or arrangements are concluded in accordance with the first indent. Any such
exports shall however be prohibited as from 1 January 1998 onwards.

The Commission, in accordance with the procedure laid down in Article 18 of Directive 75/442/EEC, shall, as soon as possible, and at the latest before 1 January 1998,
review and amend Annex V to this Regulation taking into full consideration those
wastes featuring on the list of wastes adopted in accordance with Article 1(4) of Council Directive 91/689/EEC of 12 December 1991 on hazardous waste[1] and any lists of
wastes characterized as hazardous for the purposes of the Basle Convention.
    Annex V shall be reviewed and further amended as appropriate under the same
procedure. In particular, the Commission shall review the Annex in order to give
effect to decisions of the Parties to the Basle Convention as to what waste should be
characterized as hazardous for the purposes of the Convention and to amendments
of the list of wastes adopted in accordance with Article 1(4) of Directive 91/689/EEC.
    2. The agreements and arrangements referred to in paragraph 1(b) shall guarantee
an environmentally sound management of the waste in accordance with Article 11 of
the Basle Convention and shall, in particular:

(a) guarantee that the recovery operation is carried out in an authorized centre which
    complies with the requirements for environmentally sound management;
(b) fix the conditions for the treatment of the non-recoverable components of the
    waste and, if appropriate, oblige the notifier to take them back;
(c) enable, if appropriate, the examination of the compliance of the agreements on
    the spot in agreement with the countries concerned;
(d) be subject to periodic review by the Commission and for the first time not later
    than 31 December 1996, taking into account the experience gained and the ability
    of the countries concerned to carry out recovery activities in a manner which pro-
    vides full guarantees of environmentally sound management. The Commission
    shall inform the European Parliament and the Council about the results of this
    review. If such a review leads to the conclusion that environmental guarantees
    are insufficient, the continuation of waste exports under such terms shall, on a
    proposal from the Commission, be reconsidered, including the possibility of a ban.

    3. However, without prejudice to Article 25(2) and 26(2), exports of waste for
recovery to the countries referred to in paragraph 1 shall be prohibited:

(a) where such a country prohibits all imports of such wastes or where it has not given
    its consent to their specific import;

---

[1] OJ No L 377, 31. 12. 1991, p. 20. Directive as amended by Directive 94/31/EC (OJ No L 168, 2. 7. 1994,
   p. 28).

(b) if the competent authority of dispatch has reason to believe that the waste will not be managed in accordance with environmentally sound methods in such a country.

4. The competent authority of dispatch shall require that any waste for recovery authorized for export be managed in an environmentally sound manner throughout the period of shipment and in the State of destination.

Article 17

1. In respect of waste listed in Annex II, the Commission shall notify prior to the date of application of this Regulation to every country to which the OECD Decision does not apply the list of waste included in that Annex and request written confirmation that such waste is not subject to control in the country of destination and that the latter will accept categories of such waste to be shipped without recourse to the control procedures which apply to Annex III or IV or that it indicate where such waste should be subject to either those procedures or the procedure laid down in Article 15.

If such confirmation is not received six months before the date of application of this Regulation, the Commission shall make appropriate proposals to the Council.

2. Where waste listed in Annex II is exported, it shall be destined for recovery operations within a facility which under applicable domestic law is operating or is authorized to operate in the importing country. Furthermore, a surveillance system based on prior automatic export licensing shall be established in cases to be determined in accordance with the procedure laid down in Article 18 of Directive 75/442/EEC.

Such a system shall in each case provide that a copy of the export licence be forwarded without delay to the authorities of the country in question.

3. Where such waste is subject to control in the country of destination or upon request of such a country in accordance with paragraph 1 or where a country of destination has notified under Article 3 of the Basle Convention that it regards certain kinds of waste listed in Annex II is hazardous, exports of such waste to that country shall be subjected to control. The Member State of export or the Commission shall notify all such cases to the committee established pursuant to Article 18 of Directive 75/442/EEC; the Commission shall determine in consultation with the country of destination which of the control procedures shall apply, that is those applicable to Annex III or IV or the procedure laid down in Article 15.

4. Where waste listed in Annex III is exported from the Community for recovery to countries and through countries to which the OECD Decision applies, Articles 6, 7, 8 and 9(1), (3), (4) and (5) shall apply, the provisions concerning the competent authorities of dispatch and transit applying only to the competent authorities in the Community.

5. In addition, the competent authorities of the exporting and Community-transit countries shall be informed of the decision referred to in Article 9.

6. Where the waste for recovery listed in Annex IV and waste for recovery which has not yet been assigned to Annex II, III or IV is exported for recovery to countries and through countries to which the OECD Decision applies, Article 10 shall apply by analogy.

7. In addition, where waste is exported in accordance with paragraphs 4 to 6:

– a specimen of the consignment note shall be delivered by the carrier to the last customs office of departure when the waste leaves the Community,
– as soon as the waste has left the Community, the customs office of departure shall send a copy of the consignment note to the competent authority of export,
– if, 42 days after the waste has left the Community, the competent authority of export has received no information from the consignee about this receipt of the waste, it shall inform without delay the competent authority of destination,
– the contract shall stipulate that, if a consignee issues an incorrect certificate with the consequence that the financial guarantee is released, he shall bear the costs arising from the duty to return the waste to the area of jurisdiction of the competent authority of dispatch and its disposal or recovery in an alternative and environmentally sound manner.

8. Where waste for recovery listed in Annex III and IV and waste for recovery which has not yet been assigned to Annex II, III or IV is exported to and through countries to which the OECD Decision does not apply:

– Article 15, except for paragraph 3, shall apply by analogy,
– reasoned objections may be raised in accordance with Article 7(4) only,

save as otherwise provided for in bilateral or multilateral agreements entered into in accordance with Article 16(1)(b) and on the basis of the control procedure of either paragraph 4 or 6 of this Article or Article 15.

Chapter C
Export of waste to ACP States

Article 18

1. All exports of waste to ACP States shall be prohibited.

2. This prohibition does not prevent a Member State to which an ACP State has chosen to export waste for processing from returning the processed waste to the ACP State of origin.

3. In case of re-export to ACP States, a specimen of the consignmet note, together with the stamp of authorization, shall accompany each shipment.

Title V
Imports of waste into the Community

Chapter A
Imports of waste for disposal

Article 19

1. All imports into the Community of waste for disposal shall be prohibited except those from:

(a) EFTA countries which are Parties to the Basle Convention;
(b) other countries:
   – which are Parties to the Basle Convention, or
   – with which the Community, or the Community and its Member States, have concluded bilateral or multilateral agreements or arrangements compatible with Community legislation and in accordance with Article 11 of the Basle Convention guaranteeing that the disposal operations carried out in an authorized centre and complies with the requirements for environmentally sound management, or
   – with which individual Member States have concluded bilateral agreements or arrangements prior to the date of application of this Regulation, compatible with Community legislation and in accordance with Article 11 of the Basle Convention, containing the same guarantees as referred to above and guaranteeing that the waste originated in the country of dispatch and that disposal will be carried out exclusively in the Member State which has concluded the agreement or arrangement. These agreements or arrangements shall be notified to the Commission with in three months of the date of application of the Regulation or of their date of application, whichever is the earlier, and shall expire when agreements or arrangements are concluded in accordance with the second indent, or
   – with which individual Member States conclude bilateral agreements or arrangements after the date of application of this Regulation in the circumstances of paragraph 2.

2. The Council hereby authorizes individual Member States to conclude bilateral agreements and arrangements after the date of application of this Regulation in exceptional cases for the disposal of specific waste, where such waste will not be managed in an environmentally sound manner in the country of dispatch. These agreements and arrangements shall comply with the conditions set out in paragraph 1(b), third indent and shall be notified to the Commission prior to their conclusion.

3. The countries referred to in paragraph 1(b) shall be required to present a duly motivated request beforehand to the competent authority of the Member State of destination on the basis that they do no have and cannot reasonable acquire the

technical capacity and the necessary facilities in order to dispose of the waste in an environmentally sound manner.

4. The competent authority of destination shall prohibit the bringing of waste into its area of jurisdiction if it has reason to believe that the waste will not be managed in an environmentally sound manner in its area.

Article 20

1. Notification shall be made to the competent authority of destinations by means of the consignment note in accordance with Article 3(5) with copies to the consignee of the waste and to the competent authorities of transit. The consignment note shall be issued by the competent authority of destination. On receipt of the notification, the competent authority of destination shall, within three working days, send a written acknowledgement to the notifier, with copies to the competent authorities of transit in the Community.

2. The competent authority of destination shall authorize the shipment only in the absence of objections on its part or from the other competent authorities concerned. The authorization shall be subject to any transport conditions referred to in paragraph 5.

3. The competent authorities of destination and transit in the Community may, within 60 days of dispatch of the copy of the acknowledgement, raise objections based on Article 4(3).

They may also request additional information. These objections shall be conveyed in writing to the notifier, with copies to the other competent authorities concerned in the Community;

4. The competent authority of destination shall have 70 days following dispatch of the acknowledgement to take its decision authorizing the shipment, with or without conditions, or refusing it. It may also request additional information.

It shall send certified copies of the decision to the competent authorities of transit in the Community, the consignee and the customs office of entry into the Community.

The competent authority of destination shall take its decision no earlier than 61 days following the dispatch of the acknowledgement. It may, however, take its decision earlier if it has the written consent of the other competent authorities.

The competent authority of destination shall signify its authorization by appropriately stamping the consignment note.

5. The competent authority of destination and transit in the Community shall have 60 days following dispatch of the acknowledgement to lay down conditions in respect of the shipment of the waste. These conditions, which must be conveyed to the notifier, with copies to the competent authorities concerned, may not be more stringent than those laid down in respect of similar shipments occuring wholly within the jurisdiction of the competent authority in question.

6. The shipment may be effected only after the notifier has received authorization from the competent authority of destination.

7. Once the notifier has received authorization, he shall insert the date of the shipment and otherwise complete the consignment note and send copies to the competent authorities concerned three working days before the shipment is made. A specimen of the consignment note shall be delivered by the carrier to the customs office of entry into the Community.

A copy or, if requested by the competent authorities, a specimen of the consignment note, together with the stamp of authorization, shall accompany each shipment.

All undertakings involved in the operation shall complete the consignment note at the points indicated, sign it and retain a copy.

8. Within three working days following receipt of the waste for disposal, the consignee shall send copies of the completed consignment note, except for the certificate referred to in paragraph 9, to the notifier and the competent authorities concerned;

9. As soon as possible and not later than 180 days following the receipt of the waste, the consignee shall, under his responsibility, send a certificate of disposal to the notifier and the other competent authorities concerned. This certificate shall be part of or attached to the consignment note which accompanies the shipment.

Chapter B
Imports of waste for recovery

Article 21

1. All imports of waste for recovery into the Community shall be prohibited, except those from: (a) countries to which the OECD decision applies; (b) other countries:

- which are Parties to the Basle Convention and/or with which the Community, or the Community and its Member States, have concluded bilateral or multilateral or regional agreements or arrangements compatible with Community legislation and in accordance with Article 11 of the Basle Convention, guaranteeing that the recovery operation is carried out in an authorized centre and complies with the requirements for environmentally sound management, or
- with which individual Member States have concluded bilateral agreements or arrangements prior to the date of application of this Regulation, where these are compatible with Community legislation and in accordance with Article 11 of the Basle Convention, containing the same guarantees as referred to above. These agreements or arrangements shall be notified to the Commission within three months of the date of application of this Regulation or of their date of application, whichever is the earlier, and shall expire when agreements or arrangements are concluded in accordance with the first indent, or
- with which individual Member States conclude bilateral agreements or arrangements after the date of application of this Regulation in the circumstances of paragraph 2.

2. The Council hereby authorizes individual Member States to conclude after the date of applications of this Regulation bilateral agreements and arrangements in exceptional cases for the recovery of specific waste, where a Member State deems such agreements or arrangements necessary to avoid any interruption of waste treatment before the Community has concluded those agreements and arrangements. Such agreements and arrangements shall also be compatible with Community legislation and in accordance with Article 11 of the Basle Convention; they shall be notified to the Commission prior to their conclusion and shall expire when agreements or arrangements are concluded in accordance with paragraph 1(b), first indent.

Article 22

1. Where waste is imported for recovery from countries and through countries to which the OECD Decision applies, the following control procedures shall apply by analogy:

(a) for waste listed in Annex III: Articles 6, 7, 8, 9(1), (3), (4) and (5), and 17(5);
(b) for waste listed in Annex IV and waste which has not yet been assigned to Annex II, III or IV: Article 10.

2. Where waste for recovery listed in Annexes III and IV and waste which has not yet been assigned to Annex II, III or IV is imported from and through countries to the OECD Decision does not apply:

– Article 20 shall apply by analogy,
– reasoned objections may be raised in accordance with Article 7(4) only,

save as otherwise provided for the bilateral or multilateral agreements entered into in accordance with Article 21(1)(b) and on the basis of the control procedures of either paragraph 1 of this Article or Article 20.

Title VI
Transit of waste from outside and through the Community for disposal or recovery outside the Community

Chapter A
Waste for disposal and recovery (except transit covered by Article 24)

Article 23

1. Where waste for disposal and, except in cases covered by Article 24, recovery is shipped through (a) Member State(s), notification shall be effected by means of the consignment note to the last competent authority of transit within the Community, with copies to the consignee, the other competent authorities concerned and the customs offices of entry into and departure from the Community.

2. The last competent authority of transit within the Community shall promptly inform the notifier of receipt of the notification. The other competent authorities in the Community shall, on the basis of paragraph 5, convey their reactions to the last competent authority of transit in the Community, which shall then respond in writing to the notifier within 60 days, consenting to the shipment with or without reservations; or imposing, if appropriate, conditions laid down by the other competent authorities of transit, or withholding information. Any refusal or reservations must be justified. The competent authority shall send a certified copy of the decision to both the other competent authorities concerned and the customs offices of entry into and departure from the Community.

3. Without prejudice to Articles 25(2) and 26(2), the shipment shall be admitted into the Community only if the notifier has received the written consent of the last competent authority of transit. This authority shall signify its consent by appropriately stamping the consignment note.

4. The competent authorities of transit within the Community shall have 20 days following notification to lay down, if appropriate, any conditions attached to the transport of the waste. These conditions, which must be conveyed to the notifier, with copies to the competent authorities concerned, may not be more stringent than those laid down in respect of similar shipments occurring wholly within the jurisdiction of the competent authority in question.

5. The consignment note shall be issued by the last competent authority of transit within the Community.

6. Once the notifier has received authorization, he shall complete the consignment note and send copies to the competent authorities concerned three working days before the shipment is made. A specimen of the consignment note, together with the stamp of authorization, shall accompany each shipment. A specimen of the consignment note shall be supplied by the carrier to the customs office of departure when the waste leaves the Community.

All undertakings involved in the operation shall complete the consignment note at the points indicated, sign it and retain a copy thereof.

7. As soon as the waste has left the Community, the customs office of departure shall send a copy of the consignment note to the last competent authority of transit within the Community.

Furthermore, at the latest 42 days after the waste has left the Community, the notifier shall declare or certify to that competent authority, with copies to the other competent authorities of transit, that it has arrived at its intended destination.

Chapter B
Transit of waste for recovery from and to a country to which the OECD Decision applies

Article 24

1. Transit of waste for recovery listed in Annexes III and IV from a country and transferred for recovery to a country to which the OECD Decision applies through

(a) Member State(s) requires notification to all competent authorities of transit of the Member State(s) concerned.

2. Notification shall be effected by means of the consignment note.

3. On receipt of the notification the competent authority(ies) of transit shall send an acknowledgement to the notifier and to the consignee within three working days.

4. This competent authority(ies) of transit may raise reasoned objections to the planned shipment based on Article 7(4). Any objection must be provided in writing to the notifier and to the competent authorities of transit of the other Member States concerned within 30 days of dispatch of the acknowledgement.

5. The competent authority of transit may decide to provide written consent in less than 30 days.

In the case of transit of waste listed in Annex IV and waste which has not yet been assigned to Annex II, III or IV, consent must be given in writing prior to commencement of the shipment.

6. The shipment may be effected only in the absence of any objection.

Title VII
Common provisions

Article 25

1. Where a shipment of waste to which the competent authorities concerned have consented cannot be completed in accordance with the terms of the consignment note or the contract referred to in Articles 3 and 6, the competent authority of dispatch shall, within 90 days after it has been informed thereof, ensure that the notifier returns the waste to its area of jurisdiction or elsewhere within the State of dispatch unless it is satisfied that the waste can be disposed of or recovered in an alternative and environmentally sound manner.

2. In cases referred to in paragraph 1, a further notification shall be made. No Member State of dispatch or Member State of transit shall oppose the return of this waste at the duly motivated request of the competent authority of destination and with an explanation of the reason.

3. The obligation of the notifier and the subsidiary obligation of the State of dispatch to take the waste back shall end when the consignee has issued the certificate referred to in Articles 5 and 8.

Article 26

1. Any shipment of waste effected:

(a) without notification to all competent authorities concerned pursuant to the provisions of this Regulation; or
(b) without the consent of the competent authorities concerned pursuant to the provisions of this Regulation; or

(c) with consent obtained from the competent authorities concerned through falsification, misrepresentation or fraud; or

(d) which is not specified in a material way in the consignment note; or

(e) which results in disposal or recovery in contravention of Community or international rules; or

(f) contrary to Articles 14, 16, 19 and 21

shall be deemed to be illegal traffic.

2. If such illegal traffic is the responsibility of the notifier of the waste, the competent authority of dispatch shall ensure that the waste in question is:

(a) taken back by the notifier or, if necessary, by the competent authority itself, into the State of dispatch, or if impracticable;

(b) otherwise disposed of or recovered in an environmentally sound manner,

within 30 days from the time when the competent authority was informed of the illegal traffic or within such other period of time as may be agreed by the competent authorities concerned.

In this case a further notification shall be made. No Member State of dispatch or Member State of transit shall oppose the return of this waste at the duly motivated request of the competent authority of destination and with an explanation of the reason.

3. If such illegal traffic is the responsibility of the consignee, the competent authority of destination shall ensure that the waste in question is disposed of in an environmentally sound manner by the consignee or, if impracticable, by the competent authority itself within 30 days from the time it was informed of the illegal traffic or within any such other period of time as may be agreed by the competent authorities concerned. To this end, they shall cooperate, as necessary, in the disposal or recovery of the waste in an environmentally sound manner.

4. Where responsibility for the illegal traffic cannot be imputed to either the notifier or the consignee, the competent authorities shall cooperate to ensure that the waste in question is disposed of or recovered in an environmentally sound manner. Guidelines for this cooperation shall be established in accordance with the procedure laid down in Article 18 of Directive 75/442/EEC.

5. Member States shall take appropriate legal action to prohibit and punish illegal traffic.

Article 27

1. All shipments of waste covered within the scope of this Regulation shall be subject to the provision of a financial guarantee or equivalent insurance covering costs for shipment, including cases referred to in Articles 25 and 26, and for disposal or recovery.

2. Such guarantees shall be returned when proof has been furnished, by means of:

— the certificate of disposal or recovery, that the waste has reached its destination and has been disposed of or recovered in an environmentally sound manner,
— Control copy T 5 drawn up pursuant to Commission Regulation (EEC) No 2823/87[1] that, in the case of transit through the Community, the waste has left the Community.

3. Each Member State shall inform the Commission of the provision which it makes in national law pursuant to this Article. The Commission shall forward this information to all Member States.

Article 28

1. While respecting the obligations imposed on him by the applicable Articles 3, 6, 9, 15, 17, 20, 22, 23 and 24, the notifier may use a general notification procedure where waste for disposal or recovery having the same physical and chemical characteristics is shipped periodically to the same consignee following the same route. If, in the case of unforeseen circumstances, this route cannot be followed, the notifier shall inform the competent authorities concerned as soon as possible or before the shipment starts if the need for route modification is already known at this time. Where the route modification is known before the shipment starts and this involves other competent authorities than those concerned in the general notification, this procedure shall not be used.

2. Under a general notification procedure, a single notification may cover several shipments of waste over a maximum period of one year. The indicated period may be shortened by agreement between the competent authorities concerned.

3. The competent authorities concerned shall make their agreement to the use of this general notification procedure subject to the subsequent supply of additional information. If the composition of the waste is not as notified or if the conditions imposed on its shipment are not respected, the competent authorities concerned shall withdraw their consent to this procedure by means of official notice to the notifier. Copies of this notice shall be sent to the other competent authorities concerned.

4. General notification shall be made by means of the consignment note.

Article 29

Wastes which are the subject of different notifications shall not be mixed during shipment.

Article 30

1. Member States shall take the measures needed to ensure that waste is shipped in accordance with the provisions of this Regulation. Such measures may include

---

[1] OJ No L 270, 23. 9. 1987, p. 1.

inspections of establishments and undertakings, in accordance with Article 13 of Directive 75/442/EEC, and spot checks of shipments.

2. Checks may take place in particular:

— at the point of origin, carried out with the producer, holder or notifier,
— at the destination, carried out with the final consignee,
— at the external frontiers of the Community,
— during the shipment within the Community.

3. Checks may include the inspection of documents, the confirmation of identity and, if appropriate, the physical control of the waste.

Article 31

1. The consignment note shall be printed and completed and any further documentation and information referred to in Articles 4 and 6 shall be supplied in a language which is acceptable to the competent authority of:

— dispatch, as referred to in Articles 3, 7, 15 and 17, in the case of both a shipment of waste within the Community and the export of waste,
— destination, as referred to in Articles 20 and 22, in the case of the import of waste,
— transit, as referred to in Articles 23 and 24. A translation shall be supplied by the notifier at the request of the other competent authorities concerned in a language acceptable to them.

2. Further details may be determined in accordance with the procedure laid down in Article 18 of Directive 75/442/EEC.

Title VIII
Other provisions

Article 32

The provisions of the international transport conventions listed in Annex I to which the Member States are parties shall be complied with in so far as they cover the waste to which this Regulation refers.

Article 33

1. Appropriate administrative costs of implementing the notification and supervision procedure and usual costs of appropriate analyses and inspections may be charged to the notifier.

2. Costs arising from the return of waste, including shipment, disposal or recovery of the waste in an alternative and environmentally sound manner pursuant to Articles 25(1) and 26(2), shall be charged to the notifier or, if impracticable, to the Member States concerned.

3. Costs arising from disposal or recovery in an alternative and environmentally sound manner pursuant to Article 26(3) shall be charged to the consignee.

4. Costs arising from disposal or recovery, including possible shipment pursuant to Article 26(4), shall be charged to the notifier and/or the consignee depending upon the decision by the competent authorities involved.

Article 34

1. Without prejudice to the provisions of Article 26 and to Community and national provisions concerning civil liability and irrespective of the point of disposal or recovery of the waste, the producer of that waste shall take all the necessary steps to dispose of or recover or to arrange for disposal or recovery of the waste so as to protect the quality of the environment in accordance with Directives 75/442/EEC and 91/689/EEC.

2. Member States shall take all necessary steps to ensure that the obligations laid down in paragraph 1 are carried out.

Article 35

All documents sent to or by the competent authorities shall be kept in the Community for at least three years by the competent authorities, the notifier and the consignee.

Article 36

Member States shall designate the competent authority or authorities for the implementation of this Regulation. A single competent authority of transit shall be designated by each Member State.

Article 37

1. Member States and the Commission shall each designate at least one correspondent responsible for informing or advising persons or undertakings who or which make enquiries. The Commission correspondent shall forward to the correspondents of the Member States any questions put to him which concern the latter, and *vice versa*.

2. The Commission shall, if requested by Member States or if otherwise appropriate, periodically hold a meeting of the correspondents to examine with them the questions raised by the implementation of this Regulation.

Article 38

1. Member States shall notify the Commission not later than three months before the date of application of this Regulation of the name(s), address(es) and telephone and telex/telefax number(s) of the competent authorities and of the correspondents, together with the stamp of the competent authorities. Member States shall notify the Commission annually of any changes in this information.

2. The Commission shall send the information without delay to the other Member States and to the Secretariat of the Basle Convention. The Commission shall

furthermore send to Member States the waste management plans referred to in Article 7 of Directive 75/442/EEC.

Article 39

1. Member States may designate customs offices of entry into and departure from the Community for shipments of waste entering and leaving the Community and inform the Commission thereof. The Commission shall publish the list of these offices in the *Official Journal of the European Communities* and, if appropriate, update this list.

2. If Member States decide to designate the custom offices referred to in paragraph 1, no shipment of waste shall be allowed to use any other frontier crossing points within a Member State for entering or leaving the Community.

Article 40

Member States, as appropriate and necessary in liaison with the Commission, shall cooperate with other parties to the Basle Convention and inter-State organizations directly or through the Secretariat of the Basle Convention, *inter alia*, via the exchange of information, the promotion of environmentally sound technologies and the development of appropriate codes of good practice.

Article 41

1. Before the end of each calendar year, Member States shall draw up a report in accordance with Article 13(3) of the Basle Convention and send it to the Secretariat of the Basle Convention and a copy thereof to the Commission.

2. The Commission shall, based on these reports, establish every three years report on the implementation of this Regulation by the Community and its Member States. It may request to this end additional information in accordance with Article 6 of Directive 91/692/EEC.[1]

Article 42

1. The Commission shall draw up not later than three months before the date of application of this Regulation and adapt if appropriate afterwards, in accordance with the procedure laid down in Article 18 of Directive 75/442/EEC, the standard consignment note, including the form of the certificate of disposal and recovery (either integral to the consignment note or, meanwhile, attached to the existing consignment note under Directive 84/631/EEC) taking account in particular of:

– the relevant Articles of this Regulation,
– the relevant international Conventions and agreements.

2. The existing form of the consignment note shall apply by analogy until the new consignment note has been drawn up. The form of the certificate of disposal and

---

[1] OJ No L 377, 31. 12. 1991, p. 48.

recovery to be attached to the existing consignment note shall be drawn up as soon as possible.

3. Without prejudice to the procedure laid down in Article 1(3)(c) and (d) regarding Annex II.A, Annexes II, III and IV shall be adapted by the Commission in accordance with the procedure laid down in Article 18 of Directive 75/442/EEC only to reflect changes already agreed under the review mechanism of the OECD.

4. The procedure referred to in paragraph 1 shall apply also to define environmentally sound management, taking into account the relevant international conventions and agreements.

Article 43

Directive 84/631/EEC is hereby repealed with effect from the date of application of this Regulation. Any shipment pursuant to Articles 4 and 5 of that Directive shall be completed not later than six months from the date of application of this Regulation.

Article 44

This Regulation shall enter into force on the third day following its publication in the *Official Journal of the European Communities.*

It shall apply 15 months after publication.

This Regulation shall be binding in its entirety and directly applicable in all Member States.

Annexes

[omitted]

Council Directive 1999/31/EC of 26 April 1999 on the landfill of waste (as amended)

Editorial note

Directive 1999/31 of 26 April 1999 on the landfill of waste aims to provide for measures, procedures and guidance to prevent or reduce as far as possible negative effects of the landfill of waste on the environment, in particular on surface water, groundwater, soil, air and human health and on the global environment by way of stringent operational and technical requirements on the waste and landfills (Article 1). The Directive defines, *inter alia*, the different categories of waste (waste, municipal waste, hazardous waste, non-hazardous waste and inert waste) and applies to all landfills, defined as waste disposal sites for the deposit of waste onto or into land (i.e. underground) (Article 2). The Directive applies to any landfill as defined in Article 2(g) and some exceptions to the scope of its applications are provided (Article 3). Each landfill is classified in one of three classes: landfills for hazardous waste; landfills for non-hazardous waste; landfills for inert waste (Article 4). Member States are required to set up a national strategy for the implementation of the reduction of biodegradable waste going into landfills. This strategy should include measures to achieve the specific reduction of the total amount of biodegradable waste going into landfills within specified time frames (Article 5). The Directive specifies types of waste that are not acceptable in landfills (Article 5(3)). Member States are to ensure that only waste that has been subject to treatment is landfilled (with the exception of inert waste for which treatment is not feasible) (Article 6(a)). Only hazardous waste within the meaning of the Directive may be assigned to a hazardous waste landfill; landfills for non-hazardous waste may be used for municipal waste and for non-hazardous waste; landfill sites for inert waste may be used only for inert waste (Article 6(b), (c), (d)).

The Directive establishes a regime based on a permit system for operating landfill sites. Applications for permits must contain the information specified by the Directive (Article 7). The competent authority is to issue a permit for the operation of a landfill if it is satisfied that the landfill project complies with the provisions of the Directive (Article 8). The costs involved in setting up and operating the landfill, including the estimated costs of the closure and aftercare for a period of at least thirty years, are to be covered by the price to be charged by the operator for the disposal of any type of waste in that site (Article 10). Waste acceptance procedures are established (Article 11).

Specific provisions are made for the control and monitoring of landfill sites in the operational phase (Article 12). Provisions are made for the closure and aftercare of a landfill (Article 13). Existing landfill sites may not continue operating unless they comply with measures indicated by the Directive as soon as possible and in any event within eight years starting from the deadline for its implementation in the Member States (Article 14 and Article 18(1)). Member States shall report to the Commission every three years on the implementation of the Directive. The Commission will then publish within nine months a Community report on the implementation of the Directive (Article 15).

Source: OJ L 182 16.07.1999 p. 1. Amended by: Regulation (EC) No 1882/2003 of the European Parliament and of the Council of 29 September 2003 L 284 1 31.10.2003

Council Directive 1999/31/EC of 26 April 1999 on the landfill of waste (as amended)

The Council of the European Union,

Having regard to the Treaty establishing the European Community, and in particular Article 130s(1) thereof,

Having regard to the proposal from the Commission,[1]

Having regard to the opinion of the Economic and Social Committee,[2]

Acting in accordance with the procedure laid down in Article 189c of the Treaty,[3]

(1) Whereas the Council resolution of 7 May 1990[4] on waste policy welcomes and supports the Community strategy document and invites the Commission to propose criteria and standards for the disposal of waste by landfill;

(2) Whereas the Council resolution of 9 December 1996 on waste policy considers that, in the future, only safe and controlled landfill activities should be carried out throughout the Community;

(3) Whereas the prevention, recycling and recovery of waste should be encouraged as should the use of recovered materials and energy so as to safeguard natural resources and obviate wasteful use of land;

(4) Whereas further consideration should be given to the issues of incineration of municipal and non-hazardous waste, composting, biomethanisation, and the processing of dredging sludges;

(5) Whereas under the polluter pays principle it is necessary, *inter alia*, to take into account any damage to the environment produced by a landfill;

---

[1] OJ C 156, 24.5.1997, p. 10.   [2] OJ C 355, 21.11.1997, p. 4.

[3] Opinion of the European Parliament of 19 February 1998 (OJ C 80,16.3.1998, p. 196), Council common position of 4 June 1998 (OJ C 333, 30.10.1998, p. 15) and Decision of the European Parliament of 3 February 1999 (OJ C 150, 28.5.1999, p. 78)

[4] OJ C 122, 18.5.1990, p. 2.

(6) Whereas, like any other type of waste treatment, landfill should be adequately monitored and managed to prevent or reduce potential adverse effects on the environment and risks to human health;

(7) Whereas it is necessary to take appropriate measures to avoid the abandonment, dumping or uncontrolled disposal of waste; whereas, accordingly, it must be possible to monitor landfill sites with respect to the substances contained in the waste deposited there, whereas such substances should, as far as possible, react only in foreseeable ways;

(8) Whereas both the quantity and hazardous nature of waste intended for landfill should be reduced where appropriate; whereas the handling of waste should be facilitated and its recovery enhanced; whereas the use of treatment processes should therefore be encouraged to ensure that landfill is compatible with the objectives of this Directive; whereas sorting is included in the definition of treatment;

(9) Whereas Member States should be able to apply the principles of proximity and self-sufficiency for the elimination of their waste at Community and national level, in accordance with Council Directive 75/442/EEC of 15 July 1975 on waste[1] whereas the objectives of this Directive must be pursued and clarified through the establishment of an adequate, integrated network of disposal plants based on a high level of environmental protection;

(10) Whereas disparities between technical standards for the disposal of waste by landfill and the lower costs associated with it might give rise to increased disposal of waste in facilities with low standards of environmental protection and thus create a potentially serious threat to the environment, owing to transport of waste over unnecessarily long distances as well as to inappropriate disposal practices;

(11) Whereas it is therefore necessary to lay down technical standards for the landfill of waste at Community level in order to protect, preserve and improve the quality of the environment in the Community;

(12) Whereas it is necessary to indicate clearly the requirements with which landfill sites must comply as regards location, conditioning, management, control, closure and preventive and protective measures to be taken against any threat to the environment in the short as well as in the long-term perspective, and more especially against the pollution of groundwater by leachate infiltration into the soil;

(13) Whereas in view of the foregoing it is necessary to define clearly the classes of landfill to be considered and the types of waste to be accepted in the various classes of landfill;

(14) Whereas sites for temporary storage of waste should comply with the relevant requirements of Directive 75/442/EEC;

---

[1] OJ L 194, 25.7.1975, p. 39. Directive as last amended by Commission Decision 96/350/EC (OJ L 135, 6.6.1996, p. 32).

(15) Whereas the recovery, in accordance with Directive 75/442/EEC, of inert or non-hazardous waste which is suitable, through their use in redevelopment/restoration and filling-in work, or for construction purposes may not constitute a landfilling activity;

(16) Whereas measures should be taken to reduce the production of methane gas from landfills, *inter alia*, in order to reduce global warming, through the reduction of the landfill of biodegradable waste and the requirements to introduce landfill gas control;

(17) Whereas the measures taken to reduce the landfill of biodegradable waste should also aim at encouraging the separate collection of biodegradable waste, sorting in general, recovery and recycling;

(18) Whereas, because of the particular features of the landfill method of waste disposal, it is necessary to introduce a specific permit procedure for all classes of landfill in accordance with the general licensing requirements already set down in Directive 75/442/EEC and the general requirements of Directive 96/61/EC concerning integrated pollution prevention and control[1] whereas the landfill site's compliance with such a permit must be verified in the course of an inspection by the competent authority before the start of disposal operations;

(19) Whereas, in each case, checks should be made to establish whether the waste may be placed in the landfill for which it is intended, in particular as regards hazardous waste;

(20) Whereas, in order to prevent threats to the environment, it is necessary to introduce a uniform waste acceptance procedure on the basis of a classification procedure for waste acceptable in the different categories of landfill, including in particular standardised limit values; whereas to that end a consistent and standardised system of waste characterisation, sampling and analysis must be established in time to facilitate implementation of this Directive; whereas the acceptance criteria must be particularly specific with regard to inert waste;

(21) Whereas, pending the establishment of such methods of analysis or of the limit values necessary for characterisation, Member States may for the purposes of this Directive maintain or draw up national lists of waste which is acceptable or unacceptable for landfill, or define criteria, including limit values, similar to those laid down in this Directive for the uniform acceptance procedure;

(22) Whereas for certain hazardous waste to be accepted in landfills for non-hazardous waste acceptance criteria should be developed by the technical committee;

(23) Whereas it is necessary to establish common monitoring procedures during the operation and after-care phases of a landfill in order to identify any possible adverse environmental effect of the landfill and take the appropriate corrective measures;

---

[1] OJ L 257, 10.10.1996, p. 26.

(24) Whereas it is necessary to define when and how a landfill should be closed and the obligations and responsibility of the operator on the site during the after-care period;

(25) Whereas landfill sites that have been closed prior to the date of transposition of this Directive should not be subject to its provisions on closure procedure;

(26) Whereas the future conditions of operation of existing landfills should be regulated in order to take the necessary measures, within a specified period of time, for their adaptation to this Directive on the basis of a site-conditioning plan;

(27) Whereas for operators of existing landfills having, in compliance with binding national rules equivalent to those of Article 14 of this Directive, already submitted the documentation referred to in Article 14(a) of this Directive prior to its entry into force and for which the competent authority authorised the continuation of their operation, there is no need to resubmit this documentation nor for the competent authority to deliver a new authorisation;

(28) Whereas the operator should make adequate provision by way of a financial security or any other equivalent to ensure that all the obligations flowing from the permit are fulfilled, including those relating to the closure procedure and after-care of the site;

(29) Whereas measures should be taken to ensure that the price charged for waste disposal in a landfill cover all the costs involved in the setting up and operation of the facility, including as far as possible the financial security or its equivalent which the site operator must provide, and the estimated cost of closing the site including the necessary after-care;

(30) Whereas, when a competent authority considers that a landfill is unlikely to cause a hazard to the environment for longer than a certain period, the estimated costs to be included in the price to be charged by an operator may be limited to that period;

(31) Whereas it is necessary to ensure the proper application of the provisions implementing this Directive throughout the Community, and to ensure that the training and knowledge acquired by landfill operators and staff afford them the necessary skills;

(32) Whereas the Commission must establish a standard procedure for the acceptance of waste and set up a standard classification of waste acceptable in a landfill in accordance with the committee procedure laid down in Article 18 of Directive 75/442/EEC;

(33) Whereas adaptation of the Annexes to this Directive to scientific and technical progress and the standardisation of the monitoring, sampling and analysis methods must be adopted under the same committee procedure;

(34) Whereas the Member States must send regular reports to the Commission on the implementation of this Directive paying particular attention to the national strategies to be set up in pursuance of Article 5; whereas on the basis of these reports the Commission shall report to the European Parliament and the Council;

Has adopted this Directive

Article 1
Overall objective

1. With a view to meeting the requirements of Directive 75/442/EEC, and in particular Articles 3 and 4 thereof, the aim of this Directive is, by way of stringent operational and technical requirements on the waste and landfills, to provide for measures, procedures and guidance to prevent or reduce as far as possible negative effects on the environment, in particular the pollution of surface water, groundwater, soil and air, and on the global environment, including the greenhouse effect, as well as any resulting risk to human health, from landfilling of waste, during the whole life-cycle of the landfill.

2. In respect of the technical characteristics of landfills, this Directive contains, for those landfills to which Directive 96/61/EC is applicable, the relevant technical requirements in order to elaborate in concrete terms the general requirements of that Directive. The relevant requirements of Directive 96/61/EC shall be deemed to be fulfilled if the requirements of this Directive are complied with.

Article 2
Definitions

For the purposes of this Directive:

(a) '*waste*' means any substance or object which is covered by Directive 75/442/EEC;

(b) '*municipal waste*' means waste from households, as well as other waste which, because of its nature or composition, is similar to waste from household;

(c) '*hazardous waste*' means any waste which is covered by Article 1(4) of Council Directive 91/689/EEC of 12 December 1991 on hazardous waste[1]

(d) '*non-hazardous waste*' means waste which is not covered by paragraph (c);

(e) '*inert waste*' means waste that does not undergo any significant physical, chemical or biological transformations. Inert waste will not dissolve, burn or otherwise physically or chemically react, biodegrade or adversely affect other matter with which it comes into contact in a way likely to give rise to environmental pollution or harm human health. The total leachability and pollutant content of the waste and the ecotoxicity of the leachate must be insignificant, and in particular not endanger the quality of surface water and/or groundwater;

(f) '*underground storage*' means a permanent waste storage facility in a deep geological cavity such as a salt or potassium mine;

(g) '*landfill*' means a waste disposal site for the deposit of the waste onto or into land (i.e. underground), including:
   – internal waste disposal sites (i.e. landfill where a producer of waste is carrying out its own waste disposal at the place of production), and

---

[1] OJ L 377, 31.12.1991, p. 20. Directive as last amended by Directive 94/31/EC (OJ L 168, 2.7.1994, p. 28);

- a permanent site (i.e. more than one year) which is used for temporary storage of waste, but excluding:
- facilities where waste is unloaded in order to permit its preparation for further transport for recovery, treatment or dispsal elsewhere, and
- stoarage of waste prior to recovery or treatment for a period less than three years as a general rule, or
- storage of waste prior to disposal for a period less than one year;

(h) *'treatment'* means the physical, thermal, chemical or biological processes, including sorting, that change the characteristics of the waste in order to reduce its volume or hazardous nature, facilitate its handling or enhance recovery;

(i) *'leachate'* means any liquid percolating through the deposited waste and emitted from or contained within a landfill;

(j) *'landfill gas'* means all the gases generated from the landfilled waste;

(k) *'eluate'* means the solution obtained by a laboratory leaching test;

(l) *'operator'* means the natural or legal person responsible for a landfill in accordance with the internal legislation of the Member State where the landfill is located; this person may change from the preparation to the after-care phase;

(m) *'biodegradable waste'* means any waste that is capable of undergoing anaerobic or aerobic decomposition, such as food and garden waste, and paper and paperboard;

(n) *'holder'* means the producer of the waste or the natural or legal person who is in possession of it;

(o) *'applicant'* means any person who applies for a landfill permit under this Directive;

(p) *'competent authority'* means that authority which the Member States designate as responsible for performing the duties arising from this Directive;

(q) *'liquid waste'* means any waste in liquid form including waste waters but excluding sludge;

(r) *'isolated settlement'* means a settlement:
- with no more than 500 inhabitants per municipality or settlement and no more than five inhabitants per square kilometre and,
- where the distance to the nearest urban agglomeration with at least 250 inhabitants per square kilometre is not less than 50 km, or with difficult access by road to those nearest agglomerations, due to harsh meteorological conditions during a significant part of the year.

Article 3
Scope

1. Member States shall apply this Directive to any landfill as defined in Article 2(g).

2. Without prejudice to existing Community legislation, the following shall be excluded from the scope of this Directive:

– the spreading of sludges, including sewage sludges, and sludges resulting from dredging operations, and similar matter on the soil for the purposes of fertilisation or improvement,
– the use of inert waste which is suitable, in redevelopment/restoration and filling-in work, or for construction purposes, in landfills,
– the deposit of non-hazardous dredging sludges alongside small waterways from where they have been dredged out and of non-hazardous sludges in surface water including the bed and its sub soil,
– the deposit of unpolluted soil or of non-hazardous inert waste resulting from prospecting and extraction, treatment, and storage of mineral resources as well as from the operation of quarries.

3. Without prejudice to Directive 75/442/EEC Member States may declare at their own option, that the deposit of non-hazardous waste, to be defined by the committee established under Article 17 of this Directive, other than inert waste, resulting from prospecting and extraction, treatment and storage of mineral resources as well as from the operation of quarries and which are deposited in a manner preventing environmental pollution or harm to human health, can be exempted from the provisions in Annex I, points 2, 3.1, 3.2 and 3.3 of this Directive.

4. Without prejudice to Directive 75/442/EEC Member States may declare, at their own option, parts or all of Articles 6(d), 7(i), 8(a)(iv), 10, 11(1)(a), (b) and (c), 12(a) and (c), Annex I, points 3 and 4, Annex II (except point 3, level 3, and point 4) and Annex III, points 3 to 5 to this Directive not applicable to:

(a) landfill sites for non-hazardous or inert wastes with a total capacity not exceeding 15 000 tonnes or with an annual intake not exceeding 1 000 tonnes serving islands, where this is the only landfill on the island and where this is exclusively destined for the disposal of waste generated on that island. Once the total capacity of that landfill has been used, any new landfill site established on the island shall comply with the requirements of this Directive;
(b) landfill sites for non-hazardous or inert waste in isolated settlements if the landfill site is destined for the disposal of waste generated only by that isolated settlement.

Not later than two years after the date laid down in Article 18(1), Member States shall notify the Commission of the list of islands and isolated settlements that are exempted. The Commission shall publish the list of islands and isolated settlements.

5. Without prejudice to Directive 75/442/EEC Member States may declare, at their own option, that underground storage as defined in Article 2(f) of this Directive can be exempted from the provisions in Article 13(d) and in Annex I, point 2, except first indent, points 3 to 5 and in Annex III, points 2, 3 and 5 to this Directive.

Article 4
Classes of landfill

Each landfill shall be classified in one of the following classes:

– landfill for hazardous waste,
– landfill for non-hazardous waste,
– landfill for inert waste.

Article 5
Waste and treatment not acceptable in landfills

1. Member States shall set up a national strategy for the implementation of the reduction of biodegradable waste going to landfills, not later than two years after the date laid down in Article 18(1) and notify the Commission of this strategy. This strategy should include measures to achieve the targets set out in paragraph 2 by means of in particular, recycling, composting, biogas production or materials/energy recovery. Within 30 months of the date laid down in Article 18(1) the Commission shall provide the European Parliament and the Council with a report drawing together the national strategies.

2. This strategy shall ensure that:

(a) not later than five years after the date laid down in Article 18(1), biodegradable municipal waste going to landfills must be reduced to 75% of the total amount (by weight) of biodegradable municipal waste produced in 1995 or the latest year before 1995 for which standardised Eurostat data is available

(b) not later than eight years after the date laid down in Article 18(1), biodegradable municipal waste going to landfills must be reduced to 50% of the total amount (by weight) of biodegradable municipal waste produced in 1995 or the latest year before 1995 for which standardised Eurostat data is available;

(c) not later than 15 years after the date laid down in Article 18(1), biodegradable municipal waste going to landfills must be reduced to 35% of the total amount (by weight) of biodegradable municipal waste produced in 1995 or the latest year before 1995 for which standardised Eurostat data is available.

Two years before the date referred to in paragraph (c) the Council shall reexamine the above target, on the basis of a report from the Commission on the practical experience gained by Member States in the pursuance of the targets laid down in paragraphs (a) and (b) accompanied, if appropriate, by a proposal with a view to confirming or amending this target in order to ensure a high level of environmental protection.

Member States which in 1995 or the latest year before 1995 for which standardised EUROSTAT data is available put more than 80% of their collected municipal waste to landfill may postpone the attainment of the targets set out in paragraphs (a), (b), or

(c) by a period not exceeding four years. Member States intending to make use of this provision shall inform in advance the Commission of their decision. The Commission shall inform other Member States and the European Parliament of these decisions.

The implementation of the provisions set out in the preceding subparagraph may in no circumstances lead to the attainment of the target set out in paragraph (c) at a date later than four years after the date set out in paragraph (c).

3. Member States shall take measures in order that the following wastes are not accepted in a landfill:

(a) liquid waste;
(b) waste which, in the conditions of landfill, is explosive, corrosive, oxidising, highly flammable or flammable, as defined in Annex III to Directive 91/689/EEC;
(c) hospital and other clinical wastes arising from medical or veterinary establishments, which are infectious as defined (property H9 in Annex III) by Directive 91/689/EEC and waste falling within category 14 (Annex I.A) of that Directive.
(d) whole used tyres from two years from the date laid down in Article 18(1), excluding tyres used as engineering material, and shredded used tyres five years from the date laid down in Article 18(1) (excluding in both instances bicycle tyres and tyres with an outside diameter above 1 400 mm);
(e) any other type of waste which does not fulfil the acceptance criteria determined in accordance with Annex II.

4. The dilution of mixture of waste solely in order to meet the waste acceptance criteria is prohibited.

Article 6
Waste to be accepted in the different classes of landfill

Member States shall take measures in order that:

(a) only waste that has been subject to treatment is landfilled. This provision may not apply to inert waste for which treatment is not technically feasible, nor to any other waste for which such treatment does not contribute to the objectives of this Directive, as set out in Article 1, by reducing the quantity of the waste or the hazards to human health or the environment;
(b) only hazardous waste that fulfils the criteria set out in accordance with Annex II is assigned to a hazardous landfill;
(c) landfill for non-hazardous waste may be used for:
  (i) municipal waste;
  (ii) non-hazardous waste of any other origin, which fulfil the criteria for the acceptance of waste at landfill for non-hazardous waste set out in accordance with Annex II;

(iii) stable, non-reactive hazardous wastes (e.g. solidified, vitrified), with leaching behaviour equivalent to those of the non-hazardous wastes referred to in point (ii), which fulfil the relevant acceptance criteria set out in accordance with Annex II. These hazardous wastes shall not be deposited in cells destined for biodegradable non-hazardous waste,

(d) inert waste landfill sites shall be used only for inert waste.

Article 7
Application for a permit

Member States shall take measures in order that the application for a landfill permit must contain at least particulars of the following:

(a) the identity of the applicant and of the operator when they are different entities;
(b) the description of the types and total quantity of waste to be deposited;
(c) the proposed capacity of the disposal site;
(d) the description of the site, including its hydrogeological and geological characteristics;
(e) the proposed methods for pollution prevention and abatement;
(f) the proposed operation, monitoring and control plan;
(g) the proposed plan for the closure and after-care procedures;
(h) where an impact assessment is required under Council Directive 85/337/EEC of 27 June 1985 on the assessment of the effects of certain public and private projects on the environment,[1] the information provided by the developer in accordance with Article 5 of that Directive;
(i) the financial security by the applicant, or any other equivalent provision, as required under Article 8(a)(iv) of this Directive.

Following a successful application for a permit, this information shall be made available to the competent national and Community statistical authorities when requested for statistical purposes.

Article 8
Conditions of the permit

Member States shall take measures in order that:

(a) the competent authority does not issue a landfill permit unless it is satisfied that:
  (i) without prejudice to Article 3(4) and (5), the landfill project complies with all the relevant requirements of this Directive, including the Annexes;
  (ii) the management of the landfill site will be in the hands of a natural person who is technically competent to manage the site; professional and technical development and training of landfill operators and staff are provided;

---

[1] OJ L 175, 5.7.1985, p. 40. Directive as amended by Directive 97/11/EC (OJ L 73, 14.3.1997, p. 5).

(iii) the landfill shall be operated in such a manner that the necessary measures are taken to prevent accidents and limit their consequences;

(iv) adequate provisions, by way of a financial security or any other equivalent, on the basis of modalities to be decided by Member States, has been or will be made by the applicant prior to the commencement of disposal operations to ensure that the obligations (including after-care provisions) arising under the permit issued under the provisions of this Directive are discharged and that the closure procedures required by Article 13 are followed. This security or its equivalent shall be kept as long as required by maintenance and after-care operation of the site in accordance with Article 13(d). Member States may declare, at their own option, that this point does not apply to landfills for inert waste;

(b) the landfill project is in line with the relevant waste management plan or plans referred to in Article 7 of Directive 75/442/EEC;

(c) prior to the commencement of disposal operations, the competent authority shall inspect the site in order to ensure that it complies with the relevant conditions of the permit. This will not reduce in any way the responsibility of the operator under the conditions of the permit.

Article 9
Content of the permit

Specifying and supplementing the provisions set out in Article 9 of Directive 75/442/EEC and Article 9 of Directive 96/61/EC, the landfill permit shall state at least the following:

(a) the class of the landfill;

(b) the list of defined types and the total quantity of waste which are authorised to be deposited in the landfill;

(c) requirements for the landfill preparations, landfilling operations and monitoring and control procedures, including contingency plans (Annex III, point 4.B), as well as provisional requirements for the closure and after-care operations;

(d) the obligation on the applicant to report at least annually to the competent authority on the types and quantities of waste disposed of and on the results of the monitoring programme as required in Articles 12 and 13 and Annex III.

Article 10
Cost of the landfill of waste

Member States shall take measures to ensure that all of the costs involved in the setting up and operation of a landfill site, including as far as possible the cost of the financial security or its equivalent referred to in Article 8(a)(iv), and the estimated costs of the closure and after-care of the site for a period of at least 30 years shall be covered by the price to be charged by the operator for the disposal of any type of waste in that site.

Subject to the requirements of Council Directive 90/313/EEC of 7 June 1990 on the freedom of access to information on the environment[1] Member States shall ensure transparency in the collection and use of any necessary cost information.

Article 11
Waste acceptance procedures

1. Member States shall take measures in order that prior to accepting the waste at the landfill site:

(a) before or at the time of delivery, or of the first in a series of deliveries, provided the type of waste remains unchanged, the holder or the operator can show, by means of the appropriate documentation, that the waste in question can be accepted at that site according to the conditions set in the permit, and that it fulfils the acceptance criteria set out in Annex II;

(b) the following reception procedures are respected by the operator:
  – checking of the waste documentation, including those documents required by Article 5(3) of Directive 91/689/EEC and, where they apply, those required by Council Regulation (EEC) No 259/93 of 1 February 1993 on the supervision and control of shipments of waste within, into and out of the European Community;[2]
  – visual inspection of the waste at the entrance and at the point of deposit and, as appropriate, verification of conformity with the description provided in the documentation submitted by the holder. If representative samples have to be taken in order to implement Annex II, point 3, level 3, the results of the analyses shall be kept and the sampling shall be made in conformity with Annex II, point 5. These samples shall be kept at least one month;
  – keeping a register of the quantities and characteristics of the waste deposited, indicating origin, date of delivery, identity of the producer or collector in the case of municipal waste, and, in the case of hazardous waste, the precise location on the site. This information shall be made available to the competent national and Community statistical authorities when requested for statistical purposes;

(c) the operator of the landfill shall always provide written acknowledgement of receipt of each delivery accepted on the site;

(d) without prejudice to the provisions of Regulation (EEC) No 259/93, if waste is not accepted at a landfill the operator shall notify without delay the competent authority of the non-acceptance of the waste.

2. For landfill sites which have been exempted from provisions of this Directive by virtue of Article 3(4) and (5), Member States shall take the necessary measures to provide for:

---

[1] OJ L 158, 23.6.1990, p. 56.
[2] OJ L 30, 6.2.1993, p. 1. Regulation as amended by Regulation (EC) No 120/97 (OJ L 22, 24.1.1997, p. 14).

– regular visual inspection of the waste at the point of deposit in order to ensure that only non-hazardous waste from the island or the isolated settlement is accepted at the site; and
– a register on the quantities of waste that are deposited at the site be kept.

Member States shall ensure that information on the quantities and, where possible, the type of waste going to such exempted sites forms part of the regular reports to the Commission on the implementation of the Directive.

Article 12
Control and monitoring procedures in the operational phase

Member States shall take measures in order that control and monitoring procedures in the operational phase meet at least the following requirements:

(a) the operator of a landfill shall carry out during the operational phase a control and monitoring programme as specified in Annex III;
(b) the operator shall notify the competent authority of any significant adverse environmental effects revealed by the control and monitoring procedures and follow the decision of the competent authority on the nature and timing of the corrective measures to be taken. These measures shall be undertaken at the expense of the operator.

   At a frequency to be determined by the competent authority, and in any event at least once a year, the operator shall report, on the basis of aggregated data, all monitoring results to the competent authorities for the purpose of demonstrating compliance with permit conditions and increasing the knowledge on waste behaviour in the landfills;
(c) the quality control of the analytical operations of the control and monitoring procedures and/or of the analyses referred to in Article 11(1)(b) are carried out by competent laboratories.

Article 13
Closure and after-care procedures

Member States shall take measures in order that, in accordance, where appropriate, with the permit:

(a) a landfill or part of it shall start the closure procedure:
   (i) when the relevant conditions stated in the permit are met; or
   (ii) under the authorisation of the competent authority, at the request of the operator; or
   (iii) by reasoned decision of the competent authority;
(b) a landfill or part of it may only be considered as definitely closed after the competent authority has carried out a final on-site inspection, has assessed all the reports submitted by the operator and has communicated to the operator its approval for

the closure. This shall not in any way reduce the responsibility of the operator under the conditions of the permit;

(c) after a landfill has been definitely closed, the operator shall be responsible for its maintenance, monitoring and control in the after-care phase for as long as may be required by the competent authority, taking into account the time during which the landfill could present hazards.

The operator shall notify the competent authority of any significant adverse environmental effects revealed by the control procedures and shall follow the decision of the competent authority on the nature and timing of the corrective measures to be taken;

(d) for as long as the competent authority considers that a landfill is likely to cause a hazard to the environment and without prejudice to any Community or national legislation as regards liability of the waste holder, the operator of the site shall be responsible for monitoring and analysing landfill gas and leachate from the site and the groundwater regime in the vicinity of the site in accordance with Annex III.

Article 14

Existing landfill sites

Member States shall take measures in order that landfills which have been granted a permit, or which are already in operation at the time of transposition of this Directive, may not continue to operate unless the steps outlined below are accomplished as soon as possible and within eight years after the date laid down in Article 18(1) at the latest:

(a) with a period of one year after the date laid down in Article 18(1), the operator of a landfill shall prepare and present to the competent authorities, for their approval, a conditioning plan for the site including the particulars listed in Article 8 and any corrective measures which the operator considers will be needed in order to comply with the requirements of this Directive with the exception of the requirements in Annex I, point 1;

(b) following the presentation of the conditioning plan, the competent authorities shall take a definite decision on whether operations may continue on the basis of the said conditioning plan and this Directive. Member States shall take the necessary measures to close down as soon as possible, in accordance with Article 7(g) and 13, sites which have not been granted, in accordance with Article 8, a permit to continue to operate;

(c) on the basis of the approved site-conditioning plan, the competent authority shall authorise the necessary work and shall lay down a transitional period for the completion of the plan. Any existing landfill shall comply with the requirements of this Directive with the exception of the requirements in Annex I, point 1 within eight years after the date laid down in Article 18(1);

(d) (i) within one year after the date laid down in Article 18(1), Articles 4, 5, and 11 and Annex II shall apply to landfills for hazardous waste;

(ii) within three years after the date laid down in Article 18(1), Article 6 shall apply to landfills for hazardous waste.

Article 15
Obligation to report

At intervals of three years Member States shall send to the Commission a report on the implementation of this Directive, paying particular attention to the national strategies to be set up in pursuance of Article 5. The report shall be drawn up on the basis of a questionnaire or outline drafted by the Commission in accordance with the procedure laid down in Article 6 of Directive 91/692/EEC.[1] The questionnaire or outline shall be sent to Member States six months before the start of the period covered by the report. The report shall be sent to the Commission within nine months of the end of the three-year period covered by it. The Commission shall publish a Community report on the implementation of this Directive within nine months of receiving the reports from the Member States.

Article 16
Committee

Any amendments necessary for adapting the Annexes to this Directive to scientific and technical progress and any proposals for the standardisation of control, sampling and analysis methods in relation to the landfill of waste shall be adopted by the Commission, assisted by the Committee established by Article 18 of Directive 75/442/EEC and in accordance with the procedure set out in Article 17 of this Directive. Any amendments to the Annexes shall only be made in line with the principles laid down in this Directive as expressed in the Annexes. To this end, as regards Annex II, the following shall be observed by the Committee: taking into account the general principles and general procedures for testing and acceptance criteria as set out in Annex II, specific criteria and/or test methods and associated limit values should be set for each class of landfill, including if necessary specific types of landfill within each class, including underground storage. Proposals for the standardisation of control, sampling and analysis methods in relation to the Annexes of this Directive shall be adopted by the Commission, assisted by the Committee, within two years after the entry into force of this Directive.

The Commission, assisted by the Committee, will adopt provisions for the harmonisation and regular transmission of the statistical date referred to in Articles 5, 7 and 11 of this Directive, within two years after the entry into force of this Directive, and for the amendments of such provisions when necessary.

---

[1] OJ L 377, 31.12.1991, p. 48.

Article 17

1. The Commission shall be assisted by a committee.

2. Where reference is made to this Article, Articles 5 and 7 of Decision 1999/468/EC[1] shall apply, having regard to the provisions of Article 8 thereof. The period laid down in Article 5(6) of Decision 1999/468/EC shall be set at three months.

3. The Committee shall adopt its rules of procedure.

Article 18

Transposition

1. Member States shall bring into force the laws, regulations and administrative provisions necessary to comply with this Directive not later than two years after its entry into force. They shall forthwith inform the Commission thereof. When Member States adopt these measures, they shall contain a reference to this Directive or shall be accompanied by such reference on the occasion of their official publication. The methods of making such a reference shall be laid down by Member States.

2. Member States shall communicate the texts of the provisions of national law which they adopt in the field covered by this Directive to the Commission.

Article 19

Entry into force

This Directive will enter into force on the day of its publication in the *Official Journal of the European Communities*.

Article 20

Addressees

This Directive is addressed to the Member States.

Annex 1

General requirements for all classes of landfills

1. *Location*

1.1. The location of a landfill must take into consideration requirements relating to:
  (a) the distances from the boundary of the site to residential and recreation areas, waterways, water bodies and other agricultural or urban sites;
  (b) the existence of groundwater, coastal water or nature protection zones in the area;
  (c) the geological and hydrogeological conditions in the area;

---

[1] Council Decision 1999/468/EC of 28 June 1999 laying down the procedures for the exercise of implementing powers conferred on the Commission (OJ L 184, 17.7.1999, p. 23).

(d) the risk of flooding, subsidence, landslides or avalanches on the site;

(e) the protection of the nature or cultural patrimony in the area.

1.2. The landfill can be authorised only if the characteristics of the site with respect to the abovementioned requirements, or the corrective measures to be taken, indicate that the landfill does not pose a serious environmental risk.

2. *Water control and leachate management*

Appropriate measures shall be taken, with respect to the characteristics of the landfill and the meteorological conditions, in order to:

- control water from precipitations entering into the landfill body,
- prevent surface water and/or groundwater from entering into the land-filled waste,
- collect contaminated water and leachate. If an assessment based on consideration of the location of the landfill and the waste to be accepted shows that the landfill poses no potential hazard to the environment, the competent authority may decide that this provision does not apply,
- treat contaminated water and leachate collected from the landfill to the appropriate standard required for their discharge.

The above provisions may not apply to landfills for inert waste.

3. *Protection of soil and water*

3.1. A landfill must be situated and designed so as to meet the necessary conditions for preventing pollution of the soil, groundwater or surface water and ensuring efficient collection of leachate as and when required according to Section 2. Protection of soil, groundwater and surface water is to be achieved by the combination of a geological barrier and a bottom liner during the operational/active phase and by the combination of a geological barrier and a bottom liner during the operational/active phase and by the combination of a geological barrier and a top liner during the passive phase/post closure.

3.2. The geological barrier is determined by geological and hydrogeological conditions below and in the vicinity of a landfill site providing sufficient attenuation capacity to prevent a potential risk to soil and groundwater.

The landfill base and sides shall consist of a mineral layer which satisfies permeability and thickness requirements with a combined effect in terms of protection of soil, groundwater and surface water at least equivalent to the one resulting from the following requirements:

- landfill for hazardous waste: $K \leq 1,0 \times 10^{-9}$ m/s; thickness ≥ 5 m,
- landfill for non-hazardous waste: $K \leq 1,0 \times 10^{-9}$ m/s; thickness ≥ 1 m,
- landfill for inert waste: $K \leq 1,0 \times 10^{-7}$ m/s; thickness ≥ 1 m,

m/s: meter/second.

Where the geological barrier does not naturally meet the above conditions it can be completed artificially and reinforced by other means giving equivalent protection. An artificially established geological barrier should be no less than 0,5 metres thick.

3.3. In addition to the geological barrier described above a leachate collection and sealing system must be added in accordance with the following principles so as to ensure that leachate accumulation at the base of the landfill is kept to a minimum:

Leachate collection and bottom sealing

Landfill category	non hazardous	hazardous
Artificial sealing liner	required	required
Drainage layer ≥ 0,5 m	required	required

Member States may set general or specific requirements for inert waste landfills and for the characteristics of the abovementioned technical means.

If the competent authority after a consideration of the potential hazards to the environment finds that the prevention of leachate formation is necessary, a surface sealing may be prescribed. Recommendations for the surface sealing are as follows:

Landfill category	non hazardous	hazardous
Gas drainage layer	required	not required
Artificial sealing liner	not required	required
Impermeable mineral layer	required	required
Drainage layer > 0,5 m	required	required
Top soil cover > 1 m	required	required.

3.4. If, on the basis of an assessment of environmental risks taking into account, in particular, Directive 80/68/EEC[1] the competent authority has decided, in accordance with Section 2 ('Water control and leachate management'), that collection and treatment of leachate is not necessary or it has been established that the landfill poses no potential hazard to soil, groundwater or surface water, the requirements in paragraphs 3.2 and 3.3 above may be reduced accordingly. In the case of landfills for inert waste these requirements may be adapted by national legislation.

[1] OJ L 20, 26.1.1980, p. 43. Directive as last amended by Directive 91/692/EEC (OJ L 377, 31.12.1991, p. 48).

3.5. The method to be used for the determination of the permeability coefficient for landfills, in the field and for the whole extension of the site, is to be developed and approved by the Committee set up under Article 17 of this Directive.

4. *Gas control*

4.1. Appropriate measures shall be taken in order to control the accumulation and migration of landfill gas (Annex III).
4.2. Landfill gas shall be collected from all landfills receiving biodegradable waste and the landfill gas must be treated and used. If the gas collected cannot be used to produce energy, it must be flared.
4.3. The collection, treatment and use of landfill gas under paragraph 4.2 shall be carried on in a manner which minimises damage to or deterioration of the environment and risk to human health.

5. *Nuisances and hazards*

Measures shall be taken to minimise nuisances and hazards arising from the landfill through:

– emissions of odours and dust,
– wind-blown materials,
– noise and traffic,
– birds, vermin and insects,
– formation and aerosols,
– fires.

The landfill shall be equipped so that dirt originating from the site is not dispersed onto public roads and the surrounding land.

6. *Stability*

The emplacement of waste on the site shall take place in such a way as to ensure stability of the mass of waste and associated structures, particularly in respect of avoidance of slippages. Where an artificial barrier is established it must be ascertained that the geological substratum, considering the morphology of the landfill, is sufficiently stable to prevent settlement that may cause damage to the barrier.

7. *Barriers*

The landfill shall be secured to prevent free access to the site. The gates shall be locked outside operating hours. The system of control and access to each facility should contain a programme of measures to detect and discourage illegal dumping in the facility.

Annex II
Waste acceptance criteria and procedures

1. *Introduction*

This Annex describes:

— general principles for acceptance of waste at the various classes of landfills. The future waste classification procedure should be based on these principles,
— guidelines outlining preliminary waste acceptance procedures to be followed until a uniform waste classification and acceptance procedure has been developed. This procedure will, together with the relevant sampling procedures, be developed by the technical Committee referred to in Article 16 of this Directive. The technical Committee shall develop criteria which have to be fulfilled for certain hazardous waste to be accepted in landfills for non-hazardous waste. These criteria should, in particular, take into account the short, medium and long term leaching behaviour of such waste. These criteria shall be developed within two years of the entry into force of this Directive. The technical Committee shall also develop criteria which have to be fulfilled for waste to be accepted in underground storage. These criteria must take into account, in particular, that the waste is not to be expected to react with each other and with the rock.

This work by the technical Committee, with the exception of proposals for the standardisation of control, sampling and analysis methods in relation to the Annexes of this Directive which shall be adopted within two years after the entry into force of this Directive, shall be completed within three years from the entry into force of this Directive and must be carried out having regard to the objectives set forth in Article 1 of this Directive.

2. *General principles*

The composition, leachability, long-term behaviour and general properties of a waste to be landfilled must be known as precisely as possible. Waste acceptance at a landfill can be based either on lists of accepted or refused waste, defined by nature and origin, and on waste analysis methods and limit values for the properties of the waste to be accepted. The future waste acceptance procedures described in this Directive shall as far as possible be based on standardised waste analysis methods and limit values for the properties of waste to be accepted.

   Before the definition of such analysis methods and limit values, Member States should at least set national lists of waste to be accepted or refused at each class of landfill, or define the criteria required to be on the lists. In order to be accepted at a particular class of landfill, a type of waste must be on the relevant national list or fulfil criteria similar to those required to be on the list. These lists, or the equivalent criteria, and the analysis methods and limit values shall be sent to the Commission within six months of the transposition of this Directive or whenever they are adopted at national level.

These lists or acceptance criteria should be used to establish site specific lists, i.e. the list of accepted waste specified in the permit in accordance with Article 9 of this Directive.

The criteria for acceptance of waste on the reference lists or at a class of landfill may be based on other legislation and/or on waste properties.

Criteria for acceptance at a specific class of landfill must be derived from considerations pertaining to:

— protection of the surrounding environment (in particular groundwater and surface water),
— protection of the environmental protection systems (e.g. liners and leachate treatment systems),
— protection of the desired waste-stabilisation processes within the landfill,
— protection against human-health hazards.

Examples of waste property-based criteria are:

— requirements on knowledge of total composition,
— limitations on the amount of organic matter in the waste,
— requirements or limitations on the biodegradability of the organic waste components,
— limitations on the amount of specified, potentially harmful/hazardous components (in relation to the abovementioned protection criteria),
— limitations on the potential and expected leachability of specified, potentially harmful/hazardous components (in relation to the abovementioned protection criteria),
— ecotoxicological properties of the waste and the resulting leachate.

The property-based criteria for acceptance of waste must generally be most extensive for inert waste landfills and can be less extensive for non-hazardous waste landfills and least extensive for hazardous waste landfills owing to the higher environmental protection level of the latter two.

3. General procedures for testing and acceptance of waste

The general characterisation and testing of waste must be based on the following three-level hierarchy:

Level 1: *Basic characterisation.* This constitutes a thorough determination, according to standardised analysis and behaviour-testing methods, of the short and long-term leaching behaviour and/or characteristic properties of the waste.

Level 2: *Compliance testing.* This constitutes periodical testing by simpler standardised analysis and behaviour-testing methods to determine whether a waste complies with permit conditions and/or specific reference criteria. The tests focus on key variables and behaviour identified by basic characterisation.

Level 3: *On-site verification.* This constitutes rapid check methods to confirm that a waste is the same as that which has been subjected to compliance testing and that which is described in the accompanying documents. It may merely consist of a visual inspection of a load of waste before and after unloading at the landfill site.

A particular type of waste must normally be characterised at Level 1 and pass the appropriate criteria in order to be accepted on a reference list. In order to remain on a site-specific list, a particular type of waste must at regular intervals (e.g. annually) be tested at Level 2 and pass the appropriate criteria. Each waste load arriving at the gate of a landfill must be subjected to Level 3 verification.

Certain waste types may be exempted permanently to temporarily from testing at Level 1. This may be due to impracticability to testing, to unavailability of appropriate testing procedures and acceptance criteria or to overriding legislation.

4. Guidelines for preliminary waste acceptance procedures

Until this Annex is fully completed only Level 3 testing is mandatory and Level 1 and Level 2 applied to the extent possible. At this preliminary stage waste to be accepted at a particular class of landfill must either be on a restrictive national or site-specific list for that class of landfill or fulfil criteria similar to those required to get on the list.

The following general guidelines may be used to set preliminary criteria for acceptance of waste at the three major classes of landfill or the corresponding lists.

Inert waste landfills: only inert waste as defined in Article 2(e) can be accepted on the list.

Non-hazardous waste landfills: in order to be accepted on the list a waste type must not be covered by Directive 91/689/EEC.

Hazardous waste landfills: a preliminary rough list for hazardous waste land-fills would consist of only those waste types covered by Directive 91/689/EEC. Such waste types should, however, not be accepted on the list without prior treatment if they exhibit total contents or leachability of potentially hazardous components that are high enough to constitute a short-term occupational or environmental risk or to prevent sufficient waste stabilisation within the projected lifetime of the landfill.

5. Sampling of waste

Sampling of waste may pose serious problems with respect to representation and techniques owing to the heterogeneous nature of many wastes. A European standard for sampling of waste will be developed. Until this standard is approved by Member States in accordance with Article 17 of this Directive, the Member States may apply national standards and procedures.

Annex III
Control and monitoring procedures in operation and after-care phases

1. *Introduction*

The purpose of this Annex is to provide the minimum procedures for monitoring to be carried out to check:

- that waste has been accepted to disposal in accordance with the criteria set for the category of landfill in question,
- that the processes within the landfill proceed as desired,
- that the environmental protection systems are functioning fully as intended,
- that the permit conditions for the landfill are fulfilled.

2. *Meteorological data*

Under their reporting obligation (Article 15), Member States should supply data on the collection method for meteorological data. It is up to Member States to decide how the data should be collected (*in situ*, national meteoro-logical network, etc.).

Should Member States decide that water balances are an effective tool for evaluating whether leachate is building up in the landfill body or whether the site is leaking, it is recommended that the following data are collected from monitoring at the landfill or from the nearest meteorological station, as long as required by the competent authority in accordance with Article 13(c) of this Directive:

	Operation phase	After-care phase
1.1. Volume of precipitation	daily	daily, added to monthly values
1.2. Temperature (min., max., 14.00 h CET)	daily	monthly average
1.3. Direction and force of prevailing wind	daily	not required
1.4. Evaporation (lysimeter)[1]	daily	daily, added to monthly values
1.5. Atmospheric humidity (14.00 h CET)	daily	monthly average

[1] Or through other suitable methods.

3. *Emission data: water, leachate and gas control*

Sampling of leachate and surface water if present must be collected at representative points. Sampling and measuring (volume and composition) of leachate must be performed separately at each point at which leachate is discharged from the site. Reference: general guidelines on sampling technology, ISO 5667-2 (1991).

Monitoring of surface water is present shall be carried out at not less than two points, one upstream from the landfill and one downstream.

Gas monitoring must be representative for each section of the landfill. The frequency of sampling and analysis is listed in the following table. For leachate and water, a sample, representative of the average composition, shall be taken for monitoring.

The frequency of sampling could be adapted on the basis of the morphology of the landfill waste (in tumulus, buried, etc). This has to be specified in the permit.

	Operating phase	After-care phase[3]
2.1. Leachate volume	monthly[1,3]	every six months
2.2. Leachate composition[2]	quarterly[3]	every six months
2.3. Volume and composition of surface water[7]	quarterly[3]	every six months
2.4. Potential gas emissions and atmospheric pressure[4] (CH_4, CO_2, O_2, H_2S, H_2 etc.)	monthly[3,5]	every six months[6]

[1] The frequency of sampling could be adapted on the basis of the morphology of the landfill waste (in tumulus, buried, etc.). This has to be specified in the permit.

[2] The parameters to be measured and the substances to be analysed vary according to the composition of the waste deposited; they must be laid down in the permit document and reflect the leaching characteristics of the wastes.

[3] If the evaluation of data indicates that longer intervals are equally effective, they may be adapted. For leachates, conductivity must always be measured at least once a year.

[4] Thease measurements are related mainly to the content of organic material in the waste.

[5] CH_4, CO_2, O_2, regularly, other gases as required, according to the composition of the waste deposited, with a view to reflecting its leaching properties.

[6] Efficiency of the gas extraction system must be checked regularly.

[7] On the basis of the characteristics of the landfill site, the competent authority may determine that these measurements are not required, and will report accordingly in the way laid down in Article 15 of the Directive. 2.1 and 2.2 apply only where leachate collection takes place (see Annex 1(2)).

4. *Protection of groundwater*

A. *Sampling*

The measurements must be such as to provide information on groundwater likely to be affected by the discharging of waste, with at least one measuring point in the groundwater inflow region and two in the outflow region. This number can be increased on the basis of a specific hydrogeological survey and the need for an early identification of accidental leachate release in the groundwater.

Sampling must be carried out in at least three locations before the filling operations in order to establish reference values for future sampling. Reference: Sampling Groundwaters, ISO 5667, Part 11, 1993.

B. *Monitoring*

The parameters to be analysed in the samples taken must be derived from the expected composition of the leachate and the groundwater quality in the area. In selecting the parameters for analysis account should be taken of mobility in the groundwater zone. Parameters could include indicator parameters in order to ensure an early recognition of change in water quality.[1]

	Operation phase	After-care phase
Level of groundwater	every six months[1]	every six months[1]
Groundwater composition	site-specific frequency[2,3]	site-specific frequency[2,3]

[1] If there are fluctuating groundwater levels, the frequency must be increased.

[2] The frequency must be based on possibility for remedial actions between two samplings if a trigger level is reached, i.e. the frequency must be determined on the basis of knowledge and the evaluation of the velocity of groundwater flow.

[3] When a trigger level is reached (see C), verification is necessary by repeating the sampling. When the level has been confirmed, a contingency plan (laid down in the permit) must be followed.

C. *Trigger levels*

Significant adverse environmental effects, as referred to in Articles 12 and 13 of this Directive, should be considered to have occurred in the case of groundwater, when an analysis of a groundwater sample shows a significant change in water quality. A trigger level must be determined taking account of the specific hydro-geological formations in the location of the landfill and groundwater quality. The trigger level must be laid down in the permit whenever possible.

The observations must be evaluated by means of control charts with established control rules and levels for each downgradient well. The control levels must be determined from local variations in groundwater quality.

5. *Topography of the site: data on the landfill body*

	Operating phase	After-care phase
5.1. Structure and composition of landfill body[1]	yearly	
5.2. Settling behaviour of the level of the landfill body	yearly	yearly reading

[1] Data for the status plan of the concerned landfill: surface occupied by waste, volume and composition of waste, methods of depositing, time and duration of depositing, calculation of the remaining capacity still available at the landfill.

[1] Recommended parameters: ph, TOC, phenols, heavy metals, fluoride, AS, oil/hydrocarbons.

Directive 2000/53/EC of the European Parliament and of the Council of 18 September 2000 on end-of-life vehicles (as amended)

Editorial note

Directive 2000/53 of 18 September 2000 lays down measures to prevent waste from vehicles, as a first priority, and in addition measures to re-use, recycle and recover in other forms end-of-life vehicles (Article 1). The Directive covers vehicles and end-of-life vehicles, including their components and materials (Article 3). Member States are required to promote the prevention of waste by encouraging, *inter alia*, vehicle manufacturers to limit the use of hazardous substances in vehicles, and to design and produce new vehicles which take into account and facilitate their dismantling, re-use and recovery (Article 4). Member States must ensure that economic operators set up systems for the collection of end-of-life vehicles and that collection facilities are adequately available in their territory (Article 5). All end-of-life vehicles must be stored and treated in accordance with Directive 75/442 (framework waste directive) and in compliance with the minimum technical requirements of its Annex I (Article 6(1)). Establishments carrying out the treatment operations must obtain a permit or be registered, with some exceptions (Article 6(2)). Member States are required to take the necessary measures to encourage the re-use of components which are suitable for re-use, the recovery of components which cannot be re-used and the giving of preference to recycling when environmentally viable. For this purpose, specific targets are set by the Directive (Article 7). Component and coding standards are to be used by producers, in concert with material and equipment manufacturers, to facilitate the identification of those components and materials which are suitable for re-use and recovery (Article 8). Member States are to send a report to the Commission on the implementation of the Directive (Article 9).

Source: OJ L 269 21.10.2000 p. 34. Amended by: Commission Decision 2002/525/EC of 27 June 2002 L 170 81 29.06.2002

Directive 2000/53/EC of the European Parliament and of the Council of 18 September 2000 on end-of-life vehicles (as amended)

The European Parliament and the Council of the European Union,

Having regard to the Treaty establishing the European Community, and in particular Article 175(1) thereof,

Having regard to the proposal from the Commission,[1]

Having regard to the opinion of the Economic and Social Committee,[2]

Having consulted the Committee of the Regions,

Acting in accordance with the procedure referred to in Article 251 of the Treaty in the light of the joint text approved by the Conciliation Committee on 23 May 2000,[3]

Whereas

(1) The different national measures concerning end-of-life vehicles should be harmonised in order, first, to minimise the impact of end-of-life vehicles on the environment, thus contributing to the protection, preservation and improvement of the quality of the environment and energy conservation, and, second, to ensure the smooth operation of the internal market and avoid distortions of competition in the Community.

(2) A Community-wide framework is necessary in order to ensure coherence between national approaches in attaining the objectives stated above, particularly with a view to the design of vehicles for recycling and recovery, to the requirements for collection and treatment facilities, and to the attainment of the targets for reuse, recycling and recovery, taking into account the principle of subsidiarity and the polluter-pays principle.

(3) Every year end-of-life vehicles in the Community generate between 8 and 9 million tonnes of waste, which must be managed correctly.

(4) In order to implement the precautionary and preventive principles and in line with the Community strategy for waste management, the generation of waste must be avoided as much as possible.

(5) It is a further fundamental principle that waste should be reused and recovered, and that preference be given to reuse and recycling.

(6) Member States should take measures to ensure that economic operators set up systems for the collection, treatment and recovery of end-of-life vehicles.

(7) Member States should ensure that the last holder and/or owner can deliver the end-of-life vehicle to an authorised treatment facility without any cost as a result of the vehicle having no or a negative, market value. Member States should ensure

---

[1] OJ C 337, 07.11.1997, p. 3, and OJ C 156, 03.06.1999, p. 5.   [2] OJ C 129, 27.4.1998, p. 44.

[3] Opinion of the European Parliament of 11 February 1999 (OJ C 150,28.5.1999, p. 420), Council Common Position of 29 July 1999 (OJ C 317, 04.11.1999, p. 19) and Decision of the European Parliament of 3 February 2000 (not yet published in the Official Journal). Council Decision of 20 July 2000 and Decision of the European Parliament of 7 September 2000.

that producers meet all, or a significant part of, the costs of the implementation of these measures; the normal functioning of market forces should not be hindered.

(8) This Directive should cover vehicles and end-of-life vehicles, including their components and materials, as well as spare and replacement parts, without prejudice to safety standards, air emissions and noise control.

(9) This Directive should be understood as having borrowed, where appropriate, the terminology used by several existing directives, namely Council Directive 67/548/EEC of 27 June 1967 on the approximation of laws, regulations and administrative provisions relating to the classification, packaging and labelling of dangerous substances,[1] Council Directive 70/156/EEC of 6 February 1970 on the approximation of the laws of the Member States relating to the type-approval of motor vehicles and their trailers,[2] and Council Directive 75/442/EEC of 15 July 1975 on waste.[3]

(10) Vintage vehicles, meaning historic vehicles or vehicles of value to collectors or intended for museums, kept in a proper and environmentally sound manner, either ready for use or stripped into parts, are not covered by the definition of waste laid down by Directive 75/442/EEC and do not fall within the scope of this Directive.

(11) It is important that preventive measures be applied from the conception phase of the vehicle onwards and take the form, in particular, of reduction and control of hazardous substances in vehicles, in order to prevent their release into the environment, to facilitate recycling and to avoid the disposal of hazardous waste. In particular the use of lead, mercury, cadmium and hexavalent chromium should be prohibited. These heavy metals should only be used in certain applications according to a list which will be regularly reviewed. This will help to ensure that certain materials and components do not become shredder residues, and are not incinerated or disposed of in landfills.

(12) The recycling of all plastics from end-of-life vehicles should be continuously improved. The Commission is currently examining the environmental impacts of PVC. The Commission will, on the basis of this work, make proposals as appropriate as to the use of PVC including considerations for vehicles.

(13) The requirements for dismantling, reuse and recycling of end-of-life vehicles and their components should be integrated in the design and production of new vehicles.

(14) The development of markets for recycled materials should be encouraged.

---

[1] OJ 196, 16.8.1967, p. 1. Directive as last amended by Commission Directive 98/98/EC (OJ L 355, 30.12.1998, p. 1).

[2] OJ L 42, 23.2.1970, p. 1. Directive as last amended by Directive 98/91/EC of the European Parliament and of the Council (OJ L 11, 16.1.1999, p. 25).

[3] OJ L 194, 25.7.1975, p. 39. Directive as last amended by Commission Decision 96/350/EC (OJ L 135, 6.6.1996, p. 32).

(15) In order to ensure that end-of-life vehicles are discarded without endangering the environment, appropriate collection systems should be set up.

(16) A certificate of destruction, to be used as a condition for the deregistration of end-of-life vehicles, should be introduced. Member States without a de-registration system should set up a System according to which a certificate of destruction is notified to the relevant competent authority when the end-of-life vehicle is transferred to a treatment facility.

(17) This Directive does not prevent Member States from granting, where appropriate, temporary deregistrations of vehicles.

(18) Collection and treatment operators should be allowed to operate only when they have received a permit or, in case a registration is used instead of a permit, specific conditions have been complied with.

(19) The recyclability and recoverability of vehicles should be promoted.

(20) It is important to lay down requirements for storage and treatment operations in order to prevent negative impacts on the environment and to avoid the emergence of distortions in trade and competition.

(21) In order to achieve results in the short term and to give operators, consumers and public authorities the necessary perspective for the longer term, quantified targets for reuse, recycling and recovery to be achieved by economic operators should be set.

(22) Producers should ensure that vehicles are designed and manufactured in such a way as to allow the quantified targets for reuse, recycling and recovery to be achieved. To this end the Commission will promote the preparation of European standards and will take the other necessary measures in order to amend the pertinent European vehicle type-approval legislation.

(23) Member States should ensure that in implementing the provisions of this Directive competition is preserved, in particular as regards the access of small and medium-sized enterprises to the collection, dismantling, treatment and recycling market.

(24) In order to facilitate the dismantling and recovery, in particular recycling of end-of-life vehicles, vehicle manufacturers should provide authorised treatment facilities with all requisite dismantling information, in particular for hazardous materials.

(25) The preparation of European standards, where appropriate, should be promoted. Vehicle manufacturers and material producers should use component and material coding standards, to be established by the Commission assisted by the relevant committee. In the preparation of these standards the Commission will take account, as appropriate, of the work going on in this area in the relevant international forums.

(26) Community-wide data on end-of-life vehicles are needed in order to monitor the implementation of the objectives of this Directive.

(27) Consumers have to be adequately informed in order to adjust their behaviour and attitudes; to this end information should be made available by the relevant economic operators.

(28) Member States may choose to implement certain provisions by means of agreements with the economic sector concerned, provided that certain conditions are met.

(29) The adaptation to scientific and technical progress of the requirements for treatment facilities and for the use of hazardous substances and, as well as the adoption of minimum standards for the certificate of destruction, the formats for the database and the implementation measures necessary to control compliance with the quantified targets should be effected by the Commission under a Committee procedure.

(30) The measures to be taken for the implementation of this Directive should be adopted in accordance with Council Decision 1999/468/EC of 28 June 1999 laying down the procedures for the exercise of implementing powers conferred on the Commission.[1]

(31) Member States may apply the provisions of this Directive in advance of the date set out therein, provided such measures are compatible with the Treaty,

Have adopted this Directive:

Article 1
Objectives

This Directive lays down measures which aim, as a first priority, at the prevention of waste from vehicles and, in addition, at the reuse, recycling and other forms of recovery of end-of-life vehicles and their components so as to reduce the disposal of waste, as well as at the improvement in the environmental performance of all of the economic operators involved in the life cycle of vehicles and especially the operators directly involved in the treatment of end-of-life vehicles.

Article 2
Definitions

For the purposes of this Directive:

1. 'vehicle' means any vehicle designated as category M1 or N1 defined in Annex IIA to Directive 70/156/EEC, and three wheel motor vehicles as defined in Directive 92/61/EEC, but excluding motor tricycles;

2. 'end-of-life vehicle' means a vehicle which is waste within the meaning of Article 1(a) of Directive 75/442/EEC;

---

[1] OJ L 184, 17.7.1999, p. 23.

3. 'producer' means the vehicle manufacturer or the professional importer of a vehicle into a Member State;

4. 'prevention' means measures aiming at the reduction of the quantity and the harmfulness for the environment of end-of-life vehicles, their materials and substances;

5. 'treatment' means any activity after the end-of-life vehicle has been handed over to a facility for depollution, dismantling, shearing, shredding, recovery or preparation for disposal of the shredder wastes, and any other operation carried out for the recovery and/or disposal of the end-of-life vehicle and its components;

6. 'reuse' means any operation by which components of end-of-life vehicles are used for the same purpose for which they were conceived;

7. 'recycling' means the reprocessing in a production process of the waste materials for the original purpose or for other purposes but excluding energy recovery. Energy recovery means the use of combustible waste as a means to generate energy through direct incineration with or without other waste but with recovery of the heat;

8. 'recovery' means any of the applicable operations provided for in Annex IIB to Directive 75/442/EEC;

9. 'disposal' means any of the applicable operations provided for in Annex IIA to Directive 75/442/EEC;

10. 'economic operators' means producers, distributors, collectors, motor vehicle insurance companies, dismantlers, shredders, recoverers, recyclers and other treatment operators of end-of-life vehicles, including their components and materials;

11. 'hazardous substance' means any substance which is considered to be dangerous under Directive 67/548/EEC;

12. 'shredder' means any device used for tearing into pieces or fragmenting end-of-life vehicles, including for the purpose of obtaining directly reusable metal scrap;

13. 'dismantling information' means all information required for the correct and environmentally sound treatment of end-of-life vehicles. It shall be made available to authorised treatment facilities by vehicle manufacturers and component producers in the form of manuals or by means of electronic media (e.g. CD-ROM, on-line services).

Article 3
Scope

1. This Directive shall cover vehicles and end-of-life vehicles, including their components and materials. Without prejudice to Article 5(4), third subparagraph, this shall apply irrespective of how the vehicle has been serviced or repaired during use and irrespective of whether it is equipped with components supplied by the producer or with other components whose fitting as spare or replacement parts accords with the appropriate Community provisions or domestic provisions.

2. This Directive shall apply without prejudice to existing Community legislation and relevant national legislation, in particular as regards safety standards, air emissions and noise controls and the protection of soil and water.

3. Where a producer only makes or imports vehicles that are exempt from Directive 70/156/EEC by virtue of Article 8(2)(a) thereof, Member States may exempt that producer and his vehicles from Articles 7(4), 8 and 9 of this Directive.

4. Special-purpose vehicles as defined in the second indent of Article 4(1)(a) of Directive 70/156/EEC shall be excluded from the provisions of Article 7 of this Directive.

5. For three-wheel motor vehicles only Articles 5(1), 5(2) and 6 of this Directive shall apply.

Article 4

Prevention

1. In order to promote the prevention of waste Member States shall encourage, in particular:

(a) vehicle manufacturers, in liaison with material and equipment manufacturers, to limit the use of hazardous substances in vehicles and to reduce them as far as possible from the conception of the vehicle onwards, so as in particular to prevent their release into the environment, make recycling easier, and avoid the need to dispose of hazardous waste;

(b) the design and production of new vehicles which take into full account and facilitate the dismantling, reuse and recovery, in particular the recycling, of end-of-life vehicles, their components and materials;

(c) vehicle manufacturers, in liaison with material and equipment manufacturers, to integrate an increasing quantity of recycled material in vehicles and other products, in order to develop the markets for recycled materials.

2.

(a) Member States shall ensure that materials and components of vehicles put on the market after 1 July 2003 do not contain lead, mercury, cadmium or hexavalent chromium other than in cases listed in Annex II under the conditions specified therein;

(b) in accordance with the procedure laid down in Article 11 the Commission shall on a regular basis, according to technical and scientific progress, amend Annex II, in order to:

  (i) as necessary, establish maximum concentration values up to which the existence of the substances referred to in subparagraph (a) in specific materials and components of vehicles shall be tolerated;

  (ii) exempt certain materials and components of vehicles from the provisions of subparagraph (a) if the use of these substances is unavoidable;

(iii) delete materials and components of vehicles from Annex II if the use of these substances is avoidable;

(iv) under points (i) and (ii) designate those materials and components of vehicles that can be stripped before further treatment; they shall be labelled or made identifiable by other appropriate means;

(c) the Commission shall amend Annex II for the first time not later than 21 October 2001. In any case none of the exemptions listed therein shall be deleted from the Annex before 1 January 2003.

Article 5
Collection

1. Member States shall take the necessary measures to ensure:

− that economic operators set up systems for the collection of all end of life vehicles and, as far as technically feasible, of waste used parts removed when passenger cars are repaired,
− the adequate availability of collection facilities within their territory.

2. Member States shall also take the necessary measures to ensure that all end-of-life vehicles are transferred to authorised treatment facilities.

3. Member States shall set up a system according to which the presentation of a certificate of destruction is a condition for deregistration of the end-of-life vehicle. This certificate shall be issued to the holder and/or owner when the end-of-life vehicle is transferred to a treatment facility. Treatment facilities, which have obtained a permit in accordance with Article 6, shall be permitted to issue a certificate of destruction. Member States may permit producers, dealers and collectors on behalf of an authorised treatment facility to issue certificates of destruction provided that they guarantee that the end-of-life vehicle is transferred to an authorised treatment facility and provided that they are registered with public authorities.

Issuing the certificate of destruction by treatment facilities or dealers or collectors on behalf of an authorised treatment facility does not entitle them to claim any financial reimbursement, except in cases where this has been explicitly arranged by Member States.

Member States which do not have a deregistration system at the date of entry into force of this Directive shall set up a system according to which a certificate of destruction is notified to the relevant competent authority when the end-of-life vehicle is transferred to a treatment facility and shall otherwise comply with the terms of this paragraph. Member States making use of this subparagraph shall inform the Commission of the reasons thereof.

4. Member States shall take the necessary measures to ensure that the delivery of the vehicle to an authorised treatment facility in accordance with paragraph 3 occurs

without any cost for the last holder and/or owner as a result of the vehicle's having no or a negative market value.

Member States shall take the necessary measures to ensure that producers meet all, or a significant part of, the costs of the implementation of this measure and/or take back end-of-life vehicles under the same conditions as referred to in the first subparagraph.

Member States may provide that the delivery of end-of-life vehicles is not fully free of charge if the end-of-life vehicle does not contain the essential components of a vehicle, in particular the engine and the coachwork, or contains waste which has been added to the end-of-life vehicle.

The Commission shall regularly monitor the implementation of the first subparagraph to ensure that it does not result in market distortions, and if necessary shall propose to the European Parliament and the Council an amendment thereto.

5. Member States shall take the necessary measures to ensure that competent authorities mutually recognise and accept the certificates of destruction issued in other Member States in accordance with paragraph 3. To this end, the Commission shall draw up, not later than 21 October 2001 the minimum requirements for the certificate of destruction.

Article 6

Treatment

1. Member States shall take the necessary measures to ensure that all end-of life vehicles are stored (even temporarily) and treated in accordance with the general requirements laid down in Article 4 of Directive 75/442/EEC, and in compliance with the minimum technical requirements set out in Annex I to this Directive, without prejudice to national regulations on health and environment.

2. Member States shall take the necessary measures to ensure that any establishment or undertaking carrying out treatment operations obtains a permit from or be registered with the competent authorities, in compliance with Articles 9, 10 and 11 of Directive 75/442/EEC.

The derogation from the permit requirement referred to in Article 11(1)(b) of Directive 75/442/EEC may apply to recovery operations concerning waste of end-of-life vehicles after they have been treated according to Annex 1(3) to this Directive if there is an inspection by the competent authorities before the registration. This inspection shall verify:

(a) type and quantities of waste to be treated;
(b) general technical requirements to be complied with;
(c) safety precautions to be taken,

in order to achieve the objectives referred to in Article 4 of Directive 75/442/EEC. This inspection shall take place once a year. Member States using the derogation shall send the results to the Commission.

3. Member States shall take the necessary measures to ensure that any establishment or undertaking carrying out treatment operations fulfils at least the following obligations in accordance with Annex I:

(a) end-of-life vehicles shall be stripped before further treatment or other equivalent arrangements are made in order to reduce any adverse impact on the environment. Components or materials labelled or otherwise made identifiable in accordance with Article 4(2) shall be stripped before further treatment;
(b) hazardous materials and components shall be removed and segregated in a selective way so as not to contaminate subsequent shredder waste from end-of-life vehicles;
(c) stripping operations and storage shall be carried out in such a way as to ensure the suitability of vehicle components for reuse and recovery, and in particular for recycling.
Treatment operations for depollution of end-of-life vehicles as referred to in Annex I(3) shall be carried out as soon as possible.

4. Member States shall take the necessary measures to ensure that the permit or registration referred to in paragraph 2 includes all conditions necessary for compliance with the requirements of paragraphs 1, 2 and 3.

5. Member States shall encourage establishments or undertakings, which carry out treatment operations to introduce, certified environmental management systems.

Article 7
Reuse and recovery

1. Member States shall take the necessary measures to encourage the reuse of components which are suitable for reuse, the recovery of components which cannot be reused and the giving of preference to recycling when environmentally viable, without prejudice to requirements regarding the safety of vehicles and environmental requirements such as air emissions and noise control.

2. Member States shall take the necessary measures to ensure that the following targets are attained by economic operators:

(a) no later than 1 January 2006, for all end-of-life vehicles, the reuse and recovery shall be increased to a minimum of 85 % by an average weight per vehicle and year. Within the same time limit the reuse and recycling shall be increased to a minimum of 80 % by an average weight per vehicle and year; for vehicles produced before 1 January 1980, Member States may lay down lower targets, but not lower than 75 % for reuse and recovery and not lower than 70 % for reuse and recycling. Member States making use of this subparagraph shall inform the Commission and the other Member States of the reasons therefor;
(b) no later than 1 January 2015, for all end-of-life vehicles, the reuse and recovery shall be increased to a minimum of 95 % by an average weight per vehicle and

year. Within the same time limit, the re-use and recycling shall be increased to a minimum of 85 % by an average weight per vehicle and year.

By 31 December 2005 at the latest the European Parliament and the Council shall re-examine the targets referred to in paragraph (b) on the basis of a report of the Commission, accompanied by a proposal. In its report the Commission shall take into account the development of the material composition of vehicles and any other relevant environmental aspects related to vehicles.

The Commission shall, in accordance with the procedure laid down in Article 11, establish the detailed rules necessary to control compliance of Member States with the targets set out in this paragraph. In doing so the Commission shall take into account all relevant factors, inter alia the availability of data and the issue of exports and imports of end-of-life vehicles. The Commission shall take this measure not later than 21 October 2002.

3. On the basis of a proposal from the Commission, the European Parliament and the Council shall establish targets for reuse and recovery and for reuse and recycling for the years beyond 2015.

4. In order to prepare an amendment to Directive 70/156/EEC, the Commission shall promote the preparation of European standards relating to the dismantlability, recoverability and recyclability of vehicles. Once the standards are agreed, but in any case no later than by the end of 2001, the European Parliament and the Council, on the basis of a proposal from the Commission, shall amend Directive 70/156/EEC so that vehicles type-approved in accordance with that Directive and put on the market after three years after the amendment of the Directive 70/156/EEC are re-usable and/or recyclable to a minimum of 85 % by weight per vehicle and are re-usable and/or recoverable to a minimum of 95 % by weight per vehicle.

5. In proposing the amendment to Directive 70/156/EEC relating to the ability to be dismantled, recoverability and recyclability of vehicles, the Commission shall take into account as appropriate the need to ensure that the reuse of components does not give rise to safety or environmental hazards.

Article 8
Coding standards/dismantling information

1. Member States shall take the necessary measures to ensure that producers, in concert with material and equipment manufacturers, use component and material coding standards, in particular to facilitate the identification of those components and materials which are suitable for reuse and recovery.

2. Not later than 21 October 2001 the Commission shall, in accordance with the procedure laid down in Article 11 establish the standards referred to in paragraph 1 of this Article. In so doing, the Commission shall take account of the work going on in this area in the relevant international forums and contribute to this work as appropriate.

3. Member States shall take the necessary measures to ensure that producers provide dismantling information for each type of new vehicle put on the market within six months after the vehicle is put on the market. This information shall identify, as far as it is needed by treatment facilities in order to comply with the provisions of this Directive, the different vehicle components and materials, and the location of all hazardous substances in the vehicles, in particular with a view to the achievement of the objectives laid down in Article 7.

4. Without prejudice to commercial and industrial confidentiality, Member States shall take the necessary measures to ensure that manufacturers of components used in vehicles make available to authorised treatment facilities, as far as it is requested by these facilities, appropriate information concerning dismantling, storage and testing of components which can be reused.

Article 9
Reporting and information

1. At three-year intervals Member States shall send a report to the Commission on the implementation of this Directive. The report shall be drawn up on the basis of a questionnaire or outline drafted by the Commission in accordance with the procedure laid down in Article 6 of Directive 91/692/EEC[1] with a view to establishing databases on end-of-life vehicles and their treatment. The report shall contain relevant information on possible changes in the structure of motor vehicle dealing and of the collection, dismantling, shredding, recovery and recycling industries, leading to any distortion of competition between or within Member States. The questionnaire or outline shall be sent to the Member States six months before the start of the period covered by the report. The report shall be made to the Commission within nine months of the end of the three-year period covered by it.

The first report shall cover the period of three years from 21 April 2002. Based on the above information, the Commission shall publish a report on the implementation of this Directive within nine months of receiving the reports from the Member States.

2. Member States shall require in each case the relevant economic operators to publish information on:

– the design of vehicles and their components with a view to their recoverability and recyclability,
– the environmentally sound treatment of end-of-life vehicles, in particular the removal of all fluids and dismantling,
– the development and optimisation of ways to reuse, recycle and recover end-of-life vehicles and their components,
– the progress achieved with regard to recovery and recycling to reduce the waste to be disposed of and to increase the recovery and recycling rates.

[1] OJ L 377, 31.12.1991, p. 48.

The producer must make this information accessible to the prospective buyers of vehicles. It shall be included in promotional literature used in the marketing of the new vehicle.

Article 10
Implementation

1. Member States shall bring into force the laws, regulations and administrative provisions necessary to comply with this Directive by 21 April 2002. They shall immediately inform the Commission thereof.

When Member States adopt these measures, these shall contain a reference to this Directive or shall be accompanied by such reference on the occasion of their official publication. The methods of making such a reference shall be laid down by Member States.

2. Member States shall communicate to the Commission the text of the main provisions of domestic law, which they adopt in the field governed by this Directive.

3. Provided that the objectives set out in this Directive are achieved, Member States may transpose the provisions set out in Articles 4(1), 5(1), 7(1), 8(1), 8(3) and 9(2) and specify the detailed rules of implementation of Article 5(4) by means of agreements between the competent authorities and the economic sectors concerned. Such agreements shall meet the following requirements

(a) agreements shall be enforceable;
(b) agreements need to specify objectives with the corresponding deadlines;
(c) agreements shall be published in the national official journal or an official document equally accessible to the public and transmitted to the Commission;
(d) the results achieved under an agreement shall be monitored regularly, reported to the competent authorities and to the Commission and made available to the public under the conditions set out in the agreement;
(e) the competent authorities shall make provisions to examine the progress reached under an agreement;
(f) in case of non-compliance with an agreement Member States must implement the relevant provisions of this Directive by legislative, regulatory or administrative measures.

Article 11
Committee procedure

1. The Commission shall be assisted by the committee established by Article 18 of Directive 75/442/EEC, hereinafter referred to as 'the Committee'.

2. Where reference is made to this Article, Articles 5 and 7 of Decision 1999/468/EC shall apply, having regard to the provisions of Article 8 thereof.

The period laid down in Article 5(6) of Decision 1999/468/EC shall be set at three months.

3. The Committee shall adopt its rules of procedure.

4. The Commission, according to the procedure laid down in this Article, shall adopt:

(a) the minimum requirements, as referred to in Article 5(5), for the certificate of destruction;
(b) the detailed rules referred to in Article 7(2), third subparagraph;
(c) the formats relating to the database system referred to in Article 9;
(d) the amendments necessary for adapting the Annexes to this Directive to scientific and technical progress.

Article 12
Entry into force

1. This Directive shall enter into force on the day of its publication in the *Official Journal of the European Communities.*

2. Article 5(4) shall apply:

— as from 1 July 2002 for vehicles put on the market as from this date,
— as from 1 January 2007 for vehicles put on the market before the date referred to in the first indent.

3. Member States may apply Article 5(4) in advance of the dates set out in paragraph 2.

Article 13
Addressees

This Directive is addressed to the Member States.

Annex I
Minimum technical requirements for treatment in accordance with
Article 6(1) and (3)

1. Sites for storage (including temporary storage) of end-of-life vehicles prior to their treatment:

— impermeable surfaces for appropriate areas with the provision of spillage collection facilities, decanters and cleanser-degeasers,
— equipment for the treatment of water, including rainwater, in compliance with health and environmental regulations.

2. Sites for treatment:

— impermeable surfaces for appropriate areas with the provision of spillage collection facilities, decanters and cleanser-degreasers,

- appropriate storage for dismantled spare parts, including impermeable storage for oil-contaminated spare parts,
- appropriate containers for storage of batteries (with electrolyte neutralization on site or elsewhere), filters and PCB/PCT-containing condensers,
- appropriate storage tanks for the segregated storage of end-of-life vehicle fluids: fuel, motor oil, gearbox oil, transmission oil, hydraulic oil, cooling liquids, antifreeze, brake fluids, battery acids, air-conditioning system fluids and any other fluid contained in the end-of-life vehicle,
- equipment for the treatment of water, including rainwater, in compliance with health and environmental regulations,
- appropriate storage for used tyres, including the prevention of fire hazards and excessive stockpiling.

3. Treatment operations for depollution of end-of-life vehicles: – removal of batteries and liquified gas tanks,

- removal or neutralisation of potential explosive components, (e.g. air bags),
- removal and separate collection and storage of fuel, motor oil, transmission oil, gearbox oil, hydraulic oil, cooling liquids, antifreeze, brake fluids, air-conditioning system fluids and any other fluid contained in the end-of-life vehicle, unless they are necessary for the re-use of the parts concerned,
- removal, as far as feasible, of all components identified as containing mercury.

4. Treatment operations in order to promote recycling:

- removal or catalysts,
- removal of metal components containing copper, aluminium and magnesium if these metals are not segregated in the shredding process,
- removal of tyres and large plastic components (bumpers, dashboard, fluid containers, etc), if these materials are not segregated in the shredding process in such a way that they can be effectively recycled as materials,
- removal of glass.

5. Storage operations are to be carried out avoiding damage to components containing fluids or to recoverable components and spare parts.

Annex II
Materials and components exempt from Article 4(2)(a)

Materials and components	Scope and expiry date of the exemption	To be labelled or made identifiable in accordance with Article 4(2)(b)(iv)
Lead as an alloying element		
1. Steel for machining purposes and galvanised steel containing up to 0.35% lead by weight		
2. a) Aluminium for machining purposes with a lead content up to 2% by weight	(a) 1 July 2005[1]	
b) Aluminium for machining purposes with a lead content up to 1% by weight	(b) 1 July 2008[2]	
3. Copper alloy containing up to 4% lead by weight		
4. Lead-bronze bearing shells and bushes		
Lead and lead compounds in components		
5. Batteries		X
6. Vibration dampers		X
7. Wheel balance weights	Vehicles type-approved before 1 July 2003 and wheel balance weights intended for servicing of these vehicles: 1 July 2005[3]	
8. Vulcanising agents and stabilisers for elastomers in fluid handling and powertrain applications	1 July 2005[4]	
9. Stabiliser in protective paints	1 July 2005	

(*cont.*)

(*cont.*)

Materials and components	Scope and expiry date of the exemption	To be labelled or made identifiable in accordance with Article 4(2)(b)(iv)
10. Carbon brushes for electric motors	Vehicles type-approved before 1 July 2003 and carbon brushes for electric motors intended for servicing of these vehicles: 1 January 2005	
11. Solder in electronic circuit boards and other electric applications		X[5]
12. Copper in brake linings containing more than 0,5% lead by weight	Vehicles type-approved before 1 July 2003 and servicing on these vehicles: 1 July 2004	X
13. Valve seats	Engine types developed before 1 July 2003: 1 July 2006	
14. Electrical components which contain lead in a glass or ceramic matrix compound except glass in bulbs and glaze of spark plugs		X[6] (for components other than piezo in engines)
15. Glass in bulbs and glaze of spark plugs	1 January 2005	
16. Pyrotechnic initiators	1 July 2007	
Hexavalent chromium		
17. Corrosion preventive coatings	1 July 2007	
18. Absorption refrigerators in motorcar-avans		X
Mercury		
19. Discharge lamps and instrument panel displays		X
Cadmium		
20. Thick film pastes	1 July 2006	

Materials and components	Scope and expiry date of the exemption	To be labelled or made identifiable in accordance with Article 4(2)(b)(iv)
21. Batteries for electrical vehicles	After 31 December 2005, the placing on the market of NiCd batteries shall only be allowed as replacement parts for vehicles put on the market before this date.	X

[1] By 1 January 2005 the Commission shall assess whether the phase-out time scheduled for this entry has to be reviewed in relation to the availability of substitutes for lead, taking into account the objectives of Article 4(2)(a).

[2] See footnote 1.

[3] By 1 January 2005, the Commission shall assess this exemption in relation to road safety aspects.

[4] See footnote 1.

[5] Dismantling if, in correlation with entry 14, an average threshold of 60 grams per vehicle is exceeded. For the application of this clause, electronic devices not installed by the manufacturer on the production line shall not be taken into account.

[6] Dismantling if, in correlation with entry 11, an average threshold of 60 grams per vehicle is exceeded. For the application of this clause, electronic devices not installed by the manufacturer on the production line shall not be taken into account.

Notes:

– a maximum concentration value up to 0,1% by weight and per homogeneous material, for lead, hexavalent chromium and mercury and up to 0,01% by weight per homogeneous material for cadmium shall be tolerated, provided these substances are not intentionally introduced,[1]

– a maximum concentration value up to 0,4% by weight of lead in aluminium shall also be tolerated provided it is not intentionally introduced,[2]

– a maximum concentration value up to 0,4% by weight of lead in copper intended for friction materials in brake linings shall be tolerated until 1 July 2007 provided it is not intentionally introduced,[3]

– the reuse of parts of vehicles which were already on the market at the date of expiry of an exemption is allowed without limitation since it is not covered by Article 4(2)(a),

– until 1 July 2007, new replacement parts intended for repair[4] of parts of vehicles exempted from the provisions of Article 4(2)(a) shall also benefit from the same exemptions.

[1] 'Intentionally introduced' shall mean 'deliberately utilised in the formulation of a material or component where its continued presence is desired in the final product to provide a specific characteristic, appearance or quality'. The use of recycled materials as feedstock for the manufacture of new products, where some portion of the recycled materials may contain amounts of regulated metals, is not to be considered as intentionally introduced.

[2] See footnote 1.

[3] See footnote 1.

[4] This clause applies to replacement parts and not to components intended for normal servicing of vehicles. It does not apply to wheel balance weights, carbon brushes for electric motors and brake linings as these components are covered in specific entries.

Directive 2000/76/EC of the European Parliament and of the Council of 4 December 2000 on the incineration of waste

Editorial note

Directive 2000/76 of 4 December 2000 aims to prevent or to limit as far as practicable negative effects on the environment, in particular pollution by emissions into air, soil, surface water and groundwater, and the resulting risks to human health, from the incineration and co-incineration of waste. This aim is to be met by means of stringent operational conditions and technical requirements, through setting emission limit values for waste incineration and co-incineration plants within the Community and also through meeting the requirements of Directive 75/442/EEC (Article 1). The Directive covers incineration and co-incineration plants, with some exceptions specifically listed in the instrument (Article 2).

No incineration or co-incineration plant is to operate without a permit, to be obtained from the competent authority (Article 4). Permits are given by the competent authority if the conditions laid out by the Directive are met. The competent authority shall periodically reconsider and update the permit conditions. The competent authority is to enforce compliance with the permit conditions (Article 4). The operator of the incineration or co-incineration plant is to take all necessary measures concerning the delivery and reception of waste in order to prevent or to limit as far as practicable negative effects on the environment (Article 5). Operating conditions for incineration and co-incineration plants are specified by Article 6. Incineration and co-incineration plants are to be designed, equipped, built and operated in such a way that the emission limit values set out in Annexes to the Directive are not exceeded in the exhaust gas (Article 7). Waste water from the cleaning of exhaust gases discharged from an incineration or co-incineration plant is to be subject to a permit granted by the competent authority (Article 8). Residues resulting from the operation of the incineration or co-incineration plant are to be minimised in their amount and harmfulness and recycled where appropriate (Article 9). Measurement equipment is to be installed and techniques used in order to monitor parameters, conditions and mass concentrations relevant to the incineration or co-incineration (Article 10). Applications for new permits for incineration and co-incineration are to be made available to the public for an appropriate period to enable it to comment on them before a decision is reached by the competent authority (Article 12). The competent authority shall lay down in the permit conditions allowing abnormal operation for a maximum permissible period (Article 13). Member States are to determine the penalties applicable for breaches of national provisions implementing the Directive (Article 19).

The Directive repeals as from 28 December 2005: Article 8(1) and the Annex to Directive 75/439/EEC; Directive 89/369/EEC; Directive 89/429/EEC; Directive 94/67/EC.

Source: OJ L 332 28.12.2000 p. 91. Corrected by: Corrigendum, OJ L 145 31.05.2001 p. 52

Directive 2000/76/EC of the European Parliament and of the Council of 4 December 2000 on the incineration of waste

The European Parliament and the Council of the European Union,

Having regard to the Treaty establishing the European Community, and in particular Article 175(1) thereof,

Having regard to the proposal from the Commission,[1]

Having regard to the Opinion of the Economic and Social Committee,[2]

Having regard to the Opinion of the Committee of the Regions,[3]

Acting in accordance with the procedure laid down in Article 251 of the Treaty,[4] and in the light of the joint text approved by the Conciliation Committee on 11 October 2000,

Whereas:

(1) The fifth Environment Action Programme: Towards sustainability — A European Community programme of policy and action in relation to the environment and sustainable development, supplemented by Decision No 2179/98/EC on its review,[5] sets as an objective that critical loads and levels of certain pollutants such as nitrogen oxides (NOx), sulphur dioxide (SO_2), heavy metals and dioxins should not be exceeded, while in terms of air quality the objective is that all people should be effectively protected against recognised health risks from air pollution. That Programme further sets as an objective a 90% reduction of dioxin emissions of identified sources by 2005 (1985 level) and at least 70%

---

[1] OJ C 13, 17.1.1998, p. 6 and OJ C 372, 2.12.1998, p. 11.

[2] OJ C 116, 28.4.1999, p. 40.   [3] OJ C 198, 14.7.1999, p. 37.

[4] Opinion of the European Parliament of 14 April 1999 (OJ C 219, 30.7.1999, p. 249), Council Common Position of 25 November 1999 (OJ C 25, 28.1.- 2000, p. 17) and Decision of the European Parliament of 15 March 2000 (not yet published in the Official Journal). Decision of the European Parliament of 16 November 2000 and Decision of the Council of 20 November 2000.

[5] OJ C 138, 17.5.1993, p. 1 and OJ L 275, 10.10.1998, p. 1

reduction from all pathways of cadmium (Cd), mercury (Hg) and lead (Pb) emissions in 1995.

(2) The Protocol on persistent organic pollutants signed by the Community within the framework of the United Nations Economic Commission for Europe (UN-ECE) Convention on long-range transboundary air pollution sets legally binding limit values for the emission of dioxins and furans of 0,1 ng/m; TE (Toxicity Equivalents) for installations burning more than 3 tonnes per hour of municipal solid waste, 0,5 ng/m; TE for installations burning more than 1 tonne per hour of medical waste, and 0,2 ng/m; TE for installations burning more than 1 tonne per hour of hazardous waste.

(3) The Protocol on Heavy Metals signed by the Community within the framework of the UN-ECE Convention on long-range transboundary air pollution sets legally binding limit values for the emission of particulate of 10 mg/m^3 for hazardous and medical waste incineration and for the emission of mercury of 0,05 mg/m^3 for hazardous waste incineration and 0,08 mg/m^3 for municipal waste incineration.

(4) The International Agency for Research on Cancer and the World Health Organisation indicate that some polycyclic aromatic hydrocarbons (PAHs) are carcinogenic. Therefore, Member States may set emission limit values for PAHs among other pollutants.

(5) In accordance with the principles of subsidiarity and proportionality as set out in Article 5 of the Treaty, there is a need to take action at the level of the Community. The precautionary principle provides the basis for further measures. This Directive confines itself to minimum requirements for incineration and co-incineration plants.

(6) Further, Article 174 provides that Community policy on the environment is to contribute to protecting human health.

(7) Therefore, a high level of environmental protection and human health protection requires the setting and maintaining of stringent operational conditions, technical requirements and emission limit values for plants incinerating or co-incinerating waste within the Community. The limit values set should prevent or limit as far as practicable negative effects on the environment and the resulting risks to human health.

(8) The Communication from the Commission on the review of the Community Strategy for waste management assigns prevention of waste the first priority, followed by reuse and recovery and finally by safe disposal of waste; in its Resolution of 24 February 1997 on a Community Strategy for waste management,[1] the Council reiterated its conviction that waste prevention should be the first priority of any rational waste policy in relation to minimising waste production and the hazardous properties of waste.

---

[1] OJ C 76, 11.3.1997, p. 1.

(9) In its Resolution of 24 February 1997 the Council also underlines the importance of Community criteria concerning the use of waste, the need for appropriate emission standards to apply to incineration facilities, the need for monitoring measures to be envisaged for existing incineration plants, and the need for the Commission to consider amending Community legislation in relation to the incineration of waste with energy recovery in order to avoid large-scale movements of waste for incineration or co-incineration in the Community.

(10) It is necessary to set strict rules for all plants incinerating or co-incinerating waste in order to avoid transboundary movements to plants operating at lower costs due to less stringent environmental standards.

(11) The Communication from the Commission/energy for the future: renewable sources of energy/White paper for a Community strategy and action plan takes into consideration in particular the use of biomass for energy purposes.

(12) Council Directive 96/61/EC[1] sets out an integrated approach to pollution prevention and control in which all the aspects of an installations environmental performance are considered in an integrated manner. Installations for the incineration of municipal waste with a capacity exceeding 3 tonnes per hour and installations for the disposal or recovery of hazardous waste with a capacity exceeding 10 tonnes per day are included within the scope of the said Directive.

(13) Compliance with the emission limit values laid down by this Directive should be regarded as a necessary but not sufficient condition for compliance with the requirements of Directive 96/61/EC. Such compliance may involve more stringent emissions limit values for the pollutants envisaged by this Directive, emission limit values for other substances and other media, and other appropriate conditions.

(14) Industrial experience in the implementation of techniques for the reduction of polluting emissions from incineration plants has been acquired over a period of ten years.

(15) Council Directives 89/369/EEC[2] and 89/429/EEC[3] on the prevention and reduction of air pollution from municipal waste incineration plants have contributed to the reduction and control of atmospheric emissions from incineration plants. More stringent rules should now be adopted and those Directives should accordingly be repealed.

(16) The distinction between hazardous and non-hazardous waste is based principally on the properties of waste prior to incineration or co-incineration but not on differences in emissions. The same emission limit values should apply to the incineration or co-incineration of hazardous and non-hazardous waste

---

[1] OJ L 257, 10.10.1996, p. 26.
[2] OJ L 163, 14.6.1989, p. 32. Directive as last amended by the Accession Act of 1994.
[3] OJ L 203, 15.7.1989, p. 50. Directive as last amended by the Accession Act of 1994.

but different techniques and conditions of incineration or co-incineration and different monitoring measures upon reception of waste should be retained.

(17) Member States should take into account Council Directive 1999/30/EC of 22 April 1999 relating to limit values for sulphur dioxide, nitrogen dioxide and oxides of nitrogen, particulate matter and lead in ambient air[1] when implementing this Directive.

(18) The incineration of hazardous waste with a content of more than 1% of halogenated organic substances, expressed as chlorine, has to comply with certain operational conditions in order to destroy as many organic pollutants such as dioxins as possible.

(19) The incineration of waste which contains chlorine generates flue gas residues. Such residues should be managed in a way that minimises their amount and harmfulness.

(20) There may be grounds to provide for specified exemptions to the emission limit values for some pollutants during a specified time limit and subject to specific conditions.

(21) Criteria for certain sorted combustible fraction of non-hazardous waste not suitable for recycling, should be developed in order to allow the authorisation of the reduction of the frequency of periodical measurements.

(22) A single text on the incineration of waste will improve legal clarity and enforceability. There should be a single directive for the incineration and co-incineration of hazardous and non-hazardous waste taking fully into account the substance and structure of Council Directive 94/67/EC of 16 December 1994 on the incineration of hazardous waste.[2] Therefore Directive 94/67/EC should also be repealed.

(23) Article 4 of Council Directive 75/442/EEC of 15 July 1975 on waste[3] requires Member States to take the necessary measures to ensure that waste is recovered or disposed of without endangering human health and without harming the environment. To this end, Articles 9 and 10 of that Directive provide that any plant or undertaking treating waste must obtain a permit from the competent authorities relating, *inter alia*, to the precautions to be taken.

(24) The requirements for recovering the heat generated by the incineration or co-incineration process and for minimising and recycling residues resulting from the operation of incineration or co-incineration plants will assist in meeting the objectives of Article 3 on the waste hierarchy of Directive 75/442/EEC.

(25) Incineration and co-incineration plants treating only animal waste regulated by Directive 90/667/EEC[4] are excluded from the scope of this Directive. The

---

[1] OJ L 163, 29.6.1999, p. 41.
[2] OJ L 365, 31.12.1994, p. 34.
[3] OJ L 194, 25.7.1975, p. 39. Directive as last amended by Commission Decision 350/96/EC (OJ L 135, 6.6.1996, p. 32).
[4] Council Directive 90/667/EEC of 27 November 1990, laying down the veterinary rules for the disposal and processing of animal waste, for its placing on the market and for the prevention of pathogens in feedstuffs

Commission intends to propose a revision to the requirements of Directive 90/667 with a view to providing for high environmental standards for the incineration and co-incineration of animal waste.

(26) The permit for an incineration or co-incineration plant shall also comply with any applicable requirements laid down in Directives 91/271/EEC,[1] 96/61/EC, 96/62/EC,[2] 76/464/EEC,[3] and 1999/31/EC.[4]

(27) The co-incineration of waste in plants not primarily intended to incinerate waste should not be allowed to cause higher emissions of polluting substances in that part of the exhaust gas volume resulting from such co-incineration than those permitted for dedicated incineration plants and should therefore be subject to appropriate limitations.

(28) High-standard measurement techniques are required to monitor emissions to ensure compliance with the emission limit values for the pollutants.

(29) The introduction of emission limit values for the discharge of waste water from the cleaning of exhaust gases from incineration and co-incineration plants will limit a transfer of pollutants from the air into water.

(30) Provisions should be laid down for cases where the emission limit values are exceeded as well as for technically unavoidable stoppages, disturbances or failures of the purification devices or the measurement devices.

(31) In order to ensure transparency of the permitting process throughout the Community the public should have access to information with a view to allowing it to be involved in decisions to be taken following applications for new permits and their subsequent updates. The public should have access to reports on the functioning and monitoring of the plants burning more than three tonnes per hour in order to be informed of their potential effects on the environment and human health.

(32) The Commission should present a report both to the European Parliament and the Council based on the experience of applying this Directive, the new scientific knowledge gained, the development of the state of technology, the progress achieved in emission control techniques, and on the experience made in waste management and operation of the plants and on the development of environmental requirements, with a view to proposing, as appropriate, to adapt the related provisions of this Directive.

---

of animal or fish origin and amending Directive 90/425/EEC (OJ L 363, 27.12.1990, p.51). Directive as last amended by the Accession Act of 1994.

[1] Council Directive 91/271/EEC of 21 May 1991 concerning urban waste-water treatment (OJ L 135, 30.5.1991, p. 40). Directive as amended by Directive98/15/EC (OJ L 67, 7.3.1998, p. 29).

[2] Council Directive 96/62/EC of 27 September 1996 on ambient air quality assessment and management (OJ L 296, 21.11.1996, p. 55).

[3] Council Directive 76/464/EEC of 4 May 1976 on pollution caused by certain dangerous substances discharged into the aquatic environment of the Community (OJ L 129, 18.5.1976, p. 23). Directive as last amended by the Accession Act of 1994.

[4] Directive 1999/31/EC of 26 April 1999 on the landfill of waste (OJ L 182, 16.7.1999, p. 1).

(33) The measures necessary for the implementation of this Directive are to be adopted in accordance with Council Decision 1999/468/EC of 28 June 1999 laying down the procedures for the exercise of implementing powers conferred on the Commission.[1]

(34) Member States should lay down rules on penalties applicable to infringements of the provisions of this Directive and ensure that they are implemented; those penalties should be effective, proportionate and dissuasive,

Have adopted this Directive:

Article 1
Objectives

The aim of this Directive is to prevent or to limit as far as practicable negative effects on the environment, in particular pollution by emissions into air, soil, surface water and groundwater, and the resulting risks to human health, from the incineration and co-incineration of waste.

This aim shall be met by means of stringent operational conditions and technical requirements, through setting emission limit values for waste incineration and co-incineration plants within the Community and also through meeting the requirements of Directive 75/442/EEC.

Article 2
Scope

1. This Directive covers incineration and co-incineration plants.

2. The following plants shall however be excluded from the scope of this Directive:

(a) Plants treating only the following wastes:
    (i) vegetable waste from agriculture and forestry,
    (ii) vegetable waste from the food processing industry, if the heat generated is recovered,
    (iii) fibrous vegetable waste from virgin pulp production and from production of paper from pulp, if it is co-incinerated at the place of production and the heat generated is recovered,
    (iv) wood waste with the exception of wood waste which may contain halogenated organic compounds or heavy metals as a result of treatment with wood-preservatives or coating, and which includes in particular such wood waste originating from construction and demolition waste,
    (v) cork waste,
    (vi) radioactive waste,
    (vii) animal carcasses as regulated by Directive 90/667/EEC without prejudice to its future amendments,

---

[1] OJ L 184, 17.7.1999, p. 23.

(viii) waste resulting from the exploration for, and the exploitation of, oil and gas resources from off-shore installations and incinerated on board the installation;

(b) Experimental plants used for research, development and testing in order to improve the incineration process and which treat less than 50 tonnes of waste per year.

Article 3
Definitions

For the purposes of this Directive:

1. 'waste' means any solid or liquid waste as defined in Article 1(a) of Directive 75/442/EEC;

2. 'hazardous waste' means any solid or liquid waste as defined in Article 1(4) of Council Directive 91/689/EEC of 12 December 1991 on hazardous waste.[1]

   For the following hazardous wastes, the specific requirements for hazardous waste in this Directive shall not apply:

   (a) combustible liquid wastes including waste oils as defined in Article 1 of Council Directive 75/439/EEC of 16 June 1975 on the disposal of waste oils[2] provided that they meet the following criteria:

      (i) the mass content of polychlorinated aromatic hydrocarbons, e.g. polychlorinated biphenyls (PCB) or pentachlorinated phenol (PCP) amounts to concentrations not higher than those set out in the relevant Community legislation;

      (ii) these wastes are not rendered hazardous by virtue of containing other constituents listed in Annex II to Directive 91/689/EEC in quantities or in concentrations which are inconsistent with the achievement of the objectives set out in Article 4 of Directive 75/442/EEC; and

      (iii) the net calorific value amounts to at least 30 MJ per kilogramme,

   (b) any combustible liquid wastes which cannot cause, in the flue gas directly resulting from their combustion, emissions other than those from gasoil as defined in Article 1(1) of Directive 93/12/EEC[3] or a higher concentration of emissions than those resulting from the combustion of gasoil as so defined;

3. 'mixed municipal waste' means waste from households as well as commercial, industrial and institutional waste, which because of its nature and composition is similar to waste from households, but excluding fractions indicated in the Annex

---

[1] OJ L 377, 31.12.1991, p. 20. Directive as amended by Directive 94/31/EC. (OJ L 168, 2.7.1994, p. 28).

[2] OJ L 194, 25.7.1975, p. 23. Directive as last amended by the Accession Act of 1994.

[3] Council Directive 93/12/EEC of 23 March 1993 relating to the sulphur content of certain liquid fuels (OJ L 74, 27.3.1993, p. 81). Directive as last amended by Directive 1999/32/EC (OJ L 121,11.5.1999, p. 13).

to Decision 94/3/EC[1] under heading 20 01 that are collected separately at source and excluding the other wastes indicated under heading 20 02 of that Annex;

4. 'incineration plant' means any stationary or mobile technical unit and equipment dedicated to the thermal treatment of wastes with or without recovery of the combustion heat generated. This includes the incineration by oxidation of waste as well as other thermal treatment processes such as pyrolysis, gasification or plasma processes in so far as the substances resulting from the treatment are subsequently incinerated.

   This definition covers the site and the entire incineration plant including all incineration lines, waste reception, storage, on site pretreatment facilities, waste-fuel and air-supply systems, boiler, facilities for the treatment of exhaust gases, on-site facilities for treatment or storage of residues and waste water, stack, devices and systems for controlling incineration operations, recording and monitoring incineration conditions;

5. 'co-incineration plant' means any stationary or mobile plant whose main purpose is the generation of energy or production of material products and:
   – which uses wastes as a regular or additional fuel; or
   – in which waste is thermally treated for the purpose of disposal.
   If co-incineration takes place in such a way that the main purpose of the plant is not the generation of energy or production of material products but rather the thermal treatment of waste, the plant shall be regarded as an incineration plant within the meaning of point 4.

   This definition covers the site and the entire plant including all co-incineration lines, waste reception, storage, on site pretreatment facilities, waste-, fuel- and air-supply systems, boiler, facilities for the treatment of exhaust gases, on-site facilities for treatment or storage of residues and waste water, stack devices and systems for controlling incineration operations, recording and monitoring incineration conditions;

6. 'existing incineration or co-incineration plant' means an incineration or co-incineration plant:
   (a) which is in operation and has a permit in accordance with existing Community legislation before 28 December 2002, or,
   (b) which is authorised or registered for incineration or co-incineration and has a permit issued before 28 December 2002 in accordance with existing Community legislation, provided that the plant is put into operation not later than 28 December 2003, or
   (c) which, in the view of the competent authority, is the subject of a full request for a permit, before 28 December 2002, provided that the plant is put into operation not later than 28 December 2004;

---

[1] Commission Decision 94/3/EC of 20 December 1993 establishing a list of wastes pursuant to Article 1a of Council Directive 75/442/EEC on waste (OJ L 5, 7.1.1994, p. 15).

7. 'nominal capacity' means the sum of the incineration capacities of the furnaces of which an incineration plant is composed, as specified by the constructor and confirmed by the operator, with due account being taken, in particular, of the calorific value of the waste, expressed as the quantity of waste incinerated per hour;

8. 'emission' means the direct or indirect release of substances, vibrations, heat or noise from individual or diffuse sources in the plant into the air, water or soil;

9. 'emission limit values' means the mass, expressed in terms of certain specific parameters, concentration and/or level of an emission, which may not be exceeded during one or more periods of time;

10. 'dioxins and furans' means all polychlorinated dibenzo-p-dioxins and dibenzo-furans listed in Annex I;

11. 'operator' means any natural or legal person who operates or controls the plant or, where this is provided for in national legislation, to whom decisive economic power over the technical functioning of the plant has been delegated;

12. 'permit' means a written decision (or several such decisions) delivered by the competent authority granting authorisation to operate a plant, subject to certain conditions which guarantee that the plant complies with all the requirements of this Directive. A permit may cover one or more plants or parts of a plant on the same site operated by the same operator;

13. 'residue' means any liquid or solid material (including bottom ash and slag, fly ash and boiler dust, solid reaction products from gas treatment, sewage sludge from the treatment of waste waters, spent catalysts and spent activated carbon) defined as waste in Article 1(a) of Directive 75/442/EEC, which is generated by the incineration or co-incineration process, the exhaust gas or waste water treatment or other processes within the incineration or co-incineration plant.

Article 4
Application and permit

1. Without prejudice to Article 11 of Directive 75/442/EEC or to Article 3 of Directive 91/689/EEC, no incineration or co-incineration plant shall operate without a permit to carry out these activities.

2. Without prejudice to Directive 96/61/EC, the application for a permit for an incineration or co-incineration plant to the competent authority shall include a description of the measures which are envisaged to guarantee that:

(a) the plant is designed, equipped and will be operated in such a manner that the requirements of this Directive are taking into account the categories of waste to be incinerated;

(b) the heat generated during the incineration and co-incineration process is recovered as far as practicable e.g. through combined heat and power, the generating of process steam or district heating;

(c) the residues will be minimised in their amount and harmfulness and recycled where appropriate;

(d) the disposal of the residues which cannot be prevented, reduced or recycled will be carried out in conformity with national and Community legislation.

3. The permit shall be granted only if the application shows that the proposed measurement techniques for emissions into the air comply with Annex III and, as regards water, comply with Annex III paragraphs 1 and 2.

4. The permit granted by the competent authority for an incineration or co-incineration plant shall, in addition to complying with any applicable requirement laid down in Directives 91/271/EEC, 96/61/EC, 96/62/EC, 76/464/EEC and 1999/31/EC:

(a) list explicitly the categories of waste which may be treated. The list shall use at least the categories of waste set up in the European Waste Catalogue (EWC), if possible, and contain information on the quantity of waste, where appropriate;

(b) include the total waste incinerating or co-incinerating capacity of the plant;

(c) specify the sampling and measurement procedures used to satisfy the obligations imposed for periodic measurements of each air and water pollutants.

5. The permit granted by the competent authority to an incineration or co-incineration plant using hazardous waste shall in addition to paragraph 4:

(a) list the quantities of the different categories of hazardous waste which may be treated;

(b) specify the minimum and maximum mass flows of those hazardous wastes, their lowest and maximum calorific values and their maximum contents of pollutants, e.g. PCB, PCP, chlorine, fluorine, sulphur, heavy metals.

6. Without prejudice to the provisions of the Treaty, Member States may list the categories of waste to be mentioned in the permit which can be co-incinerated in defined categories of co-incineration plants.

7. Without prejudice to Directive 96/61/EC, the competent authority shall periodically reconsider and, where necessary, update permit conditions.

8. Where the operator of an incineration or co-incineration plant for non-hazardous waste is envisaging a change of operation which would involve the incineration or co-incineration of hazardous waste, this shall be regarded as a substantial change within the meaning of Article 2(10)(b) of Directive 96/61/EC and Article 12(2) of that Directive shall apply.

9. If an incineration or co-incineration plant does not comply with the conditions of the permit, in particular with the emission limit values for air and water, the competent authority shall take action to enforce compliance.

Article 5
Delivery and reception of waste

1. The operator of the incineration or co-incineration plant shall take all necessary precautions concerning the delivery and reception of waste in order to prevent or to limit as far as practicable negative effects on the environment, in particular the pollution of air, soil, surface water and groundwater as well as odours and noise, and direct risks to human health. These measures shall meet at least the requirements set out in paragraphs 3 and 4.

2. The operator shall determine the mass of each category of waste, if possible according to the EWC, prior to accepting the waste at the incineration or co-incineration plant.

3. Prior to accepting hazardous waste at the incineration or coincineration plant, the operator shall have available information about the waste for the purpose of verifying, *inter alia*, compliance with the permit requirements specified in Article 4(5). This information shall cover:

(a) all the administrative information on the generating process contained in the documents mentioned in paragraph 4(a);
(b) the physical, and as far as practicable, chemical composition of the waste and all other information necessary to evaluate its suitability for the intended incineration process;
(c) the hazardous characteristics of the waste, the substances with which it cannot be mixed, and the precautions to be taken in handling the waste.

4. Prior to accepting hazardous waste at the incineration or coincineration plant, at least the following reception procedures shall be carried out by the operator:

(a) the checking of those documents required by Directive 91/689/EEC and, where applicable, those required by Council Regulation (EEC) No 259/93 of 1 February 1993 on the supervision, and control of shipments of waste within, into and out of the European Community[1] and by dangerous-goods transport regulations;
(b) the taking of representative samples, unless inappropriate, e.g. for infectious clinical waste, as far as possible before unloading, to verify conformity with the information provided for in paragraph 3 by carrying out controls and to enable the competent authorities to identify the nature of the wastes treated. These samples shall be kept for at least one month after the incineration.

5. The competent authorities may grant exemptions from paragraphs 2, 3 and 4 for industrial plants and undertakings incinerating or co-incinerating only their own waste at the place of generation of the waste provided that the requirements of this Directive are met.

---

[1] OJ L 30, 6.2.1993, p. 1. Regulation as last amended by Commission Regulation (EC) No 2408/98 (OJ L 298, 7.11.1998, p. 19).

Article 6
Operating conditions

1. Incineration plants shall be operated in order to achieve a level of incineration such that the slag and bottom ashes Total Organic Carbon (TOC) content is less than 3% or their loss on ignition is less than 5% of the dry weight of the material. If necessary appropriate techniques of waste pretreatment shall be used.

Incineration plants shall be designed, equipped, built and operated in such a way that the gas resulting from the process is raised, after the last injection of combustion air, in a controlled and homogeneous fashion and even under the most unfavourable conditions, to a temperature of 850°C, as measured near the inner wall or at another representative point of the combustion chamber as authorised by the competent authority, for two seconds. If hazardous wastes with a content of more than 1% of halogenated organic substances, expressed as chlorine, are incinerated, the temperature has to be raised to 1100°C for at least two seconds.

Each line of the incineration plant shall be equipped with at least one auxiliary burner. This burner must be switched on automatically when the temperature of the combustion gases after the last injection of combustion air falls below 850°C or 1100°C as the case may be. It shall also be used during plant start-up and shut-down operations in order to ensure that the temperature of 850°C or 1100°C as the case may be is maintained at all times during these operations and as long as unburned waste is in the combustion chamber.

During start-up and shut-down or when the temperature of the combustion gas falls below 850°C or 1100°C as the case may be, the auxiliary burner shall not be fed with fuels which can cause higher emissions than those resulting from the burning of gasoil as defined in Article 1(1) of Council Directive 75/716/EEC, liquefied gas or natural gas.

2. Co-incineration plants shall be designed, equipped, built and operated in such a way that the gas resulting from the co-incineration of waste is raised in a controlled and homogeneous fashion and even under the most unfavourable conditions, to a temperature of 850°C for two seconds. If hazardous wastes with a content of more than 1 % of halogenated organic substances, expressed as chlorine, are co-incinerated, the temperature has to be raised to 1100°C.

3. Incineration and co-incineration plants shall have and operate an automatic system to prevent waste feed:

(a) at start-up, until the temperature of 850°C or 1100°C as the case may be or the temperature specified according to paragraph 4 has been reached;
(b) whenever the temperature of 850°C or 1100°C as the case may be or the temperature specified according to paragraph 4 is not maintained;
(c) whenever the continuous measurements required by this Directive show that any emission limit value is exceeded due to disturbances or failures of the purification devices.

4. Conditions different from those laid down in paragraph 1 and, as regards the temperature, paragraph 3 and specified in the permit for certain categories of waste or for certain thermal processes may be authorised by the competent authority, provided the requirements of this Directive are met. Member States may lay down rules governing these authorisations. The change of the operational conditions shall not cause more residues or residues with a higher content of organic pollutants compared to those residues which could be expected under the conditions laid down in paragraph 1.

Conditions different from those laid down in paragraph 2 and, as regards the temperature, paragraph 3 and specified in the permit for certain categories of waste or for certain thermal processes may be authorised by the competent authority, provided the requirements of this Directive are met. Member States may lay down rules governing these authorisations. Such authorisation shall be conditional upon at least the provisions for emission limit values set out in Annex V for total organic carbon and CO being complied with.

In the case of co-incineration of their own waste at the place of its production in existing bark boilers within the pulp and paper industry, such authorisation shall be conditional upon at least the provisions for emission limit values set out in Annex V for total organic carbon being complied with.

All operating conditions determined under this paragraph and the results of verifications made shall be communicated by the Member State to the Commission as part of the information provided in accordance with the reporting requirements.

5. Incineration and co-incineration plants shall be designed, equipped, built and operated in such a way as to prevent emissions into the air giving rise to significant ground-level air pollution; in particular, exhaust gases shall be discharged in a controlled fashion and in conformity with relevant Community air quality standards by means of a stack the height of which is calculated in such a way as to safeguard human health and the environment.

6. Any heat generated by the incineration or the co-incineration process shall be recovered as far as practicable.

7. Infectious clinical waste should be placed straight in the furnace, without first being mixed with other categories of waste and without direct handling.

8. The management of the incineration or the co-incineration plant shall be in the hands of a natural person who is competent to manage the plant.

Article 7
Air emission limit values

1. Incineration plants shall be designed, equipped, built and operated in such a way that the emission limit values set out in Annex V are not exceeded in the exhaust gas.

2. Co-incineration plants shall be designed, equipped, built and operated in such a way that the emission limit values determined according to or set out in Annex II are not exceeded in the exhaust gas.

If in a co-incineration plant more than 40% of the resulting heat release comes from hazardous waste, the emission limit values set out in Annex V shall apply.

3. The results of the measurements made to verify compliance with the emission limit values shall be standardised with respect to the conditions laid down in Article 11.

4. In the case of co-incineration of untreated mixed municipal waste, the limit values will be determined according to Annex V, and Annex II will not apply.

5. Without prejudice to the provisions of the Treaty, Member States may set emission limit values for polycyclic aromatic hydrocarbons or other pollutants.

Article 8
Water discharges from the cleaning of exhaust gases

1. Waste water from the cleaning of exhaust gases discharged from an incineration or co-incineration plant shall be subject to a permit granted by the competent authorities.

2. Discharges to the aquatic environment of waste water resulting from the cleaning of exhaust gases shall be limited as far as practicable, at least in accordance with the emission limit values set in Annex IV.

3. Subject to a specific provision in the permit, the waste water from the cleaning of exhaust gases may be discharged to the aquatic environment after separate treatment on condition that:

(a) the requirements of relevant Community, national and local provisions are complied with in the form of emission limit values; and
(b) the mass concentrations of the polluting substances referred to in Annex IV do not exceed the emission limit values laid down therein.

4. The emission limit values shall apply at the point where waste waters from the cleaning of exhaust gases containing the polluting substances referred to in Annex IV are discharged from the incineration or co-incineration plant.

Where the waste water from the cleaning of exhaust gases is treated on site collectively with other on-site sources of waste water, the operator shall take the measurements referred to in Article 11:

(a) on the waste water stream from the exhaust gas cleaning processes prior to its input into the collective waste water treatment plant;
(b) on the other waste water stream or streams prior to its or their input into the collective waste water treatment plant;
(c) at the point of final waste water discharge, after the treatment, from the incineration plant or co-incineration plant.

The operator shall take appropriate mass balance calculations in order to determine the emission levels in the final waste water discharge that can be attributed to the waste water arising from the cleaning of exhaust gases in order to check compliance with the emission limit values set out in Annex IV for the waste water stream from the exhaust gas cleaning process.

Under no circumstances shall dilution of waste water take place for the purpose of complying with the emission limit values set in Annex IV.

5. When waste waters from the cleaning of exhaust gases containing the polluting substances referred to in Annex IV are treated outside the incineration or co-incineration plant at a treatment plant intended only for the treatment of this sort of waste water, the emission limit values of Annex IV are to be applied at the point where the waste waters leave the treatment plant. If this off-site treatment plant is not only dedicated to treat waste water from incineration, the operator shall take the appropriate mass balance calculations, as provided for under paragraph 4(a), (b) and (c), in order to determine the emission levels in the final waste water discharge that can be attributed to the waste water arising from the cleaning of exhaust gases in order to check compliance with the emission limit values set out in Annex IV for the waste water stream from the exhaust gas cleaning process.

Under no circumstances shall dilution of waste water take place for the purpose of complying with the emission limit values set in Annex IV.

6. The permit shall:

(a) establish emission limit values for the polluting substances referred to in Annex IV, in accordance with paragraph 2 and in order to meet the requirements referred to in paragraph 3(a);
(b) set operational control parameters for waste water at least for pH, temperature and flow.

7. Incineration and co-incineration plant sites, including associated storage areas for wastes, shall be designed and in such a way as to prevent the unauthorised and accidental release of any polluting substances into soil, surface water and groundwater in accordance with the provisions provided for in relevant Community legislation. Moreover, storage capacity shall be provided for contaminated rainwater run-off from the incineration or co-incineration plant site or for contaminated water arising from spillage or fire-fighting operations.

The storage capacity shall be adequate to ensure that such waters can be tested and treated before discharge where necessary.

8. Without prejudice to the provisions of the Treaty, Member States may set emission limit values for polycyclic aromatic hydrocarbons or other pollutants.

Article 9
Residues

Residues resulting from the operation of the incineration or coincineration plant shall be minimised in their amount and harmfulness. Residues shall be recycled, where appropriate, directly in the plant or outside in accordance with relevant Community legislation.

Transport and intermediate storage of dry residues in the form of dust, such as boiler dust and dry residues from the treatment of combustion gases, shall take place in such a way as to prevent dispersal in the environment e.g. in closed containers.

Prior to determining the routes for the disposal or recycling of the residues from incineration and co-incineration plants, appropriate tests shall be carried out to establish the physical and chemical characteristics and the polluting potential of the different incineration residues. The analysis shall concern the total soluble fraction and heavy metals soluble fraction.

Article 10
Control and monitoring

1. Measurement equipment shall be installed and techniques used in order to monitor the parameters, conditions and mass concentrations relevant to the incineration or co-incineration process.

2. The measurement requirements shall be laid down in the permit or in the conditions attached to the permit issued by the competent authority.

3. The appropriate installation and the functioning of the automated monitoring equipment for emissions into air and water shall be subject to control and to an annual surveillance test. Calibration has to be done by means of parallel measurements with the reference methods at least every three years.

4. The location of the sampling or measurement points shall be laid down by the competent authority.

5. Periodic measurements of the emissions into the air and water shall be carried out in accordance with Annex III, points 1 and 2.

Article 11
Measurement requirements

1. Member States shall, either by specification in the conditions of the permit or by general binding rules, ensure that paragraphs 2 to 12 and 17, as regards air, and paragraphs 9 and 14 to 17, as regards water, are complied with.

2. The following measurements of air pollutants shall be carried out in accordance with Annex III at the incineration and co-incineration plant:

(a) continuous measurements of the following substances: NOx, provided that emission limit values are set, CO, total dust, TOC, HCl, HF, SO_2;
(b) continuous measurements of the following process operation parameters: temperature near the inner wall or at another representative point of the combustion chamber as authorised by the competent authority, concentration of oxygen, pressure, temperature and water vapour content of the exhaust gas;
(c) at least two measurements per year of heavy metals, dioxins and furans; one measurement at least every three months shall however be carried out for the first 12 months of operation. Member States may fix measurement periods where

they have set emission limit values for polycyclic aromatic hydrocarbons or other pollutants.

3. The residence time as well as the minimum temperature and the oxygen content of the exhaust gases shall be subject to appropriate verification, at least once when the incineration or co-incineration plant is brought into service and under the most unfavourable operating conditions anticipated.

4. The continuous measurement of HF may be omitted if treatment stages for HCl are used which ensure that the emission limit value for HCl is not being exceeded. In this case the emissions of HF shall be subject to periodic measurements as laid down in paragraph 2(c).

5. The continuous measurement of the water vapour content shall not be required if the sampled exhaust gas is dried before the emissions are analysed.

6. Periodic measurements as laid down in paragraph 2(c) of HCl, HF and SO_2 instead of continuous measuring may be authorised in the permit by the competent authority in incineration or co-incineration plants, if the operator can prove that the emissions of those pollutants can under no circumstances be higher than the prescribed emission limit values.

7. The reduction of the frequency of the periodic measurements for heavy metals from twice a year to once every two years and for dioxins and furans from twice a year to once every year may be authorised in the permit by the competent authority provided that the emissions resulting from co-incineration or incineration are below 50% of the emission limit values determined according to Annex II or Annex V respectively and provided that criteria for the requirements to be met, developed in accordance with the procedure laid down in Article 17, are available. These criteria shall at least be based on the provisions of the second subparagraph, points (a) and (d).

Until 1 January 2005 the reduction of the frequency may be authorised even if no such criteria are available provided that:

(a) the waste to be co-incinerated or incinerated consists only of certain sorted combustible fractions of non-hazardous waste not suitable for recycling and presenting certain characteristics, and which is further specified on the basis of the assessment referred to in subparagraph (d);

(b) national quality criteria, which have been reported to the Commission, are available for these wastes;

(c) co-incineration and incineration of these wastes is in line with the relevant waste management plans referred to in Article 7 of Directive 75/442/EEC;

(d) the operator can prove to the competent authority that the emissions are under all circumstances significantly below the emission limit values set out in Annex II or Annex V for heavy metals, dioxins and furans; this assessment shall be based on information on the quality of the waste concerned and measurements of the emissions of the said pollutants;

(e) the quality criteria and the new period for the periodic measurements are specified in the permit; and

(f) all decisions on the frequency of measurements referred to in this paragraph, supplemented with information on the amount and quality of the waste concerned, shall be communicated on a yearly basis to the Commission.

8. The results of the measurements made to verify compliance with the emission limit values shall be standardised at the following conditions and for oxygen according to the formula as referred to in Annex VI:

(a) Temperature 273 K, pressure 101,3 kPa, 11% oxygen, dry gas, in exhaust gas of incineration plants;

(b) Temperature 273 K, pressure 101,3 kPa, 3% oxygen, dry gas, in exhaust gas of incineration of waste oil as defined in Directive 75/439/EEC;

(c) when the wastes are incinerated or co-incinerated in an oxygenenriched atmosphere, the results of the measurements can be standardised at an oxygen content laid down by the competent authority reflecting the special circumstances of the individual case;

(d) in the case of co-incineration, the results of the measurements shall be standardised at a total oxygen content as calculated in Annex II. When the emissions of pollutants are reduced by exhaust gas treatment in an incineration or co-incineration plant treating hazardous waste, the standardisation with respect to the oxygen contents provided for in the first subparagraph shall be done only if the oxygen content measured over the same period as for the pollutant concerned exceeds the relevant standard oxygen content.

9. All measurement results shall be recorded, processed and presented in an appropriate fashion in order to enable the competent authorities to verify compliance with the permitted operating conditions and emission limit values laid down in this Directive in accordance with procedures to be decided upon by those authorities.

10. The emission limit values for air shall be regarded as being complied with if:

(a) – none of the daily average values exceeds any of the emission limit values set out in Annex V(a) or Annex II;

– 97% of the daily average value over the year does not exceed the emission limit value set out in Annex V(e) first indent;

(b) either none of the half-hourly average values exceeds any of the emission limit values set out in Annex V(b), column A or, where relevant, 97% of the half-hourly average values over the year do not exceed any of the emission limit values set out in Annex V(b), column B;

(c) none of the average values over the sample period set out for heavy metals and dioxins and furans exceeds the emission limit values set out in Annex V(c) and (d) or Annex II;

(d) the provisions of Annex V(e), second indent or Annex II, are met.

11. The half-hourly average values and the 10-minute averages shall be determined within the effective operating time (excluding the start-up and shut-off periods if no waste is being incinerated) from the measured values after having subtracted the value of the confidence interval specified in point 3 of Annex III. The daily average values shall be determined from those validated average values.

To obtain a valid daily average value no more than five half-hourly average values in any day shall be discarded due to malfunction or maintenance of the continuous measurement system. No more than ten daily average values per year shall be discarded due to malfunction or maintenance of the continuous measurement system.

12. The average values over the sample period and the average values in the case of periodical measurements of HF, HCl and SO_2 shall be determined in accordance with the requirements of Article 10(2) and (4) and Annex III.

13. The Commission, acting in accordance with the procedure laid down in Article 17, shall decide, as soon as appropriate measurement techniques are available within the Community, the date from which continuous measurements of the air emission limit values for heavy metals, dioxins and furans shall be carried out in accordance with Annex III.

14. The following measurements shall be carried out at the point of waste water discharge:

(a) continuous measurements of the parameters referred to in Article 8(6)(b);
(b) spot sample daily measurements of total suspended solids; Member States may alternatively provide for measurements of a flow proportional representative sample over a period of 24 hours;
(c) at least monthly measurements of a flow proportional representative sample of the discharge over a period of 24 hours of the polluting substances referred to in Article 8(3) with respect to items 2 to 10 in Annex IV;
(d) at least every six months measurements of dioxins and furans; however one measurement at least every three months shall be carried out for the first 12 months of operation. Member States may fix measurement periods where they have set emission limit values for polycyclic aromatic hydrocarbons or other pollutants.

15. The monitoring of the mass of pollutants in the treated waste water shall be done in conformity with Community legislation and laid down in the permit as well as the frequency of the measurements.

16. The emission limit values for water shall be regarded as being complied with if:

(a) for total suspended solids (polluting substance number 1), 95% and 100% of the measured values do not exceed the respective emission limit values as set out in Annex IV;
(b) for heavy metals (polluting substances number 2 to 10) no more than one measurement per year exceeds the emission limit values set out in Annex IV; or, if the

Member State provides for more than 20 samples per year, no more than 5% of these samples exceed the emission limit values set out in Annex IV;

(c) for dioxins and furans (polluting substance 11), the twice-yearly measurements do not exceed the emission limit value set out in Annex IV.

17. Should the measurements taken show that the emission limit values for air or water laid down in this Directive have been exceeded, the competent authorities shall be informed without delay.

Article 12
Access to information and public participation

1. Without prejudice to Council Directive 90/313/EEC[1] and Directive 96/61/EC, applications for new permits for incineration and co-incineration plants shall be made available at one or more locations accessible to the public, such as local authority offices, for an appropriate period to enable it to comment on them before the competent authority reaches a decision. That decision, including at least a copy of the permit, and any subsequent updates, shall also be made available to the public.

2. For incineration or co-incineration plants with a nominal capacity of two tonnes or more per hour and notwithstanding Article 15(2) of Directive 96/61/EC, an annual report to be provided by the operator to the competent authority on the functioning and monitoring of the plant shall be made available to the public. This report shall, as a minimum requirement, give an account of the running of the process and the emissions into air and water compared with the emission standards in this Directive. A list of incineration or co-incineration plants with a nominal capacity of less than two tonnes per hour shall be drawn up by the competent authority and shall be made available to the public.

Article 13
Abnormal operating conditions

1. The competent authority shall lay down in the permit the maximum permissible period of any technically unavoidable stoppages, disturbances, or failures of the purification devices or the measurement devices, during which the concentrations in the discharges into the air and the purified waste water of the regulated substances may exceed the prescribed emission limit values.

2. In the case of a breakdown, the operator shall reduce or close down operations as soon as practicable until normal operations can be restored.

3. Without prejudice to Article 6(3)(c), the incineration plant or co-incineration plant or incineration line shall under no circumstances continue to incinerate waste

---

[1] Council Directive 90/313/EEC of 7 June 1990 on the freedom of access to information on the environment (OJ L 158, 23.6.1990, p. 56). Directive as last amended by the Accession Act of 1994.

for a period of more than four hours uninterrupted where emission limit values are exceeded; moreover, the cumulative duration of operation in such conditions over one year shall be less than 60 hours. The 60-hour duration applies to those lines of the entire plant which are linked to one single flue gas cleaning device.

4. The total dust content of the emissions into the air of an incineration plant shall under no circumstances exceed 150 mg/m^3 expressed as a half-hourly average; moreover the air emission limit values for CO and TOC shall not be exceeded. All other conditions referred to in Article 6 shall be complied with.

Article 14
Review clause

Without prejudice to Directive 96/61/EC, the Commission shall submit a report to the European Parliament and the Council before 31 December 2008 based on experience of the application of this Directive, in particular for new plants, and on the progress achieved in emission control techniques and experience in waste management. Furthermore, the report shall be based on the development of the state of technology, of experience in the operation of the plants, of environmental requirements. This report will include a specific section on the application of Annex II.1.1 and in particular on the economic and technical feasibility for existing cement kilns as referred to in the footnote to Annex II.1.1 of respecting the NOx emission limit value for new cement kilns set out in that Annex. The report shall, as appropriate, be accompanied by proposals for revision of the related provisions of this Directive. However, the Commission shall, if appropriate, propose an amendment for Annex II.3 before the said report, if major waste streams are directed to types of co-incineration plants other than those dealt with in Annex II.1 and II.2.

Article 15
Reporting

The reports on the implementation of this Directive shall be established in accordance with the procedure laid down in Article 5 of Council Directive 91/692/EEC. The first report shall cover at least the first full three-year period after 28 December 2002 and comply with the periods referred to in Article 17 of Directive 94/67/EC and in Article 16(3) of Directive 96/61/EC. To this effect, the Commission shall elaborate the appropriate questionnaire in due time.

Article 16
Future adaptation of the directive

The Commission shall, in accordance with the procedure laid down in Article 17(2), amend Articles 10, 11 and 13 and Annexes I and III in order to adapt them to technical progress or new findings concerning the health benefits of emission reductions.

Article 17
Regulatory committee

1. The Commission shall be assisted by a regulatory committee.

2. Where reference is made to this paragraph, Articles 5 and 7 of Decision 1999/468/EC shall apply, having regard to the provisions of Article 8 thereof.

The period laid down in Article 5(6) of Decision 1999/468/EC shall be set at three months.

3. The committee shall adopt its own rules of procedure.

Article 18
Repeal

The following shall be repealed as from 28 December 2005:

(a) Article 8(1) and the Annex to Directive 75/439/EEC;
(b) Directive 89/369/EEC;
(c) Directive 89/429/EEC;
(d) Directive 94/67/EC.

Article 19
Penalties

The Member States shall determine penalties applicable to breaches of the national provisions adopted pursuant to this Directive. The penalties thus provided for shall be effective, proportionate and dissuasive. The Member States shall notify those provisions to the Commission by 28 December 2002 at the latest and shall notify it without delay of any subsequent amendment affecting them.

Article 20
Transitional provisions

1. Without prejudice to the specific transitional provisions provided for in the Annexes to this Directive, the provisions of this Directive shall apply to existing plants as from 28 December 2005.

2. For new plants, i.e. plants not falling under the definition of 'existing incineration or co-incineration plant' in Article 3(6) or paragraph 3 of this Article, this Directive, instead of the Directives mentioned in Article 18, shall apply as from 28 December 2002.

3. Stationary or mobile plants whose purpose is the generation of energy or production of material products and which are in operation and have a permit in accordance with existing Community legislation where required and which start co-incinerating waste not later than 28 December 2004 are to be regarded as existing co-incineration plants.

Article 21
Implementation

1. Member States shall bring into force the laws, regulations and administrative provisions necessary to comply with this Directive not later than 28 December 2002. They shall forthwith inform the Commission thereof. When Member States adopt those measures, they shall contain a reference to this Directive or be accompanied by such reference on the occasion of their official publication. The methods of making such reference shall be laid down by the Member States.

2. Member States shall communicate to the Commission the text of the provisions of domestic law which they adopt in the field governed by this Directive.

Article 22
Entry into force

This Directive shall enter into force on the day of its publication in the *Official Journal of the European Communities.*

Article 23
Addressees

This Directive is addressed to the Member States.

Annexes

[Omitted]

PART VIII

Dangerous substances

Council Directive 92/3/Euratom of 3 February 1992 on the supervision and control of shipments of radioactive waste between Member States and into and out of the Community

Editorial note

Euratom Directive 92/3 applies to shipments of radioactive waste between Member States and into and out of the EC whenever the quantities and concentrations exceed the levels set by Euratom Directive 80/836 (Article 1(1)). The Directive distinguishes between shipments: between Member States; into and out of the EC; and reshipment operations. For each, transport operations must comply with EC and national provisions and international agreements (Article 3). Shipments between Member States must be authorised by the countries of origin, destination and transit (Articles 4, 6, 7). Applications may govern more than one shipment over a period of up to three years (Article 5). Imports into the EC from third countries must be authorised by the destination Member State (Article 10(1)), and rules are set forth governing the situation where an EC State is a transit State (Article 10(2)). Exports out of the EC are prohibited to the Antarctic region, to a Party to the Fourth ACP–EEC Convention which is not a Member State of the EC (unless the waste is being returned after reprocessing) or to a country which does not have the technical, legal or administrative resources to manage radioactive waste safely (Articles 11(1)–(2), 14). Radioactive waste exports to third countries require notification and authorisation (Article 12). In reshipment operations, sealed sources containing non-fissile material are not governed by the Directive (Article 13). Special rules govern processing, reprocessing and subsequent return (Article 14), and return if non-completion or non-compliance has occurred (Article 15).

Source: OJ L 35 12.02.1992 p. 24

Council Directive 92/3/Euratom of 3 February 1992 on the supervision and control of shipments of radioactive waste between Member States and into and out of the Community

The Council of the European Communities,

Having regard to the Treaty establishing the European Atomic Energy Community, and in particular Articles 31 and 32 thereof,

Having regard to the proposal from the Commission,[1] drawn up after obtaining the opinion of a group of persons appointed by the Scientific and Technical Committee from among scientific experts in the Member States,

Having regard to the opinion of the European Parliament,[2]

Having regard to the opinion of the Economic and Social Committee,[3]

Whereas on 2 February 1959 the Council adopted Directives laying down the basic standards for the protection of the health of workers and the general public against the dangers arising from ionizing radiation,[4] as amended by Directive 80/836/Euratom[5] and Directive 84/467/Euratom;[6]

Whereas, pursuant to Article 2 of Directive 80/836/Euratom, these basic safety standards apply *inter alia* to the transport of natural and artificial radioactive substances;

Whereas, pursuant to Article 3 of Directive 80/836/Euratom, each Member State must make compulsory the reporting of activities which involve a hazard arising from ionizing radiation; whereas, in the light of possible dangers and other relevant considerations these activities are subject to prior authorization in cases decided upon by each Member State;

Whereas Member States have consequently set up systems within their territories in order to meet the requirements of Article 3 of Directive 80/836/Euratom laying down basic standards in accordance with Article 30 of the Euratom Treaty; whereas, therefore, by means of the internal controls that Member States apply on the basis of national rules consistent with existing Community and any relevant international requirements, Member States continue to ensure a comparable level of protection within their territories;

Whereas the protection of the health of workers and the general public requires that shipments of radioactive waste between Member States and into and out of the Community be subject to a system of prior authorization; whereas this requirement is in line with the Community's policy of subsidiarity;

Whereas the European Parliament resolution of 6 July 1988 on the findings of the Committee of Inquiry into the Handling and Transport of Nuclear Materials[7] calls *inter alia,* for comprehensive Community rules to make transfrontier movements of nuclear waste subject to a system of strict controls and authorizations from their point of origin to their point of storage;

Whereas Council Directive 84/631/EEC of 6 December 1984 on the supervision and control within the European Community of the transfrontier shipment of hazardous waste[8] does not apply to radioactive waste;

---

[1] OJ No C 210, 23. 8. 1990, p. 7.   [2] OJ No C 267, 14. 10. 1991, p. 210.
[3] OJ No C 168, 10. 7. 1990, p. 18.   [4] OJ No 11, 20. 2. 1959, p. 221/59.
[5] OJ No L 246, 17. 9. 1980, p. 1.   [6] OJ No L 265, 5. 10. 1984, p. 4.
[7] OJ No C 235, 12. 9. 1988, p. 70.
[8] OJ No L 326, 13. 12. 1984, p. 31. Directive as last amended by Directive 86/279/EEC (OJ No L 181, 4. 7. 1986, p. 13).

Whereas by Decision No 90/170/EEC[1] the Council has decided that the Community should be Party to the Basel Convention on the control of transboundary movements of hazardous wastes and their disposal of 22 March 1989; whereas that Convention does not apply to radioactive waste;

Whereas all the Member States have subscribed to the International Atomic Energy Agency (IAEA) code of good practice on the international transboundary movement of radioactive waste;

Whereas the management of radioactive waste necessitates supervision and control including a compulsory and common notification procedure for shipments of such waste;

Whereas measures ensuring *post-factum* control of shipments are necessary;

Whereas the competent authorities of the Member States of destination of radioactive waste should be able to raise objections to shipments of radioactive waste;

Whereas it is also desirable for the competent authorities of the Member State of origin and of the Member State(s) of transit to be able, subject to certain criteria, to lay down conditions in respect of the shipment of radioactive waste on their territory;

Whereas, to protect human health and the environment against dangers arising from such waste, account must be taken of risks occurring outside the Community; whereas, therefore, in the case of radioactive waste entering and/or leaving the Community, the third country of destination or origin and any third country or countries of transit must be consulted and informed and must have given their consent;

Whereas the Fourth ACP-EEC Convention signed at Lomé on 15 December 1989 contains specific provisions governing the export of radioactive waste from the Community to non-member States party to that Convention;

Whereas radioactive waste may contain nuclear materials as defined by Commission Regulation (Euratom) No 3227/76 of 19 October 1976 concerning the application of the provisions on Euratom safeguards[2] and the transport of such substances must be subjected to the International Convention on the physical protection of nuclear materials (IAEA, 1980),

Has adopted this Directive:

Title I

Scope

Article 1

1. This Directive shall apply to shipments of radioactive waste between Member States and into and out of the Community whenever the quantities and concentration exceed the levels laid down in Articles 4(a) and (b) of Directive 80/836/Euratom.

2. Specific provisions concerning reshipment of such waste are set out in Title IV.

---

[1] OJ No L 92, 7. 4. 1990, p. 52.
[2] OJ No L 363, 31. 12. 1976, p. 1. Regulation as amended by Regulation (Euratom) No 220/90 (OJ No L 22, 27. 1. 1990, p. 56).

Article 2

For the purpose of this Directive:

- 'radioactive waste' means any material which contains or is contaminated by radio-nuclides and for which no use is foreseen,
- 'shipment' means transport operations from the place of origin to the place of destination, including loading and unloading, of radioactive waste,
- the 'holder' of radioactive waste means any natural or legal person who, before carrying out a shipment, has the legal responsibility for such materials and intends to carry out shipment to a consignee,
- the 'consignee' of radioactive waste means any natural or legal person to whom such material is shipped,
- 'place of origin' and 'place of destination' mean places situated in two different countries, either Member States of the Community or third countries, accordingly called 'country of origin' and 'country of destination',
- 'competent authorities' means any authority which, under the law or regulations of the countries of origin, transit or destination, are empowered to implement the system of supervision and control defined in Titles I to IV inclusive; these competent authorities shall be designated in accordance with Article 17,
- 'sealed source' has the meaning given to it in Directive 80/836/Euratom.

Article 3

The transport operations necessary for shipment shall comply with Community and national provisions and with international agreements on the transport of radioactive material.

Title II
Shipments between Member States

Article 4

A holder of radioactive waste who intends to carry out a shipment of such waste or to arrange for such a shipment to be carried out shall submit an application for authorization to the competent authorities of the country of origin. These competent authorities shall send such applications for approval to the competent authorities of the country of destination and of the country or countries of transit, if any.

For this purpose they shall use the standard document referred to in Article 20.

The sending of that document shall in no way affect the subsequent decision referred to in Article 7.

Article 5

1. Any application may be sent in respect of more than one shipment, provided that:

- the radioactive waste to which it relates essentially has the same physical, chemical and radioactive characteristics, and
- the shipments are to be made from the same holder to the same consignee and involve the same competent authorities, and
- where shipments involve third countries, such transit is via the same frontier post of entry to and/or exit from the Community and via the same frontier post of the third country or countries concerned, unless otherwise agreed between the competent authorities concerned.

2. The authorization shall be valid for a period of not more than three years.

Article 6

1. Not later than two months after receipt of the duly completed application, the competent authorities of the country of destination and of any country of transit shall notify the competent authorities of the country of origin of their acceptance or of the conditions which they consider necessary or of their refusal to grant approval.

For this purpose they shall use the standard document referred to in Article 20.

2. Any conditions required by the competent authorities of the Member States, whether they are the country of transit or of destination, may not be more stringent than those laid down for similar shipments within those States and must comply with existing international agreements.

Reasons shall be given for any refusal to grant approval, or the attaching of conditions to approval, in accordance with Article 3.

3. However, the competent authorities of the country of destination or of any country of transit may request a further period of not more than one month in addition to the period referred to in paragraph 1 to make their position known.

4. If upon expiry of the periods referred to in paragraph 1 and, if appropriate, paragraph 3, no reply has been received from the competent authorities of the country of destination and/or the intended countries of transit, those countries shall be deemed to have given their approval for the shipment requested, unless they have informed the Commission, in accordance with Article 17, that they do not accept this automatic approval procedure in general.

Article 7

If all the approvals necessary for shipment have been granted, the competent authorities of the Member State of origin shall be entitled to authorize the holder of the radioactive waste to ship it and inform the competent authorities of the country of destination and of the country or countries of transit, if any.

For that purpose, they shall use the standard document referred to in Article 20. Any additional requirements for such shipments shall be attached to this document.

This authorization shall not in any way affect the responsibility of the holder, the transporter, the owner, the consignee or any other natural or legal person involved in the shipment.

Article 8

Without prejudice to any other accompanying documents required under other relevant legal provisions, the documents referred to in Articles 4 and 6 shall accompany each shipment falling under the scope of this Directive, including the cases of approval of more than one transfer referred to in Article 5.

Where shipments are made by rail, these documents shall be available to the competent authorities of all the countries concerned.

Article 9

1. Within 15 days of receipt, the consignee of the radioactive waste shall send the competent authorities of its Member State an acknowledgement of receipt, using the standard document referred to in Article 20.

2. The competent authorities of the country of destination shall send copies of the acknowledgement to the other countries involved in the operation. The competent authorities of the country of origin shall send a copy of the acknowledgement to the original holder.

Title III
Imports into and exports out of the Community

Article 10

1. Where waste falling within the scope of this Directive is to enter the Community from a third country and the country of destination is a Member State, the consignee shall submit an application for authorization to the competent authorities of that Member State using the standard document referred to in Article 20. The consignee shall act as the holder and the competent authorities of the country of destination shall act as if they were the competent authorities of the country of origin referred to in Title II in respect of the country or countries of transit.

2. Where waste falling within the scope of this Directive is to enter the Community from a third country and the country of destination is not a Member State, then the Member State in whose territory the waste is first to enter the Community shall be deemed to be the country of origin for the purposes of that shipment.

3. With regard to shipments falling within paragraph 1, the intended consignee of the shipment within the Community, and with regard to shipments falling within paragraph 2, the person within the Member State in whose territory the waste is first to enter the Community who has responsibility for managing the shipment within that Member State shall inform his competent authorities in order to initiate the appropriate procedures.

Article 11

The competent authorities of Member States shall not authorize shipments:

1. either to:
   (a) a destination south of latitude 60° south;
   (b) a State party to the Fourth ACP-EEC Convention which is not a member of the Community, taking account, however, of Article 14;
2. or to a third country which, in the opinion of the competent authorities of the country of origin, in accordance with the criteria referred to in Article 20, does not have the technical, legal or administrative resources to manage the radioactive waste safely.

Article 12

1. Where radioactive waste is to be exported from the Community to a third country, the competent authorities of the Member State of origin shall contact the authorities of the country of destination regarding such a shipment.

2. If all the conditions for shipment are fulfilled, the competent authorities of Member State of origin shall authorize the holder of radioactive waste to ship it and shall inform the authorities of the country of destination about this shipment.

3. This authorization shall not in any way affect the responsibility of the holder, the transporter, the owner, the consignee or any other natural or legal person involved in the shipment.

4. For the purpose of the shipment, the standard documents referred to in Article 20 shall be used.

5. The holder of the radioactive waste shall notify the competent authorities of the country of origin that the waste has reached its destination in the third country within two weeks of the date of arrival and shall indicate the last customs post in the Community through which the shipment passed.

6. This notification shall be substantiated by a declaration or certification of the consignee of the radioactive waste stating that the waste has reached its proper destination and indicating the customs post of entry in the third country.

Title IV
Reshipment operations

Article 13

Where a sealed source is returned by its user to the supplier of the source in another country, its shipment shall not fall within the scope of this Directive.

However, this exemption shall not apply to sealed sources containing fissile material.

Article 14

This Directive shall not affect the right of a Member State or an undertaking in the Member State to which waste is to be exported for processing to return the waste after treatment to its country of origin. Nor shall it affect the right of a Member State or an undertaking in that Member State to which irradiated nuclear fuel is to be exported for reprocessing to return to its country of origin waste and/or other products of the reprocessing operation.

Article 15

1. Where a shipment of radioactive waste cannot be completed or if the conditions for shipment are not complied with in accordance with the provisions under Title II, the competent authorities of the Member State of dispatch shall ensure that the radioactive waste in question is taken back by the holder of that waste.

2. In case of shipments of radioactive waste from a third country to a destination within the Community, the competent authorities of the Member State of destination shall ensure that the consignee of that waste negotiates a clause with the holder of the waste established in the third country obliging that holder to take back the waste where a shipment cannot be completed.

Article 16

The Member State or States which approved transit for the initial shipment may not refuse to approve reshipment in the cases referred to:

– in Article 14, if the reshipment concerns the same material after treatment or reprocessing and if all relevant legislation is respected,
– in Article 15, if the reshipment is undertaken on the same conditions and with the same specifications.

Title V
Procedural provisions

Article 17

Member States shall forward to the Commission not later than 1 January 1994 the name(s) and the address(es) of the competent authorities and all necessary information for rapidly communicating with such authorities, as well as their possible non-acceptance of the automatic approval procedure referred to in Article 6(4).

Member States shall regularly forward to the Commission any changes to such data.

The Commission shall communicate this information, and any changes thereto, to all the competent authorities in the Community.

Article 18

Every two years, and for the first time on 31 January 1994, Member States shall forward to the Commission reports on the implementation of this Directive.

They shall supplement these reports by information on the situation with regard to shipments within their respective territories.

On the basis of these reports, the Commission shall prepare a summary report for the European Parliament, the Council and the Economic and Social Committee.

Article 19

The Commission shall be assisted in performing the tasks laid down in Articles 18 and 20 by a Committee of an advisory nature composed of representatives of the Member States and chaired by the representative of the Commission.

The representative of the Commission shall submit to the Committee a draft of the measures to be taken. The Committee shall deliver its opinion on the draft within a time limit which the Chairman may lay down according to the urgency of the matter, if necessary by taking a vote.

The opinion shall be recorded in the minutes; in addition, each Member State shall have the right to ask to have its position recorded in the minutes.

The Commission shall take the utmost account of the opinion delivered by the Committee. It shall inform the Committee of the manner in which its opinion has been taken into account.

Article 20

The procedure laid down in Article 19 shall in particular apply to:

- the preparation and possible updating of the standard document for applications for authorization referred to in Article 4,
- the preparation and possible updating of the standard document for granting approval referred to in Article 6(1),
- the preparation and possible updating of the standard document for acknowledgment of receipt referred to in Article 9(1),
- the establishment of criteria enabling Member States, to evaluate whether requirements for exports of radioactive waste are met, as provided for in Article 11(2),
- the preparation of the summary report referred to in Article 18.

Title VI
Final provisions

Article 21

1. Member States shall bring into force not later than 1 January 1994 the laws, regulations and administrative provisions necessary to comply with this Directive. They shall forthwith inform the Commission thereof.

2. When Member States adopt the measures referred to in paragraph 1, they shall contain a reference to this Directive or shall be accompanied by such reference on the

occasion of their official publication. The methods of making such reference shall be laid down by the Member States.

3. Member States shall communicate to the Commission the main provisions of domestic law which they adopt in the field governed by this Directive.

Article 22

This Directive is addressed to the Member States.

Done at Brussels, 3 February 1992.

Council Regulation (Euratom) No 1493/93 of 8 June 1993 on shipments of radioactive substances between Member States

Editorial note

Council Regulation Euratom/1493/93 of 8 June 1993 on shipments of radioactive substances between Member States establishes a scheme of notification and information exchange in relation to substances whose quantities exceed the levels laid down by Directive 80/836/Euratom and in relation to radioactive wastes as defined by Directive 92/3/Euratom (Article 1(1)). Each Member State is required to implement Article 3 of Directive 80/836/Euratom in respect of each recipient of a shipment of nuclear material from another Member State (Article 1(2)). The Regulation specifies that control procedures for the purpose of radiation protection are to be applied in a non-discriminatory manner (Article 3). A holder of a radioactive substance who intends to send it to another Member State must first obtain a declaration from the consignee in the form of Annexes I and II, indicating that all the provisions of Article 3 of Directive 80/836/Euratom have been complied with (Article 4(1)). The declaration must first go to the competent authority in the destination Member State and then to the holder (Article 4(2)). The Regulation permits the declaration to refer to more than one shipment under certain specified conditions for a maximum period of three years (Article 5). The Regulation requires holders of radioactive substances who have dispatched such substances to provide the competent authority of the destination Member State regularly with the particulars of the shipments (Article 6). The Regulation is without prejudice to any existing national provisions and international agreements on the transport and transit of radioactive material (Article 9) or to Directive 92/3/Euratom (Article 10). It is to cease to apply to radioactive waste on 1 January 1994, the date when Directive 92/3/Euratom enters into force (Article 11(2)).

Source: OJ L 148 19.06.1993 p. 1

Council Regulation (Euratom) No 1493/93 of 8 June 1993 on shipments of radioactive substances between Member States

The Council of the European Communities,
    Having regard to the Treaty establishing the European Atomic Energy Community, and in particular Articles 31 and 32 thereof,

Having regard to the proposal from the Commission,[1] drawn up after obtaining the opinion of a group of persons appointed by the Scientific and Technical Committee from among scientific experts in the Member States,

Having regard to the opinion of the European Parliament,[2]

Having regard to the opinion of the Economic and Social Committee,[3]

Whereas on 2 February 1959 the Council adopted directives laying down the basic standards for the protection of the health of workers and the general public against the dangers arising from ionizing radiation,[4] amended in particular by Directive 80/836/Euratom;[5]

Whereas, pursuant to Article 3 of Directive 80/836/Euratom, each Member State must make compulsory the reporting of activities which involve a hazard arising from ionizing radiation; whereas, in the light of possible dangers and other relevant considerations, these activities are subject to prior authorization in cases decided upon by each Member State;

Whereas Member States have consequently set up systems within their territories in order to meet the requirements of Article 3 of Directive 80/836/Euratom; whereas, therefore, by means of the internal controls that Member States apply on the basis of national rules consistent with existing Community and any relevant international requirements, Member States continue to ensure a comparable level of protection within their territories;

Whereas shipments of radioactive waste between Member States and into and out of the Community are subject to the specific measures laid down by Directive 92/3/Euratom;[6] whereas Member States are required to bring into force not later than 1 January 1994 the laws, regulations and administrative provisions necessary to comply with Directive 92/3/Euratom; whereas each Member State should be responsible for ensuring that its own radioactive waste is properly managed;

Whereas the removal of frontier controls in the Community as from 1 January 1993 has deprived the competent authorities of Member States of information previously received through those controls on shipments of radioactive substances; whereas there is a need for the competent authorities concerned to receive the same level of information as before to continue implementing their controls for radiation protection purposes; whereas a Community system of declaration and provision of information would facilitate the maintenance of radiation protection control; whereas a system of prior declaration is needed for shipments of sealed sources and radioactive waste;

---

[1] OJ No C 347, 31. 12. 1992, p. 17. [2] OJ No 150, 31. 5. 1993, [3] OJ No C 19, 25. 1. 1993, p. 13.

[4] OJ No L 11, 20. 2. 1959, p. 221/59.

[5] OJ No L 246, 17. 9. 1980, p. 1. Directive as amended by Directive 84/467/Euratom (OJ No L 265, 5.10.1984, p. 4).

[6] OJ No L 35, 12. 2. 1992, p. 24.

Whereas special fissile materials as defined by Article 197 of the EAEC Treaty are subject to the provisions of Title II, Chapter VII – Safeguards of that Treaty; whereas the transport of such materials is subject to the obligations of the Member States and the Commission pursuant to the International Convention on the Physical Protection of Nuclear Materials (IAEA.1980);

Whereas this Regulation is without prejudice to provision of information and to controls imposed for reasons other than radiation protection,

Has adopted this Regulation:

Article 1

This Regulation shall apply to shipments, between Member States, of sealed sources and other relevant sources, whenever the quantities and concentrations exceed the levels laid down in Article 4(a) and (b) of Directive 80/836/Euratom. It shall also apply to shipments of radioactive waste, between Member States, as covered by Directive 92/3/ Euratom.2. In the case of nuclear materials, each Member State carries out all necessary controls, within its own territory, in order to ensure that each consignee of such materials, which are the subject of a shipment from another Member State, complies with the national provisions implementing Article 3 of Directive 80/836/Euratom.

Article 2

For the purposes of this Regulation

- shipment means transport operations from the place of origin to the place of destination, including loading and unloading of radioactive substances,
- the holder of radioactive substances means any natural or legal person who, before carrying out a shipment, has the legal responsibility under national law for such materials and intends to carry out shipment to a consignee,
- the cosignee of radioactive substances means any natural or legal person to whom such material is shipped,
- sealed source has the meaning given to it in Directive 80/836/Euratom,
- other relevant source means any radioactive substance not being a sealed source intended for direct or indirect use of the ionizing radiation it emits for medical, veterinary, industrial, commercial, research or agricultural applications,
- radioactive waste has the meaning given to it in Directive 92/3/Euratom,
- nuclear materials means the special fissile materials, the source materials and the ores as defined in Article 197 of the EAEC Treaty,
- competent authorities means any authority responsible in the Member State for the application or administration of this Regulation or of any other authority designated by the Member State,
- activity has the meaning given to it in Directive 80/836/Euratom.

Article 3

Controls of shipments of sealed sources, other relevant sources and radioactive waste between Member States, pursuant to Community or national law, for the purpose of radiation protection shall be performed as part of the control procedures applied in a non-discriminatory manner throughout the territory of the Member State.

Article 4

1. A holder of sealed sources or radioactive waste who intends to carry out a shipment of such sources or waste, or to arrange for such a shipment to be carried out, shall obtain a prior written declaration by the consignee of the radioactive substances to the effect that the consignee has complied, in the Member State of destination, with all applicable provisions implementing Article 3 of Directive 80/836/Euratom and with relevant national requirements for safe storage, use or disposal of that class of source or waste.

The declaration shall be made by means of the standard documents set out in Annexes I and II to this Regulation.

2. The declaration referred to in paragraph 1 shall be sent by the consignee to the competent authority of the Member State to which the shipment is to be made. The competent authority shall confirm with its stamp on the document that it has taken note of the declaration and the declaration shall then be sent by the consignee to the holder.

Article 5

1. The declaration referred to in Article 4 may refer to more than one shipment, provided that:

– the sealed sources or radioactive waste to which it relates have essentially the same physical and chemical characteristics,
– the sealed sources or radioactive waste to which it relates do not exceed the levels of activity set out in the declaration, and
– the shipments are to be made from the same holder to the same consignee and involve the same competent authorities.

2. The declaration shall be valid for a period of not more than three years from the date of stamping by the competent authority as referred to in Article 4(2).

Article 6

A holder of sealed sources, other relevant sources and radioactive waste who has carried out a shipment of such sources or waste, or arranged for such a shipment to be carried out, shall, within 21 days of the end of each calendar quarter, provide the competent authorities in the Member State of destination with the following information in respect of deliveries during the quarter:

– names and addresses of consignees,
– the total activity per radionuclide delivered to each consignee and the number of such deliveries made,
– the highest single quantity of each radionuclide delivered to each consignee,
– the type of substance: sealed source, other relevant source or radioactive waste.

The first such return shall cover the period 1 July to 30 September 1993.

Article 7

The competent authorities of Member States shall cooperate in ensuring the application and enforcement of this Regulation.

Article 8

Member States shall forward to the Commission not later than 1 July 1993 the name(s) and the address(es) of the competent authorities as defined in Article 2 and all necessary information for rapidly communicating with such authorities.

Member States shall forward to the Commission any changes to such data.

The Commission shall communicate this information, and any changes thereto, to all competent authorities in the Community and shall publish it, and any changes thereto, in the Official Journal of the European Communities.

Article 9

Nothing in this Regulation shall effect existing national provisions and international agreements on the transport, including transit, of radioactive material.

Article 10

Nothing in this Regulation shall affect the obligations and rights resulting from Directive 92/3/Euratom.

Article 11

1. The Regulation shall enter into force on the 20th day following its publication in the Official Journal of the European Communities.

2. This Regulation shall cease to apply to radioactive waste on 1 January 1994.

This Regulation shall be binding in its entirety and directly applicable in all Member States. Done at Luxembourg, 8 June 1993.

Annex I
Shipment of sealed sources between the Member States of the European Community

Standard document to be used pursuant to Council Regulation (EEC) No 1493/93
Notice

- The consignee of sealed sources must complete boxes 1 to 5 and send this form to the relevant competent authority in his country.
- The competent authority of the consignee Member State must fill in box 6 and return this form to the consignee.
- The consignee must then send this form to the holder in the forwarding country prior to the shipment of the sealed sources.
- All sections of this form must be completed and boxes ticked, where appropriate.

1. THIS DECLARATION CONCERNS: ONE SHIPMENT (This form is valid until the shipment is completed unless otherwise stated in box 6) expected date of shipment (if available): SEVERAL SHIPMENTS (This form is valid for three years unless otherwise stated in box 6)

2. DESTINATION OF THE SOURCE(S)

Name of consignee:
Person to contact:
Address:
Tel.: Fax:

3. HOLDER OF THE SOURCE(S) IN THE FORWARDING COUNTRY

Name of holder:
Person to contact:
Address:
Tel.: Fax:

4. DESCRIPTION OF THE SOURCE(S) INVOLVED IN THE SHIPMENT(S)

(a) Radionuclide(s):
(b) Maximum activity of individual source (MBq):
(c) Number of sources:
(d) If this (these) sealed source(s) is (are) mounted in (a) machinery/device/equipment, short description of the machinery/device/equipment:
(e) Indicate (if available and requested by the competent authorities):
    - national or international technical standard with which the sealed source(s) complies(y) and certificate number:
    - date of expiry of certification:
    - name of the manufacturer and catalogue reference:

5. DECLARATION OF THE AUTHORIZED OR RESPONSIBLE PERSON

- I, the consignee, hereby certify that the information provided in this form is correct.
- I, the consignee, hereby certify that I am licensed, authorized or otherwise permitted to receive the source(s) described in this form.
- Licence, authorization or other permission number (if applicable) and validity date thereof:
- I, the consignee, hereby certify that I comply with all the relevant national requirements, such as those relating to the safe storage, use or disposal of the source(s) described in this form.
- Name: Signature: Date:

6. CONFIRMATION BY THE COMPETENT AUTHORITY OF THE CONSIGNEE COUNTRY THAT IT HAS TAKEN NOTE OF THIS DECLARATION.

Stamp: Name of the authority:
Address:
Tel.: Fax:
Date:
This declaration is valid until (if applicable):
Please see box 1, page 1, for guidance on the length of time this form is valid.

Annex II
Shipment of radioactive waste between the Member States of the European Community

Standard document to be used pursuant to Council Regulation (Euratom) No 1493/93
Notice

- The consignee of radioactive waste must complete boxes 1 to 6 and send this form to the relevant competent authority of his country.
- The competent authority of the consignee Member State must fill in box 7 and return this form to the consignee.
- The consignee must then send this form to the holder in the forwarding country prior to the shipment of the radioactive waste.
- All sections of this form must be completed and boxes ticked, where appropriate.
- This document will no longer apply from 1 January 1994.

1. THIS DECLARATION CONCERNS: ONE SHIPMENT

expected date of shipment (if available):
SEVERAL SHIPMENTS

2. DESTINATION OF THE RADIOACTIVE WASTE

Name of consignee:
Person to contact:
Address:
Tel.: Fax:

3. HOLDER OF THE RADIOACTIVE WASTE IN THE FORWARDING COUNTRY

Name of holder:
Person to contact:
Address:
Tel.: Fax:

4. NATURE OF THE RADIOACTIVE WASTE

(a) Description of waste:
(b) Origin of the waste: (e.g. medical, research, power production, etc.)
(c) Principal radionuclides:
(d) Maximum alpha activity of the shipment(s) (Bq):
(e) Maximum beta/gamma activity of the shipment(s) (Bq):
(f) Maximum quantity of waste of the shipment(s), volume or mass (m3 or kg):
(g) Number of shipments:

5. PURPOSE OF SHIPMENT
(waste conditioning, storage, disposal, etc.)

6. DECLARATION OF THE AUTHORIZED OR RESPONSIBLE PERSON

– I, the consignee, hereby certify that the information provided in this form is correct.
– I, the consignee, hereby certify that I am licensed, authorized or otherwise permitted to receive the radioactive waste described in this form.
– Licence, authorization or other permission number (if applicable) and validity date thereof:
– I, the consignee, hereby certify that I comply with all the relevant national requirements relating to the safe storage or disposal of the waste described in this form.

Name: Signature: Date:

7. CONFIRMATION BY THE COMPETENT AUTHORITY OF THE CONSIGNEE COUNTRY THAT IT HAS TAKEN NOTE OF THIS DECLARATION

Stamp: Name of the authority:
Address:
Tel.: Fax:
Date:
This declaration is valid until (if applicable):
Please see notice, page 1, for guidance on the length of time this form is valid.

Council Directive 96/82/EC of 9 December 1996 on
the control of major-accident hazards involving
dangerous substances (as amended)

Editorial note

Directive 96/82 of 9 December 1996, as amended, is aimed at the prevention of major
accidents involving hazardous substances and the limitation of their consequences
(Article 1). The Directive applies to establishments where dangerous substances are
present in the quantities it specifies (Article 2(1)). Exclusions to the application of the
Directive are provided in Article 4. The operator of an establishment or installation
subject to the provisions of the Directive is obliged to take all measures necessary to
prevent major accidents and to limit their consequences for man or the environment
and is required to prove to the competent authority that he has taken all the measures
necessary (Article 5). The operator is to send to the competent authority the notifications specified under Article 6. Operators must establish a major-accident prevention
policy and ensure its implementation (Article 7). Operators are to produce a safety
report (Article 9) and establish emergency plans (Article 11). Member States are to
ensure that the objectives of the Directive are taken into account in their land-use policies, through controlling the siting of new establishments, modifications to existing
establishments and new developments such as transport links, locations frequented
by the public and residential areas in the vicinity of existing establishments. In the
long term, such policies should ensure that appropriate distances between hazardous
establishments and residential areas are maintained (Article 12).

Information on safety measures and on the requisite behaviour in case of an accident
shall be supplied regularly to all persons liable to be affected by a major accident
(Article 13). The operator is to supply specific information following the occurrence
of a major accident (Article 14). Where the measures taken by the operator for the
prevention and mitigation of major accidents are seriously deficient, Member States
are to prohibit the use or bringing into use of any establishment, installation or
storage facility (Article 17). Competent authorities in the Member States are to set
up a system of inspections or other measures of control appropriate to the type of
establishment concerned (Article 18). Member States and the Commission are to
exchange information on the experience gained with regard to the prevention of
major accidents and the mitigation of their effects (Article 19). Information received

in the application of the Directive is to be made available to any natural or legal person who so requests, with specific provisions to safeguard confidentiality (Article 20).

Source: OJ L 10 14.01.1997 p. 13. Amended by: Regulation (EC) No 1882/2003 of the European Parliament and of the Council of 29 September 2003 L 284 1 31.10.2003; Directive 2003/105/EC of the European Parliament and of the Council of 16 December 2003 L 345 97 31.12.2003

Council Directive 96/82/EC of 9 December 1996 on the control of major-accident hazards involving dangerous substances (as amended)

The Council of the European Union,

Having regard to the Treaty establishing the European Community, and in particular Article 130s(1) thereof,

Having regard to the proposal from the Commission,[1]

Having regard to the opinion of the Economic and Social Committee,[2]

Acting in accordance with the procedure laid down in Article 189c of the Treaty,[3]

(1) Whereas Council Directive 82/501/EEC of 24 June 1982 on the major-accident hazards of certain industrial activities[4] is concerned with the prevention of major accidents which might result from certain industrial activities and with the limitation of their consequences for man and the environment;

(2) Whereas the objectives and principles of the Community's environment policy, as set out in Article 130r(1) and (2) of the Treaty and detailed in the European Community's action programmes on the environment,[5] aim, in particular, at preserving and protecting the quality of the environment, and protecting human health, through preventive action;

(3) Whereas the Council and the representatives of the Governments of the Member States, meeting within the Council, in their accompanying resolution concerning the fourth Action Programme on the Environment,[6] highlighted the need for more effective implementation of Directive 82/501/EEC and called for a review of the Directive to include, if necessary, a possible widening of its scope and a greater exchange of information on the matter between Member States; whereas the fifth Action Programme, the general approach of which was approved by

---

[1] OJ No C 106, 14. 4. 1994, p. 4 and OJ No C 238, 13. 9. 1995, p. 4.

[2] OJ No C 295, 22. 10. 1994, p. 83.

[3] Opinion of the European Parliament of 16 February 1995 (OJ No C 56, 6. 3. 1995, p. 80), Council common position of 19 March 1996 (OJ No C 120, 24. 4. 1996, p. 20) and Decision of the European Parliament of 15 July 1996 (OJ No C 261, 9. 9. 1996, p. 24).

[4] OJ No L 230, 5. 8. 1982, p. 1. Directive as last amended by Directive 91/692/EEC (OJ No L 377, 31. 12. 1991, p. 48).

[5] OJ No C 112, 20. 12. 1973, p. 1. OJ No C 139, 13. 6. 1977, p. 1. OJ No C 46, 17. 2. 1983, p. 1. OJ No C 70, 18. 3. 1987, p. 1. OJ No C 138, 17. 5. 1993, p. 1.

[6] OJ No C 328, 7. 12. 1987, p. 3.

the Council and the representatives of the Governments of the Member States, meeting within the Council, in their resolution of 1 February 1993,[1] also presses for better risk-and-accident management;

(4) Whereas, in the light of the accidents at Bhopal and Mexico City, which demonstrated the hazard which arises when dangerous sites and dwellings are close together, the Council Resolution of 16 October 1989 called on the Commission to include in Directive 82/501/EEC provisions concerning controls on land-use planning when new installations are authorized and when urban development takes place around existing installations;

(5) Whereas the said Council resolution invited the Commission to work with Member States towards greater mutual understanding and harmonization of national principles and practices regarding safety reports;

(6) Whereas it is desirable to pool the experience gained through different approaches to the control of major-accident hazards; whereas the Commission and the Member States should develop their relations with the relevant international bodies and seek to establish measures equivalent to those set out in this Directive for use in third countries;

(7) Whereas the Convention on the Transboundary Effects of Industrial Accidents of the United Nations Economic Commission for Europe provides for measures regarding the prevention of, preparedness for and response to industrial accidents capable of causing transboundary effects as well as for international cooperation in this field;

(8) Whereas Directive 82/501/EEC constituted a first stage in the harmonization process; whereas the said Directive should be revised and supplemented in order to ensure high levels of protection throughout the Community in a consistent and efficient manner; whereas the present harmonization is limited to the measures which are necessary to put in place a more effective system for preventing major accidents with widespread effects and for limiting their consequences;

(9) Whereas major accidents can have consequences beyond frontiers; whereas the ecological and economic cost of an accident is borne not only by the establishment affected but also by the Member States concerned; whereas it is therefore necessary to take measures ensuring a high level of protection throughout the Community;

(10) Whereas the provisions of this Directive must apply without prejudice to Community provisions as regards health and safety at work;

(11) Whereas use of a list specifying certain installations while excluding others with identical hazards is not an appropriate practice, and may allow potential sources of major accidents to escape regulation; whereas the scope of Directive 82/501/EEC must be altered to make the provisions applicable to

[1] OJ No C 138, 17. 5. 1993.

all establishments where dangerous substances are present in sufficiently large quantities to create a major-accident hazard;

(12) Whereas, with due regard for the Treaty and in compliance with the relevant Community legislation, Member States may retain or adopt appropriate measures for transport-related activities at docks, wharves and marshalling yards, which are excluded from this Directive, in order to ensure a level of safety equivalent to that established by this Directive;

(13) Whereas the transmission of dangerous substances through pipelines also has a potential to produce major accidents; whereas the Commission should, after collecting and evaluating information about existing mechanisms within the Community for regulating such activities and the occurrence of relevant incidents, prepare a communication setting out the case, and most appropriate instrument, for action in this area if necessary;

(14) Whereas, with due regard for the Treaty and in compliance with the relevant Community legislation, Member States may retain or adopt measures on waste land-fill, which do not come within the scope of this Directive;

(15) Whereas analysis of the major accidents reported in the Community indicates that the majority of them are the result of managerial and/or organizational shortcomings; whereas it is therefore necessary to lay down at Community level basic principles for management systems, which must be suitable for preventing and controlling major-accident hazards and limiting the consequences thereof;

(16) Whereas differences in the arrangements for the inspection of establishments by the competent authorities may give rise to differing levels of protection; whereas it is necessary to lay down at Community level the essential requirements with which the systems for inspection established by the Member States must comply;

(17) Whereas, in order to demonstrate that all that is necessary has been done to prevent major accidents, to prepare contingency plans and response measures, the operator should, in the case of establishments where dangerous substances are present in significant quantities, provide the competent authority with information in the form of a safety report containing details of the establishment, the dangerous substances present, the installation or storage facilities, possible major accidents and the management systems available, in order to prevent and reduce the risk of major accidents and to enable the necessary steps to be taken to limit the consequences thereof;

(18) Whereas, in order to reduce the risk of domino effects, where establishments are sited in such a way or so close together as to increase the probability and possibility of major accidents, or aggravate their consequences, there should be provision for the exchange of appropriate information and cooperation on public information;

(19) Whereas, in order to promote access to information on the environment, the public should have access to safety reports produced by operators, and persons

likely to be affected by a major accident should be given information sufficient to inform them of the correct action to be taken in that event;

(20) Whereas, in order to provide against emergencies, in the case of establishments where dangerous substances are present in significant quantities it is necessary to establish external and internal emergency plans and to create systems to ensure those plans are tested and revised as necessary and implemented in the event of a major accident or the likelihood thereof;

(21) Whereas the staff of an establishment must be consulted on the internal emergency plan and the public must be consulted on the external emergency plan;

(22) Whereas, in order to provide greater protection for residential areas, areas of substantial public use and areas of particular natural interest or sensitivity, it is necessary for land-use and/or other relevant policies applied in the Member States to take account of the need, in the long term, to keep a suitable distance between such areas and establishments presenting such hazards and, where existing establishments are concerned, to take account of additional technical measures so that the risk to persons is not increased;

(23) Whereas, in order to ensure that adequate response measures are taken if a major accident occurs, the operator must immediately inform the competent authorities and communicate the information necessary for them to assess the impact of that accident;

(24) Whereas, in order to provide for an information exchange and to prevent future accidents of a similar nature, Member States should forward information to the Commission regarding major accidents occurring in their territory, so that the Commission can analyze the hazards involved, and operate a system for the distribution of information concerning, in particular, major accidents and the lessons learned from them; whereas this information exchange should also cover 'near misses' which Member States regard as being of particular technical interest for preventing major accidents and limiting their consequences,

Has adopted this Directive:

Article 1
Aim

This Directive is aimed at the prevention of major accidents which involve dangerous substances, and the limitation of their consequences for man and the environment, with a view to ensuring high levels of protection throughout the Community in a consistent and effective manner.

Article 2
Scope

1. The Directive shall apply to establishments where dangerous substances are present in quantities equal to or in excess of the quantities listed in Annex I, Parts 1

and 2, column 2, with the exception of Articles 9, 11 and 13 which shall apply to any establishment where dangerous substances are present in quantities equal to or in excess of the quantities listed in Annex I, Parts 1 and 2, column 3.

For the purposes of this Directive, the 'presence of dangerous substances' shall mean the actual or anticipated presence of such substances in the establishment, or the presence of those which it is believed may be generated during loss of control of an industrial chemical process, in quantities equal to or in excess of the thresholds in Parts 1 and 2 of Annex I.

2. The provisions of this Directive shall apply without prejudice to Community provisions concerning the working environment, and, in particular, without prejudice to Council Directive 89/391/EEC of 12 June 1989 on the introduction of measures to encourage improvements in the safety and health of workers at work.[1]

Article 3

Definitions

For the purposes of this Directive:
1. 'establishment' shall mean the whole area under the control of an operator where dangerous substances are present in one or more installations, including common or related infrastructures or activities;
2. 'installation' shall mean a technical unit within an establishment in which dangerous substances are produced, used, handled or stored. It shall include all the equipment, structures, pipework, machinery, tools, private railway sidings, docks, unloading quays serving the installation, jetties, warehouses or similar structures, floating or otherwise, necessary for the operation of the installation;
3. 'operator' shall mean any individual or corporate body who operates or holds an establishment or installation or, if provided for by national legislation, has been given decisive economic power in the technical operation thereof;
4. 'dangerous substance' shall mean a substance, mixture or preparation listed in Annex 1, Part 1, or fulfilling the criteria laid down in Annex 1, Part 2, and present as a raw material, product, by-product, residue or intermediate, including those substances which it is reasonable to suppose may be generated in the event of accident;
5. 'major accident' shall mean an occurrence such as a major emission, fire, or explosion resulting from uncontrolled developments in the course of the operation of any establishment covered by this Directive, and leading to serious danger to human health and/or the environment, immediate or delayed, inside or outside the establishment, and involving one or more dangerous substances;
6. 'hazard' shall mean the intrinsic property of a dangerous substance or physical situation, with a potential for creating damage to human health and/or the environment;

[1] OJ No L 183, 29. 6. 1989, p. 1.

7. 'risk' shall mean the likelihood of a specific effect occurring within a specified period or in specified circumstances;

8. 'storage' shall mean the presence of a quantity of dangerous substances for the purposes of warehousing, depositing in safe custody or keeping in stock.

Article 4
Exclusions

This Directive shall not apply to the following:

(a) military establishments, installations or storage facilities;

(b) hazards created by ionizing radiation;

(c) the transport of dangerous substances and intermediate temporary storage by road, rail, internal waterways, sea or air, outside the establishments covered by this Directive, including loading and unloading and transport to and from another means of transport at docks, wharves or marshalling yards;

(d) the transport of dangerous substances in pipelines, including pumping stations, outside establishments covered by this Directive;

(e) the exploitation (exploration, extraction and processing) of minerals in mines, quarries or by means of boreholes, with the exception of chemical and thermal processing operations and storage related to those operations which involve dangerous substances, as defined in Annex I;

(f) the offshore exploration and exploitation of minerals, including hydrocarbons;

(g) waste land-fill sites, with the exception of operational tailings disposal facilities, including tailing ponds or dams, containing dangerous substances as defined in Annex I, in particular when used in connection with the chemical and thermal processing of minerals.

Article 5
General obligations of the operator

1. Member States shall ensure that the operator is obliged to take all measures necessary to prevent major accidents and to limit their consequences for man and the environment.

2. Member States shall ensure that the operator is required to prove to the competent authority referred to in Article 16, hereinafter referred to as the 'competent authority', at any time, in particular for the purposes of the inspections and controls referred to in Article 18, that he has taken all the measures necessary as specified in this Directive.

Article 6
Notification

1. Member States shall require the operator to send the competent authority a notification within the following time-limits:

- for new establishments, a reasonable period of time prior to the start of construction or operation,
- for existing establishments, one year from the date laid down in Article 24(1),
- for establishments which subsequently fall within the scope of this Directive, within three months after the date on which this Directive applies to the establishment concerned, as laid down in the first subparagraph of Article 2(1).

2. The notification required by paragraph 1 shall contain the following details:

(a) the name or trade name of the operator and the full address of the establishment concerned;
(b) the registered place of business of the operator, with the full address;
(c) the name or position of the person in charge of the establishment, if different from (a);
(d) information sufficient to identify the dangerous substances or category of substances involved;
(e) the quantity and physical form of the dangerous substance or substances involved;
(f) the activity or proposed activity of the installation or storage facility;
(g) the immediate environment of the establishment (elements liable to cause a major accident or to aggravate the consequences thereof).

3. In the case of existing establishments for which the operator has already provided all the information under paragraph 2 to the competent authority under the requirements of national law at the date of entry into force of this Directive, notification under paragraph 1 is not required.

4. In the event of:

- any significant increase in the quantity or significant change in the nature or physical form of the dangerous substance present, as indicated in the notification provided by the operator pursuant to paragraph 2, or any change in the processes employing it, or
- modification of an establishment or an installation which could have significant repercussions on major accident hazards, or
- permanent closure of the installation,

the operator shall immediately inform the competent authority of the change in the situation.

Article 7
Major-accident prevention policy

1. Member States shall require the operator to draw up a document setting out his major-accident prevention policy and to ensure that it is properly implemented. The major-accident prevention policy established by the operator shall be designed to guarantee a high level of protection for man and the environment by appropriate means, structures and management systems.

1a. For establishments which subsequently fall within the scope of this Directive, the document referred to in paragraph 1 shall be drawn up without delay, but at all events within three months after the date on which this Directive applies to the establishment concerned, as laid down in the first subparagraph of Article 2(1).

2. The document must take account of the principles contained in Annex III and be made available to the competent authorities for the purposes of, amongst other things, implementation of Articles 5(2) and 18.

3. This Article shall not apply to the establishments referred to in Article 9.

Article 8
Domino effect

1. Member States shall ensure that the competent authority, using the information received from the operators in compliance with Articles 6 and 9, identifies establishments or groups of establishments where the likelihood and the possibility or consequences of a major accident may be increased because of the location and the proximity of such establishments, and their inventories of dangerous substances.

2. Member States must ensure that in the case of the establishments thus identified: (a) suitable information is exchanged in an appropriate manner to enable these establishments to take account of the nature and extent of the overall hazard of a major accident in their major accident prevention policies, safety management systems, safety reports and internal emergency plans; (b) provision is made for cooperation in informing the public and in supplying information to the authority responsible for the preparation of external emergency plans.

Article 9
Safety report

1. Member States shall require the operator to produce a safety report for the purposes of:

(a) demonstrating that a major-accident prevention policy and a safety management system for implementing it have been put into effect in accordance with the information set out in Annex III;

(b) demonstrating that major-accident hazards have been identified and that the necessary measures have been taken to prevent such accidents and to limit their consequences for man and the environment;

(c) demonstrating that adequate safety and reliability have been incorporated into the design, construction, operation and maintenance of any installation, storage facility, equipment and infrastructure connected with its operation which are linked to major-accident hazards inside the establishment;

(d) demonstrating that internal emergency plans have been drawn up and supplying information to enable the external plan to be drawn up in order to take the necessary measures in the event of a major accident;

(e) providing sufficient information to the competent authorities to enable decisions to be made in terms of the siting of new activities or developments around existing establishments.

2. The safety report shall contain at least the data and information listed in Annex II. It shall name the relevant organizations involved in the drawing up of the report. It shall also contain an updated inventory of the dangerous substances present in the establishment.

Safety reports, or parts of reports, or any other equivalent reports produced in response to other legislation, may be combined to form a single safety report for the purposes of this Article, where such a format obviates the unnecessary duplication of information and the repetition of work by the operator or competent authority, on condition that all the requirements of this Article are complied with.

3. The safety report provided for in paragraph 1 shall be sent to the competent authority within the following time limits:

— for new establishments, a reasonable period of time prior to the start of construction or of operation,
— for existing establishments not previously covered by Directive 82/501/EEC, three years from the date laid down in Article 24(1),
— for other establishments, two years from the date laid down in Article 24(1),
— for establishments which subsequently fall within the scope of this Directive, without delay, but at all events within one year after the date on which this Directive applies to the establishment concerned, as laid down in the first subparagraph of Article 2(1),
— in the case of the periodic reviews provided for in paragraph 5, without delay.

4. Before the operator commences construction or operation, or in the cases referred to in the second, third, fourth and fifth indents of paragraph 3, the competent authority shall within a reasonable period of receipt of the report:

— communicate the conclusions of its examination of the safety report to the operator, if necessary after requesting further information, or
— prohibit the bringing into use, or the continued use, of the establishment concerned, in accordance with the powers and procedures laid down in Article 17.

5. The safety report shall be periodically reviewed and where necessary updated:

— at least every five years,
— at any other time at the initiative of the operator or the request of the competent authority, where justified by new facts or to take account of new technical knowledge about safety matters, for example arising from analysis of accidents or, as far as possible, 'near misses', and of developments in knowledge concerning the assessment of hazards.

6.

(a) Where it is demonstrated to the satisfaction of the competent authority that particular substances present at the establishment, or any part thereof, are in a state incapable of creating a major accident hazard, then the Member State may, in accordance with the criteria referred to in subparagraph (b), limit the information required in safety reports to those matters which are relevant to the prevention of residual major-accident hazards and the limitation of their consequences for man and the environment.

(b) Before this Directive is brought into application, the Commission, acting in accordance with the procedure laid down in Article 16 of Directive 82/501/EEC, shall establish harmonized criteria for the decision by the competent authority that an establishment is in a state incapable of creating a major accident hazard within the meaning of subparagraph (a). Subparagraph (a) shall not be applicable until those criteria have been established.

(c) Member States shall ensure that the competent authority communicates a list of the establishments concerned to the Commission, giving reasons. The Commission shall forward the lists annually to the Committee referred to in Article 22.

(d) The Commission is invited to review by 31 December 2006 in close cooperation with the Member States, the existing 'Guidance on the Preparation of a Safety Report'.

Article 10

Modification of an installation, an establishment or a storage facility

In the event of the modification of an installation, establishment, storage facility, or process or of the nature or quantity of dangerous substances which could have significant repercussions on major-accident hazards, the Member States shall ensure that the operator:

— reviews and where necessary revises the major-accident prevention policy, and the management systems and procedures referred to in Articles 7 and 9,
— reviews, and where necessary revises, the safety report and informs the competent authority referred to in Article 16 of the details of such revision in advance of such modification.

Article 11

Emergency plans

1. Member States shall ensure that, for all establishments to which Article 9 applies:

(a) the operator draws up an internal emergency plan for the measures to be taken inside the establishment,
    — for new establishments, prior to commencing operation,
    — for existing establishments not previously covered by Directive 82/501/EEC, three years from the date laid down in Article 24(1),

  - for other establishments, two years from the date laid down in Article 24(1),
  - for establishments which subsequently fall within the scope of this Directive, without delay, but at all events within one year after the date on which this Directive applies to the establishment concerned, as laid down in the first sub-paragraph of Article 2(1);

(b) the operator supplies to the competent authorities, to enable the latter to draw up external emergency plans, the necessary information within the following periods of time:
  - for new establishments, prior to the start of operation,
  - for existing establishments not previously covered by Directive 82/501/EEC, three years from the date laid down in Article 24(1),
  - for other establishments, two years from the date laid down in Article 24(1),
  - for establishments which subsequently fall within the scope of this Directive, without delay, but at all events within one year after the date on which this Directive applies to the establishment concerned, as laid down in the first sub-paragraph of Article 2(1);

(c) the authorities designated for that purpose by the Member State draw up an external emergency plan for the measures to be taken outside the establishment.

2. The emergency plans must be established with the objectives of:

- containing and controlling incidents so as to minimize the effects, and to limit damage to man, the environment and property,
- implementing the measures necessary to protect man and the environment from the effects of major accidents,
- communicating the necessary information to the public and to the services or authorities concerned in the area,
- providing for the restoration and clean-up of the environment following a major accident.

Emergency plans shall contain the information set out in Annex IV.

3. Without prejudice to the obligations of the competent authorities, Member States shall ensure that the internal emergency plans provided for in this Directive are drawn up in consultation with personnel working inside the establishment, including long-term relevant subcontracted personnel, and that the public is consulted on external emergency plans when they are established or updated.

4. Member States shall ensure that internal and external emergency plans are reviewed, tested, and where necessary revised and updated by the operators and designated authorities at suitable intervals of no longer than three years. The review shall take into account changes occurring in the establishments concerned or within the emergency services concerned, new technical knowledge, and knowledge concerning the response to major accidents.

4a. With regard to external emergency plans, Member States should take into account the need to facilitate enhanced cooperation in civil protection assistance in major emergencies.

5. Member States shall ensure that emergency plans are put into effect without delay by the operator and, if necessary by the competent authority designated for this purpose:

– when a major accident occurs, or
– when an uncontrolled event occurs which by its nature could reasonably be expected to lead to a major accident.

6. The competent authority may decide, giving reasons for its decision, in view of the information contained in the safety report, that the requirement to produce an external emergency plan under paragraph 1 shall not apply.

Article 12
Land-use planning

1. Member States shall ensure that the objectives of preventing major accidents and limiting the consequences of such accidents are taken into account in their land-use policies and/or other relevant policies. They shall pursue those objectives through controls on:

(a) the siting of new establishments,
(b) modifications to existing establishments covered by Article 10,
(c) new developments such as transport links, locations frequented by the public and residential areas in the vicinity of existing establishments, where the siting or developments are such as to increase the risk or consequences of a major accident.

Member States shall ensure that their land-use and/or other relevant policies and the procedures for implementing those policies take account of the need, in the long term, to maintain appropriate distances between establishments covered by this Directive and residential areas, buildings and areas of public use, major transport routes as far as possible, recreational areas and areas of particular natural sensitivity or interest and, in the case of existing establishments, of the need for additional technical measures in accordance with Article 5 so as not to increase the risks to people.

1a. The Commission is invited by 31 December 2006, in close cooperation with the Member States, to draw up guidelines defining a technical database including risk data and risk scenarios, to be used for assessing the compatibility between the establishments covered by this Directive and the areas described in paragraph 1. The definition of this database shall as far as possible take account of the evaluations made by the competent authorities, the information obtained from operators and all other relevant information such as the socioeconomic benefits of development and the mitigating effects of emergency plans.

2. Member States shall ensure that all competent authorities and planning authorities responsible for decisions in this area set up appropriate consultation procedures to facilitate implementation of the policies established under paragraph 1. The procedures shall be designed to ensure that technical advice on the risks arising from the establishment is available, either on a case-by-case or on a generic basis, when decisions are taken.

Article 13
Information on safety measures

1. Member States shall ensure that information on safety measures and on the requisite behaviour in the event of an accident is supplied regularly and in the most appropriate form, without their having to request it, to all persons and all establishments serving the public (such as schools and hospitals) liable to be affected by a major accident originating in an establishment covered by Article 9.

The information shall be reviewed every three years and, where necessary, repeated and updated, at least if there is any modification within the meaning of Article 10. It shall also be made permanently available to the public. The maximum period between the repetition of the information to the public shall, in any case, be no longer than five years.

Such information shall contain, at least, the information listed in Annex V.

2. Member States shall, with respect to the possibility of a major accident with transboundary effects originating in an establishment under Article 9, provide sufficient information to the potentially affected Member States so that all relevant provisions contained in Articles 11, 12 and this Article can be applied, where applicable, by the affected Member State.

3. Where the Member State concerned has decided that an establishment close to the territory of another Member State is incapable of creating a major-accident hazard beyond its boundary for the purposes of Article 11(6) and is not therefore required to produce an external emergency plan under Article 11(1), it shall so inform the other Member State.

4. Member States shall ensure that the safety report is made available to the public. The operator may ask the competent authority not to disclose to the public certain parts of the report, for reasons of industrial, commercial or personal confidentiality, public security or national defence. In such cases, on the approval of the competent authority, the operator shall supply to the authority, and make available to the public, an amended report excluding those matters.

5. Member States shall ensure that the public is able to give its opinion in the following cases:

– planning for new establishments covered by Article 9,
– modifications to existing establishments under Article 10, where such modifications are subject to obligations provided for in this Directive as to planning,
– developments around such existing establishments.

6. In the case of establishments subject to the provisions of Article 9, Member States shall ensure that the inventory of dangerous substances provided for in Article 9(2) is made available to the public subject to the provisions of paragraph 4 of this Article and Article 20.

Article 14
Information to be supplied by the operator following a major accident

1. Member States shall ensure that, as soon as practicable following a major accident, the operator shall be required, using the most appropriate means:

(a) to inform the competent authorities;
(b) to provide them with the following information as soon as it becomes available:
   – the circumstances of the accident,
   – the dangerous substances involved,
   – the data available for assessing the effects of the accident on man and the environment, and
   – the emergency measures taken;
(c) to inform them of the steps envisaged:
   – to alleviate the medium- and long-term effects of the accident,
   – to prevent any recurrence of such an accident;
(d) to update the information provided if further investigation reveals additional facts which alter that information or the conclusions drawn.

2. Member States shall require the competent authority:

(a) to ensure that any urgent, medium- and long-term measures which may prove necessary are taken;
(b) to collect, by inspection, investigation or other appropriate means, the information necessary for a full analysis of the technical, organizational and managerial aspects of the major accident;
(c) to take appropriate action to ensure that the operator takes any necessary remedial measures; and
(d) to make recommendations on future preventive measures.

Article 15
Information to be supplied by the Member States to the Commission

1. For the purpose of prevention and mitigation of major accidents, Member States shall inform the Commission as soon as practicable of major accidents meeting the criteria of Annex VI which have occurred within their territory. They shall provide it with the following details:

(a) the Member State, the name and address of the authority responsible for the report;
(b) the date, time and place of the major accident, including the full name of the operator and the address of the establishment involved;

(c) a brief description of the circumstances of the accident, including the dangerous substances involved, and the immediate effects on man and the environment;

(d) a brief description of the emergency measures taken and of the immediate precautions necessary to prevent recurrence.

2. Member States shall, as soon as the information provided for in Article 14 is collected, inform the Commission of the result of their analysis and recommendations using a report form established and kept under review through the procedure referred to in Article 22. Reporting of this information by Member States may be delayed only to allow for the completion of legal proceedings where such reporting is liable to affect those proceedings.

3. Member States shall inform the Commission of the name and address of any body which might have relevant information on major accidents and which is able to advise the competent authorities of other Member States which have to intervene in the event of such an accident.

Article 16
Competent authority

Without prejudice to the operator's responsibilities, Member States shall set up or appoint the competent authority or authorities responsible for carrying out the duties laid down in this Directive and, if necessary, bodies to assist the competent authority or authorities at technical level.

Article 17
Prohibition of use

1. Member States shall prohibit the use or bringing into use of any establishment, installation or storage facility, or any part thereof where the measures taken by the operator for the prevention and mitigation of major accidents are seriously deficient.

Member States may prohibit the use or bringing into use of any establishment, installation or storage facility, or any part thereof if the operator has not submitted the notification, reports or other information required by this Directive within the specified period.

2. Member States shall ensure that operators may appeal against a prohibition order by a competent authority under paragraph 1 to an appropriate body determined by national law and procedures.

Article 18
Inspections

1. Member States shall ensure that the competent authorities organize a system of inspections, or other measures of control appropriate to the type of establishment concerned. Those inspections or control measures shall not be dependent upon receipt of the safety report or any other report submitted. Such inspections or other control measures shall be sufficient for a planned and systematic examination of the

systems being employed at the establishment, whether of a technical, organizational or managerial nature, so as to ensure in particular:

- that the operator can demonstrate that he has taken appropriate measures, in connection with the various activities involved in the establishment, to prevent major accidents,
- that the operator can demonstrate that he has provided appropriate means for limiting the consequences of major accidents, on site and off site,
- that the data and information contained in the safety report, or any other report submitted, adequately reflects the conditions in the establishment,
- that information has been supplied to the public pursuant to Article 13(1).

2. The system of inspection specified in paragraph 1 shall comply with the following conditions:

(a) there shall be a programme of inspections for all establishments. Unless the competent authority has established a programme of inspections based upon a systematic appraisal of major-accident hazards of the particular establishment concerned, the programme shall entail at least one on-site inspection made by the competent authority every twelve months of each establishment covered by Article 9;
(b) following each inspection, a report shall be prepared by the competent authority;
(c) where necessary, every inspection carried out by the competent authority shall be followed up with the management of the establishment, within a reasonable period following the inspection.

3. The competent authority may require the operator to provide any additional information necessary to allow the authority fully to assess the possibility of a major accident and to determine the scope of possible increased probability and/or aggravation of major accidents, to permit the preparation of an external emergency plan, and to take substances into account which, due to their physical form, particular conditions or location, may require additional consideration.

Article 19
Information system and exchanges

1. Member States and the Commission shall exchange information on the experience acquired with regard to the prevention of major accidents and the limitation of their consequences. This information shall concern, in particular, the functioning of the measures provided for in this Directive.

1a. For establishments covered by this Directive, Member States shall supply the Commission with at least the following information:

(a) the name or trade name of the operator and the full address of the establishment concerned; and
(b) the activity or activities of the establishment.

The Commission shall set up and keep up to date a database containing the information supplied by the Member States. Access to the database shall be reserved to persons authorized by the Commission or the competent authorities of the Member States.

2. The Commission shall set up and keep at the disposal of Member States a register and information system containing, in particular, details of the major accidents which have occurred within the territory of Member States, for the purpose of:

(a) the rapid dissemination of the information supplied by Member States pursuant to Article 15(1) among all competent authorities;
(b) distribution to competent authorities of an analysis of the causes of major accidents and the lessons learned from them;
(c) supply of information to competent authorities on preventive measures;
(d) provision of information on organizations able to provide advice or relevant information on the occurrence, prevention and mitigation of major accidents.

The register and information system shall contain, at least:

(a) the information supplied by Member States in compliance with Article 15(1);
(b) an analysis of the causes of the accidents;
(c) the lessons learned from the accidents;
(d) the preventive measures necessary to prevent a recurrence.

3. Without prejudice to Article 20, access to the register and information system shall be open to government departments of the Member States, industry or trade associations, trade unions, non-governmental organizations in the field of the protection of the environment and other international or research organizations working in the field.

4. Member States shall provide the Commission with a three-yearly report in accordance with the procedure laid down in Council Directive 91/692/EEC of 23 December 1991 standardizing and rationalizing reports on the implementation of certain Directives relating to the environment[1] for establishments covered by Articles 6 and 9. The Commission shall publish a summary of this information every three years.

Article 20
Confidentiality

1. Member States shall ensure, in the interests of transparency, that the competent authorities are required to make information received pursuant to this Directive available to any natural or legal person who so requests.

Information obtained by the competent authorities or the Commission may, where national provisions so require, be kept confidential if it calls into question:

– the confidentiality of the deliberations of the competent authorities and the Commission,

---

[1] OJ No L 377, 31. 12. 1991, p. 48.

- the confidentiality of international relations and national defence,
- public security,
- the confidentiality of preliminary investigation proceedings or of current legal proceedings,
- commercial and industrial secrets, including intellectual property,
- personal data and/or files,
- data supplied by a third party if that party asks for them to be kept confidential.

2. This Directive shall not preclude the conclusion by a Member State of agreements with third countries on the exchange of information to which it is privy at internal level.

Article 21
Terms of reference of the Committee

The measures required to adapt the criteria referred to in Article 9(6)(b) and Annexes II to VI to technical progress and to draw up the report form referred to in Article 15(2) shall be adopted in accordance with the procedure laid down in Article 22.

Article 22
Committee

1. The Commission shall be assisted by a committee.

2. Where reference is made to this Article, Articles 5 and 7 of Decision 1999/468/EC[1] shall apply, having regard to the provisions of Article 8 thereof.

The period laid down in Article 5(6) of Decision 1999/468/EC shall be set at three months.

3. The Committee shall adopt its rules of procedure.

Article 23
Repeal of Directive 82/501/EEC

1. Directive 82/501/EEC shall be repealed 24 months after the entry into force of this Directive.

2. Notifications, emergency plans and information for the public presented or drawn up pursuant to Directive 82/501/EEC shall remain in force until such time as they are replaced under the corresponding provisions of this Directive.

Article 24
Implementation

1. Member States shall bring into force the laws, regulations and administrative provisions necessary to comply with this Directive not later than 24 months after its entry into force. They shall forthwith inform the Commission thereof. When Member

---

[1] Council Decision 1999/468/EC of 28 June 1999 laying down the procedures for the exercise of implementing powers conferred on the Commission (OJ L 184, 17.7.1999, p. 23).

States adopt these measures, they shall contain a reference to this Directive or shall be accompanied by such reference on the occasion of their official publication. The methods of making such reference shall be laid down by Member States.

2. Member States shall communicate to the Commission the main provisions of domestic law which they adopt in the field governed by this Directive.

Article 25
Entry into force

This Directive shall enter into force on the 20th day following that of its publication in the *Official Journal of the European Communities.*

Article 26

This Directive is addressed to the Member States.

List of Annexes

Annex I – Application of the Directive

Annex II – Minimum data and information to be considered in the safety report specified in Article 9

Annex III – Principles referred to in Article 7 and information referred to in Article 9 on the management system and the organization of the establishment with a view to the prevention of major accidents

Annex IV – Data and information to be included in the emergency plans specified under Article

Annex V – Items of information to be communicated to the public as provided for in Article 13(1)

Annex VI – Criteria for the notification of an accident to the Commission as provided for in Article 15(1)

Annex I
Application of the Directive

Introduction

1. This Annex applies to the presence of dangerous substances at any establishment within the meaning of Article 3 of this Directive and determines the application of the relevant Articles thereof.

2. Mixtures and preparations shall be treated in the same way as pure substances provided they remain within concentration limits set according to their properties under the relevant Directives given in Part 2, Note 1, or their latest adaptation to technical progress, unless a percentage composition or other description is specifically given.

3. The qualifying quantities set out below relate to each establishment.

4. The quantities to be considered for the application of the relevant Articles are the maximum quantities which are present or are likely to be present at any one time. Dangerous substances present at an establishment only in quantities equal to or

less than 2% of the relevant qualifying quantity shall be ignored for the purposes of calculating the total quantity present if their location within an establishment is such that it cannot act as an initiator of a major accident elsewhere on the site.

5. The rules given in Part 2, Note 4 governing the addition of dangerous substances, or categories of dangerous substances, shall apply where appropriate.

6. For the purposes of this Directive, a gas is any substance that has an absolute vapour pressure equal to or greater than 101,3 kPa at a temperature of 20°C.

7. For the purposes of this Directive, a liquid is any substance that is not defined as gas and that is not in the solid state at a temperature of 20°C and at a standard pressure of 101,2 kPa.

Part 1 & Part 2
[Omitted]

Annex II
Minimum data and information to be considered in the safety Report specified in Article 9

I. *Information on the management system and on the organization of the establishment with a view to major accident prevention*
This information shall contain the elements given in Annex III.

II. *Presentation of the environment of the establishment*
A. description of the site and its environment including the geographical location, meterological, geological, hydrographic conditions and, if necessary, its history;
B. identification of installations and other activities of the establishment which could present a major-accident hazard;
C. description of areas where a major accident may occur.

III. *Description of the installation*
A. description of the main activities and products of the parts of the establishment which are important from the point of view of safety, sources of major-accident risks and conditions under which such a major accident could happen, together with a description of proposed preventive measures;
B. description of processes, in particular the operating methods;
C. description of dangerous substances:
    1. inventory of dangerous substances including:
        – the identification of dangerous substances: chemical name, CAS number, name according to IUPAC nomenclature,
        – the maximum quantity of dangerous substances present or likely to be present;
    2. physical, chemical, toxicological characteristics and indication of the hazards, both immediate and delayed for man and the environment;
    3. physical and chemical behaviour under normal conditions of use or under foreseeable accidental conditions.

IV. *Identification and accidental risks analysis and prevention methods*
A.   detailed description of the possible major-accident scenarios and their probability or the conditions under which they occur including a summary of the events which may play a role in triggering each of these scenarios, the causes being internal or external to the installation;
B.   assessment of the extent and severity of the consequences of identified major accidents; major accidents including maps, images or, as appropriate, equivalent descriptions, showing areas which are liable to be affected by such accidents arising from the establishment, subject to the provisions of Articles 13(4) and 20;
C.   description of technical parameters and equipment used for the safety of installations.

V. *Measures of protection and intervention to limit the consequences of an accident*
A.   description of the equipment installed in the plant to limit the consequences of major accidents;
B.   organization of alert and intervention;
C.   description of mobilizable resources, internal or external;
D.   summary of elements described in A, B, and C above necessary for drawing up the internal emergency plan prepared in compliance with Article 11.

Annex III
Principles referred to in Article 7 and information referred to in Article 9 on the management system and the organization of the Establishment with a view to the prevention of major accidents

For the purpose of implementing the operator's major-accident prevention policy and safety management system account shall be taken of the following elements. The requirements laid down in the document referred to in Article 7 should be proportionate to the major-accident hazards presented by the establishment:

(a) the major accident prevention policy should be established in writing and should include the operator's overall aims and principles of action with respect to the control of major-accident hazards;
(b) the safety management system should include the part of the general management system which includes the organizational structure, responsibilities, practices, procedures, processes and resources for determining and implementing the major-accident prevention policy;
(c) the following issues shall be addressed by the safety management system:
     (i) organization and personnel – the roles and responsibilities of personnel involved in the management of major hazards at all levels in the organization. The identification of training needs of such personnel and the provision of the

training so identified. The involvement of employees and of subcontracted personnel working in the establishment;

(ii) identification and evaluation of major hazards – adoption and implementation of procedures for systematically identifying major hazards arising from normal and abnormal operation and the assessment of their likelihood and severity;

(iii) operational control – adoption and implementation of procedures and instructions for safe operation, including maintenance, of plant, processes, equipment and temporary stoppages;

(iv) management of change – adoption and implementation of procedures for planning modifications to, or the design of new installations, processes or storage facilities;

(v) planning for emergencies – adoption and implementation of procedures to identify foreseeable emergencies by systematic analysis, to prepare, test and review emergency plans to respond to such emergencies and to provide specific training for the staff concerned. Such training shall be given to all personnel working in the establishment, including relevant subcontracted personnel;

(vi) monitoring performance – adoption and implementation of procedures for the ongoing assessment of compliance with the objectives set by the operator's major-accident prevention policy and safety management system, and the mechanisms for investigation and taking corrective action in case of non-compliance. The procedures should cover the operator's system for reporting major accidents of near misses, particularly those involving failure of protective measures, and their investigation and follow-up on the basis of lessons learnt;

(vii) audit and review – adoption and implementation of procedures for periodic systematic assessment of the major-accident prevention policy and the effectiveness and suitability of the safety management system; the documented review of performance of the policy and safety management system and its updating by senior management.

Annex IV
Data and information to be included in the emergency plans specified under Article 11

1. *Internal emergency plans*

(a) Names or positions of persons authorized to set emergency procedures in motion and the person in charge of and coordinating the on-site mitigatory action.

(b) Name or position of the person with responsibility for liaising with the authority responsible for the external emergency plan.

(c) For foreseeable conditions or events which could be significant in bringing about a major accident, a description of the action which should be taken to control the conditions or events and to limit their consequences, including a description of the safety equipment and the resources available.

(d) Arrangements for limiting the risks to persons on site including how warnings are to be given and the actions persons are expected to take on receipt of a warning.

(e) Arrangements for providing early warning of the incident to the authority responsible for setting the external emergency plan in motion, the type of information which should be contained in an initial warning and the arrangements for the provision of more detailed information as it becomes available.

(f) Arrangements for training staff in the duties they will be expected to perform, and where necessary coordinating this with off-site emergency services.

(g) Arrangements for providing assistance with off-site mitigatory action.

2. *External emergency plans*

(a) Names or positions of persons authorized to set emergency procedures in motion and of persons authorized to take charge of and coordinate offsite action.

(b) Arrangements for receiving early warning of incidents, and alert and callout procedures.

(c) Arrangements for coordinating resources necessary to implement the external emergency plan.

(d) Arrangements for providing assistance with on-site mitigatory action.

(e) Arrangements for off-site mitigatory action.

(f) Arrangements for providing the public with specific information relating to the accident and the behaviour which it should adopt.

(g) Arrangements for the provision of information to the emergency services of other Member States in the event of a major accident with possible transboundary consequences.

Annex V
Items of information to be communicated to the public as provided for in Article 13(1)

1. Name of operator and address of the establishment.
2. Identification, by position held, of the person giving the information.
3. Confirmation that the establishment is subject to the regulations and/or administrative provisions implementing this Directive and that the notification referred to in Article 6(3), or the safety report referred to in Article 9(1) has been submitted to the competent authority.
4. An explanation in simple terms of the activity or activities undertaken at the establishment.
5. The common names or, in the case of dangerous substances covered by Part 2 of Annex I, the generic names or the general danger classification of the substances and preparations involved at the establishment which could give rise to a major accident, with an indication of their principal dangerous characteristics.

6. General information relating to the nature of the major-accident hazards, including their potential effects on the population and the environment.

7. Adequate information on how the population concerned will be warned and kept informed in the event of a major accident.

8. Adequate information on the actions the population concerned should take, and on the behaviour they should adopt, in the event of a major accident.

9. Confirmation that the operator is required to make adequate arrangements on site, in particular liaison with the emergency services, to deal with major accidents and to minimize their effects.

10. A reference to the external emergency plan drawn up to cope with any offsite effects from an accident. This should include advice to cooperate with any instructions or requests from the emergency services at the time of an accident.

11. Details of where further relevant information can be obtained, subject to the requirements of confidentiality laid down in national legislation.

Annex VI
Criteria for the notification of an accident to the Commission as provided for in Article 15(1)

I. Any accident covered by paragraph 1 or having at least one of the consequences described in paragraphs 2, 3, 4 and 5 must be notified to the Commission.

1. *Substances involved*

Any fire or explosion or accidental discharge of a dangerous substance involving, a quantity of at least 5% of the qualifying quantity laid down in column 3 of Annex I.

2. *Injury to persons and damage to real estate*

An accident directly involving a dangerous substance and giving rise to one of the following events:

- a death,
- six persons injured within the establishment and hospitalized for at least 24 hours,
- one person outside the establishment hospitalized for at least 24 hours,
- dwelling(s) outside the establishment damaged and unusable as a result of the accident,
- the evacuation or confinement of persons for more than 2 hours (persons × hours): the value is at least 500,
- the interruption of drinking water, electricity, gas or telephone services for more than 2 hours (persons × hours): the value is at least 1 000.

3. *Immediate damage to the environment*

- *permanent or long-term damage to terrestrial habitats:*
- 0,5 ha or more of a habitat of environmental or conservation importance protected by legislation,

– 10 or more hectares of more widespread habitat, including agricultural land,

– *significant or long-term damage to freshwater and marine habitats**
– 10 km or more of river or canal,
– 1 ha or more of a lake or pond,
– 2 ha or more of delta,
– 2 ha or more of a coastline or open sea,

– *significant damage to an aquifer or underground water***
– 1 ha or more.

4. *Damage to property*

– damage to property in the establishment: at least ECU 2 million,
– damage to property outside the establishment: at least ECU 0,5 million.

5. *Cross-border damage*
Any accident directly involving a dangerous substance giving rise to effects outside the territory of the Member State concerned.

   II. Accidents or 'near misses' which Member States regard as being of particular technical interest for preventing major accidents and limiting their consequences and which do not meet the quantitative criteria above should be notified to the Commission.

---

[*] In assessing damage, reference could be made where appropriate to Directives 75/440/EEC, 76/464/EEC and Directives adopted for its application in relation to certain substances, namely, Directives 76/160/EEC, 78/659/EEC, 79/923/EEC, or to the Lethal Concentration (LC) for 50% of the species representative of the environment affected as defined by Directive 92/32/EEC for the criterion 'dangerous for the environment'.
[**] In assessing damage, reference could be made where appropriate to Directives 75/440/EEC, 76/464/EEC and Directives adopted for its application in relation to certain substances, namely, Directives 76/160/EEC, 78/659/EEC, 79/923/EEC, or to the Lethal Concentration (LC) for 50% of the species representative of the environment affected as defined by Directive 92/32/EEC for the criterion 'dangerous for the environment'.

Directive 2001/18/EC of the European Parliament and of the Council of 12 March 2001 on the deliberate release into the environment of genetically modified organisms and repealing Council Directive 90/220/EEC

Editorial note

Directive 2001/18 is a so-called 'horizontal' Directive and aims to regulate, in accordance with the precautionary principle and to protect human health and the environment, the carrying out of deliberate release into the environment of genetically modified organisms (GMOs) for any purpose other than placing on the market within the Community and the placing on the market of genetically modified organisms as or in products within the Community (Article 1). Specific exemptions to the application of the Directive are found in Article 3. All appropriate measures shall be taken by Member States to avoid adverse effects on human health and the environment which might arise from the deliberate release or placing on the market of GMOs. GMOs can only be released or placed on the market according to the provisions of the Directive (Article 4).

Part B of the Directive regulates the deliberate release of GMOs for any purpose other than for placing on the market (Articles 5–11). Before undertaking deliberate release, any person must submit a notification to the competent authority of the Member State within whose territory the release is to take place. The notification should include, *inter alia*, a full risk assessment. The competent authority is to respond to the notifier within ninety days and either consent to or deny the proposed release (Article 6). In specific circumstances, a differentiated procedure for the release of certain GMOs is provided (Article 7). In case of modifications, unintended changes or the emergence of new information, the notifier must immediately take measures to protect human health and the environment and notify the competent authority (Article 8). The public are to be consulted and informed of the proposed deliberate release (Article 9). Notifiers shall send reports to the competent authority, after the completion of the release, in respect of any risk to human health and the environment (Article 10).

Part C of the Directive regulates the placing on the market of GMOs as or in products (Articles 12–24). Before a GMO or a combination of GMOs as or in products is placed on the market, a notification is to be submitted to the competent authority of the Member State where such a GMO is to be placed on the market for the first time. The notification must include, *inter alia*, a full risk assessment (Article 13). On receiving the notification, the competent authority is to examine it for compliance with the Directive and prepare, within ninety days after receipt of the notification, an assessment report and send it to the notifier. In case of a report indicating that the GMO(s) in question should be placed on the market, the Commission should be sent a copy of the report, which it will forward to the competent authorities of the Member States (Article 14). In the absence of any reasoned objection from a Member State or from the Commission, the competent authority of the Member State shall give its consent for placing the GMO(s) on the market throughout the Community (Article 15 and Article 19). The consent is to be given for a maximum of ten years. If the Member State to which the application was notified decides to refuse the placing on the market of the GMO(s), the request is rejected (Article 15). In case of objection by the Commission or by the authority of another Member State, the procedure outline in Article 18 is to be followed. Following the placing on the market, the notifier is to ensure monitoring and reporting as specified by Article 20. Article 21 specifies the labelling requirements for GMO(s) placed on the market. Member States may not prohibit the circulation of GMO(s) complying with the Directive (Article 22). However, a Member State may provisionally restrict or prohibit the use and/or sale of a GMO as or in a product if, as a result of new information, it has detailed grounds for considering the GMO a risk to human health or the environment. It shall inform the Commission and the other Member States (Article 23). The public are to be informed and may make comments on applications (Article 24). Confidentiality is protected (Article 25). Member States are to determine the penalties to be imposed for breaches of national legislation implementing the Directive (Article 33).

Further rules on the Community's regime on GMOs are to be found, *inter alia*, in the following instruments (not reproduced): Regulation (EC) No 1829/2003 of the European Parliament and of the Council of 22 September 2003 on genetically modified food and feed (*Official Journal L 268, 18/10/2003 p. 1*); Commission Regulation (EC) No 641/2004 of 6 April 2004 on detailed rules for the implementation of Regulation (EC) No 1829/2003 of the European Parliament and of the Council as regards the application for the authorisation of new genetically modified food and feed, the notification of existing products and adventitious or technically unavoidable presence of genetically modified material which has benefited from a favourable risk evaluation (*Official Journal L 102, 07/04/2004 p. 14*); Regulation (EC) No 1830/2003 of the European Parliament and of the Council of 22 September 2003 concerning the traceability and labelling of genetically modified organisms and the traceability of food and feed products produced from genetically modified organisms and amending Directive 2001/18/EC (*Official Journal L 268, 18/10/2003 p. 24*); Council Directive 90/219/EEC of 23 April 1990 on the contained use of genetically modified micro-organisms (*Official Journal L 117, 08/05/1990 pp. 0001–0014*) and Council Directive

98/81/EC of 26 October 1998 amending Directive 90/219/EEC on the contained use of genetically modified micro-organisms (*Official Journal L 330, 05/12/1998 p. 13*); Regulation (EC) No 1946/2003 of the European Parliament and of the Council of 15 July 2003 on transboundary movements of genetically modified organisms (*Official Journal L 287, 05.11.2003 p. 1*).

Source: OJ L 106 17.04.2001 p. 1. Amended by: Commission Decision 2002/623/EC of 24 July 2002 L 200 22 30.07.2002. Regulation (EC) No 1829/2003 of the European Parliament and of the Council of 22 September 2003 L 268 1 18.10.2003. Regulation (EC) No 1830/2003 of the European Parliament and of the Council of 22 September 2003 L 268 24 18.10.2003

Directive 2001/18/EC of the European Parliament and of the Council of 12 March 2001 on the deliberate release into the environment of genetically modified organisms and repealing Council Directive 90/220/EEC

The European Parliament and the Council of the European Union,

Having regard to the Treaty establishing the European Community, and in particular Article 95 thereof,

Having regard to the proposal from the Commission,[1]

Having regard to the opinion of the Economic and Social Committee,[2]

Acting in accordance with the procedure laid down in Article 251 of the Treaty, in the light of the joint text approved by the Conciliation Committee on 20 December 2000,[3]

Whereas:

(1) The Report of the Commission on the Review of Council Directive 90/220/EEC of 23 April 1990 on the deliberate release into the environment of genetically modified organisms,[4] adopted on 10 December 1996, identified a number of areas where improvement is needed.

(2) There is a need for clarification of the scope of Directive 90/220/EEC and of the definitions therein.

(3) Directive 90/220/EEC has been amended. Now that new amendments are being made to the Directive, it is desirable, for reasons of clarity and rationalisation, that the provisions in question should be recast.

---

[1] OJ C 139, 4.5.1998, p. 1.   [2] OJ C 407, 28.12.1998, p. 1.

[3] Opinion of the European Parliament of 11 February 1999 (OJ C 150, 28.5.1999, p. 363), Council Common Position of 9 December 1999 (OJ C 64, 6.3.2000, p. 1) and Decision of the European Parliament of 12 April 2000 (OJ C 40, 7.2.2001, p. 123). Decision of the European Parliament of 14 February 2001 and Decision of the Council of 15 February 2001.

[4] OJ L 117, 8.5.1990, p. 15. Directive as last amended by Commission Directive 97/35/EC (OJ L 169, 27.6.1997, p. 72).

(4) Living organisms, whether released into the environment in large or small amounts for experimental purposes or as commercial products, may reproduce in the environment and cross national frontiers thereby affecting other Member States. The effects of such releases on the environment may be irreversible.

(5) The protection of human health and the environment requires that due attention be given to controlling risks from the deliberate release into the environment of genetically modified organisms (GMOs).

(6) Under the Treaty, action by the Community relating to the environment should be based on the principle that preventive action should be taken.

(7) It is necessary to approximate the laws of the Member States concerning the deliberate release into the environment of GMOs and to ensure the safe development of industrial products utilising GMOs.

(8) The precautionary principle has been taken into account in the drafting of this Directive and must be taken into account when implementing it.

(9) Respect for ethical principles recognised in a Member State is particularly important. Member States may take into consideration ethical aspects when GMOs are deliberately released or placed on the market as or in products.

(10) For a comprehensive and transparent legislative framework, it is necessary to ensure that the public is consulted by either the Commission or the Member States during the preparation of measures and that they are informed of the measures taken during the implementation of this Directive.

(11) Placing on the market also covers import. Products containing and/or consisting of GMOs covered by this Directive cannot be imported into the Community if they do not comply with its provisions.

(12) Making GMOs available to be imported or handled in bulk quantities, such as agricultural commodities, should be regarded as placing on the market for the purpose of this Directive.

(13) The content of this Directive duly takes into account international experience in this field and international trade commitments and should respect the requirements of the Cartagena Protocol on Biosafety to the Convention on Biological Diversity. As soon as possible, and in any case before July 2001, the Commission should, in the context of the ratification of the Protocol, submit the appropriate proposals for its implementation.

(14) Guidance on the implementation of provisions related to the definition of the placing on the market in this Directive should be provided by the Regulatory Committee.

(15) When defining 'genetically modified organism' for the purpose of this Directive, human beings should not be considered as organisms.

(16) The provisions of this Directive should be without prejudice to national legislation in the field of environmental liability, while Community legislation in this field needs to be complemented by rules covering liability for different types of environmental damage in all areas of the European Union. To this end the Commission has undertaken to bring forward a legislative proposal on

environmental liability before the end of 2001, which will also cover damage from GMOs.

(17) This Directive should not apply to organisms obtained through certain techniques of genetic modification which have conventionally been used in a number of applications and have a long safety record.

(18) It is necessary to establish harmonised procedures and criteria for the case-by-case evaluation of the potential risks arising from the deliberate release of GMOs into the environment.

(19) A case-by-case environmental risk assessment should always be carried out prior to a release. It should also take due account of potential cumulative long-term effects associated with the interaction with other GMOs and the environment.

(20) It is necessary to establish a common methodology to carry out the environmental risk assessment based on independent scientific advice. It is also necessary to establish common objectives for the monitoring of GMOs after their deliberate release or placing on the market as or in products. Monitoring of potential cumulative long-term effects should be considered as a compulsory part of the monitoring plan.

(21) Member States and the Commission should ensure that systematic and independent research on the potential risks involved in the deliberate release or the placing on the market of GMOs is conducted. The necessary resources should be secured for such research by Member States and the Community in accordance with their budgetary procedures and independent researchers should be given access to all relevant material, while respecting intellectual property rights.

(22) The issue of antibiotic-resistance genes should be taken into particular consideration when conducting the risk assessment of GMOs containing such genes.

(23) The deliberate release of GMOs at the research stage is in most cases a necessary step in the development of new products derived from, or containing GMOs.

(24) The introduction of GMOs into the environment should be carried out according to the 'step by step' principle. This means that the containment of GMOs is reduced and the scale of release increased gradually, step by step, but only if evaluation of the earlier steps in terms of protection of human health and the environment indicates that the next step can be taken.

(25) No GMOs, as or in products, intended for deliberate release are to be considered for placing on the market without first having been subjected to satisfactory field testing at the research and development stage in ecosystems which could be affected by their use.

(26) The implementation of this Directive should be carried out in close liaison with the implementation of other relevant instruments such as Council Directive 91/414/EEC of 15 July 1991 concerning the placing of plant protection products on the market.[1] In this context the competent authorities concerned with the

---

[1] OJ L 230, 19.8.1991, p. 1. Directive as last amended by Commission Directive 1999/80/EC (OJ L 210, 10.8.1999, p. 13).

implementation of this Directive and of those instruments, within the Commission and at national level, should coordinate their action as far as possible.

(27) Concerning the environmental risk assessment for part C, risk management, labelling, monitoring, information to the public and safeguard clause, this Directive should be a point of reference for GMOs as or in products authorised by other Community legislation which should therefore provide for a specific environmental risk assessment, to be carried out in accordance with the principles set out in Annex II and on the basis of information specified in Annex III without prejudice to additional requirements laid down by the Community legislation mentioned above, and for requirements as regards risk management, labelling, monitoring as appropriate, information to the public and safeguard clause at least equivalent to that laid down in this Directive. To this end it is necessary to provide for cooperation with the Community and Member State bodies mentioned in this Directive for the purpose of its implementation.

(28) It is necessary to establish a Community authorisation procedure for the placing on the market of GMOs, as or in products, where the intended use of the product involves the deliberate release of the organism(s) into the environment.

(29) The Commission is invited to conduct a study which should contain an assessment of various options to improve further the consistency and efficiency of this framework, particularly focusing on a centralised authorisation procedure for the placing on the market of GMOs within the Community.

(30) For sectoral legislation, monitoring requirements may have to be adapted to the product concerned.

(31) Part C of this Directive does not apply to products covered by Council Regulation (EEC) No 2309/93 of 22 July 1993 laying down Community procedures for the authorisation and supervision of medicinal products for human and veterinary use and establishing a European Agency for the Evaluation of Medicinal Products,[1] provided that it includes an environmental risk assessment equivalent to that provided for by this Directive.

(32) Any person, before undertaking a deliberate release into the environment of a GMO, or the placing on the market of GMOs, as or in products, where the intended use of the product involves its deliberate release into the environment, is to submit a notification to the national competent authority.

(33) That notification should contain a technical dossier of information including a full environmental risk assessment, appropriate safety and emergency response, and, in the case of products, precise instructions and conditions for use, and proposed labelling and packaging.

(34) After notification, no deliberate release of GMOs should be carried out unless the consent of the competent authority has been obtained.

---

[1] OJ L 214, 24.8.1993, p. 1. Regulation as amended by Commission Regulation (EC) No 649/98 (OJ L 88, 24.3.1998, p. 7).

(35) A notifier should be able to withdraw his dossier at any stage of the administrative procedures laid down in this Directive. The administrative procedure should come to an end when a dossier is withdrawn.

(36) Rejection of a notification for the placing on the market of a GMO as or in products by a competent authority should be without prejudice to the submission of a notification of the same GMO to another competent authority.

(37) An agreement should be reached at the end of the mediation period when no objections remain.

(38) Rejection of a notification following a confirmed negative assessment report should be without prejudice to future decisions based on the notification of the same GMO to another competent authority.

(39) In the interests of the smooth functioning of this Directive, Member States should be able to avail themselves of the various provisions for the exchange of information and experience before having recourse to the safeguard clause in this Directive.

(40) In order to ensure that the presence of GMOs in products containing, or consisting of, genetically modified organisms is appropriately identified, the words 'This product contains genetically modified organisms' should appear clearly either on a label or in an accompanying document.

(41) A system should be designed using the appropriate committee procedure, for the assignment of a unique identifier to GMOs, taking into account relevant developments in international fora.

(42) It is necessary to ensure traceability at all stages of the placing on the market of GMOs as or in products authorised under part C of this Directive.

(43) It is necessary to introduce into this Directive an obligation to implement a monitoring plan in order to trace and identify any direct or indirect, immediate, delayed or unforeseen effects on human health or the environment of GMOs as or in products after they have been placed on the market.

(44) Member States should be able, in accordance with the Treaty, to take further measures for monitoring and inspection, for example by official services, of the GMOs as or in products placed on the market.

(45) Means should be sought for providing possibilities for facilitating the control of GMOs or their retrieval in the event of severe risk.

(46) Comments by the public should be taken into consideration in the drafts of measures submitted to the Regulatory Committee.

(47) The competent authority should give its consent only after it has been satisfied that the release will be safe for human health and the environment.

(48) The administrative procedure for granting consents for the placing on the market of GMOs as or in products should be made more efficient and more transparent and first-time consent should be granted for a fixed period.

(49) For products for which consent has been granted for a fixed period a streamlined procedure should apply as regards the renewal of consent.

(50) The existing consents granted under Directive 90/220/EEC have to be renewed in order to avoid disparities between consents granted under that Directive and those pursuant to this Directive and in order to take full account of the conditions of consent under this Directive.

(51) Such renewal requires a transitional period during which existing consents granted under Directive 90/220/EEC remain unaffected.

(52) When a consent is renewed, it should be possible to revise all the conditions of the original consent, including those related to monitoring and the time limitation of the consent.

(53) Provision should be made for consultation of the relevant Scientific Committee(s) established by Commission Decision 97/579/ EC[1] on matters which are likely to have an impact on human health and/or the environment.

(54) The system of exchange of information contained in notifications, established under Directive 90/220/EEC, has been useful and should be continued.

(55) It is important to follow closely the development and use of GMOs.

(56) When a product containing a GMO, as or in products, is placed on the market, and where such a product has been properly authorised under this Directive, a Member State may not prohibit, restrict or impede the placing on the market of GMOs, as or in products, which comply with the requirements of this Directive. A safeguard procedure should be provided in case of risk to human health or the environment.

(57) The Commission's European Group on Ethics in Science and New Technologies should be consulted with a view to obtaining advice on ethical issues of a general nature regarding the deliberate release or placing on the market of GMOs. Such consultations should be without prejudice to the competence of Member States as regards ethical issues.

(58) Member States should be able to consult any committee they have established with a view to obtaining advice on the ethical implications of biotechnology.

(59) The measures necessary for the implementation of this Directive are to be adopted in accordance with Council Decision 1999/468/EC of 28 June 1999 laying down the procedures for the exercise of implementing powers conferred on the Commission.[2]

(60) The information exchange set up under this Directive should also cover experience gained with the consideration of ethical aspects.

(61) In order to increase the effective implementation of the provisions adopted under this Directive it is appropriate to provide

(62) A report to be issued every three years by the Commission, taking into account the information provided by Member States, should contain a separate chapter

---

[1] OJ L 237, 28.8.1997, p. 18.
[2] OJ L 184, 17.7.1999, p. 23. For penalties to be applied by Member States, including in the event of release or placing on the market contrary to the provisions of this Directive, particularly as a result of negligence.

regarding the socioeconomic advantages and disadvantages of each category of GMOs authorised for placing on the market, which will take due account of the interest of farmers and consumers.

(63) The regulatory framework for biotechnology should be reviewed so as to identify the feasibility of improving further the consistency and efficiency of that framework. Procedures may need to be adapted so as to optimise efficiency, and all options which might achieve that should be considered,

Have adopted this Directive:

Part A
General provisions

Article 1
Objective

In accordance with the precautionary principle, the objective of this Directive is to approximate the laws, regulations and administrative provisions of the Member States and to protect human health and the environment when:

– carrying out the deliberate release into the environment of genetically modified organisms for any other purposes than placing on the market within the Community,
– placing on the market genetically modified organisms as or in products within the Community.

Article 2
Definitions

For the purposes of this Directive:

(1) 'organism' means any biological entity capable of replication or of transferring genetic material;
(2) 'genetically modified organism (GMO)' means an organism, with the exception of human beings, in which the genetic material has been altered in a way that does not occur naturally by mating and/ or natural recombination; Within the terms of this definition:
   (a) genetic modification occurs at least through the use of the techniques listed in Annex I A, part 1;
   (b) the techniques listed in Annex I A, part 2, are not considered to result in genetic modification;
(3) 'deliberate release' means any intentional introduction into the environment of a GMO or a combination of GMOs for which no specific containment measures are used to limit their contact with and to provide a high level of safety for the general population and the environment;

(4) 'placing on the market' means making available to third parties, whether in return for payment or free of charge; The following operations shall not be regarded as placing on the market:
  – making available genetically modified microorganisms for activities regulated under Council Directive 90/219/EEC of 23 April 1990 on the contained use of genetically modified microorganisms[1] including culture collections,
  – making available GMOs other than microorganisms referred to in the first indent, to be used exclusively for activities where appropriate stringent containment measures are used to limit their contact with and to provide a high level of safety for the general population and the environment, the measures should be based on the same principles of containment as laid down in Directive 90/219/EEC,
  – making available GMOs to be used exclusively for deliberate releases complying with the requirements laid down in part B of this Directive;
(5) 'notification' means the submission of the information required under this Directive to the competent authority of a Member State;
(6) 'notifier' means the person submitting the notification;
(7) 'product' means a preparation consisting of, or containing, a GMO or a combination of GMOs, which is placed on the market;
(8) 'environmental risk assessment' means the evaluation of risks to human health and the environment, whether direct or indirect, immediate or delayed, which the deliberate release or the placing on the market of GMOs may pose and carried out in accordance with Annex II.

Article 3

Exemptions

1. This Directive shall not apply to organisms obtained through the techniques of genetic modification listed in Annex I B.

2. This Directive shall not apply to the carriage of genetically modified organisms by rail, road, inland waterway, sea or air.

Article 4

General obligations

1. Member States shall, in accordance with the precautionary principle, ensure that all appropriate measures are taken to avoid adverse effects on human health and the environment which might arise from the deliberate release or the placing on the market of GMOs. GMOs may only be deliberately released or placed on the market in conformity with part B or part C respectively.

---

[1] OJ L 117, 8.5.1990, p. 1. Directive as amended by Directive 98/81/EC (OJ L 330 5.12.1998, p. 13).

2. Any person shall, before submitting a notification under part B or part C, carry out an environmental risk assessment. The information which may be necessary to carry out the environmental risk assessment is laid down in Annex III. Member States and the Commission shall ensure that GMOs which contain genes expressing resistance to antibiotics in use for medical or veterinary treatment are taken into particular consideration when carrying out an environmental risk assessment, with a view to identifying and phasing out antibiotic resistance markers in GMOs which may have adverse effects on human health and the environment. This phasing out shall take place by the 31 December 2004 in the case of GMOs placed on the market according to part C and by 31 December 2008 in the case of GMOs authorised under part B.

3. Member States and where appropriate the Commission shall ensure that potential adverse effects on human health and the environment, which may occur directly or indirectly through gene transfer from GMOs to other organisms, are accurately assessed on a case-by case basis. This assessment shall be conducted in accordance with Annex II taking into account the environmental impact according to the nature of the organism introduced and the receiving environment.

4. Member States shall designate the competent authority or authorities responsible for complying with the requirements of this Directive. The competent authority shall examine notifications under part B and part C for compliance with the requirements of this Directive and whether the assessment provided for in paragraph 2 is appropriate.

5. Member States shall ensure that the competent authority organises inspections and other control measures as appropriate, to ensure compliance with this Directive. In the event of a release of GMO(s) or placing on the market as or in products for which no authorisation was given, the Member State concerned shall ensure that necessary measures are taken to terminate the release or placing on the market, to initiate remedial action if necessary, and to inform its public, the Commission and other Member States.

Part B
Deliberate release of GMOs for any other purpose than for placing on the market

Article 5

1. Articles 6 to 11 shall not apply to medicinal substances and compounds for human use consisting of, or containing, a GMO or combination of GMOs provided that their deliberate release for any purpose other than that of being placed on the market is authorised by Community legislation which provides:

(a) for a specific environmental risk assessment in accordance with Annex II and on the basis of the type of information specified in Annex III without prejudice to additional requirements provided for by the said legislation;
(b) for explicit consent prior to release;

(c) for a monitoring plan in accordance with the relevant parts of Annex III, with a view to detecting the effects of the GMO or GMOs on human health or the environment;

(d) in an appropriate manner for requirements relating to treatment of new items of information, information to the public, information on the results of releases, and exchanges of information at least equivalent to those contained in this Directive and in the measures taken in accordance therewith.

2. Assessment of the risks to the environment presented by such substances and compounds shall be carried out in coordination with the national and Community authorities mentioned in this Directive.

3. Procedures ensuring conformity of the specific environmental risk assessment and equivalence with the provisions of this Directive must be provided for by the said legislation, which must refer to this Directive.

Article 6
Standard authorisation procedure

1. Without prejudice to Article 5, any person must, before undertaking a deliberate release of a GMO or of a combination of GMOs, submit a notification to the competent authority of the Member State within whose territory the release is to take place.

2. The notification referred to in paragraph 1 shall include:

(a) a technical dossier supplying the information specified in Annex III necessary for carrying out the environmental risk assessment of the deliberate release of a GMO or combination of GMOs, in particular:

  (i) general information including information on personnel and training,
  (ii) information relating to the GMO(s),
  (iii) information relating to the conditions of release and the potential receiving environment,
  (iv) information on the interactions between the GMO(s) and the environment,
  (v) a plan for monitoring in accordance with the relevant parts of Annex III in order to identify effects of the GMO(s) on human health or the environment,
  (vi) information on control, remediation methods, waste treatment and emergency response plans,
  (vii) a summary of the dossier;

(b) the environmental risk assessment and the conclusions required in Annex II, section D, together with any bibliographic reference and indications of the methods used.

3. The notifier may refer to data or results from notifications previously submitted by other notifiers, provided that the information, data and results are non confidential or these notifiers have given their agreement in writing, or may submit additional information he considers relevant.

4. The competent authority may accept that releases of the same GMO or of a combination of GMOs on the same site or on different sites for the same purpose and within a defined period may be notified in a single notification.

5. The competent authority shall acknowledge the date of receipt of the notification and, having considered, where appropriate, any observations by other Member States made in accordance with Article 11, shall respond in writing to the notifier within 90 days of receipt of the notification by either:

(a) indicating that it is satisfied that the notification is in compliance with this Directive and that the release may proceed; or
(b) indicating that the release does not fulfil the conditions of this Directive and that notification is therefore rejected.

6. For the purpose of calculating the 90 day period referred to in paragraph 5, no account shall be taken of any periods of time during which the competent authority:

(a) is awaiting further information which it may have requested from the notifier, or
(b) is carrying out a public inquiry or consultation in accordance with Article 9; this public inquiry or consultation shall not prolong the 90 day period referred to in paragraph 5 by more than 30 days.

7. If the competent authority requests new information it must simultaneously give its reasons for so doing.

8. The notifier may proceed with the release only when he has received the written consent of the competent authority, and in conformity with any conditions required in this consent.

9. Member States shall ensure that no material derived from GMOs which are deliberately released in accordance with part B is placed on the market, unless in accordance with part C.

Article 7
Differentiated procedures

1. If sufficient experience has been obtained of releases of certain GMOs in certain ecosystems and the GMOs concerned meet the criteria set out in Annex V, a competent authority may submit to the Commission a reasoned proposal for the application of differentiated procedures to such types of GMOs.

2. Following its own initiative or at the latest 30 days following the receipt of a competent authority's proposal, the Commission shall,

(a) forward the proposal to the competent authorities, which may, within 60 days, present observations and at the same time;
(b) make available the proposal to the public which may, within 60 days, make comments; and

(c) consult the relevant Scientific Committee(s) which may, within 60 days give an opinion.

3. A decision shall be taken on each proposal in accordance with the procedure laid down in Article 30(2). This decision shall establish the minimum amount of technical information from Annex III necessary for evaluating any foreseeable risks from the release, in particular:

(a) information relating to the GMO(s);
(b) information relating to the conditions of release and the potential receiving environment;
(c) information on the interactions between the GMO(s) and the environment;
(d) the environmental risk assessment.

4. This decision shall be taken within 90 days of the date of the Commission's proposal or of receipt of the competent authority's proposal. This 90 day period shall not take into account the period of time during which the Commission is awaiting the observations of competent authorities, the comments of the public or the opinion of Scientific Committees, as provided for in paragraph 2.

5. The decision taken under paragraphs 3 and 4 shall provide that the notifier may proceed with the release only when he has received the written consent of the competent authority. The notifier shall proceed with the release in conformity with any conditions required in this consent.

The decision taken under paragraphs 3 and 4 may provide that releases of a GMO or of a combination of GMOs on the same site or on different sites for the same purpose and within a defined period may be notified in a single notification.

6. Without prejudice to paragraphs 1 to 5, Commission Decision 94/730/EC of 4 November 1994 establishing simplified procedures concerning the deliberate release into the environment of genetically modified plants pursuant to Article 6(5) of Council Directive 90/220/EEC[1] shall continue to apply.

7. Where a Member State decides to make use or not of a procedure established in a decision taken in accordance with paragraphs 3 and 4 for releases of GMOs within its territory, it shall inform the Commission thereof.

Article 8
Handling of modifications and new information

1. In the event of any modification of, or unintended change to, the deliberate release of a GMO or of a combination of GMOs which could have consequences with regard to risks for human health and the environment after the competent authority has given its written consent, or if new information has become available on such risks, either while the notification is being examined by the competent authority of a

---

[1] OJ L 292, 12.11.1994, p. 31.

Member State or after that authority has given its written consent, the notifier shall immediately:

(a) take the measures necessary to protect human health and the environment;
(b) inform the competent authority in advance of any modification or as soon as the unintended change is known or the new information is available;
(c) revise the measures specified in the notification.

2. If information becomes available to the competent authority referred to in paragraph 1 which could have significant consequences with regard to risks for human health and the environment or under the circumstances described in paragraph 1, the competent authority shall evaluate such information and make it available to the public. It may require the notifier to modify the conditions of, suspend or terminate the deliberate release and shall inform the public thereof.

Article 9
Consultation of and information to the public

1. Member States shall, without prejudice to the provisions of Articles 7 and 25, consult the public and, where appropriate, groups on the proposed deliberate release. In doing so, Member States shall lay down arrangements for this consultation, including a reasonable time-period, in order to give the public or groups the opportunity to express an opinion.

2. Without prejudice to the provisions of Article 25:

– Member States shall make available to the public information on all part B releases of GMOs in their territory;
– the Commission shall make available to the public the information contained in the system of exchange of information pursuant to Article 11.

Article 10
Reporting by notifiers on releases

After completion of a release, and thereafter, at any intervals laid down in the consent on the basis of the results of the environmental risk assessment, the notifier shall send to the competent authority the result of the release in respect of any risk to human health or the environment, with, where appropriate, particular reference to any kind of product that the notifier intends to notify at a later stage. The format for the presentation of this result shall be established in accordance with the procedure laid down in Article 30(2).

Article 11
Exchange of information between competent authorities and the Commission

1. The Commission shall set up a system of exchange of the information contained in the notifications. The competent authorities shall send to the Commission, within

30 days of its receipt, a summary of each notification received under Article 6. The format of this summary shall be established and modified if appropriate in accordance with the procedure laid down in Article 30(2).

2. The Commission shall, at the latest 30 days following their receipt, forward these summaries to the other Member States, which may, within 30 days, present observations through the Commission or directly. At its request, a Member State shall be permitted to receive a copy of the full notification from the competent authority of the relevant Member State.

3. The competent authorities shall inform the Commission of the final decisions taken in compliance with Article 6(5), including where relevant the reasons for rejecting a notification, and of the results of the releases received in accordance with Article 10.

4. For the releases of GMOs referred to in Article 7, once a year Member States shall send a list of GMOs which have been released on their territory and a list of notifications that were rejected to the Commission, which shall forward them to the competent authorities of the other Member States.

Part C
Placing on the market of GMOs as or in products

Article 12
Sectoral legislation

1. Articles 13 to 24 shall not apply to any GMO as or in products as far as they are authorised by Community legislation which provides for a specific environmental risk assessment carried out in accordance with the principles set out in Annex II and on the basis of information specified in Annex III without prejudice to additional requirements provided for by the Community legislation mentioned above, and for requirements as regards risk management, labelling, monitoring as appropriate, information to the public and safeguard clause at least equivalent to that laid down in this Directive.

2. As far as Council Regulation (EEC) No 2309/93 is concerned, Articles 13 to 24 of this Directive shall not apply to any GMO as or in products as far as they are authorised by that Regulation provided that a specific environmental risk assessment is carried out in accordance with the principles set out in Annex II to this Directive and on the basis of the type of information specified in Annex III to this Directive without prejudice to other relevant requirements as regards risk assessment, risk management, labelling, monitoring as appropriate, information to the public and safeguard clause provided by Community legislation concerning medicinal products for human and veterinary use.

3. Procedures ensuring that the risk assessment, requirements regarding risk management, labelling, monitoring as appropriate, information to the public and

safeguard clause are equivalent to those laid down in this Directive shall be introduced, in a Regulation of the European Parliament and of the Council. Future sectoral legislation based on the provisions of that Regulation shall make a reference to this Directive. Until the Regulation enters into force, any GMO as or in products as far as they are authorised by other Community legislation shall only be placed on the market after having been accepted for placing on the market in accordance with this Directive.

4. During evaluation of the requests for the placing on the market of the GMOs referred to in paragraph 1, the bodies established by the Community under this Directive and by Member States for the purpose of implementing this Directive shall be consulted.

Article 12a
Transitional measures for adventitious or technically unavoidable presence of genetically modified organisms having benefited from a favourable risk evaluation

1. Placing on the market of traces of a GMO or combination of GMOs in products intended for direct use as food or feed or for processing shall be exempted from Articles 13 to 21 provided that they meet the conditions referred to in Article 47 of Regulation (EC) No 1829/2003 of the European Parliament and of the Council of 22 September 2003 on genetically modified food and feed.[1]

2. This Article shall be applicable for a period of three years after the date of application of Regulation (EC) No 1829/2003.

Article 13
Notification procedure

1. Before a GMO or a combination of GMOs as or in products is placed on the market, a notification shall be submitted to the competent authority of the Member State where such a GMO is to be placed on the market for the first time.

The competent authority shall acknowledge the date of receipt of the notification and immediately forward the summary of the dossier referred to in paragraph 2(h) to the competent authorities of the other Member States and the Commission. The competent authority shall without delay examine whether the notification is in accordance with paragraph 2 and shall, if necessary, ask the notifier for additional information.

When the notification is in accordance with paragraph 2, and at the latest when it sends its assessment report in accordance with Article 14(2), the competent authority shall forward a copy of the notification to the Commission which shall, within 30 days of its receipt, forward it to the competent authorities of the other Member States.

2. The notification shall contain:

(a) the information required in Annexes III and IV. This information shall take into account the diversity of sites of use of the GMO as or in a product and shall include

---

[1] OJ L 268, 18.10.2003, p. 1.

information on data and results obtained from research and developmental releases concerning the impact of the release on human health and the environment;

(b) he environmental risk assessment and the conclusions required in Annex II, section D;

(c) the conditions for the placing on the market of the product, including specific conditions of use and handling;

(d) with reference to Article 15(4), a proposed period for the consent which should not exceed ten years;

(e) a plan for monitoring in accordance with Annex VII, including a proposal for the time-period of the monitoring plan; this time-period may be different from the proposed period for the consent;

(f) a proposal for labelling which shall comply with the requirements laid down in Annex IV. The labelling shall clearly state that a GMO is present. The words 'this product contains genetically modified organisms' shall appear either on a label or in an accompanying document;

(g) a proposal for packaging which shall comprise the requirements laid down in Annex IV;

(h) a summary of the dossier. The format of the summary shall be established in accordance with the procedure laid down in Article 30(2).

If on the basis of the results of any release notified under part B, or on other substantive, reasoned scientific grounds, a notifier considers that the placing on the market and use of a GMO as or in a product do not pose a risk to human health and the environment, he may propose to the competent authority not to provide part or all of the information required in Annex IV, section B.

3. The notifier shall include in this notification information on data or results from releases of the same GMOs or the same combination of GMOs previously or currently notified and/or carried out by the notifier either inside or outside the Community.

4. The notifier may also refer to data or results from notifications previously submitted by other notifiers or submit additional information he considers relevant, provided that the information, data and results are non-confidential or these notifiers have given their agreement in writing.

5. In order for a GMO or combination of GMOs to be used for a purpose different from that already specified in a notification, a separate notification shall be submitted.

6. If new information has become available with regard to the risks of the GMO to human health or the environment, before the written consent is granted, the notifier shall immediately take the measures necessary to protect human health and the environment, and inform the competent authority thereof. In addition, the notifier shall revise the information and conditions specified in the notification.

Article 14
Assessment report

1. On receipt and after acknowledgement of the notification in accordance with Article 13(2), the competent authority shall examine it for compliance with this Directive.

2. Within 90 days after receipt of the notification the competent authority shall:

– prepare an assessment report and send it to the notifier. A subsequent withdrawal by the notifier shall be without prejudice to any further submission of the notification to another competent authority;
– in the case referred to in paragraph 3(a), send its report, together with the information referred to in paragraph 4 and any other information on which it has based its report, to the Commission which shall, within 30 days of its receipt, forward it to the competent authorities of the other Member States.

In the case referred to paragraph 3(b), the competent authority shall send its report, together with the information referred to in paragraph 4 and any other information on which it has based its report, to the Commission no earlier than 15 days after sending the assessment report to the notifier and no later than 105 days after receipt of the notification. The Commission shall, within 30 days of its receipt, forward the report to the competent authorities of the other Member States.

3. The assessment report shall indicate whether:

(a) the GMO(s) in question should be placed on the market and under which conditions; or
(b) the GMO(s) in question should not be placed on the market.

The assessment reports shall be established in accordance with the guidelines laid down in Annex VI.

4. For the purpose of calculating the 90 day period referred to in paragraph 2, any periods of time during which the competent authority is awaiting further information which it may have requested from the notifier shall not be taken into account. The competent authority shall state the reasons in any request for further information.

Article 15
Standard procedure

1. In the cases referred to in Article 14(3), a competent authority or the Commission may ask for further information, make comments or present reasoned objections to the placing on the market of the GMO(s) in question within a period of 60 days from the date of circulation of the assessment report.

Comments or reasoned objections and replies shall be forwarded to the Commission which shall immediately circulate them to all competent authorities.

The competent authorities and the Commission may discuss any outstanding issues with the aim of arriving at an agreement within 105 days from the date of circulation of the assessment report.

Any periods of time during which further information from the notifier is awaited shall not be taken into account for the purpose of calculating the final 45 day period for arriving at an agreement. Reasons shall be stated in any request for further information.

2. In the case referred to in Article 14(3)(b), if the competent authority which prepared the report decides that the GMO(s) should not be placed on the market, the notification shall be rejected. This decision shall state the reasons.

3. If the competent authority which prepared the report decides that the product may be placed on the market, in the absence of any reasoned objection from a Member State or the Commission within 60 days following the date of circulation of the assessment report referred to in Article 14(3)(a) or if outstanding issues are resolved within the 105 day period referred to in paragraph 1, the competent authority which prepared the report shall give consent in writing for placing on the market, shall transmit it to the notifier and shall inform the other Member States and the Commission thereof within 30 days.

4. The consent shall be given for a maximum period of ten years starting from the date on which the consent is issued.

For the purpose of approval of a GMO or a progeny of that GMO intended only for the marketing of their seeds under the relevant Community provisions, the period of the first consent shall end at the latest ten years after the date of the first inclusion of the first plant variety containing the GMO on an official national catalogue of plant varieties in accordance with Council Directives 70/457/EEC[1] and 70/458/EEC.[2] In the case of forest reproductive material, the period of the first consent shall end at the latest ten years after the date of the first inclusion of basic material containing the GMO on an official national register of basic material in accordance with Council Directive 1999/105/EC.[3]

Article 16
Criteria and information for specified GMOs

1. A competent authority, or the Commission on its own initiative, may make a proposal on criteria and information requirements to be met for the notification, by

---

[1] Council Directive 70/457/EEC of 29 September 1970 on the common catalogue of varieties of agricultural plant species (OJ L 225, 12.10.1970, p. 1). Directive as last amended by Directive 98/96/EC (OJ L 25, 1.2.1999, p. 27).

[2] Council Directive 70/458/EEC of 29 September 1970 on the marketing of vegetable seed (OJ L 225, 12.10.1970, p. 7). Directive as last amended by Directive 98/96/EC.

[3] Council Directive 1999/105/EC of 22 December 1999 on the marketing of forest reproductive material (OJ L 11, 15.1.2000, p. 17).

way of derogation from Article 13, for the placing on the market of certain types of GMOs as or in products.

2. These criteria and information requirements as well as any appropriate requirements for a summary shall be adopted, after consultation of the relevant Scientific Committee(s), in accordance with the procedure laid down in Article 30(2). The criteria and the information requirements shall be such as to ensure a high level of safety to human health and the environment and be based on the scientific evidence available on such safety and on the experience gained from the release of comparable GMOs.

The requirements set out in Article 13(2) shall be replaced by those adopted above, and the procedure set out in Article 13(3), (4), (5) and (6) and Articles 14 and 15 shall apply.

3. Before the procedure laid down in Article 30(2) for a decision on criteria and information requirements referred to in paragraph 1 is initiated, the Commission shall make the proposal available to the public. The public may make comments to the Commission within 60 days. The Commission shall forward any such comments, together with an analysis, to the Committee set up pursuant to Article 30.

Article 17
Renewal of consent

1. By way of derogation from Articles 13, 14 and 15, the procedure set out in paragraphs 2 to 9 shall be applied to the renewal of:

(a) consents granted under part C; and
(b) before 17 October 2006 of consents granted under Directive 90/220/EEC for placing on the market of GMOs as or in products before 17 October 2002.

2. At the latest nine months before the expiry of the consent, for the consents referred to in paragraph 1(a), and before 17 October 2006, for the consents referred to in paragraph 1(b), the notifier under this Article shall submit a notification to the competent authority which received the original notification, which shall contain:

(a) a copy of the consent to the placing on the market of the GMOs;
(b) a report on the results of the monitoring which was carried out according to Article 20. In the case of consents referred to in paragraph 1(b), this report shall be submitted when the monitoring was carried out;
(c) any other new information which has become available with regard to the risks of the product to human health and/or the environment; and
(d) as appropriate, a proposal for amending or complementing the conditions of the original consent, *inter alia* the conditions concerning future monitoring and the time limitation of the consent.

The competent authority shall acknowledge the date of receipt of the notification and when the notification is in accordance with this paragraph it shall without delay forward a copy of the notification and its assessment report to the Commission, which shall, within 30 days of their receipt, forward them to the competent authorities of the other Member States. It shall also send its assessment report to the notifier.

3. The assessment report shall indicate whether:

(a) the GMO(s) should remain on the market and under which conditions; or
(b) the GMO(s) should not remain on the market.

4. The other competent authorities or the Commission may ask for further information, make comments, or present reasoned objections within a period of 60 days from the date of circulation of the assessment report.

5. All comments, reasoned objections and replies shall be forwarded to the Commission which shall immediately circulate them to all competent authorities.

6. In the case of paragraph 3(a) and in the absence of any reasoned objection from a Member State or the Commission within 60 days from the date of circulation of the assessment report, the competent authority which prepared the report shall transmit to the notifier the final decision in writing and shall inform the other Member States and the Commission thereof within 30 days. The validity of the consent should not, as a general rule, exceed ten years and may be limited or extended as appropriate for specific reasons.

7. The competent authorities and the Commission may discuss any outstanding issues with the aim of arriving at an agreement within 75 days from the date of circulation of the assessment report.

8. If outstanding issues are resolved within the 75 day period referred to in paragraph 7, the competent authority which prepared the report shall transmit to the notifier its final decision in writing and shall inform the other Member States and the Commission thereof within 30 days. The validity of the consent may be limited as appropriate.

9. Following a notification for the renewal of a consent in accordance with paragraph 2, the notifier may continue to place the GMOs on the market under the conditions specified in that consent until a final decision has been taken on the notification.

Article 18
Community procedure in case of objections

1. In cases where an objection is raised and maintained by a competent authority or the Commission in accordance with Articles 15, 17 and 20, a decision shall be adopted and published within 120 days in accordance with the procedure laid down in Article 30(2). This decision shall contain the same information as in Article 19(3).

For the purpose of calculating the 120 day period, any period of time during which the Commission is awaiting further information which it may have requested from the notifier or is seeking the opinion of the Scientific Committee which has been consulted in accordance with Article 28 shall not be taken into account. The Commission shall state reasons in any request for further information and inform the competent authorities of its requests to the notifier. The period of time during which the Commission is awaiting the opinion of the Scientific Committee shall not exceed 90 days.

The period of time that the Council takes to act in accordance with the procedure laid down in Article 30(2) shall not be taken into account.

2. Where a favourable decision has been taken, the competent authority which prepared the report shall give consent in writing to the placing on the market or to the renewal of the consent, shall transmit it to the notifier and shall inform the other Member States and the Commission thereof within 30 days following the publication or notification of the decision.

Article 19
Consent

1. Without prejudice to requirements under other Community legislation, only if a written consent has been given for the placing on the market of a GMO as or in a product may that product be used without further notification throughout the Community in so far as the specific conditions of use and the environments and/or geographical areas stipulated in these conditions are strictly adhered to.

2. The notifier may proceed with the placing on the market only when he has received the written consent of the competent authority in accordance with Articles 15, 17 and 18, and in conformity with any conditions required in that consent.

3. The written consent referred to in Articles 15, 17 and 18 shall, in all cases, explicitly specify:

(a) the scope of the consent, including the identity of the GMO(s) to be placed on the market as or in products, and their unique identifier;

(b) the period of validity of the consent;

(c) the conditions for the placing on the market of the product, including any specific condition of use, handling and packaging of the GMO(s) as or in products, and conditions for the protection of particular ecosystems/environments and/or geographical areas;

(d) that, without prejudice to Article 25, the notifier shall make control samples available to the competent authority on request;

(e) the labelling requirements, in compliance with the requirements laid down in Annex IV. The labelling shall clearly state that a GMO is present. The words 'This product contains genetically modified organisms' shall appear either on a label or in a document accompanying the product or other products containing the GMO(s);

(f) monitoring requirements in accordance with Annex VII, including obligations to report to the Commission and competent authorities, the time period of the monitoring plan and, where appropriate, any obligations on any person selling the product or any user of it, *inter alia*, in the case of GMOs grown, concerning a level of information deemed appropriate on their location.

4. Member States shall take all necessary measures to ensure that the written consent and the decision referred to in Article 18, where applicable, are made accessible to the public and that the conditions specified in the written consent and the decision, where applicable, are complied with.

Article 20
Monitoring and handling of new information

1. Following the placing on the market of a GMO as or in a product, the notifier shall ensure that monitoring and reporting on it are carried out according to the conditions specified in the consent. The reports of this monitoring shall be submitted to the Commission and the competent authorities of the Member States. On the basis of these reports, in accordance with the consent and within the framework for the monitoring plan specified in the consent, the competent authority which received the original notification may adapt the monitoring plan after the first monitoring period.

2. If new information has become available, from the users or other sources, with regard to the risks of the GMO(s) to human health or the environment after the written consent has been given, the notifier shall immediately take the measures necessary to protect human health and the environment, and inform the competent authority thereof.

In addition, the notifier shall revise the information and conditions specified in the notification.

3. If information becomes available to the competent authority which could have consequences for the risks of the GMO(s) to human health or the environment, or under the circumstances described in paragraph 2, it shall immediately forward the information to the Commission and the competent authorities of the other Member States and may avail itself of the provisions in Articles 15(1) and 17(7) where appropriate, when the information has become available before the written consent.

When the information has become available after the consent has been given, the competent authority shall within 60 days after receipt of the new information, forward its assessment report indicating whether and how the conditions of the consent should be amended or the consent should be terminated to the Commission which shall, within 30 days of its receipt, forward it to the competent authorities of the other Member States.

Comments or reasoned objections to further placing on the market of the GMO or on the proposal for amending the conditions of the consent shall, within 60 days following the circulation of the assessment report, be forwarded to the Commission which shall immediately forward them to all competent authorities.

The competent authorities and the Commission may discuss any outstanding issues with the aim of arriving at an agreement within 75 days from the date of circulation of the assessment report.

In the absence of any reasoned objection from a Member State or the Commission within 60 days following the date of circulation of the new information or if outstanding issues are resolved within 75 days, the competent authority which prepared the report shall amend the consent as proposed, shall transmit the amended consent to the notifier and shall inform the other Member States and the Commission thereof within 30 days.

4. So as to ensure its transparency, the results of the monitoring carried out under part C of the Directive shall be made publicly available.

Article 21
Labelling

1. Member States shall take all necessary measures to ensure that at all stages of the placing on the market, the labelling and packaging of GMOs placed on the market as or in products comply with the relevant requirements specified in the written consent referred to in Articles 15(3), 17(5) and (8), 18(2) and 19(3).

2. For products where adventitious or technically unavoidable traces of authorised GMOs cannot be excluded, a minimum threshold may be established below which these products shall not have to be labelled according to the provision in paragraph 1. The threshold levels shall be established according to the product concerned, under the procedure laid down in Article 30(2).

3. For products intended for direct processing, paragraph 1 shall not apply to traces of authorised GMOs in a proportion no higher than 0,9% or lower thresholds established under the provisions of Article 30(2), provided that these traces are adventitious or technically unavoidable.

Article 22
Free circulation

Without prejudice to Article 23, Member States may not prohibit, restrict or impede the placing on the market of GMOs, as or in products, which comply with the requirements of this Directive.

Article 23
Safeguard clause

1. Where a Member State, as a result of new or additional information made available since the date of the consent and affecting the environmental risk assessment or reassessment of existing information on the basis of new or additional scientific knowledge, has detailed grounds for considering that a GMO as or in a product which has been properly notified and has received written consent under this Directive constitutes a risk to human health or the environment, that Member State may provisionally restrict or prohibit the use and/or sale of that GMO as or in a product on its territory.

The Member State shall ensure that in the event of a severe risk, emergency measures, such as suspension or termination of the placing on the market, shall be applied, including information to the public.

The Member State shall immediately inform the Commission and the other Member States of actions taken under this Article and give reasons for its decision, supplying its review of the environmental risk assessment, indicating whether and how the conditions of the consent should be amended or the consent should be terminated, and, where appropriate, the new or additional information on which its decision is based.

2. A decision shall be taken on the matter within 60 days in accordance with the procedure laid down in Article 30(2). For the purpose of calculating the 60 day period, any period of time during which the Commission is awaiting further information which it may have requested from the notifier or is seeking the opinion of the Scientific Committee(s) which has/have been consulted shall not be taken into account. The period of time during which the Commission is awaiting the opinion of the Scientific Committee(s) consulted shall not exceed 60 days.

Likewise, the period of time the Council takes to act in accordance with the procedure laid down in Article 30(2) shall not be taken into account.

Article 24
Information to the public

1. Without prejudice to Article 25, upon receipt of a notification in accordance with Article 13(1), the Commission shall immediately make available to the public the summary referred to in Article 13(2)(h). The Commission shall also make available to the public assessment reports in the case referred to in Article 14(3)(a). The public may make comments to the Commission within 30 days. The Commission shall immediately forward the comments to the competent authorities.

2. Without prejudice to Article 25, for all GMOs which have received written consent for placing on the market or whose placing on the market was rejected as or in products under this Directive, the assessment reports carried out for these GMOs and the opinion(s) of the Scientific Committees consulted shall be made available to the public. For each product, the GMO or GMOs contained therein and the use or uses shall be clearly specified.

Part D
Final provisions

Article 25
Confidentiality

1. The Commission and the competent authorities shall not divulge to third parties any confidential information notified or exchanged under this Directive and shall protect intellectual property rights relating to the data received.

2. The notifier may indicate the information in the notification submitted under this Directive, the disclosure of which might harm his competitive position and which should therefore be treated as confidential. Verifiable justification must be given in such cases.

3. The competent authority shall, after consultation with the notifier, decide which information will be kept confidential and shall inform the notifier of its decisions.

4. In no case may the following information when submitted according to Articles 6, 7, 8, 13, 17, 20 or 23 be kept confidential:

– general description of the GMO or GMOs, name and address of the notifier, purpose of the release, location of release and intended uses;
– methods and plans for monitoring of the GMO or GMOs and for emergency response;
– environmental risk assessment.

5. If, for whatever reasons, the notifier withdraws the notification, the competent authorities and the Commission must respect the confidentiality of the information supplied.

Article 26
Labelling of GMOs referred to in Article 2(4), second subparagraph

1. The GMOs to be made available for operations referred to under Article 2(4), second subparagraph, shall be subject to adequate labelling requirements in accordance with the relevant sections of Annex IV in order to provide for clear information, on a label or in an accompanying document, on the presence of GMOs. To that effect the words 'This product contains genetically modified organisms' shall appear either on a label or in an accompanying document.

2. The conditions for the implementation of paragraph 1 shall, without duplicating or creating inconsistencies with existing labelling provisions laid down in existing Community legislation, be determined in accordance with the procedure laid down in Article 30(2). In doing so, account should be taken, as appropriate, of labelling provisions established by Member States in accordance with Community legislation.

Article 26a
Measures to avoid the unintended presence of GMOs

1. Member States may take appropriate measures to avoid the unintended presence of GMOs in other products.

2. The Commission shall gather and coordinate information based on studies at Community and national level, observe the developments regarding coexistence in the Member States and, on the basis of the information and observations, develop guidelines on the coexistence of genetically modified, conventional and organic crops.

Article 27
Adaptation of Annexes to technical progress

Sections C and D of Annex II, Annexes III to VI, and section C of Annex VII shall be adapted to technical progress in accordance with the procedure laid down in Article 30(2).

Article 28
Consultation of Scientific Committee(s)

1. In cases where an objection as regards the risks of GMOs to human health or to the environment is raised by a competent authority or the Commission and maintained in accordance with Article 15(1),17(4), 20(3) or 23, or where the assessment report referred to in Article 14 indicates that the GMO should not be placed on the market, the relevant Scientific Committee(s) shall be consulted by the Commission, on its own initiative or at the request of a Member State, on the objection.

2. The relevant Scientific Committee(s) may also be consulted by the Commission, on its own initiative or at the request of a Member State, on any matter under this Directive that may have an adverse effect on human health and the environment.

3. The administrative procedures laid down in this Directive shall not be affected by paragraph 2.

Article 29
Consultation of Committee(s) on Ethics

1. Without prejudice to the competence of Member States as regards ethical issues, the Commission shall, on its own initiative or at the request of the European Parliament or the Council, consult any committee it has created with a view to obtaining its advice on the ethical implications of biotechnology, such as the European Group on Ethics in Science and New Technologies, on ethical issues of a general nature.

This consultation may also take place at the request of a Member State.

2. This consultation is conducted under clear rules of openness, transparency and public accessibility. Its outcome shall be accessible to the public.

3. The administrative procedures provided for in this Directive shall not be affected by paragraph 1.

Article 30
Committee procedure

1. The Commission shall be assisted by a committee.

2. Where reference is made to this paragraph, Articles 5 and 7 of Decision 1999/468/EC shall apply, having regard to the provisions of Article 8 thereof.

The period laid down in Article 5(6) of Decision 1999/468/EC shall be set at three months.

3. The committee shall adopt its own rules of procedure.

Article 31
Exchange of information and reporting

1. Member States and the Commission shall meet regularly and exchange information on the experience acquired with regard to the prevention of risks related to the release and the placing on the market of GMOs. This information exchange shall also cover experience gained from the implementation of Article 2(4), second subparagraph, environmental risk assessment, monitoring and the issue of consultation and information of the public.

Where necessary, guidance on the implementation of Article 2(4), second subparagraph, may be provided by the committee established under Article 30(1).

2. The Commission shall establish one or several register(s) for the purpose of recording the information on genetic modifications in GMOs mentioned in point A No 7 of Annex IV. Without prejudice to Article 25, the register(s) shall include a part which is accessible to the public. The detailed arrangements for the operation of the register(s) shall be decided in accordance with the procedure laid down in Article 30(2).

3. Without prejudice to paragraph 2 and point A No 7 of Annex IV,

(a) Member States shall establish public registers in which the location of the release of the GMOs under part B is recorded.

(b) Member States shall also establish registers for recording the location of GMOs grown under part C, *inter alia* so that the possible effects of such GMOs on the environment may be monitored in accordance with the provisions of Articles 19(3)(f) and 20(1). Without prejudice to such provisions in Articles 19 and 20, the said locations shall:
   – be notified to the competent authorities, and
   – be made known to the public in the manner deemed appropriate by the competent authorities and in accordance with national provisions.

4. Every three years, Member States shall send the Commission a report on the measures taken to implement the provisions of this Directive. This report shall include a brief factual report on their experience with GMOs placed on the market in or as products under this Directive.

5. Every three years, the Commission shall publish a summary based on the reports referred to in paragraph 4.

6. The Commission shall send to the European Parliament and the Council, in 2003 and thereafter every three years, a report on the experience of Member States with GMOs placed on the market under this Directive.

7. When submitting this report in 2003, the Commission shall at the same time submit a specific report on the operation of part B and part C including an assessment of:

(a) all its implications, particularly to take account of the diversity of European ecosystems and the need to complement the regulatory framework in this field;

(b) the feasibility of various options to improve further the consistency and efficiency of this framework, including a centralised Community authorisation procedure and the arrangements for the final decision making by the Commission;

(c) whether sufficient experience has accumulated on the implementation of part B differentiated procedures to justify a provision on implicit consent in these procedures and on part C to justify the application of differentiated procedures; and

(d) the socioeconomic implications of deliberate releases and placing on the market of GMOs.

8. The Commission shall send to the European Parliament and the Council every year, a report on the ethical issues referred to in Article 29(1); this report may be accompanied, if appropriate, by a proposal with a view to amending this Directive.

Article 32
Implementation of the Cartagena Protocol on biosafety

1. The Commission is invited to bring forward as soon as possible and in any case before July 2001 a legislative proposal for implementing in detail the Cartagena Protocol on biosafety. The proposal shall complement and, if necessary, amend the provisions of this Directive.

2. This proposal shall, in particular, include appropriate measures to implement the procedures laid down in the Cartagena Protocol and, in accordance with the Protocol, require Community exporters to ensure that all requirements of the Advance Informed Agreement Procedure, as set out in Articles 7 to 10, 12 and 14 of the Cartagena Protocol, are fulfilled.

Article 33
Penalties

Member States shall determine the penalties applicable to breaches of the national provisions adopted pursuant to this Directive. Those penalties shall be effective, proportionate and dissuasive.

Article 34
Transposition

1. Member States shall bring into force the laws, regulations and administrative provisions necessary to comply with this Directive by 17 October 2002. They shall forthwith inform the Commission thereof.

When Member States adopt these measures they shall contain a reference to this Directive or shall be accompanied by such reference on the occasion of their official publication. The methods of making such a reference shall be laid down by the Member States.

2. Member States shall communicate to the Commission the texts of the main provisions of domestic law which they adopt in the field covered by this Directive.

Article 35
Pending notifications

1. Notifications concerning placing on the market of GMOs as or in products received pursuant to Directive 90/220/EEC, and in respect of which the procedures of that Directive have not been completed by 17 October 2002 shall be subject to the provisions of this Directive.

2. By 17 January 2003 notifiers shall have complemented their notification in accordance with this Directive.

Article 36
Repeal

1. Directive 90/220/EEC shall be repealed on 17 October 2002.

2. References made to the repealed Directive shall be construed as being made to this Directive and should be read in accordance with the correlation table in Annex VIII.

Article 37

This Directive shall enter into force on the day of its publication in the *Official Journal of the European Communities.*

Article 38

This Directive is addressed to the Member States.

Annex I A
Techniques referred to in Article 2(2)

Part 1
Techniques of genetic modification referred to in Article 2(2)(a) are *inter alia:*

(1) recombinant nucleic acid techniques involving the formation of new combinations of genetic material by the insertion of nucleic acid molecules produced by whatever means outside an organism, into any virus, bacterial plasmid or other vector system and their incorporation into a host organism in which they do not naturally occur but in which they are capable of continued propagation;

(2) techniques involving the direct introduction into an organism of heritable material prepared outside the organism including micro-injection, macro-injection and micro-encapsulation;

(3) cell fusion (including protoplast fusion) or hybridisation techniques where live cells with new combinations of heritable genetic material are formed through the fusion of two or more cells by means of methods that do not occur naturally.

Part 2
Techniques referred to in Article 2(2)(b) which are not considered to result in genetic modification, on condition that they do not involve the use of recombinant nucleic acid molecules or genetically modified organisms made by techniques/methods other than those excluded by Annex I B:

(1) in vitro fertilisation,
(2) natural processes such as: conjugation, transduction, transformation,
(3) polyploidy induction.

Annex I B
Techniques referred to in Article 3

Techniques/methods of genetic modification yielding organisms to be excluded from the Directive, on the condition that they do not involve the use of recombinant nucleic acid molecules or genetically modified organisms other than those produced by one or more of the techniques/methods listed below are:

(1) mutagenesis,
(2) cell fusion (including protoplast fusion) of plant cells of organisms which can exchange genetic material through traditional breeding methods.

Annex II
Principles for the environmental risk assessment

This Annex describes in general terms the objective to be achieved, the elements to be considered and the general principles and methodology to be followed to perform the environmental risk assessment (e.r.a.) referred to in Articles 4 and 13. It will be supplemented by guidance notes to be developed in accordance with the procedure laid down in Article 30(2). These guidance notes shall be completed by 17 October 2002.

With a view to contributing to a common understanding of the terms 'direct, indirect, immediate and delayed' when implementing this Annex, without prejudice to further guidance in this respect and in particular as regards the extent to which indirect effects can and should be taken into account, these terms are described as follows:

— 'direct effects' refers to primary effects on human health or the environment which are a result of the GMO itself and which do not occur through a causal chain of events;

- 'indirect effects' refers to effects on human health or the environment occurring through a causal chain of events, through mechanisms such as interactions with other organisms, transfer of genetic material, or changes in use or management. Observations of indirect effects are likely to be delayed;
- 'immediate effects' refers to effects on human health or the environment which are observed during the period of the release of the GMO. Immediate effects may be direct or indirect;
- 'delayed effects' refers to effects on human health or the environment which may not be observed during the period of the release of the GMO, but become apparent as a direct or indirect effect either at a later stage or after termination of the release.

A general principle for environmental risk assessment is also that an analysis of the 'cumulative long-term effects' relevant to the release and the placing on the market is to be carried out. 'Cumulative long-term effects' refers to the accumulated effects of consents on human health and the environment, including *inter alia* flora and fauna, soil fertility, soil degradation of organic material, the feed/food chain, biological diversity, animal health and resistance problems in relation to antibiotics.

A. *Objective*

The objective of an e.r.a. is, on a case by case basis, to identify and evaluate potential adverse effects of the GMO, either direct and indirect, immediate or delayed, on human health and the environment which the deliberate release or the placing on the market of GMOs may have. The e.r.a. should be conducted with a view to identifying if there is a need for risk management and if so, the most appropriate methods to be used.

B. *General principles*

In accordance with the precautionary principle, the following general principles should be followed when performing the e.r.a.:

- identified characteristics of the GMO and its use which have the potential to cause adverse effects should be compared to those presented by the non-modified organism from which it is derived and its use under corresponding situations;
- the e.r.a. should be carried out in a scientifically sound and transparent manner based on available scientific and technical data;
- the e.r.a. should be carried out on a case by case basis, meaning that the required information may vary depending on the type of the GMOs concerned, their intended use and the potential receiving environment, taking into account, i.a., GMOs already in the environment;
- if new information on the GMO and its effects on human health or the environment becomes available, the e.r.a. may need to be readdressed in order to:
  - determine whether the risk has changed;
  - determine whether there is a need for amending the risk management accordingly.

C. Methodology

C.1. Characteristics of GMOs and releases

Depending on the case the e.r.a. has to take into account the relevant technical and scientific details regarding characteristics of:

- the recipient or parental organism(s);
- the genetic modification(s), be it inclusion or deletion of genetic material, and relevant information on the vector and the donor;
- the GMO;
- the intended release or use including its scale;
- the potential receiving environment; and
- the interaction between these.

Information from releases of similar organisms and organisms with similar traits and their interaction with similar environments can assist the e.r.a.

C.2. Steps in the e.r.a.

In drawing conclusions for the e.r.a. referred to in Articles 4, 6, 7 and 13 the following points should be addressed:

1. Identification of characteristics which may cause adverse effects:

Any characteristics of the GMOs linked to the genetic modification that may result in adverse effects on human health or the environment shall be identified. A comparison of the characteristics of the GMO(s) with those of the non-modified organism under corresponding conditions of the release or use, will assist in identifying the particular potential adverse effects arising from the genetic modification. It is important not to discount any potential adverse effect on the basis that it is unlikely to occur.

Potential adverse effects of GMOs will vary from case to case, and may include:

- disease to humans including allergenic or toxic effects (see for example items II.A.11. and II.C.2(i) in Annex III A, and B 7 in Annex III B);
- disease to animals and plants including toxic, and where appropriate, allergenic effects (see for example items II.A.11. and II.C.2(i) in Annex III A, and B 7 and D 8 in Annex III B);
- effects on the dynamics of populations of species in the receiving environment and the genetic diversity of each of these populations (see for example items IV B 8, 9 and 12 in Annex III A);
- altered susceptibility to pathogens facilitating the dissemination of infectious diseases and/or creating new reservoirs or vectors;
- compromising prophylactic or therapeutic medical, veterinary, or plant protection treatments, for example by transfer of genes conferring resistance to antibiotics used in human or veterinary medicine (see for example items II.A.11(e) and II.C.2(i)(iv) in Annex III A);

– effects on biogeochemistry (biogeochemical cycles), particularly carbon and nitrogen recycling through changes in soil decomposition of organic material (see for example items II.A.11(f) and IV.B.15 in Annex III A, and D 11 in Annex III B).

Adverse effects may occur directly or indirectly through mechanisms which may include:

– the spread of the GMO(s) in the environment,
– the transfer of the inserted genetic material to other organisms, or the same organism whether genetically modified or not,
– phenotypic and genetic instability,
– interactions with other organisms,
– changes in management, including, where applicable, in agricultural practices.

2. *Evaluation of the potential consequences of each adverse effect, if it occurs*
The magnitude of the consequences of each potential adverse effect should be evaluated.

This evaluation should assume that such an adverse effect will occur.

The magnitude of the consequences is likely to be influenced by the environment into which the GMO(s) is (are) intended to be released and the manner of the release.

3. *Evaluation of the likelihood of the occurrence of each identified potential adverse effect*
A major factor in evaluating the likelihood or probability of adverse effects occurring is the characteristics of the environment into which the GMO(s) is intended to be released, and the manner of the release.

4. *Estimation of the risk posed by each identified characteristic of the GMO(s)*
An estimation of the risk to human health or the environment posed by each identified characteristic of the GMO which has the potential to cause adverse effects should be made as far as possible, given the state of the art, by combining the likelihood of the adverse effect occurring and the magnitude of the consequences, if it occurs.

5. *Application of management strategies for risks from the deliberate release or marketing of GMO(s)*
The risk assessment may identify risks that require management and how best to manage them, and a risk management strategy should be defined.

6. *Determination of the overall risk of the GMO(s)*
An evaluation of the overall risk of the GMO(s) should be made taking into account any risk management strategies which are proposed.

D. Conclusions on the potential environmental impact from the release or the placing on the market of GMOs

On the basis of an e.r.a. carried out in accordance with the principles and methodology outlined in sections B and C, information on the points listed in sections D1 or D2 should be included, as appropriate, in notifications with a view to assisting in drawing conclusions on the potential environmental impact from the release or the placing on the market of GMOs:

D.1. In the case of GMOs other than higher plants

1. Likelihood of the GMO to become persistent and invasive in natural habitats under the conditions of the proposed release(s).
2. Any selective advantage or disadvantage conferred to the GMO and the likelihood of this becoming realised under the conditions of the proposed release(s).
3. Potential for gene transfer to other species under conditions of the proposed release of the GMO and any selective advantage or disadvantage conferred to those species.
4. Potential immediate and/or delayed environmental impact of the direct and indirect interactions between the GMO and target organisms (if applicable).
5. Potential immediate and/or delayed environmental impact of the direct and indirect interactions between the GMO with non-target organisms, including impact on population levels of competitors, prey, hosts, symbionts, predators, parasites and pathogens.
6. Possible immediate and/or delayed effects on human health resulting from potential direct and indirect interactions of the GMO and persons working with, coming into contact with or in the vicinity of the GMO release(s).
7. Possible immediate and/or delayed effects on animal health and consequences for the feed/food chain resulting from consumption of the GMO and any product derived from it, if it is intended to be used as animal feed.
8. Possible immediate and/or delayed effects on biogeochemical processes resulting from potential direct and indirect interactions of the GMO and target and non-target organisms in the vicinity of the GMO release(s).
9. Possible immediate and/or delayed, direct and indirect environmental impacts of the specific techniques used for the management of the GMO where these are different from those used for non-GMOs.

D.2. In the case of genetically modified higher plants (GMHP)

1. Likelihood of the GMHP becoming more persistent than the recipient or parental plants in agricultural habitats or more invasive in natural habitats.
2. Any selective advantage or disadvantage conferred to the GMHP.
3. Potential for gene transfer to the same or other sexually compatible plant species under conditions of planting the GMHP and any selective advantage or disadvantage conferred to those plant species.
4. Potential immediate and/or delayed environmental impact resulting from direct and indirect interactions between the GMHP and target organisms, such as predators, parasitoids, and pathogens (if applicable).
5. Possible immediate and/or delayed environmental impact resulting from direct and indirect interactions of the GMHP with non-target organisms, (also taking into account organisms which interact with target organisms), including impact

on population levels of competitors, herbivores, symbionts (where applicable), parasites and pathogens.

6. Possible immediate and/or delayed effects on human health resulting from potential direct and indirect interactions of the GMHP and persons working with, coming into contact with or in the vicinity of the GMHP release(s).

7. Possible immediate and/or delayed effects on animal health and consequences for the feed/food chain resulting from consumption of the GMO and any products derived from it, if it is intended to be used as animal feed.

8. Possible immediate and/or delayed effects on biogeochemical processes resulting from potential direct and indirect interactions of the GMO and target and non-target organisms in the vicinity of the GMO release(s).

9. Possible immediate and/or delayed, direct and indirect environmental impacts of the specific cultivation, management and harvesting techniques used for the GMHP where these are different from those used for non-GMHPs.

Guidance notes on the objective, elements, general principles and methodology of the environmental risk assessment referred to in Annex II to Directive 2001/18/EC

[Omitted]

Annex III
Information required in the notification

A notification referred to in part B or part C of the Directive is to include, as appropriate, the information set out below in the sub-Annexes.

Not all the points included will apply to every case. It is to be expected that individual notifications will address only the particular subset of considerations which is appropriate to individual situations.

The level of detail required in response to each subset of considerations is also likely to vary according to the nature and the scale of the proposed release.

Future developments in genetic modification may necessitate adapting this Annex to technical progress or developing guidance notes on this Annex.

Further differentiation of information requirements for different types of GMOs, for example single celled organisms, fish or insects, or for particular use of GMOs like the development of vaccines, may be possible once sufficient experience with notifications for the release of particular GMOs has been gained in the Community.

The description of the methods used or the reference to standardised or internationally recognised methods shall also be mentioned in the dossier, together with the name of the body or bodies responsible for carrying out the studies.

Annex III A applies to releases of all types of genetically modified organisms other than higher plants. Annex III B applies to release of genetically modified higher plants.

The term 'higher plants' means plants which belong to the taxonomic group Spermatophytae (Gymnospermae and Angiospermae).

Annex III A
Information required in notifications concerning releases of genetically modified organisms other than higher plants

I. General information

A. Name and address of the notifier (company or institute)
B. Name, qualifications and experience of the responsible scientist(s)
C. Title of the project

II. Information relating to the GMO

A. Characteristics of (a) the donor, (b) the recipient or (c) (where appropriate) parental organism(s):

1. scientific name,
2. taxonomy,
3. other names (usual name, strain name, etc.),
4. phenotypic and genetic markers,
5. degree of relatedness between donor and recipient or between parental organisms,
6. description of identification and detection techniques,
7. sensitivity, reliability (in quantitative terms) and specificity of detection and identification techniques,
8. description of the geographic distribution and of the natural habitat of the organism including information on natural predators, preys, parasites and competitors, symbionts and hosts,
9. organisms with which transfer of genetic material is known to occur under natural conditions,
10. verification of the genetic stability of the organisms and factors affecting it,
11. pathological, ecological and physiological traits:
    (a) classification of hazard according to existing Community rules concerning the protection of human health and/or the environment;
    (b) generation time in natural ecosystems, sexual and asexual reproductive cycle;
    (c) information on survival, including seasonability and the ability to form survival structures;
    (d) pathogenicity: infectivity, toxigenicity, virulence, allergenicity, carrier (vector) of pathogen, possible vectors, host range including non-target organism. Possible activation of latent viruses (proviruses). Ability to colonise other organisms;
    (e) antibiotic resistance, and potential use of these antibiotics in humans and domestic organisms for prophylaxis and therapy;
    (f) involvement in environmental processes: primary production, nutrient turnover, decomposition of organic matter, respiration, etc.

12. Nature of indigenous vectors:
    (a) sequence;
    (b) frequency of mobilisation;
    (c) specificity;
    (d) presence of genes which confer resistance.
13. History of previous genetic modifications.

B. *Characteristics of the vector*

1. nature and source of the vector,
2. sequence of transposons, vectors and other non-coding genetic segments used to construct the GMO and to make the introduced vector and insert function in the GMO,
3. frequency of mobilisation of inserted vector and/or genetic transfer capabilities and methods of determination,
4. information on the degree to which the vector is limited to the DNA required to perform the intended function.

C. *Characteristics of the modified organism*
1. Information relating to the genetic modification:

(a) methods used for the modification;
(b) methods used to construct and introduce the insert(s) into the recipient or to delete a sequence;
(c) description of the insert and/or vector construction;
(d) purity of the insert from any unknown sequence and information on the degree to which the inserted sequence is limited to the DNA required to perform the intended function;
(e) methods and criteria used for selection;
(f) sequence, functional identity and location of the altered/inserted/deleted nucleic acid segment(s) in question with particular reference to any known harmful sequence.

2. Information on the final GMO:

(a) description of genetic trait(s) or phenotypic characteristics and in particular any new traits and characteristics which may be expressed or no longer expressed;
(b) structure and amount of any vector and/or donor nucleic acid remaining in the final construction of the modified organism;
(c) stability of the organism in terms of genetic traits;
(d) rate and level of expression of the new genetic material. Method and sensitivity of measurement;
(e) activity of the expressed protein(s);

(f) description of identification and detection techniques including techniques for the identification and detection of the inserted sequence and vector;

(g) sensitivity, reliability (in quantitative terms) and specificity of detection and identification techniques;

(h) history of previous releases or uses of the GMO;

(i) considerations for human health and animal health, as well as plant health:

    (i) toxic or allergenic effects of the GMOs and/or their metabolic products;

    (ii) comparison of the modified organism to the donor, recipient or (where appropriate) parental organism regarding pathogenicity;

    (iii) capacity for colonisation;

    (iv) if the organism is pathogenic to humans who are immunocompetent:

        – diseases caused and mechanism of pathogenicity including invasiveness and virulence,

        – communicability,

        – infective dose,

        – host range, possibility of alteration,

        – possibility of survival outside of human host,

        – presence of vectors or means of dissemination,

        – biological stability,

        – antibiotic resistance patterns,

        – allergenicity,

        – availability of appropriate therapies.

    (v) other product hazards.

III. Information relating to the conditions of release and the receiving environment

A. *Information on the release*

1. description of the proposed deliberate release, including the purpose(s) and foreseen products,
2. foreseen dates of the release and time planning of the experiment including frequency and duration of releases,
3. preparation of the site previous to the release,
4. size of the site,
5. method(s) to be used for the release,
6. quantities of GMOs to be released,
7. disturbance on the site (type and method of cultivation, mining, irrigation, or other activities),
8. worker protection measures taken during the release,
9. post-release treatment of the site,
10. techniques foreseen for elimination or inactivation of the GMOs at the end of the experiment,

11. information on, and results of, previous releases of the GMOs, especially at different scales and in different ecosystems.

B. *Information on the environment (both on the site and in the wider environment):*

1. geographical location and grid reference of the site(s) (in case of notifications under part C the site(s) of release will be the foreseen areas of use of the product),
2. physical or biological proximity to humans and other significant biota,
3. proximity to significant biotopes, protected areas, or drinking water supplies,
4. climatic characteristics of the region(s) likely to be affected,
5. geographical, geological and pedological characteristics,
6. flora and fauna, including crops, livestock and migratory species,
7. description of target and non-target ecosystems likely to be affected,
8. a comparison of the natural habitat of the recipient organism with the proposed site(s) of release,
9. any known planned developments or changes in land use in the region which could influence the environmental impact of the release.

IV. Information relating to the interactions between the GMOs and the environment

A. *Characteristics affecting survival, multiplication and dissemination*

1. biological features which affect survival, multiplication and dispersal,
2. known or predicted environmental conditions which may affect survival, multiplication and dissemination (wind, water, soil, temperature, pH, etc.),
3. sensitivity to specific agents.

B. *Interactions with the environment*

1. predicted habitat of the GMOs,
2. studies of the behaviour and characteristics of the GMOs and their ecological impact carried out in simulated natural environments, such as microcosms, growth rooms, greenhouses,
3. genetic transfer capability
   (a) postrelease transfer of genetic material from GMOs into organisms in affected ecosystems;
   (b) postrelease transfer of genetic material from indigenous organisms to the GMOs;
4. likelihood of postrelease selection leading to the expression of unexpected and/or undesirable traits in the modified organism,
5. measures employed to ensure and to verify genetic stability. Description of genetic traits which may prevent or minimize dispersal of genetic material. Methods to verify genetic stability,

6. routes of biological dispersal, known or potential modes of interaction with the disseminating agent, including inhalation, ingestion, surface contact, burrowing, etc.,
7. description of ecosystems to which the GMOs could be disseminated,
8. potential for excessive population increase in the environment,
9. competitive advantage of the GMOs in relation to the unmodified recipient or parental organism(s),
10. identification and description of the target organisms if applicable,
11. anticipated mechanism and result of interaction between the released GMOs and the target organism(s) if applicable,
12. identification and description of non-target organisms which may be adversely affected by the release of the GMO, and the anticipated mechanisms of any identified adverse interaction,
13. likelihood of post-release shifts in biological interactions or in host range,
14. known or predicted interactions with non-target organisms in the environment, including competitors, preys, hosts, symbionts, predators, parasites and pathogens,
15. known or predicted involvement in biogeochemical processes,
16. other potential interactions with the environment.

V. Information on monitoring, control, waste treatment and emergency response plans

A. *Monitoring techniques*

1. methods for tracing the GMOs, and for monitoring their effects,
2. specificity (to identify the GMOs, and to distinguish them from the donor, recipient or, where appropriate, the parental organisms), sensitivity and reliability of the monitoring techniques,
3. techniques for detecting transfer of the donated genetic material to other organisms,
4. duration and frequency of the monitoring.

B. *Control of the release*

1. methods and procedures to avoid and/or minimise the spread of the GMOs beyond the site of release or the designated area for use,
2. methods and procedures to protect the site from intrusion by unauthorised individuals,
3. methods and procedures to prevent other organisms from entering the site.

C. *Waste treatment*

1. type of waste generated,
2. expected amount of waste,
3. description of treatment envisaged.

D. Emergency response plans

1. methods and procedures for controlling the GMOs in case of unexpected spread,
2. methods for decontamination of the areas affected, for example eradication of the GMOs,
3. methods for disposal or sanitation of plants, animals, soils, etc., that were exposed during or after the spread,
4. methods for the isolation of the area affected by the spread,
5. plans for protecting human health and the environment in case of the occurrence of an undesirable effect.

Annex III B
Information required in notifications concerning releases of genetically modified higher plants (GMHPs) (Gymnospermae and Angiospermae)

A. *General information*

1. Name and address of the notifier (company or institute),
2. Name, qualifications and experience of the responsible scientist(s),
3. Title of the project,

B. *Information relating to (a) the recipient or (b) (where appropriate) parental plants*

1. Complete name:
   (a) family name
   (b) genus
   (c) species
   (d) subspecies
   (e) cultivar/breeding line
   (f) common name.
2. (a) Information concerning reproduction:
       (i) mode(s) of reproduction
      (ii) specific factors affecting reproduction, if any
      (iii) generation time.
   (b) Sexual compatibility with other cultivated or wild plant species, including the distribution in Europe of the compatible species.
3. Survivability:
   (a) ability to form structures for survival or dormancy
   (b) specific factors affecting survivability, if any.
4. Dissemination:
   (a) ways and extent (for example an estimation of how viable pollen and/or seeds declines with distance) of dissemination
   (b) specific factors affecting dissemination, if any.

5. Geographical distribution of the plant.
6. In the case of plant species not normally grown in the Member State(s), description of the natural habitat of the plant, including information on natural predators, parasites, competitors and symbionts.
7. Other potential interactions, relevant to the GMO, of the plant with organisms in the ecosystem where it is usually grown, or elsewhere, including information on toxic effects on humans, animals and other organisms.

C. *Information relating to the genetic modification*

1. Description of the methods used for the genetic modification.
2. Nature and source of the vector used.
3. Size, source (name) of donor organism(s) and intended function of each constituent fragment of the region intended for insertion.

D. *Information relating to the genetically modified plant*

1. Description of the trait(s) and characteristics which have been introduced or modified.
2. Information on the sequences actually inserted/deleted:
   (a) size and structure of the insert and methods used for its characterisation, including information on any parts of the vector introduced in the GMHP or any carrier or foreign DNA remaining in the GMHP;
   (b) in case of deletion, size and function of the deleted region(s);
   (c) copy number of the insert;
   (d) location(s) of the insert(s) in the plant cells (integrated in the chromosome, chloroplasts, mitochondria, or maintained in a non-integrated form), and methods for its determination.
3. Information on the expression of the insert:
   (a) information on the developmental expression of the insert during the lifecycle of the plant and methods used for its characterisation;
   (b) parts of the plant where the insert is expressed (for example roots, stem, pollen, etc.).
4. Information on how the genetically modified plant differs from the recipient plant in:
   (a) mode(s) and/or rate of reproduction;
   (b) dissemination;
   (c) survivability.
5. Genetic stability of the insert and phenotypic stability of the GMHP.
6. Any change to the ability of the GMHP to transfer genetic material to other organisms.
7. Information on any toxic, allergenic or other harmful effects on human health arising from the genetic modification.

8. Information on the safety of the GMHP to animal health, particularly regarding any toxic, allergenic or other harmful effects arising from the genetic modification, where the GMHP is intended to be used in animal feedstuffs.
9. Mechanism of interaction between the genetically modified plant and target organisms (if applicable).
10. Potential changes in the interactions of the GMHP with non-target organisms resulting from the genetic modification.
11. Potential interactions with the abiotic environment.
12. Description of detection and identification techniques for the genetically modified plant.
13. Information about previous releases of the genetically modified plant, if applicable.

E. *Information relating to the site of release (only for notifications submitted pursuant to Articles 6 and 7)*

1. Location and size of the release site(s).
2. Description of the release site ecosystem, including climate, flora and fauna.
3. Presence of sexually compatible wild relatives or cultivated plant species.
4. Proximity to officially recognised biotopes or protected areas which may be affected.

F. *Information relating to the release (only for notifications submitted pursuant to Articles 6 and 7)*

1. Purpose of the release.
2. Foreseen date(s) and duration of the release.
3. Method by which the genetically modified plants will be released.
4. Method for preparing and managing the release site, prior to, during and post release, including cultivation practices and harvesting methods.
5. Approximate number of plants (or plants per m^2).

G. *Information on control, monitoring, postrelease and waste treatment plans (only for notifications submitted pursuant to Articles 6 and 7)*

1. Any precautions taken:
   (a) distance(s) from sexually compatible plant species, both wild relatives and crops
   (b) any measures to minimise/prevent dispersal of any reproductive organ of the GMHP (for example pollen, seeds, tuber).
2. Description of methods for post-release treatment of the site.
3. Description of post-release treatment methods for the genetically modified plant material including wastes.
4. Description of monitoring plans and techniques.
5. Description of any emergency plans.
6. Methods and procedures to protect the site.

Annex IV
Additional information

This Annex describes in general terms the additional information to be provided in the case of notification for placing on the market and information for labelling requirements regarding GMOs as or in product to be placed on the market, and GMO exempted under Article 2(4), second subparagraph. It will be supplemented by guidance notes, as regards i.a. the description of how the product is intended to be used, to be developed in accordance with the procedure laid down in Article 30(2). The labelling of exempted organisms as required by Article 26 shall be met by providing appropriate recommendations for, and restrictions on, use:

A. The following information shall be provided in the notification for placing on the market of GMOs as or in product in addition to that of Annex III:

1. proposed commercial names of the products and names of GMOs contained therein, and any specific identification, name or code used by the notifier to identify the GMO. After the consent any new commercial names should be provided to the competent authority,
2. name and full address of the person established in the Community who is responsible for the placing on the market, whether it be the manufacturer, the importer or the distributor,
3. name and full address of the supplier(s) of control samples,
4. description of how the product and the GMO as or in product are intended to be used. Differences in use or management of the GMO compared to similar non-genetically modified products should be highlighted,
5. description of the geographical area(s) and types of environment where the product is intended to be used within the Community, including, where possible, estimated scale of use in each area,
6. intended categories of users of the product e.g. industry, agriculture and skilled trades, consumer use by public at large,
7. information on the genetic modification for the purposes of placing on one or several registers modifications in organisms, which can be used for the detection and identification of particular GMO products to facilitate post-marketing control and inspection. This information should include where appropriate the lodging of samples of the GMO or its genetic material, with the competent authority and details of nucleotide sequences or other type of information which is necessary to identify the GMO product and its progeny, for example the methodology for detecting and identifying the GMO product, including experimental data demonstrating the specificity of the methodology. Information that cannot be placed, for confidentiality reasons, in the publicly accessible part of the register should be identified,

8. proposed labelling on a label or in an accompanying document. This must include, at least in summarised form, a commercial name of the product, a statement that 'This product contains genetically modified organisms', the name of the GMO and the information referred to in point 2, the labelling should indicate how to access the information in the publicly accessible part of the register.

B. The following information shall be provided in the notification, when relevant, in addition to that of point A, in accordance with Article 13 of this Directive:

1. measures to take in case of unintended release or misuse,
2. specific instructions or recommendations for storage and handling,
3. specific instructions for carrying out monitoring and reporting to the notifier and, if required, the competent authority, so that the competent authorities can be effectively informed of any adverse effect. These instructions should be consistent with Annex VII part C,
4. proposed restrictions in the approved use of the GMO, for example where the product may be used and for what purposes,
5. proposed packaging,
6. estimated production in and/or imports to the Community,
7. proposed additional labelling. This may include, at least in summarised form, the information referred to in points A 4, A 5, B 1, B 2, B 3 and B 4.

Annex V
Criteria for the application of differentiated procedures (Article 7)

The criteria referred to in Article 7(1) are set out below.

1. The taxonomic status and the biology (for example mode of reproduction and pollination, ability to cross with related species, pathogenecity) of the nonmodified (recipient) organism shall be well-known.
2. There shall be sufficient knowledge about the safety for human health and the environment of the parental, where appropriate, and recipient organisms in the environment of the release.
3. Information shall be available on any interaction of particular relevance for the risk assessment, involving the parental, where appropriate, and recipient organism and other organisms in the experimental release ecosystem.
4. Information shall be available to demonstrate that any inserted genetic material is well characterised. Information on the construction of any vector systems or sequences of genetic material used with the carrier DNA shall be available. Where a genetic modification involves the deletion of genetic material, the extent of the deletion shall be known. Sufficient information on the genetic modification shall

also be available to enable identification of the GMO and its progeny during a release.

5. The GMO shall not present additional or increased risks to human health or the environment under the conditions of the experimental release that are not presented by releases of the corresponding parental, where appropriate, and recipient organisms. Any capacity to spread in the environment and invade other unrelated ecosystems and capacity to transfer genetic material to other organisms in the environment shall not result in adverse effects.

Annex VI
Guidelines for the assessment reports

The assessment report provided for by Articles 13, 17, 19 and 20 should include in particular the following:

1. Identification of the characteristics of the recipient organism which are relevant to the assessment of the GMO(s) in question. Identification of any known risks to human health and the environment resulting from the release into the environment of the recipient non-modified organism.
2. Description of the result of the genetic modification in the modified organism.
3. Assessment of whether the genetic modification has been characterised sufficiently for the purpose of evaluating any risks to human health and the environment.
4. Identification of any new risks to human health and the environment that may arise from the release of the GMO(s) in question as compared to the release of the corresponding non-modified organism(s), based on the environmental risk assessment carried out in accordance with Annex II.
5. A conclusion on whether the GMO(s) in question should be placed on the market or as (a) product(s) and under which conditions, whether the GMOs in question shall not be placed on the market or whether the views of other competent authorities and the Commission are sought for on specific issues of the e.r.a.. These aspects should be specified. The conclusion should clearly address the use proposed, risk management and the monitoring plan proposed. In the case that it has been concluded that the GMOs should not be placed on the market, the competent authority shall give reasons for its conclusion.

Annex VII
Monitoring plan

This Annex describes in general terms the objective to be achieved and the general principles to be followed to design the monitoring plan referred to in Articles 13(2), 19(3) and 20. It will be supplemented by guidance notes to be developed in accordance with the procedure laid down in Article 30(2). These guidance notes shall be completed by 17 October 2002.

A. *Objective*

The objective of a monitoring plan is to:

- confirm that any assumption regarding the occurrence and impact of potential adverse effects of the GMO or its use in the e.r.a. are correct, and
- identify the occurrence of adverse effects of the GMO or its use on human health or the environment which were not anticipated in the e.r.a.

B. *General principles*

Monitoring, as referred to in Articles 13, 19 and 20, takes place after the consent to the placing of a GMO on the market.

The interpretation of the data collected by monitoring should be considered in the light of other existing environmental conditions and activities. Where changes in the environment are observed, further assessment should be considered to establish whether they are a consequence of the GMO or its use, as such changes may be the result of environmental factors other than the placing of the GMO on the market.

Experience and data gained through the monitoring of experimental releases of GMOs may assist in designing the post marketing monitoring regime required for the placing on the market of GMOs as or in products.

C. *Design of the monitoring plan*

The design of the monitoring plan should:

1. be detailed on a case by case basis taking into account the e.r.a.,
2. take into account the characteristics of the GMO, the characteristics and scale of its intended use and the range of relevant environmental conditions where the GMO is expected to be released,
3. incorporate general surveillance for unanticipated adverse effects and, if necessary, (case-) specific monitoring focusing on adverse effects identified in the e.r.a.:
    3.1. whereas case-specific monitoring should be carried out for a sufficient time period to detect immediate and direct as well as, where appropriate, delayed or indirect effects which have been identified in the e.r.a.,
    3.2. whereas surveillance could, if appropriate, make use of already established routine surveillance practices such as the monitoring of agricultural cultivars, plant protection, or veterinary and medical products. An explanation as to how relevant information collected through established routine surveillance practices will be made available to the consent-holder should be provided.
4. facilitate the observation, in a systematic manner, of the release of a GMO in the receiving environment and the interpretation of these observations with respect to safety to human health or the environment,
5. identify who (notifier, users) will carry out the various tasks the monitoring plan requires and who is responsible for ensuring that the monitoring plan is set into

place and carried out appropriately, and ensure that there is a route by which the consent holder and the competent authority will be informed on any observed adverse effects on human health and the environment. (Time points and intervals for reports on the results of the monitoring shall be indicated.),

6. give consideration to the mechanisms for identifying and confirming any observed adverse effects on human health and environment and enable the consent holder or the competent authority, where appropriate, to take the measures necessary to protect human health and the environment.

Annex VIII
Correlation table

[Omitted]

PART IX

Water quality

Council Directive 75/440/EEC of 16 June 1975 concerning the quality required of surface water intended for the abstraction of drinking water in the Member States (as amended)

Editorial note

Council Directive 75/440/EEC of 16 June 1975 concerning the quality required of surface water intended for the abstraction of drinking water in the Member States seeks to harmonise national legislation and establish quality standards. The Directive applies only to surface water intended for use in the abstraction of drinking water, although all surface water intended for human consumption and supplied for public use is to be considered drinking water (Article 1). The Directive sets out in its annexes the limit values for different qualities of surface water (Article 2), so that those listed in the 'I' columns of Annex II are minimum values which Member States must establish and those in the 'G' columns represent guidelines which Member States must endeavour to respect (Article 3). Member States are required to ensure that the Directive applies without distinction to national or international waters (Article 4(1)). Those surface waters which do not meet the mandatory minimum values in the Directive are not to be used, save for exceptional circumstances, whereupon suitable processes must be introduced to bring the quality up to standard and the Commission is to be notified (Article 4(3)). Member States are also required to take all necessary measures to improve the environment continuously, including drawing up a systematic plan of action along with a timetable (Article 4(2)). The Directive sets forth detailed measurement and sampling provisions to ensure compliance (Article 5), although Member States are permitted to set more stringent requirements for surface water than those in the Directive (Article 6). Implementation of the Directive in a manner that leads to the direct or indirect deterioration of the quality of surface water is prohibited (Article 7). The Directive sets out several specific circumstances in which its provisions may be waived, although in any event public health is not to be disregarded and the Commission must be notified (Article 8). The Directive provides for amendment of the numerical values and parameters set forth in Annex II (Article 9) and establishes detailed arrangements by which Member States are to keep the Commission informed about the implementation of the Directive (Article 9a). The Directive will be repealed in December 2007 as specified by Article 21(1) of Directive 2000/60/EC (see below).

Source: Originally published in OJ L 194 25.07.1975 p. 26. Amended by: Council Directive of 9 October 1979 (79/869/EEC) (OJ L 271 29.10.1979 p. 44); Council Directive of 23 December 1991 (91/692/EEC) (OJ L 377 31.12.1991 p. 59)

Council Directive 75/440/EEC of 16 June 1975 concerning the quality required of surface water intended for the abstraction of drinking water in the Member States (as amended)

The Council of the European Communities,

Having regard to the Treaty establishing the European Economic Community, and in particular Articles 100 and 235 thereof;

Having regard to the proposal from the Commission;

Having regard to the Opinion of the European Parliament;[1]

Having regard to the Opinion of the Economic and Social Committee;[2]

Whereas the increasing use of water resources for the abstraction of water for human consumption necessitates a reduction in the pollution of water and its protection against subsequent deterioration;

Whereas it is necessary to protect public health and, to this end, to exercise surveillance over surface water intended for the abstraction of drinking water and over the purification treatment of such water;

Whereas any disparity between the provisions on the quality required of surface water intended for the abstraction of drinking water already applicable or in preparation in the various Member States may create unequal conditions of competition and thus directly affect the functioning of the common market; whereas it is therefore necessary to approximate laws in this field as provided for in Article 100 of the Treaty;

Whereas it seems necessary for this approximation of laws to be accompanied by Community action so that one of the aims of the Community in the sphere of protection of the environment and improvement of the quality of life can be achieved by wider regulations; whereas certain specific provisions to this effect should therefore be laid down; whereas Article 235 of the Treaty should be invoked as the powers required for this purpose have not been provided by the Treaty;

Whereas the programme of action of the European Communities on the environment[3] provides that quality objectives are to be jointly drawn up fixing the various requirements which an environment must meet *inter alia* the definition of parametric values for water, including surface water intended for the abstraction of drinking water;

Whereas the joint fixing of minimum quality requirements for surface water intended for the abstraction of drinking water precludes neither more stringent

---

[1] OJ No C 62, 30. 5. 1974, p. 7.   [2] OJ No C 109, 19. 9. 1974, p. 41.   [3] OJ No C 112, 20. 12. 1973, p. 3.

requirements in the case of such water otherwise utilized nor the requirements imposed by aquatic life;

Whereas it will be necessary to review in the light of new technical and scientific knowledge the parametric values defining the quality of surface water used for the abstraction of drinking water;

Whereas the methods currently being worked out for water sampling and for measuring the parameters defining the physical, chemical and microbiological characteristics of surface water intended for the abstraction of drinking water are to be covered by a Directive to be adopted as soon as possible,

Has adopted this Directive:

Article 1

1. This Directive concerns the quality requirements which surface fresh water used or intended for use in the abstraction of drinking water, hereinafter called 'surface water', must meet after application of appropriate treatment.

Ground water, brackish water and water intended to replenish water-bearing beds shall not be subject to this Directive.

2. For the purposes of applying this Directive, all surface water intended for human consumption and supplied by distribution networks for public use shall be considered to be drinking water.

Article 2

For the purposes of this Directive surface water shall be divided according to limiting values into three categories, A1, A2 and A3, which correspond to the appropriate standard methods of treatment given in Annex I. These groups correspond to three different qualities of surface water, the respective physical, chemical and microbiological characteristics of which are set out in the table given in Annex II.

Article 3

1. Member States shall set, for all sampling points, or for each individual sampling point, the values applicable to surface water for all the parameters given in Annex II.

Member States may refrain from setting the values of parameters in respect of which no value is shown, in the table in Annex II, pursuant to the first subparagraph pending determination of the figures in accordance with the procedure under Article 9.

2. The values set pursuant to paragraph 1 may not be less stringent than those given in the 'I' columns of Annex II.

3. Where values appear in the 'G' columns of Annex II, whether or not there is a corresponding value in the 'I' columns of that Annex, Member States shall endeavour to respect them as guidelines, subject to Article 6.

Article 4

1. Member States shall take all necessary measures to ensure that surface water conforms to the values laid down pursuant to Article 3. Each Member State shall apply this Directive without distinction to national waters and waters crossing its frontiers.

2. In line with the objectives of this Directive, Member States shall take the necessary measures to ensure continuing improvement of the environment. To this end, they shall draw up a systematic plan of action including a timetable for the improvement of surface water and especially that falling within category A3. In this context, considerable improvements are to be achieved under the national programmes over the next 10 years.

The timetable referred to in the first subparagraph will be drawn up in the light of the need to improve the quality of the environment, and of water in particular, and the economic and technical constraints which exist or which may arise in the various regions of the Community.

The Commission will carry out a thorough examination of the plans referred to in the first subparagraph, including the timetables, and will, if necessary, submit appropriate proposals to the Council.

3. Surface water having physical, chemical and microbiological characteristics falling short of the mandatory limiting values corresponding to treatment type A3 may not be used for the abstraction of drinking water. However, such lower quality water may, in exceptional circumstances, be utilized provided suitable processes – including blending – are used to bring the quality characteristics of the water up to the level of the quality standards for drinking water.

The Commission must be notified of the grounds for such exceptions, on the basis of a water resources management plan within the area concerned, as soon as possible, in the case of existing installations, and in advance, in the case of new installations. The Commission will examine these grounds in detail and, where necessary, submit appropriate proposals to the Council.

Article 5

1. For the purposes of Article 4 surface water shall be assumed to conform to the relevant parameters if samples of this water taken at regular intervals at the same sampling point and used in the abstraction of drinking water show that it complies with the parametric values for the water quality in question, in the case of:

– 95% of the samples for parameters conforming to those specified in the 'I' columns in Annex II,
– 90% of the samples in all other cases, and if in the case of the 5 or 10% of the samples which do not comply:

(a) the water does not deviate from the parametric values in question by more than 50%, except for temperature, pH, dissolved oxygen and microbiological parameters;
(b) there can be no resultant danger to public health;
(c) consecutive water samples taken at statistically suitable intervals do not deviate from the relevant parametric values.

(... deleted)

3. Higher values than the parametric values for the water quality in question, shall not be taken into consideration in the calculation of the percentages referred to in paragraph 1 when they are the result of floods or natural disasters or abnormal weather conditions.

4. Sampling shall mean the place at which surface water is abstracted before being sent for purification treatment.

Article 6

Member States may at any time fix more stringent values for surface water than those laid down in this Directive.

Article 7

Implementation of the measures taken pursuant to this Directive may under no circumstances lead either directly or indirectly to deterioration of the current quality of surface water.

Article 8

This Directive may be waived:

(a) in the case of floods or other natural disasters;
(b) in the case of certain parameters marked (O) in Annex II because of exceptional meteorological or geographical conditions;
(c) where surface water undergoes natural enrichment in certain substances as a result of which it would exceed the limits laid down for categories A1, A2 and A3 in the table in Annex II;
(d) in the case of surface-water in shallow lakes or virtually stagnant surface water, for parameters marked with an asterisk in the table in Annex II, this derogation being applicable only to lakes with a depth not exceeding 20 m, with an exchange of water slower than one year, and without a discharge of waste water into the water body.

Natural enrichment means the process whereby, without human intervention, a given body of water receives from the soil certain substances contained therein.

In no case may the exceptions provided for in the first subparagraph disregard the requirements of public health protection.

Where a Member State waives the provisions of this Directive, it shall forthwith notify the Commission thereof, stating its reasons and the periods anticipated.

Article 9

The numerical values and the list of parameters given in the table in Annex II, defining the physical, chemical and microbiological characteristics of surface water may be revised either at the request of a Member State or on a proposal from the Commission, whenever technical and scientific knowledge regarding methods of treatment is extended or drinking water standards are modified.

Article 9a

At intervals of three years the Member States shall send information to the Commission on the implementation of this Directive, in the form of a sectoral report which shall also cover other pertinent Community Directives. This report shall be drawn up on the basis of a questionnaire or outline drafted by the Commission in accordance with the procedure laid down in Article 6 of Directive 91/692/EEC.[1] The questionnaire or outline shall be sent to the Member States six months before the start of the period covered by the report. The report shall be sent to the Commission within nine months of the end of the three-year period covered by it.

The first report shall cover the period from 1993 to 1995 inclusive.

The Commission shall publish a Community report on the implementation of the Directive within nine months of receiving the reports from the Member States.

Article 10

Member States shall bring into force the laws, regulations and administrative provisions needed in order to comply with this Directive within two years of its notification.

They shall forthwith inform the Commission thereof.

Article 11

This Directive is addressed to the Member States.

Annexes

[Omitted]

[1] OJ No L 377, 31. 12. 1991, p. 48.

Council Directive 76/160/EEC of 8 December 1975 concerning the quality of bathing water (as amended)

Editorial note

Council Directive 76/160 requires Member States to set the values applicable to bathing water. The Directive applies to bathing water as defined in Article 1(2), with the exclusion of water intended for therapeutic purposes and water used in swimming pools (Article 1(1)). The Directive indicates in its Annex the physical, chemical and microbiological parameters applicable to bathing water (Article 2). Member States must set values applicable to bathing waters. Such values may not be less stringent than those given in the Annex (in case of values found in column I). Values appearing in column G of the Annex are to be used as guidelines (Article 3). Member States had until December 1985 to ensure that bathing water quality conformed to the limit values in the Annex, subject to derogations granted by them and communicated to the Commission (Article 4). The Directive requires Member States to carry out sampling operations (Article 6). More stringent values can be set by the Member States (Article 7). The Directive may be waived in exceptional circumstances (Article 8). Article 9 specifies that amendments to the Directive are to be adopted according to the procedure set out in Article 11. For this purpose a Committee on Adaptation to Technical Progress (Article 10) is to assist the Commission (Article 11).

Source: Originally published in OJ L 31 05.02.1976 p. 1. Amended by: Council Directive of 23 December 1991 (91/692/EEC) L 377 48 31.12.1991; Council Regulation (EC) No 807/2003 of 14 April 2003 L 122 36 16.05.2003. Amended by: Act of Accession of Greece L 291 17 19.11.1979; Act of Accession of Spain and Portugal L 302 23 15.11.1985; Act of Accession of Austria, Sweden and Finland C 241 21 29.08.1994 (adapted by Council Decision 95/1/EC, Euratom, ECSC) L 1 1 01.01.1995

Council Directive 76/160/EEC of 8 December 1975 concerning the quality of bathing water (as amended)

The Council of the European Communities,

Having regard to the Treaty establishing the European Economic Community, and in particular Articles 100 and 235 thereof,

Having regard to the proposal from the Commission,

Having regard to the opinion of the European Parliament,[1]

Having regard to the opinion of the Economic and Social Committee,[2]

Whereas, in order to protect the environment and public health, it is necessary to reduce the pollution of bathing water and to protect such water against further deterioration;

Whereas surveillance of bathing water is necessary in order to attain, within the framework of the operation of the common market, the Community's objectives as regards the improvement of living conditions, the harmonious development of economic activities throughout the Community and continuous and balanced expansion;

Whereas there exist in this area certain laws, regulations or administrative provisions in Member States which directly affect the functioning of the common market; whereas, however, not all the powers needed to act in this way have been provided for in the Treaty;

Whereas the programme of action of the European Communities on the environment[3] provides that quality objectives are to be jointly drawn up fixing the various requirements which an environment must meet *inter alia* the definition of parameters for water, including bathing water; whereas, in order to attain these quality objectives, the Member States must lay down limit values corresponding to certain parameters;

Whereas bathing water must be made to conform to these values within 10 years following the notification of this Directive;

Whereas it should be provided that bathing water will, under certain conditions, be deemed to conform to the relevant parametric values even if a certain percentage of samples taken during the bathing season does not comply with the limits specified in the Annex;

Whereas, to achieve a certain degree of flexibility in the application of this Directive, the Member States must have the power to provide for derogations; whereas such derogations must not, however, disregard requirements essential for the protection of public health;

Whereas technical progress necessitates rapid adaptation of the technical requirements laid down in the Annex; whereas, in order to facilitate the introduction of the measures required for this purpose, a procedure should be provided for whereby close cooperation would be established between the Member States and the Commission within a Committee on Adaptation to Technical Progress;

Whereas public interest in the environment and in the improvement of its quality is increasing; whereas the public should therefore receive objective information on the quality of bathing water,

---

[1] OJ No C 128, 9. 6. 1975, p. 13.   [2] OJ No C 286, 15. 12. 1975, p. 5.   [3] OJ No C 112, 20. 12. 1973, p. 3.

Has adopted this Directive:

Article 1

1. This Directive concerns the quality of bathing water, with the exception of water intended for therapeutic purposes and water used in swimming pools.

2. For the purposes of this Directive:

(a) 'bathing water' means all running or still fresh waters or parts thereof and sea water, in which:
  – bathing is explicitly authorized by the competent authorities of each member State, or
  – bathing is not prohibited and is traditionally practised by a large number of bathers;
(b) 'bathing area' means any place where bathing water is found;
(c) 'bathing season' means the period during which a large number of bathers can be expected, in the light of local custom, and any local rules which may exist concerning bathing and weather conditions.

Article 2

The physical, chemical and microbiological parameters applicable to bathing water are indicated in the Annex which forms an integral part of this Directive.

Article 3

1. Member States shall set, for all bathing areas or for each individual bathing area, the values applicable to bathing water for the parameters given in the Annex.

In the case of the parameters for which no values are given in the Annex, Member States may decide not to fix any values pursuant to the first subparagraph, until such time as figures have been determined.

2. The values set pursuant to paragraph 1 may not be less stringent than those given in column I of the Annex.

3. Where values appear in column G of the Annex, whether or not there is a corresponding value in column I of the Annex, Member States shall endeavour, subject to Article 7, to observe them as guidelines.

Article 4

1. Member States shall take all necessary measures to ensure that, within 10 years following the notification of this Directive, the quality of bathing water conforms to the limit values set in accordance with Article 3.

2. Member States shall ensure that, in bathing areas specially equipped for bathing to be created by the competent authorities of the Member States after the notification of this Directive, the 'I values' laid down in the Annex are observed from the time when bathing is first permitted. However, for bathing areas created during the two

years following the notification of this Directive, these values need not be observed until the end of that period.

3. In exceptional circumstances Member States may grant derogations in respect of the 10-year time limit laid down in paragraph 1.

Justifications for any such derogations based on plans for the management of water within the area concerned must be communicated to the Commission as soon as possible and not later than six years following the notification of this Directive. The Commission shall examine these justifications in detail and, where necessary, make appropriate proposals concerning them to the Council.

4. As regards sea water in the vicinity of frontiers and water crossing frontiers which affect the quality of the bathing water of another Member State, the consequences for the common quality objectives for bathing areas so affected shall be determined in collaboration by the riparian Member States concerned.

The Commission may participate in these deliberations.

Article 5

1. For the purposes of Article 4, bathing water shall be deemed to conform to the relevant parameters:
if samples of that water, taken at the same sampling point and at the intervals specified in the Annex, show that it conforms to the parametric values for the quality of the water concerned, in the case of:

— 95% of the samples for parameters corresponding to those specified in column I of the Annex;
— 90% of the samples in all other cases with the exception of the 'total coliform' and 'faecal coliform' parameters where the percentage may be 80% and if, in the case of the 5, 10 or 20% of the samples which do not comply:
— the water does not deviate from the parametric values in question by more than 50%, except for microbiological parameters, pH and dissolved oxygen;
— consecutive water samples taken at statistically suitable intervals do not deviate from the relevant parametric values.

2. Deviations from the values referred to in Article 3 shall not be taken into consideration in the calculation of the percentage referred to in paragraph 1 when they are the result of floods, other natural disasters or abnormal weather conditions.

Article 6

1. The competent authorities in the Member States shall carry out sampling operations, the minimum frequency of which is laid down in the Annex.

2. Samples should be taken at places where the daily average density of bathers is highest. Samples should preferably be taken 30 cm below the surface of the water except for mineral oil samples which shall be taken at surface level. Sampling should begin two weeks before the start of the bathing season.

3. Local investigation of the conditions prevailing upstream in the case of fresh running water, and of the ambient conditions in the case of fresh still water and sea water should be carried out scrupulously and repeated periodically in order to obtain geographical and topographical data and to determine the volume and nature of all polluting and potentially polluting discharges and their effects according to the distance from the bathing area.

4. Should inspection by a competent authority or sampling operations reveal that there is a discharge or a probable discharge of substances likely to lower the quality of the bathing water, additional sampling must take place. Such additional sampling must also take place if there are any other grounds for suspecting that there is a decrease in water quality.

5. Reference methods of analysis for the parameters concerned are set out in the Annex. Laboratories which employ other methods must ensure that the results obtained are equivalent or comparable to those specified in the Annex.

Article 7

1. Implementation of the measures taken pursuant to this Directive may under no circumstances lead either directly or indirectly to deterioration of the current quality of bathing water.

2. Member States may at any time fix more stringent values for bathing water than those laid down in this Directive.

Article 8

This Directive may be waived:

(a) in the case of certain parameters marked (0) in the Annex, because of exceptional weather or geographical conditions;
(b) when bathing water undergoes natural enrichment in certain substances causing a deviation from the values prescribed in the Annex.

Natural enrichment means the process whereby, without human intervention, a given body of water receives from the soil certain substances contained therein.

In no case may the exceptions provided for in this Article disregard the requirements essential for public health protection.

Where a Member State waives the provisions of this Directive, it shall forthwith notify the Commission thereof, stating its reasons and the periods anticipated.

Article 9

Such amendments as are necessary for adapting this Directive to technical progress shall relate to:

– the methods of analysis
– the G and I parameter values set out in the Annex.

They shall be adopted in accordance with the procedure laid down in Article 11.

Article 10

1. A Committee on Adaptation to Technical Progress (hereinafter called 'the committee') is hereby set up. It shall consist of representatives of the Member States and be chaired by a representative of the Commission.

Article 11

1. The Commission shall be assisted by the Committee on Adaptation to Technical Progress.

2. Where reference is made to this Article, Articles 5 and 7 of Decision 1999/468/EC[1] shall apply. The period laid down in Article 5(6) of Decision 1999/468/EC shall be set at three months.

3. The committee shall adopt its rules of procedure.

Article 12

1. Member States shall bring into force the laws, regulations and administrative provisions necessary to comply with this Directive within two years of its notification. They shall forthwith inform the Commission thereof.

2. Member States will communicate to the Commission the texts of the main provisions of national law which they adopt in the field covered by this Directive.

Article 13

Every year, and for the first time by 31 December 1993, the Member States shall send to the Commission a report on the implementation of this Directive in the current year. The report shall be drawn up on the basis of a questionnaire or outline drafted by the Commission in accordance with the procedure laid down in Article 6 of Directive 91/692/EEC.[2] The questionnaire or outline shall be sent to the Member States six months before the start of the period covered by the report. The report shall be made to the Commission before the end of the year in question. The Commission shall publish a Community report on the implementation of the Directive within four months of receiving the reports from the Member States.

Article 14

This Directive is addressed to the Member States.

Annex

Quality requirements for bathing water

[Omitted]

---

[1] OJ L 184, 17.7.1999, p. 23.   [2] OJ No L 377, 31.12.1991, p. 48.

Council Directive 91/271/EEC of 21 May 1991
concerning urban waste water treatment
(as amended)

Editorial note

Directive 91/271 of 21 May 1991, as amended, concerns the collection, treatment and discharge of urban waste water and waste water from certain industrial sectors (Article 1). All urban areas must be provided with collection systems for urban waste water by 31 December 2000 for those with a population equivalent (p.e.) of more than 15,000 and by 31 December 2005 for those with a p.e. of between 2,000 and 15,000 (Article 3(1)).

Urban waste water entering collecting systems is to be subject before discharge to secondary treatment (Article 4(1)). Discharges from sensitive areas are subject to even more stringent treatment (Article 5). Member States are required to make sure that urban waste water treatment plants built to comply with the Directive are designed, constructed and operated and maintained to ensure performance under all normal climatic circumstances (Article 10). Treated waste water is to be re-used where appropriate and disposal routes must minimise the adverse effects on the environment (Article 12). The Directive establishes monitoring and other basic implementation requirements (Articles 15–17).

Source: OJ L 135 30.05.1991 p. 40. Amended by: Commission Directive 98/15/EC of 27 February 1998 L 67 29 07.03.1998; Regulation (EC) No 1882/2003 of the European Parliament and of the Council of 29 September 2003 L 284 1 31.10.2003. Corrected by: Corrigendum, OJ L 139 02.06.1999 p. 34 (98/15/EC)

Council Directive 91/271/EEC of 21 May 1991 concerning urban waste water treatment (as amended)

The Council of the European Communities,

Having regard to the Treaty establishing the European Economic Community, and in particular Article 130s thereof,

Having regard to the proposal from the Commission,[1]

---

[1] OJ No C 1, 4. 1. 1990, p. 20 and OJ No C 287, 15. 11. 1990, p. 11.

Having regard to the opinion of the European Parliament,[1]

Having regard to the opinion of the Economic and Social Committee,[2]

Whereas the Council Resolution of 28 June 1988 on the protection of the North Sea and of other waters in the Community[3] invited the Commission to submit proposals for measures required at Community level for the treatment of urban waste water;

Whereas pollution due to insufficient treatment of waste water in one Member State often influences other Member States' waters; whereas in accordance with Article 130r, action at Community level is necessary;

Whereas to prevent the environment from being adversely affected by the disposal of insufficiently-treated urban waste water, there is a general need for secondary treatment of urban waste water;

Whereas it is necessary in sensitive areas to require more stringent treatment; whereas in some less sensitive areas a primary treatment could be considered appropriate;

Whereas industrial waste water entering collecting systems as well as the discharge of waste water and disposal of sludge from urban waste water treatment plants should be subject to general rules or regulations and/or specific authorizations;

Whereas discharges from certain industrial sectors of biodegradable industrial waste water not entering urban waste water treatment plants before discharge to receiving waters should be subject to appropriate requirements;

Whereas the recycling of sludge arising from waste water treatment should be encouraged; whereas the disposal of sludge to surface waters should be phased out;

Whereas it is necessary to monitor treatment plants, receiving waters and the disposal of sludge to ensure that the environment is protected from the adverse effects of the discharge of waste waters;

Whereas it is important to ensure that information on the disposal of waste water and sludge is made available to the public in the form of periodic reports;

Whereas Member States should establish and present to the Commission national programmes for the implementation of this Directive;

Whereas a Committee should be established to assist the Commission on matters relating to the implementation of this Directive and to its adaptation to technical progress,

Has adopted this Directive:

Article 1

This Directive concerns the collection, treatment and discharge of urban waste water and the treatment and discharge of waste water from certain industrial sectors.

---

[1] OJ No C 260, 15. 10. 1990, p. 185.   [2] OJ No C 168, 10. 7. 1990, p. 36.   [3] OJ No C 209, 9. 8. 1988, p. 3.

The objective of the Directive is to protect the environment from the adverse effects of the abovementioned waste water discharges.

Article 2

For the purpose of this Directive:

1. 'urban waste water' means domestic waste water or the mixture of domestic waste water with industrial waste water and/or run-off rain water;
2. 'domestic waste water' means waste water from residential settlements and services which originates predominantly from the human metabolism and from household activities;
3. 'industrial waste water' means any waste water which is discharged from premises used for carrying on any trade or industry, other than domestic waste water and run-off rain water;
4. 'agglomeration' means an area where the population and/or economic activities are sufficiently concentrated for urban waste water to be collected and conducted to an urban waste water treatment plant or to a final discharge point;
5. 'collecting system' means a system of conduits which collects and conducts urban waste water;
6. '1 p.e. (population equivalent)' means the organic biodegradable load having a five-day biochemical oxygen demand (BOD5) of 60g of oxygen per day;
7. 'primary treatment' means treatment of urban waste water by a physical and/or chemical process involving settlement of suspended solids, or other processes in which the BOD5 of the incoming waste water is reduced by at least 20% before discharge and the total suspended solids of the incoming waste water are reduced by at least 50%;
8. 'secondary treatment' means treatment of urban waste water by a process generally involving biological treatment with a secondary settlement or other process in which the requirements established in Table 1 of Annex I are respected;
9. 'appropriate treatment' means treatment of urban waste water by any process and/or disposal system which after discharge allows the receiving waters to meet the relevant quality objectives and the relevant provisions of this and other Community Directives;
10. 'Sludge' means residual sludge, whether treated or untreated, from urban waste water treatment plants;
11. 'eutrophication' means the enrichment of water by nutrients, especially compounds of nitrogen and/or phosphorus, causing an accelerated growth of algae and higher forms of plant life to produce an undesirable disturbance to the balance of organisms present in the water and to the quality of the water concerned;
12. 'estuary' means the transitional area at the mouth of a river between fresh-water and coastal waters. Member States shall establish the outer (seaward) limits of

estuaries for the purposes of this Directive as part of the programme for implementation in accordance with the provisions of Article 17(1) and (2);

13. 'coastal waters' means the waters outside the low-water line or the outer limit of an estuary.

Article 3

1. Member States shall ensure that all agglomerations are provided with collecting systems for urban waste water,

– at the latest by 31 December 2000 for those with a population equivalent (p.e.) of more than 15 000, and
– at the latest by 31 December 2005 for those with a p.e. of between 2 000 and 15 000.

For urban waste water discharging into receiving waters which are considered 'sensitive areas' as defined under Article 5, Member States shall ensure that collection systems are provided at the latest by 31 December 1998 for agglomerations of more than 10 000 p.e.

Where the establishment of a collecting system is not justified either because it would produce no environmental benefit or because it would involve excessive cost, individual systems or other appropriate systems which achieve the same level of environmental protection shall be used.

2. Collecting systems described in paragraph 1 shall satisfy the requirements of Annex I(A). These requirements may be amended in accordance with the procedure laid down in Article 18.

Article 4

1. Member States shall ensure that urban waste water entering collecting systems shall before discharge be subject to secondary treatment or an equivalent treatment as follows:

– at the latest by 31 December 2000 for all discharges from agglomerations of more than 15 000 p.e.,
– at the latest by 31 December 2005 for all discharges from agglomerations of between 10 000 and 15 000 p.e.,
– at the latest by 31 December 2005 for discharges to fresh-water and estuaries from agglomerations of between 2 000 and 10 000 p.e.

2. Urban waste water discharges to waters situated in high mountain regions (over 1 500 m above sea level) where it is difficult to apply an effective biological treatment due to low temperatures may be subjected to treatment less stringent than that prescribed in paragraph 1, provided that detailed studies indicate that such discharges do not adversely affect the environment.

3. Discharges from urban waste water treatment plants described in paragraphs 1 and 2 shall satisfy the relevant requirements of Annex I.B. These requirements may be amended in accordance with the procedure laid down in Article 18.

4. The load expressed in p.e. shall be calculated on the basis of the maximum average weekly load entering the treatment plant during the year, excluding unusual situations such as those due to heavy rain.

Article 5

1. For the purposes of paragraph 2, Member States shall by 31 December 1993 identify sensitive areas according to the criteria laid down in Annex II.

2. Member States shall ensure that urban waste water entering collecting systems shall before discharge into sensitive areas be subject to more stringent treatment than that described in Article 4, by 31 December 1998 at the latest for all discharges from agglomerations of more than 10 000 p.e.

3. Discharges from urban waste water treatment plants described in paragraph 2 shall satisfy the relevant requirements of Annex I B. These requirements may be amended in accordance with the procedure laid down in Article 18.

4. Alternatively, requirements for individual plants set out in paragraphs 2 and 3 above need not apply in sensitive areas where it can be shown that the minimum percentage of reduction of the overall load entering all urban waste water treatment plants in that area is at least 75% for total phosphorus and at least 75% for total nitrogen.

5. Discharges from urban waste water treatment plants which are situated in the relevant catchment areas of sensitive areas and which contribute to the pollution of these areas shall be subject to paragraphs 2, 3 and 4.

In cases where the above catchment areas are situated wholly or partly in another Member State Article 9 shall apply.

6. Member States shall ensure that the identification of sensitive areas is reviewed at intervals of no more than four years.

7. Member States shall ensure that areas identified as sensitive following review under paragraph 6 shall within seven years meet the above requirements.

8. A Member State does not have to identify sensitive areas for the purpose of this Directive if it implements the treatment established under paragraphs 2, 3 and 4 over all its territory.

Article 6

1. For the purposes of paragraph 2, Member States may by 31 December 1993 identify less sensitive areas according to the criteria laid down in Annex II.

2. Urban waste water discharges from agglomerations of between 10 000 and 150 000 p.e. to coastal waters and those from agglomaterions of between 2 000 and 10 000 p.e. to estuaries situated in areas described in paragraph 1 may be subjected to

treatment less stringent than that prescribed in Article 4 providing that:

– such discharges receive at least primary treatment as defined in Article 2(7) in conformity with the control procedures laid down in Annex I D,
– comprehensive studies indicate that such discharges will not adversely affect the environment. Member States shall provide the Commission with all relevant information concerning the abovementioned studies.

3. If the Commission considers that the conditions set out in paragraph 2 are not met, it shall submit to the Council an appropriate proposal.

4. Member States shall ensure that the identification of less sensitive areas is reviewed at intervals of not more than four years.

5. Member States shall ensure that areas no longer identified as less sensitive shall within seven years meet the requirements of Articles 4 and 5 as appropriate.

Article 7

Member States shall ensure that, by 31 December 2005, urban waste water entering collecting systems shall before discharge be subject to appropriate treatment as defined in Article 2(9) in the following cases:

– for discharges to fresh-water and estuaries from agglomerations of less than 2 000 p.e.,
– for discharges to coastal waters from agglomerations of less than 10 000 p.e.

Article 8

1. Member States may, in exceptional cases due to technical problems and for geographically defined population groups, submit a special request to the Commission for a longer period for complying with Article 4.

2. This request, for which grounds must be duly put forward, shall set out the technical difficulties experienced and must propose an action programme with an appropriate timetable to be undertaken to implement the objective of this Directive. This timetable shall be included in the programme for implementation referred to in Article 17.

3. Only technical reasons can be accepted and the longer period referred to in paragraph 1 may not extend beyond 31 December 2005.

4. The Commission shall examine this request and take appropriate measures in accordance with the procedure laid down in Article 18.

5. In exceptional circumstances, when it can be demonstrated that more advanced treatment will not produce any environmental benefits, discharges into less sensitive areas of waste waters from agglomerations of more than 150 000 p.e. may be subject to the treatment provided for in Article 6 for waste water from agglomerations of between 10 000 and 150 000 p.e.

In such circumstances, Member States shall submit beforehand the relevant documentation to the Commission. The Commission will examine the case and take appropriate measures in accordance with the procedure laid down in Article 18.

Article 9

Where waters within the area of jurisdiction of a Member State are adversely affected by discharges of urban waste water from another Member State, the Member State whose waters are affected may notify the other Member State and the Commission of the relevant facts.

The Member States concerned shall organize, where appropriate with the Commission, the concertation necessary to identify the discharges in question and the measures to be taken at source to protect the waters that are affected in order to ensure conformity with the provisions of this Directive.

Article 10

Member States shall ensure that the urban waste water treatment plants built to comply with the requirements of Articles 4, 5, 6 and 7 are designed, constructed, operated and maintained to ensure sufficient performance under all normal local climatic conditions. When designing the plants, seasonal variations of the load shall be taken into account.

Article 11

1. Member States shall ensure that, before 31 December 1993, the discharge of industrial waste water into collecting systems and urban waste water treatment plants is subject to prior regulations and/or specific authorizations by the competent authority or appropriate body.

2. Regulations and/or specific authorization shall satisfy the requirements of Annex I C. These requirements may be amended in accordance with the procedure laid down in Article 18.

3. Regulations and specific authorization shall be reviewed and if necessary adapted at regular intervals.

Article 12

1. Treated waste water shall be reused whenever appropriate. Disposal routes shall minimize the adverse effects on the environment.

2. Competent authorities or appropriate bodies shall ensure that the disposal of waste water from urban waste water treatment plants is subject to prior regulations and/or specific authorization.

3. Prior regulations and/or specific authorization of discharges from urban waste water treatment plants made pursuant to paragraph 2 within agglomerations of 2 000 to 10 000 p.e. in the case of discharges to fresh waters and estuaries, and of 10 000 p.e. or more in respect of all discharges, shall contain conditions to satisfy the relevant

requirements of Annex I B. These requirements may be amended in accordance with the procedure laid down in Article 18.

4. Regulations and/or authorization shall be reviewed and if necessary adapted at regular intervals.

Article 13

1. Member States shall ensure that by 31 December 2000 biodegradable industrial waste water from plants belonging to the industrial sectors listed in Annex III which does not enter urban waste water treatment plants before discharge to receiving waters shall before discharge respect conditions established in prior regulations and/or specific authorization by the competent authority or appropriate body, in respect of all discharges from plants representing 4 000 p.e. or more.

2. By 31 December 1993 the competent authority or appropriate body in each Member State shall set requirements appropriate to the nature of the industry concerned for the discharge of such waste water.

3. The Commission shall carry out a comparison of the Member States' requirements by 31 December 1994. It shall publish the results in a report and if necessary make an appropriate proposal.

Article 14

1. Sludge arising from waste water treatment shall be re-used whenever appropriate. Disposal routes shall minimize the adverse effects on the environment.

2. Competent authorities or appropriate bodies shall ensure that before 31 December 1998 the disposal of sludge from urban waste water treatment plants is subject to general rules or registration or authorization.

3. Member States shall ensure that by 31 December 1998 the disposal of sludge to surface waters by dumping from ships, by discharge from pipelines or by other means is phased out.

4. Until the elimination of the forms of disposal mentioned in paragraph 3, Member States shall ensure that the total amount of toxic, persistent or bioaccumulable materials in sludge disposed of to surface waters is licensed for disposal and progressively reduced.

Article 15

1. Competent authorities or appropriate bodies shall monitor:

- discharges from urban waste water treatment plants to verify compliance with the requirements of Annex I.B in accordance with the control procedures laid down in Annex I.D,
- amounts and composition of sludges disposed of to surface waters.

2. Competent authorities or appropriate bodies shall monitor waters subject to discharges from urban waste water treatment plants and direct discharges as described

in Article 13 in cases where it can be expected that the receiving environment will be significantly affected.

3. In the case of a discharge subject to the provisions of Article 6 and in the case of disposal of sludge to surface waters, Member States shall monitor and carry out any other relevant studies to verify that the discharge or disposal does not adversely affect the environment.

4. Information collected by competent authorities or appropriate bodies in complying with paragraphs 1, 2 and 3 shall be retained in the Member State and made available to the Commission within six months of receipt of a request.

5. Guidelines on the monitoring referred to in paragraphs 1, 2 and 3 may be formulated in accordance with the procedure laid down in Article 18.

Article 16

Without prejudice to the implementation of the provisions of Council Directive 90/313/EEC of 7 June 1990 on the freedom of access to information on the environment,[1] Member States shall ensure that every two years the relevant authorities or bodies publish situation reports on the disposal of urban waste water and sludge in their areas.

These reports shall be transmitted to the Commission by the Member States as soon as they are published.

Article 17

1. Member States shall by 31 December 1993 establish a programme for the implementation of this Directive.

2. Member States shall by 30 June 1994 provide the Commission with information on the programme.

3. Member States shall, if necessary, provide the Commission by 30 June every two years with an update of the information described in paragraph 2.

4. The methods and formats to be adopted for reporting on the national programmes shall be determined in accordance with the procedure laid down in Article 18. Any amendments to these methods and formats shall be adopted in accordance with the same procedure.

5. The Commission shall every two years review and assess the information received pursuant to paragraphs 2 and 3 above and publish a report thereon.

Article 18

1. The Commission shall be assisted by a committee.

2. Where reference is made to this Article, Articles 5 and 7 of Decision 1999/468/EC[2] shall apply, having regard to the provisions of Article 8 thereof.

---

[1] OJ No L 158, 23. 6. 1990, p. 56.

[2] Council Decision 1999/468/EC of 28 June 1999 laying down the procedures for the exercise of implementing powers conferred on the Commission (OJL 184, 17.7.1999, p.23).

The period laid down in Article 5(6) of Decision 1999/468/EC shall be set at three months.

3. The Committee shall adopt its rules of procedure.

Article 19

1. Member States shall bring into force the laws, regulations and administrative provisions necessary to comply with this Directive no later than 30 June 1993. They shall forthwith inform the Commission thereof.

2. When Member States adopt the measures referred to in paragraph 1, they shall contain a reference to this Directive or shall be accompanied by such a reference on the occasion of their official publication.

The methods of making such a reference shall be laid down by the Member States.

3. Member States shall communicate to the Commission the texts of the main provisions of national law which they adopt in the field governed by this Directive.

Article 20

This Directive is addressed to the Member States.

Annex I
Requirements for urban waste water

A. *Collecting systems*[1]

Collecting systems shall take into account waste water treatment requirements.

The design, construction and maintenance of collecting systems shall be undertaken in accordance with the best technical knowledge not entailing excessive costs, notably regarding:

– volume and characteristics of urban waste water,
– prevention of leaks,
– limitation of pollution of receiving waters due to storm water overflows.

B. *Discharge from urban waste water treatment plants to receiving waters*[1]

1. Waste water treatment plants shall be designed or modified so that representative samples of the incoming waste water and of treated effluent can be obtained before discharge to receiving waters.

2. Discharges from urban waste water treatment plants subject to treatment in accordance with Articles 4 and 5 shall meet the requirements shown in Table 1.

---

[1] Given that it is not possible in practice to construct collecting systems and treatment plants in a way such that all waste water can be treated during situations such as unusually heavy rainfall, Member States shall decide on measures to limit pollution from storm water overflows. Such measures could be based on dilution rates or capacity in relation to dry weather flow, or could specify a certain acceptable number of overflows per year.

3. Discharges from urban waste water treatment plants to those sensitive areas which are subject to eutrophication as identified in Annex II.A (a) shall in addition meet the requirements shown in Table 2 of this Annex.

4. More stringent requirements than those shown in Table 1 and/or Table 2 shall be applied where required to ensure that the receiving waters satisfy any other relevant Directives.

5. The points of discharge of urban waste water shall be chosen, as far as possible, so as to minimize the effects on receiving waters.

C. *Industrial waste water*

Industrial waste water entering collecting systems and urban waste water treatment plants shall be subject to such pre-treatment as is required in order to:

– protect the health of staff working in collecting systems and treatment plants,
– ensure that collecting systems, waste water treatment plants and associated equipment are not damaged,
– ensure that the operation of the waste water treatment plant and the treatment of sludge are not impeded,
– ensure that discharges from the treatment plants do not adversely affect the environment, or prevent receiving water from complying with other Community Directives,
– ensure that sludge can be disposed of safety in an environmentally acceptable manner.

D. *Reference methods for monitoring and evaluation of results*

1. Member States shall ensure that a monitoring method is applied which corresponds at least with the level of requirements described below.

Alternative methods to those mentioned in paragraphs 2, 3 and 4 may be used provided that it can be demonstrated that equivalent results are obtained.

Member States shall provide the Commission with all relevant information concerning the applied method. If the Commission considers that the conditions set out in paragraphs 2, 3 and 4 are not met, it will submit an appropriate proposal to the Council.

2. Flow-proportional or time-based 24-hour samples shall be collected at the same well-defined point in the outlet and if necessary in the inlet of the treatment plant in order to monitor compliance with the requirements for discharged waste water laid down in this Directive.

Good international laboratory practices aiming at minimizing the degradation of samples between collection and analysis shall be applied.

3. The minimum annual number of samples shall be determined according to the size of the treatment plant and be collected at regular intervals during

the year:

– 2 000 to 9 999 p.e.:   12 samples during the first year.
                              four samples in subsequent years, if it can be shown that
                              the water during the first year complies with the
                              provisions of the Directive; if one sample of the four fails,
                              12 samples must be taken in the year that follows.
– 10 000 to 49 999 p. e.:   12 samples.
– 50 000 p.e. or over: 24 samples.

4. The treated waste water shall be assumed to conform to the relevant parameters
if, for each relevant parameter considered individually, samples of the water show that
it complies with the relevant parametric value in the following way:

(a) for the parameters specified in Table 1 and Article 2(7), a maximum number of
    samples which are allowed to fail the requirements, expressed in concentrations
    and/or percentage reductions in Table 1 and Article 2(7), is specified in Table 3;
(b) for the parameters of Table 1 expressed in concentrations, the failing samples
    taken under normal operating conditions must not deviate from the parametric
    values by more than 100%. For the parametric values in concentration relating to
    total suspended solids deviations of up to 150% may be accepted;
(c) for those parameters specified in Table 2 the annual mean of the samples for each
    parameter shall conform to the relevant parametric values.

5. Extreme values for the water quality in question shall not be taken into consideration when they are the result of unusual situations such as those due to heavy
rain.

Tables
[omitted]

Annex II
Criteria for identification of sensitive and less sensitive areas

A. *Sensitive areas*
A water body must be identified as a sensitive area if it falls into one of the following
groups:

(a) natural freshwater lakes, other freshwater bodies, estuaries and coastal waters
    which are found to be eutrophic or which in the near future may become eutrophic
    if protective action is not taken.
        The following elements might be taken into account when considering which
    nutrient should be reduced by further treatment:
    (i) lakes and streams reaching lakes/reservoirs/closed bays which are found to
        have a poor water exchange, whereby accumulation may take place. In these

areas, the removal of phosphorus should be included unless it can be demonstrated that the removal will have no effect on the level of eutrophication. Where discharges from large agglomerations are made, the removal of nitrogen may also be considered;

(ii) estuaries, bays and other coastal waters which are found to have a poor water exchange, or which receive large quantities of nutrients. Discharges from small agglomerations are usually of minor importance in those areas, but for large agglomerations, the removal of phosphorus and/or nitrogen should be included unless it can be demonstrated that the removal will have no effect on the level of eutrophication;

(b) surface freshwaters intended for the abstraction of drinking water which could contain more than the concentration of nitrate laid down under the relevant provisions of Council Directive 75/440/EEC of 16 June 1975 concerning the quality required of surface water intended for the abstraction of drinking water in the Member States[1] if action is not taken;

(c) areas where further treatment than that prescribed in Article 4 of this Directive is necessary to fulfil Council Directives.

B. *Less sensitive areas*

A marine water body or area can be identified as a less sensitive area if the discharge of waste water does not adversely affect the environment as a result of morphology, hydrology or specific hydraulic conditions which exist in that area.

When identifying less sensitive areas, Member States shall take into account the risk that the discharged load may be transferred to adjacent areas where it can cause detrimental environmental effects. Member States shall recognize the presence of sensitive areas outside their national jurisdiction.

The following elements shall be taken into consideration when identifying less sensitive areas: open bays, estuaries and other coastal waters with a good water exchange and not subject to eutrophication or oxygen depletion or which are considered unlikely to become eutrophic or to develop oxygen depletion due to the discharge of urban waste water.

Annex III
Industrial sectors

1. Milk-processing
2. Manufacture of fruit and vegetable products
3. Manufacture and bottling of soft drinks
4. Potato-processing
5. Meat industry

[1] OJ No L 194, 25. 7. 1975, p. 26 as amended by Directive 79/869/EEC (OJ No L 271, 29. 10. 1979, p. 44).

  6. Breweries
  7. Production of alcohol and alcoholic beverages
  8. Manufacture of animal feed from plant products
  9. Manufacture of gelatine and of glue from hides, skin and bones
10. Malt-houses
11. Fish-processing industry

Council Directive 98/83/EC of 3 November 1998 on the quality of water intended for human consumption (as amended)

Editorial note

Directive 98/83 of 3 November 1998 concerns the quality of water intended for human consumption and its objective is the protection of human health from adverse effects of any contamination of water intended for human consumption (Article 1). Article 3 sets out the exceptions to the application of the Directive. Member States are to take the measures necessary to ensure that water intended for human consumption is wholesome and clean (Article 4). Member States are to set values applicable to water intended for human consumption (Article 5). Article 6 sets out the points of compliance for the parameters established according to Article 5. Regular monitoring of the quality of water intended for human consumption is to be carried out (Article 7). Failure to meet the parametric values established is to be investigated and remedial actions are to be taken (Article 8). Information and reporting obligations are set out in Article 13.

Source: OJ L 330 05.12.1998 p. 32. Amended by: Regulation (EC) No 1882/2003 of the European Parliament and of the Council of 29 September 2003 L 284 1 31.10.2003. Corrected by: Corrigendum, OJ L 111 20.04.2001 p. 31 (98/83/EC)

Council Directive 98/83/EC of 3 November 1998 on the quality of water intended for human consumption (as amended)

The Council of the European Union,

Having regard to the Treaty establishing the European Community and, in particular, Article 130s(1) thereof,

Having regard to the proposal from the Commission,[1]

Having regard to the opinion of the Economic and Social Committee,[2]

Having regard to the opinion of the Committee of the Regions,[3]

---

[1] OJ C 131, 30.5.1995, p. 5 and OJ C 213, 15.7.1997, p. 8.   [2] OJ C 82, 19.3.1996, p. 64.
[3] OJ C 100, 2.4.1996, p. 134.

Acting in accordance with the procedure laid down in Article 189c,[1]

(1) Whereas it is necessary to adapt Council Directive 80/778/EEC of 15 July 1980 relating to the quality of water intended for human consumption[2] to scientific and technological progress; whereas experience gained from implementing that Directive shows that it is necessary to create an appropriately flexible and transparent legal framework for Member States to address failures to meet the standards; whereas, furthermore, that Directive should be re-examined in the light of the Treaty on European Union and in particular the principle of subsidiarity;

(2) Whereas in keeping with Article 3b of the Treaty, which provides that no Community action should go beyond what is necessary to achieve the objectives of the Treaty, it is necessary to revise Directive 80/778/EEC so as to focus on compliance with essential quality and health parameters, leaving Member States free to add other parameters if they see fit;

(3) Whereas, in accordance with the principle of subsidiarity, Community action must support and supplement action by the competent authorities in the Member States;

(4) Whereas, in accordance with the principle of subsidiarity, the natural and socio-economic differences between the regions of the Union require that most decisions on monitoring, analysis, and the measures to be taken to redress failures be taken at a local, regional or national level insofar as those differences do not detract from the establishment of the framework of laws, regulations and administrative provisions laid down in this Directive;

(5) Whereas Community standards for essential and preventive health-related quality parameters in water intended for human consumption are necessary if minimum environmental-quality goals to be achieved in connection with other Community measures are to be defined so that the sustainable use of water intended for human consumption may be safeguarded and promoted;

(6) Whereas, in view of the importance of the quality of water intended for human consumption for human health, it is necessary to lay down at Community level the essential quality standards with which water intended for that purpose must comply;

(7) Whereas it is necessary to include water used in the food industry unless it can be established that the use of such water does not affect the wholesomeness of the finished product;

(8) Whereas to enable water-supply undertakings to meet the quality standards for drinking water, appropriate water-protection measures should be applied to

---

[1] Opinion of the European Parliament of 12 December 1996 (OJ C 20, 20.1.1997, p. 133), Council common position of 19 December 1997 (OJ C 91, 26.3.1998, p. 1) and Decision of the European Parliament of 13 May 1998 (OJ C 167, 1.6.1998, p. 92).

[2] OJ L 229, 30.8.1980, p. 11. Directive as last amended by the 1994 Act of Accession.

ensure that surface and groundwater is kept clean; whereas the same goal can be achieved by appropriate water-treatment measures to be applied before supply;

(9) Whereas the coherence of European water policy presupposes that a suitable water framework Directive will be adopted in due course;

(10) Whereas it is necessary to exclude from the scope of this Directive natural mineral waters and waters which are medicinal products, since special rules for those types of water have been established;

(11) Whereas measures are required for all parameters directly relevant to health and for other parameters if a deterioration in quality has occurred; whereas, furthermore, such measures should be carefully coordinated with the implementation of Council Directive 91/414/EEC of 15 July 1991 concerning the placing of plant protection products on the market[1] and Directive 98/8/EC of the European Parliament and of the Council of 16 February 1998 concerning the placing of biocidal products on the market;[2]

(12) Whereas it is necessary to set individual parametric values for substances which are important throughout the Community at a level strict enough to ensure that this Directive's purpose can be achieved;

(13) Whereas the parametric values are based on the scientific knowledge available and the precautionary principle has also been taken into account; whereas those values have been selected to ensure that water intended for human consumption can be consumed safely on a life-long basis, and thus represent a high level of health protection;

(14) Whereas a balance should be struck to prevent both microbiological and chemical risks; whereas, to that end, and in the light of a future review of the parametric values, the establishment of parametric values applicable to water intended for human consumption should be based on public-health considerations and on a method of assessing risk;

(15) Whereas there is at present insufficient evidence on which to base parametric values for endocrine-disrupting chemicals at Community level, yet there is increasing concern regarding the potential impact on humans and wildlife of the effects of substances harmful to health;

(16) Whereas in particular the standards in Annex I are generally based on the World Health Organisation's 'Guidelines for drinking water quality', and the opinion of the Commission's Scientific Advisory Committee to examine the toxicity and ecotoxicity of chemical compounds;

(17) Whereas Member States must set values for other additional parameters not included in Annex I where that is necessary to protect human health within their territories;

---

[1] OJ L 230, 19.8.1991, p. 1. Directive as last amended by Commission Directive 96/68/EC (OJ L 277, 30.10.1996, p. 25).
[2] OJ L 123, 24.4.1998, p. 1.

(18) Whereas Member States may set values for other additional parameters not included in Annex I where that is deemed necessary for the purpose of ensuring the quality of the production, distribution and inspection of water intended for human consumption;

(19) Whereas, when Member States deem it necessary to adopt standards more stringent than those set out in Annex I, Parts A and B, or standards for additional parameters not included in Annex I but necessary to protect human health, they must notify the Commission of those standards;

(20) Whereas Member States are bound, when introducing or maintaining more stringent protection measures, to respect the principles and rules of the Treaty, as they are interpreted by the Court of Justice;

(21) Whereas the parametric values are to be complied with at the point where water intended for human consumption is made available to the appropriate user;

(22) Whereas the quality of water intended for human consumption can be influenced by the domestic distribution system; whereas, furthermore, it is recognised that neither the domestic distribution system nor its maintenance may be the responsibility of the Member States;

(23) Whereas each Member State should establish monitoring programmes to check that water intended for human consumption meets the requirements of this Directive; whereas such monitoring programmes should be appropriate to local needs and should meet the minimum monitoring requirements laid down in this Directive;

(24) Whereas the methods used to analyse the quality of water intended for human consumption should be such as to ensure that the results obtained are reliable and comparable;

(25) Whereas, in the event of non-compliance with the standards imposed by this Directive the Member State concerned should investigate the cause and ensure that the necessary remedial action is taken as soon as possible to restore the quality of the water;

(26) Whereas it is important to prevent contaminated water causing a potential danger to human health; whereas the supply of such water should be prohibited or its use restricted;

(27) Whereas, in the event of non-compliance with a parameter that has an indicator function, the Member State concerned must consider whether that non-compliance poses any risk to human health; whereas it should take remedial action to restore the quality of the water where that is necessary to protect human health;

(28) Whereas, should such remedial action be necessary to restore the quality of water intended for human consumption, in accordance with Article 130r(2) of the Treaty, priority should be given to action which rectifies the problem at source;

(29) Whereas Member States should be authorised, under certain conditions, to grant derogations from this Directive; whereas, furthermore, it is necessary to establish

a proper framework for such derogations, provided that they must not consti-tute a potential danger to human health and provided that the supply of water intended for human consumption in the area concerned cannot otherwise be maintained by any other reasonable means;

(30) Whereas, since the preparation or distribution of water intended for human consumption may involve the use of certain substances or materials, rules are required to govern the use thereof in order to avoid possible harmful effects on human health;

(31) Whereas scientific and technical progress may necessitate rapid adaptation of the technical requirements laid down in Annexes II and III; whereas, furthermore, in order to facilitate application of the measures required for that purpose, pro-vision should be made for a procedure under which the Commission can adopt such adaptations with the assistance of a committee composed of representatives of the Member States;

(32) Whereas consumers should be adequately and appropriately informed of the quality of water intended for human consumption, of any derogations granted by the Member States and of any remedial action taken by the competent author-ities; whereas, furthermore, consideration should be given both to the technical and statistical needs of the Commission, and to the rights of the individual to obtain adequate information concerning the quality of water intended for human consumption;

(33) Whereas, in exceptional circumstances and for geographically defined areas, it may be necessary to allow Member States a more extensive timescale for compliance with certain provisions of this Directive;

(34) Whereas this Directive should not affect the obligations of the Member States as to the time limit for transposition into national law, or as to application, as shown in Annex IV,

Has adopted this Directive:

Article 1
Objective

1. This Directive concerns the quality of water intended for human consumption.

2. The objective of this Directive shall be to protect human health from the adverse effects of any contamination of water intended for human consumption by ensuring that it is wholesome and clean.

Article 2
Definitions

For the purposes of this Directive:

1. 'water intended for human consumption' shall mean:
   (a) all water either in its original state or after treatment, intended for drinking, cooking, food preparation or other domestic purposes, regardless of its origin

and whether it is supplied from a distribution network, from a tanker, or in
bottles or containers;

  (b) all water used in any food-production undertaking for the manufacture, pro-
      cessing, preservation or marketing of products or substances intended for
      human consumption unless the competent national authorities are satisfied
      that the quality of the water cannot affect the wholesomeness of the foodstuff
      in its finished form;

2. 'domestic distribution system' shall mean the pipework, fittings and appliances
   which are installed between the taps that are normally used for human consumption and the distribution network but only if they are not the responsibility of the
   water supplier, in its capacity as a water supplier, according to the relevant national
   law.

Article 3
Exemptions

  1. This Directive shall not apply to:

  (a) natural mineral waters recognised as such by the competent national authorities,
      in accordance with Council Directive 80/777/EEC of 15 July 1980 on the approxi-
      mation of the laws of the Member States relating to the exploitation and marketing
      of natural mineral waters;[1]
  (b) waters which are medicinal products within the meaning of Council Directive
      65/65/EEC of 26 January 1965 on the approximation of provisions laid down by
      law, regulation or administrative action relating to medicinal products.[2]

  2. Member States may exempt from the provisions of this Directive:

  (a) water intended exclusively for those purposes for which the competent authorities
      are satisfied that the quality of the water has no influence, either directly or
      indirectly, on the health of the consumers concerned;
  (b) water intended for human consumption from an individual supply providing less
      than 10 mZ3 a day as an average or serving fewer than 50 persons, unless the water
      is supplied as part of a commercial or public activity.

  3. Member States that have recourse to the exemptions provided for in paragraph
2(b) shall ensure that the population concerned is informed thereof and of any action
that can be taken to protect human health from the adverse effects resulting from
any contamination of water intended for human consumption. In addition, when a
potential danger to human health arising out of the quality of such water is apparent,
the population concerned shall promptly be given appropriate advice.

---

[1] OJ L 229, 30.8.1980, p. 1. Directive as last amended by Directive 96/70/EC (OJ L 299, 23.11.1996, p. 26).
[2] OJ 22 9.2.1965, p. 369. Directive as last amended by Directive 93/39/EEC (OJ L 214, 24.8.1993, p. 22).

Article 4
General obligations

1. Without prejudice to their obligations under other Community provisions, Member States shall take the measures necessary to ensure that water intended for human consumption is wholesome and clean.

For the purposes of the minimum requirements of this Directive, water intended for human consumption shall be wholesome and clean if it:

(a) is free from any micro-organisms and parasites and from any substances which, in numbers or concentrations, constitute a potential danger to human health, and
(b) meets the minimum requirements set out in Annex I, Parts A and B;

and if, in accordance with the relevant provisions of Articles 5 to 8 and 10 and in accordance with the Treaty, Member States take all other measures necessary to ensure that water intended for human consumption complies with the requirements of this Directive.

2. Member States shall ensure that the measures taken to implement this Directive in no circumstances have the effect of allowing, directly or indirectly, either any deterioration of the present quality of water intended for human consumption so far as that is relevant for the protection of human health or any increase in the pollution of waters used for the production of drinking water.

Article 5
Quality standards

1. Member States shall set values applicable to water intended for human consumption for the parameters set out in Annex I.

2. The values set in accordance with paragraph 1 shall not be less stringent than those set out in Annex I. As regards the parameters set out in Annex I, Part C, the values need be fixed only for monitoring purposes and for the fulfilment of the obligations imposed in Article 8.

3. A Member State shall set values for additional parameters not included in Annex I where the protection of human health within its national territory or part of it so requires. The values set should, as a minimum, satisfy the requirements of Article 4(1)(a).

Article 6
Point of compliance

1. The parametric values set in accordance with Article 5 shall be complied with:

(a) in the case of water supplied from a distribution network, at the point, within premises or an establishment, at which it emerges from the taps that are normally used for human consumption;

(b) in the case of water supplied from a tanker, at the point at which it emerges from the tanker;

(c) in the case of water put into bottles or containers intended for sale, at the point at which the water is put into the bottles or containers;

(d) in the case of water used in a food-production undertaking, at the point where the water is used in the undertaking.

2. In the case of water covered by paragraph 1(a), Member States shall be deemed to have fulfilled their obligations under this Article and under Articles 4 and 8(2) where it can be established that noncompliance with the parametric values set in accordance with Article 5 is due to the domestic distribution system or the maintenance thereof except in premises and establishments where water is supplied to the public, such as schools, hospitals and restaurants.

3. Where paragraph 2 applies and there is a risk that water covered by paragraph 1(a) would not comply with the parametric values established in accordance with Article 5, Member States shall nevertheless ensure that:

(a) appropriate measures are taken to reduce or eliminate the risk of non-compliance with the parametric values, such as advising property owners of any possible remedial action they could take, and/or other measures, such as appropriate treatment techniques, are taken to change the nature or properties of the water before it is supplied so as to reduce or eliminate the risk of the water not complying with the parametric values after supply; and

(b) the consumers concerned are duly informed and advised of any possible additional remedial action that they should take.

Article 7
Monitoring

1. Member States shall take all measures necessary to ensure that regular monitoring of the quality of water intended for human consumption is carried out, in order to check that the water available to consumers meets the requirements of this Directive and in particular the parametric values set in accordance with Article 5. Samples should be taken so that they are representative of the quality of the water consumed throughout the year. In addition, Member States shall take all measures necessary to ensure that, where disinfection forms part of the preparation or distribution of water intended for human consumption, the efficiency of the disinfection treatment applied is verified, and that any contamination from disinfection by-products is kept as low as possible without compromising the disinfection.

2. To meet the obligations imposed in paragraph 1, appropriate monitoring programmes shall be established by the competent authorities for all water intended for human consumption. Those monitoring programmes shall meet the minimum requirements set out in Annex II.

3. The sampling points shall be determined by the competent authorities and shall meet the relevant requirements set out in Annex II.

4. Community guidelines for the monitoring prescribed in this Article may be drawn upin accordance with the procedure laid down in Article 12.

5. (a) Member States shall comply with the specifications for the analyses of parameters set out in Annex III.

   (b) Methods other than those specified in Annex III, Part 1, may be used, providing it can be demonstrated that the results obtained are at least as reliable as those produced by the methods specified.

   Member States which have recourse to alternative methods shall provide the Commission with all relevant information concerning such methods and their equivalence.

   (c) For those parameters listed in Annex III, Parts 2 and 3, any method of analysis may be used provided that it meets the requirements set out therein.

6. Member States shall ensure that additional monitoring is carried out on a case-by-case basis of substances and micro-organisms for which no parametric value has been set in accordance with Article 5, if there is reason to suspect that they may be present in amounts or numbers which constitute a potential danger to human health.

Article 8
Remedial action and restrictions in use

1. Member States shall ensure that any failure to meet the parametric values set in accordance with Article 5 is immediately investigated in order to identify the cause.

2. If, despite the measures taken to meet the obligations imposed in Article 4(1), water intended for human consumption does not meet the parametric values set in accordance with Article 5, and subject to Article 6(2), the Member State concerned shall ensure that the necessary remedial action is taken as soon as possible to restore its quality and shall give priority to their enforcement action, having regard *inter alia* to the extent to which the relevant parametric value has been exceeded and to the potential danger to human health.

3. Whether or not any failure to meet the parametric values has occurred, Member States shall ensure that any supply of water intended for human consumption which constitutes a potential danger to human health is prohibited or its use restricted or such other action is taken as is necessary to protect human health. In such cases consumers shall be informed promptly thereof and given the necessary advice.

4. The competent authorities or other relevant bodies shall decide what action under paragraph 3 should be taken, bearing in mind the risks to human health which would be caused by an interruption of the supply or a restriction in the use of water intended for human consumption.

5. Member States may establish guidelines to assist the competent authorities to fulfil their obligations under paragraph 4.

6. In the event of non-compliance with the parametric values or with the specifications set out in Annex I, Part C, Member States shall consider whether that non-compliance poses any risk to human health. They shall take remedial action to restore the quality of the water where that is necessary to protect human health.

7. Member States shall ensure that, where remedial action is taken, consumers are notified except where the competent authorities consider the non-compliance with the parametric value to be trivial.

Article 9

Derogations

1. Member States may provide for derogations from the parametric values set out in Annex I, Part B, or set in accordance with Article 5(3), up to a maximum value to be determined by them, provided no derogation constitutes a potential danger to human health and provided that the supply of water intended for human consumption in the area concerned cannot otherwise be maintained by any other reasonable means. Derogations shall be limited to as short a time as possible and shall not exceed three years, towards the end of which a review shall be conducted to determine whether sufficient progress has been made.

Where a Member State intends to grant a second derogation, it shall communicate the review, along with the grounds for its decision on the second derogation, to the Commission. No such second derogation shall exceed three years.

2. In exceptional circumstances, a Member State may ask the Commission for a third derogation for a period not exceeding three years. The Commission shall take a decision on any such request within three months.

3. Any derogation granted in accordance with paragraphs 1 or 2 shall specify the following:

(a) the grounds for the derogation;
(b) the parameter concerned, previous relevant monitoring results, and the maximum permissible value under the derogation;
(c) the geographical area, the quantity of water supplied each day, the population concerned and whether or not any relevant food-production undertaking would be affected;
(d) an appropriate monitoring scheme, with an increased monitoring frequency where necessary;
(e) a summary of the plan for the necessary remedial action, including a timetable for the work and an estimate of the cost and provisions for reviewing;
(f) the required duration of the derogation.

4. If the competent authorities consider the non-compliance with the parametric value to be trivial, and if action taken in accordance with Article 8(2) is sufficient to

remedy the problem within 30 days, the requirements of paragraph 3 need not be applied.

In that event, only the maximum permissible value for the parameter concerned and the time allowed to remedy the problem shall be set by the competent authorities or other relevant bodies.

5. Recourse may no longer be had to paragraph 4 if failure to comply with any one parametric value for a given water supply has occurred on more than 30 days on aggregate during the previous 12 months.

6. Any Member State which has recourse to the derogations provided for in this Article shall ensure that the population affected by any such derogation is promptly informed in an appropriate manner of the derogation and of the conditions governing it. In addition the Member State shall, where necessary, ensure that advice is given to particular population groups for which the derogation could present a special risk.

These obligations shall not apply in the circumstances described in paragraph 4 unless the competent authorities decide otherwise.

7. With the exception of derogations granted in accordance with paragraph 4 a Member State shall inform the Commission within two months of any derogation concerning an individual supply of water exceeding $1\,000\,\text{m}^3$ a day as an average or serving more than 5 000 persons, including the information specified in paragraph 3.

8. This Article shall not apply to water intended for human consumption offered for sale in bottles or containers.

Article 10
Quality assurance of treatment, equipment and materials

Member States shall take all measures necessary to ensure that no substances or materials for new installations used in the preparation or distribution of water intended for human consumption or impurities associated with such substances or materials for new installations remain in water intended for human consumption in concentrations higher than is necessary for the purpose of their use and do not, either directly or indirectly, reduce the protection of human health provided for in this Directive; the interpretative document and technical specifications pursuant to Article 3 and Article 4(1) of Council Directive 89/106/EEC of 21 December 1988 on the approximation of laws, regulations and administrative provisions of the Member States relating to construction products[1] shall respect the requirements of this Directive.

Article 11
Review of Annexes

1. At least every five years, the Commission shall review Annex I in the light of scientific and technical progress and shall make proposals for amendments, where necessary, under the procedure laid down in Article 189c of the Treaty.

---

[1] OJ L 40, 11.2.1989, p. 12. Directive as last amended by Directive 93/68/EEC (OJ L 220, 30.8.1993, p. 1).

2. At least every five years, the Commission shall adapt Annexes II and III to scientific and technical progress. Such changes as are necessary shall be adopted in accordance with the procedure laid down in Article 12.

Article 12

1. The Commission shall be assisted by a committee.

2. Where reference is made to this Article, Articles 4 and 7 of Decision 1999/468/EC[1] shall apply, having regard to the provisions of Article 8 thereof.

The period laid down in Article 4(3) of Decision 1999/468/EC shall be set at three months.

3. The Committee shall adopt its rules of procedure.

Article 13
Information and reporting

1. Member States shall take the measures necessary to ensure that adequate and up-to-date information on the quality of water intended for human consumption is available to consumers.

2. Without prejudice to Council Directive 90/313/EEC of 7 June 1990 on the freedom of access to information on the environment,[2] each Member State shall publish a report every three years on the quality of water intended for human consumption with the objective of informing consumers. The first report shall cover the years 2002, 2003 and 2004. Each report shall include, as a minimum, all individual supplies of water exceeding 1 000 m^3 a day as an average or serving more than 5 000 persons and it shall cover three calendar years and be published within one calendar year of the end of the reporting period.

3. Member States shall send their reports to the Commission within two months of their publication.

4. The formats and the minimum information for the reports provided for in paragraph 2 shall be determined having special regard to the measures referred to in Article 3(2), Article 5(2) and (3), Article 7(2), Article 8, Article 9(6) and (7) and 15(1), and shall if necessary be amended in accordance with the procedure laid down in Article 12.

5. The Commission shall examine the Member States' reports and, every three years, publish a synthesis report on the quality of water intended for human consumption in the Community. That report shall be published within nine months of the receipt of the Member States' reports.

6. Together with the first report on this Directive as mentioned in paragraph 2, Member States shall also produce a report to be forwarded to the Commission on the

---

[1] Council Decision 1999/468/EC of 28 June 1999 laying down the procedures for the exercise of implementing powers conferred on the Commission (OJ L 184, 17.7.1999, p. 23).

[2] OJ L 158, 23.6.1990, p. 56.

measures they have taken or plan to take to fultil their obligations pursuant to Article 6(3) and Annex I, Part B, note 10. The Commission shall submit, as appropriate, a proposal on the format of this report in accordance with the procedure laid down in Article 12.

Article 14
Timescale for compliance

Member States shall take the measures necessary to ensure that the quality of water intended for human consumption complies with this Directive within five years of its entry into force, without prejudice to Notes 2, 4 and 10 in Annex I, Part B.

Article 15
Exceptional circumstances

1. A Member State may, in exceptional circumstances and for geographically defined areas, submit a special request to the Commission for a period longer than that laid down in Article 14. The additional period shall not exceed three years, towards the end of which a review shall be carried out and forwarded to the Commission which may, on the basis of that review, permit a second additional period of up to three years. This provision shall not apply to water intended for human consumption offered for sale in bottles or containers.

2. Any such request, grounds for which shall be given, shall set out the difficulties experienced and include, as a minimum, all the information specified in Article 9(3).

3. The Commission shall examine that request in accordance with the procedure laid down in Article 12.

4. Any Member State which has recourse to this Article shall ensure that the population affected by its request is promptly informed in an appropriate manner of the outcome of that request. In addition, the Member State shall, where necessary, ensure that advice is given to particular population groups for which the request could present a special risk.

Article 16
Repeal

1. Directive 80/778/EEC is hereby repealed with effect from five years after the entry into force of this Directive. Subject to paragraph 2, this repeal shall be without prejudice to Member States' obligations regarding deadlines for transposition into national law and for application as shown in Annex IV.

Any reference to the Directive repealed shall be construed as a reference to this Directive and shall be read in accordance with the correlation table set out in Annex V.

2. As soon as a Member State has brought into force the laws, regulations and administrative provisions necessary to comply with this Directive and has taken the measures provided for in Article 14, this Directive, not Directive 80/778/EEC, shall

apply to the quality of water intended for human consumption in that Member State.

Article 17
Transposition into national law

1. Member States shall bring into force the laws, regulations and administrative provisions necessary to comply with this Directive within two years of its entry into force. They shall forthwith inform the Commission thereof.

When the Member States adopt those measures, these shall contain references to this Directive or shall be accompanied by such references on the occasion of their official publication. The methods of making such references shall be laid down by the Member States.

2. The Member States shall communicate to the Commission the texts of the provisions of national law which they adopt in the field covered by this Directive.

Article 18
Entry into force

This Directive shall enter into force on the 20th day following its publication in the *Official Journal of the European Communities*.

Article 19
Addressees

This Directive is addressed to the Member States.

Annexes

[Omitted]

Directive 2000/60/EC of the European Parliament and of the Council of 23 October 2000 establishing a framework for Community action in the field of water policy (as amended)

Editorial note

Directive 2000/60 of 23 October 2000, as amended, establishes a framework for the protection of inland surface waters, transitional waters, coastal waters and groundwater (Article 1). Member States are to identify the individual river basins lying within their national territory and assign them to individual basin districts. Appropriate administrative arrangements are to be made for the application of the Directive within each river basin district (Article 3(1) and (2)). River basins covering the territory of more than one Member State are to be assigned to an international river basin district. If the river basin extends beyond the territory of the Community, appropriate coordination with relevant non-Member States is to be sought (Article 3(3) and (5)).

The Directive specifies the environmental objectives to be achieved through its implementation and sets timescales for their achievement for surface waters (Article 4(1)(a)); groundwater (Article 4(1)(b)); and protected areas (Article 4(1)(c)). Member States are to ensure that, for each river basin district, an analysis of its characteristics, a review of the impact of human activities, and an economic analysis of its use is undertaken (Article 5). Register(s) shall be established of all areas within each river basin district which have been designated as requiring special protection (Article 6). All bodies of water intended for the abstraction of water intended for human consumption are to be identified (Article 7). Programmes for the monitoring of water status in order to establish a coherent and comprehensive overview of water status within each river basin district are to be set up (Article 8). Member States are to take into account the principle of the recovery of the costs of water services and the polluter pays principle. They shall ensure that, by 2010, their water pricing policies provide, *inter alia*, adequate incentives for users to use water efficiently (Article 9). All discharges into surface waters are to be controlled according to the combined approach set out in Article 10.

Each Member State should establish for each river basin district a programme of measures aimed at achieving the environmental objectives established under Article 4. Each programme is to include basic and supplementary measures (Article 11).

A river basin management plan is to be produced for each river basin (Article 13).
The public should have an active involvement in the implementation of the Directive
and in particular in the production, review and updating of the river basin management plans (Article 14). Copies of the river basin management plans are to be
sent to the Commission and to other Member States concerned (Article 15). The
European Parliament and the Council are to adopt specific measures against pollution of water by individual pollutants or groups of pollutants and to prevent and
control groundwater pollution on the basis of a proposal presented by the Commission (Articles 16 and 17). The Commission is to publish a report on the implementation of the Directive at the latest twelve years after its entry into force (Article 18). The Directive lists a number of existing Directives which will be gradually repealed after its entry into force (Article 22). Penalties for breaches of national
provisions implementing the Directive are to be determined by the Member States
(Article 23).

Source: OJ L 327 22.12.2000 p. 1. Amended by: Decision No 2455/2001/EC of the
European Parliament and of the Council of 20 November 2001 L 331 1 15.12.2001

Directive 2000/60/EC of the European Parliament and of the Council of 23 October 2000 establishing a framework for Community action in the field of water policy (as amended)

The European Parliament and the Council of the European Union,
  Having regard to the Treaty establishing the European Community, and in partic-
ular Article 175(1) thereof, Having regard to the proposal from the Commission,[1]
  Having regard to the opinion of the Economic and Social Committee,[2]
  Having regard to the opinion of the Committee of the Regions,[3]
  Acting in accordance with the procedure laid down in Article 251 of the Treaty,[4]
and in the light of the joint text approved by the Conciliation Committee on 18 July
2000,
  Whereas:

(1) Water is not a commercial product like any other but, rather, a heritage which
    must be protected, defended and treated as such.
(2) The conclusions of the Community Water Policy Ministerial Seminar in Frank-
    furt in 1988 highlighted the need for Community legislation covering ecological

---

[1] OJ C 184, 17.6.1997, p. 20, OJ C 16, 20.1.1998, p. 14 and OJ C 108, 7.4.1998, p. 94.
[2] OJ C 355, 21.11.1997, p. 83.   [3] OJ C 180, 11.6.1998, p. 38.
[4] Opinion of the European Parliament of 11 February 1999 (OJ C 150, 28.5.1999, p. 419) confirmed on
    16 September 1999, and Council Common Position of 22 October 1999 (OJ C 343, 30.11.1999, p. 1).
    Decision of the European Parliament of 7 September 2000 and Decision of the Council of 14 September
    2000.

quality. The Council in its resolution of 28 June 1988[1] asked the Commission to submit proposals to improve ecological quality in Community surface waters.

(3) The declaration of the Ministerial Seminar on groundwater held at The Hague in 1991 recognised the need for action to avoid long-term deterioration of freshwater quality and quantity and called for a programme of actions to be implemented by the year 2000 aiming at sustainable management and protection of freshwater resources. In its resolutions of 25 February 1992,[2] and 20 February 1995,[3] the Council requested an action programme for groundwater and a revision of Council Directive 80/68/EEC of 17 December 1979 on the protection of groundwater against pollution caused by certain dangerous substances,[4] as part of an overall policy on freshwater protection.

(4) Waters in the Community are under increasing pressure from the continuous growth in demand for sufficient quantities of good quality water for all purposes. On 10 November 1995, the European Environment Agency in its report 'Environment in the European Union – 1995' presented an updated state of the environment report, confirming the need for action to protect Community waters in qualitative as well as in quantitative terms.

(5) On 18 December 1995, the Council adopted conclusions requiring, *inter alia*, the drawing up of a new framework Directive establishing the basic principles of sustainable water policy in the European Union and inviting the Commission to come forward with a proposal.

(6) On 21 February 1996 the Commission adopted a communication to the European Parliament and the Council on European Community water policy setting out the principles for a Community water policy.

(7) On 9 September 1996 the Commission presented a proposal for a Decision of the European Parliament and of the Council on an action programme for integrated protection and management of groundwater.[5] In that proposal the Commission pointed to the need to establish procedures for the regulation of abstraction of freshwater and for the monitoring of freshwater quality and quantity.

(8) On 29 May 1995 the Commission adopted a communication to the European Parliament and the Council on the wise use and conservation of wetlands, which recognised the important functions they perform for the protection of water resources.

(9) It is necessary to develop an integrated Community policy on water.

(10) The Council on 25 June 1996, the Committee of the Regions on 19 September 1996, the Economic and Social Committee on 26 September 1996, and the European Parliament on 23 October 1996 all requested the Commission to come

---

[1] OJ C 209, 9.8.1988, p. 3. [2] OJ C 59, 6.3.1992, p. 2. [3] OJ C 49, 28.2.1995, p. 1.
[4] OJ L 20, 26.1.1980, p. 43. Directive as amended by Directive 91/692/EEC (OJ L 377, 31.12.1991, p. 48).
[5] OJ C 355, 25.11.1996, p. 1.

forward with a proposal for a Council Directive establishing a framework for a European water policy.

(11) As set out in Article 174 of the Treaty, the Community policy on the environment is to contribute to pursuit of the objectives of preserving, protecting and improving the quality of the environment, in prudent and rational utilisation of natural resources, and to be based on the precautionary principle and on the principles that preventive action should be taken, environmental damage should, as a priority, be rectified at source and that the polluter should pay.

(12) Pursuant to Article 174 of the Treaty, in preparing its policy on the environment, the Community is to take account of available scientific and technical data, environmental conditions in the various regions of the Community, and the economic and social development of the Community as a whole and the balanced development of its regions as well as the potential benefits and costs of action or lack of action.

(13) There are diverse conditions and needs in the Community which require different specific solutions. This diversity should be taken into account in the planning and execution of measures to ensure protection and sustainable use of water in the framework of the river basin. Decisions should be taken as close as possible to the locations where water is affected or used. Priority should be given to action within the responsibility of Member States through the drawing up of programmes of measures adjusted to regional and local conditions.

(14) The success of this Directive relies on close cooperation and coherent action at Community, Member State and local level as well as on information, consultation and involvement of the public, including users.

(15) The supply of water is a service of general interest as defined in the Commission communication on services of general interest in Europe.[1]

(16) Further integration of protection and sustainable management of water into other Community policy areas such as energy, transport, agriculture, fisheries, regional policy and tourism is necessary. This Directive should provide a basis for a continued dialogue and for the development of strategies towards a further integration of policy areas. This Directive can also make an important contribution to other areas of cooperation between Member States, *inter alia*, the European spatial development perspective (ESDP).

(17) An effective and coherent water policy must take account of the vulnerability of aquatic ecosystems located near the coast and estuaries or in gulfs or relatively closed seas, as their equilibrium is strongly influenced by the quality of inland waters flowing into them. Protection of water status within river basins will provide economic benefits by contributing towards the protection of fish populations, including coastal fish populations.

[1] OJ C 281, 26.9.1996, p. 3.

(18) Community water policy requires a transparent, effective and coherent legislative framework. The Community should provide common principles and the overall framework for action. This Directive should provide for such a framework and coordinate and integrate, and, in a longer perspective, further develop the overall principles and structures for protection and sustainable use of water in the Community in accordance with the principles of subsidiarity.

(19) This Directive aims at maintaining and improving the aquatic environment in the Community. This purpose is primarily concerned with the quality of the waters concerned. Control of quantity is an ancillary element in securing good water quality and therefore measures on quantity, serving the objective of ensuring good quality, should also be established.

(20) The quantitative status of a body of groundwater may have an impact on the ecological quality of surface waters and terrestrial ecosystems associated with that groundwater body.

(21) The Community and Member States are party to various international agreements containing important obligations on the protection of marine waters from pollution, in particular the Convention on the Protection of the Marine Environment of the Baltic Sea Area, signed in Helsinki on 9 April 1992 and approved by Council Decision 94/157/EC,[1] (1) the Convention for the Protection of the Marine Environment of the North-East Atlantic, signed in Paris on 22 September 1992 and approved by Council Decision 98/249/EC,[2] and the Convention for the Protection of the Mediterranean Sea Against Pollution, signed in Barcelona on 16 February 1976 and approved by Council Decision 77/585/EEC,[3] and its Protocol for the Protection of the Mediterranean Sea Against Pollution from Land-Based Sources, signed in Athens on 17 May 1980 and approved by Council Decision 83/101/EEC.[4] This Directive is to make a contribution towards enabling the Community and Member States to meet those obligations.

(22) This Directive is to contribute to the progressive reduction of emissions of hazardous substances to water.

(23) Common principles are needed in order to coordinate Member States' efforts to improve the protection of Community waters in terms of quantity and quality, to promote sustainable water use, to contribute to the control of transboundary water problems, to protect aquatic ecosystems, and terrestrial ecosystems and wetlands directly depending on them, and to safeguard and develop the potential uses of Community waters.

(24) Good water quality will contribute to securing the drinking water supply for the population.

[1] OJ L 73, 16.3.1994, p. 19. [2] OJ L 104, 3.4.1998, p. 1.
[3] OJ L 240, 19.9.1977, p 1. [4] OJ L 67, 12.3.1983, p. 1.

(25) Common definitions of the status of water in terms of quality and, where relevant for the purpose of the environmental protection, quantity should be established. Environmental objectives should be set to ensure that good status of surface water and groundwater is achieved throughout the Community and that deterioration in the status of waters is prevented at Community level.

(26) Member States should aim to achieve the objective of at least good water status by defining and implementing the necessary measures within integrated programmes of measures, taking into account existing Community requirements. Where good water status already exists, it should be maintained. For groundwater, in addition to the requirements of good status, any significant and sustained upward trend in the concentration of any pollutant should be identified and reversed.

(27) The ultimate aim of this Directive is to achieve the elimination of priority hazardous substances and contribute to achieving concentrations in the marine environment near background values for naturally occurring substances.

(28) Surface waters and groundwaters are in principle renewable natural resources; in particular, the task of ensuring good status of groundwater requires early action and stable long-term planning of protective measures, owing to the natural time lag in its formation and renewal. Such time lag for improvement should be taken into account in timetables when establishing measures for the achievement of good status of groundwater and reversing any significant and sustained upward trend in the concentration of any pollutant in groundwater.

(29) In aiming to achieve the objectives set out in this Directive, and in establishing a programme of measures to that end, Member States may phase implementation of the programme of measures in order to spread the costs of implementation.

(30) In order to ensure a full and consistent implementation of this Directive any extensions of timescale should be made on the basis of appropriate, evident and transparent criteria and be justified by the Member States in the river basin management plans.

(31) In cases where a body of water is so affected by human activity or its natural condition is such that it may be unfeasible or unreasonably expensive to achieve good status, less stringent environmental objectives may be set on the basis of appropriate, evident and transparent criteria, and all practicable steps should be taken to prevent any further deterioration of the status of waters.

(32) There may be grounds for exemptions from the requirement to prevent further deterioration or to achieve good status under specific conditions, if the failure is the result of unforeseen or exceptional circumstances, in particular floods and droughts, or, for reasons of overriding public interest, of new modifications to the physical characteristics of a surface water body or alterations to the level of bodies of groundwater, provided that all practicable steps are taken to mitigate the adverse impact on the status of the body of water.

(33) The objective of achieving good water status should be pursued for each river basin, so that measures in respect of surface water and groundwaters belonging to the same ecological, hydrological and hydrogeological system are coordinated.

(34) For the purposes of environmental protection there is a need for a greater integration of qualitative and quantitative aspects of both surface waters and groundwaters, taking into account the natural flow conditions of water within the hydrological cycle.

(35) Within a river basin where use of water may have transboundary effects, the requirements for the achievement of the environmental objectives established under this Directive, and in particular all programmes of measures, should be coordinated for the whole of the river basin district. For river basins extending beyond the boundaries of the Community, Member States should endeavour to ensure the appropriate coordination with the relevant non-member States. This Directive is to contribute to the implementation of Community obligations under international conventions on water protection and management, notably the United Nations Convention on the protection and use of transboundary water courses and international lakes, approved by Council Decision 95/308/EC[1] and any succeeding agreements on its application.

(36) It is necessary to undertake analyses of the characteristics of a river basin and the impacts of human activity as well as an economic analysis of water use. The development in water status should be monitored by Member States on a systematic and comparable basis throughout the Community. This information is necessary in order to provide a sound basis for Member States to develop programmes of measures aimed at achieving the objectives established under this Directive.

(37) Member States should identify waters used for the abstraction of drinking water and ensure compliance with Council Directive 80/778/EEC of 15 July 1980 relating to the quality of water intended for human consumption.[2]

(38) The use of economic instruments by Member States may be appropriate as part of a programme of measures. The principle of recovery of the costs of water services, including environmental and resource costs associated with damage or negative impact on the aquatic environment should be taken into account in accordance with, in particular, the polluter-pays principle. An economic analysis of water services based on long-term forecasts of supply and demand for water in the river basin district will be necessary for this purpose.

(39) There is a need to prevent or reduce the impact of incidents in which water is accidentally polluted. Measures with the aim of doing so should be included in the programme of measures.

[1] OJ L 186, 5.8.1995, p. 42.
[2] OJ L 229, 30.8.1980, p. 11. Directive as last amended by Directive 98/83/ EC (OJ L 330, 05.12.1998, p. 32).

(40) With regard to pollution prevention and control, Community water policy should be based on a combined approach using control of pollution at source through the setting of emission limit values and of environmental quality standards.

(41) For water quantity, overall principles should be laid down for control on abstraction and impoundment in order to ensure the environmental sustainability of the affected water systems.

(42) Common environmental quality standards and emission limit values for certain groups or families of pollutants should be laid down as minimum requirements in Community legislation. Provisions for the adoption of such standards at Community level should be ensured.

(43) Pollution through the discharge, emission or loss of priority hazardous substances must cease or be phased out. The European Parliament and the Council should, on a proposal from the Commission, agree on the substances to be considered for action as a priority and on specific measures to be taken against pollution of water by those substances, taking into account all significant sources and identifying the cost-effective and proportionate level and combination of controls.

(44) In identifying priority hazardous substances, account should be taken of the precautionary principle, relying in particular on the determination of any potentially adverse effects of the product and on a scientific assessment of the risk.

(45) Member States should adopt measures to eliminate pollution of surface water by the priority substances and progressively to reduce pollution by other substances which would otherwise prevent Member States from achieving the objectives for the bodies of surface water.

(46) To ensure the participation of the general public including users of water in the establishment and updating of river basin management plans, it is necessary to provide proper information of planned measures and to report on progress with their implementation with a view to the involvement of the general public before final decisions on the necessary measures are adopted.

(47) This Directive should provide mechanisms to address obstacles to progress in improving water status when these fall outside the scope of Community water legislation, with a view to developing appropriate Community strategies for overcoming them.

(48) The Commission should present annually an updated plan for any initiatives which it intends to propose for the water sector.

(49) Technical specifications should be laid down to ensure a coherent approach in the Community as part of this Directive. Criteria for evaluation of water status are an important step forward. Adaptation of certain technical elements to technical development and the standardisation of monitoring, sampling and analysis methods should be adopted by committee procedure. To promote a thorough understanding and consistent application of the criteria for characterisation of

the river basin districts and evaluation of water status, the Commission may adopt guidelines on the application of these criteria.

(50) The measures necessary for the implementation of this Directive should be adopted in accordance with Council Decision 1999/468/EC of 28 June 1999 laying down the procedures for the exercise of implementing powers conferred on the Commission.[1]

(51) The implementation of this Directive is to achieve a level of protection of waters at least equivalent to that provided in certain earlier acts, which should therefore be repealed once the relevant provisions of this Directive have been fully implemented.

(52) The provisions of this Directive take over the framework for control of pollution by dangerous substances established under Directive 76/464/EEC.[2] That Directive should therefore be repealed once the relevant provisions of this Directive have been fully implemented.

(53) Full implementation and enforcement of existing environmental legislation for the protection of waters should be ensured. It is necessary to ensure the proper application of the provisions implementing this Directive throughout the Community by appropriate penalties provided for in Member States' legislation. Such penalties should be effective, proportionate and dissuasive,

Have adopted this Directive:

Article 1
Purpose

The purpose of this Directive is to establish a framework for the protection of inland surface waters, transitional waters, coastal waters and groundwater which:

(a) prevents further deterioration and protects and enhances the status of aquatic ecosystems and, with regard to their water needs, terrestrial ecosystems and wetlands directly depending on the aquatic ecosystems;

(b) promotes sustainable water use based on a long-term protection of available water resources;

(c) aims at enhanced protection and improvement of the aquatic environment, *inter alia*, through specific measures for the progressive reduction of discharges, emissions and losses of priority substances and the cessation or phasing-out of discharges, emissions and losses of the priority hazardous substances;

(d) ensures the progressive reduction of pollution of groundwater and prevents its further pollution, and

---

[1] OJ C 184, 17.7.1999, p. 23.
[2] OJ L 129, 18.5.1976, p. 23. Directive as amended by Directive 91/692/EEC (OJ L 377, 31.12.1991, p. 48).

(e) contributes to mitigating the effects of floods and droughts and thereby contributes to:
  – the provision of the sufficient supply of good quality surface water and groundwater as needed for sustainable, balanced and equitable water use,
  – a significant reduction in pollution of groundwater,
  – the protection of territorial and marine waters, and
  – achieving the objectives of relevant international agreements, including those which aim to prevent and eliminate pollution of the marine environment, by Community action under Article 16(3) to cease or phase out discharges, emissions and losses of priority hazardous substances, with the ultimate aim of achieving concentrations in the marine environment near background values for naturally occurring substances and close to zero for man-made synthetic substances.

Article 2
Definitions

For the purposes of this Directive the following definitions shall apply:

1. 'Surface water' means inland waters, except groundwater; transitional waters and coastal waters, except in respect of chemical status for which it shall also include territorial waters.
2. 'Groundwater' means all water which is below the surface of the ground in the saturation zone and in direct contact with the ground or subsoil.
3. 'Inland water' means all standing or flowing water on the surface of the land, and all groundwater on the landward side of the baseline from which the breadth of territorial waters is measured.
4. 'River' means a body of inland water flowing for the most part on the surface of the land but which may flow underground for part of its course.
5. 'Lake' means a body of standing inland surface water.
6. 'Transitional waters' are bodies of surface water in the vicinity of river mouths which are partly saline in character as a result of their proximity to coastal waters but which are substantially influenced by freshwater flows.
7. 'Coastal water' means surface water on the landward side of a line, every point of which is at a distance of one nautical mile on the seaward side from the nearest point of the baseline from which the breadth of territorial waters is measured, extending where appropriate up to the outer limit of transitional waters.
8. 'Artificial water body' means a body of surface water created by human activity.
9. 'Heavily modified water body' means a body of surface water which as a result of physical alterations by human activity is substantially changed in character, as designated by the Member State in accordance with the provisions of Annex II.

10. 'Body of surface water' means a discrete and significant element of surface water such as a lake, a reservoir, a stream, river or canal, part of a stream, river or canal, a transitional water or a stretch of coastal water.

11. 'Aquifer' means a subsurface layer or layers of rock or other geological strata of sufficient porosity and permeability to allow either a significant flow of groundwater or the abstraction of significant quantities of groundwater.

12. 'Body of groundwater' means a distinct volume of groundwater within an aquifer or aquifers.

13. 'River basin' means the area of land from which all surface run-off flows through a sequence of streams, rivers and, possibly, lakes into the sea at a single river mouth, estuary or delta.

14. 'Sub-basin' means the area of land from which all surface run-off flows through a series of streams, rivers and, possibly, lakes to a particular point in a water course (normally a lake or a river confluence).

15. 'River basin district' means the area of land and sea, made up of one or more neighbouring river basins together with their associated groundwaters and coastal waters, which is identified under Article 3(1) as the main unit for management of river basins.

16. 'Competent Authority' means an authority or authorities identified under Article 3(2) or 3(3).

17. 'Surface water status' is the general expression of the status of a body of surface water, determined by the poorer of its ecological status and its chemical status.

18. 'Good surface water status' means the status achieved by a surface water body when both its ecological status and its chemical status are at least 'good'.

19. 'Groundwater status' is the general expression of the status of a body of groundwater, determined by the poorer of its quantitative status and its chemical status.

20. 'Good groundwater status' means the status achieved by a groundwater body when both its quantitative status and its chemical status are at least 'good'.

21. 'Ecological status' is an expression of the quality of the structure and functioning of aquatic ecosystems associated with surface waters, classified in accordance with Annex V.

22. 'Good ecological status' is the status of a body of surface water, so classified in accordance with Annex V.

23. 'Good ecological potential' is the status of a heavily modified or an artificial body of water, so classified in accordance with the relevant provisions of Annex V.

24. 'Good surface water chemical status' means the chemical status required to meet the environmental objectives for surface waters established in Article 4(1)(a), that is the chemical status achieved by a body of surface water in which concentrations of pollutants do not exceed the environmental quality standards established in Annex IX and under Article 16(7), and under other relevant Community legislation setting environmental quality standards at Community level.

25. 'Good groundwater chemical status' is the chemical status of a body of groundwater, which meets all the conditions set out in table 2.3.2 of Annex V.

26. 'Quantitative status' is an expression of the degree to which a body of groundwater is affected by direct and indirect abstractions.

27. 'Available groundwater resource' means the long-term annual average rate of overall recharge of the body of groundwater less the long-term annual rate of flow required to achieve the ecological quality objectives for associated surface waters specified under Article 4, to avoid any significant diminution in the ecological status of such waters and to avoid any significant damage to associated terrestrial ecosystems.

28. 'Good quantitative status' is the status defined in table 2.1.2 of Annex V.

29. 'Hazardous substances' means substances or groups of substances that are toxic, persistent and liable to bio-accumulate, and other substances or groups of substances which give rise to an equivalent level of concern.

30. 'Priority substances' means substances identified in accordance with Article 16(2) and listed in Annex X. Among these substances there are 'priority hazardous substances' which means substances identified in accordance with Article 16(3) and (6) for which measures have to be taken in accordance with Article 16(1) and (8).

31. 'Pollutant' means any substance liable to cause pollution, in particular those listed in Annex VIII.

32. 'Direct discharge to groundwater' means discharge of pollutants into groundwater without percolation throughout the soil or subsoil.

33. 'Pollution' means the direct or indirect introduction, as a result of human activity, of substances or heat into the air, water or land which may be harmful to human health or the quality of aquatic ecosystems or terrestrial ecosystems directly depending on aquatic ecosystems, which result in damage to material property, or which impair or interfere with amenities and other legitimate uses of the environment.

34. 'Environmental objectives' means the objectives set out in Article 4.

35. 'Environmental quality standard' means the concentration of a particular pollutant or group of pollutants in water, sediment or biota which should not be exceeded in order to protect human health and the environment.

36. 'Combined approach' means the control of discharges and emissions into surface waters according to the approach set out in Article 10.

37. 'Water intended for human consumption' has the same meaning as under Directive 80/778/EEC, as amended by Directive 98/83/EC.

38. 'Water services' means all services which provide, for households, public institutions or any economic activity:
    (a) abstraction, impoundment, storage, treatment and distribution of surface water or groundwater,
    (b) waste-water collection and treatment facilities which subsequently discharge into surface water.

39. 'Water use' means water services together with any other activity identified under Article 5 and Annex II having a significant impact on the status of water. This concept applies for the purposes of Article 1 and of the economic analysis carried out according to Article 5 and Annex III, point (b).

40. 'Emission limit values' means the mass, expressed in terms of certain specific parameters, concentration and/or level of an emission, which may not be exceeded during any one or more periods of time. Emission limit values may also be laid down for certain groups, families or categories of substances, in particular for those identified under Article 16. The emission limit values for substances shall normally apply at the point where the emissions leave the installation, dilution being disregarded when determining them. With regard to indirect releases into water, the effect of a waste-water treatment plant may be taken into account when determining the emission limit values of the installations involved, provided that an equivalent level is guaranteed for protection of the environment as a whole and provided that this does not lead to higher levels of pollution in the environment.

41. 'Emission controls' are controls requiring a specific emission limitation, for instance an emission limit value, or otherwise specifying limits or conditions on the effects, nature or other characteristics of an emission or operating conditions which affect emissions. Use of the term 'emission control' in this Directive in respect of the provisions of any other Directive shall not be held as reinterpreting those provisions in any respect.

Article 3
Coordination of administrative arrangements within river basin districts

1. Member States shall identify the individual river basins lying within their national territory and, for the purposes of this Directive, shall assign them to individual river basin districts. Small river basins may be combined with larger river basins or joined with neighbouring small basins to form individual river basin districts where appropriate. Where groundwaters do not fully follow a particular river basin, they shall be identified and assigned to the nearest or most appropriate river basin district. Coastal waters shall be identified and assigned to the nearest or most appropriate river basin district or districts.

2. Member States shall ensure the appropriate administrative arrangements, including the identification of the appropriate competent authority, for the application of the rules of this Directive within each river basin district lying within their territory.

3. Member States shall ensure that a river basin covering the territory of more than one Member State is assigned to an international river basin district. At the request of the Member States involved, the Commission shall act to facilitate the assigning to such international river basin districts. Each Member State shall ensure the appropriate administrative arrangements, including the identification of the appropriate competent authority, for the application of the rules of this Directive within the portion of any international river basin district lying within its territory.

4. Member States shall ensure that the requirements of this Directive for the achievement of the environmental objectives established under Article 4, and in particular all programmes of measures are coordinated for the whole of the river basin district. For international river basin districts the Member States concerned shall together ensure this coordination and may, for this purpose, use existing structures stemming from international agreements. At the request of the Member States involved, the Commission shall act to facilitate the establishment of the programmes of measures.

5. Where a river basin district extends beyond the territory of the Community, the Member State or Member States concerned shall endeavour to establish appropriate coordination with the relevant non- Member States, with the aim of achieving the objectives of this Directive throughout the river basin district. Member States shall ensure the application of the rules of this Directive within their territory.

6. Member States may identify an existing national or international body as competent authority for the purposes of this Directive.

7. Member States shall identify the competent authority by the date mentioned in Article 24.

8. Member States shall provide the Commission with a list of their competent authorities and of the competent authorities of all the international bodies in which they participate at the latest six months after the date mentioned in Article 24. For each competent authority the information set out in Annex I shall be provided.

9. Member States shall inform the Commission of any changes to the information provided according to paragraph 8 within three months of the change coming into effect.

Article 4
Environmental objectives

1. In making operational the programmes of measures specified in the river basin management plans:

(a) for surface waters
   (i) Member States shall implement the necessary measures to prevent deterioration of the status of all bodies of surface water, subject to the application of paragraphs 6 and 7 and without prejudice to paragraph 8;
   (ii) Member States shall protect, enhance and restore all bodies of surface water, subject to the application of subparagraph (iii) for artificial and heavily modified bodies of water, with the aim of achieving good surface water status at the latest 15 years after the date of entry into force of this Directive, in accordance with the provisions laid down in Annex V, subject to the application of extensions determined in accordance with paragraph 4 and to the application of paragraphs 5, 6 and 7 without prejudice to paragraph 8;

    (iii) Member States shall protect and enhance all artificial and heavily modified bodies of water, with the aim of achieving good ecological potential and good surface water chemical status at the latest 15 years from the date of entry into force of this Directive, in accordance with the provisions laid down in Annex V, subject to the application of extensions determined in accordance with paragraph 4 and to the application of paragraphs 5, 6 and 7 without prejudice to paragraph 8;

    (iv) Member States shall implement the necessary measures in accordance with Article 16(1) and (8), with the aim of progressively reducing pollution from priority substances and ceasing or phasing out emissions, discharges and losses of priority hazardous substances without prejudice to the relevant international agreements referred to in Article 1 for the parties concerned;

(b) for groundwater

    (i) Member States shall implement the measures necessary to prevent or limit the input of pollutants into groundwater and to prevent the deterioration of the status of all bodies of groundwater, subject to the application of paragraphs 6 and 7 and without prejudice to paragraph 8 of this Article and subject to the application of Article 11(3)(j);

    (ii) Member States shall protect, enhance and restore all bodies of groundwater, ensure a balance between abstraction and recharge of groundwater, with the aim of achieving good groundwater status at the latest 15 years after the date of entry into force of this Directive, in accordance with the provisions laid down in Annex V, subject to the application of extensions determined in accordance with paragraph 4 and to the application of paragraphs 5, 6 and 7 without prejudice to paragraph 8 of this Article and subject to the application of Article 11(3)(j);

    (iii) Member States shall implement the measures necessary to reverse any significant and sustained upward trend in the concentration of any pollutant resulting from the impact of human activity in order progressively to reduce pollution of groundwater. Measures to achieve trend reversal shall be implemented in accordance with paragraphs 2, 4 and 5 of Article 17, taking into account the applicable standards set out in relevant Community legislation, subject to the application of paragraphs 6 and 7 and without prejudice to paragraph 8;

(c) for protected areas

    Member States shall achieve compliance with any standards and objectives at the latest 15 years after the date of entry into force of this Directive, unless otherwise specified in the Community legislation under which the individual protected areas have been established.

2. Where more than one of the objectives under paragraph 1 relates to a given body of water, the most stringent shall apply.

3. Member States may designate a body of surface water as artificial or heavily modified, when:

(a) the changes to the hydromorphological characteristics of that body which would be necessary for achieving good ecological status would have significant adverse effects on:
   (i) the wider environment;
   (ii) navigation, including port facilities, or recreation;
   (iii) activities for the purposes of which water is stored, such as drinking-water supply, power generation or irrigation;
   (iv) water regulation, flood protection, land drainage, or
   (v) other equally important sustainable human development activities;
(b) the beneficial objectives served by the artificial or modified characteristics of the water body cannot, for reasons of technical feasibility or disproportionate costs, reasonably be achieved by other means, which are a significantly better environmental option. Such designation and the reasons for it shall be specifically mentioned in the river basin management plans required under Article 13 and reviewed every six years.

4. The deadlines established under paragraph 1 may be extended for the purposes of phased achievement of the objectives for bodies of water, provided that no further deterioration occurs in the status of the affected body of water when all of the following conditions are met:

(a) Member States determine that all necessary improvements in the status of bodies of water cannot reasonably be achieved within the timescales set out in that paragraph for at least one of the following reasons:
   (i) the scale of improvements required can only be achieved in phases exceeding the timescale, for reasons of technical feasibility;
   (ii) completing the improvements within the timescale would be disproportionately expensive;
   (iii) natural conditions do not allow timely improvement in the status of the body of water.
(b) Extension of the deadline, and the reasons for it, are specifically set out and explained in the river basin management plan required under Article 13.
(c) Extensions shall be limited to a maximum of two further updates of the river basin management plan except in cases where the natural conditions are such that the objectives cannot be achieved within this period.
(d) A summary of the measures required under Article 11 which are envisaged as necessary to bring the bodies of water progressively to the required status by the extended deadline, the reasons for any significant delay in making these measures operational, and the expected timetable for their implementation are set out in the

river basin management plan. A review of the implementation of these measures and a summary of any additional measures shall be included in updates of the river basin management plan.

5. Member States may aim to achieve less stringent environmental objectives than those required under paragraph 1 for specific bodies of water when they are so affected by human activity, as determined in accordance with Article 5(1), or their natural condition is such that the achievement of these objectives would be infeasible or disproportionately expensive, and all the following conditions are met:

(a) the environmental and socioeconomic needs served by such human activity cannot be achieved by other means, which are a significantly better environmental option not entailing disproportionate costs;
(b) Member States ensure,
  – for surface water, the highest ecological and chemical status possible is achieved, given impacts that could not reasonably have been avoided due to the nature of the human activity or pollution,
  – for groundwater, the least possible changes to good groundwater status, given impacts that could not reasonably have been avoided due to the nature of the human activity or pollution;
(c) no further deterioration occurs in the status of the affected body of water;
(d) the establishment of less stringent environmental objectives, and the reasons for it, are specifically mentioned in the river basin management plan required under Article 13 and those objectives are reviewed every six years.

6. Temporary deterioration in the status of bodies of water shall not be in breach of the requirements of this Directive if this is the result of circumstances of natural cause or *force majeure* which are exceptional or could not reasonably have been foreseen, in particular extreme floods and prolonged droughts, or the result of circumstances due to accidents which could not reasonably have been foreseen, when all of the following conditions have been met:

(a) all practicable steps are taken to prevent further deterioration in status and in order not to compromise the achievement of the objectives of this Directive in other bodies of water not affected by those circumstances;
(b) the conditions under which circumstances that are exceptional or that could not reasonably have been foreseen may be declared, including the adoption of the appropriate indicators, are stated in the river basin management plan;
(c) the measures to be taken under such exceptional circumstances are included in the programme of measures and will not compromise the recovery of the quality of the body of water once the circumstances are over;
(d) the effects of the circumstances that are exceptional or that could not reasonably have been foreseen are reviewed annually and, subject to the reasons set out in

paragraph 4(a), all practicable measures are taken with the aim of restoring the body of water to its status prior to the effects of those circumstances as soon as reasonably practicable, and

(e) a summary of the effects of the circumstances and of such measures taken or to be taken in accordance with paragraphs (a) and (d) are included in the next update of the river basin management plan.

7. Member States will not be in breach of this Directive when:

− failure to achieve good groundwater status, good ecological status or, where relevant, good ecological potential or to prevent deterioration in the status of a body of surface water or groundwater is the result of new modifications to the physical characteristics of a surface water body or alterations to the level of bodies of groundwater, or
− failure to prevent deterioration from high status to good status of a body of surface water is the result of new sustainable human development activities and all the following conditions are met:

(a) all practicable steps are taken to mitigate the adverse impact on the status of the body of water;
(b) the reasons for those modifications or alterations are specifically set out and explained in the river basin management plan required under Article 13 and the objectives are reviewed every six years;
(c) the reasons for those modifications or alterations are of overriding public interest and/or the benefits to the environment and to society of achieving the objectives set out in paragraph 1 are outweighed by the benefits of the new modifications or alterations to human health, to the maintenance of human safety or to sustainable development, and
(d) the beneficial objectives served by those modifications or alterations of the water body cannot for reasons of technical feasibility or disproportionate cost be achieved by other means, which are a significantly better environmental option.

8. When applying paragraphs 3, 4, 5, 6 and 7, a Member State shall ensure that the application does not permanently exclude or compromise the achievement of the objectives of this Directive in other bodies of water within the same river basin district and is consistent with the implementation of other Community environmental legislation.

9. Steps must be taken to ensure that the application of the new provisions, including the application of paragraphs 3, 4, 5, 6 and 7, guarantees at least the same level of protection as the existing Community legislation.

Article 5
Characteristics of the river basin district, review of the environmental
impact of human activity and economic analysis of water use

1. Each Member State shall ensure that for each river basin district or for the portion
of an international river basin district falling within its territory:

– an analysis of its characteristics,
– a review of the impact of human activity on the status of surface waters and on
   groundwater, and
– an economic analysis of water use

is undertaken according to the technical specifications set out in Annexes II and III
and that it is completed at the latest four years after the date of entry into force of this
Directive.

2. The analyses and reviews mentioned under paragraph 1 shall be reviewed, and
if necessary updated at the latest 13 years after the date of entry into force of this
Directive and every six years thereafter.

Article 6
Register of protected areas

1. Member States shall ensure the establishment of a register or registers of all
areas lying within each river basin district which have been designated as requiring
special protection under specific Community legislation for the protection of their
surface water and groundwater or for the conservation of habitats and species directly
depending on water. They shall ensure that the register is completed at the latest four
years after the date of entry into force of this Directive.

2. The register or registers shall include all bodies of water identified under Article 7(1) and all protected areas covered by Annex IV.

3. For each river basin district, the register or registers of protected areas shall be
kept under review and up to date.

Article 7
Waters used for the abstraction of drinking water

1. Member States shall identify, within each river basin district:

– all bodies of water used for the abstraction of water intended for human consumption providing more than 10 m3 a day as an average or serving more than 50 persons,
   and
– those bodies of water intended for such future use.

Member States shall monitor, in accordance with Annex V, those bodies of water
which according to Annex V, provide more than 100 m^3 a day as an average.

2. For each body of water identified under paragraph 1, in addition to meeting the objectives of Article 4 in accordance with the requirements of this Directive, for surface water bodies including the quality standards established at Community level under Article 16, Member States shall ensure that under the water treatment regime applied, and in accordance with Community legislation, the resulting water will meet the requirements of Directive 80/778/EEC as amended by Directive 98/83/EC.

3. Member States shall ensure the necessary protection for the bodies of water identified with the aim of avoiding deterioration in their quality in order to reduce the level of purification treatment required in the production of drinking water. Member States may establish safeguard zones for those bodies of water.

Article 8
Monitoring of surface water status, groundwater status and protected areas

1. Member States shall ensure the establishment of programmes for the monitoring of water status in order to establish a coherent and comprehensive overview of water status within each river basin district:

– for surface waters such programmes shall cover:

  (i) the volume and level or rate of flow to the extent relevant for ecological and chemical status and ecological potential, and
  (ii) the ecological and chemical status and ecological potential;

– for groundwaters such programmes shall cover monitoring of the chemical and quantitative status,
– for protected areas the above programmes shall be supplemented by those specifications contained in Community legislation under which the individual protected areas have been established.

2. These programmes shall be operational at the latest six years after the date of entry into force of this Directive unless otherwise specified in the legislation concerned. Such monitoring shall be in accordance with the requirements of Annex V.

3. Technical specifications and standardised methods for analysis and monitoring of water status shall be laid down in accordance with the procedure laid down in Article 21.

Article 9
Recovery of costs for water services

1. Member States shall take account of the principle of recovery of the costs of water services, including environmental and resource costs, having regard to the economic analysis conducted according to Annex III, and in accordance in particular with the polluter pays principle.

Member States shall ensure by 2010:

– that water-pricing policies provide adequate incentives for users to use water resources efficiently, and thereby contribute to the environmental objectives of this Directive,
– an adequate contribution of the different water uses, disaggregated into at least industry, households and agriculture, to the recovery of the costs of water services, based on the economic analysis conducted according to Annex III and taking account of the polluter pays principle. Member States may in so doing have regard to the social, environmental and economic effects of the recovery as well as the geographic and climatic conditions of the region or regions affected.

2. Member States shall report in the river basin management plans on the planned steps towards implementing paragraph 1 which will contribute to achieving the environmental objectives of this Directive and on the contribution made by the various water uses to the recovery of the costs of water services.

3. Nothing in this Article shall prevent the funding of particular preventive or remedial measures in order to achieve the objectives of this Directive.

4. Member States shall not be in breach of this Directive if they decide in accordance with established practices not to apply the provisions of paragraph 1, second sentence, and for that purpose the relevant provisions of paragraph 2, for a given water-use activity, where this does not compromise the purposes and the achievement of the objectives of this Directive. Member States shall report the reasons for not fully applying paragraph 1, second sentence, in the river basin management plans.

Article 10
The combined approach for point and diffuse sources

1. Member States shall ensure that all discharges referred to in paragraph 2 into surface waters are controlled according to the combined approach set out in this Article.

2. Member States shall ensure the establishment and/or implementation of:

(a) the emission controls based on best available techniques, or
(b) the relevant emission limit values, or
(c) in the case of diffuse impacts the controls including, as appropriate, best environmental practices set out in:
  – Council Directive 96/61/EC of 24 September 1996 concerning integrated pollution prevention and control,[1]
  – Council Directive 91/271/EEC of 21 May 1991 concerning urban waste-water treatment,[2] – Council Directive 91/676/EEC of 12 December 1991 concerning

[1] OJ L 257, 10.10.1996, p. 26.
[2] OJ L 135, 30.5.1991, p. 40. Directive as amended by Commission Directive 98/15/EC (OJ L 67, 7.3.1998, p. 29).

the protection of waters against pollution caused by nitrates from agricultural sources,[1]
- the Directives adopted pursuant to Article 16 of this Directive,
- the Directives listed in Annex IX,
- any other relevant Community legislation at the latest 12 years after the date of entry into force of this Directive, unless otherwise specified in the legislation concerned.

3. Where a quality objective or quality standard, whether established pursuant to this Directive, in the Directives listed in Annex IX, or pursuant to any other Community legislation, requires stricter conditions than those which would result from the application of paragraph 2, more stringent emission controls shall be set accordingly.

Article 11
Programme of measures

1. Each Member State shall ensure the establishment for each river basin district, or for the part of an international river basin district within its territory, of a programme of measures, taking account of the results of the analyses required under Article 5, in order to achieve the objectives established under Article 4. Such programmes of measures may make reference to measures following from legislation adopted at national level and covering the whole of the territory of a Member State. Where appropriate, a Member State may adopt measures applicable to all river basin districts and/or the portions of international river basin districts falling within its territory.

2. Each programme of measures shall include the 'basic' measures specified in paragraph 3 and, where necessary, 'supplementary' measures.

3. 'Basic measures' are the minimum requirements to be complied with and shall consist of:

(a) those measures required to implement Community legislation for the protection of water, including measures required under the legislation specified in Article 10 and in part A of Annex VI;
(b) measures deemed appropriate for the purposes of Article 9;
(c) measures to promote an efficient and sustainable water use in order to avoid compromising the achievement of the objectives specified in Article 4;
(d) measures to meet the requirements of Article 7, including measures to safeguard water quality in order to reduce the level of purification treatment required for the production of drinking water;
(e) controls over the abstraction of fresh surface water and groundwater, and impoundment of fresh surface water, including a register or registers of water

---

[1] OJ L 375, 31.12.1991, p. 1.

abstractions and a requirement of prior authorisation for abstraction and impoundment. These controls shall be periodically reviewed and, where necessary, updated. Member States can exempt from these controls, abstractions or impoundments which have no significant impact on water status;

(f) controls, including a requirement for prior authorisation of artificial recharge or augmentation of groundwater bodies. The water used may be derived from any surface water or groundwater, provided that the use of the source does not compromise the achievement of the environmental objectives established for the source or the recharged or augmented body of groundwater. These controls shall be periodically reviewed and, where necessary, updated;

(g) for point source discharges liable to cause pollution, a requirement for prior regulation, such as a prohibition on the entry of pollutants into water, or for prior authorisation, or registration based on general binding rules, laying down emission controls for the pollutants concerned, including controls in accordance with Articles 10 and 16. These controls shall be periodically reviewed and, where necessary, updated;

(h) for diffuse sources liable to cause pollution, measures to prevent or control the input of pollutants. Controls may take the form of a requirement for prior regulation, such as a prohibition on the entry of pollutants into water, prior authorisation or registration based on general binding rules where such a requirement is not otherwise provided for under Community legislation. These controls shall be periodically reviewed and, where necessary, updated;

(i) for any other significant adverse impacts on the status of water identified under Article 5 and Annex II, in particular measures to ensure that the hydromorphological conditions of the bodies of water are consistent with the achievement of the required ecological status or good ecological potential for bodies of water designated as artificial or heavily modified. Controls for this purpose may take the form of a requirement for prior authorisation or registration based on general binding rules where such a requirement is not otherwise provided for under Community legislation. Such controls shall be periodically reviewed and, where necessary, updated;

(j) a prohibition of direct discharges of pollutants into groundwater subject to the following provisions: Member States may authorise reinjection into the same aquifer of water used for geothermal purposes. They may also authorise, specifying the conditions for:

   – injection of water containing substances resulting from the operations for exploration and extraction of hydrocarbons or mining activities, and injection of water for technical reasons, into geological formations from which hydrocarbons or other substances have been extracted or into geological formations which for natural reasons are permanently unsuitable for other purposes. Such injections shall not contain substances other than those resulting from the above operations,

- reinjection of pumped groundwater from mines and quarries or associated with the construction or maintenance of civil engineering works,
- injection of natural gas or liquefied petroleum gas (LPG) for storage purposes into geological formations which for natural reasons are permanently unsuitable for other purposes,
- injection of natural gas or liquefied petroleum gas (LPG) for storage purposes into other geological formations where there is an overriding need for security of gas supply, and where the injection is such as to prevent any present or future danger of deterioration in the quality of any receiving groundwater,
- construction, civil engineering and building works and similar activities on, or in the ground which come into contact with groundwater. For these purposes, Member States may determine that such activities are to be treated as having been authorised provided that they are conducted in accordance with general binding rules developed by the Member State in respect of such activities,
- discharges of small quantities of substances for scientific purposes for characterisation, protection or remediation of water bodies limited to the amount strictly necessary for the purposes concerned,

  provided such discharges do not compromise the achievement of the environmental objectives established for that body of groundwater;
(k) in accordance with action taken pursuant to Article 16, measures to eliminate pollution of surface waters by those substances specified in the list of priority substances agreed pursuant to Article 16(2) and to progressively reduce pollution by other substances which would otherwise prevent Member States from achieving the objectives for the bodies of surface waters as set out in Article 4;
(l) any measures required to prevent significant losses of pollutants from technical installations, and to prevent and/or to reduce the impact of accidental pollution incidents for example as a result of floods, including through systems to detect or give warning of such events including, in the case of accidents which could not reasonably have been foreseen, all appropriate measures to reduce the risk to aquatic ecosystems.

4. 'Supplementary' measures are those measures designed and implemented in addition to the basic measures, with the aim of achieving the objectives established pursuant to Article 4. Part B of Annex VI contains a non-exclusive list of such measures.

Member States may also adopt further supplementary measures in order to provide for additional protection or improvement of the waters covered by this Directive, including in implementation of the relevant international agreements referred to in Article 1.

5. Where monitoring or other data indicate that the objectives set under Article 4 for the body of water are unlikely to be achieved, the Member State shall ensure that:

- the causes of the possible failure are investigated,
- relevant permits and authorisations are examined and reviewed as appropriate,

- the monitoring programmes are reviewed and adjusted as appropriate, and
- additional measures as may be necessary in order to achieve those objectives are established, including, as appropriate, the establishment of stricter environmental quality standards following the procedures laid down in Annex V.

Where those causes are the result of circumstances of natural cause or *force majeure* which are exceptional and could not reasonably have been foreseen, in particular extreme floods and prolonged droughts, the Member State may determine that additional measures are not practicable, subject to Article 4(6).

6. In implementing measures pursuant to paragraph 3, Member States shall take all appropriate steps not to increase pollution of marine waters. Without prejudice to existing legislation, the application of measures taken pursuant to paragraph 3 may on no account lead, either directly or indirectly to increased pollution of surface waters. This requirement shall not apply where it would result in increased pollution of the environment as a whole.

7. The programmes of measures shall be established at the latest nine years after the date of entry into force of this Directive and all the measures shall be made operational at the latest 12 years after that date.

8. The programmes of measures shall be reviewed, and if necessary updated at the latest 15 years after the date of entry into force of this Directive and every six years thereafter. Any new or revised measures established under an updated programme shall be made operational within three years of their establishment.

Article 12
Issues which can not be dealt with at Member State level

1. Where a Member State identifies an issue which has an impact on the management of its water but cannot be resolved by that Member State, it may report the issue to the Commission and any other Member State concerned and may make recommendations for the resolution of it.

2. The Commission shall respond to any report or recommendations from Member States within a period of six months.

Article 13
River basin management plans

1. Member States shall ensure that a river basin management plan is produced for each river basin district lying entirely within their territory.

2. In the case of an international river basin district falling entirely within the Community, Member States shall ensure coordination with the aim of producing a single international river basin management plan. Where such an international river basin management plan is not produced, Member States shall produce river basin management plans covering at least those parts of the international river basin district falling within their territory to achieve the objectives of this Directive.

3. In the case of an international river basin district extending beyond the boundaries of the Community, Member States shall endeavour to produce a single river basin management plan, and, where this is not possible, the plan shall at least cover the portion of the international river basin district lying within the territory of the Member State concerned.

4. The river basin management plan shall include the information detailed in Annex VII.

5. River basin management plans may be supplemented by the production of more detailed programmes and management plans for sub-basin, sector, issue, or water type, to deal with particular aspects of water management. Implementation of these measures shall not exempt Member States from any of their obligations under the rest of this Directive.

6. River basin management plans shall be published at the latest nine years after the date of entry into force of this Directive.

7. River basin management plans shall be reviewed and updated at the latest 15 years after the date of entry into force of this Directive and every six years thereafter.

Article 14
Public information and consultation

1. Member States shall encourage the active involvement of all interested parties in the implementation of this Directive, in particular in the production, review and updating of the river basin management plans. Member States shall ensure that, for each river basin district, they publish and make available for comments to the public, including users:

(a) a timetable and work programme for the production of the plan, including a statement of the consultation measures to be taken, at least three years before the beginning of the period to which the plan refers;

(b) an interim overview of the significant water management issues identified in the river basin, at least two years before the beginning of the period to which the plan refers;

(c) draft copies of the river basin management plan, at least one year before the beginning of the period to which the plan refers. On request, access shall be given to background documents and information used for the development of the draft river basin management plan.

2. Member States shall allow at least six months to comment in writing on those documents in order to allow active involvement and consultation.

3. Paragraphs 1 and 2 shall apply equally to updated river basin management plans.

Article 15
Reporting

1. Member States shall send copies of the river basin management plans and all subsequent updates to the Commission and to any other Member State concerned within three months of their publication:

(a) for river basin districts falling entirely within the territory of a Member State, all river management plans covering that national territory and published pursuant to Article 13;

(b) for international river basin districts, at least the part of the river basin management plans covering the territory of the Member State.

2. Member States shall submit summary reports of:

– the analyses required under Article 5, and
– the monitoring programmes designed under Article 8

undertaken for the purposes of the first river basin management plan within three months of their completion.

3. Member States shall, within three years of the publication of each river basin management plan or update under Article 13, submit an interim report describing progress in the implementation of the planned programme of measures.

Article 16
Strategies against pollution of water

1. The European Parliament and the Council shall adopt specific measures against pollution of water by individual pollutants or groups of pollutants presenting a significant risk to or via the aquatic environment, including such risks to waters used for the abstraction of drinking water. For those pollutants measures shall be aimed at the progressive reduction and, for priority hazardous substances, as defined in Article 2(30), at the cessation or phasing-out of discharges, emissions and losses. Such measures shall be adopted acting on the proposals presented by the Commission in accordance with the procedures laid down in the Treaty.

2. The Commission shall submit a proposal setting out a list of priority substances selected amongst those which present a significant risk to or via the aquatic environment. Substances shall be prioritised for action on the basis of risk to or via the aquatic environment, identified by:

(a) risk assessment carried out under Council Regulation (EEC) No 793/93,[1] Council Directive 91/414/EEC,[2] and Directive 98/8/ EC of the European Parliament and of the Council,[3] or

---

[1] OJ L 84, 5.4.1993, p. 1.
[2] OJ L 230, 19.8.1991, p. 1. Directive as last amended by Directive 98/47/EC (OJ L 191, 7.7.1998, p. 50).
[3] OJ L 123, 24.4.1998, p. 1.

(b) targeted risk-based assessment (following the methodology of Regulation (EEC) No 793/93) focusing solely on aquatic ecotoxicity and on human toxicity via the aquatic environment. When necessary in order to meet the timetable laid down in paragraph 4, substances shall be prioritised for action on the basis of risk to, or via the aquatic environment, identified by a simplified risk-based assessment procedure based on scientific principles taking particular account of:
  - evidence regarding the intrinsic hazard of the substance concerned, and in particular its aquatic ecotoxicity and human toxicity via aquatic exposure routes, and
  - evidence from monitoring of widespread environmental contamination, and
  - other proven factors which may indicate the possibility of widespread environmental contamination, such as production or use volume of the substance concerned, and use patterns.

3. The Commission's proposal shall also identify the priority hazardous substances. In doing so, the Commission shall take into account the selection of substances of concern undertaken in the relevant Community legislation regarding hazardous substances or relevant international agreements.

4. The Commission shall review the adopted list of priority substances at the latest four years after the date of entry into force of this Directive and at least every four years thereafter, and come forward with proposals as appropriate.

5. In preparing its proposal, the Commission shall take account of recommendations from the Scientific Committee on Toxicity, Ecotoxicity and the Environment, Member States, the European Parliament, the European Environment Agency, Community research programmes, international organisations to which the Community is a party, European business organisations including those representing small and medium-sized enterprises, European environmental organisations, and of other relevant information which comes to its attention.

6. For the priority substances, the Commission shall submit proposals of controls for:

  - the progressive reduction of discharges, emissions and losses of the substances concerned, and, in particular
  - the cessation or phasing-out of discharges, emissions and losses of the substances as identified in accordance with paragraph 3, including an appropriate timetable for doing so. The timetable shall not exceed 20 years after the adoption of these proposals by the European Parliament and the Council in accordance with the provisions of this Article.

In doing so it shall identify the appropriate cost-effective and proportionate level and combination of product and process controls for both point and diffuse sources and take account of Community-wide uniform emission limit values for process controls. Where appropriate, action at Community level for process controls may be established on a sector-by-sector basis. Where product controls include a review of the relevant authorisations issued under Directive 91/414/EEC and Directive 98/8/EC, such reviews shall be carried out in accordance with the provisions of those Directives. Each proposal for controls shall specify arrangements for their review, updating and for assessment of their effectiveness.

7. The Commission shall submit proposals for quality standards applicable to the concentrations of the priority substances in surface water, sediments or biota.

8. The Commission shall submit proposals, in accordance with paragraphs 6 and 7, and at least for emission controls for point sources and environmental quality standards within two years of the inclusion of the substance concerned on the list of priority substances. For substances included in the first list of priority substances, in the absence of agreement at Community level six years after the date of entry into force of this Directive, Member States shall establish environmental quality standards for these substances for all surface waters affected by discharges of those substances, and controls on the principal sources of such discharges, based, *inter alia*, on consideration of all technical reduction options. For substances subsequently included in the list of priority substances, in the absence of agreement at Community level, Member States shall take such action five years after the date of inclusion in the list.

9. The Commission may prepare strategies against pollution of water by any other pollutants or groups of pollutants, including any pollution which occurs as a result of accidents.

10. In preparing its proposals under paragraphs 6 and 7, the Commission shall also review all the Directives listed in Annex IX. It shall propose, by the deadline in paragraph 8, a revision of the controls in Annex IX for all those substances which are included in the list of priority substances and shall propose the appropriate measures including the possible repeal of the controls under Annex IX for all other substances. All the controls in Annex IX for which revisions are proposed shall be repealed by the date of entry into force of those revisions.

11. The list of priority substances of substances mentioned in paragraphs 2 and 3 proposed by the Commission shall, on its adoption by the European Parliament and the Council, become Annex X to this Directive. Its revision mentioned in paragraph 4 shall follow the same procedure.

Article 17
Strategies to prevent and control pollution of groundwater

1. The European Parliament and the Council shall adopt specific measures to prevent and control groundwater pollution. Such measures shall be aimed at achieving the objective of good groundwater chemical status in accordance with Article 4(1)(b) and shall be adopted, acting on the proposal presented within two years after the entry into force of this Directive, by the Commission in accordance with the procedures laid down in the Treaty.

2. In proposing measures the Commission shall have regard to the analysis carried out according to Article 5 and Annex II. Such measures shall be proposed earlier if data are available and shall include: (a) criteria for assessing good groundwater chemical status, in accordance with Annex II.2.2 and Annex V 2.3.2 and 2.4.5; (b) criteria for the identification of significant and sustained upward trends and for the definition of starting points for trend reversals to be used in accordance with Annex V 2.4.4.

3. Measures resulting from the application of paragraph 1 shall be included in the programmes of measures required under Article 11.

4. In the absence of criteria adopted under paragraph 2 at Community level, Member States shall establish appropriate criteria at the latest five years after the date of entry into force of this Directive.

5. In the absence of criteria adopted under paragraph 4 at national level, trend reversal shall take as its starting point a maximum of 75% of the level of the quality standards set out in existing Community legislation applicable to groundwater.

Article 18
Commission report

1. The Commission shall publish a report on the implementation of this Directive at the latest 12 years after the date of entry into force of this Directive and every six years thereafter, and shall submit it to the European Parliament and to the Council.

2. The report shall include the following:

(a) a review of progress in the implementation of the Directive;
(b) a review of the status of surface water and groundwater in the Community undertaken in coordination with the European Environment Agency;
(c) a survey of the river basin management plans submitted in accordance with Article 15, including suggestions for the improvement of future plans;
(d) a summary of the response to each of the reports or recommendations to the Commission made by Member States pursuant to Article 12;
(e) a summary of any proposals, control measures and strategies developed under Article 16;
(f) a summary of the responses to comments made by the European Parliament and the Council on previous implementation reports.

3. The Commission shall also publish a report on progress in implementation based on the summary reports that Member States submit under Article 15(2), and submit it to the European Parliament and the Member States, at the latest two years after the dates referred to in Articles 5 and 8.

4. The Commission shall, within three years of the publication of each report under paragraph 1, publish an interim report describing progress in implementation on the

basis of the interim reports of the Member States as mentioned in Article 15(3). This shall be submitted to the European Parliament and to the Council.

5. The Commission shall convene when appropriate, in line with the reporting cycle, a conference of interested parties on Community water policy from each of the Member States, to comment on the Commission's implementation reports and to share experiences. Participants should include representatives from the competent authorities, the European Parliament, NGOs, the social and economic partners, consumer bodies, academics and other experts.

Article 19
Plans for future Community measures

1. Once a year, the Commission shall for information purposes present to the Committee referred to in Article 21 an indicative plan of measures having an impact on water legislation which it intends to propose in the near future, including any emerging from the proposals, control measures and strategies developed under Article 16. The Commission shall make the first such presentation at the latest two years after the date of entry into force of this Directive.

2. The Commission will review this Directive at the latest 19 years after the date of its entry into force and will propose any necessary amendments to it.

Article 20
Technical adaptations to the Directive

1. Annexes I, III and section 1.3.6 of Annex V may be adapted to scientific and technical progress in accordance with the procedures laid down in Article 21, taking account of the periods for review and updating of the river basin management plans as referred to in Article 13. Where necessary, the Commission may adopt guidelines on the implementation of Annexes II and V in accordance with the procedures laid down in Article 21.

2. For the purpose of transmission and processing of data, including statistical and cartographic data, technical formats for the purpose of paragraph 1 may be adopted in accordance with the procedures laid down in Article 21.

Article 21
Regulatory committee

1. The Commission shall be assisted by a committee (hereinafter referred to as 'the Committee').

2. Where reference is made to this Article, Articles 5 and 7 of Decision 1999/468/EC shall apply, having regard to the provisions of Article 8 thereof. The period laid down in Article 5(6) of Decision 1999/468/EC shall be set at three months.

3. The Committee shall adopt its rules of procedure.

Article 22
Repeals and transitional provisions

1. The following shall be repealed with effect from seven years after the date of entry into force of this Directive:

- Directive 75/440/EEC of 16 June 1975 concerning the quality required of surface water intended for the abstraction of drinking water in the Member States,[1]
- Council Decision 77/795/EEC of 12 December 1977 establishing a common procedure for the exchange of information on the quality of surface freshwater in the Community,[2]
- Council Directive 79/869/EEC of 9 October 1979 concerning the methods of measurement and frequencies of sampling and analysis of surface water intended for the abstraction of drinking waters in the Member States.[3]

2. The following shall be repealed with effect from 13 years after the date of entry into force of this Directive:

- Council Directive 78/659/EEC of 18 July 1978 on the quality of freshwaters needing protection or improvement in order to support fish life,[4]
- Council Directive 79/923/EEC of 30 October 1979 on the quality required of shellfish waters,[5]
- Council Directive 80/68/EEC of 17 December 1979 on the protection of groundwater against pollution caused by certain dangerous substances,
- Directive 76/464/EEC, with the exception of Article 6, which shall be repealed with effect from the entry into force of this Directive.

3. The following transitional provisions shall apply for Directive 76/464/EEC:

(a) the list of priority substances adopted under Article 16 of this Directive shall replace the list of substances prioritised in the Commission communication to the Council of 22 June 1982;
(b) for the purposes of Article 7 of Directive 76/464/EEC, Member States may apply the principles for the identification of pollution problems and the substances causing them, the establishment of quality standards, and the adoption of measures, laid down in this Directive.

4. The environmental objectives in Article 4 and environmental quality standards established in Annex IX and pursuant to Article 16(7), and by Member States under

---

[1] OJ L 194, 25.7.1975, p. 26. Directive as last amended by Directive 91/692/ EEC.
[2] OJ L 334, 24.12.1977, p. 29. Decision as last amended by the 1994 Act of Accession.
[3] OJ L 271, 29.10.1979, p. 44. Directive as last amended by the 1994 Act of Accession.
[4] OJ L 222, 14.8.1978, p. 1. Directive as last amended by the 1994 Act of Accession.
[5] OJ L 281, 10.11.1979, p. 47. Directive as amended by Directive 91/692/ EEC.

Annex V for substances not on the list of priority substances and under Article 16(8) in respect of priority substances for which Community standards have not been set, shall be regarded as environmental quality standards for the purposes of point 7 of Article 2 and Article 10 of Directive 96/61/EC.

5. Where a substance on the list of priority substances adopted under Article 16 is not included in Annex VIII to this Directive or in Annex III to Directive 96/61/EC, it shall be added thereto.

6. For bodies of surface water, environmental objectives established under the first river basin management plan required by this Directive shall, as a minimum, give effect to quality standards at least as stringent as those required to implement Directive 76/464/EEC.

Article 23
Penalties

Member States shall determine penalties applicable to breaches of the national provisions adopted pursuant to this Directive. The penalties thus provided for shall be effective, proportionate and dissuasive.

Article 24
Implementation

1. Member States shall bring into force the laws, regulations and administrative provisions necessary to comply with this Directive at the latest 22 December 2003. They shall forthwith inform the Commission thereof. When Member States adopt these measures, they shall contain a reference to this Directive or shall be accompanied by such a reference on the occasion of their official publication. The methods of making such a reference shall be laid down by the Member States.

2. Member States shall communicate to the Commission the texts of the main provisions of national law which they adopt in the field governed by this Directive. The Commission shall inform the other Member States thereof.

Article 25
Entry into force

This Directive shall enter into force on the day of its publication in the *Official Journal of the European Communities.*

Article 26
Addressees

This Directive is addressed to the Member States.

Annex I

Information required for the list of competent authorities

As required under Article 3(8), the Member States shall provide the following information on all competent authorities within each of its river basin districts as well as
the portion of any international river basin district lying within their territory.

  (i) *Name and address of the competent authority* – the official name and address of
      the authority identified under Article 3(2).
 (ii) *Geographical coverage of the river basin district* – the names of the main rivers
      within the river basin district together with a precise description of the bound-
      aries of the river basin district. This information should as far as possible be
      available for introduction into a geographic information system (GIS) and/or
      the geographic information system of the Commission (GISCO).
(iii) *Legal status of competent authority* – a description of the legal status of the com-
      petent authority and, where relevant, a summary or copy of its statute, founding
      treaty or equivalent legal document.
 (iv) *Responsibilities* – a description of the legal and administrative responsibilities of
      each competent authority and of its role within each river basin district.
  (v) *Membership* – where the competent authority acts as a coordinating body for
      other competent authorities, a list is required of these bodies together with a
      summary of the institutional relationships established in order to ensure coor-
      dination.
 (vi) *International relationships* – where a river basin district covers the territory of
      more than one Member State or includes the territory of non-Member States,
      a summary is required of the institutional relationships established in order to
      ensure coordination.

Annex II

1. Surface waters

1.1. *Characterisation of surface water body types*

Member States shall identify the location and boundaries of bodies of surface water
and shall carry out an initial characterisation of all such bodies in accordance with
the following methodology. Member States may group surface water bodies together
for the purposes of this initial characterisation.

  (i) The surface water bodies within the river basin district shall be identified as
      falling within either one of the following surface water categories – rivers, lakes,
      transitional waters or coastal waters – or as artificial surface water bodies or
      heavily modified surface water bodies.
 (ii) For each surface water category, the relevant surface water bodies within
      the river basin district shall be differentiated according to type. These

types are those defined using either 'system A' or 'system B' identified in section 1.2.

(iii) If system A is used, the surface water bodies within the river basin district shall first be differentiated by the relevant ecoregions in accordance with the geographical areas identified in section 1.2 and shown on the relevant map in Annex XI. The water bodies within each ecoregion shall then be differentiated by surface water body types according to the descriptors set out in the tables for system A.

(iv) If system B is used, Member States must achieve at least the same degree of differentiation as would be achieved using system A. Accordingly, the surface water bodies within the river basin district shall be differentiated into types using the values for the obligatory descriptors and such optional descriptors, or combinations of descriptors, as are required to ensure that type specific biological reference conditions can be reliably derived.

(v) For artificial and heavily modified surface water bodies the differentiation shall be undertaken in accordance with the descriptors for whichever of the surface water categories most closely resembles the heavily modified or artificial water body concerned.

(vi) Member States shall submit to the Commission a map or maps (in a GIS format) of the geographical location of the types consistent with the degree of differentiation required under system A.

1.2. Ecoregions and surface water body types

1.2.1 Rivers

System A

Fixed typology	Descriptors
Ecoregion	Ecoregions shown on map A in Annex XI
Type	Altitude typology high: > 800 m mid-altitude: 200 to 800 m lowland: < 200 m Size typology based on catchment area small: 10 to 100 km^2 medium: > 100 to 1 000 km^2 large: $> 1 000$ to 10 000 km^2 very large: $> 10 000$ km^2 Geology calcareous siliceous organic

System B

Alternative characterisation	Physical and chemical factors that determine the characteristics of the river or part of the river and hence the biological population structure and composition
Obligatory factors	altitude latitude longitude geology size
Optional factors	distance from river source energy of flow (function of flow and slope) mean water width mean water depth mean water slope form and shape of main river bed river discharge (flow) category valley shape transport of solids acid neutralising capacity mean substratum composition chloride air temperature range mean air temperature precipitation

1.2.2. Lakes

System A

Fixed typology	Descriptors

Ecoregion
Type
	Ecoregions shown on map A in Annex XI
	Altitude typology
	    high: > 800 m
	    mid-altitude: 200 to 800 m
	    lowland: < 200 m
	Depth typology based on mean depth
	    < 3 m
	    3 to 15 m
	    > 15 m

Fixed typology	Descriptors

	Size typology based on surface area
	    0,5 to 1 km^2
	    1 to 10 km^2
	    10 to 100 km^2
	    > 100 km^2

	Geology
	    calcareous
	    siliceous
	    organic

System B

Alternative characterisation	Physical and chemical factors that determine the characteristics of the lake and hence the biological population structure and composition
Obligatory factors	altitude latitude longitude depth geology size
Optional factors	mean water depth lake shape residence time mean air temperature air temperature range mixing characteristics (e.g. monomictic, dimictic, polymictic) acid neutralising capacity background nutrient status mean substratum composition water level fluctuation

1.2.3. Transitional Waters

System A

Fixed typology	Descriptors
Ecoregion	The following as identified on map B in Annex XI: Baltic Sea Barents Sea Norwegian Sea North Sea North Atlantic Ocean Mediterranean Sea
Type	Based on mean annual salinity $< 0{,}5\%c$: freshwater 0,5 to $< 5\%c$: oligohaline 5 to $< 18\%c$: mesohaline 18 to $< 30\%c$: polyhaline 30 to $< 40\%c$: euhaline Based on mean tidal range < 2 m: microtidal 2 to 4 mmesotidal > 4 m: macrotidal

System B

Alternative characterisation	Physical and chemical factors that determine the characteristics of the transitional water and hence the biological population structure and composition
Obligatory factors	latitude longitude tidal range salinity
Optional factors	depth current velocity wave exposure residence time mean water temperature mixing characteristics turbidity mean substratum composition shape water temperature range

1.2.4. Coastal Waters

System A

Fixed typology	Descriptors
Ecoregion	The following as identified on map B in Annex XI: Baltic Sea Barents Sea Norwegian Sea North Sea North Atlantic Ocean Mediterranean Sea
Type	Based on mean annual salinity $< 0,5‰$: freshwater 0,5 to $< 5‰$ oligohaline 5 to $< 18‰$: mesohaline 18 to $< 30‰$: polyhaline 30 to $< 40‰$: euhaline Based on mean depth shallow waters: < 30 m intermediate: (30 to 200 m) deep: > 200 m

System B

Alternative characterisation	Physical and chemical factors that determine the characteristics of the coastal water and hence the biological community structure and composition
Obligatory factors	latitude longitude tidal range salinity
Optional factors	current velocity wave exposure mean water temperature mixing characteristics turbidity retention time (of enclosed bays) mean substratum composition water temperature range

1.3. Establishment of type-specific reference conditions for surface water body types

(i) For each surface water body type characterised in accordance with section 1.1, type-specific hydromorphological and physicochemical conditions shall be established representing the values of the hydromorphological and physico-chemical quality elements specified in point 1.1 in Annex V for that surface water body type at high ecological status as defined in the relevant table in point 1.2 in Annex V. Type-specific biological reference conditions shall be established, representing the values of the biological quality elements specified in point 1.1 in Annex V for that surface water body type at high ecological status as defined in the relevant table in section 1.2 in Annex V.

(ii) In applying the procedures set out in this section to heavily modified or artificial surface water bodies references to high ecological status shall be construed as references to maximum ecological potential as defined in table 1.2.5 of Annex V. The values for maximum ecological potential for a water body shall be reviewed every six years.

(iii) Type-specific conditions for the purposes of points (i) and (ii) and type-specific biological reference conditions may be either spatially based or based on mod-elling, or may be derived using a combination of these methods. Where it is not possible to use these methods, Member States may use expert judgement to establish such conditions. In defining high ecological status in respect of con-centrations of specific synthetic pollutants, the detection limits are those which can be achieved in accordance with the available techniques at the time when the type-specific conditions are to be established.

(iv) For spatially based type-specific biological reference conditions, Member States shall develop a reference network for each surface water body type. The network shall contain a sufficient number of sites of high status to provide a sufficient level of confidence about the values for the reference conditions, given the variability in the values of the quality elements corresponding to high ecological status for that surface water body type and the modelling techniques which are to be applied under paragraph (v).

(v) Type-specific biological reference conditions based on modelling may be derived using either predictive models or hindcasting methods. The methods shall use historical, palaeological and other available data and shall provide a sufficient level of confidence about the values for the reference conditions to ensure that the conditions so derived are consistent and valid for each surface water body type.

(vi) Where it is not possible to establish reliable type-specific reference conditions for a quality element in a surface water body type due to high degrees of natural variability in that element, not just as a result of seasonal variations, then that element may be excluded from the assessment of ecological status for that surface water type. In such circumstances Member States shall state the reasons for this exclusion in the river basin management plan.

1.4. Identification of Pressures

Member States shall collect and maintain information on the type and magnitude of the significant anthropogenic pressures to which the surface water bodies in each river basin district are liable to be subject, in particular the following.

Estimation and identification of significant point source pollution, in particular by substances listed in Annex VIII, from urban, industrial, agricultural and other installations and activities, based, *inter alia,* on information gathered under:

  (i) Articles 15 and 17 of Directive 91/271/EEC;

 (ii) Articles 9 and 15 of Directive 96/61/EC;[1]

and for the purposes of the initial river basin management plan:

 (iii) Article 11 of Directive 76/464/EEC; and

 (iv) Directives 75/440/EC, 76/160/EEC,[2] 78/659/EEC and 79/923/ EEC.[3]

Estimation and identification of significant diffuse source pollution, in particular by substances listed in Annex VIII, from urban, industrial, agricultural and other installations and activities; based, *inter alia,* on information gathered under:

  (i) Articles 3, 5 and 6 of Directive 91/676/EEC;[4]

 (ii) Articles 7 and 17 of Directive 91/414/EEC;

 (iii) Directive 98/8/EC;

and for the purposes of the first river basin management plan:

 (iv) Directives 75/440/EEC, 76/160/EEC, 76/464/EEC, 78/659/EEC and 79/923/EEC.

Estimation and identification of significant water abstraction for urban, industrial, agricultural and other uses, including seasonal variations and total annual demand, and of loss of water in distribution systems.

Estimation and identification of the impact of significant water flow regulation, including water transfer and diversion, on overall flow characteristics and water balances.

Identification of significant morphological alterations to water bodies.

Estimation and identification of other significant anthropogenic impacts on the status of surface waters.

---

[1] OJ L 135, 30.5.1991, p. 40. Directive as last amended by Directive 98/15/EC (OJ L 67, 7.3.1998, p. 29).

[2] OJ L 31, 5.2.1976, p. 1. Directive as last amended by the 1994 Act of Accession.

[3] OJ L 281, 10.11.1979, p. 47. Directive as amended by Directive 91/692/EEC (OJ L 377, 31.12.1991, p. 48).

[4] OJ L 375, 31.12.1991, p. 1.

Estimation of land use patterns, including identification of the main urban, industrial
and agricultural areas and, where relevant, fisheries and forests.

1.5. Assessment of Impact

Member States shall carry out an assessment of the susceptibility of the surface water
status of bodies to the pressures identified above.

Member States shall use the information collected above, and any other relevant
information including existing environmental monitoring data, to carry out an assessment of the likelihood that surface waters bodies within the river basin district will
fail to meet the environmental quality objectives set for the bodies under Article 4.

Member States may utilise modelling techniques to assist in such an assessment.

For those bodies identified as being at risk of failing the environmental quality
objectives, further characterisation shall, where relevant, be carried out to optimise
the design of both the monitoring programmes required under Article 8, and the
programmes of measures required under Article 11.

2. Groundwaters

2.1. Initial characterization

Member States shall carry out an initial characterisation of all groundwater bodies to
assess their uses and the degree to which they are at risk of failing to meet the objectives
for each groundwater body under Article 4. Member States may group groundwater
bodies together for the purposes of this initial characterisation. This analysis may
employ existing hydrological, geological, pedological, land use, discharge, abstraction
and other data but shall identify:

- the location and boundaries of the groundwater body or bodies,
- the pressures to which the groundwater body or bodies are liable to be subject
  including:
  - diffuse sources of pollution
  - point sources of pollution
  - abstraction
  - artificial recharge,
- the general character of the overlying strata in the catchment area from which the
  groundwater body receives its recharge,
- those groundwater bodies for which there are directly dependent surface water
  ecosystems or terrestrial ecosystems.

2.2. Further characterisation

Following this initial characterisation, Member States shall carry out further characterisation of those groundwater bodies or groups of bodies which have been identified
as being at risk in order to establish a more precise assessment of the significance of

such risk and identification of any measures to be required under Article 11. Accordingly, this characterisation shall include relevant information on the impact of human activity and, where relevant, information on:

– geological characteristics of the groundwater body including the extent and type of geological units,
– hydrogeological characteristics of the groundwater body including hydraulic conductivity, porosity and confinement,
– characteristics of the superficial deposits and soils in the catchment from which the groundwater body receives its recharge, including the thickness, porosity, hydraulic conductivity, and absorptive properties of the deposits and soils,
– stratification characteristics of the groundwater within the groundwater body,
– an inventory of associated surface systems, including terrestrial ecosystems and bodies of surface water, with which the groundwater body is dynamically linked,
– estimates of the directions and rates of exchange of water between the groundwater body and associated surface systems,
– sufficient data to calculate the long term annual average rate of overall recharge,
– characterisation of the chemical composition of the groundwater, including specification of the contributions from human activity. Member States may use typologies for groundwater characterisation when establishing natural background levels for these bodies of groundwater.

2.3. Review of the impact of human activity on groundwaters

For those bodies of groundwater which cross the boundary between two or more Member States or are identified following the initial characterisation undertaken in accordance with paragraph 2.1 as being at risk of failing to meet the objectives set for each body under Article 4, the following information shall, where relevant, be collected and maintained for each groundwater body:

(a) the location of points in the groundwater body used for the abstraction of water with the exception of:
– points for the abstraction of water providing less than an average of 10 m^3 per day, or,
– points for the abstraction of water intended for human consumption providing less than an average of 10 m^3 per day or serving less than 50 persons,
(b) the annual average rates of abstraction from such points,
(c) the chemical composition of water abstracted from the groundwater body,
(d) the location of points in the groundwater body into which water is directly discharged,
(e) the rates of discharge at such points,
(f) the chemical composition of discharges to the groundwater body, and

(g) land use in the catchment or catchments from which the groundwater body receives its recharge, including pollutant inputs and anthropogenic alterations to the recharge characteristics such as rainwater and run-off diversion through land sealing, artificial recharge, damming or drainage.

2.4. Review of the impact of changes in groundwater levels

Member States shall also identify those bodies of groundwater for which lower objectives are to be specified under Article 4 including as a result of consideration of the effects of the status of the body on:

  (i) surface water and associated terrestrial ecosystems
 (ii) water regulation, flood protection and land drainage
(iii) human development.

2.5 Review of the impact of pollution on groundwater quality

Member States shall identify those bodies of groundwater for which lower objectives are to be specified under Article 4(5) where, as a result of the impact of human activity, as determined in accordance with Article 5(1), the body of groundwater is so polluted that achieving good groundwater chemical status is infeasible or disproportionately expensive.

Annex III
Economic analysis

The economic analysis shall contain enough information in sufficient detail (taking account of the costs associated with collection of the relevant data) in order to:

(a) make the relevant calculations necessary for taking into account under Article 9 the principle of recovery of the costs of water services, taking account of long term forecasts of supply and demand for water in the river basin district and, where necessary:
    – estimates of the volume, prices and costs associated with water services, and
    – estimates of relevant investment including forecasts of such investments;
(b) make judgements about the most cost-effective combination of measures in respect of water uses to be included in the programme of measures under Article 11 based on estimates of the potential costs of such measures.

Annex IV
Protected areas

1. The register of protected areas required under Article 6 shall include the following types of protected areas:

 (i) areas designated for the abstraction of water intended for human consumption under Article 7;

(ii) areas designated for the protection of economically significant aquatic species;
(iii) bodies of water designated as recreational waters, including areas designated as bathing waters under Directive 76/160/EEC;
(iv) nutrient-sensitive areas, including areas designated as vulnerable zones under Directive 91/676/EEC and areas designated as sensitive areas under Directive 91/271/EEC; and
(v) areas designated for the protection of habitats or species where the maintenance or improvement of the status of water is an important factor in their protection, including relevant Natura 2000 sites designated under Directive 92/43/EEC[1] and Directive 79/409/EEC.[2]

2. The summary of the register required as part of the river basin management plan shall include maps indicating the location of each protected area and a description of the Community, national or local legislation under which they have been designated.

Annex V

---

[1] OJ L 206, 22.7.1992, p. 7. Directive as last amended by Directive 97/62/EC (OJ L 305, 08.11.1997, p. 42).
[2] OJ L 103, 25.4.1979, p. 1. Directive as last amended by Directive 97/49/EC (OJ L 223, 13.8.1997, p. 9).

1. Surface water status

1.1. *Quality elements for the classification of ecological status*

1.1.1. Rivers

Biological elements

Composition and abundance of aquatic flora

Composition and abundance of benthic invertebrate fauna

Composition, abundance and age structure of fish fauna

Hydromorphological elements supporting the biological elements
Hydrological regime
    quantity and dynamics of water flow
    connection to groundwater bodies

River continuity

    Morphological conditions
        river depth and width variation
        structure and substrate of the river bed
        structure of the riparian zone

Chemical and physico-chemical elements supporting the biological elements

General
Thermal conditions
Oxygenation conditions
Salinity
Acidification status
Nutrient conditions

Specific pollutants
Pollution by all priority substances identified as being discharged into the body of
    water
Pollution by other substances identified as being discharged in significant quantities
    into the body of water

1.1.2. Lakes

Biological elements
Composition, abundance and biomass of phytoplankton
Composition and abundance of other aquatic flora
Composition and abundance of benthic invertebrate fauna
Composition, abundance and age structure of fish fauna

Hydromorphological elements supporting the biological elements
Hydrological regime
    quantity and dynamics of water flow
    residence time
    connection to the groundwater body

Morphological conditions
    lake depth variation
    quantity, structure and substrate of the lake
    bed structure of the lake shore

Chemical and physico-chemical elements supporting the biological elements

General
Transparency
Thermal conditions
Oxygenation conditions
Salinity
Acidification status
Nutrient conditions

Specific pollutants
Pollution by all priority substances identified as being discharged into the body of
water
Pollution by other substances identified as being discharged in significant quantities
into the body of water

1.1.3. Transitional waters

Biological elements
Composition, abundance and biomass of phytoplankton
Composition and abundance of other aquatic flora
Composition and abundance of benthic invertebrate fauna
Composition and abundance of fish fauna

Hydro-morphological elements supporting the biological elements
Morphological conditions
    depth variation
    quantity, structure and substrate of the bed
    structure of the intertidal zone

Tidal regime
    freshwater flow
    wave exposure

Chemical and physico-chemical elements supporting the biological elements

General
Transparency
Thermal conditions
Oxygenation conditions
Salinity
Nutrient conditions

Specific pollutants
Pollution by all priority substances identified as being discharged into the body of
water
Pollution by other substances identified as being discharged in significant quantities
into the body of water

1.1.4. Coastal waters

Biological elements
Composition, abundance and biomass of phytoplankton
Composition and abundance of other aquatic flora
Composition and abundance of benthic invertebrate fauna

Hydromorphological elements supporting the biological elements
Morphological conditions
depth variation
structure and substrate of the coastal bed
structure of the intertidal zone

Tidal regime
direction of dominant currents
wave exposure

Chemical and physico-chemical elements supporting the biological elements

General
Transparency
Thermal conditions
Oxygenation conditions
Salinity
Nutrient conditions

Specific pollutants
Pollution by all priority substances identified as being discharged into the body of
water
Pollution by other substances identified as being discharged in significant quantities
into the body of water

1.1.5. Artificial and heavily modified surface water bodies

The quality elements applicable to artificial and heavily modified surface water bodies shall be those applicable to whichever of the four natural surface water categories above most closely resembles the heavily modified or artificial water body
concerned.

1.2. *Normative definitions of ecological status classifications*

Table 1.2. *General definition for rivers, lakes, transitional waters and coastal waters*

The following text provides a general definition of ecological quality. For the purposes of classification the values for the quality elements of ecological status for each surface water category are those given in tables 1.2.1 to 1.2.4 below.

Element	High status	Good status	Moderate status
General	There are no, or only very minor, anthropogenic alterations to the values of the physico-chemical and hydromorphological quality elements for the surface water body type from those normally associated with that type under undisturbed conditions.	The values of the biological quality elements for the surface water body type show low levels of distortion resulting from human activity, but deviate only slightly from those normally associated with the surface water body type under undisturbed conditions.	The values of the biological quality elements for the surface water body type deviate moderately from those normally associated with the surface water body type under undisturbed conditions. The values show moderate signs of distortion resulting from human activity and are significantly more disturbed than under conditions of good status.
	The values of the biological quality elements for the surface water body reflect those normally associated with that type under undisturbed conditions, and show no, or only very minor, evidence of distortion.		
	These are the type-specific conditions and communities.		

Waters achieving a status below moderate shall be classified as poor or bad.

Waters showing evidence of major alterations to the values of the biological quality elements for the surface water body type and in which the relevant biological communities deviate substantially from those normally associated with the surface water body type under undisturbed conditions, shall be classified as poor.

Waters showing evidence of severe alterations to the values of the biological quality elements for the surface water body type and in which large portions of the relevant biological communities normally associated with the surface water body type under undisturbed conditions are absent, shall be classified as bad.

1.2.1. Definitions for high, good and moderate ecological status in rivers

Biological quality elements

Element	High status	Good status	Moderate status
Phytoplankton	The taxonomic composition of phytoplankton corresponds totally or nearly totally to undisturbed conditions. The average phytoplankton abundance is wholly consistent with the type-specific physico-chemical conditions and is not such as to significantly alter the type-specific transparency conditions. Planktonic blooms occur at a frequency and intensity which is consistent with the type-specific physico-chemical conditions.	There are slight changes in the composition and abundance of planktonic taxa compared to the type-specific communities. Such changes do not indicate any accelerated growth of algae resulting in undesirable disturbances to the balance of organisms present in the water body or to the physico-chemical quality of the water or sediment. A slight increase in the frequency and intensity of the type-specific planktonic blooms may occur.	The composition of planktonic taxa differs moderately from the type-specific communities. Abundance is moderately disturbed and may be such as to produce a significant undesirable disturbance in the values of other biological and physico-chemical quality elements. A moderate increase in the frequency and intensity of planktonic blooms may occur. Persistent blooms may occur during summer months.
Macrophytes and phytobenthos	The taxonomic composition corresponds totally or nearly totally to undisturbed conditions. There are no detectable changes in the average macrophytic and the average phytobenthic abundance.	There are slight changes in the composition and abundance of macrophytic and phytobenthic taxa compared to the type-specific communities. Such changes do not indicate any accelerated growth of phytobenthos or higher forms plant life resulting in undesirable	The composition of macrophytic and phytobenthic taxa differs moderately from the type-specific community and is significantly more distorted than at good status. Moderate changes in the average macrophytic and the average of phytobenthic

Element	High status	Good status	Moderate status
		disturbances to the balance of organisms present in the water body or to the physico-chemical quality of the water or sediment.	abundance are evident.
			The phytobenthic community may be interfered with and, in some areas, displaced by bacterial tufts and coats present as a result of anthropogenic activities.
		The phytobenthic community is not adversely affected by bacterial tufts and coats present due to anthropogenic activity.	
Benthic invertebrate fauna	The taxonomic composition and abundance correspond totally or nearly totally to undisturbed conditions.	There are slight changes in the composition and abundance of invertebrate taxa from the type-specific communities.	The composition and abundance of invertebrate taxa differ moderately from the type-specific communities.
	The ratio of disturbance sensitive taxa to insensitive taxa shows no signs of alteration from undisturbed levels.	The ratio of disturbance-sensitive taxa to insensitive taxa shows slight alteration from type-specific levels.	Major taxonomic groups of the type-specific community are absent.
	The level of diversity of invertebrate taxa shows no sign of alteration from undisturbed levels.	The level of diversity of invertebrate taxa shows slight signs of alteration from type-specific levels.	The ratio of disturbance-sensitive taxa to insensitive taxa, and the level of diversity, are substantially lower than the type-specific level and significantly lower than for good status.
Fish fauna	Species composition and abundance correspond totally or nearly totally to undisturbed conditions.	There are slight changes in species composition and abundance from the type-specific communities attributable to anthropogenic impacts on physico-chemical	The composition and abundance of fish species differ moderately from the type-specific communities attributable to anthropogenic impacts on physico-chemical
	All the type-specific disturbance-sensitive species are present.		

Element	High status	Good status	Moderate status
	The age structures of the fish communities show little sign of anthropogenic disturbance and are not indicative of a failure in the reproduction or development of any particular species.	and hydromorphological quality elements.	or hydromorphological quality elements.
		The age structures of the fish communities show signs of disturbance attributable to anthropogenic impacts on physico-chemical or hydromorphological quality elements, and, in a few instances, are indicative of a failure in the reproduction or development of a particular species, to the extent that some age classes may be missing.	The age structure of the fish communities shows major signs of anthropogenic disturbance, to the extent that a moderate proportion of the type specific species are absent or of very low abundance.

Hydromorphological quality elements

Element	High status	Good status	Moderate status
Hydrological regime	The quantity and dynamics of flow, and the resultant connection to groundwaters, reflect totally, or nearly totally, undisturbed conditions.	Conditions consistent with the achievement of the values specified above for the biological quality elements.	Conditions consistent with the achievement of the values specified above for the biological quality elements.
River continuity	The continuity of the river is not disturbed by anthropogenic activities and allows undisturbed migration of aquatic organisms and sediment transport.	Conditions consistent with the achievement of the values specified above for the biological quality elements.	Conditions consistent with the achievement of the values specified above for the biological quality elements.

Element	High status	Good status	Moderate status
Morphological conditions	Channel patterns, width and depth variations, flow velocities, substrate conditions and both the structure and condition of the riparian zones correspond totally or nearly totally to undisturbed conditions.	Conditions consistent with the achievement of the values specified above for the biological quality elements.	Conditions consistent with the achievement of the values specified above for the biological quality elements.

Physico-chemical quality elements[1]

Element	High status	Good status	Moderate status
General conditions	The values of the physico-chemical elements correspond totally or nearly totally to undisturbed conditions. Nutrient concentrations remain within the range normally associated with undisturbed conditions. Levels of salinity, pH, oxygen balance, acid neutralising capacity and temperature do not show signs of anthropogenic disturbance and remain within the range normally associated with undisturbed conditions.	Temperature, oxygen balance, pH, acid neutralising capacity and salinity do not reach levels outside the range established so as to ensure the functioning of the type specific ecosystem and the achievement of the values specified above for the biological quality elements. Nutrient concentrations do not exceed the levels established so as to ensure the functioning of the ecosystem and the achievement of the values specified above for the biological quality elements.	Conditions consistent with the achievement of the values specified above for the biological quality elements.

Element	High status	Good status	Moderate status
Specific synthetic pollutants	Concentrations close to zero and at least below the limits of detection of the most advanced analytical techniques in general use.	Concentrations not in excess of the standards set in accordance with the procedure detailed in section 1.2.6 without prejudice to Directive 91/414/EC and Directive 98/8/EC. (< EQS)	Conditions consistent with the achievement of the values specified above for the biological quality elements.
Specific non-synthetic pollutants	Concentrations remain within the range normally associated with undisturbed conditions (background levels = bgl).	Concentrations not in excess of the standards set in accordance with the procedure detailed in section 1.2.6[2] without prejudice to Directive 91/414/EC and Directive 98/8/EC. (< EQS)	Conditions consistent with the achievement of the values specified above for the biological quality elements.

[1] The following abbreviations are used: bgl = background level, EQS = environmental quality standard.

[2] Application of the standards derived under this protocol shall not require reduction of pollutant concentrations below background levels: (EQS > bgl).

1.2.2. Definitions for high, good and moderate ecological status in lakes

Biological quality elements

Element	High status	Good status	Moderate status
Phytoplankton	The taxonomic composition and abundance of phytoplankton correspond totally or nearly totally to undisturbed conditions. The average phytoplankton biomass is consistent with the type-specific physico-chemical	There are slight changes in the composition and abundance of planktonic taxa compared to the type-specific communities. Such changes do not indicate any accelerated growth of algae resulting in undesirable disturbance to the balance of	The composition and abundance of planktonic taxa differ moderately from the type-specific communities. Biomass is moderately disturbed and may be such as to produce a significant undesirable disturbance in the condition of other biological quality

Element	High status	Good status	Moderate status
	conditions and is not such as to significantly alter the type-specific transparency conditions.	organisms present in the water body or to the physico-chemical quality of the water or sediment.	elements and the physico-chemical quality of the water or sediment.
	Planktonic blooms occur at a frequency and intensity which is consistent with the type specific physico-chemical conditions.	A slight increase in the frequency and intensity of the type specific planktonic blooms may occur.	A moderate increase in the frequency and intensity of planktonic blooms may occur. Persistent blooms may occur during summer months.
Macrophytes and phytobenthos	The taxonomic composition corresponds totally or nearly totally to undisturbed conditions.	There are slight changes in the composition and abundance of macrophytic and phytobenthic taxa compared to the type-specific communities. Such changes do not indicate any accelerated growth of phytobenthos or higher forms of plant life resulting in undesirable disturbance to the balance of organisms present in the water body or to the physico-chemical quality of the water.	The composition of macrophytic and phytobenthic taxa differ moderately from the type-specific communities and are significantly more distorted than those observed at good quality.
	There are no detectable changes in the average macrophytic and the average phytobenthic abundance.		Moderate changes in the average macrophytic and the average phytobenthic abundance are evident.
		The phytobenthic community is not adversely affected by bacterial tufts and coats present due to anthropogenic activity.	The phytobenthic community may be interfered with, and, in some areas, displaced by bacterial tufts and coats present as a result of anthropogenic activities.
Benthic invertebrate fauna	The taxonomic composition and abundance correspond totally or nearly totally	There are slight changes in the composition and abundance of	The composition and abundance of invertebrate taxa differ moderately from the

Element	High status	Good status	Moderate status
	to the undisturbed conditions. The ratio of disturbance sensitive taxa to insensitive taxa shows no signs of alteration from undisturbed levels. The level of diversity of invertebrate taxa shows no sign of alteration from undisturbed levels.	invertebrate taxa compared to the type-specific communities. The ratio of disturbance sensitive taxa to insensitive taxa shows slight signs of alteration from type-specific levels. The level of diversity of invertebrate taxa shows slight signs of alteration from type-specific levels.	type-specific conditions. Major taxonomic groups of the type-specific community are absent. The ratio of disturbance sensitive to insensitive taxa, and the level of diversity, are substantially lower than the type-specific level and significantly lower than for good status.
Fish fauna	Species composition and abundance correspond totally or nearly totally to undisturbed conditions. All the type-specific sensitive species are present. The age structures of the fish communities show little sign of anthropogenic disturbance and are not indicative of a failure in the reproduction or development of a particular species.	There are slight changes in species composition and abundance from the type-specific communities attributable to anthropogenic impacts on physico-chemical or hydromorphological quality elements. The age structures of the fish communities show signs of disturbance attributable to anthropogenic impacts on physico-chemical or hydromorphological quality elements, and, in a few instances, are indicative of a failure in the reproduction or development of a particular species, to the extent that some age classes may be missing.	The composition and abundance of fish species differ moderately from the type-specific communities attributable to anthropogenic impacts on physico-chemical or hydromorphological quality elements. The age structure of the fish communities shows major signs of disturbance, attributable to anthropogenic impacts on physico-chemical or hydromorphological quality elements, to the extent that a moderate proportion of the type specific species are absent or of very low abundance.

Hydromorphological quality elements

Element	High status	Good status	Moderate status
Hydrological regime	The quantity and dynamics of flow, level, residence time, and the resultant connection to groundwaters, reflect totally or nearly totally undisturbed conditions.	Conditions consistent with the achievement of the values specified above for the biological quality elements.	Conditions consistent with the achievement of the values specified above for the biological quality elements.
Morphological conditions	Lake depth variation, quantity and structure of the substrate, and both the structure and condition of the lake shore zone correspond totally or nearly totally to undisturbed conditions.	Conditions consistent with the achievement of the values specified above for the biological quality elements.	Conditions consistent with the achievement of the values specified above for the biological quality elements.

Physico-chemical quality elements[1]

Element	High status	Good status	Moderate status
General conditions	The values of physico-chemical elements correspond totally or nearly totally to undisturbed conditions. Nutrient concentrations remain within the range normally associated with undisturbed conditions.	Temperature, oxygen balance, pH, acid neutralising capacity, transparency and salinity do not reach levels outside the range established so as to ensure the functioning of the ecosystem and the achievement of the values specified above for the biological quality elements.	Conditions consistent with the achievement of the values specified above for the biological quality elements.

Element	High status	Good status	Moderate status
	Levels of salinity, pH, oxygen balance, acid neutralising capacity, transparency and temperature do not show signs of anthropogenic disturbance and remain within the range normally associated with undisturbed conditions.	Nutrient concentrations do not exceed the levels established so as to ensure the functioning of the ecosystem and the achievement of the values specified above for the biological quality elements.	
Specific synthetic pollutants	Concentrations close to zero and at least below the limits of detection of the most advanced analytical techniques in general use.	Concentrations not in excess of the standards set in accordance with the procedure detailed in section 1.2.6 without prejudice to Directive 91/414/EC and Directive 98/8/EC. (<EQS)	Conditions consistent with the achievement of the values specified above for the biological quality elements.
Specific non-synthetic pollutants	Concentrations remain within the range normally associated with undisturbed conditions (background levels = bgl).	Concentrations not in excess of the standards set in accordance with the procedure detailed in section 1.2.6[2] without prejudice to Directive 91/414/EC and Directive 98/8/EC. (< EQS)	Conditions consistent with the achievement of the values specified above for the biological quality elements.

[1] The following abbreviations are used: bgl = background level, EQS = environmental quality standard.

[2] Application of the standards derived under this protocol shall not require reduction of pollutant concentrations below background levels: (EQS > bgl).

1.2.3. Definitions for high, good and moderate ecological status in transitional waters

Biological quality elements

Element	High status	Good status	Moderate status
Phytoplankton	The composition and abundance of the phytoplanktonic taxa are consistent with undisturbed conditions. The average phytoplankton biomass is consistent with the type-specific physico-chemical conditions and is not such as to significantly alter the type-specific transparency conditions. Planktonic blooms occur at a frequency and intensity which is consistent with the type specific physico-chemical conditions.	There are slight changes in the composition and abundance of phytoplanktonic taxa. There are slight changes in biomass compared to the type-specific conditions. Such changes do not indicate any accelerated growth of algae resulting in undesirable disturbance to the balance of organisms present in the water body or to the physico-chemical quality of the water. A slight increase in the frequency and intensity of the type specific planktonic blooms may occur.	The composition and abundance of phytoplanktonic taxa differ moderately from type-specific conditions. Biomass is moderately disturbed and may be such as to produce a significant undesirable disturbance in the condition of other biological quality elements. A moderate increase in the frequency and intensity of planktonic blooms may occur. Persistent blooms may occur during summer months.
Macroalgae	The composition of macroalgal taxa is consistent with undisturbed conditions. There are no detectable changes in macroalgal cover due to anthropogenic activities.	There are slight changes in the composition and abundance of macroalgal taxa compared to the type-specific communities. Such changes do not indicate any accelerated growth of phytobenthos or higher forms of plant life resulting in undesirable disturbance to the balance of organisms	The composition of macroalgal taxa differs moderately from type-specific conditions and is significantly more distorted than at good quality. Moderate changes in the average macroalgal abundance are evident and may be such as to result in an undesirable disturbance to the

Element	High status	Good status	Moderate status
		present in the water body or to the physico-chemical quality of the water.	balance of organisms present in the water body.
Angiosperms	The taxonomic composition corresponds totally or nearly totally to undisturbed conditions. There are no detectable changes in angiosperm abundance due to anthropogenic activities.	There are slight changes in the composition of angiosperm taxa compared to the type-specific communities. Angiosperm abundance shows slight signs of disturbance.	The composition of the angiosperm taxa differs moderately from the type-specific communities and is significantly more distorted than at good quality. There are moderate distortions in the abundance of angiosperm taxa.
Benthic invertebrate fauna	The level of diversity and abundance of invertebrate taxa is within the range normally associated with undisturbed conditions. All the disturbance-sensitive taxa associated with undisturbed conditions are present.	The level of diversity and abundance of invertebrate taxa is slightly outside the range associated with the type-specific conditions. Most of the sensitive taxa of the type-specific communities are present.	The level of diversity and abundance of invertebrate taxa is moderately outside the range associated with the type-specific conditions. Taxa indicative of pollution are present. Many of the sensitive taxa of the type-specific communities are absent.
Fish fauna	Species composition and abundance is consistent with undisturbed conditions.	The abundance of the disturbance-sensitive species shows slight signs of distortion from type-specific conditions attributable to anthropogenic impacts on physico-chemical or hydromorphological quality elements.	A moderate proportion of the type-specific disturbance-sensitive species are absent as a result of anthropogenic impacts on physicochemical or hydromorphological quality elements.

Hydromorphological quality elements

Element	High status	Good status	Moderate status
Tidal regime	The freshwater flow regime corresponds totally or nearly totally to undisturbed conditions.	Conditions consistent with the achievement of the values specified above for the biological quality elements.	Conditions consistent with the achievement of the values specified above for the biological quality elements.
Morphological conditions	Depth variations, substrate conditions, and both the structure and condition of the intertidal zones correspond totally or nearly totally to undisturbed conditions.	Conditions consistent with the achievement of the values specified above for the biological quality elements.	Conditions consistent with the achievement of the values specified above for the biological quality elements.

Physico-chemical quality elements[1]

Element	High status	Good status	Moderate status
General conditions	Physico-chemical elements correspond totally or nearly totally to undisturbed conditions. Nutrient concentrations remain within the range normally associated with undisturbed conditions. Temperature, oxygen balance and transparency do not show signs of anthropogenic disturbance and remain within the range normally associated with undisturbed conditions.	Temperature, oxygenation conditions and transparency do not reach levels outside the ranges established so as to ensure the functioning of the ecosystem and the achievement of the values specified above for the biological quality elements. Nutrient concentrations do not exceed the levels established so as to ensure the functioning of the ecosystem and the achievement of the values specified above for the biological quality elements.	Conditions consistent with the achievement of the values specified above for the biological quality elements.

Element	High status	Good status	Moderate status
Specific synthetic pollutants	Concentrations close to zero and at least below the limits of detection of the most advanced analytical techniques in general use.	Concentrations not in excess of the standards set in accordance with the procedure detailed in section 1.2.6 without prejudice to Directive 91/414/EC and Directive 98/8/EC. (< EQS)	Conditions consistent with the achievement of the values specified above for the biological quality elements.
Specific non-synthetic pollutants	Concentrations remain within the range normally associated with undisturbed conditions (background levels = bgl).	Concentrations not in excess of the standards set in accordance with the procedure detailed in section 1.2.6[2] without prejudice to Directive 91/414/EC and Directive 98/8/EC. (< EQS)	Conditions consistent with the achievement of the values specified above for the biological quality elements.

[1] The following abbreviations are used: bgl = background level, EQS = environmental quality standard.

[2] Application of the standards derived under this protocol shall not require reduction of pollutant concentrations below background levels: (EQS > bgl).

1.2.4. Definitions for high, good and moderate ecological status in coastal waters

Biological quality elements

Element	High status	Good status	Moderate status
Phytoplankton	The composition and abundance of phytoplanktonic taxa are consistent with undisturbed conditions. The average phytoplankton biomass is consistent with the type-specific	The composition and abundance of phytoplanktonic taxa show slight signs of disturbance. There are slight changes in biomass compared to type-specific conditions. Such	The composition and abundance of planktonic taxa show signs of moderate disturbance. Algal biomass is substantially outside the range associated with type-specific conditions, and is

Element	High status	Good status	Moderate status
	physico-chemical conditions and is not such as to significantly alter the type-specific transparency conditions. Planktonic blooms occur at a frequency and intensity which is consistent with the type-specific physico-chemical conditions.	changes do not indicate any accelerated growth of algae resulting in undesirable disturbance to the balance of organisms present in the water body or to the quality of the water. A slight increase in the frequency and intensity of the type-specific planktonic blooms may occur.	such as to impact upon other biological quality elements. A moderate increase in the frequency and intensity of planktonic blooms may occur. Persistent blooms may occur during summer months.
Macroalgae and angiosperms	All disturbance-sensitive macroalgal and angiosperm taxa associated with undisturbed conditions are present. The levels of macroalgal cover and angiosperm abundance are consistent with undisturbed conditions.	Most disturbance-sensitive macroalgal and angiosperm taxa associated with undisturbed conditions are present. The level of macroalgal cover and angiosperm abundance show slight signs of disturbance.	A moderate number of the disturbance-sensitive macroalgal and angiosperm taxa associated with undisturbed conditions are absent. Macroalgal cover and angiosperm abundance is moderately disturbed and may be such as to result in an undesirable disturbance to the balance of organisms present in the water body.

Hydromorphological quality elements

Element	High status	Good status	Moderate status
Benthic invertebrate fauna	The level of diversity and abundance of invertebrate taxa is within the range normally associated with undisturbed conditions.	The level of diversity and abundance of invertebrate taxa is slightly outside the range associated with the type-specific conditions.	The level of diversity and abundance of invertebrate taxa is moderately outside the range associated with the type-specific conditions.
	All the disturbance-sensitive taxa associated with undisturbed conditions are present.	Most of the sensitive taxa of the type-specific communities are present.	Taxa indicative of pollution are present. Many of the sensitive taxa of the type-specific communities are absent.
Tidal regime	The freshwater flow regime and the direction and speed of dominant currents correspond totally or nearly totally to undisturbed conditions.	Conditions consistent with the achievement of the values specified above for the biological quality elements.	Conditions consistent with the achievement of the values specified above for the biological quality elements.
Morphological conditions	The depth variation, structure and substrate of the coastal bed, and both the structure and condition of the inter-tidal zones correspond totally or nearly totally to the undisturbed conditions.	Conditions consistent with the achievement of the values specified above for the biological quality elements.	Conditions consistent with the achievement of the values specified above for the biological quality elements.

Physico-chemical quality elements[1]

Element	High status	Good status	Moderate status
General conditions	The physico-chemical elements correspond totally or nearly totally to undisturbed conditions.\n\nNutrient concentrations remain within the range normally associated with undisturbed conditions.\n\nTemperature, oxygen balance and transparency do not show signs of anthropogenic disturbance and remain within the ranges normally associated with undisturbed conditions.	Temperature, oxygenation conditions and transparency do not reach levels outside the ranges established so as to ensure the functioning of the ecosystem and the achievement of the values specified above for the biological quality elements.\n\nNutrient concentrations do not exceed the levels established so as to ensure the functioning of the ecosystem and the achievement of the values specified above for the biological quality elements.	Conditions consistent with the achievement of the values specified above for the biological quality elements.
Specific synthetic pollutants	Concentrations close to zero and at least below the limits of detection of the most advanced analytical techniques in general use.	Concentrations not in excess of the standards set in accordance with the procedure detailed in section 1.2.6 without prejudice to Directive 91/414/EC and Directive 98/8/EC. ($<$ EQS)	Conditions consistent with the achievement of the values specified above for the biological quality elements.
Specific non-synthetic pollutants	Concentrations remain within the range normally associated with undisturbed conditions (background levels = bgl).	Concentrations not in excess of the standards set in accordance with the procedure detailed in section 1.2.6[2] without prejudice to Directive 91/414/EC and Directive 98/8/EC. ($<$ EQS)	Conditions consistent with the achievement of the values specified above for the biological quality elements.

[1] The following abbreviations are used: bgl = background level, EQS = environmental quality standard.

[2] Application of the standards derived under this protocol shall not require reduction of pollutant concentrations below background levels: (EQS $>$ bgl).

1.2.5. Definitions for maximum, good and moderate ecological potential for heavily modified or artificial water bodies

Element	Maximum ecological potential	Good ecological potential	Moderate ecological potential
Biological quality elements	The values of the relevant biological quality elements reflect, as far as possible, those associated with the closest comparable surface water body type, given the physical conditions which result from the artificial or heavily modified characteristics of the water body.	There are slight changes in the values of the relevant biological quality elements as compared to the values found at maximum ecological potential.	There are moderate changes in the values of the relevant biological quality elements as compared to the values found at maximum ecological potential. These values are significantly more distorted than those found under good quality.
Hydromorpho-logical elements	The hydromorphological conditions are consistent with the only impacts on the surface water body being those resulting from the artificial or heavily modified characteristics of the water body once all mitigation measures have been taken to ensure the best approximation to ecological continuum, in particular with respect to migration of fauna and appropriate spawning and breeding grounds.	Conditions consistent with the achievement of the values specified above for the biological quality elements.	Conditions consistent with the achievement of the values specified above for the biological quality elements.
Physico-chemical elements			

Element	Maximum ecological potential	Good ecological potential	Moderate ecological potential
General conditions	Physico-chemical elements correspond totally or nearly totally to the undisturbed conditions associated with the surface water body type most closely comparable to the artificial or heavily modified body concerned. Nutrient concentrations remain within the range normally associated with such undisturbed conditions. The levels of temperature, oxygen balance and pH are consistent with the those found in the most closely comparable surface water body types under undisturbed conditions.	The values for physico-chemical elements are within the ranges established so as to ensure the functioning of the ecosystem and the achievement of the values specified above for the biological quality elements. Temperature and pH do not reach levels outside the ranges established so as to ensure the functioning of the ecosystem and the achievement of the values specified above for the biological quality elements. Nutrient concentrations do not exceed the levels established so as to ensure the functioning of the ecosystem and the achievement of the values specified above for the biological quality elements.	Conditions consistent with the achievement of the values specified above for the biological quality elements.
Specific synthetic pollutants	Concentrations close to zero and at least below the limits of detection of the most advanced analytical techniques in general use.	Concentrations not in excess of the standards set in accordance with the procedure detailed in section 1.2.6 without prejudice to Directive 91/414/EC and Directive 98/8/EC. (< EQS)	Conditions consistent with the achievement of the values specified above for the biological quality elements.

Element	Maximum ecological potential	Good ecological potential	Moderate ecological potential
Specific non-synthetic pollutants	Concentrations remain within the range normally associated with the undisturbed conditions found in the surface water body type most closely comparable to the artificial or heavily modified body concerned (background levels = bgl).	Concentrations not in excess of the standards set in accordance with the procedure detailed in section 1.2.6[1] without prejudice to Directive 91/414/EC and Directive 98/8/EC. (< EQS)	Conditions consistent with the achievement of the values specified above for the biological quality elements.

[1] Application of the standards derived under this protocol shall not require reduction of pollutant concentrations below background levels.

1.2.6. Procedure for the setting of chemical quality standards by Member States

In deriving environmental quality standards for pollutants listed in points 1 to 9 of Annex VIII for the protection of aquatic biota, Member States shall act in accordance with the following provisions. Standards may be set for water, sediment or biota.

Where possible, both acute and chronic data shall be obtained for the taxa set out below which are relevant for the water body type concerned as well as any other aquatic taxa for which data are available. The 'base set' of taxa are:

– algae and/or macrophytes
– daphnia or representative organisms for saline waters
– fish.

Setting the environmental quality standard

The following procedure applies to the setting of a maximum annual average concentration:

(i) Member States shall set appropriate safety factors in each case consistent with the nature and quality of the available data and the guidance given in section 3.3.1 of Part II of 'Technical guidance document in support of Commission Directive 93/67/EEC on risk assessment for new notified substances and Commission Regulation (EC) No 1488/94 on risk assessment for existing substances' and the safety factors set out in the table below:

	Safety factor
At least one acute $L(E)C_{50}$ from each of three trophic levels of the base set	1 000
One chronic NOEC (either fish or daphnia or a representative organism for saline waters)	100
Two chronic NOECs from species representing two trophic levels (fish and/or daphnia or a representative organism for saline waters and/or algae)	50
Chronic NOECs from at least three species (normally fish, daphnia or a representative organism for saline waters and algae) representing three trophic levels	10
Other cases, including field data or model ecosystems, which allow more precise safety factors to be calculated and applied	Case-by-case assessment

(ii) where data on persistence and bioaccumulation are available, these shall be taken into account in deriving the final value of the environmental quality standard;

(iii) the standard thus derived should be compared with any evidence from field studies. Where anomalies appear, the derivation shall be reviewed to allow a more precise safety factor to be calculated;

(iv) the standard derived shall be subject to peer review and public consultation including to allow a more precise safety factor to be calculated.

1.3. *Monitoring of ecological status and chemical status for surface waters*

The surface water monitoring network shall be established in accordance with the requirements of Article 8. The monitoring network shall be designed so as to provide a coherent and comprehensive overview of ecological and chemical status within each river basin and shall permit classification of water bodies into five classes consistent with the normative definitions in section 1.2. Member States shall provide a map or maps showing the surface water monitoring network in the river basin management plan.

On the basis of the characterisation and impact assessment carried out in accordance with Article 5 and Annex II, Member States shall for each period to which a river basin management plan applies, establish a surveillance monitoring programme and an operational monitoring programme. Member States may also need in some cases to establish programmes of investigative monitoring. Member States shall monitor parameters which are indicative of the status of each relevant quality element. In selecting parameters for biological quality elements Member States shall identify the appropriate taxonomic level required to achieve adequate confidence and precision in the classification of the quality elements. Estimates of the level of confidence and precision of the results provided by the monitoring programmes shall be given in the plan.

1.3.1. Design of surveillance monitoring

Objective

Member States shall establish surveillance monitoring programmes to provide information for:

- supplementing and validating the impact assessment procedure detailed in Annex II,
- the efficient and effective design of future monitoring programmes,
- the assessment of long-term changes in natural conditions, and
- the assessment of long-term changes resulting from widespread anthropogenic activity.

The results of such monitoring shall be reviewed and used, in combination with the impact assessment procedure described in Annex II, to determine requirements for monitoring programmes in the current and subsequent river basin management plans.

Selection of monitoring points

Surveillance monitoring shall be carried out of sufficient surface water bodies to provide an assessment of the overall surface water status within each catchment or subcatchments within the river basin district. In selecting these bodies Member States shall ensure that, where appropriate, monitoring is carried out at points where:

- the rate of water flow is significant within the river basin district as a whole; including points on large rivers where the catchment area is greater than 2 500 km^2,
- the volume of water present is significant within the river basin district, including large lakes and reservoirs,
- significant bodies of water cross a Member State boundary,
- sites are identified under the Information Exchange Decision 77/795/EEC, and

at such other sites as are required to estimate the pollutant load which is transferred across Member State boundaries, and which is transferred into the marine environment.

Selection of quality elements

Surveillance monitoring shall be carried out for each monitoring site for a period of one year during the period covered by a river basin management plan for:

- parameters indicative of all biological quality elements,
- parameters indicative of all hydromorphological quality elements,
- parameters indicative of all general physico-chemical quality elements,
- priority list pollutants which are discharged into the river basin or sub-basin, and
- other pollutants discharged in significant quantities in the river basin or sub-basin,

unless the previous surveillance monitoring exercise showed that the body concerned reached good status and there is no evidence from the review of impact of human activity in Annex II that the impacts on the body have changed. In these cases, surveillance monitoring shall be carried out once every three river basin management plans.

1.3.2. Design of operational monitoring

Operational monitoring shall be undertaken in order to:

- establish the status of those bodies identified as being at risk of failing to meet their environmental objectives, and
- assess any changes in the status of such bodies resulting from the programmes of measures.

The programme may be amended during the period of the river basin management plan in the light of information obtained as part of the requirements of Annex II or as part of this Annex, in particular to allow a reduction in frequency where an impact is found not to be significant or the relevant pressure is removed.

Selection of monitoring sites
Operational monitoring shall be carried out for all those bodies of water which on the basis of either the impact assessment carried out in accordance with Annex II or surveillance monitoring are identified as being at risk of failing to meet their environmental objectives under Article 4 and for those bodies of water into which priority list substances are discharged. Monitoring points shall be selected for priority list substances as specified in the legislation laying down the relevant environmental quality standard. In all other cases, including for priority list substances where no specific guidance is given in such legislation, monitoring points shall be selected as follows:

- for bodies at risk from significant point source pressures, sufficient monitoring points within each body in order to assess the magnitude and impact of the point source. Where a body is subject to a number of point source pressures monitoring points may be selected to assess the magnitude and impact of these pressures as a whole,
- for bodies at risk from significant diffuse source pressures, sufficient monitoring points within a selection of the bodies in order to assess the magnitude and impact of the diffuse source pressures. The selection of bodies shall be made such that they are representative of the relative risks of the occurrence of the diffuse source pressures, and of the relative risks of the failure to achieve good surface water status,
- for bodies at risk from significant hydromorphological pressure, sufficient monitoring points within a selection of the bodies in order to assess the magnitude and impact of the hydromorphological pressures. The selection of bodies shall be indicative of the overall impact of the hydromorphological pressure to which all the bodies are subject.

Selection of quality elements

In order to assess the magnitude of the pressure to which bodies of surface water are subject Member States shall monitor for those quality elements which are indicative of the pressures to which the body or bodies are subject. In order to assess the impact of these pressures, Member States shall monitor as relevant:

– parameters indicative of the biological quality element, or elements, most sensitive to the pressures to which the water bodies are subject,
– all priority substances discharged, and other pollutants discharged in significant quantities,
– parameters indicative of the hydromorphological quality element most sensitive to the pressure identified.

1.3.3. Design of investigative monitoring

Objective

Investigative monitoring shall be carried out:

– where the reason for any exceedances is unknown,
– where surveillance monitoring indicates that the objectives set out in Article 4 for a body of water are not likely to be achieved and operational monitoring has not already been established, in order to ascertain the causes of a water body or water bodies failing to achieve the environmental objectives, or
– to ascertain the magnitude and impacts of accidental pollution, and shall inform the establishment of a programme of measures for the achievement of the environmental objectives and specific measures necessary to remedy the effects of accidental pollution.

1.3.4. Frequency of monitoring

For the surveillance monitoring period, the frequencies for monitoring parameters indicative of physico-chemical quality elements given below should be applied unless greater intervals would be justified on the basis of technical knowledge and expert judgement.

For biological or hydromorphological quality elements monitoring shall be carried out at least once during the surveillance monitoring period.

For operational monitoring, the frequency of monitoring required for any parameter shall be determined by Member States so as to provide sufficient data for a reliable assessment of the status of the relevant quality element. As a guideline, monitoring should take place at intervals not exceeding those shown in the table below unless greater intervals would be justified on the basis of technical knowledge and expert judgement.

Frequencies shall be chosen so as to achieve an acceptable level of confidence and precision. Estimates of the confidence and precision attained by the monitoring system used shall be stated in the river basin management plan.

Monitoring frequencies shall be selected which take account of the variability in parameters resulting from both natural and anthropogenic conditions. The times at which monitoring is undertaken shall be selected so as to minimise the impact of seasonal variation on the results, and thus ensure that the results reflect changes in the water body as a result of changes due to anthropogenic pressure. Additional monitoring during different seasons of the same year shall be carried out, where necessary, to achieve this objective.

Quality element	Rivers	Lakes	Transitional	Coastal
Biological				
Phytoplankton	6 months	6 months	6 months	6 months
Other aquatic flora	3 years	3 years	3 years	3 years
Macro invertebrates	3 years	3 years	3 years	3 years
Fish	3 years	3 years	3 years	
Hydromorphological				
Continuity	6 years			
Hydrology	continuous	1 month		
Morphology	6 years	6 years	6 years	6 years
Physico-chemical				
Thermal conditions	3 months	3 months	3 months	3 months
Oxygenation	3 months	3 months	3 months	3 months
Salinity	3 months	3 months	3 months	
Nutrient status	3 months	3 months	3 months	3 months
Acidification status	3 months	3 months		
Other pollutants	3 months	3 months	3 months	3 months
Priority substances	1 month	1 month	1 month	1 month

1.3.5. Additional monitoring requirements for protected areas

The monitoring programmes required above shall be supplemented in order to fulfil the following requirements:

Drinking water abstraction points
Bodies of surface water designated in Article 7 which provide more than 100 m^3 a day as an average shall be designated as monitoring sites and shall be subject to such additional monitoring as may be necessary to meet the requirements of that Article. Such bodies shall be monitored for all priority substances discharged and all other substances discharged in significant quantities which could affect the status of the body of water and which are controlled under the provisions of the Drinking Water Directive. Monitoring shall be carried out in accordance with the frequencies set out below:

Community served	Frequency
< 10 000	4 per year
10 000 to 30 000	8 per year
> 30 000	12 per year.

Habitat and species protection areas

Bodies of water forming these areas shall be included within the operational monitoring programme referred to above where, on the basis of the impact assessment and the surveillance monitoring, they are identified as being at risk of failing to meet their environmental objectives under Article 4. Monitoring shall be carried out to assess the magnitude and impact of all relevant significant pressures on these bodies and, where necessary, to assess changes in the status of such bodies resulting from the programmes of measures. Monitoring shall continue until the areas satisfy the water-related requirements of the legislation under which they are designated and meet their objectives under Article 4.

1.3.6. Standards for monitoring of quality elements

Methods used for the monitoring of type parameters shall conform to the international standards listed below or such other national or international standards which will ensure the provision of data of an equivalent scientific quality and comparability.

Macroinvertebrate sampling

ISO 5667-3:1995	Water quality – Sampling – Part 3: Guidance on the preservation and handling of samples
EN 27828:1994	Water quality – Methods for biological sampling – Guidance on hand net sampling of benthic macroinvertebrates
EN 28265:1994	Water quality – Methods of biological sampling – Guidance on the design and use of quantitative samplers for benthic macroinvertebrates on stony substrata in shallow waters
EN ISO 9391:1995	Water quality – Sampling in deep waters for macroinvertebrates – Guidance on the use of colonisation, qualitative and quantitative samplers
EN ISO 8689-1:1999	Biological classification of rivers PART I: Guidance on the interpretation of biological quality data from surveys of benthic macroinvertebrates in running waters
EN ISO 8689-2:1999	Biological classification of rivers PART II: Guidance on the presentation of biological quality data from surveys of benthic macroinvertebrates in running waters

Macrophyte sampling
Relevant CEN/ISO standards when developed

Fish sampling
Relevant CEN/ISO standards when developed

Diatom sampling
Relevant CEN/ISO standards when developed

Standards for physico-chemical parameters
Any relevant CEN/ISO standards

Standards for hydromorphological parameters
Any relevant CEN/ISO standards

1.4. *Classification and presentation of ecological status*

1.4.1. Comparability of biological monitoring results

(i) Member States shall establish monitoring systems for the purpose of estimating the values of the biological quality elements specified for each surface water category or for heavily modified and artificial bodies of surface water. In applying the procedure set out below to heavily modified or artificial water bodies, references to ecological status should be construed as references to ecological potential. Such systems may utilise particular species or groups of species which are representative of the quality element as a whole.

(ii) In order to ensure comparability of such monitoring systems, the results of the systems operated by each Member State shall be expressed as ecological quality ratios for the purposes of classification of ecological status. These ratios shall represent the relationship between the values of the biological parameters observed for a given body of surface water and the values for these parameters in the reference conditions applicable to that body. The ratio shall be expressed as a numerical value between zero and one, with high ecological status represented by values close to one and bad ecological status by values close to zero.

(iii) Each Member State shall divide the ecological quality ratio scale for their monitoring system for each surface water category into five classes ranging from high to bad ecological status, as defined in Section 1.2, by assigning a numerical value to each of the boundaries between the classes. The value for the boundary between the classes of high and good status, and the value for the boundary between good and moderate status shall be established through the intercalibration exercise described below.

(iv) The Commission shall facilitate this intercalibration exercise in order to ensure that these class boundaries are established consistent with the normative definitions in Section 1.2 and are comparable between Member States.

(v) As part of this exercise the Commission shall facilitate an exchange of information between Members States leading to the identification of a range of sites in each ecoregion in the Community; these sites will form an intercalibration network. The network shall consist of sites selected from a range of surface water body types present within each ecoregion. For each surface water body type selected, the network shall consist of at least two sites corresponding to the boundary between the normative definitions of high and good status, and at least two sites corresponding to the boundary between the normative definitions of good and moderate status. The sites shall be selected by expert judgement based on joint inspections and all other available information.

(vi)   Each Member State monitoring system shall be applied to those sites in the intercalibration network which are both in the ecoregion and of a surface water body type to which the system will be applied pursuant to the requirements of this Directive. The results of this application shall be used to set the numerical values for the relevant class boundaries in each Member State monitoring system.

(vii) Within three years of the date of entry into force of the Directive, the Commission shall prepare a draft register of sites to form the intercalibration network which may be adapted in accordance with the procedures laid down in Article 21. The final register of sites shall be established within four years of the date of entry into force of the Directive and shall be published by the Commission.

(viii) The Commission and Member States shall complete the intercalibration exercise within 18 months of the date on which the finalised register is published.

(ix)   The results of the intercalibration exercise and the values established for the Member State monitoring system classifications shall be published by the Commission within six months of the completion of the intercalibration exercise.

1.4.2. Presentation of monitoring results and classification of ecological status and ecological potential

(i)   For surface water categories, the ecological status classification for the body of water shall be represented by the lower of the values for the biological and physico-chemical monitoring results for the relevant quality elements classified in accordance with the first column of the table set out below. Member States shall provide a map for each river basin district illustrating the classification of the ecological status for each body of water, colour-coded in accordance with the second column of the table set out below to reflect the ecological status classification of the body of water:

Ecological status classification	Colour code
High	Blue
Good	Green
Moderate	Yellow
Poor	Orange
Bad	Red

(ii) For heavily modified and artificial water bodies, the ecological potential classification for the body of water shall be represented by the lower of the values for
the biological and physicochemical monitoring results for the relevant quality
elements classified in accordance with the first column of the table set out below.
Member States shall provide a map for each river basin district illustrating the
classification of the ecological potential for each body of water, colour-coded, in
respect of artificial water bodies in accordance with the second column of the
table set out below, and in respect of heavily modified water bodies in accordance
with the third column of that table:

| | Colour code | |
Ecological potential classification	Artificial Water Bodies	Heavily Modified
Good and above	Equal green and light grey stripes	Equal green and dark grey stripes
Moderate	Equal yellow and light grey stripes	Equal yellow and dark grey stripes
Poor	Equal orange and light grey stripes	Equal orange and dark grey stripes
Bad	Equal red and light grey stripes	Equal red and dark grey stripes

(iii) Member States shall also indicate, by a black dot on the map, those bodies of
water where failure to achieve good status or good ecological potential is due
to non-compliance with one or more environmental quality standards which
have been established for that body of water in respect of specific synthetic and
non-synthetic pollutants (in accordance with the compliance regime established
by the Member State).

1.4.3. Presentation of monitoring results and classification of chemical status

Where a body of water achieves compliance with all the environmental quality standards established in Annex IX, Article 16 and under other relevant Community legislation setting environmental quality standards it shall be recorded as achieving good
chemical status. If not, the body shall be recorded as failing to achieve good chemical
status.

Member States shall provide a map for each river basin district illustrating chemical
status for each body of water, colour-coded in accordance with the second column of
the table set out below to reflect the chemical status classification of the body of water:

Chemical status classification	Colour code
Good	Blue
Failing to achieve good	Red

2. Groundwater

2.1. *Groundwater quantitative status*

2.1.1. Parameter for the classification of quantitative status

Groundwater level regime

2.1.2. Definition of quantitative status

Elements	Good status
Groundwater level	The level of groundwater in the groundwater body is such that the available groundwater resource is not exceeded by the long-term annual average rate of abstraction. Accordingly, the level of groundwater is not subject to anthropogenic alterations such as would result in: – failure to achieve the environmental objectives specified under Article 4 for associated surface waters, – any significant diminution in the status of such waters, – any significant damage to terrestrial ecosystems which depend directly on the groundwater body, and alterations to flow direction resulting from level changes may occur temporarily, or continuously in a spatially limited area, but such reversals do not cause saltwater or other intrusion, and do not indicate a sustained and clearly identified anthropogenically induced trend in flow direction likely to result in such intrusions.

2.2. *Monitoring of groundwater quantitative status*

2.2.1. Groundwater level monitoring network

The groundwater monitoring network shall be established in accordance with the requirements of Articles 7 and 8. The monitoring network shall be designed so as to provide a reliable assessment of the quantitative status of all groundwater bodies or groups of bodies including assessment of the available groundwater resource. Member States shall provide a map or maps showing the groundwater monitoring network in the river basin management plan.

2.2.2. Density of monitoring sites

The network shall include sufficient representative monitoring points to estimate the groundwater level in each groundwater body or group of bodies taking into account short and long-term variations in recharge and in particular:

— for groundwater bodies identified as being at risk of failing to achieve environmental objectives under Article 4, ensure sufficient density of monitoring points to assess the impact of abstractions and discharges on the groundwater level,
— for groundwater bodies within which groundwater flows across a Member State boundary, ensure sufficient monitoring points are provided to estimate the direction and rate of groundwater flow across the Member State boundary.

2.2.3. Monitoring frequency

The frequency of observations shall be sufficient to allow assessment of the quantitative status of each groundwater body or group of bodies taking into account short and long-term variations in recharge. In particular:

— for groundwater bodies identified as being at risk of failing to achieve environmental objectives under Article 4, ensure sufficient frequency of measurement to assess the impact of abstractions and discharges on the groundwater level,
— for groundwater bodies within which groundwater flows across a Member State boundary, ensure sufficient frequency of measurement to estimate the direction and rate of groundwater flow across the Member State boundary.

2.2.4. Interpretation and presentation of groundwater quantitative status

The results obtained from the monitoring network for a groundwater body or group of bodies shall be used to assess the quantitative status of that body or those bodies. Subject to point 2.5. Member States shall provide a map of the resulting assessment of groundwater quantitative status, colour-coded in accordance with the following regime:

Good: green
Poor: red

2.3. *Groundwater chemical status*

2.3.1. Parameters for the determination of groundwater chemical status

Conductivity
Concentrations of pollutants

2.3.2. Definition of good groundwater chemical status

Elements	Good status
General	The chemical composition of the groundwater body is such that the concentrations of pollutants: – as specified below, do not exhibit the effects of saline or other intrusions – do not exceed the quality standards applicable under other relevant Community legislation in accordance with Article 17 – are not such as would result in failure to achieve the environmental objectives specified under Article 4 for associated surface waters nor any significant diminution of the ecological or chemical quality of such bodies nor in any significant damage to terrestrial ecosystems which depend directly on the groundwater body
Conductivity	Changes in conductivity are not indicative of saline or other intrusion into the groundwater body

2.4. *Monitoring of groundwater chemical status*

2.4.1. Groundwater monitoring network

The groundwater monitoring network shall be established in accordance with the requirements of Articles 7 and 8. The monitoring network shall be designed so as to provide a coherent and comprehensive overview of groundwater chemical status within each river basin and to detect the presence of long-term anthropogenically induced upward trends in pollutants.

On the basis of the characterisation and impact assessment carried out in accordance with Article 5 and Annex II, Member States shall for each period to which a river basin management plan applies, establish a surveillance monitoring programme.

The results of this programme shall be used to establish an operational monitoring programme to be applied for the remaining period of the plan. Estimates of the level of confidence and precision of the results provided by the monitoring programmes shall be given in the plan.

2.4.2. Surveillance monitoring

Objective
Surveillance monitoring shall be carried out in order to:

– supplement and validate the impact assessment procedure,
– provide information for use in the assessment of long-term trends both as a result of changes in natural conditions and through anthropogenic activity.

Selection of monitoring sites
Sufficient monitoring sites shall be selected for each of the following:

- bodies identified as being at risk following the characterisation exercise undertaken in accordance with Annex II,
- bodies which cross a Member State boundary.

Selection of parameters
The following set of core parameters shall be monitored in all the selected groundwater bodies:

- oxygen content
- pH value
- conductivity
- nitrate
- ammonium

Bodies which are identified in accordance with Annex II as being at significant risk of failing to achieve good status shall also be monitored for those parameters which are indicative of the impact of these pressures.

Transboundary water bodies shall also be monitored for those parameters which are relevant for the protection of all of the uses supported by the groundwater flow.

2.4.3. Operational monitoring

Objective
Operational monitoring shall be undertaken in the periods between surveillance monitoring programmes in order to:

- establish the chemical status of all groundwater bodies or groups of bodies determined as being at risk,
- establish the presence of any long term anthropogenically induced upward trend in the concentration of any pollutant.

Selection of monitoring sites
Operational monitoring shall be carried out for all those groundwater bodies or groups of bodies which on the basis of both the impact assessment carried out in accordance with Annex II and surveillance monitoring are identified as being at risk of failing to meet objectives under Article 4. The selection of monitoring sites shall also reflect an assessment of how representative monitoring data from that site is of the quality of the relevant groundwater body or bodies.

Frequency of monitoring

Operational monitoring shall be carried out for the periods between surveillance monitoring programmes at a frequency sufficient to detect the impacts of relevant pressures but at a minimum of once per annum.

2.4.4. Identification of trends in pollutants

Member States shall use data from both surveillance and operational monitoring in the identification of long term anthropogenically induced upward trends in pollutant concentrations and the reversal of such trends. The base year or period from which trend identification is to be calculated shall be identified. The calculation of trends shall be undertaken for a body or, where appropriate, group of bodies of groundwater. Reversal of a trend shall be demonstrated statistically and the level of confidence associated with the identification stated.

2.4.5 Interpretation and presentation of groundwater chemical status

In assessing status, the results of individual monitoring points within a groundwater body shall be aggregated for the body as a whole. Without prejudice to the Directives concerned, for good status to be achieved for a groundwater body, for those chemical parameters for which environmental quality standards have been set in Community legislation:

- the mean value of the results of monitoring at each point in the groundwater body or group of bodies shall be calculated, and
- in accordance with Article 17 these mean values shall be used to demonstrate compliance with good groundwater chemical status.

Subject to point 2.5, Member States shall provide a map of groundwater chemical status, colour-coded as indicated below:

Good: green
Poor: red

Member States shall also indicate by a black dot on the map, those groundwater bodies which are subject to a significant and sustained upward trend in the concentrations of any pollutant resulting from the impact of human activity. Reversal of a trend shall be indicated by a blue dot on the map. These maps shall be included in the river basin management plan.

2.5 *Presentation of Groundwater Status*

Member States shall provide in the river basin management plan a map showing for each groundwater body or groups of groundwater bodies both the quantitative status and the chemical status of that body or group of bodies, colour-coded in accordance with the requirements of points 2.2.4 and 2.4.5. Member States may choose not to provide separate maps under points 2.2.4 and 2.4.5 but shall in that case also provide an indication in accordance with the requirements of point 2.4.5 on the map required under this point, of those bodies which are subject to a significant and sustained upward trend in the concentration of any pollutant or any reversal in such a trend.

Annex VI
Lists of measures to be included within the programmes of measures

Part A
Measures required under the following Directives:

   (i) The Bathing Water Directive (76/160/EEC);
  (ii) The Birds Directive (79/409/EEC);[1]
 (iii) The Drinking Water Directive (80/778/EEC) as amended by Directive (98/83/EC);
 (iv) The Major Accidents (Seveso) Directive (96/82/EC);[2]
  (v) The Environmental Impact Assessment Directive (85/337/EEC);[3]
 (vi) The Sewage Sludge Directive (86/278/EEC);[4]
(vii) The Urban Waste-water Treatment Directive (91/271/EEC);
(viii) The Plant Protection Products Directive (91/414/EEC);
 (ix) The Nitrates Directive (91/676/EEC);
  (x) The Habitats Directive (92/43/EEC);[5]
 (xi) The Integrated Pollution Prevention Control Directive (96/61/EC).

Part B
The following is a non-exclusive list of supplementary measures which Member States within each river basin district may choose to adopt as part of the programme of measures required under Article 11(4):

   (i) legislative instruments
  (ii) administrative instruments
 (iii) economic or fiscal instruments
 (iv) negotiated environmental agreements
  (v) emission controls
 (vi) codes of good practice
(vii) recreation and restoration of wetlands areas
(viii) abstraction controls

[1] OJ L 103, 25.4.1979, p. 1.
[2] OJ L 10, 14.1.1997, p. 13.
[3] OJ L 175, 5.7.1985, p. 40. Directive as amended by Directive 97/11/EC (OJ L 73, 14.3.1997, p. 5).
[4] OJ L 181, 8.7.1986, p. 6.   [5] OJ L 206, 22.7.1992, p. 7.

  (ix) demand management measures, *inter alia*, promotion of adapted agricultural production such as low water requiring crops in areas affected by drought
   (x) efficiency and reuse measures, *inter alia*, promotion of water-efficient technologies in industry and water-saving irrigation techniques
  (xi) construction projects
 (xii) desalination plants
(xiii) rehabilitation projects
 (xiv) artificial recharge of aquifers
  (xv) educational projects
 (xvi) research, development and demonstration projects
(xvii) other relevant measures

Annex VII
River basin management plans

A. River basin management plans shall cover the following elements:

1. a general description of the characteristics of the river basin district required under Article 5 and Annex II.
   This shall include:
   1.1. for surface waters:
      – mapping of the location and boundaries of water bodies,
      – mapping of the ecoregions and surface water body types within the river basin,
      – identification of reference conditions for the surface water body types;
   1.2. for groundwaters:
      – mapping of the location and boundaries of groundwater bodies;
2. a summary of significant pressures and impact of human activity on the status of surface water and groundwater, including:
   – estimation of point source pollution,
   – estimation of diffuse source pollution, including a summary of land use,
   – estimation of pressures on the quantitative status of water including abstractions,
   – analysis of other impacts of human activity on the status of water;
3. identification and mapping of protected areas as required by Article 6 and Annex IV;
4. a map of the monitoring networks established for the purposes of Article 8 and Annex V, and a presentation in map form of the results of the monitoring programmes carried out under those provisions for the status of:
   4.1. surface water (ecological and chemical);
   4.2. groundwater (chemical and quantitative);
   4.3. protected areas;

5. a list of the environmental objectives established under Article 4 for surface
   waters, groundwaters and protected areas, including in particular identification
   of instances where use has been made of Article 4(4), (5), (6) and (7), and the
   associated information required under that Article;

6. a summary of the economic analysis of water use as required by Article 5 and
   Annex III;

7. a summary of the programme or programmes of measures adopted under Article
   11, including the ways in which the objectives established under Article 4 are
   thereby to be achieved;

   7.1. a summary of the measures required to implement Community legislation
        for the protection of water;

   7.2. a report on the practical steps and measures taken to apply the principle of
        recovery of the costs of water use in accordance with Article 9;

   7.3. a summary of the measures taken to meet the requirements of Article 7;

   7.4. a summary of the controls on abstraction and impoundment of water,
        including reference to the registers and identifications of the cases where
        exemptions have been made under Article 11(3)(e);

   7.5. a summary of the controls adopted for point source discharges and other
        activities with an impact on the status of water in accordance with the
        provisions of Article 11(3)(g) and 11(3)(i);

   7.6. an identification of the cases where direct discharges to groundwater have
        been authorised in accordance with the provisions of Article 11(3)(j);

   7.7. a summary of the measures taken in accordance with Article 16 on priority
        substances;

   7.8. a summary of the measures taken to prevent or reduce the impact of acci-
        dental pollution incidents;

   7.9. a summary of the measures taken under Article 11(5) for bodies of water
        which are unlikely to achieve the objectives set out under Article 4;

   7.10. details of the supplementary measures identified as necessary in order to
         meet the environmental objectives established;

   7.11. details of the measures taken to avoid increase in pollution of marine waters
         in accordance with Article 11(6);

8. a register of any more detailed programmes and management plans for the river
   basin district dealing with particular sub-basins, sectors, issues or water types,
   together with a summary of their contents;

9. a summary of the public information and consultation measures taken, their
   results and the changes to the plan made as a consequence;

10. a list of competent authorities in accordance with Annex I;

11. the contact points and procedures for obtaining the background documentation
    and information referred to in Article 14(1), and in particular details of the
    control measures adopted in accordance with Article 11(3)(g) and 11(3)(i) and
    of the actual monitoring data gathered in accordance with Article 8 and Annex V.

B. The first update of the river basin management plan and all subsequent updates shall also include:

1. a summary of any changes or updates since the publication of the previous version of the river basin management plan, including a summary of the reviews to be carried out under Article 4(4), (5), (6) and (7);
2. an assessment of the progress made towards the achievement of the environmental objectives, including presentation of the monitoring results for the period of the previous plan in map form, and an explanation for any environmental objectives which have not been reached;
3. a summary of, and an explanation for, any measures foreseen in the earlier version of the river basin management plan which have not been undertaken;
4. a summary of any additional interim measures adopted under Article 11(5) since the publication of the previous version of the river basin management plan.

Annex VIII
Indicative list of the main pollutants

1. Organohalogen compounds and substances which may form such compounds in the aquatic environment.
2. Organophosphorous compounds.
3. Organotin compounds.
4. Substances and preparations, or the breakdown products of such, which have been proved to possess carcinogenic or mutagenic properties or properties which may affect steroidogenic, thyroid, reproduction or other endocrine-related functions in or via the aquatic environment.
5. Persistent hydrocarbons and persistent and bioaccumulable organic toxic substances.
6. Cyanides.
7. Metals and their compounds.
8. Arsenic and its compounds.
9. Biocides and plant protection products.
10. Materials in suspension.
11. Substances which contribute to eutrophication (in particular, nitrates and phosphates).
12. Substances which have an unfavourable influence on the oxygen balance (and can be measured using parameters such as BOD, COD, etc.).

Annex IX
Emission limit values and environmental quality standards

The 'limit values' and 'quality objectives' established under the re Directives of Directive 76/464/EEC shall be considered emission limit values and environmental quality standards, respectively, for the purposes of this Directive. They are established in the following Directives:

(i) The Mercury Discharges Directive (82/176/EEC);[1]
(ii) The Cadmium Discharges Directive (83/513/EEC);[2]
(iii) The Mercury Directive (84/156/EEC);[3]
(iv) The Hexachlorocyclohexane Discharges Directive (84/491/EEC);[4] (4) and
(v) The Dangerous Substance Discharges Directive (86/280/EEC).[5]

[1] OJ L 81, 27.3.1982, p. 29.
[2] OJ L 291, 24.10.1983, p. 1.
[3] OJ L 74, 17.3.1984, p. 49.
[4] OJ L 274, 17.10.1984, p. 11.
[5] OJ L 181, 4.7.1986, p. 16.

Annex X
*List of priority substances in the field of water policy**

	CAS number[1]	EU number[2]	Name of priority substance	Identified as priority hazardous substance
(1)	15972–60–8	240–110–8	Alachlor	
(2)	120–12–7	204–371–1	Anthracene	(X)***
(3)	1912–24–9	217–617–8	Atrazine	(X)***
(4)	71–43–2	200–753–7	Benzene	
(5)	not applicable	not applicable	Brominated diphenylethers**	(X)****
(6)	7440–43–9	231–152–8	Cadmium and its compounds	X
(7)	85535–84–8	287–476–5	C_{10-13}-chloroalkanes**	X
(8)	470–90–6	207–432–0	Chlorfenvinphos	
(9)	2921–88–2	220–864–4	Chlorpyrifos	(X)***
(10)	107–06–2	203–458–1	1,2-Dichloroethane	
(11)	75–09–2	200–838–9	Dichloromethane	
(12)	117–81–7	204–211–0	Di(2-ethylhexyl)phthalate (DEHP)	(X)***
(13)	330–54–1	206–354–4	Diuron	(X)***
(14)	115–29–7	204–079–4	Endosulfan	(X)***
	959–98–8	not applicable	(alpha-endosulfan)	
(15)	206–44–0	205–912–4	Fluoranthene*****	
(16)	118–74–1	204–273–9	Hexachlorobenzene	X
(17)	87–68–3	201–765–5	Hexachlorobutadiene	X
(18)	608–73–1	210–158–9	Hexachlorocyclohexane	X
	58–89–9	200–401–2	(gamma-isomer, Lindane)	
(19)	34123–59–6	251–835–4	Isoproturon	(X)***
(20)	7439–92–1	231–100–4	Lead and its compounds	(X)***
(21)	7439–97–6	231–106–7	Mercury and itrs compounds	X

	CAS number[1]	EU number[2]	Name of priority substance	Identified as priority hazardous substance
(22)	91–20–3	202–049–5	Naphthalene	(X)***
(23)	7440–02–0	231–111–4	Nickel and its compounds	
(24)	25154–52–3	246–672–0	Nonylphenols	X
	104–40–5	203–199–4	(4-(para)-nonylphenol)	
(25)	1806–26–4	217–302–5	Octylphenols	(X)***
	140–66–9	not applicable	(para-tert-octylphenol)	
(26)	608–93–5	210–172–5	Pentachlorobenzene	X
(27)	87–86–5	201–778–6	Pentachlorophenol	(X)***
(28)	not applicable	not applicable	Polyaromatic hydrocarbons	X
	50–32–8	200–028–5	(Benzo(a)pyrene),	
	205–99–2	205–911–9	(Benzo(b)fluoranthene),	
	191–24–2	205–883–8	(Benzo(g,h,i)perylene),	
	207–08–9	205–916–6	(Benzo(k)fluoranthene),	
	193–39–5	205–893–2	(Indeno(1,2,3-cd)pyrene)	
(29)	122–34–9	204–535–2	Simazine	(X)***
(30)	688–73–3	211–704–4	Tributyltin compounds	X
	36643–28–4	not applicable	(Tributyltin-cation)	
(31)	12002–48–1	234–413–4	Trichlorobenzenes	(X)***
	120–82–1	204–428–0	(1,2,4-Trichlorobenzene)	
(32)	67–66–3	200–663–8	Trichloromethane (Chloroform)	
(33)	1582–09–8	216–428–8	Trifluralin	(X)***

    * Where groups of substances have been selected, typical individual representatives are listed as indicative parameters (in brackets and without number). The establishment of controls will be targeted to these individual substances, without prejudicing the inclusion of other individual representatives, where appropriate.

    ** These groups of substances normally include a considerable number of individual compounds. At present, appropriate indicative parameters cannot be given.

    *** This priority substance is subject to a review for identification as possible 'priority hazardous substance'. The Commission will make a proposal to the European Parliament and Council for its final classification not later than 12 months after adoption of this list. The timetable laid down in Article 16 of Directive 2000/60/EC for the Commission's proposals of controls is not affected by this review.

    **** Only Pentabromobiphenylether (CAS-number 32534–81–9).

    ***** Fluoranthene is on the list as an indicator of other, more dangerous Polyaromatic Hydrocarbons.

[1] CAS: Chemical Abstract Services.

[2] EU-nummer: European Inventory of Existing Commercial Chemical Substances (EINECS) or European List of Notified Chemical Substances (ELINCS).

Annex XI

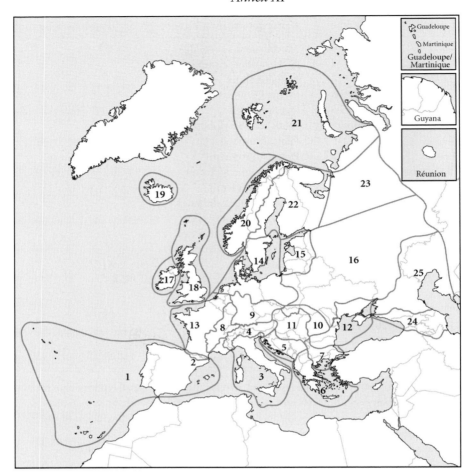

1. Iberic-Macaronesian region
2. Pyrenees
3. Italy, Corsica and Malta
4. Alps
5. Dinaric western Balkan
6. Hellenic western Balkan
7. Eastern Balkan
8. Western highlands
9. Central highlands
10. The Carpathians
11. Hungarian lowlands
12. Pontic province
13. Western plains
14. Central plains
15. Baltic province
16. Eastern plains
17. Ireland and Northern Ireland
18. Great Britain
19. Iceland
20. Borealic uplands
21. Tundra
22. Fenno-Scandian shield
23. Taiga
24. The Caucasus
25. Caspic depression

Map A
System A: Ecoregions for rivers and lakes.

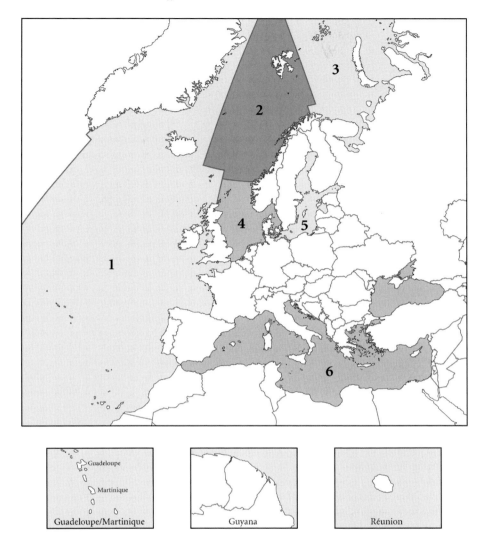

1. Atlantic Ocean
2. Norwegian Sea
3. Barents Sea
4. North Sea
5. Baltic Sea
6. Mediterranean Sea

Map B
System A: Ecoregions for transitional waters and coastal waters.